RECLAIMING FEMALE AGENCY

RECLAIMING FEMALE AGENCY

FEMINIST ART HISTORY AFTER POSTMODERNISM

Edited by Norma Broude and Mary D. Garrard

UNIVERSITY OF CALIFORNIA PRESS BERKELEY LOS ANGELES LONDON

The publisher gratefully acknowledges the generous
contribution to this book provided by the Art
Endowment Fund of the University of California
Press Associates.

University of California Press
Berkeley and Los Angeles, California

University of California Press, Ltd.
London, England

Library of Congress Cataloging-in-Publication Data

Reclaiming female agency : feminist art history after postmodernism / edited
by Norma Broude and Mary D. Garrard.
    p. cm.
Includes bibliographical references and index.
ISBN 0-520-24251-3 (cloth : alk. paper)—ISBN 0-520-24252-1 (pbk. : alk. paper)
    1. Feminism and art. I. Broude, Norma. II. Garrard, Mary D. III. Title.
N72.F45R43   2005
704'.042—dc22   2004016111

Manufactured in Canada

14 13 12 11 10 09 08 07 06 05
10 9 8 7 6 5 4 3 2

CONTENTS

PREFACE AND ACKNOWLEDGMENTS

THIS IS THE THIRD COLLECTION of essays in feminist art history that we two have coedited, following *Feminism and Art History: Questioning the Litany* (1982) and *The Expanding Discourse: Feminism and Art History* (1992). Considering the time frame that this series brackets with the publication of the present volume, we now look back to a period of politically engaged feminist writing that spans nearly a quarter century. We are proud to have shared in the identification and consolidation of a rich and creative body of scholarship that has substantially affected the course of art history. It is especially rewarding to know that these collections and their users trace a genealogy: people who used the first two volumes as students then assigned them to their own students, who in turn have assigned them to their students. Thus it is that the books are still in print and still find a readership at all levels of the academic spectrum. To those generations of readers, we are indebted for your thoughtful reception and long-term supportive commitment.

Readers may note that there are more essays on women artists in this volume than in the previous ones. Taken together, the three books contain essays on twenty-five individual female artists, a few of them treated more than once from different perspectives. There are also essays in each volume that examine the art of various women artists in groups. But, once more, we would reiterate that this is not primarily a book on women artists. Rather, like its predecessors, it examines the art of both women and men, conceptual frameworks and social constructs, to challenge art history as a disciplinary practice that has reified the asymmetrical power positions determined by gender.

More than the preceding volumes, the present book has a theme, which is the issue of female agency and its repression, both in public life and the cultural record. As a disciplinary intervention at a particular time in cultural and political history, this volume differs from the earlier ones in this and other significant ways. *Questioning the Litany* was a pioneering effort that was fueled by the political energies of a growing feminist political movement in the United States and Western Europe. *The Expanding Discourse* reflects the engagement of a maturing feminist art history with postmodern critical perspectives and theories. With the twenty-three essays in *Reclaiming Female Agency*, we showcase the work of recent writers whose concerns revive the political urgency of first-generation feminist art history. It may be no coincidence that the book makes its appearance at a time when personal and political freedoms for women are being both fiercely threatened and heroically claimed worldwide.

The subtitle of the present book, *Feminist Art History after Postmodernism*, reflects a spirit that pervades the essays we have chosen and that is also to be found in the larger intellectual community—a spirit of dissatisfaction with the often narrow, self-limiting, and self-reflexive concerns of academic theory and a desire to return to real-world issues. Many of these writers use and build on the sophisticated tools of postmodern thought; yet their work often exposes its limitations for feminism and sharply critiques some of its premises, showing more directly than before how postmodernism, as a patriarchal tool of analysis that has denied the very possibility of individual agency, has become part of the larger historical problem for women. The essays in this volume demonstrate what will be surprising to some readers: that women have worked consistently and self-consciously across time to prevent their own erasure, and that their strategies and assertions, even if taken only on the level of threats to be resisted, have immeasurably affected and belied the hegemonic metanarratives of patriarchal culture.

In producing this book, we have received consistent support and encouragement from the University of California Press in countless ways and human forms. Our greatest debt is to Stephanie Fay, our editor, for her engaged and proactive interest in our project, her wise judgment in all matters, and her steadfast commitment to bringing this book to fruition. We also thank her superbly capable assistant, Erin Marietta, for shepherding us through the assembling of the manuscript and for her exceptional skill in rounding up errant lambs of all kinds. Our special thanks and appreciation go to Sue Heinemann, project manager for this volume, for her enthusiasm about the book, her experienced help at a critical juncture of the process, and her sharp editorial eye. We thank Victoria Kuskowski for a powerful and creative design, and we are grateful to the team as a whole for including us in the decision-making process of design and layout.

A particular debt of gratitude goes to Cass Canfield, Jr., our editor for the first two books, published by HarperCollins. It was he who first encouraged us to produce a third volume, and he continued to do so even after his retirement, when he knew he would not be the one to publish it. Cass's vision has been a continuing inspiration to us throughout the creation of all three books and, were it not a gender stereotype, we would gladly call him our muse.

Gratitude of a different kind is owed our contributors. First, we thank our eighteen collaborators in *Reclaiming Female Agency* for their warm and enthusiastic support of the enterprise from the outset and their cooperative participation in getting the manuscript into swift production, cheerfully and efficiently meeting our draconian deadlines. Beyond the immediate moment, we extend our deepest appreciation to the fifty-seven authors whose work comprises all three volumes, for their visionary and insightful scholarship, which has created, built upon, and articulated the still-growing and changing entity known as feminist art history. Your work is the meat of this trilogy, in which we can collectively take pride.

Finally, once again, we thank each other, longtime personal and professional partners, for the joy that we have shared in working together to create these books.

INTRODUCTION

RECLAIMING FEMALE AGENCY

Norma Broude and Mary D. Garrard

OVER THE PAST three decades, feminist art history has undergone both radical growth and subtle transformation. Originating in women's political self-discovery, feminist art history in the 1970s aimed to correct historical gender inequities by recovering women's history and revealing gender distortion in the canonical record. Early feminist art history interrogated and challenged culture as a whole, exposing its biases and hierarchies of value, from the near-monolithic standpoint of an undifferentiated feminist impulse.

In the 1970s and 1980s British and American feminists gradually refined and expanded their original mission to challenge sexist culture. First as independent forerunners and then as heirs of the postmodern and poststructuralist thinkers, we set out at the same time, on different sides of the Atlantic, to question existing systems—above all, patriarchy. Like other feminist scholars, feminist art historians have built our work upon the postmodern precept that the circulation of power in society is not natural but culturally manipulated and directed. This and other postmodern axioms proved to be invaluable tools in the early 1980s and beyond, as the feminist project to deconstruct patriarchal power structures continued, now with more sophisticated theoretical equipment at its disposal.[1]

Another development of the 1980s was the gradual absorption of feminist art history within the academy into the postmodern rubric of gender studies, now broadened to include men's studies, gay and lesbian perspectives, and queer theory. Under the impetus of poststructuralist theory, the notion of a unitary feminism yielded to feminism*s*, whose agendas were differentiated by race, class, and ethnicity, and the very concept of gender came to be problematized as a socially constructed entity. As feminist art historians began to recognize the larger scope and complexities of the power relationships that feminism interrogates and challenges, feminist art history came increasingly to situate female experience within a larger framework of multiple and fluid gendered identities and positions, and to consider gender as only one of many factors in a constantly shifting and evolving, often tensely balanced, pattern of power relationships. Yet as feminist art history changed direction, splintering under the impact of postmodern gender studies into differing and contentious theoretical positions, it risked losing its original feminist political urgency.[2]

The first casualty of poststructuralist gender studies was the possibility of women's agency. In an influential article of 1988, Lisa Tickner claimed that the question was no longer "why are there no great women artists?" but "how are the processes of sexual differentiation played out across the representations of art and art history?"[3] Tickner aligned herself with other British feminists who had moved away from a feminist art history concerned with women's experiential differences from men to focus instead on their "positional" difference in a "relational system." Emphasizing that gender is a "semiotic category," she shifted the discussion away from female agency into a realm that assumes no agency on anyone's part, only (here quoting Griselda Pollock's definition of patriarchy) "a web of psycho-social relationships which institute a socially significant difference on the axis of sex."[4] Citing the work of Pollock, Kathleen Adler, and Tamar Garb on Mary Cassatt, Berthe Morisot, and Marie Bashkirtseff as appropriate models for the study of women artists, Tickner advocated the study of the marginal and negotiated *place* of the woman artist in a particular social system and the ways in which her *position* as a woman is "repressed, refracted or revealed in her work."[5]

The critical emphasis of recent decades on the cultural impasse for women has created, we believe, a distorted picture of female participation in culture, one that portrays women as paralyzed within and by an abstract system of social relationships and representational constructs. The current of feminist scholarship and theory that found its touchstones in Freud, Lacan, and Saussure, in systems of psychology and linguistics grounded in masculinist principles, has in effect, if not by intention, reified existing power structures, often producing an elaborate justification of the status quo. More generally, art historians working in the gender studies mode, deferential to postmodern skepticism about the modernist heroizing of individual artists, have focused less and less on the work and agency of individual women artists, shying away especially from the idea of a feminist expression grounded in women's real life experiences. The result has been the steady erosion and suppression of an activist, reformist feminism within an increasingly theoretical and largely masculinist postmodernism.

Whether in politics or art, women's agency has been detrimentally circumscribed by the idea that the coherent identity of the category "woman" is a theoretical impossibility. This restriction sprang in part from the crippling prohibition against "essentialism," whose opponents learned to spot trouble in any text that hinted at the possibility that women as a group might act (or think or behave) in a particular, identifiable way.[6] The idea that there might be an identifiable female point of view in art, first presented in 1970s feminist art history, was doubted even at the outset;[7] but in the 1980s this idea was roundly discredited as "essentialist" by writers attuned to the postmodern precept that "woman" is a social, not a biological, construct.

The anti-essentialist position in turn came under criticism, most effectively from Diana Fuss, who, in an influential book of 1989, pointed out that a fundamental essentialism was actually at work in the theories of social constructionism forged or endorsed by anti-essentialists. Fuss also noted the latter's virtual invention of an essentialism that in fact few feminists claimed or practiced.[8] Nevertheless, she embraced what has been called the "risk of essence," pointing to the political value of an essentializing identity claim when coalition politics are practiced, and the political usefulness of thinking of women as a group, even at the expense of minimizing their differences. Defending Luce Irigaray's strategic use of a "language of essence," Fuss declared: "The point, for Irigaray, of defining women from an essentialist standpoint is not to imprison women within their bodies but to rescue them from enculturating definitions by men. An essentialist definition of 'woman' implies that there will always remain some part of 'woman' which resists masculine imprinting and socialization."[9]

But, of course, essentialism—defined as an unfounded belief in the natural and permanent nature of gender traits and the social positions they mark— is a fundamental characteristic of patriarchy itself. Thus, for many feminist art historians of the 1990s and later, the most productive and influential aspects of anti-essentialist theory have been those that critiqued *masculinist* essentialisms. Judith Butler, for example, has emphasized gender's liminality and performative enforcement, in the interest of breaking down totalizing or essentializing worldviews.[10] Similarly, Homi Bhabha has examined the colonial/postcolonial discourse of power from a psychological perspective.[11] Criticizing Edward Said's argument that colonialist power was maintained through an uncomplicated will and ability to dominate the powerless and passive oppressed, Bhabha points instead to a core ambivalence or unconscious anxiety on the part of the dominators, which threatens their power from the inside and admits the potential of resistance from the marginalized. Feminist art historians can certainly learn from the example of postcolonial discourse, in which the dominant-and-oppressed model has been replaced with theories, by Bhabha and others, that postulate agency on the part of the repressed and unconscious fear on the part of the dominators, or from Epifanio San Juan Jr., who wants to move beyond language-based theory to concentrate on the histories of particular "subalterns" who have resisted colonial repression.[12]

Within feminist art history as well, the idea of a history consisting of monolithic patriarchal control over women as passive victims, interrupted by sporadic feminist interventions, has been discredited by many recent writers. Several decades of feminist scholarship have already shown that women have exercised agency as artists, patrons, viewers, and taste-makers. What is different about the new scholarship is that it focuses upon the continuous destabilizing pressure that women's agency has exerted upon culture: women's efforts to resist masculinist cultural hegemony produced counterefforts to absorb, counteract, and appropriate their resistances. And some distinctly female points of view, we now know, were so different from the prevailing male paradigms that they could not be comfortably absorbed and assimilated.

The issue of *female agency*, both its presence and its repression, emerged as a strong current in feminist art-historical literature of the 1990s and has provoked, in our view, the most advanced and fruitful thinking of the present moment. In reaction to the dominant theoretical positions of the 1980s, which can be seen in retrospect to have been conservative positions, many feminist art historians began in the 1990s to look more closely at the agency of specific women in history, uncovering the subversive power they actually wielded, as measured by visible cultural efforts to suppress or neutralize them. The subject of this book, then, is how women attempted to claim power and agency, and how masculinist culture acted and continues to act to negate and neutralize those efforts.

The essays included here trace that dialogue and struggle in Western visual culture from the Renaissance to the present. We begin with the sixteenth century, when women artists and patrons became visible enough to constitute a threatening and destabilizing cultural force, and we focus on literature generated in the 1990s by the visual arts—primarily painting and the graphic arts, but also sculpture, photography, and film. The dialectical discourse between "high art" and "crafts," so important a part of the feminist art-historical project in the 1970s and 1980s, is no longer so central in the literature, perhaps because it is considered a battle already won. Its resonances nevertheless continue to be heard here in the ongoing critical debates over Judy Chicago's *Dinner Party*. Finally, this book is not about, nor could it be about, all cultures. We have focused, as in our previous volumes, on art and artists in Western Europe and North America.[13] Such recent artists as Hung Liu and Shirin Neshat are considered from their positions as American artists who act out of a liminal multicultural experience that is specifically Western.

In the sections that follow, we take up some of the major theoretical constructs of 1980s feminist art history that have been challenged and critically reconsidered by the contributors to this volume.

FEMALE SUBJECTIVE AGENCY
AND ITS REPRESSION

One of the foundational critical tenets in recent decades has been the notion of gendered subjectivity—the idea that every artist or writer responds to the world and represents it in artistic constructions, consciously or unconsciously, from the position of gendered experience. In principle, the gender positions of male and female are equivalent, since social rules for gender performance have been codified in equally elaborate forms for both sexes. In practice, however, it has been only for women that gender expectations conflicted with a desire for cultural achievement or a public voice. In the early modern period, the social casting of the female as passive counterpart to the active male, whether as silent and obedient wife, exemplum of beauty, or sexual object, could not easily accommodate the independent artistic activity of living women, especially when they produced images that challenged or complicated cultural norms. (The theoretical situation for female artistic subjectivity has, ironically, not been much better in the postmodern era, when Lacanian psychoanalytic and postfeminist theories have jointly postulated the impossibility of women's subjective agency in a symbolic order dominated by a masculine universal and in a discourse of power in which, as Others, women have no speaking position.)

The very existence of female artists in the Renaissance was deeply problematic for male artists, as can be seen in the theoretical claims designed to contain them. Women could not produce art, it was said, only children; women were thought to be incapable of divine artistic genius because they were allegedly farther than men from God.[14] When artists such as Sofonisba Anguissola, Artemisia Gentileschi, and Elisabetta Sirani opposed the socially constituted definitions of their sex, producing paintings that reversed normative female models, they set in motion cultural resistance to their agency. It is important to see that a dynamic is involved: the artistic agendas of these painters were formed in part by their personal responses to existing gender structures. Their art initiated a transgressive dialogue with culture that implicitly questioned the status quo, and some of them were culturally punished for their transgressions.

As Mary Garrard shows in "Here's Looking at Me: Sofonisba Anguissola and the Problem of the Woman Artist," Anguissola, an Italian Renaissance painter, confronted the seeming impossibility in the sixteenth century of presenting an image of a female self that could be interpreted as active subject rather than passive object, as primarily the image of an empowered artist and not a beautiful woman. Her *Bernardino Campi Painting Sofonisba Anguissola* is, Garrard argues, a picture that thematizes this dilemma, for Anguissola has constructed an image that seems to authorize Campi (Anguissola's teacher), yet slyly subordinates him both to her own painted face on the easel and to the woman outside the frame who painted this picture, whose presence is invoked by gazes and whose

"perspective encompasses the whole scene." In this work, Anguissola took a subtle course, exaggerating masculinist typologies of female images to the point of parody and gentle ridicule. In *The Chess Game*, she quietly championed the alternative values of female kinship networks. Her reformulations were subtle and sometimes polyvalent; that they might also be interpreted as consistent with dominant gender models may explain how their subversive thrust could have been ignored for so long.

In seventeenth-century Italy, Artemisia Gentileschi and Elisabetta Sirani reacted against models of sexualized or pacified females, models so predominant in the art of their time that even biblical or mythical heroines such as Judith or Cleopatra were routinely disempowered. First Gentileschi, then Sirani (perhaps in emulation of Artemisia's example) produced images of aggressively agile women whose ability to act and accomplish deeds is emphasized and even imaginatively enlarged. In "The Antique Heroines of Elisabetta Sirani," Babette Bohn examines Sirani as one of an unusually large number of female artists, writers, and musicians active in early modern Bologna, noting that Sirani chose to depict female protagonists from ancient history who modeled virtues, such as courage and heroism, that were atypical in images of women.

Like Anguissola, and also like her own Bolognese predecessor Lavinia Fontana, Sirani deliberately eschewed eroticized female images. She offers an exceptionally empowered Timoclea, a formidably heroic Judith, and an image of the Roman matron Portia proving her courage rather than the more common scene of her suicide. Another famous suicide, Cleopatra, was depicted by several Bolognese women artists; Sirani and Fontana present Cleopatra as a fully clothed and dignified woman, in sharp divergence from the normative eroticized temptress. Bohn argues persuasively that Bologna provided an unusually supportive and inspiring environment for the creative and intellectual achievements of women; their sheer numbers fostered an unusually receptive public and vice versa.

By contrast, the especially transgressive power of Artemisia Gentileschi's art has brought forth cultural repression from her day to ours, as Mary Garrard and Sheila ffolliott demonstrate in their essays. In "Artemisia's Hand," Garrard focuses on the strong hands and forceful gestures of Artemisia's depicted female characters, in order to demonstrate the artist's abiding interest in expressing female agency and to address the connoisseurship problem of authorship, that is, the artist's "hand." Garrard points to recent attributions to the artist that, in effect if not intention, work to replace the image of an empowered Artemisia with a more conventional feminized identity, as expressed through putative self-representations. Not incidentally, these paintings, whose attributions to Artemisia are here rejected, show female characters with unusually weak hands or none at all. Against the tendency of both Artemisia's contemporaries and modern art historians to minimize and suppress Artemisia's agency, whether real or figured in her art, Garrard adduces three new examples, in works by or about Artemisia, in which the painter signals her artistic presence to us through subtle and witty gestures of the hand.

In "Learning to Be Looked At: A Portrait of (the Artist as) a Young Woman in Agnès Merlet's *Artemisia*," ffolliott shows how the contemporary French filmmaker Merlet, in making her film on Artemisia, was impelled to sexualize and distort the artist's persona, just as her male predecessors had done. This time, however, it was accomplished through the visually persuasive medium of cinema. Ffolliott shows how Merlet's filmic devices work to contain Gentileschi, reinscribing her within traditional viewing structures as object of the male gaze rather than as authorial subject of the film. She quotes the filmmaker's avowed intention to present the artist as "a great romantic heroine," whose "destiny is to learn about passion in a painful way," and points to the film's operatic devices that support this vision. Yet, as ffolliott notes, Merlet also makes mischievous use of art history, employing and distorting the Vasarian model of master-pupil artist genealogy, in which the pupil surpasses his teacher, to position Artemisia between two male-artist rivals, her father-teacher and her rapist-"teacher," whose dual authorities she is never permitted (in the film) to challenge or escape.

Throughout history, it would seem, the more powerfully a woman asserted her agency, the more vigorous was its repression. Marie de' Medici, queen of France during the rule of her husband, Henri IV, and one of the grandest female art patrons in Western history, is herself commemorated in the cycle of paintings she commissioned for the Luxembourg Palace. Yet, as Geraldine Johnson shows, in "Pictures Fit for a Queen: Peter Paul Rubens and the Marie de' Medici Cycle," a conflict emerged in that cycle between the discourse of allegorical female nudes that Rubens habitually employed and the message of her own heroic agency that the queen wished to project in her effort to regain power from her son Louis XIII. The queen's image in the paintings is compromised by double-edged feminine signifiers, such as the exposed female breast, meant as positive and powerful yet read as negative and dangerous, interpretatively downgraded by male viewers in general and by Marie de' Medici's critics in particular into tropes of female seductiveness and vanity. In Johnson's analysis, the Medici cycle exemplifies the "complicated and often contradictory notions of the nature of female sexuality and its relationship to power."

Over the course of his work for Marie de' Medici, Rubens seems to have modified his iconography and imagery to suit the queen's wishes, yet as Johnson points out, given the delicacy of her adversary being her son, the most that she could triumph over was her own gender and its perceived limitations. In the *Presentation of the Portrait*, Henri IV views Marie de' Medici in a mirror-like portrait—probably intended, from her perspective, to express the idea that he sees himself and his own virtues in her, a way of supporting her claim to succeed him. Her strong gaze and the assertive role implied by the arrangement would have ideally fulfilled the conditions for representation's ability to confer and legitimize power, had she been male. Yet these features of the picture worked against her because they could be conformed to a gender stereotype: Marie de' Medici's face was compared by contemporary critics to the deceitful and evil head of Medusa, who turns men to stone.

In "The Portrait of the Queen: Elisabeth Vigée-Lebrun's *Marie-Antoinette en chemise*," Mary Sheriff also deals with the suppression of a powerful female historical subject and the complex relationship that existed between politics, gender, and representation within the French monarchy. While conflicts of will and style between Marie de' Medici and Rubens were resolved to the queen's political detriment, the accord between Queen Marie-Antoinette and her painter Elisabeth Vigée-Lebrun was considerably more harmonious. Yet the painter may have served her queen all too well. Sheriff examines the genesis and reception of Vigée-Lebrun's portrait of Marie-Antoinette *en chemise* (1783) in relation to accepted traditions of representing French queens. In contrast to portraits of French kings, which seamlessly constituted and legitimized their absolutist authority, portraits of queens normally conformed to Salic law. Provisions of this law excluded females from royal succession, presenting them as dependent wives with no power or property of their own, and with attire and attributes that mirrored their identity as the king's possession and progenitor of his dynasty.

Vigée-Lebrun's transgressive portrait of Marie-Antoinette, painted in accord with the private tastes of the queen and her powerful Hapsburg mother, Marie-Thérèse, presented her as a private individual *en chemise*, an image that mirrored the intimate private life at Trianon that Marie-Antoinette had defiantly created for herself. The portrait had to be withdrawn from the Salon because of inflamed public reactions to its informality and perceived immodesty, as well as inflated public perceptions of the foreign-born queen's power. In Sheriff's reading, Marie-Antoinette's sexual body was seen to corrupt the body politic. The Austrian-born queen brought alien style (English gardens and the *chemise*) into the heart of French sacred space; she offended further by feminizing that space, both in the gender of her preferred guests and in the lesbian sexuality rumored to have been practiced at Trianon. Her embrace of the *robe en chemise* and her preference for escaping to a female social world provided fuel for her enemies, and the portrait precipitated a host of libelous charges from the court, ranging from extravagance to sexual promiscuity, tribadism, and even incest.

As Sheriff explains, the queen's mortal body became a symbol of aristocratic vice and sexual deviance, and she herself became an early scapegoat for the monarchy's moral corruption and decline. Jacques-Louis David's quick sketch of Marie-Antoinette on the way to her execution effectively countered Vigée-Lebrun's image of the queen as a powerful nonconformist, offering instead "a public woman vanquished," stripped of her power and made to exhibit behavior appropriate to feminine and aristocratic stereotypes—as a lesson, perhaps, to women who attempt to overstep the bounds of their prescribed and "natural" roles.

Taken as a group, these early modern examples demonstrate the risks, for women, of trying to claim power through self-representation—at least when a male viewer is posited. Marie-Antoinette's image as the "tribade of Trianon" may have been admired by her female followers, but it fostered her downfall with the larger masculine and heterosexist public. The quietly feminist paintings of Sofonisba Anguissola and Elisabetta Sirani may have evoked pride in the small circle of women who saw them, yet these artists' strategies to escape sexualization under the masculinist gaze had, in order to succeed, to be nuanced and intentionally ambiguous, perhaps deliberately kept just beneath the threshold of risk. Anguissola relied on semiotic ambiguity, embedding her claim of artistic agency within conventional, but polysemous, emblems of feminine virtue (the virginals), while Sirani cloaked a vision of female triumph in the garments of antique heroic prototypes. Artemisia Gentileschi's more strident assertions were dealt harder blows, as measured in near-hysterical efforts, both in her day and our own, to sexualize, distort, or otherwise suppress the empowered, virilized women represented in her images and by her authorial identity.

As these essays show, women artists and public

figures who seek agency through art do not occupy immutable positions defined by permanent gender structures; rather, they enter and affect gendered discourses of representation whose standards of what is "natural" or appropriate are so precarious, so inherently unstable, that their rules and codes must be perpetually policed. Every action, every image, that threatens the masculinist status quo apparently must be resisted. The most persistent strategy of suppression has been to eroticize strong women, in an effort to limit and demonize their power. Although this has not had the effect of stopping women from claiming cultural agency, it has shaped the expressive substance of their aesthetic performances in art and public action.

Indeed, as this collection of essays demonstrates, the *threat* of female power circulates around all representations constructed by and about women. It is masculine fear of this threat—not so much what women do as what they might do—that makes women artists both especially vulnerable and especially dangerous. They enter a masculine art scene preconditioned to dismiss them on arrival, as "merely" women whose production is to be judged apart, who are either too beautiful and virtuous to do heavy (artistic) lifting or too tainted by eroticism and sexuality to be taken seriously as artists. We must learn to regard these slights of the female not as the disdain of the inferior by those justly ensconced in power, but as expressions of fear (albeit of phantasms, such as the castrated and castrating woman), which have turned into strategies for those insecure about their power. The essays gathered here offer evidence for the working postulate that patriarchy wants to inscribe itself most forcefully at the times when it is most under threat.

In "Depoliticizing Women: Female Agency, the French Revolution, and the Art of Boucher and David," Erica Rand reveals the extent to which fears of female power and agency transcended boundaries of class and politics to inform images that were produced both before and after the social upheavals of the French Revolution. She reverses the traditional oppositional stance of Boucher and David to demonstrate the strategies that permitted both to "defuse female agency." Boucher eroticized the female image for masculine visual pleasure, naturalizing his female protagonists in effective response to the period's widespread fear of women's cultural power, especially as mistresses and *salonières*. In his *Venus and Vulcan*, for example, Boucher displays the goddess's body for the viewer's gaze, presenting female agency in a negative light: women who deploy their bodies opportunistically and decadently are implicitly indicted. Similarly, David's presentation of women who transgressed the boundaries of traditional gender roles served a prescriptive republican agenda, functioning to direct women away from the arena of public politics and back to the private sphere of motherhood and family.

In the *Death of Marat*, for example, the self-constructed image of Charlotte Corday as a political heroine of high principle is both erased and politically neutralized. Though she herself is not seen in this image of the man she assassinated, her bodiless presence is nevertheless an important and carefully orchestrated aspect of the painting, taking the form of the letter that Marat holds, purposefully edited to characterize her as a deceptive and unnatural woman and to discredit her own interpretation of her act.[15] In the context of revolutionary-era fears of women's political activity, Rand argues that David, "a delegate to the National Convention and one of its primary crafters of gender ideology," used related tactics in other images to deauthorize and redirect Revolutionary female political activism. Thus, the political engagement of the Sabine women and the contemporary women of the October riots is presented in David's imagery as wholly framed and motivated by their commitment to preserving the private values of home and family.

The question of whether or to what extent David was motivated by an antifeminist political agenda, and how successful that agenda may have been, has been recently complicated by Darcy Grimaldo Grigsby, who, in "Nudity *à la grecque* in 1799," examines the controversial reception of David's *Intervention of the Sabine Women* and concludes that, whatever David's intentions may have been, he was unable to control the readings of his painting in his own time. Pointing to the tension in the painting between fashionable, scantily dressed women and male nudes who "now appeared undressed" and "as objects of women's vision," Grigsby asserts that David's tableau newly and shockingly foregrounded the female spectator as a "viewer of male flesh," a viewer whose gaze was capable of compromising the masculine *beau idéal*.

The fluid meanings of sartorial signifiers pictured in the painting further complicated its readings and confused its message. For during the Directory period, while men were increasingly covering their bodies to excess, women were electing a mode of Greek attire that revealed the female body and was seen by contemporaries as an exhibitionist and immoral fashion choice. When Directory women appropriated men's cultural signifiers through antique dress, they were perceived as sexualizing that dress and thereby debasing Republican iconography, threatening to corrupt the (fraternal) Republic by depriving its symbols of their cultural and political power.

Grigsby's analysis provides an important intervention in a dominant feminist discourse, one that has assumed the absolute and gendered separation between public and private spheres during and following the French Revolution, with David as the central figure and cultural enforcer of this separation. David's inability to control contemporary readings of the *Sabines* as a result of real women's intervention and co-option of sartorial symbolism is a revelation that would seem, on the face of it, to refute Rand's more traditional feminist claim, which uses intention rather than reception to uncover gender politics in specific historical periods and situations. In our view, however, these readings support and do not invalidate one another. For both writers would surely agree that cultural rhetoric and imagery designed to reinforce conservative positions about women's place is likely to be a defensive response to a threatening assertion of power and agency. In the words of Grigsby, "Modern scholarship that takes for granted women's role as representatives of the private sphere is . . . repeating

a reactionary prescription, not a reality of post-Revolutionary society."

Feminist analyses such as Rand's, however, reveal the recurring pattern of these reactionary prescriptions in every era and the recurring double bind: women assert a tenuous freedom that never becomes real power and whose effects are thus easily manipulated out of our received histories. Although the appropriation of Greek dress by women during the Directory may have briefly interfered with political readings of David's image, for the past two hundred years it is the "reactionary prescription" assigned to David's narrative by the conservative party line that has been consistently attached to the *Sabines*, disguising the diversity of competing gender positions in his own period in the interest of a patriarchy that has the power to naturalize, control, and rewrite the historical metanarrative over time. This power makes the feminist political analysis of the images and their cultural operation accurate still. For no matter how many competing voices and strands may have existed and interacted in any period, it is the conservative position, useful for supporting the continuing status quo of the patriarchal political and family structure, that is most apt to survive in the historical record.

In "Conduct Unbecoming: Daumier and *Les Bas-Bleus*," Janis Bergman-Carton broadens the limited typologies used by earlier feminist scholars to categorize and discuss women and their cultural representations in nineteenth-century France (primarily courtesans and women victimized into prostitution) to include the "woman of letters" and the "woman of ideas," women who were referred to derogatorily during the period as *bas-bleus*, or "bluestockings." The subversive power and potentially destabilizing presence of these women of letters in the social, political, and intellectual life of France during the period of the July Monarchy is revealed and measured, she shows, by the efforts that were made to denigrate and discredit them. In particular, Bergman-Carton encourages her readers to look directly at the gendered meanings of Daumier's caricatures of the *bas-bleus* and at the role these images played in helping to discourage social and political change for women in his era and beyond. The bluestockings were ridiculed and satirized by Daumier as sexually deviant home-wreckers and child-neglecters, antithetical to the feminine ideal. Modern Daumier scholars have argued that the artist himself was not against feminist reform per se, but rather aimed his satire at its "sententious high priestesses and camp followers." Yet, as Bergman-Carton succinctly observes: "Representing women writers not as women who write but as sexless hags and promiscuous shrews is not a neutral act. To ignore the cultural and political content of these images by studying them as benign scenes of everyday life is not a neutral act either."

If Daumier's nineteenth-century *Bas-Bleus* lithographs represent the power of popular imagery to repress female political agency, the twentieth-century reception of Judy Chicago's *The Dinner Party* could be said to represent a related phenomenon in opposite terms: the power of politically motivated critics to repress female agency expressed in art. In her essay "The 'Sexual Politics' of *The Dinner Party:* A Critical Context," Amelia Jones examines critical responses to the work that has become the "central icon" of the early feminist movement in the United States, a highly visible and controversial monument that was wildly popular yet sharply criticized by both conservative antifeminists and diverse feminist factions. Advocates of avant-garde high modernism faulted *The Dinner Party*'s populist, "low-art" appeal to the masses, its perceived lack of "quality," and its association with women's tastes and domestic crafts. The strategies of journalists were not unlike those of Daumier, to repress by caricature and ridicule; thus, descriptions of *The Dinner Party* linked it with the appalling values of kitsch art and emphasized the "vulgarity" and "bad taste" of the vulviform images seen in the thirty-nine large plates on the dinner table. So offensive were Chicago's abstracted images of female genitalia to masculinist political conservatives that *The Dinner Party* was "hysterically denounced for its obscenity" by right-wing members of Congress. What was in bad taste for these critics, Jones leads us to see, was Chicago's insistence on her right to use the female body, not for masculine viewing pleasure but for feminist political expression.

Some feminists, on the other hand, found *The Dinner Party*'s overt female imagery to represent an essentializing reduction of women—including "bluestockings" such as Mary Wollstonecraft and Virginia Woolf—to a biological feminine dubiously limited to wombs and vaginas. Characterizing this critique as insufficiently informed about the theory and practice of 1970s feminist activists and artists, Jones argues that supposedly "essentialist" artists such as Chicago and Miriam Schapiro were in reality reclaiming degraded "feminine" forms for political purposes. It was a crucial first step for feminism, Jones says, "to mark gender as informative of cultural practice, to refuse the masculinist notion of 'universality' that guaranteed the privileging of male-invented forms and themes as neutrally aesthetic," and to create a self-affirming "women's art" that "became a unifying factor, a means of binding together an infinitely variable group of practices." For the pioneers, this meant the recuperation of the female body long held hostage by men, so that it might be turned into a group-specific signifier *for* women, rather than *about* them.

The early feminists' idealist vision of a sisterhood that transcended the barriers of class, race, and sexual preference was perhaps inherently unstable. Examining critiques of *The Dinner Party* that came from Hispanic women, women of color, lesbians, and those critical of Chicago's personal celebrity in a collaborative feminist project, Jones exposes "the pitfalls of identity politics" that have plagued feminism increasingly since the 1970s. Poststructuralist feminists criticized *The Dinner Party* for its reduction of feminism to a biological common denominator; for these critics, its gender-universalizing was its weakness. But criticism also came from feminist groups who saw no place, or an inappropriately marked place, at the dinner table for lesbians and women of color—from this viewpoint, the project was unsatisfactory because it was not universal enough.

The sharply polarized reception of *The Dinner Party*, especially from feminists, forms an important and instructive chapter in the history of feminism. For ironically, in the late twentieth century, women seem to have done to ourselves what artists like Boucher, David, and Daumier did to their female contemporaries: using or allowing imagery to divide women into camps of "good" and "bad," right- and wrong-minded, on the basis of feminist or antifeminist propriety and theoretical decorum, and thus helping to break up the collective power of women who wield agency as a political group.

CHALLENGING MASCULINIST PSYCHOANALYSIS

For many, though not all, feminists, psychoanalysis has been an especially problematic methodological category. Feminism and psychoanalysis are, on the surface, at odds with each other because of the strongly patriarchal nature of Freudian psychology, in particular Freud's definition of human sexuality according to a masculine model.[16] Perhaps more patriarchalist than Freud, and certainly more influential in the postmodern era, was Jacques Lacan, who began as a Freudian psychoanalyst but grounded himself in structuralism and semiotics. Lacan famously pronounced that the symbolic order is patriarchal, with the phallus as the transcendental signifier, and that the unconscious is structured by language, which is masculine. Lacan's theories were challenged by French feminists such as Hélène Cixous, Julia Kristeva, and especially Luce Irigaray; they were more vigorously contested by American and British feminists, notably Nancy Chodorow, Jane Gallop, and to some extent, Alice Jardine.[17] At the same time, Lacanian theory was embraced in France by the women who formed the *psych et po* group, and it has continued to be the dominant model for many British feminist thinkers.[18] Despite its enduring appeal to some feminists, however, Lacanian theory would radically repress female agency, and it stands as a hostile interdiction to activist feminism.

In "Louise Bourgeois's *Femmes-Maisons:* Confronting Lacan," Julie Nicoletta presents the sculptor Bourgeois as an artist who critiqued Lacan's ideas about gender and the unconscious. Nicoletta explains that, in her art of the 1940s and 1950s, when Lacan was writing his theories, Bourgeois was dealing with the same issues that he addressed—specifically, gender differentiation in the context of Freudian psychology. Although Bourgeois may not have read Lacan until the 1970s, Nicoletta suggests that she is likely to have known his ideas (and perhaps Lacan himself) as early as the 1930s, when they participated in the same intellectual and artistic circles in Paris. As if in direct refutation of Lacan's theoretical pronouncements about the masculine nature of the unconscious and the symbolic order, Bourgeois expressed interest in overcoming patriarchal dominance through the *combination* of the sexes. As she put it in an interview, "We are all vulnerable in some way and we are all male-female."[19]

Nicoletta first examines Bourgeois's *Femmes-Maisons* paintings of the 1940s, which present images of nude females with houses that cover their heads and sometimes their bodies, as ambivalent expressions of woman's relation to the house as a symbol of the domestic. Some of the *Femmes-Maisons* express anxiety and a desire for escape; one hints at female contentment in her social role. Yet, for Bourgeois, the house may be not only a social but also a psychic signifier. In the context of Nicoletta's argument, it is suggestive that the sculptor chose houses, which in Freudian psychology often represent the psyche, or whole self, or even the unconscious. Does she address in these images woman's confinement in men's (Lacan's) ideas? Or does Bourgeois feminize the symbolic order defined by Lacan as masculine? In either case, she would seem to practice *gynesis*, the term used by Alice Jardine (with whom Nicoletta compares Bourgeois) for "the putting into discourse of 'woman' as that process beyond the Cartesian Subject, the Dialectics of Representation, or Man's Truth."[20]

Nicoletta points out further that, whereas Lacan insists upon the linguistic structuring of the unconscious and explores the mind through language, Bourgeois explores problems of communication through the visual or the semiotic, with a particular penchant for gender duality and ambiguity. This aligns her, in Nicoletta's reading, with Kristeva's idea of the semiotic as prepatriarchal and pre-Oedipal, feminine but also bisexual, and hence capable of breaking down gendered binaries. Kristeva, however, ascribed the power of semiotic disruption only to male writers; the fact that her own orientation was fundamentally phallic[21] leads us to value all the more the originality and daring of Louise Bourgeois's precocious critique of Lacanian phallogocentrism in semiotic terms.

LIFE AFTER DEATH (OF THE AUTHOR): WOMEN AS PATRONS, TASTEMAKERS, AND INTERPRETERS

We might take a second look at another influential postmodern principle, that the "author" is not the sole creator of culture but merely the delivery agent at the end of a long chain of causation, in which many cultural entities play roles. Roland Barthes's notion of the "death of the author," which was especially influential for the theorists of art history in the 1980s and 1990s, has been protested by many feminists, including ourselves, on the grounds that the exaggerated adulation of heroic authorship was declared to be passé just when women began to take the stage as authors/artists.[22] But perhaps we have been identifying with the wrong part of this equation. To apply this principle *on behalf of* women, we might point out that women have played major cultural roles according to the revised value system of postmodernism, not only as "authors" but also in the increasingly esteemed category of those "causal factors that helped produce the work."[23] We do not have in mind helpmeets or muses; instead, we look to women who have shaped taste and cultural values, sometimes by articulating new ones as patrons and consumers, and sometimes by posing a perceived threat to masculinist values so dangerous that men made art about it.

In this respect, we must question the myth that males have driven art history. If the subject of our study is visual cultural production, it is obvious from at least two perspectives that women have directed the course of culture as much as men. One of these is that of the non-fine-art categories such as crafts, photography, and other genres in which women have played a major role—or, in the case of genres such as quilts, an ascendant one.[24] The other perspective arises from the intersection of psychology and power. "Woman" as a principle, to be envied for her procreative power, feared for her dangerous sexuality, or fetishized for her beauty, has haunted the art of men since the Bronze Age, forming its dominant themes and images. It is true that this Woman is a chimera, the product of men's imaginations. But in many instances, some of them detailed in this book, real women were the agents who precipitated masculine resistances and fears: Marie-Antoinette, nineteenth-century bluestocking feminists, Judy Chicago, to name only the most obvious.

In the 1990s, much work was done to recover the histories of women active as patrons and tastemakers. The literature on female patronage in particular has burgeoned, and numerous recent books have effectively gathered new scholarship, especially for the early modern period, the golden age of patronage by rulers, monarchs, and clergy. We now know considerably more, not only about famous female patrons such as Isabella d'Este, duchess of Ferrara; Giovanna da Piacenza, abbess of a Benedictine nunnery in Parma; or Marie de' Medici, queen of France; but also about previously anonymous women across Europe whose art patronage, emanating from convents, courts, and palaces, has been estimated to account for as much as 10 percent of all Renaissance art production.[25]

Several articles in this volume deal with women's patronage and support of the arts, in instances where their individual preferences for artists or styles may be said to have shaped taste in their time or to have complicated our understanding of gendered values. In her essay, "A Woman's Pleasure: Ingres's *Grande Odalisque*," Carol Ockman examines a nexus of female patronage in the early nineteenth century, including prominent figures such as Juliette Récamier and Paolina Borghese, and she reveals that a woman, Caroline Bonaparte Murat, queen of Naples and sister of Paolina Borghese, was the patron behind the commission for Ingres's *Grande Odalisque*. This is a revelation that changes our understanding of Ingres's painting, which feminists had formerly viewed with discomfort as a piece of orientalizing exotica for the male gaze, and it engages, in Ockman's words, "notions of female spectatorship and 'feminine' taste that complicate assumptions about pleasure and power." For although the piece was commissioned as a gift for the queen's husband and envisioned as a pendant to the so-called *Sleeper of Naples*, an earlier Ingres painting in his collection, there are distinct differences between that frontal and conventionally langorous female nude painted for a male patron and this odalisque. Her inverted posture and clear gaze toward the viewer deprive that viewer of full visual access to and enjoyment of her body, a change attributable to an intervening female taste, which Ockman claims played an important role in shaping the art of this period.

Ockman suggests that "there was a pictorial language during this period that was created in large part by women," a dialogue among works women commissioned that enunciated their own tastes and interests over and above those of the diverse artists who painted the works. Although women like Paolina Borghese and Mme Récamier were made famous by their eroticized images in works by Canova and Gérard, respectively, Ockman leads us to see that these very sensualized images—and the "feminine," or anacreontic, taste they represented—though seemingly natural to women from an essentialist perspective, became culturally transgressive when women sponsored them, since "as soon as female agency acquired connotations of power and control—control over one's body, power over a state—the imagery itself constituted a threat." Ockman's interpretation resonates historically, both in the early modern and present periods. Recent scholars have pointed out a similar taste for sensual feminine imagery on the part of female patrons in sixteenth-century Italy,[26] and the political resistance to Judy Chicago's *Dinner Party* can similarly be understood as a reaction to the threat posed by female control of the imaged female body.

Influential writings of the 1980s, such as Janet Wolff's work on "the invisible *flâneuse*,"[27] have led to categorical assumptions in the feminist art-histor-ical literature about female disempowerment, assumptions that flattened what was in reality a far more complex social dynamic and that ignored or underestimated the resisted but inexorable emergence of female spectatorship in nineteenth-century consumer society. In "Selling, Seduction, and Soliciting the Eye: Manet's *Bar at the Folies-Bergère*," Ruth Iskin presents an interpretation of Manet's much contested painting that is rooted in the emerging culture of mass consumption and display in late-nineteenth-century Paris and that offers to the female spectator a position of agency denied by earlier feminist analyses. Replacing the notion of a single, mastering male gaze (fetishized in the feminist literature) with the notion of crowd spectatorship that included the active presence of women and the female gaze, Iskin invokes the "contesting codes of a multiplicity of gazes." She argues that far from being objectified or identified with consumer products, woman's "spectator/consumer status implied some measure of agency," reflected in the advertisements for department stores and upscale café-concerts that were increasingly designed to solicit their gaze. Iskin challenges what had become an orthodoxy in feminist analysis—in Griselda Pollock's description, the "spaces of femininity" and the middle-class woman's stifling confinement to the private sphere.[28] She confirms that respectable middle-class women did attend café-concerts (they are visible in the crowd at the Folies-Bergère), a venue that actively marketed to this audience. Iskin writes: "Women's visibility in visual representations of the period suggests that their presence in public was far more extensive than the oft-cited doctrine of separate spheres would have us believe."

Iskin also provides new tools for interpreting the *Bar*'s conflicting semiotic codes, using the perspectives of the mixed audience to explain the painting's multiple and contradictory points of view. Pointing to Manet's signature on a bottle that stands for sale on the bar, she posits Manet's identification with the barmaid and the "collapsed distinctions between painter, painting, and goods for sale at the bar." The way is thus open for us to consider the possibility that, as an artist in an increasingly commercialized art world, Manet might have identified with the female café worker and the ambiguity of her position in a situation where agency is undermined by commodification. This, too, complicates conventional notions, even feminist ones, of the relation between gender and power.

Studies such as those by Grigsby, Ockman, and Iskin present a picture of women's growing cultural power as viewers and consumers. And, as Iskin shows, in the later nineteenth century, women began to exercise consumer power in the real world, at the point where economics, fashion, and style intersect. Yet this was not an unqualified advance, in part because, as in the case of women's political assertions, such agency led to the production of cultural rhetoric designed to reinforce conservative positions about women's place. Also, when linked with each other, femininity, commodification, and consumerism could all acquire fatal downward mobility, especially when aligned with the gendered structures of artistic style (discussed below).

The death of the author, as good postmoderns know, is accompanied by the birth of the reader. In the 1990s, some feminist art historians have taken this liberating principle to mean that the interpreting reader, like the viewing subject, can be female as well as male. In her essay "New Encounters with *Les Demoiselles d'Avignon:* Gender, Race, and the Origins of Cubism," Anna Chave presents an alternative interpretation of an art-historical icon, which she deliberately grounds in her gendered difference as a female interpreting eye.

Here, some background may be useful. In a groundbreaking essay of 1973, Carol Duncan applied the tools of Marxism and feminism to identify the "femme fatale" and "new, primitive woman" archetypes that structure Pablo Picasso's *Demoiselles d'Avignon*, asserting that "no other modern work reveals more of the rock foundation of sexist anti-humanism or goes further and deeper to justify and celebrate the domination of woman by man."[29] Since then, efforts have abounded to redeem and recuperate this threatened icon and wellspring of the phallocentric modernist enterprise, and to preserve Picasso

as a cultural hero and restore him as a champion of individual freedom and creativity—reviving the very same avant-garde myth that Duncan's critique had unmasked. These efforts have ranged from Patricia Leighten's contention that Picasso's painting was an "anarchist manifesto" that sympathetically linked the plight of colonized Africans with that of European prostitutes and expressed outrage over the exploitation of both, to Tamar Garb's more recent consideration of the appreciative response to the *Demoiselles* by a single historical reader, the lesbian and male-identified writer Gertrude Stein. Stein's ability to empathize "with Picasso as a radical artist rather than the 'demoiselles' as victimised 'women'" is implicitly taken by Garb to counter and discredit earlier feminist readings of the painting's misogynist core and its ideological exclusion of women as agents from the mainstream of modernist production.[30]

Uniquely building on Duncan's feminist reading, Anna Chave privileges reception over production to offer a postmodern and postcolonial reading of the *Demoiselles*. Declining at the outset to explore Picasso's "intentions," she pits her own "unauthorized" reactions to the painting against those of its presumed core audience of heterosexual white males and removes from their control the cultural meanings and power of the image. Confronting the confusion and exaggerated fear with which the latter group has persistently responded to the *Demoiselles*, and attempting from her own position as a heterosexual feminist to identify with the painting's female protagonists, she characterizes and repositions the demoiselles not as subjugated victims but as ultimately powerful women who act "as lightning rods for *fear* of the empowerment of women and peoples of color." Following Homi Bhabha (and implicitly countering Leighten's argument), Chave characterizes Picasso's appropriation of sacred African masks as a disrespectful act of mimicry, a strategy initially deployed, according to Bhabha, to control and disempower colonized peoples. But, measured in terms of reception and by their ability over the years to instill a disproportionate amount of fear in male viewers, these "grotesque" masks may be seen to function ultimately, Chave suggests, as tools of empowerment for the painting's newly defined and critically repositioned female protagonists. By extension, also empowered is the female spectator, who is authorized by Chave to interpret pictures like the *Demoiselles* from the viewpoint of positions and values that are invoked but not championed in the painting, reading "against the grain" of intentionality so that the work of art might address larger segments of its wider audience.

In her essay, "The New Woman in Hannah Höch's Photomontages: Issues of Androgyny, Bisexuality, and Oscillation," Maud Lavin examines the art of Hannah Höch from the standpoint of female spectatorship. Höch's androgynous photomontages deliberately interrogated gender identities in 1920s Weimar Germany, where intense theoretical speculation about homosexuality was rampant. Yet, unlike contemporary androgynous imagery in art and film, Höch's art did not offer a masculinized image of women that might be understood within largely acceptable frameworks such as the New Woman, nor did she show women "improved" through masculinization, such as were seen in print media. Höch, who was in a lesbian relationship during this period, instead made images that "depict a pleasure in the movement between gender positions and a deliberate deconstruction of rigid masculine and feminine identities." Lavin explores Höch's use of irony and her bigendered references within the same composition, finding in her art an "oscillation between polarized positions of masculinity and femininity" and a shifting of subject-object positions. These, Lavin claims, are "fundamental conditions of female spectatorship." Because female viewers often experience anxiety when looking at images that present a choice between identifying with male or female characters, oscillation between the two positions can resolve that conflict, offering women "multiple pleasures," including "destabilization of the hierarchy itself."

Lesbians in particular, Lavin postulates, might find affirmation of identity in androgynous images. Yet lesbian agency, when overtly asserted, could meet silent resistance, as Lavin shows in her discussion of the film *Mädchen in Uniform*, whose producer and director were lesbian collaborators. Despite its explicitly lesbian content, the film was never reviewed or discussed in those terms, and was received instead as an anti-authoritarian protest against Prussian militarism. In Weimar culture, gender confusion was popular, but, as Michel Foucault warned, speaking about alternative sexualities may not be liberating but merely "repressive tolerance." Lavin speculates that *Mädchen in Uniform*'s "stereotypical representation of alternative sexuality" was a more limited strategy for liberalizing public attitudes than Höch's use of the principle of oscillation, which, by eliciting viewer participation from a fluidly gendered person, could be more effective "in linking gender subjectivity to nonhierarchical social change."

Though it effectively presents issues of both female agency and female spectatorship, Julie Cole's essay, "Claude Cahun, Marcel Moore, and the Collaborative Construction of a Lesbian Subjectivity," is appropriately juxtaposed with Lavin's, since both concern the work and reception of lesbian-identified artists. Claude Cahun (née Lucy Schwob), a French artist who has been associated with Surrealism, created a photographic series of so-called self-portraits in collaboration with her stepsister and lesbian partner Marcel Moore (Suzanne Malherbe). In most of these works, we see only Cahun's image, yet as Cole observes, since Moore took and presumably helped stage the photographs, she was equally involved in their creation. Because the photographs were not produced for public consumption but instead remained in the couple's private possession, Cole argues that they are best understood as the result of a collaborative project, and that the intended audience of that project was themselves alone.

In these photographs, which Cole explains to have been mistakenly connected with the goals and interests of the Surrealists, Cahun and Moore explore the performative nature of gender identity and play with gender ambiguity; they frequently use mirrored or doubled images, as if to emphasize the private and interactive nature of their collaboration. Despite the seeming innocence of their private expression, however, Cahun/Moore's representation of themselves can be understood as highly transgressive in a society that continuously monitored female imagery. In Cole's interpretation, Cahun made the subversive decision to appear in her only published "self-portrait" as a (masculinized) "monstrous distortion," who "flaunted her refusal to participate in a compulsively heterosexual culture, and announced her identity as lesbian without providing (straight male) viewers with the opportunity to appropriate, sexualize, or exoticize her lesbian body for their own purposes."

THE GENDERING OF STYLE

An important issue for feminist art history has been the hierarchical gendering of artistic styles. Traditional art history normatively concerns itself with style wars, such as that between drawing and color, which originated as a theoretical opposition in sixteenth-century Italy and resurfaced in subsequent periods, most famously in nineteenth-century France as an opposition of the partisans of the classicist Ingres (line) and the Romantic Delacroix (color). It has long been understood that power was at stake in this discourse, for proponents of one faction (usually drawing) proclaimed its hierarchic superiority over the other. Yet it remained for feminists to identify the fundamental role of gender in the status and value assigned to certain styles. In an essay in *The Expanding Discourse*, Patricia Reilly looked at the controversy of *disegno* versus *colore* in Italian Renaissance art theory from this perspective, noting the elevating association of line or design with masculinity and the stigmatizing association of color with femininity—a binary paradigm that invoked other weighted binaries, such as mind versus body, reason versus emotion, or culture versus nature.[31]

In this volume, several writers resume the discourse of gendered style in ways that deepen our understanding of its political power. In her essay, "The Gendering of Impressionism," Norma Broude examines the crucial role played by gender in the critical reception and art-historical reshaping of Western art history's most enduringly popular style. Challenging the equally enduring misinterpretation of Impressionism as an art that was motivated by a rational and scientifically based quest for optical realism (a reading still alive in art history textbooks today), Broude points to the Romantic roots of the Impressionist landscape painters, who prioritized light and color over drawing and whose approach to a female-identified natural world, she says, was responsive rather than aggressive, aiming not to control or "master" nature but "simply to fix upon canvas the artist's response to the stimulus that nature has provided."

At stake for Impressionism, Broude contends, ever since its late-nineteenth-century emergence in a world marked by the growing prestige of a masculine-identified, positivist science, has been the need to rescue the style from the cultural feminization of its origins in Romantic landscape painting and to create for it instead an identity endowed with the stereotypical attributes of masculinity. Asking why Impressionism, "an art that was based on the subjectivity of vision and that emphasized the expression of feeling and emotion generated by contact with nature, [came] to be seen in the twentieth century as an art of optical realism and 'scientific objectivity,' devoid of feeling," she proceeds to trace a dynamic pattern of cultural mythmaking and to show how the gendered identity of Impressionism was continually destabilized and reconfigured by partisans of subsequent styles.

It was the Symbolist artists and critics, she argues, who needed Impressionism to be their feminized Other, and who first attempted, in the 1890s, to codify the feminine gendering of the Impressionist style. Seizing upon earlier critics' efforts to justify the unorthodox aspects of the Impressionist style by linking them to scientific explanations of how the human eye works, the Symbolists recast gendered subjectivity in new terms. Turning away from the material world of nature and denigrating positivist science, they claimed for themselves the presumably superior (masculine) position of conceptual creativity, generated in the mind, as contrasted with the passive and mechanical (feminine) recording of mere sensory impressions.

But in the early twentieth century, as Impressionism gained commercial value and was collected by industrialists and entrepreneurs, it was reclaimed by the masculine realm, as a style suitably virile for its new category of advocates. Once more, Impressionism's presumed scientific affinities were trotted out, now joining the heroic metanarrative of modernism itself. In Broude's interpretation, the remasculinization of Impressionism in the early twentieth century was consonant with the agenda of modernist abstraction and with "art's withdrawal from the traditional arena of struggle with female nature and its safe removal to a 'higher' plane." Thus it was that Clement Greenberg could praise Monet's late work for its formalist impassivity, claiming it as the radical precursor to modernism in general and to Abstract Expressionism in particular.

In her essay, "Reconsidering the Stain: On Gender and the Body in Helen Frankenthaler's Painting," Lisa Saltzman takes up the next chapter, as it were. She identifies in the rhetoric that circulated around Abstract Expressionism a strategic intention to masculinize the well-known subjectivity of the Abstract Expressionist painters and to protect it from the taint of femininity. This was accomplished, in part, by exaggerating the differences between the male New York School painters and the female artists who breached their ranks in the postwar years, such as Helen Frankenthaler, Grace Hartigan, Lee Krasner, and Joan Mitchell. In the critical reception of Frankenthaler's work in particular, Saltzman finds a pervasive reliance upon bodily metaphors and gendered descriptions of her style to set her apart from her male colleagues. Thus Frankenthaler's innovative use of the "stain" was characterized in gendered terms, as though it were an act of nature lacking in creative control. She was described as passively and decoratively "staining the linen," while Jackson Pollock was typically described as "actively impregnating the virgin canvas." Although the forms and tech-

niques of Morris Louis were derived from those of Frankenthaler, his works were nevertheless differentiated as virile and supremely masculine, and his "feminine delicacy" was valued and applauded as a sort "that only a man could produce."[32]

Saltzman sees essentialized gender difference as an unmarked but necessary underpinning of the theoretical rhetoric of high modernist painting. She notes that in post–World War II America, when the dissolution of rigid boundaries between the sexes produced anxieties in both art and life, one could find an urgency expressed in art criticism to maintain aesthetic and qualitative differences between the male and female artists of the New York School. Saltzman observes: "Feminist readings of social and cultural history have sought to demonstrate that when a threat to patriarchal society is perceived, an attempt is made to preserve the social order, to reconstitute its boundaries and hierarchies."

Saltzman further distinguishes the original critics of Abstract Expressionism, who used fluidity and bodily metaphors in order to segregate and denigrate the abstract paintings produced by women, from later French feminist theorists such as Luce Irigaray, who celebrate and valorize these differences. She also contrasts the anxious responses of the original critics of the 1950s—who faced a shifting cultural terrain and sought to preserve the gendered social order by imposing binary coding and the metaphorics of the body on New York School painting—with contemporary abstract practice at the turn of the twenty-first century, which self-consciously invokes the body and its essential fluids, she says, in order to emphasize human similarities and deconstruct gender difference.

The essays by Broude and Saltzman together create a picture of successive modernist styles marked by constantly shifting gender identifications. Yet as Broude notes,

While the particular phenomena to which patriarchal culture attaches masculine and feminine labels may change over time, what remains constant is the privileging of whatever happens at the moment to hold the masculine—

usually the "objective"—position. Romanticism and modernism problematized this traditional arrangement by regendering subjectivity, predictably privileging masculine subjectivity over feminine subjectivity, but nonetheless conferring new validity upon subjectivity as a cultural position.

In "Minimalism and Biography," Anna Chave considers the gendering of subjectivity in personal as well as stylistic terms. She addresses the mythic construction of Minimalism in the critical literature as a cool, anti-expressive, and impersonal practice to expose its gender-laden bases and biases. She points in particular to the critical reception of Robert Morris and Carl Andre, artists widely credited with inaugurating Minimalism, which has consistently spared them the biographical treatment that would have threatened their mythic status. The opposite has been true of the reception of women artists, such as the sculptor Eva Hesse and modern dance pioneers Simone Forti and Yvonne Rainer, who have been treated critically as peripheral to the Minimalist movement. Asserting the existence of "multiple Minimalisms," Chave invokes biography to reverse these critical constructions and unmask their creation by self-interested individuals, critics implicated in very personal terms with the male Minimalist artists whose reputations they built. She proposes "to turn biography to oppositional ends, exploring what has been at stake, and for whom, in the exempting of certain artists from biographical scrutiny," and in the mythic creation of the Minimalist hero as a man "without a body or a biography, and certainly without any private history."

In the 1960s, the material and the social were elevated over the individual and the subjective, while the expressive and the personal were denigrated as feminine. Marxist criticism aligned itself with Minimalist initiatives and poststructuralist art criticism, in an extreme separation of the personal and the social (which feminists in the early 1970s would counter with the insight that the personal *is* the political). But, as Chave points out, although this critical paradigm shift should theoretically have led to the unseating of the artist/hero, male Minimalist artists were no less heroized than their predecessors in the art-historical canon had been.

Women associated with Minimalism, by contrast, were persistently tainted by the charge of excessive subjectivity. Even though Hesse used the grid and the cube, seriality and repetition, industrial materials and methods—all the elements of a Minimalist-identified practice—the personal dimensions of her art nevertheless exacted a critical price and ensured her secondary status as an artist. Hesse's protofeminist art and metaphoric, tactile forms, unlike the alienating, distancing, and antimetaphorical strategies of the canonical Minimalists, were "more idiosyncratic, more suggestive of the body . . . more expressive . . . more aligned with values the society codes as feminine." Chave argues for the innovational priority and greater influence of Hesse's sculpture, and of the dance constructions and theatrical props of Forti (Morris's first wife), in order to correct the "critical asymmetry that allows [Morris's] production to figure as an impersonal, towering cultural force while Forti's pathbreaking experiments are eclipsed to little more than footnotes, and Hesse's hugely influential enterprise is still considered liable to being depreciated as 'purely personal.'"

The issue of gendered expectations in both style and subject has produced minefields for many women artists. In this volume, two essays in particular demonstrate how some of them have negotiated this problem. In the nineteenth century, when line and color were widely regarded as gendered elements in art, Mary Cassatt's strong draftsmanship challenged the notion of what a woman artist was supposed to be biologically capable of achieving. Like the women in her 1893 *Modern Woman* mural, Cassatt openly desired and pursued autonomy, success, and fame as a professional in the public sphere; but as a respectable upper-middle-class woman, in an era of dynamic social change, she had nevertheless to accommodate her era's notions of proper femininity and woman's "natural" place. In "Mary Cassatt: Modern Woman or the Cult of True Womanhood?" Norma Broude traces Cassatt's efforts to negotiate these conflicting models and recognizes in the personal and professional strategies she deployed a "pattern of resistance on the one hand and simultaneous complicity on the other." This pattern, she observes, was "typical of many Euro-American women artists and intellectuals who achieved fairly notable positions during the nineteenth century," and it is a pattern that is shown in these essays to be equally applicable to the situation of women artists such as Sofonisba Anguissola in the sixteenth century and Marie Laurencin in the twentieth.

Thus it is that, in Cassatt's art, striking images of modern woman's agency share the stage with repeated images of mothers and children, many in traditional Madonna and Child and Holy Family configurations—a genre to which the artist turned (after initial reluctance) from the 1880s on, and for which she received widespread approval. Broude examines and challenges the essentialist assumptions that underpin the successful reception of Cassatt's signature images of mothers and children, both in her day, when they were regarded as natural expressions of the artist's femininity, and in our own, when they have come to be interpreted, additionally, as psychological projections of this childless and unmarried woman artist's own experiences as a daughter. Characterizing Cassatt as an ambitious, "self-conscious and skillful player in a game of professionalism and identity that was still constructed in the nineteenth century to exclude women," Broude presents the mother and child images as a calculated, market-driven choice, an emblem of Cassatt's professional ambition and agency, and she asks: "Why can we not consider the possibility that, in painting mothers and children, Cassatt functioned as a male artist might have done, looking at but not necessarily identifying with a subject that was 'Other' to 'Self'?" "For Mary Cassatt," she concludes, "was an artist and a woman who sought to challenge the phallic public order by actively laying claim to it. To ignore this as the foun-

dation of the choices that supported her work and her life is to practice a binary essentialism that co-opts her and denies her her true voice."

In "The 'Strength of the Weak' as Portrayed by Marie Laurencin," Bridget Elliott takes on an artist who was scorned both in her time and after for the signs of femininity she projected: "Grace and charm rather than genius, narcissistic self-absorption, surface without substance." Along with Coco Chanel, Colette, and Valentine Tessier, Laurencin and her work "have been figured as the feminized bodies of commodified mass culture," "soft and saleable," to be sharply contrasted with the image of a pure, scientific, and intense (masculine) avant-garde. Elliott does not claim that Laurencin was really a more avant-garde artist than we had thought, but rather points out ways in which she cannot be explained by familiar feminist models. She neither advanced a transgressive *écriture/peinture feminine* nor stood entirely outside a canonical modernism that excluded women.

Laurencin's extreme cultivation of feminine identity, through her dress and the decor of her home and in her depictions of "active and relatively unfragmented female subjects," Elliott argues, should not be viewed as naively essentialist and compromising, but instead as "tactical incursions into avant-garde space." Indeed, Laurencin insisted that her art was both "thoroughly modern *and* completely feminine," neatly skewering a familiar binary. A contemporary critic, Dorothy Todd, characterized her as both feminine and feminist, "probably the strangest feminist the world has ever seen."

Elliott shows that Marie Laurencin had a "constantly shifting and ambivalent relation to the Cubist avant-garde," even as her femininity was exploited by both the artist herself and her critics. In Elliott's view, the alleged weakness of Laurencin's femininity proved to be an unexpected source of strength and cultural resistance. Her extreme cultivation of her feminine identity fit into some definitions of modernity that were not at odds with femininity—Apollinaire, for example, encouraged artists of both sexes to "take up the new decorative aesthetic and its commercial opportunities." But to other dedicated modernists, it was Laurencin's insistent and commercially successful engagement with the decorative and the fashionable that was threatening. Elliott contrasts her business acumen, her ability to call the tune, with (in Laurencin's scornful description) Picasso's childlike toadying to dealers. Laurencin's slyly subversive tactics brought her a certain immunity from criticism, as well as a positioning vis-à-vis the avant-garde that Elliott connects with Michel de Certeau's "tactical indeterminacy, where alternative meanings slip into the system under the guise of social conformity."

INTERSECTIONS
OF GENDER AND ETHNICITY

In the late twentieth century, as globalism brought multicultural self-consciousness to Western Europe and North America, the Western perception of the gendered binary of male and female became increasingly complicated by the factor of cultural difference. In the context of this book, the Chinese American artist Hung Liu and the Iranian-born artist Shirin Neshat are appropriately considered as artists who identify deeply with their countries of origin, yet whose point of view and strategies for representation are derived in large measure from their experiences of living and working in the United States. Each of these artists has been deeply engaged with her native culture—indeed, it is for each her primary subject matter—but from a perspective distinctly outside that culture, whose repressive attitudes and practices toward women her Western context permits her to critique. At the same time, these artists' interjection of Chinese and Iranian cultural issues and practices into Western discourse offers to Western women a perspective on themselves as well. As Hung Liu has put it, "I am an artist from China and in China the terms by which I am defined here make little sense."

In her essay, "Cultural Collisions: Identity and History in the Work of Hung Liu," Allison Arieff examines the liminal position and art of Hung Liu, who was born in China in 1948 and spent her early adult years as an art student under a Communist regime that fostered the use of an officially sanctioned Soviet Realist art for propaganda purposes. Constrained by a system that did not value individual creativity, Liu came to the United States in 1984. Developing her art and thought in the context of Western modernism and postmodernism, she has combined photographic images and other contemporary materials and practices with traditionally sanctioned Chinese art practices (such as copying) to express the collision she feels in her own person between ancient Chinese tradition and modern Western society, and to use her art to make that cultural clash vivid in our eyes. As she puts it, in words used as text in one of her pieces: "Five-thousand-year-old culture on my back. Late-twentieth-century world in my face."

Arieff examines Hung Liu's full frontal images that foreground the practice of female footbinding—to Western feminist eyes the most sorrowful and outrageous practice of traditional Chinese misogyny—a practice that was meant to have been but was not eliminated with Communist reform. Yet Liu also critiques Western representational practices by replicating the poses of odalisques in figures who recline in Chinese dress, seeking at the same time to empower the Chinese women she depicts by giving them a confrontational gaze. In doing this, Arieff argues, Liu has taken up the agenda encouraged by feminist art historians—to counteract the ideological power that gender-differentiated representation wields in culture by giving depicted females an agency and subjectivity that would replace their pervasive objectification in images.

Because Hung Liu has been concerned with race as much as gender in the objectification of Asian women, Arieff considers her strategies for countering "Orientalism," or the projection of Western fantasies upon its binary opposite, the East, which in the colonialist mentality was perceived as inferior. It is a difficult issue to mediate for one in Liu's position, caught between known Western stereotypes about the East and a reality she no longer knows directly. Yet one might also say that she is uniquely positioned to do so. Liu has used "found" photographs to re-present images of Asian women as seen through Western photographers' eyes, adducing these for her American-born audiences so that they may recognize how they have come to accept a construction of an Orient that never was. The project of Hung Liu and other Asian American artists has been to confront race and gender stereotypes through images that embody the perspectives of their bicultural experience.[33]

Shirin Neshat, an Iranian-born artist and filmmaker who has lived in exile in the United States since 1974, and in New York since 1983, sees herself similarly as a hybrid, living between two cultures. "I can never call any place home, I will forever be in a state of in-between," she has said, yet she also emphasizes that "my work reflects who I am, as a person who is bi-cultural . . . someone who loves and hates both worlds."[34] John Ravenal addresses this central feature of Neshat's identity in his essay in this volume, "Shirin Neshat: Double Vision." It was the culture shock she experienced when revisiting Iran after its transformation into a fundamentalist Islamic state in the 1980s, Ravenal explains, that triggered Neshat's decision to represent women in Islamic culture in photography and film. Profiting from her liminal position, like Hung Liu, Shirin Neshat does not aim for a more "accurate" representation of Muslim women; rather, she explores existing stereotypes to reveal their constructed, artificial nature.[35]

Neshat's films deal with binary oppositions between masculine and feminine, expressed in visually powerful images of groups—women in black *chador*s, men in black and white—that move through architectural spaces or stark landscapes of shore and sea in patterns that articulate gendered power structures. Rituals are evoked, whether Islamic or generic, only to be subverted. *Rapture*, for example, begins with gendered expectations—active men at the center, passive women at the margins—then reverses. Gradually, the women assume agency, speaking, interrupting, moving out to sea in boats, while the men's world contracts. They act from a position of power, yet, as Ravenal observes, "[The men] are masters of their structure, but their ardent embrace of its boundaries suggests imprisonment in its confines." It is the women who are able to rise to meaningful action. Ravenal quotes Neshat's explanation: "This all ties

back to what I believe is a type of feminism that comes from such cultures; on a daily basis the resistance you sense from the women is far higher than that of the men. Why? Because the women are the ones who are under extreme pressure; they are repressed and therefore they are more likely to resist and ultimately to break free."[36]

In *Rapture*, the audience is positioned between two projectors, bringing Western viewers into a dialogue with their Iranian female and male counterparts, who sometimes seem to stare at them, putting the audience under scrutiny. The very act of watching the film carries ideological implications, for, as Neshat points out, "You decide which side you are going to look at and which to deny."[37] As with Hung Liu, Western audiences are prompted to consider the social manipulation of gender roles in their own culture through the reflecting mirror of another. Even the vaunted superior position of women in Western democracies may come under scrutiny, for Neshat's lens is wide-angle: she is concerned not just with Islamic societies but, more generally, with "what it is like to live under repression and be a woman." Although her avowed subject is women, she emphasizes that it is not her tactic to alienate men from her work, and indeed, one writer has advanced the idea that Neshat is a "visual theorist of the body" seen through female eyes; "as she gives agency to the feminine, the masculine is re/articulated."[38]

The commitments of Hung Liu and Shirin Neshat to feminist issues in a multicultural world, and in particular their critique of their native cultures from the position of Western values, take on additional political significance at the present time, when the principle of cultural diversity is sometimes claimed to outweigh the universal rights of women. The question has been posed provocatively by Susan Moller Okin in a book entitled *Is Multiculturalism Bad for Women?*[39] Okin's own answer is yes, when the "group rights" of minority cultures struggling to preserve their own values and practices (such as polygamy or cliterodectomy) are allowed to take precedence over the human rights of women who are damaged by those cultural practices. Yet other contributors to Okin's volume, such as Homi Bhabha and Azizah Y. al-Hibri, dismiss her Western liberal position as a patronizing, colonialist mentality that shares patriarchalist views of the Other and/or fails to recognize the different forms of feminism to be found in Islamic countries and within Islam itself. The tension between feminism and multiculturalism is all the more troubling to feminists when it is perceived as a gendered construct, with feminism now in the masculinist position. This subject, which is gaining urgency in today's world, may seem to take us far afield from the history of art, but it also brings us back to some of the touchstones of this volume: the manipulation of history by the gendering of style or conceptual entities; the division of reality into binarized opposites of Self and Other; and the conflict between essentializing and social constructionist ideals.

RECLAIMING FEMALE AGENCY: A STRATEGY FOR THE FUTURE

The essays in this volume offer a nuanced and critical view of some of the foundational premises of earlier feminist art history. Yet, collectively, they also demonstrate the existence of a continuing feminist position in art-historical scholarship, one that resists the postmodern effort to absorb and neutralize feminism by welcoming its fragmentation into multiple "others." Whereas we used to say that feminist and "mainstream" art historical approaches should be integrated, it now seems more urgent to ensure that feminism is not assimilated and flattened out into just another postmodernism. For it is feminism's difference, we now recognize, that allows it to monitor a culture that is still not neutral or impartial about gender.

Within a patriarchy that has not yet fully ended, woman's alleged inferiority has been inscribed in art in depressingly consistent terms. (In this sense, the charge of essentialism leveled at early feminists might better be aimed at masculinists of limited imagination.) Women who have resisted or rebelled against their characterization have necessarily operated within the terms of the existing discourse. Their responses—whether political (as in feminist movements) or aesthetic (feminist art movements, but also individual expressive gestures)—could be seen as forming an interest group position, opposed to that formed by and for men. From the female perspective, male culture's continuing suppression of female agency has been a negative and repressive force (though from the male standpoint, a utilitarian and positive one). In the traditional art-historical narrative, repressive forces are identified and catalogued, usually as interest groups that resist change: in the sixteenth century, a newly puritanical Counter-Reformation Church took a stand against libertine currents in Renaissance humanism; nineteenth-century art academies opposed the avant-garde. If it is commonplace to speak in art history of factional interaction in the political, theological, and aesthetic spheres, why should we not also trace the interaction of gender interest groups in the discourse of art?

Such analysis would give us a way to understand cultural repression as a reaction to a power threat: whether it comes from women like Marie-Antoinette or Marie de' Medici, or a style like Impressionism—in each case, men or a masculine principle is undermined by a danger from "the feminine," and in each case the response is the same: to preserve masculine power by imposing negativizing gender stereotypes on the Other and putting it/her at a safe distance, in a lesser category. This gambit has worked for a long time, and the self-claimed masculine control of culture has been so successful that many women including high-profile artists such as Helen Frankenthaler and Georgia O'Keeffe—have not wished to be perceived as part of a female interest group, reluctant to be associated with a subgroup countenanced by the patriarchy as lesser. But it is one thing to find (and one always does) individual women eager to be on the side of power, like "trusties" in the prison system, who are naive enough to believe that they can personally escape the limiting category *Woman* by identifying with and supporting patriarchal values. It is considerably more destructive when this form of self-interest motivates and clouds women's professional judgments, leading them to espouse and enunciate such patent nonsense as the idea that only males are capable of using symbolic language, that females are psychologically crippled from birth, or that femininity is socially constructed while masculinity is innately the default gender for the human race.

Poststructuralism, by insisting on the impossibility of fixing meaning outside language, or even of getting from here to there, and certainly by teaching us to distrust metanarratives, has paralyzed our original feminist effort to challenge standing art-historical accounts that were narrow, distorted, or inaccurate. Thirty years later, many of art history's metanarratives are still in place, and the real cultural power that women have demonstrably wielded continues to be suppressed in history's masculinist accounts. An important result of the most recent decade of work in feminist art history has been to call *all* of our metanarratives into question, even feminist ones, but most significantly, to expose the continuing masculinism of interpretation, which, even in the face of contradictory evidence, has ensured that masculinist metanarratives tend to survive or become reimposed.

Nevertheless, the right strategy for feminists now, in our view, is not to complain that we don't have access to cultural power, but simply to recognize and claim the power and agency that women have had and continue to exercise. What needs now to be further explored is the interplay between women's cultural assertion and the erasure or resistance that both followed and preceded it. We must rebalance the larger picture, describing a cultural dynamic that consisted not of men's cultural dominance and women's occasional achievements, but rather of a steady and ongoing participation of women in culture, as active agents at every level—from artistic creation to patronage and reception, and as a conceptual force that threatened a fragile and sometimes desperate masculine hegemony. In order to reclaim women's history, we will need to rewrite men's history.

NOTES

1. For our earlier discussion of the relationship between feminist art history and foundational poststructuralist writers, see "Introduction," in Norma Broude and Mary D. Garrard, eds., *The Expanding Discourse* (New York: HarperCollins, 1992).

2. For analogous developments in the fields of literary criticism and history, see Barbara Johnson, "Introduction," in *The Feminist Difference: Literature, Psychoanalysis, Race, and Gender* (Cambridge, Mass.: Harvard University Press, 1998); and Joan Hoff, "The Pernicious Effects of Poststructuralism," in Diane Bell and Renate Klein, eds., *Radically Speaking: Feminism Reclaimed* (North Melbourne, Australia: Spinifex Press, 1996), 393–412. Hoff argues vigorously that poststructuralism has been "no friend" of feminism in numerous ways, especially through the ahistoricism of its theoretical and linguistic turn. She locates a precedent for the ability of masculinist discourses such as poststructualism to paralyze feminist agendas in the observation of Carroll Smith-Rosenberg that women in the 1920s and 1930s, especially literary figures and psychoanalysts, "stopped speaking to each other in a common language," rejecting their own original intention to challenge trendy scientific and Freudian terminology in feminist terms and adopting these constructs instead (Hoff, 410–11).

3. Lisa Tickner, "Feminism, Art History, and Sexual Difference," *Genders* 3 (1988): 92–128.

4. Tickner, "Feminism, Art History, and Sexual Difference," 106; Griselda Pollock, "Vision, Voice and Power," *Block* 6 (1982): 10. Although Tickner discussed three different feminist methodologies in her article, in categories of sexual difference adapted from Michèle Barrett, her own sympathies with positional difference and difference explained by psychoanalysis were clear.

5. Tickner, "Feminism, Art History, and Sexual Difference," 102.

6. Conspicuous among the anti-essentialist feminist writers in the 1980s was Chris Weedon, *Feminist Practice and Poststructuralist Theory* (Oxford: Blackwell, 1987).

7. For example, Shulamith Firestone, writing in 1970, said that there cannot be a truly female point of view in a male culture (from *The Dialectic of Sex*, quoted in Hilary Robinson, *Feminism-Art-Theory: An Anthology 1968–2000* [Oxford: Blackwell, 2001], 15).

8. Diana Fuss, *Essentially Speaking: Feminism, Nature, and Difference* (New York: Routledge, 1989), ch. 1.

9. Ibid., 61. It was Stephen Heath who suggested that "the risk of essence may have to be taken" ("Difference," *Screen* 19 [1978]: 99, quoted by Fuss, 18). Despite Irigaray's conspicuous claiming of an essential feminine, many writers have attempted, in Jan Campbell's description, to "rescue her from an essentialist collapse into biological or ontological notions of the body" (Jan Campbell, *Arguing with the Phallus: Feminist, Queer and Postcolonial Theory, A Psychoanalytic Contribution* [London: Zed Books, 2000], 116–18), a fact that reveals the continuing danger of "essentialism" in postmodern perceptions. By now, a number of other writers have pricked the bubble of anti-essentialist positioning; see especially Somer Brodribb, *Nothing Mat(t)ers: A Feminist Critique of Postmodernism* (Melbourne: Spinifex Press, 1992).

10. Judith Butler, *Gender Trouble: Feminism and the Subversion of Identity* (New York: Routledge, 1990), and *Bodies That Matter: On the Discursive Limits of "Sex"* (New York: Routledge, 1994).

11. Homi Bhabha, *The Location of Culture* (London: Routledge, 1994). See also the useful analysis by Campbell, *Arguing with the Phallus*, ch. 7, esp. 194.

12. Epifanio San Juan Jr., *Beyond Postcolonial Theory* (New York: St. Martin's Press, 1998).

13. Norma Broude and Mary D. Garrard, *Feminism and Art History: Questioning the Litany* (New York: Harper and Row, 1982); Broude and Garrard, *Expanding Discourse*.

14. See Fredrika H. Jacobs, *Defining the Renaissance* Virtuosa*: Women Artists and the Language of Art History and Criticism* (Cambridge: Cambridge University Press, 1997).

15. See Helen Weston, "The Corday-Marat Affair: No Place for a Woman," in *Jacques-Louis David's Marat*, ed. William Vaughan and Helen Weston (Cambridge: Cambridge University Press, 2000), 128–52. Weston expands upon part of the argument first advanced by Rand (whom she fails to acknowledge or name), but takes the position that Corday was ultimately complicit in her own erasure.

16. There have been numerous feminist critics of Freud, but especially important early figures were Karen Horney, Melanie Klein, and more recently, Nancy Chodorow, who have each questioned the centrality of the phallus in Freud's theory, and offered nonmasculinist models of child development.

17. Useful compendiums are Susan Seller, ed., *The Hélène Cixous Reader* (London: Routledge, 1994); Margaret Whitford, ed., *The Irigaray Reader* (Oxford: Blackwell, 1991); and Toril Moi, ed., *The Kristeva Reader* (Oxford: Blackwell, 1986). See also Jane Gallop, *The Daughter's Seduction: Feminism and Psychoanalysis* (Ithaca, N.Y.: Cornell University Press, 1982), and *Thinking through the Body* (New York: Columbia University Press, 1988); Nancy Chodorow, *Feminism and Psychoanalytic Theory* (New Haven, Conn.: Yale University Press, 1990); Teresa Brennan, ed., *Between Feminism and Psychoanalysis* (London: Routledge, 1990); and Richard Feldstein and Judith Roof, eds., *Feminism and Psychoanalysis* (Ithaca, N.Y.: Cornell University Press, 1990).

18. On *psych et po*, see Christine Delphy, "Les Origines du mouvement de libération des femmes en France," *Nouvelles Questions Feministes* 16, 17, 18 (1991): 137–48; and [Delphy], "French Feminism: An Imperialist Invention," in Bell and Klein, *Radically Speaking*, 383–92. In the latter, Delphy criticizes Americans' blind-faith adoption of "French feminism," as does Laura Cottingham in "Just a Sketch of What a Feminist Art, or Feminism, Could or Ever Did Mean before or after Whatever Is Implied by the Present," in Susan Bee and Mira Schor, eds., *M/E/A/N/I/N/G: An Anthology of Artists' Writings, Theory, and Criticism* (Durham, N.C.: Duke University Press, 2000), 77 and note 4. Writers for the Britist film journal *Screen*, including leading feminists such as Griselda Pollock, drew heavily on Lacanian psychoanalytic theory. An exception is Stephen Heath's critique of Lacan's masculinist ideology ("Difference," *Screen* 19 [1978]: 50–112). More recently, Pollock has invoked Bracha Lichtenbeg Ettinger's idea of Matrix to suggest that "the feminine" might be thought of as a "site of resistance to the existing phallic order of the Symbol"; in this theory, however, Pollock explains that Matrix is not postulated as "the opposite of the Phallus; it is rather a supplementary perspective" (Pollock, *Differencing the Canon: Feminist Desire and the Writing of Art's Histories* [London: Routledge, 1999], 210–13.

19. Dorothy Seiberling, "The Female View of Erotica," *New York Times*, 11 February 1974, cited in Lucy R. Lippard, "Louise Bourgeois: From the Inside Out," *Artforum*, March 1975, 31.

20. Alice A. Jardine, "Gynesis" (1982), in *Critical Theory since 1965*, ed. Hazard Adams and Leroy Searle (Tallahassee: Florida State University Press, 1986), 564.

21. Julia Kristeva, *Revolution in Poetic Language* (New York: Columbia University Press, 1984); see also Campbell, *Arguing with the Phallus*, 102–108.

22. Roland Barthes, "The Death of the Author," in *Image, Music, Text*, essays selected and trans. Stephen Heath (New York: Hill and Wang, 1977). See also Mieke Bal and Norman Bryson, "Semiotics and Art History," *Art Bulletin* 73 (1991): 174–208.

23. Bal and Bryson, "Semiotics and Art History," 183.

24. A groundbreaking introduction to what has become a large category of feminist analysis was Patricia Mainardi, "Quilts: The Great American Art," in *Questioning the Litany: Feminism and Art History*, ed. Norma Broude and Mary D. Garrard (New York: Harper and Row, 1982), ch. 17.

25. Jaynie Anderson, "Rewriting the History of Art Patronage," *Renaissance Studies* 10 (1996): 129–38, introduces a group of papers on female patronage in the fourteenth to sixteenth centuries, and provides a useful overview. She gives evidence that 10 percent of Renaissance patronage came from women, mostly widows and nuns. See also Catherine King, "Medieval and Renaissance Matrons, Italian-Style," *Zeitschrift für Kunstgeschichte* 55 (1992): 372–93; [Catherine King], *Renaissance Women Patrons: Wives and Widows in Italy, c. 1300–1550* (Manchester: Manchester University Press, 1998); Cynthia Lawrence, ed., *Women and Art in Early Modern Europe: Patrons, Collectors and Connoisseurs* (University Park: Pennsylvania University Press, 1997); and David Wilkins and Sheryl Reiss, eds., *Beyond Isabella: Secular Women Patrons of Art in Renaissance Italy* (Kirksville, Mo.: Truman State University, 2001).

In several important articles, Carolyn Valone has documented some fifty sixteenth-century Roman women active as architectural patrons: "Roman Matrons as Patrons: Various Views of the Cloister Wall," in *The Crannied Wall: Women, Religion and the Arts in Early Modern Europe*, ed. Craig Monson (Ann Arbor: University of Michigan Press, 1992); "Piety and Patronage: Women and the Early Jesuits," in *Creative Women in Medieval and Early Modern Italy: A Religious and Artistic Renaissance*, ed. E. Ann Matter and John Coakley (Philadelphia: University of Pennsylvania Press, 1994), 157–84; and "Women on the Quirinal Hill: Patronage in Rome, 1560–1630," *Art Bulletin* 76 (1994): 129–46.

26. See Marjorie Och, "Vittoria Colonna and the Commission for a *Mary Magdalene* by Titian," and Mary Vaccaro, "Dutiful Widows: Female Patronage and Two Marian Altarpieces by Parmigianino," both articles in Wilkins and Reiss, *Beyond Isabella*.

27. Janet Wolff, "The Invisible Flâneuse: Women and the Literature of Modernity," *Theory, Culture, and Society* 2–3 (1985); reprinted in Janet Wolff, *Feminine Sentences: Essays on Women and Culture* (Berkeley: University of California Press, 1990), 34–50.

28. Griselda Pollock, "Modernity and the Spaces of Femininity," in *Vision and Difference: Femininity, Feminism and the Histories of Art* (London: Routledge, 1988), 50–90; reprinted in Broude and Garrard, *The Expanding Discourse*, 245–67.

29. Carol Duncan, "Virility and Domination in Early Twentieth-Century Vanguard Painting," in Broude and Garrard, *Feminism and Art History*, 305.

30. Patricia Leighten, "The White Peril and L'Art Nègre: Picasso, Primitivism, and Anti-Colonialism," *Art Bulletin* 72 (December 1990): 609–30; Tamar Garb, "'To Kill the Nineteenth Century': Sex and Spectatorship with Gertrude and Pablo," in *Picasso's "Les Demoiselles d'Avignon,"* ed. Christopher Green (Cambridge: Cambridge University Press, 2001), 55–76; this quote, 59.

31. Patricia L. Reilly, "The Taming of the Blue: Writing Out Color in Renaissance Theory," in Broude and Garrard, *The Expanding Discourse*, ch. 4.

32. This particularly deft appropriation of female subjectivity, now recast as a male virtue, is a good example of what Elaine Showalter and others have called the "Tootsie syndrome," after the film in which Dustin Hoffman, dressed as a woman, proved himself a "better" woman than real ones; see Hoff, in *Radically Speaking*, 400.

33. See Elaine H. Kim, "'Bad Women': Asian American Visual Artists Hanh thi Pham, Hung Liu, and Yong Soon Min," *Feminist Studies* 22 (Fall 1996): 573–602.

34. The first of these quotes comes from Susan Horsburgh, "Middle East Daily," *Time Europe*, 31 January 2001 (online at www.time.com/time/europe/webonly/mideast/2000/08/neshat.html); the second quote comes from an interview with Neshat by Feri

Daftari, in the Seventh Annual Artists' Interviews, College Art Association conference, New York, 21 February 2003.

35. Igor Zabel, "Women in Black," *Art Journal* 60 (2001): 17–25; this citation, 17.

36. Arthur Danto, "Shirin Neshat," *Bomb* 73 (Fall 2000): 65.

37. Neshat interview, College Art Association, 2003.

38. Hamid Dashabi, "Bordercrossings: Shirin Neshat's Body of Evidence," in *Shirin Neshat*, exhibition catalogue, Castello di Rivoli Museo d'Arte Contemporanea, Rivoli-Torino, 30 January–5 May 2002 (Milan: Edizioni Charta, 2002), 59.

39. Susan Moller Okin, ed., *Is Multiculturalism Bad for Women?* (Princeton, N.J.: Princeton University Press, 1999), 9–24.

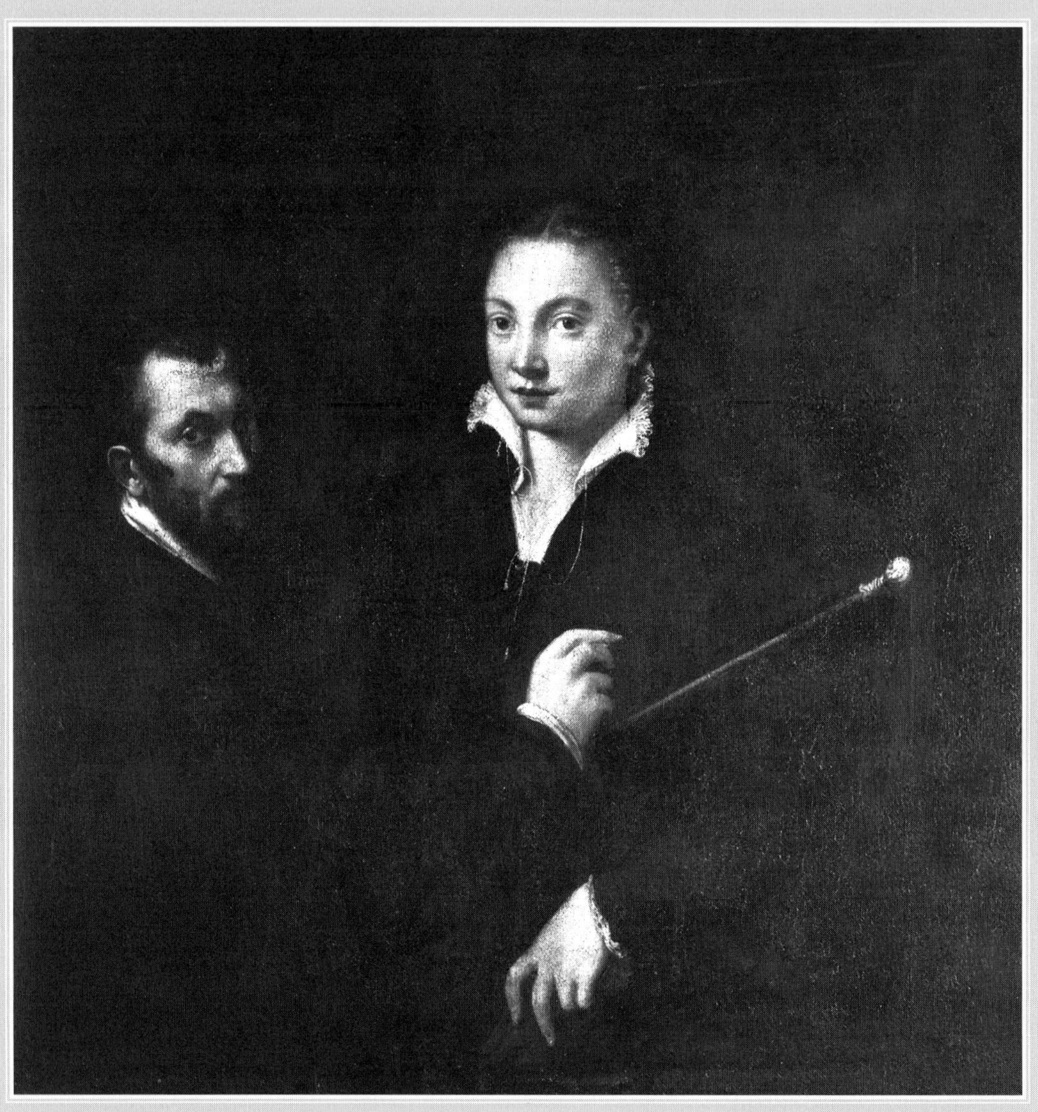

1

HERE'S LOOKING AT ME

Sofonisba Anguissola and the Problem of the Woman Artist

Mary D. Garrard

AN UNUSUAL PORTRAIT by Sofonisba Anguissola gained new prominence from its illustration in color in Whitney Chadwick's *Women, Art, and Society* (1990). Chadwick claimed of the portrait in question, *Bernardino Campi Painting Sofonisba Anguissola* (fig. 1.1), that in presenting herself in the guise of a portrait being painted by her teacher, Anguissola produced "the first historical example of the woman artist consciously collapsing the subject-object position."[1] Chadwick's observation opens up the possibility of understanding the painting in a new way, for she points to the peculiar conflation of subject and object that uniquely befell women artists in the Renaissance and complicates their art, especially their self-portraits. From this starting point, I will here explore the form of self-presentation offered by Anguissola in the Siena portrait and several other works in the context of a fundamental problem for the Renaissance female artist: the differentiation of herself as artist (the subject position) from herself as trope and theme for the male artist (the object position).

The double portrait of Anguissola and Campi is a prime example of the artist's vaunted ability to create what Vasari called "breathing likenesses," images of persons who "appear alive and lacking speech only."[2] The two figures emerge from a dark void, their rosy flesh modeled in a warm light, caught in an arrested moment that is heightened by the double set of penetrating gazes aimed at the viewer. Drawing us into their own psychological space and time, the figures offer a singularly effective example of the "speaking likeness," a rhetorical genre that originated in antiquity and extended, in the Renaissance humanist tradition, from Donatello's *Zuccone* (whose maker implored the statue to "speak, speak") to John Singleton Copley's portraits (of which John Adams wrote that "you can scarcely help discoursing with them, asking questions and receiving answers").[3] The genre of the psychologically engaging subject found special application in northern Italy in the sixteenth century in the work of artists such as Lotto, Savoldo, Anguissola, and Moroni.

But although the barrier between viewer and viewed is dissolved in the Siena painting through the rapport established across the picture plane, it is not entirely accurate to say that the subject-object relationship is collapsed. Such a conflation does occur in a straightforward self-portrait by Anguissola, her

Figure 1.1. Sofonisba Anguissola, *Bernardino Campi Painting Sofonisba Anguissola*, late 1550s. Oil on canvas. Pinacoteca Nazionale, Siena. (Photo: Alinari/Art Resource, New York.)

earliest securely dated self-portrait in Vienna, painted in 1554. Here the artist's dual self-presentation as painter and model is emphasized by the inscription in the book she holds, at once an identity tag and a signature, which reads: SOPHONISBA ANGUISSOLA VIRGO SE IPSAM FECIT 1554.[4] In the Siena canvas, however, which is signed less conspicuously,[5] Anguissola might be said to be intensifying, not collapsing, the distance between herself as artist (subject) and herself as model (object) through the inclusion of a third character sandwiched between the two. His presence has the effect of doubly distancing the painted image of Anguissola on an easel, since within the fictive realm he is more "real" than she is. The two depicted figures play out the theme of active and passive—he paints, she is painted—a theme summarized in the alignment of their hands, one working and the other in repose. In one sense, Campi himself is objectified, for his image is the product of the unseen artist's hand. But since the unseen artist is the model for the depicted painter, the fictive Campi (subject) is empowered, while the living painter (object) is diminished. If subject and object are in any way collapsed here, it is into object, since each of the three figures—Campi, painted Anguissola, and invisible Anguissola—is the object of another's scrutiny. We might well conclude that the painter who contrived this image has willingly relinquished the subject role.

Does such a renunciation spring from stereotypical female timidity, a fear of speaking in one's own right? Certainly, the painter's inclusion of Campi seems self-effacing and has the effect of concealing her own pride and ambition. It is he who calls our attention to this woman artist, he who commemorates her identity by painting an image of her. Her identity thereby acquires greater significance than if she presented herself directly or showed herself in the act of painting, for his action indicates exterior validation of her merit by one whose judgment is implicitly worth more than her own. And since Campi was Anguissola's teacher, the image might be an elaborate deferential conceit, presenting him as a kind of Pygmalion who has brought to life a successful painter with a coherent identity out of the inert raw material of a girl's

unformed talent. Such a reading of Sofonisba as Campi's creation would gain support from the cultural construct pervasive in the Renaissance that cast males as subjective agents with creative powers and females as passive vessels, objects acted upon by men, a construct that the Pygmalion myth itself reflects.[6]

The Pygmalion reading could also be supported by a telling contemporary document. In 1554 the painter Francesco Salviati wrote a letter to Bernardino Campi praising some works by Sofonisba Anguissola that had recently appeared in Rome. Describing the artist as "the beautiful Cremonese painter, your creation," Salviati characterized Anguissola's art as the product of Campi's own "beautiful intellect," a contribution to his already well-established artistic reputation.[7] To some extent Salviati's crediting of the young artist's achievement to her teacher is justifiable, considering that he undoubtedly helped to shape her talent. Yet it is curious that this construction of the two artists' relationship should have been perpetuated in the Siena canvas, which was painted by a mature Sofonisba, postdating Salviati's description by several years. (Although the date of the painting cannot be precisely established, both Anguissola's apparent age and the painting's assured style point to a date several years later than the Uffizi self-portrait of 1552 and the Vienna self-portrait of 1554.[8] A *terminus ante* is given by the artist's departure for Spain in 1559 to enter the service of Philip II; thus, the canvas may be safely assigned to the last years of the 1550s.)

How could Anguissola have deliberately constructed an image that falsely demeaned her position and undermined her own worth? Before we dismiss her as having internalized female inferiority, as having blindly accepted and passed along a masculinist ideology, let us consider this unusual painting in the light of modern critical perspectives. Might the Pygmalion conceit be a kind of disguise? Might we have here an example of female "mimicry," as defined by Luce Irigaray, in which a woman artist mimics or acts out the roles of femininity, in order to expose, subversively, the thing that she mimics. For if, as Irigaray has argued, women have access only to masculine linguistic (or, we can add, pictorial) structures, their only means of gaining critical distance from them is to "play with mimesis . . . in order to make 'visible' by an effect of playful repetition what should have remained hidden."[9] The analogy is more apt than it might seem, for the postmodern emphasis upon the social construction of personal identity and gender roles was anticipated in the sixteenth century, a period defined by its own concepts of self-fashioning, dissimulation and masking, and the artificial crafting of behavior.[10]

We need not invoke cultural conditions to justify a more subtle reading of this painting, however, for it projects its own clues. Although Campi is shown as the creative agent in one sense, in other respects it is he who is diminished, and even used transactionally. The image of Anguissola is larger than his own, something fairly rare in pictures that show artists painting or displaying paintings. Anguissola's image competes with Campi's in importance, not only from its larger size but also from its position in the design. Higher on the surface, she seems taller. Aligned with the central axis that is emphasized by the vertical stack of hands and head, she is more imposing. And the quadrated image of Anguissola is as fully present, as fully empowered, as the "real" image of Campi, since she too gazes directly at the viewer, and she maintains her presence through exactly as many particular features—a lighted face, a collar and throat, a single hand.

More important than either depicted character, however, is the invisible Sofonisba Anguissola who is both artist and subject. This ghostly larger presence—and she is clearly larger, because both Campi and the painted Anguissola look up at her—distinctly one-ups Campi, for while he paints only her, she paints both him and herself, and her perspective encompasses the whole scene. Moreover, as Fredrika Jacobs has observed, Anguissola's image of Campi is more "living," less static than the image he has made of her.[11] A similar point was made by Germaine Greer, who remarked that "the head of Campi is subtly expressive, in [Sofonisba's] own best manner, while her version of his version of herself is blank and moon-faced, larger than life."[12]

Correspondingly, it is significant that Bernardino is shown using a mahlstick, the artist's tool to steady the hand. Sofonisba depicts herself using this device in her early self-portraits, but never again after she matured as an artist. In Renaissance art the mahlstick sometimes connoted artistic timidity or preoccupation with detail. In his *Dialogo* of 1548, Paolo Pini claimed that the practice of steadying oneself with the mahlstick was in fact a shameful thing, not followed by the ancients. The mahlstick is presented as an instrument of slavish work on a medal commemorating Lavinia Fontana, whose verso presents the inspired Allegory of Painting casting aside her mahlstick to work freehand.[13] Sofonisba may then have provided Bernardino with a mahlstick in her double portrait to suggest that he was an uncreative imitator. Thus, if we take all these pictorial cues into account, we must alter our original reading: Bernardino is present only to define by contrast the thematically more important figure of Anguissola and to establish his own artistic worth as less than hers.

Moreover, we may ask of this slavish copyist, what is your model for the image on the easel? It cannot be the unseen Sofonisba before him, for she would not have been standing inert like this while she was painting him. And since no portrait of Anguissola by Campi is known, whereas the depicted portrait generically resembles many of her own self-portraits (approximately five predate this painting),[14] the image on the easel is likely to represent a work by Anguissola herself. We have here, then, a built-in falsification, an internal deception: Campi playing at making an image that the artist has already made. *He* thus becomes the unnecessary element, not Pygmalion but pseudo-Pygmalion, presenting himself as the creator of an artistic persona that is actually the creation of the artist herself. From this viewpoint, pace Lacan, she is the subject, both speaking and spoken. As the "spoken," however, she is not object but subject, because her creative Self is the theme of this painting.

What makes the painting work in this way is Campi's over-the-shoulder gaze at the invisible artist, a bit of staging that evokes her presence more effectively than if she were shown standing there paint-

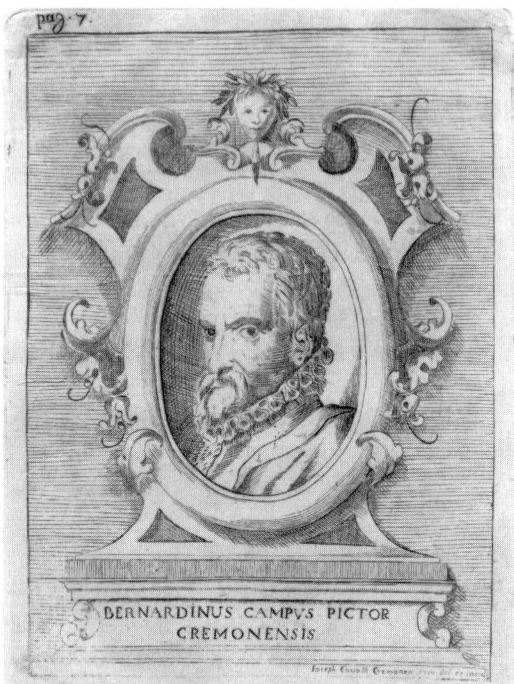

Figure 1.2. Joseph Cavalli, engraving after sixteenth-century portrait of Bernardino Campi. From Giambattista Zaist, *Notizie istoriche de' pittori, scultori, ed architetti cremonese*, 1774. (Photo: Dean Beesom.)

by which time Anguissola had left for Spain. By the time the Siena portrait was painted, Bernardino was no longer Sofonisba's teacher and was long gone. It is thus another curious artifice that she should have brought him into the work at all, nearly a decade after her apprenticeship ended, at a stage of her life when she really did not need his validation.

The head of Campi in Anguissola's painting was probably taken from a portrait now lost, whose appearance is recorded, in reverse, in the engraved frontispiece to the first volume of Giambattista Zaist's chronicle of Cremonese artists published in 1774 (fig. 1.2). Zaist took the engraved image of Campi, as well as his account of the lives of Campi and the Anguissola sisters, from Alessandro Lamo's *Discorso* of 1584.[15] The reversed relationship between the engraved portrait and Anguissola's Siena double portrait suggests that both were based upon another painted depiction of Campi, perhaps a self-portrait (though none is known at present). We are now in a position to see that the lifelike immediacy of the Siena painting is a contrivance, since the picture was constructed from an existing self-portrait by each artist, and we can recognize Anguissola's appropriation of Bernardino Campi's self-image for her own more expansive purposes.

ing. With this stroke Anguissola thematizes the subject of the male artist/active agent combined with his subject/passive product, while enframing it within a larger discourse—one that is generated from the viewpoint of the painter who is the invisible model for the image being created on the easel by Campi, and whom, as we have seen, he falsely presents as a static object. The invisible artist is therefore witness to the deception that she records in her larger image. But to be more precise, she does not really document a deception, she constructs one. For just as the image on Campi's canvas was probably not painted from life by Campi, Campi himself was probably not painted from life by Anguissola. He left Cremona in 1549, the year that her three-year apprenticeship with him ended, to spend the next thirteen years working for patrons in Milan and various north Italian courts, a sojourn that kept him away from Cremona until 1562,

For what audience was so subtle a form of self-promotion intended? To answer this question, we must reconstruct the problematic world of the Renaissance woman artist, beginning with a clue in an important document produced close to the genesis of the Siena painting. In a letter of December 23, 1558, the writer Annibale Caro asserted to Sofonisba's father, Amilcare Anguissola, that as a connoisseur of art he took special pleasure in self-portraits by women artists such as Amilcare's daughters, particularly Sofonisba, since he could exhibit them as "two marvels," one the work itself, the other its painter.[16] Caro's letter reflects two commonly held ideas of the period. One was that the exceptional existence of a woman artist in Renaissance Italy was a social "marvel." The other was that while a beautiful woman might be a marvel of nature, the image of a beautiful woman was a marvel of art. As an extension of the latter idea, imaged female beauty had become in sixteenth-century art theory a synecdoche for art itself.[17]

Caro's esteem for the image of the female painter reflects a theoretical commonplace of his day, that the special connection between art and female beauty could be symbolized in a portrait of a woman. The attributes of female beauty were set down by Agnolo Firenzuola in his widely influential treatise on the beauty of women published in 1548: thick, golden, curly hair; ample, swelling breasts; long slender legs.[18] These features were popularized, even standardized, in the treatises of Paolo Pino (1548), Federigo Luigini (1554), and others, and they even became the basis of a parlor game described by Innocentio Ringhieri in 1551.[19] Several sixteenth-century female portraits— foremost among them Titian's *La Bella*, Giorgione's *Laura*, Raphael's *La Fornarina*, and Parmigianino's *Antea*—seem to have been perceived, if not created, as generic images of beautiful women rather than specific individuals.[20] Indeed, there was a conflict between these categories, since the construct of the perfect woman was purely theoretical, not to be found in real life. Firenzuola describes it as the Chimera of Beauty because, like the Chimera, "that fair one whom we will devise may be imagined but never found."[21] Assembled from the separate beautiful features of many human women (no one of whom possesses perfect beauty), the ideal beauty created by the theorist or the artist transcends all imperfect particularity. And thus, in metaphoric terms, the beautiful woman, whether in idea or in image, was like art itself: both were created by perfecting the incomplete, fragmentary, and perishable elements found in nature.

Increasingly in the sixteenth century, portraits that projected the image of ideal beauty were sexually charged, whether they were understood to represent the artist's own beloved, such as Parmigianino's *Antea;* anonymous paragons of beauty, such as Titian's *La Bella* (which was purchased from the painter by a patron not acquainted with its sitter); or images of courtesans, such as Palma Vecchio's *Flora*, which might trail thin allegorical veils but were basically eroticized dream images, possessable by the patron as commodities for his fantasy life of eroticism and power.[22] The sexual dynamic that powered the four-way relationship between artist, patron, model, and image of ideal beauty was both influenced and symbolized by the story of Apelles' depiction of Campaspe, the mistress of his patron Alexander the Great, a story frequently depicted in Renaissance art. As Castiglione tells the story, Apelles' desire for his model Campaspe led Alexander to give his mistress to the painter, since Apelles could discern her beauty more perfectly than he.[23] In this story and its Renaissance representations, both the model to be improved upon and the new creation that displaces her are the exchangeable possessions of men, whether patron or artist.

The sexualization of the artist-patron-model relationship was mirrored in the sexualization and gender-structuring of the creative process itself. In the writings of Pino (1548), Vasari (1568), Dolce (1557), and Boschini (1660), as Patricia Reilly has observed, "Colors were described as the body through which the painter was literally able to reproduce life."[24] The ascription to men of creative artistic powers virtually identical to the creation of human life found philosophical support in the Aristotelian dictum pervasive in Renaissance Italy that human procreation was in fact male-generated: "The female always provides the material, the male that which fashions it."[25] Thus the male artist was presented as the creative shaper of the material model that he turned into art, just as man was understood to inseminate woman physically with his life force.

Many a male artist fashioned his identity on such concepts. If the painted image of a beautiful woman served to remind him of his special creative potential (and of his sexual virility), to support this fantasy women in general were cast onto the passive side of the metaphorical equation, consigned either to the realm of the material—lifeless, meaningless matter out of which man made art—or to the possessable, whether as real-life courtesan or portable imaged beauty. The self-definition of the male artist depended heavily upon the construction of a negativized and fantastical creature that was woman as Other, or alien. As Stephen Greenblatt put it, the self-fashioning of the Renaissance man was "achieved in relation to something perceived as alien, strange, or hostile. This threatening Other—heretic, savage, witch, adulteress, traitor, Antichrist—must be discovered or invented in order to be attacked and destroyed."[26]

But the excessive argumentation devoted to the construction of woman-as-passive-matter opened up an avenue for potential counterattack from the quarter of the female artist, whose very existence threatened the myth. For if only men possessed the creative spark, how could one explain the phenomenon of the woman artist? The strategies of defense employed on behalf of the male artist myth against this potential sabotage were few but effective. Women artists were brought under theoretical control by (1) explaining them as exceptional to the natural order of things, marvels of nature, and (2) defining them in terms that reinforced their similarity to other women rather than to men, specifically by emphasizing their beauty and their virtue. Although it is true that male artists too were sometimes described as "miracles of nature" or "virtuous," the meaning of the terms shifted when applied to the opposite sex. The possession of *virtù* meant something quite different for Renaissance men, invoking heroism, bravery, and cultural achievement, rather than chastity, purity, and virginity—aspects of expansive individualism rather than patriarchal control.[27]

Applying the first of these strategies of containment, the poet Angelo Grillo described Sofonisba Anguissola in 1589 as a "miracle of nature."[28] The second category is exemplified by contemporary descriptions of Anguissola as "la bella pittrice" (Salviati) or as "virtuosa"(Vasari), feminizing labels that work to subtly erode her artistic agency. An analogous instance of the renaturalizing of the Renaissance woman painter is found in Ridolfi's description of Marietta Robusti as "a model of womanly virtue," a characterization preceded by the statement that "in spite of man the female sex triumphs, armed as it is by the beauty that serves it well."[29] Examined closely, the

two strategies of containment of the woman artist seem to contradict each other: is she an unnatural phenomenon of nature or a natural exponent of femininity? Occasionally we glimpse a writer struggling to resolve this contradiction in terms that will keep the woman artist in a nonthreatening position. A telling example is Vasari's explanation of Anguissola's achievement: "If women know so well how to make living men, what marvel is it that those who wish to do so are also so well able to make them in painting?"[30] Vasari here wields the double-edged sword with anxious energy, implying that women's art-making is a natural anatomical function—thus less creative an act than men's cerebral art-making—while simultaneously situating Anguissola, an unmarried non-mother at that time, within her sex on the very terms by which she might be judged deficient.

For the female artist, special problems ensue from the male artist myth, its impingement upon and inapplicability to her own situation. Who will be *her* Other? What metaphor enables her creative act? There is no category above which she might be elevated and, worse, the male metaphor poses a considerable threat to her already unstable identity. Salviati's description of Anguissola's work and her entire artistic self as a creation and achievement of Bernardino Campi works to cancel that identity, for the present and the future. (Salviati had added in his letter that, in times to come, Campi would represent Cremona, preceding all other artists.)[31] Caro's interpretation of Sofonisba's self-image as yet another emblem of the beauty-art equation points up further dangers of that equation for the woman artist. She paints her own face at great risk, since it will be taken not as herself but as the sign of an idea. How can she show that she is an artist, not an emblem? How can she avoid being joined to the wrong discourse when even straightforward portraits of intellectually distinguished women are rendered in terms of a beauty so tinged with sexuality that they can be mistaken for courtesans?[32] The problem of the woman artist in the Renaissance was, consequently, her inability to claim artistic subjectivity because of continuous theoretical displacement and her inability to escape the topos that colored and dominated her self-presentations: feminine beauty as a metaphor for the beauty of art.

It is impossible to know, in the absence of any written statement, exactly how Anguissola felt about the situation of the woman artist. But it would be naive to take her silence for apathy or indifference. Sofonisba and her sisters, daughters of a nobleman who fostered their study of art, music, and letters, were women of a higher social class than most male artists, and they were said to have received a good education.[33] One privilege of the protected, leisure-filled life that an upper-class unmarried woman enjoyed was the freedom to read and think as well as to paint—and the sharp mind that Anthony Van Dyck observed in Anguissola when she was in her nineties was surely just as sharp in her twenties.[34] Were she so inclined, the painter could have found readings in the 1550s that challenged the masculine mystique, for the Renaissance debate on woman had by this time produced texts offering a protofeminist position on patriarchy.

A particularly important example, recently adduced by Constance Jordan, was Ortensio Landi's *Lettere di molte valorose donne* of 1549, a collection of the correspondence of literate noble and middle-class women in the Veneto. Although Jordan took these letters to be authentic, they are now considered the fictional creation of Landi himself. Even so, they offer an acute recognition of the professional limitations confronting women.[35] Landi's "authors" produced imaginative texts that could help women transcend the limitations imposed on them, constructing (in Jordan's words) "fictions that express their own empowerment . . . imagining themselves in male roles and performing in situations usually closed to women." Some of them challenge the authority of masculine authorship. Ippolita Crema asks, "Why do [men] insist so brazenly that all wit belongs only to them? that all strength belongs to them and finally also all value?" A current of exhortation runs through other letters. They call for women to awaken from their profound sleep (Beatrice Pia), to pursue their studies and take up a literary life (Lucietta Soranza), so as to engage in the rewriting of history that would,

in effect, deconstruct patriarchal ideology. Livia d'Arco wrote: "Let us not fear their pens, let us study eloquence together with wisdom, and even we may write blaming men, how they have been against us for so long, and even to this day."[36]

The critical and rebellious spirit of these letters would have been thought-provoking. And even if Anguissola never read them, their very existence demonstrates the level of independent critical judgment on the subject of gender to be found among literate noblewomen of her day. If we try to imagine what feelings and thoughts the authoritative discourse on male creativity might have elicited in an intelligent and educated woman such as Sofonisba Anguissola, we can better understand the Siena double portrait as a commentary on the subject of the woman artist from the viewpoint of a woman artist. I propose that we consider it as a response, if not to the particular letter written by Caro, then to the prevailing attitudes about women artists that the letter represents. However unscholarly such an approach might seem, it surely can be no worse than one that assumes women artists were oblivious to what was said about them by men.

As an educated woman in a gender-conscious and gender-critical age, Anguissola may well have felt negated—erased and deprived of artistic agency—by the attitudes represented in Salviati's description of her as Campi's product and in Caro's reduction of her identity to an emblem of (male) creativity. If so, then the Siena painting may have been designed to problematize the topos of the woman artist, to prevent the viewer from conflating the artist-agent with her image as a symbol of beauty. The picture's very construction, with its built-in contradiction, suggests that she intended to alert a thoughtful viewer to the issues. On the primary level, it is a self-portrait. On the secondary level, she is a metaphor for Campi's artistic creativity. But on the tertiary level, the model that he imitates and ostensibly improves upon is more ontologically real and artistically greater than he is. She who is the painter of this picture, whatever else she may be, is a separate entity from the flat image Campi paints, and it is the artist, triumphantly detached from oppressive metaphor, with whom the spectator must ultimately deal.

The image on Campi's easel is Sofonisba's own creation, the face that up to the making of this picture she has presented to the world. Let us now define the nature of Sofonisba's self-image—how she presents herself and how she protects her self-image from undesirable associations—deconstructing, in effect, a self-image carefully constructed to negotiate the gender minefields here described. We will then be in a better position to determine how she could have come to ironize that self-image.

In life, Sofonisba Anguissola was protected from association with the wrong class of women (i.e., prostitutes or courtesans) by her position within the nobility. It was probably in deference to their class status as unmarried noblewomen, *gentildonne*, that Vasari described two of the Anguissola sisters as "the most virtuous daughters," and Lamo called them "le due virtuose Gentildonne."[37] The term *virtuous*, applied to Sofonisba when she was in her thirties and still unmarried, would have underlined her virginal and celibate status. However, Sofonisba herself embraced the descriptor *virgo*—the word forms part of her signature in as many as eight of her paintings[38]—a fact suggesting that it must have been for her a positive term of self-definition. In the first place, the word called attention to her impeccable morals, effectively countering any possible association of her image with courtesan portraits. And the word *virgo* also carried in the Renaissance the implication of independence and self-possession, a broader metaphoric dimension that may have appealed to this female artist.

Learned women were frequently likened to paragons of chastity from antiquity: in the fifteenth century, Angelo Poliziano compared Cassandra Fedele to Camilla, the virginal warrior of the *Aeneid*; Antonio Loschi compared the book-lined cell of Maddalena Scrovegni with Scythia, the home of the Amazons. As Margaret King has observed, behind all these figures was Athena, "martially armed, unnaturally born, coldly virginal, and though female, de-

fined not by sex but by intellect."[39] Although the militant virgin analogy was more fervently embraced by male writers than by females, some examples of women's enthusiasm for it can be found. Isotta Nogarola, for instance, celebrates women's knowledge and virtue by adducing Camilla, Penthesilea, and the Amazons.[40] A different set of associations for the category *virgo*—richer, less austere, and without the taint of unnaturalness—was available within the golden-age tradition of Greek and Latin poetry in which the constellation Virgo was identified with Astraea, the powerful and just virgin. Astraea/Virgo, widely celebrated in Renaissance literature and in the popular realm through the zodiacal figure, was distantly linked with the fertility goddesses Isis, Atargatis, and Venus. She is a complex deity whom Frances Yates has described as "fertile and barren at the same time; orderly and righteous."[41]

Queen Elizabeth I of England drew these two currents together. Quite early in her reign, she was characterized as both Virgo and Amazon. The associations of Virgo-Astraea with power, justice, virginity, and a golden age were especially appropriate to that unmarried female monarch, but Elizabeth's depiction as an Amazon in literature and imagery and her description as a manly and invincible virago went against the grain of these terms' usually negative connotations when applied to "normal" women. It was the Virgin Queen's stunning exceptionality that made the difference, for she was popularly exempted from the female sex altogether as one "gifted with the desirable qualities of men."[42] In her case, the positive turn given to the Amazon association and the connection of virginity with empowerment were expedient since they fortified national identity, but the example demonstrates how, under the right circumstances, the term *virgo* could evoke heroic virility rather than female constraint. This was put directly by William Gager, who wrote to the queen in the 1580s that he hoped she would "be not so much a virgin as a virago: away with female terrors."[43] To the Renaissance ear, one presumes, the idea of virago was always present in the shadow of the word *virgo*, to be adduced for an exceptional queen but

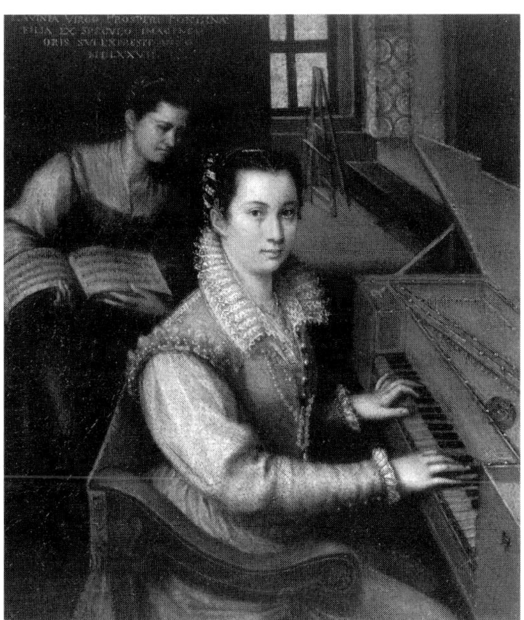

Figure 1.3. Lavinia Fontana, *Self-Portrait*, signed and dated 1577. Oil on canvas. Galleria dell'Accademia di San Luca, Rome. (Photo: author.)

under normal circumstances to be suppressed as its dangerous opposite.

Sofonisba Anguissola's choice of the appellation *virgo* for herself, shortly before Queen Elizabeth's ascent to the throne in 1558, may have been based on similar cultural associations. Like Elizabeth, she could have viewed the word *virgo* as empowering. Certainly, Sofonisba's decision not to marry for a large part of her life (she was about forty when she married for the first time)[44] is consistent with the valorization of independence that the term *virgo* may have connoted for her. Indeed, in this respect she set the tone for her five younger sisters, only two of whom married (Europa and Anna Maria). Three of Sofonisba's sisters became artists (Lucia, Europa, and Anna Maria), and one (Elena) entered a convent—perhaps another independent choice.[45] Lucia Anguissola followed Sofonisba in signing two of her pictures with the word *virgo*. On two more Anguissola paintings, one by Lucia and one by Sofonisba, the variant *adolescens* appears. It is implausible that this word was meant to signify youth and immaturity, as some scholars have

suggested,[46] since when the paintings were executed, the artists were about twenty and twenty-seven respectively. The word *adolescens* is likely instead to have carried its Latin thrust as a present active participle: "growing" (into maturity and independence), and in this sense a word somewhat analogous to *virgo*. The apparently proud use of the term *virgo* by another female painter of the Renaissance, Lavinia Fontana, inscribed by the artist on a self-portrait painted in the year of her marriage (fig. 1.3), indicates that for these women the word must have referred to something other than the state of their wombs.[47]

In her dress and hairstyle, Sofonisba Anguissola fashioned herself—presumably in life as well as art— as a dignified, serious, and self-possessed woman. In individual self-portraits painted from 1554 through 1561, she presents herself wearing black or near-black jackets *(corpetti)* with high-necked white lace collars beneath. Her hair is austerely decorous—parted in the middle, pulled back and arranged in braids that conform closely to the head. She wears no necklace or earrings. In an age of flamboyant clothing and jewelry and celebrated feminine display, Sofonisba conspicuously avoided the associations with vanity and luxury traditionally ascribed to women, for the sumptuary laws of sixteenth-century Cremona permitted a woman of her class more luxurious clothing than she allowed herself. This is evident in the colorful and ornate dresses worn by her younger sisters and other women in portraits.[48] The color black, which Sofonisba chose to wear long before she joined the Spanish court of Philip II (where black was mandated for both sexes), was worn increasingly in the sixteenth century by members of the nobility, but in the 1550s it was still worn primarily by noblemen.

Sofonisba's self-fashioning is more in keeping with the associations given to dark clothing in Castiglione's *Il Cortegiano*, where it is recommended for the ideal courtier, to convey his inner worth.[49] This prescription is, of course, for men only—Castiglione gives women no advice on how to dress. Sofonisba's attire, allowing for differences between the sexes in collar styles, is far closer to that of males of the period than of females, down to the restless and energetic white collar strings that hang at the throat. This style of dress, connoting noble status and association with the liberal arts and cultural pursuits, was recommended as appropriate for artists by Paolo Pino in his treatise of 1548.[50] As an artist of noble birth, Sofonisba boldly appropriated all the elevating signifiers that the male courtier model had to offer, a female adaptation just within the parameters of femininity.[51] (The analogy in our own time is the "dress-for-success" woman's suit composed of a skirt and a masculinized jacket.)

In her self-portraits, then, Anguissola presents herself as "like a man," avoiding feminine signifiers that might link her with paragons of beauty or courtesans and emphasizing features associated with independence, self-possession, and maturity. Such a self-presentation carried risks for a woman in Sofonisba's position. In the Renaissance (but not uniquely), women of achievement who remained unmarried tended to produce irrational anxiety in men. A well-known example is Isotta Nogarola, the brilliant humanist of fifteenth-century Verona. Like Sofonisba, Isotta was praised by male humanists for her virginity and esteemed above her equally learned sister Ginevra, whose marriage and loss of virgin status were taken to indicate her loss of a "flair" for humanistic studies.[52] Yet Isotta's very achievements and the independence that supported them had a threatening edge. Criticized by one male humanist as improperly talkative, she was also excoriated by an anonymous pamphleteer for sexual deviancy (on an invented charge of incest). The latter singled out her alleged sexual misconduct to demonstrate a common saying, "The woman of fluent speech is never chaste," which, he says, "can be supported by the example of the greatest number of learned women."[53]

The exaggerated sexualizing of intellectual or creative women worked to render them unexceptional, "only a woman." The opposite face of this, exaggerated praise of their chastity, stressed their exceptional nature. The latter position has been described as "not-woman,"[54] women mythologized as sexually perfect—which was another form of sexualizing them, of course, and had the equally useful

effect of distracting attention from their threatening achievements. The problem for the woman artist or writer in the Renaissance was to create a self-image that avoided evoking the extremes of "only a woman" and "not-woman." Anguissola rejected decisively the "only a woman" casting. Yet in playing down her femininity, Sofonisba had also to seek a safe position between "not-woman" and "like a man": not so much virility as to offend, but enough to stake her serious claim on culture. Such a safe zone is not easily found; there is, in fact, no space between these two overlapping positions. For Sofonisba's self-image and male writers' perception of her might actually converge, their meanings becoming confused. Her proclamation of virgin status, for example, would fit a man's perspective as well as her own—for her, it expresses creative expansion, while he might use it to contain her creativity.

Yet these are the very conditions that foster subversive acts. Without suggesting that Anguissola had anything like a radical agenda, I propose that she intentionally created images that had different meanings for differently gendered audiences. Precisely because the common outward markings of "like a man" and "not-woman" are ambiguous as to which is meant, Sofonisba and other women artists could go quite far in coded self-expression disguised as proper femininity. One signifier with polyvalent meaning is the spinet or virginal that Sofonisba included in at least two portraits, the Capodimonte *Portrait of Sofonisba (or Lucia)* and the Spencer *Self-Portrait* of 1561 (fig. 1.4). Virginals appear as well in female portraits or self-portraits by Caterina van Hemessen, Lavinia Fontana, and Marietta Robusti (figs. 1.3 and 1.5).[55] The attribute has been explained as a sign that these artists were also proficient in music, as young noblewomen often were (though we do not know as a fact that Lavinia Fontana was musical).[56] Yet considering that this keyboard instrument was particularly associated with women in the Renaissance[57] and that virginals and the label *virgo* were combined in two of the four paintings here discussed, we might also read it as a metaphorical statement about the self.

Another vein of Renaissance signification connects

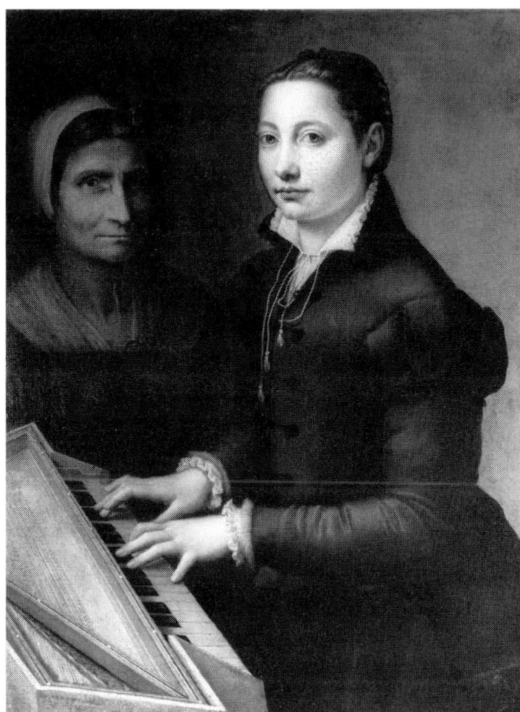

Figure 1.4. Sofonisba Anguissola, *Self-Portrait*, signed and dated 1561. Oil on canvas. The Collection at Althorp Park. (Photo: Photographic Survey, Courtauld Institute of Art.)

music with sexuality, however, and certain musical instruments, such as organs and spinets, with the female body.[58] The masculinist position on this is exemplified by Titian's Prado *Venus and Cupid with an Organist*, in which the organist's stare at the woman's naked body establishes the metaphor of her body as the instrument upon which he conducts his sexual performance.[59] In other musical imagery, a woman plays the instrument to establish an erotic context, as we see in a painting by the Bergamasque Bernardino Licinio, in which a woman playing a spinet and wearing a suggestively low-cut dress is approached by a man with money in his hand.[60] Anguissola and Fontana take special care to distinguish themselves from this type by emphasizing their independence of men, dignity in dress, and the seriousness of the musical performance. In their paintings the attending maidservant no longer resembles a procuress, as she does in Licinio's picture.

An opposing musical model linking the organ or spinet with female chastity existed in the figure of Saint Cecilia, the early Christian martyr who renounced sex on the eve of her marriage. Reginia Stefaniak has traced Cecilia's association with a musical instrument back to Methodius's metaphor of the virginal body as a well-tempered instrument whose harmony was not disturbed by the distempering influence of sexual intercourse.[61] Saint Cecilia was shown from the Trecento onward with musical instruments, particularly the organetto. When female artists such as Anguissola and Fontana showed themselves playing the musical instrument identified in popular thought with the female body, they did not merely depart from the sexualizing tradition to connect instead with the virginal Saint Cecilia. In the secular and contemporary contexts in which they join their self-images with musical instruments, Anguissola and Fontana emphasize not the form of the instrument but their own act of playing it, thus conveying the idea of self-possession and self-management. At the same time, they extend the range of the synecdoche so that the virginal represents not only body but also mind, talent, and abilities.

These portraits of women with virginals thus call up multiple associations, differently weighted in different viewers. The expressive tone of a picture ascribed to Marietta Robusti (fig. 1.5) is more conventional than those of Anguissola and Fontana, and could appeal to many men as a juxtaposition of a beautiful woman and a musical instrument, which recalls the admirable purity of Saint Cecilia yet pleasantly mingles in the imagination with the erotic accessibility of another kind of woman altogether. Simultaneously, it might be understood by many women as representing a female who manages her sexuality as competently as she performs upon the musical instrument that symbolizes her total creative potential.[62] There are comparable signifiers in other images. We might read Sofonisba Anguissola's many images of herself and her sisters with musical instruments, palettes, brushes, and books as expressions of self-confidence and ambition, which both fuel and justify her desire to join the masculine sphere of serious cre-

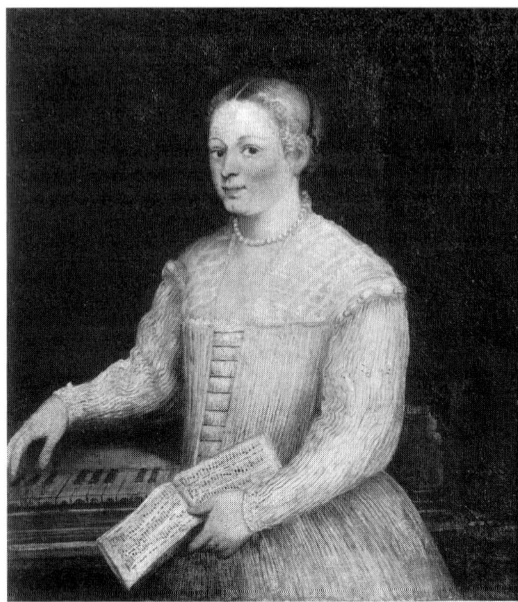

Figure 1.5. Ascribed to Marietta Robusti, called Tintoretta, *Self-Portrait* (?), ca. 1580. Oil on canvas. Uffizi, Florence. (Photo: Alinari/Art Resource, New York.)

ative and intellectual achievement. And once we concede such intention on her part, we acquire the key to understanding Sofonisba's best-known painting, *The Chess Game*.

In *The Chess Game* of 1555 (fig. 1.6) three of the Anguissola sisters are gathered at a chess table as their nurse looks on. This painting has justly been regarded as an innovative contribution to the emerging categories of genre painting and the conversation piece.[63] But more is at stake here. It is important to know that the ancient game of chess had undergone a major rules change, initiated in Italy in the late fifteenth century and well established there by 1510, which revolutionized the game and produced its modern form, called by chess historians "the new chess." The difference was in the capability of the pieces: to speed up the game, pawns could now advance two spaces rather than one in their initial move, bishops could move an unlimited number of spaces along their diagonal axes rather than only one, and the queen be-

came the most powerful piece on the board, now capable of moving not just one space but an unlimited number of spaces in any direction, horizontally, vertically, or diagonally.[64] The new status and power of the queen, now greater than that of the king himself, was the most noteworthy result of the rules change, as is indicated in sixteenth-century descriptions of the game: the Italians called it *dela donna* (or *dama*), the French, *eschecs de la dame enragée*.

I suggest that we see a commentary on the "new chess" in a painting from Anguissola's Cremonese circle, formerly believed to be hers but now ascribed to Giulio Campi (fig. 1.7). Here, an elegantly dressed, imperious woman sweeps the board with a commanding gesture—she appears to have taken her opponent's king—to the apparent consternation of a group of male figures that includes a soldier.[65] Although the painting has been interpreted Neoplatonically as the conquest of Mars by Venus, it seems likely that it may instead express the new superior power of the queen over knights or pawns (foot soldiers), either of which could be represented by the figure in armor. (The jester or fool at lower right may refer to another Italian name for the new game, *ala rabiosa*, mad chess.) In a painting of a chess game of 1521 by Lucas van Leyden, a work that has been identified as Giulio Campi's pictorial source,[66] the roles are reversed. The female player makes her move timidly, with some coaching, as her male opponent relaxes, bored and self-satisfied. The slow pace of the game is implied by the distracted conversations that go on around them. This painting depicts an especially slow version known as courier chess, which lingered long in Germany and was played by the old rules.[67] In changing the gender roles, Campi seems to comment on the difference between the games—a commentary that Anguissola, as a member of the Campi circle, may well have had in mind when she rehearsed the chess theme herself.

With its military and feudal imagery, the game of chess has long been compared metaphorically with war.[68] The rules change that produced a newly empowered queen brought the dimension of gender to the game's metaphoric powers, an expanded applica-

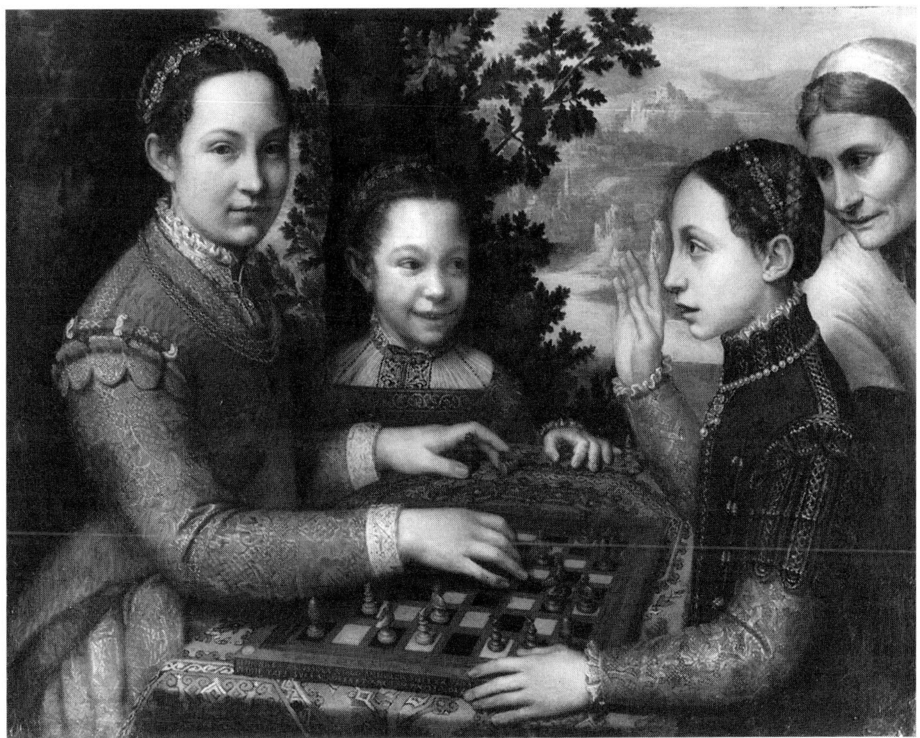

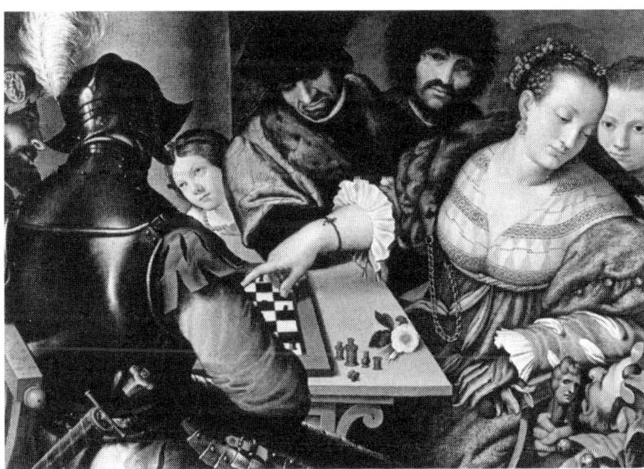

Figure 1.6 (TOP). Sofonisba Anguissola, *The Chess Game* (Lucia, Europa, and Minerva Anguissola and nurse), signed and dated 1555. Oil on canvas. Muzeum Narodowe, Poznan. (Photo: Erich Lessing/Art Resource, New York.)

Figure 1.7 (LEFT). Giulio Campi, *The Chess Game*, 1530s or 1540s. Oil on canvas. Musei Civici, Turin. (Photo: Torino, Museo Civico d'Arte Antica e Palazzo Madama; courtesy of Fondazione Torino Musei.)

tion that is reflected in the chess paintings of Lucas van Leyden, Giulio Campi, and Sofonisba Anguissola, though from different perspectives. Lucas and Giulio offer, through vignettes of buffoonery, a comic joining of the rules of chess, old and new, with the battle of the sexes. By contrast, Sofonisba presents a rare and perhaps unique image of a chess game whose participants and observers are all female, a statement that must be seen as, above all, an affirmation of female intelligence. (Chess-playing was already perceived as a highly intellectual activity in the Renaissance; Castiglione disparages the game as demanding disproportionate time and study from the well-rounded courtier.)[69]

Yet one may ask whether the Anguissola sisters are playing only chess. For if playing the spinet or virginal is a metaphor for self-possession and creative achievement, playing chess may represent something similar, particularly when the game's only female piece has been elevated to a position of great power. Playing chess, with its intellectual demands and strategies, is like playing a musical instrument or playing the game of art, a connection underlined by the visual analogy between the spinet-playing Lavinia Fontana (fig. 1.4) and the chess-playing Lucia, the eldest of Sofonisba's group. Lucia has won the game, to the surprise and admiring concession of the loser, Europa, who receives a teasing grin from Minerva. Lucia's triumph is shared with the spectator, at whom she smiles, who is also the painter Sofonisba. In the art of painting, it is suggested, these sisters both compete with one another (the only arena in which competition was available to them) and look to each other as role models and teachers. Thus Europa, whose future as a painter is forecast here, looks to Lucia, who had already completed her artistic apprenticeship under Sofonisba, to whom she looks in deference or for approval. The youngest of the four, Minerva, though no more than seven in 1555, is imagined to find her role model in Europa.

The chain of influence and connection among the sisters implied in *The Chess Game* is echoed in the art produced by the elder two. What has been considered a problem for Anguissola connoisseurship—the differentiation of the artists' individual styles and the identification of individual sisters in portrait images— may in fact result from their intentional imitation and replication of one another's style and imagery.[70] In attempting to sort out the hands, we may be barking up the wrong tree. It would be equally productive to accept the images as they are given us: of the Anguissola sisters as a family of artists, an ideal female community, bonded with each other through their kinship and artistic aspirations, whose images of each other pay tribute to their solidarity and mutual support, even as they present a collective self-image under collective construction.

The inner dynamic of *The Chess Game* depends upon and is revealed through the sequence of gazes that leads from figure to figure and, finally, out of the picture space to the viewer. Its meaning is complete only when we realize that the artist Sofonisba, the eldest artist-sister and teacher of the others, is the culmination of the sequence. Thus her artistic sisters might be thought of as Sofonisba's creation, as she was said to be Campi's, and they are part of her self-image. As in the Siena *Campi Painting Anguissola,* the invisible painter holds the controlling viewpoint on the subject, since only she has a perspective on the whole. Yet the painter is not only an observer but also a participant in this portrait narrative, included by the gazes of her painted characters, with whom she shares a private history. Through her carefully composed self-revealing presentation, the artist further extends an invitation to the spectator to join in, not as controlling master of the gaze but as a secret sharer in the standpoint of the artist and collaborator in the creation of meaning. A connection between the artist and the spectator is presumed because the image can be understood fully only by one who knows what the invisible painter knows about these people, their relationships, and their aspirations. We might then say that the artist herself and her subject-sisters form the primary audience for Sofonisba's art. On a secondary level, we are invited into their world, but explicitly on their terms.

In the light of this reading of *The Chess Game*, it seems clear that Anguissola's "genre" scenes are not casual glimpses of family life but images with typological significance. The extent to which "genre" was taken on a serious level in the mid sixteenth century is implied in Michelangelo's reported response to Sofonisba's drawing of a laughing girl (fig. 1.8), that the image of a crying boy would have been better.[71] Since the former can hardly have been easier to draw than the latter, the real difference for Michelangelo was the importance of the theme: boys were better than girls, and tragedy was better than comedy. Sofonisba evidently complied with his advice (fig. 1.9), but the fact that she had drawn the laughing girl first says something about the difference between their perspectives. Significantly, there is hardly a laughing figure in all of Michelangelo's art—and some would say there is not a (real) female in it either. One wonders what *il divino* made of Sofonisba's crying boy, who does not

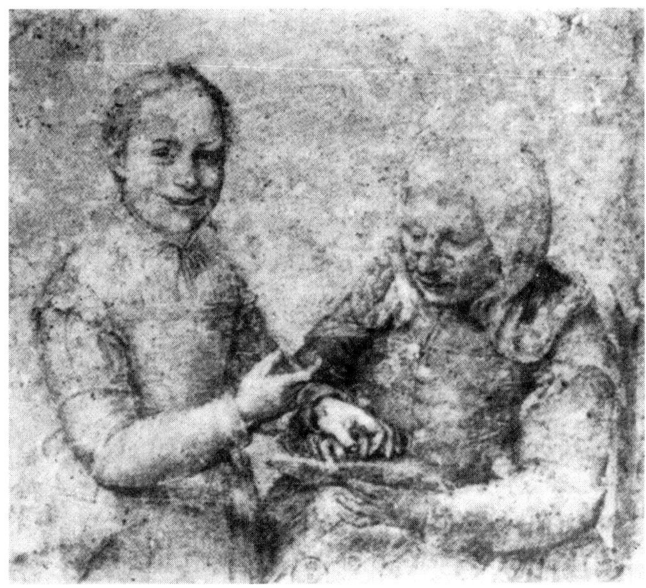

Figure 1.8. Sofonisba Anguissola, *Old Woman Studying the Alphabet Instructed by a Girl*, 1550s. Drawing. Uffizi, Florence. Gabinetto dei Disegni e Stampe. By permission of Ministero dei Beni e le Attività Culturali; all rights reserved. (Photo: Gabinetto Fotografico della Soprintendenza Speciale per il Polo Museale Fiorentino.)

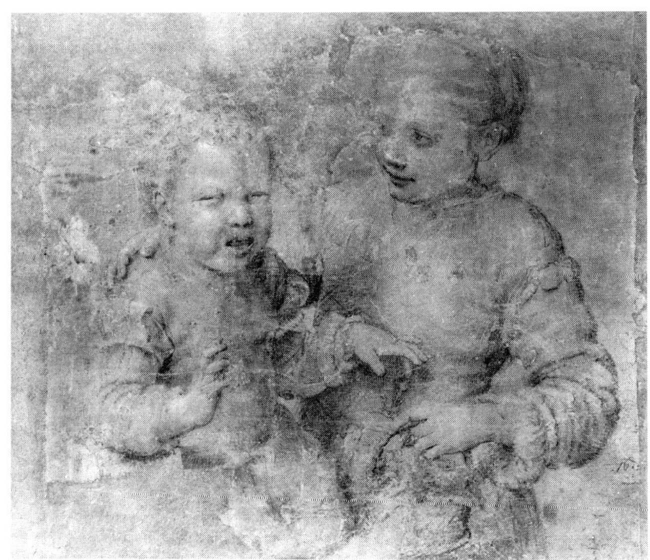

Figure 1.9. Sofonisba Anguissola, *Boy Bitten by a Crab*, 1550s. Drawing. Naples, Capodimonte Museum. By permission of Ministero dei Beni e le Attività Culturali. (Photo: Soprintendenza Speciale per il Polo Museale Napoletano.)

weep the tragic tears of a Laocoön, only those of a child who needs a Band-Aid. The amused response of his older sister sets in comic perspective the mishap of a little boy who is no hero and not even brave. It is an ignoble position for a male, one that Caravaggio, when he borrowed the motif, was careful to dignify by eroticizing.[72]

If Michelangelo recognized the masculine ignominy of the crying boy in Sofonisba's drawing, he kept his literary silence. He could have objected to the laughing girl for another reason, however, for surely this is the more deeply subversive drawing. The girl who instructs her old nurse in the alphabet does not ridicule the old woman, as the drawing's usual title indicates; rather, she proudly points to her own unlikely pupil, naively exulting in a role traditionally forbidden to her, that of mentor and initiator into culture of her own nurturing nurse. Appropriating male cultural agency for her young surrogate while positioning it firmly within a female context, Sofonisba effectively reformulates the nature-culture construct on new terms, comically reversing—and thereby ridiculing—the masculinist hierarchic model that she replaces with a model of symbiotic interchange.

The comparison of Sofonisba with Michelangelo, prompted by their documented relationship, points up the unusual nature of Sofonisba's audience, or audiences, which in turn helps account for her new expressive key. Though saturated with personal expression, Michelangelo's art was, like the work of most male artists, largely produced for the public sphere. Sofonisba Anguissola produced some portraits and a few religious paintings on commission, but her paintings of herself and her sisters, as well as her "genre" portraits, originated in the private realm. Although some of the self-portraits found an outside market, which in turn stimulated their production, the fact that Vasari saw both *The Chess Game* and *The Family Group* in the Anguissola home in 1566, a decade after they were painted, indicates that they had no original patron and no immediate market.[73] Sofonisba's two drawings and three portrait narratives posed an implicit challenge to the hierarchy of values of sixteenth-century Italian art. In place of male heroism and the celebration of religion and state, they advance an art focused upon secluded family life, kinship networks, private history—the quotidian, but not necessarily the insignificant—while implicitly questioning the patriarchalism from which they depart. Her subversive challenge was not recognized in Sofonisba's lifetime. It was undoubtedly too coded, as well as too marginal and unthreatening, to affect a culture so deeply involved in sustaining its mythic structures of gentleman-artist-hero and the patriarchal family. In the end, her art was purchased and admired by male connoisseurs as expressions of their values, not hers.

On the other hand, as a woman whose family sta-

tus in the 1550s ensured that she needed neither to work for a living nor to marry, Sofonisba Anguissola enjoyed a rare privilege. Her condition may have excluded her from much in the world, but it provided her one thing of inestimable value: the proverbial Woolfian "room of her own." She enjoyed both the physical and the psychological space to create images for the private delectation of herself and her sisters, images that might function for them as symbols of their achievement and promise, as talismans for their creative development, and as commentaries on the world in which they lived. Thus the paintings had dual meanings: one for the patron or outsider who interpreted their expression in conventional terms, and another as daring, socially heretical critiques of those very conventions. Although her private discourse was not valued by Anguissola's contemporaries, it is fortunately recognizable to today's student of women's history, and in that sense joins the metahistorical discourse of feminism.

Indeed, one can read the images here discussed as an evolving sequence in which Sofonisba's growing sense of independence and self-worth meshes with her growing enlightenment about the patriarchal world into which she was born. We move from the early self-portraits, projections of a strong and confident psyche, to *The Chess Game*, a kind of female Eden and a celebration of women's accomplishments and talent. Next comes *The Family Group*, which in emblematizing the patriarchal family acknowledges the marginal position of even a brilliant female artist in the larger world.[74] But then, in *Campi Painting Anguissola*, the tables are turned, and the woman artist establishes herself as transcendent over the male painter who would claim her imaged persona as his own creation. Common to all of these works is the inclusion of the unseen self in the picture's meaning as both participant and commentator. Thus in the largest sense, they are all self-images.

If *Campi Painting Anguissola* represents a form of getting even, of reframing reality so as to ironize the construct of the woman artist as masculine creation, its terms were surely justifiable, for in 1559, on the brink of her departure for Spain, Sofonisba Anguissola's worth, measured in the status of her patrons, was greater than that of Bernardino Campi. She took one more opportunity to point this out, in a letter she wrote to Campi from Madrid in 1561. Writing in response to a letter from him (the first she has received, she complains), she regrets that she cannot send him the portrait of the king he has requested because she has not yet painted it, being presently occupied in painting a portrait of the king's sister for the pope.[75] She promises to send a portrait of the queen, however, as soon as she finishes the other one. Though perhaps meant in straightforward terms, the letter effectively crystallizes the difference in their positions: he was painting portraits for modestly eminent north Italian princesses, while she was in the service of the most powerful monarch in Europe.

We feminists today may have been complicit in drawing too sharp a line between the achievements of Renaissance women as exotic exceptions and so-called "real" achievement. For, though we lack full knowledge of Anguissola's years in Spain, she seems to have been successful there by every contemporary measure. She was court painter and lady-in-waiting to the queen, Isabella of Valois, whom she taught to paint, and though Sofonisba's Spanish oeuvre has not been firmly established, she manifestly had royal commissions.[76] She was rewarded lavishly with extravagant gifts, dowry, and a substantial annual stipend, with which she supported her father and the family in Cremona and, after Amilcare's death in 1573, her brother Asdrubale.[77] Sofonisba's two marriages do not seem to have interfered with her painting and other cultural activity; if anything, they provided new environments for their practice. In Palermo, where she resided part-time with her first husband between 1571 and 1579, she continued to paint and perhaps to teach painting.[78] And in Genoa, where she lived with her second husband, Orazio Lomellini, from 1584 to 1616–20, her household is said to have been the center of salons and artists' gatherings.[79]

Of course, if Anguissola had been born male with the same talents and creative originality, she would have had an expanded range of patrons and subjects, and she would have enjoyed a different kind of fame in posterity. The nature of her achievement was shaped by the limitations she experienced. But if she had to market her own self-image as an exceptional woman artist, she nevertheless found a position to take on this and a way of imaging it that permitted her to escape to a degree the problematic position of the woman artist. In her three narrative portraits—*The Chess Game*, *The Family Group*, and *Campi Painting Anguissola*—she claims artistic subjectivity through the mask of invisibility. Concealing those female attributes that would subsume her into objectified beauty, and registering her presence on the unseen side of the picture plane, she ensures that she cannot be pinned by the viewer's gaze. In this floating position, a looming absence whose real appearance is left to our imagination, she may be said to carry "not-woman" to the ultimate extreme, yet she escapes confinement in a demeaning conceptual category. In such a situation, perhaps even better than being larger than life is being larger than art.

NOTES

1. Siena, Pinacoteca Nazionale (o.c., 43⅝ × 43⅛ inches). Whitney Chadwick, *Women, Art, and Society* (London: Thames and Hudson, 1990), 70; color reproduction, fig. 37. Documentation for the painting is given by Flavio Caroli, *Sofonisba Anguissola e le sue sorelle* (Milan: Arnoldo Mondadori Editore, 1987), 102.

2. Giorgio Vasari, *Le vite de' più eccellenti pittori, scultori ed architettori* (Florence: Ed. Gaetano Milanesi, 1875–85), 7: 498.

3. H. W. Janson, *The Sculpture of Donatello* (Princeton, N.J.: Princeton University Press, 1963), 35 and 40; Virgil Barker, *American Painting, History and Interpretation* (New York: Macmillan, 1950), 134.

4. See Caroli, *Anguissola*, 98.

5. The painting is signed in the lower right corner, in faint lettering that includes "VIRGO" and ". . . SSOLA," according to Ilya Sandra Perlingieri, *Sofonisba Anguissola: The First Great Woman Artist of the Renaissance* (New York: Rizzoli, 1992), 52.

6. The gendered construction of artistic creativity in the Renaissance is examined in Fredrika Jacobs, "Woman's Capacity to Create: The Unusual Case of Sofonisba Anguissola," *Renaissance Quarterly* 47 (1994); and in her *Defining the Renaissance Virtuosa: Women Artists and the Language of Art History and Criticism* (Cambridge: Cambridge University Press, 1997).

7. For the text of Salviati's letter of 28 April 1554, see Caroli, *Anguissola*, 36. Sofonisba and her sister Elena studied painting with Bernardino Campi from 1545 to 1549.

8. The Siena museum dates the double portrait c. 1558; Perlingieri has unconvincingly proposed a date of 1550.

9. Luce Irigaray, "Pouvoir du discours, subordination du féminin," in *Ce sexe qui n'en est pas un* (Paris: Editions de Minuit, 1977), 74.

10. See Stephen Greenblatt, *Renaissance Self-Fashioning, from More to Shakespeare* (Chicago: University of Chicago Press, 1980), 20 and 162 ff.

11. Fredrika Jacobs, personal communication, 1991.

12. Germaine Greer, *The Obstacle Race: The Fortunes of Women Painters and Their Work* (New York: Farrar, Straus, Giroux, 1979), 181.

13. On the iconography of the Fontana medal, see Mary D. Garrard, *Artemisia Gentileschi: The Image of the Female Hero in Italian Baroque Art* (Princeton, N.J.: Princeton University Press, 1980), 339. For Pino's text, see Mary Pardo, "Paolo Pino's 'Dialogo di Pittura': A Translation with Commentary" (Ph.D. diss., University of Pittsburgh, 1984), 340.

14. See Caroli, *Anguissola*, cats. 2, 3, 4, 8, and 9.

15. Alessandro Lamo, *Discorso intorno alla scolari, e pittura . . . e nobile pittore cremonese M. Bernardino Campi* (Cremona, 1584), in Giambattista Zaist, *Notizie istoriche de' pittori, scultori, ed architetti cremonese* (Cremona: A. M. Panni, 1774).

16. Caro's letter is quoted in full in Caroli, *Anguissola*, 37.

17. On the theme of female beauty as a synecdoche for art, see Elizabeth Cropper, "The Beauty of Woman: Problems in the Rhetoric of Renaissance Portraiture," in *Rewriting the Renaissance: The Discourse of Sexual Difference in Early Modern Europe*, ed. Margaret W. Ferguson, Maureen Quilligan, and Nancy J. Vickers (Chicago: University of Chicago Press, 1986), 175–90.

18. For Firenzuola's treatise, *Discorsi delle bellezze delle donne*, see Agnolo Firenzuola, *On the Beauty of Women*, trans. and ed. Konrad Eisenbichler and Jacqueline Murray (Philadelphia: University of Pennsylvania Press, 1971). On this and other Renaissance treatises on female beauty, see Elizabeth Cropper, "On Beautiful Women: Parmigianino, Petrarchismo and the Vernacular Style," *Art Bulletin* 58 (1976): 374–94; Mary Rogers, "The Decorum of Women's Beauty: Trissino, Firenzuola, Luigini and the Representation of Women in Sixteenth-Century Painting," *Renaissance Studies* 2 (1988): 47–87; and Jacqueline Murray, "Agnolo Firenzuola on Female Sexuality and Women's Equality," *Sixteenth-Century Journal* 20 (1991): 199–213.

19. Cropper, "Parmigianino," esp. 384–85.

20. Cropper, "The Beauty of Woman," esp. 176–79.

21. Dedicatory letter to *Bellezze delle donne* (quoted by Murray, "Firenzuola," 200). The idea that beauty does not reside in a single example is traceable to the topos of Zeuxis recounted by (among others) Alberti and Castiglione.

22. On Antea and *La Bella*, see Cropper, "The Beauty of Woman," 178–79.

23. Baldassare Castiglione, *The Book of the Courtier*, trans. C. S. Singleton (Garden City, N.Y.: Doubleday, 1959), 80–82.

24. Patricia Reilly, "The Taming of the Blue: Writing Out Color in Italian Renaissance Theory," in *The Expanding Discourse: Feminism and Art History*, ed. Norma Broude and Mary D. Garrard (New York: Harper-Collins, 1992), 92.

25. Jacobs, "Woman's Capacity," 80; see also Mary D. Garrard, "Leonardo da Vinci: Female Portraits, Female Nature," in *Expanding Discourse*, ed. Broude and Garrard, 69–70.

26. Greenblatt, *Renaissance Self-Fashioning*, 9.

27. On sixteenth-century definitions of *virtú*, see Hannah F. Pitkin, *Fortune Is a Woman: Gender and Politics in the Thought of Niccolò Machiavelli* (Berkeley: University of California Press, 1984), esp. ch. 6; on its application for women, see Ian Maclean, *The Renaissance Notion of Woman* (Cambridge: Cambridge University Press, 1980), 49–67.

28. Grillo's description is quoted by Rossana Sacchi, "Documenti per Sofonisba Anguissola," *Paragone* 39 (1988): 79. On Renaissance women artists as exceptions, see Ann Sutherland Harris and Linda Nochlin,

Women Artists: 1550–1950 (Los Angeles: Los Angeles County Museum of Art and New York: Alfred A. Knopf, 1976), 26–35; Mary D. Garrard, "Re-view of Laura M. Ragg, *The Women Artists of Bologna*," *Woman's Art Journal* 1 (1980–81); Chadwick, *Women, Art, and Society*, 26–32, 66 ff; and Jacobs, "Woman's Capacity."

29. Carlo Ridolfi, *The Life of Tintoretto, and of His Children Domenico and Marietta*, trans. and intro. Catherine Enggass and Robert Enggass (University Park: Pennsylvania State University Press, 1984), 98. On the strategy of conflating women artists with other women, see Garrard, *Gentileschi*, 173–74. Artemisia Gentileschi, whose reputation for virtue suffered from the infamy of her rape trial, was nevertheless frequently acclaimed for her beauty.

30. Vasari, 6: 502. This enigmatic statement is also discussed by Jacobs, "Woman's Capacity," 83.

31. Caroli, *Anguissola*, 36.

32. This was the case with Leonardo's portrait of Cecilia Gallerani; see Garrard, "Leonardo da Vinci: Female Portraits, Female Nature," in *Expanding Discourse*, ed. Broude and Garrard, 59–85.

33. Vasari, 6: 498; Zaist, *Notizie*, 189–90; Vincenzo Lancetti, *Biografia Cremonese ossia Dizionario storico delle famiglie e persone . . .* (Milan: G. Borsani, 1819, in 3 vols.), 1: 250; Filippo Baldinucci, *Notizie de' professori del disegno da Cimabue in Qua*, 14 vols. (Milan: Società Tipografica de' Classici Italiani, 1811), 8: 211; see also Harris and Nochlin, *Women Artists*, 30, 106; and Perlingieri, *Anguissola*, 30–33.

34. Van Dyck met Sofonisba Anguissola in Palermo on July 12, 1624, an event he commemorated in a sketch and a written account. He described her as "still having her memory and an exceedingly quick mind" (Harris and Nochlin, *Women Artists*, 106).

35. Constance Jordan, *Renaissance Feminism: Literary Texts and Political Models* (Ithaca, N.Y.: Cornell University Press, 1990), 138–43. Anne Jacobson Schutte, "Irene di Spilimbergo: The Image of a Creative Woman in Late Renaissance Italy," *Renaissance Quarterly* 44 (1991): 47, believed the letters to be fictional, and that has recently been confirmed. See Meredith Kennedy Ray, "'A gloria del sesso feminile': Epistolary Constructions of Gender in Early Modern Italian Letter Collections," Ph.D. diss., University of Chicago, 2002, ch. 2.

36. These passages are quoted from Jordan, *Renaissance Feminism*.

37. Vasari, 6: 498; Lamo, *Discorso*, 36. (Vasari refers to Sofonisba and Elena, the two eldest daughters, who studied with Bernardino Campi.)

38. Caroli, *Anguissola*, cats. 1, 3–5, 7–8, 11, and 14.

39. Margaret L. King, "Book-Lined Cells: Women and Humanism in the Early Italian Renaissance," in *Beyond Their Sex: Learned Women of the European Past*, ed. Patricia H. Labalme (New York: New York University Press, 1980), 79–80; see also Anthony Grafton and Lisa Jardine, "Women Humanists: Education for What?" in Grafton and Jardine, *From Humanism to the Humanities: Education and the Liberal Arts in Fifteenth- and Sixteenth-Century Europe* (Cambridge, Mass.: Harvard University Press, 1986), 36.

40. From a letter of 1439 or 1440; see Isotta Nogarola, *Complete Writings: Letterbook, Dialogue on Adam and Eve, Orations*, ed. and trans. Margaret L. King and Diana Robin (Chicago: University of Chicago Press, 2004), 99.

41. Frances Yates, *Astraea: The Imperial Theme in the Sixteenth Century* (London: Routledge and Kegan Paul, 1975), esp. 30–37 and 59–79.

42. Winifred Schleiner, "*Divina virago:* Queen Elizabeth as an Amazon," *Studies in Philology* 75 (1978): 172.

43. Ibid., 164.

44. Sofonisba's marriage in about 1570 to a Sicilian nobleman, Fabrizio de Moncada, arranged by her Spanish patrons, took her from Madrid to Palermo.

45. The second Anguissola daughter, Elena (born 1534/35), became a nun. Lucia (1536/38–1565) completed her apprenticeship under Sofonisba at age fifteen. Europa (1542/43–1572) was also trained in painting by Sofonisba, and married in the early 1560s. Minerva, born in 1548/49, did not pursue her study of art. Anna Maria (born 1555/58) became a painter and married in 1585. On the oeuvres of Lucia, Europa, and Anna Maria, see Harris and Nochlin, *Women Artists*, 109–14; Caroli, *Anguissola*, 149–75; and Lancetti, *Biografia Cremonese*, 247–50.

46. For example, Carlo Bonetti, "Varietà, Nel centenario di Sofonisba Anguissola," *Archivio storico lombardo* 55 (1928), part 1, 292, trying to explain why she would sign *adolescens* at twenty-seven, calls it "a pardonable, small feminine vanity."

47. The painting in the Accademia di San Luca bears the

date 1577 (the year of Fontana's marriage). A variant version in the Uffizi, long considered the artist's own replica, was catalogued by Maria Teresa Cantaro, *Lavinia Fontana bolognese "pittora singolare," 1552–1614* (Milan: Jandi Sapi Editori, 1989), 72–74, as a nonautograph copy. Cantaro suspected its authenticity in part because the word *virgo* was repeated in its inscription, while the date was changed from 1577 to 1578, when *virgo* should no longer have been applicable. Still unanswered is why a copyist would have changed the date.

48. For portraits of young northern Italian women, see Rosita Levi Pisetzky, *Storia del costume in Italia*, vol. 3 (Milan: Istituto editoriale italiano, 1966); and Ferruccia Cappi Bentivegna, *Abbigliamento e costume nella pittura Italiana*, vol. 1 (Rome: C. Bestetti, 1962).

49. Castiglione, *The Courtier*, 121–23.

50. See Pardo, *Pino*, 380.

51. Cf. the distinction drawn by Lisa Jardine between "fashionably 'masculine' female dress" and the transvestite, role-transgressive wearing of men's clothes, *Still Harping on Daughters: Women and Drama in the Age of Shakespeare* (Sussex, England: Harvester Press, 1983), 159–61.

52. Grafton and Jardine, *Humanism*, 35–36, esp. n. 16.

53. Ibid., 40–41.

54. Ibid., 48.

55. The probable influence of Anguissola on Fontana in the creation of this type of musical self-portrait, inscribed *virgo*, has been acknowledged; see Cantaro, *Fontana*, 74.

56. E.g., Harris and Nochlin, *Women Artists*, 108; and Chadwick, *Women, Art, and Society*, 72. Although Cantaro, *Fontana*, 6, alleges that Lavinia Fontana was instructed in letters and music, this is not stated in any of the early biographies. Lavinia may have studied music but not to the level of proficiency that would make the virginal her distinguishing attribute. Baldinucci, *Notizie*, 8:211, says that the Anguissola sisters were trained in music but radically subordinates this accomplishment to their practice of painting. The extent of Caterina van Hemessen's known association with music is that she married a musician.

57. The connection of virginals with women is widely acknowledged by music historians; see Sibyl Marcuse, *Musical Instruments: A Comprehensive Dictionary* (New York: Doubleday, 1975), 581.

58. E. Winternitz, *Musical Instruments and Their Symbolism in Western Art: Studies in Musical Iconography* (New Haven, Conn.: Yale University Press, 1979), 48–56, discusses the sexual symbolism of musical instruments.

59. See David Rosand, "*Ermeneutica Amorosa:* Observations on the Interpretation of Titian's Venuses," in *Tiziano e Venezia: Convegno internazionale di studi* (Vicenza: N. Pozza, 1980), 375–81.

60. See *I pittori bergamaschi* (Bergamo: Bolis, 1979), 3: 418–19.

61. Regina Stefaniak, "Raphael's *Santa Cecilia:* A Fine and Private Vision of Virginity," *Art History* 14 (1991): 360.

62. The Uffizi painting's attribution has been questioned, but it was first identified as Robusti's self-portrait by Marco Boschini (1675). The young woman holds a book of madrigals by a French composer, here open to the madrigal "Madonna per voi ardo" (*Painters by Painters*, exhibition catalogue [Florence: Uffizi Gallery and New York: National Academy of Design, 1988], cat. 6).

If gender conventions were not involved, women's self-portraits with musical instruments might more easily be read as metaphors for artistic creativity on the model of a prominent contemporary analogy: Veronese's *Marriage at Cana* (1563) features a string quartet at its center, whose musicians have been identified as Veronese, Titian, Tintoretto, and Jacopo Bassano. See Terisio Pignatti, *Veronese* (Venice: Alfieri, 1976), 126.

63. For example, Harris and Nochlin, *Women Artists*, 106. *The Chess Game* was seen by Vasari in the Anguissola home in 1566. For its subsequent provenance, see Caroli, *Anguissola*, 104.

64. Richard Eales, *Chess: The History of a Game* (New York: Oxford University Press, 1985), ch. 3; and Harry Golombek, *Chess: A History* (London: Putnam, 1976), chs. 7 and 8.

65. On the attributions of the Turin painting once ascribed to Sofonisba, see Caroli, *Anguissola*, 178; and *I Campi e la cultura artistica cremonese del Cinquecento* (Milan: Electa, 1985), 133–34.

66. Bert W. Meijer, "Cremona e i Paesi Bassi," in Caroli, *I Campi*, 25.

67. Golombek, *Chess*, 95–96. The interest of Campi and Anguissola in chess games could have been sparked by

their Cremonese compatriot Marco Girolamo Vida, who in 1527 published his *Scacchia Ludus,* a widely popular mock-heroic poem that described the new rules.

68. E.g., Machiavelli's "Comparison of the Game of Chess with the Notable Treatises of War," a manuscript dedicated to Cosimo I de' Medici. Cited by Eales, *Chess,* 91.

69. Castiglione, *The Courtier,* 127–28.

70. For Anguissola portraits that present problems of identification and authorship, see Caroli, *Anguissola,* cats. 37, 3, and 34.

71. For Tommaso Cavalieri's letter to Cosimo I de' Medici of 20 January 1562, and the accompanying two drawings, see Charles de Tolnay, "Sofonisba Anguissola and Her Relations with Michelangelo," *Journal of the Walters Art Gallery* 4 (1941): 115–19. Cavalieri writes that "the divine Michelangelo having seen a drawing done by her hand of a smiling girl, said that he would have liked to see a weeping boy, as a subject more difficult to draw . . . [after hearing this], she [Sofonisba] sent to him this drawing which was a portrait of her brother, whom she has intentionally shown as weeping." The incident was also mentioned by Vasari, 5: 81.

72. As Roberto Longhi first observed, Caravaggio is likely to have taken from Anguissola the finger-biting motif in his *Boy Bitten by a Lizard;* the point is reiterated in recent literature. The image was identified as homoerotic by Donald Posner, "Caravaggio's Homoerotic Early Works," *Art Quarterly* 34 (1971): 305.

73. *The Family Group* was described by Vasari when he visited the Anguissola house in 1566 (6: 498–99). By the mid seventeenth century the painting had come to Rome, where it was admired in the Villa Borghese by Baldinucci, among others.

74. *The Family Group* was discussed in these terms in the original, longer version of this essay.

75. Anguissola's letter to Campi (21 October 1561) is quoted in full by Caroli, *Anguissola,* 53–54; and in translation by Perlingieri, *Anguissola,* 126.

76. On Anguissola's Spanish portraits, see Marianne Haraszti-Takács, "Nouvelles Données relatives à la vie et à l'oeuvre de Sofonisba Anguissola," *Bulletin du Musée Hongrois des Beaux-Arts* 31 (1968): 53–67; and Caroli, *Anguissola.* Perlingieri provides valuable new documentation for Sofonisba's Spanish period, but many of her attributions are controversial.

77. Baldinucci, *Notizie,* 8:224.

78. See Harris and Nochlin, *Women Artists,* 107. Perlingieri, *Anguissola,* ch. 8, has claimed that the painter remained through the 1570s at the Spanish court, where she continued to receive commissions.

79. Returning to Cremona in late 1579, Anguissola met and shortly married Lomellini, who was captain of the ship. For new information on this marriage, see Perlingieri, *Anguissola,* 169–73. On Anguissola in Spain and Genoa, see Haraszti-Takács, "Nouvelles Données," 55–56; and Bonetti, "Varietà," esp. 292–95. There remains some confusion about Anguissola's whereabouts in the last decade of her life, but she was certainly in Genoa around 1624–25. Artists who met at her home included Procaccini, Gentileschi (presumably Orazio), Roncalli, and others. Lancetti spoke of the painters (in Genoa) "who went to admire and consult her" (Bonetti, "Varietà," 293).

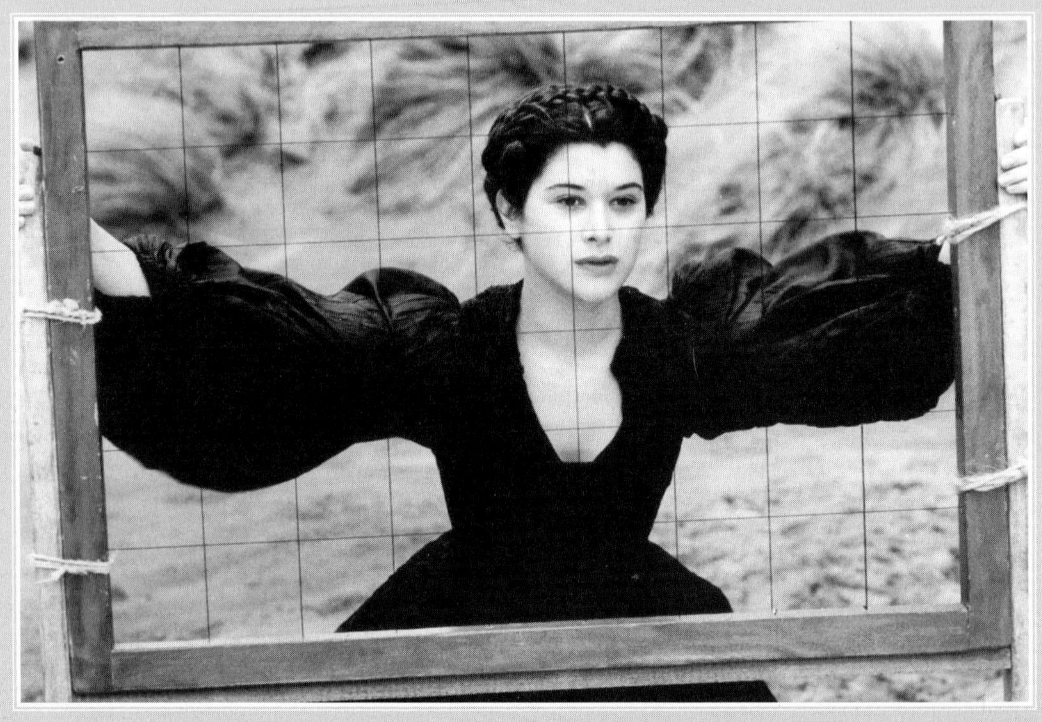

2

LEARNING TO BE LOOKED AT

*A Portrait of (the Artist as) a Young Woman
in Agnès Merlet's* Artemisia

Sheila ffolliott

AGNÈS MERLET'S 1997 FILM, *Artemisia,* opens with a full-screen tight close-up of an eye, under a sepia veiling effect that prevents it from appearing overly clinical.[1] The image provides an effective introduction to issues explored in this film about a seventeenth-century woman artist.[2] We might expect a film about a visual artist to concern that person's eye. We also expect film, itself a visual medium, to fascinate the eye of the spectator. Rather than simply confirm such expectations, this filmic eye unsettles. First, because of the extremity of the close-up, we see only part of the eye. Then, although it stares directly and fixedly forward, the eye blinks, and the pupil dilates and contracts, reacting to light. Finally, the camera itself is seldom still, adding to the nervousness generated by the image and the somewhat frenzied soundtrack.

Are we then to read this eye (staring directly forward) as that of the surveying *looker,* by which I mean—in the sixteenth-century sense—the viewer, the active agent (the "one who looks") choosing and controlling what is seen?[3] Or are we rather to see it (blinking, moving, and agitated) as the eye of the *lookee,* someone aware of being looked at or with the potential for being examined? While it flies in the face of conventional notions of the artist's eye, such an eye serves, in fact, as an effective emblem for the story of a woman artist in early modern Europe. For all women, following the strictures of the honor culture that obtained, were under constant scrutiny, their behavior monitored and apt to be criticized.[4] My use of the word *looker* to denote someone who looks will, in fact, seem archaic. By the end of the nineteenth century, *viewer* had replaced the earlier usage of *looker,* while *looker* now meant "a person, usually a woman, of particularly pleasing appearance."[5] The active agent has become just the opposite: a beautiful woman worthy of being looked at. This film, despite the filmmaker's assertions that she articulated the "inner struggle of an artistic voice," in fact, does the same thing, ultimately relegating her artist protagonist (the looker) to the more usual female position as the object of someone else's gaze (the looker, when female).

Over the past decade, early modern culture has come to the silver screen with a spate of productions of Shakespeare plays, the Oscar-winning *Shakespeare in Love* (1998), plus a recent efflorescence of films cen-

This essay was first published in *Quidditas: Journal of the Rocky Mountain Medieval and Renaissance Association* 20 (1999): 95–116. Reprinted courtesy of *Quidditas: Journal of the Rocky Mountain Medieval and Renaissance Association.*

Figure 2.1. Valentina Cervi in Agnès Merlet's *Artemisia*. Miramax Zoë. (Photo: Umberto Montiroli.)

tering upon early modern women: *Queen Margot* (1994), *Dangerous Beauty* (1998), *Elizabeth* (1999), and *Artemisia* (1997).[6] At the time of its 1998 United States premiere, this last film, ostensibly about the seventeenth-century Italian painter Artemisia Gentileschi, garnered a great deal of comment, not only in the press but also in more informal venues. A handout entitled "Now That You've Seen the Film, Meet the Real Artemisia Gentileschi," prepared by art historian and Artemisia Gentileschi scholar Mary D. Garrard with Gloria Steinem, was distributed at theaters and disseminated on listserves. Adrienne DeAngelis maintains a web site on the film, with links to reviews and related material.[7] Reviews appeared in the film press, and Garrard published a further review in *Art in America*.[8] Additionally, the Internet Movie Database (IMDb) facilitated the popular democracy of the web by providing a forum for self-generated evaluations and comment, and even a vote.[9]

Those commentators critical of the film have correctly pointed out serious problems in the trite, simplistic portrait of a female artist that *Artemisia* presents. Many focused on the historical inaccuracy of the portrayal, justifiably calling into question director and screenwriter Agnès Merlet's interpretation of Artemisia Gentileschi's life. Merlet, a 1982 graduate of the prestigious Ecole Nationale des Beaux-Arts in Paris, said that she was inspired to make this film after seeing Artemisia Gentileschi's painting of *Judith Slaying Holofernes* (presumably the Uffizi version, ca. 1620, because it figures in the film) in class and, replicating an experience common to many students of art history, feeling stunned to learn that a woman had painted this forceful and accomplished work.

In this essay I begin with a brief reference to the plot-based criticism of the film and then turn to comment on the cinematography, which, I argue—by drawing upon standard representations of women in sixteenth- and seventeenth-century works of art—contributes substantially to the problematic portrayal of this woman artist. On almost every occasion when Artemisia is shown making art, the camerawork undermines her artistic authority, relegating her to the more usual female position of the model.

Artemisia Gentileschi (1593–1652/3) was the first of four children born in Rome to Tuscan painter Orazio Gentileschi and Prudentia Montone.[10] Her mother died when Artemisia was twelve, and Orazio did not remarry. In terms of early modern European society, this created a practical problem (irrespective of any culturally appropriate sense of loss that father or children may have felt, about which we can only speculate). In the honor culture that obtained, an unprotected girl's chastity—the prime measure of a woman's virtue—was invariably suspect, and therefore needed shielding. While her father, a painter in oils, worked in his studio at home, all was well. Artemisia was protected and, like other early modern women artists, learned about art from her father.[11] When Artemisia was about eighteen, however, Orazio received a prestigious commission to undertake frescoes at the Quirinal palace (a papal residence). This medium required painting on location, which would, of necessity, remove him from the house. Orazio needed to provide for Artemisia's "protection," so, in 1611, he seemingly arranged for their neighbor, a woman called Tuzia, to move in with the family and chaperone his daughter.[12] Shortly thereafter, Agostino Tassi, her father's coworker on the fresco project, raped the young painter in her house. Elizabeth Cohen, who has drawn from the archival evidence of rape and other trials before the papal magistrates to illuminate the world of women in sixteenth- and seventeenth-century Rome, has set this event into its historical context.[13] As she demonstrates, seventeenth-century law did not consider rape a crime of violence against an individual, nor were its potentially traumatic effects on the victim understood in such terms. Rather, rape was a matter of honor: the rape of a virgin, in particular, compromised the woman and her family. Tassi was brought to trial and jailed, but only as the result of a suit put forward by Orazio about a year later.[14] The trial transcripts record the sometimes conflicting testimony of

Artemisia, Tassi, and several witnesses. Artemisia claimed that, scheming with Tuzia, Tassi took her by force although she fought back with a knife.

After the rape, however, Artemisia continued to have sex with Tassi because, she said, he promised to marry her, and that would have reinstated her honor in the public eye. Orazio too probably hoped for this "solution," but Tassi had not revealed that he was already married. At the trial, he admitted no wrongdoing and, in fact, to diminish the effects of his action, claimed that Artemisia was not a virgin. Witnesses supported both positions. Instead of delving into this complexity, however, Merlet took the easy way out. Jurisprudence employed torture to test the veracity of testimony when "he said/she said" versions remained at odds. In Tassi's trial, Artemisia was tortured, not he, and she did not recant. In the film, however, Merlet contrived a scene in which Tassi watches Artemisia's torture and then, because he cannot stand his "love object's" suffering, confesses. Her torture enables him to play the hero rather than confirming— in conformity with Roman legal theory—that she spoke the truth.[15] Tassi was jailed and we now know, thanks to new evidence unearthed by Alexandra LaPierre and Patrizia Cavazzini, that he was sentenced to five years' exile but evaded punishment with the help of his powerful patrons.[16]

Artemisia did eventually marry (not Tassi), had four children, then separated from her husband, and lived and worked in Florence, Rome, Naples, and England.[17] She achieved professional recognition on a par with her male peers, having been appointed a member of the Florentine artistic academy, the Accademia del Disegno, in 1616, and having executed work for, among other patrons, the grand dukes of Tuscany (as did Pietro da Cortona), Queen Henrietta Maria of England (as did van Dyck), and Don Antonio Ruffo of Messina, Sicily (as did Rembrandt). The number of works currently attributed to her hovers at around fifty.

Director Merlet, who also wrote the screenplay, chose to focus on the period around 1610–12, when Artemisia painted her earliest works and when she was raped.[18] This conforms to the pattern of the other films about early modern women: *Dangerous Beauty*, *Elizabeth*, *Queen Margot*, and *Artemisia* all focus on their protagonists' youths and emerging sexuality. As others have pointed out, what documentary evidence we have about the life of Artemisia Gentileschi relates overwhelmingly to the rape trial. It remains a matter of debate how much this experience, as it has been interpreted, affected her artistic production at the time and for the rest of her life.[19] The film's plot, however, links her emergence as an artist to what Merlet recasts as her sexual awakening, calling it "A Double Initiation: The Art of Painting and the Art of Loving."[20] Merlet portrays Agostino unequivocally as her teacher/lover.[21]

To provide a narrative framework to link the documented vestiges of the painter's life, Merlet, "in fleshing out [*sic*] Artemisia's character," looked rather to literary heroines. "I saw from the beginning that she was a great romantic heroine," Merlet said. "She reminded me of a character that the Brontës might have created or Thomas Hardy. Her destiny is to learn about passion in a painful way." Merlet thus projected the plot of a nineteenth-century heroine of romantic novels—that is, willful girl escapes the clutches of her father to follow her creative destiny; tragic lover helps her gain her "freedom," but they cannot marry—onto that of a seventeenth-century woman artist. The film also verges on full-blown grand opera. Aided by the Verdian strings of the overture, the film's plot resembles an admixture of *Rigoletto* and *Tosca*.[22] Such an anachronistic conceptualization begs all sorts of questions: primarily, why impose such fictional models when we have historical evidence about Artemisia herself and about the social milieu in which she lived and worked?

Merlet's acknowledged historical sources include Eva Menzio, who transcribed many of the trial documents, and Germaine Greer's study of women artists across time, *The Obstacle Race*.[23] Greer's characterization certainly contributes to the romantic narrative. On the set, moreover, Merlet must have engendered a climate of ignoring history for myth, for the actress who played Artemisia, Valentina Cervi, when interviewed, attested to having read about her character, but then having largely dismissed such research in favor of what she describes as a direct artist-to-artist intuition (completely ignoring what mediates such experience for her): "Books merely tell us what others think of her [Artemisia], but in her paintings I could feel her emotions, how she would react in each moment." Such naive essentialist claims have produced a film that clings to a decontextualized myth of the "artist" as someone (male) driven by a post-Romantic understanding of sex and passion.

Granted it is difficult to make a story about a woman artist simply by grafting a female protagonist onto the male master plot of the artist's life.[24] The Italian artist and historian Giorgio Vasari perfected the story line of the Renaissance artist's life in his 1550/68 collection of biographies of individual artists. These *Lives* (as biographies of heroized individuals) draw their plot structure from several literary genres, including epic.[25] Although there are variations in this enduring master narrative of art history, it is the artist's singular genius that eventually propels him to surpass his master. This master plot / plot of mastery (adopted as well by those writers succeeding Vasari who wrote on seventeenth-century artists) is still alive and well and informing the practice of art history.[26] In fact, the desire to surpass was not limited to the master-pupil relationship; it was the governing metaphor of art in the early modern period, based upon the *paragone* (comparison) that was played out in several categories of relationship: between pupil and master, between artists, between art forms (for example, painting and poetry), and ultimately between art and nature.

As Fredrika Jacobs makes clear, Vasari and his contemporaries employed different, distinctly female models to describe and evaluate women artists and art by women: models like the procreative one ("If women know so well how to make living men, what marvel is it that those who wish are also so well able to make them in painting?"), which, ironically, keeps women out of the male-only master-pupil genealogy.[27] Merlet's plot situates Artemisia between two male artist-rivals, her father-teacher and her rapist-teacher. There are times in the film when the young Artemisia claims that she will surpass her teachers, but in terms of the action, she rather leaves the authority of one male teacher for that of another. Even when it is clear at the end of the film that she and Tassi cannot marry, and Artemisia tells her father that the rape experience has hardened her and prepared her for the realities of life, she still hears Tassi's voice when she begins to paint.

Now I shall turn to an analysis of the way in which the cinema itself works to present this woman artist as the subject of an artwork rather than its maker. While others have concentrated their critiques on the script, I argue here that the camerawork by Benoît Delhomme further plots Artemisia into stereotype. A publicity photograph distributed by Miramax and captioned "Director Agnès Merlet on location for Artemisia" shows her at work, looking out at and holding up her hands to place within a frame the object of her sight, which is congruent with the viewer (fig. 2.2). On her right is, presumably, the cinematographer Benoît Delhomme, looking out from behind his camera, in an arrangement reminiscent of self-portraits like that of Velázquez in *Las Meninas*, where he stands beside his easel and looks out at the viewer, who is simultaneously in the position of his subject.

As the director/screenwriter confirms having drawn inspiration from nineteenth-century literature, the cinematographer acknowledges his inspiration from works of art. Delhomme, primitivist painter and cinematographer of *The Winslow Boy* (1999) and other films, has acknowledged looking at art for insight into the worlds he portrays.[28] The look of *The Winslow Boy* is informed, he says, by the works of John Singer Sargent. Other cinematographers have consciously or unconsciously, admittedly or not, done the same thing for films set in the early modern era. Scenes from *The Return of Martin Guerre*, for example, resonate with overtones from depictions of French peasants by the brothers LeNain and other images gleaned from sixteenth- and seventeenth-century painters, and Eric Rohmer's *Marquise d'O* is filled with

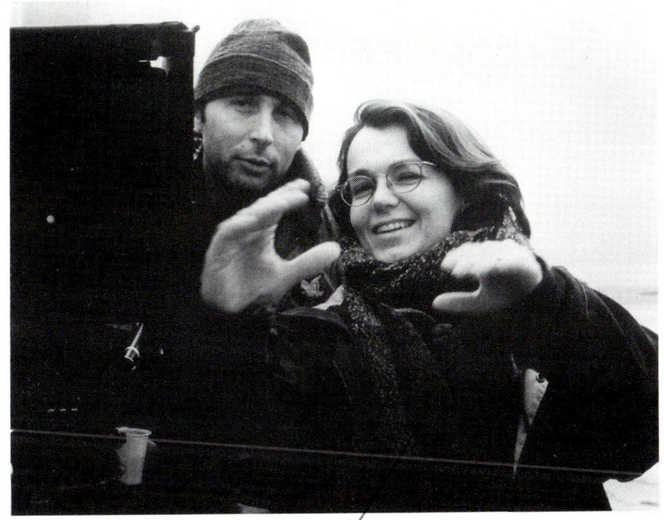

references to Greuze and other eighteenth-century painters.[29] Delhomme admits, in the case of *Artemisia*, to having been inspired by the work of Caravaggio, as was Artemisia Gentileschi herself. He must also have looked closely at portraits by artists like Dürer, who would create tiny highlights in the eyes of his subjects reflecting specific objects, like a window.[30] In the eye scene at the beginning of *Artemisia*, in fact, we see candles reflected on the eye's surface.

While useful in creating an atmosphere suggestive of the early seventeenth century (because this is how it seems to us), what other effects does drawing inspiration from sixteenth- and seventeenth-century paintings have on this portrayal of the life of Artemisia Gentileschi? This is not the space to rehearse the entire history of debate about the theory of the "gaze," but I refer to it here in order to contemplate the problem of representing a woman artist when employing models from seventeenth-century painting, which embody the "male gaze." Considering the implications of this notion for Renaissance art, Paolo Berdini argued, "As man is the subject of the look, woman is the object of the gaze, two complementary positions that constitute identity in the field of vision."[31] Such a formation not only has implications for gender but also sets these up as opposing positions

that one person cannot simultaneously occupy, even though, several decades after the appearance of Laura Mulvey's "Visual Pleasure and Narrative Cinema," which was highly influential in defining representation in terms of the presumably male-gendered gaze, we now acknowledge more fluid relationships with what we see.[32] Rather than assume an essential male gaze, postmodern notions of subjectivity present different opportunities for spectators to project and identify with what is seen. In other words, in a particular situation, spectators of either sex may assume male or female subject positions.

Whoever is responsible for the vision inherent in this film (and I do not want to speculate on intentionality or the respective gender expectations of a female director and a male cinematographer), there are moments in *Artemisia* in which the viewer sees and identifies with Artemisia Gentileschi as the owner of the artist's sovereign gaze, such as when we see her standing erect as she sizes up a young, awkwardly naked man posing for her sketch (fig. 2.3). More often, however, at the very moment when she is shown practicing her art (when she generates a gaze), the film all too quickly moves to reposition Artemisia as the object of someone else's gaze (fig. 2.1). Gaze theory, as originally articulated, is therefore doubly germane to an analysis of this film, with its acknowledged use of

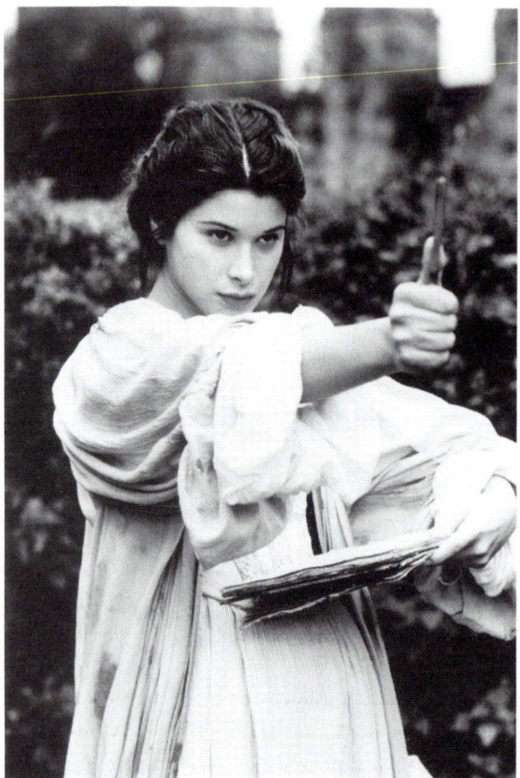

Figure 2.3. Valentina Cervi in Agnès Merlet's *Artemisia*. Miramax Zoë. (Photo: Umberto Montiroli.)

seventeenth-century paintings as inspiration for the look.[33] I shall consider two particular cases; both center on artistic practice.

Practically at the start of the film (before the main title), we see the young Artemisia drawing herself. She does this in secret to escape the prying glances of those in an invented convent school.[34] Such a setting for the young Artemisia Gentileschi is consistent with Merlet's vision of her as a Jane Eyre–like romantic heroine. Merlet stages Artemisia's self-study as a stolen moment (but, significantly, with the audience let in as voyeurs), a bit of private rebellion away from those who would discourage her incipient artistic interest, manifest in her (improper) interest in the body. The scene begins with her on her bed wearing (and partially removing) her chemise. She takes a small oval mirror and moves it and herself around to exam-ine (and display to the viewer) various parts of her body—shoulder, chest, and leg—with the aid of a candle. She then sets the mirror against a pillow and draws herself.

The mirror, of course, is emblematic of the artist's mimetic practice, but it was also practical, and many artists (e.g., Alberti and Leonardo) advocated its use for a variety of purposes. The mirror was used in particular for depicting oneself, whether for studies or finished self-portraits.[35] We have no evidence that Artemisia drew herself at all; but if she had, she would not have been the only artist to do so. At its most basic, the practice of drawing oneself provided an economical and expedient way to study the body (knowledge of the male body was considered fundamental to artistic practice), and probably many artists did it.[36] The sixteenth-century German artist Albrecht Dürer made several drawings of himself and acknowledged the use of a mirror.[37] He inscribed one portrait drawing: "This I fashioned after myself out of a mirror in the year 1484 when I was still a child."[38] Later, in 1513, as a more developed artist, he drew his own left hand, then analyzed its dimensions and used the result in his systematic studies of proportions.[39] In fact, there are no extant drawings by Artemisia or her father. Somewhat ironically, therefore, in 1625 another artist, Pierre Dumonstier le Neveu, portrayed Artemisia's frilly-cuffed raised right hand (British Museum, London) wielding a paintbrush, and inscribed the drawing with fulsome praise, not of the beauty of the hand itself but rather of the beauty that it could render.[40]

The more highly finished self-portrait often employed the fiction of the artist looking in the mirror. In *De Claris Mulieribus*, Boccaccio provided a biography of Marcia, an ancient woman artist who composed her self-portrait by looking in the mirror, and the episode was illustrated in fourteenth- and fifteenth-century manuscripts of that text. The sixteenth-century Italian painter Sofonisba Anguissola (like Dürer) inscribed a small self-portrait in which she holds an anagram of her father's name (Museum of Fine Arts, Boston) with the claim that it had been "painted from a mirror with her own hand," although the mirror does not appear in the portrait itself.[41] Another sixteenth-century Italian painter, Lavinia Fontana, produced a self-portrait with a mirror. Perhaps the most famous early modern self-portrait involving the looking glass is that by the young Parmigianino (Kunsthistorisches Museum, Vienna), made to resemble a convex mirror; this work is not a study, but a theorized tour-de-force intended to impress.[42]

But while there is a tradition of the self-portrait using the device of the mirror, there is an important difference between those portraits and the way in which Delhomme and Merlet present Artemisia's examination and drawing of herself in the film. Their portrayal presents us with a seminude Artemisia looking at herself in order to sketch. The drawings resulting from this study that we are shown are not complete portraits but studies of parts of her anatomy. Here too, the film fits right into Mulvey's gendered categorizations, in that Artemisia's body is presented in parts, both in the film itself and in the sketches.

There is, in fact, one example of an early modern nude self-portrait, Dürer's of 1503 (Staatliche Kunstsammlung, Weimar).[43] Joseph Koerner notes that the artist represents himself in three-quarter length, with his locks pulled back in a hairnet, which shifts attention away from the usual focus of self-portraiture—the face and hands—to what he calls "his naked and exposed private body."[44] In these images, significantly, Dürer faces the viewer and, even when nude, retains some authority—because he stands. Our glimpse into the filmic Artemisia's self-study, however, shows her unaware of our presence, as she intently poses for herself and the viewer.

Not only is the experience of viewing her at work not similar to self-portraits; it also does not conform to contemporary depictions of the artist's studio, where clothed apprentices sit in chairs around a table sketching after casts. Of course, Merlet's staging underscores the fact that Artemisia was excluded, by virtue of her sex, from such places of organized study. But recall that, in fact, she learned her art in her father's studio. In the film, however, her gratuitous secret study provides views of her entire body, or its

parts, on her bed, bathed in candlelight—and thus recalls another painting tradition, that of women simply looking at themselves. Some of these include a mirror, in subjects like "Venus at Her Toilette" (the mirror also serves as an attribute of Venus), so Artemisia's staging reminds the knowledgeable viewer of depictions of nude or seminude women contemplating themselves in the mirror, like those by Bellini (Kunsthistorisches Museum, Vienna), Titian (Louvre, Paris, and National Gallery, Washington), Rubens (Prince of Liechtenstein, Vaduz), Annibale Carracci (National Gallery, Washington), and Velázquez (National Gallery, London).[45] Therefore, when confronted with an image of a woman looking into a mirror, the viewer, prepared by the image tradition, sees her activity not as that of an artist, but rather more as someone concerned for her looks and preparing to receive a male visitor. In others of these images, allegory kicks in, the woman's mirror-gazing alluding to the vice of vanity.[46]

As the camera glances over Artemisia's body, it does not always show the mirror. Thus this scene features a nude female without a mirror but looking at her body bathed in candlelight—for example, Caravaggesque works on the nocturnal "Flea Hunt" theme. In fact, John F. Moffitt's description of Gerard Honthorst's *Merry Flea Hunt* (Kunstmuseum, Basel) and of Georges de La Tour's *La Femme à la puce/The Flea Catcher* (Musée Historique Lorrain, Nancy) could, in fact, just as aptly apply to the scene of Artemisia drawing herself in the Merlet film: "We voyeur-like, eavesdrop upon the boudoir of a voluptuous, solitary maiden seated upon a rumpled bed and barely clad in a clinging peignoir . . . in which (Honthorst) a woman pulls back the bedclothes or (Georges de la Tour) sits by the light of the candle to inspect herself."[47] This subject has, in fact, been related to classical and French erotic poetry on the topic of the nocturnal flea, which enjoys unimpeded access to the female body. Moffitt concludes his article on the literary meaning of the "amorous flea" by relating the artist's task to the flea: "The painter takes on the role of the . . . flea. The color-daubed tip of

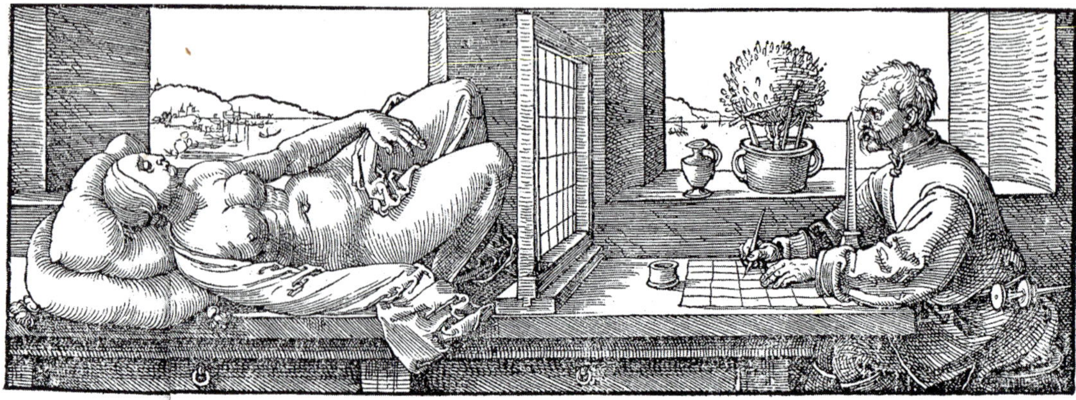

Figure 2.4. Albrecht Dürer, *Unterweisung des Messung*. By permission of the Folger Shakespeare Library, Washington, D.C.

the painter's brush becomes the microcosmic amorous adventurer, scaling the breathtaking scenes of the swelling hills and dales of his recumbent mistress's roseate body."[48] In neither of these prototypes is the woman's self-scrutiny connected with her own artistic endeavor; rather it is related to her being looked at by others. Because of the representational tradition, the combination of her being nude, in bed, using a mirror, and lit by a candle robs Artemisia of whatever artistic authority she might possess.

Later on in the film, Artemisia has begun lessons with Tassi. He introduces his young pupil to an optical device—a grid of strings suspended horizontally and vertically in a frame—used to translate what is viewed to what is depicted. This grid recurs at several subsequent moments in the film. The device, a lattice of strings called a *velo* or *vela,* is mentioned by Alberti and Leonardo da Vinci.[49] While a mimetic imperative drove the practice of art in the early modern era, theories about how it might be achieved varied. In the fifteenth century, stemming from an attempt to be more scientific about their practice, artists sought to give their art a rational (ergo mathematical) basis. Tools were devised to facilitate artistic practice that regarded the painted surface / picture plane as a window to be looked through to see the world that artists created. A gridded frame permitted artists to replicate more precisely what they saw in each square through

transcription to similar squares drawn on the surface upon which they worked.

A well-known sixteenth-century woodcut illustration by Dürer (made for his how-to book on the mathematical practice of art) shows a male artist looking through such a grid at a seminude female model reclining before him (fig. 2.4). The text accompanying this illustration describes the practice and includes the following: "Then place the object [in this case, of course, a female model] to be drawn a good distance away. Move it or bend it as you like . . . so as to please you."[50] If you put yourself into the position of the artist, you can imagine the view of the female model that you would have, as several art historians have described.

In the film, Tassi instructs Artemisia in the use of various optical instruments.[51] Then they go outdoors and she, used to working indoors and close to her subject matter, claims she cannot see anything worthy of painting, while Tassi tells her that the "world is vast" and proceeds to try to teach her, we could say, to adopt a male gaze (the ability to identify with figures positioned outdoors in landscape and in action).[52] The grid is set up to frame a view of ocean and sky. At first we see both teacher and pupil on the land side (where the artist would normally stand), but then Tassi tells Artemisia to close her eyes, and he describes what she'll see when she opens them ("The sea pushes at the horizon . . ."). At the conclusion of his narration, he has moved to the other side of the frame. We see her through the grid as she opens her eyes and "sees," or at least articulates what he has told her to see. His description becomes her vision. And he has assumed the position of the artist and she the model.

I was reminded here of the narrative created by the installation in Washington's National Gallery of Art of its first one-woman exhibition almost fifty years after it opened: the 1987 show devoted to the nineteenth-century French painter Berthe Morisot. The first painting confronting the viewer entering that exhibition was Manet's *Le Repos: Portrait of Berthe Morisot* (Museum of Art, Rhode Island School of Design, Providence), not a work by the artist herself. The initial impression, then, was that of another—more canonical—artist's representation of the woman artist as model. Only after taking this in did one turn to Morisot's own works. Having been duly "framed" by a superior masculine artist, Morisot's own production was, even if unwittingly, prejudiced by a museum so committed to the canon that it could not see her otherwise.[53]

To return to Merlet's film, the gridded frame recurs at two other points in the film. First, during the rape trial, when Artemisia visits Tassi in jail. She inquires if his cell has a window and, if so, what he sees from it. He begins to describe the landscape ("two hills . . ."), using the sort of artistic-poetic language he had employed earlier, and she closes her eyes. The camera then moves to the view from his cell window, seen through a grid of iron bars. The artificial gridded frame appearing in Dürer's "how-to" book has its window-based equivalent in a contemporary treatise on the practice of perspective by Johann II von Pfälz-Simmeren.[54] It contains an illustration of a young draftsman transcribing the landscape he sees through a reticulated window onto a gridded surface.[55] However, in the film the gridded window serves to intensify the mythmaking rather than to illustrate artistic practice, for it replays a prototype from the life of the ur-romantic artist, Vincent Van Gogh, who painted his expressionistic vision, *Starry Night* (Museum of Modern Art, New York), from the barred window of his cell in the mental hospital at St. Rémy.

The gridded frame makes a final appearance at the end of the film. Artemisia breaks into Tassi's studio and takes the frame outdoors. She sets it up facing the sea, as Tassi had originally done. We are behind her, looking with her through the grid as she makes adjustments and ponders her potential subject matter. But then the camera switches position and we view her, like a model rather than an artist, through the squares of the frame. Once on the "model" side, she bends over to reposition it and, as she does so, the camera catches a privileged perspective view of her cleavage (fig. 2.1). Then we return to a position behind her as she recites Tassi's description of his view from his jail cell ("two hills . . ."), while we view the ocean.

Although we see her initially using the device to size up the world to produce an image, our view *with* her is shortly transformed into a view *of* her through the squares. Artemisia practically assumes the position of the female model in Dürer's woodcut. She is thereby returned to the more conventional location for a female—as a model in a picture seen/made by someone else rather than the originator of the image. Moreover, although Artemisia stands, unlike Dürer's recumbent model seen through the grid, the cinematographer's gaze is directed right at her chemise-less cleavage, as Dürer's artist's gaze had been directed at his model's sex. The final impression of Merlet's film is of Artemisia not as the "looker" but rather as the "lookee." Once again, her being on view, her body constantly scrutinized, undermines her being taken seriously as the image-maker.

Dürer's woodcut image of the female model under the methodical scrutiny of the new Renaissance artist has been employed frequently in art history books to serve as an uncomplicated illustration of scientifically based artistic practice, even serving as the cover for Joshua Taylor's influential primer, *Learning to Look*, an introduction to visual analysis first published in 1957. That book was intended, as its author states, to teach a basic appreciation of art. By employing that image for the cover, it also teaches about gender roles in artistic practice.

It was only in the 1970s that the Dürer began to be deconstructed, and, whereas the woodcut appeared uncomplicatedly before, it now appears frequently to illustrate points about gender, power, and representation.[56] H. Diane Russell observed, "The reclining figure is a half-nude female who has her eyes closed. She is an object on a table, just as are a lute and a vase that are shown in two other perspective woodcuts in the treatise."[57] In his analysis of this image, Joseph Koerner makes the following observation: "Dürer has articulated the various zones of representation—artist, model, image, and viewer—classifying them through a system of antitheses: female and male, supine and upright, naked and clothed, rounded and square."[58] In this system, you cannot be artist and model at the same time. Referring to Dürer's self-portraits, mentioned earlier, however, Koerner argues that his "self-portrait studies highlight the tension between looking and representing and unite maker and model."[59] But, because of gender ideologies and the representational tradition, this cannot be true for the filmed Artemisia: she must oscillate between the two positions. Artemisia may have the power to attract looks, but in so doing she loses artistic authority. She remains an object rather than a subject or a maker of meaning. Merlet's film doesn't show Artemisia learning to look so much as learning to be looked at.[60]

NOTES

1. I am particularly indebted to Sharon Beehler, Peter Brunette, Elizabeth Cohen, Diane Dillon, Claire Farago, Ann ffolliott, Susan Frye, Mary D. Garrard, Peter Lukehart, Sara Jayne Steen, Ellen Todd, and Georgianna Ziegler for their help.
2. John C. Tibbetts, "Artemisia," H-Net Reviews, http://www.h-net.msu.edu/reviews/exhibit/showrev.cgi?path=142, also noticed the significance of the eye close-up, calling it "a perfect précis for the entire film." We disagree, however, on how the eye emblematizes what goes on in the film.
3. *OED*, 1556; J. Heywood, *Spider & Flie*, xcii, 181.
4. Paolo Berdini, "Women under the Gaze: A Renaissance Genealogy," *Art History* 21 (1998): 576: "To be under the gaze is for woman the consequence of the Fall, a form of punishment for that act of transgression."
5. *OED*, 1893; S. Crane, *Maggie*, v. 41.
6. The Internet Movie Database (IMDb) lists 118 film and television productions of Shakespeare plays since 1990.
7. The web site can be found at http://www.efn.org/~acd/Artemisia.html.
8. Mary D. Garrard, "Artemisia's Trial by Cinema," *Art in America* 86 (1998): 65–69; republished in *Singular Women*, ed. Kristen Frederickson and Sarah Webb (Berkeley: University of California Press, 2003).
9. The Internet Movie Database recorded a total of 418 votes, generating an average response of 6.7/10: a D+.
10. Biographical details about Artemisia appear in Mary D. Garrard, *Artemisia Gentileschi: The Image of the Female Hero in Baroque Painting* (Princeton, N.J.: Princeton University Press, 1989); R. Ward Bissell, *Artemisia Gentileschi and the Authority of Art* (University Park: Pennsylvania State University Press, 1999); Elizabeth Cropper, "Gentileschi, Artemsia," in *Dictionary of Women Artists*, ed. Delia Gaze (London: Fitzroy Dearborn Publishers, 1997), 1: 565–70; and "Life on the Edge: Artemisia Gentileschi, Famous Woman Painter," in Keith Christiansen and Judith W. Mann, *Orazio and Artemisia Gentileschi* (New York: Metropolitan Museum of Art and New Haven: Yale University Press, 2001).
11. Lavinia Fontana's father was a painter, but Sofonisba Anguissola's father was not, and he arranged for her to receive instruction from a male professional. Young boys were simply apprenticed to established masters.
12. Cropper, "Gentileschi," 576.
13. Elizabeth Cohen, "The Trials of Artemisia Gentileschi: A Rape as History," *Sixteenth Century Journal* 31 (2000): 47–76. She argues that only two categories of rape received adjudication: *stupro* (forcible defloration of a virgin) and adultery.
14. Cohen, "Trials," 59–60. The trial began in March 1612 and lasted seven months.
15. This analysis derives from Garrard, "Trial."
16. Alexandra LaPierre, *Artemisia: Un duel pour l'immortalité* (Paris: R. Laffont, 1998); Patrizia Cavazzini, *Palazzo Lancelotti ai Coronari* (Rome: Istituto Poligrafico e Zecca dello Stato, 1998), 175–76, cited by Cohen, "Trials," 49.

17. Her arranged marriage to Pietro Antonio di Vincenzo Stiattesi took place on November 29, 1612.

18. The Miramax credits list, "Original screenplay by Agnès Merlet, with the collaboration of Christine Miller; Adaptation and Dialogue, Agnès Merlet and Patrick Amos."

19. Cohen, "Trials," 47, argues that overly presentist interpretations of rape have affected the interpretation of her paintings.

20. This and later quotations attributed to the director and the actress playing Artemisia appeared in "Production Notes" included in the publicity packet distributed by Miramax-Zoë, unpaginated.

21. For his basic biography, see Antonietta dell'Agli, "Tassi [Buonamici], Agostino," *The Dictionary of Art*, ed. Jane Shoaf Turner (New York: Grove's Dictionaries, 1996), 30: 355–56.

22. *Rigoletto* in that it involves a widower concerned for his daughter's honor; *Tosca* in that the filmed Artemisia behaves more like someone who would sing "Vissi d'Arte, Vissi d'Amore" ("I lived for my art, I lived for love") than the innocent Gilda. Krishna Levy composed the score for *Artemisia*.

23. Germaine Greer, "The Magnificent Exception," in *The Obstacle Race: The Fortunes of Women Painters and Their Work* (New York: Farrar, Straus, Giroux, 1979), 189–207; Eva Menzio, ed., *Artemisia Gentileschi/Agostino Tassi, Atti di un processo per stupro* (Milan: Edizione dell Donne), 1981.

24. The *locus classicus* of this argument appeared in Linda Nochlin's pioneering "Why Have There Been No Great Women Artists?" *Art News* 69 (1970–71): 22–45 and 62–71. Cropper, "Edge," forcefully reasserted the impossibility of studying Artemisia Gentileschi simply as an "artist," as if that term were gender-neutral.

25. See Patricia Rubin, "What Men Saw: Vasari's Life of Leonardo da Vinci and the Image of the Renaissance Artist," *Art History* 13 (1990): 34–46; and Corine Schleif, "The Roles of Women in Challenging the Canon of 'Great Master' Art History," in *Attending to Early Modern Women*, ed. Susan D. Amussen and Adele Seeff (Newark: University of Delaware Press, 1998), 74–92. For insights on Vasari, thanks also to Leonard Barkan and the members of his 1993 Folger Institute seminar "The Language and History of the Arts: Vasari and His Tradition."

26. Most introductory art history survey books reproduce a Vasarian structure. See Sheila ffolliott, "Putting Women into the Picture: Gender and Art History in the Classroom," in Amussen and Seeff, *Attending to Women*, 74–92.

27. Fredrika H. Jacobs, *Defining the Renaissance Virtuosa: Women Artists and the Language of Art History and Criticism* (Cambridge: Cambridge University Press, 1997), esp. ch. 3, "(Pro) creativity," 27–63. For the sixteenth century, drawing from antiquity, in procreation men provided the form and women merely the matter. Frances Borzello, *Seeing Ourselves: Women's Self Portraits* (New York: Henry N. Abrams, 1998), 28, refers to the same passage.

28. Laura Winters, "A Risk-Taking Perfectionist behind the Camera," *New York Times*, 5 December 1999, 36.

29. See Craig Eliason's website "Art History Goes to the Movies," http://www.rci.rutgers.edu/~eliason/ahgttm.htm.

30. Dürer's *Self Portrait as Christ* (Munich: Alte Pinakotek) and his *Portrait of Hieronymus Holzschner* (Berlin: Staatliche Museum) both display this ruse.

31. Berdini, "Women under the Gaze," 566.

32. Laura Mulvey, "Visual Pleasure and Narrative Cinema," in *Visual and Other Pleasures* (Bloomington: Indiana University Press, 1989), 14–26.

33. Margaret Olin, "Gaze," in *Critical Terms for Art History*, ed. Robert S. Nelson and Richard Shiff (Chicago: University of Chicago Press, 1996), 208–19, informs much of this discussion.

34. Cropper, "Gentileschi," 576, mentions Orazio's "proposal that she [Artemisia] become a nun." This would have obviated the problem of dealing with a motherless daughter.

35. Heinrich Schwarz, "Schicle, Dürer, and the Mirror," *Art Quarterly* 30 (1967): 217.

36. Bellori, a seventeenth-century art critic, wrote of Caravaggio that he was too poor to use models, so he drew himself. See also Borzello, *Seeing Ourselves*, 26, about artists' self-depictions.

37. Joseph Leo Koerner, *The Moment of Self-Portraiture in German Renaissance Art* (Chicago: University of Chicago Press, 1993), discusses these drawings in detail.

38. Koerner, *Moment of Self-Portraiture*, 47.

39. Ibid., 156–57, where Koerner notes Dürer's making his own hand exemplary of his ideal in these proportion studies.

40. Joanna Woods-Marsden, *Renaissance Self-Portraiture: The Visual Construction of Identity and the Social Status of the Artist* (New Haven, Conn.: Yale University Press, 1998), 195; and Garrard, *Female Hero*, 64. This too is a topos: Koerner, *Moment of Self-Portraiture*, 156, discusses Dürer's hand as the creator of beauty.

41. Woods-Marsden, *Renaissance Self-Portraiture*, 203: SOPHONISBA ANGUISSOLA VIR[GO] IPSIUS MANU EX [S]PECULO DEPICTAM CREMONAE.

42. Ibid., 133–37.

43. Illustrated in Koerner, *Moment of Self-Portraiture*, fig. 120. Women would do nude self-portraits only in the twentieth century; see Borzello, *Seeing Ourselves*, 139ff.

44. Koerner, *Moment of Self-Portraiture*, 239, notes further that this drawing displays "the body with a frankness that is without antecedent or successor within the western tradition until this century."

45. See, for example, Rona Goffen, "Bellini's *Nude with Mirror,*" *Venezia Cinquecento: Studi di storia dell'arte e della cultura* 1 (1991): 185–99.

46. Woods-Marsden, *Renaissance Self-Portraiture*, 33, citing Benjamin Goldberg, *The Mirror and the Man* (Charlottesville: University Press of Virginia, 1985). Other categories of picture feature women looking at mirrors, e.g., Allegories of Vanity and images of Mary Magdalene. Melancholy, an important feature of the artistic temperament generally denied to women, also requires an introspective female figure for its iconography. See Jacobs, *Defining the Renaissance* Virtuosa, 64–84; Juliana Schiesari and Marilyn Miguel, eds., *The Gendering of Melancholy: Feminism, Psychoanalysis and the Symbolics of Loss in Renaissance Literature* (Ithaca, N.Y.: Cornell University Press, 1992); and, with regard to Artemisia Gentileschi's own art, Mary D. Garrard, *Artemisia Gentileschi around 1622: The Shaping and Reshaping of an Artistic Identity* (Berkeley: University of California Press, 2001).

47. John F. Moffitt, "*La Femme à la puce:* The Textual Background of Seventeenth-Century Painted 'Flea Hunts,'" *Gazette des Beaux-Arts* 6, no. 110 (1987): 99; Barry Wind, "Close Encounters of the Baroque Kind: Amatory Paintings by Terbrugghen, Baburen, and La Tour," *Studies in Iconography* 4 (1978): 115–24.

48. Moffitt, "*La Femme à la puce,*" 102.

49. Thanks to Clare Farago for clarification on these points. See Martin Kemp, *The Science of Art: Optical Themes in Western Art from Brunelleschi to Seurat* (New Haven, Conn.: Yale University Press, 1990), 171; and Mary Pardo, "Veiling the *Venus of Urbino,*" in *Titian's The Venus of Urbino,* ed. Rona Goffen (Cambridge: Cambridge University Press, 1997), 108–28.

50. Albrecht Dürer, *The Painter's Manual: A Manual of Measurement of Lines, Areas, and Solids by Means of Compass and Ruler* (1538), trans. Walter L. Strauss (New York: Abaris Books, 1977).

51. These conform to artistic practice as described by scholars like Martin Kemp, *The Science of Art*, and more recently by artist David Hockney, *Secret Knowledge: Rediscovering the Lost Techniques of the Old Masters* (New York: Viking Studio), 2001.

52. Olin, "Gaze," 211.

53. Shortly after the Morisot exhibit, the National Gallery of Art held a one-person exhibition of Georgia O'Keeffe. Apparently there was discussion about mounting a simultaneous "complementary" exhibition of Alfred Stieglitz's portrait photographs of O'Keeffe, many of which depicted the artist/model in the nude.

54. Johann II von Pfalz-Simmeren, *Eyn schön nützlich Büchlein under Underweisung der Kunst des Messens, mit dem Zirckel, Richtscheidt, oder Linial . . .* (Simmern, 1531). Facsimile edition, ed. Trude Aldrian, *Instrumentaria artium,* 4 (Graz: Akademische Druck-und Verlagsanstalt, 1970).

55. James Elkins, *The Poetics of Perspective* (Ithaca, N.Y.: Cornell University Press, 1994), 51.

56. Some examples: John Berger, *Ways of Seeing* (Harmondsworth: BBC and Penguin Books, 1972); and Lynda Nead, *The Female Nude: Art, Obscenity, and Sexuality* (London: Routledge, 1992).

57. H. Diane Russell, *Eva/Ave: Woman in Renaissance and Baroque Prints* (Washington, D.C.: National Gallery of Art and New York: Feminist Press at the City University of New York, 1990), 23. She contrasts this image with one of a male artist similarly employing instruments to make a portrait of a man: "In the portrait illustration, by contrast, the subject is a man. He is fully dressed and sits upright in a chair, a posture that bespeaks inherent dignity. He, moreover, looks directly and alertly back at the artist."

58. Koerner, *Moment of Self-Portraiture*, 446.

59. Koerner characterized the self-portrait in Erlangen, ca. 1491, as "an anatomy of the tensions that attend the double activity of looking and representing"

(ibid., 239). See also, in this context, Woods-Marsden, *Renaissance Self-Portraiture*, 37.

60. Although this remains a matter of debate, Borzello, *Seeing Ourselves*, 43, interprets Sofonisba Anguissola's *Bernardino Campi Painting Sofonisba Anguissola,* an image in which we see her as the subject of a portrait being painted by her teacher, as "defining the conflict inherent in the unnaturalness of being a female artist in the sixteenth century . . . making herself as pretty as a picture—the object of the gaze and not the maker of the object." See also Woods-Marsden, *Renaissance Self-Portraiture*, 208–209; and chapter 1, this volume.

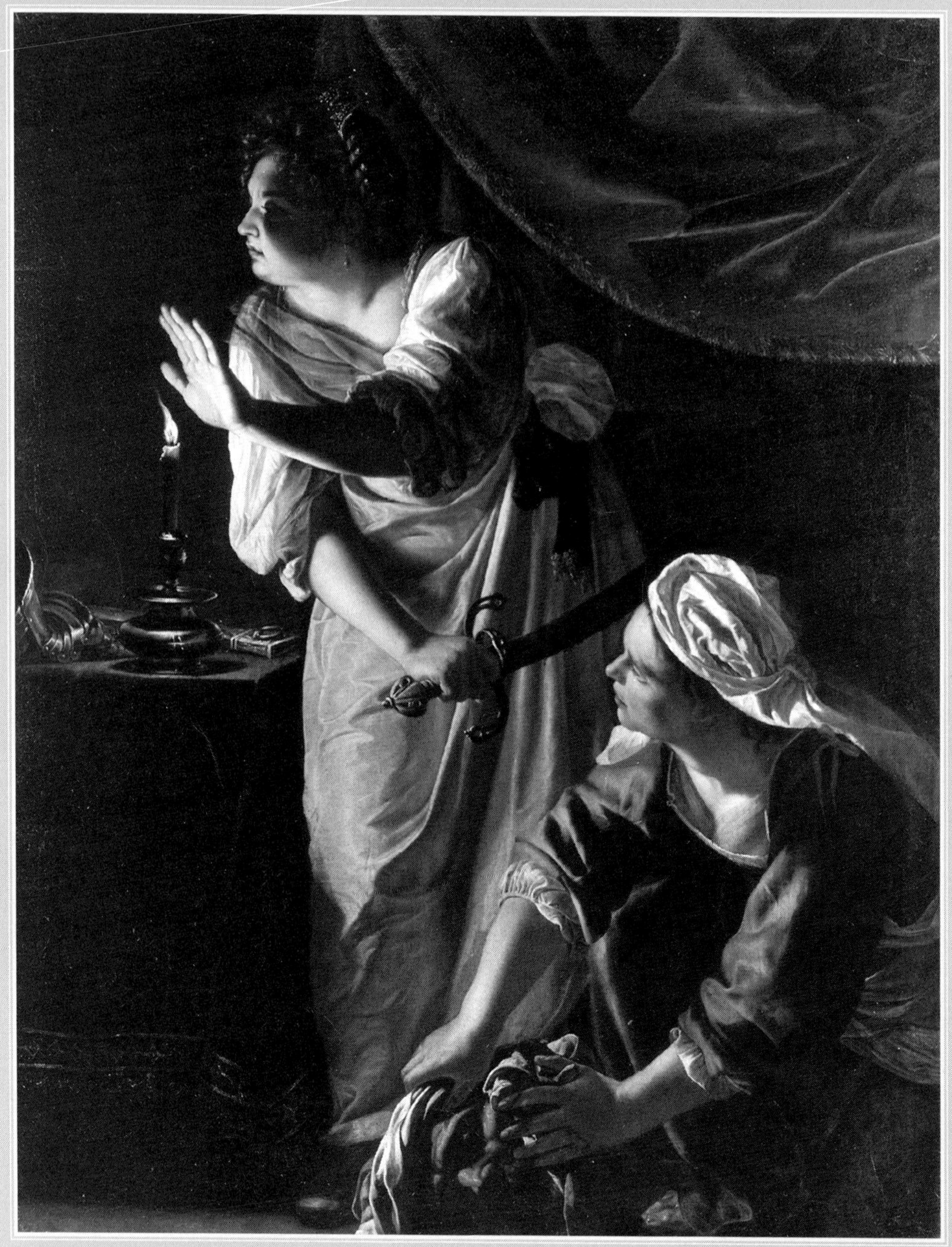

3

ARTEMISIA'S HAND

Mary D. Garrard

ART HISTORIANS who are normally careful connoisseurs seem to crumble at the alleged sight of Artemisia's face. The Hugford *Female Martyr* (fig. 3.2) is one of several paintings that have recently been attributed to Artemisia Gentileschi and identified as images of the artist herself. Another is the *Woman Playing a Lute* now in Minneapolis (fig. 3.3), presented in the 2002 *Orazio and Artemisia Gentileschi* exhibition and its catalogue as a self-portrait of the artist.[1] These two works are very different in style, however, and the faces somewhat divergent in physiognomy. The very possibility of recognizing Artemisia's image in a painting, it appears, must trump serious considerations of style and other factors.

We may reasonably ask whether there are quite so many self-portraits and self-images as have been claimed. The compulsion to identify Artemisia herself in every woman's face she painted, despite the lack of resemblance among the faces in these images, may well be influenced by gendered preconceptions. One is the cultural habit of seeing woman as object-to-be-looked-at, the site of scopophilic pleasure. A preoccupation with the female body in these terms led many early modern writers to fixate upon women artists as objects of beauty rather than as active agents, a way of thinking that has by no means disappeared

in today's world. A related gender stereotype, female narcissism, lurks behind the suggestion that Artemisia, locked in a claustrophobic Roman household, became obsessed with her own features and painted them repeatedly (this was recently proposed by one art historian and hinted at by another). Such gendered assumptions are all the more dangerous when unacknowledged, because they silently buttress attributions presented as value-neutral and thus affect the defining of Artemisia's oeuvre and artistic identity.

As a way of challenging certain recent attributions and establishing broader criteria, I propose that we turn away from faces and look at *hands,* an unexamined aspect of Artemisia's distinctive style. It is a tenet of traditional connoisseurship that the depiction of hands can be an identifying trait of an artistic "hand." Giovanni Morelli and Bernard Berenson argued that the hand ranked somewhere below the eyes and mouth in revealing the descriptive habits of individual artists. These connoisseurs focused, however, on the static details of fingernails, wrinkles, or the shape of a thumb. Max Friedländer, another eminent connoisseur, more astutely observed that "the hand speaks more through its movement than through its shape."[2] Indeed, the hand speaks through *both* its movement and its shape, but we in the twenty-first

This essay is adapted from a paper given at the international symposium "Artemisia Gentileschi: Taking Stock," held at the St. Louis Art Museum, St. Louis, Missouri, 13 September 2002. For reproductions of the many paintings by Artemisia discussed here that could not be illustrated, see Mary D. Garrard's 1989 *Artemisia Gentileschi,* Ward Bissell's *Artemisia Gentileschi and the Authority of Art,* or Keith Christiansen and Judith W. Mann's *Orazio and Artemisia Gentileschi* (cited in notes).

Figure 3.1. Artemisia Gentileschi, *Judith and Her Maidservant with the Head of Holofernes,* ca. 1625. Oil on canvas. The Detroit Institute of Arts, gift of Leslie H. Green.

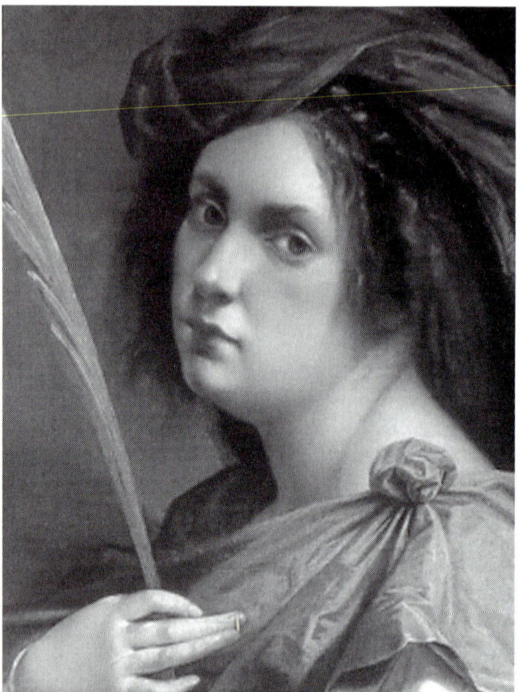

Figure 3.2. Attributed to Artemisia Gentileschi, *Female Martyr*, ca. 1615? Oil on panel. Private collection. (Photo: owner.)

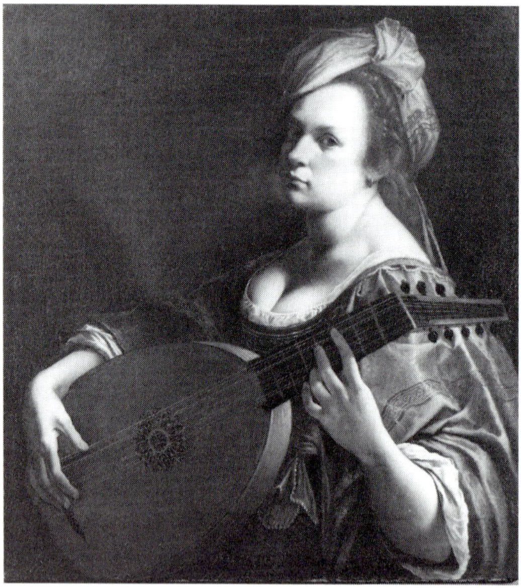

Figure 3.3. Attributed to Artemisia Gentileschi, *Portrait of a Woman Playing a Lute*, ca. 1615–17. Oil on canvas. Curtis Galleries, Minneapolis, Minnesota. (Photo: Curtis Galleries.)

century are positioned to take this consideration further, for hands in art are shaped and move according to a variety of social preconceptions.

Like faces, hands have a gender dimension. They are the locus of agency, both literally and symbolically. In the early modern period, when the only female agency that signified was located in the womb, it is not surprising that some female artists, as if to compensate, depicted female characters with unusually strong forearms and firm hands, whose agility and grip express the women's power to act upon the world. Artemisia, above all, gives us such figures. It is through their hands that Artemisia's women take on the world and confront adversity. Looking at the Uffizi *Judith*, we fixate upon the bloody decapitation, achieved with surgical skill by two coldly detached women, but we rarely comment on those supremely competent hands, wrists, and forearms that carry out the determined minds' command. In Artemisia's world, female figures hammer and paint, grab and hold, push and shove, with extraordinary ease. Their hands and arms are exceptionally strong, more than adequate for the job to be done. Lucretia, for instance, clutches both breast and sword with an anxious energy that doubles the tension shown in her face. The midwives in the *Birth of the Baptist* barely *have* faces, but they all have powerful forearms that move the basins around the space as capably as they got that baby born.

Perhaps the most capable hands in all of Artemisia's oeuvre are those of Abra in the Detroit *Judith* (fig. 3.1). These large, strong hands lead us into the picture at its base, the viewer's point of entry into this large painting, establishing the theme of female power to be amplified above. Gently but firmly, and with an ease that bespeaks self-confidence, Abra's hands close the sack around the ashen head, indifferent to the blood that stains their fingers. Our eyes are led from Abra's hands through her arms and gaze, upward, to the most dramatic display of gestural rhetoric in Artemisia's art. Judith's flamboyant gestures are dramatic, but also subtle. With her right hand, she claims authority, gripping Holofernes' sword with unusual determination. The angle of her wrist echoes that of the defeated general's empty gauntlet on the table, as if to mock

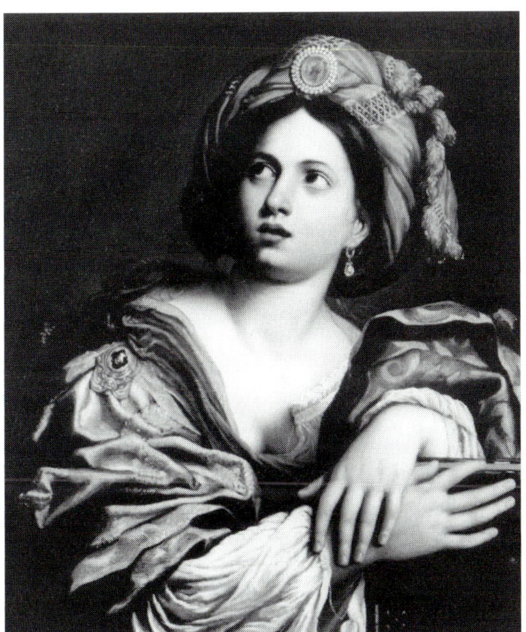

Figure 3.4. Domenichino, *The Persian Sibyl*, ca. 1620s. Oil on canvas. Wallace Collection, London. (Reproduced by permission of the Trustees of the Wallace Collection, London.)

his loss of power and flaunt her gain of it. Judith's left hand sweeps expansively across her body, impelled by the blade-like curve of her shadowed arm; her flat palm rises rhetorically into strong light to shout, "Stop, I hear something." This arresting gesture dramatizes not the women's power but their vulnerability. It's a visual cry of alarm at a moment of danger.

Artemisia's women exert pressure with their hands. Their fingers grasp objects firmly and make a fist. They have full rotary motion in the wrist, and their wrists break backward to show the strain of exertion, just as men's hands do. If, as seems likely, Artemisia modeled Judith's hand in the Naples and Uffizi pictures on the male figures in Orazio's *Crowning with Thorns*, this proved to be an effective strategy for empowering her women. For, more than anything, it's the breaking wrist that convincingly signifies both *agility* and *agency*, words linked by their common root, *agere*—to set in motion, to drive, construct, or build. Orazio treats female hands differently. His

women are typically given light work; they have a soft touch. With very few exceptions, Orazio shows women with hands that hang relaxed and graceful, bend forward limply, or barely grasp a heavy object. His tendency to turn active figures into still lifes has been noted,[3] but not the gendered differential that exaggerates this effect in his female figures. Artemisia's women have normal human hands that function as signs of female agency; Orazio's women have feminine hands, signs of female passivity.

In presenting women's hands as objects of beauty or signs of passivity, Orazio follows the lead of many a Renaissance artist—Raphael and Bronzino, for instance—who give us female hands that are white, smooth, and soft, their fingers long and delicate, tapering toward the tips, just as the Cinquecento theorist Agnolo Firenzuola prescribes in his treatise on the beauty of women.[4] The self-conscious display of a woman's beautiful hands, sustained in the Seicento by artists such as Guido Reni and Domenichino (fig. 3.4), was fueled by a literary tradition derived from Petrarch,[5] in which the perfect woman is described through poetic tributes to the beauty of her body parts, itemized fetishistically. In art influenced by this tradition, when women do things with their hands, it must be ineffectively.

Orazio's *Lute Player* in the National Gallery in Washington (fig. 3.5) seems disposed for the display of one beautiful hand. What action we see is barely credible, for it's not easy to play a lute while supporting it lightly with a thumb on the back. Male lutists, whether seen frontally or, like Orazio's lute player, from the back, as in Paul Bril's *Self-Portrait* in the Rhode Island School of Design, typically grasp the instrument more vigorously and have actively moving, jointed fingers. The hands of female lute players, by contrast, as in Carlo Saraceni's Palazzo Barberini *St. Cecilia and Angel*, are arranged to show off their beauty; they barely move, and pose self-consciously.[6] (One qualification: in the pictorial world of Roman Caravaggesque realism, "low-life" women often have strong hands, and they sometimes play lusty songs on lutes, just like the men, but largely they do nefarious or shady things, like picking pockets or

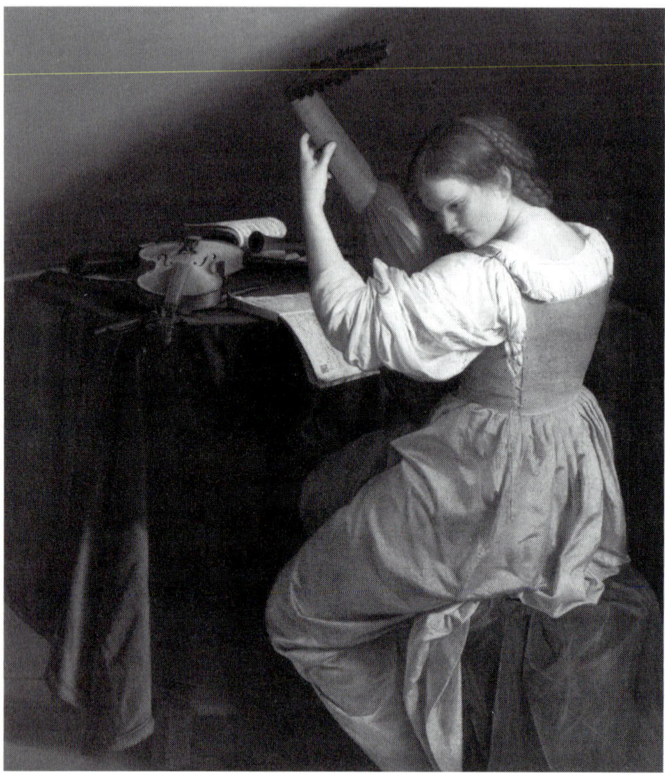

Figure 3.5. Orazio Gentileschi, *The Lute Player*, ca. 1612–15. Oil on canvas. National Gallery of Art, Washington, D.C., Ailsa Mellon Bruce Fund. (Image © 2005 Board of Trustees, National Gallery of Art, Washington, D.C.)

telling fortunes—female agency here is shaded by moralizing stereotype.)

Artemisia's Spada *Lute Player* (fig. 3.6) is another matter. In the context of gendered norms, this woman's hands are extraordinary. Firmly modeled, with knuckles and jointed fingers, these agile hands credibly play the instrument. They seem almost more alive than the woman's face. Jointed hands and articulated knuckles link the Spada figure with the newly discovered *Woman Playing a Lute* (fig. 3.3), which is identified in the Gentileschi exhibition catalogue as a self-portrait of the artist on the strength of its presumed identity with a self-portrait of Artemisia playing a lute that was mentioned in a Villa Medici inventory of 1638.[7] The hands of these two lute players are not identical in shape and coloration, yet they share the qualities of mobility and agility that are relatively rare in images of female hands—one indication that the new painting could be by Artemisia.

More troubling for the Artemisia attribution is the eroticized décolletage of the *Woman Playing a Lute*, something rarely seen in Artemisia's clothed women. (In the *Esther*, or the *Self-Portrait as the Allegory of Painting*, the neckline is as low, but the breasts do not heave out of it. Uniquely, the Naples and Uffizi *Judith*s display a sensuous, swelling curve in a single breast, yet this feature could refer to the seductive role the heroine assumed to snare Holofernes.) The sensuality of the *Woman Playing a Lute* was emphasized in the wall label at the Metropolitan Museum's installation of the *Orazio and Artemisia Gentileschi* exhibition, where we read that the painting's erotic overtones were appropriate both to the traditional association of music and love and to Artemisia's reputation "not simply as a painter," but as a beautiful and seductive woman. Here again, a scopophilic bias interferes with good reasoning. Would the Artemisia who escaped from gossip-ridden Rome to the relative dignity of marriage and court status in Florence risk restigmatization as a seductive woman by presenting herself

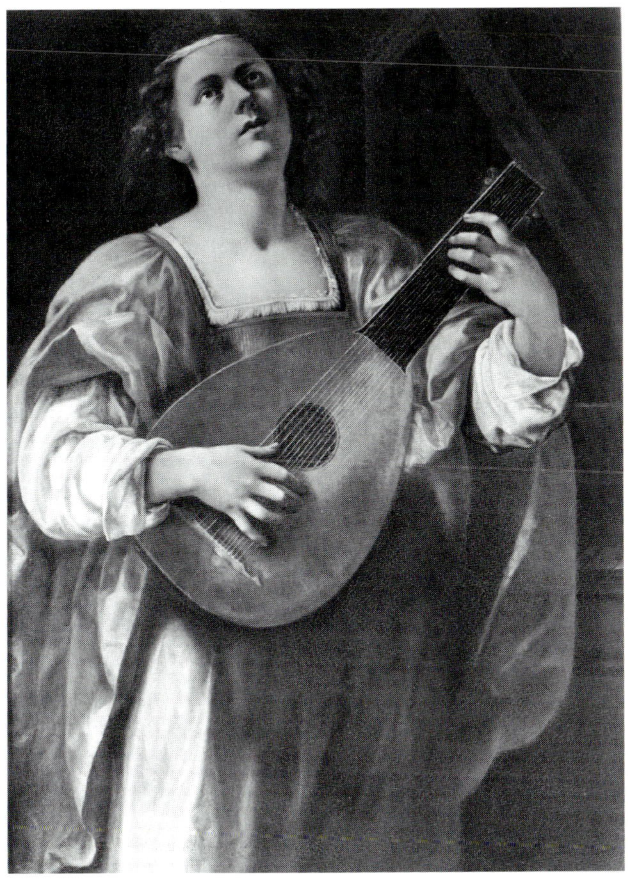

Figure 3.6. Artemisia Gentileschi,
The Lute Player, 1610s. Oil on canvas.
Galleria Spada, Rome. (Photo: Alinari/
Art Resource, New York.)

in this guise? It's certainly not impossible that Artemisia might have sexualized her own image, yet if we have to choose, it's much more probable that she did not. Conceivably, this is Artemisia's portrait of another woman, perhaps contextualized by some theatrical performance at the Florentine court (as Judith Mann suggests, though she proposes Artemisia in that role).[8] Or, it might represent Artemisia herself, painted as another artist wished to present her, driven by the same eroticizing impulses that shaped the Metropolitan Museum wall label.

The latter possibility comes to mind when we consider the *Female Martyr* also newly identified as Artemisia and ascribed to her (fig. 3.2). This woman slightly resembles the *Woman Playing a Lute,* and also the Artemisia of Jerome David's portrait engraving, in the set of the eyes, nose, and mouth. Moreover, an inscription on the back of the panel identifies the work as by the hand of Artemisia—though the accuracy of this inscription might be questioned, considering that the inscriber also claimed that Artemisia was a "niece of Orazio."[9] A more reliable signifier than an inscription of uncertain vintage, it seems to me, is the telltale hand. For there is not so dainty and formless a hand in all of Artemisia's established oeuvre, no hand so relentlessly feminine, so lacking in structure.

In the exhibition catalogue entry, the *Martyr* is compared to Artemisia's Florentine *St. Catherine*, a painting that combines two of the artist's hand types in the same image. Yet the *Martyr*'s hand bears no resemblance to either of these hands. It displays neither the articulated knuckles of Catherine's right hand, nor what I once called the "dimpled knuckles" of her left hand. It is also inconceivable that the artist who

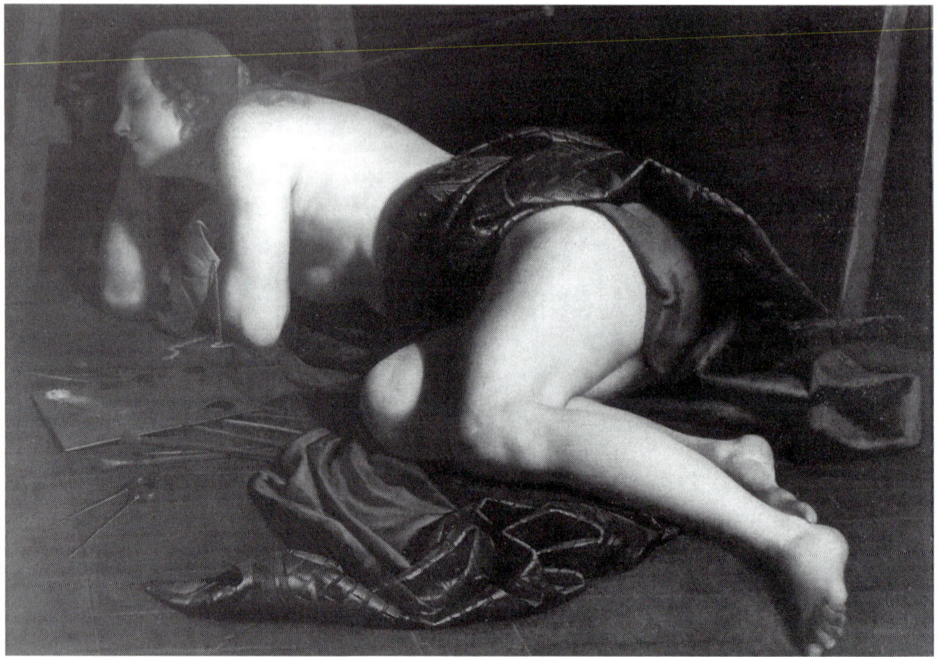

Figure 3.7. Attributed to Artemisia Gentileschi, *Allegory of Painting*, 1620s. Oil on canvas. Musée de Tessé, Le Mans. (Photo: Musées du Mans.)

painted that flabby hand with its wayward tapering fingers could have painted the strong, jointed, firmly structured hands of the Villa Medici *Woman Playing a Lute*. This might be an image of Artemisia as a martyr, possibly even a copy of a painting by Artemisia, but it was surely painted by another artist. Given the stylistic divergence between the *Martyr* and the *Woman Playing a Lute*, it seems to me that the echo of facial type from one to the other can only be explained by postulating that an ur-image of Artemisia's face lies behind the play with her identity in both pictures.[10]

When painting hands, Artemisia appears to think from inside her own body. It's not necessarily that she copies her own hands (though an artist always has this option), but when she draws a female hand, she seems to experience it kinesthetically, feeling its capacity to move. Artemisia's male hands are much less anatomically convincing. In the Bologna *Gonfaloniere*, for example, one hand touches a table, yet without exerting pressure; the other hangs, graceful but lifeless, like an empty glove. Artemisia never painted a female figure who did not have at least one, and usually two, visible hands. In her pictorial world, where female protagonists succeed in their quests through manual dexterity and the hand is a synecdoche for female capability, women without hands would be disabled.

This is among the reasons why we should firmly reject the attribution to Artemisia of the Le Mans *Allegory of Painting* (fig. 3.7), an attribution re-supported by the inclusion of the picture in the Gentileschi exhibition. In his catalogue raisonné of Artemisia's paintings, Ward Bissell has rightly protested this attribution, arguing that its "openly obscene" presentation of a reclining female nude from a viewpoint that emphasizes her buttocks would be unthinkable for Artemisia.[11] This is particularly the case because the figure represented is the Allegory of Painting, accompanied by the mask, brushes, and palette that are her attributes, an allegorical figure that was by the 1620s already identified with Artemisia herself.[12] Bis-

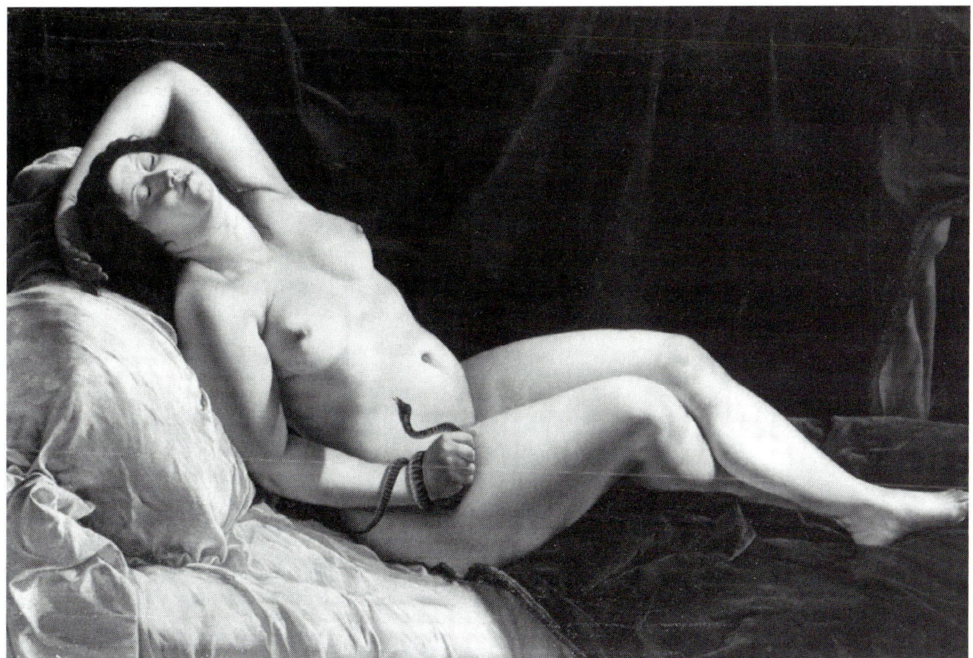

Figure 3.8. Artemisia Gentileschi, *Cleopatra*, ca. 1621–22, detail. Oil on canvas. Amedeo Morandotti, Milan. (Photo: owner.)

sell claims that Artemisia would hardly invoke so compromising a self-reference, and argues instead that the painter may have been Giovanni Baglioni, an earlier antagonist of Orazio who, as a man with an agenda, may have intended to wound Orazio by insulting his daughter.

If the painter of this objectified, debased, and disarmed *Pittura* did intend to evoke Artemisia in the image, as Bissell suggests and I think likely, then I would say the indignity was aimed not at her father but at Artemisia herself, for it clearly fantasizes the repression of her artistic agency, through figurative disempowerment and sinister sexualizing. The figure's arms are visually cut off at the elbow by objects or shadows—a form of castration in this context. Her visible body parts include long, inactive legs, a partially hidden but clearly reddened anus (as Bissell says, hinting at an intercourse that preceded the woman's sleep), and finally, diminished by the telescoping perspective, the truncated arms and a head

that ostensibly rests on the lower strut of an easel, yet floats awkwardly like the organically disconnected elbow and knee. More truly obscene than the painting, and effectively more malicious than the artist's probable intent, is the notion still seriously entertained in the Gentileschi exhibition and its catalogue, that Artemisia herself might have painted what would have been a deeply self-debasing picture.

What's to gain by ascribing this painting to Artemisia? We might ask a similar question about the disputed *Cleopatra* (fig. 3.8) attribution: what's at stake in denying her authorship of this work? In both cases, though in reverse terms, the painter's artistic subjectivity is compromised by the identification of the depicted body as her own. In both cases, as in that of the Villa Medici *Woman Playing a Lute*, Artemisia the sex object supplants Artemisia the artist. Just for the record, the attribution of the *Cleopatra* to Orazio has been supported by an all-male cast of writers (Erich Schleier, Carlo Volpe, and most recently, Ward Bissell and Keith Christiansen). Writers who support the attribution to Artemisia have been mostly, though not exclusively, female (the women include Ann Sutherland Harris, Mina Gregori, myself, and most recently, Judith Mann).[13] I hesitate to invoke the specter of gendered scholarship, but gender-weighted attention to the relative importance of experience versus desire may have led the women, but not the men, to reject the Orazio attribution on the grounds of anatomical description. One has only to compare Cleopatra's breasts, which are at least minimally flattened by gravity, with the perfect domical cupcakes that sit on the chests of Orazio's Danae and other nudes, to see radically divergent mentalities about female anatomy at work.

The attribution of the *Cleopatra* to Orazio is also fueled by the woman-is-to-be-looked-at preconception, since some of its proponents presume that Artemisia must have been the model for the nude Cleopatra. Christiansen suggested this interpretation in the Metropolitan wall labels; he was a bit more circumspect in his catalogue entry, yet he was quick to connect Cleopatra's portrait-like face with the rumor that Artemisia sometimes posed nude for her father.[14] Not so subtly, this unsupported rumor, when combined with the identification of Cleopatra as "really" Artemisia, renders seemingly credible the slanderous hint, by one of Tassi's defenders in the rape trial, of unseemly behavior between father and daughter.[15] Missing is the consideration that if Orazio had been engaging in funny business with his daughter, putting her face on a female nude would be incredibly self-incriminating.

Of course, the *Cleopatra* is equally unseemly as a painting by Artemisia, as long as we insist that the face of this nude woman pinned to the bed and displayed for the gaze must be the artist's own. Indeed, many feminists have expressed discomfort with the attribution of the painting to Artemisia because of its repetition of the pornographically flavored reclining female nude. I continue to believe that its homely realism tends to subvert rather than reify the eroticized type that may have been specified by her patron, and

that the painting is entirely comprehensible, and even complex, if interpreted in a straightforward way as an image of Cleopatra, queen of Egypt, directing her own suicide.[16] In further support of the Artemisia attribution, I would emphasize one neglected consideration: agency in this painting is expressed in the steady fist that grips the asp and controls the narrative.

The hand test alone would place this disputed picture firmly in Artemisia's oeuvre. There are no other Cleopatras in art who clutch the asp so forcefully, as Mann notes in the Gentileschi catalogue.[17] And there is no female hand in Orazio's art comparable to Cleopatra's tightly gripping fist, whose intensity is punctuated by a protruding thumb. I count two fists in his entire oeuvre, neither with a clearly visible or prominent thumb, and both of these belong to figures for which Artemisia may have posed (the Detroit *Violinist* and the Houston *Sibyl*). To find this hand in Artemisia's work, however, we have only to look to the Naples, Pitti, Uffizi, and Detroit *Judith*s. The fact that Orazio never used the gesture, while Artemisia made it a virtual trademark, joins many other considerations to support the probability that it was she who painted the *Cleopatra*. The prominence of female fists in Artemisia's oeuvre runs considerably against the cultural grain, for, according to representational norms, a fist is masculine, an open hand feminine. He who brandishes a fist threatens, asserts force or, in the gestural world of modern sport, asserts victory as an achievement specifically linked to his manhood. (At a recent Wimbledon tournament, for instance, Lleyton Hewitt and Serena Williams both frequently made a victory fist when they won a point or a game. Nevertheless, the championship photographs gave us gender-appropriate gestures for each: he pumped, she waved.)

Artemisia knew quite well what female hands are supposed to do. She could produce the pampered hand or the graceful hand with the best of them, especially in the Casa Buonarroti *Inclination* and the Pitti *Magdalen*, paintings in which grace distinctly overtakes dexterity. But hands are shaped by class as well as gender. Artemisia's Florentine characters, echoing the lifestyles of their courtly patrons, sustain the Petrarchan ideal of feminine beauty quite late into an age that had in Rome been radically disarranged by the new working-class aesthetic of Caravaggism. A trace memory of her Roman origins may explain the fact that even Artemisia's comely hands are attached to rather muscular forearms, which she usually contrives to expose. The strange awkwardness of the *Magdalen*'s left hand may have resulted from a head-on collision between the Florentine beauty convention that called for long tapered fingers and Artemisia's naturalist impulse to articulate the joints of a moving hand. Yet its exaggerated jointing borders on parody, hinting at a resistance to the conventions of gender and class.

Later, in Naples, Artemisia joined women of different classes in the same painting. The servant at lower left in the Columbus *Bathsheba* is a reprise of a figure in the *Birth of the Baptist*, both assertively defined as working class by their rolled-up sleeves, muscular forearms, and reddened skin. Similar servant women discover the dead queen in the Roman *Cleopatra*. In the *Bathsheba*, the prominently positioned working woman is strongly contrasted in type with the beautiful and opulent white-skinned heroine, a juxtaposition that is highly unusual in Neapolitan painting of this period. It is a form of *contrapposto*, to be sure—a pleasing contrasting of opposites that might have been encouraged by her patron. Yet one wonders whether the artist's own sympathies might have intruded. Positioned by her liminality as an artist to know the worlds of both workers and aristocrats, Artemisia could present both from experienced knowledge. We might surmise that in those pictures that increasingly present glamorous and passive heroines, she included the working women, voluntarily, as displaced models of female agency.

In a broader sense, even when detached from specific gestures, the hand functions as a gendered signifier of cultural prowess. From antiquity through the Renaissance, hands were considered to represent the brain, an organ that was effectively masculine. As we learn from Claire Sherman's recent exhibition and catalogue devoted to the hand, terms like "to grasp" or "to apprehend" show how persistently the intellectual is expressed through the manual. "Taking hold" means "understanding new ideas." For Aristotle, man's hand distinguished him from animals: "The hand is for the body as the intellect is for the soul."[18] In the art of painting, the hand is the visual voice of the intellect; Leonardo da Vinci famously avowed that the motions of the mind must be expressed by the motions of the body. The Renaissance artist's hand was both agent and sign of his creative ability. In Giotto's time, an artist was celebrated for his *manus et ingenium*, skill and talent.[19] Two centuries later, when the craftsman's talent had been magnified into the artist's genius, Dürer was praised for his "divine hand." As Richard Spear has noted, this figure of speech and its counterparts—divine brush, divine art, or the learned hand, *dotta mano*—all were used to refer to a nexus of artistic genius, divinity, and imagination only found in the greatest artists: Raphael, Michelangelo, and Titian.[20]

What of the hand of the woman artist? Elisabetta Sirani was praised by a contemporary Bolognese poet in masculine terms, as Babette Bohn points out (see chapter 4, this volume). He called her *pittore*, not *pittrice* (male, not female painter), and described her as empowered by a *destra armata*, her strong right arm. Sirani's heroic images of Judith and Timoclea exhibit a commanding dexterity that may have been inspired by Artemisia's strong-handed women, yet the Bolognese painter received different critical treatment. The virilizing of Sirani distinctly differs from Artemisia's positioning by an anonymous Venetian poet who juxtaposed Artemisia *pittrice* with a hypothetical *pittore* to contrast their depictions of an *amoretto*. The imaginary male painter is fortified with a *dotta man virile*, a learned masculine hand; Artemisia, by contrast, has the (more limited) power to create a lifelike image, an unsurprising achievement for a woman who can, after all, give birth to a real child—that is to say, whose natural sphere is not artistic creation but maternal procreation.[21]

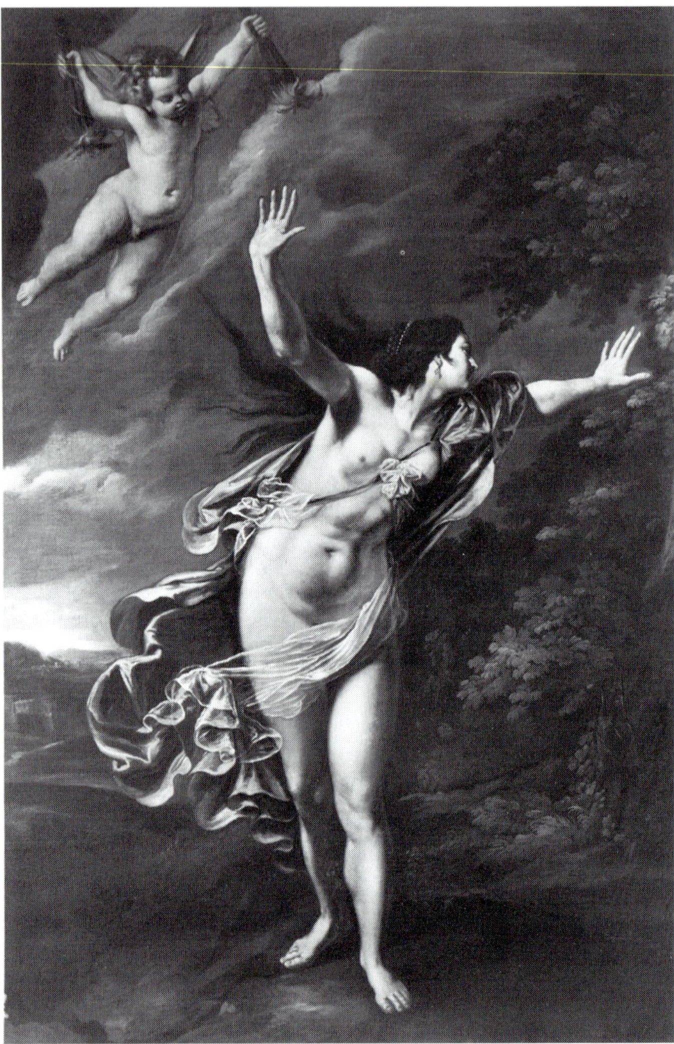

Figure 3.9. Artemisia Gentileschi, *Aurora*, ca. 1625–27. Oil on canvas. Maurizio and Alessandra Marini Collection. (Photo: owners.)

We see Artemisia's unlearned hand holding a paintbrush in the well-known drawing by her contemporary Pierre Dumonstier le Neveu. In an accompanying text, the draftsman tells us that Artemisia's hand stands for her ability to create ravishing images for discerning eyes.[22] There is a hint of Petrarchan fetishizing here, since male artists blessed with divine hands were rarely if ever represented by their hands per se. (In the early modern period, when artists were engaged in a campaign to elevate the intellectual status of their practice, this would have been a reminder of the very thing upwardly mobile artists were trying to make people forget—that great art might be generated in the mind but had to be executed by the lowly hand.) If the highest praise possible for a woman artist is honorary masculinity, something that the lower-keyed Elisabetta Sirani received fully in the poetic tribute to her *destra armata*, in the case of the more threatening Artemisia Gentileschi, the homage is qualified by gender, both in the anonymous Venetian poem and in Dumonstier's drawing.

Dumonstier associates Artemisia with the idea of

beauty, not only in his image of her hand alone but also in his text, which links Artemisia's right hand with the much-praised beauty of the hands of Aurora. This might be a conventional allusion to Homer's "rosy-fingered dawn," but it must also indirectly refer to Artemisia's own painting of Aurora, known from its description by the seventeenth-century Florentine writer Filippo Baldinucci, which Bissell has recently identified with a painting in a Roman private collection (fig. 3.9).[23] I would support the *Aurora* attribution (with some reservations about the handling of the putto and the landscape), for what is most persuasively Artemisian about this image is the pair of prominent and active hands. In significant contrast to contemporary images of Aurora, such as Guido Reni's version at the Casino Rospigliosi, which presents the goddess of dawn floating like a ship's figurehead, with floral wreaths in her arms, or as in Guercino's Casino Ludovisi goddess, who is seated in a chariot strewing flowers—in contrast to these, Artemisia's Aurora steps free of her chariot, a full-bodied striding personification. Again, her agency is emphasized: the muscular goddess physically parts the sky with her hands, her flattened palms pressing firmly against the dark walls of night, just as Baldinucci describes. Unusually, Baldinucci praises both the *ingegno* and *mano* of Artemisia, an even-handed gesture that differentiates him from Dumonstier and the Venetian poet, who qualify Artemisia's artistic hand by its gender, subtly repressing all memory of the virile hands she actually painted.[24]

I have written before about the interactive dynamic that seems invariably to develop between Artemisia Gentileschi's art and its reception, both in her time and ours.[25] Writers then and now have reacted to her strong women and their aggressive deeds with praise for the beauty of the artist and her ravishing imagery, and with innuendoes about her eroticized reputation. So it is not surprising that in the Gentileschi exhibition of 2002, the largest and most widely viewed display of Artemisia's art ever mounted, and at the symposium in St. Louis that was the climax of the Gentileschi year,

once again Artemisia's artistic assertion—claiming power for her female heroes and artistic identity for herself—met cultural repression. Nobody meant to do her harm, but many are complicit in undermining Artemisia's artistic agency. It is not only those who enthusiastically support dubious attributions to Artemisia that would demean and belittle her as an artist. Nor is it only Keith Christiansen, who produced the dismissive and defamatory wall labels at the Met (yet in his paper at the Artemisia symposium in St. Louis tacked surprisingly, offering readings of Artemisia's paintings that fully credited her with intention and purpose), nor Ward Bissell, who at the symposium decided to reattribute virtually all of Artemisia's early paintings to Orazio, to the mystification of symposium participants and audience alike. It is also that, throughout the catalogue essays, one finds a systematic denial of independent agency to Artemisia, a habit of looking at her as always reactive—to artists such as Orazio, Reni, Vouet, or Guercino, or to her patrons' demands—but rarely as proactive. The first English-language exhibition catalogue devoted to Artemisia's art is an impressive and useful volume in many respects, yet it is disappointing to see in it so little attention given to her creative originality.

This brings me again to Artemisia's depiction of hands, for it is here especially that she talks back to her critics, speaking to the agency of women in a gestural voice that cannot be repressed. As Artemisia herself promised her patron Don Antonio Ruffo in March 1649, "The works will speak for themselves."[26] To facilitate their doing so, I will close with several examples of Artemisia's manual telegraphy, instances in which she expresses identity or undermines convention through coded gestures of hand and arm. One I have previously noted is the protagonist of the Seville *Magdalen*, whose head is supported by an awkwardly bent wrist. I have recently argued that this is an intentional allusion to artistic melancholy, on the model of Michelangelo, who is seen in the same pose in a sixteenth-century engraving, following his own use of the pose to signify the melancholic temperament. With a single gesture, I proposed, Artemisia

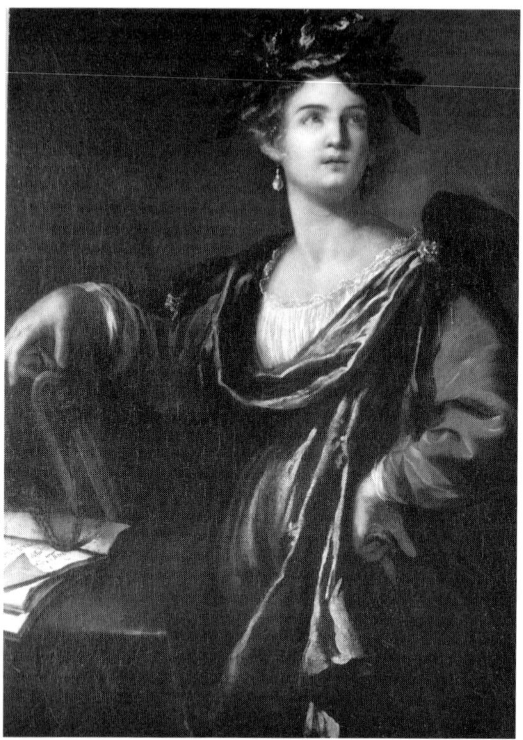

Figure 3.10. Artemisia Gentileschi, *Clio, Muse of History*, 1632. Oil on canvas. Private collection. (Photo: owner.)

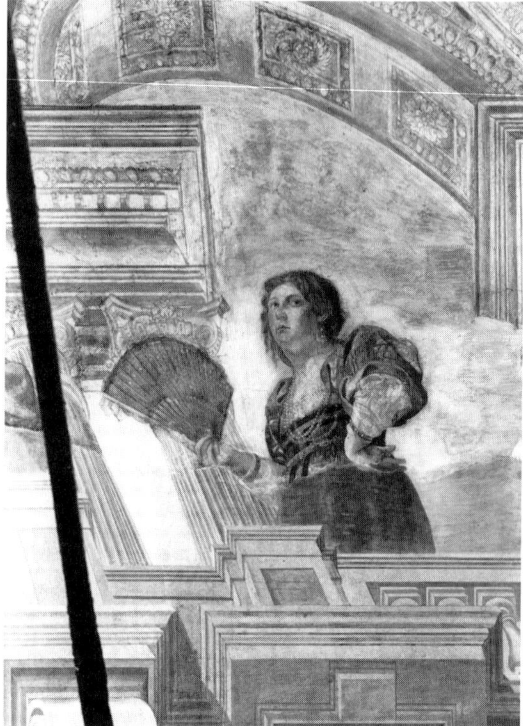

Figure 3.11. Orazio Gentileschi and Agostino Tassi, *A Musical Concert with Apollo and the Muses*, 1611, detail of a woman holding a fan. Fresco. Palazzo Pallavicini-Rospigliosi, Casino delle Muse, Rome. (Photo: Istituto Centrale per il Catalogo e la Documentazione, Rome.)

brought the concept of creative melancholia to her *Magdalen*, to convey something about her own creative powers as an artist.[27]

If the turn of a hand could carry private meaning for Artemisia, then perhaps significance is also to be found in a half-hidden gesture in the painting of *Clio* (fig. 3.10). Artemisia inserts herself into this image of the muse of history, as Elizabeth Cropper and I have each observed, for by placing her signature on the page of history, along with the name of her patron, she intertwines the agenda of her patron's fame with her own.[28] Unlike Cropper, I doubt that the face of Clio should be interpreted as an Artemisian self-portrait, yet the figure's akimbo left arm and bent wrist might have been an imprint of self as legible (to those in the know) as the artist's signature on the page. For

is there not the ghost of a familiar image of Artemisia embedded in Clio's pose? A number of writers have identified Artemisia's face in the woman holding a fan who looks down at us in Orazio's fresco at the Casino of the Muses (fig. 3.11). We can't be sure about the face, but I do think that we may see Artemisia's own body language here. As Joaneath Spicer has pointed out, the hand-on-hip, jutting-elbow stance is a very unusual pose for a woman to strike in art. By contrast, male figures often display themselves in this pose (think of Donatello's bronze *David*), which connotes self-assertion, cocky confidence, or elegant showing off.[29]

The rare assumption of such a posture by two female figures linked with Artemisia suggests her presence in both instances. Though not a self-portrait, the

Clio bears a clear conceptual relationship to Artemisia's identity. Here as elsewhere, the artist's sense of herself invades the female characters she invents. The figure in the Casino of the Muses is unlikely to "represent" the eighteen-year-old Artemisia, but perhaps she served as Orazio's model (a very different thing from posing in the nude). And if so, why not imagine that she struck her own pose? She was, after all, not a professional model but by all accounts a feisty and self-assertive young woman. It seems to me entirely possible that the woman in the fresco, only subtextually Artemisia when painted, might have later been claimed by the artist herself as a signature posture.

Another work that has been persistently connected with Artemisia is the Palazzo Barberini *Allegory of Painting* (fig. 3.12). There is general consensus that the picture may represent Artemisia as Pittura, though some writers, including myself, have doubted that she painted the portrait.[30] But look at this figure's painting hand, and its lifted little finger—the ear finger, as it was called in Artemisia's time. According to John Bulwer's *Chirologia*, a seventeenth-century vocabulary of gestures based on common usage in gestural discourse, the raised ear-finger (in Bulwer's illustration, it is raised as high as in the *Allegory*) represents contemptuous provocation, a dare or challenge advanced by those confident in the strength of their abilities.[31] Once we realize that this Allegory of Painting is challenging the viewer, our understanding of the picture is changed. If painted by Artemisia, this would be an allegorized self-image of an aggressively competitive artist who challenges her male peers—an image that corresponds to both her known ambition and her reception. More likely, it was another painter who fixed this image of Artemisia as a competitor in the world of art. But, either way, the picture is *about* her artistic ambition. It is not far-fetched to imagine that it was Artemisia the model who initiated the gestural challenge preserved by the artist who painted her.

Finally, even *Corisca* (fig. 3.13) may subtend a coded gesture. In this painting, Artemisia presents a scene from Battista Guarini's *Il Pastor Fido* in which a nymph cleverly escapes a lecherous satyr. The beautiful hair that attracted him turns out to be a wig, Corisca makes her getaway, and the joke is on the satyr. Artemisia's very choice of this rarely depicted episode reveals her feminist sensibilities.[32] But take a good look at Corisca's left hand. The play of shadow blurs the fingers so that only three are clearly visible, yet two of these, the index and ear fingers, are prominent and slightly advanced. Bulwer explains the meaning of this gesture in its more obvious form: "To present the index and ear-finger wagging," he says, is a sign of folly on the part of its recipient. "It implies such men to be asses," to have wagging asses' ears. (It is also, of course, a sign of cuckoldry, as Bulwer notes.)[33]

Now, Artemisia did not go so far as to have Corisca wag her fingers at the lecherous satyr, for that would distort the narrative. But a visually literate Italian would surely pick up on this hint of the ass-eared insult, especially the wit of its relevance to the goat-eared satyr. Those who imagine the satyr to be the hero of this painting and Corisca the wicked villain—as certain modern art historians have insisted[34]—might not have noticed this subtle detail. But contemporaries of Artemisia such as Isabella Andreini and Valeria Miani, women who wrote pastoral dramas that relish the topos of nymphs outwitting and humiliating satyrs,[35] would surely have shared the painter's glee in showing us what Corisca thought of the satyr, and whose story this really is.

In the wake of the Gentileschi exhibition, our ongoing project of defining Artemisia's oeuvre has become increasingly problematic and, so, has acquired growing urgency. As with other artists whose oeuvres are known insufficiently, it's a chicken-and-egg situation: in deciding what paintings are by her hand, we must be guided by our sense of her artistic identity, yet that identity can only be created out of the aggregate of her known works. At present, there is no consensus about Artemisia's identity, and recent writers sharply disagree, perhaps most notably about the

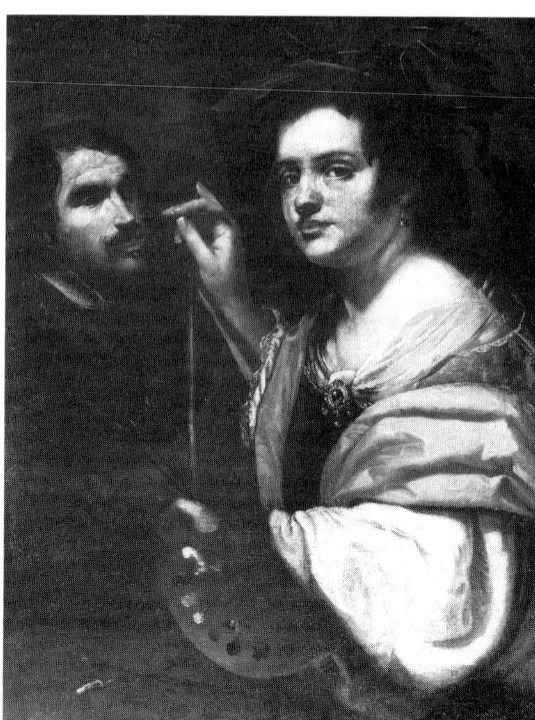

Figure 3.12. Attributed to Artemisia Gentileschi, *Portrait of a Woman Artist as the Allegory of Painting*, ca. 1630? Oil on canvas. Galleria Nazionale d'Arte Antica, Palazzo Barberini, Rome. (Photo: Istituto Centrale per il Catalogo e la Documentazione, Rome.)

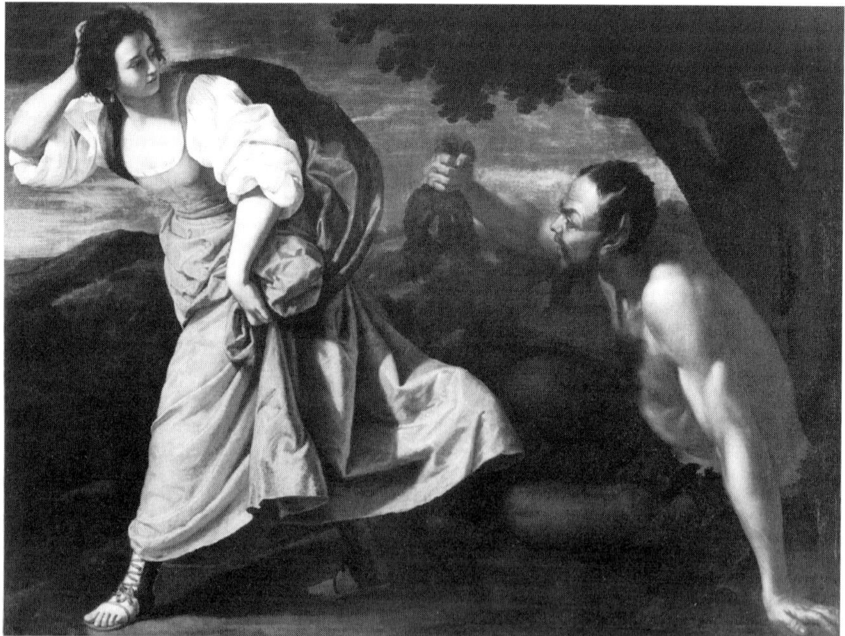

Figure 3.13. Artemisia Gentileschi, *Corisca and the Satyr*, 1630s or 1640s. Oil on canvas. Private collection. (Photo: owner.)

relevance of gender considerations for her work. I have long argued that gender issues and even feminism, understood in its broadest definition, are not extrinsic to Artemisia's art but are manifestly at its heart. Those who perceive in this a feminist bias should also recognize the more pernicious forms of gender bias that go unacknowledged. For, as the examples discussed in this essay show, gender stereotypes can be used to diminish Artemisia and deny her cultural agency, sometimes by the very writers who deny gender's relevance for her art.

Because connoisseurship is not a socially neutral practice, it is necessary to question attributions that seem suspicious or ill-founded—certainly those that are incompatible with what we know of Artemisia's style, but also those that are inconsistent with her conceptualization of female characters and their action in the narrative world. Part of the questioning is deconstructive: *cui bono?* what's at stake? From what definition of the artist, we must ask, does a particular attribution derive?

Yet our work must also be constructive, for if we believe that Artemisia's art is more important for art history than the issues of her putative personal beauty presently being exploited and the cultural sexualization presently being imposed on her, then it's time to shift attention back to the paintings and their participation—perhaps better is Griselda Pollock's word, their *intervention*—in the discourses of art and art history. As we see especially in her gestural rhetoric, Artemisia was an artist of great expressive subtlety and visual wit, and she disrupted the art-world dialogue by presenting an exemplum of female agency that upset gender expectations, in both her own time and ours. Artemisia's intervention sparked an intense critical debate that has not ceased, and we owe it to her to keep this debate on track.

NOTES

1. Keith Christiansen and Judith W. Mann, eds., *Orazio and Artemisia Gentileschi* (New York: Metropolitan Museum of Art and New Haven, Conn.: Yale University Press, 2002), cats. 56 (the *Martyr*) and 57 (the *Lute Player*).

2. Bernard Berenson (whose connoisseurship principles were founded on those of Morelli), "Rudiments of Connoisseurship (A Fragment)," in *The Study and Criticism of Italian Art* (London: George Bell and Sons, 1902), 134–36; Max J. Friedländer, *On Art and Connoisseurship*, trans. Tancred Borenius (London: B. Cassirer, 1942), reprinted in *Historical and Philosophical Issues in the Conservation of Cultural Heritage*, ed. Nicholas S. Price, M. Kirby Talley, Jr., and Alessandra M. Vaccaro (Los Angeles: Getty Conservation Institute, 1996), 148.

3. See Christiansen and Mann, *Gentileschi*, cat. 16, for the still-life reading; cat. 23, for Orazio's *Crowning with Thorns*; and for prime examples of the female hands Orazio developed in his maturity, see cats. 24, 28, 34, and 35.

4. Agnolo Firenzuola, *On the Beauty of Women* (1541), trans. and ed. Konrad Eisenbichler and Jacqueline Murray (Philadelphia: University of Pennsylvania Press, 1992), 67.

5. Elizabeth Cropper, "On Beautiful Women, Parmigianino, Petrarchismo, and the Vernacular Style," *Art Bulletin* 58 (1976): 374–94.

6. For the images of lute players by Bril and Saraceni, see Beverly Louise Brown, ed., *The Genius of Rome, 1592–1623* (London: Royal Academy of the Arts, 2001), nos. 31 and 48.

7. Christiansen and Mann, *Gentileschi*, cat. 57. The picture, which was unknown until its appearance at auction in 1998, corresponds roughly in dimensions to the work described in the inventory, a "portrait of Artemisia playing the lute by her own hand."

8. Ibid., entry by Mann.

9. Christiansen and Mann, *Gentileschi*, cat. 56. The inscription reads (in translation): "By the hand of Artemisia, daughter of A[u]r[e]li[o] Lomi / Pisan, niece of Orazio." The painting, which turned up at auction in 1995, has been connected with a work owned by eighteenth-century English collector Ignazio Hugford.

10. The existence of a variant of the *Female Martyr* in the Zeri Collection also points to the possibility of a missing work by Artemisia's hand. See Roberto Contini and Gianni Papi, *Artemisia* (Florence: Casa

Buonarroti and Leonardo-De Luca Editori, 1991), cat. 16. Contini and Papi accepted both versions as by Artemisia; Mann doubts the Zeri version. In the Zeri picture, the martyr wears a crown of flowers, and her hand is less suspect than that in the Hugford version, yet these works differ considerably from each other, and neither is by Artemisia in my opinion.

11. Christiansen and Mann, *Gentileschi*, cat. 64. R. Ward Bissell, *Artemisia Gentileschi and the Authority of Art* (University Park: Pennsylvania State University Press, 1999), cat. X-1 (pp. 299–301).

12. Bissell cites the Barberini *Allegory of Painting* believed to represent Artemisia (discussed later in this essay) and Artemisia's own *Self-Portrait as the Allegory of Painting* of 1630 or later. But there is reason to believe that the association of Artemisia with the Allegory of Painting began during her Florentine period, in the years 1612 to 1620; see Mary D. Garrard, *Artemisia Gentileschi around 1622: The Shaping and Reshaping of an Artistic Identity* (Berkeley: University of California Press, 2001), 55–61, and fig. 31.

13. For differing opinions about the attribution of the *Cleopatra*, see Christiansen and Mann, *Gentileschi*, cat. 17. Unusually, the painting is included in both the Orazio and Artemisia sections of the exhibition catalogue, where the co-authors present opposing positions, but the edge is given to Orazio (Christiansen provides the more complete entry and the full-size reproduction; Mann reproduces the picture in half-length detail).

14. Christiansen and Mann, *Gentileschi*, cat. 17.

15. On Artemisia's alleged posing nude for Orazio, see Christiansen, in Christiansen and Mann, *Gentileschi*, 98, and Cropper, "On Beautiful Women," 274–75. The rumor that Orazio had improper relations with his daughter, or wished to, can be found in the rape trial testimony. It was suggested by Marco Antonio Coppino, a witness for Tassi's defense, and stated by Tassi himself (Mary D. Garrard, *Artemisia Gentileschi: The Image of the Female Hero in Italian Baroque Art* [Princeton, N.J.: Princeton University Press, 1989], 481 and 453).

16. See Garrard, *Artemisia*, 1989, 244 ff.

17. Mann, in Christiansen and Mann, *Gentileschi*, 304.

18. Claire Richter Sherman with Peter M. Lukehart, with contributions by Brian P. Copenhaver et al., *Writing on Hands: Memory and Knowledge in Early Modern Europe* (Carlisle, Pa.: Dickinson College, Trout Gallery, and Washington, D.C: Folger Shakespeare Library, 2000), 22 (entry by Martin Kemp).

19. Michael Baxandall, *Giotto and the Orators* (Oxford: Clarendon Press, 1971), 15–16.

20. Richard E. Spear, *The "Divine" Guido: Religion, Sex, Money and Art in the World of Guido Reni* (New Haven, Conn.: Yale University Press, 1997), ch. 14, "Di Sua Mano," esp. 259–65.

21. For the poem, and a different interpretation, see Bissell, *Artemisia*, 355–56.

22. For discussion of Dumonstier's drawing and its texts, see Garrard, *Artemisia*, 1989, 63–64; and Bissell, *Artemisia*, 221–22.

23. Baldinucci, writing in the 1680s, as cited in Bissell, *Artemisia*, cat. 15.

24. See ibid. for Baldinucci's text. Another tribute to Artemisia rare for its lack of gender stereotype came from the Venetian writer Antonio Colluraffi, who in 1628 compared her to Apelles and Parrhasius. See Patrizia Costa, "Artemisia Gentileschi in Venice," *Source* 19, no. 3 (2000): 28–36, cited by Cropper in Christiansen and Mann, *Gentileschi*, 268–69.

25. See Garrard, *Artemisia*, 2001, "Conclusion," esp. 118–23.

26. Garrard, *Artemisia*, 1989, 391–92.

27. Garrard, *Artemisia*, 2001, ch. 1.

28. Cropper, in Christiansen and Mann, *Gentileschi*, 267–68; Garrard, *Artemisia*, 1989, 90–96.

29. Joaneath Spicer, "The Renaissance Elbow," in *A Cultural History of Gesture*, ed. Jan Bremmer and Herman Roodenburg (Ithaca, N.Y.: Cornell University Press, 1991), 84–128.

30. For a review of the literature, see the exhibition catalogue, Claudio Strinati and Rossella Vodret, *Caravaggio and His Italian Followers, from the Collections of the Galleria Nazionale d'Arte Antica di Roma* (Venice: Marsilio Editori, 1998), cat. no. 19.

31. John Bulwer, *Chirologia: Or, The Natural Language of the Hand*, and *Chironomia: Or, The Art of Manual Rhetoric* (1644), ed. James W. Cleary (Carbondale: Southern Illinois University Press, 1974), 136.

32. For the identification of this painting's subject and interpretation, see Mary D. Garrard, "Artemisia Gentileschi's *Corisca and the Satyr*," *Burlington Magazine* 135 (1993): 34–38.

33. Bulwer, *Chirologia*, 138–39.

34. E.g., Bissell, *Artemisia*, 76–77.

35. Isabella Andreini, *La Mirtilla* [Verona, 1588], ed. Maria Luisa Doglio (Lucca: Maria Pacini Fazzi Editore, 1995); for discussion of the parodic tone of this pastoral work and Valeria Miani's *Amorosa speranza* of 1604, see Virginia Cox, "Fiction, 1560–1650," in *A History of Women's Writing in Italy*, ed. Letizia Panizza and Sharon Wood (Cambridge: Cambridge University Press, 2000), 55.

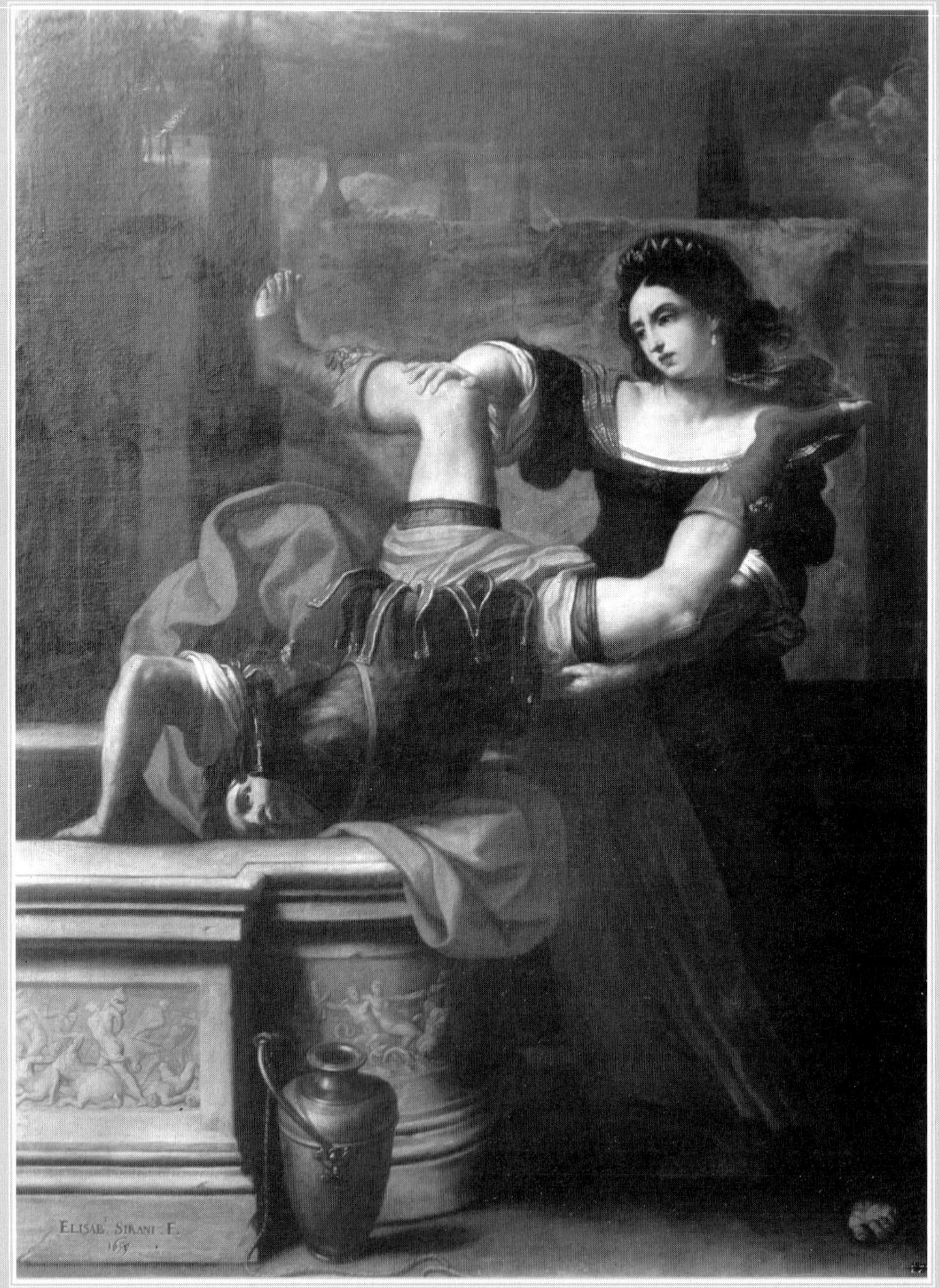

ELISAB. SIRANI. F.
165

THE ANTIQUE HEROINES OF ELISABETTA SIRANI

Babette Bohn

DESPITE THE BREVITY of her career, the painter Elisabetta Sirani (1638–65) contributed significantly to the evolution of painting in her native city of Bologna.[1] A pivotal figure in promoting the prominence of women artists in Bologna, Sirani was also innovative in developing new interpretations of female figures in her paintings. This pattern of interpretation is particularly discernible in her works portraying heroines from antique history, who lack the eroticism generally employed by her male compatriots in such portrayals and are characterized instead by virtues more commonly associated with men than women during the early modern period in Italy.

Bologna, to be sure, provided a receptive environment for Sirani's achievements. The second city of the papal states and site of the oldest university in Europe, it was arguably the leading Italian city during the sixteenth and seventeenth centuries in sustaining the success of secular women artists. This achievement may be linked to many factors, including a relatively favorable attitude toward female education,[2] the role of university scholars as art patrons, extensive private and ecclesiastical patronage, and the prevalence of family workshops, where artists' female relatives frequently had access to artistic training. The latter phenomenon is particularly marked during the Seicento, when at least six artists' daughters (including Sirani),

two wives, one sister, and one niece became painters or printmakers in Bologna, thanks to the family connections that made training available.[3]

Also influential, beginning in the late sixteenth century, was Caterina Vigri (1413–63), founder of the Corpus Domini, Bologna's Poor Clares convent, and the first known female painter in the city. Vigri's beatification in 1592 launched her popular local cult and marked the beginning of her impact on Bolognese women painters. Although no extant written sources confirm the interest of later Bolognese women painters in their Quattrocento predecessor, at least two Seicento women depicted Vigri in paintings; one provided a picture for her convent; and Elisabetta Sirani lived just around the corner from the Corpus Domini.[4] During the early eighteenth century, Vigri was canonized and established as the patron saint of the Bolognese artists' academy, making Bologna the only Italian city with its own female saint associated with the art of painting.[5]

Vigri was also a writer whose example inspired other female writers in Bologna. Her best-known work, *Le Sette Armi spirituali*, was conceived as a spiritual guide for the novices of her order.[6] The number of known Bolognese women writers increased dramatically after Vigri's death in 1463, tripling from ten during the Quattrocento to thirty during the

An earlier version of this essay, with the same title, was published in *Renaissance Studies* 16, no. 1 (2002): 52–79. Reprinted by permission of Blackwell Publishing.

Figure 4.1. Elisabetta Sirani, *Timoclea*, 1659. Oil on canvas. Museo Nazionale di Capodimonte, Naples. By permission of Ministero dei Beni e le Attività Culturali. (Photo: Soprintendenza Speciale per il Polo Museale Napoletano.)

Cinquecento, and dwindling slightly to twenty during the Seicento.[7] An increase in secular writing by women and in literary efforts by women who were not nuns is particularly marked during the seventeenth century in Bologna, when only eight of the twenty women writers cited by Fantuzzi and Orlandi were nuns. Four other women wrote on religious subjects; and eight Bolognese women wrote secular poetry.[8] This evidence of increased education among non-monastic women, which made their literary activity possible, parallels the increased availability of artistic training during the seventeenth century to non-monastic women, who became active in greater numbers, more or less simultaneously, in Elisabetta Sirani's school of painting.

Craig Monson has shown that musical renown was also achieved by Bolognese nuns during the seventeenth century, despite the severe restrictions on Bolognese convent music after the Council of Trent (1545–63). In the Camaldolese convent of Santa Cristina della Fondazza, the Bolognese convent that was most famous for its music during the early Seicento, Lucrezia Orsina Vizzana (1590–1662) became the first Bolognese nun musician to publish her own musical compositions.[9] Thus women made significant advances in early modern Bologna in the literary, musical, and artistic realms.

The achievements of Bolognese women were praised by local writers, beginning in the late sixteenth century. In his poem of 1590, *La Gloria delle donne*, the great Bolognese poet Giulio Cesare Croce celebrated women from antiquity to the present, culminating in Croce's own female contemporaries in Bologna.[10] During the seventeenth century, two key Bolognese writers on art, Malvasia and Masini, included discussions of Bolognese women painters in their accounts of Bolognese art. Malvasia, the biographer of the Bolognese painters, focused primarily on Lavinia Fontana (1552–1614) and Elisabetta Sirani in his *Felsina pittrice* of 1678, but Masini in 1690 expanded his considerations to include some seventeen mostly seventeenth-century women painters and printmakers.[11] This growing attention to Bolognese women artists continued during the eighteenth and early nineteenth centuries, when local writers like Alessandro Macchiavelli, Marcello Oretti, Luigi Crespi, Gaetano Giordani, and Carolina Bonafede chronicled the artistic achievements of Bolognese women. The last notable work in this tradition was published in 1907 by Laura Ragg, an English-speaking author.[12]

Although the importance of Bologna's women artists is widely recognized, their works have always been understood in the context of stylistic developments shaped by their male compatriots. One recent text justified this approach by observing that works by Bolognese women relate "more directly to that of their male contemporaries than to that of other women."[13] Thus Lavinia Fontana is understood as the disciple of her father, Prospero, and Elisabetta Sirani is seen as a follower of Guido Reni.[14] Sirani's association with Reni dates back to her own contemporaries, who buried Elisabetta, after her premature death at the age of twenty-seven, in the same tomb as Guido, so that they might be united in death as they had been in life.[15] Presumably based upon stylistic similarities, a few writers even wrongly supposed her to have been Reni's pupil or assistant, a clear historical impossibility since Reni died in 1642, when Sirani was only four years old.[16] Thus the historical construction of Bolognese women's art as homogeneous with the art of their male contemporaries has a long and uniform pedigree.

This essay presents a different view. Although stylistic affinities between Bolognese women and their male compatriots are evident, I argue that Bolognese female artists often adopted a fundamentally different approach to portrayals of female protagonists, frequently choosing and interpreting subjects quite differently from male painters in Bologna. These differences will be examined in a group of pictures illustrating subjects from classical history. In some cases, Elisabetta Sirani chose subjects that were rarely if ever depicted by male artists. In other instances, Sirani and her predecessor Lavinia Fontana portrayed popular subjects innovatively, rejecting traditionally eroticized portrayals and instead depicting female protagonists with an emphasis on such virtues as courage and intelligence—characteristics then generally understood as atypical of women.

Moreover, I suggest that during the seventeenth century, when Bolognese women first became significant producers of history paintings, Elisabetta Sirani and her female followers developed a subspecialization in pictures of heroines from antiquity, produced for a small group of Bolognese private collectors whose taste for such subjects is documented in inventories and in a few extant works. Antique heroines were of course popularly depicted by many artists, male and female, during the Seicento.[17] However, the high percentage of such subjects among the works of seventeenth-century Bolognese female painters suggests that patrons found particular appeal in having heroic women painted by women artists whose own achievements may have been seen as analogous to accomplishments by ancient women that were also viewed as atypical of their sex.

Before beginning an analysis of these works, it is worth noting that such unconventional rejections of eroticism for female protagonists are not universal in the works of the female artists discussed here. Neither Lavinia Fontana nor Elisabetta Sirani, the only two painters whose works survive in significant numbers, consistently avoided eroticism in their depictions of women. For both artists, part of the explanation for this inconsistency must be sought in the differing attitudes of diverse patrons, whenever the original patrons can be identified. However, Sirani's extant works suggest that she was more consistent in creating innovatively virtuous interpretations of heroines from classical history than in other subjects. Traditional religious figures, such as Mary Magdalen, in contrast, were often portrayed by Sirani with the same eroticism typically employed by her male contemporaries.[18] Sirani may have found greater latitude for original interpretations in secular subjects, and particularly in uncommon themes for which firm pictorial traditions were not established. Moreover, Bologna's tradition of antiquarianism promoted the receptivity of local patrons to such subjects.

With a history that predated the Etruscans, the oldest university in Europe, and a thriving community of humanists and collectors of ancient art, Bologna enjoyed a strong tradition of antiquarianism from the Quattrocento. The works of Marcantonio Raimondi (c. 1470/82–1527/34), Amico Aspertini (1474–1552), and Francesco Francia (c. 1450–1517), among others, testify to the formidable impact of antique art, mythology, and history on local artists. As is well known, Marcantonio's antiquarian interests are conspicuous throughout his career, in prints after antique sculptures and in prints that treat antique subjects.[19] An example of the close connections between humanists and artists in Bologna is provided by the Bolognese poet Giovanni Achillini's relationships with Marcantonio, Francia, and Aspertini. Both Aspertini and Marcantonio made portraits of Achillini, who in turn praised the two artists in his poetry, emphasizing their knowledge of antiquity. Achillini, who owned a collection of medals and other antique works, established a prototype that continued in Bologna for the next few centuries: that of the learned literary collector with an interest in the ancient world.[20]

During the late sixteenth and seventeenth centuries, the antiquarian interests of artists and collectors continued. Although antique subjects and formal quotations may be found in the works of many artists, the three Carracci and Domenichino are the artists whose iconographic and formal connections to the ancient world are most conspicuous during this period. Among the leading art collectors in Bologna during Sirani's day, Francesco Cospi (1606–86) exemplifies the learned literary collector with a taste for antiquity. The son of a Bolognese father and a Florentine mother, Cospi, thanks to the connections of his Medici mother, became the Medici agent who collected Bolognese art for the grand duke, for whom Cospi acquired works by Elisabetta Sirani and her father, Giovanni Andrea, among others.[21] Cospi's own collection included four pictures by Elisabetta Sirani, three by Giovanni Andrea, nineteen by Guido Reni, and more than a hundred other pictures, mostly by Bolognese artists. He also collected ancient medals, antique sculptures, and natural wonders in his "Museo Cospiano," now in the Museo Civico Medioevale in

Bologna. All the natural and artistic works in Cospi's collection were catalogued in a publication of 1677 that was dedicated to Ferdinand III de' Medici.[22]

Given the strong tradition for antiquarianism in Bologna, antique subjects proliferated in Bolognese painting during the sixteenth and seventeenth centuries. Bologna was a large and prosperous city during this period, and its wealthy families erected thirty-nine palaces in the city during the sixteenth century alone.[23] Many of these were decorated with frescoed scenes from ancient history or mythology, as exemplified by Pellegrino Tibaldi's frescoes in the Palazzo Poggi and frescoes by the three Carracci for the Palazzo Magnani. In the early seventeenth century, fewer frescoes with antique subjects were produced for Bolognese palaces, although Bolognese painters like Reni and Domenichino painted such works for patrons outside Bologna. During the second half of the Seicento, many frescoes with ancient subjects were again produced for Bolognese palaces, as exemplified by Giovanni Antonio Burrini's mythological frescoes for the Albergati, Bugami, and Alamandini palaces (1659–1690) and the mythological frescoes in Palazzo Pepoli by Domenico Maria Canuti (1669–71) and Giuseppe Maria Crespi (1690s). In addition to monumental fresco cycles, easel pictures with antique subjects were also extremely popular among Bolognese collectors.[24] Since, apart from the aptly named Teresa Muratori (1662–1708), women are not known to have painted in fresco in Bologna, it is these smaller oil paintings that this essay considers.[25]

Before turning to a discussion of specific works, however, one final issue must be addressed: the production of history paintings by male and female artists. In Italy, women artists did not generally specialize in history painting, the broad category that included religious, historical, and literary subjects. Such subjects demanded superior erudition of the artist, just as they (allegedly) produced greater edification in the viewer. As Jacobs has shown, since women were considered biologically incapable of true creation and portraits were seen as replications of nature rather than inventions, portraiture was viewed as the most appropriate female métier, avoiding, as it allegedly did, any necessity for real creativity.[26] Thus Lavinia Fontana specialized in portraiture, the favored genre for women in the Renaissance. Fontana's detailed renderings of rich fabrics and jewels attracted many wealthy female patrons in Bologna.[27] She was evidently less prolific and less successful as a history painter than as a portraitist, although, as will be seen below, she produced some genuinely innovative history paintings.[28]

It is only in the seventeenth century in Bologna that women artists began to specialize in history painting—a landmark achievement, since history painting was widely regarded as the most important and intellectual branch of art. This development is connected to many factors, including the evolving acceptance of professional women painters in the city and improvements in female education. It is tempting to speculate that it may also be related to the conspicuous increase in the number of women writers in Bologna during the Cinquecento.

The first woman in Bologna to specialize in history painting was Elisabetta Sirani, whose extraordinary career during the mid seventeenth century marks the pinnacle of the female artistic trajectory in Bologna. Sirani made every effort to transform the prospects for women artists in Bologna and to ensure her own fame. She founded the first school of painting for women outside a convent in Europe, training a dozen women and making painting available not only to daughters of painters, like Sirani herself, but also to women without family connections, like Ginevra Cantofoli, Lucrezia Scarfaglia, Vincenza Fabri, Veronica Franchi, and Maria Elena Panzacchia. Unlike any of her contemporaries, Sirani's concern with posterity prompted her to compile a list of nearly two hundred of her paintings, and she often signed and dated her pictures.[29] Despite a short career of scarcely more than a decade, she may also have been the most prolific woman artist in Europe before 1700, producing over two hundred paintings, ten etchings, and many drawings.[30] Sirani became a celebrity in Bologna, and her studio was visited by such eminent tourists as Cosimo de' Medici, grand duke of Tuscany; Cosimo's uncle Leopoldo; the duchess of

Braunschweig; and the duke of Mirandola.[31] Her patrons included the latter four figures as well as papal legates, Bolognese senators, cardinals, and many leading aristocratic Bolognese families, including the Guidotti, Pietramellara, Ercolani, Albergati, Cospi, Sampieri, and Ranuzzi.

The variety of Sirani's subjects is unusual among women painters. Resisting the typical specialization for Italian women, she produced only about fifteen portraits. Religious subjects comprised the largest category of her paintings, some 69 percent. Many of these religious pictures were paintings of the Madonna and Child that were made as private devotional pictures for Bolognese patrons, although Sirani also produced altarpieces and paintings of saints and Old Testament subjects. Seventeen percent of her pictures portrayed allegories and subjects from classical history and mythology. Thus Sirani was above all a history painter, a distinction that also characterized most of her female followers.[32]

Did Sirani possess a level of erudition sufficient to foster her creation of history paintings? Although no letters by the artist survive to elucidate this issue, the 1666 inventory of her father's possessions, made the year after Elisabetta's death, supplies the interesting information that he owned a collection of twenty antique and modern books, a library to which his daughter, who lived with her father throughout her short life, demonstrably had access. Sirani's library included ancient works like Pliny's *Natural History*, Ovid's *Metamorphoses*, and Plutarch's *Lives*. Among its modern holdings were Vasari's *Lives*, Boccaccio's *La genealogia de gli dei de gentili*, a book on the saints, a handbook on medals, and Cesare Ripa's *Iconologia*.[33] Thus Elisabetta had access to iconographic works that provided information essential for her history paintings.

Two of Sirani's portrayals of women from the ancient world are evidently unique in seventeenth-century Italian painting. The first is her *Timoclea* (fig. 4.1), painted in 1659 for the Bolognese banker Andrea Cattalani, as a pendant for her painting of *Judith Showing the Head of Holofernes to the Israelites* (fig. 4.2).[34] Cattalani, who owned seven paintings by Elisabetta Sirani and fifteen by her father, Giovanni

Andrea, is typical of several collectors who took a particular interest in Elisabetta's work: he was a local businessman who collected primarily Bolognese seventeenth-century art, most of it probably commissioned directly from the artists; and he evidently lacked any broad interest in women artists, since the 1668 inventory of his collection lists no works by any woman painter other than Sirani.[35] Although there is no evidence that Cattalani collected pictures by women artists apart from Sirani, he was interested in portrayals of heroic women from antiquity. In addition to Sirani's *Timoclea*, the 1668 inventory of his ninety-eight-item collection lists nine other pictures with subjects from antique history or mythology, four of them featuring heroic women: a *Lucrezia* and a *Sibyl* by Giovanni Andrea Sirani, a *Story of Atalanta* by "Francesco Milanese," and a *Tarquin Raping Lucrezia* by Palma.[36]

The Sirani library included a copy of Plutarch's *Lives*, which Elisabetta evidently consulted for several of her paintings.[37] One of these, the *Timoclea*, depicts a rare subject from Plutarch's *Life of Alexander*. In Plutarch's account, Alexander led his Macedonian army to put down the rebellion of Thebes. In the wake of the city's almost total destruction by Alexander's army, a Thracian captain broke into the house of Timoclea, "a matron of high character and repute." After raping her, the unnamed captain asked Timoclea where her money was concealed. She led him to a well in the garden, into which she claimed that she had thrown her most valuable possessions. When the greedy Thracian leaned over to view the treasure, Timoclea pushed him into the well and then flung great stones upon him, until she had killed him. It is this act—a courageous woman throwing her male adversary into a well—that is portrayed by Sirani.[38]

Presumably encouraged by Cattalani's interest in heroic women from antiquity, Sirani chose a subject that is not known to have been depicted by any other Italian painter.[39] Timoclea's courage and assertiveness were virtues associated by classical and early modern writers with men, not women. Aristotle argued that the perfection of masculine virtue was in commanding and that of female virtue was in obedience (*Pol-*

itics 1.12), and most Italian writers of the early modern period agreed. Boccaccio's introduction to 104 biographies of famous women refers to women as the "weaker sex," and maintains a traditional valuing of female chastity, despite the inclusion of biographies of "flawed" characters with other strengths.[40] Alberti suggested that in choosing a wife, a man should look for beauty, parentage, riches, and an honorable manner that entailed modesty and purity.[41] For Torquato Tasso, each sex had a dominant virtue: courage for men and chastity for women.[42] Even among Bolognese women writers, to judge from surviving works, heroic women were rarely praised. Only Bartolomea da Mantugliano, in a poem of 1406, praised a group of virtuous women from antiquity that included Penthesilea, Camilla, Sofonisba, and Portia.[43] Giulio Cesare Croce, writing in Bologna nearly two hundred years later to praise women, singled out many of the same figures from antiquity, but praised them for such feminine-identified qualities as honesty, chastity, innocence, and piety.[44] Thus Timoclea's actions and character as described by Plutarch and portrayed by Sirani violated traditional stereotypes of female virtue.

Other parts of the Timoclea story do occasionally appear in Italian art.[45] Sirani's Bolognese compatriot Domenichino painted a picture in circa 1615 of *Alexander and Timoclea* (Louvre, Paris), part of a series of pictures depicting events from the life of Alexander the Great, for Cardinal Alessandro Peretti Montalto.[46] Domenichino's picture portrayed the deeds of one Alexander to honor the patron, a "second" Alexander; and thus his picture is less concerned with Timoclea's heroism than with Alexander's. To this end, Domenichino depicted a different point in the story: After killing the captain, Timoclea was brought before Alexander, who was immediately impressed by her dignity and courage. When Alexander asked who she was, Timoclea identified herself as "the sister of Theagenes, who fought the battle of Chaeronea with your father Philip, and fell there in command for the liberty of Greece." Plutarch reported that Alexander was so impressed by Timo-

clea that he granted freedom to her and her children.[47] Instead of portraying Timoclea's heroic actions, Domenichino shows her as a statuesque and dignified figure before a generous and noble Alexander.

Sirani's *Timoclea* portrays a dispassionate female protagonist whose erect posture and unruffled demeanor contrast with the ungainly pose of the captain, who tumbles, heels over head and legs askew, into the well. Timoclea's modest dress and orderly hair betray nothing of the recent rape and eschew any sensuality that would distract from her portrayal as the "matron of high character and repute" described by Plutarch.[48] Such elimination of any salacious references to the recent rape, through full or partial nudity, is not conventional in Italian art, as a comparison with representations of Lucretia makes clear.[49]

This avoidance of eroticism and emotionality also characterizes *Timoclea*'s pendant, the *Judith Showing the Head of Holofernes to the Israelites* (fig. 4.2). As with her Timoclea, Sirani represents her Judith at a less popularly depicted moment of the story. Instead of showing Judith decapitating Holofernes, an event that, suggestively, took place in the Assyrian general's tent, Sirani shows the moment of Judith's greatest triumph, when she displays the head of her male adversary to the Israelite people. Instead of portraying Judith as a beautiful woman standing near a bed, in proximity to a half-clad Holofernes, Sirani's Judith is a weighty figure who towers over the cityscape and other figures, centered and brightly illuminated by a light that signifies divine favor.[50] Although she is richly attired, the medallion on Judith's bodice is decorated with the ferocious features of Medusa, another formidable female who killed men. Significantly, it is at this moment in the biblical text that Judith reaffirms her chastity: "I swear that it was my face that seduced him to his destruction, and that he committed no sin with me, to defile and shame me" (Judith 13:16). Sirani's *Judith* is faithful to the text's message of female chastity, but it also conveys female potency. Sirani's *Judith* has been denigrated by modern critics for its unemotional heroine, who contrasts markedly with Artemisia Gentileschi's more dramatic Judiths. It

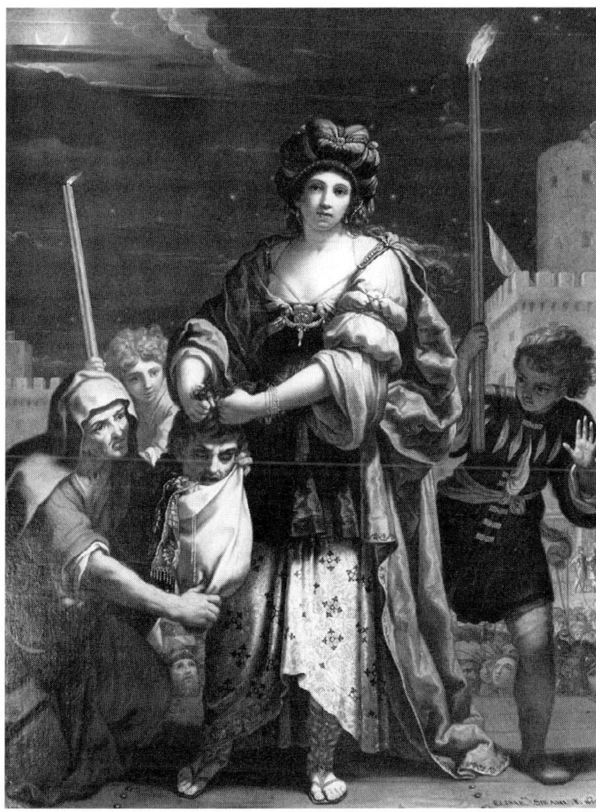

Figure 4.2. Elisabetta Sirani, *Judith Showing the Head of Holofernes to the Israelites*, 1658. Oil on canvas. The Burghley House Collection, Stamford, U.K. (Photo: Photographic Survey, Courtauld Institute of Art.)

seems likely, however, that the unemotionalism of Sirani's female protagonists, like their large bodies and modest clothing, is part of the artist's deliberate strategy to eliminate the sexuality that typified such heroines in Italian art. Instead of beauty, emotion, and sexuality, Sirani's Timoclea and Judith are characterized by dispassionate courage, strength, dignity, and fortitude—the very qualities that impressed Alexander the Great with Timoclea, according to Plutarch.

Sirani's anomalous agenda, in her atypical depictions of women, is also reflected in her unusual pairing of Timoclea, a woman from ancient history, with Judith, a woman from the Old Testament Apocrypha. I know of no other instance in Italian painting of the period in which these two subjects were pendants. The decision of Sirani and Cattalani to combine the popular subject of Judith with the uncommon narrative of Timoclea may well have been intended to reinforce

the message of female virtue. Judith, the heroic Israelite woman who saved her people by courageously decapitating the Assyrian general Holofernes, was understood by the church as a prefiguration of the Virgin. Judith's chaste triumph over Holofernes, the devil's agent, paralleled Mary's chaste conception of Christ, who triumphed over the devil. Thus she was also a symbol of patriotism and virtue, although an alternative tradition linked her with Delilah and other "scheming females" who had triumphed unnaturally over powerful men. A poem contemporary with Sirani's picture by the Bolognese writer Giovanni Luigi Piccinardi expresses this conception of Judith as a woman whose virtue is unusual for her sex. The poem, entitled "Se Giuditta trionfasse d'Oloferne con la Bellezza, pure con l'Eloquenza," argues that both beauty and eloquence were prerequisite to Judith's triumph, and that each reinforced the other:

Without Beauty Eloquence is silent,
Since Beauty is mute Eloquence,
And Eloquence is loquacious Beauty.[51]

Early modern women were not expected to possess eloquence, since this virtue had no application within the convent or household. Leonardo Bruni argued:

For why should the subtleties of . . . rhetorical conundrums consume the powers of a woman, who never sees the forum? The art of delivery . . . [is] so far . . . from being the concern of a woman that if she should gesture energetically with her arms as she spoke and shout with violent emphasis, she would probably be thought mad and put under restraint. The contests of the forum, like those of warfare and battle, are the sphere of men.[52]

Sirani's Judith, like her Timoclea, combines virtues generally ascribed to men (eloquence and fortitude) with the beauty and chastity traditionally associated with women.

A second anomalous depiction by Sirani of a heroic woman from antiquity is her *Portia Wounding Her Thigh* (fig. 4.3), an overdoor picture painted in 1664 for Simone Tassi and now in a private collection. Like Cattalani, Tassi was a rich Bolognese business-man who collected primarily Bolognese pictures. An inventory of his collection in 1671 included five pictures by Elisabetta Sirani among the sixty-six lots; and Sirani's *Portia*, appraised at five hundred lire, was the most valuable item in the collection (no. 49).[53] All five of Tassi's pictures by Sirani were history paintings, and three portrayed subjects from antiquity, also including a *Venus* (no. 32) and a *Sibyl* (no. 57).[54] Tassi evidently shared Cattalani's interest in pictures of heroic women from antiquity, since twelve of his sixty-six pictures treated antique subjects, and five of these featured heroic women, including Sirani's *Portia; a Lucrezia,* a *Cleopatra with Mark Antony,* and a *Circe* by unidentified artists (nos. 7, 45, and 53); and a *Semiramis* by Giovanni Andrea Sirani (no. 50) that is now lost. The latter hung next to Sirani's *Portia* and was probably its companion piece. In addition to

Tassi's five works ascribed to Elisabetta Sirani, he owned at least one work by another Bolognese woman: a *Portrait of a Woman* by Lavinia Fontana (no. 17).[55]

Sirani's *Portia*, like her *Timoclea*, substitutes an unusual moment in the story for a more commonly represented episode. Portia's history was recounted by several ancient Roman writers, including Q. Valerius Maximus and Plutarch, who discussed Portia in his life of her husband, Brutus. Most Italian artists represented the suicide of Portia, who took her own life by swallowing hot coals after the death of her husband at the Battle of Philippi.[56] In Bologna, the subject was probably popularized by Guido Reni, whose half-length *Portia* of circa 1625–26 (Durazzo-Pallavicini Collection, Genoa), with her low-cut dress, uplifted eyes, and dish of hot coals, exemplifies Reni's formula for the portrayal of ancient heroines like Lucretia, Artemisia, Cleopatra, and Portia.[57] Reni generally positioned these figures in a strong light near the picture plane, with minimal clothing and historical details, as eroticized offerings to the male gaze. With their scant iconography, Reni's pictures scarcely qualify as genuine history paintings.

In her *Portia*, as in other works, Sirani portrayed her heroine in a wholly different light. Instead of the more common subject of Portia's suicide, Sirani depicted Portia wounding her thigh to prove her courage to her husband, Brutus.[58] The only other painting of the subject known to this writer, Ercole de' Roberti's picture of circa 1490 (Kimbell Art Museum, Fort Worth, Texas), which was probably made for a female patron, Eleonora of Aragon, shows Portia articulating the reasons for her wound to Brutus.[59] Instead of placing Portia's wound in her foot, like Roberti, Sirani located the wound in Portia's thigh, following the account of Plutarch, the only ancient writer to specify this location.[60] Thus for her *Portia*, as for her *Timoclea*, Elisabetta presumably consulted the copy of Plutarch's *Lives* in the Sirani library.

Roberti focused on the relationship between Portia and her husband and the contrast between her active demonstration of valor and his quiet expression of foolishness. Sirani's approach is quite different.

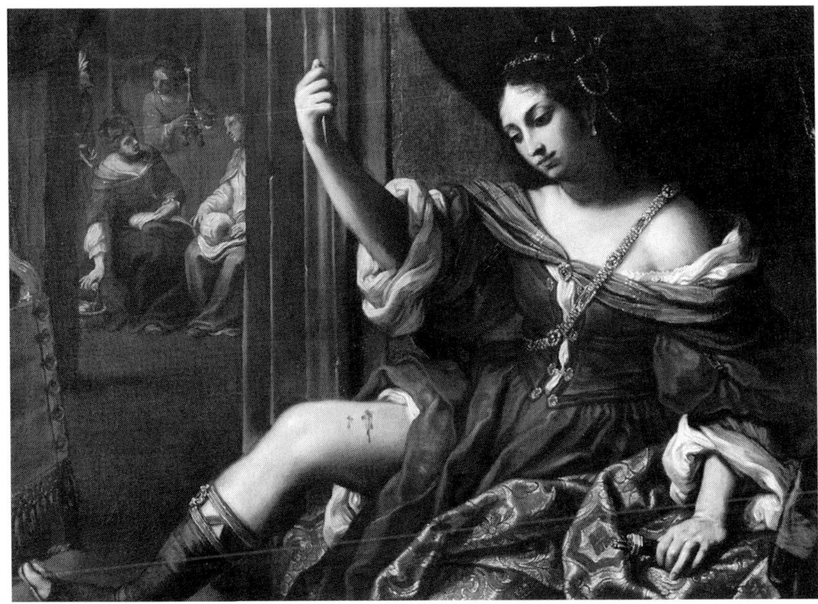

Figure 4.3. Elisabetta Sirani, *Portia Wounding Her Thigh*, 1664. Oil on canvas. Stephen Warren Miles and Marilyn Ross Miles Foundation, Houston, Texas. (Photo: Herbert F. Johnson Museum of Art, Cornell University.)

Her Portia is not accompanied by Brutus; instead, she is juxtaposed with other women, whose conventional female pursuits (in the background) underscore Portia's exceptional nature. Portia's fortitude, a virtue associated with men, is demonstrated in a female figure whose elaborate, brightly colored feminine clothing emphasizes her gender. Sirani's juxtaposition of her heroine with more ordinary women rather than with her husband calls attention to the remarkable coexistence of Portia's femininity and fortitude. If Elisabetta's *Portia* was the companion piece for Giovanni Andrea's painting of *Semiramis*, the iconographic scheme depicting strong women from antiquity is even clearer, since Semiramis was an Assyrian queen who famously donned her son's costume to continue her late husband's military conquests for another forty-two years.[61] Both Portia and Semiramis exemplified the masculine virtue of fortitude, and both were consequently included by Christine de Pizan among the admirable women from early history in her *City of Women*.[62] Unlike Timoclea, both Portia and Semiramis were among the female exemplars from antiquity included by the Bolognese poet Giulio Cesare Croce in *La Gloria delle donne*, of 1590.[63]

A more popular subject in art was provided by the Egyptian queen Cleopatra VII, whose story captured the imagination of numerous artists and writers throughout Europe during the early modern period.[64] Cleopatra inherited the throne of Egypt with her brother Ptolemy XIII in 51 B.C. at the age of seventeen. Her reign lasted about two decades, until she and her Roman husband, Mark Antony, were defeated by Octavian in 31 B.C. at the battle of Actium. Both Cleopatra and Antony committed suicide in 30 B.C.

Although Cleopatra was the last of the Ptolemies and a great political leader, it was her sexual liaisons with Mark Antony and Julius Caesar that generally attracted attention in art and literature. Egypt allowed women greater rights of inheritance and public visibility than ancient Rome or Israel, a discrepancy that, Mary Hamer has argued, contributed to Western misinterpretations of Cleopatra as conveying sexual availability in a display that in Egypt was merely appropriate to the ruler.[65] Thus Cleopatra is "other," both as female and as non-Roman.

Western writers developed an increasingly negative view of Cleopatra. The earliest full account of her life, written nearly two hundred years after her death, comes from Plutarch, who had allegedly read her now-lost memoirs.[66] He wrote that Cleopatra's charisma derived not from her beauty, which was un-exceptional, but from her forceful personality.[67] His description of Cleopatra as not beautiful is consistent with her depiction on coins, which portray a woman with a low forehead, jutting chin, and large hooked nose.[68] In the mid-fourteenth century, however, Giovanni Boccaccio emphasized her beauty, greed, and lustfulness. His account begins:

> Cleopatra was an Egyptian woman who became an object of gossip for the whole world. Although she was the descendant of Ptolemy, the son of Lagus and king of Macedonia through a long line of kings . . . , she nevertheless came to rule through crime. She gained glory for almost nothing else than her beauty, while on the other hand she became known throughout the world for her greed, cruelty and lustfulness.[69]

Boccaccio's negative view and ahistorical notion of Cleopatra's beauty influenced most subsequent Italian painters, who almost invariably portrayed her as beautiful and seductive.

Cleopatra is rare in Bolognese painting before 1620, although she appears in several sixteenth-century works on paper.[70] A drawing by Giacomo Francia in the Princeton University Art Museum, an engraving by Francia, and several engravings by Marcantonio Raimondi provide some examples.[71] All depict what became a popular subject in art: Cleopatra's suicide, after her defeat at the battle of Actium. Like the suicides of Lucretia, Portia, Dido, and others, the subject exemplifies the popularity of female self-destruction in Western art.[72] These Bolognese examples eroticize female suicide, portraying Cleopatra as a nude with snakes who attack her breasts, a motif that became remarkably persistent in art, in light of Plutarch's and Boccaccio's accounts that Cleopatra's arms received the fatal bites. Plutarch also specified that Cleopatra died in all her royal ornaments, befitting her queenly status, so both the nudity and the emphasis on breasts were evidently artistic inventions to provide an erotic stimulus for a male audience.[73] Cleopatra's portrayal as a nude figure with

a snake in a landscape also links her suggestively with Eve, the archetypal female sexual temptress.

In Bologna, the subject of Cleopatra's suicide was popularized by Guido Reni in at least six pictures painted between 1625 and 1642 (fig. 4.4).[74] The numerous studio copies after these works testify to their popularity. Most of Reni's Cleopatras depict half-length women, strongly illuminated and close to the picture plane before a neutral or minimal background. All portray women whose exposed breasts are attacked by phallic snakes. Private collectors evidently appreciated Reni's sexy Cleopatras, who are almost indistinguishable from his sexy Lucretias, presented in a similar format. Both lack details to elucidate historical significance, apart from Lucretia's knife and Cleopatra's snake. Thus little distracts the male viewer from the half-clad woman whose open mouth and uplifted eyes might just as well be construed as an expression of sexual passion as of final anguish. Other male artists of the Bolognese school were stimulated by Reni's example to produce pictures that are more erotic than historical. Guercino's early *Cleopatra* of circa 1621 (Norton Simon Museum of Art, Pasadena, California) probably predates the known examples by Reni; but his two later *Cleopatras,* of 1639 (private collection, Ferrara) and 1648 (Galleria d'arte del Comune in Palazzo Rosso, Genoa) demonstrate Reni's influence, with their nudity and eroticism.[75] Guido Cagnacci produced at least five *Cleopatra* pictures between circa 1635 and circa 1662, each one more salacious than the last. Cagnacci's naturalistic female nudes either sink back into their chairs in limp, receptive surrender (Brera Museum, Milan) or writhe and cry out in a semblance of pain that is strongly suggestive of sexual ecstasy (Salamon collection, Milan).[76] His erotic agenda and basic format, with a strong light emphasizing the figure, which is placed close to the picture plane and set against a darkened background, derive from Reni's prototypes, although his figures are more naturalistic than Reni's generalized women.

Although at least two Cleopatra paintings by Bolognese women painters are lost today,[77] both Lavinia Fontana and Elisabetta Sirani represented

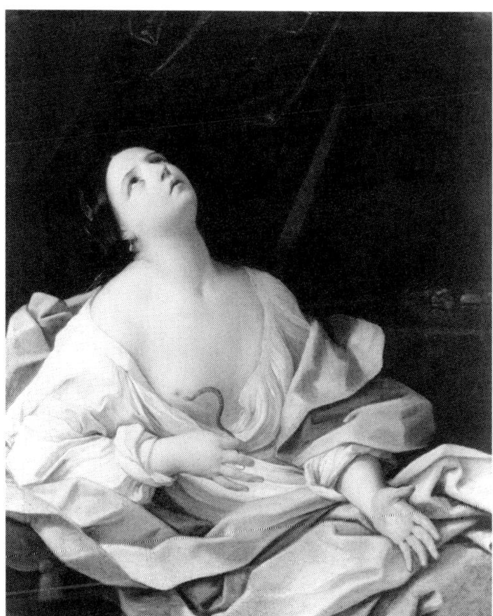

Figure 4.4. Guido Reni, *Cleopatra*, ca. 1631–32. Oil on canvas. The Royal Collection © 2005, Her Majesty Queen Elizabeth II.

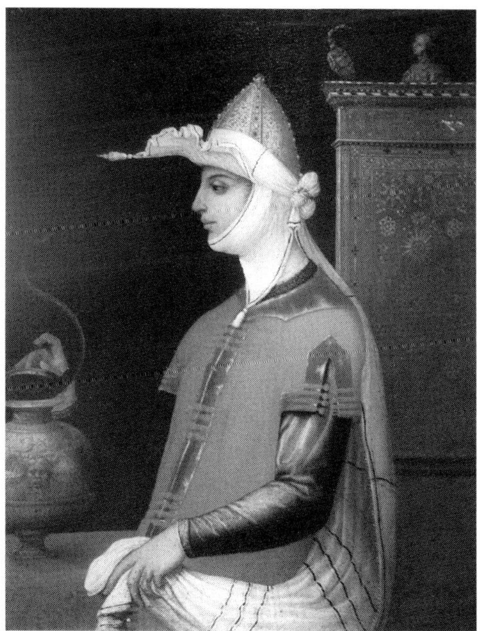

Figure 4.5. Lavinia Fontana, *Cleopatra*, ca. 1585–1614. Oil on canvas. Galleria Spada, Rome. By permission of Ministero dei Beni e le Attività Culturali. (Photo: Archivio Fotografico Soprintendenza Speciale per il Polo Museale Romano.)

the subject in extant paintings. The differences between their portrayals and those of their male contemporaries are striking. Fontana's *Cleopatra* in the Galleria Spada, Rome (fig. 4.5), variously dated between 1585 and 1614,[78] is portrayed in the moments before her actual suicide, as she releases the poisonous snake from a vase. She is fully clothed and is not voluptuous, with loosely fitting robes that do not even curve to suggest the presence of breasts underneath. Her jeweled hat and rich red garment attest to her lofty rank and veil both body and hair, eliminating the traditional attributes of erotic femininity. Cleopatra's impassive profile contrasts strongly with Reni's impassioned Cleopatras. The exotic vase and armoire, surmounted with a three-legged vessel, a long-necked bird, and a bust,[79] provide an unconventional attention to iconography by denoting Cleopatra's Near Eastern origins, an attention that has been linked with the renewed interest in the East stimulated by the wars of the early 1570s against the Turks and the Battle of Lepanto.[80] Fontana's untraditional attention to Cleopatra's high rank and geographical origins, combined with an equally unusual avoidance of nudity, conveys female power and control in lieu of sexuality.

The patron of Sirani's *Cleopatra* (fig. 4.6) is unknown, since it was mentioned neither in the artist's list of works nor by any of her early biographers.[81] This exceptional painting avoids the subject of Cleopatra's suicide altogether, illustrating instead a subject that became popular only during the eighteenth century in Italian painting.[82] Pliny and Boccaccio both related the story: to exhibit her extraordinary wealth to Mark Antony, Cleopatra promised to expend an unprecedented sum at a banquet. To achieve her goal, she dissolved a priceless pearl in vinegar and drank it, thereby winning her wager with Antony and demonstrating her cleverness and vast wealth.[83] As Hamer explains, such a display of opulence signified political power in Egyptian culture but was misinterpreted by Western writers as erotic and excessive.[84] Boccaccio's account perfectly exemplifies this skewed interpretation; the adjectives he employs for Cleopatra in this short section include *covetous, greedy,*

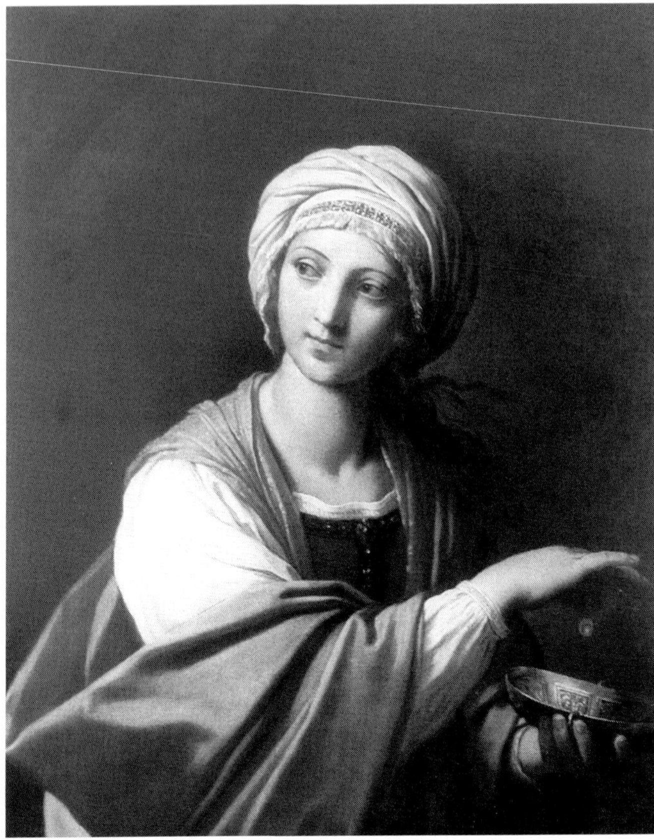

Figure 4.6. Elisabetta Sirani, *Cleopatra*, ca. 1662–63. Oil on canvas. Private collection, Chicago.

seductive, and *lewd*.[85] Tiepolo's opulent painting from the 1740s in the Palazzo Labia in Venice highlights the interaction with Antony of a provocatively bare-breasted Cleopatra.[86] Sirani's Cleopatra, in contrast, is an isolated figure whose simple juxtaposition to the pearl expresses her wealth and cleverness without reference to male companions. Like Fontana's Cleopatra, she is unemotional, fully clothed, and not voluptuous, avoiding any erotic charge. Sirani's untraditional interpretation of Cleopatra probably influenced Donato Creti's painting of circa 1700–1710 (Collezione Hercolani Fava Simonetti, Bologna), which also portrays a solitary, half-length Cleopatra, fully clothed, impassive, and devoid of erotic appeal, holding the cup and pearl. With the emerging taste for neoclassicism

in Bolognese art, painters like Creti rejected the Reniesque emotional eroticism that had dominated such subjects in Bologna for two generations, turning instead to Sirani's cooler, quieter models.

The *Cleopatra* paintings of Fontana and Sirani portray unemotional, heroic figures without erotic overtones, whose quiet dignity and elegance are appropriate to their royal status. This characterization distinguishes them definitively from the Cleopatras of their male compatriots. It also differs from Artemisia Gentileschi's portrayals of Cleopatra (see fig. 3.8, p. 69) and other antique heroines, who also express untraditional potency but without eschewing nudity and emotion.[87]

Sirani portrayed many exceptional women from

antiquity. Apart from Timoclea, Portia, and Cleopatra, she also painted Iole, Pamphile, who invented the art of weaving silk, Galatea, sibyls, and others.[88] Many of these pictures are now unknown; and all recorded paintings of such subjects by her female followers are lost.[89] Perhaps, like the literary women humanists who preceded them, Sirani and her circle cultivated demonstrations of classical learning to prove their parity with male colleagues.[90] The extant examples further suggest that women interpreted these subjects differently from male artists in early modern Bologna. Fontana's and Sirani's heroines eschew the sensuality and emotionality typically assigned to women by male artists, in favor of a portrayal characterized instead by strength, intelligence, and detachment—virtues associated during the early modern period with men. For Sirani, who has always been misunderstood as a follower of Guido Reni, these depictions were part of a strategy to elevate the stature of women in Bolognese culture, aspirations that were thwarted by her premature death at the age of twenty-seven.

Did Elisabetta Sirani's unconventional characterizations of female protagonists shape the language of male contemporaries who wrote descriptions of her artistry? Her first biographer, Count Carlo Cesare Malvasia, who knew both Elisabetta and her father personally, admired Elisabetta's virile and monumental manner of painting, which, for Malvasia, clearly distinguished her works from those of her female predecessors.[91] Similar gender reversals also characterize the language of Giovanni Luigi Piccinardi, a Bolognese poet who celebrated Sirani's achievements in a poem written in 1665, the year of her death. In it, he compares her to the (masculine) Sun, identifies her with the masculine term for painter, *pittore*, rather than the feminine *pittrice*, and describes her in virile terms as "armed" with her brush:

> Emulating the sun, with golden hair
> The luminous painter colors the rainbow
> Paint, Sirani, and your right hand armed
> With the ingenious brush makes the canvas
> blossom.[92]

Thus Sirani, like the heroines she portrayed in painting, was seen by contemporaries as possessing attributes that connected her to a tradition of masculine virtue. Such gender reversals in the language of art produced some paradoxical results: they distinguished Sirani for her exceptional gifts but helped to confuse her contributions with those of her male compatriots.

NOTES

1. Although Sirani has been the subject of little modern critical study, two important essays are Fiorella Frisoni, "La vera Sirani," *Paragone* 29 (1978): 3–18; and idem, "Elisabetta Sirani," in *La Scuola di Guido Reni*, ed. Emilio Negro and Massimo Pirondini (Modena: Artioli Editore, 1992), 343–64.

2. The education of girls was encouraged by Bolognese bishop Gabriele Paleotti, whose mother was renowned for her learning. Paleotti's promotion of female education was expressed in his "Ordine delle Scuole delle Putte che vanno ad imparare la Dottrina Christiana le domeniche e feste nella Città di Bologna," 16–18. See Paolo Prodi, *Il Cardinale Gabriele Paleotti (1522–1597)* (Rome: Edizioni di storia e letteratura, 1959–67), 1: 38–40.

3. The six artists' daughters are Elisabetta Sirani, Anna Maria Sirani (1645–1715), Barbara Sirani (1641–1692), Veronica Fontana (1619–1690), Teresa Coriolani (active c. 1627–1676), and Maria Oriana Galli (1656–1749). Francesca Fantoni (active late seventeenth to early eighteenth century?) was an artist's niece; Giulia Canuti (fl. 1684) was an artist's sister; and Antonia Pinelli Bertusio (d. 1644) and Lucia Casalini Torelli (1677–1762) were both married to painters. Most Italian women artists during this period were the wives and daughters of painters, so it is not the existence of this phenomenon in Bologna but rather its frequency that was unusual.

4. Among the numerous lost works by Bolognese women painters cited by early writers, two were paintings depicting Vigri. Elisabetta Sirani's sister Anna Maria (1645–1715) painted a canvas "for Malta . . . with the Beata Caterina Vigri of Bologna." Carlo Cesare Malvasia, *Felsina pittrice, Vite de' pit-*

tori bolognesi, ed. G. P. Zanotti (Bologna: Tipografia Guidi all'Ancora and Forni Editore, 1678 and 1841), 2: 412; Antonio di Paolo Masini, *Aggiunte alla Bologna Perlustrata*, unpublished notes of 1690, published in Adriana Arfelli, "'Bologna Perlustrata,' di Antonio di Paolo Masini e l' 'Aggiunta' del 1690," *L'Archiginnasio* 12 (1957): 188–237; and Luigi Crespi, *Felsina pittrice: Vite de' pittori bolognesi* (Bologna: Marco Pagliarini, 1769), 75. Elisabetta's pupil Lucrezia Scarfaglia (active c. 1677) painted a "Beata Caterina di Bologna" for the Bolognese Albergati family and a now lost *San Pasquale* for the Corpus Domini. Marcello Oretti, *Notizie de' professor del dissegno cioè pittori scultori ed architetti bolognesi e de forestieri di sua scuola raccolte da Marcello Oretti bolognese*, unpublished manuscript in the Biblioteca Comunale dell'Archiginnasio, Bologna, n.d., B 129, 121; Crespi, *Felsina pittrice*, 119.

5. Recent studies of Vigri include Mary Martin McLaughlin, "Creating and Recreating Communities of Women: The Case of Corpus Domini, Ferrara, 1406–1452," *Signs* 14 (1989): 293–320; Serena Spanò Martinelli, "La biblioteca del 'Corpus Domini' bolognese: L'inconsueto spaccato di una cultura monastica femminile," *La Bibliofilia* 88 (1986): 1–21; Jeryldene M. Wood, *Women, Art, and Spirituality: The Poor Clares of Early Modern Italy* (Cambridge: Cambridge University Press, 1996); and Vera Fortunati, ed., *Vita artistica nel monastero femminile* (Bologna: Editrice Compositori, 2002).

6. See Caterina Vigri, *Le Sette Armi spirituali*, ed. Cecilia Foletti (Padua: Editrice Antenore, 1985).

7. These statistics were compiled by the author. Some information on Bolognese women writers is in Giovanni Fantuzzi, *Notizie degli scrittori bolognesi* (Bologna: Stamperia di S. Tommaso d'Aquino, 1781); Fr. Pellegrino Antonio Orlandi, *Notizie degli scrittori bolognesi e dell'opere loro stampate e manoscritte* (Bologna: Costantino Pisarri, 1714); Luisa Bergalli, *Componimenti poetici delle più illustri rimatrici d'ogni secolo, fino all'anno 1575* (Venice: Antonio Mora, 1726); and Elisabetta Graziosi, *Avventuriere a Bologna: Due storie esemplari* (Modena: Mucchi, 1998), 141–238; but most works are no longer traceable.

8. The eight (or nine) secular women writers cited by Fantuzzi and Orlandi are Laura or Lavinia Danielli, Laura Felice Ghirardelli, Elisabetta Gondi/Isabella Gondi (possibly the same person), Ippolita Ludovisi, Giulia Ruini Musotti, Laura Felice Nannini, Giulia Ruini, and Teresa Zani.

9. See Craig Monson, *Disembodied Voices: Music and Culture in an Early Modern Italian Convent* (Berkeley: University of California Press, 1995), 2–3, 6, and 17.

10. Giulio Cesare Croce, *La Gloria delle donne* (Bologna: Alessandro Benaci, 1590), 1–31; Properzia de' Rossi and Lavinia Fontana are praised on 18–19. For other sixteenth-century works praising Bolognese women, see Caroline Murphy, "'In Praise of the Ladies of Bologna': The Image and Identity of the Sixteenth-Century Bolognese Female Patriciate," *Renaissance Studies* 13 (1999): 440–54.

11. Malvasia wrote full biographies of Lavinia Fontana (*Felsina pittrice*, 1: 173–80) and Elisabetta Sirani (ibid., 2: 385–407) and briefly mentioned painters like Antonia Pinelli (ibid., 2: 270), Ginevra Cantofoli (ibid., 2: 407), and Teresa Coriolani (ibid.). Masini's unpublished *Aggiunte* of 1690 to his *Bologna Perlustrada* provided the first detailed information on Anna Maria and Barbara Sirani (Arfelli, "Bologna Perlustrata," 205 and 209–10) and discussed Teresa Muratori, Ginevra Cantofoli, Lucrezia Scarfaglia, Veronica Fontana, and others.

12. Alessandro Macchiavelli, *Delle Donne bolognesi per letteratura e disegno illustri*, unpublished manuscript in the Biblioteca Comunale dell'Archiginnasio, Bologna (B 1331), 1741; Oretti, *Notizie* (undated, but probably 1770s); Crespi, *Felsina pittrice*; Gaetano Giordani, *Notizie delle donne pittrici di Bologna* (Bologna: Tipografia Nobili e Comp., 1832); Carolina Bonafede, *Cenni biografici e ritratti d'insigni: Donne bolognesi* (Bologna: Tipografia Sassi nelle Spaderie, 1845); Laura M. Ragg, *The Women Artists of Bologna* (London: Methuen, 1907).

13. Whitney Chadwick, *Women, Art, and Society* (London: Thames and Hudson, 1996), 92.

14. On Fontana, see Ragg, *Women Artists*, esp. 201–203; and Vera Fortunati, *Lavinia Fontana of Bologna 1552–1614* (Milan: Electa, 1998), 14. Sirani was linked with Reni by Ragg, *Women Artists*, 290–91; Ann Sutherland Harris and Linda Nochlin, *Women Artists: 1550–1950* (Los Angeles: Los Angeles County Museum of Art and New York: Alfred A. Knopf, 1976), 148; and others.

15. This is paraphrased from Giovanni Luigi Piccinardi,

quoted in Malvasia, *Felsina pittrice*, 2: 403. The artists were buried together in the Guidotti chapel, San Domenico, Bologna, where Elisabetta's godfather, Senator Saulo Guidotti, was also buried. The original inscription is lost but was recorded by Amico Ricci, *Iscrizione sepolcrale di Guido Reni ed Elisabetta Sirani esistente in San Domenico di Bologna* (Bologna: Tipografia Marsigli, 1842). Giovanni Luigi Piccinardi also wrote a poem honoring Elisabetta in the year of her death (*Poesie* [Bologna: Evangelista Dozza, 1665], 51).

16. See Michelangelo Gualandi, *Elisabetta Sirani pittrice, intagliatrice, musicista bolognese* (Bologna: Marsigli e Rocchi, 1853), 1–2. During the late eighteenth century, Marcello Oretti termed this a common misconception (*Notizie*, B.129, 68ter).

17. See the many antique heroines treated in Bettina Baumgärtel and Silvia Neysters, eds., *Die Galerie der Starken Frauen* (Munich: Klinkhardt and Biermann, 1995).

18. Two examples are Sirani's *Magdalen*s in the Pinacoteca Nazionale in Bologna and the Musée des Beaux-Arts in Besançon, both bare-breasted figures with long hair and a tactile interest that enhances their sensuality.

19. See Marzia Faietti, Konrad Oberhuber, et al., *Bologna e l'umanesimo 1490–1510* (Bologna: Nuova Alfa Editoriale, 1988), esp. 17–44, 52–55, 99, and 144–46.

20. Ibid., 31–32; and David Landau and Peter Parshall, *The Renaissance Print 1470–1550* (New Haven, Conn.: Yale University Press, 1994), 99.

21. See Miriam Filetti Mazza, *Archivio del Collezionismo Mediceo: Il Cardinal Leopoldo, 2: Rapporti con il mercato emiliano* (Milan: Riccardo Ricciardi Editore, 1993), 1: 3–7, and 20–25; and Edward L. Goldberg, *Patterns in Late Medici Art Patronage* (Princeton, N.J.: Princeton University Press, 1983), 34–53.

22. Lorenzo Legati, *Museo Cospiano* (Bologna: Giacomo Monti, 1677).

23. Giancarlo Roversi, *Palazzi e case nobili del '500 a Bologna: La storia, le famiglie, le opere d'arte* (Bologna: Casalecchio di Reno, 1986).

24. This is illustrated by five inventories of Bolognese art collections dated during Elisabetta Sirani's lifetime. See Raffaella Morselli and Anna Cera Sones, *Documents for the History of Collecting, Italian Inventories 3: Collezioni e quadrerie nella Bologna del Seicento, in-*ventari *1640–1707* (Los Angeles: Getty Information Institute, 1998), nos. 4, 31, 43, 52, and 55.

25. On Muratori, see Crespi, *Felsina pittrice*, 155–57; and Anna Maria Degli Angeli, "Il mito della donna artista nella Bologna del Seicento," *Il Carrobbio* 13 (1987): 124–27.

26. Fredrika H. Jacobs, *Defining the Renaissance* Virtuosa: *Women Artists and the Language of Art History and Criticism* (Cambridge: Cambridge University Press, 1997), 40–47.

27. Caroline Murphy, "Lavinia Fontana: The Making of a Woman Artist," in *Women of the Golden Age: An International Debate on Women in Seventeenth-Century Holland, England, and Italy*, ed. Els Kloek, Nicole Teeuwen, and Marijke Huisman (Hilversum: Verloren, 1994), 179–80.

28. Maria Teresa Cantaro, *Lavinia Fontana bolognese 'pittora singolare' 1552–1614* (Milan: Jandi Sapi Editori, 1989), catalogues about fifty history paintings with plausible attributions to Fontana.

29. Her list was published by Malvasia, *Felsina pittrice*, 2: 393–400. The works are arranged in chronological order, and the list usually specifies the patron.

30. Artemisia Gentileschi, for example, produced 161 paintings, according to R. Ward Bissell (*Artemisia Gentileschi and the Authority of Art* [University Park: University of Pennsylvania Press, 1999]); and no prints or drawings by Artemisia are known. Cantaro *(Lavinia Fontana)* catalogued 105 paintings and 38 drawings by Lavinia Fontana, in addition to fourteen questionable attributions.

31. Malvasia, *Felsina pittrice*, 2: 399–400.

32. Most of the works by Sirani's female followers are lost, apart from a handful of paintings and drawings by Ginevra Cantofoli, Lucrezia Scarfaglia, and Elisabetta's sisters Barbara and Anna Maria. Information on these works derives from the early writers (particularly Antonio Masini, Carlo Cesare Malvasia, Marcello Oretti, and Luigi Crespi) and from surviving inventories of Bolognese collections. Based on these sources, Anna Maria Sirani, Vincenza Fabri, Francesca Fantoni, Veronica Franchi, Maria Oriana Galli, Camilla Lauteri, and Caterina Mongardi were known exclusively as history painters; and Barbara Sirani and Ginevra Cantofoli were known predominantly as such. Only Maria Elena Panzacchia (d. 1737) was singled out by Luigi Crespi for her portraits in

pastel (*Felsina pittrice*, 155). The later Bolognese painter Lucia Casalini Torelli (1677–1762) produced both portraits and altarpieces.

33. Morselli and Sones, *Collezioni*, 414.

34. Sirani cited both works in her list of her paintings, listing the *Judith* (now Burghley House, England) as a work of 1658 and the *Timoclea* (now Museo di Capodimonte, Naples) as a work of 1659 (Malvasia, *Felsina pittrice*, 2: 394). Both works are also signed and dated by the artist. For a discussion of the *Judith* as a self-portrait of the artist, see Babette Bohn, "Female Self-Portraiture in Early Modern Bologna," *Renaissance Studies* 18 (2004).

35. Sirani cites only three pictures for Cattalani in her list of works (Malvasia, *Felsina pittrice*, 2: 394 and 397); but the 1668 inventory of Cattalani's collection lists seven works by Elisabetta and fifteen by Giovanni Andrea (Morselli and Sones, *Collezioni*, 153–58).

36. Morselli and Sones, *Collezioni*, 156, item nos. 6, 8, 12, and 23.

37. Ibid., 414.

38. Plutarch, *The Lives of the Noble Grecians and Romans*, trans. John Dryden (Chicago: Encyclopedia Britannica, 1952), 454–546. Plutarch gives another version of the story in "Concerning the Virtues of Women" (*The Complete Writings of Plutarch*, ed. William Goodwin [New York: Colonial, 1906], 376–78), but Sirani's picture is based on the version in Plutarch's *Lives*, which was in her father's library.

39. No other example is listed by A. Pigler, *Barockthemen* (Budapest: Verlag der Ungarischen Akademie der Wissenshaften, 1956), 2: 438.

40. Giovanni Boccaccio, *Concerning Famous Women*, trans. Guido A. Guarino (New Brunswick, N.J.: Rutgers University Press, 1963), xxxiii and xxxvii.

41. Leon Battista Alberti, *The Family in Renaissance Florence*, trans. Renée Neu Watkins (Columbia: University of South Carolina Press, 1969), 115.

42. *Discorso della virtù feminile e donnesca*, 1582. See Ian Maclean, *The Renaissance Notion of Woman: A Study in the Fortunes of Scholasticism and Medical Science in European Intellectual Life* (Cambridge: Cambridge University Press, 1980), 50–67.

43. Bartolomea's untitled poem of 1406 was published by Bergalli, *Componimenti*, 7–15.

44. Croce, *Gloria*, 10–11.

45. See Pigler, *Barockthemen*, 2: 362–63.

46. See Richard Spear, *Domenichino* (New Haven, Conn.: Yale University Press, 1982), no. 43 and plate 156.

47. Plutarch, *Lives*, 546.

48. Ibid., 545.

49. See Rona Goffen, "Lotto's Lucretia," *Renaissance Quarterly* 52 (1999): 742–81.

50. The modern attribution to Elisabetta Sirani of a more traditional painting of *Judith and Holofernes* in the Walters Art Gallery, Baltimore (inv. no. 37.253) seems questionable. It was catalogued by Federico Zeri as "attributed to Elisabetta Sirani," in lieu of its former identification as a German picture (*Italian Paintings in the Walters Art Gallery* [Baltimore: Trustees of the Walters Art Gallery, 1976], no. 359). However, Judith's face and the smooth paint surface are both atypical of the artist; and the composition replicates an etching ascribed to Giovanni Andrea Sirani. The etching (not listed by Bartsch) is inscribed "G.R.I" (Guido Reni invenit). An impression in the Pinacoteca Nazionale, Bologna (PN 23106) is inscribed: "G. And. Sirani inciso." Bettina Baumgärtel published this etching as Elisabetta or Giovanni Andrea in Baumgärtel and Neysters, *Die Galerie der Starken Frauen*, 267; but Elisabetta, unlike her father, made no reproductive prints after other artists.

51. "Senza Beltade l'Eloquenza tace, / Che la Beltade è un Eloquenza muta, / E l'Eloquenza è una Beltà loquace Piccinardi." *Poesie*, 30–31.

52. Quoted in Margaret Leah King, *Women of the Renaissance* (Chicago: University of Chicago Press, 1991), 194.

53. Morselli and Sones, *Collezioni*, 420, lot no. 49. The picture, which is signed "ELISABA SIRANI 1664" on the chair at lower left, is cited in Sirani's list as an overdoor for Simone Tassi, painted in 1664 (Malvasia, *Felsina pittrice*, 2: 399). According to the Herbert F. Johnson Museum of Art at Cornell University, where the picture was formerly on loan, the picture passed into the Bonfiglioli family collection before it was purchased by Spencer A. Samuels & Co., who sold it to the present owner.

54. Sirani's list does not mention the *Venus*, *Geometry*, and *Sibyl* noted in the 1671 inventory (nos. 32, 33, and 57), but cites four pictures painted for Tassi between 1660 and 1664: the *Portia*, two paintings of the *Virgin* (only one is cited in the inventory), and a *St. Anthony of Padua* (Malvasia, *Felsina pittrice*, 2: 395, 397, and

399). The *St. Anthony* was painted for San Leonardo, passed to Tassi's heirs in the Gessi family, and is now in the Pinacoteca Nazionale di Bologna.

55. This may be the picture by Fontana described by Malvasia as the "ritratto di Lindra, madre di Simon Tassi" (*Felsina pittrice*, 1: 178).

56. See Pigler, *Barockthemen*, 2: 415.

57. See D. Stephen Pepper, *Guido Reni* (New York: Phaidon Press, 1984), no. 107 and fig. 132.

58. Pigler listed sixteen paintings of Portia's suicide (*Barockthemen*, 2: 415).

59. See Ruth Wilkins Sullivan, "Three Ferrarese Panels on the Theme of 'Death rather than Dishonour' and the Neapolitan Connection," *Zeitschrift für Kunstgeschichte* 57 (1994): 610.

60. Bernadette Perrin, ed., *Plutarch's Lives* (Cambridge, Mass.: Harvard University Press, 1970), 153.

61. See Irene Samuel, "Semiramis in the Middle Ages: History of a Legend," *Medievalia et Humanistica* 2 (1944): 32–44.

62. Christine de Pizan, *The Book of the City of Ladies*, trans. Earl Jeffrey Richards (New York: Persea Books, 1998), I.15.1–2, II.25.2. Most of the ancient heroines represented by Sirani are discussed in this work, but it is not mentioned in the inventory of her father's library.

63. Croce, *Gloria*, 10.

64. On the numerous literary treatments of Cleopatra during the period, see Marilyn L. Williamson, *Infinite Variety: Antony and Cleopatra in Renaissance Drama and Earlier Tradition* (Mystic, Conn.: Lawrence Verry, 1974). On Cleopatra's historical significance and artistic treatment in antiquity, see Susan Walker and Peter Higgs, eds., *Cleopatra of Egypt: From History to Myth* (London: British Museum Publications, 2001).

65. Mary Hamer, *Signs of Cleopatra* (London: Routledge, 1993), 18–20.

66. Lucy Hughes-Hallett, *Cleopatra: History, Dreams, and Distortions* (New York: Harper and Row, 1990), 17.

67. Plutarch, *Lives*, 757. See also Hughes-Hallett, *Cleopatra*, 17.

68. Ibid., fig. 2; but see Guy Weill Goudchaux, "Was Cleopatra Beautiful? The Conflicting Answers of Numismatics," in Walker and Higgs, eds., *Cleopatra*, 210–16.

69. Boccaccio, *Concerning Famous Women*, 192.

70. The only two paintings known to me are Lavinia Fontana's picture, discussed below, and a *Suicide of Cleopatra* ascribed to Denys Calvaert in the Cassa di Risparmio, Cesena.

71. Felton Gibbons, *Catalogue of Italian Drawings in the Art Museum, Princeton* (Princeton, N.J.: Princeton University Press, 1977), no. 219; Bartsch 15.459.5, reproduced in Suzanne Boorsch and John Spike, *Italian Artists of the Sixteenth Century* (*The Illustrated Bartsch*, vol. 31) (New York: Abaris Books, 1980), 294; and Bartsch 14.158–63.193 and 197–211, reproduced in Konrad Oberhuber, *The Works of Marcantonio Raimondi and of His School* (*The Illustrated Bartsch*, vol. 26) (New York: Abaris Books, 1978), 190–97. Bartsch no. 193 is signed with Agostino Veneziano's monogram.

72. See Mary D. Garrard, *Artemisia Gentileschi: The Image of the Female Hero in Italian Baroque Art* (Princeton, N.J.: Princeton University Press, 1989), 213.

73. Plutarch, *Lives*, 779; and Boccaccio, *Concerning Famous Women*, 196.

74. See Pepper, *Guido Reni*, nos. 106, 111, 136, 181, 189, and 210; and Richard Spear, *The Divine Guido: Religion, Sex, Money and Art in the World of Guido Reni* (New Haven, Conn.: Yale University Press, 1997), 77–100.

75. See David Stone, *Guercino: Catalogo completo dei dipinti* (Florence: Cantini, 1991), nos. 76, 162, and 235.

76. See Daniele Benati and Marco Bona Catellotti, *Guido Cagnacci* (Milan: Electa, 1993), nos. 3, 17, 18, 39, and 42.

77. *Cleopatra* paintings by Veronica Franchi, a disciple of Elisabetta Sirani, and by Francesca Fantoni, a niece of Giovanni Gioseffo dal Sole, are mentioned by Oretti (*Notizie*, B129, 124 and B132, 271–72); and Crespi (*Felsina pittrice*, 76 and 27).

78. Cantaro suggested a date between 1604 and 1614 (*Lavinia Fontana*, no. 4a.98), but Fortunati and Ghirardi dated it around 1585 (Fortunati, *Lavinia Fontana*, no. 15). The patron is unknown. The picture was attributed to Andrea del Sarto in a 1759 inventory of the Spada collection and was ascribed to Fontana by Federico Zeri, whose attribution has been accepted by all subsequent writers (*Galleria Spada in Roma: Catalogo dei dipinti* [Florence: Sansoni, 1954], 80).

79. Cantaro identified the bird as an ibis, which was worshipped by the ancient Egyptians for its destruction of insects and serpents, and suggested that the bust

represented the Roman goddess Diana (*Lavinia Fontana*, no. 41.98).

80. Fortunati, *Lavinia Fontana*, no. 15.

81. The painting is not signed or dated, but its style suggests a date of c. 1662–63. Only the modern provenance of the work is recorded: the collection of Lord Belper, Kingston Hall, Nottinghamshire, until 1976, when it was sold by Christie's; a private collection in London; Guarisco Gallery, Washington, D.C.; and its current location in a private collection. Despite the absence of a signature or early record, the characteristic style led Christie's and later Frisoni to publish it as Sirani's work ("La vera Sirani," 11). A second autograph version of the picture is now in the Flint Institute of Arts (Flint, Michigan).

82. In Italy, the subject appears earliest in Venice, including examples by Leandro Bassano, Sebastiano Mazzoni, and Giulio Carpioni, setting the stage for the great Cleopatra pictures of Tiepolo during the eighteenth century. See Pigler, *Barockthemen*, 396–97. The only Bolognese example known to this writer that predates Sirani's is Alessandro Tiarini's picture of c. 1647 in a private collection (see Emilio Negro and Massimo Pirondini, *La Scuola dei Carracci dall' Accademia alla Bottega di Ludovico* [Modena: Artioli Editore, 1994], 301, 306 n. 120, and 311 fig. 391).

83. Pliny reported that she removed a priceless pearl earring, dissolved it in vinegar, drank it, and was about to do the same with the second pearl when she was stopped by the judge of the wager, who pronounced that Cleopatra had already won (Paul Turner, ed., *Selections from the History of the World, commonly called The Natural History of C. Plinius Secundus* [Carbondale: Southern Illinois University Press, 1962], 105–106). See also Boccaccio, *Concerning Famous Women*, 194–95.

84. Hamer, *Signs*, 18–21 and 30–33.

85. Boccaccio, *Concerning Famous Women*, 194–95.

86. See Michael Levey, *Giambattista Tiepolo: His Life and Art* (New Haven, Conn.: Yale University Press, 1986), 143–66 and fig. 135.

87. Garrard (*Artemisia Gentileschi*, 244–47) argues that Artemisia's picture formerly in Milan (Amedeo Morandotti) is untraditional in its unidealized handling of the nude figure and her firm grip on the snake, which suggests Cleopatra's control and power. Bissell (*Artemisia Gentileschi*, no. X-6) interprets the figure more erotically and ascribes the painting to Orazio Gentileschi. He attributes two other *Cleopatra*s to Artemisia (fig. 110, no. 22; and color plate XIX, no. 29). Bissell's no. 22 is also accepted by Garrard (fig. 242); his no. 29 is a less convincing attribution.

88. Sirani noted three paintings of Iole in her list of works: one in 1659 for the count of Novellara, and two for Berlingiero Gessi, both made in 1662 (Malvasia, *Felsina pittrice*, 2: 394 and 397). The third picture, which Gessi sent as a gift to Cesare Leopardi, with the lion's skin altered to a leopard's skin, is now in the Cassa di Risparmio, Bologna; the two others are lost.

    Sirani included a lost picture of Pamphile in her list, describing it as a tondo painted for Abbot Certani in 1664 (Malvasia, *Felsina pittrice*, 2: 399). This may have been in the collection of Ferdinando Cospi, where Legati noted "Una Panfilia, che pettina Bombage" (*Museo Cospiano*, 517) by Giovanni Andrea Sirani, but it seems likely that he confused Elisabetta's work with her father's. Although no other paintings of Pamphile are known, she was described by Boccaccio (*Concerning Famous Women*, 95) and Christine de Pizan (*City of Ladies*, I.40.1).

    Sirani's *Galatea*, noted in her list as a work of 1664 for Marchese Ferdinando Cospi, is in a private collection and is signed and dated 1664 (Malvasia, *Felsina pittrice*, 2: 399; Frisoni, *Scuola di Guido Reni*, plate 345).

    Two *Sibyls* in the Pinacoteca Nazionale, Bologna, that are signed and dated 1660 are the two pictures cited by Sirani from that year (Malvasia, *Felsina pittrice*, 2: 395). Sirani also listed a *Circe* from 1657 and two paintings of Venus, one painted in 1663 for Annibale Dovara and the other in 1665 for Annibale Ranuzzi (Malvasia, *Felsina pittrice*, 2: 394, 398, and 399). All three works are now lost.

89. Francesca Fantoni painted a *Rape of Europa*, an *Artemisia*, and a *Cleopatra* (noted by Crespi, *Felsina pittrice*, 27; and Oretti, *Notizie*, B132, 271–72); and Veronica Franchi painted a *Lucrezia*, an *Artemisia*, a *Rape of Helen*, and a *Cleopatra* (cited by Crespi, *Felsina pittrice*, 76; and Oretti, *Notizie*, B129, 1240). None of these pictures is still known today. Other Sirani followers, including her two sisters and Ginevra Cantofoli, produced almost exclusively religious pictures, according to the early writers.

90. See Margaret Leah King, "Thwarted Ambitions: Six Learned Women of the Italian Renaissance," *Soundings* 59 (1976): 280–304.

91. He says that Elisabetta worked in "un modo, che ebbe del virile e del grande" (Malvasia, *Felsina pittrice*, 2: 385–86). Jacobs (*Renaissance* Virtuosa, 26) discusses how anomalous such language was in biographies of female artists during the period.

92. *Poesie*, 51. In the title, Piccinardi employed the conventional feminine *pittrice*: "Alla Signora Elisabetta Sirana Pittrice famosissima." I am grateful to Francesca D'Alessandro Behr for her assistance with this translation. The original Italian reads: "Emula al Sol, che con la chioma aurata / Luminoso Pittor l'Iri colora / Pingi, Sirana, e la tua destra armata / D'ingegnoso Pennello i Lini infiora. Piccinardi."

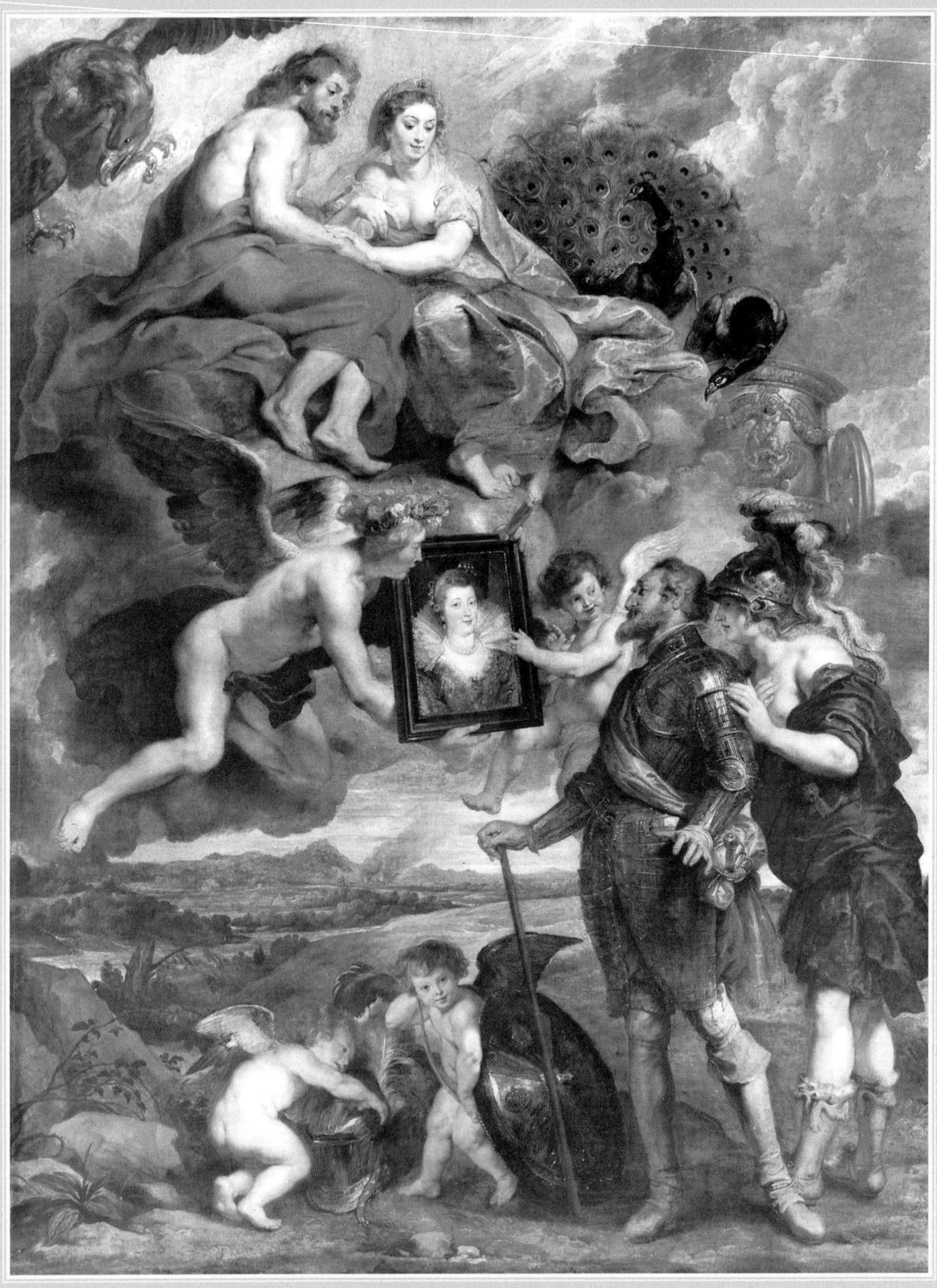

5

PICTURES FIT FOR A QUEEN

Peter Paul Rubens and the Marie de' Medici Cycle

Geraldine A. Johnson

PETER PAUL RUBENS devoted a significant portion of his artistic career to painting images either for or of women. He painted his two wives on many occasions, and he was commissioned to paint religious works and portraits for important female patrons such as Archduchess Isabella, ruler of the Spanish Netherlands, and the countess of Arundel. At the same time, in his mythological-allegorical works created almost exclusively for male patrons, Rubens painted innumerable nymphs and goddesses, often nude or only partially clad. Indeed, Rubens's development of a pictorial rhetoric based primarily on the display of the bare female body is so closely tied to his artistic identity that the adjective *Rubensian* is still current. It was only in the twenty-four canvases he painted for one of the two long galleries of Marie de' Medici's newly built Luxembourg Palace in Paris, however, that Rubens combined these two aspects of his art: a female patron and his usual visual language.[1] The Medici cycle is the only major example in this period of a large-scale, semipublic cycle dedicated exclusively to glorifying the life of a contemporary woman. When Rubens fulfilled this unusual commission by using a visual rhetoric of exposed female bodies to represent history as allegory or myth, he inadvertently created

a situation in which the cultural presuppositions of the cycle's contemporary viewers—mainly members of the French court and important visitors from abroad—ran headlong into the personal and political messages the queen had hoped the cycle would project.[2] It is precisely the uniqueness of the Medici cycle in terms of what is represented as well as how it is represented that reveals the gender-specific nature of Rubens's strategies for visual representation in general.

The Medici cycle's tensions are particularly well illustrated by one of the most interesting images in the series, the *Presentation of Marie de' Medici's Portrait to Henri IV.*[3] This painting demonstrates the consequences of Rubens's decision to use his usual visual rhetoric in the special case of a woman who was both the patron and the portrayed, the viewer as well as the viewed (fig. 5.1). In this image, the French king, Henri IV, gazes adoringly at the portrait of his bride-to-be, Marie de' Medici, proffered to him by a group of heavenly deities. Marie de' Medici, meanwhile, stares directly at the outside viewer. The queen is circumscribed by the black painted frame around her image which serves to turn her presence into a "mere" work of art, which can be scrutinized at lei-

This essay was first published in *Art History* 16 (September 1993): 447–69. Copyright © Association of Art Historians 1993. Reprinted by permission of the Association of Art Historians and Blackwell Publishing.

Figure 5.1. Peter Paul Rubens, *The Presentation of Marie de' Medici's Portrait to Henri IV,* 1622–25. Oil on canvas. Musée du Louvre, Paris. (Photo: Réunion des Musées Nationaux/Art Resource, New York.)

sure by the outside beholder, by Henri IV, and by the gods and goddesses. At the same time, Marie de' Medici breaks out of being "merely" artificial and decorative through her confident and unflinching outward gaze, which gives her the power of direct communication with the audience, a power denied most of the other figures in the image, including the king himself. Male and female, subject and object, levels of reality and artifice: the complexities of the *Presentation of the Portrait* can serve as an introduction to the ambiguities that exist between the representation of women and women as representation in seventeenth-century culture.

Ever since the seventeenth century, viewers of Rubens's Medici cycle have commented on the contrasts between the artist's imagery and the historical circumstances surrounding his patron, Marie de' Medici. In the later part of the century, Félibien lamented: "For, I beg you, just what do Cupid, Hymen, Mercury, the Graces, Tritons, [and] Nereids have to do with . . . Marie de Médicis?"[4] More recent critics have also remarked on the disjunctions between Rubens's rhetoric of allegory and the historical realities of Marie de' Medici's life.[5] Even Rubens himself complained that some visitors to the Medici gallery had "not grasped the true meaning" of some of the paintings and had "taken amiss" certain subjects.[6] One important factor in these problems—indeed, an important factor in the cycle's lack of immediate influence both artistically and politically—is the inherent conflict between Rubens's visual language and the fact that his patron was a woman.[7] Although some scholars have explored Marie de' Medici's role as a female patron, most of the extensive research on the cycle has concentrated on deciphering what its individual images mean. The personal and political references of the allegorical figures, the links to classical texts and emblem books, and the relationship to traditional "female" iconographies have all been assessed, but even recent studies have largely ignored how Rubens's language of visual representation was itself also affected by his patron's history and gender and how this in turn might have affected contemporary viewers of the cycle.[8] In other words, deciphering *what* the im-

ages mean is not enough; one must also explore *how* they mean.[9]

The Medici cycle, completed in 1625, falls roughly at the midpoint of Rubens's artistic career.[10] The apparent contradictions between Rubens's representational strategies and the special demands of having a female patron can be explained in part by the history and circumstances of the commission. The surviving contracts and correspondence suggest that the project was to a certain extent a commission by committee.[11] Abbé Maugis, Richelieu, Peiresc, Rubens, and Marie de' Medici herself, as well as others at the French court, all played at least some role in the final choice of subjects. In addition, the fact that much of the planning and execution had to be done in two different places, Paris and Antwerp, over more than three years (January 1622 to May 1625), further explains some of the cycle's inconsistencies. Even more importantly, over the course of the project, the delicate political situation between Marie de' Medici and her son, Louis XIII, was in constant flux, and her aims and tactics for personal propaganda through the Medici cycle were repeatedly adapted to the changing political climate.

Following the assassination in 1610 of her husband, Henri IV, Marie de' Medici ruled as regent for her minor son for four years until he attained his majority. At first, Louis XIII was content to allow his mother to continue to exercise her power, and he readily praised the "widow who happily governs the people, . . . sends the armies, . . . chooses the captains, . . . goes on campaign, . . . [and] directs the triumphs."[12] By 1617, however, relations between mother and son had deteriorated to the point that Marie de' Medici had been banished to Blois, and in 1619 she was openly supporting the grandees who were trying to start a rebellion against the king. By 1620, Louis XIII and his mother had reconciled, and in 1621, Marie de' Medici was asked to rejoin the king's council. It was during this truce that the queen mother commissioned Rubens to paint his series of large canvases for the main west gallery of her new Parisian palace, the Luxembourg, a space that was to serve as a grand approach and waiting area for visitors to her state apartments.[13] She chose this prominent setting in order to impress upon visitors from the French court and especially upon her son the king the veracity of her carefully selected and edited version of her life's main events, an important part of her attempts to regain her son's trust and hence some of her former power and influence.[14] The reconciliation of mother and son was only temporary, however, for by 1631, Marie de' Medici was forced to flee permanently from France and had to live out her days in exile.[15] In terms of solidifying her personal and political position in France, the Medici cycle had not been effective or, at least, not effective enough as an act of visual propaganda.[16]

Before the cycle and continuing after its completion, Rubens developed a pictorial language for allegory that was ultimately based on the symbolic display of nude female bodies. When he adapted this rhetoric to the Medici cycle commission in which the primary heroic subject was a woman, Rubens's deployment of nude female bodies as allegorical figures inevitably created friction between the messages he and his patron intended the paintings to project and the visual language used to represent them. In the *Education of Marie de' Medici*, for example, Rubens used the instantly recognizable image of the nude Three Graces as an attribute of the queen's childhood education (fig. 5.2). The instrument-playing male god, Orpheus,[17] assumes the role of the implied heterosexual male viewer by gazing directly at the nude women, whose bare flesh is highlighted all the more by the sharp contrast between their brightly lit pale skin and the much darker surrounding space. One of the Graces looks coyly out at the viewer, and it is she alone, the only one implying an awareness of the presence of the beholder standing before the painting, who teasingly tries to hide her nudity.[18]

The *Education of Marie de' Medici* seems to illustrate the relationship found in many of Rubens's mythological-allegorical works in which a male viewer (implicitly standing before the work and, in many cases, explicitly depicted within the work) scrutinizes a female nude. Unlike Rubens's many *Judgments of Paris* or his *Nymph and Satyr* or *Shepherd*

paintings intended primarily for the decoration of the private apartments of male patrons, however, the projected audience for the *Education of Marie de' Medici* included two very different categories of viewers—namely, the queen herself as patron of the cycle and, equally importantly, the male courtiers of the French court, who made formal visits to the Luxembourg Palace. The inclusion of the Three Graces was a means of asserting the queen's femininity. At the same time, the young Marie de' Medici is depicted turning her back on these women and instead concentrating intensely on the lessons of the goddess of wisdom, Minerva, who is dressed in armor. It is the figure of Orpheus who summarizes the inherent problems of using nude female bodies in conjunction with a message about a woman pursuing the then still primarily masculine arts of learning:[19] like the implied heterosexual male viewers of the painting as envisioned by Rubens, Orpheus can only concentrate his gaze on the enticing nude Graces, not on the young Marie de' Medici, who should be the work's main focus. Thus, by using his usual visual rhetoric of the allegorical female nude and by including a viewer in the person of Orpheus who acts out the normative heterosexual male response to this visual language, Rubens has unwittingly demonstrated how distracting his representational strategy based on the nude female body can be to the painting's viewers. Rather than proving to the French courtiers that Marie de' Medici's primary interest lies in learning the art of wise government, Rubens's nude female allegorical figures act instead as distractions from the queen's intended message by reminding male viewers of the dangers associated with female sexuality in seventeenth-century culture in general.

The motif of the exposed female body, especially the exposed breast, occurs in several other paintings in the Medici cycle. In the *Meeting of Marie de' Medici and Henri IV in Lyons*, Marie de' Medici looks down submissively and presents her bare breast to her husband as a sign of her acceptance of her role as wife and mother subservient to her king.[20] The composition echoes a coronation of the Virgin and, in fact, Marie de' Medici's exposed breast is Virgin-like, the

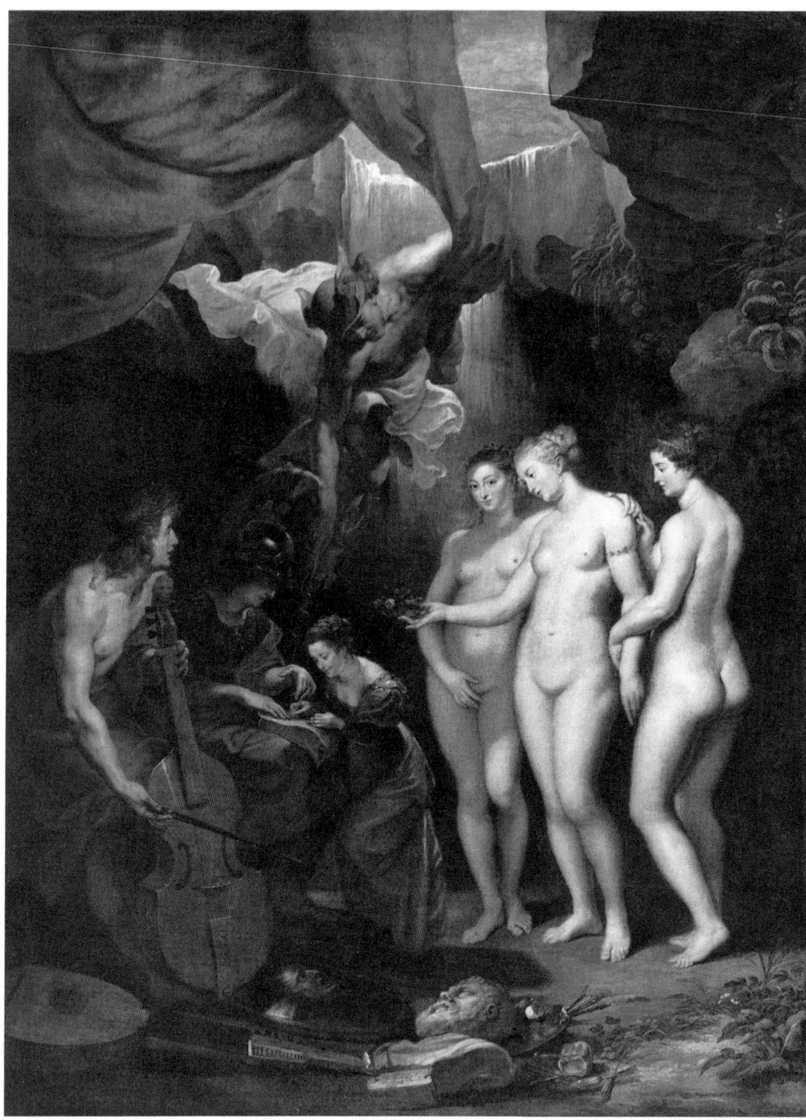

Figure 5.2. Peter Paul Rubens, *The Education of Marie de' Medici*, 1622–25. Oil on canvas. Musée du Louvre, Paris. (Photo: Réunion des Musées Nationaux/Art Resource, New York.)

ultimate symbol of woman as nurturer and procreator in an ordered, male-dominated universe.[21] Indeed, this image is one of several in the cycle that explicitly link Marie de' Medici to her namesake, the Virgin Mary.[22] In the *Peace of Marie de' Medici and Louis XIII Confirmed in Heaven*, the allusion is to an assumption of the Virgin. Like the Virgin, Marie de' Medici becomes both the mother and mystical bride of her son, her bare breast acting as a sign of this dual role. Rubens in fact used the bare breast as an attrib-

ute of the Virgin in several paintings he produced on the theme of the Virgin and Child.[23] In both the *Meeting in Lyons* and the *Peace Confirmed in Heaven*, the queen mother's bare breast emphasizes her feminine and motherly qualities. Rubens used these attributes to depict Marie de' Medici as powerful precisely because of her gender, because of her ability to bear and nurture the king's children, thereby ensuring the continuation of the dynasty.[24] This image of a woman defined, empowered, and sanctified through the attributes of her gender appears in other works painted by Rubens throughout his career that also accentuate the nurturing breast as the principal attribute of such a woman. In the Dulwich *Mars, Venus and Cupid* or the Rijksmuseum *Cimon and Pero,* a woman's breast gives life to both a young male child and an old male prisoner. In paintings such as the *Allegory of Peace and War* in London or the *Origins of the Milky Way* in Madrid, the mother's breast is the symbol of the establishment (or reestablishment) of an ordered world—indeed, an ordered universe.

In other paintings by Rubens, however, bare breasts carry much more negative associations. Instead of being positive symbols of the submissive and nurturing wife and mother, bare breasts allude to the dangers of female seduction. This is seen perhaps most powerfully in Rubens's London *Samson and Delilah.*[25] In this painting, Delilah's provocatively bared breasts, emphasized by the luminously painted flesh tones, which are highlighted all the more by the contrast with the much darker surrounding space, are symbols of a woman's ability to use her sexuality to incapacitate and emasculate an unwary man. Delilah uses her passive female sexuality, symbolized by her bare breasts, in order to exercise vengeance and control, traits associated in this period primarily with active male heroes and a very different type of meaning for the exposed female breast than that associated with the Virgin as wife and mother.[26]

Seventeenth-century culture in general seems to have held similarly ambiguous views about the significance of the bare female breast.[27] The bare breast was depicted as a positive attribute in images of the Virgin Mary as well as in the tradition of heroic female portraiture. Moralizing works, such as Juvernay's *Discours particulier contre la vanité des femmes de ce temps,* on the other hand, stressed the horrible fate that awaited any woman who dared to bare her breasts in public.[28] The frontispiece of this book shows a woman baring her breasts in a low-cut dress who is about to be attacked by a devil rising up out of the mouth of Hell. Other works, such as Polman's 1635 sermon *Le Chancre ou Couvre-sein féminin,* viciously attacked women who displayed their bare breasts in

public, calling them whores who "fling out carnal thoughts between those two mounds of flesh; they let villainous desires lodge in the trough between those bare breasts."[29] This type of vitriolic assault on the bare female breast crops up in French texts published throughout the seventeenth century.[30] In addition to the textual evidence provided by sermons and pamphlets, the pervasive notion in this period that the female breast was something powerful and potentially dangerous can be detected in the widespread practice of putting babies out to nurse, often to wet nurses in the country, thereby keeping even the nursing breast of middle- and upper-class women controlled by husbands and hidden from public view.[31] Thus, although Rubens and his patron certainly intended the queen's bare breasts in paintings such as the *Meeting at Lyons* and the *Peace Confirmed in Heaven* to be viewed positively as signs of her submissive and nurturing role as wife and mother, seventeenth-century culture in general and Rubens in works such as his *Delilah* in particular would have conditioned male viewers to see this attribute as potentially negative in its dangerous associations with female seduction, sexuality, and power.

The problems contemporary visitors to the Medici gallery faced in trying to interpret Marie de' Medici's bare breasts are intimately related to the question of context: if the queen was clearly portrayed as exclusively Virgin-like when exposing her breasts, the cycle's viewers would have understood this display in a positive context. In several of the images, however, Rubens and his patron chose to pair bare female breasts with attributes normally associated in the seventeenth century with male power, a combination that would have reminded viewers instead of the well-known topos of the dangerous power of women.[32] In the *Felicity of the Regency* and the portrait of *Marie de' Medici as Queen Triumphant,* for example, the queen's exposed breast is juxtaposed with attributes usually associated with male rulers (scales of justice, scepter, orb, throne) in the case of the former and with male warriors (helmet, armor, cannon, guns) in the latter (fig. 5.3). Although Rubens and his patron clearly wanted these paintings to act as positive affir-

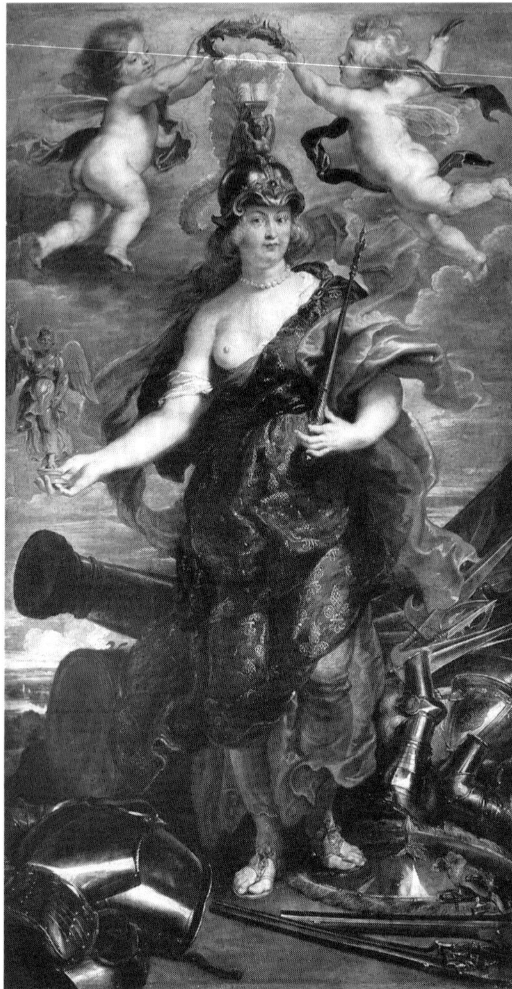

Figure 5.3. Peter Paul Rubens, *Marie de' Medici as Queen Triumphant*, 1622–25. Oil on canvas. Musée du Louvre, Paris. (Photo: Réunion des Musées Nationaux/Art Resource, New York.)

mations of the queen's abilities, in spite of her gender, to govern wisely and lead France to glory, the seventeenth-century view of women as potentially dangerous temptresses like Delilah who used their femininity to gain power over men meant that these images at the same time inadvertently allowed for very negative interpretations of Marie de' Medici's intentions.

In France, the Salic law specifically prohibited women from inheriting the throne.[33] The fact that this

law was circumvented three times in less than a century—for the regencies of Catherine and Marie de' Medici and for Anne of Austria later in the seventeenth century—simply confirmed male courtiers' fears of women gaining power at their expense.[34] A text published at the time that Rubens was working on the Medici cycle made clear allusion to the perceived dangers of Marie de' Medici's assumption of power when it condemned the

> true trickery [of] that superb Assyrian queen Semiramis, who massacred her husband and son . . . in order to rule over men and, so much did she want to imitate men's actions, she even dared to renounce woman's dress and clothe herself in the royal mantle.[35]

The combination of bare female breasts with clothing and attributes normally associated with male rulers in paintings such as the *Felicity of the Regency* or the *Queen Triumphant* would thus have reminded contemporary viewers of the then-current topos of the queen as a woman trying to usurp traditional male power. The fact that some of the cycle's images could easily have been (mis)interpreted in this way points to a fundamental problem: as an unusual—indeed, unique—type of project in this period, the Medici cycle as a whole was unable to provide its seventeenth-century viewers with a sufficiently stable or unambiguous context to prevent such negative readings of its images and its patron's intentions.

This friction between Marie de' Medici's desire to regain political power and the suspicion seventeenth-century patriarchal culture had of powerful women is reflected in the conflicting portrayals of women in printed books of the period. A popular literary genre in the seventeenth century was the so-called "gallery" of famous women—biographical compilations of the lives of female "worthies" from the Bible, mythology, and history that served as positive examples for contemporary women.[36] At the same time that authors such as Pierre Le Moyne in *La Gallerie des femmes fortes* (1647) and Jacques Du Bosc in *La Femme héroïque* (1645) used women of the past as heroic examples for the female sex, other texts of the period afforded much more negative readings of many of these same exemplary women. In works such as the anonymous *Les Singeries des femmes de ce temps descouvertes* and the *Tableau historique des ruses et subtilitez des femmes*, both published in 1623 while Rubens was designing the Medici cycle, famous women from the past were presented as dangerous figures whose deceitful seductions allowed them to tempt and then triumph over men.[37] Thus, while the biblical Susanna or Judith or the ancient Queen Semiramis could be praised as worthy models in some (con)texts, they could also serve as dire warnings of the dangers of female sexuality and power in other (con)texts. By combining images of female nudity with images of female power on behalf of a female patron, the Medici cycle therefore inevitably created a context that evoked many of this period's complicated and often contradictory notions of the nature of female sexuality and its relationship to power.

The wide range of meanings associated with female nudity can be further illustrated by another project undertaken by Rubens shortly before he began the Medici cycle. In about 1620, Rubens designed an engraving of *Susanna and the Elders* that he dedicated to Anna Roemer Visscher, an important member of Dutch humanist-literary circles who was also particularly admired for her virtue.[38] The dedication included an appropriately chaste and moralizing inscription calling Susanna, whose nude body forms the focal point of the composition, a "Pudicitiae exemplar." Originally, however, Rubens had planned to dedicate a different *Susanna* print to Anna Visscher. This print was finally executed in 1624, but, instead of a chaste dedication to Anna Visscher, it had a rather bawdy inscription that would have been much less appropriate for association with a highly respected woman, even though the nude figure of Susanna remained basically the same in both prints.[39] Instead of a comment about female chastity and virtue, this latter print was inscribed with the motto "Turpe Senilis Amor," a warning about the absurdity of old men being tempted to lust after pretty young girls.[40] The heterosexual male viewer, included symbolically within

these images in the figures of the lecherous old men about to assault the cowering Susanna, could have interpreted either depiction of female nudity as potentially dangerous. It was only thanks to the prints' different inscriptions that a viewer was able to determine whether Susanna's nudity was to be understood as a sign of innocent virtue or as a sign of seductive vice. Rubens was able to use very similar compositions for quite different purposes only because a text was included in order to provide the interpretive context necessary for a "correct" reading of the significance of each image's nudity.

In other instances, even the presence of an inscribed text was inadequate for ensuring that an exposed female body was understood "correctly." This appears to have been the case in Rubens's title-page design for Balthasar Cordier's edition of commentaries on St. Luke's Gospel, the *Catena sexaginta quinque graecorum patrum in S. Lucam*, published in Antwerp in 1628. Here, even the context provided by the title page's text was not enough to prevent Cordier from misreading the exposed legs and breasts of the figure of Truth negatively and demanding that the figure be covered up.[41] With neither a single, authoritative text to accompany it nor previous painted examples of this type of project to refer to, the context for interpreting the entire Medici cycle was inevitably much less clear than in the case of the title page of a religious treatise. The ever-changing personal and political situation of Marie de' Medici, as evidenced by the continuous modifications made to the list of subjects she wished to have painted, meant that a certain degree of ambiguity in the cycle was probably willed by both patron and painter. Nevertheless, the volatility inherent in using a visual rhetoric based on the nude female body in a cycle commissioned by a woman seeking to regain power meant that the positive context in which the queen wished her cycle to be framed could easily have been misunderstood by contemporary male viewers conditioned to view female nudity as something potentially dangerous and threatening.

In creating the Medici cycle, Marie de' Medici and Rubens must have been aware to a certain degree of the possible problems involved in developing a series of paintings that would extol the queen's ability to govern France without suggesting that she was a dangerously aggressive woman intent on seizing traditional male power. The original plans for both the Marie de' Medici gallery and the never-executed parallel gallery planned for Henri IV called for the "heroic deeds" of the queen and the "triumphs" of her dead husband to be the main themes of the cycles.[42] This theme of triumph is made more explicit in the second plan of April 1622, when the most prominent position on the far end wall of the queen's gallery was reserved for Marie de' Medici's *Triumph at Jülich*, a painting in the tradition of the quasi-historical royal equestrian portrait.[43] This initially clear focus on Marie de' Medici as a triumphant queen, however, became increasingly obscured as modifications were made to the subjects and their placement in the gallery in response to changing political circumstances. For instance, the ignoble *Flight from Paris* (which, in the end, was never executed), the *Escape from Blois,* and the *Full Reconciliation of Hostilities* were subjects suggested for the cycle later in 1622 that depicted the recent low points in the queen's relations with her son, followed by the current truce.[44] These subjects were unlikely to enhance the theme of the Queen Triumphant, but signaled instead a new, perhaps less aggressive approach by the patron to regaining the king's confidence. As the queen's political aims and tactics changed, Rubens modified his original plan to represent Marie de' Medici as a clearly heroic and triumphant ruler and instead added scenes that would have been less threatening to the cycle's most important male viewer, Louis XIII.

The essence of the problem facing both Marie de' Medici and Rubens in creating a gallery dedicated to a queen seeking to regain her lost powers can be reduced to a single question: over what could and should Marie de' Medici be shown to be triumphant? In the course of the Medici cycle project, answers to this question fluctuated, leading to a sense of uncertainty in the message projected by the gallery as a whole. In scenes such as the *Triumph at Jülich*, the *Consignment of the Regency,* or the *Exchange of Prin-*

cesses (a painting of Marie de' Medici's carefully arranged political marriages for her children), the triumphs of the queen were clearly military or political. Like any male ruler, Marie de' Medici demonstrated through these paintings her ability to soldier, govern, and negotiate marital alliances. In other paintings in the cycle, the queen's triumph was over her own gender and its limitations in the eyes of seventeenth-century patriarchal culture. As previously discussed, Marie de' Medici turns her back on the nude Graces in the *Education of Marie de' Medici* and focuses instead on the lessons of the armor-clad Minerva. Similarly, in the *Disembarkation in Marseilles*, Marie de' Medici not only symbolically walks away from her earlier political attachments to Tuscany but also literally walks over the frothy nude Nereids frolicking in the sea below (fig. 5.4). In the *Apotheosis of Henri IV and the Assumption of the Regency*, the disheveled, nearly nude female Victory in the center of the long rectangular canvas is a sign of the disordered world that Marie de' Medici's enthronement as regent on the right side of the painting is meant to reorder.[45] The violently abducted nude female figure of Truth in the *Triumph of Truth* and the bare-breasted female Virtues who row the symbolic ship of state in the *Majority of Louis XIII* are depicted literally beneath the person of Marie de' Medici, thus signaling that, like any male ruler, she too can use the visual rhetoric of the nude female allegorical figure to signify her power over her sex as well as over truth and virtue.[46]

Unlike a man, however, Marie de' Medici's use of nudity in the context of a series dedicated to returning a woman to a position of power left her open to highly critical interpretations of her intentions by the male courtiers from the French court who came to visit the Luxembourg Palace and who were used to equating certain kinds of female nudity and seductiveness with a dangerous loss of male potency and power. Even without reading the paintings in such a negative context, the implied heterosexual male viewers, like Orpheus gazing at the nude Graces, could have been distracted altogether from the personal and political messages the queen was trying to put forth

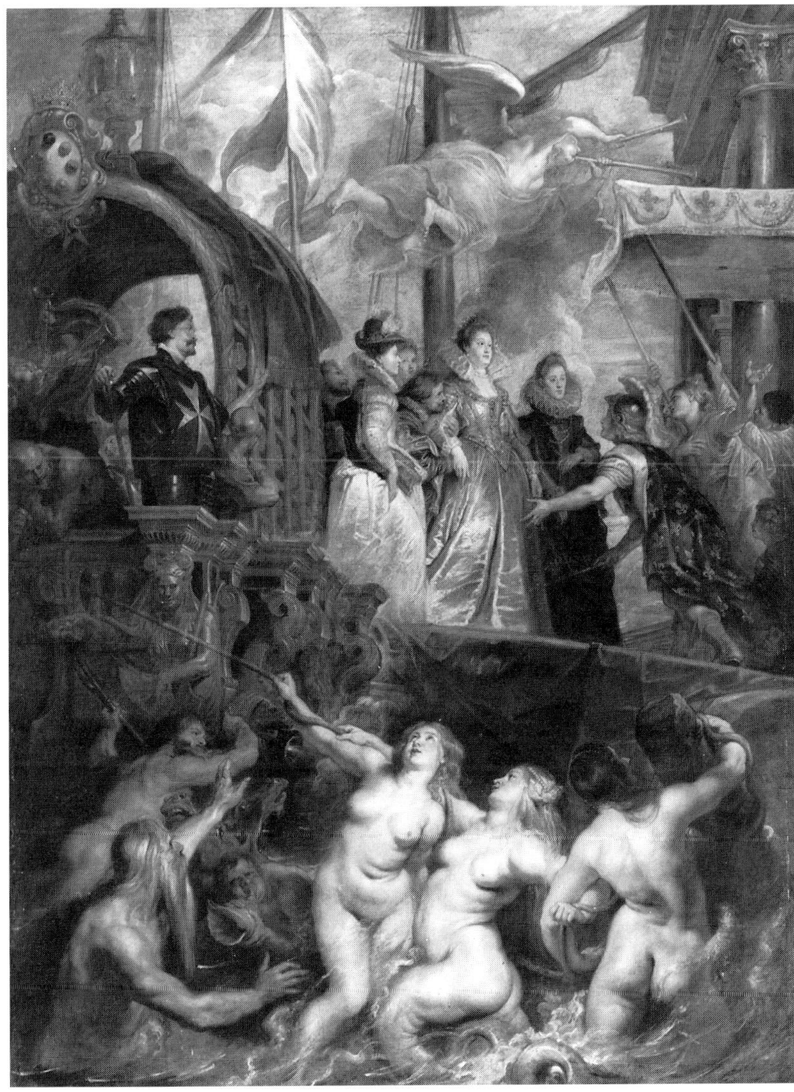

Figure 5.4. Peter Paul Rubens, *The Disembarkation of Marie de' Medici in Marseilles*, 1622–25. Oil on canvas. Musée du Louvre, Paris. (Photo: Réunion des Musées Nationaux/Art Resource, New York.)

in the cycle by the repeated display of nude female bodies in one painting after another. This emphasis on female nudity was heightened by the formal strategies used by Rubens, strategies that are particularly important when one considers the fact that these canvases, measuring nearly four meters in height, would have been viewed mainly from below by the gallery's visitors.[47] Many of the nude women in the Medici cycle are either near the center or in the forwardmost plane of the image, as, for example, in the *Education of Marie de' Medici*, the *Disembarkation in Marseilles*, the *Apotheosis and Assumption of the Regency*, and the *Triumph of Truth*. Rubens further accentuated the bare female bodies he painted in luminous shades of pink and white by contrasting them with often much darker surrounding spaces. By using these types of compositional and coloristic tactics, Rubens in effect was privileging a reading of these nudes as merely seductively painted bodies prominently displayed for the heterosexual male gaze's visual consumption rather

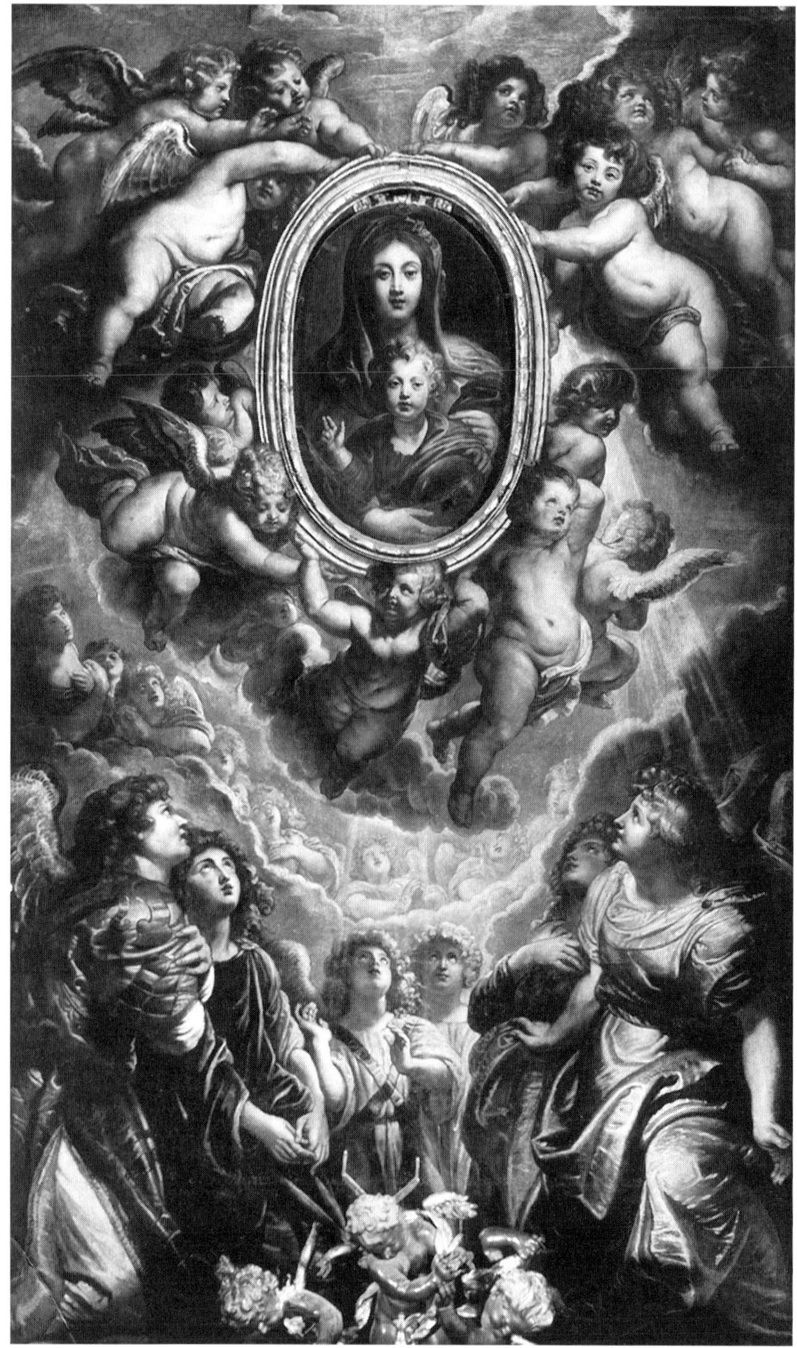

Figure 5.5. Peter Paul Rubens, *Icon of the Virgin and Child Adored by Angels*, 1608. Oil on canvas and on copper plate (over older fresco). S. Maria in Vallicella, Rome. (Photo: Alinari/Art Resource, New York.)

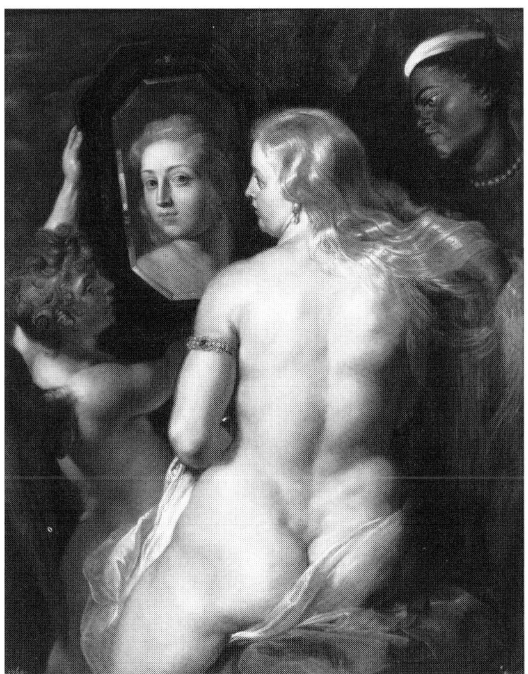

Figure 5.6. Peter Paul Rubens, *Venus at Her Mirror*, ca. 1616. Oil on panel. Collection of the Prince of Liechtenstein, Vaduz Castle.

than as essential figures in a complex iconography devised to vindicate the queen.

This problematic relationship between female subject and male viewer, between art and beholder, is made most explicit in the Medici cycle in the *Presentation of Marie de' Medici's Portrait to Henri IV* discussed briefly above. It is in this scene that the problems of viewing, and in particular of viewing a woman who is both subject and patron, are brought most clearly to the surface. In the *Presentation of the Portrait*, the two opposed ends of the spectrum of the woman as object of the male gaze are condensed into a single image: woman as seductive Venus and woman as chaste Virgin. Even Rubens's formal approach stresses this duality with the restrained color and composition of Marie de' Medici's portrait, contrasting sharply with the exuberantly painted barebreasted figure of Juno floating directly above the queen's image. Unlike earlier allusions in the cycle to Marie de' Medici's sacred namesake, the portrait

within the painting does not recall the historical events associated with the Virgin Mary's life but rather refers specifically to other depictions of the Virgin in works of art—namely, in icons. Rubens's painting for the Roman church of S. Maria in Vallicella, for instance, is one of several works by him that are actually paintings about paintings of the Virgin (fig. 5.5).[48] In this image, putti hold up a painting of the Virgin and Child for both the outside viewer and the angels within the composition to adore. The Medici cycle's *Presentation of the Portrait* echoes this type of painting: winged deities hold up the portrait of Marie de' Medici as Virgin Mary to be admired from below by the outside viewer as well as by the figures within the image, including her future husband, Henri IV.

In addition to the references to Marian prototypes, the *Presentation of the Portrait* also recalls traditional depictions of the Virgin's pagan opposite, Venus. In Rubens's *Venus at Her Mirror* in Vaduz (Liechtenstein), for instance, the mirror reflection of the goddess looks out directly at the viewer with a knowing and almost challenging gaze, much as Marie de' Medici looks out from her portrait (fig. 5.6).[49] The allusions to the dangers of feminine vanity and the seductiveness of the female gaze that are implicit in such depictions of Venus and her mirror are somewhat lessened in the *Presentation of the Portrait* by the fact that the person who looks into the mirror-like painting is not a woman but the king of France, Henri IV. Indeed, the composition may well allude to the literary genre known as the "Mirror of the Prince," a type of book devoted to describing appropriate royal conduct. The title page of one such book published in Brussels in 1655, Belluga's *Speculum Principum*, in fact depicts a prince looking into a black-framed mirror in which he sees a reflection of himself accompanied by Virtues.[50] By seeing Marie de' Medici in the painting-as-mirror, the implication is that Henri IV sees himself in her, a point the queen was eager to stress in her claims to be her husband's legitimate successor. While paintings such as the *Consignment of Government*, the *Coronation*, and the *Apotheosis and Assumption of the Regency* all overtly sought to legitimize Marie de' Medici's claims to the regency, it is only in the *Presentation of the Portrait* that she is transformed into the mirror image of the king, a somewhat subtler but perhaps even more effective plea for the legitimacy of her rule than the depiction of any single historical event could ever be.

Early-seventeenth-century texts and images took up this notion of Marie de' Medici as the mirror image of her husband, the king, and made it explicit. Even before the death of Henri IV, emblems were designed that emphasized this mirror-like relationship. An emblem of 1609, for example, shows a sun reflected in a rectangular framed mirror, with a somewhat later description explaining that this scene "allegorically represents the [queen's] . . . wise recognition that all her luster comes from that of the king . . . [who] planned to make her regent in his absence and to give her all the honors that she could hope for."[51] In the 1615 *Harangue panegyrique a la reine sur l'heureux succeʒ de sa regence,* the author Balzac wrote that it "seems to us that he [Henri IV] reigns still under a face of a woman and such that we must call him Queen in you, or call you King."[52] A pamphlet extolling the queen's virtues that was published in 1612 asserts that "our King is not dead, but seeing himself decaying, he wanted . . . to take new life . . . in order to lengthen the stretch of his years . . . [therefore] you [Marie de' Medici] seeing him before your eyes, only hav[e] . . . changed of degree."[53] And Jean Prévost's 1613 text *Apothéose du très chrestien Roy de France et de Navarre Henri IIII* says that Henri IV has built his mausoleum in the very person of Marie de' Medici.[54]

At the same time that the king seems to search for a mirror image of himself in the portrait of his bride-to-be, Marie de' Medici's own gaze in the *Presentation of the Portrait* is self-consciously directed outward: she is a woman who is fully aware of being looked at both from within the painting and from without by the outside viewer. In one sense, as the patron of the cycle, the represented Marie de' Medici's outward gaze acts as a kind of mirror reflection of the real Marie de' Medici standing before the painting. As importantly, however, her unflinching gaze serves to acknowledge the other key viewers of the cycle—namely, the male courtiers on official visits to her palace and especially her son, the king. It is through her awareness of her position as the object of the male gazes of her courtiers and king (Henri IV as well as Louis XIII) that Marie de' Medici gains power. By calmly and steadily returning the outside viewer's gaze, Marie de' Medici adopts a position that is equal to that of the men who view her. Indeed, as the only figure in the scene (besides the putto directly beneath her) who seems to be aware of the presence of an outside viewer, it is she who communicates most powerfully and directly with the spectator, like an icon of the Virgin whose outward gaze allows her to affect directly the worshipful viewers gathered before her image.[55] The force of Marie de' Medici's gaze should have played an important role in her attempts to use the Medici cycle in her quest to regain the personal and political authority she had recently lost.

In fact, the theme of Marie de' Medici's powerful and empowering gaze was developed in several texts published during her regency. The queen is described as the "Beautiful regent of our lands / Whose rich gazes of female charms / . . . Gives life or death" and "Her favorable gaze is all powerful / May it pour over us a saintly influence."[56] But, in the same way that seventeenth-century culture could read the biographies of famous women of the past or could view bare breasts in negative as well as in positive terms, Marie de' Medici's gaze was also described very critically by some contemporary writers, especially after her first fall from power. *Les Singeries des femmes de ce temps descouvertes*, published in 1623, says in a passage alluding to Marie de' Medici that "the woman hides under a deceitful face all that one can imagine in this world that is perfidious and evil . . . there is nothing more inconstant than her face . . . the head of Medusa turns all things to stone . . . [including] men."[57] In an anonymous text published while Marie de' Medici was still in power, she is described as "this beautiful French Astraea [who] has totally changed: she has removed her blindfold, *she now sees clearly* . . . her [outer] dress is . . . chameleon-like in order to allow her to take on whatever colors her passion demands."[58] The gaze of the powerful woman could be threatening as well as life-giving in the opinion of seventeenth-century writers.

One must assume that both Rubens and Marie de' Medici intended her assertive outward gaze in the *Presentation of the Portrait* to be interpreted in a positive manner. One of the problems faced by contemporary viewers of the painting, however, was trying to determine the appropriate context in which to place the portrait of the bride-to-be who eventually ruled as regent. Marie de' Medici's portrait collapses within itself two quite distinct portrait traditions: depictions of beautiful women intended to be admired by their male lovers as well as portraits commemorating male patrons who wanted a visual affirmation of their worldly fame and power that would impress their peers.[59] This ambiguity about how to understand the queen's portrait in terms of its implied function and audience could, of course, be seen as a felicitous combination of the two roles—loving wife and mother as well as powerful ruler—Marie de' Medici wished to adopt at the time of the cycle's commission. Once again, however, the patron's lack of control over her audience's actual responses could just as well have led contemporary male viewers to regard very negatively her attempts to mask her quest for power under the guise of the seductive female gaze. It is perhaps ironic, then, that Marie de' Medici's empowering gaze out toward the male viewers in front of the painting is only effected through the mediation of artifice: like the painting of the *Icon of the Virgin and Child* in S. Maria in Vallicella or the Liechtenstein *Venus,* the queen's assertive gaze seems to be possible only when it issues forth from a painting within a painting, from a mirror within art's mirror.

The ambiguities associated with the female gaze, with the role of art in depicting female sexuality and power, are also part of the broader issue of Rubens's understanding of visual representation in general. The fact that the black frame around the queen's portrait in the *Presentation of the Portrait* echoes the black frames that encased the entire Medici cycle allows this particular image to function even more explicitly as a painting that mirrors the painted cycle as a whole.[60] Like Gide's "mise en abyme," the text that includes

within itself a representation of itself, or Schlegel's notion of a "poetry of poetry," Rubens's *Presentation of the Portrait* recapitulates in the painting within the painting some of the artist's ideas on the nature of visual representation.[61] While the "mise en abyme" usually is used to highlight the internal structure of a text or other work of art, in the case of the *Presentation of the Portrait,* it also acts to bring to the surface the gender-specific tensions inherent in Rubens's strategies of visual representation and in seventeenth-century culture in general.

Rubens produced other images that illustrate his ongoing interest in thematizing the problems of representing representation and of exploring the relationship between art and the viewer. One of these is the title page he designed for Blosius's *Opera* in 1632. Like the painting within the painting in the *Presentation of the Portrait,* this engraving depicts an open book on the title page of the book the reader holds in his or her hands.[62] It too includes an active viewer-reader within the composition who looks up to the book held aloft by heavenly beings, a book that echoes the larger opus the reader is about to peruse. In the *Christ and Doubting Thomas* triptych painted for Nicolaas Rockox in circa 1613–15, Rubens used a sacred narrative to represent the ideal relationship between image and spectator (fig. 5.7).[63] At the same time, this work could also be interpreted as a comment on the relative positions of male versus female viewers. St Thomas and the other apostles gathered around Christ have direct physical as well as visual access to the subject itself, while secular viewers, both those standing implicitly before the painting and the two donors depicted explicitly in the side panels, are relegated to a space clearly outside the sacred scene. The apostles' gazes and gestures demonstrate the properly reverential viewing relationship the spectator should have to Christ's sacred body. The viewers before the painting, however, are also made aware of the distance between themselves and this image by the separated figures of Nicolaas Rockox and his wife, Adriana Perez. The spectator is both drawn into the work by Adriana Perez's inviting outward gaze and simultaneously excluded from the sacred central core to

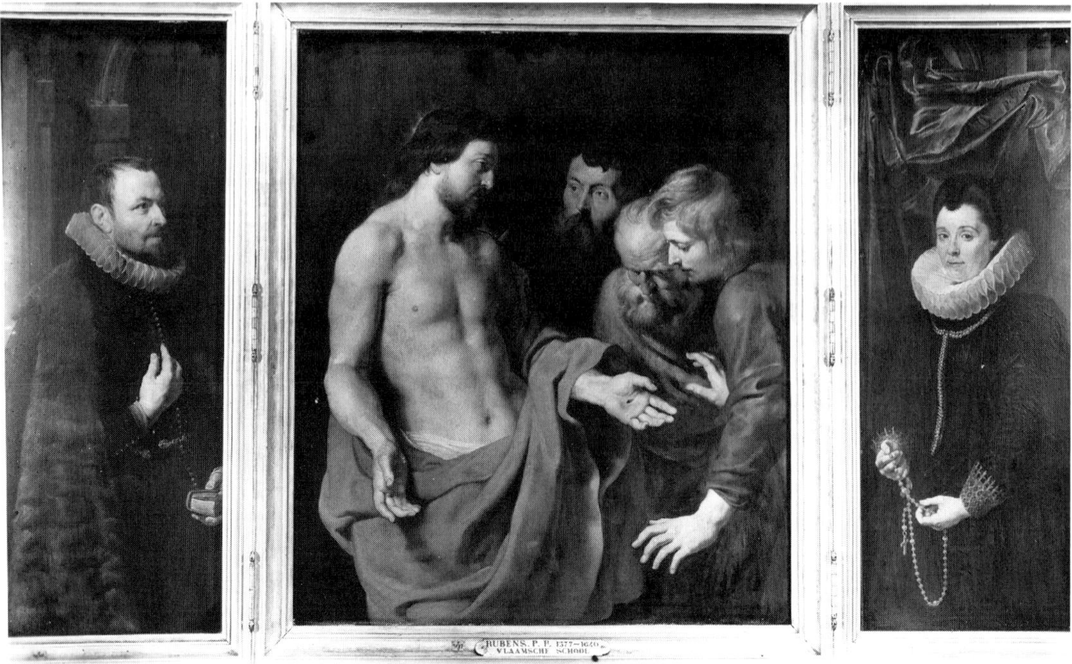

Figure 5.7. Peter Paul Rubens, *The Rockox Triptych: Christ and Doubting Thomas* (center), *Nicolaas Rockox* (left), and *Adriana Perez* (right), ca. 1613–15. Oil on panel. Koninklijk Museum voor Schone Kunsten, Antwerp.

which only Nicolaas Rockox, intensely gazing at Christ's body, seems to have visual access. Adriana Perez is empowered by her direct visual communication with the outside viewer, but at the same time she remains excluded from the true center of power, the sacred body of Christ, which is accessible only to the male gazes of her husband and the apostles.

In projects such as the Rockox triptych or the Blosius title page, as Frank Stella has accurately observed, "Rubens came to believe that he could make painting about painting."[64] The crucial difference between such images and the *Presentation of the Portrait*, however, is that in the latter work, Rubens creates a painting not about representation in general but about a very particular problem, namely, how to depict a woman seeking power in seventeenth-century France. As the first (and only) example in this period of a large-scale series dedicated to glorifying the life of a contemporary woman, the Medici cycle had no precedents. Its viewers therefore had no frame of reference, no clearly defined context in which to interpret the cy-

cle. Indeed, the ever-varying combinations of female imagery, from the queen's assertive gaze and occasionally bared breast to the nude Graces and Nereids, could easily have been misinterpreted by seventeenth-century male visitors to the gallery conditioned to assess the female gaze as well as the female body in highly ambiguous ways. To understand the elusive relationships between gender and representation brought to the surface by the Medici cycle, one must go beyond deciphering its classical and Christian iconography, beyond trying to determine *what* individual images mean, and instead focus on *how* they mean, that is, on the mechanisms that create meaning. Rubens's essentially patriarchal visual rhetoric encompasses not just iconography but also the dynamic interaction of allegory, myth, and history, the tactical use of color and composition, and references to the repertoire of female images available to his contemporaries. It is only by dissecting these strategies for visual representation and analyzing them within the context of seventeenth-century culture that one can begin to understand the inevitable problems that arose when Rubens applied this rhetoric to the project of depicting a once-powerful woman trying to regain her influence in a male-dominated society.

NOTES

This essay was first published with additional illustrations and more extensive notes. I would like to thank Joseph Koerner and Simon Schama for invaluable advice and encouragement in preparing the original article. I am also grateful for the comments provided by R. Stanley Johnson and Ursula Gustorf Johnson on an earlier version of this essay.

1. The Medici gallery was a well-lit and richly decorated space measuring 58 by 7.60 meters. Rubens's paintings would have towered over the gallery's visitors: most are nearly 4 meters high with the bottom edges of the frames originally at least 1.30 meters above the floor. Twenty of the canvases were hung between the windows on the long sides of the gallery with the remaining four on the two short ends of the space. See Deborah Marrow, "The Art Patronage of Maria de' Medici" (Ph.D. diss., University of Pennsylvania, 1978), 66–69; Marie-Noëlle Baudouin-Matuszek et al., *Marie de Médicis et le Palais du Luxembourg* (Paris: Délégation à l'action artistique de la ville de Paris, 1991), 220 and 225; and Jacques Thuillier and Jacques Foucart, *Le storie di Maria de' Medici di Rubens al Lussemburgo* (Milan: Rizzoli Editore, 1967), 65–66, and the illustrations on 33, 35, and 68–69.

2. On seventeenth-century visitors to the gallery, see Baudouin-Matuszek, *Marie de Médicis*, 218–22; and Thuillier and Foucart, *Le storie*, 10, 120, 122–26, and 130ff. Except for the queen herself and the female members of the court mentioned in a description of the gallery's opening in 1625, only male visitors are recorded in the surviving documents. One assumes, however, that female members of the court continued to visit the cycle as well. In any case, the queen's primary concern would have been to impress the male courtiers who, in a highly patriarchal culture, wielded the most power and influence. On the women in the queen's entourage and her relationship to the male grandees, see Baudouin-Matuszek, *Marie de Médicis*, 125–30.

3. Portraits of potential brides were often sent to kings and noblemen in this period. Marie de' Medici herself requested such works for her second son. See Marrow, "Art Patronage," 107–11. Ronald F. Millen and Robert E. Wolf, *Heroic Deeds and Mystic Figures: A New Reading of Rubens' Life of Maria de' Medici* (Princeton, N.J.: Princeton University Press, 1989), 49–50, mention portraits of Marie de' Medici sent to Henri IV during marriage negotiations. Some portraits of the queen similar to the one in the *Presentation of the Portrait* survive. See Karla Langedijk, *The Portraits of the Medici: 15th-18th Centuries*, vol. 2 (Florence: Studio per edizioni scelte, 1983), 1245 and 1250–51.

4. Marrow, "Art Patronage," 105.

5. For example, see Svetlana Alpers, "Manner and Meaning in Some Rubens Mythologies," *Journal of the Warburg and Courtauld Institutes* 30 (1967): 295; and Thuillier and Foucart, *Le storie*, 36.

6. From letters to Jacques Dupuy in 1626 and to Peiresc in 1625, respectively. See Ruth Saunders Magurn, *The Letters of Peter Paul Rubens* (Cambridge, Mass.: Harvard University Press, 1955), 149 and 109.

7. Alpers, "Manner and Meaning," 295, calls the cycle a "striking failure." Politically, the series was unable to solidify Marie de' Medici's precarious position at the French court. Millen and Wolf, *Heroic Deeds*, 13, suggest that if the queen's "fall can be attributed to any single misstep, it would be the overconfidence with which she commissioned and conceived the Luxembourg paintings." Thuillier and Foucart, *Le storie*, 38–40; Marrow, "Art Patronage," 105; and Anthony Blunt, *Art and Architecture in France 1500–1700* (London: Penguin Books, 1982), 361, all comment on the cycle's failure to inspire any contemporary artistic imitations.

8. For instance, Millen and Wolf, *Heroic Deeds*; and Susan Saward, *The Golden Age of Marie de' Medici* (Ann Arbor: University of Michigan Research Press, 1982), have seen emblems and classical literature, respectively, as the iconographic keys that will unlock the cycle's meaning. Beverly Heisner, "Marie de Medici: Self-Promotion through Art," *Feminist Art Journal* 6, no. 2 (1977): 21–26; Marrow, "Art Patronage"; idem, "Marie de' Medici and the Decoration of the Luxembourg Palace," *Burlington Magazine* 121 (1979): 783–91; Elaine Rhea Rubin, "The Heroic Image: Women

and Power in Early-Seventeenth Century France, 1610–1661" (Ph.D. diss., George Washington University, 1977); and Mary D. Garrard, *Artemisia Gentileschi* (Princeton, N.J.: Princeton University Press, 1989), 157–59, have analyzed the queen as a female patron and her use of "female" iconographies.

9. See Joseph L. Koerner, "The Mortification of the Image: Death as a Hermeneutic in Hans Baldung Grien," *Representations* 10 (1985): 52–101, on the notion of *how* images mean as opposed to *what* they mean.

10. There is a vast literature on Rubens. For overviews of his career, see Christopher White, *Peter Paul Rubens: Man & Artist* (New Haven, Conn.: Yale University Press, 1987); and Michael Jaffé, *Catalogo completo: Rubens* (Milan: Rizzoli, 1989). See also the ongoing *Corpus Rubenianum Ludwig Burchard*, begun in 1968.

11. The project is well documented by Thuillier and Foucart, *Le storie*, esp. 131 and 91ff. See also Ewald M. Vetter, "Rubens und die Genese des Programms der Medicigalerie," *Pantheon* 32 (1974): 355–73; and Marrow, "Art Patronage," 92–99.

12. Rubin, "Heroic Image," 84–85.

13. On the gallery as a waiting area for visitors, see Marrow, "Art Patronage," 66; and Thuillier and Foucart, *Le storie*, 31.

14. Rubens describes Louis XIII's first visit to the gallery in a letter to Peiresc on May 13, 1625. See Magurn, *Letters*, 109.

15. On Marie de' Medici's relationship to Louis XIII, see Victor-L. Tapié, *France in the Age of Louis XIII and Richelieu*, trans. D. M. Lockie (Cambridge: Cambridge University Press, 1984); and Geoffrey Parker, *Europe in Crisis: 1598–1648* (Ithaca, N.Y.: Cornell University Press, 1979), 128ff.

16. See note 7 above.

17. Although early guides to the cycle call this figure both Apollo and Orpheus, a text possibly dictated by Rubens himself calls him by the latter name. See Jacques Thuillier, "La 'Galerie de Médicis' de Rubens et sa genèse: Un document inédit," *Revue de l'art* 4 (1969): 56.

18. Rubens's interest in exploring the nuances of the female gaze is suggested by the preparatory oil sketches for the *Education of Marie de' Medici* and the *Presentation of the Portrait*, which do not yet show either the Grace or the queen looking outward. See Julius Held, *The Oil Sketches of Peter Paul Rubens* (Princeton, N.J.: Princeton University Press, 1980).

19. Although Marie de' Medici had a relatively liberal education for a woman of her time, the emphasis was mainly on the visual arts and skills such as precious stone connoisseurship rather than on history, literature, or politics. On her education and cultural formation in Florence, see Thuillier and Foucart, *Le storie*, 13; Marrow, "Art Patronage," 7–13; Baudouin-Matuszek, *Marie de Médicis*, 38–84; and Sara Mamone, *Firenze e Parigi: Due capitali dello spettacolo per una regina: Maria de' Medici* (Milan: Silvana Editoriale, 1987).

20. The queen's interest in emphasizing her position as wife as well as mother is demonstrated by her commissioning numerous images of marriages and mothers. See Marrow, "Art Patronage," 48–49, 71–73, and 155–59.

21. John B. Knipping, ed., *Iconography of the Counter Reformation in the Netherlands*, vol. 2 (Leiden: De Graff, 1974), 258 and 263ff; and Margaret R. Miles, "The Virgin's One Bare Breast: Female Nudity and Religious Meaning in Tuscan Early Renaissance Culture," in *The Female Body in Western Culture*, ed. S. R. Suleiman (Cambridge, Mass.: Harvard University Press, 1986), 193–208, explore the sometimes ambiguous meanings associated with the Madonna's bare breast in art.

22. *The Birth of Marie de' Medici*, the *Education of Marie de' Medici*, the *Marriage by Proxy*, the *Birth of Louis XIII*, the *Coronation*, and the *Apotheosis of Henri IV and Assumption of the Regency*, which shows the queen enthroned, all recall a traditional iconography of the Virgin. On the cycle's Marian imagery, see Heisner, "Marie de Medici," 23–24; Marrow, "Art Patronage," 149–55; F. Hamilton Hazlehurst, "Additional Sources for the Medici Cycle," *Bulletin: Musées Royaux des Beaux-Arts de Belgique* 6 (1967): 114; Millen and Wolf, *Heroic Deeds*, 34, 61–62, and 217–18; and Robert W. Berger, "Rubens and Caravaggio: A Source for a Painting from the Medici Cycle," *Art Bulletin* 54 (1972): 473–77.

23. See, for example, Rubens's c.1635 painting of the *Virgin and Child* in Cologne.

24. It is ironic but not unexpected that the queen was never the principal wet nurse or caretaker of her son. On Louis XIII's childhood, see Elizabeth Wirth Marvick, *Louis XIII: The Making of a King* (New Haven, Conn.: Yale University Press, 1986).

25. See White, *Rubens*, 99–102, on this commission.

26. A similarly dangerous display of female breasts is seen in Rubens's *Judith* in Braunschweig. Knipping, *Iconography*, 1: 47, discusses the popular theme of "the fatal influence of women." See also H. Diane Russell, *Eva/ Ave: Woman in Renaissance and Baroque Prints* (Washington, D.C.: National Gallery of Art, 1990), 147ff; and Simon Schama, "Wives and Wantons: Versions of Womanhood in Seventeenth Century Dutch Art," *Oxford Art Journal* 3 (1980): 9. On the notion of the passive female versus the active male hero, see Rubin, "Heroic Image," passim.

27. Anne Hollander, *Seeing through Clothes* (New York: Viking Press, 1978), 187–99, suggests that bare breasts went from alluding primarily to virtuous maternity in fifteenth-century art to being increasingly associated with sexual pleasure and desire by the seventeenth century.

28. First published in 1635. See Ian Maclean, *Woman Triumphant: Feminism in French Literature 1610–1652* (Oxford: Clarendon Press, 1977), 218. This book was so popular that a third edition had been printed by 1637 with a different title, *Discours particulier contre les femmes desbraillees de ce temps*, which focused even more clearly on the dangers of female nudity.

29. Cited in Pierre Darmon, *Mythologie de la femme dans l'ancienne France, XVIe-XIXe siècle* (Paris: Editions du Seuil, 1983), 42 (my translation).

30. For example, see the anonymous 1617 texts *Discours nouveau de la mode* and *La Courtisane déchiffrée* or the 1675 books by Père Louis de Bouvignes *(Le Miroir de la vanité des femmes mondaines)* and Jacques Boileau *(Abus des nudités de gorge)*, which all continue to harangue women who bare their breasts. Darmon, *Mythologie*, 41–43. Although it is unclear whether Marie de' Medici or Rubens knew the specific texts cited here, the fact that a work like the *Discours particulier* had three editions in as many years, as mentioned in note 28 above, does imply a relatively widespread interest in such tracts. In addition, the queen's active promotion of the Catholic reform and her links to Catholic devotional politics in Paris speak to an interest on her part in the kinds of issues raised by these types of religious sermons and moralizing works. On the queen's religious habits and pro-Catholic policies, see Baudouin-Matuszek, *Marie de Médicis*, 108–109, 112–13, 121–22, 134–36, and 139–45.

31. On the use of wet nurses by even the artisan class in the early modern period, see Christiane Klapisch-Zuber, "Blood Parents and Milk Parents: Wet Nursing in Florence, 1300–1530," in *Women, Family, and Ritual in Renaissance Italy*, trans. L. Cochrane (Chicago: University of Chicago Press, 1985), 132–64; and Jaques Gélis, "L'Individualisation de l'enfant," in *Histoire de la vie privée: De la Renaissance aux Lumières*, vol. 3, ed. P. Ariès and G. Duby (Paris: Seuil, 1986), 315 and 320–21. See also note 24 above.

32. On this topos, see note 26 above.

33. See Rubin, "Heroic Image," 8–10; and Maclean, *Woman Triumphant*, 58–62.

34. On earlier French female rulers, see Marian F. Facinger, "A Study of Medieval Queenship: Capetian France 987–1237," *Studies in Medieval and Renaissance History* 5 (1968): 1–48; and Claire R. Sherman, "Taking a Second Look: Observations on the Iconography of a French Queen, Jeanne de Bourbon (1338–1378)," in *Feminism and Art History: Questioning the Litany*, ed. N. Broude and M. Garrard (New York: Harper and Row, 1982), 100–117. Marrow, "Art Patronage," 159–60, discusses Marie de' Medici's interest in earlier French queens.

35. *Les Singeries des femmes de ce temps descouvertes* (1623), 12 (my translation). See Rubin, "Heroic Image," 105–106; and Garrard, *Artemisia*, 156–57.

36. On this literary genre, see Maclean, *Woman Triumphant*; Rubin, "Heroic Image"; and Marrow, "Art Patronage," 160–61. Some of these texts included engravings that depicted each woman in a full-length portrait. Several painted galleries dedicated to women "worthies" were also commissioned in this period, but, despite their "female" iconography, they differed from the Medici cycle, which alone focused on the life of a contemporary woman rather than on virtuous women from the past. On these galleries, see Maclean, *Woman Triumphant*, 210–11; Marrow, "Art Patronage," 162–65; Garrard, *Artemisia*, 158; and Bernard Dorival, "Art et politique en France au XVIIe siècle: La galerie des hommes illustres du Palais Cardinal," *Bulletin de la société de l'histoire de l'art français* (1973): 43–60.

37. See Rubin, "Heroic Image," 104–109 and passim; Maclean, *Woman Triumphant*; and Darmon, *Mythologie*, on seventeenth-century "anti-feminist" texts.

38. See Simon Schama, *The Embarrassment of Riches*

(Berkeley: University of California Press, 1988), 408–10.

39. Susanna is placed a bit further back in space and her crouching pose is reversed in the later engraving, but the overall compositions of the two prints are quite similar.

40. See Elizabeth McGrath, "Rubens's 'Susanna and the Elders' and Moralizing Inscriptions on Prints," in *Wort und Bild in der Niederländischen Kunst und Literatur des 16. und 17. Jahrhunderts*, ed. H. Vekeman and J. M. Hofstede (Erftstadt: Lukassen Verlag, 1984), 81–85, on these inscriptions.

41. Cordier's condemnation of Truth's nudity is known from a letter to him by his publisher, Moretus. See J. Richard Judson and Carl van de Velde, *Book Illustrations and Title-Pages (Corpus Rubenianum, Part XXI)* (London: Harvey Miller, 1978), 2: 382 and 1: 249–53, figs. 199–200. See also Knipping, *Iconography*, 1: 63.

42. See Thuillier and Foucart, *Le storie*, 95–96 and 68–70, for the first contract of February 1622 and for the plans for the Henri IV gallery. See also Ingrid Jost, "Bemerkungen zur Heinrichsgalerie des P. P. Rubens," *Nederlands Kunsthistorisch Jaarboek* 15 (1964): 175–219; and Baudouin-Matuszek, *Marie de Médicis*, 222–23.

43. Thuillier and Foucart, *Le storie*, 85–86; Millen and Wolf, *Heroic Deeds*, 155–59; Marrow, "Art Patronage," 166–74; and Otto von Simson, "Politische Symbolik im Werk Rubens," in *Rubens: Kunstgeschichtliche Beiträge*, ed. E. Hubala (Constance: L. Leonhardt, 1979), 26–27, discuss this painting and the theme of triumph throughout the cycle.

44. See Thuillier and Foucart, *Le storie*, 12, and the chart on 131.

45. On the "disorderly" or "misused" woman as a sign of societal disarray, see Natalie Zemon Davis, "Women on Top," in *Society and Culture in Early Modern France* (Stanford, Calif.: Stanford University Press, 1975), 124–51.

46. On the violently abducted or "rapt" woman in seventeenth-century culture, see Sarah Hanley, "Family and State in Early Modern France: The Marriage Pact," in *Connecting Spheres: Women in the Western World, 1500 to the Present*, ed. M. J. Boxer and J. H. Quataert (New York: Oxford University Press, 1987), 58–61; and Margaret D. Carroll, "The Erotics of Absolutism: Rubens and the Mystification of Sexual Violence," *Representations* 25 (1989): 3–30.

47. See notes 1 and 2 above.

48. The icon of the Virgin and Child was painted on a removable copper plate beneath which was an allegedly miraculous fresco of the Madonna. On this project, see Fernanda Castiglioni, "'Non sono, dunque, si' mala cosa le immagini' (C. Baronio). Stato degli studi, considerazioni e ipotesi sui Rubens della Vallicella," *Annuario dell'Istituto di Storia dell'Arte, Università degli Studi di Roma*, n.s. 2 (1982–83): 14–22; Michael Jaffé, "Peter Paul Rubens and the Oratorian Fathers," *Proporzioni* 4 (1963): 209–41; White, *Rubens*, 50–51; Kerry Downes, *Rubens* (London: Jupiter Books, 1980), 68–72; Pierre Georgel and Anne-Marie Lecoq, *La peinture dans la peinture* (Dijon: Le musée, 1983), 63; and Hans Belting, *Bild und Kult: Eine Geschichte des Bildes vor dem Zeitalter der Kunst* (Munich: C. H. Beck'sche Verlagsbuchhandlung, 1990), 541–45.

49. Edward Snow, "Theorizing the Male Gaze: Some Problems," *Representations* 25 (1989): 32–34, emphasizes the male viewer–female object relationship in the Liechtenstein *Venus*. G. F. Hartlaub, *Zauber des Spiegels: Geschichte und Bedeutung des Spiegels in der Kunst* (Munich: R. Piper, 1951), 79–80 and 107–108, examines the role of mirrors in this and other images of Venus.

50. On this genre, see J. A. Emmens, "Les Menines de Velasquez: Miroir des princes pour Philippe IV," *Nederlands Kunsthistorisch Jaarboek* 12 (1961), esp. 60–62.

51. Jacques De Bie, *La France metallique* (Paris: Jean Camusat, 1636), 309 (my translation). Illustrated as medal IX (Marie de' Medici section). See also Millen and Wolf, *Heroic Deeds*, 141. Another emblem in De Bie on the theme of the king's reflection in a mirror is medal LXXXV (Henri IV section). The queen is said to reflect her son, Louis XIII, in medal XXXI (Marie de' Medici section).

52. Rubin, "Heroic Image," 75.

53. From the anonymous pamphlet *Prosopopée historique et alitographie du bon heur de regente de Frances*. Rubin, "Heroic Image," 71.

54. Ibid., 79. In François de Rosset's 1612 text, *Le Romant des chevaliers . . .*, Morpheus appears before Marie de' Medici's eyes as Henri IV. See ibid., 71–72.

55. See Belting, *Bild und Kult*, passim, on the intercessory functions of Madonna icons and on the power of the Virgin's gaze.

56. The first passage is from the 1614 *Vers divers sur le Bal-*

let des dix Verds; the second is from the 1615 *Ballet de Madame, soeur aisnée du roi*. Rubin, "Heroic Image," 76 and 87.

57. *Les singeries*, 9–10 (my translation). See Rubin, "Heroic Image," 104–105.

58. *La Cassandre françoise* (1615), 14–15, with emphasis added in my translation. See also Rubin, "Heroic Image," 88.

59. Elizabeth Cropper, "The Beauty of Woman: Problems in the Rhetoric of Renaissance Portraiture," in *Rewriting the Renaissance: The Discourse of Sexual Difference in Early Modern Europe*, ed. M. W. Ferguson et al. (Chicago: University of Chicago Press, 1986), 175–90; and Patricia Simons, "Women in Frames: The Gaze, the Eye, the Profile in Renaissance Portraiture," *History Workshop* 25 (1988): 4–30, explore issues of gender in Italian portraiture.

60. Unlike the present frames, the original black wood frames also had some decorative motifs in gold painted on them. See Thuillier and Foucart, *Le storie*, 131–32.

61. On Andre Gide's theory of the "mise en abyme," see Lucien Dällenbach, *The Mirror in the Text* (Cambridge: Polity Press, 1989), who also quotes Friedrich Schlegel on poetry, 175–76.

62. Julius S. Held, "Rubens and the Book," in *Rubens and His Circle: Studies by Julius Held*, ed. A. W. Lowenthal et al. (Princeton, N.J.: Princeton University Press, 1982), 179, says that "the very book . . . has become its own title page." See also Judson and van de Velde, *Book Illustrations*, 1: 260–65 and 2: figs. 208–11.

63. See White, *Rubens*, 102–106, on this commission. Rockox also owned Rubens's *Samson and Delilah*. Both works are shown in an imaginary view of Rockox's collection by Frans Franken the Younger. Gerard Thomas included the triptych's central panel in another imaginary gallery with an artist pointing at Christ, thus further supporting a reading of this work as a paradigmatic image on the relation between art and the viewer. See Zirka Z. Filipczak, *Picturing Art in Antwerp: 1550–1700* (Princeton, N.J.: Princeton University Press, 1987), 58–59, figs. 30 and 94; and White, *Rubens*, 99–100, fig. 115.

64. Frank Stella, *Working Space* (Cambridge, Mass.: Harvard University Press, 1986), 40.

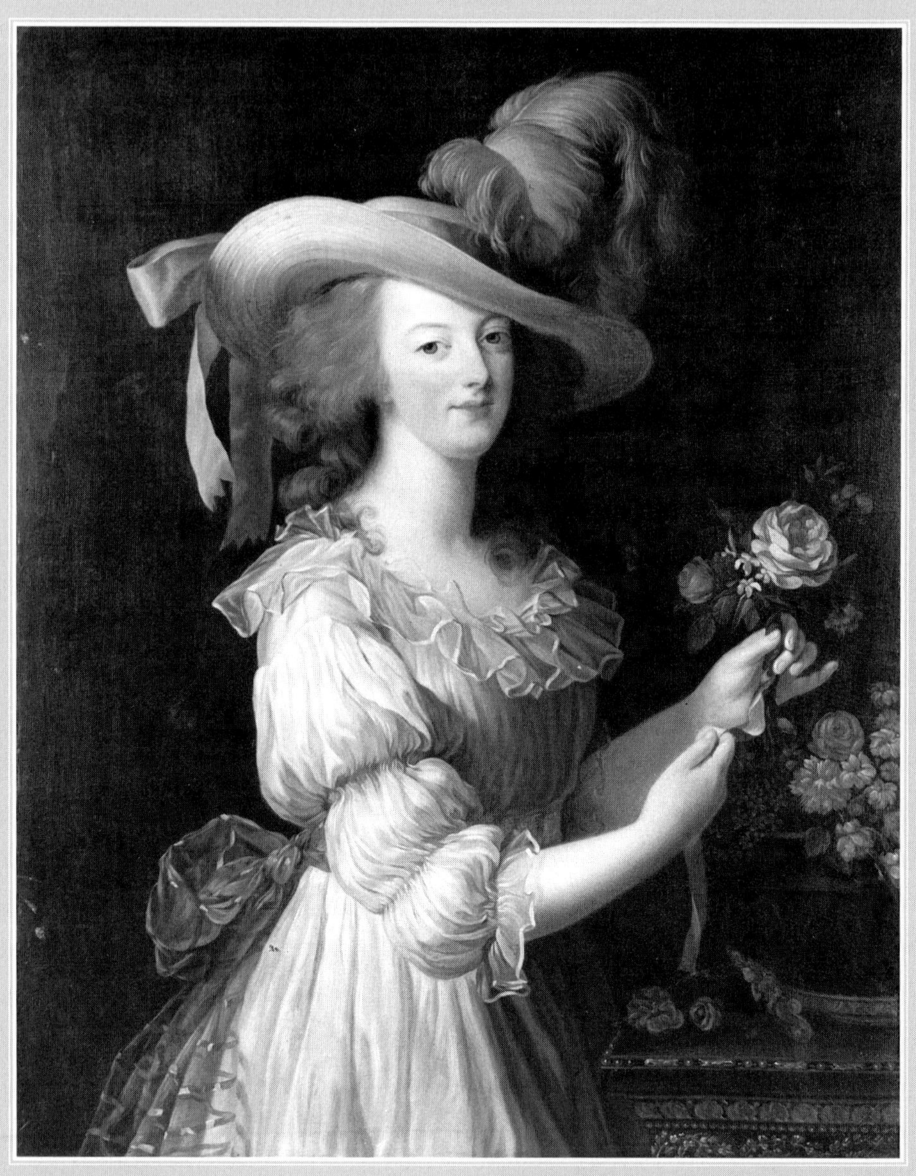

6

THE PORTRAIT OF THE QUEEN

Elisabeth Vigée-Lebrun's Marie-Antoinette en chemise

Mary D. Sheriff

THE QUEEN'S NEW CLOTHES

Imagine yourself a visitor to the Salon of 1783 gazing at the portrait of Marie-Antoinette painted by Elisabeth Vigée-Lebrun (fig. 6.1). You see the queen sporting a straw hat and dressed fashionably in a simple gown of white muslin. How are you responding to the image? What story are you generating from the portrait? Ah, but you cannot have a response, you cannot generate a story until I tell you just what sort of visitor, even which particular visitor, you are; until you can measure your distance from the viewer generated by the portrait itself. Marie-Antoinette appears at the Salon, but for whom, and as whom, is she appearing?

Vigée-Lebrun's portrait particularly raises these questions because the public descried it, even forced Vigée-Lebrun to remove it from the Salon. Why did this portrait disturb? What of queenship was or was not represented there? The immediate answer isolates the unsuitability of the costume *en lévite* or *en chemise* for public appearance. Imported from England in the 1780s, and adapted by the famous dressmaker Rose Bertin, the *robe en chemise* was made from sheer white muslin, fastened down the back, and caught at the

waist with a sash. The underskirt and corset, which ordinarily showed through the transparent muslin, were often of blue or pink silk. A soft fichu, usually of linen gauze, and a straw hat completed the ensemble. The style was immensely popular in England, where it made a fashion statement for the "natural woman," suggesting simplicity and honest sentiment. In France, however, the formalities of court made these simple styles less acceptable; for public appearances the *robe en chemise* was considered immodest, even though it revealed far less of the body than traditional court dresses with deeply scooped necklines. The *Cabinet des Modes* of 1786 included the *robe en chemise* under informal wear, and if worn outside the private chambers, such dress was reserved for walks in the park, for picnics, or for playing milkmaid with a few friends. Because this dress became closely associated with Marie-Antoinette, many called it the *chemise à la reine*.[1] As simple as these lingerie frocks might seem, in the early 1780s they were a luxury garment, made from very fine cotton fabric and purchased only at considerable expense.

The *Correspondance littéraire* suggests that the Salon public was shocked by the impropriety, the im-

This essay is adapted from chapter 5 in my book *The Exceptional Woman: Elisabeth Vigée-Lebrun and the Cultural Politics of Art* (Chicago: University of Chicago Press, 1996). Reprinted by permission of the University of Chicago Press.

Figure 6.1. Elisabeth Vigée-Lebrun, *Marie-Antoinette en chemise*, Salon of 1783. Oil on panel. Kunsthistorisches Museum, Vienna. (Photo: Bridgeman-Giraudon/Art Resource, New York.)

modesty of the queen appearing publicly in such attire: "Earlier one noticed among the portraits of this amiable artist that of the *Queen en lévite,* but because the public seemed to disapprove of a costume unworthy of Her Majesty, [Vigée-Lebrun] was pressed to substitute for it another with an attire more analogous to the dignity of the throne."[2] The *Mémoires secrets,* always quick to publish the latest gossip on Vigée-Lebrun, complained about showing an august person in garments reserved for the palace interior. The article went on, however, to shift the blame away from the artist, assuming that the painter was not authorized to take such a "liberty" without the consent of her sitter.[3]

Other pamphleteers were clever in their criticism. In *La Morte de trois mille ans,* for example, comments about the queen's attire were indirect but nonetheless censorious. Simultaneously reporting and commenting on the reactions of the Greek maiden Dibutadis visiting the sculpture court, the narrator tells his reader that

> although it was an ancient practice, she found the fierce Achilles a bit too familiar for appearing nude before the ladies. He draws his sword undoubtedly to frighten those who would disapprove of his nudity. At least his attitude pleases. The ladies who appear in public *en chemise* cannot be overly critical of his attire. Their own contrasts with the noble simplicity that was the adornment of the beautiful Greek maiden.[4]

Seen in public and in mixed company, a woman garbed *en chemise* is as inappropriate as a nude man—and much less pleasing. Her dress is no more modest than his nakedness, and it stands in pointed contrast to the Greek maiden's "noble simplicity." Armed with his sword, Achilles can fend off all critics, but the woman *en chemise* is defenseless; she cannot even point a finger at the warrior's undress.

A second pamphlet, *Momus au Salon,* is even more subtle, including a character described as a "marquise en chemise." The marquise plays the role of fashionable woman, at least as that role was described in moralizing tracts: she goes to the theater, sleeps until noon, and seduces the men around her. At one point while she is boasting about her ability to judge painting, the marquise declares herself "not modest," a comment that has a resonance beyond claiming her expertise as a connoisseur. As to her preferences, the marquise loves the soft touch that is perceptible in works by Vigée-Lebrun. Her taste is thus far distanced from the "noble simplicity" favored by the Greek maiden.[5]

Years later Vigée-Lebrun described the controversy surrounding this portrait of Marie-Antoinette: "One [portrait] represented her donning a straw hat and garbed in a dress of white muslin with sleeves folded up, but quite orderly; when it was shown at the Salon, the malicious did not refrain from saying that the queen was represented in her underwear."[6] These reports of negative responses, however, contrast with other recorded ones, underlining the obvious point that reaction to the queen's portrait depended on who was looking when and where. The queen herself apparently admired the work; she sent three versions of it to close women relatives and in 1786 judged it the most resembling of all her portraits.[7] Vigée-Lebrun's *Souvenirs,* in addition, include a report of another public's response to the image:

> This portrait in any case was not less of a great success. Toward the end of the exhibition there was a small piece at the Vaudeville which, I believe, was titled "The Union of the Arts." Brongniart, the architect, and his wife, whom the author had taken into his confidence, had reserved a box in the front and came to find me on the opening day to take me to the spectacle. As nothing prepared me for the surprise that awaited me, you can imagine my emotion when Painting arrived, and I saw the actress who represented her imitate me in a surprising manner in painting the queen's portrait. At that moment everyone in the parterre and in the boxes turned toward me and broke into applause. I do not believe that one could ever be so touched, so recognized, as I was that night.[8]

Although the divergence of these responses leads to the obvious question of what these audiences saw when they looked at the queen's portrait, a more fundamental question might be: what did they expect to see in a publicly exhibited portrait of the queen? If a portrait of Caesar was Caesar, and a portrait of Louis was Louis, what then was a portrait of Marie-Antoinette, a particular queen of France? To ask this question is to call forth a narrative that aligns Vigée-Lebrun's portrait of the queen and Louis Marin's *Portrait of the King*. I set these as companion pieces to explore the queen's portrait as it relates to Marin's chiasmus: representation of power and power of representation.

THE REPRESENTATION OF POWER AND THE POWER OF REPRESENTATION

In his now classic text, Louis Marin considered the face of absolute monarchy, Louis XIV, whose cultural ministers and painters deployed the power of representation to maintain a political imaginary suited to the pleasures/demands of the state.[9] Sustaining this imaginary was an official aesthetics that Marin summarizes in three statements: the king's motto "L'état, c'est moi," the Catholic maxim "Ceci est mon corps," and the Port Royalist's utterance "Le portrait de César, c'est César."[10] Playing on Kantorowicz's notion of the king's two bodies as the essence of a medieval theological kingship, Marin proposes for classical absolutism: "The king has only one body left, but this sole body, in truth, unifies three, a physical historical body, a juridico-political body, and a semiotic sacramental body, the sacramental body, the 'portrait,' operating the exchange without remainder (or attempting to eliminate all remainder) between the historical and political bodies."[11]

In attempting "an exchange without remainder," the portrait, the king's sacramental body, is the site where the physical body of a man-king and the theoretical body of a nation-state are married. Indeed, the man-king is only "absolute monarch" in images. Marin concludes that a belief in the effectiveness of these iconic signs is obligatory, or the monarch is emptied of substance. The portrait is thus both semiotic—that is, constituted of signs—and sacramental, a political Eucharist in which the king is truly present.[12]

Three terms—*representation*, *power*, and *imagination*—emerge as central to Marin's thesis. In his definition, the representational framework has both the "effect and power of presence instead of absence and death and the effect of subject, the power of institution, authorization, and legitimization."[13] Representation does not simply signify a preexisting subject who is elsewhere—it constitutes its own legitimate and authorized subject by exhibiting qualifications, justifications, and titles of the present. Power is the *ability* to exert an action on someone or something, and as Marin defines it, power stands in a constant and shifting relation with its own potentiality, force, and representability. Power valorizes potential as obligatory constraint, and "in this sense power means to institute potential as law."[14] More important to Marin's argument, force represented is potential and power, because representation, which has the power of presence and the power of institution, puts force in signs. In other words, the representation of force is doubly forceful; force is both the signified of representation and an attribute intrinsic to it.[15]

Marin considers representation as a "delegate of force" because it institutes an imaginary order of relations between the king's subjects and the state. What gives power to power's discourse is the imagination's potential power; through imagination subjects internalize the master's discourse as a representation of obligatory belief. The portrait of the king, then, represents (constitutes and authorizes) the relations that different subjects imagine themselves to have with the king-state.[16]

At first glance, Marin's text, dealing as it does with Louis XIV and classic absolutism, may seem remote from the portrait of a reputedly frivolous queen made when the French monarchy, greatly desacralized, had lost much of its mystical power. Yet the framing of this particular queenly portrait mediates between the Sun King and the ill-fated queen. The portrait appeared in the Salon of 1783, a salon the Comte d'Angiviller, Surintendant des Bâtiments, conceived as a move in his plans to revive the *gloire* of French art during the reign of Louis XIV. Fashioning himself as the new Colbert, d'Angiviller wanted to restore power to representation, a power he perceived it had lost during the reign of Louis XV, and to make art once again an important instrument of state. In this Salon, however, a portrait of the queen exhibited by a woman both stole the show and embarrassed the monarchy. Not only the power of the artist but also the power of the queen was implicated when the *Mémoires secrets* pronounced that at the Salon, the scepter of Apollo had fallen to the distaff side. Take away the qualification "of Apollo," and the phrase is identical to that used to describe female rule. Thus there is an implicit parallel between the reputed triumph of her woman painter and the imagined ascendancy of the female monarch.

Marin's text provokes significant questions when read in tandem with Vigée-Lebrun's portrait of Marie-Antoinette. How does a portrait of the *queen* serve the aims of state? What relations of representation, power, and imagination are at work in the queen's portrait? What does it mean to represent the queen? In his *Portrait of the King*, Marin explicated a system of power and representation in which each portrait of Louis XIV meant the same thing, and seemed to mean it absolutely—that is, for every viewer at every moment. The central chiasmus (representation of power and power of representation) figures a closed system, for it places the two terms as mirror images of one another. Figuring the relation between the king and his image as a chiasmus, Marin uses the figure to explicate how belief is structured by representation and to elucidate the repressive structure of absolute monarchy in colonizing the subject's imagination. In Marin's text, the chiasmus defines absolutism played out in/on the represented body—the portrait—of the king. Marin demonstrates how through representation the king is authorized as subject, as absolute transcendent Subject. In Marin's analysis, there is an implicit filiation between "absolute monarch" and signifieds like Law, God, and Phallus.

SALIC/PHALLIC LAW

It should surprise no one that the French monarchy depended on the suppression of women's claims to the scepter. Indeed, one could suggest three sentences that characterize this gendered side of absolutist aesthetics. The first of these comes from Antoine Loisel's maxims and condenses the Salic law (1607): "The kingdom cannot fall to the distaff side."[17] The second, drawn from Bignon's *De l'excellence des Roys et du Royaume de France* (1610), justifies that law: "This is not a written law but one that was born with us that we have not invented but drawn from nature itself."[18] And the third, from Guy Coquille, *Institution du droit de Français* (1588), separates the queen—the king's wife—from the body of the king and hence from state power: "The king is monarch and has no companion in his royal majesty. External honors can be communicated to the wives of kings, but that which is of his majesty, representing his power and dignity, resides inextricably in his person alone."[19]

Salic law determined kingship by the right of succession and excluded from succession females and males descended in the female line. Whereas there were queens of France, there were no French queens. The queen of France signified the wife of the king, and *queen* had no meaning except in relation to *king*. Salic law was considered first among the fundamental laws of France, which were laws perceived as anterior to all other laws and hence constitutional of the nation. Although the sacredness of monarchy and its mystical character were widely challenged in the Enlightenment—at least in philosophical circles—part of the Salic law and its seventeenth-century justifications fit well with thinking on women that crossed political boundaries during the ancien régime and Revolution. Jurists such as Le Bret in his *Traité de la Souveraineté du roi* justified the exclusion of women on the basis of natural law. Salic law, he argued, conformed

> to the law of nature which, having decreed woman imperfect, weak, and debilitated, as much in body as in mind, has submitted her to the power of man, whom she (nature) has . . . enriched with a stronger judgment, more assured courage, and a stronger physical force. Also we see that divine law wants a wife to recognize and render obedience to her husband as to her master and to her King.[20]

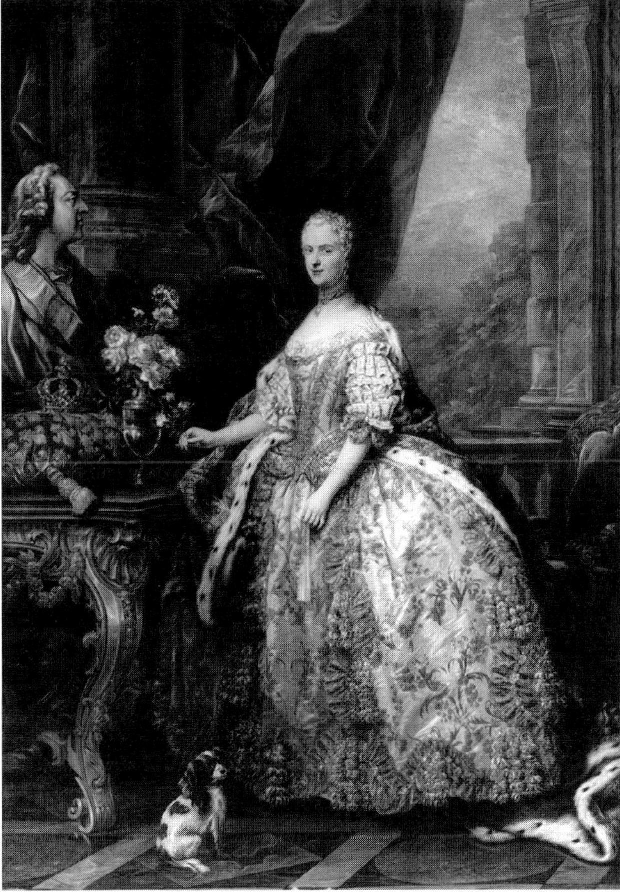

Figure 6.2. Carle Van Loo, *Portrait of Marie Leszczynska*, 1747. Oil on canvas. Château de Versailles, Versailles. (Photo: Réunion des Musées Nationaux/Art Resource, New York.)

The fundamental law of France, Salic law, is thus justified along the same lines as those laws that prescribed a wife's *état* as one of subservience to her husband. State portraits, moreover, represented this relation, and they remained fairly constant in type from Louis XIV to Louis XVI. A queen is a wife, and an official portrait of the queen shows the wife of the king; it is always a (possible) companion piece to the king's portrait.

Carle Van Loo's portrait of Queen Marie Lesczynska (fig. 6.2), commissioned for the royal collection and shown in the Salon of 1747, represents the type for the queen's public portrait. The painting is large-scale and shows the full-length standing figure. The pose, although formal, is not stiff, and the attitude suggests regal bearing in its straight lines and stability. Indeed, the portraitist establishes a virtual line that runs the length of the body through the boned bodice, which comes to a point at the center of the queen's waist, and the highlighted crease at the front of her dress. The downturned folded fan she clutches in her left hand emphasizes this line, which can also be imagined as extending upward from the point of her bodice, through the middle of her jeweled pendant and face. Thus centered, the queen becomes one of three strong verticals that define the picture; she is as solid as the columns to her right and left. In what is something of a tour de force, Van Loo manages to associate the queen, standing before us in her elaborate and frilled court dress, with these strong verticals, rather than with the ornately carved rococo table leg curving prominently in the left foreground. We imagine her not as serpentine and seductive, but as standing straight and erect underneath the mounds of costume. The overall shape of her dressed body, moreover, tends toward a stable triangle, with the curve of her waist more or less straightened out by the fall of her cape. Comparing this type of queen's portrait to state portraits of the king, say Van Loo's *Louis XV* (Musée du Château, Versailles), shows a gendered contrast also at work. Kings look active and queens immobile. Kings partake of the energy encoded in the agitated drapery that swirls around them, and their visibly protruding, taut leg muscles suggest the force attributed to the male body.

As is typical in official portraits, the queen, Marie Leszczynska, is displayed in elaborate court costume, and the room is as ornamented as the queen. Marin suggested that to be elegant is to show that a great number of people have worked to produce the effect. Hair, embroidery, ribbons, and the like are in the people's eyes effects of force—signs of work at work to show how one can make others work.[21] The queen's portrait, however, points not to her own force and power, but to that of the king. The markers of high status are clarified by the attributes of queenship—Marie's crown resting on a nearby table and her ermine-trimmed cape with fleur-de-lys lining. The defining quality of queenship—her relation to the king—is signified twice, first because the image appeared as a companion piece to Van Loo's portrait of Louis XV, and second because Louis appears within the painting as a portrait bust on the table. The king seems to be gazing down at his queen as she looks out at the audience. Although viewers cannot share the king's gaze, they can imagine themselves exchanging glances with the queen. At the same time, they see him looking at her, and can envision him as re-presenting, or authorizing, or even authoring her. Through the king's gaze, the whole top half of the

composition—the queen's face and upper body—is framed in a space defined by his triangle of vision.

The problem in making a state portrait of the queen is how to eulogize the absolute monarch through a portrait of his wife, how to show the king's force in the queen's portrait. Marin has argued that in representation, to be elegant is to show and to be one's appearance, and also to present oneself to others and by that to represent oneself through one's image in the gaze of others.[22] The queen here is represented through her image as the regal and elegant consort not only in the gaze of her subjects (those who are the real viewers of the painting), but also in the gaze of her husband, the king—who is the real Subject in and of the painting. Although Marin argues that to be elegant is to show and be shown, to assume both the subject and the object position, here the queen is the object of the king's showing. Marie Leszczynska is represented to us as queen, but the authority that allows her representation is vested elsewhere; her image always refers to that authority.

The portrait of the queen, then, creates a subject "queen of France" that refers to a position a woman holds because she is wife to the king of France. Not an accident of birth but a legal contract changes the historical woman into a queen. The title *queen* held no authority or right to govern. And the queen held no relation to the kingdom independent of her relation to the king. The wife of the king, a queen was expected to be the mother of a king, and her function was to produce sons. As Marie-Thérèse wrote to Marie-Antoinette: "To bear children, that is why you have been summoned; it is by bearing children that your happiness will be secured."[23] The queen's fertility was a major concern, but as only the father could confer royalty, she was the medium through which power was exchanged between father and son. Power passed through the queen's body but was not part of her.

This point returns me to the third and final proposition of the aesthetics of queenship: "The king is monarch and has no companion in his royal majesty. External honors can be communicated to the wives of kings, but that which is of his majesty, representing his power and dignity, resides inextricably in his person alone." In terms of the relation between king and queen, the third proposition is very significant. In some respects they did not have the same relation as other married couples, especially when marriage was conceptualized as a uniting of two individuals into one "body," with the husband as the head. This view of marriage could not obtain for the king and queen, because only in *his* person, thought by tradition to be united to the state, resided majesty, power, and dignity.

The queen, moreover, did not share community property with the king. Another of the fundamental laws of France conceptualized the king's domain as an attribute of sovereignty, and sovereignty could not be subdivided or alienated, that is, shared with the queen or anyone else. What the king acquired went to the profit of his kingdom, which came to be thought of as the king's "most privileged spouse."[24] Thus the king had two spouses—the privileged one, or the kingdom, which shared his sovereignty, and the alienated one, or the queen, who was separated from it. Indeed, since the sixteenth century, various marriage metaphors described the king's relation to the kingdom: "The king is the *husband and political spouse* of the *chose publique* (the kingdom) which brings to him at his *sacre* and Coronation the said *domain as the dowry* of this Crown. And kings swear solemnly at their sacre and Coronation never to alienate that dowry."[25] Not only did the marriage metaphor persist through the eighteenth century, but also from the union between the king and the kingdom came the tradition of calling the king's children the children of France.[26]

When the king is married to the nation and his children are the children of France, the queen is—at least metaphorically—displaced as mother of the (future) king. There could be no coordination between the queen's body and that of the other wife— the *royaume*, or France. Queens are theoretically and symbolically foreign to the kingdom, so the portrait of the queen operates no exchange between the real historical woman and the political body/state. Unless the presence of the king is indicated, nothing

closes the representational play of the queen's portrait. This is perhaps why all queens, as Hunt and Revel respectively have said of Marie-Antoinette, have "many bodies" or are "paper queens."[27] Indeed, their queenship exists only on paper—on marriage documents.

Although the queen had no relation of her own to the kingdom, she was fated to live in the gaze of court and populace. As the king's consort, she was the object of elaborate court rituals and spectacles of viewing, and she had little or no private life, in the sense of a life apart from her position as queen. At court the queen did not own her own body. She was dressed and undressed in elaborate ceremony; her giving birth was a major public spectacle. Yet she was not as completely a public person, or as completely the public's person, as was the king, for her theoretical relation to court and nation was that of outsider alien to the *chose publique*.

As an outsider, the queen could raise fears of overstepping her boundaries, of having too much power over the king her husband, or the king her son. In the first case, her power could come from the place where women were perceived to exercise their authority—the bedroom. Historically, however, this sort of female power was fragmented because the king took various official and unofficial mistresses. Louis XVI, however, was not a womanizer, and he had no official mistresses. Thus his queen, Marie-Antoinette, seemed to be the only influential woman in his life, and her influence was undiluted, a situation complicated by the perception that Louis was a weak ruler and man. Marie-Antoinette was an archduchess and daughter of an empress; she presented the real and imagined threat of allegiance to her mother's house.

MARIE-ANTOINETTE PORTRAYED

In the French imaginary, royalty was incestuous. The dauphin, the child of France, fulfilled the Oedipal fantasy of marrying his mother, France, at his coronation, when she became his privileged spouse. In practice, the historical woman who became queen of France, at least in the seventeenth and eighteenth centuries, represented a principle of exogamy. Because the importation of a (foreign) woman was necessary to the proper running of the monarchy, the queen of France can be construed as a sign of political alliance between two families or houses. The portrait of the queen can underscore and/or mask this meaning of queenship.

Consider, for example, the image of Marie de' Medici in *The Presentation of the Portrait* from Rubens's famous series (Louvre, Paris; fig. 5.1, p. 100). In that panel, Juno and Jupiter watch as putti present to Henri IV the portrait of Marie. Although in reality she was chosen as a wife because of political needs and in exchange for debt relief, the king seems immediately smitten with her image, gazing at it like a lovestruck suitor. Marie's position in a dynasty is not visible in the bust portrait, and her personal attributes are left to attract the king. The portrait presents itself as a representation of Marie's charms, and it seems to elicit from Henri the effects of love. Rubens hides the exchange value of the queen and attributes power to her representation not as dynastic symbol but as desirable woman. Bear in mind, however, that Marie de' Medici's portrait was presented in a work designed for her; as regent, her interest was to underplay her outsider status and position as an object of diplomatic exchange. The image of a close and trusting relationship between herself and the deceased king could only help secure her position.

In relation to queenship as diplomatic exchange, the making and viewing of Marie-Antoinette's portrait has an important history. Before Louis XV would close the deal with Marie-Thérèse, he wanted to see a portrait of the young archduchess. We cannot really know why Louis insisted on having this portrait. Perhaps he understood it as his prerogative, since it was traditional to be supplied with such an image. Perhaps he, sly old fox, was also drawing out the negotiations, extending the courtship. For her part, Marie-Thérèse seems never to have been satisfied with any portrait, and she repeatedly delayed sending a definitive one, as if no artist could really capture the beauty of her daughter—always implying that there was more, something that could not be represented.[28] Al-

ways leaving something to the old king's imagination. Perhaps she knew the value of prolonging the anticipation. The impatient Louis wanted to send France's most distinguished portrait painter, the academician François-Hubert Drouais. But Drouais overestimated the king's desire and asked too high a price. In the end, in late January of 1769, Louis sent Joseph Ducreux to do the job. A hairdresser went with him because Marie-Thérèse wanted her daughter to look as French as possible.[29]

The portrait that sealed the deal is now lost, but Jacques Gautier-Dagoty represented it in an engraving that shows the duc de Choiseul, who brokered the marriage, holding the long-sought likeness (*Louis XV Presenting the Portrait of Marie-Antoinette to the Dauphin*; fig. 6.3). The success of frenchification is evident here, as the woman seen in the portrait (Marie-Antoinette) is nearly the mirror image of the court lady (the king's sister?) standing nearby. Although this similarity can be attributed to the artist's mediocre skills, the effect of sameness is appreciable whether or not it was intended. Not only does the young woman resemble the image of Marie-Antoinette, but her hands and fan are held to frame her upper body in an oval shape mimicking the portrait's format. Glancing back toward the dauphin, she assesses the effect of her portrait double. But all this builds from the periphery inward. Louis XV holds the center with his grandson alongside him. They are holding hands—a sign of dynastic continuity—and behind them hangs a portrait of the deceased queen surmounted by a double portrait of king and queen. Busts of Henri IV and Louis XIV are also evident in the background. Gautier-Dagoty's work is a portrait of dynastic succession and diplomatic mission. The work focuses on Louis XV, who appears not only as the leading character, but also as the principal spectator of the event. If one speculates that not only Marie-Thérèse but both aging monarchs pinned their hopes of peace on the alliance between their houses, this painting represents the last great diplomatic initiative of Louis XV's reign.

If the history of making Marie-Antoinette's portrait is bound on one side by the French king, it is determined on the other by the Hapsburg empress. The

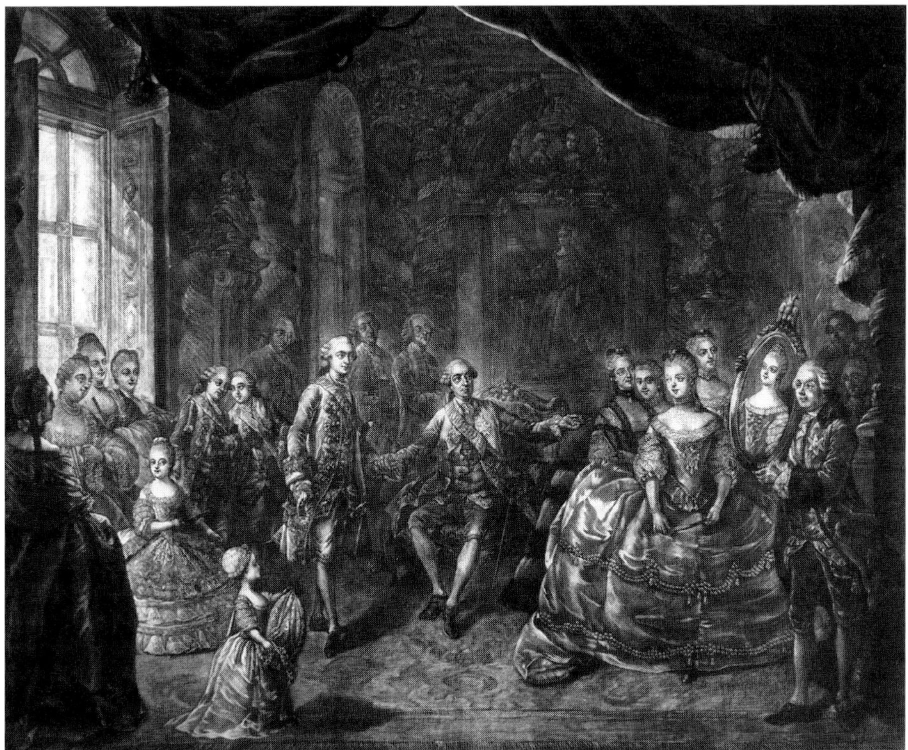

Figure 6.3. Jacques Gautier-Dagoty, *Louis XV Presenting the Portrait of Marie-Antoinette to the Dauphin*, 1769. Oil on canvas. (Photo: Bibliothèque nationale de France, Paris.)

approval of Marie-Thérèse seems to have secured Vigée-Lebrun her position as favored portraitist. The correspondence of Marie-Thérèse, her agent Count Mercy, and Marie-Antoinette shows the empress anxious to have appropriate images of her daughter. As a mother, she wanted private portraits to remind her of the child sent away; as empress, she wanted public statements of her daughter's position first as dauphine, then as queen. It was in conjunction with the latter that Vigée-Lebrun was first successful. Why and how Vigée-Lebrun was called to paint the queen from life is not clear, but it is evident that the official images made by other painters exasperated both queen and empress.

Marie-Thérèse spent nearly a decade trying to obtain an official portrait of her daughter (as dauphine or queen) that pleased her. After commissioning a work from the painter Jean-Etienne Liotard, she wrote to Marie-Antoinette in December of 1770: "I await the painting of Liotard with great expectations, but in your finery not in casual dress nor in a man's outfit. I want to see you in your proper place."[30] The work has been lost, but we know from correspondence that Liotard did not satisfy the empress's expectations. Her comment, however, also points to another aspect of the story. Smaller, private images of Marie-Antoinette did satisfy the mother who, making a distinction between them and official portraits, allowed them more leeway in terms of costume. Her remark about not wanting to see her daughter in a man's outfit recalls Joseph Krantzinger's famous 1771 portrait of Marie-Antoinette *en amazone*, that is, in a costume resembling a man's riding coat. Marie-Thérèse expressed her pleasure even at this portrait since it represented her daughter as she was, enjoying her activities.[31] Thus even as she warned Marie-

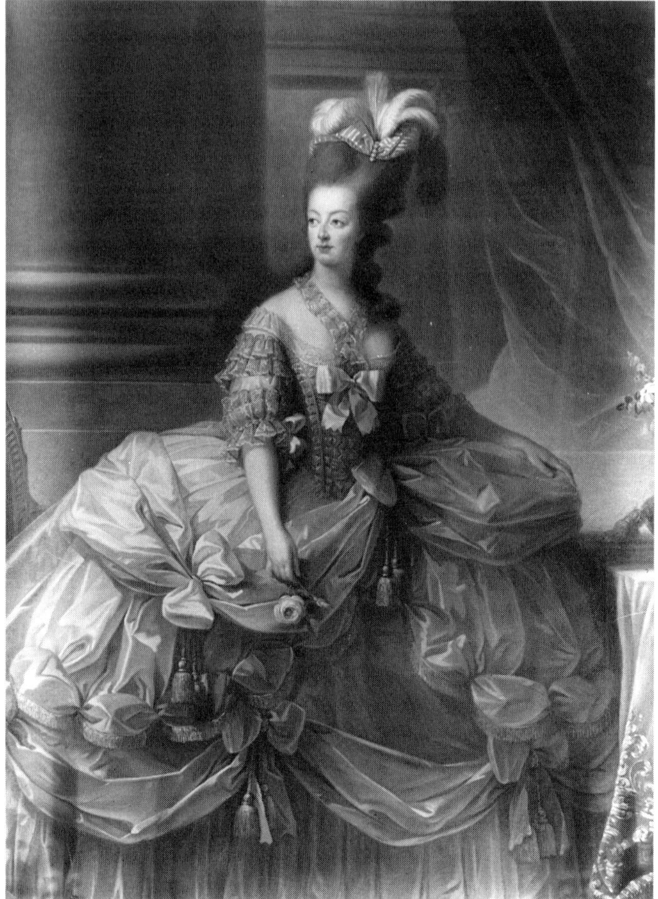

Figure 6.4. Elisabeth Vigée-Lebrun, *Portrait of Marie-Antoinette*, 1778–79. Oil on canvas. Collection Hesse. (Photo: Bridgeman-Giraudon/Art Resource, New York.)

Antoinette against the dangers of horse riding— especially of riding *en homme*, which she found hazardous for future fertility—she relished these images and used them in her private spaces.[32] In August 1771, she wrote to her daughter, "I have received your portrait in pastel, it is quite resembling and it pleases me and the whole family. It is in the cabinet where I work, and the [second] framed image is in my bedroom, where I work in the evenings, so I have you with me before my eyes and you are always profoundly in my heart."[33]

The search for a suitable official portrait went on for years, however, much to both women's exasperation. In 1774, Marie-Antoinette wrote to Marie-Thérèse: "It quite saddens me not to have been able to find a painter who catches my resemblance; if I found one I would give him all the time he wanted, and although he would be able to make only a bad copy, I would have a great pleasure in dedicating it to my dear mama."[34] The letter responds to the unrealized desire of the mother, and three years later the daughter wrote to her in a similar vein: "I put myself at the discretion of the painter, for as long as he wanted and in the attitude that he wished. I would give everything for him to be able to succeed and to satisfy my dear mama."[35] Several days later, Marie-

Thérèse wrote to Marie-Antoinette about two official portraits—one as wife of the king, the other as daughter of the empress—that she had requested:

> Excuse my impatience for your large portrait. Mercy received today the measurements for it. The [other one] will be for my cabinet, so that you can be there with the king. But this large one will be for a room where all the family is in large portraits. Must not this charming queen also be there? Must her mother alone be deprived of this dear daughter? I would like to have your face and court dress; even if the expression is not too resembling. So as not to inconvenience you too much, it satisfies me to have your face and demeanor, which I do not know and with which everyone is pleased. Having lost my dear daughter when she was such a small child, this desire to know how she is formed must excuse my impatience, coming from a most lively fund of maternal tenderness.[36]

Finally, two years later, a portrait arrived that suited Marie-Thérèse, a portrait painted by Elisabeth Vigée-Lebrun (fig. 64). Here is how the empress responded after receiving the work in April 1779: "Your large portrait pleases me! Ligne has found it resembling, but it is enough for me that it represents your face, with which I am quite happy."[37] Given that Vigée-Lebrun's image succeeded where so many others had failed, is it any surprise that Marie-Antoinette became attached to the painter who finally pleased her dear mama?

The work sent by Vigée-Lebrun is well within the tradition of the queen's official portrait. The symbolic accessories duplicate many of those seen in Van Loo's portrait of Marie Leszczynska. The queen is standing near a table on which rests a crown placed on a pillow decorated with fleur-de-lys. The curving figure that signaled a woman's body is presented within a more stable triangular form. On one side the queen's extended arm masks the round of her hip, and on the other a virtual diagonal runs from her headdress down the slope of her shoulders and through her skirt.

That diagonal is emphasized by the direction of her gaze. As in Van Loo's portrait, the vertical accents—the straight arm and the hanging tassels adorning her dress—reinforce the stabilizing effect of the massive columns. Moreover, the artist uses to positive effect the long Hapsburg face. The right side is rendered in a sharp, straight profile; on the left, her hair is pulled well back, and the vertical shadow cast along temple and neck stands out against the rounded and lightly rouged cheeks and chin. The hair, underplayed and kept in shadow, acts as a frame for the face. Despite her plumed headdress and wavy hair, Marie-Antoinette's highlighted face rises from her neck with a verticality nearly as regular and definite as that of the column beside her. Moreover, she holds the center of the composition easily. Her face is isolated against a rectangular space articulated by the door frame in the background, and light reflected from her white neck and chest, which are bare of necklace, pendant, or other jewels, ensures her maximum visibility.

Marie-Antoinette's image in this work is simplified in comparison to that of Louis XV's queen, although it is still opulent enough to bespeak royal status. Similarly, the artist maintains certain traditional elements, such as the swag of drapery that both adds complexity to the composition and theatricalizes the sitter. However, even the drapery swag is made to seem less self-consciously dramatic by reducing the complexity of its folds and tracing a more or less vertical fall rather than a diagonal sweep. It is not enough to attribute this difference to a change in taste, since in other images Marie-Antoinette was even more decorated than Marie Leszczynska. Overly embellished images of her daughter drew criticism from Marie-Thérèse, who felt they made Marie-Antoinette look like an actress. In March 1776, she found the dress and hairstyle of her daughter represented in a work by Drouais (now lost) outré and "too inferior for the rank of a great princess."[38] I prefer to believe that Vigée-Lebrun's simplifications represent the artist's appeal to the recipient of the portrait, Marie-Thérèse, who had repeatedly complained about overly decorated images. Given the numbers of painters called to represent the queen, the quest for the proper image of Marie-Antoinette could hardly have been news to the artistic community.

In her portrait of the queen, Vigée-Lebrun reduces the ornamentation by restricting the number of different elements in the painting (elements are repeated rather than varied) and by making these less decorative. She uses one dominant color for the costume, which makes this dress seem more austere, and she restricts the color range of the entire composition, relying primarily on an overall white with strong red accents and more muted ones of gold and blue. Even the headdress is simplified, and because the hat's plume harmonizes in overall shape with the flowers on the nearby table, it seems integrated with the overall composition and not singled out as an attention-grabbing flourish. Vigée-Lebrun, moreover, has made the queen look serious and august. Marie-Antoinette does not engage the viewer; rather than acknowledge anyone's gaze, she stares out of the painting. Her expression resembles that usually reserved for important male sitters—for example, the king. Focused as it is on some thing—or some history—we cannot see, her look recapitulates that which Vigée-Lebrun gives to a bust of Louis XVI positioned on a plinth in the painting's upper right corner.

"MALICIOUS PEOPLE SAID THE QUEEN APPEARED IN HER UNDERWEAR"

The portrait of Marie-Antoinette *en chemise* is obviously not a state portrait, although a successful state portrait was probably Vigée-Lebrun's license to make this one. As we have seen, there was a tradition of depicting the queen more informally, but such portraits did not often appear "in public" at the Salon, as did the image of Marie-Antoinette *en chemise*. In this portrait, Vigée-Lebrun shows the queen standing at a table, but set against a blank background so it is not clear if the sitter is positioned in an interior or exterior space. Marie-Antoinette poses as she wraps a blue satin ribbon around a small nosegay, which includes her signature flower—the rose. A few flowers lie on the table and a larger bouquet stands in a blue Sèvres vase decorated with a gilded satyr's head. For whom, one wonders, does the queen wind the ribbon as she looks out of the composition with a lopsided glance? Her person, moreover, is pushed up to the picture plane so that the viewer can fancy herself in intimate conversation with the monarch. The entire image is coded for informality and refers to the artful naturalness of the picturesque. Marie-Antoinette's face is skillfully framed in a C-curve formed by arms, ribbon, and hat plume, and her straw hat breaks the contours of the long Hapsburg face in a pleasing way. Her soft, unpowdered hair, lack of jewelry, and seemingly simple costume also betoken a studied naturalness associated with the look *en chemise*.

The image that reworked the portrait *en chemise*, Vigée-Lebrun's *Marie-Antoinette with a Rose* (fig. 6.5), lacks the intimacy of close contact with the sitter as well as the naturalness implied by composition and dress. Although the portrait is set in the informal space of a garden, the sitter is distanced from her audience, set back from the picture plane. Her eyes are bright and blue, but not as large or as inviting as those in the earlier version, and now it is decidedly more difficult to imagine exchanging glances with the figure. Her satin court costume; formal, powdered coiffure; and elaborate headdress change the tone of the piece, since the queen no longer wears the dress characteristic of private spaces shared with friends.

Why make the portrait *en chemise?* The letters between Marie-Antoinette and Marie-Thérèse suggest that even early on Marie-Antoinette wanted to see herself painted in her favorite costumes, undertaking her favorite activities. What does Marie-Antoinette want to be in the portrait *en chemise?* What desire is Vigée-Lebrun representing to her? What trap for her desire, as Louis Marin would say, is she presenting the queen? In showing the queen as a fashionable lady, Vigée-Lebrun has imaged, perhaps without realizing it, Marie-Antoinette's desire not to be queen of France. I am not suggesting anything like a wish for abdication, but rather a desire to separate herself, if only temporarily, from the demands of the office. I would like to distinguish this desire—if it is possible

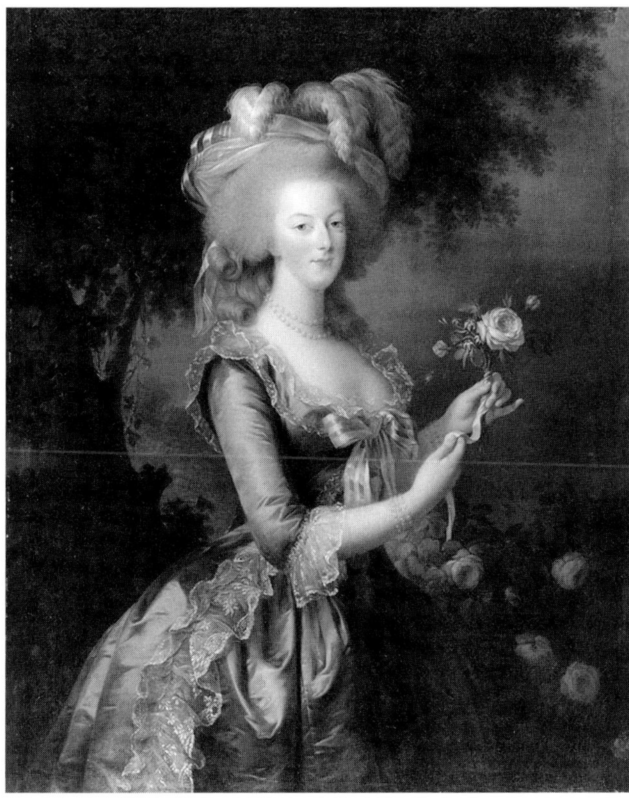

Figure 6.5. Elisabeth Vigée-Lebrun, *Portrait of Marie Antoinette with a Rose*, 1784. Oil on canvas. Château de Versailles, Versailles. (Photo: Réunion des Musées Nationaux/Art Resource, New York.)

to do so—from the vision of Marie-Antoinette's escapist tendencies well represented in all kinds of writing, from serious historical studies to Hollywood movie scripts, and reworked every day for the visitors tromping through her private apartments at Versailles.

What I have in mind is a bit more sympathetic toward this admittedly spoiled woman; for while Marie-Antoinette likely wanted sometimes to escape her position, she certainly had no desire to be less than a queen, even for a day. She wanted to be what she—willful woman that she was—wanted to be, not what French etiquette would make her. It was a revolt, of sorts, but hardly a profound political one. Jacques Revel has well articulated the dilemma of Marie-Antoinette in writing of her pretension to conduct her life as she wished. Marie-Antoinette "forgot the maxim that royalty has no right to private life."[39]

Revel goes on, analyzing her wish to create a private space symbolized by Trianon: "In this case, the staging of the private sphere is at the origin of a degradation of the representation that it renders trivial, even ridiculous."[40] It is a joke, maybe even an outrage, a queen playing milkmaid with her Sèvres buckets and golden implements. We see class anger and anticipate the final dramatization of the distinction between the queen playing at being a peasant and the real state of the French people. It is easy to imagine the queen, dressed as a milkmaid, uttering that apocryphal line: "Let them eat cake!"

Yet we forget today what other messages other audiences might have constructed from this portrait and the remaking of the space at Versailles. What if one looks at this portrait from a perspective other than that of the Revolution? How might a "public" of 1783 still attached to the monarchy, *patrimoine*, and *gloire* have read the desire encoded in the queen's portrait and at Trianon? How they read these could, for a segment of the public, have been directed by the queen's enemies at court, for libels issuing from the court forged the first of the caricatures that were to haunt the queen through the Revolution.[41]

If Trianon was an escape from anything, it was an escape from the court with all its formality and, one imagines, tedium. In the portrait Marie-Antoinette represents herself not in terms of a position at court, but in terms of a position in a larger society—as a fashionable woman. The portrait confuses boundaries; the queen *en chemise* is a queen in masquerade. In this work the queen appropriates the right to pose publicly as a private individual, a fashionable woman. Taking the authority not to occupy her position as queen, Marie-Antoinette defies the sacrosanct laws of French court etiquette.

A WOMAN JUDGED

Although it is clear that Marie-Antoinette enjoyed close friendships with women at court and supported women artists, the queen showed no solidarity with women of different classes. This, however, does not mean that French women did not have some stake—no matter how remote—in the queen's status. At least some commentators argued that the Salic law had a negative impact on all women. In his *Histoire des Amazones anciennes et modernes* of 1740, the abbé Guyon wrote that the Salic law "which has excluded them [women] from the throne of France, in our minds has made them lose a part of the esteem that several among them rightfully merit."[42]

Feminist historians and critics writing today increasingly draw attention to the relation between Marie-Antoinette's fate and that of all French women. Lynn Hunt, for example, writes: "The question of Marie-Antoinette and the issue of the status of women more generally were closely connected, even though Marie-Antoinette herself probably had no interest in women's rights and early French feminists had little concern for the queen."[43] Madelyn Gutwirth

uses her analysis of Germaine de Staël's *Réflexions sur le procès de la reine* (1793) to demonstrate that Staël understood much of what was at stake for women in the queen's trial and execution: "Whereas the courtly code had maintained a semblance of social integration for the women of the privileged class, the new republican code promises women honor as mothers. Staël clearly perceived that in killing the queen, a people 'neither just nor generous' was expressing both the death of the old and the feebleness of the new dispensation."[44]

Indeed, Staël addressed her defense of Marie-Antoinette to women and stressed their common cause with her: "Oh! you, women of all countries, of all classes of society, listen to me with the emotion I experience. The fate of Marie-Antoinette contains everything that can touch your heart: if you are happy, so was she."[45] In her *Réflexions*, Staël exonerates the queen of the many crimes—and especially that of bad mother—charged against her, and concludes by suggesting to women not their collectivity in difference, but their similarity in sharing a single fate: "I return to you, women whose lives are all sacrificed with [that of] so tender a mother, whose lives are all sacrificed in the outrage that would be perpetrated against weakness by the annihilation of pity. It is the end of your dominion if ferocity reigns, it is the end of your destiny if your tears flow in vain."[46] Staël here panders to some of the most conservative clichés about woman's nature, but at the same time warns women of their vulnerable position in the social order. Marie-Antoinette's impending fate symbolizes that position, and earlier in the pamphlet Staël had reminded her readers that the slander used to damn Marie-Antoinette was the sort that could be used to ruin any woman.[47]

A decade before Marie-Antoinette's trial constructed her as the quintessential bad mother, Vigée-Lebrun unwittingly showed her as an immodest woman, providing enemies with yet more evidence against her.[48] Showing the work was perhaps a tactical error. Maybe the artist was captivated by a certain image of the queen or by her desire to please a patron captivated by a certain image of herself. So captivated that she "forgot" what everyone knew by 1783: the Salon was becoming a school for virtue and morality increasingly intolerant of immodest depictions. Or maybe the artist just counted on art critics devoted to the monarchy to ensure the proper reception for her work. Aside from these possibilities, Vigée-Lebrun likely considered a Salon entry as a portrayal of her talent. This was, after all, the response to the portrait *en chemise* of the circles she frequented, the response she represented in the *Souvenirs*.

In 1783, however, paintings were also judged according to the moral effect of their subject matter, according to how they could influence future action. In a Salon where critics found the most up-to-date history paintings to be those dedicated to great men, to heroic action, to women sacrificed for their virtue—how would this portrait of the queen of France signify? What future did the queen *en chemise* suggest? Not the future of the past—the *gloire* of the French monarchy—but a future symbolized by the world of Trianon. The emblem of Trianon was the dress *en chemise*, as commentators, including the Royalist Rose Campan, have noted.[49] It was as the queen of Trianon that Marie-Antoinette was displayed, judged, and condemned at the Salon of 1783. Although her condemnation then was not as consequential as it would be in 1793, there is an underlying similarity in the charges against her. At her trial Marie-Antoinette was accused of damaging her son's sexual potency.[50] As the queen *en chemise*, she was castigated for feminizing a sacred space of the virile French monarchy with her society of women at Trianon. This violation—like that of her son—was all the more egregious because engineered by a foreign woman, by the *Autrichienne*.

TRIANON

Both Trianons, the grand and the petit, were conceived as resting places for the king to shelter him during the summer's heat, but each took on other functions, both practical and symbolic. The Grand Trianon became a stage setting for Louis XIV. There the Sun King entertained his court and offered himself to the court as spectacle.[51] The Petit Trianon has a different history, but it too participated in the French monarchy's symbolics. Its domain was carved out in 1750 with the establishment of a botanical garden, which Louis XV entrusted to Claude Richard. The cultivation of different species of plants extended the symbolism of the seventeenth-century gardens in which Versailles contained the entire cosmos. Jacques-Ange Gabriel designed the garden pavilion built in 1750, which again was the king's resting place on his garden walks. The Château du Petit Trianon (1763–68), built by the same architect, allowed Louis more extended visits and became the place where he met Mme de Pompadour and where they entertained. His next mistress, Mme du Barry, later occupied the Trianon palace. Although the domain of the Petit Trianon was generally associated with the symbolics of Versailles, its palace was associated with the king's pleasure.

In 1774 Louis XVI gave the Petit Trianon to Marie-Antoinette, who transformed the grounds into an English garden, which we can take as a symbol of the freedom and liberty she hoped to obtain there. With its aesthetics mimicking the look of natural growth through planned disorder, the English garden has long symbolized these values.[52] More important, perhaps, is that the English garden (like the English dress *en chemise*) was a foreign import into the heart of the French symbolic space. Replanting these gardens coincided with a general replanting of the estate after the trees had been cut down and sold for timber. As head of the Bâtiments, d'Angiviller was in charge of this project. Susan Taylor Leduc has argued that the practical reason for the replanting was hidden under royal propaganda designed to influence public opinion. D'Angiviller wanted the replantation to be perceived as "a restoration of a symbolic space that would signal a return to a golden age of Bourbon rule under the young monarchs, Louis XVI and the queen, Marie-Antoinette."[53] D'Angiviller's fantasy of the replanting was hardly supported by the queen's *jardin anglais* at Trianon, with its serpentine paths, surprising views, and architectural follies. As Taylor-Leduc has argued, Trianon negated d'Angiviller's hope for restoring the park as a sign of royal and national power.[54] The English garden represented what was fashionable and modern, not the French tradition and Bourbon rule.[55] The court's malice took aim at these gardens and accused Marie-Antoinette of changing the name of her domain to "little Vienna." Mme Campan recalls these rumors in her memoirs, and although the particulars of the story may be unreliable, the tale jibes well with the other charges emanating from the court:

> From the moment she was in possession of the Petit Trianon, it was spread about in some societies that she had changed the name of the pleasure pavilion that the king had just given her and had substituted that of little Vienna or little Schönbrun. A man of the court, simple enough to believe the rumor and desiring to enter into her society at the Petit Trianon, wrote to M. Campan to ask permission of the queen. He had in his letter called Trianon little Vienna.[56]

The image of Trianon as "little Schönbrun" may have been highlighted by copies of paintings that Marie-Antoinette had sent from Vienna and whose subjects recalled her childhood there. In particular, a copy by Wuchart represented the opera and ballet performed by the young archdukes and archduchesses at the marriage of Joseph II. It pictured Marie-Antoinette as a young girl dancing a minuet with her brothers. The French accused her of still dancing to their tune.

In its association with Trianon, the portrait *en chemise* could be, and indeed was, read as indicating the queen's desire to escape being French, to bring what was alien into the heart of the French realm. Two other comments about the dress make this point. One appeared in a court libel, the *Correspondance secrète inédites sur Louis XVI, Marie-Antoinette et La Cour et La Ville de 1777–1792*, which reported that the queen's fashion angered the silk makers at Lyon, who charged her with ruining a national industry for the profit of her brother Joseph, the Hapsburg ruler.[57] A second remark directed to the portrait retitled it "France as Austria reduced to covering herself with straw."[58]

It is difficult to exaggerate how much clothing mattered in the symbolic economy; its importance for Marie-Antoinette was established with the elaborate etiquette designed to ensure that neither the Hapsburg empress nor the Bourbon king would be slighted when the guardianship of an adolescent girl—the future queen of France—was transferred from Vienna to Paris. The transfer took place in 1770 on neutral territory, on an island in the Rhine under the domain of neither empire, where the French erected tents and other portable shelters. In one of those shelters the young Marie-Antoinette performed the ceremony of the toilette (or rather had it performed on her). She was divested of all her Austrian garb, stripped of all of her clothing, and redressed in garments fabricated entirely in France. She emerged from the tent as if reborn, or at least converted.[59]

The portrait *en chemise* flaunted the conventions of French etiquette and French dress and opened Marie-Antoinette to the charge that her conversion was not sincere. Even if she had fully assimilated French culture, however, Marie-Antoinette would always be foreign to it. The portrait *en chemise*—or the libels it provoked—brought to light what was fundamental about the queen of France: she was alien to the kingdom. Marie-Antoinette the *Autrichienne* was not invented by the revolutionaries or even by her enemies at court. She was conceived with the fundamental laws of France.

But more was encoded in Marie-Antoinette's portrait than the *Autrichienne*, and indeed, the portrait came to stand for some of the most common themes of the libels emanating from the court: the queen's foreign character, her extravagant spending, and her uncontrolled sexuality. The association with her spending was evident in 1783, for the queen was reputed to have dispensed outrageous sums for the decoration of Trianon. As to the queen's sexuality, the dress signaled the costume worn by Marie-Antoinette's friends, whom libelists characterized as the "tribades of Trianon." This last association was damning not so much because people necessarily believed that lovemaking between women was rampant in the queen's circle, but because the queen had made a location associated with the king and the French domain not only foreign but also feminine. Intimacy among women replaced male desire at Trianon.

Although men were among the invited guests, women and children dominated Trianon, and they stayed there without the ceremony or etiquette normally associated with the court. The king regularly visited the queen at Trianon, but he never slept there. By representing Marie-Antoinette as the queen of Trianon, Vigée-Lebrun made a portrait of the queen for which one can imagine no companion portrait of the king, who was alien to that realm. In fact, a counterpart to the portrait of the queen *en gaulle* could be found among Vigée-Lebrun's Salon entries in her portrait of the marquise de la Guiche, a member of the queen's intimate circle, as a milkmaid.

The image of Trianon, with its aura of female intimacy, lingered long after the Revolution, and as Terry Castle has shown, women in the nineteenth century called up this myth to manufacture a lesbian identity. Castle writes:

> And yet one cannot help but feel in the end, perhaps, that there is also something bizarrely liberating, if not revolutionary, about the transmogrification of Marie-Antoinette into a lesbian heroine. It is true that there is a nostalgic element in her cult: women who thought they "saw" her, like Hélène Smith, the "Dream Romances" writer, and Moberly and Jourdain, were in one sense flagrantly retreating into the past, into a kind of psychic old regime. But in the act of conjuring up her ghost, they were also, I think, conjuring something new into being—a poetics of possibility. It is perhaps not too much to say that in her role as idealized martyr, Marie-Antoinette functioned as a kind of lesbian Oscar Wilde: a rallying point for sentiment and collective emotional intransigence. She gave those who idolized her a way of thinking about themselves. And out of such reflection—peculiar as its manifestations may often look to us now—something of the modern lesbian identity was born.[60]

OTHER POSSIBILITIES

Castle's notion of the poetics of possibility leads me to wonder if other women besides Smith, Moberly, and Jourdain saw other sorts of possibilities in the figure of Marie-Antoinette. I am thinking here of women like Olympe de Gouges, who dedicated to the queen her Declaration of the Rights of Woman. This is not to argue that the queen in any way supported or sympathized with the political goals of the French Revolution or generally supported women's rights, but with Olympe de Gouges, advocates for women could imagine the queen as a potential ally. Moreover, Marie-Antoinette provided for some women during the old regime the image of an exceptional woman, a powerful woman descended from an even more powerful woman, who proved herself a supporter of women's endeavors. Under Marie-Antoinette's protection, for example, the *Journal des Dames* reappeared in 1774, five years after its suspension. Mme de Montanclos (then, baronne de Prinzen) dedicated the new publication to Marie-Antoinette, who lent her support in late 1773, when she was still dauphine. Although Marie-Antoinette may not have advocated the political and moral stances taken by much of what appeared in the *Journal des Dames*, she maintained her patronage of the publication. Nina Gelbart speculates that the queen was grateful to Mme de Montanclos, who seemed eager to uphold her as "an intelligent and virtuous model for the whole female sex."[61]

In the visual arts, not only did the queen advance Vigée-Lebrun's career, but she was also a strong supporter of the artist Anne Vallayer-Coster. On September 15, 1779, Mercy reports to Marie-Thérèse that Marie-Antoinette left Versailles only to go to Paris to see the Salon. In that Salon was Vallayer-Coster's image of a vestal crowned with roses, which belonged

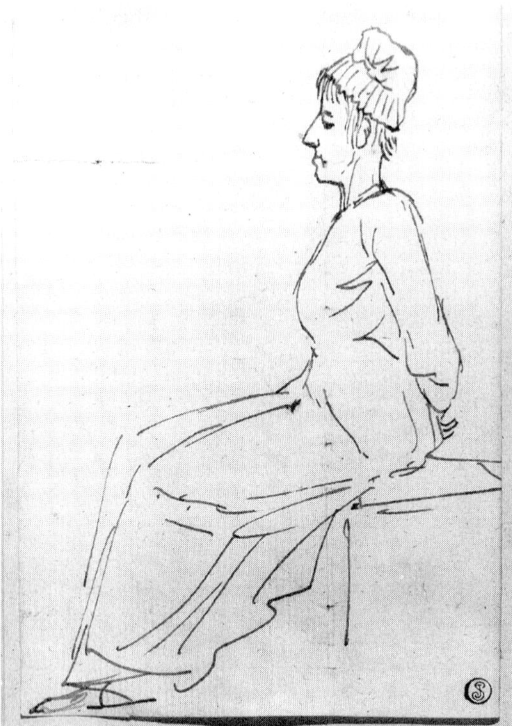

Figure 6.6. Jacques-Louis David, *Marie-Antoinette*, 1793. Drawing. Musée du Louvre, Paris. (Photo: Réunion des Musées Nationaux/Art Resource, New York.)

David's work, finding the real queen in neither the portrait she found most resembling nor the one her mother found most pleasing. These authors were perhaps led by the immediacy the rapid sketch suggested; or maybe the reputation of the great male artist seduced them; or it could be that the tendency to view Marie-Antoinette from the perspective of the Revolution motivated them. On the other hand, David's drawing may have seemed the most "resembling" because it so well fits the stereotype of a royal person as one who acts with great dignity in the face of imminent annihilation. Finally following the proper etiquette, in David's image Marie-Antoinette is resigned to her fate. Here is how Henri Bouchot characterized the work:

> David had the last sitting with the queen, he saw her for a few seconds before him more majestic and more sovereign than Madame Le Brun or the others had known her. No rouge on her cheeks, no powder in her hair. A linen bonnet has replaced the toque of velvet, a little white robe garbs her miserably; it is again a portrait "en gaulle," the last one this time.[64]

to the queen.[62] And today the Bibliothèque Nationale houses many novels from the eighteenth century written by women and bound with the arms of Marie-Antoinette. It is not so important for the queen actually to have read the books; it was enough that she owned them to enhance a writer's reputation. French women, at least some of them, had a very specific stake in the queen's fate.

In view of this admittedly far less revolutionary poetics of possibility, it seems particularly ironic that those who wrote the first histories of representing this queen installed as her true portrait Jacques-Louis David's sketch of her on the way to the guillotine (fig. 6.6). Georges Duploooio, for example, believed he found her "authentic likeness" in David's work, particularly in the bone structure.[63] Writing at about the same time, other historians also selected

Finding David's portrait the most majestic seems to me a misogynistic and perversely Royalist gesture. In this image, the woman-queen can be safely majestic and sovereign precisely because she has no power. Her hands tied behind her back, Marie-Antoinette is not threatening to the French republic as the daughter of the Hapsburg empress, nor to her viewers as an unruly woman. She is here resigned to the role that, perhaps even more than the part of mother, patriarchy has reserved for woman—that of victim. I am not suggesting that she was the Revolution's victim, as Royalist sympathizers would portray her, but rather that she occupies the position of victim, the "feminine" place of the one destined to be attacked.[65]

From the standpoint of many French citizens in 1793, Marie-Antoinette certainly represented the indecent privileges of aristocracy and the bankrupt principles of monarchy. It would be folly to deny that she is entitled to represent a share of that meaning. But such a reading of the queen's image can no longer be cited, at least not after the work of Hunt, Maza, Gutwirth, Colwill, and others, without also noting that she more than other likely candidates came to embody "the possible profanation of everything the nation held sacred."[66] In this context, David's sketch can be viewed as one more example of the interest focused on the queen's body and, more specifically, as part of the attention that accompanied her on the road to the scaffold.

Vigée-Lebrun's portrait of Marie-Antoinette and David's sketch of her must be read according to the different political circumstances in which they were produced. Marie-Antoinette in 1783 posed a threat not to the new French republic, but to certain interests at court and within the governing elite. What ties the two images together, however, is that in different ways each presents Marie-Antoinette not simply as the king's wife, but as the most notorious, dangerous, and powerful public woman in France. And a woman who acted in public—both in 1783 and 1793—not only raised fears of sexual dedifferentiation, but also bore the blame for society's moral decline.

David's portrait pictures not so much an absolute monarch—for the queen could never be that in France—but a public woman vanquished, paying equally for her real and imagined political sins and gender-bendings. In contrast is Vigée-Lebrun's 1783 portrait, which transgresses, first by showing the queen in a private role, and second by showing her as a woman with the will to reconfigure associations within the elite, to ignore the rules of court life and etiquette, to reconsecrate part of the king's domain. Of the two images, I prefer the one made in 1783; it lends Marie-Antoinette not the political power of a monarch's wife anxious to quell a popular revolution, and not the authority of the austere queen-mother who sits with her children in the official portrait Vigée-Lebrun made in 1787 (Musée du Château, Versailles). I prefer the portrait that allows Marie-Thérèse's daughter the power to define herself against estab-lished norms of seemly, modest, womanly behavior. I prefer Vigée-Lebrun's unofficial portrait, the one the sitter chose as her image, the one that shows Marie-Antoinette as the tribade of Trianon.

NOTES

1. David Russell, *Costume History and Style* (Englewood Cliffs, N.J.: Prentice-Hall, 1983), 302–305.

2. *Correspondance littéraire, philosophique et critique par Grimm, Diderot, Raynal, Meister, etc*, ed. Maurice Tourneux, 16 vols. (Paris: Garnier Frères, 1880), 13: 441–42.

3. *Mémoires secrets pour servir à l'histoire de la république des lettres en France depuis MDCCLXII jusqu'à nos jours, ou Journal d'un observateur*, 36 vols. (London: J. Adamson, 1780–89), 24: 9.

4. *La Morte de trois milles ans au Salon de 1783*, Collection Deloynes, 286: 6.

5. *Momus au Sallon*, Collection Deloynes, 292: 16, 21, 43, and 45.

6. Elisabeth Vigée-Lebrun, *Souvenirs*, ed. Claudine Herrmann, 2 vols. (Paris: Des Femmes, 1986), 1: 65–66.

7. Maxime de la Rocheterie and the Marquise de Beaucourt, eds., *Lettres de Marie-Antoinette* (Paris: Alphonse Picard et fils, 1895), 89.

8. Vigée-Lebrun, *Souvenirs*, 1: 66.

9. Louis Marin, *Portrait of the King*, trans. Martha Houle (Minneapolis: University of Minnesota Press, 1988), vii. Audiences, however, did not always interpret representations as those who constructed them expected.

10. Ibid., 11–12.

11. Ibid., 14.

12. Ibid., 3–15.

13. Ibid., 5. Representation in Marin's text is both a substitution and an official showing, as when the term means to represent or to show one's documents.

14. Ibid., 6.

15. Ibid.

16. Whether or not this actually happens in the imagination of an individual subject is a different question.

17. As quoted from Antoine Loysel, *Institutes coutumières*, ed. Michel Reulos (Paris, 1935) in Roland E. Mousnier, *The Institutions of France under the Absolute Monarchy 1598–1789*, trans. Arthur Goldhammer, 2

vols. (Chicago: University of Chicago Press, 1979), 2: 87.

18. Mousnier, *Institutions*, 1: 650.

19. Ibid., 2: 88.

20. As quoted in Marcel Marion, *Dictionnaire des Institutions de la France aux XVIIIe et XVIIIe siècles* (Paris, 1923; rpt. New York: Burt Franklin, 1963), 340.

21. Marin, *Portrait of the King*, 27–28.

22. Ibid., 26.

23. *Correspondance sècrete entre Marie-Thérèse et le Cte de Mercy-Argenteau*, intro. and notes, M. Le Chevalier Alfred d'Arneth and M. A. Geffroy, 3 vols. (Paris: Didot, 1874), 1: 104.

24. Sarah Hanley, *The Lit de Justice of the Kings of France: Constitutional Ideology in Legend, Ritual, and Discourse* (Princeton, N.J.: Princeton University Press, 1983), 91–95; and Mousnier, *Institutions*, 2: 87.

25. Hanley, *Lit de Justice*, 95.

26. Ibid., 97–98; and Mousnier, *Institutions*, 2: 89–90.

27. Jacques Revel, "Marie-Antoinette in Her Fictions: The Staging of Hatred," in *Fictions of the French Revolution*, ed. Bernadette Fort (Evanston, Ill.: Northwestern University Press, 1991), 114; and Lynn Hunt, "The Many Bodies of Marie-Antoinette," in *Eroticism and the Body Politic*, ed. Lynn Hunt (Baltimore: Johns Hopkins University Press, 1991), 111–12.

28. Even after Louis received Ducreux's portrait, Marie-Thérèse's agent in Paris let it be understood that Marie-Antoinette's beauty was superior to that represented. J. Flammermot, "Les Portraits de Marie-Antoinette," *Gazette des Beaux-Arts* 18 (1897): 5–21.

29. Marguerite Jallut, *Marie-Antoinette et ses peintres* (Paris: Noyer, 1955), 10; Flammermont, "Les Portraits de Marie-Antoinette," 16.

30. Letter dated December 1770. *Correspondance secrète*, 1: 105.

31. *Correspondance secrète*, 1: 157. Marie-Thérèse liked the work so well she gave Kratzinger a bonus. *Marie-Antoinette: Archiduchesse, Dauphine et Reine* (Paris: Editions des Musées Nationaux, 1955), 29.

32. On Marie-Thérèse's warnings about riding "en homme," see *Correspondence secrète*, 1: 104.

33. Letter dated 17 August 1771. Ibid., 1: 196.

34. Letter of 18 October 1774. Ibid., 2: 248.

35. Letter of 16 June 1777. Ibid., 3: 85.

36. Letter of 20 June 1777. Ibid., 3: 87.

37. Letter of 1 April 1779. Ibid., 3: 303.

38. Letter from Marie-Thérèse to the Count de Mercy, 18 March 1775. Ibid., 2: 310.

39. Revel, "Marie-Antoinette in Her Fictions," 120.

40. Ibid., 123.

41. Lynn Hunt, *The Family Romance of the French Revolution* (Berkeley: University of California Press, 1992), 103–104.

42. Jean-Baptiste Guyon, *Historie des Amazones Anciennes et Modernes*, 2 vols. (Paris: Chez Jean Vilette, 1740), 1: 52–53.

43. Hunt, *The Family Romance*, 89–90.

44. Madelyn Gutwirth, *The Twilight of the Goddesses* (New Brunswick, N.J.: Rutgers University Press, 1992), 301.

45. Madame de Staël, *Réflexions sur les procès de la reine par une femme*, intro. Monique Cottret (Montpellier: Les Presses du Languedoc, 1994), v.

46. Ibid., xxx.

47. Ibid., xvi; and Gutwirth, *Twilight*, 301.

48. On the trial of Marie-Antoinette, see Hunt, *The Family Romance*, 92–95; and Elisabeth Colwill, "Just Another *Citoyenne*? Marie-Antoinette on Trial 1790–1793," *History Workshop* 28 (Autumn 1989): 63–87.

49. Rose Campan, *Mémoires de Madame Campan, Première Femme de Chambre de Marie-Antoinette*, ed. Jean Chalon, notes by Carlos de Angulo (Paris: Mercure de France, 1988), 149–50.

50. Hunt, *The Family Romance*, 101.

51. As quoted by Marin, *Portrait of the King*, 205.

52. Susan Taylor-Leduc, "Louis XVI's Public Gardens: The Replantation of Versailles in the Eighteenth Century," *Journal of Garden History* (Summer 1994): 82–86.

53. Ibid.

54. Ibid., 87.

55. I owe this observation to Nicholas Mirzoeff.

56. Campan, *Mémoires*, 84.

57. *Correspondance secrète inédite sur Louis XVI, Marie-Antoinette et la Cour et la ville de 1777–1792*, 2 vols. (Paris: Henri Plon, 1866), 2: 228.

58. Quoted in Henri Bouchot, "Marie-Antoinette et ses peintres," *Les Lettres et les Arts* 1 (1 January 1887): 46.

59. Stefan Zweig, *Marie-Antoinette: Portrait of an Average Woman* (New York: Garden City Publishing, 1933), 13 ff.

60. Terry Castle, "Marie-Antoinette Obsession," *Representations* 38 (Spring 1992): 31.

61. Nina Rattner Gelbart, *Feminine and Opposition Journalism in Old Regime France: Le Journal des Dames* (Berkeley: University of California Press, 1987), 179.

62. The letter appears in *Correspondance secrète*, 3: 250.

63. Georges Duplessis, "Introduction," *Iconographie de Marie-Antoinette*, n.p.

64. Bouchot, "Marie-Antoinette," 58.

65. For a discussion of political attacks on wives and mistresses of rulers, see Sarah Maza, "The Diamond Necklace Affair," in *Eroticism and the Body Politic*, ed. Hunt, 63–70. For a comparison of Marie-Antoinette to the "scapegoat," see Hunt, *The Family Romance*, 114.

66. Hunt, *The Family Romance*, 95.

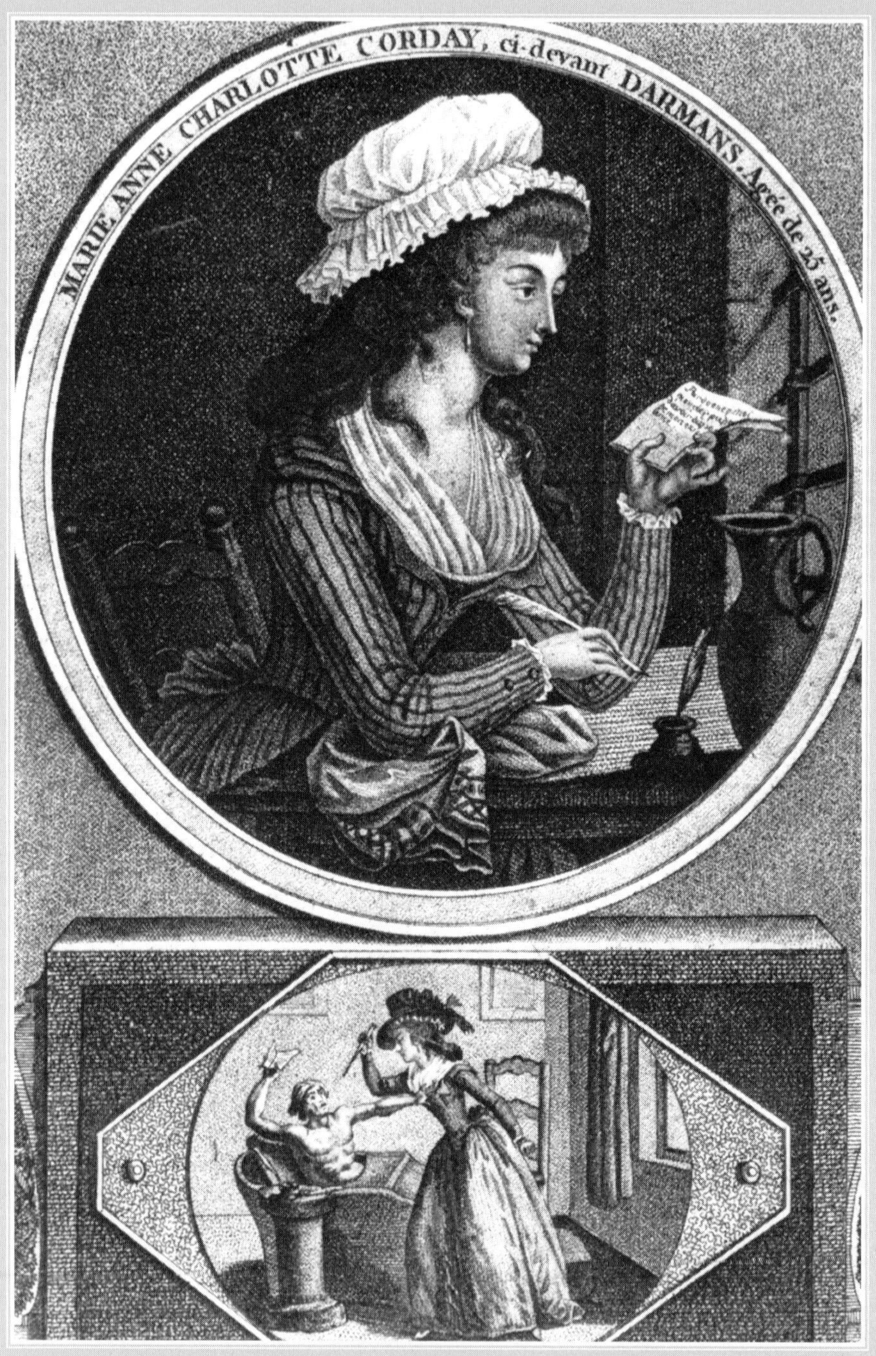

MARIE ANNE CHARLOTTE CORDAY, ci-devant DARMANS, Agée de 25 ans.

7

DEPOLITICIZING WOMEN

Female Agency, the French Revolution, and the Art of Boucher and David

Erica Rand

To appreciate, that is, to sense this canvas, you do not have to be an artist, or art initiate; it is enough to be a husband and father, a man of feeling and a citizen. . . .

As [the painting] inflamed my imagination, I thought I saw Frenchmen of different factions ready to strangle each other, and the Mother-Country herself between them, and crying: stop.

PIERRE-JEAN-BAPTISTE CHAUSSARD, *On the Painting of the Sabine Women by David* (1800)

ALTHOUGH THIS PASSAGE on Jacques-Louis David's *Intervention of the Sabine Women* (1799; fig. 7.2) may be little known outside art history, Chaussard's interpretive move is all too familiar. He ostensibly wants only to translate past into present, to reveal the contemporary subject in classical guise. Notice, however, that when Chaussard envisions contemporary politics, he does not see contemporary women. Outside the canvas: husband, father, man, and citizen. On the canvas: only contemporary men. The Roman and Sabine men become political antagonists of the French Revolution who reconcile during the Directory; the Sabine women are abstracted into the "Mother Country." Through an erasure passing as transfiguration, Chaussard removes women as material, historical beings from the political stage.

In this essay, I reassess the disjunction between women and politics in David's work. As historians have recently emphasized, Revolutionary leaders marshaled propaganda, legislation, and force to achieve precisely the effect Chaussard ascribes to sincere feeling. Faced with the specter of female power-brokering under the monarchy and with ongoing female participation in Revolutionary events, they struggled to position women and the feminine outside—often billed as above—the public sphere.[1] Revolutionary festivals enshrined mothers of heroes and female allegories of Liberty, while Revolutionary law increasingly constrained women who resisted these domesticating ideals. Yet scholars who have debated David's political involvement usually presume—as Chaussard appears to presume—that the significant actors in the

Figure 7.1. François-Marie-Isidore Queverdo, *Marie-Anne-Charlotte Corday*, 1793. Engraving. (Photo: Bibliothèque nationale de France, Paris.)

143

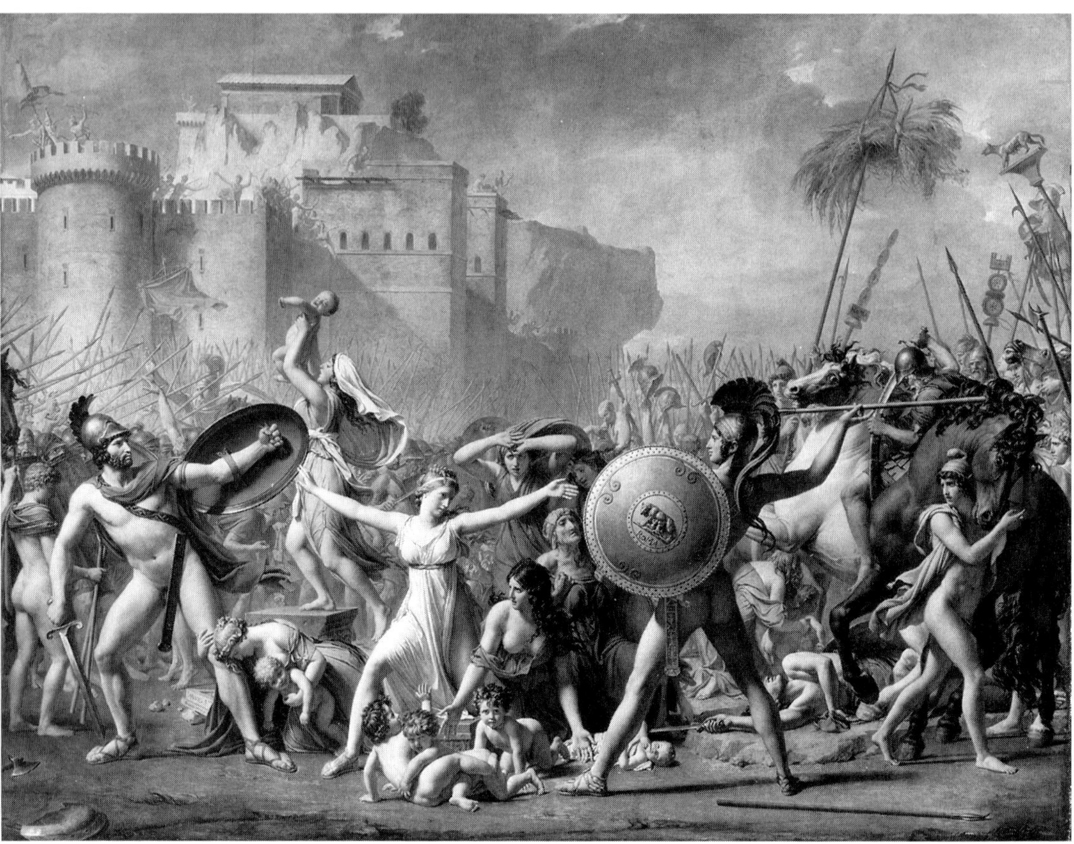

Figure 7.2. Jacques-Louis David, *Intervention of the Sabine Women*, 1799. Oil on canvas. Musée du Louvre, Paris. (Photo: Réunion des Musées Nationaux/Art Resource, New York.)

political arena were (or are) male; indeed, David's attention to women and gender is often used to prove that David was politically unengaged or to defend psychoanalytic interpretations that detach the images from the historical particulars of David's political context.[2] But David, who was a delegate to the National Convention and one of its primary crafters of gender ideology, could make no such presumption. Instead, I will argue, far from merely presenting domestically circumscribed women and a masculine public sphere, as is usually thought, David both registers and works to deauthorize Revolutionary female political activism.

I want first, however, to posit a related process of female disempowerment in the Rococo paintings of François Boucher. Boucher has traditionally been seen to represent everything David repudiated, including female influence over art and politics. By reapposing the two artists, I intend both to underscore the historical specificity of David's depoliticizing project and to suggest some general conclusions about the means through which cultural products delegitimate women's place in the public sphere and the critical strategies through which this ideological work remains invisible.

Boucher, like David, is generally seen to separate women from politics, but through a different maneuver: while David circumscribes women, Boucher, reputedly to suit female desire, abandons politics. His art seems to operate in a gap between two periods in which history painting bears witness to important po-

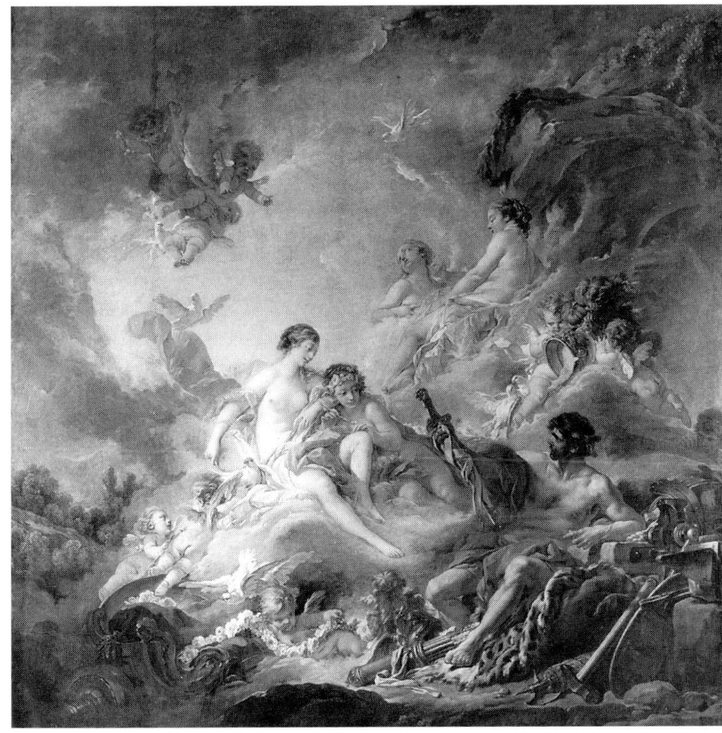

Figure 7.3. François Boucher, *Venus at Vulcan's Forge*, 1757. Oil on canvas. Musée du Louvre, Paris. (Photo: Réunion des Musées Nationaux/Art Resource, New York.)

litical transformations, between "after me the deluge" and "liberty, equality, fraternity, or death." In the interval occur a political regime and an artistic style widely believed to be controlled by women: Louis XV's government and Rococo art, which seems stylistically and thematically to signal a flight into play, with artifice the main aesthetic and erotics the main subject. Boucher's *Venus at Vulcan's Forge* (1757; fig. 7.3) shows why the Rococo has been characterized this way. Dominated by voluptuous bodies, pale colors, and ambiguous, ethereal spaces, the painting might well be said to picture the simultaneous victory of women and sex over men and politics, since the ascendance of Venus and her coterie has shunted the production of martial weapons to the margins.

Yet the painting might be construed quite differently to be about, not against, political matters if we consider it in relation to one widely attested, though partly illusory, phenomenon that Montesquieu memorably termed a "republic of women." In his 1721 novel *The Persian Letters*, Montesquieu has his fic-

tional visitor to Paris observe that every French man in a position of power, including the king, is actually controlled by a woman, probably his mistress, "through whose hands pass all the favors and sometimes the injustices that he may perform."[3] So, too, in *Venus at Vulcan's Forge*, female sexual allure, uncircumscribed by marital ties, is used for political ends. Venus, violating once again the bonds of marital possession by displaying her body for the voyeuristic gaze of all, has persuaded her husband to forge arms for Aeneas, who is her son by another man and destined to make the first conquests toward the founding of Rome.[4] In the painting, as in Montesquieu's scenario, the political sphere has been erotically infested, and a particular form of female agency characterizes and epitomizes its decay: women deploy their bodies opportunistically in the bed of one man to benefit other men of their own choosing.

If Boucher, then, engages not only female sexual license but through it contemporary forms of female political intrusion, he also works to block the per-

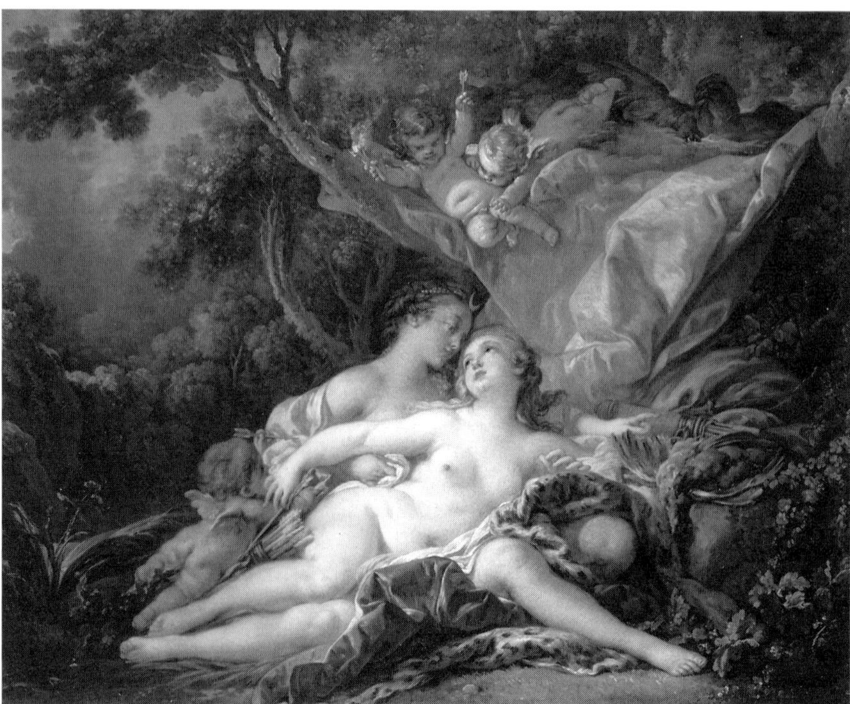

Figure 7.4. François Boucher, *Jupiter in the Guise of Diana and the Nymph Callisto*, 1759. Oil on canvas. The Nelson-Atkins Museum of Art, Kansas City, Missouri (Purchase: Nelson Trust), 32-29.

ception that men cannot control women. A crucial aspect of this effect is a displacement of disruptive content. Boucher does not directly depict the heterosexual transactions upon which the story hinges. Instead, sexual contact is displaced to two embracing female figures, an erotic transfer that occurs in many Rococo paintings but which Boucher especially moves to center stage. The device appears, for instance, in *Leda and the Swan* (1741), in *Apollo Revealing His Divinity to Issé* (1750), and, most interestingly, perhaps, in his paintings of Jupiter and Callisto, such as the 1759 version (fig. 7.4). Here, Jupiter takes the form of Diana in order to seduce her nymph Callisto; quite literally, a male achieves power through female wiles.[5]

Now, in several ways, these erotically enlaced fe males represent female power to act politically. Besides simply multiplying the presence of female sexual allure—the source, reputedly, of women's power to intervene in the masculine pursuits of war and government—they stand for and invoke the hetero-

sexual act, which as we have seen, stands for women's mode of intervention. The painting of Jupiter and Callisto especially alludes to its disguised heterosexual coupling, as Boucher signals the identity of Zeus iconographically through the presiding eagle, and uses a characteristic differentiation of skin tone so that the male-roled Diana/Jupiter has, as heterosexual tradition would dictate, darker skin.[6]

Yet the embracing female group also undercuts the appearance of female power. This is partly because Boucher's nude women are portrayed for male erotic visual appropriation. Boucher critics concur on this point; even those who think Boucher painted to please women assume that women were satisfied when female figures on the canvas looked delectable to men. The more women, and the more erotically depicted, the more males will be pleased; a heterosexual optic is consistently presumed.[7]

Furthermore, throughout Boucher's career, what might anachronistically be termed lesbian behavior is particularly associated with manless structures, which themselves signal female oppression under corrupt social orders. For instance, Montesquieu's *Persian Letters*, Mme de Graffigny's *Peruvian Letters* of 1747, and Diderot's *The Nun*, written in 1760, all include critiques of harems and/or convents, two female communities frequently attacked as the scourges, respectively, of despotism and aristocracy.[8] It is primarily in these groups that lesbianism finds its place, sometimes portrayed as a source of microresistance, always as a source of male titillation, ultimately, though, as a sign of desperation.[9] Overall, for Boucher's contemporaries, the image of women together points to unfair enclosure far more than rebellion.

Boucher's art, like its most famous patron, Louis XV's mistress Mme de Pompadour, symbolizes the power of women during the so-called century of women and the infestation through women of politics with sex. Yet even as female figures dominate the canvas in ways that refer to women's perceived mode of political intervention, female power is simultaneously disarticulated by being configured to invite erotic appropriation and to signal female enclosure. Although Montesquieu's Persian visitor uses a metaphor of female collectivity, a republic, to describe the appearance of female power, for Montesquieu, as for other social critics of the period, women do not primarily transgress male rules or enter the political sphere as a group but rather individually, through transactions with individual men: one might say that women deploy power heterosocially rather than homosocially.[10] With the corruption of the male political sphere displaced to female erotic, and homoerotic, excess, women appear to be no longer threatening. The representation of women in power, then, does not necessarily significantly rupture the tradition of male control—over politics, over painting, over women—but sometimes, as here, provides an opportunity to reinstate male mastery.

With this point in mind, let us turn to David. On most matters of politics and gender, the two artists seem to diverge. Boucher paints for aristocrats, David for Revolutionaries. Boucher avoids serious topics; David paints political virtue. Boucher depicts mostly women for female or female-dominated patrons; David's significant viewers and actors seem to have thrown off the yoke of female influence. These oppositions, though, hinge on a key point of agreement. In Boucher's art women have empire, but empires are not the subject of art; in David's art the reverse is true. Both artists, then, present politics as a male realm. With Boucher, though, the disempowerment of women occurs as effect rather than strategy; with David, I will argue, the disarticulation of female political power has the status of a project.

There are two generally accepted premises about *Oath of the Horatii* (1785; fig. 7.5) and *Brutus* (1789). The first is that they anticipate Revolutionary events. The dramatic act of oath-taking in the earlier work calls to mind numerous ceremonial oaths sworn in national and regional festivals, as well as the Tennis Court Oath of June 1789, which David was later commissioned to paint. The story of Brutus, who overthrows a monarchy deemed sexually depraved, installs a republican government, and sacrifices everything necessary to defend it from royalist conspiracies, contains obvious parallels to the French situation.[11]

The second premise is that, roughly speaking, men represent the public sphere and women represent the private sphere. In *Oath of the Horatii*, three brothers, arms taut, swear to defend Rome upon swords held by their father, while the women of the family, enervated by despair, bemoan the inevitable impending loss of a loved one.[12] Here, despite the shared domestic setting, men and women embody antithetical concerns, and David indicates no apparent way to span the spatial and psychic distance between them.[13] In *Brutus*, a bit differently, the grieving but stoic father/ruler, like the women, feels the pull to protect family. But the crossover ends there. The emotional, wilting women bear no sign of the strength required to make the painful decisions that public responsibilities entail; it is not that men have no ties to the private sphere, but that women have no place in the public one.

Less often articulated is that the truth of the second premise compromises the accuracy of the first. For while David's male characters do what many men later did during the Revolution, Revolutionary

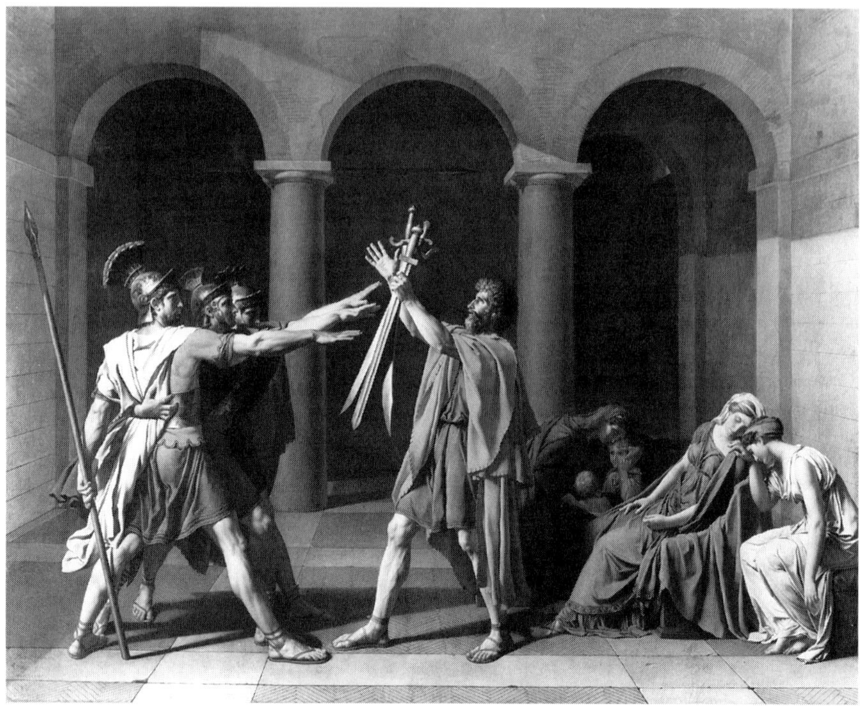

Figure 7.5. Jacques-Louis David, *The Oath of the Horatii*, 1785. Oil on canvas. Musée du Louvre, Paris. (Photo: Réunion des Musées Nationaux/Art Resource, New York.)

women did far more than weep in wilting masses at home.[14] Even if they largely defined themselves as wives and mothers, women early entered the public sphere in those roles to support the Revolutionary cause. Women attended political assemblies until they were expelled from them and not infrequently made and were lauded for patriotic speeches. Women also massed in groups that were not limited to members of a single family, and in these female groups performed highly visible actions. They made patriotic donations and participated in largely female riots, including the October Days of 1789, the Sugar Crisis of 1792, and the February Days of 1793. Moreover, when women stood to the side while men swore patriotic oaths, it was not because they were reluctant, unmoved, or unable to support or comprehend political ideals but because men had refused to allow women to identify themselves, even ceremonially, as political actors.

I do not want to imply that David's women in *Oath of the Horatii* and *Brutus* lost relevance during the Revolution. Far from it. David fixes women in the private sphere, occupied with relational ties. In this, he anticipates a key feature of Revolutionary law and ideology, which was increasingly directed toward making the family women's primary focus.[15] David's prescience on this matter, though, is hardly as noteworthy as his decision to paint Brutus in 1788, because the idea that women belong far from politics is far from Revolutionary. What changes during the Revolution is less the message than the context in which it was articulated. By the time David redisplayed the paintings at the Salon of 1791, female political actors had become a highly visible phenomenon. And in 1793, at the height of David's involvement in Revolutionary politics, he undertook two projects that dealt directly with the problem: *The Death of Marat* (fig. 7.6), in which he handles the anomaly of a female assassin; and his Festival of the Constitution, in which he finds a safe place in Revolutionary history for the Heroines of October.

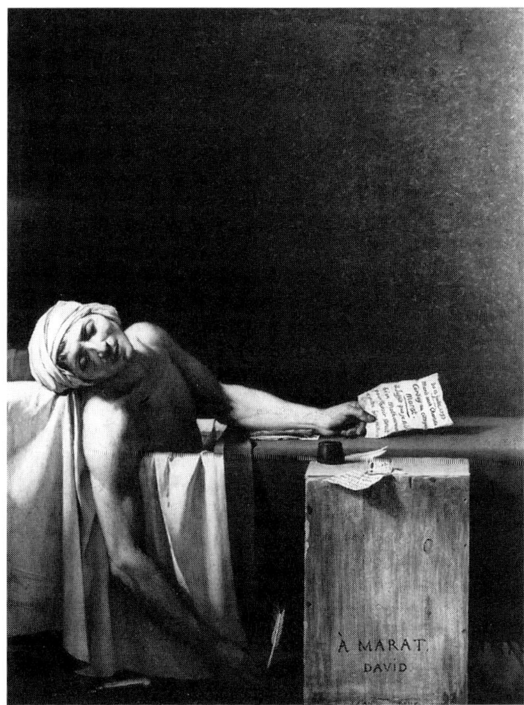

Figure 7.6. Jacques-Louis David, *The Death of Marat*, 1793. Oil on canvas. Royal Museum of Fine Arts of Belgium, Brussels.

Six weeks after Charlotte Corday assassinated Marat on July 13, 1793, her unorthodox position in the world of men found visual representation in a two-scene engraving by Queverdo (fig. 7.1). The lower scene portrays the moment just before the murder: Marat futilely recoils in his sabot-shaped tub, while Corday prepares to plunge in the knife. As Queverdo depicts them, victim and assassin come from different, oppositely gendered realms of meaning and action that ordinarily ought not to overlap. Marat's gesture and half-visible nudity allude, through David, to Socrates, the prototypical protagonist of the male sanctum.[16] But Marat will not die nobly among men like the embattled political philosopher who came before him, but at the hands of a woman of fashion. Leaning over Marat in three-quarter profile, Corday is posed to reveal her costume and fine figure as much as her fatal intention: fancy hat, striped décolleté dress, newly redone hairdo, slim waist. The engraving's larger scene depicts Corday writing to her fa-

ther in prison the day before she was guillotined: "Forgive me, dear father, for having disposed of my existence [myself]."[17] By committing a crime that resulted in her death, she had usurped her father's right to dispense her future according to his choice and for his own benefit.

The engraving points to a consistent feature of Corday representation. Virtually all who judged her, no matter what the verdict, saw her act as a violation of gender norms. People either saw a woman and could not see a political actor or saw a political assassin and could not quite call her a woman. The deputy Chabot, describing her crime at the National Convention, called her one of those monsters vomited forth by nature from time to time, a deadly hybrid of male courage and female delirium masquerading as fully female.[18] Her prosecutors swore that she must have been a vehicle of male plotters; her eulogizer called her an angel.[19] An article disseminated by Parisian officials creatively implied both positions: "Sentimental love and its soft emotions no longer approach the heart of a woman who has the pretension to knowledge, to wit, and to free thought, to the politics of nations. . . . Sensible and amiable men do not like women of this type."[20] The text manages to suggest simultaneously that Corday acted like a man, thus separating political assassination from womanly conceptions, and that she could not successfully act like a man, thus discouraging the idea that gender-appropriate behavior was in some sense optional.

These early textual recuperations concur on one point: the body of a woman cannot adequately represent Corday. So it is appropriate that David does not give her bodily form in his painting *Death of Marat*, although Corday's physical absence has other sources. Having recently completed for the National Convention a painting of Lepelletier de Saint-Fargeau, who had been killed by a Royalist soldier for voting the death of the king, David was immediately called to immortalize Marat. And, since *The Death of Marat* was to be a pendant, David followed the Lepelletier portrait's general format. As in the Lepelletier portrait, David does not picture the act of assassination in progress. Instead, he lays out the political martyr in a Christ-like, iconic pose, alluding through objects and settling to the circumstances of death. Accordingly, David includes Corday only by placing a letter from her in Marat's hand; he does not portray her in body.

If gender ideology cannot be termed the cause of Corday's absence, it certainly contributes to the particular form of her presence. As he had done in *Oath of the Horatii* and *Brutus*, David works in *Marat* to take the woman out of the political sphere. To do this, he obscures the political dimension of Corday's purpose by twisting the form of her own masquerade. Corday had actually intended to kill Marat openly on the Convention floor, adhering to the values of transparent and open political self-representation promoted during the Revolution.[21] Since he was at home ill, however, she had had to resort to what she termed an *"artifice perfide"*: she composed several letters to him in which she pretended to share Marat's political allegiance, when she actually intended to kill him in the name of his Girondin opposition.[22] In the first note, which Marat received, Corday promises to reveal details about a Girondin counterrevolutionary plot. The second letter, which Corday never had to deliver, appeals similarly to shared political goals: "I have secrets to reveal that are most important for the health of the Republic. I have already been persecuted for the cause of liberty. I am miserable; it is enough that I am so to have the right to your protection." Although David gleans his reference to Corday from these letters, he does not transmit her anti-Girondin ruse. The note in Marat's hand, dated "13 juillet 1793" and addressed "Marie Anne Charlotte Corday au citoyen Marat," says: "Il suffit que je sois bien malheureuse pour avoir droit à votre bienveillance" (It is enough that I am truly miserable to have the right to your goodwill). David has dropped from the note any clue of Corday's avowedly political purpose.[23]

Nor does David stop at removing politics from the letter. He also includes a misleading hint about the letter's now cryptic meaning. On Marat's table rest an *assignat* and the note: "Vous donnerez cet assignat à cette mère de 5 enfants et dont le mari est mort pour la défense de la patrie" (You will give this bill to this

mother with five children whose husband has died defending the country). Of course, this multivalent note characterizes Marat as well as Corday. Implying (fictively) that Marat died while performing an act of charity for a destitute mother, it testifies to both the general moral goodness and specific class allegiance of "l'ami du peuple."[24] At the same time, it appears to supply the meaning of Corday's text. Because the concepts "poor widowed mother" and "charitable donation" in the note can so easily explain the words *malheureuse* and *bienveillance* in the letter, the viewer is invited to read in Corday's plea a request for a similar donation. With no other clues in the painting, Corday's *artifice perfide* appears to be a matter of gender, not of politics. Instead of being a Girondin in the guise of a Montagnard, Corday seems to be a bad woman disguised as a good woman—as a mother who comes to public attention only through the deeds of her husband. And since Corday only appears through her artifice, the political implications of the murder appear to consist wholly in the political identity of Marat, rather than in a conflict between two political antagonists, Marat and Corday.

David, then, makes it possible to recuperate the conceptual dilemma of the female political assassin through the main strategies employed by others: depoliticizing the woman or defeminizing the patriot killer. On the one hand, the painting's internal discourse suggests that Corday's ruse and motivations can be completely understood without reference to contemporary politics and through the network of significations that traditionally delimit the category *woman* within the private sphere. On the other, David situates Corday in violation of that category. Whether or not the viewer accepts David's fiction that Corday was no political activist, Corday appears to have violated women's intended role, of which David conveniently includes a textual reminder, purportedly penned by Marat himself.

Yet we cannot leave David's interpretation without asking why David included Corday at all. Why not simply omit her, rather than perpetuate her notoriety? Because, perhaps, by the time David painted *Marat*, she already seemed destined for a long sojourn in the collective imagination. Corday is one of many women who came to public attention singly or in groups during the Revolution and whose deeds were immediately publicized through newspapers, journals, and popular prints. David could only hope to manage the representation of her; he could hardly expect to erase or cover her imprint. The still-erect pen in Marat's hand stands as the symbol of this strategy. David has given Marat what he tried to appropriate from Corday: the last word on Corday's meaning. In Queverdo's print, that honor had gone to Corday, and to opposite effect. Corday's apology for transgressing paternal authority plants her final state of mind in the realm of ideal womanhood, so that the murder seems either to be regretted or to have issued from a noble mind. In David's painting, Marat—with whom David aligns himself through the signature "A Marat, David"—supplies the definition of ideal womanhood, the apparent meaning of Corday's prose, and consequently, the depoliticization of Corday's act.[25] David transmits Corday to posterity with his own interpretation firmly attached.

He takes a similar approach to the Women of October. On July 11, 1793, three days before he undertook *Marat,* David presented to the National Convention his plan for the upcoming Fête de la Réunion Républicaine, also called the Festival of the Constitution, to be held on August 10.[26] The complex program entailed a procession through five stations that was designed to retell the history of the Republic as the triumph of the people, from the fall of the Bastille to the adoption of the new constitution. The second station commemorated the October Days (October 5–6, 1789), when a largely female procession marched to Versailles and forced the king to return to Paris. In David's plan, women who had participated would be seated on cannons under a triumphal arch. Some would hold branches, others trophies—unequivocal praise, David wrote, for the striking victory of these courageous citizens over the servile royal guard. Harangues, cries of joy, and artillery salvos would underscore their triumph, and the women would receive laurels from the president of the National Convention.

David's text, more widely viewed than the festival itself,[27] constitutes one of the most unqualified celebrations of female political activism to be produced during the Revolution, and certainly by David. It also contains another affirmation. Some of the October heroines now belonged to the Society of Revolutionary Republican Women, an organization of radical women that both worked for women's rights and had contributed, as a group, to the May ouster of the Girondins, the event that had motivated Corday's actions.[28] Thus, in the process of honoring female activism of the past, David's ceremony would indirectly honor female activists of the present.

Yet this celebration was undermined in two ways. In the president's speech, he advised the women to channel their courage into motherhood: "Women! Liberty, attacked by tyrants, needs heroes to defend her. It's your job to give birth to them. May all the generous and warrior virtues flow, with mother's milk, into the heart of all French infants."[29] This textual implantation of motherhood over activism reflects disintegrating Jacobin support for the Society of Revolutionary Republican Women in particular and for female political practice in general. Yet it also encapsulates Revolutionary attitudes from the start. Confronted with female political activism, successive Revolutionary governments tried, on the one hand, to promote the fulfillment of marital and maternal duties as the only legitimate outlets for female patriotism and, on the other, to legally prevent women from meeting outside the family for political purposes. In 1793, women were put under virtual house arrest, prohibited from congregating in groups of five or more. The speech, then, returns this portion of the festival to the Revolutionary mainstream.

More importantly, it rehearses a message that David has displaced and dispersed to other parts of the festival. When the president used the metaphor of mother's milk to express his desire to see courage flowing out of women into boys, he echoed a metaphor that David had dramatically ritualized at the first station, where government representatives from the eighty-four districts drank water issuing from the breasts of a large, hieratically posed statue of Nature. The October heroines, then, were preceded by a female figure that authorized the president's domesticating admonitions, being simultaneously greater than life and grounded in motherhood. The women were followed by symbols and rites that further discounted them. At the fourth station, a distinctly masculine image of force represented "le Peuple français": a male colossus, unnamed but iconographically identified as Hercules, smashing the monster of Federalism with his club. The fifth station confirmed that maleness was crucial to David's "Peuple." Here, at an altar to the nation, offerings symbolized the labor by which "the People provides for his wife and children." Ignoring the contributions of women both to the political effectiveness of "le peuple" and, of necessity, to the family economy, David idealizes a situation in which men negotiate the world outside the family for women and children at home.

As Lynn Hunt points out, David conceives of his history on one level as a chronology of ascending political formations.[30] For David, the colossus at Station Four represents a higher stage of the Revolution than the three female-centered symbols before it: the fountain of Nature, the Women of October, and the statue of Liberty. From this standpoint, the festival narrates the erasure of the 1789 heroines from the story of the Revolution. From another standpoint, it might be more fruitful to think of David's treatment of the October heroines as a way to accomplish the difficult task of representation without reproduction. That is, David had good reason to depict the Women of October and to specify their laudable action. The royal family's forced return to Paris was an important early step, impossible to neglect, toward the triumph of the people, the festival's most explicit narrative. But he did not want to generate imitations, either in action or in potentially action-generating imagery.[31] So he described one type of female behavior and works, to prescribe another. David also arrested reproduction through his form of presentation. By having the Women of October stand for themselves in this living tableau, he manages to dramatize their achievement without involving additional women in the celebration of female activism; no new women would be honored in the activist role as some would be honored for acting out the allegorical role of Liberty.[32]

Having examined David's approach to "real" women, I want to return to the *Sabines* and consider ways in which formal compositional strategies of history painting enhance his political project. Chaussard's interpretation, which has been widely accepted over the past two centuries, identifies the underlying subject as male political antagonists in the Revolution reconciled by the "Mother-Country."[33] The apparent subject concerns the founding of Rome. Three years after the armies of Romulus had abducted a number of Sabine women to populate his new settlement, the Sabine men, led by Tatius, came to retrieve them forcibly. By this point, however, the abducted women had become wives and mothers of Romans and were loath to be rescued. They rushed distraught onto the battlefield, infants in tow, and with Hersilia, the wife of Romulus, as their most eloquent speaker begged the men to respect the family ties that now bound Romans and Sabines. The men were so moved that they not only ceased fighting but agreed to form one people.[34]

Why would David use a story about female political intervention to depict a contemporary political scenario, such as the one Chaussard presents, from which earthly women are absent? Indeed, David seems to emphasize compositionally the remarkable mingling of genders on male ground. In both *Oath of the Horatii*, recalled here for the viewer by the pose of Romulus, and in *Brutus*, David had used visual gender segregation to denote women's unfitness for public service. In the *Sabines* too, David concentrates the women in one location, but now he places them at the center rather than the margin of male activity. And they no longer form an isolated, imploded group. Hersilia can almost touch the shields of the two male principals, while on her right a woman clings to Tatius's leg. No unbridgeable gap separates male and female here. Yet David also implies that in an ideal society, none but allegorical females actually belong in Hersilia's place. The Sabine women enter the battlefield conspicuously without weapons and only as wives and mothers. Holding, pointing to, or standing near their children, they simultaneously dramatize the family at risk and manifest their own primary identification within it.

How can we understand this particular combination of conflictual signals in a painted account of ideal female behavior? We can begin, I suggest, by focusing on a feature of the *Sabines* that also occurred in the work of Boucher: a slipperiness with regard to female allegiance. In Boucher's paintings *Venus and Vulcan* and *Jupiter and Callisto,* the dialectical conflict between female power and male mastery depends in part on a simultaneous imaging of homosexual and heterosexual configurations. David, too, keeps a dual female alliance before the viewer: women with women, now in the form of a political group; and women with men, now in the form of the family. To underscore the former, David highlights the necessarily collective nature of the action. He distributes among a central group of women four different actions constitutive of one intervention: separating the men, pointing to the children, crying out, and displaying female wretchedness. As Norman Bryson points out, David also twins the women's poses so that one woman begins arm movements that another appears to terminate, again suggesting that the task demands coordinated labor.[35] (Note here, however, how the varied roles suggest differences as well as alliances among women, partly through the racialized convention whereby Hersilia, the woman of highest status, who is designated as such partly by her light skin, has the role most suggestive of self-control: not for her the flying drapery, breast-baring, loose hair, or active child endangerment that other interveners manifest.) Underscoring the latter is the adjacent grouping of Tatius, his female supplicant, and her child, next to which David signs his name, who model the family unit that the women hope to preserve. In addition, the position of Hersilia, who is compositionally enmeshed at the center of both an X formed by the women interveners and a recurring V foreground pattern formed with the two male protagonists, underscores the centrality of both formations.

Note, also, that these two configurations already had currency in accounts of recent types of female behavior that David had confronted and re-presented during the Revolution. David's description of frenzied and disheveled women with wild hair (*échevellées*) running through the fray, screaming and wail-ing, bears a remarkable resemblance to contemporary descriptions of the Women of October. The family picture, with father minding the sword and mother minding the child, reproduces an omnipresent ideological construction used in numerous ways during the Revolution to rationalize or restrict women's political activism. As importantly, there already existed a tradition of superimposing the mother image upon the female rioter image to place the latter in a better light. During the Old Regime, authorities rarely prosecuted women who were mothers for participating in bread riots, setting a precedent of leniency that benefited the Women of October.[36] The most positive accounts of the October Days emphasize the women's quest for bread, suggesting that they should be viewed as an agglomeration of desperate mothers, each forced to leave home and take temporary collective possession of the public space in order to fulfill roles that ordinarily occupied them elsewhere.

This is precisely the narrative and structure of *Intervention of the Sabine Women,* which constitutes, I argue, David's second gloss on the Women of October, the first having occurred in the Festival of the Constitution of 1793. In the painting, David again portrays women agitators with a maternal overlay that justifies past actions and proscribes future repetitions. But the ancient trappings add several comforting twists, which are telescoped in the image of the mothers surrounded by swords. Instead of using violence against others, the Sabines invited violence against themselves. And they only transgressed traditional gender boundaries out of an intense desire to maintain them; their purpose was to withdraw from the battlefield. This could not be said of all the October heroines representing themselves in 1793, since some were still enthusiastic political activists.

David's painting foreshadows this wholly male political sphere of the future through the poses of Romulus and Tatius, who mirror each other in stance and also complement each other through the sexually allusive opposition of spear and shield. Bryson, who also notes this aspect of the *Sabines,* argues to the contrary that the women will break rather than reconstitute this male order. The women's true accomplishment, according to Bryson, is to reorient men locked into a homoerotic parody of sexual difference: "They are driving a wedge into the dyadic vision of the men; they introduce true difference, differently gendered bodies."[37] This interpretation seems to me to entail an undue, and insufficiently analyzed, privileging of heterosexual/heterosocial structures. It is more plausible to conclude that the women make possible, rather than thwart, male bonding. Before the women's intervention, male homosociality is fraught with danger for men: Romulus manages to shield his genitals but cannot, as it were, cover his rear. The empty sheath that now falls across Tatius's genitals offers dubious protection, either physical or symbolic. As Darcy Grimaldo Grigsby notes, however, David added the sheath in 1808; in 1799 Tatius lacked even that.[38] The women's intervention functions to redirect male violence away from other men. The men must either plunge their weapons into women or lay down their arms and let the women conserve their homes; in either scenario, the battlefield is safer for men and the women are under erasure.

Chaussard was right to suggest that although the *Sabines* appears to signal David's retreat from Revolutionary politics into a classical world of idealized nudity, it actually addresses topical political matters. But the *Sabines* is about contemporary women at least as much as it is about contemporary men. It does not just depict the reconciliation of male factions so that peace may reign in *la mère patrie*. It also reengages one of the most disturbing configurations of Revolutionary female political activism—the rioting group. Refracting previous representations of female rioting through the medium of ancient history, David manages to imply that even when they most intruded onto the political stage, women essentially possessed an unwavering, single-focused commitment to the concerns of the private sphere. Given his artistic and political history, David was uniquely positioned to craft such an image. *Oath of the Horatii* and *Brutus* reveal him to be an advocate of separate spheres before the Revolution, while his Revolutionary activities involved him in the creative dissemination of gender ideology. Dramatic maternal enshrinements and confinements were one of his

specialties, and the *Sabines* cannot be understood without taking into account previous labors of domestication performed upon Charlotte Corday and, especially, upon the Women of October. Unlike *Oath of the Horatii* and *Brutus,* the *Sabines* is the work of a man who had to paint women onto the political stage in order to keep them off of it. Yet David does not quite erase the signs of Revolutionary gender disarray. In the process of superimposing motherly domestic allegiance onto female political alliance, David presents a sight that signals the very opposite of women's internalization of male rules: the spectacle of women prepared to be the agents of their own children's deaths. A dangerously thin conceptual veneer distinguishes the barbarian Medea from what one admirer of the *Sabines* called a "gate of respectability that no soldier would dare pass!"[39] The allegiance of the mother in David's painting, like Boucher's adulterous Venus, remains ultimately unguaranteed.

In the art of Boucher and David, the appearance of female power bears witness in historically particular forms to the perception that women can occupy and transform the male political world. If their images demonstrate that the representation of women outside the political sphere is often difficult to achieve in eighteenth-century visual culture, these examples also suggest why such depoliticizing maneuvers have often eluded attention. Both artists defuse female agency by placing female figures simultaneously within and outside configurations through which women deployed power at the time. These dual imagings cannot be recognized unless the historical referents of female political activism and of female affiliation are interrogated. Such a query must also attend to the assumptions about configuration and affiliation that underly critical approaches to gender. During the Revolution, for instance, the privileging of women's family role was partly a strategy to disperse politically active women into isolated domestic units. Consequently, when critics presume heterosexual/heterosocial structures to be normative or primary for women, they begin with a model that Revolutionary leaders worked hard to inscribe. Recognizing and challenging such models must be a central feminist project.

The epigraph is from [Pierre-Jean-Baptiste] Chaussard, *Sur le Tableau des Sabines par David* (Paris: Charles Pougens, 1800), 4. For their engagement with this project in various earlier manifestations, I thank Elizabeth Helsinger, Linda Seidel, Lise Kildegaard, and Andrew Parker. Many thanks to Sallie Hackett for her help in preparing the manuscript.

1. On the gendering of the Revolutionary public sphere, see, for instance, Lynn Hunt, *Politics, Culture, and Class in the French Revolution* (Berkeley: University of California Press, 1984); Joan B. Landes, *Women and the Public Sphere in the Age of the French Revolution* (Ithaca, N.Y.: Cornell University Press, 1988).

2. Foremost among advocates of David's political disengagement is Anita Brookner, *Jacques-Louis David* (New York: Thames and Hudson, 1980). Psychoanalytic readings include Norman Bryson, *Tradition and Desire: From David to Delacroix* (Cambridge: Cambridge University Press, 1984); and Ronald Paulson, *Representations of Revolution* (New Haven, Conn.: Yale University Press, 1983). The tendency to lose sight of Revolutionary female political activism is not limited to writers on David. For instance, in "Medusa's Head: Male Anxiety under Political Pressure" (in *The End of the Line: Essays on Psychoanalysis and the Sublime* [New York: Columbia University Press, 1985], 165–93, 249–56), Neil Hertz reads several images of female activists of 1789 and 1848 as apotropaic symbolizations of male castration anxiety during political crisis; although the images actually depict female activists, he does not consider whether the images are informed by the actions and status of contemporary women. The most fruitful treatments of politics and gender in David's art have been Thomas E. Crow, *Painters and Public Life in Eighteenth-Century Paris* (New Haven, Conn.: Yale University Press, 1985); and Carol Duncan, "Fallen Fathers: Images of Authority in Pre-Revolutionary French Art," *Art History* 4, no. 2 (June 1981): 186–202. Duncan's early work on domesticating female imagery in eighteenth-century French art should also be cited here. See "Happy Mothers and Other New Ideas in French Art," *Art Bulletin* 55 (December 1973): 570–83, reprinted in *Feminism and Art History: Questioning the Litany*, ed. Norma Broude and Mary D. Garrard (New York: Harper and Row, 1982), 201–19.

3. Montesquieu, *Les Lettres persanes*, ed. Paul Vernière (Paris: Garnier Frères, 1960), letter 107.

4. The story comes from the *Aeneid*, 8: 485–533.

5. This story, too, which appears in Ovid *(Metamorphoses*, trans. Mary M. Innes [Harmondsworth: Penguin Books, 1986], 61–62), has a narrative affinity to Montesquieu's republic of women. In both Ovid and Montesquieu, a male confronts a female group defined by ordinarily male concerns—hunting and politics, respectively—and infiltrates it with weapons labeled feminine in the eighteenth century: for Montesquieu, personal relations; for Jupiter, the female body, artifice, and disguise.

6. Contrast in skin tone, of course, may be used to underscore various contrasts among women as well as between women and men, as I discuss later regarding the *Sabines*.

7. Edmond and Jules de Goncourt, whose assessment of Boucher has remained standard, exemplify this tendency. Passionate same-sex relationships were clearly within the Goncourts' conceptual framework for the eighteenth century. They had earlier discussed "romantic friendship" between women in *La Femme au dix-huitième siècle*, rev. ed., 2 vols. (Paris: Flammarion and Fasquelle, n.d. [1862]), 91–94, and they had read texts, such as Diderot's *La Religieuse*, that consider female homoerotic episodes. Yet they did not view female homoerotics as a referent for the relation of viewer to image, although they attributed much of Boucher's success to female patronage and taste. *L'Art du dix-huitième siècle*, rev. ed., 2 vols. (Paris: Rapilly, 1873), 177–254.

8. Madame de Graffigny, *Lettres d'une péruvienne*, in *Oeuvres complètes de Mme de Grafigny* (Paris: Lelong, 1821); Denis Diderot, *The Nun*, trans. Leonard Tancock (Harmondsworth: Penguin, 1974).

9. In the *Lettres persanes*, letters 4 and 147 discuss lesbian behavior in the harem as a (futile and temporary) violation of the sultan's power. Diderot primarily treats lesbianism as one of the unhealthy by-products of female segregation, although as Eve Kosofsky Sedgwick has recently discussed, lesbian practices in *The Nun* are also the occasion for complex—and equally partial and fleeting—manipulations of power by its participants. "Privilege of Unknowing," *Genders* 1 (March 1988): 112–17. The *Peruvian Letters* does not depict lesbianism.

10. I use here the terminology developed by Sedgwick in

Between Men: English Literature and Male Homosocial Desire (New York: Columbia University Press, 1985). On the lack of female solidarity among French women in the salon setting, a primary site of female engagement with political and social matters, see Evelyn Gordon Bodec, "Salonnières and Blue Stockings: Educated Obsolescence and Burgeoning Feminism," *Feminist Studies* 3 (Spring–Summer 1976): 191–93.

11. Consequently, the painting and person of Brutus were often invoked during the Revolution. See Robert L. Herbert, *David, Voltaire, "Brutus," and the French Revolution: An Essay in Art and Politics* (New York: Viking, 1972).

12. The women include the mother of the Horatii, a woman who is both the wife of a Horatius brother and a sister of the three Curatius brothers who will soon fight the Horatii, and Camilla, a Horatius sister betrothed to a Curatius brother. Since all of the brothers of one family will die, bereavement is inevitable.

13. As Crow eloquently states, "The picture refuses to find form for the relationships between men and women which are central to its narrative content." *Painters and Public Life*, 236.

14. On women's political activism during the French Revolution, see Jane Abray, "Feminism in the French Revolution," *American Historical Review* 80, no. 1 (February 1975): 43–62; Darlene Gay Levy, Harriet Branson Applewhite, and Mary Durham Johnson, eds. and trans., *Women in Revolutionary Paris, 1789–1795, Selected Documents* (Urbana: University of Illinois Press, 1979); Landes, *Women and the Public Sphere*, 93–168.

15. This process of circumscription included reward as well as punishment. Women acquired new rights under Revolutionary family law: to enter and exit marriages more freely, to administer the property they brought into a marriage, to expect and question their husband's fidelity. See James F. Traer, *Marriage and the Family in Eighteenth-Century France* (Ithaca, N.Y.: Cornell University Press, 1980), 94–95, 118–21; and Roderick Phillips, *Family Breakdown in Late Eighteenth-Century France: Divorces in Rouen, 1792–1803* (Oxford: Clarendon Press, 1980), 11–12. At the same time, state-directed festivals and state-approved cultural products extolled motherhood and wifehood as patriotic roles. Against the background of women's actual political influence, however, according women better status in the home emerges as

an attempt not to enfranchise women but to gild a cage of sharply decreasing diameter. I argue this point more fully in "Boucher, David, and the French Revolution: Politics and Gender in Eighteenth-Century French History Painting" (Ph.D. diss., University of Chicago, 1989), 59–78.

16. David's painting *The Death of Socrates* (1787), which had been re-exhibited with the *Oath* and *Brutus* at the Salon of 1791, was well known.

17. The legible text of the print paraphrases the letter of July 16 that Corday actually wrote: "Forgive me, dear father, for having disposed of my life without your consent. I have avenged many innocent victims; I have forestalled many disasters." Quoted in Adolphe Huard, *Mémoires sur Charlotte Corday, d'après des documents authentiques et inédits* (Paris: Léon Roudiez, 1866), 239–40. For illustrations of other contemporary images generated by the assassination, see Georges de Batz, "History, Truth, and Art," *Art Quarterly* 8, no. 4 (Autumn 1945): 249–60; and Michael Marrinan, "Images and Ideas of Charlotte Corday: Texts and Contexts of an Assassination," *Arts* 54, no. 8 (April 1980): 158–61.

18. "Séance du dimanche 14 juillet," *Moniteur Universal*, no. 197, 16 July 1793, in vol. 17 of *Réimpression de l'Ancien Moniteur* (Paris: Henri Plon, 1860), 17: 129.

19. *Deuxième interrogatoire de Charlotte Corday*, reproduced in Huard, *Mémoires*, 234; Adam Lux, *Charlotte Corday*, reproduced in ibid., 223–28.

20. Quoted and translated by Marrinan, "Corday," 160–61, from a facsimile of the handbill.

21. On Revolutionary transparency, see Hunt, *Politics, Culture, and Class*, 42–46, 72–74.

22. On May 31, 1793, the Montagnards had taken control of the National Convention from the more moderate Girondin party, also referred to as "Federalists." Several days later, after *sans culottes* demanded the Girondins' arrest, many of the Girondin leaders fled to Caen, where Corday lived. It was then that she conceived the idea of assassinating Marat, whose journalism had contributed to the Girondins' retreat. Corday discusses her *artifice perfide* in a letter to her Girondin compatriot Barbaroux written in prison. Quoted in Huard, *Mémoires*, 199.

23. For the texts of these letters, see de Batz, "History," 250, 260.

24. For a good account of how Marat's identity as a "friend of the people" contributes to the painting's

meaning, see William Olander, "Pour transmettre à la posterité: French Painting and Revolution, 1774–1795" (Ph.D. diss., New York University, 1983), 249–53.

25. The textuality of these strategies might also be related to the new importance of the publicized text in Revolutionary juridical practices and concepts, as discussed with regard to Marat in Marie-Hélène Huet, *Rehearsing the Revolution: The Staging of Marat's Death, 1793–1797*, trans. Robert Hurley (Berkeley: University of California Press, 1982), 5–7, 56–58.

26. *Rapport et décret sur la Fête de la Réunion républicaine du 10 Août, présentés au nom du Comité d'Instruction publique, par David, Député du Département de Paris. Imprimé par ordre de la Convention Nationale, & envoyé aux Départements & aux Armées* (Paris: Imprimerie Nationale, 1793), 5–6. The text is reproduced in Daniel and Guy Wildenstein, *Documents complémentaires au catalogue de l'oeuvre de Louis David* (Paris: Bibliothèque des Arts, 1973), no. 459. On David's role in organizing Revolutionary festivals, see David L. Dowd, *Pageant Master of the Republic: Jacques-Louis David and the French Revolution* (Lincoln: University of Nebraska Press, 1948). See Mona Ozouf, *La Fête révolutionnaire, 1789–1799* (Paris: Gallimard, 1976), on the festival phenomenon in general.

27. Besides being sent to the *départments* and armies, the proposal was also reprinted in the *Moniteur* on July 17. *Réimpression* 17: 119–21.

28. Marie Cerati, *Le Club des citoyennes révolutionnaires* (Paris: Editions Sociales, 1966), 101.

29. Quoted in ibid., 102.

30. Hunt, *Politics, Culture, and Class*, 98.

31. The behavior David wanted to generate finds typical expression in this stage direction from his plan, presented to the convention on July 11, 1794, for the festival to render Pantheon honors to the teenage martyrs Barra and Viala. "Let every mother to whom the heavens have refused male children say to her daughters: Today, you see, a great people pays homage to heroic devotion; tomorrow it will celebrate modesty *[pudeur]* and filial piety. Make yourselves worthy, my daughters, to become the object of its admiration." The speech goes on to promote Cornelia, a Roman matron famous for preferring her children to jewelry, as a model. Wildenstein, *David*, no. 1096.

32. On Revolutionary living allegories, see Maurice Ag-

ulhon, *Marianne into Battle: Republican Imagery and Symbolism in France, 1789* (Cambridge: Cambridge University Press, 1981), 27–30; and Ozouf, *La Fête*, 116–20. Agulhon notes that the women who portrayed political concepts such as Liberty were often permanently marked by the role: some perished in the White Terror as a result, while others were regarded with reverence and awe into old age.

33. Texts that reaffirm Chaussard's interpretation include Jules Renouvier, *Histoire de l'art pendant la Révolution* (Paris: Veuve Jules Renouard, 1863), 82–83; James H. Rubin, "Oedipus, Antigone, and Exiles in Post-Revolutionary France," *Art Quarterly* 36, no. 3 (Autumn 1973): 149–51; and Albert Boime, *Art in an Age of Revolution* (Chicago: University of Chicago Press, 1987), 483. For a slightly different version of the argument that the women are allegories of France and the men represent Frenchmen, see Norman Bryson, "Centres and Margins in David," *Word and Image* 4, no. 1 (January–March 1988): 48. The widespread acceptance of Chaussard's view can be partly explained by the next paragraph in the text, in which Chaussard claims that, after he offered David his interpretation, David replied: "Such was my thought when I seized the paintbrushes; I've been heard!" (Chaussard, *Sabines*, 4). Surely, however, a critic's testimonial to his own critical talent cannot be considered authoritative. Also cited is the widely circulated story that David was inspired to paint the *Sabines* by the generosity of his wife, who set aside their political differences and marital estrangement to intervene on his behalf when he was imprisoned in 1794 and 1795. Another tale of a woman outside of politics mediating between male political antagonists, it is of dubious origin and uncertain truth.

34. David, whose primary literary source was Plutarch's *Romulus*, clearly wanted his viewers to know the story, which he retold in the pamphlet he distributed to viewers when he exhibited the painting in his studio in 1799. Wildenstein, *David*, no. 1326.

35. Bryson, *Tradition and Desire*, 91–93.

36. Olwen Hufton, "Women in the French Revolution," *Past and Present* 53 (November 1971): 104.

37. Bryson, *Tradition and Desire*, 92–93.

38. See chapter 8, this volume.

39. A.D., "Examen du tableau des Sabines," *La Décade philosophique* (10 pluviose an VII [30 January 1800]): 228.

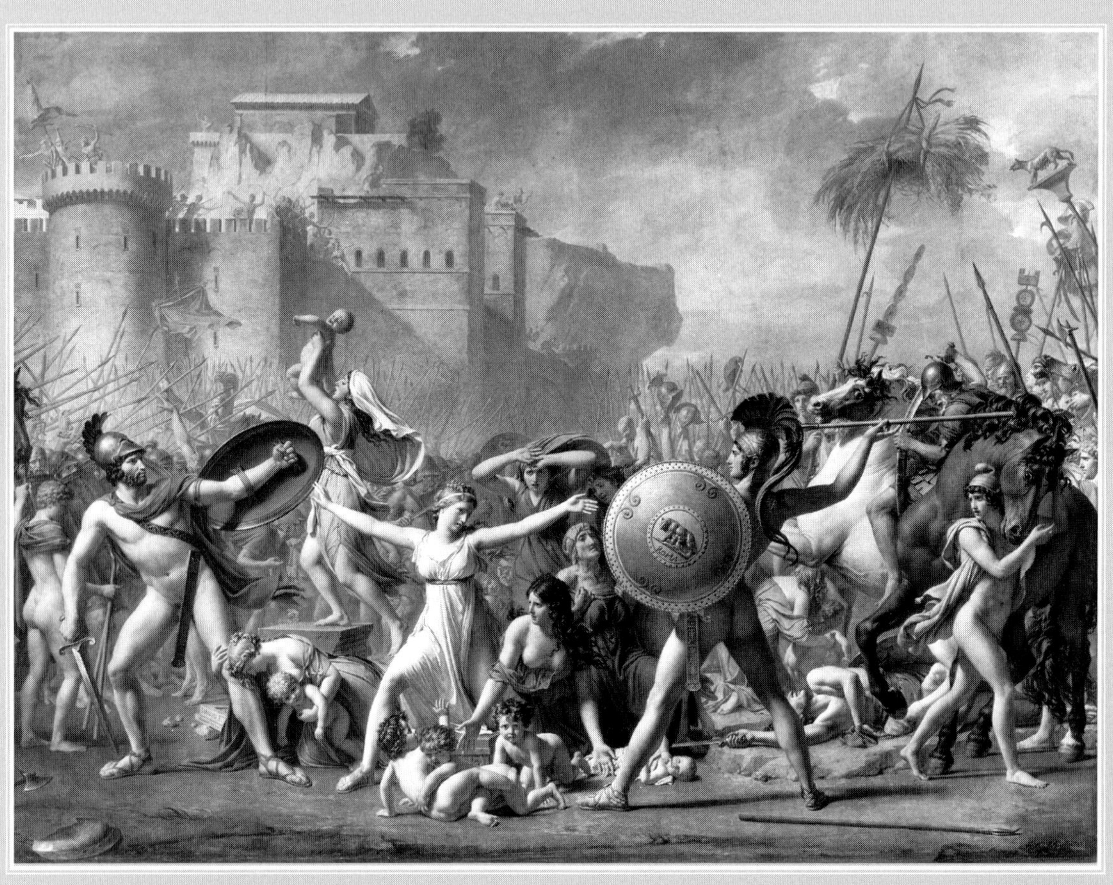

8

NUDITY *À LA GRECQUE* IN 1799

Darcy Grimaldo Grigsby

WAKE UP the women at the right of Jacques-Louis David's *Oath of the Horatii* of 1785 and place them between the male warriors. Now remove the men's clothes. This is the startling, even preposterous double move of David's *Intervention of the Sabine Women* of 1799 (fig. 8.1). If David's martyr portraits of isolated, unconscious, and eroticized male bodies, like his *Bara* of 1793, astutely and economically offered an iconography for the radical fraternal Republic, his transposition of the solitary male nude into a composition that prominently included dressed women proved problematic. The painting's awkwardness derives from the tensions not only between female dress and male nudity, but between the women's action and the men's friezelike stasis, between the pathos now displaced onto the female figures and the technical precision lavished on the evacuated husks of the standing male *académies*.

Scholarship has for the most part treated the novel conjunction of naked male bodies and newly central female protagonists as separate issues. While the nudes have been cited as evidence of David's stylistic shift toward a classical Greek purism, the Sabine women's prominence has been interpreted as affording a familial basis for the reconciliation of a divided and warring post-Revolutionary France. Aesthetic priorities (male nudity) and narrative saliency (female intervention) have often been held asunder.

Historians have also emphasized the success rather than the controversy of David's stilted and theatrical painting. That success, we have been told, hinged on the artist's reliance on women to integrate a fractured society. As daughters of the Sabines and wives of the Romans, the Sabine women were objects of exchange that unified a new people. Marginalized from the public sphere of the radical Jacobin fraternity, women during the Directory could be shuffled onto center stage in order strategically to represent another familial basis for community. This has been the emphasis of scholars like Stefan Germer, who has argued that "women's confinement all along to the private sphere" permitted their embodiment of "a new ethical foundation for society," and Dorothy Johnson, who has characterized the work as an "image of savage and primordial maternity" that celebrates "women's primordial and essential role in the creation of civilization."[1] By contrast, Ewa Lajer-Burcharth has importantly emphasized women's feminist activism during the French Revolution and David's reliance upon women as figurations of disorder. However, she too has argued that the *Sabines* ultimately contains the threat posed by women by binding them

This is an abridged version of an essay of the same title first published in the *Art Bulletin* 80, no. 2 (June 1998): 311–35. Copyright © 1998 by Darcy Grimaldo Grigsby. Reprinted by permission of the author and courtesy of the College Art Association.

Figure 8.1. Jacques-Louis David, *Intervention of the Sabine Women*, 1799. Oil on canvas. Musée du Louvre, Paris. (Photo: Réunion des Musées Nationaux/Art Resource, New York.)

to the roles of mothers and wives, effectively circumscribing their activity within a family configuration. According to Lajer-Burcharth, David's painting represents above all a "defense of the patrilinearity of the family" and thereby functions as a "safeguard image, indeed 'a salutary imago' of male republican self at the end of the revolution."[2]

These accounts take as their premise the success of David's tableau. Their deconstructions of its ideological workings depend upon the assumption that the painting matched its audience's needs, that David with characteristic savvy enabled a society undergoing rapid change to redefine itself. Indeed, we rely upon David's paintings to tell us about those social and political transformations. We understand them to be constitutive of such shifts. Problems arise, however, when the paintings are extricated from the field of contention in which they were made and received. In his best pictures, David almost always took risks that were hotly debated. This was part and parcel of his art's productive work; its eloquence and intelligence resided in David's capacity to locate such hot spots, such vital sites of dissension and anxiety. In fact, David's *Intervention of the Sabines* did *not* reconcile its fractured audience. Displayed at eye level, opposite a mirror, in a commercial exhibition, the painting was certainly a box-office success, attracting some fifty thousand visitors over its unprecedented five-year run.[3] But the votes made by admission fees are evidence less of consensus than of interest, and that interest derived from the work's controversy, its failure to deploy antiquity as a unifying metaphorical language. Ironically, David's very success in giving the Revolution antique form ultimately led to classicism's loss of authority. *Nudité à la grecque* in 1799 could not be disengaged from the dramatic return of women to center stage.

THE NUDITY OF HEROES

The controversies surrounding David's picture are well known, if not sufficiently interrogated. Indeed, David himself mapped them out in a brochure distributed to all paying visitors, thereby situating the painting within a frame of dissension. The artist felt compelled to offer long, erudite textual arguments replete with important antecedents to defend his innovative entrepreneurial exhibition as well as the nudity of his picture's male protagonists.[4] David's text arguably attempted both to control debate and to instantiate it. In fact, contemporaries seized his terms and continued to argue about both choices for years.[5] I believe that the controversies were interrelated and that the scandal of David's tableau resided in the ways it made *nudité à la grecque* the centerpiece of a public spectacle. Indeed, it was the spectacularization of antiquity as a site of nakedness and the mingling of genders and classes that made David's epic painting such a provocation to his critics.

For David, the nude signified art because it signified antiquity. In his "Note on the Nudity of My Heroes," the painter described the nude as a greater artistic achievement than the clothed figure and offered a classical pedigree for the ideal form. He explicitly stated that his goal was to paint a work that the Greeks and Romans would not have found foreign to their customs. Significantly, the artist presumed that authenticity, even transparency, to the classical world would be valued in modern France. To speak to the ancients was to speak to Frenchmen, yet he also felt the need to defend the signs of that veracity (male nudity). David was caught in a bind: he admitted the possibility of disparate cultural boundaries, but he wanted to believe that Frenchmen would respect and understand the language of the ancients. The painter appears to have been blind to the contradiction between universalist and relativist models of culture.

As a classical ideal, nudity promised universality. For David, nudity was the guarantor of art's power to transcend the messy particularities of actual social relations. During the Directory, in spite of the crisis of the Terror, it was still possible to believe in the unified, whole body as a transparent emblem of truth. Here is the Idéologue Amaury Duval: "The dressed man is a mask; he is only himself undressed; it is men one must paint and not the simulacra of men."[6] Nonetheless, the faith expressed by David and Duval was under siege in 1799. For some of their contemporaries, nudity exacerbated rather than alleviated class tensions. While Lajer-Burcharth has asserted that David's male nudes offered the bourgeois male viewer an illusory fiction of ideal wholeness, a number of David's critics believed the nudity of his tableau's figures to be in conflict with bourgeois interests and taste.

Most simply, the bourgeoisie—famously invested in portraiture—could not be relied on to appreciate the artistic language of antiquity. Take for example "C.Z.," the reviewer for *Le Courrier des Spectacles* who vehemently attacked the nudity in the *Sabines*. Permitting art no metaphorical latitude, the author could not forgive David for portraying warriors unrealistically: no people, antique or "savage," placed naked men in circumstances requiring clothing.[7] For literal-minded post-Revolutionary critics like C.Z., classicism was no more than a foreign affectation alien to French habits and values. Moreover, the risk posed by a painting like the *Sabines* was not simply that it was anachronistic but that it rendered the ruling class vulnerable, all too easily provoking working-class ridicule of bourgeois pretensions. C.Z., tongue in cheek, evokes the stuff of panicky nightmares: "A dressed hero is far more imposing. If you send him nude in the middle of a public place, I strongly doubt that the dressed people who surround him, will see him with eyes other than those of his valet de chambre, and you know how difficult it is to be a hero in the eyes of the latter."[8]

C.Z. astutely denigrated the classical hero by redefining him in specifically contemporary French terms. Romulus and Tatius become vulnerable, naked Frenchmen stripped of clothing and class authority before a (disrespectful) crowd of dressed domestic servants. David had argued that it was customary among ancient artists to represent gods and heroes nude. C.Z., by contrast, assumed that such a custom inverted class prerogatives: so the elite must go bare while the common people enjoy the privilege of clothing! If the reasoning is unsophisticated, it better underscores the extent to which the reception of nudity could be a matter of class standing.

Between David's text and the critics of nudity there is an incommensurable gap. If the artist privileged classical aesthetic criteria with little thought to the discrepancy between ancient cultures and his own, the hostile critics privileged French social practices as the circumscribing conditions of art-making and feigned ignorance of the French classical tradition. David's most eloquent Republican champion, the Idéologue Pierre-Jean-Baptiste Chaussard, offered a more complex assessment of the *Sabines*.[9] In contrast to David, who presumed that the painting could produce a unified public appreciative of his antiquarian deployment of nudity, Chaussard argued that the controversial reception of the male nudes appropriately differentiated strata of French society.[10] The Republican critic admitted that David's sublime language of antiquity, particularly his male nudes, would be understood only by an elite, but he believed the painting reconciled a divided society by offering different bases of appeal: "While [David's] enemies go to the painting to seek flaws; his rivals to seek torments; his emulators to seek lessons; the philosopher to seek an object of profound meditation; the friend of the arts to seek pleasure mixed with admiration; the multitude throngs to find new and lively sensations. For [the multitude], it is really only a spectacle."[11] Appreciation of antiquity requires sophistication, but the touching narrative of family strife and reconciliation appeals to the crowd, since "man is above all avid for strong sensations or emotions."[12]

Yet even as he praised David's accomplishment, Chaussard betrayed his ambivalence: "The vulgar only seize expressions of a common and trivial nature; those [expressions] of a superior order and *le beau idéal* escape them by their elevation, or overpower and humiliate them by their grandeur. It is the pathos of the subject that attracts the crowd around this tableau."[13] Thus, while an educated segment of the audience could appreciate *le beau idéal* and the painting's elevated style and message, the multitude is hungry only for "strong sensations." Chaussard referred to David's work as a "drama," but he at-

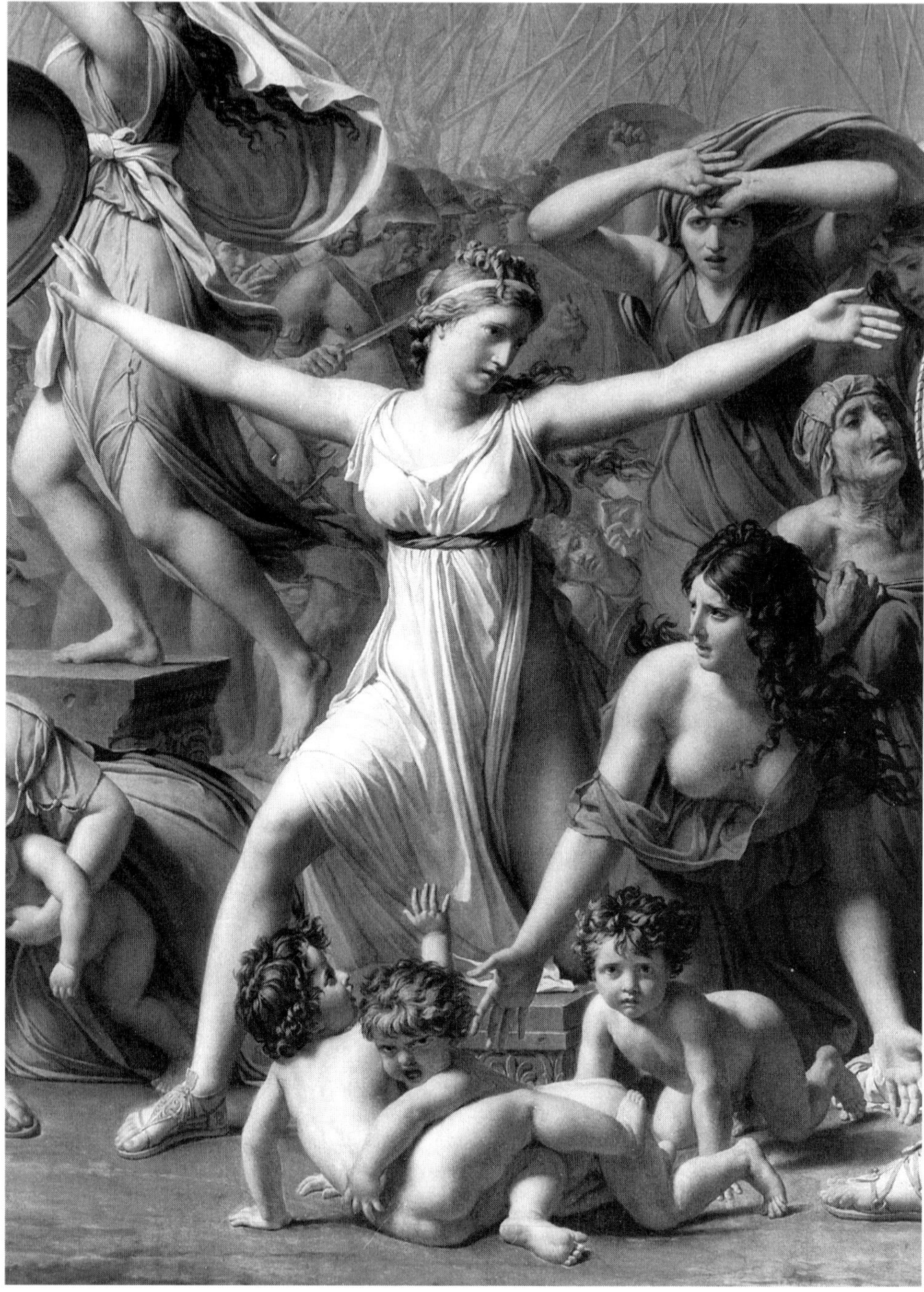

Figure 8.2. Jacques-Louis David, *Intervention of the Sabine Women*, 1799, detail. Oil on canvas. Musée du Louvre, Paris. (Photo: Réunion des Musées Nationaux/Art Resource, New York.)

tempted to distance its effect from the unruly reception of popular spectacle; the *Sabines*, he argued,
stunned the multitude into "religious silence."[14] Thus
David's painting at once revealed and reconciled
class divisions, not only by gathering all people before the painting but by transforming the behavior of
the "crowd" into something more closely resembling
dignity. The familial drama—women's emotional
intervention between ennobled men *à l'antique*—
drew the crowd before the painting, and this was
good. But the fit between crowd and female emotional
expressivity needed to be mediated, even transformed, by an intervening model of appropriate noble behavior. That onerous burden was born by Hersilia (fig. 8.2).

Like other critics, Chaussard praised this woman
in white for her noble status.[15] Hersilia was distinguished from the women who surround her not only
by her ideal character and beauty but by "the dignity
of her suffering, the highest trait characterizing a being and a spirit outside the common condition." By
contrast, the women who rush forward, disheveled,
with burning tears and uncovered breasts expressed
"passions in common conditions or vulgar persons."[16]
Chaussard was right to differentiate Hersilia from her
emotive chorus. In David's painting, the central heroine at once divides the warring men from each other
and protects the audience from the hurling propulsion
of the expressive female figures. Hersilia stands, legs
and arms outstretched, like a dam containing the tor-
rent of disorder behind her. Only her left hand fails
to reach Romulus's shield; this is the weakest point of
containment, and the women and children pour forth
through the opening, the babies tumbling like waves
onto the foreground strip of earth.

Chaussard and David alike relied on Hersilia to
mediate between nobility and vulgarity, between the
inexpressive, stilted male heroes and the emotional female chorus. Given her pivotal role in the reconciliation of antitheses, it comes as no surprise that David
struggled long and hard to give her form and was
never fully satisfied. In a series of preparatory drawings, the painter progressively tidied up and contained
the agitated rhythms of her figure. While her flapping

hair and the rippling waves of her bodice initially ra-
diated out from her form, in the final painting hair and
costume are circumscribed, polished, and made to adhere closely to the smooth orbs of her head and
breasts. Hersilia is increasingly likened to the two
male protagonists in position, scale, and pose, the parallel disposition of their legs establishing a powerful
rhythm across the picture's surface (with a final pi-
quant note sounded by the leg of the twisting ephebe
who retreats at right). Conjoining the painting's female and male perpendicular axes, Hersilia's cruci-
form figure is, therefore, the very fulcrum of the composition. As the solitary embodiment of feminine
nobility, she alone forces women's propelling expressivity into the static horizontal frieze of artful
masculine display.

Chaussard's criticism of the *Sabines* offered a subtle defense of David's classicizing idiom by empty-
ing the male nudes of narrative signification and displacing expressivity as well as temporality onto the
female figures. The women act—they intervene—in
order that the men stop acting and thereby attain the
stasis identified with art. The suspension of the men's
action, the transformation of war into display, permits
the male bodies to become *le beau idéal*. Hersilia's
contradictory role is both to enact intervention and
to stop time. She serves to arrest the male protagonists' activity but also to dam up women's emotive
narrative momentum. In so doing, she is meant to
reconcile the splitting of painting's function into elite
aesthetics (statuary) and popular expressivity (drama).
There were risks to this double move, however. As
the hostile criticism of the *Sabines* attests, Hersilia
could not reliably metamorphose naked men into an
autonomous realm of art, nor could she deflect criticism from her own form. A heroine's noble status at
the interstices of (high) art and (popular) spectacle
was not so easily secured.

Chaussard effectively accommodated the dissension between David and C.Z. concerning male nudity
by reading their aesthetic disagreement as a matter of
class difference. The "grandeur" of nudity, Chaussard implied, went over C.Z.'s head, but the drama of
David's painting was pitched downward to his (unini-

tiated) level. Chaussard attempted to defend classical nudity by segregating it from the wider society as an inviolate realm of *le beau idéal*. For the Republican critic, the greatest achievement of David's painting was its capacity to preserve the (masculine) classical ideal by offering another axis of (feminine) spectacular pathos. But Chaussard's argument ultimately failed to preserve the aesthetic isolation of David's male nudes. Indeed, C.Z.'s voice erupted at the end of his text even as he attempted to refute it. Suddenly, Chaussard, like C.Z., conjured the abhorrent vision of the Frenchman robbed of clothes:

> There is a man who must dread to see himself nude; it is the man of our modern ages, it is the person degraded physically as well as morally, deformed by swaddling, by all the bonds by which he is and continues to be strangled, compressed by his clothes, bent under the ridicule of fashions, branded by idleness, by pleasures and vices.[17]

Nothing could be more loathsome than the sight of modern man stripped bare, not because he would be humiliated before his servants but because his body had been permanently inscribed by his (vulgar) cultural practices, particularly fashion. Unlike David's figures, contemporary man had been degraded physically as well as morally by his sartorial habits, by swaddling clothes, by all his confining bonds. The male body of the French nation was deformed, bent, branded, and strangled. Chaussard's rhetorical violence, recalling the character of Revolutionary debates, bespoke particular anxiety concerning the bodies of France's newborn male citizens.[18]

During the Revolutionary period, pleasure and vice had been associated with the falsity of the aristocracy's makeup and powdered wigs, but Chaussard's rhetoric does not target specific social classes. Instead, his criticism is leveled at the deformation of a whole and intact masculinity by a commodified fashion available to all members of society. Among other things, the Revolution was supposed to have liberated the bodies of French citizens heretofore oppressed by the artifice and social stratification of

ancien régime dress.[19] The paradox, however, was that the Revolutionary investment in the body as a natural sign had ushered in an increasingly arbitrary and ephemeral system of fashion. Unmoored from traditional class privileges, clothing became a matter of invention.[20] Lynn Hunt has described the Revolutionary preoccupation with the decoration of the body as an attempt to achieve transparency (clothing directly signifying the interiority of the Revolutionary self).[21] But to invent Revolutionary signs— whether sartorial or political—was to engender an atmosphere of intense competition and rapid obsolescence, a habitual restless revolution. Although the Republic expended enormous resources to legitimate itself, the result was a more conspicuous notion of transience.

Fashion's pace of innovation and obsolescence further accelerated during the Directory. Never before had dress changed so quickly. In 1799, one critic bemoaned the speed with which *la mode* ruined families, marriages, and virtuous women.[22] Chaussard too, in a social commentary of 1798, likened fashion to the winds.[23] The provisionality and arbitrariness of fashion did not represent an evacuation of political signification, however. Indeed, dress during the Directory became an explicit marker of political allegiances. While the male members of the Royalist so-called golden youth, those post-Thermidor dandies known as the *muscadins* and *incroyables*, expressed their resistance to the Republican government by a flamboyant elaboration of English styles, the radical *exclusifs* flaunted an opposing set of sartorial signifiers. Within this highly inventive and politicized semiotic system, the Royalists' black collars were read against the Jacobins' red collars, the counter-revolutionaries' long hairstyles, replete with *oreilles de chien*, against the Jacobins' short haircuts *(les têtes tondues)*.[24] In such a factionalized climate of rapid experimentation, contemporary dress clearly offered no single "national" set of markers. Like French society, it was splintered into dissenting camps.

No wonder Chaussard celebrated David's male nudes! Here was an ideal distanced from the volatile inconstancy of ephemeral social practices, fashion foremost among them. Nudity *à l'antique* proposed a certainty, a truth untouched by the continual revolution of style.[25] Nudity, so the argument went, stood outside time. Nonetheless, Chaussard's outburst betrays him: "There is a man who must dread to see himself nude; it is the man of our modern ages, . . . bent under the ridicule of fashions." To describe nudes in terms of contemporary Frenchmen's bodies, even in order to oppose them, is to admit to their relation. Nudity *à la grecque* inevitably leads to the specter of nakedness in turn-of-the-century France. And even the naked body, according to Chaussard, was inscribed by its cultural and historical specificity; it was branded and deformed by its social practices. There was no retrievable general, ideal sign among real bodies. David's shift to male nudity from the antique dress of his pre-Revolutionary paintings, such as *Oath of the Horatii* and *Brutus*, appears to have been difficult to defend.

DAVID'S NUDES

In the criticism of David's *Sabines*, the nude male heroes were viewed, on the one hand, as metaphoric idealizations, whole and complete classical nudes; on the other hand, as literal and veristic men stripped of clothes. David's painting itself must be held responsible for the polarized interpretations it engendered: the *Sabines* provoked debate about the status of nudity by juxtaposing two very different naked male figures. One of these differences has been lost due to modifications David made to the canvas in 1808. Until that date, the frontal figure of Tatius displayed genitals. Although the painting now deploys the scabbard like the almost comical contrivances of drapery featured in *académies*, there was initially no such phallic displacement. Today the plunging penile scabbard draws rather than deflects attention, particularly given the pendulous descent of no less than three legs from Tatius's covered genitals, but in 1799 Tatius's uncensored nudity also elicited comment, for instance by the English visitor Henry Redhead Yorke: "Tatius is displayed full to the view *in puris naturalibus*. He also wears not only a helmet and san-

dals, but carries a shield and a scarlet mantle buckled upon the breast, but so contrived as to exhibit his whole body in a state of nature."[26] In a tradition in which shading and drapery served gently to veil the genitals, David's use of props accentuated their presence in a way that seemed to Yorke less natural than contrived.

Before the 1808 modifications, the Sabine warrior Tatius was a far more exposed and vulnerable figure than Romulus, the Roman half-god. All that remains hidden to the spectator in the back view of Romulus was displayed in the frontal figure of Tatius. Although the two men stand in mirrored opposition, with Hersilia as the whitened screen between them (and their ephebic equerries as their bracketing complements), their intimate pairing only highlights their differences.[27] Tatius, the mortal man, consists of an awkward, disjointed set of limbs appended to a short and broad stump of a torso. He is, moreover, strangely asymmetrical. His bent right arm and leg compress that side of his body into a compact unit enclosed by the length of the extended sword. By contrast, his left arm and leg are extended but appear no less awkward; both their lengths are segmented by the straps of the shield and the clinging woman. Our view of Tatius's grasp of the underside of the shield underscores his full visibility—we see the length of his arm submitted to the mechanical requirements of his armor (like a mounted specimen in a trompe-l'oeil painting). Such details imbue this slightly scowling, naked warrior with a poignantly prosaic quality. Gravity and tactility play their part. Tatius's disproportioned but volumetric body seems cumbersome, a burden to move through space, and the metal weapons such heavy and unforgiving weights. David's technical difficulties further exacerbate our sense of the figure's awkwardness. The arm holding the shield is ambiguously attached to the oversize shoulder; the diminutive head appears to retreat from the clumsy tangle of drapery, straps, and bulging muscles at right.

The half-god Romulus, by contrast, is quite successfully understated. Our sense of his completeness and perfection is produced, paradoxically, by the concealment of his body seen from the back. Deep shadows and a series of substitute forms occlude the visibility of his anatomy. Unlike the dark, concave oval held by Tatius (is it an oval or a foreshortened circle?), Romulus's luminous and beautifully convex circular shield hides most of his torso as well as his left shoulder and arm. Gently kissing the graceful curve of his silhouetted waist, the perfect circle stops exquisitely short of severing his body in two and casts the right half in shadow, rendering it an abstracted and graceful set of undulating contours. While Tatius is evenly lit, only a slicing edge of Romulus catches the light and offers a glimpse of flesh. The flat treatment, even tonality, and apparent lack of acuity in the shaded side of his body muffle his corporality, but nonetheless heighten the eroticism of the softly modeled orbs of his buttocks—so perfectly echoing the softly protruding sphere of the shield as well as the vertically disposed sword's sheath. By contrast, the harshly thrusting sword and scabbard that bracket Tatius's genitals underscore rather than mitigate our sense of his vulnerability. The juxtaposition of implements of war and naked male anatomy makes Tatius seem more defenseless. His flesh is assailable. Romulus is protected and fortified by the phallic substitutes for mere anatomy because the all-too-human referents of corporal specificity are cloaked.[28]

If David's brochure assimilated Tatius and Romulus as antique nudes, his painting provoked argument about nudity by offering disparate models of the unclothed body. Unlike Romulus, Tatius failed to repress the artist's toil before a weary model encumbered by props. By betraying his status as a naked model, the Sabine warrior proved to be no more than what C.Z. suspected: an undressed Frenchman, Chaussard's body branded and inscribed by the deformations of contemporary practices. Thus, while Romulus's seamless figure bolstered classicists' arguments about nudity's ideality, Tatius's clumsy form fueled critics' hostility regarding the absurdities of nakedness. David's painting was far more complex than his published defense would allow. It seems that neither David nor critics like C.Z. were capable of addressing both Tatius and Romulus at once.

If the male nudes were inherently controversial, Hersilia draped in white, like her sisters in David's pictures of the 1780s, would seem to offer an acceptably chaste classical counterpoint. Here, at least, David seems to have taken no risks and sustained his pre-Revolutionary iconography of female dress. While nudity could not keep contemporary references at bay, authentic archaeology might. Significantly, however, the English visitor Henry Redhead Yorke was compelled to slip into modish French in order to describe Hersilia's dress: "Between these two figures stands Hersilia; she is robed in white *à la grecque*, in other words according to the present fashion."[29]

David maintained his pre-Revolutionary style of female costume in *Intervention of the Sabines*, but Frenchwomen's clothing practices had changed radically since the mid 1780s. In 1783, a critic could oppose contemporary women's toilette to the noble simplicity of an ancient statue "*à la grecque*, very beautiful, with an antique air, costume and form of the most exquisite purity, a virginal and primitive expression, and who seemed to be neither of our nation nor of our century."[30] But by the late 1790s, the woman attired *à la grecque* was removed neither in space nor in time. Far from securing history painting's decorous distance from current social practices, classical garb offered a point of contact between past and present. David himself was largely responsible for this collapse of high art and ephemeral fashion. The example of his paintings combined with his impact as Revolutionary iconographer had encouraged a pervasive adoption of classical dress, particularly by women. Fashionable women were consciously modeling themselves on the female protagonists populating David's major pre-Revolutionary tableaux.[31] Paris was filled with Camillas and the daughters of Brutus. Portraits like David's *Henriette de Verninac* (1799) corroborate the evidence of contemporary fashion plates that Frenchwomen had appropriated the antique attire previously adorning allegorical personifications and classical history painting's heroines (fig. 8.3). Prior to the Revolution, women had mas-

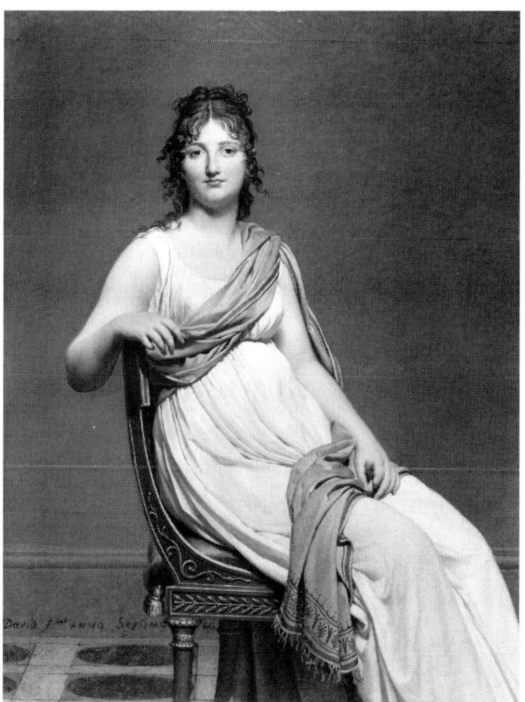

Figure 8.3. Jacques-Louis David, *Portrait of Henriette de Verninac*, 1799. Oil on canvas. Musée du Louvre, Paris. (Photo: Réunion des Musées Nationaux/Art Resource, New York.)

queraded as Flora for their portraits or had theatrically enacted the classical past at parties, most notably, Elisabeth Vigée-Lebrun's famous *souper à la grecque* in 1788.[32] By the late 1790s, however, dress *à l'antique* had become everyday garb rather than an elite's occasional fantasy costume.

Hersilia stands, therefore, not only as the solitary embodiment of ennobled femininity in David's picture but also as its most chic protagonist. Of all the figures within the painting, she most closely resembles members of the audience. If Hersilia bore the burden of integrating elite and popular viewers, what are the implications of her attire's simultaneous reference to the past and to the present? How did her up-to-date stylishness *à la grecque* inflect her status as ennobled heroine? And what was the relationship between her contemporaneity and the volatile interpretations of the male nudes who bracket her?

Nudity *à la grecque* has seemed thus far to concern

the status of male nudes. However, within Directory debates about fashion, classical nudity was associated above all with the increasing visibility of female, not male, bodies. Women's negating sartorial strategies at the very outset of the French Revolution had metamorphosed in the late 1790s into a flirtation with dress that approached undress. On September 7, 1789, women had donned simple white gowns and donated their ornaments to the state in an attempt to distance themselves from compromising associations of femininity with aristocratic ostentation.[33] However, renunciation too is a fashion choice. Negation leads from the excesses of ornamentation to the excesses of revealed flesh; modesty occupies some indeterminable midpoint. During the Directory, the appropriation of Greek attire evoked the Revolutionary prescription of female chastity but transgressed it, playfully manipulating but quite wittily rejecting the virtuous role imposed on women throughout the Revolution. The staid, classically draped figure of Republican Liberty had always been vulnerable to mocking commentary about women's lasciviousness (fig. 8.4).[34] During the hedonistic days of the Directory, the shift from liberty to license seemed all too inevitable. Much ink was spent mocking women's "liberty" to be seen in public *sans chemise*, that is, without underclothing.[35] In addition, Grecian gowns had become increasingly light and transparent, as can be seen in numerous portraits, including a 1799 portrait by Eulalie Morin of Juliette Récamier (Château de Versailles) dressed in such a thin robe *à la grecque* that her breasts and nipples, like Hersilia's, are quite clearly visible. In a witticism of the period, women were flattered for being "well undressed" rather than "well dressed."[36] A party game involved disrobing in order to determine which woman's costume, including shoes, weighed the least.[37] A number of contemporary paintings, including those by Louis-Léopold Boilly (see fig. 8.6 below), feature women whose gauzy outfits and abbreviated undergarments reveal not only arms and cleavage but also, through the transparent fabric, the fleshy length of their legs, in some cases deceptively covered by flesh-colored tights.[38]

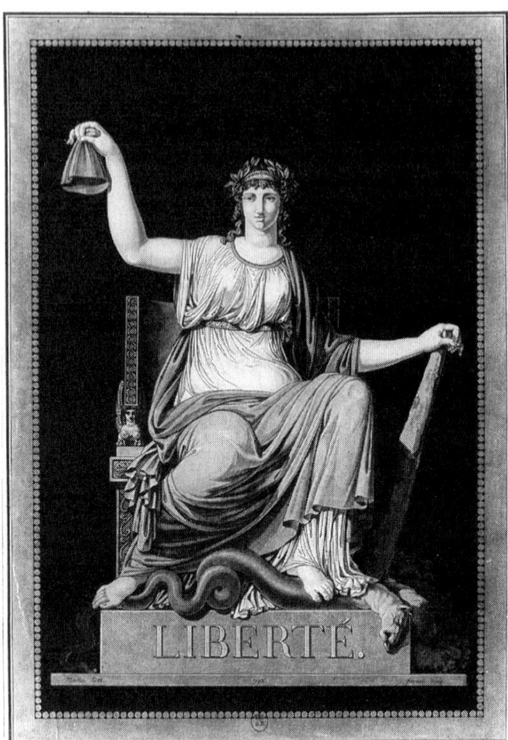

Figure 8.4. Jean-François Janinet after Jean Guillaume Moitte, *Liberty*, 1792. Engraving. (Photo: Bibliothèque nationale de France, Paris.)

In the late 1790s, nudity was self-consciously performed by women as an intriguing game of revelation and deception. The scandals associated with the period's most fashionable women are famous. Was it Mme Hamelin or Mme Tallien who promenaded in the Champs-Elysées "half-nude," arms and throat revealed, a gauzy cloth covering flesh-colored stockings in order to fabricate a glimpse of her nakedness? That an honest man was forced to rescue this exhibitionist from a jeering crowd offered the press a moralizing pretext to tell the story.[39] But other reports indicate that this fashion was hardly circumscribed to the chic elite: "Nine-tenths of women are dressed in white and very negligently assembled. A very small number seem to be occupied with their toilette, and they are distinguished by bearing their shoulders and a part of their back nude."[40]

Not surprisingly, the *citoyennes* who walked through the public gardens in transparent, gauzy draperies invited denunciations of the classical style on the basis of extra-aesthetic criteria. In such attacks, classical garb was deemed inappropriate to the French climate because it belonged to a different geography and therefore a different culture. In 1798, for example, a doctor named Désessarts argued in the press that "he had seen more young girls die since the [adoption] of *nudités gazées* than in the last forty years."[41] In 1799 another physician, Victor Broussonet, condemned the unhealthiness of women's appropriation of flimsy classical garb in his brochure *De la mode et des habillements*. Broussonet argued that Frenchwomen were foolish to adopt the minimal cladding of ancient Mediterranean cultures in the chilly climate of Paris: "Respiratory inflammation, colds, the suppression of menses have been the result of these *revolting nudities*. Our women, in imitation of the Romans, have discovered breasts and shoulders."[42] On September 7, 1799, only months before the exhibition of the *Sabines*, the journal *Le Publiciste* described another doctor's attempt to dissuade women from exposing themselves to such dangers: "In order to dissuade women from the furor of appearing almost nude in our gardens, doctor Angrand . . . is going to collect a great number of histories of grave illnesses, often fatal, occasioned by the usage of clothing *à la grecque*."[43] Less than two weeks later, the *Journal de Paris* published a letter to the editor from the Institut member Louis-Mathieu Langlès, who, despite his Republican commitments, expressed hostility toward women's adoption of antique costume.[44] Again medical reasons were marshaled, but Langlès emphasized morality rather than health.

> For a long time the moral and physical disadvantages of the Greek costume when worn in a humid and variable climate like ours have been pronounced by men of art and men of good sense. Women themselves have more facts and observations about this than those collected by all the doctors of this *Faculté*; but experience is of no use to them just as it often is no use to us, and nothing is less astonishing. What do dangers and even death

mean to those who dare to risk modesty, a sentiment more important to this [feminine] sex than self-preservation? Whether one dresses *à la grecque* or *à la romaine*, I dare predict it will never produce Cornelias.[45]

Langlès's argument registers the contradictions of post-Revolutionary French culture: the experimental identification with antiquity as an exemplary model coexisted with an increasing suspicion of its outward signs. Cornelia is virtuous, but dressing like her has its moral and physical risks. Appropriating gowns *à l'antique* will not transform Frenchwomen into their virtuous ancient counterparts; in fact, quite the contrary. The mere choice to dress *à la grecque* was proof of a lack of modesty. If women's donation of jewels in 1789 had equated the virtuous self-sacrifice of Roman women with their simple white clothes, such a conflation of antique clothing and exemplary behavior was no longer possible in 1799. Classical dress now appeared as a particularly exhibitionist and immoral fashion choice, and one, moreover, that leveled the differences between women in troubling ways.

In 1799, Pierre-Louis Roederer, one of the most eloquent critics of women's classicizing fashion, conjured the dissolution of traditional distinctions among women in the new circulation of revealed body parts. According to this Republican theorist, all women were far too willing to flaunt their flattering features: "The assembly of women is not as varied. There are no longer the old, no longer the ugly. Those who do not have a figure have such a beautiful throat! Those who do not have a [beautiful] throat have such beautiful arms! Here, all is youth, from the age of sixteen to sixty years."[46] Whether young or old, Frenchwomen were being sexualized by their titillatingly skimpy and diaphanous garb. Of course, the effaced distinctions between women were not only those of age and relative beauty. A woman's virtue also could no longer be read by her dress. Flesh apparently eroticized women equivalently; differences of morality were not inscribed upon their bodies. As a government surveillance report of 1798 made clear, all women, whether prostitutes at the Palais Royal or vir

tuous daughters and wives, were revealing themselves. The honest woman had ceased to offer the dishonest woman a model for emulation.[47]

Ultimately, however, the greatest threat posed by women's new exhibitionism was not their impact upon other women, but the power they inappropriately wielded over men. Roederer, for one, understood fashion to be the means by which women exercised their "empire."[48] This was not merely a matter of women's seduction of men, but of their substitution of tyranny for Republicanism. Ephemeral fashion is by definition antithetical to timeless law. The stakes were self-evident: as long as women— immoral, fashionable, fickle, and tyrannical—were prominent there could be no (fraternal) Republic.

> It is the independence of women's morals that has given them the authority of fashion *[la mode]*. As long as women are spectacles in performances, nymphs in promenades, and goddesses in their palace, there will not be a republic in France. In vain will the constitution have been established in accordance with the distinction of political powers; there will always be a power opposed to all others, and that is fashion. Fashion will always combat laws, because laws, if only because they are always a serious thing, can never be *à la mode*. One can attribute the morals of the European republics of Switzerland and Holland to the impotence of women to exercise the empire of fashion.[49]

What particularly disturbed Roederer was the way women insidiously exercised power in culture that they were not allowed to wield in Republican government. "What a contradiction! You refuse women all political existence, which is very just, and yet you permit all our habits to be based on their example!"[50]

By allowing women to exercise their empire over fashion, men were following their example. If we think back to Chaussard's invective concerning degraded modern man, we can better appreciate his emphasis on the Frenchman suffocating under his stylish layers. However, to argue that man was emas

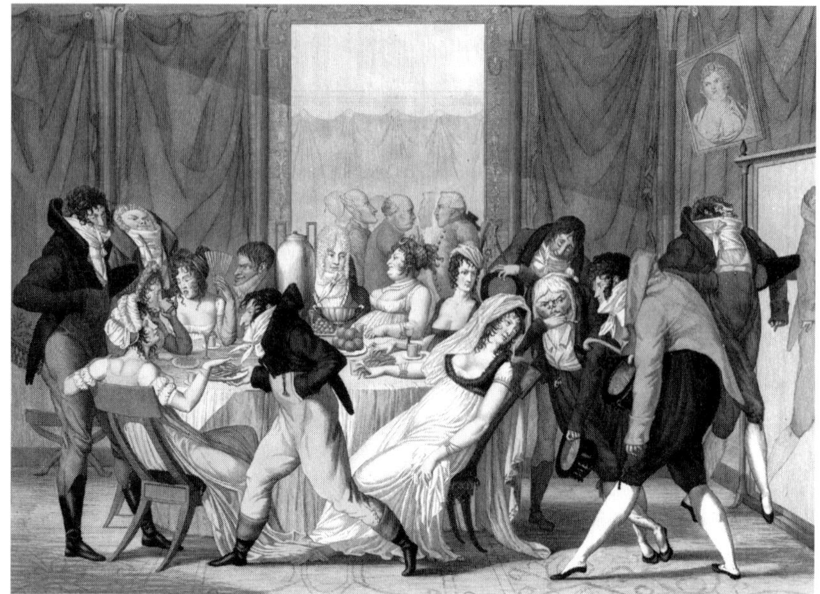

Figure 8.5. Adrien Godefroy after E. J. Harriet, *The Parisian Tea*, ca. 1799. Engraving. (Photo: Bibliothèque nationale de France, Paris.)

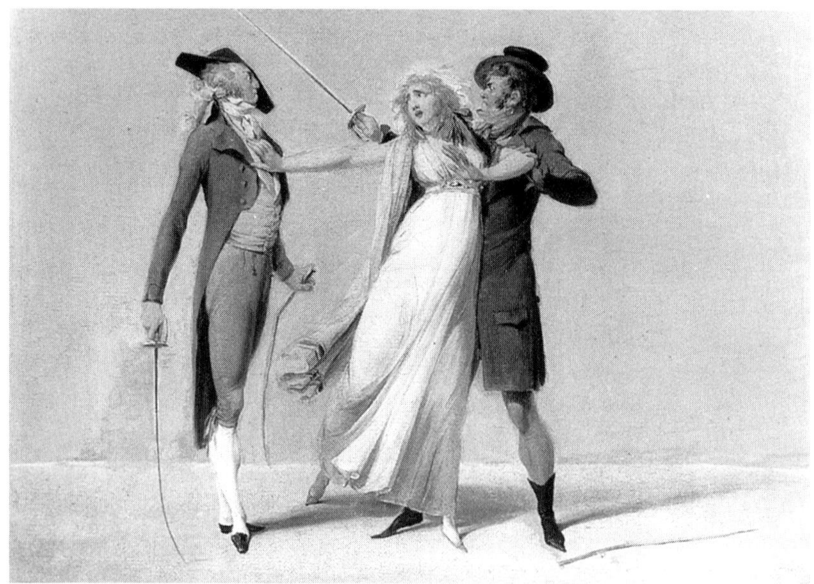

Figure 8.6. Louis-Léopold Boilly, *Make Peace*, from the series *Follies of the Day*, 1797. Oil on canvas. Private collection.

culated by succumbing to feminine fashion is to occlude a source of greater anxiety during this period. In fact, the Directory witnessed a dramatic divergence in female and male fashion (figs. 8.5, 8.6).[51] Men were drowning under their accretions of fabric, while women increasingly discarded them. Even as female citizens approached a state of nudity, men were encasing their bodies, eclectically appropriating English fashion either as a sober self-presentation or, through exaggeration, as the contrary: an excessively self-indulgent and effete sensuality that emphatically renounced Republican sobriety. The male *incroyables*, admittedly the most extreme example, swaddled their outsize physiques in ample layers of clothing and loosely fitting boots and wrapped their "delicate" necks in voluminous scarves, framed by huge collars that rose up the backs of their heads. Though clean-shaven, the *incroyables'* faces were hidden by long fluffy hair, which hung down in strands along the jaw like "dogs' ears," and sometimes by large circular eye-glasses (worn whether needed or not). An *incroyable's* attire and coiffure covered most of his face and body, rendering the protruding nose and jaw excessively prominent, penile and obscene—tips of flesh emerging from the swaddled and exaggerated length of the neck. During the Directory, there was reason to believe that men's bodies had been deformed (and perversely eroticized) by the accretions that enveloped and all but overwhelmed them.

Fashion, then, may have been associated with women, but a most disturbing deception had been enacted. Men's bodies, not women's, were bearing the weight of artifice; they were sinking within its perverse folds and crevices, while women had co-opted the masculine Republic's vision of classical simplicity. To condemn women's preoccupation with fashion was partly to deflect attention from the ways in which male bodies had been more dramatically transformed by *la mode*. If men were being suffocated by artifice, women had gallingly appropriated nudity, that former signifier of the masculine *beau idéal*.

This had no small implications for the authority of classicism in post-Revolutionary France. The status of *nudité à l'antique* was profoundly compromised by its appropriation by women. No longer a term outside contemporary social practices, nudity itself had been subsumed within the provisional, politicized, and arbitrary semiotics of a feminized fashion. Certainly, nudity was thereby trivialized, but it was also subjected to criticism on the basis of pragmatic criteria. How startling to worry that classical figures might become chilly or catch cold! Associated with modish strategies of female seduction, antique signifiers like nudity were now condemned on the basis of their inappropriateness to post-Revolutionary France, a place at once cold, damp, and desperately in need of a stringent morality to replace the loss of the Church.

By donning classical attire, women had complicated and intensified long-standing debates France was in the process of deciding. Could classicism represent the French nation? Was classicism universal in purchase, as David assumed, or only archaeologically specific to a time and place? Could it represent all people or only an initiated elite? Did classicism offer a secular moral foundation in place of religion? When women put on transparent white antique gowns in the 1790s, they rendered frivolous, ephemeral, and interchangeable French culture's most serious, ambitious, and purportedly universal style. They also redefined its politics. For Roederer, nudity was Republican only if it was male. When female, it smacked of the ancien régime. Indeed, Roederer saw the female usurpation of nudity as a desperate attempt on the part of women to recuperate power lost during the Revolution. Women were not only prone to tyranny, they were regressive, wishing no less than a return to France's forsaken past:

> Women have abused clothing to ruin and oppress men . . . but, in abusing nudity, they lose, or at least risk the empire and rights of their charms.
>
> It is because women have seen their domination in France vanish with the monarchy that they have risked even their existence. They did not want the modest happiness of an American, a Swiss, a Genevan; to regain all they have lost, they have staked everything they have, down to their health and soon this everything-goes attitude will [also] be gone.[52]

Roederer spells it out. Women were drawing attention to themselves in order to regain the prominence they had enjoyed under the ancien régime. They would risk anything—even their health—to "ruin and oppress men." Roederer understood nudity to be one step too far in a continuum of fashion wielded by women to dominate men. For women to abuse nudity was to risk their empire, but whether they maintained their power or not, significant damage had been done to the Republic's iconography: nudity *à l'antique* had been metamorphosed into a sign of (feminine) tyranny rather than (masculine) liberty.

The problem, of course, was that classicism had always been Janus-faced: gallant mythologies *à la rococo* competing with stoic and austere histories. David's achievement of a piercingly lucid "virile" idiom capable of representing grave Revolutionary certainties was formidable because it was convincing, but it must be seen as relatively short-lived, bracketed on either side by women's competing appropriations of antiquity. If antiquity in the hands of David could signify the austere absolute truths of Corneille, it could also be Racinian—elegant, pretty, decorative, lightly worn, full of innuendo, playful, witty, even humorous.[53] Behind Apollo Belvedere and heroic Davidian *académies* lurked the specter of Mme du Barry, seeking attention yet again. Less than thirty years had elapsed since her pretentious, oversize portrait "as Muse" had been removed from the Salon walls because of its overly transparent classical gown. What was unacceptable was the way the king's mistress had audaciously mapped antiquity's highest claims onto her own sexualized body.[54]

In discussions of fashion in the press and other ephemeral literature, debates about nudity were commonplace, but within the context of fashion, classicizing nudity was associated with women, not their overdressed male counterparts. In David's *Intervention of the Sabines*, women whose antique gowns fall aside to reveal breasts, legs, and thighs are placed in the midst of naked men. In the painting, women become the dressed term opposed to male nudity, yet their clothing could elicit concerns about current enthusiasms for a lascivious nudity *à la grecque*. How should David's choice simultaneously to invert and to evoke contemporary practices be interpreted? Certainly, the painter's decision to depict his male heroes nude can be seen as an attempt to define nudity *à l'antique* in masculine terms, to salvage *le beau idéal* as a masculine artistic tradition rather than a feminine sartorial invention. The consequences in 1799 of maintaining his pre-Revolutionary female iconography can also be seen as inadvertent: David believed in male nudity, and the moral ambiguity of his female figures was an unintended result of changed circumstances; it was Frenchwomen who

had changed by habitually dressing like his painting's female protagonists.

Nonetheless, David's preparatory drawings suggest that he purposefully modified Hersilia's attire, transforming the flapping layers of her bodice into the final painting's streamlined, clinging white gown, which not only reveals rosy nipples but opens to show the expanse of hips and thigh. If the modifications served partly to circumscribe Hersilia's "vulgar" expressivity, they also made her more fashionable, paradoxically—and here is David's inescapable quandary—both more antique and more up-to-date. The brooch at the shoulder, the enhancement of a sleeveless look, the simple band below her breasts, the archaeological sandals: these were all details recounted in the fashion pages of journals as well as contemporary descriptions of Paris's most visible women.[55] David chose to make Hersilia more chic— more like Mme Hamelin and Mme Tallien promenading in the Tuileries, more like Louis-Léopold Boilly's socialites in his series *Follies of the Day* of 1797 (fig. 8.6).[56] In a series of fine-tuned modifications, the painter enhanced his heroine's resemblance to a community of controversial exhibitionists.

That association of Sabines and prominent, morally ambiguous Directory women could only have been intensified by the circulation of stories concerning the identity of David's nonprofessional female models. Like many of the period's most celebrated women, the sisters de Bellegarde enjoyed the celebrity of beauty wed to scandalous sexual mores. Together, they were famous for their compromising attachment to the world of the studio; they were known, in Etienne-Jean Delécluze's words, "by the singular life they led in the midst of artists of all genres."[57] Brunette Adèle had left her husband and children in the provinces to become a highly visible Parisian mistress. While it was generally acknowledged that she had sat for the bare-breasted, kneeling woman in the *Sabines*, the extent to which she had exposed her body to the painter was a matter of rumor.[58] Jules David even claimed that Adèle, "vain" about her role as model, enjoyed appearing in public with her hair arranged to match that of David's disheveled figure.[59] Married to a defrocked priest, her blonde sister Aurore inevitably invited stories that she had posed for Hersilia.[60] She may have had some competition. According to Jules David, three society ladies volunteered for the part. These then were some of the women of fashion who would have inflected the reception of a painting often characterized as evidence of David's newly purified, aesthetic classicism.[61] Imagine such nouveaux riches moving through the *Sabines* exhibition space, appreciating their chic couture and their resemblance to David's heroine reflected in the wall-length mirror, all for the price of a ticket. Could there have been a better showplace to celebrate the spectacular, exhibitionist pleasures of fashion and the erotics of public sociability?

To simplify David's painting into an image of a fractured public sphere reconciled by the intervention of the Sabine women's "private" familial claims is therefore to ignore the controversies surrounding women during the Directory. Although David's painting has been seen as a powerful repression of Revolutionary feminist claims in its alignment of femininity and maternity, that latter equation of women and motherhood was undermined by the painting's foregrounding of women's prominence as public spectacle in Directory France. In late-1790s Paris, women were visibly disrupting the Revolutionary fraternity but not necessarily as mothers. Indeed, this was the source of anxiety. Roaming spaces outside the home, women seemed neither securely constituted by nor constitutive of familial bonds. Modern scholarship that takes for granted women's role as representatives of the private sphere is therefore repeating a reactionary prescription, not a reality of post-Revolutionary society.[62] Thinkers like Roederer and Louis-Sébastien Mercier championed female domesticity in response to Frenchwomen's perceived failure to identify themselves with such duties. Ultimately, *Intervention of the Sabines* could not circumscribe women's prominence to their familial roles. Hersilia and her emotive chorus were, above all, offering a public performance of those bonds. Unlike the women in *Oath of the Horatii* and *Brutus,* who were confined to domestic spaces, the Sabine women

were intended to be moving spectacles within the public sphere of the ancient battleground as well as the Directory entrepreneurial exhibition space.

In post-Thermidor France, women's visibility seemed not only to flaunt their difference from men but also to be the very source of their power and dominance. For a Revolutionary like Roederer, the difference of women only too clearly represented a difference of politics, the haunting specter of the fraternal Republic's antithesis: women's lawlessness—like fashion, like tyranny, like immorality—fully outside men's lawful governance. How, then, could David's *Intervention of the Sabines* propose that the fashionable woman serve as an exemplary model? Was this what Revolutionary utopian aspirations had come to? Was France now hostage to promiscuous, unregulated women like the Bellegarde sisters, Fortunée Hamelin, Thérésia Tallien, Josephine Beauharnais, and Anne-Françoise Lange?[63] It was only too evident that dress, not virtue, was inspiring general imitation. And the distinction of modishness, unlike that of virtue, perpetually needed to outrun those "nine-tenths" of Frenchwomen who acted as copycats. To be a role model because one is chic is to keep moving at the head of a crowd. The exemplarity of fashion, rather than offering France a bedrock foundation of values, only perpetuated a meaningless overturning of signs.

David was working with volatile materials here: at once exploiting antiquity's fashionability and, like Chaussard, trying desperately to buttress a tradition of the classical masculine *beau idéal* that had long served as the foundation of his art as well as his politics. In 1799, Hersilia would not behave herself. There was no way David could make her into the "neutral" emblem of noble maternal femininity that she has come to represent for many modern scholars. This is not to say that David as painter and as author of the accompanying brochure did not try to control her disruptive and competing force by diminishing its value relative to the masculine nudes. As Chaussard noted, *Intervention of the Sabines* aligns masculinity with timelessness and femininity with temporality.[64] The picture not only opposes masculine stasis (the horizontal frieze) to female action (the intersecting narrative eruption), but also male nudity to female fashion. It is against women's ephemeral appropriation of nudity that David's publication on "the nudity of [his] heroes" must be interpreted. The painter's text directs attention to the male nudes and renders the female figures invisible. According to David's brochure, women's choices were not at issue. Instead, viewers were invited to contemplate, admire, discuss, even debate male nudity. If the picture's female protagonists could elicit much informal commentary—gossip—about their dress and identity, the male bodies, David cues us, warrant serious critical discussion. Both painting and brochure spotlighted Hersilia's bracketing male counterpoints, but they did so partly by heightening their controversy. Tatius particularly was meant to goad. David relied upon the shock value of men's exposed flesh and genitals in the midst of dressed figures to direct his startled audience's attention toward his male heroes.

But this reliance on shocking masculine display points to the instability of the painting's gendered structural oppositions. For Chaussard, stasis signified a realm of aesthetic ideality contrasted to women's vulgar and disorderly activity; yet that stillness also resembled the exhibitionism associated with fashion. Tatius and Romulus were subject to being read, like fashionable women, as flamboyant if foolish exhibitionists, resorting to extremism to draw attention to themselves. Given the fashionability of the Sabine women and the prevalence of images like Boilly's *Make Peace* (fig. 8.6), would not viewers have been predisposed to see Hersilia as a chic Frenchwoman separating her competing lovers, who suddenly, inexplicably, and quite extravagantly discard their suits? Would not that wall-length mirror opposite the painting only enhance this sense of the painted men's suddenly exposed nakedness? David, Chaussard, and Roederer may have insisted that the male nudes were like law—that is, timeless and universal—but these heroes could also be interpreted as men who strove to make the most ostentatious of fashion choices.[65]

WHEN MALE AND FEMALE NUDITIES MEET

In *Intervention of the Sabines*, David offered an unstable encounter and made it the very basis of his work's controversy, as well as its success. This was a risqué confrontation between competing gendered aesthetic and political models: between contemporaneity and history, between fashion and *le beau idéal*, between the ancien régime and the Republic. But the multivalence of the term *nudité à la grecque* in 1799 attests to the incapacity of such categories to remain discrete. Even if attention could be diverted from the spectacle of women to the male nudes, those nudes were now embedded within a public sphere (and pictorial syntax) newly defined to include women, and women, moreover, who were *à la mode*. The presence of stylish women inflected the ways the male nudes were received. Next to fashionable females, the standing male *académies* now appeared undressed. They also appeared as objects of women's vision.

Thus far, my argument has for the most part treated the masculine and feminine versions of nudity *à la grecque* as independent entities, but David's painting is about their intimate if anxious confrontation. Note, for instance, Hersilia's guarded, strangely birdlike, darting glance at that peacock Romulus. One pupil distended, the other diminished and rushing away, her glassy-eyed gaze fails to cohere. While her near eye seems directed toward us, the far eye retreats to the side, its iris sitting up too high and too small, cut both by its profile edge and the overemphasized slice of white. Stare too closely and Hersilia appears wall-eyed. Look also at the similarly hooded and ambiguously muffled, asymmetrical gaze of the older woman who faces Romulus and threatens to tear off her gown and expose her breasts. Here are women in states of undress looking upon a displayed male nude; in fact, they are the only figures gazing at Romulus's exposed body. It is difficult, however, to assess precisely where they look and what they see there. They alone enjoy access to Romulus's other side, that presence or absence lurking behind (or eclipsed by?)

shield and sheath. As viewers by proxy, they heighten the suspense attending Romulus's withheld body. Their oddly uninformative but directed gazes, coupled with Tatius's frontality, compel the question: should the viewer project Tatius's anatomy onto the half-god's front, assembling his body part by part (shoulder, arm, chest, hardened stomach, genitals) in an attempt to reconstruct the man as seen by the women? To do so is to enact imaginatively a homoerotic identification of the two men's bodies, but such a projection also subtly compromises the half-god with the doubts unfurled by the awkward, "naked" specificities and vulnerabilities of his foil. Undermined is Romulus's status as an indivisible, autonomous signifier of phallic perfection, completeness, and power. Significantly, women's viewing initiates the process.

In David's painting, women are the privileged beholders not only of a god (and rapist cum husband) but also of the masculine *beau idéal*. While the homoerotic appeal of solitary naked male figures like *Bara* rendered the female viewer invisible and irrelevant, David's insertion of the Sabine women into the frame of male nudity—indeed, a masculinity wavering between ideality and genital particularity seems to have necessitated an anxious appraisal of the relationship of women, sexuality, and the public sphere. If much feminist scholarship has been preoccupied with the male gaze on the female object, especially the female nude, and recent inquiries have focused on the circuit of homoerotic desire for the male viewer of the male nude, the *Sabines* configures a differently gendered confrontation. Few paintings have catalyzed such an anxious contemporary preoccupation with the female viewer of masculine flesh.

David's picture foregrounds the female spectator not only in its privileged positioning of women as viewers of Romulus, but also in its very centerpiece, the explosive woman in red who conspicuously and directly stares at us, thereby wedding aggressivity and female viewing. The confrontational character of her level frontal gaze serves as a counterpoint to both Hersilia's skittish deflected regard and the rolling asymmetry of the old woman's eyes. The power as well as the menace of the woman in red resides in the riveting directness of her stare. But David, even as he so effectively conveys the compelling intercourse between women's viewing and our own, registers the question of its eclipse (or the power of its revelation). Beneath the billowing tent of drapery, the woman's clenched hands, hovering precisely at eye level, threaten to drop (or rise) like a shade over her eyes.

Ultimately, however, the relation between women viewers and the real world appears to have been far less fraught than women's regard of (men's) art. Significantly, the fashionable woman appeared in *Sabines* criticism not as a visible object and erotic spectacle, but as a viewer of art's male nudity. Male critics, both negative and positive, were obsessed with the encounter between actual women and art's male nudes. It is easy to discern the specter of Frenchwomen's confrontation with Tatius's exposed genitals in these interchanges. While negative critics predictably denounced the painting's capacity to compromise female members of its audience, David's supporters repeatedly described the painting's opponents as prudish, unsophisticated, and hypocritical women. For instance, in his review of the *Sabines*, Charles Landon produced a fastidious female spectator in order to dismantle her position. According to Landon, some women wanted Tatius to be further covered, but they were hypocritical in as much as they did not protest the comparable nudity of antique sculptures. If society was to follow the reasoning of these female spectators, it would be necessary to censor all the sculptures in public civic spaces, including the recently arrived spoil of Napoleonic conquest, the *Laocoön*.[66] (Precisely this confrontation between fashionable female viewer and the *Laocoön*'s bulging anatomy delighted Fuseli during the early 1800s [fig. 8.7].) The Royalist critic for the *Journal des Débats*, Jean-Baptiste-Bon Boutard, made a similar point about those who believed that male nudity produced dangerous impressions: "If David's tableau is immoral, it would be necessary to relegate to the shadows of storerooms and museums all the statues

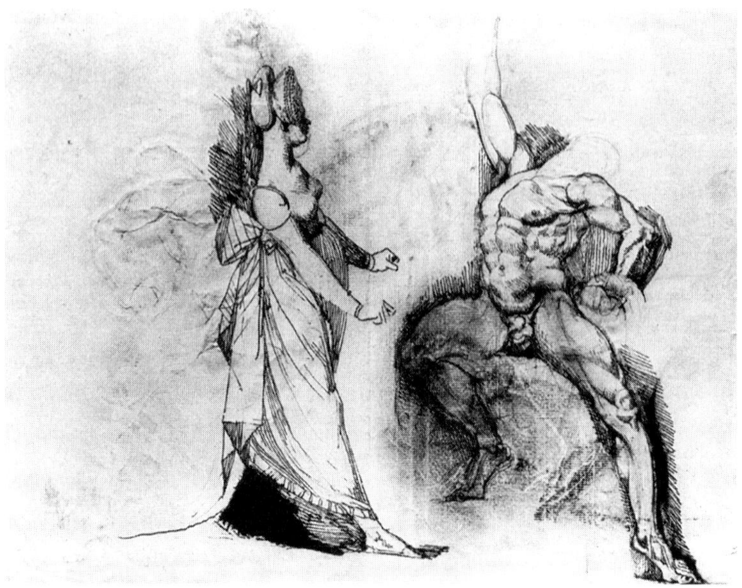

Figure 8.7. Henry Fuseli, Untitled, ca. 1800–1805. Ink on paper. Kunsthaus, Zurich. (Photo: Kunsthaus, Zurich.)

that decorate our public gardens and embellish our palaces."[67]

At stake in these arguments seems to be the status of art itself. Was the presence of the female spectator so decisive that all male nudes could be subject to removal on the basis of morality? Lest one assume that David's supporters exaggerated the extent to which censorship could be enlisted in the name of female modesty, listen to the polemicist Louis-Sébastien Mercier, who, besides condemning women's current antique fashion, also boldly denounced public sculpture by conjuring a young girl's encounter with a titillated Bacchus on the verge of an erection:

> Morality and statues are two incompatible things. And can one regard as illustrious geniuses, or rather as legislators of modesty, those artists whose immodest chisel not only reproduced but even enlarged the sexual parts of statues mutilated by time?
>
> No! It is not a weakness to be scandalized by such nudities. One does not have the right to represent to the eyes of a mother of a family that which one would not dare make audible to her ears; her young daughter walking at her side should not raise her eyes below the lily, symbol of her innocence, to contemplate nude the rounded buttocks of a Bacchus in the spring of his life, and whose amorous visage indicates that he feels the movement of voluptuousness spring up.[68]

Through the young girl's eyes, Mercier sees antique marble metamorphose into pulsating sexual arousal. Whether because of their modesty, their hypocritical prudery, or their licentiousness, women rewrote art and male nudity by (hetero)sexualizing them. Indeed, according to David's negative and positive critics alike, women saw sex everywhere. While the prude may seem the antithesis of the promiscuous undressed woman, both attest to women's incapacity to leave inviolate an aesthetic sphere. Of course, there is no such autonomous realm of "purity." The tension between ideality and eroticism is intrinsic to the representation of naked bodies. But in post-Revolutionary France, the pressure to acknowledge the presence of women viewers made the tensions (and capacious multivalences) inherent in *le beau idéal*—that cobbled-together but cherished fiction—crudely manifest. High art and somatic low could not be held asunder. Perhaps women's presence simply provided a vehicle for men to voice their own fantasies, but the shift from a masculine homoerotic to a feminine heterosexual model of viewing seems to have been decisive. If the antiquarian Winckelmann could eloquently evoke his own "rising" and "heaving" reaction to the sensual pleasures afforded by the *Apollo Belvedere* without compromising the status of aesthetic discourse, no such erotic responsiveness on the part of women could be subsumed within the rubric of aesthetic discrimination in 1790s France.[69] Because it was inextricably bound up with women's sexuality, women's spectatorship threatened to wrench the heroic male nude into the tawdry realm of pornography. Did the mere presence of Hersilia, like Mercier's young girl, elicit imaginings of Romulus's springing "movement of voluptuousness," a movement, moreover, over which he had no control?[70]

Not surprisingly, women's power to compromise the masculine *beau idéal* elicited anger on the part of male critics. Roederer, for one, believed that Mercier's preoccupation with public sculpture was misguided. Women, not male statues, were the problem. In a published letter, he expressed his impatience: "Citizen, you complain to yourself of encountering entirely nude statues of marble or bronze in our public promenades; haven't you seen in our spectacles, our balls, in society, a crowd of figures who were neither of marble nor bronze, even more nude than these statues?"[71] According to Roederer, Bacchus and his inanimate companions had been upstaged. Neither marble nor bronze, women had made themselves into living nudes, nudes moreover who seemed to be proliferating, literally taking over the public spaces of Paris: "Our spectacles, our balls, in society, a crowd." Here was the real irritation. Women were not only competing for attention with male art, they were also pretending to require its removal from view. What! Should gardens no longer feature art's heroic male nudes but become instead the sole province of a crowd of undressed women? Was there no place any longer for art, for marble, for bronze? Had female flesh simultaneously made marble seem flesh, undone its independent status, and in a hypocritical feint, taken its very place? Was this the conspiratorial intention of the alluring half-naked Frenchwomen who hypocritically demanded the covering of Tatius's exposed genitals even as they sought a glimpse in mirrors hidden within their fluttering fans?[72] Certainly the writer of a letter ("To Women dressed *à la Grecque* and *à la Romaine*") published in the *Journal des Dames et des modes* in 1799 recognized their ploy and held them responsible:

> Women have chosen the costume of Psyche, Venus and her nymphs. Dressed in an enchanting manner, they attract and hold our regard. Their breasts whose movements give birth to our desires, whose delicious forms are hardly concealed by a light fabric . . . in order better to draw their voluptuous contours, everything in this new fashion provokes voluptuousness; and yet women complain of the little decency that is preserved near them.[73]

Involuntarily seduced, unfairly accused of indecency, the male critic holds women fully responsible for fixing his regard.

Roederer conflated the nudity of art and the nudity of Frenchwomen. He saw Mercier as a dupe, scapegoating Bacchus in the name of women who themselves made a spectacle of nakedness. Chaussard, by contrast, rebutted accusations that the nudity of David's male protagonists endangered female spectators by significantly differentiating between women's nakedness and art's nudity. Rather than simply claiming superiority to the inhibitions of polite female society, Chaussard was willing to address explicitly the intimate relationship between women's viewing and fears of unregulated female sexuality. The critic who attended to the chorus of "vulgar" women in the picture also spent a great deal of time addressing the effects of David's painting on their female counterparts milling about in front of the picture. Indeed, his defense of nudity solely considered the woman spectator.

With Rousseau and Montaigne to bolster his position, Chaussard argued that the impact of the unknown upon a female imagination was far more dan-

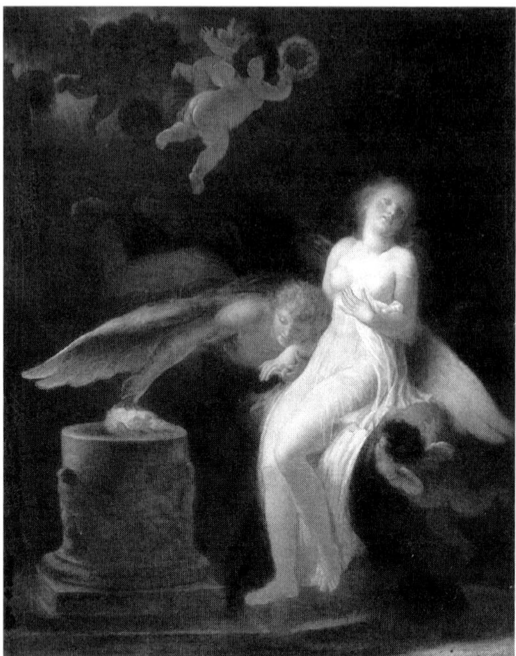

Figure 8.8. Jean-Honoré Fragonard, *Sacrifice of the Rose*, ca. 1785–88. Oil on canvas. Private collection.

gerous than a direct confrontation with the naked male body. A nude fully exposed to the light leads to indifference. Chaussard quoted Rousseau to argue that the partially draped nude produced other effects: "Isn't it known that statues and paintings only offend the eyes when a mixture of clothing renders nudities obscene? The immediate power of the senses is weak and limited: it is by the mediation of the imagination that they make their greatest ravages."[74] David's nudity is opposed to the obscene "mixture" of garments in other kinds of art. The partially clad figure invites the dangers of women's fantasies. Consistent with sensationalist theories of the eighteenth century, Chaussard claimed that habit blunts the power of sense impressions, while imagination is capaciously damaging. Offering a panoply of authorities from Greek philosophy to ethnography to solve the problem of women's "heated" arousal and extravagances, Chaussard emphasized that the education of women was far better than leaving them to guess "according

to the liberty and heat of their fantasy. In place of true parts, women substitute by heat and by hope other parts triply extravagant."[75] (Am I "imagining" this "triply extravagant" version of Tatius's genitals in the trio of legs so weirdly hanging beneath his scabbard?) Confronted with the philosophical and social problem of the female gaze, a revered lineage of great male thinkers all agreed it was better that there be no surprises. Women's presence in David's exhibition space was justified as an Enlightenment project of education.

Chaussard's enlightened sexual discourse inherited the Revolutionary concern that private conduct be transparent to public virtue. His most powerful barbs were reserved for those male hypocrites who, while anxious about the virtue of women in the public exhibition, nonetheless exposed their mothers, wives, and daughters to the lascivious pictures of their private cabinet. Comparing the *Sabines* to Fragonard's *Sacrifice of the Rose*, Chaussard contrasted the public address and virility of classicism's male nudity to the private and libertine Rococo preoccupation with female seduction (fig. 8.8). Produced just before the Revolution and engraved in 1790, Fragonard's lucrative tableau celebrates the loss of a woman's virginity by representing the swooning ecstasy of a female nude whose transparent draperies slide down from her uncovered breasts to wrap around her inner thighs.[76] Eyes rolled back, mouth partly open, the woman's face mimics Greuze's formulaic money-makers, those endlessly insipid, coy girls whose mobile features seem to have lost their anatomical moorings and threaten to slip away (the pictorial melting metaphorically enacting a lubricated onanism). Visually, the contrast to the *Sabines* could not be more startling nor, for David's defender, more effective. How could one accuse David's male nudes of being obscene

when on the contrary it is figures veiled from head to foot who express the action most at odds with decency? Such is this figure who, in the *Sacrifice of the Rose*, swoons next to an altar; such are all these compositions so modern, so libertine, in which preside, for lack of true genius, gross equivocation, and more dangerous than the cynical paintings of Aretino, address themselves less to the senses of vision than to vicious thought, re-awakening all disorders with the aid of seductive allusions, voluptuous signs, sometimes vague and devious, always expressive and licentious. Here, here are indecent compositions that corrupt the heart and trick and pervert the spirit. This man who deploys them in his cabinet under the eyes of his mother, wife and daughter does not fail to proscribe with indignation the nudity of all these half-gods of antiquity who, in their general expression, only recall dignity, virtue, heroism.[77]

So this is the hypocrisy of C.Z.! Indulging in private pornographic debauchery while publicly pretending moral outrage before antique half-gods like Romulus! Lajer-Burcharth has astutely pointed out the ways classicism accrued authority in Chaussard's text by its gendered opposition to Rococo works.[78] But Fragonard's paintings were not the only term against which David's nudes were understood. Chaussard opposed David's forthright nudes to the erotic metonymics of diaphanous garments. If the sensual narratives of those flowing fabrics were expertly enacted by Fragonard's fluid brushwork, they were also, as we know, performed in the promenades of Paris by Frenchwomen dressed *à la grecque*. Significantly, the *nudités gazées* of fashionable *Parisiennes* were less about total revelation (although this was apparently attempted) than about the seductiveness of bodies all but revealed through fabric. In Chaussard's text, the dangers of veiled seduction evoke not only Rococo libertinism but current feminine fashion, that style *à la grecque* now made Rococo, that perversion of the former marker of virtue into a new kind of libertinism.

Roederer was therefore wrong to confuse the nudity of art and the nudity of partly veiled Frenchwomen. Chaussard was not duped by Frenchwomen's appropriation of Greek nudity. Instead, he seized on the differences between female and male nudity *à la grecque* and polarized them: Frenchwomen's half-draped bodies were not the same as marble or painted fully nude gods. Gauzy drapery is seductive because it obscures; it renders unknown—private—parts of the body while teasingly implying their presence and accessibility. Full nudity renders the body public because nothing is hidden from full communal view. C.Z. believed David's figures to be "gratuitously indecent" because they transposed a private state—nakedness (upon which even a servant's gaze impinged)—into a public spectacle. For C.Z., privacy made public was indecent. Chaussard, good Revolutionary that he was, eloquently proposed the inverse: it is privacy—the hidden, the veiled—that is obscene. For Chaussard, even a classically draped heroic male figure could not embody virtue in the ways that a nude could. Only the body revealed speaks truth—particularly, I would add, at a time when even drapery *à l'antique* had become compromised by female sexuality and the license, superficiality, and ephemerality associated with not only the ancien régime but also post-Revolutionary fashion. (Note that Chaussard's opposition of veiled and fully revealed refuses to acknowledge the extent to which Romulus's body was cloaked by his armor. Metal weapons, we must presume, do not "deceive" like the folds of soft muslin.)

Chaussard discussed solely women viewers of male nudity. Rather than valorizing the male viewer of female objects, he was concerned to direct attention to the pictured men as appropriate objects of sight for both sexes. Like David, he seemed to say: look, look at men. Come out, Frenchwomen, from the dangerously secretive viewing afforded by your duplicitous fans. Instead, in public view, look directly at men. Significantly, however, Chaussard's discussion of women's viewing of male nudes led inexorably back to women's draped bodies; female bodies necessarily served as the negative example. In Chaussard's text, women were conjured as veiled bodies and as veiled vision. But while Chaussard attempted to emancipate women's looking, he and his contemporaries could not so much as entertain the notion of women's full nudity. Hersilia may have been compromised dressed *à la grecque*, but no one, not even the committed classicist Chaussard, could "imagine" her stripped bare. If women's gazes could be pedagogically sanitized, there seems to have been no solution to the ways women's bodies were permanently inscribed by sexuality. Draped or bared, woman was never fully public. The Republican valiantly attempted to salvage Romulus and Tatius; he attempted to salvage an audience in which genders and classes mingled; he tried to salvage women's viewing; but the spectacle of Hersilia, the great mediator and intervener in her clinging white gown, continued to pose perplexing problems.

WOMEN'S INTERVENTION

Intervention is no small matter. Women had intervened in 1799, compromising classicism, compromising nudity, compromising the (fraternal) Republic. Women had looked to an artistic tradition that was meant to be exemplary and had imitated its example, but that imitation seemed to many contemporaries to be confined to dress, not virtuous conduct. And to make dress exemplary was fundamentally to overturn the notion of exemplarity as a permanent foundation of timeless values. Much has been made of the ways David's painting inspired masculine emulation on the part of young artists, but that Bloomian tale of sons imitating fathers is not the story most relevant to an understanding of *Intervention of the Sabines*.[79] Women too can emulate, but in 1799 their emulation challenged a lineage—men begetting men, men looking at men—that had bracketed them out. Theirs was not the story admirable Republicans like Chaussard and Roederer hoped to tell their male progeny.

But it is wrong in the end to conflate intervention and emulation; the latter can too easily be denigrated as mindless aping. Women may have appropriated Republican iconography and thereby corrupted it, but even Roederer, who so explicitly denounced women's new tyrannical empire over *la mode,* believed that women were not ultimately their own iconographers.

Their power was not of their making. In 1798, Roederer laid the blame at the door of painters.

> In a promenade, a half-nude woman and others dressed in gauze are more than nude. . . . Yet one must agree that artists have also contributed to this revolution. At the birth of the Republican system, they spoke a lot of Greek girls, and our women took them at their word, for fear that one would speak to them next of Roman women. They were so lovable, these Greek girls, and so boring, these Roman women! One can raise one's daughter to be a Roman woman, but one prefers, oneself, to be a Greek girl.
>
> Truthfully, citizen, there is something very harsh and tyrannical in the authority of painters. Four years ago, they wanted to make us change our habits because ours were not picturesque; they arranged the nation for painting, rather than arranging painting for the nation. Now they amuse themselves dressing our women as models, chilling them, giving them colds, in order more easily to observe the purity of forms in their paintings. Will art benefit from this? I doubt it. It is very agreeable, I imagine, to draw beautiful contours; but isn't it also agreeable to express modesty, chastity, their triumphs, their difficulties, their surrender? Painters of talent! it is in virtues, and not in the license of nudity, that there are treasures for you.[80]

Frenchwomen may have flattered their vanity by fashioning themselves as lissome Greek nymphs rather than sturdy Roman paragons, but, in truth, "tyrannical" painters had initiated this national makeover. In search of sinuous contours, artists were responsible for (un)dressing women, risking their health, and dangerously promoting "the license of nudity" instead of virtue. Women, the author decides, were ultimately the malleable subjects of the dictatorial artist.

There can be little doubt that Roederer writing in the spring of 1798 had David in mind. I do not need to rehearse David's central role as iconographer of the Revolution and pageant-master for Robespierre. During the Directory, "tyrannical painter" would have conjured his name above all. Despite Roederer's certainty that women *à la mode* conspired for power, he finds a way to make David their puppet master. But even as Roederer's text robs women of authorial agency, it also registers the impact of their mimicry. To the extent that "nudity" was now bound to "license," it was also bound to fashionable French-women undressed *à la grecque*. In the controversial reception of David's *Sabines,* theirs was perhaps the most formidable intervention. Of course, what Republican classicism and the masculine *beau idéal* lost in terms of authority, David's coffers won in box-office sales. Although he would not exhibit another classical male nude for fifteen years, the scandal of nudity *à la grecque* in turn-of-the-century Paris amply paid for his country house.[81]

Who, then, risked whose health? At the onset of the Napoleonic Empire, the author of *The Friend of Women, or Letters of a Doctor concerning the influence of the clothing of women upon their morals and health . . .* offered David's example to justify his denunciation of women's loose and revealing clothing, but his parable of 1804 inverts Roederer's tale of 1798. According to this author, the *Sabines* may have made David wealthy, but he had paid the price of his own physical well-being:

> I can only cite with some confidence the works of doctors who are especially devoted to proving the dangers of immorality. Yet there is some reason to infer from the slackness *[la mollesse]* of clothing that of morals, and from the latter a bad influence upon health, when we see David, surrounded by royal luxury and fallen women, struck by a shameful affliction.[82]

By 1804, it seemed clear that Roederer's tyrannical puppet master had fallen into the seductive and regal fold of loose and luxuriant women. Hersilia, it turns out, had led ineluctably to the coronation of Joséphine by a wan, swaddled, and ermine-blanketed

hero. Sick, royal, and feminine, David was ready to paint the *Coronation* for the Salon of 1808. The same year, David, in the midst of painting flowing satins, velvets, and the fashionable stuffs of Empire, succumbed to public approbation and painted over Tatius's genitals.

NOTES

For Gregoria. This essay was based on chapter 4 of my dissertation, "Classicism, Nationalism and History: The *Prix Décennaux* of 1810 and the Politics of Art under Post-Revolutionary Empire," University of Michigan, Ann Arbor, 1995. Scholars seeking more complete documentation, especially additional primary sources and images, should consult the original *Art Bulletin* article. Translations are mine unless otherwise indicated.

1. Stefan Germer, "In Search of a Beholder: On the Relation of Art, Audiences and Social Spheres in Post-Thermidor France," *Art Bulletin* 79 (March 1992): 19–36; Dorothy Johnson, *Jacques-Louis David: Art in Metamorphosis* (Princeton, N.J.: Princeton University Press, 1993), 124–26.

2. Ewa Lajer-Burcharth, "David's *Sabine Women:* Body, Gender and Republican Culture under the Directory," *Art History* 14 (September 1991): 397–430, 413, 424; also see her later revised *Necklines: The Art of Jacques-Louis David after the Terror* (New Haven, Conn.: Yale University Press, 1999); and Erica Rand's 1990 essay "Depoliticizing Women" (chapter 7 in this volume).

3. Musée du Louvre, *Jacques-Louis David, 1748–1825,* exh. cat. (Paris: Réunion des Musées Nationaux, 1989), 336.

4. *Le tableau des Sabines, exposé publiquement au palais national des sciences et des arts . . .* (Paris, an VIII [1799–1800]), 15; cited in Daniel Wildenstein, *Documents complémentaires au catalogue de l'oeuvre de Louis David* (Paris: Fondation Wildenstein, 1973), 150.

5. Several journals assimilated David's private entrepreneurial exhibition to spectacular entertainments subject to a government tax; by 1801, even David's supporter Chaussard criticized such exhibitions. Musée du Louvre, *Jacques-Louis David,* 328–32; for

later controversies, see my "Classicism, Nationalism, and History."

6. *La Décade philosophique* 13 (10 pluviose an VIII [30 January, 1800]). Duval argued that clothed figures should be painted by women and mediocre painters. The Idéologues were self-appointed inheritors of the Enlightenment philosophes who dominated the Institut's Class of Moral and Political Sciences and who lost favor under Napoleon. Concerning the masculine *beau idéal* in this period, see Régis Michel, *Le beau idéal*, exh. cat., Musée du Louvre (Paris: Réunion des Musées Nationaux, 1989); Alex Potts, *Flesh and the Ideal: Winckelmann and the Origins of Art History* (New Haven, Conn.: Yale University Press, 1994); Thomas Crow, *Emulation: Making Artists for Revolutionary France* (New Haven, Conn.: Yale University Press, 1995); Abigail Solomon-Godeau, *Male Trouble: A Crisis in Representation* (London: Thames and Hudson, 1997); Carol Ockman, *Ingres's Eroticized Bodies: Retracing the Serpentine Line* (New Haven, Conn.: Yale University Press, 1995).

7. *Le Courrier des Spectacles*, 8 frimaire an IX (29 November 1800), 3.

8. Ibid.

9. *Sur le tableau des Sabines, par David* (Paris, an VIII [1799–1800]), Collection Deloynes (Paris: Bibliothèque Nationale, 1980), 21, no. 597. An Idéologue, Pierre-Jean-Baptiste Chaussard embraced the Revolution as a moderate Girondin. His Enlightenment faith in rationality accompanied a profound commitment to antiquity and a complete disavowal of Christianity.

10. Stefan Germer and Hubert Kohle emphasize the split address of the painting in "From the Theatrical to the Aesthetic Hero: On the Idea of Virtue in David's *Brutus* and *Sabines*," *Art History* 9, no. 2 (June 1986): 168–84.

11. *Sabines*, 39.

12. Ibid., 3.

13. Ibid., 38.

14. Ibid., 39.

15. See Amaury Duval, *La Décade philosophique* 13, 10 pluviose an VIII (30 January 1800), 228: "Each of these women has a particular expression that indicates the rank she occupies in society. The suffering of Hersilia is noble."

16. Chaussard, *Sabines*, 8–9.

17. Ibid., 39.

18. Chausssard argued that the French people did not enjoy the physical vigor of the Greeks and exhorted David to go to Greece; ibid., 30. See also Doctor Clairian, *Recherches et considérations médicales sur les vêtements des hommes particulièrement sur les -culottes . . .* (Paris, 1803).

19. See, for example, Société Populaire et Républicaine des Arts, *Considérations sur les avantages de changer le costume français* (Paris, n.d.); and the Convention's decree of October 29, 1793.

20. See Jules Renouvier, *Histoire de l'art pendant la révolution* (Paris, 1863), 463–80; Aileen Ribeiro, *Fashion in the French Revolution* (New York: Holmes and Meier, 1988); Lynn Hunt, "Révolution française et vie privée," in *Histoire de la vie privée*, ed. Philippe Ariès and Georges Duby (Paris: Seuil, [1985]), 21–52; Margaret Waller, "Disembodiment as a Masquerade: Fashion Journalists and Other 'Realist' Observers in Directory Paris," *L'Esprit Créateur* 37, no. 1 (Spring 1997): 50–60.

21. "The Rhetoric of Revolution in France," *History Workshop Journal* 15 (Spring 1983): 78–94; and Hunt, "Révolution française," 24–26.

22. Poultier, "Physionomie de Paris," *Amis des Lois* (30 ventôse an VI [20 March 1799]); cited in Alphonse Aulard, *Paris pendant la réaction thermidorienne et sous le directoire: Recueils de documents*, 5 vols. (Paris, 1898), 4: 578.

23. *Le Nouveau Diable Boiteux, Tableau philosophique et moral de Paris* (Paris, an VII [1798–99]), 2: 233.

24. See the Bureau Central report on 29 prairial an VI (16 June 1798); cited in Aulard, *Paris pendant la réaction*, 4: 720. Also see Philippe Séguy, *Histoire des modes sous l'Empire* (Paris: Promodis, 1988), 34; and Edmond and Jules de Goncourt, *Histoire de la société française pendant le Directoire* (Paris: Gallimard, 1992), 304–305.

25. See also Cartellier's complaint about fashion in an 1804 letter to a fellow sculptor; Henri Jouin, "Lettres inédits d'artistes français du XIX siècle," *Nouvelles archives de l'art français*, 3d ser., 16 (1900): 7–8.

26. *France in Eighteen Hundred and Two*, ed. J. A. C. Sykes (London, 1806), 124.

27. These differences resemble but also deviate from the paradigm of the older active partner *(erastes)* and the passive youthful love object *(eromenos)* characteristic of ancient vase painting; see Ockman, *Ingres's Eroticized Bodies*.

28. Romulus's figure accords therefore with Jacques Lacan's assertion that "the phallus can only play its role as veiled"; "The Meaning of the Phallus," in Juliet Mitchell and Jacqueline Rose, eds., *Feminine Sexuality: Jacques Lacan and the 'Ecole Freudienne'* (New York: Norton, 1982), 74–85.

29. *France in Eighteen Hundred and Two*, 124.

30. *La Morte de trois milles ans au Salon de 1783* (1783), 4; Collection Deloynes 13, no. 286, 178.

31. Jules David, *Le peintre Louis David 1748–1825: Souvenirs et documents inédits* (Paris, 1880–82), 1: 336.

32. See Elisabeth Vigée-Lebrun, *Souvenirs*, ed. Claudine Herrmann (Paris: Des Femmes, 1984) 1: 85–88; Mary Sheriff, *The Exceptional Woman: Elisabeth Vigée-Lebrun and the Cultural Politics of Art* (Chicago: University of Chicago Press, 1996), 47–48.

33. As widely noted by contemporaries, the women—artists and wives of artists—were self-consciously performing history paintings like Nicholas-Guy Brenet's *Piety and Generosity of Roman Women*, which hung next to David's painting of masculine martial sacrifice, *Oath of the Horatii*, in the Salon of 1785. I interpret the act of the donation as a double move, distancing both women and art from ornament and luxury. However, if the women's sacrifice was likened to men's sacrifice to the state, it was far less sustainable: the negation of ornament can only be performed once. See Vivian Cameron, "Approaches to Narrative and History: The Case of the Donation of September 7, 1789 and Its Images," *Studies in Eighteenth-Century Culture* 19 (1989): 413–32.

34. Female sign and abstract signified could not be held asunder: see a contemporary's protest that a young woman could only represent Liberty, not Reason, at the Festival of Reason. Mona Ozouf, *Festivals and the French Revolution*, trans. A. Sheridan (Cambridge, Mass.: Harvard University Press, 1988), 101–102.

35. Charlemagne, "Le Monde incroyable"; cited in Renouvier, *Histoire de l'art pendant la révolution*, 476.

36. Walter Markov, *Grand Empire: Virtue and Vice in the Napoleonic Era* (New York: Hippocrene, 1990), 204.

37. Ibid.

38. See *Journal des Dames et des Modes*, 9 pluviose an VI (28 January 1798); Ribeiro, *Fashion in the French Revolution*, 153 n. 31.

39. *La petite poste de Paris*, 3 messidor an V (21 June 1797); cited in Maurice Lescure, *Madame Hamelin: Merveilleuse et turbulent Fortunée (1776–1851)* (Paris: L'Harmattan, 1995), 38. A few days later, *L'Ami du peuple* of 5 messidor an V (23 June 1797) exhorted "the imprudent" "at least to respect the people, . . . if one is dissolute, it is necessary to hide it; if one is well behaved, it is necessary to appear so." Aulard, *Paris pendant la réaction*, 4: 189.

40. *Courrier des Spectacles*, 11 thermidor an V (28 July 1797), 251. Charlemagne's poem "Le Monde incroyable" also points to this pervasive adoption of Greek costume when he discovers that the "Greek with big arms" is Mme Angot, a popular symbol of the crude female *arriviste*.

41. Paris, October 1798; cited in Séguy, *Histoire des modes*, 51

42. Victor Broussonet, *De la mode et des habillements* (Paris, 1799, 2d ed. 1806).

43. 21 fructidor an VII (7 September 1799); cited in Aulard, *Paris pendant la réaction*, 5: 715.

44. In his *Voyage de Thunberg au cap de Bonne-Espérance, aux îles de la Sonde et au Japon* (Paris, 1796), 4: 59.

45. 3e jour complémentaire an VII (19 September 1799); cited in Aulard, *Paris pendant la réaction*, 5: 737.

46. *Journal de Paris*, 15 fructidor an VII (1 September 1799); cited in *Oeuvres du Comte P. L. Roederer* (Paris, 1856), 4: 396. Called "chef des philosophes" by a contemporary, Roederer embraced the Revolution as a moderate member of the Jacobin club. After the fall of the Girondins, he went into hiding, only to re-emerge after Thermidor.

47. Bureau Central Report, 4 messidor an VI (22 June 1798), 745.

48. See Elizabeth Colwill, "Transforming Women's Empire: Representations of Women in French Political Culture, 1770–1807" (Ph.D. diss., SUNY Binghamton, 1990).

49. *Journal d'économie publique, de morale et de politique*, 10 frimaire an V (31 October 1796); Roederer, *Oeuvres*, 4: 382.

50. Ibid., 4: 383.

51. Chaussard himself recognized the Directory's striking opposition of male and female fashion in *Le Nouveau Diable*, 2: 232–33; a woman asks: "And if I tremble from cold, don't you suffocate from heat?"

52. Letter addressed to L.-S. Mercier, *Journal de Paris*, 13 germinal an VI (2 April 1798), 807–808; Roederer, *Oeuvres*, 4: 382. Roederer's statement was also re-

ported in *L'Ami des Lois*, 14 germinal an VI (3 April 1798); cited in Aulard, *Paris pendant la réaction*, 4: 595.

53. On the opposition of Corneille and Racine in the late eighteenth century, see Crow, *Emulation*, 33–45.

54. See Thomas Crow, *Painters and Public Life in Eighteenth-Century Paris* (New Haven, Conn.: Yale University Press, 1985), 176–77.

55. See, for example, *Tableau général du goût, des modes et costumes de Paris par une société d'artistes et gens de lettres*, 1 vendémiaire an VII (22 September 1798); and *Journal de Paris*, 21 fructidor an IX (8 September 1801); Roederer, *Oeuvres*, 4: 400–401.

56. See Susan Siegfried, *The Art of Louis-Léopold Boilly: Modern Life in Napoleonic France* (New Haven, Conn.: Yale University Press, 1995), 70–75.

57. *Journal de Delécluze 1824–1828*, ed. R. Baschet (Paris: Bernard Grosset, 1948), 338.

58. Louis Hautecoeur, *Louis David* (Paris: La Table Ronde, 1954), 180.

59. Jules David, *Le Peintre Louis David*, 1: 336.

60. Truthful ones, according to Delafontaine's manuscript at the Bibliothèque de l'Institut, ms. 3784; see also Hautecoeur, *Louis David*, 180 n. 40.

61. See Norman Bryson, *Tradition and Desire: From David to Delacroix* (Cambridge: Cambridge University Press, 1984), 88–95; Germer and Kohle, "From the Theatrical to the Aesthetic Hero," 179–80.

62. On women's relation to the public sphere during the Revolutionary period, see, for example, Joan Landes, *Women and the Public Sphere in the Age of the French Revolution* (Ithaca, N.Y.: Cornell University Press, 1988); Madelyn Gutwirth, *The Twilight of the Goddesses: Women and Representation in the French Revolutionary Era* (New Brunswick, N.J.: Rutgers University Press, 1992); Lynn Hunt, *The Family Romance of the French Revolution* (Berkeley: University of California Press, 1993); Geneviève Fraisse, *Reason's Muse: Sexual Difference and the Birth of Democracy*, trans. Jane Marie Todd (Chicago: Chicago University Press, 1989).

63. Concerning Girodet's revenge against one such fashionable parvenu, Mlle Lange, at the Salon of 1799, see Crow, *Emulation*, 233–36; Ewa Lajer-Burcharth, "Le Rhétorique du corps féminin sous le Directoire: Le cas d'Anne-Françoise Elizabeth Lange en Danaë," in Marie-France Brive, ed., *Les Femmes et la Révolution française* (Toulouse: Presses Universitaire de Miraie, 1990), 2: 221–25.

64. I am indebted to Stefan Germer's discussion of the painting's two axes, which he relates to Benveniste's distinction between *récit* and *discours*; "In Search of a Beholder," 33–34.

65. Indeed Romulus, despite his nudity, still bears the traces of the *incroyable*'s foppish elegance with his "dog's ears" sideburns, distinctive full-lipped profile, and ornamentation condensed into serpentine red feather and luxuriant gold accessories.

66. *Journal des arts* 34 (20 nivôse an VIII [10 January 1800]): 4.

67. *Journal des Débats*, 13 ventose an VIII (4 March 1800), 2–3; Collection Deloynes 21, no. 598, 787–88.

68. Ch. 180, "Nudité," in *Le Nouveau Paris*, ed. J.-C. Bonnet (Paris: Mercure de France, 1994), 649, which was largely based on two articles in *Journal de Paris* on 9 and 12 germinal an V (29 March and 1 April 1797), 790–91 and 803–804 respectively.

69. Of course, homoerotic readings could also at particular historical junctures require similar censorship or obfuscation. Nevertheless, I would insist that in late-eighteenth-century France the homoerotic, exclusively masculine paradigm of viewing dominated aesthetic discourse. On the restraints placed upon homoerotic readings of art, see, for example, Potts, *Flesh and the Ideal*, esp. 118–31; Louis Crompton, *Byron and Greek Love: Homophobia in Nineteenth Century England* (Berkeley: University of California Press, 1985).

70. See Sheriff, *The Exceptional Woman*, 115–20, for the eighteenth-century preoccupation with the female gaze upon the male object, including Diderot's account of embarrassing sexual arousal while modeling nude for the female painter Mme Terborch.

71. *Journal de Paris*, 13 germinal an VI (2 April 1798), 807; Roederer, *Oeuvres*, 4: 386.

72. Jules David, *Le Peintre Louis David*, 1: 360, states that fashionable women feigned modesty and embarrassment by covering their eyes with a fan that cleverly concealed a viewing glass, thereby at once hiding and directing their gaze. Without clothing that differentiated the wife from the whore, women were called upon to perform their virtue. Standing between mirror and picture, these women's sense of surveillance must have been heightened, but so too would have been their titillating sense of risk and illicit pleasure.

73. De Cailly, *Journal des Dames* 25 (10 pluviose an VII [29 January 1799]): 398–400.

74. Chaussard, *Sabines,* 34.

75. Ibid., 43–44.

76. Pierre Rosenberg, *Fragonard,* exh. cat. (New York: Metropolitan Museum of Art, 1988), 548–53.

77. Chaussard, *Sabines,* 33.

78. Lajer-Burcharth, "David's *Sabine Women,*" 412.

79. Harold Bloom, *The Anxiety of Influence: A Theory of Poetry* (New York: Oxford University Press, 1973); Bryson, *Tradition and Desire*; and Crow, *Emulation.*

80. *Journal de Paris,* 13 germinal an VI (2 April 1798); Roederer, *Oeuvres,* 4: 386–87.

81. Musée du Louvre, *Jacques-Louis David,* 335.

82. P. J. Marie de Saint-Ursin, *L'Ami des femmes, ou lettre d'un médecin, concernant l'influence de l'habillement des femmes sur leurs moeurs et leur santé . . .* (Paris, 1804), 46.

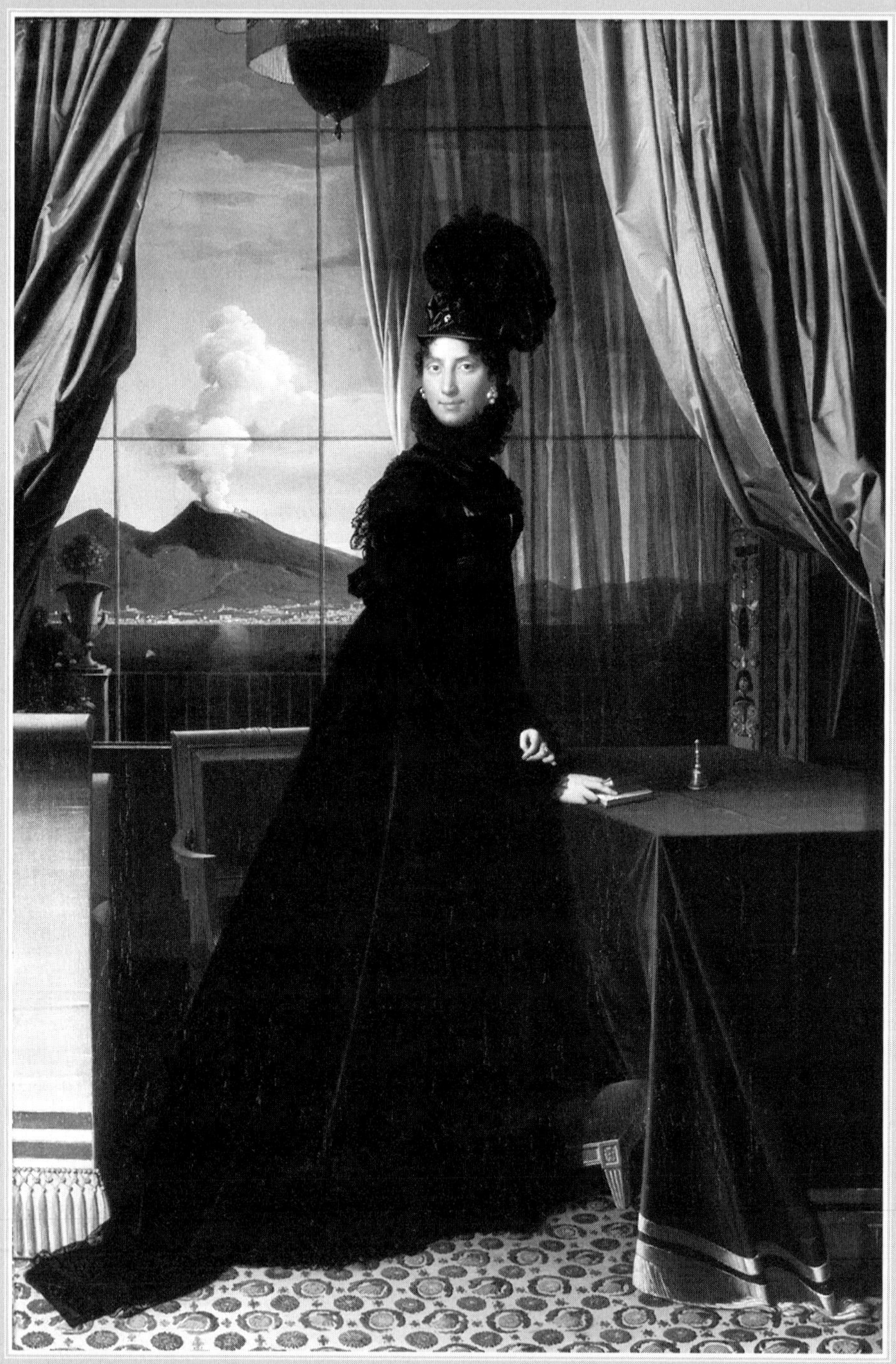

9

A WOMAN'S PLEASURE

Ingres's Grande Odalisque

Carol Ockman

THE *GRANDE ODALISQUE* is among the most famous of Ingres's productions, precisely because it uses serpentine line so dramatically to sensualize the female body (fig. 9.2). For the same reason, it is an image that has troubled some nineteenth- and twentieth-century viewers.[1] One of the most startling aspects about the painting is the fact that it was commissioned by a woman. In addition to raising questions about who commissioned and collected erotic paintings in the early nineteenth century, this information engages notions of female spectatorship and "feminine" taste that complicate assumptions about pleasure and power.

The *Grande Odalisque* was commissioned not by just any woman, but by Caroline Bonaparte Murat, the youngest of Napoleon's three sisters. In 1800, Caroline Bonaparte married Joachim Murat, then Bonaparte's aide-de-camp, a man whose image as a dashing, if slightly sinister, military officer was later immortalized in Gros's *Battle of Aboukir* (1806; Detroit Institute of Arts) and *Battle of Eylau* (1808; Louvre). Under Napoleon's regime, Joachim and Caroline Murat ruled as king and queen of Naples from 1808 to 1815. Queen Caroline commissioned Ingres to paint the *Grande Odalisque* in 1814. The work was intended as a pendant to an earlier Ingres painting, now lost, the so-called *Sleeper of Naples*, painted in 1808 and purchased in Rome by Murat in 1809 (see fig. 9.3).

The contrasts between the two paintings are plain: the reclining nude female in the *Sleeper* is shown frontally in a posture of sleepy languor; the seated nude woman in the *Grande Odalisque* is seen from behind and directs her gaze, at least in part, toward the viewer. Although it would be difficult to argue that the *Grande Odalisque* forecloses voyeurism, the openness of the pose of the woman in the *Sleeper* and her apparent obliviousness to being viewed provide a distinct alternative to the demure subject of the *Grande Odalisque*. Certainly such oppositions are frequently found in pendants; Murat himself owned two strikingly different versions of *Cupid and Psyche* by Canova, the one horizontal and unabashedly carnal (1787–93; Louvre), the other vertical and more restrained (1796–1800; Louvre). Given such precedents already in the king's collection, it is certainly plausible that the queen meant the *Grande Odalisque*, like the standing version of Canova's *Cupid and Psyche*, as a chaste antipode to its unabashedly sexy pendant.[2]

Inasmuch as the *Grande Odalisque* forms a pendant

A longer version of this essay was originally published as "A Woman's Pleasure: The *Grande Odalisque*," in Carol Ockman, *Ingres's Eroticized Bodies: Retracing the Serpentine Line* (New Haven, Conn.: Yale University Press, 1995), 32–65. Copyright © 1995 by Carol Ockman. Reprinted by permission of the author and courtesy of Yale University Press.

Figure 9.1. Jean-Auguste-Dominique Ingres, *Queen Caroline Murat*, 1814. Oil on canvas. Private collection. (Photo: author.)

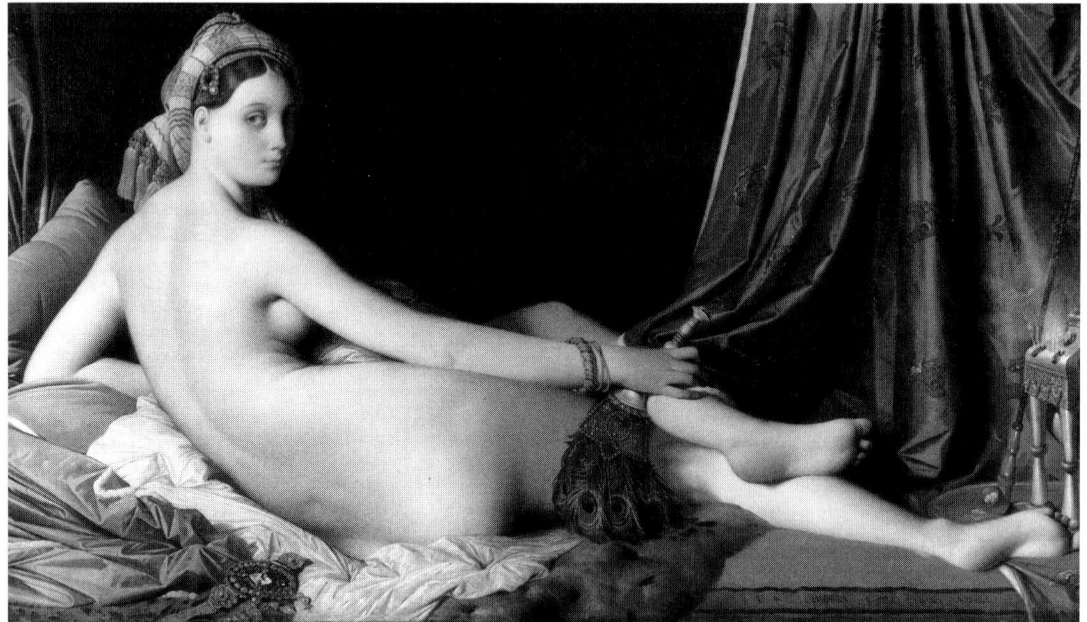

Figure 9.2. Jean-Auguste-Dominique Ingres, *Grande Odalisque*, 1814. Oil on canvas. Musée du Louvre, Paris. (Photo: Réunion des Musées Nationaux/Art Resource, New York.)

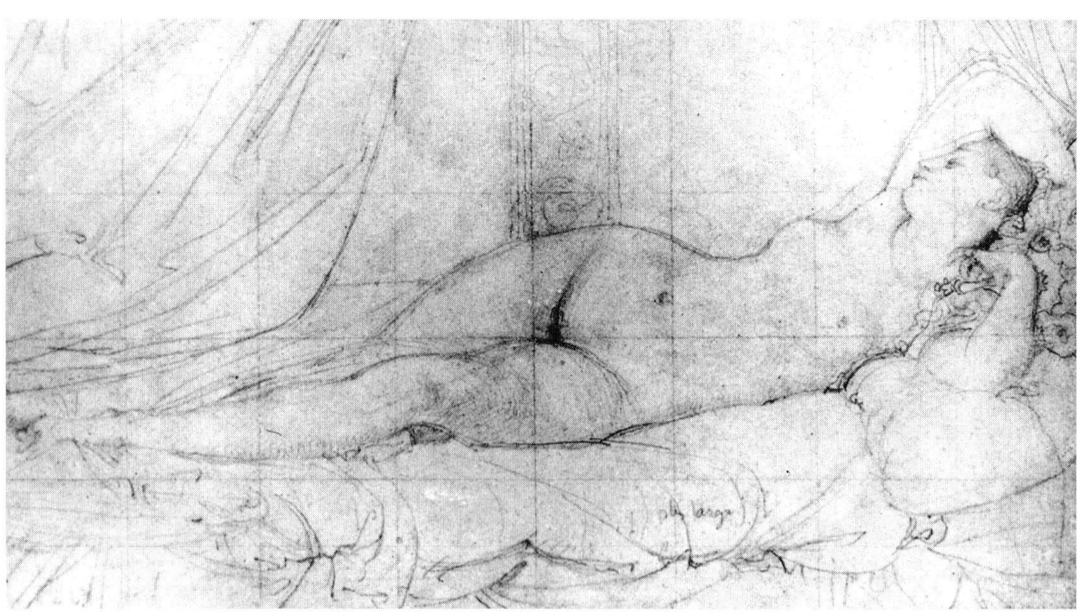

Figure 9.3. Jean-Auguste-Dominique Ingres, *Reclining Odalisque* (drawing for lost *Sleeper of Naples*). Graphite. Private collection.

to the *Sleeper,* which the king had purchased five years before, it seems most likely that the new painting was intended as a gift for Murat. And, given the king's well-known predilection for works of art depicting an aloof sensuality (works for which Mario Praz long ago coined the term "erotic frigidaire"),[3] it also seems clear that the *Grande Odalisque* was entirely consistent with the king's tastes. But the problem with this presumption is that it effectively evacuates the queen's agency either in commissioning the painting or in enjoying it herself. The tendency to construct female agency solely in relation to men does more than circumscribe Caroline Murat's role; it denies an entire constellation of relationships existing between imagery and patronage in which women played a dominant role. How, then, do we talk about this gift to the king commissioned by the queen? In exploring this question, I hope to suggest, first, how Caroline Murat's gift might be read as a statement of gender politics of sorts and, second, how the image attests to important relationships among women, the artists they patronized, and the works that were produced.

We might begin by asking if in its time the *Grande Odalisque* was a naughty painting, inappropriate for a queen to commission. This is a very difficult question to answer, but fortunately for our purposes, some primary evidence survives regarding the reception of its pendant. In a letter Ingres wrote in 1815 in a vain attempt to buy back his *Sleeper of Naples,* he speculates that his patrons might regard the picture as a bit outré: "This painting may seem a little too voluptuous for this court, [so I propose] to make another one of an entirely different subject, religious or otherwise." Given the self-serving purposes of his letter, Ingres may be granted a certain amount of exaggeration or dissembling, but there is little doubt that for him the question of appropriateness centered on the distinctly sensualized character of the painting.[4] In specifying the court as the potentially offended audience, Ingres did not anticipate greater or lesser offense to either sex. Still, it is tempting to think that Ingres had the queen's taste in mind, or that of other women of the court, since the king's earlier art purchases, including Canova's reclining *Cupid and Psyche,* made clear that he did not find voluptuousness inappropriate.

In addition, there is evidence, again in the form of a letter from Ingres, that the *Grande Odalisque* called into question the propriety of the queen herself—and by extension that of the artist. Ingres wrote to the ambassador to Naples, "Some kind people, of whom there are many in this world, have spread the word that I intended to depict Mme Murat in this painting. This is absolutely false; my model is in Rome, it's a ten-year-old little girl who modeled, and besides, those who knew Mme Murat can judge me."[5] Given that the letter focuses on the issue of verisimilitude, it seems strange that Ingres claims that the model for this bizarre but definitely adult body was a ten-year-old girl. Less puzzling perhaps, but also problematic, is the claim that *knowing* Mme Murat was somehow enough to dispel the accusation that she was the subject of the *Grande Odalisque.* Ingres's double disclaimer attempts to deny the picture's sexuality, first by making the model prepubescent (therefore not yet fully sexed), and second, by assuming that a vaguely suggested moral persona effectively cancels the possibility of representation as a sexed being. Behind the gossip that the *Grande Odalisque* might portray Caroline Murat lurks the transgressive potential of the sexed female body.

Certainly the clearest and most stunning contemporary example of the dilemmas posed by female agency and sexed bodies, however, was provided by Caroline's older sister Pauline. In 1804, Pauline had caused a minor contretemps by commissioning and apparently posing for Canova's *Paolina Borghese as Venus Victrix* (fig. 9.4). The rumor that the divine Pauline posed nude for this statue is a constant subject in the literature about Canova and the princess. Even the eminent art historian Gérard Hubert, in his scholarly study *La Sculpture dans l'Italie Napoléonienne,* felt the need to detail the positions of early-nineteenth-century scholars on the matter.[6] His catalogue of moralizing points of view is of interest today primarily because it is symptomatic of both the

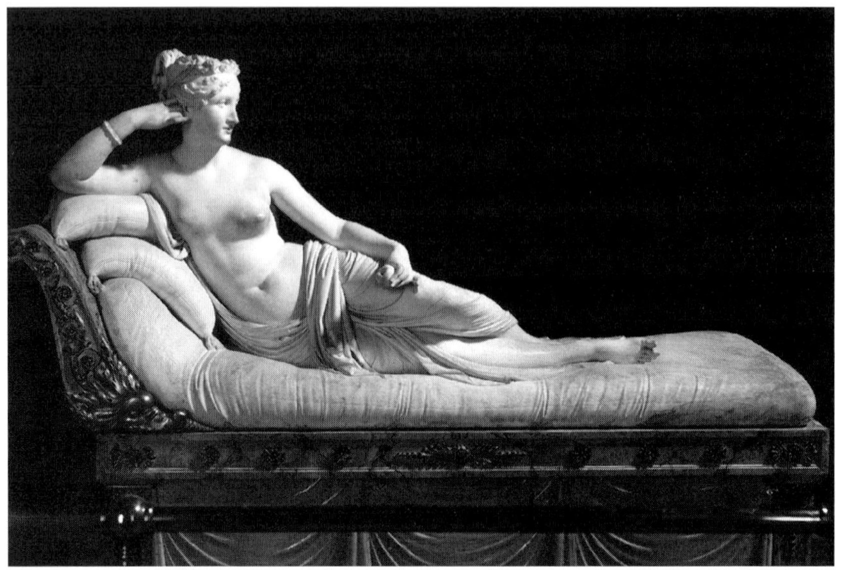

Figure 9.4. Antonio Canova, *Paolina Borghese as Venus Victrix*, 1804–8. Marble. Galleria Borghese, Rome. (Photo: Alinari/Art Resource, New York.)

desire for certainty about woman's sexual propriety and the universal titillation of illicit sexual imagery. The ongoing fascination with the sex lives of royalty and art patrons is encapsulated by the near-legendary status critics have accorded Pauline Borghese's putative retort to a skeptical *dame d'honneur*. When asked whether she actually posed nude for the sculptor, the sitter supposedly responded that Canova's studio was well heated. The shock that greeted Borghese's bold reply, much like the decision to have herself represented as Venus, the goddess of love (and not Diana, as Canova had proposed), was overwhelmingly linked to the belief that sexual display was inappropriate for a woman of her position.[7] This subtext of transgression contributed, at least in part, to the work's extraordinary popularity. The triumphant public reception of the finished sculpture was described at the time by Quatremère de Quincy:

> The *Venus Victrix* has just had a new triumph
> at the Palazzo Borghese, where it was exhibited
> for a limited time to the public. The procession
> of amateurs, as much from Rome as abroad, con-
> tinually pressed around it. Daytime was not enough
> for their admiration; they got permission to study
> the statue at night, by torch light, which, as you

know, accentuates and allows one to see the smallest nuances in the handling, and also shows up the smallest faults. It was necessary to set up an enclosure to protect the work from the crowd that constantly pushed against it.[8]

As my brief discussion of the responses to *Paolina Borghese as Venus Victrix* suggests, we need to broaden our field of inquiry in order to determine what nineteenth-century viewers considered appropriate in representations of women commissioned by women. How was artistic taste and patronage defined during the Consulate and the Empire? By way of an answer, I would suggest that there was a pictorial language during this period that was created in large part by women. This pictorial language included a dialogue among works of art, in which new commissions were planned as responses to previous commissions. In commissioning the *Grande Odalisque*, for example, Caroline Murat initiated a dialogue with other works of art that was similar to the competitive spirit Ingres assumed in making the painting. But in suggesting a parallel between rivalries among artists and rivalries among patrons, my goal is neither to reinscribe linear histories nor to offer some sort of alternative "female" taste as a complement to the extant history of

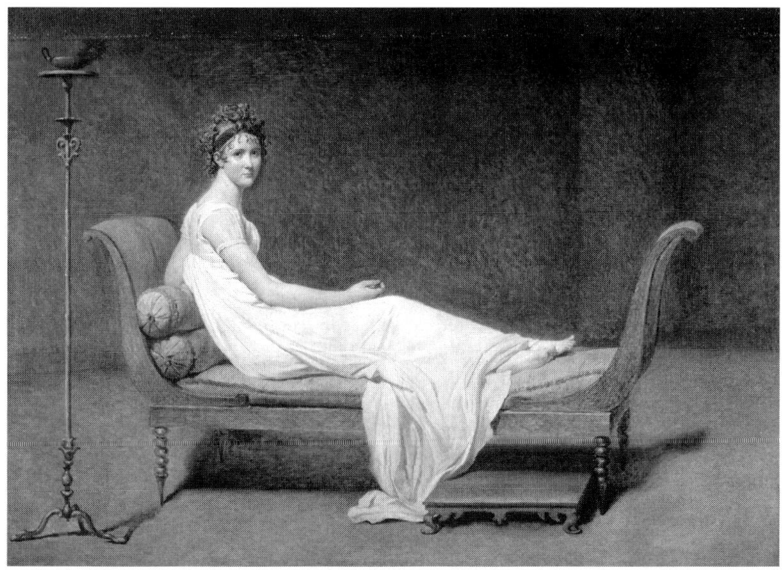

Figure 9.5. Jacques-Louis David, *Mme Récamier*, 1800. Oil on canvas. Musée du Louvre, Paris. (Photo: Réunion des Musées Nationaux/Art Resource, New York.)

largely "male" taste. Rather, my intent is to show how the introduction of gender confounds the binarism embedded in these very ways of thinking. In outlining a model for a history of patronage predicated on female agency, I am positing a relationship among a group of odalisques commissioned by women in the early nineteenth century. This series creates a genealogy of masterworks capable of being read both within a history of female patronage and within the traditional history of male artistic creation.

This brief history of early-nineteenth-century odalisques might begin with David's *Mme Récamier* (fig. 9.5), and include Gérard's portrait of the same sitter (1805; Musée Carnavalet), Canova's *Paolina Borghese as Venus Victrix* (fig. 9.4), and Ingres's *Grande Odalisque* (fig. 9.2). The clear formal connections among these works immediately endow the Récamier-Borghese-Murat model with an internal logic. Yet, at the same time, the generic logic of the model makes this particular grouping arbitrary. Other iconographic examples could easily be included—for instance, Prud'hon's well-known *Portrait of the Empress Josephine* (1805; Louvre) or even the curious nude miniature of the infant king of Rome on the lid of a small box (Château de Malmaison). The fact that this model has such flexibility and variety does not deny

its legitimacy, but rather argues for the strength of the formal connections among these images. In addition, the close personal ties among the patrons of these works suggest that a deliberate iconographic dialogue was being enunciated through the works themselves.

Socializing between Mme Récamier and the Bonaparte sisters began at least as early as 1800, so it is quite possible that Caroline Murat and Paolina Borghese were aware of Mme Récamier's portrait commissions from David in that year. Whether or not they were aware of these specific works, it is clear that the three women shared a standard of artistic taste and participated in the social activities of the royal court. Like Mme Récamier, Caroline Murat and Paolina Borghese were represented by David in his *Coronation of Napoleon* (1806; Louvre). Also like Mme Récamier, Caroline Murat commissioned a painting of herself from Gérard, that tireless portraitist of *napoléonides*; in this, her most famous portrait, she appears with her children (Château de Malmaison). Mme Récamier and the Bonaparte sisters also shared in the widespread enthusiasm for Canova's works. Not only did Paolina Borghese owe her audacious portrait as *Venus Victrix* to Canova, but the Murats, her sister and brother-in-law, followed the lead of other *napoléoni-*

des and had him sculpt their own conventional portrait busts. Finally, Mme Récamier, friend and muse more than patron to Canova, inspired at least two works by him, and he is said to have given her the first version of his *Three Graces*.[9]

In order to understand more specifically how this network of artistic patronage functioned, we might look at the activities of this circle of patrons and artists from 1813 to 1814, the year in which Caroline Murat commissioned the *Grande Odalisque*. Canova was in Naples that winter to model the portraits of Caroline and Joachim Murat.[10] During Canova's absence, Mme Récamier arrived in Rome and set up a salon that included among its regular guests the painter Granet and the director of police in Napoleonic Rome, Baron Norvins, both of whom had had their portraits painted by Ingres. Shortly after Canova's return, Mme Récamier summered with him at his house in Albano and then traveled to Naples at the invitation of the king and queen. That spring, Paolina Borghese lived at the Murats' villa in Portici for five months. Meanwhile, in Rome on December 4, 1813, Ingres was married to Madeleine Chapelle, the cousin of Josephine Niçaise-Lacroix, who was engaged to Ingres's friend, the architect François Mazois. It was Mazois, an intimate of the royal family, who introduced Ingres to the queen of Naples.[11] As a result of these interconnections, in February 1814, Ingres visited Naples for the first and only time. There, he saw his *Sleeper of Naples* hanging in Murat's private apartments, and he may actually have crossed paths with Mme Récamier. Ingres returned to Rome several months later with commissions from the Murat family for the *Grande Odalisque*, a portrait of Caroline Murat, and a portrait of the royal family.[12]

Caroline Murat's motivations in commissioning the *Grande Odalisque* may also have been affected by the circumstances surrounding the commission of its pendant, the *Sleeper*. In 1808, the year that Ingres painted it, two other important works were completed: Canova's marble version of *Paolina Borghese as Venus Victrix* and Ingres's *Bather of Valpinçon* (1808; Louvre). Canova's sculpture was exhibited briefly in Rome, then shipped to the Borghese residence in Torino; Ingres's *Bather* was sent to Paris for its mandatory review by the Academy. But the *Sleeper of Naples* mysteriously remained in Rome, where the following year Murat purchased it from an exhibition in the *sale del Campidoglio*.[13] Given the links among these three works, is it any wonder that in creating a pendant for the *Sleeper* six years later, Mme Murat or Ingres decided on an odalisque seen from the back? Might we view her commission as an in-family joke about her sister's scandalous portrait in the round? Could we see it as a sly comment on her husband's tastes, or his reputed affection for her sister? Might we view Ingres's role as reiterating the formal concerns of his *Bather*, while creating a pendant to the *Sleeper of Naples*? Were the *Grande Odalisque* and the *Sleeper of Naples*, taken together, intended to offer differing viewpoints and thereby vie with the three-dimensionality of sculpture like Canova's?

On one level, the progression from Mme Récamier's famous portraits by David and Gérard to Paolina Borghese's portrait as Venus by Canova to Caroline Murat's commission for the *Grande Odalisque* may seem obvious or oversimplified, the stuff of art history survey courses. But as an aspect of the history of patronage, it is less obvious and has broader implications. While Mme Récamier, Paolina Borghese, and Caroline Bonaparte have hardly been consigned to oblivion, their roles as art patrons have been virtually subsumed by their quasi-mythic personae.

For Mme Récamier and Paolina Borghese, it was their beauty, above all, that was legendary; for Caroline Murat, it was her supposed lust for power. In each case, the woman was believed to have the power to incite crowds. Numerous eyewitness accounts report how Mme Récamier literally stopped traffic in London; in Rome, Paolina Borghese's statue as *Venus Victrix* needed to be protected from the crowds desperate to see it. After the fall of the emperor, Caroline Murat was considered so dangerous that she, alone among the *napoléonides*, was forbidden to live south of Trieste. Central to the representation of all three women was the power of their sexuality. If the sexual charms of Mme Récamier were enhanced by her putative purity, those of Paolina Borghese were boosted by her celebrated availability. And as for Caroline Murat, hers was regarded as a case of sexual charms gone awry as she entered the public realm.[14]

Famous images of these women perpetuated their particular myths and ensured that Mme Récamier and Paolina Borghese were considered the undisputed beauties of their time. Mme Récamier purportedly preferred Gérard's more sensual portrait of herself to David's classical image,[15] and Paolina Borghese enhanced her sexy public image by having herself represented by Canova as *Venus Victrix*. Caroline Murat's portraits do not highlight her sensual charms as single-mindedly as do the famous portraits of Mme Récamier and Paolina Borghese. Although from all reports Caroline Murat was quite attractive, she was also a mother of four, and she was often pictured with her children.[16] She also generally was regarded by her contemporaries as an ambitious woman who was the power behind the throne. Madame Cavaignac wrote, "Madame Murat especially had a mania to rule." In a letter to Metternich, Count Niepperg, who led the Austrian advance guard into Naples in 1815, referred to "the queen, who is much more the king of this country than her fool of a husband."[17] As for the queen herself, caught in the bind between positive and negative stereotypes of womanhood, she apparently alternated between playing the role of self-effacing and devoted wife and that of a powerful political figure in her own right. The king's power to rule had been seriously compromised in favor of his wife by Article IV of the Bayonne treaty of July 15, 1808. In this treaty, Napoleon transferred his brother Joseph to Spain and ceded the realm of Sicily to Joachim Murat. In doing so, however, he stipulated "the eventual rights of succession of Queen Caroline" and declared that "the transfer of land had been made specifically in her interest."[18] The difficulties inherent in this proviso had direct repercussions. Correspondence between Ambassador of the Head of Household La Feuillade d'Aubusson and the emperor indicates that Murat placed restrictions on the queen so that she would not interfere with government.[19] Lurking beneath this conflict between king and queen were the contradictions that bound Caroline Murat, contradictions inherent in being a woman in the private *and* public realms.

During the Napoleonic Empire, a woman in the public arena was regarded as unnatural. The pithiest statement about that monstrous misfit—the powerful public woman—was offered by Napoleon in speaking of his sister Caroline: "She has Cromwell's head on a pretty woman's body."[20] In this context, it is particularly interesting to examine Ingres's portrait of *Queen Caroline Murat*, a painting that is surprising on virtually every level (fig. 9.1). By any standard, the royal commission was an important one for Ingres. Along with the *Grande Odalisque* and a projected portrait of the Murat family, it represented crucial patronage at a time when Ingres's French patrons were leaving Rome. Missing since 1814, the painting was rediscovered by an art dealer in 1987 and was reproduced in print for the first time in 1990.[21] As unusual as its provenance is its format, a less-than-life-size, full standing figure set in an interior, with a landscape seen through the window. But perhaps the most striking and unusual feature is that in this portrayal of a female monarch, the ideology of domesticity is not dominant.

What has not been noted in previous discussions of this resurfaced work is the painting's relationship with another portrait by Ingres, *Napoléon Bonaparte, First Consul* (fig. 9.6). In fact, *Queen Caroline Murat* bears such an uncanny resemblance to the 1804 portrait of Napoleon that they could almost be pendants were it not for the great disparity in their sizes and the ten-year difference in dates of execution. The composition of the two works is similar, with the figure positioned between a table and flanking chair and a curtain parted to reveal a landscape. Furthermore, both paintings are executed in a precise, quasi-miniaturist manner that to some extent belies their scale.[22] By clearly recalling the earlier painting of her brother, the portrait of Caroline Murat emphasizes her relation to Napoleon as well as her own role as autonomous ruler. In Ingres's painting, Caroline Murat is represented in a much more decisive pose than in the watercolor that served as Ingres's source for the setting, Clarac's maternalistic *Caroline Murat and Her*

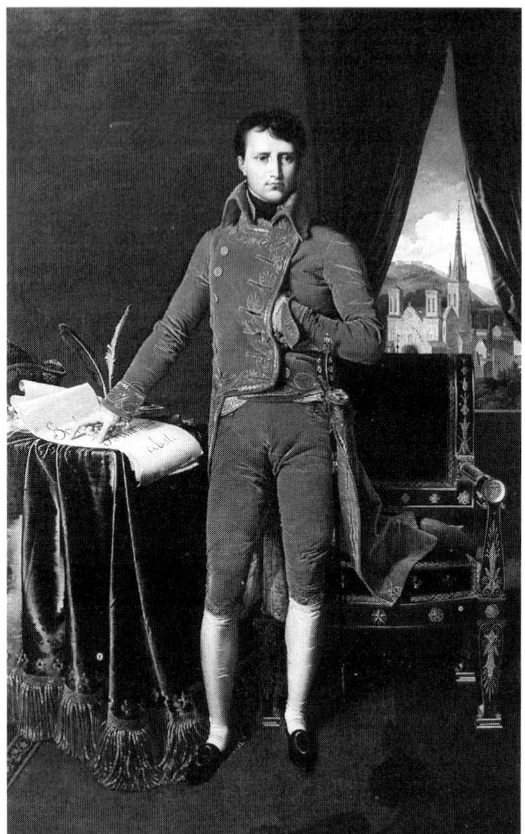

Figure 9.6. Jean-Auguste-Dominique Ingres, *Napoléon Bonaparte, First Consul*, 1804. Oil on canvas. Musée d'Armes, Liège. (Musée d'Art moderne et d'Art contemporain de la Ville de Liège.)

Children at the Royal Palace in Naples (formerly collection G. B. Spalletti Trivelli, Rome). The queen's role as ruler is admittedly qualified in Ingres's picture, however. Unlike Napoleon, who points to a decree on the table in his portrait, Caroline marks a place with her finger in a small book next to which is a diminutive bell. Nevertheless, the associations with her brother's image, as well as the similar composition, are reinforced by the viewing angle and the elongated body of the queen, which, much as in Bronzino's *Portrait of a Young Man* (c.1540; Metropolitan Museum of Art), lend a slight superciliousness to her even gaze and suggest a powerful public personage. The spectacular image of Vesuvius erupting, whose billowing smoke resembles the curling feathers of the

sitter's hat, confirms that power while adding a potentially terrifying and distinctly gendered dimension to it: the menace of nature unleashed. Ingres's comparably assertive image was, in some sense, a statement of public truth in 1814, a year in which Caroline Murat actually ruled Naples as regent during her husband's absence. Paradoxically, though, in suggesting an ongoing Napoleonic dynasty at the very moment of its collapse, the portrait also served as a supreme statement of wish fulfillment.[23]

There is no evidence to suggest that Caroline Murat was involved in the conception of her portrait. Nor do we have any indication of the queen's response other than Ingres's brief mention of the sovereign's unspecified dissatisfaction.[24] But even if the queen were directly responsible for the way she was depicted by Ingres and she was satisfied by the result, it is still difficult to separate that notion of agency from stereotypes about powerful women as unnatural. This is an issue I would like to develop in discussing the *Grande Odalisque*, a case in which there is a great deal of evidence to suggest that the image did indeed please its patron.

In commissioning the *Grande Odalisque*, Caroline Murat exhibited the same taste for highly sensualized imagery that had been evinced earlier by Mme Récamier and Paolina Borghese in their portraits by Gérard and Canova. Given the evidence that women liked this kind of imagery, the existence of a painting like the *Grande Odalisque* is hardly surprising. Even if our own "shock" about Caroline Murat's commission is due to lingering Victorian attitudes, questioning the significance of women's commissioning of sexy images of female nudes during the early nineteenth century can hardly be reduced to ahistorical prudery. I would argue that the commissions of sensualized portraits by Mme Récamier and Paolina Borghese were rather less shocking than Caroline Murat's for the *Grande Odalisque*. Given the scandal surrounding the *Venus Victrix*, this may seem a bold statement at first. But there is a difference between the commissioning by women of images in which they *appear* to define themselves as they have generally been constructed—as sexual objects—and the actual consumption of those images by women. It is precisely because Paolina Borghese's image comes to stand for a real-life persona considered sexually outré that the *Venus Victrix* has a greater power to shock than Gérard's portrait of Mme Récamier. Paradoxically, the very fact that the *Grande Odalisque* is not a portrait of a famous personage gives the image an incendiary dimension. Here, the powerful female patron cannot be reduced to a sexual object, as is the case with the portraits of Mme Récamier and Paolina Borghese. The commission for the *Grande Odalisque* thus raises the question of woman as the consumer of an erotic image in slightly different terms.

In exploring the question of the "feminine" taste for such sensualized imagery, what turns out to be most surprising about works like the *Venus Victrix* and the *Grande Odalisque* is the potential collision of female agency and sexed bodies. This dangerous mix is less troublesome when clearly defined social roles conform to their stereotypic representations, as when Mme Récamier's depiction as a Napoleonic beauty is linked to her public image of mythic virginity, or when Paolina Borghese's representation as a vamp is used to support her mythic infidelity. But the ability to use cultural representations to transgress proper feminine behavior, particularly as realized by Princess Paolina and Queen Caroline, began to inform the ways that images commissioned by them were perceived. In other words, as soon as female agency acquired connotations of power and control—control over one's body, power over a state—the imagery itself constituted a threat.

Any history of female patronage must address the historically specific development of what has been called feminine taste. In considering *le goût féminin* during the Empire, for instance, we might consider what art historian René Schneider refers to as anacreontism or alexandrianism, stylistic terms for an art that he claims appeals especially to women. Schneider defines *anacréontisme* as "a taste for mythology at once graceful, tender and voluptuous and consequently for form that is pretty, often to the point of being mannered." He further points out:

The inspiration for this taste comes from eastern Greece, on the one hand, from the Greece of Anacreon of Teos and Sappho of Lesbos, who lived in the sixth century, and, on the other, from the Hellenistic and Greco-Roman epochs where the Alexandrin spirit held sway. The Empire's greatest enthusiasm is for the period after the death of Alexander, when Hellenism, tired of epic but accustomed to Roman conquest, abandoned itself to the sweetness of life in the privileged sites of Asia Minor, Egypt, and Campania. This was a time of charmed fables in which Eros played the central role, ingenious abstractions, and pastorales in which rusticity is just an assortment of clichés. France, living out its own imperial epic, not only resembled the Alexandrine epoch but consciously evoked it.[25]

Anacreontism, as Schneider elucidates it, then, is virtually synonymous with our notion of sensualized classicism. Although Schneider first applies the term to Canova, he quickly notes its relevance to the work of Girodet, Prud'hon, Gérard, and Chaudet. The concept might also be used to describe much of Ingres's art, including the *Grande Odalisque*.

Central to any discussion of anacreontism is the quality of grace. The term is key to Schneider's conception, and it appears with some frequency in the Ingres literature as well. While the *Grande Odalisque* was not publicly exhibited in Italy when it was painted, its pendant was shown in Rome, where it was purchased by Murat in 1809. In praising the *Sleeper of Naples*, Filippo Aurelio Visconti, co-editor of *Il Museo Chiaromonti aggiunto al Pio Clementino*, singled out grace as its preeminent quality: "The vivaciousness, the grace, with which the life-size sleeping nude woman is painted is worthy of admiration."[26] However, it is in the critical writings about Canova's work that grace is most often evoked, usually in contradistinction to beauty. For example, Quatremère de Quincy, whose influential roles as doyen of neoclassical doctrine and Canova champion are well known, summed up the principal merits of Canova's art: "I do not hesitate to say that one will always find in him two distinguishing merits, that of giving life to his figures and that of grace. Of the latter one can say that in sculpture it is sometimes more beautiful than beauty itself."[27]

Leopoldo Cicognara, whose notions of beauty and *grazia* are very close to those of Canova, made a similar distinction: "I must admit that while the perfect fills us with the greatest admiration, we are inclined to love and prefer the graceful."[28] Grace is often juxtaposed with the real *(il terreno, la vie . . .),* as opposed to the ideal *(il bello ideale, le beau idéal)* with its connotations of abstraction from the real world. For Quatremère, "la grâce" and the ability "to give life to his figures" were Canova's principal merits. Like many of his contemporaries, Quatremère linked grace and sentiment. Discussing the four works that Canova exhibited in the Salon of 1808, he described the *Penitent Magdalene* as "a morsel of nothing but feeling" and continued:

> Who is to say if it isn't precisely this grace that enchants us in his works, the languid poses, the amiable physiognomies, those graceful movements, those soft forms and the pleasant handling of the marble that distinguishes his work and which one admires in his group of *Cupid and Psyche.*[29]

In describing Canova's *Venere Italica* (1804–12; Galleria Palatina, Florence), the poet and sometime critic Ugo Foscolo also emphasized the capacity of grace and the real to heighten feeling:

> But it seems as if Canova feared the awesome competition with the art of the Greek sculptor, so he embellished his new goddess with all those graces which breathe a "je ne sais quoi" of the earthly, but which more easily move the heart which, like the statue is made of clay.[30]

Although the taste for anacreontism and for the qualities of grace, lifelikeness, and feeling embodied by it was not the sole province of women, Schneider hastens to inform us that

naturally it is among women especially that the contagion spread. Canova, Chinard, Prud'hon are the favorites of Mesdames de Groslier, Récamier, and Regnault de St-Jean-d'Angély. Gérard is equally seductive for them. But the most taken with this art is the wife of the master himself: Josephine. She has made of Malmaison a sanctuary of *alexandrinisme,* where her innate taste for abandoned grace is joined with mythological sentimentalism of the late eighteenth century and Campanian Hellenism.[31]

Schneider has a monolithic conception of feminine taste, a taste ultimately rooted in biological essentialism. For women, Schneider claims, the appeal of anacreontism was natural ("naturally it is among women especially that the contagion spreads") and innate ("her [Josephine's] innate taste for abandoned grace is joined with mythological sentimentalism"). For men, on the other hand, it was a relief from the rigors of war:

> When the troops return from a campaign, they enjoy the distraction of graceful and amorous mythology at home. The emperor commissions Callamard's statue of *The Wounded Hyacinth* (1811). Murat is pleased to exhibit two groups of Canova's *Cupid and Psyche* (1802) in his château at Villiers.[32]

Thus, if anacreontic taste in women resembled nothing so much as a biological urge, in Schneider's view, in men it was more like cross-dressing—a chance to throw off one's boots and rest from the exertions of unremitting maleness.

The dangers intrinsic to a notion of "feminine" taste that complements the "masculine" have been amply demonstrated by feminist scholarship.[33] As a diehard constructionist, sensitive, I hope, to the dangers of abolishing difference, I would like to shift the question of feminine taste away from notions of the natural. Rather, what interests me about the taste for anacreontism among privileged women is the possibility it afforded them to experience sensual pleasure.

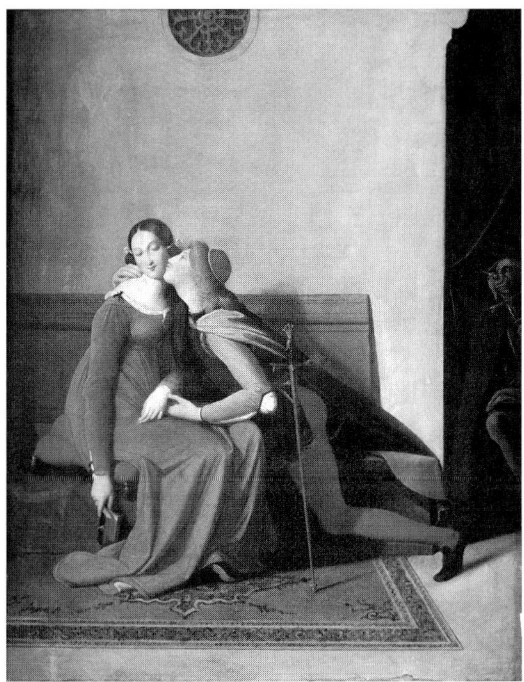

Figure 9.7. Jean-Auguste-Dominique Ingres, *Paolo and Francesca*, 1814. Oil on wood. Musée Condé, Chantilly. (Photo: Réunion des Musées Nationaux/Art Resource, New York.)

There is much evidence to suggest that many women did in fact purchase and commission anacreontic works (as did men: witness Murat). Josephine's collection, for instance, contained many striking examples of *anacréontisme*, including Canova's standing *Cupid and Psyche*, *Hebe*, the *Dancer* and *Paris*, Cartellier's *Modesty*, Antoine-Denis Chaudet's *Cyparisse*, Bosio's *Love Shooting an Arrow*, Jeanne-Elisabeth Chaudet's *Young Girl Feeding Chickens* and *Young Girl before the Statue of Minerva, Sacrificing the Gifts of Love*, Guérin's *Anacreon Rekindling Love*, and Constance Mayer's *Repose of Venus*. Based on watercolor views of the installation of Josephine's collection and a precisely documented catalogue published during the empress's lifetime, we know that her collection was eclectic with a strong bias toward old masters and modern paintings.[34] We also find that Josephine's own acquisitions outweighed the gifts to the collection. These acquisitions were generally made for Josephine in her own name, and only sometimes "un-

der the auspices of Napoleon."[35] Whatever the case, we can conclude that Josephine played a major role in forming the collection and that it is a fair index of her taste. Though the empress certainly had artistic advisors—her curator at Malmaison was no less a personage than Alexandre Lenoir, the founder of the Musée des Monuments Français—we can still recognize Josephine's taste. Like taste in general, it was simply conditioned by what others thought.

It is more difficult to speak about Caroline Murat's taste. In most instances her own purchases of artworks cannot be readily distinguished from her husband's. There are some notable exceptions, however, including three extant works by Ingres. Besides the *Grande Odalisque*, we know that Caroline Murat personally acquired the first oil version of *Paolo and Francesca* (fig. 9.7), the *Betrothal of Raphael* (Museum of Fine Arts, Baltimore), and her own portrait of 1814.[36] The genre scenes are particularly interesting for our discussion because, along with the *Grande Odalisque*, they serve as indices of the queen's anacreontic taste.

Certainly Ingres's many repetitions of the *Paolo and Francesca* theme, all of which "depict the instant of their 'innocent love,'" warrant the rubric *anacreontic*.[37] The series as a whole conforms to Schneider's criteria for anacreontic works: they demonstrate "form that is pretty, often to the point of being mannered," and they are also "beautiful fables in which the best part is reserved for Eros itself."[38] The paintings all show the moment when a kiss between the diminutive figures interrupts their reading; most of them focus exclusively on this romantic moment, while others also show the intrusion of the jealous Malatesta, who slays them for betraying him. Although no fan of Ingres's "taste for the Middle Ages," the critic Edmond About clearly appreciated the role of passion in *Paolo and Francesca* when he quipped, "Paolo is not a man, he's a kiss."[39] By extending Schneider's notion of anacreontism to encompass works associated with genres other than history, we begin to see the continuities between neoclassical and romantic, classical and orientalist, orientalist and troubadour.[40] Anacreontism promotes the strange mix of aesthetic opposites that shaped Ingres's hybrid classicism, helping to explain, for example, how he could recast his neo-classical *Sleeper of Naples* as the exoticized *Odalisque with Slave* (1839; Fogg Art Museum). Finally, the composite nature of anacreontism also helps to explain the constant oscillations between the moral and the voluptuous in Ingres's work and to make clearer the apparent contradictions in these works and in the writings about them.

The attraction of anacreontic imagery for French viewers and patrons cannot be disassociated from the effects of revolution at home and unremitting war abroad or from the ways in which women increasingly lost credibility in the public sphere under the evolving Empire. Schneider summarizes the anxieties implicit in a "feminine" art:

> Now here's a feminine artist, feminine in spite of the colossal, of the Hercules and Lycas and of the Boxer, feminine to the tip of his chisel. Woman reigns in [Canova's] oeuvre, which she has moreover spontaneously adopted: Josephine, Marie-Louise, Elisa, Pauline, Caroline, Mme Récamier, Mme de Staël-Corinne, Mme de Groslier, Mme Vigée-Lebrun, the Countess Albany, all of them recognize and love themselves there. Hair, ears, extremities are attended to in detail and with coquetry. The eye and the hand slide over the round, soapy forms, without encountering any of the projections of life—muscles, folds, or veins. Adolescence and ephebes beguile him as much as woman, androgyny attracts this emasculated modeling: the sleeping Nymph is a barely disguised reminiscence of the Hermaphrodite. He likes alabaster, which is less male than marble.[41]

For Schneider, this is a world in which the familiar binary oppositions anchoring sexual difference have been set on their head, first by invoking an extended pleiad of powerful women, then by conjoining adolescence, androgyny, and women. The specter behind his list of empresses, artists, and *salonnières* is nothing less than the reversal of order itself, signified by women's control of the means of representation.

What is represented by the feminine here is the antithesis of the heroic: the emphasis on detail, round and vaporous forms, furtive eyes, slippery hands, forms devoid of muscles, folds, or veins. It is a world from which "masculine" heroism has been expunged. If the masculine exists at all in Schneider's description, it is defined solely by negation, in opposition to what it is not. A "plastique emasculée," it has lost the capacity to signify the masculine ("féminin en dépit du colossal"). A similar thing seems to happen in much of the nineteenth-century criticism of the works by Canova that he discusses. Despite the urge to codify sexual difference through recourse to strategies of opposition, even the most exaggerated signifiers of the "masculine" in Canova's work—the *Hercules and Lycas*, the *Boxer*—are not convincing.

Ingres would seem to have experienced a similar anxiety about "the expression of force and energetic character." In his various series, he frequently chose to depict the moment of "innocent love" to the exclusion of other narrative episodes that were originally part of the project. For instance, despite repeated mentions in his notebooks, there is no evidence that Ingres ever undertook a composition for Hercules and the Pygmies. Ingres's predilection for "innocent love" also helps explain his failure to complete the pendant murals of *The Golden Age* and *The Iron Age* for the Château de Dampierre, where he worked for ten years on the idyllic scene while barely beginning its fearsome counterpart. But there are instances in which Ingres tried to express "force and energetic character": the overdetermined binary oppositions in a work like *Achilles Receiving the Ambassadors of Agamemnon* (1801; Ecole Nationale Supérieure des Beaux-Arts, Paris) certainly represent one; the inflated torso of the king of the gods in *Jupiter and Thetis* (1811; Musée Granet, Aix) is another. The exaggerated musculature in the *Saint Symphorian* (1834; Cathedral of Autun), which was criticized almost to the point of ridicule, similarly betrays anxiety about sexual difference. Ingres's failure to stabilize difference on male bodies is as instructive as his success in equating the female body with the sensual, and with the nude itself.[42]

NOTES

1. See Carol Ockman, *Ingres's Eroticized Bodies: Retracing the Serpentine Line* (New Haven, Conn.: Yale University Press, 1995), chs. 4 and 6.

2. According to Leopoldo Cicognara, Murat commissioned the standing version, symbolizing innocence, as a pendant to the reclining version, symbolizing *volupté* (Cicognara, *Storia della scultura dal suo risorgimento in Italia fino al secolo di Canova* [Prato: I Fratelli Giachetti, 1824], 7: 259).

3. Mario Praz, "Canova, or the Erotic Frigidaire," *Art News* 56 (November 1957): 24–27+.

4. Cited in Hans Naef, "La Dormeuse de Naples: Un dessin inédit d'Ingres," *Revue de l'art*, nos. 1–2 (1968): 102. This and subsequent translations are the author's. For the original texts, see Ockman, *Ingres's Eroticized Bodies*, 152–58. On Ingres's attempts to recover the *Sleeper of Naples*, see Nouvelles Acquisitions Françaises 22817, fol. 241, Salle des Manuscrits, Bibliothèque Nationale, Paris; and Hans Naef, "Un Chef-d'oeuvre retrouvé: *Le Portrait de la reine Caroline Murat* par Ingres," *Revue de l'art*, no. 88 (1990): 11–20.

5. Letter to the count of Narbonne-Pelet, French ambassador to Naples, cited in Naef, "Deux dessins d'Ingres, Monseigneur Cortois de Pressigny et le chevalier de Fontenay," *Revue de l'art*, no. 6 (1957): 248.

6. Gérard Hubert, *La Sculpture dans l'Italie Napoléonienne* (Paris: Editeur E. de Boccard, 1964), 152.

7. Virtually all of the literature on Paolina Borghese includes discussion of her amorous adventures with men other than her two husbands, General Victor-Emmanuel Leclerc, who died in 1802, and Prince Camillo Borghese, whom she married in 1804.

8. Quatremère de Quincy, *Canova et ses ouvrages* (Paris: Adrien Le Clere et Cie, 1834), 149. Quatremère is undoubtedly referring to the moment when the statue was transferred from Paolina Borghese's residence in Torino, where the statue was displayed in her private apartment, to the Galleria Borghese in 1814.

9. For socializing between Récamier and the Bonaparte sisters, see Edouard Herriot, *Madame Récamier et ses amis* (Paris: Plon, 1905), 1: 60. Eight surviving letters, written by Caroline Murat to Mme Récamier from 1824 to 1838, now in the Archives Nationales (31 AP 28 d. 598), indicate the longevity of their friendship. See also Jeanne-Françoise Récamier, *Souvenirs et correspondance tirés des papiers de Madame Récamier* (Paris: Michel Lévy Frères, 1859), 1: 275–76, 279–81; 2: 143–46, 173–74, 177–78. Mme Récamier also visited the queen during her reign in Naples and subsequently during her exile in Trieste in May 1825.

One of the two busts inspired by Mme Récamier was later recast as *Beatrice* (Ennio Francia, "Madame Récamier a Roma e l'amicizia con Canova," *Strenna dei romanisti* 50 [1989]: 195–96).

10. Angelo Borzelli, *Le Relazioni del Canova con Napoli al tempo di Ferdinando I e di Gioacchino Murat* (Napoli: Emilio Prass, 1901), 21–28.

11. Mazois excavated Pompei under a contract from the queen and published his findings in *Les Ruines de Pompei*, 2 vols. (Paris: Firmin Didot, 1824). (See Hans Naef, *Die Bildniszeichnungen* [Bern: Benteli Verlag, 1978], 1: 344ff.)

12. For their chronologies, see Francia, *Delfina de Custine, Luisa Stolberg, Giulietta Récamier a Canova: Lettere inedite* (Roma: Edizioni di Storia e Letteratura, 1972), 127–28; and Naef, "Un Chef-d'oeuvre retrouvé," 12. On the recently rediscovered portrait of the queen of Naples, see below. Ingres made several drawings for "un petit tableau de la noble famille." See Daniel Ternois, *Les Dessins d'Ingres au Musée de Montauban, les portraits* (Paris: Presses Artistiques, 1939), vol. 3, nos. 139–148; Naef, *Die Bildniszeichnungen* 4: 210–21; and Henry Lapauze, *Le Roman d'amour de M. Ingres* (Paris: P. Lafitte et Cie., 1910), 268, cited in Naef, "Un Chef-d'oeuvre retrouvé," 12.

13. For 1808 works, see François Boyer, "Autour de Canova et de Napoléon," *Revue des études italiennes* (July–September 1937), 215; and Italo Faldi, *Galleria Borghese: Le Sculture dal secolo XVI al XIX* (Roma: Istituto Poligrafico dello Stato, 1954), 46. A drawing by Pelagio Palagi illustrates the visit of Murat to the exhibition the morning of November 14, 1809 (reproduced in Elena di Majo et al., *Bertel Thorvaldsen* [Roma: De Luca Edizioni d'Arte, 1989], 8).

14. On Mme Récamier, see Francia, *Delfina de Custine*, 122. On Paolina Borghese's statue, see Quatremère de Quincy, *Canova et ses ouvrages*, 149; on Caroline Murat, see Margery Weiner, *The Parvenu Princesses* (London: John Murray, 1964), 211. For an analysis of the inappropriateness of women in the public sphere, see Sarah Maza, "The Diamond Necklace Affair Revisited (1785–1786): The Case of the Missing Queen,"

and Lynn Hunt, "The Many Bodies of Marie Antoinette: Political Pornography and the Problem of the Feminine in the French Revolution," both in *Eroticism and the Body Politic*, ed. Lynn Hunt (Baltimore: Johns Hopkins University Press, 1991), 63–89 and 108–30. See also Joan Landes, *Women and the Public Sphere in the Age of the French Revolution* (Ithaca, N.Y.: Cornell University Press, 1988), 93ff.

15. On Mme Récamier's preference for Gérard's portrait, see Anita Brookner, *Jacques-Louis David* (New York: Harper and Row, 1980), 145.

16. See Gérard, *Portrait of Caroline Murat with Her Children Achille and Laetitia*, 1803, reproduced in Comtesse Rasponi, *Souvenirs d'enfance d'une fille de Joachim Murat, La Princesse Louise Murat Comtesse Rasponi 1805–1815* (Paris: Perrin et Cie., 1929), facing 20; and Vigée-Lebrun, *Portrait de Caroline Murat avec sa fille Laetitia*, reproduced in Hubert Cole, *The Betrayers Joachim and Caroline Murat* (London: Eyre Methuen, 1972), plate 10. For an analysis of portraits of women emphasizing their maternal role, see Carol Duncan, "Happy Mothers and Other New Ideas in Eighteenth-Century French Art," in *Feminism and Art History*, ed. Norma Broude and Mary D. Garrard (New York: Harper and Row, 1982), 200–219.

17. Cavaignac in Mme Cavaignac, *Mémoires d'une inconnue, 1718–1816* (Paris: Plon, 1894), 231. Niepperg cited in Cole, *The Betrayers*, 240.

18. Cited in Albert Vandal, "Le Roi et la Reine de Naples (1801–1812)," *Revue des deux mondes*, 1 February 1910, 488. For the queen's roles, see ibid., 15 February 1910, 767, 771–72.

19. La Feuillade d'Aubusson, "Murat et Caroline en 1809," *Feuilles d'histoire* (1910). A copy of this article, in longhand, is in the Archives Nationales, Paris: 31 AP 47: 1–13.

20. Cited in Comtesse Rasponi, *Souvenirs d'enfance*, 83.

21. Naef, "Un Chef-d'oeuvre retrouvé," 11–20.

22. The portrait of *Napoléon Bonaparte, First Consul* is much larger (225.7 × 144.2 cm) than *Queen Caroline Murat* (92 × 60 cm).

23. See Cole, *The Betrayers*, 202 ff., for regency. Given both Ingres's increasing reliance on the *napoléonides* for patronage and certain events in his private life—his father's death in March 1814, the stillbirth of his first and only child in August—there was a distinctly personal component to this wish for continuity.

24. See Lapauze, *Le Roman d'amour*, 267.

25. Quoted passages are from René Schneider, "L'Art anacréontique ou alexandrin sous l'Empire," *Revue des études napoléoniennes* 2 (1916): 258. On anacreontism, see also Schneider, "L'art de Canova," 36–57.

26. Visconti, cited in Elena di Majo et al., *Bertel Thorvaldsen*, 22 n. 12.

27. Quatremère de Quincy, "Sur M. Canova, et les quatre ouvrages qu'on voit de lui à l'exposition publique de 1808," *Le Moniteur universel*, 28 December 1808, 1429–30.

28. From "Della Grazia," fifth argument in *Del Bello*, cited in Leopoldo Cicognara, *Lettere ad Antonio Canova*, ed. Gianni Venturi (Urbino: Argagli Editore, 1973), xvi. Begun in 1802, *Del Bello* was first published in Florence in 1808.

29. Quotations from Quatremère de Quincy, "Sur M. Canova," 1429.

30. Foscolo, cited in Francesca Romana Fratini, "Opere di scultura e plastica di Antonio Canova, di Isabella Teotochi Albrizzi," *Studi canoviani [Quaderni sul neoclassico]* (Rome: Bulzoni, 1973), 45 n. 5. The *Venus Italica*, which Napoleon commissioned to replace the *Medici Venus* in the Pitti Palace, arrived in Florence on 29 April 1812, approximately ten years after the ancient work was taken to Paris as the "bride" for the *Apollo Belvedere* (Hugh Honour, "Canova's Statues of Venus," *Burlington Magazine* 114 [October 1972]: 658, 665–66).

31. Schneider, "L'Art anacréontique," 259.

32. Ibid., 258.

33. For the approach emphasizing feminine taste, see Eleanor Tufts, *Our Hidden Heritage* (London: Paddington Press, 1974); Karen Petersen and J. J. Wilson, *Women Artists: Recognition and Reappraisal from the Early Middle Ages to the Twentieth Century* (New York: Harper and Row, 1976); Ann Sutherland Harris and Linda Nochlin, *Women Artists, 1550–1950* (Los Angeles: Los Angeles County Museum of Art and New York: Alfred A. Knopf, 1976). For a critique, see Lisa Tickner, "Feminism, Art History, and Sexual Difference," *Genders* 3 (Fall 1988): 93–128; and Diana Fuss, *Essentially Speaking: Feminism, Nature and Difference* (New York: Routledge, 1989).

34. On the *napoléonides* and patronage, see especially Paul Marmottan, *Les Arts en Toscane sous Napoléon: La Princesse Elisa* (Paris: H. Champion, 1901), and *Murat à l'Elysée* (Paris: P. Chéronnet, 1912); Ross E.

Taggart, *The Taste of Napoleon* (Kansas City, Mo.: Nelson Gallery and Atkins Museum of Fine Arts, 1969); Williams Buchanan, *Memoirs of Painting with a chronological history of the Importation of Pictures by the Great Masters into England* (London: R. Ackerman, 1824), 2: 269–94; and François Piétri, *Lucien Bonaparte* (Paris: Plon, 1939). On Josephine's collection in particular, see *Catalogue des tableaux de sa majesté l'impératrice Joséphine* (Paris: Imprimerie de Didot Jeune, 1811); Alain Pougetoux, *La Collection de peintures de l'impératrice Josephine* (Paris: Réunion des Musées Nationaux, 2003); M. de Lescure, *Le Château de Malmaison* (Paris: Plon, 1867); and Serge Grandjean, *Inventaire après le décès de l'impératrice Joséphine à Malmaison* (Paris: Réunion des Musées Nationaux, 1964). Auguste Garnerey's watercolor view of the music room (1812; Château de Malmaison), containing many of the empress's paintings, is reproduced in ibid. and in Pougetoux.

35. Grandjean, *Inventaire*, 37.

36. For the Murats' purchases, see Marmottan, *Murat à l'Elysée*, 23–34. For the Ingres paintings, see Patricia Condon, with Marjorie B. Cohn and Agnes Mongan, *In Pursuit of Perfection: The Art of J.-A.-D. Ingres* (Louisville, Ky.: J. B. Speed Art Museum, 1983), 70; and Wendy Leeks, "The 'Family Romance' and Repeated Themes in the Work of J.-A.-D. Ingres" (Ph.D. diss., University of Leeds, 1990), 222–24.

37. Ingres used the phrase "innocent love" in his ninth notebook, cited in Condon et al., *Pursuit of Perfection*, from which I draw the larger quotation, 70.

38. Schneider, "L'Art anacréontique," 258.

39. About, cited in Marie-Claude Chaudonneret, "Ingres: Paolo et Francesca," Galérie d'Essai, Ville de Bayonne, Musée Bayonne (dossier), n.p.

40. Indeed, the Hellenizing classicism described by Schneider *is* Asian; while the classical pedigree in no way diminishes the ideological imperialism at the heart of the *Grande Odalisque* and other orientalist works, it does soften the timeworn distinction between the *Sleeper of Naples* as classical nude and the *Grande Odalisque* as orientalist nude.

41. Schneider, "L'Art de Canova," 55. See also David d'Angers's response to Canova's works, originally published in 1844, and cited in Henry Jouin, *David d'Angers: Sa Vie, son oeuvre, ses écrits et ses contemporains* (Paris: Plon et Cie, 1878), 1: 76–77.

42. "The expression of force and energetic character" is a phrase Quatremère de Quincy used in his defense of Canova ("Sur Canova," 1430). For Hercules and the Pygmies, see Cahier 1, fol. 118v., Musée Ingres, Montauban, France. For the Château of Dampierre, see Ockman, "*Astraea Redux*: A Monarchist Reading of Ingres' Unfinished Murals at Dampierre," *Arts* (October 1986): 21–27; and "The Restoration of the Château of Dampierre: Ingres, the Duc de Luynes and an Unrealized Vision of History" (Ph.D. diss., Yale University, 1982). When *Jupiter and Thetis* was submitted as an *envoi* in 1811, the judges at the Institut de France considered the god's torso to be "d'une largeur exagerée dans sa partie supérieure, et étroit à l'attache des hanches" (Archives de l'Académie des Beaux-Arts: Procès verbaux de la Classe des Beaux-Arts, 5 E5 28 December 1811). For the exaggerated musculature in the *Saint Symphorian*, see Ockman, *Ingres's Eroticized Bodies*, ch. 4.

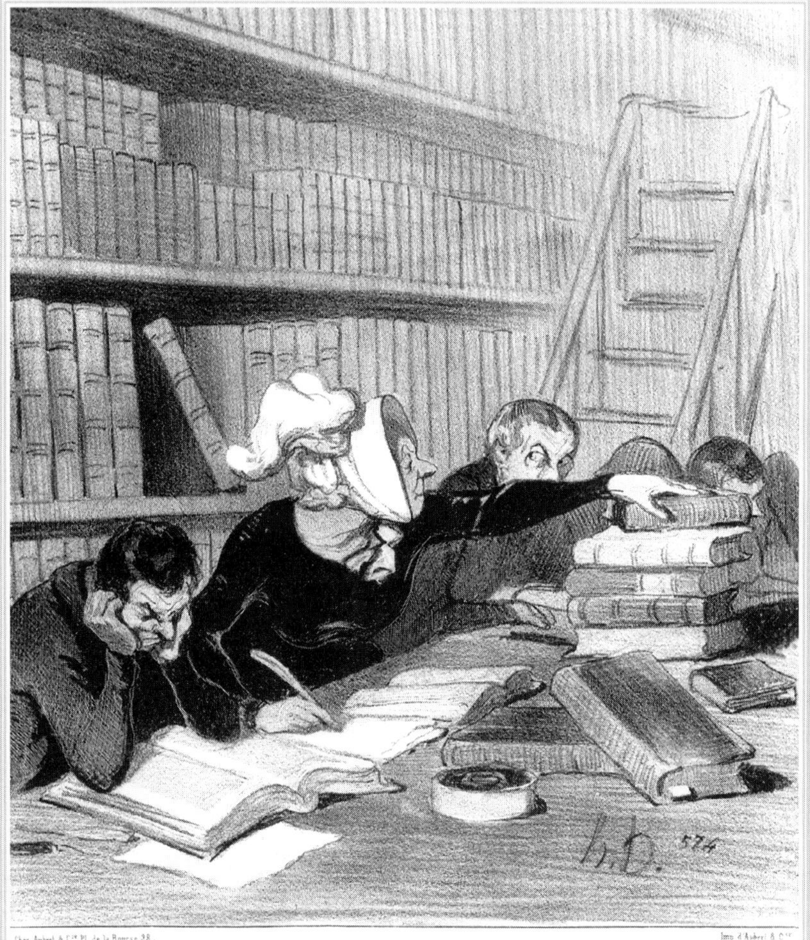

Chez Aubert & Cie Pl. de la Bourse 28. Imp. d'Aubert & Cie

– Monsieur, pardon si je vous gêne un peu . . . . mais vous comprenez qu'écrivant en ce moment un roman nouveau, je dois consulter une foule d'auteurs anciens ! . . . . . .

– (Le Monsieur à part.) Des auteurs anciens ! . . . parbleu elle aurait bien dû les consulter de leur vivant, car elle a dû être leur contemporaine ! . . . .

IO

CONDUCT UNBECOMING

Daumier and Les Bas-Bleus

Janis Bergman-Carton

THE LAST FEW decades have produced numerous iconographical studies of female typological imagery in nineteenth-century French caricature and painting. Dominated by accounts of courtesans and women victimized into prostitution by social or economic constraints, these studies usefully call attention to the obsession with the urban reality of French working-class women. But their focus principally on victimized women perpetuates a single model of female identity at the expense of more complex and equally historical ones. This essay resurrects an alternative model, prevalent in nineteenth-century art and life yet ignored in twentieth-century critical literature—that of the intellectual or political woman, what I call "the woman of ideas."

Though the concept of the woman of ideas in France is centuries old, the classification is not. More commonly and derogatorily labeled *le bas-bleu, la femme-homme,* or *l'amazon littéraire,* the woman of ideas is a female type born of the success and notoriety of such figures as Christine de Pizan and Mme de Staël, whose published works were viewed by many as invasions of traditionally masculine public realms

of literature and politics. The phrase *woman of ideas* refers to a figure principally identified by her nineteenth-century contemporaries (satirically or not) as an intellectual being who recognizes and utilizes the power of words to influence public opinion. It does not refer to the scores of talented women with careers in painting and music, areas in which women were able to function more easily without challenging male assessments of the feminine nature. Rather, the label is intended exclusively to describe women operating in the fields of literature and politics—two highly valued aspects of French public life for which women were considered ill-suited.

In the nineteenth century, the woman of ideas became an increasingly popular target for visual and literary satires. One of the most extensive caricatural treatments of the subject is found in the oeuvre of Honoré Daumier. Between 1837 and 1849, Daumier devoted over seventy lithographs to the subject. The one or two paragraphs by previous Daumier scholars who discuss these images at all range from unselfconscious restatements of Daumier's antifeminist sentiments to assurances that Daumier was offended not

This essay was first published in *Femmes d'Esprit: Women in Daumier's Caricature,* ed. Kirsten Powell and Elizabeth C. Childs, exh. cat. (Middlebury, Vt.: Christian A. Johnson Memorial Art Gallery, Middlebury College, 1990), 65–86. Reprinted by permission of the Christian A. Johnson Memorial Art Gallery and the author.

Figure 10.1. Honoré Daumier, *Monsieur, pardon si je vous gêne un peu* . . . From *Le Charivari,* 8 March 1844. Lithograph. Print Collection, Miriam and Ira D. Wallach Division of Art, Prints, and Photographs, The New York Public Library, Astor, Lenox, and Tilden Foundations.

by feminist theory but by the feminists themselves. Arsène Alexandre's 1888 characterization of Daumier's "Bas-Bleus" concludes simply that these are "women who do not want to resign themselves to being women."[1] More than a century later, the criticism of these series is barely more substantive. Howard Vincent writes that Daumier's attitude reflects nothing more than "dislike of the anti-feminine woman, the enthusiast . . . who is, after all . . . a natural target for the satirist's laughter."[2] Oliver Larkin explains in *Daumier: Man of His Time* that Daumier's ridicule is directed not at the notion of reform but at its sententious high priestesses and camp followers.[3]

Of the few essays devoted exclusively to Daumier's caricatures of the woman of ideas, most were written, not surprisingly, in the mid 1970s, the period in which the impact of feminism on art history and criticism was first registered.[4] Françoise Parturier's *Intellectuelles ("Les Bas-Bleus" et "Femmes socialistes")* and Cäcilia Rentmeister's more scholarly "Daumier und das hässliche Geschlect," for example, provide contextual enrichment essential to the reading of Daumier's imagery. But these texts are principally concerned with elucidating the present through the resurrection of a comparable historical moment. They neither analyze the lithographs in any detail nor examine these works' power to reinforce and generate social mythologies of gender.

During the July Monarchy, the avenues of expression for women had expanded, owing in part to opportunities generated by industrialization in France. Not only traditional gender distinctions but class boundaries as well were rendered more fluid by the new outlets for female expression and the material and political rewards they entailed. Daumier's caricatures of the woman of ideas deny or discredit this fluidity by reducing the female form to the dichotomous alternatives of angelic mother or demonic whore.[5] This essay examines Daumier's largest series on the subject, *Les Bas-Bleus*, which formed part of the cultural mechanism that undermined the literary and political achievements of women after 1830. It analyzes the way in which Daumier trivialized what was genuinely powerful about the woman of ideas by figuring her as a deviant, a creature who disrupts households, neglects children, and uses her fame to satisfy unnatural sexual appetites.

The principal arenas for the intellectual woman in the July Monarchy of concern here are the reemergence of a women's emancipation movement in the context of utopian socialist reform rhetoric and the burgeoning popular press. The impetus for feminist activities during the July Monarchy derived from the male leaders of the emerging French socialist movements, who tended to associate women's rights with workers' rights and general political reform. Charles Fourier and the Saint-Simonist leader Prosper Enfantin, for example, viewed female liberation as the natural measure of the humanist ideal of general emancipation, as part of the larger struggle to achieve a communal society free of all inequities.[6]

The woman of ideas also flourished within the rapid growth of the periodical press. Middle- and working-class women, to whom most respectable professional careers had been closed because of legal, economic, or educational restrictions, were able to claim a career in letters after 1830 thanks to the fundamental changes taking place within what became known as the "French literary industry." As a serialized novelist, a *chroniqueuse,* an editor or publisher of literary or political magazines, and the targeted reader of the numerous *modiste* journals, during the July Monarchy the woman of ideas became a fashionable female model and favorite subject for caricatural attack. The activities of women like George Sand, Marie d'Agoult, and Flora Tristan inspired hundreds of caricatures by Daumier, Gavarni, Cham, de Beaumont, and others.

While Daumier's series *Les Bas-Bleus* must be seen as part of the general response in the popular press to the increased visibility of the woman of ideas, its fundamental context remains the antifeminist policies of *Le Charivari*, the journal in which all of the lithographs appeared, and its forerunner, *La Caricature*.[7] The first textual references to the woman of ideas in these publications appeared in nonsatirical book reviews that were descriptive and promotional rather than analytical. In fact, many titles among the books reviewed reappear on page four, in the section devoted to advertisements.[8]

Although accounts of books by women by and large were friendly in the early 1830s, they were supplanted later in the decade by hostile satirical articles on the woman of ideas. The change is due in part to Louis-Philippe's censorial September Laws of 1835, which forced the journal's editor, Charles Philipon, to redirect the satirical focus of *Le Charivari* from the *juste-milieu* government to less overtly political subject matter.[9] Following the imposition of these restrictions, Philipon found it necessary to alter the focus of *Le Charivari* to include art and literary criticism and social caricature. Daumier's series on the woman of ideas, like most of his lithographic work between 1835 and 1848, has been relegated to this so-called lesser aspect of his oeuvre, to the period when the artist was forced to suppress his political concerns in favor of benign scenes of everyday life.

The number of articles on the woman of ideas in *Le Charivari* increased dramatically after 1835. The legally mandated shift in editorial focus from the government of Louis-Philippe to such subjects as the plays of Virginie Ancelot must have foregrounded an inequitable situation: the avenues for women writers to publicize women's issues were growing just as the opportunities for Philipon and his staff to exercise their own political agenda were waning. Unable to express their anger at Louis-Philippe, the source of their disempowerment, male journalists redirected a portion of their wrath toward a figure they saw as the female usurper of the male place, the newly professionalized *femme-auteur*. The most offensive of these usurpers was the increasingly successful *femme de lettres*.[10]

A female literary tradition had existed in France since the fifteenth century, but, until the nineteenth century, it had been aristocratic and tied principally to the institution of the salon. The hostility toward the nineteenth-century woman of ideas derived from her increasing enjoyment of the financial and critical rewards once reserved exclusively for men. It also responded to her evolution in this period from *femme-auteur* to what the nineteenth-century playwright and essayist Frédéric Soulié labeled *le bas-bleu militant*.[11]

The personality who appears to have emblematized the bourgeois *bas-bleu militant* and whose activities prompted the first sustained attack on the woman of ideas in *Le Charivari* was Mme Marie-Madeleine Poutret de Mauchamp, who in 1836 established a moderate republican "journal de législation et de jurisprudence" called *Gazette des femmes*. The model for the *Gazette des femmes* was Desirée Veret and Reine Guidorf's Saint-Simonist newspaper *La Femme libre* (1832–34). Although the writers for *La Femme libre* were harangued constantly in the legitimist and *juste-milieu* press in the early 1830s, they barely received mention in Philipon's publications. Their working-class origins seem to have ensured the benign neglect if not the sympathy of Philipon, who reserved his contempt for the bourgeois women whom he accused of arrogating the feminist rhetoric of Veret and Guindorf and capitalizing on the vogue of *la femme emancipée*.[12]

Mme Poutret de Mauchamps's purpose, articulated in the first issue of the *Gazette des Femmes*, was to educate women about legal issues and provide a platform to agitate for reform in the areas of political and civil rights. Her journal flourished between 1836 and 1838, until she, like the Saint-Simonist guru Père Enfantin, was officially silenced after being tried and convicted on fabricated morals charges.[13]

The *Gazette des Femmes* was prominent during the years when *Le Charivari* first began to mock the woman of ideas. One of the earliest attacks appears in a review of Théodore Muret's comedy *Les Droits de la femme*, which opened at the Théâtre Français in May 1837. The reviewer analyzes the female protagonist's development, under the influence of Poutret de Mauchamp, from innocent to *bas-bleu militant*: "Madame reads the novels of George Sand, she cries at performances of *Marie* [a highly publicized play by Virginie Ancelot],[14] she is up to date on all of the demonstrations and insurrections recently publicized by women through the press and the popular theater."[15] The paradigm to which the play and its review conforms—the impressionable victim manipulated by an evil female mentor—is reproduced often in the

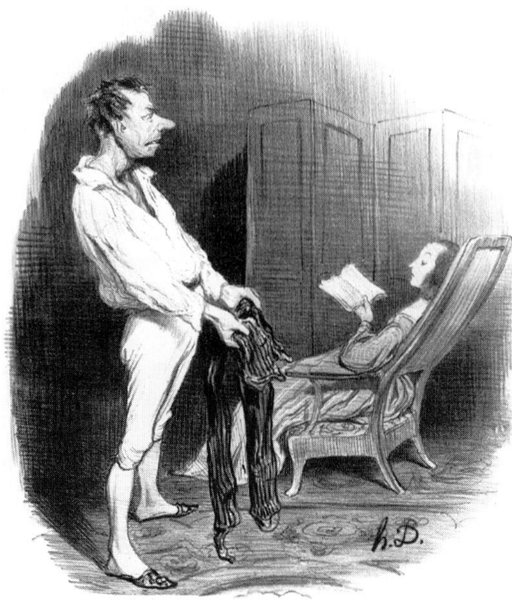

Figure 10.2. Honoré Daumier, *Je me fiche bien de votre Mme SAND* . . . From *Le Charivari*, 30 June 1839. Lithograph. Bibliothèque nationale de France, Cabinet des estampes, Paris. (Photo: Bibliothèque nationale de France, Paris.)

pages of *Le Charivari* to account for the evolution of the woman of ideas.[16]

The review of Muret's play is followed, several issues later, by a lengthy article, "Curiosités littéraires: Les Demoiselles de lettres," which describes the phenomenon of the provincial woman of ideas.[17] In a scenario that bears a striking resemblance to the sad tale of Daumier's father, she is said to discover one morning that life in the provinces is too limited.[18] She flees to Paris, where she makes the ritualistic visit to George Sand, who does not receive her, and Mme de Poutret de Mauchamps, who welcomes her with open arms. A week later, *la demoiselle de lettres* is no longer recognizable, "preaching the liberation of woman and the enslavement of man."[19]

Throughout 1837, the invectives in *Le Charivari* against the woman of ideas intensify. The journal features mock petitions from Poutret de Mauchamps to Louis-Philippe and expands the rubric of the woman

of ideas to include current female heads of state like Queen Victoria of England and Queen Maria Christina of Spain. In diatribes that give thanks for the French *lois saliques* as they ridicule Victoria's and Maria Christina's incompetence and unnatural relations with men, articles in *Le Charivari* warn of the fate of France should Poutret de Mauchamps's efforts to empower women succeed.[20] The journal uses the same rhetorical formulae to describe women as different in stature and responsibility as Poutret de Mauchamps and Queen Victoria, demonstrating how the woman of ideas evolved during the July Monarchy as the typological evocation of female deviance.

The impulse to diminish the reality of the woman of ideas by casting her as a type antithetical and dangerous to a female ideal is nowhere more explicit than in the work of Honoré Daumier.[21] Daumier's first representation of the intellectual woman appeared in 1839 as part of the *Moeurs conjugales* series. It images the threat posed by the woman of ideas rather than the writer herself, including her as an objectified concept rather than a physical entity. *Je me fiche bien de votre Mme SAND* (fig. 10.2) focuses on the impotent husband of a wife who has fallen under the spell of the unscrupulous George Sand, who here exists only as a disembodied presence. In the lithograph, a man holding a pair of trousers stands before his wife, who is seated in an easy chair absorbed in a novel. Their torsos incline backward, his in a gesture of indignant disbelief and hers slovenly conforming to the angle of her chair, punctuating the physical and psychic distance between them. His unmended pants are held in front of his genitals and mark the center of the composition, in counterpoint to the book. With disheveled hair, grimacing mouth, and protruding nose, he is the emasculated, ineffectual fool. She is individuated only by her dress and posture, her blurred and undistinguished facial features likened to the white pages of the text that assumes and becomes her identity.

"I don't give a damn about your Mme SAND," the husband declares in the legend, "who prevents women from mending pants and darning socks! . . . We must reestablish divorce or suppress those authors!" As Philippe Roberts-Jones notes, this image was published on June 28, 1839, around the same time that Sand's novel *Spiridion* was published, the same year that her portrait by Auguste Charpentier was hung at the Salon (and, in fact, reproduced in *Le Charivari*, just two and a half weeks earlier), and the same year that her most provocative book, *Lélia*, was re-released[22]—a book that incited critics like Capo de Feuillades to advise his readers to lock it away so that it could contaminate no one, especially young girls, whose virgin souls need protection from a text as perverse in places as the works of the marquis de Sade.[23]

A similar marital encounter is the subject of *Un intérieur parisien*, a lithograph from the lengthy *Moeurs conjugales* series published in May 1842, a full three years later. Like the first, it reenacts a scene of domestic disorder engendered by a woman who has been corrupted by novels. What is different, however, is that the husband no longer complains; he too appears bloodless and inanimate. Furthermore, the legend in this later work is descriptive rather than dialogic: "Monsieur is the homemaker; Madame is thinking of being the home-wrecker." The husband quietly mops the floor and attempts to maintain the very domestic order that the wife's novel encourages her to disrupt.

By 1842 the association of women reading and writing with domestic disarray had become a commonplace. Neither the text nor the author needs identification, nor is a description of the husband's misfortune necessary. The scenario would have been instantly recognized by an audience in 1842 that had been inundated since 1840 with similar parables in the popular theater and press concerning the French version of the British bluestocking.[24]

The *bas-bleu* was the subject of a number of plays in the early 1840s, including Ferdinand Langlé and F. de Villeneuve's *Le Bas-Bleu* at the Théâtre des Variétés, Pacini's opéra-séria *Saffo* (the celebrated *bas-bleu* from the island of Lesbos) at the Théâtre des Italiens, and de Veau and Brisson's *La Fille aux bas-bleus* at the Théâtre Français. Most were variations on the theme of misguided women who, after having followed the example of an unethical *bas-bleu*, were saved from humiliation and destitution by a wise man. And most ended in marriage—the institution ma-

ligned by the female protagonists in the early moments of the play—with a promise, like that made by Athenais in Langlé and de Villeneuve's comedy, that from now on pants will be worn only by husbands and "I will use my quill only for my hats."[25]

Daumier's caricatural series, the content of which appears to have been in large part dictated by the editorial board of *Le Charivari*, often capitalized on well-received themes from the popular theater. But the decision to develop *Les Bas-Bleus* seems to have been a response principally to the success of several *physiologies* published between 1840 and 1842. *Les Bas-Bleus*, Daumier's first and largest series on the woman of ideas, consists of forty lithographs issued intermittently in *Le Charivari* between January 30 and August 7, 1844. The series draws extensively from Frédéric Soulié's *Physiologie du bas-bleu* (1841–42), Edmund Texier's *Physiologie du poète* (1841), and Jules Janin's "Un Bas-Bleu," a typological essay included in Louis Curmer's *Les Français peints par eux-mêmes* (1842).[26]

Almost all of the lithographs in Daumier's *Les Bas-Bleus* visualize and embellish clichés or anecdotes from one of these three sources. The first plate of the series, for instance, *C'est singulier comme ce miroir m'applatit . . .* (fig. 10.3), concretizes Frédéric Soulié's description of *le bas-bleu véritable* "who floats between forty-five and fifty-five years old, . . . [who has] a skinny body, . . . a sad smile, . . . [and] an emaciated bosom."[27] The lithograph features a woman examining herself in a full-length mirror. Behind her hangs a painting that invokes Daumier's engraving of *la dixième muse* (the name assigned female poets during the Restoration and July Monarchy), published three years earlier as the frontispiece to Texier's *Physiologie du poète*. She is surrounded by discarded clothing that had padded her straight silhouette to make it appear curvaceous and conventionally female. Having removed the false garments, she is shown to be vainly and foolishly attributing her sexlessness to the mirror's inadequacies rather than her own. She stands facing us, glancing over her left shoulder to see the "distorted" reflection of her curveless back. A literal embodiment of the popular phrase *la femme-*

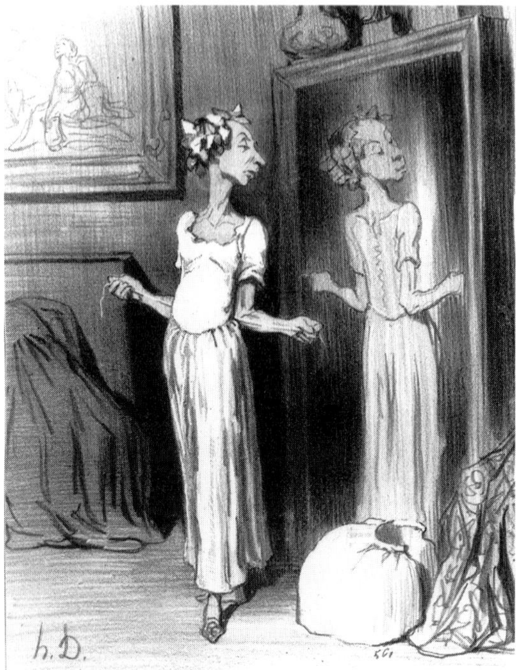

Figure 10.3. Honoré Daumier, *C'est singulier comme ce miroir m'applatit la taille* . . . From *Le Charivari*, 30 January 1844. Lithograph. Bibliothèque nationale de France, Cabinet des estampes, Paris. (Photo: Bibliothèque nationale de France, Paris.)

homme de lettres, this long-nosed, weak-chinned figure marvels at the "distortions" of her mirror: "How strange the way this mirror makes my figure appear straight and my bosom meager! What do I care anyway? Mme de Staël and M. de Buffon have proclaimed that genius has no sex." We, who are given a direct frontal view of the *bas-bleu*, are privy to the visual joke that her chest is a mirror image of her curveless back—in or out of the reflection. Daumier and his legend writer pun on the famous phrase "genius has no sex"—intended by Mme de Staël to assert the intellectual equality of women—to shift focus from the *bas-bleu*'s success as a thinker to her failures as a woman. The lithograph offers its audience a moral lesson: women who substitute the life of the mind for the life of the home are no longer women.

Over half of Daumier's *bas-bleus* are berated for their dearth of sexual and intellectual powers. Within that genre, most are also maligned for their role in denigrating the literary arts. During the July Monarchy, the literary establishment debated the merits of the growing commercialization of literature. The success of the woman of ideas was often part of that debate. For instance, in Daumier's *Monsieur, pardon si je vous gêne un peu . . .* (fig. 10.1), a foolish old woman consumed by her desire for fame fails to recognize the inappropriateness of her aggressive behavior. She dominates the table of a library reading room. Her right elbow intrudes on one neighbor's space, as her other arm reaches out unself-consciously toward a stack of books, blocking the man to her left. The tidy arrangement of the volumes on the shelves behind the readers echoes the self-contained dignity of the men, just as the only book that is askew, disrupting the order, is the one behind the *bas-bleu*'s head. Its irregularity underscores hers, the only woman and presumably the only nonintellect in the library.

In the early 1840s, prior to Daumier's series, *Le Charivari* published many articles on the women with whom male writers had to compete for jobs and government subsidies. The most venomous attacks focused on the phenomenon of journalistic nepotism—the practice of giving women undeserved publishing opportunities that they abused by sentimentalizing and cheapening literature.[28]

The identification of the *bas-bleu* with the bourgeois *femme-auteur*, who subverts the concept of family and corrupts the conventions of literature, pervades the typological studies of Texier, Soulié, and Janin. Texier's *Physiologie du poète*, for example, a project to which Daumier contributed forty-one woodcut illustrations, classifies the various types of poets writing in Paris. The range of male poets—from aristocratic gentlemen to members of the proletariat—is striking in its economic and social diversity. Furthermore, though each is vulnerable to charges of vanity and self-absorption, none is accused of subverting the social order. Conversely, the discussion of female poets is relegated to the final two chapters and makes no such class distinction. Texier's representation of *la dixième muse* is uniformly bourgeois. Moreover, when the charges of self-centeredness are levied against her rather than her male counterpart, the tone is harsh and moralizing: "The tenth muse has multiplied at a terrifying rate. She has grown without cultivation like a fungus . . . in the pages of serialized novels and on page four of the daily newspapers."[29]

Soulié's pseudohistorical survey, *Physiologie du bas-bleu*, also focuses on the dangers of the bourgeois *femme-auteur* whose ascendancy he dates to the Revolution of 1830.[30] Like most *physiologies*, Soulié disguises an idiosyncratic choice of content with a veneer of scientific classification and the rhetoric of social truism. The arbitrariness of what purports to be a legitimate categorization of the contemporary bourgeois *bas-bleu* is revealed in chapter 6, "Bas-Bleus mariées, deuxième espèce," a figure who is, according to Soulié, " the most evil of all."[31] In this chapter claiming to describe a type of *bas-bleu*, there is only the story of an ambitious wife who offers herself to a cabinet minister to obtain a position for her husband as consul of state. Absolutely nothing in the chapter beyond its title would prompt the identification of the woman as a *bas-bleu*. The label often was used indiscriminately in journalism and popular literature during the July Monarchy as a synonym for the aggressive female. It signified the freedom and confidence with which many women were operating in the public arena more than their involvement in literary activities per se. Soulié makes explicit this opposition between "le bas-bleu contemporain" and her aristocratic ancestors, whose influence was restricted to the private sphere of the salon. He asserts that the contemporary bourgeois *bas-bleu* is contemptible, "like everything that falls in the public domain."[32]

Jules Janin also credits the Revolution of 1830 with the sudden glorification of the written and spoken word and the hideous metamorphosis of the once-charming *salonnière* into an obsessive, fame-hungry *bas-bleu*. In "Un Bas-Bleu," Janin charges that modern journalism, the progeny of the French Revolution, has cheapened and corrupted literature. His essay alternates between a fiery assault on the preoccupation of the modern writer with issues of sala-

bility and an unfocused description of the bourgeois *bas-bleu*, whom he implicitly holds responsible for this situation.

Male writers, undoubtedly angered by the greater freedom, notoriety, and often financial rewards enjoyed by some of their female competition, maligned the literary achievements of the woman of ideas as tainted and artistically bankrupt. Often that judgment was reinforced with the more conventional but damaging accusation that the woman of ideas was both a literary whore and a sexual deviant responsible for the corruption of art and the dissolution of the bourgeois household.

The self-absorbed creatures who opt for the life of the spirit instead of the joys of marriage and maternity are merely foolish in Daumier's classification of *les bas-bleus*. Those who try to have it all are insidious. When Daumier's earlier depictions of the woman of ideas in the *Moeurs conjugales* series presage the theme of family ruin, they invoke the *bas-bleu* only as a sinister offstage presence manipulating female puppets. By 1844, however, the corruption is complete. Women are no longer passively absorbing their lessons from novels. They have put down their books and are out of their chairs acting out the once fictive scenarios of the sexual revolution.

Daumier's first allusion to the monstrous *bas-bleu* who violates the integrity of both family and literature occurs in his final woodcut for Texier's *Physiologie du poète*, in which a husband in his dressing gown feeds gruel to his child and the mother is nowhere to be found. We are to presume from Texier's prose that she is out cavorting with publishers while her husband fulfills her domestic responsibilities: "The muse's husband," he writes, "the same husband who devotes himself to the care of the household while the wife engages in adulterous business with Apollo, must resign himself to the complete loss of his individuality . . . he is only an object to his wife, . . . her number one domestic."[33]

The degeneration of the family forms the subject of nineteen of Daumier's forty lithographs in the series *Les Bas-Bleus*. Several draw directly on the emasculated figure of "le mari de la muse." In *Depuis que*

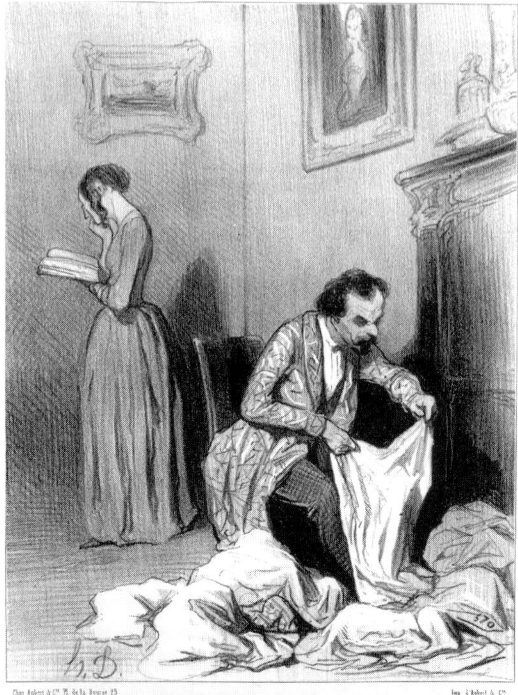

Figure 10.4. Honoré Daumier, *Depuis que Virginie a obtenu la septième accessit de poésie* . . . From *Le Charivari*, 18 April 1844. Lithograph. Print Collection, Miriam and Ira D. Wallach Division of Art, Prints, and Photographs, The New York Public Library, Astor, Lenox, and Tilden Foundations.

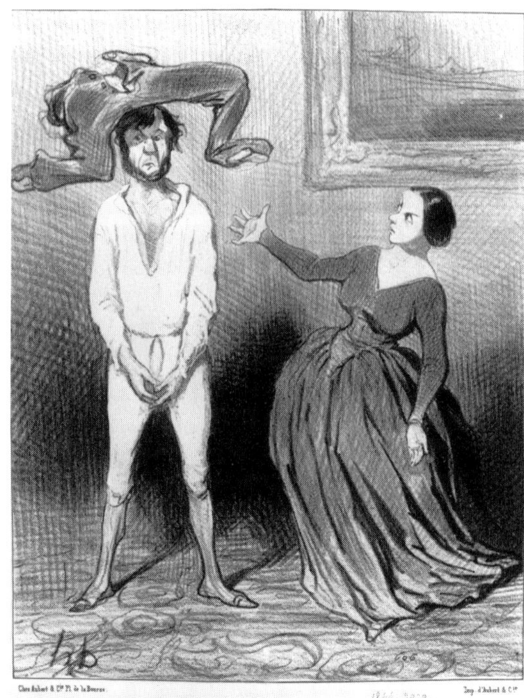

Figure 10.5. Honoré Daumier, *Une femme comme moi* . . . From *Le Charivari*, 23 May 1844. Lithograph. Honoré Daumier Lithographs, Robert D. Farber University Archives & Special Collections Department, Brandeis University Libraries.

Virginie a obtenu la septième accessit . . . (fig. 10.4), for example, the husband is shown sorting through mounds of dirty linen while his wife, hand to her chin, stands absorbed in a book. Not only has Virginia's literary award made her husband a domestic slave, but the prize itself—as Daumier's audience would have recognized—comes from an unworthy imitation of the Académie Française, the Académie des Femmes, founded by Louis-Joseph-Alphonse-Jules de Castellane in 1843.[34]

Another lithograph from *Les Bas-Bleus* engages the popular metaphorical question of who wears the pants. In *Une femme comme moi* . . . (fig. 10.5), an incredulous wife, having just flung her husband's pants in his face, shouts, "A woman like me . . . sew on a button? . . . You're crazy!" Her torso, arms, and dress—curved and animated as if by a wind of fury—contrast with the stable vertical of her husband's humbled and pantless figure. His fingertips touch embarrassedly before his genitals in a gesture of shame, while his pants, which in tonality and animation of line appear to belong more appropriately to the wife, seem to wear him. The pants hovering above his head read at once as controlling vise and a ridiculous woman's bonnet.

Daumier's most damning critiques of the bourgeois *bas-bleu* extend her domestic crimes to include maternal irresponsibility. Eight of the lithographs in

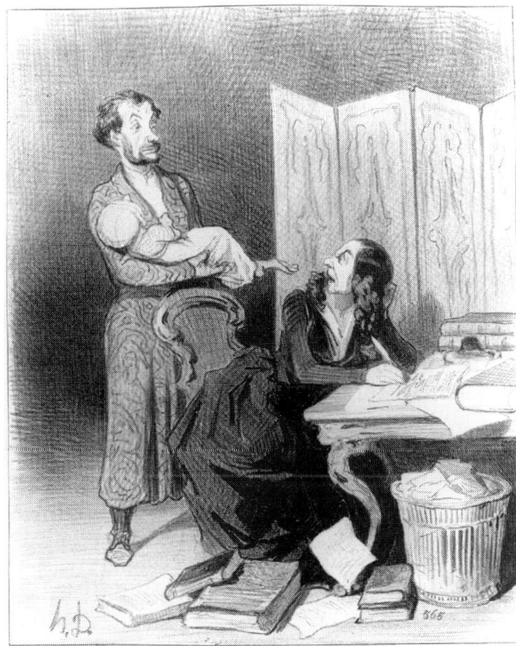

Figure 10.6. Honoré Daumier, *Emportez donc ça plus loin . . .* From *Le Charivari*, 2 March 1844. Lithograph. Print Collection, Miriam and Ira D. Wallach Division of Art, Prints, and Photographs, The New York Public Library, Astor, Lenox, and Tilden Foundations.

the series feature some variation on this subject: women giving daughters the wrong kind of education, children drowning in bathtubs as their mothers sit absorbed in thought, or shrews screaming at their husbands to take their children elsewhere so that they can finish their odes to maternity. In an image of the last type, *Emportez donc ça plus loin . . .* (fig. 10.6), a husband stands with baby in arms behind the lyre-backed chair in which his wife sits. The chair-lyre emasculates him, as does his willingness to stay home in his dressing gown and care for his child (who even appears to nurse at his breast). The wife, seated among the clutter she calls her work (though there is more paper crumpled up in the trash than there on the

desk before her), shouts for her husband to take that thing away. She threatens in the legend, "It's your first child, but I swear it will be your last!"

Daumier's most cynical figuration of the unfit mother features a pregnant woman blowing smoke rings in the face of her husband cum house-servant. In *Dis donc . . . mon mari*, a husband polishes a bowl as his wife pontificates about her various creative projects. In a reversal of conventional gender signs, his body is self-contained and likened to the round vessel shape usually associated with the female form; the *bas-bleu*, meanwhile, is a pastiche of extrusions: her left hand, a cigarette, her profile features, and an enormous belly that points accusingly toward her husband. "Say, husband," she informs him dispassionately, "I have a mind to call my play *Arthur* and entitle my child Oscar! . . . but no . . . all things considered, I will decide nothing before consulting my collaborator." Punning on the idea of a collaborator who is insinuated to have spawned both the play and the child, the lithograph demeans the woman of ideas as both untalented and unfaithful. Her husband stands passively by, symbolically robbed of his virility by the dust rag, which is arranged to suggest impotence juxtaposed with the protrusion of his wife's belly, for which he can claim no responsibility.

The association of the woman of ideas with domestic disarray and sexual promiscuity is common in caricatures and textual descriptions during the July Monarchy. The duped husband and the provocative verb "collaborate" are staple features of such prints. In another image from the series, *Ma bonne amie*, for instance, a woman writer and a male companion are startled and appear to recover from a compromising position, as the husband tentatively pokes his head in the room. He asks, "My dear, may I come in? . . . Have you finished collaborating with Monsieur?"[35]

Within the genre of the *physiologie*, Jules Janin's "Un Bas-Bleu" most strikingly and viciously literalizes this equation of literary and sexual transgression. The woman of ideas is paid handsomely, Janin complains, "to write the most abominable invectives, which offend principles of grammar and common sense."[36] If the public wants dramas, he continues, she writes a drama, choosing her subject carefully to maximize opportunities for blood and violence. She is, in other words, a literary whore who, in the name of providing bread and a good education for her beloved children, will write a story of infanticide.[37] It is bearable, he explains, when male writers sell out, because they are not the ones charged with moral education of the next generation. The danger is when those who are the teachers of our children prostitute themselves while they write of virtue, when "what she has sold all her life in bedrooms and taverns she will even sell in books."[38]

Representing women writers not as women who write but as sexless hags and promiscuous shrews is not a neutral act. To ignore the cultural and political content of these images by studying them as benign scenes of everyday life is not a neutral act either. Daumier's figurations of the woman of ideas were far more complex and politically damaging than his renderings of Louis-Philippe as Gargantua, precisely because they appeared so conventional, so "everyday." The lithographs of *Les Bas-Bleus* deny individual achievement and censor the details of a new female reality with which others might identify; they transmute an arena of power into a tired and destructive paradigm of female deviance.

As I have tried to suggest, Daumier did not work in isolation. If his antipathy toward the woman of ideas is consistent with the few details of his biography that we have,[39] it seems to have been encouraged and shaped by the policies and sensibilities of those for whom he worked in the offices of *Le Charivari* at La Maison Aubert. La Maison Aubert, which by 1841 had become the premier lithographic printer-publisher in Paris,[40] played a dominant role in the enormously lucrative *physiologie* trade that spawned Daumier's series *Les Bas-Bleus*. The development of *Les Bas-Bleus* was consistent with Philipon's shrewd rethinking of his financial and editorial position after 1835 and the redirection of his business toward its natural audience, the haute bourgeoisie, the class that produced most of the women writers in this period.

Like all good entrepreneurs, Philipon had it both ways: he at once denigrated and cultivated the bourgeois women of ideas who composed a significant portion of his audience. He published texts and images that trivialized their achievements and flattered them with attention. Philipon's awareness of the need to balance ridicule with flattery is suggested by one of *Le Charivari*'s rare serious essays that appeared midway through Daumier's series. "Salon de 1844" is an article whose ostensible purpose was to call for Salon criticism devoted exclusively to women artists, but its subtext seems to have been an attempt to appease an audience unsettled by Daumier's treatment of the woman of ideas. The article differentiates the woman of ideas from other women with professional identities; it elucidates the differences between real women of talent and "les bas-bleus."

"Salon de 1844" contrasts Daumier's unfaithful wives and irresponsible mothers who "scribble poems and novels" with women who exercise more appropriate talents. "A woman painting or singing," tends to be attractive, the article explains, whereas "a drinker of ink . . . is as disagreeable to the sight as to the mind."[41] This is true, we are told, because women are by nature creatures of feeling rather than knowledge. Therefore, since being a *savante* requires learning and thought and being an artist above all requires emotion, women are more suited to the latter. Logically, we are attracted to *la femme-artiste* because "she seems to obey her nature," unlike *la femme-homme de lettres*, who repulses us and seems "a sort of monster."[42]

"Salon de 1844" seems to be a conciliatory effort to suggest an alternative and acceptable type with whom his female readership might safely identify. It signals the desire of *Le Charivari* to participate in the vogue of ridiculing *la femme pensée* without risking the loss of her subscription fees. But to target the woman of ideas for satirical attack after 1835 was logical for another reason as well. *Le Charivari*, like La Maison Aubert, was an organization composed of male writers who undoubtedly were ambivalent about their own complicity in *la littérature industrielle* and threatened by their female competition. To identify the woman of ideas with the prostitution of literature allowed them to deflect anxiety about their own role in the commodification of literary culture. Jules Janin's significant comparison, in its very imperiousness, betrays this anxiety. The French man of letters, compliant with the September Laws and suppliant to a degraded popular taste, may have sold out. But, compared with his new women colleagues and competitors, he might not seem so diminished in moral, literary, and sexual stature. For even if both men and women writers were working for the same market, it could not so easily be said of the former that they "sell in books what they have sold all their lives in bedrooms and taverns."

NOTES

1. "Femmes qui ne veulent pas se résigner à être femmes" (Arsène Alexandre, *Honoré Daumier: L'Homme et l'oeuvre* [Paris: H. Laurens, 1888], 263). Champfleury provides another contemporary account of the series in his *Exposition des peintures et dessins de Honoré Daumier* (Paris: Gauthiers-Villars, 1878). Though he too reaffirms Daumier's prejudices against *les femmes pensées,* he is the first to attempt to contextualize it.

2. Howard Vincent, *Daumier and His World* (Evanston, Ill.: Northwestern University Press, 1968), 125.

3. Oliver Larkin, *Daumier: Man of His Time* (New York: McGraw-Hill, 1966), 50.

4. See Françoise Parturier and Jacqueline Armingeat, *Daumier: Intellectuelles ("Les Bas Bleus" et "Femmes socialistes")* (Paris: Editions Vilo-Paris, 1974); and Cäcilia Rentmeister, "Daumier und das hässliche Geschlect," in *Honoré Daumier und die ungelösten Probleme der bürgerlichen Gesellschaft,* exh. cat. (Berlin: Neue Desellschaft fur bildende Kunst for the Schloss, Charflottenburg, 1974), 57–79. See also proceeding from *Die Karikatur Zwischen Republik und Zensur: Bildsatire in Frankreich 1830 bis 1880—eine Sprache des Widerstands?* ed. Jonas Verlag. Beiträge und Kommentar zum internationalen und interdisziplinären Kolloquium über den satirischen Bildjournalismus im 19. Jahrhundert an der Universität Frakfurt, 24–27 Mai 1988.

5. This phenomenon is explored in Walter Benjamin, "Paris of the Second Empire in Baudelaire," in his *Charles Baudelaire: A Lyric Poet in the Era of High Capitalism,* trans. Harry Zohn (London: N.L.B., 1973), 12.

6. For a complete discussion, see Claire Moses, *French Feminism in the Nineteenth Century* (Albany: SUNY Press, 1984), ch. 4.

7. In any discussion of caricature, it is essential to consider the collaborative nature of the process and the many different hands involved in the conception and elaboration of an image. In the case of Daumier, the most cogent discussion can be found in Elizabeth Childs, "Honoré Daumier and the Exotic Vision: Studies in French Caricature and Culture, 1830–1870" (Ph.D. diss., Columbia University, 1989), ch. 1.

8. See, for example, Eugène Morisseau, "Indiana par George Sand," *La Caricature,* 23 May 1833, 1062.

9. For an examination of the repercussions of the September Laws, see Edwin T. Bechtel, *Freedom of the Press and l'Association Mensuelle—Philipon versus Louis-Philippe* (New York: Grolier Club, 1952). One must also take into consideration a change in personnel after 1835. In part because of economic problems that were inevitably related to Louis-Philippe's restrictive policies, *Le Charivari* was sold in 1835 and again in 1836. See the discussion of changes in *Le Charivari*'s editorial board and editorship in Jules Brisson and Félix Ribèyre, *Grands Journaux de France* (Paris: Jouast Père, 1862).

10. The hostility of male journalists toward the bourgeois *femme de letters* is most explicit in Grandville and Traviés's caricature "Les Feuilles publiques," published in *La Caricature* (26 September 1833). The image depicts the newspapers that marketed serialized novels as prostitutes.

11. Frederic Soulié, *Physiologie du bas-bleu* (Paris: Aubert et Cie, 1841–42), 19.

12. See Laure Adler, *A l'aube du féminisme: Les Premières Journalistes, 1830–1850* (Paris: Payot, 1979). The trendiness of *la femme emancipée* in the mid nineteenth century is suggested by her frequent characterization in fiction. Flaubert's La Vatnaz in *L'Education sentimentale,* for example, is based on Eugénie Niboyet and Jeanne Déroin, two prominent feminist activists of the 1840s. Many of Balzac's novels also feature a *femme-auteur.* In *Béatrix* (1840), for instance, Félicités des Touches is modeled after George Sand, and the marquise de Rochefide after Marie d'Agoult. Mme de la

Baudraye in Balzac's *La Muse du departement* was also inspired by Sand.

13. The details of Poutret de Mauchamp's activities are discussed by Marie-Louise Puesch, "Une Supercherie littéraire: Le Véritable Rédacteur de la *Gazette des femmes*, 1836–1838," *La Révolution de 1848* 32 (June–August 1935): 303–12; and Evelyne Sullerot, *Histoire de la presse féminine en France, des origins à 1848* (Paris: Armand Colin, 1966). For a discussion of Père Enfantin's leadership of the Saint-Simonist community and his imprisonment for corruption of public morals, see Moses, *French Feminism*, ch. 3.

14. The female playwright Virginie Ancelot was often maligned in the popular press for the state subsidies she received. *Marie* opened at the Théâtre Français in October 1836.

15. "Madame a lu les romans de George Sand, elle a pleuré aux représentations de Marie, elle est au courant de toutes les protestations et de toutes les motions insurrectionelles que les femmes, depuis quelques temps, publient par la voie de la presse et du théâtre" (*Le Charivari*, no. 136 [17 May 1836], 2).

16. This paradigm is also used during the July Monarchy to explain aberrant male behavior, especially that of Louis-Philippe. Between 1839 and 1848, for instance, a sequence of articles in the legitimist journal *La Mode* assigned blame for the sins of Louis-Philippe alternately to his much despised sister Adelaide and to his former governess, (the poet) Stéphanie de Genlis. See *La Mode*, February 1848, 449.

17. "Curiosités littéraires: Les Demoiselles de lettres," *Le Charivari*, 30 May 1837, 1–2.

18. Jean-Baptiste Daumier was an artisan with artistic aspirations. A glazier and a poet, Jean-Baptiste had little success in the Parisian literary community and was financially dependent on his son. For the details of his decline and commitment to an asylum, see B. Lehmann, "Daumier père et Daumier fils," *Gazette des Beaux-Arts* 1 (May 1945): 297–316. The literary and financial rewards received by such undeserving *demoiselles de provinces* as Delphine de Girardin must have been irritating to Daumier, who saw his father emasculated by the loss of his livelihood and his inability to attain recognition as an artist.

19. "Prêchant la liberté de la femme et l'asservissement de l'homme" ("Curiosités littéraires," 2).

20. See, for example, "Les Femmes ne peuvent pas avoir l'art de régner, puisqu'il n'a pas le moindre rapport avec l'art de plaire" (*Le Charivari*, 8 September 1837, 1).

21. Daumier never grants any female writer the exposure and authority of a portrait likeness. This is particularly striking given his talent for the genre, exercised in such series as *Les Représentants représentés*. Linda Nochlin's 1988 essay "Women, Art and Power," from her anthology of the same title, identifies the two feminists in Daumier's image *V'la une femme*, from the series *Les Divorceuses*, as Eugènie Niboyet and probably Jeanne Déroin. Though other caricaturists do feature actual feminists, Daumier does not. In fact, I know of no caricature from any of his series that includes a portrait charge of a female celebrity. To individuate them would have been to grant them stature and legitimacy. Furthermore, by August 1848, when this lithograph was published, Niboyet and Déroin had parted company in a fairly public manner. Articles such as "Banquet féminin de la Gaité," in *Journal pour rire*, another Maison Aubert publication, celebrated the rift between the two women and delighted in the fact that Déroin excluded Niboyet from banquets sponsored by the organization she had helped found (25 November 1848, 1).

22. Philippe Roberts-Jones, *Daumier: Humours of Married Life*, trans. Angus Malcolm (Boston: Boston Book and Art Shop, 1968), 150.

23. Capo de Feuillade, "Lélia, "*L'Europe littéraire*, 22 August 1833, 3.

24. *Le Charivari* first appropriated the term *bas-bleu* as the standard referent for the woman of ideas in the late 1830s, the same period in which invectives against her intensified. *Bluestocking* is a British term, coined in the eighteenth century to describe a circle of women who gathered regularly in the home of Elizabeth Montague (1720–1830). One of the few males allowed, Benjamin Stillingfleet, always wore blue stockings. For *Le Charivari* to have used the label *femme de lettres* would have been to continue to associate women writers like Delphine de Girardin with the historic and esteemed tradition of the French *homme de lettres*. *Le Charivari*'s sudden and widespread deployment of the term *bas-bleu* (a term that can only be seen as derogatory) in the late 1830s coincided with the ascendance of the bourgeois *femme-auteur*, with whom the label is most closely associated.

25. Ferdinand Langlé and F. de Villeneuve, *Un Bas-Bleu*

(Paris: Marchant, 1844), 12. Athenais is a barmaid seeking to escape the constraints of her class through an unexpected inheritance. One avenue of class mobility for a woman in the July Monarchy appears to have been to become a *bas-bleu*, a female type identified principally with the haute bourgeoisie.

26. The *physiologie*, a genre popular in the late 1830s and 1840s, is an extended typological essay classifying Parisian professions, avocations, and types. One of the most successful publishers of the *physiologie* was Charles Philipon. The three that appear to have shaped Daumier's series *Les Bas-Bleus* are Frédéric Soulié, *Physiologie du bas-bleu* (Paris: Aubert et Cie, 1841); Edmond Texier, *Physiologie du poète* (Paris: J. Laisne, 1841); and Jules Janin, "Un Bas-Bleu," in *Les Français peints par eux-mêmes* (Paris: Louis Curmer, 1842).

27. "Qui flotte entre quarante-cinq et cinquante-cinq ans . . . [qui a] un corps maigre, . . . le sourire douloureux, . . . [et] une poitrie decharnée" (Soulié, *Physiologie du bas-bleu*, 68).

28. This practice is documented in such sources as *Physiologie de la presse* (Paris: Jules Laisne, 1841). In the staff listings it publishes for *Le Constitutionnel* and *La Presse*, for instance, it includes the editors' wives, Mmes Charles Reynaud and Delphine de Girardin respectively. Sophie Gay, Emile de Girardin's mother-in-law, is also cited in the staff list for *La Presse*. Louise Bertin, daughter of the *Journal des débats'* editor, Louis Bertin, was the target of the most biting satires. See, for example, "L'Ombre d'Euterpe, " *Le Charivari*, 13 January 1842, 1

29. "La dixième muse s'est multipliée dans un proportion effrayante; elle a poussé sans culture, comme les champignons, . . . dans les colonnes des feuilletons, et à la quatrième page des journaux" (Texier, *Physiologie du poète*, 118).

30. The editor of Soulié's *Physiologie du bas-bleu* was Charles Philipon. It is not surprising that the text recapitulates many of the characterizations of the bourgeois woman of ideas first explored in *Le Charivari* in the late 1830s. Though Philipon had sold *Le Charivari* in 1835, he remained a powerful presence at La Maison Aubert, which continued to publish the journal.

31. "La plus méchante de toutes" (Soulié, *Physiologie du bas-bleu*, 52).

32. "Comme tout ce qui tombe dans le domain public" (ibid., 15).

33. "Le mari de la muse, ce même mari qui vaque aux soins du ménage pendant que sa femme entretient un commerce adultère avec Apollon, doit se résigner à perdre tout à fait sa personnalité . . . il n'est que la chose de sa femme, . . . c'est-à-dire son premier domestique" (ibid., 118). A related image, *Le Mari du bas-bleu*, was also published on April 10, 1842, in *Le Charivari* as part of the *Moeurs conjugales* series. A husband holding an infant explains to a gentleman that his wife is in the middle of an inspiration and cannot see him.

34. The Académie des Femmes received a great deal of attention in Maison Aubert publications and elsewhere. Jules de Castellane was a Saint-Simonist, and *Le Charivari*'s interest in belittling him by exposing his ties to the utopian socialist movement are explicit in an essay entitled "Cancans de presse" (25 March 1844). The article, which appeared midway through the run of Daumier's *Les Bas-Bleus*, exposes the fact that instead of the newspaper paying its female writers, "as has been the practice since the invention of the printing press," the writers pay the newspapers" (1).

35. The caricature may have been inspired by an identical anecdote that concludes chapter five of Soulié's *Physiologie du bas-bleu*, 50.

36. "A écrire les plus abominables invectives contre la grammaire et le sens commun" (Janin, "Un Bas-Bleu," 376).

37. Ibid., 378.

38. "Ce qu'elle a vendu toute sa vie dans les boudoirs ou dans les taverns, elle le vendra encore dans les livres" (ibid., 380).

39. In the meager biographical material, the only descriptive detail regularly invoked by friends and admirers concerns Daumier's fierce commitment to privacy and family. Thus, his attack on women who argued in favor of the right to work and the right to divorce seems consistent with his personal ideals.

40. See James Cuno, "Charles Philipon, La Maison Aubert, and the Business of Caricature in Paris, 1829–1841," *Art Journal* 43, no. 4 (Winter 1983): 352–53.

41. "Une femme peignant ou chantant . . . une buveuse d'encre . . . est désagréable à la vue comme à l'esprit" ("Salon de 1844," *Le Charivari*, 10 May 1844, 1).

42. "Semble obéir à sa nature . . . une sorte de monstre" (ibid., 1).

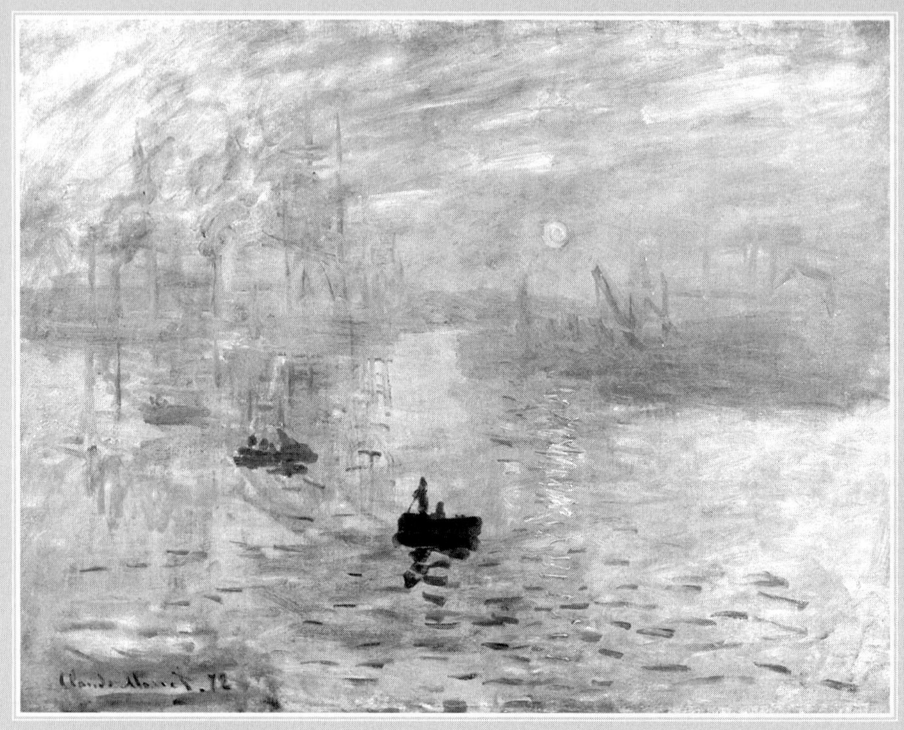

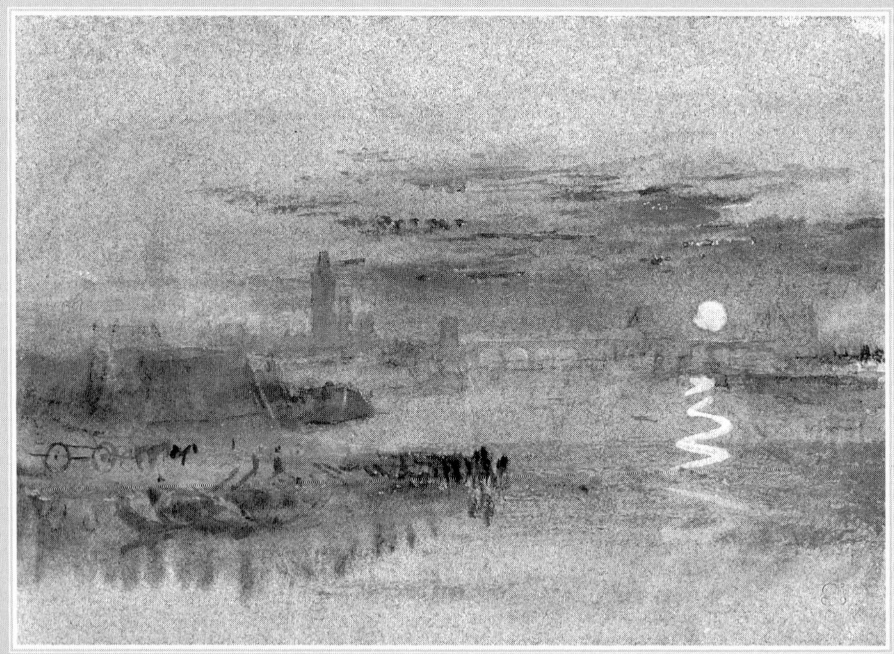

11

THE GENDERING OF IMPRESSIONISM

Norma Broude

IN THE CANONICAL story of nineteenth-century French art, the Impressionist landscape painters, exemplified by Claude Monet, were long described as artists who painted exclusively outdoors, before the motif in nature, so that they might be objectively, even scientifically, true to visual reality. According to this view, the motifs before which these artists set up their easels were of no intrinsic interest or importance to them, because they cared only about recording their optical sensations as accurately and as immediately as possible. This popular understanding of Impressionism, as a scientifically motivated form of optical realism and as an art that rejected the expressive goals of the earlier Romantic movement, remained remarkably stable throughout much of the twentieth century. And even in the relatively recent literature, we can still read that the Impressionists were artists who "eliminated the reflection of human feelings in nature."[1]

The only exception to this view of the Impressionist landscape was the late work of Claude Monet, particularly the series paintings done from the early 1890s onward, where expressive elements were long recognized and acknowledged. In 1959, the scholar George Heard Hamilton argued for detaching these paintings from Monet's earlier, Impressionist work and for grafting them instead onto the history of Postimpressionism. Citing Monet's own stated "need to render what I feel" (from a letter of 1890 when he was working on the "Haystacks"), Hamilton rightly concluded that "the true subject of the 'Haystacks' is not the stacks themselves or the weather or even the light . . . but the painter's experience, the projection of his particular feelings."[2]

Monet's late series paintings were seen by Hamilton as products of the dominant Symbolist milieu of the 1890s, and as such they represented for him a belated rejection on Monet's part of his earlier, Impressionist—for which read "objective and realist"—point of view. The problem with this still widely accepted position, however, is that there is nothing really comparable to Monet's work of the 1890s, either visually or emotionally, in Symbolist and Postimpressionist painting of the same period. To find a parallel for Monet's tonal poetry, for his attentiveness to coloristic and tonal effects of atmosphere, and

This essay is adapted from my book *Impressionism, A Feminist Reading: The Gendering of Art, Science, and Nature in the Nineteenth Century* (New York: Rizzoli International Publications, 1991, and Westview Press, 1997). The arguments it presents are drawn principally from the book's introduction and from part 3, "The Gendering of Impressionism." Text copyright © 1991 by Norma Broude. Reprinted by permission of the author.

Figure 11.1 (TOP). Claude Monet, *Impression, Sunrise*, 1873 (signed and dated lower left at a later time: "Claude Monet, 72"). Oil on canvas. Musée Marmottan–Claude Monet, Paris. (Photo: Réunion des Musées Nationaux/Art Resource, New York.)

Figure 11.2 (BOTTOM). J. M. W. Turner, *The Scarlet Sunset*, ca. 1830–40. Watercolor and gouache on paper. Tate Gallery, London. (Photo: Clore Collection, Tate Gallery, London/Art Resource, New York.)

his creation of effects of light that range from the bold and spectacular to the ethereal and evanescent in his paintings of the 1870s as well as the 1890s, it is not, I have argued, to Symbolism that we must turn, but to the Romantic landscape traditions of the 1830s (figs. 11.1 and 11.2).[3] The continuities are visually clear. But in 1959, when Hamilton was redefining Monet's late work as a projection of his personal feelings and experiences, such a broader connection with historical Romanticism was strangely inadmissible in the art-historical literature. And it remained so during the decades that followed, as art historians struggled to preserve the dualistic pattern of heroic struggle and reversal that long governed our understanding of nineteenth-century French art historiography: Romanticism in opposition to Neoclassicism, Realism and Impressionism aligning themselves against Romanticism, and then Realism and Impressionism themselves overthrown by their opposites in Symbolism and Postimpressionism.

It is instructive to compare the comments of twentieth-century writers on Monet's work of the 1870s with those of his nineteenth-century contemporaries. Hamilton described the Gare St. Lazare paintings of that decade as being merely "pictures of places," "intellectually and emotionally restricted," precluding "any possibility of reminiscence and reflection."[4] But of these same pictures, when they were shown in 1877 at the third Impressionist exhibition, Georges Rivière, a sympathetic critic and friend of the Impressionists, said: "Looking at this magnificent painting, one is seized by the same emotion as before nature, and this emotion is perhaps stronger still, for in the painting there is that of the artist as well."[5] About the viewer of the painting, Rivière wrote: "This painting addresses itself to his heart; if he is moved, the objective is fulfilled."[6] Rivière was not alone in describing the Impressionists as artists who wanted to convey their emotional experiences and responses to nature. Moreover, in many of these contemporary writings, we find that the expressive intentions of these artists are directly and sometimes exclusively linked with their concern for light—for rendering what were called the "effects" of nature's light outdoors. As one

critic put it (Alexandre Pothey, writing of the group exhibit in 1877): "Everyone knows that this group of . . . artists was formed with a single goal: to render the effect and the emotion that nature produces directly in the heart or in the soul."[7]

Why, then, did Impressionism, an art that was based on the subjectivity of vision and that emphasized the expression of feeling and emotion generated by contact with nature, come to be seen in the twentieth century as an art of optical realism and "scientific objectivity," devoid of feeling? On what has the persistent connection between Impressionism and rational science been based?

In the 1870s and 1880s, the authority of science was invoked by a few of the early supporters of Impressionism, who attempted to justify this unorthodox style by linking it to current scientific explanations of how the human eye operates. For example, some of these early defenders of Impressionism made use of the work of the German physiologist Hermann von Helmholtz, who had established that the human eye itself distinguishes only sensations of color and tone, thus demoting "line," in scientific terms, to the level of perceptual illusion.[8]

Because Impressionist paintings lacked conventional drawing and perspective and because of their loose and broken brushwork, they were often criticized in the 1870s for being unnatural, "formless," and untrue to human vision and "reality." Much of the early literature written in defense of Impressionism attempted to counter these criticisms by trying to show that Impressionism was in fact far truer to the appearances of nature than any earlier style of painting had been. And in order to accomplish this, a few of these early defenders of Impressionism invoked the authority of science in support of their argument. The principal texts are in fact only three: by the critics Edmond Duranty in 1876, Diego Martelli in 1879, and Jules Laforgue in 1883. Although these writers used the then fashionable and prestigious language of contemporary science to justify some of the unusual stylistic features of Impressionism, they each, nevertheless, emphasized the expressive and subjective nature of the Impressionists' goals. They never suggested that the Impressionists had been consciously motivated in their work by scientific ideas, nor did they ever describe Impressionism as an art of impassive optical imitation ruled by scientific objectivity.[9]

Nevertheless, this mistaken notion about Impressionism took hold and survived tenaciously throughout the twentieth century. To understand why, I have proposed, we must address the complex—and gendered—relationship that existed between art, science, and nature in the nineteenth century. And in so doing, we must recast our original question to ask why it was that Impressionism, an art gendered as female both by its conservative critics and by its avant-garde competitors at the turn of the century, was effectively regendered in the art history and criticism of the twentieth century and endowed with the stereotypical attributes of masculinity. This artificial separation of Impressionism from Romanticism and its equally artificial attachment to science have been the result, I will now argue, of the movement's feminine gendering in the nineteenth century and the next century's increasingly pressing need to regender this most valued of modern art movements as masculine.

THE GENDERING
OF ART, SCIENCE, AND NATURE

The idea that nature is to culture as female is to male has been an influential formulation in Western thought for many centuries. In the dualistic Western philosophical tradition, the idea that nature is female can be traced back to the writings of Plato and Aristotle. Over the centuries, nature, gendered as female, has been regarded as passive, but also as mysterious and secretive. "She" has thus served as the primary object of scrutiny and investigation for science, which has been characterized as "active" and "objective" and thus gendered as male. Nature, of course, has also been the primary subject of art, whose gendered identity in relation both to female nature and to male science has been far less secure and has undergone constant revision.

During the Renaissance, art aligned itself with rational science, and there emerged the view that art, like science, could master and transcend nature by discovering her secrets. A well-known sixteenth-century woodcut by the German Renaissance artist Albrecht Dürer, in which an artist is shown practicing the system of one-point perspective, clearly illustrates these ambitions and the gendered dualities that were commonly used to naturalize them (see fig. 2.4, p. 56). Here, a semidraped female model, who serves as the object of the male artist's rational and scientific perspectival investigation, can be seen as the personification of female nature.[10] And in this image, she—Nature—has become both literally and metaphorically the passive female object of the controlling male gaze.

In the seventeenth century, the desire for domination over nature emerged as the central project of the new science, and the language of science in this period was replete with gendered metaphors of aggression, sexual penetration, and conquest. In the words of the scientist Francis Bacon, nature was a bride who was to be unveiled, exposed, and penetrated even in her "innermost chambers."[11] The survival of these attitudes into the nineteenth century and beyond is amply demonstrated by the statue *Nature Unveiling Herself before Science* by the French sculptor Louis Ernest Barrias (fig. 11.3). Completed in 1899 and placed on exhibition at the medical faculty in Paris, the statue personifies nature as a beautiful young woman, her breasts bared and her hands raised to remove the veil that still covers her head. And it implies that science is a male viewer who anticipates full knowledge of nature, presented here as the passive and naked female body.

More than at any other time since the Renaissance virilization of art, Romantic landscape painters in the nineteenth century defined themselves as social outcasts in relation to this traditionally gendered paradigm. Because they took a "passive" and responsive, rather than aggressive and controlling, attitude toward their subjects in nature, they risked—and inevitably invited for themselves and for art in general—stereotypical feminization. Of course, in the larger and more simplistic, dualistic patterning of art history, Romanticism, as distinct from Neoclassicism,

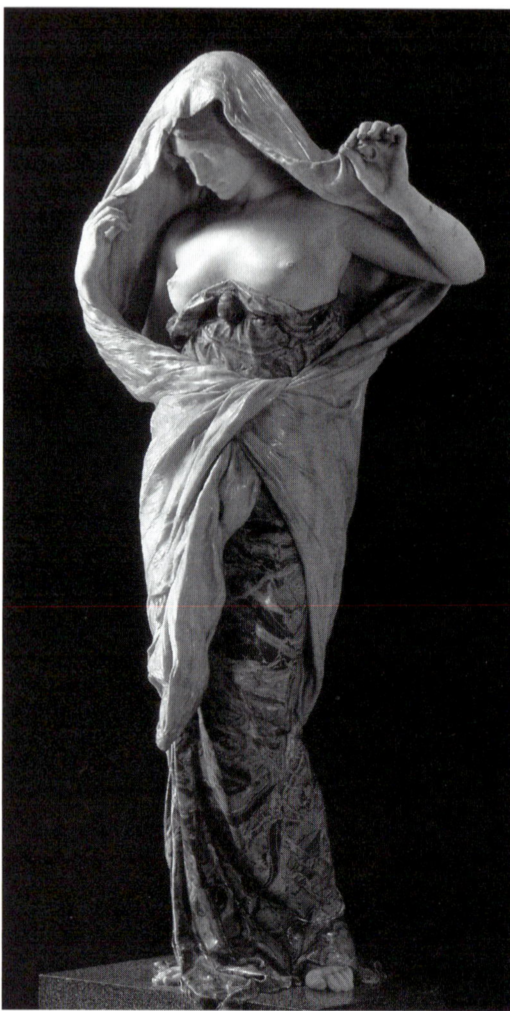

Figure 11.3. Louis Ernest Barrias, *Nature Unveiling Herself before Science*, 1899. Polychrome marble, onyx, malachite, and lapis lazuli on gray granite pedestal. Musée d'Orsay, Paris. (Photo: Réunion des Musées Nationaux/Art Resource, New York.)

has been consistently assigned a feminized cultural identity and role. This has been due in large measure to Romanticism's emphasis on color rather than drawing, and to the polarized gendering of these elements of style that was already commonplace in the nineteenth century. In the words of Charles Blanc, the nineteenth-century Beaux-Arts administrator and historian: "Drawing is the masculine sex of art and color the feminine one."[12] That is to say, drawing is regarded as rational and color as emotional.

But during the Romantic era itself, a further though equally gendered distinction was made between Romantic painters of the human figure, such as Eugène Delacroix, and painters of the same period, such as Théodore Rousseau, who devoted themselves to the landscape. These landscape painters were described by the poet and critic Charles Baudelaire as artists "whose specialty brings them closer to what is called inanimate nature." Baudelaire described them, with great scorn, as "those who have no imagination" and who therefore simply "copy the dictionary" that nature provides.[13] The distinction being made, of course, was between those who, like Delacroix, set out to "capture" and control female nature in an active and aggressive sense—which is perhaps ludicrously but nevertheless effectively illustrated in paintings such as his *Death of Sardanapalus*—as opposed to what may be seen in the work of the Barbizon landscape painters such as Rousseau: an effort not to capture or to alter or to control nature "herself," but simply to fix upon canvas the artist's response to the stimulus that nature has provided.

The gendered basis of this distinction between landscape and figurative schools of Romantic painting in France persisted throughout the nineteenth century, and it became a familiar part of the discourse surrounding the highly diverse group of artists who came to be known as the "Impressionists." An American critic writing about them in 1886, for example, talked about the "masculine principle" that informed the figure paintings of Manet, Degas, Renoir, Caillebotte, and Seurat, while he found the "feminine" in the landscape paintings of Monet, Boudin, Sisley, and Pissarro. "The tenderness and grace of Impressionism," he said, "are reserved for its landscapes," while "for humanity there is only the hard reality of naked truth."[14]

This critic's characterization of Impressionist landscape painting as a feminine art may be partly explained by the preference of these artists for the tranquility of country and suburban settings, their attraction to a domestic iconography, and their relative lack of interest in socially problematic themes (which would distinguish in many cases the work of a Monet from that of a Caillebotte). But the perception of the feminized character of this branch of Impressionism was widespread, and it had to do not so much with the subjects these artists chose—although that was part of it—but more with what was considered to be their passive and hence unmanly attitude toward nature. And this was exemplified by the very techniques these artists chose to employ, in particular their quick and fluid brushwork and lack of conventional draftsmanship, which many critics of the period objected to, in gendered terms, as feminine and suitable only to the limited intellectual capabilities of women.

However, there existed two competing forms of critical discourse that affected the gendering of Impressionism during the second half of the nineteenth century. On the one hand, the absence of conventional drawing and spatial organization in Impressionist landscape painting clearly served, in traditional terms, to feminize the movement for many of its contemporary detractors. But at the same time, during the second half of the nineteenth century, the science of physiological optics was discovering that there are in fact no forms or lines in nature. Science itself, in other words—that ultimate representative of masculinized reason and objectivity—appeared to be reversing the familiar stereotype and revising the terms of the traditionally gendered relationship between line and color, the basic elements of artistic representation and style. As the supporters of Impressionism were quick to realize, the discoveries of contemporary science in this realm could be used to sanction Impressionism's unorthodox manner of imaging nature in terms that were accessible to the positivist mainstream of thought in France during the Third Republic but that did not do violence to the original intentions of these still-Romantic painters of nature. If the patchy and sketchy technique of the Impressionist painter could now be justified in scientific terms as true to human vision in general and at the same time as the product of a physiologically unique

eye, this was an art that could now suddenly be seen both as universally objective and as subjectively expressive.

But the objectivity with which Impressionism might now be credited could at the same time be equated with passivity in relation to nature. It was essentially for this, as we shall see, that the Symbolists criticized Impressionism. For in their efforts to supplant Impressionism in the avant-garde at the end of the nineteenth century, it was the Symbolists, I shall now argue, who reintroduced and reinforced the rhetoric of mastery as the key to a newly regendered relationship between art and nature.

IMPRESSIONISM AND SYMBOLISM

It was the Symbolist critics in the 1890s who first began to redefine Impressionism for posterity. They developed and helped to propagate some of the mythic ideas about Impressionism that remained with us throughout the twentieth century, the most influential of which have been the image of the Impressionist painter as a passive recorder of optical sensations and the notion of Impressionism's objectivity and affinity with science.

Although the theory of Symbolist painting was not the invention of one person, it can be argued that it was set down and articulated most fully in the writings of the Symbolist poet, novelist, and art critic Albert Aurier (1865–92), whose pronouncements and attitudes were pivotal to the development of the movement's identity. An early supporter of Vincent Van Gogh and Paul Gauguin, Aurier published influential essays on these painters in 1890 and 1891, respectively, essays in which he developed a basic theory and definition of Symbolism in painting, in contradistinction to Impressionism. An Impressionist, according to Aurier, was an artist who sought to render "an exclusively sensory impression," generated from without, while the Symbolist sought to give form to internalized ideas, to emotions generated from within, and in so doing to reveal the essence of objects. In defense of Gauguin, Aurier further argued that the greatest art is inspired by an artist's inner mystical vision and not by a transient and external material reality.[15]

The driving forces behind Aurier's Symbolist aesthetic, it may be argued, were his deep contempt for external material reality—that is, for nature—and his equally vehement aversion to positivist science and its promotion of a materialist mentality. Aurier saw science as the enemy and the rival of art, responsible for its impoverishment in the modern world. "The limits of art," he wrote, "shrink back as science widens its domain."[16] But the twentieth century, he predicted, would be "the century of Art, of joy, of truth, following upon the century of Science, of despair, of falsehood."[17] But despite his rejection of science and the scientific method, Aurier had nevertheless absorbed many of its habits of thought, particularly its propensity for categorization and dualistic opposition and struggle. In her study of Aurier (written as an appreciation of his contributions to modernist art theory and not as a feminist critique), Patricia Mathews points this out and notes: "Aurier uses analogies of battle and combat to describe the reaction of the new artists against the old: 'In vain, exclusively materialistic art . . . struggles against the attacks of a new art.' He sees the history of art in terms of the rivalry of naturalism and idealism as well."[18]

Aurier's contempt for "detestable nature," as he termed it, his hierarchic subordination in the Neoplatonic tradition of matter to spirit, his aversion to sensuality in both life and art, and his deeply misogynist and typically fin-de-siècle distaste for what he called "the bestiality and dirty tricks" of women all helped to generate and shape his influential conception of a Symbolist art of painting.[19] Aurier's attitudes toward nature and science in particular have a direct bearing on an issue that was to become recurrent and consuming for art critics during the 1890s: the question of whether an artist is to be seen as one who controls and acts upon nature (the Symbolist) or as one who is instead acted upon by nature—a passive and feminized observer and recorder of the sensations that are generated by an external natural world (the Impressionist).

In the 1890s the Symbolists virilized art by reimposing a masculinist mode of possessing female nature upon the theory and criticism of avant-garde painting. A classic statement of this gendered attitude, as it came to be used to distinguish the Symbolists from the Impressionists, is provided by the critic Octave Mirbeau. Writing about Van Gogh in 1891, Mirbeau said of this artist:

[He] did not allow himself to become absorbed into nature. He had absorbed nature into himself; he had forced her to bend to his will, to be molded to the forms of his thought, to follow him in his flights of imagination, to submit even to those distortions *[déformations]* that specifically characterized him. Van Gogh had, to a rare degree, what distinguishes one man from another: style . . . that is, the affirmation of the personality.[20]

In the 1890s much emphasis was placed upon an artist's personal style and handwriting—"what distinguishes one man from another," according to Mirbeau. In order to affirm his personality, the artist has "to bend [nature] to his will." The Impressionists, on the other hand, were increasingly perceived in the 1890s as artists who had allowed themselves "to become absorbed into nature," who did not impose their will upon her, and who thus did not express their individual personalities through a readily identifiable and accentuated style. So quickly did this attitude take hold and affect critical judgment and vision in relation to Impressionist painting that by 1908 even a presumably sensitive observer such as Henri Matisse could write of the Impressionists (in a pronouncement that can cause only amazement today): "The Impressionist painters, Monet, Sisley especially, had delicate, vibrating sensations; as a result their canvases are all alike. The word 'impressionism' perfectly characterizes their intentions, for they register fleeting impressions."[21]

It was Roger Fry who organized the first group exhibition of works by artists whom he called the "Postimpressionists" and whose lineage he traced back to Manet (that is, to the "masculine" side of Impressionism). In the introductory essay to the catalogue of that show, which opened at the Grafton Galleries in London in November 1910, Fry and Desmond MacCarthy codified the notion of opposition and conflict between Impressionists and those who followed them, as that notion had been promulgated by the Symbolists. "The Post-Impressionists," Fry and MacCarthy declared, "consider the Impressionists too naturalistic."[22] And for these writers as well, the issue of whether an artist's stance before nature is an active or a passive one was key:

> The impressionists were artists and their imitations of appearances were modified, consciously or unconsciously, in the direction of unity and harmony; being artists they were forced to select and arrange. But the receptive, passive attitude towards the appearances of things often hindered them from rendering their real significance.[23]

The Symbolists scorned the Impressionists for their submissive attitude toward nature. They wished to eliminate nature as the prime agent in the creative process and to reinstate the artist's mind as the active and generating source of the sensation that becomes the work of art. But while they and the generations that followed them might denigrate the passivity of being "only an eye," we must keep in mind today that from this passivity and responsiveness to nature sprang originality, according to the nineteenth-century Romantic view that had nurtured both Monet and Paul Cézanne. This view was to be superseded in the twentieth century by a more traditional and conventionally gendered understanding of the avant-garde artist's relationship to nature, and this change was set into motion by the Symbolists. We should not be misled by their concern for subjective feeling and expression, a concern that they shared with the Impressionists. For the real issue at stake in defining the relationship and the differences between Symbolism and Impressionism is not the subjective/objective dichotomy that formerly structured

critical debate on this subject. The underlying issue is that of control or, to put it in terms of yet another of the gendered dualisms of patriarchal discourse, domination/submission—male art controlling female nature. When seen in these terms, Symbolism is not a continuation of Impressionist subjectivity, but rather a masculinization of it.

It is the consistent gendering as female and feminine of both the technique of Impressionism in general and the landscape school in particular in the critical literature from the late 1880s on that announces the basis for Symbolism's assertion of a subjectivity that is conceptual rather than emotional, universalizing rather than personal. The feminine gendering of Impressionism by critics seems to occur most frequently, in fact, during the decades of Symbolism's rise and ascendancy among the French avant-garde, in the late 1880s and throughout the 1890s. Its survival into the early years of the twentieth century is illustrated in the writings of such critics as Claude Roger-Marx, who asserted in 1907: "The term impressionist announces a manner of perception in noting what is beautiful which corresponds so well to the hyperaesthesia and sensitivity of women."[24] In this climate and within this context, the reimposition of a masculinist mode of possessing nature became a prime objective for Symbolist theorists and artists in the 1890s. And in these terms, I would argue, the critical and theoretical literature of Symbolism and Postimpressionism should be seen in part as a backlash against the feminizing threat of a particular aspect of the Romantic tradition—an aspect of that tradition that had threatened to gain ascendancy in nineteenth-century French painting with the ever-increasing popularity of the landscape school.

While the Symbolists expressed scorn for science, they nevertheless shared fully in its masculinist assumptions about the world of nature. For this reason, Symbolism's attitude toward science is one that is best understood in terms of a competition rather than a rejection. Not incidentally, the language of Symbolist aesthetic theory and criticism is as gendered as the language of the sciences that Symbolism scorned. In particular, the terms in which the Symbolists were inclined to cast their agenda in regard to nature often echo the gendered metaphors that attended, as we have seen, upon the "birth" of modern science in the seventeenth century. Like Francis Bacon, who envisioned the scientific enterprise as "a chaste and lawful marriage between Mind and Nature,"[25] the Symbolist painters believed that "the impression of nature must be wedded to the esthetic sentiment which chooses, arranges, simplifies and synthesizes. The painter ought not to rest until he has given birth to the child of his imagination . . . begotten by the union of his mind with reality."[26]

With such statements, Symbolism privileged artistic conceptualization (gendered in the nineteenth century as masculine) over the sensory response to nature (gendered as feminine) and used this as a strategy to distance itself from the femininity associated with the Romantic and Impressionist landscape schools. But this strategy functioned simultaneously as a bid to surpass the masculinity of science itself by asserting the priority of art over science in the realm of their shared preoccupation—the domination and transcendence over female nature. For, by definition, the scientific method of observation and experimentation remained dependent upon the base "matter" of "detestable nature," as Aurier termed it. The Symbolists, on the other hand, claimed to give form to ideas and feelings that were generated from within; and while not dependent for inspiration upon external reality, they nevertheless believed themselves capable of revealing and fixing its very essence. Thus, Symbolism regendered art as male in relation to female nature, rejecting Impressionism's feminized role, but also rejecting science and asserting its own superiority over a science that still depended for its raison d'être upon the material world.

In terms of the gender metaphor, then, Symbolism's scorn for science may be interpreted as an attempt to reverse the hierarchic positions that had been assigned by positivism to science and art in nineteenth-century France. The Symbolists' simultaneous rejection of both science and Impressionism

was based ostensibly on what the latter two shared—that is, a dependence (albeit of a very different sort) upon nature. But at heart, this dual rejection grew out of Symbolism's desire to claim for itself what science possessed and what Impressionism most conspicuously lacked—a masculinized position of dominance over the natural world, one that might in turn endow the artist and art in general with a position of cultural superiority in relation to science.

THE REGENDERING OF IMPRESSIONISM

The Symbolists' efforts to establish themselves as a recognizable entity distinct from the Impressionist movement—a process that involved the casting of Impressionism as the inferior "other"—have reinforced the tendency of later historians to write the history of this period in dualistic terms, as a narrative of conflict in which the Symbolists' scorn for science implied—and eventually, in the literature, "proved"—the Impressionists' abiding attachment to it.

During the first half of the twentieth century, a period when "objectivity" was not generally valued as a criterion for avant-garde art, the presumption of an alliance between Impressionism and positivist science was stubbornly maintained in the critical literature, even though the effect of such an alliance on Impressionism as art was often judged in negative rather than positive terms. Thus it was that in 1932 Roger Fry said of Monet that he "cared only to reproduce on his canvas the actual visual sensation as far as that was possible," describing him as an artist who "aimed almost exclusively at a scientific documentation of appearances."[27] And in 1934 James Johnson Sweeney wrote critically of Monet's Impressionism and of the positivist milieu that had given rise to it that "the encouragement of a scientific, detached impassivity struck directly at any link with the emotions."[28]

That the historically specious association of Impressionism with the objectivity of science would have nevertheless persisted in such a hostile critical climate—and at a time, moreover, when Impressionism already enjoyed widespread popularity as the modern style of choice among the middle classes—appears perplexing at first. But it becomes less so when one recognizes that this critical stance may well have been the lesser of two evils—the greater of the two being the accusations of passivity before nature and the resulting association with femininity, which the rhetoric of Symbolism had helped to promote for Impressionism in the 1890s. It was this troubling association that the mythic connection between Impressionism and science was instrumental in dissipating, so that Impressionism might be appropriately regendered for a century that had come to place upon it both enormous monetary and cultural value.

The feminine gendering of the Impressionist style and attitude, though widespread in the criticism of the 1890s, did not in fact survive into the later twentieth century. It seems to have dropped out of the literature fairly early in the century, although it was still apparently being combated, even as late as 1928, by Georges Clemenceau, whose *Claude Monet, Les Nymphéas* (an extended appreciation published as a memorial to Monet) is filled with gratuitous and in all probability compensatory assertions about the "virility" of both Monet and his enterprise. Early on in Clemenceau's book there are many physical descriptions of Monet that stress his power and manhood, his ability to impose his will (not on nature, significantly, but on the marshaling of his own powers), as well as many descriptions of the act of painting as a battle or a duel.[29]

This countering insistence upon the virility of Impressionism and the Impressionists may have become increasingly necessary in the first years of the twentieth century to support the style's early and astounding commercial success with entrepreneurial collectors both in France and elsewhere in the world, particularly in the United States.[30] In France itself, among the earliest collectors and supporters of Impressionism in the 1870s, 1880s, and 1890s were department store magnates such as Ernest Hoschedé, industrialists such as Henri Rouart, textile manufacturers such as Jean Dollfus, and bankers such as Isaac

de Camondo.[31] Innovators in business and industry, these men saw in the fluid, unstable, and wholly untraditional style of the Impressionists a vanguard art that reflected the modern spirit of entrepreneurial initiative and originality, an art that responded to and depicted the changing and dynamic modern world they had been instrumental in shaping. Ironically, then—in a striking demonstration of the way in which distinctly different and even opposing interpretations of the same phenomena can exist side by side within the same culture—the very elements of style and attitude that had made Impressionism a feminine art in the eyes of its earliest, culturally conservative detractors (its fluidity and instability) seem to have made it a masculine and virile art for this at first small but steadily growing group of independent-minded patron-collectors, captains of industry who valued Impressionism for its originality and modernity. Many of these men, interestingly enough, had collected the art of the Barbizon painters before collecting Impressionist paintings, finding in both the expression of a unique temperament and sensibility—the expression, if you will, of Romantic individualism. And that single aspect of the Romantic ethos, pervasive throughout the modern era, has indeed continued to adhere to Impressionism and to color our responses to it to the present day.

Impressionism, then, gendered as female by its conservative critics and its Symbolist rivals in the 1890s, was regendered and restored to masculinity in the twentieth century by virtue of its mythic connection with science, a connection that, in turn, was supported by the ideological concerns and outlook of capitalist collectors who identified with Impressionism and invested it with their own image. In spite of this, however, it should be noted that Impressionism continued to be the subject of a precarious duality of gendering in the art criticism, art history, and art markets of the late-twentieth-century world.

As the much sought-after possession of the entrepreneurial classes, the monetary value of Impressionist paintings steadily, indeed astronomically, increased in the second half of the twentieth century.

It is in this role as the visible sign of the wealth and power of its individual and corporate owners that Impressionism—like all art in the technological twentieth century (as in the positivist nineteenth)—has functioned as the stereotypical female in the male entrepreneurial world. In this sense, its function as a commodity in the twentieth century did not differ radically from the traditional social role assigned to actual females, despite the shifting inroads made by an active feminist movement during both the early and later decades of the twentieth century.

At the same time, however, in our commodified world, greater monetary and prestige value has been assigned consistently to art that is understood in some way to exemplify or privilege the socially constructed attributes of masculinity—for example (to use the value-laden descriptive terms of standard twentieth-century critical accounts), the scientifically based rigor of Renaissance art over the sensual playfulness and perversity of Mannerism; Neoclassical virility and moral fervor over the feminine frivolity, superficiality, and amorality of the Rococo; or twentieth-century conceptual abstraction versus what in the days before feminist enlightenment used to be called "mere" decoration.

Thus it is not really surprising that the "feminine" side of Impressionism's relationship with nature was buried and transformed over the course of the twentieth century. The anxiety that it left behind, however, continued to resurface in the art-historical and critical literature, where it took the form of exaggerated efforts to establish and defend the masculinity of the movement. In this category, broadly speaking, I would place art history's recent emphasis on the political and sociohistoric interpretation of Impressionist painting, most clearly exemplified by the influential work of T. J. Clark, whose analysis of the "bourgeois" art of the Impressionists emphasizes the contextual phenomena of popular culture and class identity in a Paris that had been transformed and "modernized" by the building campaigns of Baron Haussmann during the Second Empire.[32] Insofar as this approach seeks to objectify Impressionism and to place its meaning outside the artist, it preserves and reinforces the movement's "masculine" identity by continuing its alignment with stereotypically gendered notions about Realism in nineteenth-century French painting. Also in this category I would place recent scholarship's insistence upon searching for signs of urban and industrial elements—factory chimneys, railroad bridges, and the like—in even the most bucolic of Monet's landscapes. These issues and the social dynamic they are said to have supported as well as reflected have been foregrounded in Impressionist scholarship by writers such as Clark and Paul Hayes Tucker despite the fact that Monet himself clearly sought to ignore and evade these signs of urban encroachment, as he retreated first from Argenteuil to Vétheuil and then finally to his own protected garden at Giverny. Given the gender symbolism implicit in the urbanized landscape—the imposition of factories and railroads upon female nature by male technology—these preoccupations, too, might be seen as yet another instance of our own era's unceasing efforts to virilize the Impressionist movement.[33]

These efforts to masculinize Impressionism, of course, have also included continuing scholarly attempts to forge connections between the methods and attitudes of the Impressionists on the one hand and the way in which science was being practiced in their day on the other. Consider, for example, Joel Isaacson's proposed analogy between Monet's working methods in the 1860s and the scientific method outlined by the physiologist Claude Bernard in his *Introduction à l'étude de la médecine experimentale* of 1865. Still struggling, unself-consciously, with the Symbolists' gendered characterization of Monet as "only an eye," Isaacson, writing in the 1980s, set out to prove that Monet was, so to speak, a thinking eye, an artist whose stance in regard to nature was active, not passive. "He was a positivist," Isaacson asserts, "in the sense of a commitment to science, data, experimental investigation. . . . His primary instrument was the eye, guided by a mind that reached out, probed, questioned, and tested what he saw." Attempting to turn Monet into a cerebral and active investigator, Isaacson cites the distinction made by Bernard and Auguste Comte before him in the nineteenth century between observation and experiment. The observer, wrote Bernard, "listens to nature and writes under its dictation," while "the mind of the experimenter must be active, which is to say, it must interrogate nature." In accordance with this distinction, one that we may now recognize as traditionally gendered in both the arts and the sciences, it was Monet's aim, according to Isaacson, "to take painting beyond observation, to claim for it, by his actions, a more deliberate experimental role in the continuing realist inquiry into the appearances and understanding of nature."[34]

In the more popular critical literature, contemporary efforts to virilize Impressionism can take the form of far more direct assertions of the masculinity not only of the Impressionists but also, at times, of those who have devoted themselves to the study and interpretation of their nature-dependent art. In a review of the exhibition *Monet in the '90s: The Series Paintings,* for example, the novelist John Updike wrote of "the strenuous lessons in boldness Monet gave himself" and felt compelled to comment upon the exhibition's organizer, Paul Hayes Tucker, in surprisingly personal terms. Gendering the art historian cum scientist in this case as male and the work of art cum nature as female, Updike wrote: "Paul Tucker, a six-foot-six former all–New England tackle, now an art professor in Boston, used all his muscular powers of research and persuasion to draw over ninety of the series paintings from their hiding places on four continents over the last four years."[35]

The persistent anxiety over the unstable gendering of Impressionism that underlies such scholarly projects and critical statements is clearly pertinent to our inquiry, for they simultaneously reveal and attempt to counter deeply ingrained cultural fears. And they draw, no doubt unconsciously, upon what we may now clearly recognize as an ancient and influential system of signification that has gendered a passive natural world as female and an active, experimental science as male—a hierarchical language that

was used extensively in the twentieth century to re-gender Impressionism.

IMPRESSIONISM AND MODERNISM

The narrative of mainstream modernism has been described by the art historian Carol Duncan as a progression in which art "gradually emancipates itself from the imperative to represent convincingly or coherently a natural, presumably objective world." Duncan has pointed to the prevalence of images of women at all the critical junctures in this modernist drive toward a transcendent abstraction—in particular, images of threatening, repellent, or physically dismembered women, such as those in Pablo Picasso's *Demoiselles d'Avignon* (see fig. 15.1, p. 300) or in Willem de Kooning's *Woman* series. Pointing to the gendered basis of the modernist enterprise, Duncan asks: "What, if anything, do nudes and whores have to do with modern art's heroic renunciation of representation?" And in answer she suggests that for male artists and historians, these paintings have functioned as important symbols of a struggle that has defined modern art's most prestigious undertaking: the struggle to achieve transcendence over a material nature, long gendered as female and regarded as both threatening and inferior, in order to reach the so-called higher realms of abstraction.[36]

It was the formalist critic Clement Greenberg, writing in the 1950s, who first appropriated the late art of Monet to serve as a radical precursor to modernism in general and to Abstract Expressionism in particular. Long discredited among the avant-garde supporters of Cubism and Surrealism, Monet's late works, with their suppression of value contrast and illusionism and their resulting emphasis on surface and foreground, were validated and "made possible" once again in the eyes and words of Greenberg by the emergence of the work of Clyfford Still and Barnett Newman, both of whom admired Monet.[37] Although Greenberg assumed, along with his contemporaries, that Monet's aim was to record visual experience impassively and that his motives were "quasi-scientific," the critic nevertheless dismissed Monet's own intentions vis-à-vis nature—whatever they might have been—as irrelevant, and instead used abstraction and what he took to be Monet's inadvertent rejection of nature as the criteria by which the artist's modernity and his historical importance for the twentieth century might be defined. On the relation of Monet's art to nature and science, Greenberg wrote:

> The quasi-scientific aim he set himself in the 1890s—to record the effects of light on the same subject at different times of day and in different weather—may have involved a misconception of the purposes of art; but it was also, and more fundamentally, part of an effort to find a new principle of consistency for art . . . a more comprehensive principle; and it lay not in Nature, as he thought, but in the essence of art itself, in art's "abstractness." That he himself could not recognize this makes no difference.[38]

While Monet's efforts to capture the effects of Mediterranean light with "incandescent" colors may have resulted in pictures that "conveyed the truth of sub-tropical air and sun as never before, . . . the result as art," Greenberg maintained, "was cloying." "Monet's example," he declared, "shows as well as any how abysmally untrustworthy a mistress Nature can be for the artist who would make her his only one."[39] Yet according to Greenberg, Monet's art was unexpectedly and fortuitously saved from subservience to this "untrustworthy mistress." He explained:

> The literalness with which Monet registered his "sensations" could become an hallucinated literalness and land him on the far side of expected reality, in a region where visual fact turned into phantasmagoria that became all the more phantasmagorical because it was without a shred of fantasy. . . . Nature, prodded by an eye obsessed with the most naive kind of exactness, responded in the end with textures of color that could be managed

on canvas only by invoking the autonomous laws of the medium—which is to say Nature became the springboard for an almost abstract art.[40]

Interpreting the narrowed range of value contrasts to be found in Monet's late work not as an expressive choice but as a way of "returning painting to the surface," Greenberg then made the influential pronouncement: "The first seed of modernism, planted by the Impressionists, has turned out to be the most radical of all."[41]

Is Impressionism the foundation for modernism in painting—as has so often been claimed in the wake of Greenbergian formalism in the second half of the twentieth century? I would argue that it is not, and I would offer the artist's attitude toward nature and the gendered dichotomies that attitude has traditionally been called upon to reflect and reinforce as the keys to the assignment of the "modernist" designation. These are criteria that we can use as well to question and refine broader philosophical definitions of modernism, which have privileged as its source not Impressionism per se but Romanticism. In the view of twentieth-century cultural historians and philosophers—from Arthur O. Lovejoy to Morse Peckham to Michel Foucault—the modernist twentieth century, with its emphasis on personal expression and originality, can itself be regarded as part of the Romantic era, an era that banished the normative values and universalizing attitudes of the "classical episteme" (Foucault's term) that had preceded it.[42]

But even though Romanticism was unquestionably a major influence on art throughout the nineteenth and twentieth centuries, Romanticism itself, as we have seen, was not monolithic. On the basis of art's gendered attitude toward nature, we have isolated and defined a minority current within Romantic painting, one that surfaced primarily among the landscape painters as opposed to the figurative painters of heroic narrative (e.g., Rousseau versus Delacroix). Both valued originality, but each had a very different understanding of what it was and how it was to be achieved. Among the landscape painters, truth to a living nature—in subjective terms, according to the unique character of each artist's eye and sensibility—was viewed as the prerequisite for personal expression and personal style. The other and ultimately dominant current saw originality residing in transcendence over a mindless and inferior natural world.

The lesson learned and taught by the Romantic and Impressionist landscape painters of the nineteenth century—the lesson that nature cannot be dominated or possessed—led in the twentieth century to a rejection of nature that was presaged and prepared for by the Symbolists and their drive to transcend the physical, material world—the world of female nature. If the artist could not actively possess nature, then he could reject her. But on no account could he acknowledge—as, in the view of their critics, the "passive" landscape painters of Romanticism and Impressionism came perilously close to doing—her hegemony as the source of human sensation and art.

Symbolism might thus be viewed as the nineteenth century's final effort to reimpose intellectual control on nature and to "reveal her secrets" in the traditional terms of the gendered dialogue that has conventionally supported art's efforts to rival the active and masculinized enterprise of the sciences. In this sense, a major turning point in the history of art may indeed be seen to occur in the early twentieth century in the "primitivism" of Picasso and the Expressionists, where nature (often embodied as woman) is presented as a threatening, ferocious, and untamable force. Such imagery provides a fitting prelude to twentieth-century art's decisive turn in the direction of abstraction and nonobjectivity, a move that may be understood in part as modernism's rejection of a female nature that could not otherwise be dominated and controlled.[43]

In a 1949 essay entitled "On the Role of Nature in Modernist Painting," Clement Greenberg set forth a theoretical argument for this transition from the older Albertian position that the artist can rival and transcend nature by discovering and taking possession of her secrets to the modernist rejection of nature—

art's withdrawal from the traditional arena of struggle with female nature and its safe removal to a "higher" plane. But even here, embedded in the rhetoric of high modernism, the idea of possessing nature and of going her one better persists, albeit as a submerged undercurrent in a formalist theory that pretends to have set for itself a very different agenda. Greenberg wrote:

> When Braque and Picasso stopped trying to imitate the normal appearance of a wineglass, and tried instead to approximate, by analogy, the way nature opposed verticals in general to horizontals in general—at that point, art caught up with a new conception and feeling of reality that was already emerging in general sensibility as well as in science.

This "new conception and feeling of reality" is defined by Greenberg as a new conception of space, "an uninterrupted continuum that connects instead of separating things," providing an experience that is "far more intelligible to sight than to touch." By implication, sight is something that Greenberg associates with the conceptual (and masculine) undertakings of the artist and the scientist, while touch belongs traditionally to the material world of female nature—"detestable nature," to borrow the language of the symbolist critic Aurier. And indeed Greenberg's attitude has much in common with that of the Symbolists, for he continues: "We no longer peer through the object-surface into what is not itself; now the unity and integrity of the visual continuum, as a continuum, supplants tactile nature as the model of the unity and integrity of pictorial space." This proves, according to Greenberg, that abstract art is still "naturalistic," for now, instead of merely imitating visual experience, "the picture plane as a total object represents space as a total object." Thus, he concludes, "Art and nature confirm one another as before." We cannot help but notice, however, that the nature of which Greenberg speaks must still depend for its definition upon science, and it is a nature whose secrets are still to be stolen and revealed by art—an art that, as in the Renaissance, still seeks to rival and supplant "her."[44]

At issue today in the philosophical identification of modernism with Romanticism is the changing status of subjectivity, which, as poststructuralist analysis has taught us to recognize, is an issue of power. In the Romantic/modernist tradition, subjectivity has been a privileged attribute of art only when it has taken a masculinized form. From the figurative painters of the Romantic movement in the nineteenth century to the Abstract Expressionists of the twentieth century, male artists have appropriated and absorbed into their own domain traits of feeling and sensibility conventionally gendered as female, which they have regendered by linking their own identities as artists to an intensified assertion of art's "active" and masculinized dominance over female nature. In view of what constitutes originality in these terms (i.e., in terms of the artist's relationship to nature), Romantic and Impressionist landscape painting presented, as we have seen, an aberrant discourse, one that set out to challenge establishment values in the nineteenth century but that in the twentieth century was absorbed and pressed into the service of those very same hierarchic and gender-laden values.

While the particular phenomena to which patriarchal culture attaches masculine and feminine labels may change over time, what remains constant is the privileging of whatever happens at the moment to hold the masculine—usually the "objective"—position. Romanticism and modernism problematized this traditional arrangement by regendering subjectivity, predictably privileging masculine subjectivity over feminine subjectivity, but nonetheless conferring new validity upon subjectivity as a cultural position. While we owe to postmodern and poststructuralist analysis the exposure of this mechanism, it is one that, ironically, may hold a key to the feminist deconstruction of postmodernism itself. For in its relation to modernism (as in Symbolism's relation to Impressionism), postmodernism has played the same old game of attempting to discredit what came before it by feminizing it. While modernism associated itself with the

gendered subjectivity of a masculinized Romanticism in positive terms, postmodernism has equated modernism with Romanticism in an entirely pejorative sense. By elevating indeterminacy and interpretive multiplicity, by demonstrating the impossibility of an autonomous subjectivity, and by thus declaring that in older Romantic terms the author is dead, postmodernism has set itself to dismantling the subjectivity of modernism, thus assuming for itself a position of superior objectivity. While it purports to expose and discredit polarizing dichotomies, then, postmodernism exploits and relies on them in order to position (and privilege) itself in relation to the modernist "other," to which it has thus assigned the female role in patriarchal culture's ongoing and still powerful system of binary and gendered oppositions.

The struggle of nineteenth-century artists to define their position and the position of art in general in relation to nature and to science was complex. Over the course of the twentieth century, the history and dimensions of that struggle were flattened by an essentially masculinist criticism that sought to assimilate Impressionism into our culture's dominant view of a natural world, gendered as female, conquered and dominated not only by a male science and technology but also by art. Seeking to legitimize not only Impressionism but art itself, which had been cast in the nineteenth century as the stereotypical female in a male scientific world, art historians have missed or misread the tensions that were inherent in the dialogue between art and positivist science in the nineteenth century and have mistakenly and misleadingly described the Impressionists as artists who self-consciously adopted the teachings and methods of modern science and who attempted to be "objective" in relation to a passive and mechanistic natural world.

There is a fundamental irony, of course, in the twentieth century's alignment of Impressionism with a Baconian/Cartesian conception of the goals and procedures of an objective science. Unlike the positivist heirs to this science in the nineteenth century, who saw themselves in archetypally dualistic terms as separate from nature in a subject/object relationship that aimed for mastery and domination over a passive natural world whose "secrets" had to be "unveiled" and controlled, the Impressionists (like the Romantic landscape painters who preceded them) were artists who saw themselves as a receptive and responsive part of the natural world, thus assuming an attitude toward nature that was at once more humble and more assertively individualistic.

It was from this "passive" attitude toward nature, as their contemporaries deemed it, that the widespread characterization in the 1890s of Impressionist landscape painting as a "feminine" art was derived. As Impressionism's acceptance and value have grown over the last one hundred years, that characterization, in turn, has given rise to art-historical and critical efforts to bestow legitimacy upon Impressionism in more conventionally acceptable and prestigious terms—to regender it, in other words, by endowing it with the culturally defined attributes of masculinity; and these efforts have distorted our understanding of both the artists and their art. From the late nineteenth century on, a variety of competing interests and modes of interpretation have in fact been brought to bear upon the reception and interpretation of Impressionism. But the one consistent point of reference, as we have seen, has been the perception and evaluation of the movement in terms of the socially constructed attributes of gender.

NOTES

1. Scott Schaefer, "The French Landscape Sensibility," in *A Day in the Country: Impressionism and the French Landscape* (Los Angeles: Los Angeles County Museum of Art, 1984), 57.

2. George Heard Hamilton, *Claude Monet's Paintings of Rouen Cathedral*, Charlton Lectures on Art (Newcastle upon Tyne, England: University of Newcastle upon Tyne, 1959), 15, 18.

3. For a discussion of the formal and thematic continuities between Romantic and Impressionist landscape painting, see Norma Broude, *Impressionism, A Feminist Reading: The Gendering of Art, Science and Nature in the Nineteenth Century* (New York: Rizzoli International Publications, 1991, and New York: Westview Press, 1997), 17–80.

4. Hamilton, *Monet's Paintings of Rouen Cathedral*, 14.

5. Georges Rivière, "L'Esposition des Impressionistes," *L'Impressionniste*, no. 1 (6 April 1877): 2–6; reprinted in Lionello Venturi, *Les Archives de l'Impressionnisme*, 2 vols. (Paris: Durand Ruel, 1939), 2: 312.

6. Ibid., 2: 311.

7. Alexandre Pothey, "Beaux-Arts," *Le Petit Parisien*, 7 April 1877; reprinted in Venturi, *Les Archives de l'Impressionnisme*, 2: 303.

8. Hermann von Helmholtz, *Optique physiologique*, trans. Emie Javal and N. Th. Klein (Paris, 1867).

9. For a detailed review and contextual reinterpretation of the late-nineteenth-century literature upon which connections between Impressionism and positivist science have been based, see Broude, *Impressionism, A Feminist Reading*, part 2, "Impressionism and Science," 110–43.

10. Observed by Mary D. Garrard. See her "Leonardo da Vinci: Female Portraits, Female Nature," in *The Expanding Discourse: Feminism and Art History*, ed. Norma Broude and Mary D. Garrard (New York: HarperCollins, 1992), 72.

11. J. Spedding, R. L. Ellis, and D. D. Heath, eds., *The Works of Francis Bacon*, 14 vols. (1857–74; rpt. Stuttgart: F. F. Verlag, 1963), 5: 506.

12. Charles Blanc, *Grammaire des arts du dessin* (Paris, 1867), 22.

13. Baudelaire, "The Life and Work of Eugene Delacroix," in *The Painter of Modern Life and Other Essays*, trans. Jonathan Mayne (Oxford: Phaidon Press, 1964), 46.

14. William H. Gerdts, "Impressionism in the United States," in *World Impressionism*, ed. Norma Broude (New York: Abrams, 1990), 36. The comments quoted by Gerdts are from "The Fine Arts: The French Impressionists," *The Critic* 120 (17 April 1886): 195–96.

15. Albert Aurier, "Le Symbolisme en peinture: Paul Gauguin," *Mercure de France* 2 (March 1891), rpt. in *oeuvres posthumes*, ed. Remy de Gourmont (Paris: Mercure de France, 1893), 205, 208–11; as cited by

Richard Shiff, *Cézanne and the End of Impressionism* (Chicago: University of Chicago Press, 1984), 45, 46.

16. Aurier, "Essai sur une nouvelle méthode de critique" (1892), in *oeuvres posthumes*, 176; as cited by Patricia Townley Mathews, *Aurier's Symbolist Art Theory and Criticism* (Ann Arbor: UMI Research Press, 1986), 22.

17. Aurier, "Les Peintres symbolistes" (1892), in *oeuvres posthumes*, 294; as cited by Mathews, *Aurier's Symbolist Art Theory*, 22.

18. Mathews, *Aurier's Symbolist Art Theory*, 22.

19. On "detestable nature," see Aurier, "Eugène Carrière" (1891), in *oeuvres posthumes*, 279; as cited by Mathews, *Aurier's Symbolist Art Theory*, 46; on aversion to sensuality, see Mathews, *Aurier's Symbolist Art Theory*, 46; on misogyny, see Aurier, "Raffaelli" (1890), in *oeuvres posthumes*, 250; as cited by Mathews, *Aurier's Symbolist Art Theory*, 110.

20. Octave Mirbeau, "Vincent van Gogh," *L'Echo de Paris*, 31 March 1891, 1; as cited by Shiff, *Cézanne*, 50.

21. Henri Matisse, "Notes of a Painter" (1908), trans. in Alfred H. Barr, Jr., *Matisse, His Art and His Public* (New York: Museum of Modern Art, 1951), 120.

22. Roger Fry and Desmond MacCarthy, "The Post-Impressionists," in *Manet and the PostImpressionists* (London: Grafton Galleries, 1910), 7; as cited by Shiff, *Cézanne*, 158.

23. Fry and MacCarthy, "The Post-Impressionists," 8–9; as cited by Shiff, *Cézanne*, 158.

24. Claude Roger-Marx, *Gazette des Beaux-Arts* (1907): 507; as cited by Griselda Pollock, *Mary Cassatt* (London: Jupiter Books, 1980), 21.

25. Francis Bacon, *The Refutation of Philosophies*, trans. B. Farrington, in *The Philosophy of Francis Bacon*, 131.

26. Gauguin's instructions to his disciple Paul Sérusier, as reported in W. Verkade, *Le Tourment de Dieu* (Paris, 1926), 75–76; as cited in John Rewald, *Post-Impressionism* (New York: Museum of Modern Art, 1956), 206.

27. Roger Fry, *Characteristics of French Art* (London: Chatto and Windus, 1932), 127.

28. James Johnson Sweeney, *Plastic Redirections in Twentieth-Century Painting* (Chicago: University of Chicago Press, 1934), 6.

29. See, e.g., Clemenceau's description of Renoir's portrait of Monet at work in 1875, *Claude Monet, Les Nymphéas* (Paris: Plon, 1928), 23.

30. On Monet's commercial and critical successes from 1889 on, see Steven Z. Levine, *Monet and His Critics* (New York: Garland Publishing, 1976), 95 ff, 181 ff; and Paul Hayes Tucker, *Monet in the '90s: The Series Paintings* (New Haven, Conn.: Yale University Press, 1989). On the worldwide impact and popularity of French Impressionism, see Norma Broude, "A World in Light: France and the International Impressionist Movement, 1860–1920," in *World Impressionism* (New York: Abrams, 1990), 8–35, and passim.

31. See Albert Boime, "Entrepreneurial Patronage in Nineteenth-Century France," in *Enterprise and Entrepreneurs in Nineteenth- and Twentieth-Century France*, ed. Edward C. Carter II, Robert Forster, and Joseph N. Moody (Baltimore: Johns Hopkins University Press, 1976), 137–207.

32. Timothy J. Clark, *The Painting of Modern Life: Paris in the Art of Manet and His Followers* (New York: Alfred A. Knopf, 1985).

33. See Clark's discussion of "The Environs of Paris," in *The Painting of Modern Life*, 147–204; and Paul Hayes Tucker, *Monet at Argenteuil* (New Haven, Conn.: Yale University Press, 1982).

34. Joel Isaacson, "Observation and Experiment in the Early Work of Monet," in *Aspects of Monet: A Symposium on the Artist's Life and Times*, ed. John Rewald and Frances Weitzenhoffer (New York: Abrams, 1984), 17, 24–25, 34 n. 29.

35. John Updike, "Monet Isn't Everything: An Orgy of Impressionism in Boston," *New Republic*, 19 March 1990, 28, 30.

36. Carol Duncan, "The MoMA's Hot Mamas," *Art Journal* 48 (Summer 1989): 171–73, 176; reprinted in Broude and Garrard, eds., *The Expanding Discourse: Feminism and Art History* (New York: HarperCollins, 1992).

37. Clement Greenberg, "'American-Type' Painting" (1955/1958), in *Art and Culture* (Boston: Beacon Press, 1961), 221.

38. Clement Greenberg, "The Later Monet" (1956/1959), in *Art and Culture*, 41.

39. Ibid., 41–42.

40. Ibid., 42.

41. Ibid., 44.

42. Arthur O. Lovejoy, *The Great Chain of Being* (Cambridge: Harvard University Press, 1966 [1936]); Morse Peckham, "Toward a Theory of Romanticism," *PMLA* 66 (1951): 5–23; Michel Foucault, *The Order of*

Things: An Archaeology of the Human Sciences (New York: Vintage/Random House, 1973).

43. Surrealism, which equated the unconscious with female nature (fearing its eruptive powers but desiring at the same time to harness and control those powers through art), presents a different but not unrelated side of art's attitude toward nature in the twentieth century, one that also had a major impact on the art of the Abstract Expressionists, whom Greenberg championed. On the importance of psychoanalytic discourses for painters of the New York School, see Michael Leja, "Jackson Pollock: Representing the Unconscious," *Art History* 13 (December 1990): 542–65.

44. Clement Greenberg, "On the Role of Nature in Modernist Painting" (1949), in *Art and Culture*, 171–74.

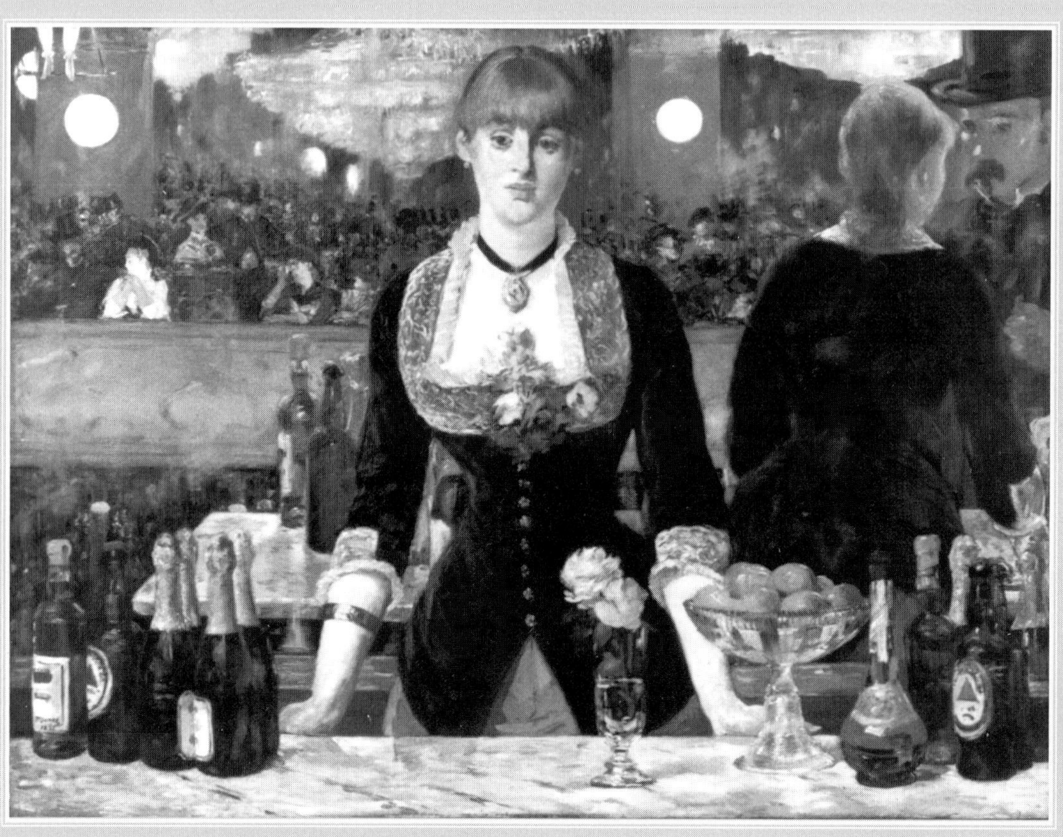

12

SELLING, SEDUCTION, AND SOLICITING THE EYE

Manet's Bar at the Folies-Bergère

Ruth E. Iskin

MOST INTERPRETERS of Edouard Manet's *Bar at the Folies-Bergère* (fig. 12.1) have assumed that the man whose face we see in the mirror is propositioning the young woman at the counter.[1] If he is not soliciting her "sexual favors" outright, it is generally assumed that her body is for sale.[2] Seduction and selling are indeed at the center of this painting, as this essay argues, though their object is not just the fashionable woman at the counter. That the barmaid is a salesgirl and the situation at hand primarily a sales transaction of the goods on the counter has not played more than a marginal role in previous discussions of the painting.

While the woman, the man, and even the mirror itself have been given center stage in interpretations of *Bar at the Folies-Bergère* for good reason, the prominent display of goods in front and the packed crowd of spectators in the back have barely been addressed.[3] No doubt, they were considered peripheral to the main scenario. But if this were the case, why is the display on the counter so provocatively positioned to beckon us as if from the threshold of the painting? And why does the radically miniaturized dense crowd in the far back take up such a large portion of the canvas? The goods on the counter and the crowd are the primary clues for my interpretation. This essay aims to revisit modernity by reviewing *Bar at the Folies-Bergère* in light of historically specific discourses of mass consumption, the changing roles of women, and the development of the modern public/crowd.

To understand Manet's painting and modernity, we must extend the circumference of our interests from the immediate history of the café-concert, and the rhetoric of pleasure, leisure, and entertainment, to broader discourses of mass consumption.[4] As Andreas Huyssen has noted, "From its beginnings the autonomy of art has been related dialectically to the commodity form."[5] The cultural history of modernity and the avant-garde painting of Manet and the Impressionists were interrelated with discourses of mass consumption. Not only was art for sale in exhibits, a fact that in the eyes of many reduced it to the level of bazaar goods, but art shows in world exhibitions also existed in the context of displays of industrial goods and the advertising of department stores and other prominent commercial enterprises. Most important, both department stores and modern artists positioned themselves in a culture of display and

This is an abridged version of an essay of the same title first published in the *Art Bulletin* 77, no. 1 (March 1995): 25–44. Copyright © 1995 by Ruth E. Iskin. Reprinted by permission of the author and courtesy of the College Art Association.

Figure 12.1. Edouard Manet, *Bar at the Folies-Bergère*, 1882. Oil on canvas. Courtauld Institute Gallery, London. (Photo: Courtauld Institute Gallery.)

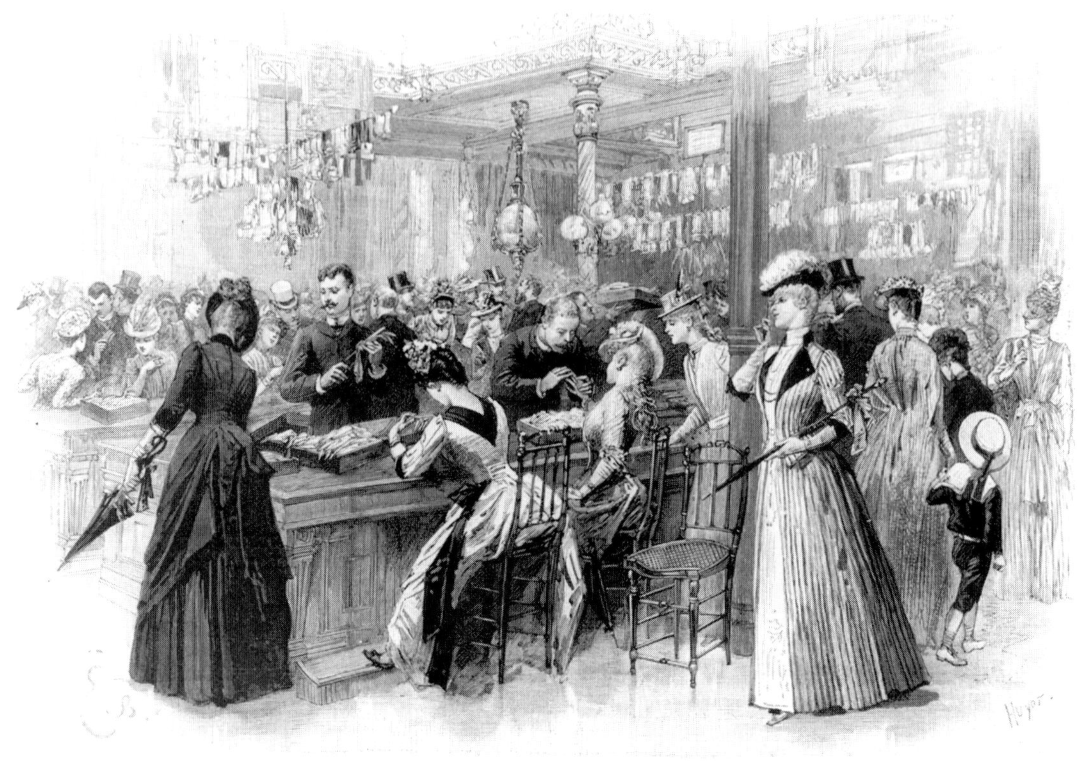

Figure 12.2. Emile Bayard, *Le Bon Marché: Au comptoir de ganterie*, from *L'Illustration*, 1889. (Photo: Research Library, The Getty Research Institute, Los Angeles.)

commodities, soliciting the eyes of consuming spectators who were part of a mass public.[6]

Though scholars may differ on when exactly the age of mass consumption began in Paris, few would dispute that it was well under way by 1882.[7] This date marked an important moment in the evolution of literary and artistic discourses about modern consumer society for Parisian audiences. It was the year in which Emile Zola's novel *Au Bonheur des dames* first appeared, in serial form, and in which Manet's *Bar at the Folies-Bergère* was exhibited in the Salon.[8] Zola's realist study of the Parisian department store features Denise Baudu, a young woman from the provinces who finds employment in Au Bonheur des Dames, where she gradually rises from lowly shop girl to top-level manager and eventually becomes coproprietor as the wife of the owner, Octave Mouret. Though the goods sold by Manet's woman at the bar differ from

the clothing sold by Zola's Denise Baudu, both works portray modern salesgirls. Denise serves customers at counters overflowing with clothes in need of being folded at the end of crowded promotional sales, while in Manet's painting, the fashionably dressed *marchande* stands behind a counter with a glittery display of bottles containing alcoholic beverages.

Counters filled with products, with salesmen or saleswomen standing behind them and one or more consumers in front, were often depicted in magazines throughout the second half of the nineteenth century; examples are Nadar's 1853 illustration with a caption reading, "From two to five she visits the stores for drapery and fancy goods, fashions, and lace," and Emile Bayard's view of the glove counter at the Bon Marché (fig. 12.2). As Novelene Ross has demonstrated, an iconography of the *dame de comptoir* receiving orders or payment in cafés, bars, or restaurants was well established by the time Manet painted *Bar at the Folies-Bergère*.[9] It is important to recognize, however, that the *dame de comptoir* in cafés and restaurants was part of a much broader discourse of mass consumption in which the counter transaction was central.

That selling and consumption qualify as the most compelling context for understanding Manet's painting is supported by the fact that some contemporary critics referred to the woman at the bar as *la marchande*, that is, "the salesgirl" or "saleswoman."[10] The class ambiguity of the fashionably dressed woman at the bar, noted by T. J. Clark, was not a failure on Manet's part to be explicit. A necessary part of the day-to-day discourse of selling and consumption at the time required of saleswomen a dress code that would be pleasing to a bourgeois clientele. Furthermore, salesgirls formed part of the aspiring new class of the *petite bourgeoisie*. A passage by Zola articulates this: "Nearly all the saleswomen, by their daily contact with the rich customers, assumed certain graces, and finished by forming a vague nameless class, something between a work-girl and a middle-class lady."[11] The type of dress worn by the woman at the counter in Manet's painting, like that of the department-store salesgirl, was presumably mandated by the establishment that hired her and was geared toward making her appealing to the public in order to further sales. It was "the costume of her employment," as A. Tabarant specifically described the dress worn by the model, Suzon—selected for this painting by Manet because she was employed as a *serveuse* at the Folies-Bergère.[12]

SOLICITING THE EYE: SEDUCTION AND CONSUMER DISPLAY

Writing in 1882 about Manet's *Bar at the Folies-Bergère*, the critic Henri Houssaye located the painting, albeit disparagingly, in the context of the modern and, by his judgment, vulgar aesthetics of Parisian shop-window displays:

It appears that this painting represents a bar at the Folies-Bergère; that this gaudy blue dress, topped by a cardboard head like those one used to see in milliners' shop windows, represents a woman; that this vaguely shaped mannequin whose face has been dashed in with three brush strokes represents a man.[13]

The large mirror that appears to extend beyond the width of Manet's painting and the glitter of reflected lights could well have provoked the association with shop windows that attracted spectators with striking displays (which often included mirrors). Lit shop windows characterized the display of high art as well during this period in Paris. "The rue Lafitte," Théophile Gautier noted, "is a permanent Salon, an exhibition of painting that lasts the whole year round. Five of the six shops show pictures in their windows. They are regularly changed and illuminated at night."[14] Manet himself reacted to the Salon's rejection of *Nana* in 1877 by showing the painting in the window of Giroux et Cie., a large dealer in objets d'art and luxury items whose windows attracted a great deal of public attention.[15]

Sumptuous displays of goods in the context of gigantic exhibition spaces with large crowds were at the core of the emerging discourse of mass consumption during the second half of the nineteenth century in Paris, both in department stores and in the world expositions. The latter, as Walter Benjamin noted, "were places of pilgrimage to the fetish commodity," and as Hippolyte Taine wrote in 1855, "All of Europe has been on the move to see commodities."[16] *Etalage*, the display of goods in commercial settings, had much in common with exhibit design at world fairs, where the vitrines often looked like shop windows or, in some instances, actually simulated them. Moreover, displaying products from specific stores was common practice at such events; the display itself often mimicked a shop window, as illustrations in magazines from that period demonstrate (fig. 12.3). At the same time, the Bon Marché was described by the press as "veritable permanent expositions,"[17] and in an article on the opening of new departments the writer referred to an earlier, memorable installation of Chinese and Japanese ob-

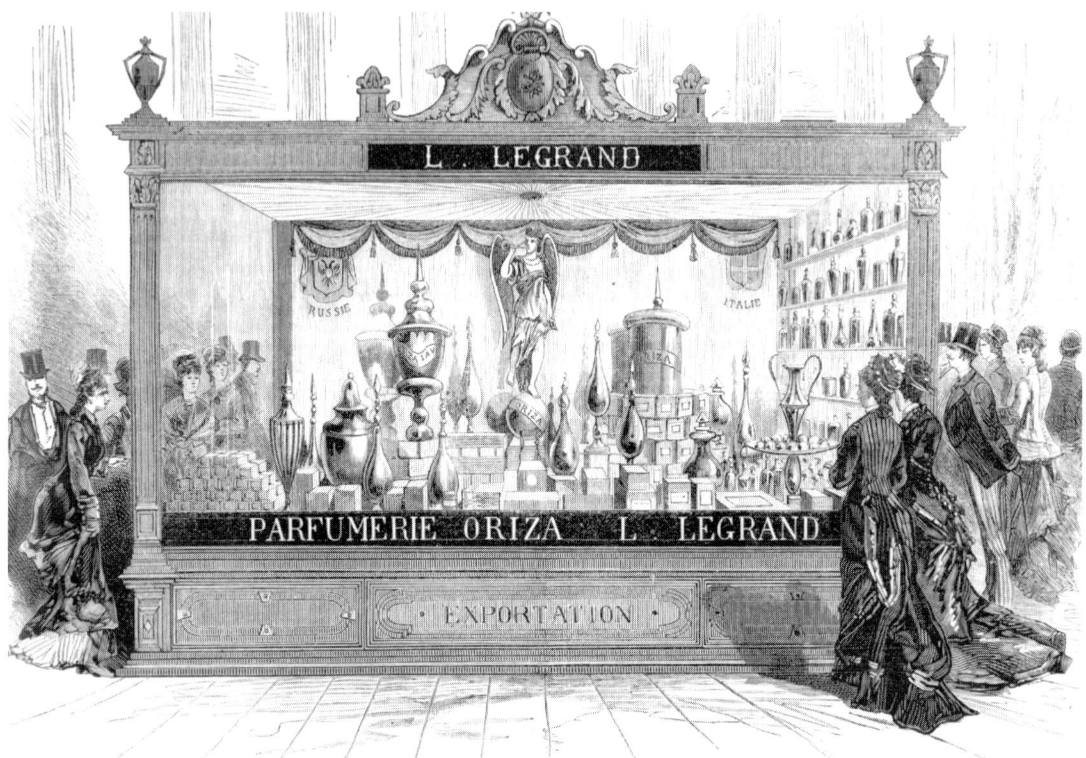

Figure 12.3. *The Parfumerie Oriza's Display*, Exposition Universelle, Paris, from *Le Monde illustré*, 1878. (Photo: Research Library, The Getty Research Institute, Los Angeles.)

jects as "a vast Asian museum" where "all of Paris, artist and amateur" met.[18]

French department stores at this time normally referred to their displays of merchandise as "expositions," to which they often invited the public through advertising in the press. An abundance of imported goods characterized many such displays, implying that commodities were accessible riches for the public in an age of industry, mass consumption, and colonialism. The Salon itself, as Patricia Mainardi has pointed out, was criticized throughout the period as "a permanent bazaar," because the art on exhibition was available for sale, in contrast to the pre-Revolutionary system, in which art was commissioned in advance and its exhibition for sale was looked down upon.[19] Thus, a government report of 1856 denounced the Salon for its "superficial little works suitable to all apartments, all purses, all tastes."[20] Art collecting was

becoming speculative and when paid admission was instituted for the Exposition Universelle of 1855, viewing exhibitions became similar to theater shows.[21] Fine art itself was shown in a commercial environment, as Edmond About wrote in reference to the 1868 Salon: "Today, in the corner of an all-purpose building, neither greenhouse nor hall but used for both, a simultaneous exhibition is thrown together of fine arts and fine vegetables, between a show of carriage makers and, no doubt, an exposition of cheese."[22]

Contemporary commentators were fully aware of the manipulations of commercial displays. The 1866 Larousse compares the *étalagiste*'s triumph to that of the "fisherman whose line is vigorously jerked by a large fish. . . . He is highly skilled in the art of arousing temptation, inciting the desires, unsettling wills and mind-sets, fascinating the undecided."[23] One of the chief strategies of the *étalagiste* was to over-

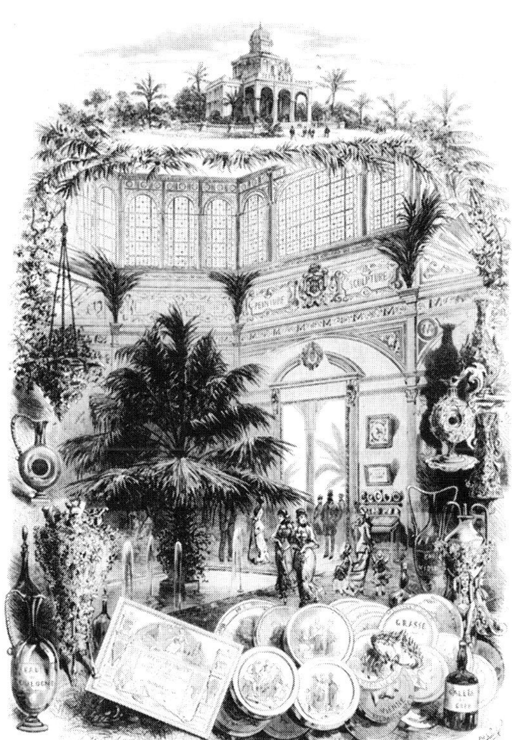

Figure 12.4. *Exposition Universelle: Le Pavillion de Monaco*, from *Le Monde illustré*, 1878. (Photo: Research Library, The Getty Research Institute, Los Angeles.)

whelm female consumers with gigantic displays of merchandise. Zola described this kind of display inside the department store as deliberately assaulting the eye, causing consumers "sore eyes." Octave Mouret, the innovative owner of Au Bonheur des Dames, was

> the best displayer in Paris, of a regular revolutionary stamp, who had founded the brutal and colossal school in the science of displaying. He delighted in a tumbling of stuffs, as if they had fallen from the crowded shelves by chance, making them glow with the most ardent colors, lighting each other up by contrast, declaring that the customers ought to have sore eyes on going out of the shop.[24]

Zola's description of Mouret in action as "lighting up this fire of stuff on a table" is comparable to Manet's

depiction of the glittering mirror and bar with the chandelier above and the light globes in the back.[25]

In contrast to the older mode of selling, where goods were neatly tucked away out of the reach of consumers, the guiding principle of modern display in department stores, as Zola described it, was to make the merchandise accessible and close to the consumer's senses. It was displayed to stimulate the desire to touch, and then buy. Illustrations of both department stores and exhibitions in magazines of the 1870s adapted this principle to the flat page by highlighting selected objects on display, placing them in the foreground while the space of the exhibition hall or department store extends toward the back; a view of the Monaco Pavilion in 1878 is a case in point (fig. 12.4).

The bold composition of Manet's *Bar at the Folies-Bergère*, too, pushes the goods up to the foreground of the painting, to confront the spectator with the utmost visual proximity, as if the products on the counter were actually within reach. It goes further by positioning the *marchande* as if ready to wait on the spectators in front of the painting. Manet's emphasis on the encounter with the goods becomes clear when his work is compared with the view of the bar from the side, in Jean-Louis Forain's small gouache *The Bar at the Folies-Bergère* of 1878.[26] Forain avoids the head-on confrontation between spectators and the bar with its goods. In contrast, the composition in Manet's painting resembles the kind of direct appeal to the spectator that was common in posters and illustrations—for example, the illustration that promoted a charity event at the opera in 1879 (fig. 12.5). The fashionably dressed Mlle Théo posing as an alluring salesgirl points to a bottle of perfume she holds up while casting an inviting look at the reader from behind a counter laden with enticing products. This illustration has much in common with the kind of visual advertising that characterized posters in Paris during the second half of the nineteenth century. As will be shown, posters promoting alcoholic and nonalcoholic beverages similarly positioned the bottles close to the spectator and next to an attractive woman. Associating goods with a beautiful woman and using both to lure spectators became a common

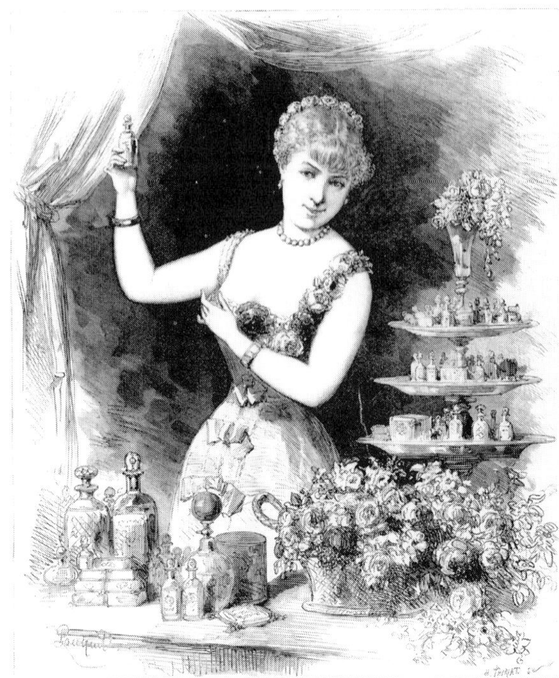

Figure 12.5. *Mlle Théo, en marchande de parfums, dans la Grande Kermesse,* cover of *L'Illustration,* 1879. (Photo: Research Library, The Getty Research Institute, Los Angeles.)

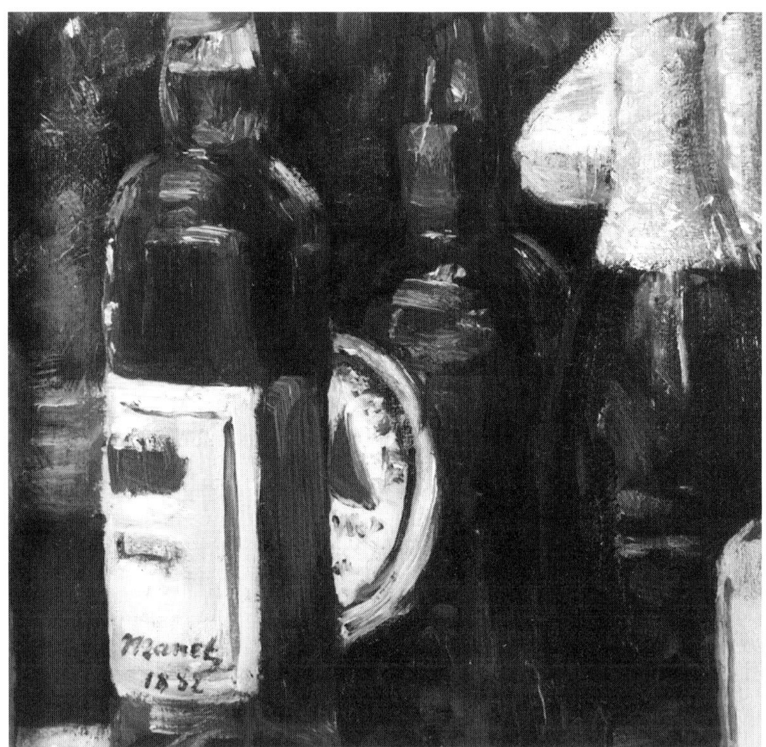

Figure 12.6. Edouard Manet, *Bar at the Folies-Bergère*, 1882, detail. Oil on canvas. Courtauld Institute Gallery, London. (Photo: Courtauld Institute Gallery.)

strategy in the evolving advertising culture of mass consumption, and it is in this context that Manet's *Bar at the Folies-Bergère* is best understood. Similarly, its composition equates encountering the painting with seeing an actual display of goods alongside its attractive saleswoman behind the bar. Moreover, the audience that Manet depicted in the mirror appears to reflect the spectators in front of his painting, because the mirror is positioned to "capture" the image of anyone standing before it. It is another device through which the spectator is virtually "hooked" into the painting.

The *marchande*'s direct address to the public, displaying goods for sale, parallels the situation of the modern artist, who, lacking government patronage, had to sell art on the open market. The painting itself reveals Manet's identification of his art with products for sale. Consider, for example, a small but meaningful detail: Manet's signature and the date of the painting, 1882, are inscribed on the label of the bottle of rosé wine or reddish liqueur that stands at the extreme left of the counter (fig. 12.6).[27]

By simultaneously signing the bottle label and the canvas, Manet playfully alludes to the discourse of selling and consumption that invades not only everyday goods but works of fine art as well. Situating his signature on the lower edge of the label, as if it were a tiny painting within the larger one, makes the label, which in the consumer age is identified with the commodity, a symbolic site of modern painting.[28] Thus placed, Manet's signature pictorially engenders a fiction of collapsed distinctions between painter, painting, and goods for sale at the bar. The date of the painting next to his signature humorously marks *Bar at the Folies-Bergère* as his own Salon vintage of 1882 and painting of *la vie moderne*.

Manet's display of bottles in this painting is radically new in the context of high art and resembles less the tradition of Western still life than advertising images of alcoholic beverages visible in Paris during the 1860s, 1870s, and 1880s. His urban "still life" of commodities signifies consumption in the public place, meant to attract the spectator, a potential customer, a consumer. Drawn in with a hint of pleasure, the con-

suming male spectator at the bar, like the potential shopper at the department store, typically female, is enticed by artful means of display. Our view of the barmaid (and of the entire painting) is mediated through the sumptuous "still life" on the counter. The shiny bottles, mandarins in a bowl, and delicate roses in a glass are all prominently positioned to evoke the senses of smell, taste, and touch, visually luring the viewer into approaching the bar, and thus the painting. In effect, Manet positions the painting as if it were a counter displaying goods, soliciting the eyes of the Salon spectators while ironically commenting on the artwork's own commercial status. Manet makes the "still life" central by painting it in relatively large dimensions and with an articulation of depth nowhere else repeated in the picture. The "still life" thus appears "real" in comparison to the images "reproduced" in the mirror.

In *Bar at the Folies-Bergère*, the bottles of champagne, Bass Pale Ale, and a reddish liqueur are presented as repeated items, mass-produced commodities in a commercial setting.[29] (With the exception of the crème de menthe on the right, none of the bottles on the counter is unique, and their "serial" nature is further underscored by their reflections in the mirror.) That the character of the "still life" in *Bar at the Folies-Bergère* is shaped by mass-produced goods for sale becomes clear when we compare it to Manet's still life in *Le Déjeuner dans l'atelier* of 1868, which depicts luncheon remains spread on a white cloth in a domestic environment; each item, whether food, china, glass, or cutlery, is presented as unique.

If the bottles collectively signify commodities in a public space, the fruit and roses on the bar belong to a well-established repertoire of domestic still life. Here they fulfill a decorative purpose, connoting, along with the image of the woman near them, an older regime of domesticity deployed to promote sales in the public environment. It is this double code of the "still-life" arrangement that acts as a decoy attracting consumers. Thus, in *Bar at the Folies-Bergère*, the lure is a complex set of codes that mixes sensual pleasures with sexual allusions, domestic plenitude with industrial mass-produced commodities on public display, and the tradition of still life with the emerging visual discourse of advertising commodities.

Benjamin's statement that Baudelaire's poetry was inspired by the poet's social experiences "of the big-city dweller, and of the customer" applies to Manet, who like Baudelaire was of a generation of artists who throughout their lives struggled in a new system of market competition.[30] Thus Baudelaire's parallel between the status of the courtesan and the poet is applicable to the modern artist as well. Poet, artist, actress, and courtesan—all had to appeal to the public, to attract admirers and buyers. As Baudelaire recognized, it was both a psychic and economic condition: "In order to have shoes she has sold her soul; but the Good Lord would laugh if, close to that vile person, I played hypocrite and mimicked loftiness, I who sell my thought and want to be an author."[31]

In this context it is not too far-fetched to suggest that both Manet's *Olympia* and his *marchande* at the Folies-Bergère bar represent the modern artist's condition in addition to their own; for women who sell themselves or other goods are a locus of identification for vanguard male artists seeking admirers for their art in the modern art market.[32] Zola's comment about Manet's paintings returning the gaze of the ignorant public "with solemn and proud disdain" is particularly apt for the confrontational gaze of *Olympia*;[33] the *marchande*'s aloofness constitutes another kind of response, and it might be argued that it is in the gazes of both of these women that Manet inscribes the gaze of the avant-garde artist at the modern public. Staring into the void with glazed eyes, the salesgirl at the counter is less a spectator than a figure on show herself. Her "sore eyes" signify the kind of loss of control inflicted by an overwhelming environment of display, usually associated with women shoppers in department stores, as Zola's *Au Bonheur des dames* so well describes. The blank gaze of Manet's *marchande* befits the weariness that working in this kind of hectic, crowded space was bound to produce.[34]

The discourse of women's looking undergoes significant changes in Paris during the second half of the nineteenth century. This is visible both in avant-garde paintings such as Manet's *Bar at the Folies-Bergère* and in the expanded visual culture of modernity from advertising posters to illustrations in mass-media journals of the time. Female spectatorship, I will contend, was not only present but also played a crucial part in the visual culture of modernity, despite a long-standing social etiquette that trained women to avert their eyes. Rather than argue for a paradigmatic "female gaze" to counter the famous "male gaze" (associated with Laura Mulvey),[35] this essay historicizes and particularizes "the" gaze, showing that modern women enacted a range of gazes depending on their social status and that representations of female gazes were exploited in advertising as well as represented in high art. Such specificities of different kinds of women's gazes notwithstanding, women, as a whole, were called upon to exercise their gazes as part of the development of the system of mass consumption. As the consumer body upon which the industrial society of the second half of the nineteenth century was founded, they played a crucial, albeit stereotyped role. And it was to a large extent through visual images that women's spectatorial consumer roles were promoted.

For these reasons, a neat division between women as display and men as possessing the gaze is not adequate to account for the historical developments of modernity. True, women's role as spectacle for male desires continues to dominate much of the visual culture of the period, from the high art of nudes erotically displayed in so many academic paintings to the low end of pornography. Nevertheless, it is important to realize that female spectators/consumers are paradigmatic of a modern type of looking—a browsing performed in crowds and characteristic of the age of mass consumption. Though excluded from Baudelaire's all-male concept of the flâneur, women were the featured spectators/consumers in Zola's novel *Au*

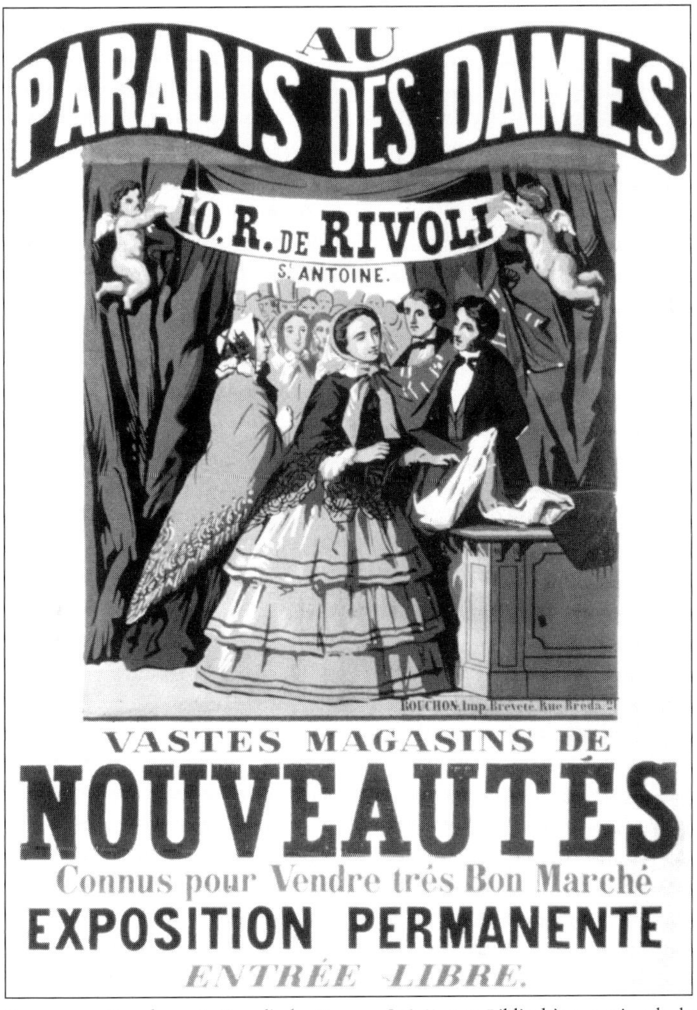

Figure 12.7. Rouchon, *Au Paradis des Dames*, 1856. Poster. Bibliothèque nationale de France, Paris. (Photo: Bibliothèque nationale de France, Paris.)

Bonheur des dames; here women make up the "nation of customers." While these women were not endowed with the kind of mastery most often associated with Baudelaire's flâneur, the fact is that women were represented not only as objects on display, but also as themselves looking.

The iconography of women consumers appears as early as 1856 in a poster by Rouchon that was one of the first commercial posters promoting a store, *Au Paradis des Dames* (fig. 12.7). It depicts a dense throng of women shoppers, followed by a few men in the distance, and, in front, two women being shown some fabric by salesmen behind a counter. The crowding of female consumers characterizes the illustration of women at the counter in the Bon Marché some three and a half decades later as well (fig. 12.2), but there we see a further articulation of the singular, if typical, bourgeois female spectator. Somewhat set apart from the rest of the crowd, this fashionably dressed Parisian is distinguished by her

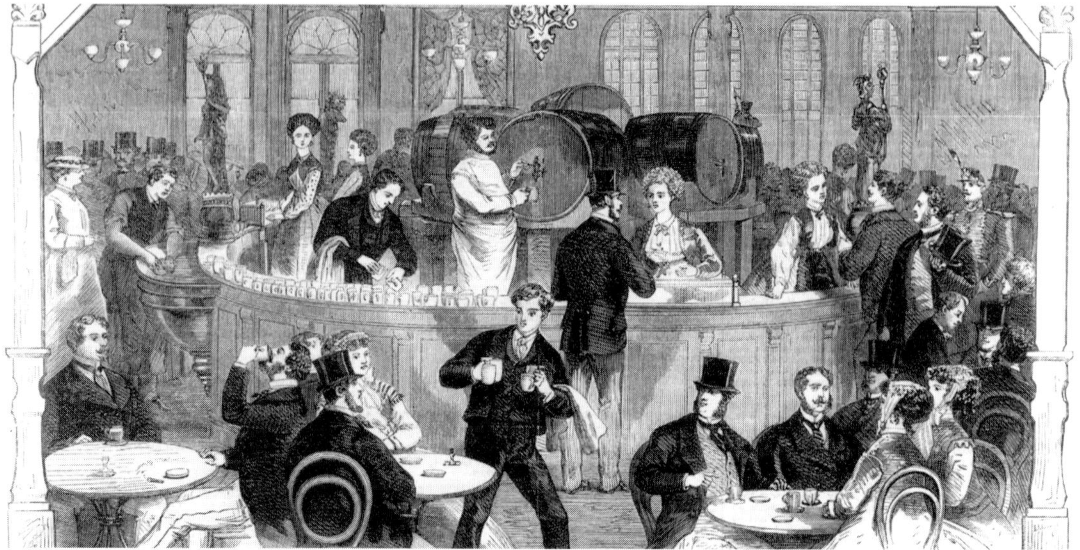

Figure 12.8. *The International Cafés in the Park at the 1867 International Exhibition in Paris*, detail: *The Austrian Café*, from *The Illustrated London News*, 1867. (Photo: Research Library, The Getty Research Institute, Los Angeles.)

interested gaze exercised through the lorgnette in her hand.

The presence of women as spectators/consumers was linked to changes in the status of women in French society during the second half of the nineteenth century and the evolving debates about their rights in areas such as divorce, secondary and higher education, access to the professions, work, better wages, and, toward the end of the century, the vote.[36] The *marchande* and the female spectators on the balcony of *Bar at the Folies-Bergère* are both exemplary of the fact that women increasingly participated in the public sphere: women of the lower classes were wage-earning workers outside the home; women of the bourgeoisie, the *petite bourgeoisie*, and to an extent, the working class shopped in department stores and consumed a variety of entertainments. Despite the ideology of domesticity (promoted in France by Jules Michelet, among others),[37] which celebrated women's labor in the home but objected to their working outside, the number of wage-earning women in France was increasing. By 1872 women constituted 29.6 percent of the paid workforce in France; in 1891, 31.4 percent.[38]

Paris in the second half of the nineteenth century offered numerous sites for women's viewing, browsing, and shopping.[39] Women's visibility in visual representations of the period suggests that their presence in public was far more extensive than the oft-cited doctrine of separate spheres would have us believe.[40] They were depicted promenading, stopping for coffee, visiting department stores and exhibitions, and depending on their class, serving customers.[41] Women are shown both behind and in front of the counters in cafés, for example, in a view of one of the cafés at the 1867 International Exhibition in Paris (fig. 12.8) and in Jean Béraud's painting of the Pâtisserie Gloppe on the Champs-Elysées, 1889.[42] Of course, respectable women mostly attended these places with friends, family members, spouses, or their children.

In 1867 the presence of ladies at the Folies-Bergère was still a shocking novelty. In the words of one writer:

For the first time I had seen women in a cafe with smoking permitted. All around us there were not just women, but Ladies. . . . the ladies themselves seemed hardly out of their

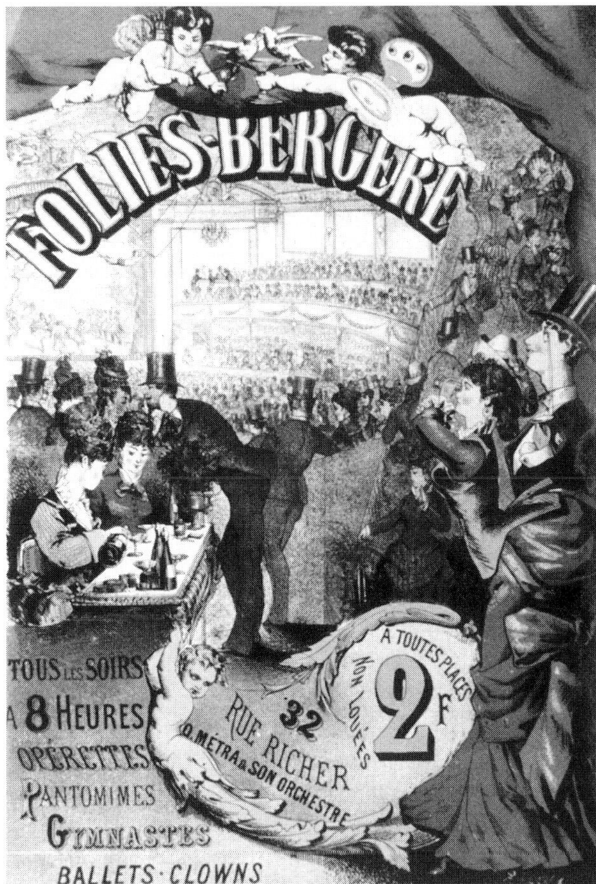

Figure 12.9. Emile Lévy, *Folies-Bergère*, 1875. Poster. Bibliothèque nationale de France, Paris. (Photo: Bibliothèque nationale de France, Paris.)

element. . . . The presence of these "well-bred" women gave the audience a quite particularly slovenly appearance.[43]

By 1882, the Folies-Bergère was clearly targeting female customers, as it advertised its evening entertainment program in *La Gazette des Femmes*, a feminist publication that promoted women's achievements in the arts.[44] Times had indeed changed by 1893, when Theodore Child accepted as a matter of fact that men and women of different classes attended establishments such as the Folies-Bergère:

The café-concert has become the chief distraction of the Parisians both of the lower and the middle classes. . . . The shopkeepers of the neighborhood,

their wives, and their daughters, their cook-maids and their clerks, the working-men, the washerwomen, the girls who toil all day in manufactories, all patronize the cafés-concerts steadily night after night.[45]

When Manet included two fashionable women, one of them looking through opera glasses, in the front of the balcony at the Folies-Bergère, he was not alone in representing the "new woman" as spectator. His avant-garde colleagues, including Mary Cassatt and Edgar Degas, did so as well, but Manet's painting also shows a conceptual common ground with the visual codes of contemporary posters—the discourse of mass consumption par excellence. One example is Emile Lévy's *Folies-Bergère* poster of 1875 (fig. 12.9),

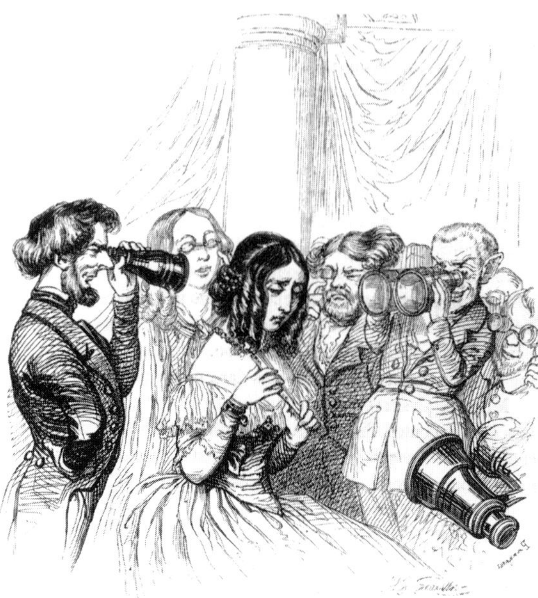

Figure 12.10. Grandville, caricature in *Petites Misères de la vie humaine*, 1843. (Photo: Research Library, The Getty Research Institute, Los Angeles.)

which includes several features that appear seven years later in Manet's painting.

Within the context of art history, discussion of nineteenth-century posters in relationship to avant-garde paintings has most often focused on examples from the 1890s and on their modern style.[46] Posters were prominent in Paris throughout the second half of the century, during the very same decades that Manet and the Impressionists were formulating their avant-garde art—the 1860s, 1870s, and 1880s. It is, of course, important to remember that posters were an emerging, thoroughly modern form of advertising that embodied a new visual discourse of mass consumption. They also had a day-to-day presence, since they were widely posted on streets. Manet himself did some lithographs and posters, notably his poster for Champfleury's book *Les Chats*, in 1868.

Though it is likely that Manet would have seen Lévy's poster, among many others, my argument does not depend on his having used this particular poster as an iconographic source.[47] Rather, I want to

draw attention to Manet's general familiarity with an emerging visual discourse of mass consumption in contemporary posters and illustrations. Lévy's poster includes a fashionable woman looking at the entertainment through her opera glasses and features her looking as prominently as her monocled male companion. Such posters were immediately related to sales strategies, and by depicting women spectators alongside men, they appealed to a public that included both genders. While Manet's painting did not, of course, take upon itself the advertising function of a poster, it did include at least some women in the spectrum of modern spectatorship.

The fact that a significant shift took place when women were represented in the role of spectators can best be appreciated by examining Grandville's pointed caricature of 1843 (fig. 12.10), in which a young woman at the opera is surrounded by men, closed in under the siege of their armed gazes: one of them scrutinizes her through his monocle, another aims a spyglass at her, and still another observes her at close range through a gigantic pair of binoculars. These technological prostheses portray looking as a virtual scopic attack whose phallic overtones are boldly stated. (Note that the authorial signatures are placed near a pair of large and disembodied binoculars that are pointed at the young woman from the lower right corner of the drawing—a strategic position that lends them a surrogate presence and makes them available for any potential, preferably male, spectator outside the caricature.)

In sharp contrast, Manet's fashionable female spectator on the balcony is looking through her opera glasses, presumably at the popular café-concert entertainment (fig. 12.11). Nevertheless, it can be argued that even her magnified gaze retains traces of the averted-gaze tradition. True, the woman is depicted in the act of looking, but she aims her opera glasses to the side, away from any engagement with the eyes of men and women in the painting and even with viewers of the painting. She is thus not depicted as challenging head-on the good manners imparted to French girls, whose gazes were strictly regulated: "The girl must above all guard against

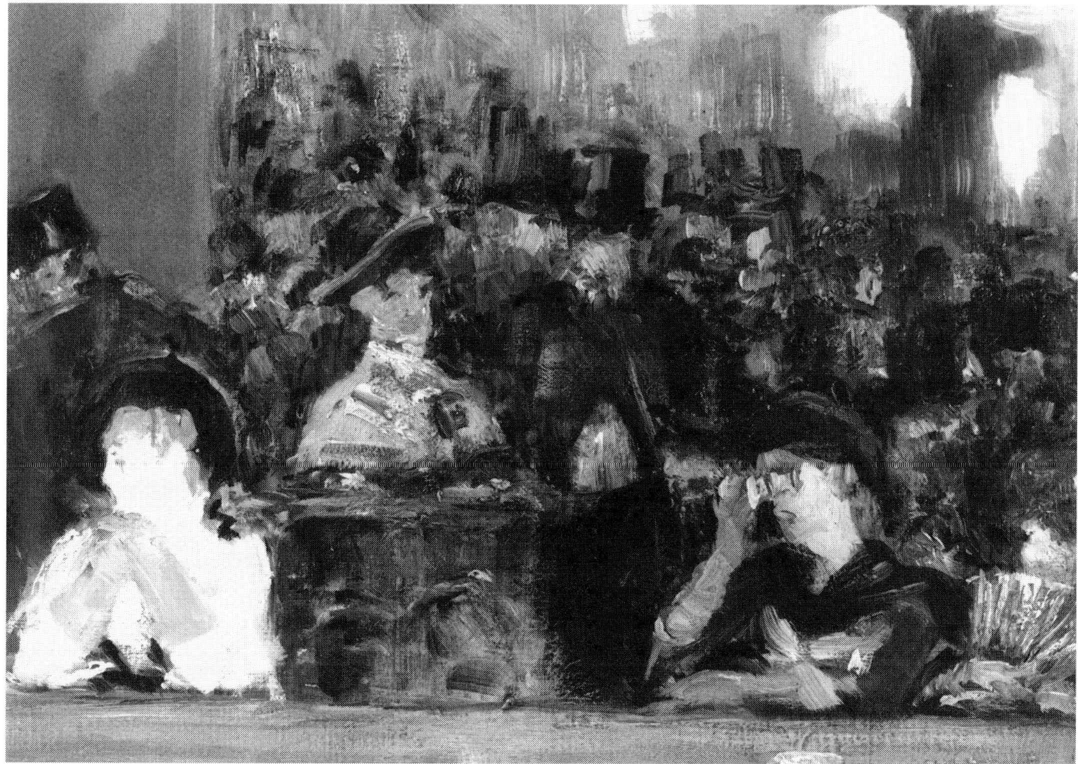

Figure 12.11. Edouard Manet, *Bar at the Folies-Bergère*, 1882, detail. Oil on canvas. Courtauld Institute Gallery, London. (Photo: Courtauld Institute Gallery.)

looking *[regarder]* fixedly, eye to eye, at the one she speaks with, and to express herself 'lowering her gaze and looking up again from time to time' which is the infallible mark of good education."[48] Nineteenth-century etiquette books advocated specific strategies for how women were to exercise their gazes, or rather how to *avoid* looking. French etiquette prescribed that when walking down the street, "Women must avoid looking people in the eye *[regarder en face]* especially men who pass near them. This would be a mark of incivility and impudence *[effronterie]*."[49]

On the other side of a bourgeois etiquette of femininity that insisted on women averting their eyes, yet accepted their increasingly necessary role as spectators and consumers, lies the transgressive gaze of the courtesan. Zola describes it in *Nana*, his novel of 1880, in the scene at the races, where "Nana scanned the scene with a huge pair of field-glasses."[50] In addition to crossing physical boundaries by making her way into a section from which courtesans were barred, "Nana looked all the ladies in the face, and made a point of staring hard at the Comtesse Sabine."[51] The dazzling and crass Parisian courtesan who takes such liberties is exercising the kind of bold gazes of momentary mastery normally the exclusive province of men. Manet had depicted this kind of confrontational gaze in *Olympia* and again in *Nana*. The latter features an actress/courtesan in the midst of her toilette in the presence of a gentleman, as she looks straight out at the spectator of the painting. The fact that the artist exhibited this painting in Giroux's shop window in 1877 only compounded the transgression, for Nana's enticing gaze was thus cast at any passerby on the boulevard des Capucines. Though the gaze of the woman at the counter in *Bar at the Folies-Bergère* is blank rather than brazen, she too looks out into the crowd. But neither her gaze nor the gazes of the women on the balcony behind her are the kind of sexually provocative, transgressive gazes characteristic of the courtesan.

The two women spectators on the balcony in *Bar at the Folies-Bergère* who have been identified are Méry Laurent and Jeanne de Marsy (fig. 12.11); they appear along with painters Gaston La Touche and Henry Dupray.[52] Laurent helped Manet at a time toward the end of his life when he needed money, by facilitating the sale of one of his pictures, and Manet's depiction of the sparkling mandarins on the bar may have been associated with his fond memories of that event.[53] Laurent and de Marsy were among the intimate circle of spectators of Manet's painting at this time. By making them a bit more legible than the rest of the people on the balcony, Manet clearly inserts their spectatorial gazes into a sketchier crowd, highlighting their presence as members of the modern public.

THE GAZES OF THE PUBLIC
IN THE "ERA OF CROWDS"

The crowd in the background of Manet's painting is best understood within the context of modern spectatorship in the second half of the nineteenth century, the era of crowds, in which the individual, male or female, becomes submerged in a mass public. Manet's reflection of the crowd in the mirror achieves a powerful effect—it implies that the actual crowds in front of the painting in the Salon coincide with those depicted as spectators of the Folies-Bergère. More than that, the vantage point of the crowd is literally structured into the painting by staging the mirror to reflect the crowd, thereby implying that our own point of view as spectators of Manet's *Bar at the Folies-Bergère* is as members of such a crowd.

The public on the balcony in Manet's painting evokes the large urban crowds that had become common at entertainment venues such as the Folies-Bergère and in department stores (by 1877 the Bon Marché's 3,500 employees served some 16,000 clients daily). On occasion the department store was depicted as bursting with crowds, much as Zola had described it and as we can see it visualized in numerous illustrations. The masses who frequented the Paris Salon and fine-arts exhibitions made even the experience of viewing officially sanctioned high art an event of popular culture. On Sundays often twenty thousand people attended the Exposition Universelle of fine arts in 1855, and more than two hundred thousand came to see several thousand artworks at the Salon during a fifty-five-day period in 1884.[54] Such exhibitions were, above all, fashionable social occasions, as an illustration of the throng at Henry Regnault's exhibit in 1872 makes clear (fig. 12.12).

The viewpoint of the crowd mediates the singular male gaze, residues of which are powerfully inscribed in the man's stare at the *marchande* in *Bar at the Folies-Bergère*. What distinguishes Manet's crowd in the back from the customer in the front is the sketchy, abstracted, and generally uniform presentation of a multiplicity. Manet, in fact, visualizes an impressionistic modern crowd as an indistinguishable mass, in a manner that is strikingly similar to Zola's description of Nana's view as she surveys the crowd at the races: "Nana looked at them through her field-glasses. At that distance, she could only distinguish a compact, confused mass of people, piled up in row upon row, a dark background relieved by pale patches which were human faces."[55] The sketchy means with which Manet indicates people as barely distinguishable units in a mass are apt for the paradigm of the modern crowd. Like the Impressionist brushstroke, each member of the crowd plays a small part in the construction of a whole.

In "The Work of Art in the Age of Mechanical Reproduction," Benjamin delineates what he characterizes as the "polar opposites" of spectatorship.[56] While premodern spectatorship is "concentration," "contemplation," and being "absorbed," modern spectatorship is "absent-minded," a "reception in the state of distraction," and an "appropriation" formed by "habit" rather than "attentive concentration."[57] Though Benjamin here contrasts the absorbed spectator of painting with the distracted spectator (at-

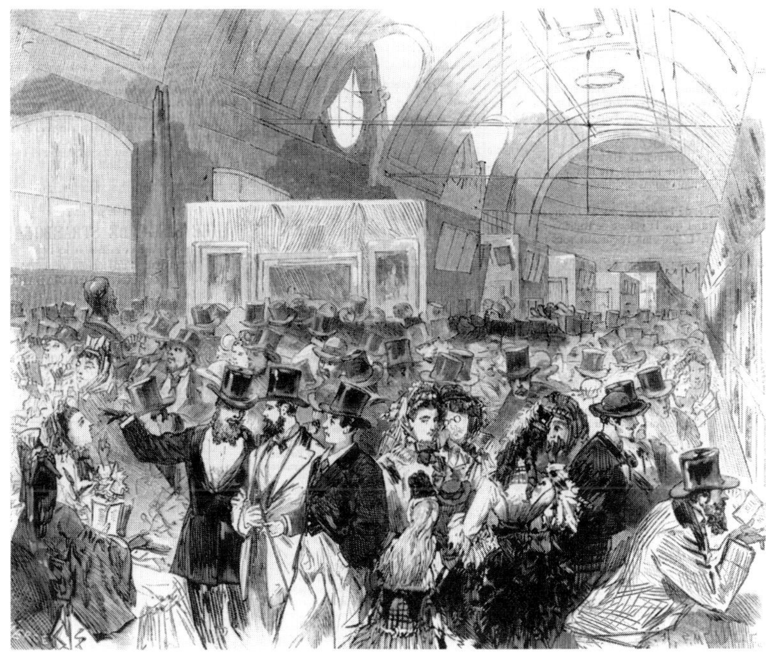

Figure 12.12. *Paris—The Crowd in the Gallery of Works by Henry Regnault at the Palais des Beaux Arts*, from *Le Monde illustré*, 1872. (Photo: Research Library, The Getty Research Institute, Los Angeles.)

tributing the change in part to the medium of film), his comments about "the distracted mass" have a great deal of validity for urban spectatorship during the late nineteenth century. Changes in viewing habits at that time were not necessarily limited to any one artistic medium. Rather, they were related to a multifaceted historical development inscribed in a mixed-gender public that was evolving in the age of mass consumption and the "era of crowds": "The greatly increased mass of participants has produced a change in the mode of participation. . . . The public is an examiner, but an absent-minded one."[58]

What exactly do the distracted gazes of the crowd in *Bar at the Folies-Bergère* signify, and how are they defined by mass consumption? Like the actual spectators of the painting in the Paris Salon, members of the crowd of the Folies-Bergère are, first of all, consumers of urban pleasures and spectacle. Their gazes do not engage in private contemplation and singular judgment but rather are an integral part of a multisensorial social interaction. As Zola complained (and countless illustrations and caricatures confirm), the browsing spectators of the Salon who look at artworks while walking, talking, seeing, and being seen

are less involved in aesthetic judgment than in mundane pleasures, expressing opinions, laughing, or flirting.[59] The modern experience of viewing art, like viewing commodities in department stores, takes place in a lively social scene in which selling is the implicit raison d'être of the event. Individual contemplative experience of art has been supplanted by pleasures of public spectatorship of objects for sale, where the primary mode is participation and interaction.

Manet's depiction of the crowd/public must also be considered within the context of the increasing representation of crowds in literature,[60] and that of an evolving crowd psychology, due especially to Gustave Le Bon's influential book *La Psychologie des foules*, published in Paris in 1895. Le Bon and others perceived modern crowds as a threat to the family spirit of preindustrial urban life and as a means of bringing about a social and political leveling.[61] Le Bon warned against their destructive influence:

While all our ancient beliefs are tottering and disappearing, while the old pillars of society are collapsing one by one, the power of crowds is the only force which is threatened by nothing and whose prestige will only be magnified. The age we are about to enter will truly be the ERA OF CROWDS.[62]

In contrast to the cultured and rational individual, crowds of men (as well as of women, and mixed crowds) were frequently characterized as barbarian: "Isolated, he is perhaps a cultivated individual; in a crowd, he is *a* barbarian, that is, a creature of instinct."[63]

The thrust of these negative theories, which were to crystallize by the end of the century, was already present in Zola's 1867 essay championing Manet; the essay included a separate section on the public.[64] But while Manet, like Zola, recognized the central role played by the modern public, his painting did not cast it in a negative light. The spectators in *Bar at the Folies-Bergère* are represented as a disciplined crowd, consuming entertainment en masse. They are seated in rows crowned by chandeliers as in so many other ticketed events that occurred in large halls, such as the Pasdeloup concerts seen in a stereoscopic photograph.[65]

For Manet and other avant-garde artists of his time, it was essential that the public become interested in an artist's work in order to ensure sufficient recognition to compete in a market system.[66] The dealer/critic system was in formation, and Durand-Ruel, the dealer known for his support of the Impressionists, made a substantial purchase of Manet's works in 1871.[67] Manet, however, never had a dealer who regularly exhibited or sold his paintings, and though he came from a family of means, he depended to a certain extent on finding buyers; at one point he was almost forced to give up his studio to cut down on expenses, and at the end of his life, he again depended on selling his paintings to pay for medical treatment.[68] Thus, Manet's status as an artist and his struggle for recognition were very much shaped by his experience of the modern condition of dependence on "the public."

Though Manet refused to join the Impressionists' alternative exhibits and insisted on seeking official Salon recognition, he pursued his own alternative exhibits throughout his career, attempting to reach the public directly.[69] True, while some of the Impres-

sionists boycotted the Salon and agreed to show exclusively in their own group exhibitions, for Manet independent exhibition strategies were supplementary to Salon exposure and validation. Above all, Manet was keenly aware of his need for an audience; he was determined to reach it and harbored a hope that if only the public could see his art unencumbered by the interference of the conservative jury or hostile critics, it would respond favorably.[70] Ironically, when he exhibited *Bar at the Folies-Bergère* during the last year of his life, it was the first time that he was no longer at the mercy of the Salon jury (a belated circumstance that came too late to affect his lifelong struggle as an artist). Having first been awarded a medal and then, in 1881, the Legion of Honor, Manet could at last count on having any painting he submitted to the Salon exhibited. Thus, he painted *Bar at the Folies-Bergère* with the intention of exhibiting it at the Salon and in the knowledge that it would be hung.

"Today the multitude demands to see with its own eyes," wrote Stéphane Mallarmé in his article on Manet, thereby recasting the negative view of the crowd into a positive notion of a multiplicity of gazes characteristic of modernity.[71] This multitude's seeing with "its own eyes" is at once a subject of Manet's painting, its addressee, and its vantage point. The crowd with its multiplicity of gazes as depicted in the mirror suggests that spectators in the front of the painting can identify with the viewpoint of the crowd. In effect, there are several points of spectatorial identification embodied in the painting: the male customer in the mirror, the woman looking through the opera glasses, and the crowd looking at the spectacle. This built-in multiplicity of gazes is, I believe, the raison d'être of the spatial "incoherence" for which *Bar at the Folies-Bergère* is well known, namely, the fact that the mirror reflection does not match what is depicted in front of it.[72] But it appears as such only to the extent that the viewer's pattern of acculturated vision expects a single viewpoint, based on well-established pictorial codes of Western art.[73] If we perceive the painting as depicting, indeed as originating from, several viewpoints rather than one, the painting makes sense differently. According to this interpretation, Manet's *Bar at the Folies-Bergère* marks a shift of pictorial codes of representation from an exclusive single male gaze to an accompanying female spectatorial gaze and a new paradigm of crowd spectatorship that includes some women alongside men.

LOOKING BEYOND THE MALE GAZE

The intense gaze of the man, cast at a suggestive proximity to the barmaid, exercises power over its female object. Manet carefully chose this dynamic after completing an earlier sketch, *Bar at the Folies-Bergère* of 1881.[74] In the sketch, the power relations are reversed: the tall blonde woman is looking downward at a diminutive male figure who appears in the mirror, and who, rather than confronting her closely, keeps a reserved distance. His blatant gaze at the woman at the counter notwithstanding, the male customer in the final version of Manet's painting is a far cry from an established regime of male spectatorship. Engaged in the public space of popular urban entertainment and stationed half inside the painting's mirror, half outside its parameters, as if he were one of a crowd in front of the painting itself, he is exercising neither individual mastery nor aloof contemplation in the tradition of the Kantian paradigm of the "disinterested" spectator. Rather, conflated with the mirror of modern life, he is a consumer in the process of buying a drink, and perhaps more. In some ways this male spectator/consumer is like Baudelaire's flâneur whose "passion and . . . profession are to become one flesh with the crowd."[75] Manet's painting depicts the man at the bar as Baudelaire described his famed flâneur in "The Painter of Modern Life": "We might liken him to a mirror as vast as the crowd itself; or to a kaleidoscope gifted with consciousness responding to each one of its movements and reproducing the multitude of life."[76] As a member of the crowd, he is no longer of the singular, aristocratic tradition of the male gaze. His privileged viewpoint has been relativized along with a partial loss of mastery, and the hermetically defined territory of an individual subject has been redefined by an urban intercourse with the crowd. By the same token, the tradition of the contemplative gaze at art was undermined both by the mass public and by the mixing of art and industry at the universal expositions. The age of industrialism and mass consumption radically changed the experience of viewing art, as one writer complained: "The marvelous spectacle of tongs and soaps, of wheelbarrows and of warming pans, all side by side with works of art, . . . the screech of machinery . . . disturbs the tranquility so desirable for those who really want to study a statue or a painting."[77]

The modernity of *Bar at the Folies-Bergère* lies in its inclusion of the points of view of both the crowd and the modern individual (male and female), marking a moment of transition in which residues of an established paradigm of a male gaze are mixed with contesting codes of a multiplicity of gazes. In contrast to a binary opposition of female spectacle and male gaze, the issue is more complicated, as is evident when one considers the evolving identities of men and women during the latter part of the nineteenth century in Paris. In this context, let me restage Baudelaire's enthusiastic endorsements of the "passion for roaming" of a solitary male stroller,[78] that famous intoxication of the flâneur with incognito gazing in the city—a myth that became practically synonymous with modernity—in light of a little-known passage in one of his letters. Baudelaire's letter surely describes a feeling quite different from stereotypical male flânerie, and one that must have been no less typical of the experiences of young men (not to mention women) in Paris at the time. The poet writes of his yearning to share his gaze with a particular woman, and to buy with her what both of their gazes desire: "I catch myself thinking as I look at some handsome object or beautiful scenery or anything at all agreeable, 'Why isn't she with me, why isn't she here to admire that with me or to buy that with me?'"[79] In this discourse of romance in the age of consumption, Baudelaire's fantasy suggests that both he and she enjoy being seduced together by "some handsome object" in a shop window.

During the last decade of the century, a stereotyping discourse that associated women with spectacle and seduction reasserted itself with new vigor in both fin-de-siècle high art and advertising posters. The latter commonly featured a woman's seductive image on display next to the product. Nevertheless, women continued to be frequently represented as spectators in contemporary posters, attesting to their newer role as consumers, and serving to attract them. Though no less exploitative than depicting women as objects on display, imaging them as spectators represented a shift in how their subjectivity was being addressed. Rather than identifying woman exclusively with object/product, her spectator/consumer status implied some measure of agency. Eugène Grasset's poster for the Odéon theater (used for different events by changing the text in the upper right) features a fashionably dressed young woman seated in a loge;[80] the large pair of opera glasses on the ledge in front of her announces her role as spectator, though its position, as if staring back at her, is a subtle trace of the tradition that deprived woman of her own gaze.

Many posters used blatantly seductive images of women even as they appealed primarily to them as consumers. One example from a rich variety of posters advertising alcoholic and nonalcoholic beverages at the turn of the century is Francisco Tamagno's *La Framboisette*.[81] A modern woman winks at the spectator, flaunting her attractions and referring to the product in the foreground with her unabashedly flirtatious look. The poster was probably intended to reach female consumers, because the sweet-tasting Framboisette was popular with them. Implied is the suggestion that a woman's state of bliss and seductive powers can be acquired simply by drinking Framboisette. In addition, the poster may appeal to male consumers by implying that her intoxicating favors accompany the purchase of the drink. That the bottles in *Bar at the Folies-Bergère* cannot be read as a still life but rather are radically positioned as products for sale situates them in the commercial discourse of *étalage* and advertising, and calls attention to the fact that the discourse of mass consumption already resided even in avant-garde art during the time of Manet and the Impressionists. Manet's last major statement, *Bar at the Folies-Bergère* powerfully visualizes this discourse, and in no small

measure this is what makes it such a striking painting of modernity.[82]

If we ask whether *Bar at the Folies-Bergère* was critical of mass consumption, was complicit with it, or even celebrated it, an argument could be made in favor of each of these possibilities, though it would be misleading to cast the debate in such "either/or" terms. Avant-garde painting was inevitably both immersed in the contemporaneous scene of mass consumption and an agent in it. Manet's painting operated within this emerging paradigm, which, in the visual culture of Paris in the last decades of the nineteenth century, was boldly spelled out in posters and illustrations. Deviating from academic traditions, which attempted to be oblivious to modernity, *Bar at the Folies-Bergère* was innovative precisely for inscribing the new paradigm simultaneously into its style, composition, and mode of address.

Manet's painting literally foregrounds selling and seduction. Yet it steers clear of the overt seduction of advertising posters like *La Framboisette*. Instead, the attractive *marchande* at the bar possesses the remote gaze that Benjamin finds in Baudelaire's poetry, eyes that "have lost their ability to look."[83] Manet's painting, like Baudelaire's poetry, has evoked desire by portraying a "mirror-like blankness," for, "the deeper the remoteness which a glance has to overcome, the stronger will be the spell that is apt to emanate from the gaze. In eyes that look at us with a mirror-like blankness the remoteness remains complete."[84] Seduction may be most successful when undetected by its object of desire. In this context, the pervasive allusions to the man in the mirror as seducing the woman in so many interpretations of *Bar at the Folies-Bergère* may be a displacement that attests to the success of the other seamless seduction that Manet's painting performs—the seduction of its spectators as much as of the customers at the bar. For it is the crowd/public both in the mirror and in front of the picture—our eyes—that are solicited by Manet's dazzling painting, we who are (pro)positioned by the lusciously rendered "still life" of commodities on the counter, under the spell of eyes that do not return our gazes in this image of the modern age of mass consumption.

1. The issues discussed in this essay are further addressed in my forthcoming book *Impressionism, Parisian Consumer Culture and Modern Women* (Cambridge: Cambridge University Press). My thanks to Debora L. Silverman, Donald Preziosi, Cécile Whiting, and Richard Shiff for their helpful comments during the revisions of the essay and to Ann Bermingham, Sam Weber, and Albert Boime, for reading and commenting on the original paper. My gratitude to Nancy Troy for her helpful comments on the essay while serving as editor of the *Art Bulletin*. Finally my thanks to the Research Library, Getty Research Institute, Los Angeles, and to the staff of the library and special collections. (For recent interpretations of Manet's *Bar*, see also Bradford Collins, ed., *Twelve Views of Manet's Bar* [Princeton, N.J.: Princeton University Press, 1996], which was not available before the original publication of this essay.) Translations are by the author unless otherwise noted.

2. Both recent and nineteenth-century commentators have shared this assumption. The catalogue entry in *Manet, 1832–1883*, exh. cat. (New York: Metropolitan Museum of Art 1983), 478, goes against the grain, arguing that the barmaid was no fallen woman; and Robert Herbert's interpretation of the painting (in *Impressionism: Art, Leisure, and Parisian Society* [New Haven, Conn.: Yale University Press, 1988], 81) differentiates between the woman at the counter, whom he identifies as a server of drinks, and her probable behavior. Suzon (the woman who worked at the bar at the Folies-Bergère and acted as the model for the painting, which Manet did in his studio) insisted on being accompanied by her boyfriend to the sessions, as reported by Manet's biographer, Tabarant.

3. See T. J. Clark, "The Bar at the Folies-Bergère," in *The Wolf and the Lamb: Popular Culture in France*, ed. Jacques Beauroy, Marc Bertrand, and Edward T. Gragan (Saratoga, Calif.: Anma Libri, 1977), 233–52; and T. J Clark, *The Painting of Modern Life: Paris in the Art of Manet and His Followers* (New York: Knopf, 1985), 205–58.

4. The history of the café-concert figures prominently in Clark, "The Bar at the Folies-Bergère," in Clark, *The Painting of Modern Life*; and in Herbert, *Impressionism*.

5. Andreas Huyssen, *After the Great Divide: Modernism, Mass Culture, Postmodernism* (Bloomington: Indiana University Press, 1986), 17.

6. For discussion of how the Impressionists presented their exhibitions to the public, see Martha Ward, "Impressionist Installations and Private Exhibitions," *Art Bulletin* 73, no. 4 (1991): 599–622.

7. Rosalind H. Williams (in *Dream Worlds: Mass Consumption in Late Nineteenth-Century France* [Berkeley: University of California Press, 1982], 9) locates the consumer revolution between 1850 and World War I in France. Nicholas Green (in *The Spectacle of Nature: Landscape and Bourgeois Culture in Nineteenth-Century France* [Manchester: Manchester University Press, 1990], 17–65) argues that metropolitan ideology associated with consumption was forged between 1820 and 1840 in Paris.

8. Emile Zola, *Au Bonheur des dames* (1883; serialized in *Gil Blas*, 1882); trans. as *The Ladies' Paradise* (1886), intro. Kristin Ross (Berkeley: University of California Press, 1992), 16. Set in the 1860s, the novel was based on Zola's study of the Bon Marché and other department stores. On the Bon Marché, see Michael Miller, *The Bon Marché, Bourgeois Culture and the Department Store, 1869–1920* (Princeton, N.J.: Princeton University Press, 1981).

9. Novelene Ross, *Manet's Bar at the Folies-Bergère and the Myths of Popular Illustration* (Ann Arbor, Mich.: UMI Research Press, 1982), 75–92. Despite her discussion of the iconographic tradition of the *dame de comptoir* in magazine illustrations, Ross ultimately interprets the barmaid in the familiar context of leisure, entertainment, and pleasure.

10. See, e.g., quotations from C. Flor, in *Le National de 1869*, C. de Beaulieu (no source given), and Le Senne in *Le Télégraphe*, 2 May 1882, all of whom call the woman at the counter in Manet's painting *la marchande*; cited in Clark, *The Painting of Modern Life*, 242. Clark does not comment on the use of the term but quotes these passages as part of a range of contemporary critical responses referring to the emotional tenor of the barmaid's expression and pose and to the question "what was it she was selling, after all?" (ibid.).

11. Zola, *Ladies' Paradise*, 138.

12. Adolphe Tabarant, *Manet et ses oeuvres* (Paris: Librairie Hachette, 1947), 424.

13. *Revue des deux mondes* 51 (1882): 583.

14. *L'Artiste*, 3 January 1858; cited in Nicholas Green, "Circuits of Production, Circuits of Consumption: The Case of Mid-Nineteenth-Century French Art Dealing," *Art Journal* 48, no. 1 (1989): 29.

15. Kathleen Adler, *Manet* (Oxford: Phaidon, 1986), 104. On Giroux, see Green, *Spectacle of Nature*, 25–26.

16. Walter Benjamin, *Charles Baudelaire: A Lyric Poet in the Era of High Capitalism*, trans. H. Zohn (London: New Left Books, 1973), 165. "L'Europe s'est déplacé pour voir des marchandises," cited in ibid. (translation adapted).

17. *Le Monde illustré* 1 (1875): 182.

18. "Les Agrandissements du Bon Marché," *L'Illustration*, 9 October 1880, 245.

19. Patricia Mainardi, "The Double Exhibition in Nineteenth-Century France," *Art Journal* 47, no. 1 (1989): 24, 25, 21. See also Patricia Mainardi, *Art and Politics of the Second Empire: The Universal Expositions of 1855 and 1867* (New Haven, Conn.: Yale University Press, 1987); and Nicholas Green, "Dealing in Temperaments: Economic Transformation of the Artistic Field in France during the Second Half of the Nineteenth Century," *Art History* 10, no. 1 (March 1987): 59–77.

20. L. de Laborde, cited in Mainardi, *Art and Politics*, 21.

21. Ibid., 45

22. Edmond About, "Le Salon de 1868," *Revue des deux mondes*, 1 June 1868, 720, cited in Mainardi, *Art and Politics*, 194–95.

23. Pierre Larousse, *Grand Dictionnaire universel du XIXe siècle* (1866, 79), reprint, Geneva-Paris: Slatkine, 1982, 7: 997.

24. Zola, *Ladies' Paradise*, 45.

25. Ibid.

26. See illustration in original publication of this essay in *Art Bulletin* 77, no. 1 (March 1995): 30.

27. There was plenty of room for Manet to have placed his signature in that corner of the painting, on the counter as he did in several other instances.

28. Jean Baudrillard's analysis, which places the emphasis on consumption rather than production as the dominant ideology in the twentieth century, applies to some extent also to the late nineteenth century. Jean Baudrillard, "The Political Economy of the Sign," in *Selected Writings*, ed. and intro. Mark Poster (Stanford, Calif.: Stanford University Press, 1988).

29. Although foodstuffs may be repeated in market-type displays of fruits and vegetables in earlier paintings, such items differ from mass-produced commodities in that the latter repeat each other exactly, excluding the variety and singularity that characterize organic produce.

30. Benjamin, *Charles Baudelaire*, 106.

31. Cited in ibid., 34.

32. This avenue was, of course, not available to contemporary avant-garde women painters such as Mary Cassatt or Berthe Morisot, who had to be intent on preserving their reputations. See, e.g., Anne Higonnet, *Berthe Morisot's Images of Women* (Cambridge, Mass.: Harvard University Press, 1992); and Griselda Pollock, "Modernity and the Spaces of Femininity," in *Vision and Difference: Femininity, Feminism, and Histories of Art* (London: Routledge, 1988), 50–90.

33. Cited in George Heard Hamilton, *Manet and His Critics* (New Haven, Conn.: Yale University Press, 1954), 126.

34. Working in this kind of environment precipitated a fatigue attributed to modernity, as discussed in medical literature from the 1870s; see Anson Rabinbach, *The Human Motor: Energy, Fatigue and the Origins of Modernity* (New York: Basic Books, 1990), 19–44; and T. M. McBride, "A Woman's World: Department Stores and the Evolution of Women's Employment, 1870–1920," *French Historical Studies* 10 (1978): 673.

35. Laura Mulvey, "Visual Pleasure and Narrative Cinema" (1975), in *Art after Modernism: Rethinking Representation*, ed. Brian Wallis (New York: New Museum of Contemporary Art, 1984). Mulvey's article is based on a psychoanalytic analysis of the male gaze in contrast to woman as object on display in the framework of film. See also Rachel Bowlby's analysis of Zola's *Au Bonheur des dames*, in *Just Looking: Consumer Culture in Dreiser, Gissing and Zola* (New York: Methuen, 1985), 18–34, 66–82. Pollock, *Vision*, 87, addresses women's objectification in both art and art history and argues that female artists such as Cassatt and Morisot produced paintings that represent women as subjects rather than as objectified by and for a male gaze.

36. On French feminism in the nineteenth century, see Claire Goldberg Moses, *French Feminism in the Nineteenth Century* (Albany: State University of New York Press, 1984), 203; and Patrick Kay Bidelman, *Pariahs Stand Up!: The Founding of the Liberal Feminist Movement in France, 1858–1889* (Westport, Conn.: Greenwood Press, 1982).

37. Jules Michelet, *Woman* (1860), trans. J. W. Palmer (New York, 1873). Michelet's and others' promotion of female domesticity must be seen as a counterdiscourse in the context of the advocacy of women's rights in the nineteenth century. It was an antifeminist position. For an analysis of the latter, see Deborah L. Silverman, *Art Nouveau in Fin-de-Siècle France: Politics, Psychology, and Style* (Berkeley: University of California Press, 1989), 63–74.

38. The percentage of wage earners in the total female population in France in 1872 was 23.7, and in 1891 it was 26.6; see Paul Bairoch, *The Working Population and Its Structure: International Historical Statistics*, vol. 1, ed. T. Deldycke et al. (Brussels: Institut de Sociologie, Université Libre, 1968), cited by Leslie Parker Hume and Karen M. Offen, "The Adult Woman: Work," in *Victorian Women: A Documentary Account*, ed. Erna Olafson Hellerstein, Leslie Parker Hume, and Karen M. Offen (Stanford, Calif.: Stanford University Press, 1981), 273.

39. On the *flâneuse*, see Ruth E. Iskin, "The Pan-European Flâneuse in Fin-de-Siècle Posters: Advertising Modern Women in the City," *Nineteenth-Century Contexts* 25, no. 4 (2003): 333–56; and "The Flâneuse in Fin-de-Siècle French Posters: Advertising Images of Modern Women in Paris," in *The Invisible Flâneuse? Art, Gender and Nineteenth Century Paris*, ed. Aruna D'Souza and Tom McDonough (Manchester: Manchester University Press, forthcoming).

40. For the predominance of the male flâneur's gaze, arguments on the impossibility of the flâneuse, and the influence of the separate spheres of men and women, see Janet Wolff, "The Invisible Flâneuse: Women and the Literature of Modernity," in *Feminine Sentences: Essays on Women and Culture* (Berkeley: University of California Press, 1990), 34–50; and Pollock, *Vision*, 50–90.

41. Linda Nochlin makes the point that "men's leisure is produced and maintained by women's work, disguised to look like pleasure." Referring to Manet's *Bar at the Folies-Bergère* and *Beer Server*, Nochlin states that "from the vantage point of the new women's history . . . middle- and upper-class men's leisure is sustained and enlivened by the labor of women—by entertainment and service workers like these represented by Manet"; see Linda Nochlin, "Morisot's Wet Nurse: The Construction of Work and Leisure in Impres-

sionist Painting," in *Perspectives on Morisot*, ed. T. J. Edelstein (New York: Hudson Hills Press, 1990), 94.

42. See illustration in original publication of this essay, *Art Bulletin* 77, no. 1 (March 1995): 34.

43. Louis Veuillot, *Odeurs de Paris* (Paris, 1867; emphasis in original); cited in Clark, *The Painting of Modern Life*, 208. This quotation exemplifies a Catholic extremist response to the loss of an all-male public in popular entertainment. Jurgen Habermas, *The Structural Transformation of the Public Sphere*, trans. Thomas Burger (Cambridge, Mass.: MIT Press, 1989), deplores the loss of the "coherence" of a highly cultured public engaged in critical debate during the age of Enlightenment, and contrasts this idealized public (which to a large extent excluded women) to the vulgar modern public of consumption in the nineteenth century.

44. *La Gazette des Femmes*, 10 March 1882, under the heading "Théatre et musique."

45. Theodore Child, *The Praise of Paris* (New York: Harper, 1893), 185.

46. For example, the decorative style and surface qualities of some of Seurat's paintings have been analyzed as having been influenced by Jules Chéret's posters; see Robert Herbert et al., *Georges Seurat, 1859–1891*, exh. cat. (New York: Metropolitan Museum of Art, 1991), 342, 361–62. Herbert also mentions Chéret's 1875 poster *Aux Folies-Bergère* in connection with Manet's *Bar at the Folies-Bergère*, referring to the mirrors on the walls of the establishment, which are visible in the poster, Herbert, *Impressionism*, 79.

47. From the relatively small size of the poster, we can conclude that it was used for display on the premises of the Folies-Bergère rather than outdoors. Street posters were larger, since they had to be seen from a greater distance. I am indebted to Rejane Bargiel, curator of the Musée de la Publicité, Paris, for this information, and to her as well as to Anne-Marie Sauvage and Mme Jestaz, curators at the Cabinet des Estampes, Bibliothèque Nationale, for making nineteenth-century posters available for my viewing.

48. J.-B.-J. Champagnac [J.-B.-J. de Chantal], *La Civilité des jeunes personnes* (Paris, 1843), 102; cited in Isabelle Bricard, *Saintes ou pouliches: L'Education des jeunes filles au XIXe siècle* (Paris: Michel, 1985), 119.

49. J. B. J. de Chantal, *La Civilité des jeunes personnes* (Paris, 1859), 48, 50.

50. Emile Zola, *Nana* (1880; serialized in 1879), trans. with intro. George Holden (Harmondsworth, England: Penguin, 1972), 348.

51. Ibid., 365.

52. Tabarant, *Manet et ses ouevres*, 424. Laurent, an inspiration for Odette, a character in Marcel Proust's novel *A la recherche du temps perdu*, was a leading courtesan whose friends included some of the most distinguished artists and men of letters of her time. Manet and Mallarmé were probably among her *amants de coeur*. For George Moore's recollections of Laurent and her relationship with Manet, see Adolphe Tabarant, *Manet: Histoire catalographique* (Paris: Editions Montaigne, 1931), 416. For an analysis of avant-garde art and historically specific conditions of women's prostitution during this period, see Hollis Clayson, *Painted Love: Prostitution in French Art and the Impressionist Era* (New Haven, Conn.: Yale University Press, 1991), 113–53, which discusses *Bar at the Folies-Bergère* in terms of the barmaid as prostitute.

53. Laurent's involvement in the sale (and later an exchange of the original painting by Manet for another one) to Etienne Barroil occurred during 1879–80, when Manet's need for money was great because of treatment he was undergoing at a clinic in Bellevue. See Manet's letter to Laurent, June? 1880, cited in J. Wilson Bareau, ed., *Manet by Himself: Correspondence and Conversation, Paintings, Pastels, Prints and Drawings* (Boston: Little, Brown, 1991), 247.

54. F. B. de Mercey, "L'Exposition Universelle des Beaux-Arts en 1855," *Revue contemporaine* 31 (1857): 486; cited in Mainardi, *Art and Politics*, 46. Figures for 1884 cited in Theodore Zeldin, *France, 1848–1945* (Oxford: Oxford University Press, 1977), 2: 445.

55. Zola, *Nana*, 357.

56. Walter Benjamin, "The Work of Art in the Age of Mechanical Reproduction," in *Illuminations*, ed. and intro. Hannah Arendt, trans. Harry Zohn (New York: Schocken Books, 1968), 239–41.

57. Ibid. Michael Fried, *Absorption and Theatricality: Painting and Beholder in the Age of Diderot* (Chicago: University of Chicago Press, 1980), addresses issues of the beholder in eighteenth-century French painting. Idem, "Manet in His Generation: The Face of Painting in the 1860s," *Critical Inquiry* 19, no. 1 (1992): 22–69, analyzes the relationship between painting and beholder in Manet's paintings of the 1860s within the frameworks of absorption, theatricality, and the generation of 1863.

58. Benjamin, *The Work of Art*, 239–41.

59. The public figured centrally in Zola's writing about Manet in the 1860s. Significantly, his 1867 publication on Manet included a section titled "The Public"; see Emile Zola, "Édouard Manet," in *Portrait of Manet by Himself and His Contemporaries*, ed. Pierre Courthion and Pierre Cailler, trans. Michael Ross (London: Cassell, 1966), 134–39.

60. Baudelaire, Zola, Hugo, and Poe all wrote about the crowd; see Benjamin, *Charles Baudelaire*, 35–66. On Zola, see Naomi Schor, *Zola's Crowds* (Baltimore: Johns Hopkins University Press, 1978).

61. See Susanna Barrows, *Distorting Mirrors: Visions of the Crowd in Late Nineteenth-Century France* (New Haven, Conn.: Yale University Press, 1981), 140.

62. Gustave Le Bon, *La Psychologie des foules* (Paris, 1895), 3; cited in ibid., 172

63. Le Bon, *Psychologie*, 20; cited in ibid., 169.

64. For example, defending Manet, Zola describes how a group that does not understand new paintings and pokes fun at them can, when joined by various idlers and passersby, turn into a mad crowd; Zola, "Edouard Manet," in *Portrait of Manet*, 135.

65. See illustration in original publication of this essay, *Art Bulletin* 77, no. 1 (March 1995): 40. Jules Pasdeloup founded a series of *concerts populaires* in 1861; see Michel Cabaud, *Paris et les parisiens sous le Second Empire* (Paris: Belfond, 1982), 136.

66. For Zola's description of Manet's attitude to Parisian high society—"This revolutionary painter, who adored the fashionable world"—see "The Influence of Manet," in *Portrait of Manet*, ed. Courthion and Cailler, 162 (preface to *Exposition des oeuvres de Manet* [Paris, 1884], 14).

67. On the dealer/critic system, see Harrison C. White and Cynthia A. White, *Canvases and Careers: Institutional Change in the French Painting World* (New York: Wiley, 1965).

68. *The Correspondence of Berthe Morisot*, ed. Denis Rouart, trans. Betty W. Hubbard (New York: Weyhe, 1959), 98. In September 1874 Eugène Manet, the artist's brother, wrote to his wife, Berthe Morisot: "The entire tribe of painters is in distress. The dealers are overstocked. Edouard talks of cutting down expenses and giving up his studio." In 1881 he wrote: "Business is bad. Every-

one is penniless as a result of the recent financial events, and painting is feeling the effect" (ibid., 104). Manet's letter of 1880 to Méry Laurent (cited in Wilson-Bareau, *Manet by Himself*, 247) confirms his dependence on the sale of his work even at the end of his life, when his reputation was established.

69. For Manet's exhibitions, see Adler, *Manet*, 95–106. In the 1860s Manet exhibited several times in the Martinet gallery, despite the fact that critics thought it would harm his chances at the Salon (ibid., 97). In 1867, at great expense, Manet rented a large space close to Courbet's pavilion in order to mount a major exhibition of some fifty-three works. He organized the show and its publication himself. In 1876 he opened his studio to the public, garnering some seventy-eight press notices. In 1877 he exhibited *Nana* (after it was rejected by the Salon) in the window of Giroux et Cie. The most unusual of his alternative exhibition strategies was developed when, in 1879, realizing that political constraints would prevent him from exhibiting *The Execution of the Emperor Maximilian* in France, he sent it on tour to the United States with singer Emile Ambré; through Ambré's efforts, the painting was seen in theater lobbies and was a center of attention at press conferences. Finally, in 1880, at the height of his success, Manet had a one-man exhibition in the offices of the new magazine *La Vie Parisienne* (Hamilton, *Manet*, 227).

70. His 1867 catalogue (see n. 59) articulated his wish to reach the public directly: "It is said that 'official' recognition, encouragement, and rewards are actually guarantee of talent in the eyes of a certain part of the public. . . . In these circumstances the artist has been advised to wait. To wait for what? Until there is no jury? He has preferred to settle the question with the public. . . . To exhibit is to find friends and allies for the struggle" (Hamilton, *Manet*, 106). Hamilton notes (105) that the unsigned preface in this catalogue, which has been attributed to Zacharie Astruc, has "much about it which suggests a collaborative undertaking between Zola and Manet."

71. Stéphane Mallarmé, "The Impressionists and Edouard Manet," *Art Monthly Review* 30 (September 1876); reprinted in *The New Painting: Impressionism, 1874–1886*, ed. Charles S. Moffett et al., exh. cat. (San Francisco: Fine Arts Museums of San Francisco, 1986), 33.

72. See Clark, *The Painting of Modern Life*, 250–53, for a different interpretation.

73. Herbert's interpretation (*Impressionism*, 81) of two viewpoints (those of the barmaid and the man in the mirror) is of interest in this context.

74. See illustration in original publication of this essay, *Art Bulletin* 77, no. 1 (March 1995): 42.

75. Charles Baudelaire, "The Painter of Modern Life" ("Le Peintre de la vie moderne," *Le Figaro*, 26 November, 28 November, 3 December 1863), rpt. in *The Painter of Modern Life and Other Essays*, trans. and ed. Jonathan Mayne (London: Phaidon, 1965), 9–10 (written between 1859 and 1860; see ibid., xviii), 9.

76. Ibid., 9–10.

77. E. Galichon (editor of the *Gazette des Beaux-Arts*), "Les Beaux-arts à l'Exposition Universelle," *Gazette des Beaux-Arts* 1 (May 1867): 409–14; cited in Mainardi, *Art and Politics*, 128.

78. Charles Baudelaire, "Crowds," in *Paris Spleen, 1869*, trans. Louise Varèse (New York: New Directions, 1970), 20.

79. Baudelaire, letter to Mme Aupick, 11 September 1856; cited in Michelle Perrot, "Roles and Characters," in *A History of Private Life*, vol. 4, ed. Michelle Perrot (Cambridge, Mass.: Harvard University Press, 1990), 186.

80. See illustration in original publication of this essay, *Art Bulletin* 77, no. 1 (March 1995): 43.

81. For further discussion of this poster and for its illustration, see Ruth E. Iskin, "Popularizing New Women in Belle Époque Advertising Posters," in *A Belle Époque? Women and Feminism in French Society and Culture, 1890–1910*, ed. Diana Holmes and Carrie Tarr (Oxford: Berghahn Books, forthcoming).

82. This is not to suggest that Manet's painting was *the* source that influenced the entire discourse of visual advertising in the later nineteenth century. Rather, paintings and posters were participating in an evolving discourse.

83. Walter Benjamin, "Some Motifs in Baudelaire," in *Illuminations*, 189.

84. Ibid., 190.

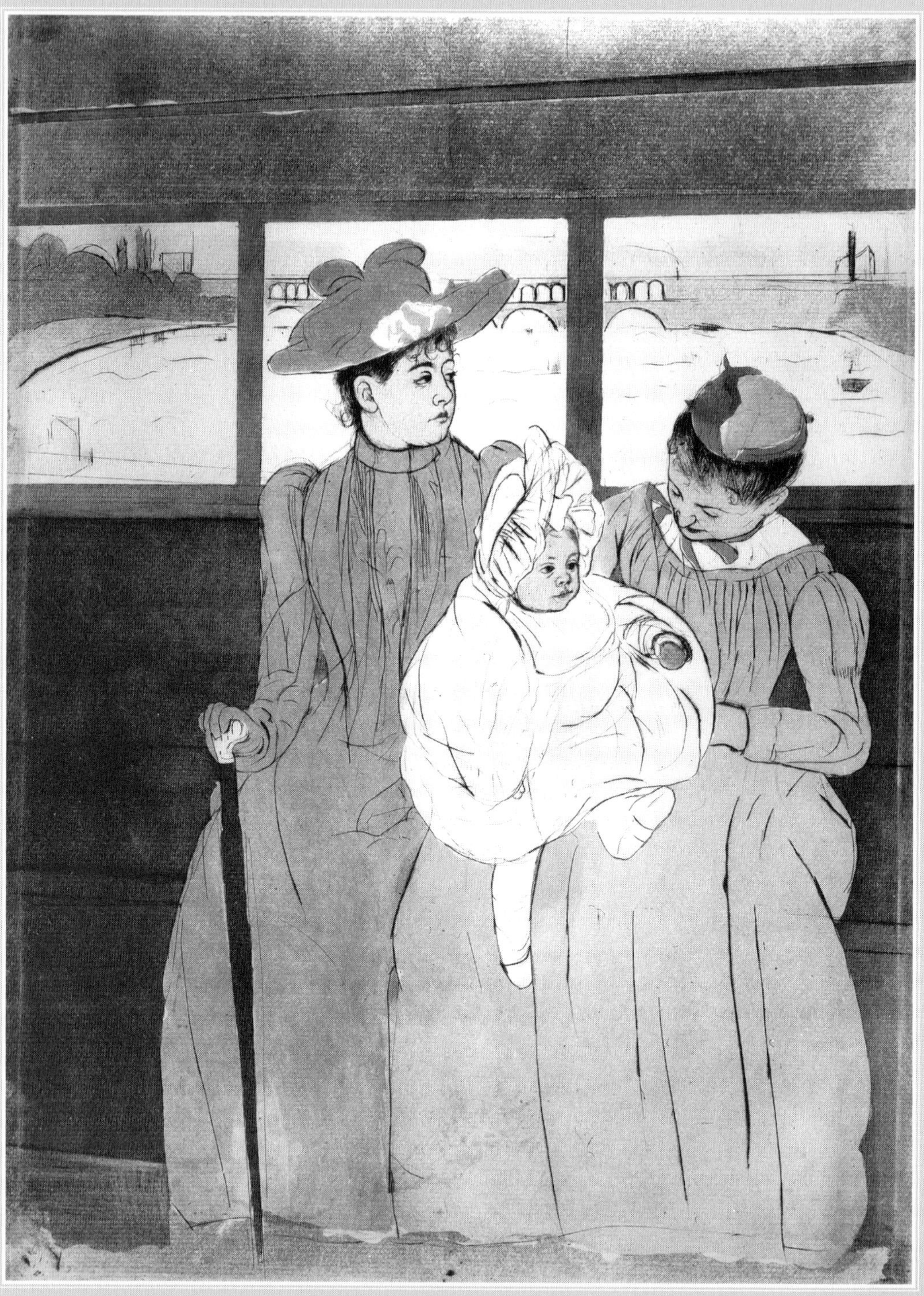

13

MARY CASSATT

Modern Woman or the Cult of True Womanhood?

Norma Broude

"MARY CASSATT: MODERN WOMAN" was the title of an impressive and long-overdue exhibition of the work of this American expatriate artist, mounted by the Art Institute of Chicago in the fall of 1998. That title, apparently a provocative one in some quarters because of the extra-aesthetic issues it raised,[1] both referred to and was derived from the title of the ambitious *Modern Woman* mural painted by Cassatt to decorate one of the lunettes in the central Gallery of Honor of the Woman's Building at the Chicago Columbian Exposition of 1893 (fig. 13.2).[2] Needless to say, it was most unusual in that period for a woman to receive a commission to decorate a public building. For this and other reasons, the segregated Woman's Building provided an important professional opportunity for Cassatt, who was still little known in America at this time. Largely responsible for her selection was Bertha Palmer (Mrs. Potter Palmer), a prominent social leader and philanthropist in Chicago, who was president of the Board of Lady Managers authorized by Congress to oversee the Woman's Building. It was the energy and determi-

nation of Mrs. Palmer that persuaded Cassatt to accept the commission in spite of what she perceived as American hostility to women artists. "After all," Cassatt wrote a friend in 1894, "speak to me of France. Women do not have to fight for recognition here if they do serious work. I suppose it is Mrs. Potter's French blood," she continued, " which gives her her organizing powers and her determination that women should be *someone* and not *something*."[3]

That determination was also very much Cassatt's own. Nearly fifty years old in 1892 when she was offered the commission, Cassatt had never married and lived what we might today regard as an alternative lifestyle for a woman of her period. Her own mother had recently described her as a woman who was "intent on fame and money." "After all," her mother had added, pragmatically and perhaps somewhat defensively, "a woman who is not married is lucky if she has a decided love for work of any kind and the more absorbing it is the better."[4]

Cassatt's mural in three panels, an allegory in modern dress, shows the freedom of modern woman

This essay is based on my lecture "The Woman Artist and Nineteenth-Century Culture," delivered as the keynote address for the symposium "Woman as Artist and Subject: Mary Cassatt, Julia Margaret Cameron, and Nineteenth-Century Art and Culture," held in association with an exhibition at the Art Institute of Chicago (13 November 1998), and for the opening at the National Gallery of Art, Washington, D.C. (6 June 1999). It appeared under the present title in *Woman's Art Journal* 21 (Fall–Winter 2001): 36–43, and is reprinted here, in a revised and expanded form, by permission of the author and the *Woman's Art Journal*.

Figure 13.1. Mary Cassatt, *In the Omnibus*, ca. 1890–91. Etching, drypoint, and aquatint, 14⅜ × 10⅜ in. National Gallery of Art, Washington, D.C.; Rosenwald Collection. (Image © Board of Trustees, National Gallery of Art, Washington, D.C.)

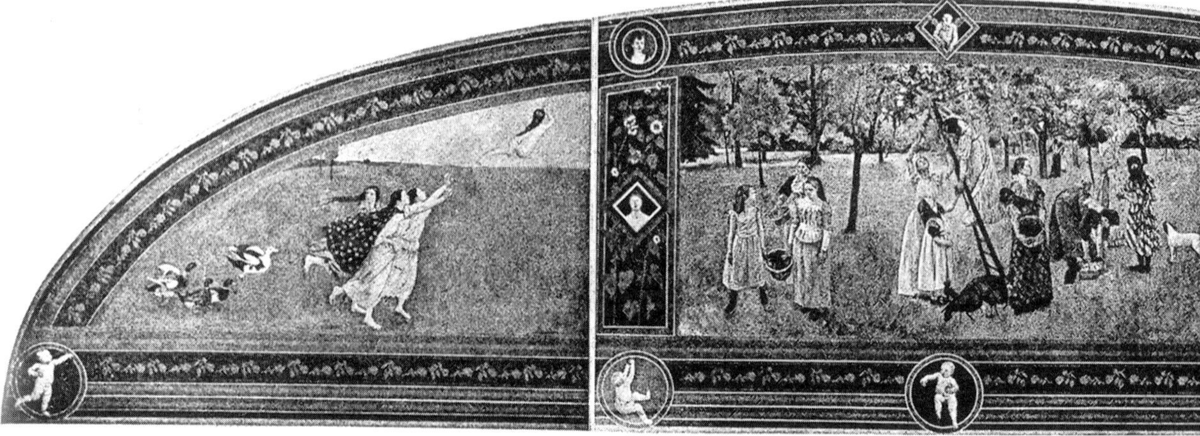

to pursue knowledge, art, and fame. In the panel on the left, young girls pursue fame, with fame as a nude female child who leads them upward and onward as she flies freely through the sky. I would point out that this allegorical image relates to and may make self-conscious reference to one of the "Vending of Cupids" motifs from the well-known wall paintings at Pompeii, an image in which young women are shown pursuing a putto, a symbol of love in flight (fig. 13.3). Here, Cassatt plays audaciously on an ancient image and a traditional stereotype of femininity, inverting it meaningfully for the "modern woman." In the panel at the right, three modern young women are presented as the arts, music, and the dance. And in the central and largest panel, Cassatt takes as her subject "Young Women Plucking the Fruits of Knowledge and Science." In an outdoor setting, women working together carry baskets, climb ladders, and reach to pluck and eat the ripe fruit that swings overhead, which they then pass on to the next generation of young girls. In this central panel, Cassatt again boldly inverts the gendered meanings of familiar imagery and iconography—in this case, the innumerable fin-de-siècle Garden of Eden images by such artists as Edvard Munch and Paul Gauguin, in which woman or Eve is presented in various guises as the evil femme fatale, the instrument of the devil who caused man's fall by

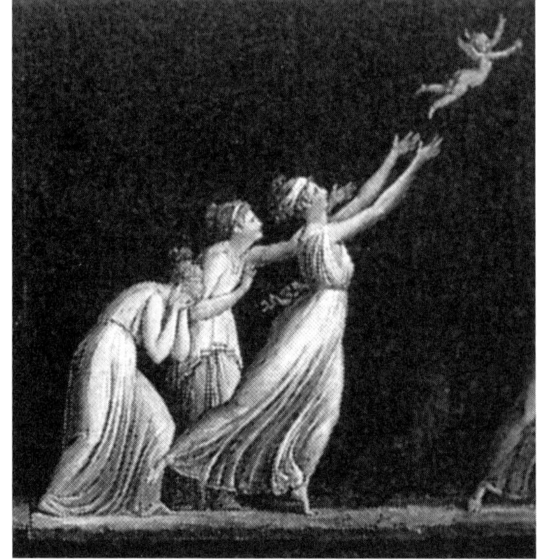

Figure 13.3. *Cupid in Flight*, fresco from Pompeii, before A.D. 79, detail, from a copy by Antonio Canova, ca. 1799. From *La Gipsoteca Canoviana di Possagno* (1992), 114.

tempting him to eat the fruit of the tree of knowledge. At the end of the nineteenth century, of course, the fruits that were now at stake, the fruits of contemporary knowledge and science, were still widely regarded as forbidden fruits for women and girls, for this was an era when expert medical opinion held that

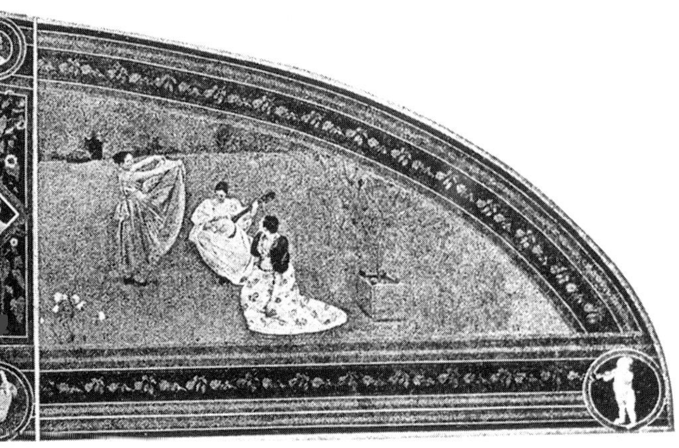

Figure 13.2 (ACROSS SPREAD). Mary Cassatt, *Modern Woman*, 1892–93. Oil on canvas, 12 × 58 ft. (presumed destroyed). Mural for the Woman's Building, World's Columbian Exposition, Chicago, 1893. (Photo: Chicago Historical Society.)

education and intellectual exertion might make women infertile or even drive them insane.

Cassatt's *Modern Woman* mural was not a critical success, not least of all because there were no male figures in it. This caused one critic to comment that, as a result, the painting "seems too trivial and below the dignity of a great occasion."[5] The absence of male figures had been an issue for some even while the work was still in progress. In a letter to Mrs. Palmer, Cassatt had reported: "An American friend asked me in rather a huffy tone the other day, 'Then this is woman apart from her relations to man!' I told him it was. Men I have no doubt are painted in all their vigor on the walls of the other buildings."[6] A witty retort, certainly, and one that was entirely worthy of Cassatt's "modern woman." But then she went on to soften, qualify, and justify it in terms that may no longer seem so modern, and which can begin to illuminate Cassatt's predicament as a woman artist, even a relatively emancipated and successful one, at the end of the nineteenth century. Men may be depicted in all their vigor on the walls of the other buildings, she says, but then continues: "To us the sweetness of childhood, the charm of womanhood, if I have not conveyed some sense of that charm, in one word, if I have not been absolutely feminine, then I have failed."[7]

These statements deserve sustained attention because they present some revealing contradictions. Despite Cassatt's own resistance to patriarchal norms of proper femininity—her mother described her as a woman who wanted to achieve fame and money through her own accomplishments—and in spite of the recognition that she enjoyed in Europe, she here cloaks and masks those unseemly ambitions in conventionally gendered language. She walks a fine line, one that respectable women of her class apparently still had to negotiate even at the end of the century. In her mural, Cassatt gives expression to the modern woman's desire for autonomy and access to the public sphere, a desire based on modern doctrines of rationality, progress, and ambitious individualism. But her words betray signs of a conventional, almost essentialist belief in "women's qualities," a femininity of sweetness and charm, an acceptance of the gender stereotypes that the mural seems to defy. What we see here, I propose, is an important and widespread pattern of resistance on the one hand and simultaneous complicity on the other, a pattern typical of many Euro-American women artists and intellectuals who achieved fairly notable positions during the nineteenth century. Like Cassatt, these women desired autonomy, success, and fame, but they had also absorbed the patriarchal values of their bourgeois, Victorian era.[8] And in a century of dynamic and discomforting social change, their own ambivalence, I would suggest, may have been the necessary price or even the necessary condition for their extraordinary achievements.

Despite Cassatt's view of France, her adopted country, as a place where "women do not have to fight for recognition . . . if they do serious work," that was not and had never been universally the case. For in France, as elsewhere during the nineteenth century, women were defined primarily by their maternal capacities, and motherhood within the parameters of the patriarchal family was the virtuous norm for the respectable woman. To the extent that education was advocated at all for women, it was justified, by liberals and conservatives alike, only as a tool that could better enable women to fulfill their roles as wives and mothers. Whereas in the eighteenth century women had been denigrated by philosophers such as Jean-Jacques Rousseau for their lesser nature and weaker characters, in the nineteenth century, as the historian Joan B. Landes has observed, social philosophers such as Auguste Comte and historians such as Jules Michelet began to credit women's nature "as a source of difference *and* as the cause of their superiority, a superiority that was nonetheless reckoned only in the moral and spiritual domain." In Comte's Positive system, which had a Cult of Woman at its core, a gendered, bourgeois order was inscribed as the modern ideal for French society; women were praised "as the vehicles of feeling over reason, morality over politics," and they were assigned the special mission of moralizing society and guarding the domestic realm. Women's presumed weaknesses thus became their strengths, and they were placed on a pedestal that effectively barred them not only from equal citizenship but also from professionalism and from any real voice in the public realm.[9]

As an upper-middle-class woman who, atypically, became a professional artist in the public realm—and not what was far more common in her day, an amateur "lady painter"—Mary Cassatt had to negotiate very carefully her relationship to this "cult of true womanhood." Nevertheless, in an era of change and

transition, Cassatt did occasionally use her art to challenge or at least to wryly expose an aspect of the gendered social relations of her era. For example, *At the Opera* (1877–78; Museum of Fine Arts, Boston), one of the most widely discussed and analyzed of her works in recent feminist literature, is certainly a self-conscious statement about the gendered experience of looking and being looked at in public from the female point of view. In the foreground, a mature and sedate woman in black looks out toward the stage through her opera glasses, while a man in a distant box has his glasses focused on her—or, more likely, it now seems, on another woman, in daring décolleté, whom we glimpse sitting in the box immediately behind her.[10] And in a similarly transgressive spirit, in the late 1870s, Cassatt chose to paint pictures of her sister Lydia (*Lydia Reading in a Garden*, 1878–79; Art Institute of Chicago) and her mother (*The Artist's Mother Reading "Le Figaro,"* 1878; private collection), both shown to be utterly absorbed in reading the daily newspaper. While this activity, as a subject, may seem entirely normal and harmless to us today, we must bear in mind that, within the context of this period and its debates over woman's capabilities and natural place, Cassatt was in fact making a particular kind of claim in these pictures for the educated woman—a claim that, in some quarters, could still cause discomfort and could still be viewed as a daring and destabilizing statement. For even though 1880 was the year in which a controversial education law was passed in France, authorizing for the first time the establishment of secondary schools for girls, that law, the Camille Sée law, carefully defined a course of study for girls that would not prepare them for the baccalaureat examination, consequently barring them from higher education and access to the professions.[11] In a political climate that thus effectively acted to preserve the long-standing definition of education for women as education for submissive motherhood, the activity of reading—in particular the reading of newspapers—could still be regarded as problematic, implying gender role reversal through an "unnatural" engagement with the public and the political sphere.

At other times, of course, especially from the late 1880s on, Cassatt produced images that supported and that continue to support a far more conservative view of woman's nature and position: those attractive and sometimes powerfully evocative but nevertheless basically repetitive images of happily sequestered mothers and children, which have been emphasized and made so familiar to us by the subsequent literature. It was Cassatt's own political astuteness, I believe, at least in equal measure to the conservatism of her social and class conditioning, that was responsible for this complex pattern that I would here identify and emphasize in her art, a pattern of guarded social resistance on the one hand and complicity on the other. And this ambivalence can also be observed in the multiple, shifting identities that Cassatt assumed in representing herself, as well as other women.

For despite her own very modern ambitions and her undeniable political skills in negotiating a professional world still constructed to exclude women, Cassatt's social conditioning as an upper-middle-class woman could still make it very difficult for her to reconcile her personal and professional identities. She insisted at all times, for example, on preserving the public facade, or masquerade if you will, of proper femininity in her own self-presentations. Nevertheless, Cassatt's self-portraits communicate the self-conscious anxiety of self-presentation that must have existed for her in a world where men normally possessed the gaze and women were its objects, a world where men were the artists and women their models. In a small watercolor self-portrait of about 1880 (National Portrait Gallery, Washington, D.C.), she presents herself absorbed in the work on her drawing board, barely suggested by a few diagonal lines at the right. With her face obscured in shadow, the features smudged and imprecise, she seems withdrawn and inaccesssible to the viewer. In another, more formal self-portrait of about 1878 (fig. 13.4), Cassatt gives herself firmer but not conventionally pretty facial features; but she is no less ambivalent about the production of her own body image, as woman and as artist. She places herself here in the role not of a

working artist but of a prettily attired feminine object who leans against the arm of an overstuffed chair. Nevertheless, she once again eludes the male viewer's gaze, this time through a twisted and somewhat uncomfortable body placement that masks and obscures her female attributes. She does not look out at the viewer but instead stares resolutely beyond the frame, deflecting the viewer's gaze from her own person and thus helping to reinscribe for herself, in some measure, the masculine subject position of being the one who looks rather than the one who is looked at—the position that was essential to her identity as an artist but at odds with her classed notions of femininity and decorum.

Those standards of decorum were undoubtedly at the root of Cassatt's professed aversion to the portrait that Edgar Degas painted of her in the early 1880s (National Portrait Gallery, Washington, D.C.). It shows her seated indecorously and informally, bent forward with legs spread and elbows on knees as she pauses in her examination of some cards, variously identified as tarot cards and as *cartes de visites*, which she holds fanned out in her hands. Similar tensions involving issues of identity and decorum were addressed in an even more unconventional way by Degas in his several images of Mary Cassatt at the Louvre. In figure 13.5, for example, Cassatt is seen from the rear and presents a corsetted and exaggeratedly feminine body type. But in her black suit, she is dressed far more simply and severely than was the norm for ladies of her era, and she leans not on a woman's parasol but on a man's umbrella.[12] In this subtle but critically destabilized image of the artist as *femme-homme*, Degas seems to have been seeking a different way of balancing Cassatt's position as feminine model—and hence, in this instance, as object of the gaze—with a suggestion of the more masculine subject position that she did perforce assume in her professional life, a position that was integral to her unconventional identity as an artist.

As a woman artist in the late nineteenth century, Cassatt was obliged to negotiate not only her relationship to the "cult of true womanhood" but also her

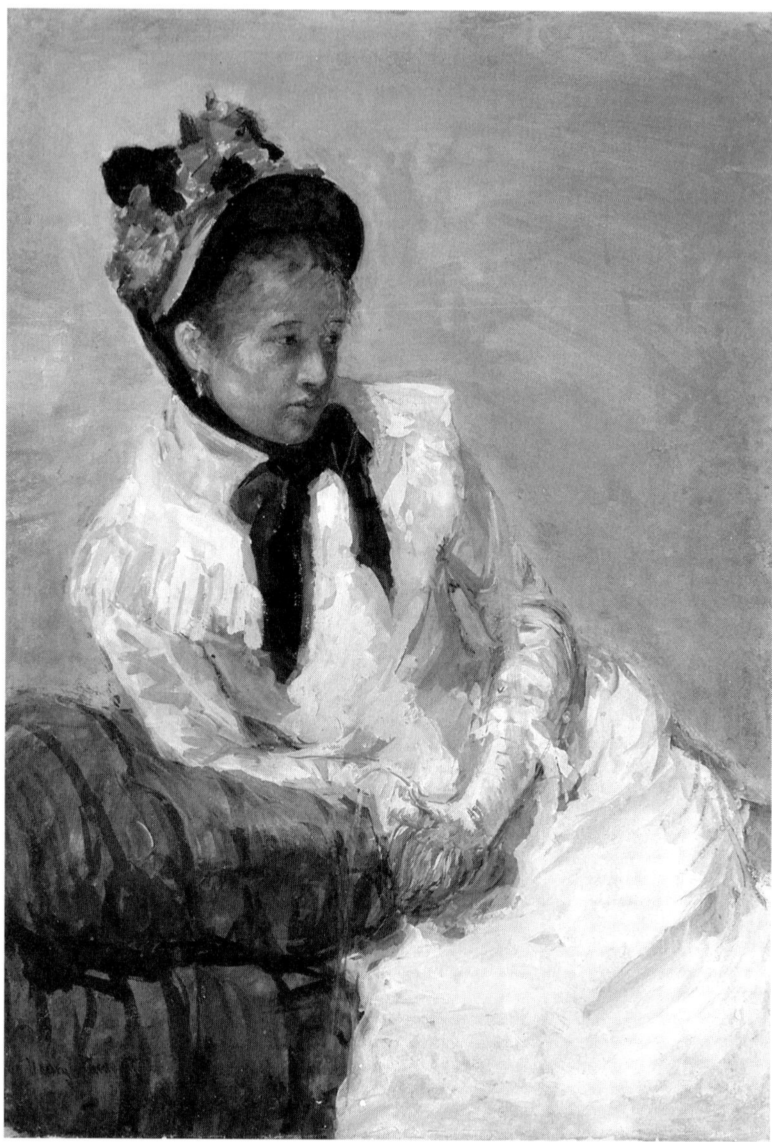

Figure 13.4. Mary Cassatt, *Self-Portrait*, 1878. Gouache on paper, 23⅜ × 16⁹⁄₁₆ in. The Metropolitan Museum of Art; Bequest of Edith H. Proskauer, 1975 (1975.319.1). All rights reserved, The Metropolitan Museum of Art.

special relationship to the gendered and hierarchized concepts of artistic style that prevailed during her era.[13] In nineteenth-century France, for example, scientific opinion held that women were physiologically less capable of rational and creative thought than were men, and that women were, by their very bio-logical nature, more given to imitation, emotionalism, and superficiality. Thus it was that the work of Berthe Morisot, who along with Cassatt and Marie Bracquemond exhibited on a fairly regular basis with the Impressionists, could be consistently praised by critics for the same qualities that they objected to in the work

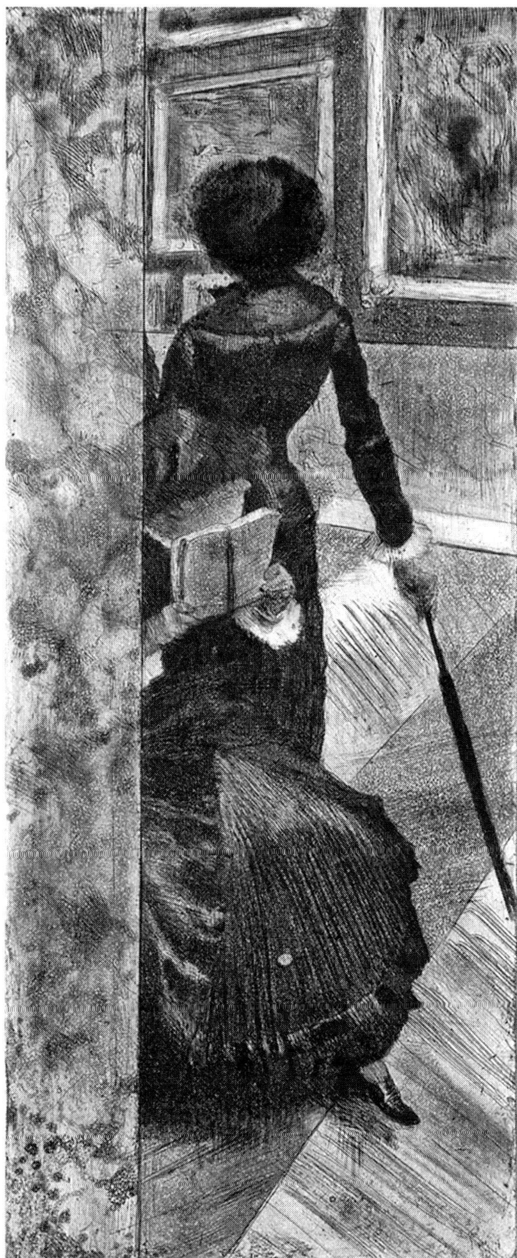

Figure 13.5. Edgar Degas, *Mary Cassatt at the Louvre: The Paintings Gallery*, ca. 1879–80. Etching, drypoint, and aquatint, 14⁵⁄₁₆ × 8¹³⁄₁₆ in. National Gallery of Art, Washington, D.C.; Rosenwald Collection. (Image © Board of Trustees, National Gallery of Art, Washington, D.C.)

of her male colleagues. These qualities included the quickness and fluidity of Morisot's brushwork, what was described as her exclusive concern for superficial sensation rather than draftsmanship and compositional structure, and her responsive and imitative facility. For art critics of the period, Morisot's Impressionist paintings therefore seemed a perfectly natural and appropriate expression of the artist's femininity, for which she should be praised and approved. But it was only in those terms, they made clear, as an art for and by women, that Impressionism in general could be justified. For men to work in this manner—as the male Impressionists did—was an unsuitable abdication of their God-given intellectual gifts, a betrayal of their very biological identity as men, and hence a threat to the social order.[14]

Mary Cassatt's stylistic choices and strengths were also in this sense a threat to the social order. For her strong drawing, which distinguished her style from that of Morisot, was not what a woman was supposed to be biologically capable of doing. According to Cassatt's own report, Degas once said of her work that "no woman has a right to draw like that,"[15] an admiring comment, certainly, but at best a backhanded compliment that reflects the prejudices and assumptions of this era. Degas admired Cassatt's strengths as a draftsman, but saw them as an exception to what were widely assumed to be the limits of creativity and achievement for women.

Both Cassatt and Morisot were born into an era when a respectable lady was not supposed to go about unchaperoned in public; nor, if she were suitably modest, would she allow her eyes to meet the gaze of a man who was not a member of her immediate family. Despite their status as exceptional women, functioning as professionals in a wider arena, these artists were forced to negotiate such conventional notions of respectable behavior for women of their class. And their professional identities and careers were inevitably shaped by these classed notions of feminine propriety, which limited their choice of subjects for the most part to the domestic realm and also limited the kinds of professional contacts they might have with their male colleagues. Rarely, for example, did these artists paint the adult male, and when they did, their models were usually members of their own family, as in Morisot's painting of 1883, in which she depicted her husband, Eugène Manet, overseeing their daughter Julie at play outdoors (private collection), or in Cassatt's portrait of 1884, of her brother Alexander J. Cassatt, who sits reading the newspaper while his young son Robert looks over his shoulder (Philadelphia Museum of Art). Although intimate depictions of mothers and children have long been a staple of art and artists in the Western tradition, the subject of fathers and children, and in particular fathers and daughters, has been a rare and unusual one outside the realm of the formal family portrait. In the late nineteenth century, though no less rare as a subject, fathers and children did appear in the work of Degas in the 1870s, and in the 1880s more predictably in the work of women artists such as Cassatt and Morisot. Here, then, is a notable example of how these women were able to turn their cultural limitations into an advantage, creating unorthodox images that uniquely defied the cultural stereotypes and that began to explore in a contemporary manner the nature of fathering as a role for men—or, more specifically, for upper-middle-class men—in the modern world.

But it was for their more culturally orthodox and more numerous representations of mothers and children that these artists were best known and most appreciated, in their own time and for long afterward. The title of the first monograph on Cassatt, published in 1913 by Achille Segard, *Un peintre des enfants et des mères—Mary Cassatt*, says it all. Much earlier, in 1881, the critic Joris Karl Huysmans had written of Cassatt that only a woman could so successfully paint children, a remark that had reportedly annoyed her.[16] But, nevertheless, from the 1880s on, she turned her attention in large measure to the subject of motherhood, garnering wide success and approval for images that often had unabashed overtones of traditional Madonna and Child and Holy Family imagery.

Why the repeated images of mothers and children from an artist who was not a mother and who in her own life was reported to have taken note of children only insofar as they could serve her as models?[17] To begin to answer this complicated question, we must get beyond the usual cant that has been promoted since the nineteenth century, the myth that these happy mothers and beautiful children are natural expressions of Cassatt's femininity and therefore more truthful as images of the mother-child bond than any previously painted. And we must consider instead the very specific social and market contexts that framed Cassatt's choices and the reception of her work.

On one level, in the surprisingly seductive and even Michelangelesque babies sometimes portrayed by Cassatt in their mothers' arms—for example, *The Caress* (1902; fig. 13.6)—we may be seeing, in a guarded and limited form, this upper-middle-class woman artist's only respectable access to the unclad figure and to the high art tradition of the nude. But in more far-reaching terms, I would reiterate that Cassatt was a self-conscious and skillful player in a game of professionalism and identity that was still constructed in the nineteenth century to exclude women. And in light of what we know about the network of discourses—philosophical, moral, medical, and aesthetic—that defined the female creative subject, the woman artist in the nineteenth century, Cassatt's choices are really not surprising ones. In that context, we may readily see how the subject of mothers and children—at first apparently resisted, then later embraced by this artist—would have provided for Cassatt one of the few, narrow gaps of possibility within which she, as an ambitious woman artist of the upper classes, could fully grasp and define for herself a socially acceptable professional status and identity. And the success of her strategy—as strategy I believe it was—is easily measured by the sudden outpouring of articles and in particular by the proliferation of reproductions of Cassatt's works that began to appear in popular journals both in France and the United States from the turn of the century onward. These included such diverse publications as *Scribner's Magazine* (1896), *Brush and Pencil* (1900), *L'Art décoratif* (1902), *La Revue de l'art ancien et moderne* (1908), *Les Modes* (1904), *Harper's Bazaar* (1911), *Les Arts* (1912), *Arts and Decoration* (1915), *Town and Country* (1916), and many others.[18]

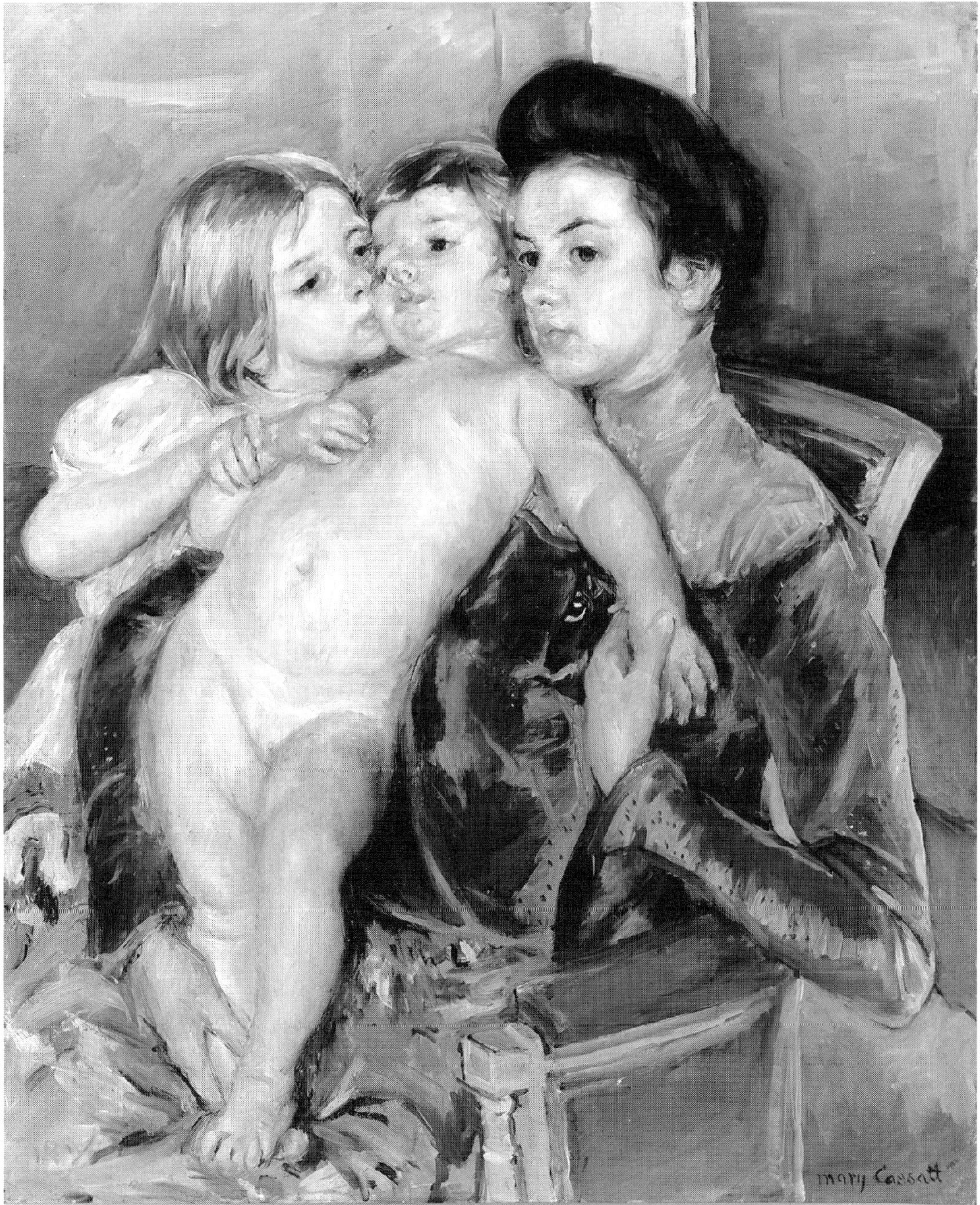

Figure 13.6. Mary Cassatt, *The Caress*, 1902. Oil on canvas, 32½ × 27 in. Smithsonian American Art Museum, Washington, D.C.; Gift of William T. Evans. (Photo: Smithsonian American Art Museum, Washington, D.C./Art Resource, New York.)

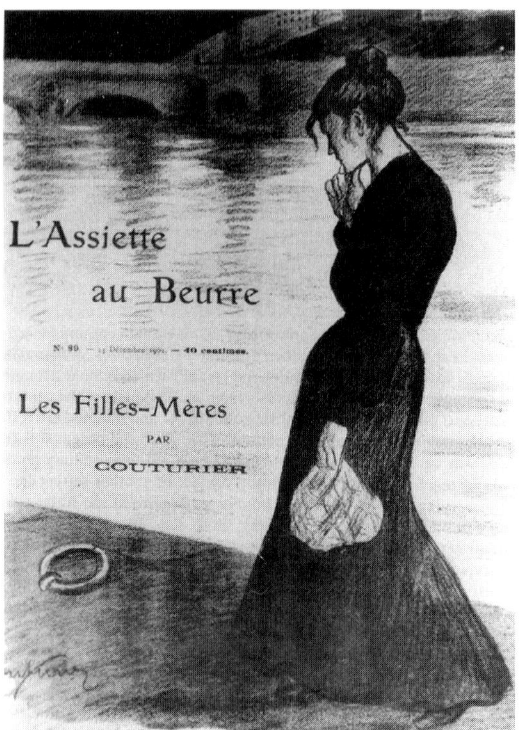

Figure 13.7. Couturier, *The Unwed Mothers*, cover of *L'Assiette au Beurre*, 13 December 1902. From Fuchs, *Poor and Pregnant in Paris* (1992), 2.

If Cassatt's presumably natural and spontaneous images of mothers embraced by children who hang affectionately upon their necks remind us not only of Renaissance madonnas but also of the happy mothers of eighteenth-century bourgeois art, that, too, is not accidental. The oeuvres of many late-eighteenth-century painters, from Sir Joshua Reynolds to Elisabeth Vigée-Lebrun, graphically portray the joys and rewards of family life and particularly of motherhood, often depicting physical intimacy between mother and child or showing us the adoration of a secular infant. And as we now know, such images were part of a wider late-eighteenth-century program of moral edification and reform that encouraged women to assume and indeed to wallow in the joys of maternal responsibility, at a time when such behavior had not, in fact, been the cultural norm.[19] A century later, during the 1880s and 1890s, when Cassatt began to devote her-

self so successfully to the production of similar images, it may have been, in large measure, because a similar kind of social problem existed again in France, and visual representation was once again being called upon to play an important propagandistic role in helping to redefine and reshape the social order.

Cassatt's images of happy and fulfilled mothers surrounded by children who are personifications of goodness and innocence, these pictures that deify motherhood and its joys, were painted in an era of great—one might even say, hysterical—public concern over declining birthrates in France, when the issue of motherhood and family had taken on special political and social significance for the nation. In this time of change, as middle-class women were gradually gaining legal access to education and even, after 1884, divorce, debates over the *femme nouvelle* suddenly flooded the Parisian press; and the "new woman's" desire for independence and education over traditional values of marriage and family was not only seen as a threat to the structure of the family but was also publicly blamed for the declining birthrate. Images proliferated during this period, in the popular press and magazines as well as in high art, equating motherhood with patriotism and promoting women's traditional role in the home as the anchor of bourgeois domesticity.

The good of family and country was thus used as a persuasive argument in efforts to control and limit women's access to higher education and the public sphere. But depending on who was doing the arguing, the good of family and country could also be used as an argument for cautiously widening that access, and it frequently was so employed during the 1890s by liberals and by some feminist women. Interestingly enough, French feminists of the 1890s included many wives and relatives of prominent republican statesmen and educators. Predictably, these well-placed, upper-middle-class women were no friend to the *femme nouvelle*. Instead they embraced the concept of "equality in difference" and advocated the sexual division of labor in society and the family.[20] And like their counterparts in the United States, women such as Louisine Havemeyer and Bertha Palmer, these conservative feminists constituted an affluent seg-

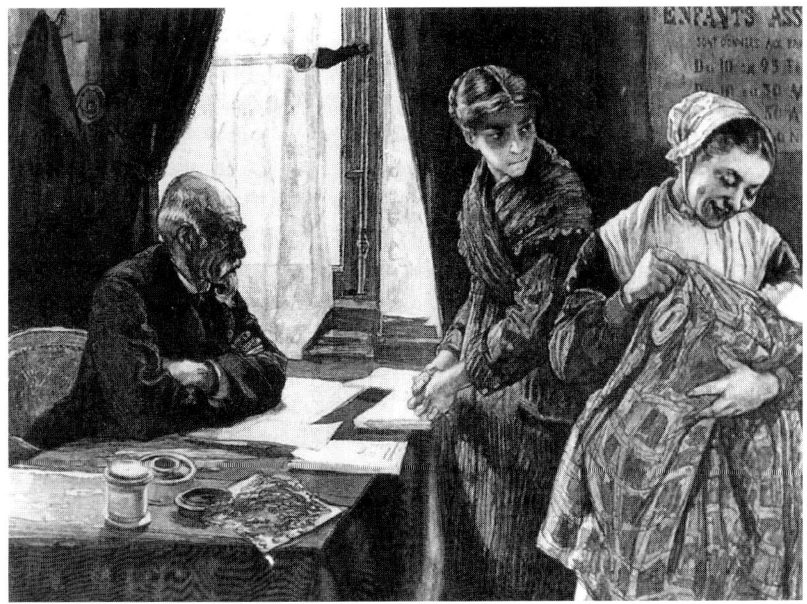

Figure 13.8. Jean Geoffroy, *At the Hospice des Enfants Assistés*, from *L'Illustration*, 1882. From Fuchs, *Poor and Pregnant in Paris* (1992), 223.

ment of the market that might be counted on to welcome images like Cassatt's, images that enhanced the role of motherhood and that acknowledged women's presumably "natural" place in the home.

Although one might never know it from Cassatt's paintings of mothers and children, even those for which she often used her servants as models, being poor and pregnant in Paris in the nineteenth century was not an uplifting experience for women. The realities of infanticide and infant abandonment are graphically suggested by a chilling cover illustration (fig. 13.7) for a story on unwed mothers that appeared in the magazine *L'Assiette au Beurre* in 1902. Despite the development of social welfare programs designed to prevent it, infanticide was very much a class issue in France and had a great deal to do with the phenomenon of depopulation that so obsessed the national leadership at the end of the century. A less desperate and more common solution to the problem of unwanted pregnancies for poor working-class women is seen in an image by Jean Geoffroy, "At the Hospice des Enfants Assistés," which appeared in the Parisian journal *L'Illustration* in 1882, in which a distraught working-class woman legally abandons her child to the state-run Hospice for Needy Children (fig. 13.8).

Throughout the nineteenth century, a high proportion of children born out of wedlock, as well as large numbers of legitimate children born to poor families who simply could not support them—as many as 31 percent of such births in 1869—were abandoned to a state-run foundling home system that many did not survive.[21] In this light, then, we might view Cassatt's famous images of motherhood not so much as "truthful" re-creations of a universal feminine experience at the end of the nineteenth century—as art audiences are today prone to do—but rather as a classed projection of a conservative and repressive social ideal, an ideal that existed in fact for relatively few women, and certainly not for the working poor, during this era.

Much has been made in recent feminist studies on Cassatt and Morisot of the conventional notions of feminine respectability that denied these upper-middle-class women artists access to the wider public sphere—the streets and cafés and music halls that were the prime subjects of modernity for their male colleagues in the avant-garde, while their own experience limited them and their art to the domestic realm. These so-called "spaces of femininity" have even been seen to impact compositionally upon the carefully delimited spatial stages on which women artists often placed their female

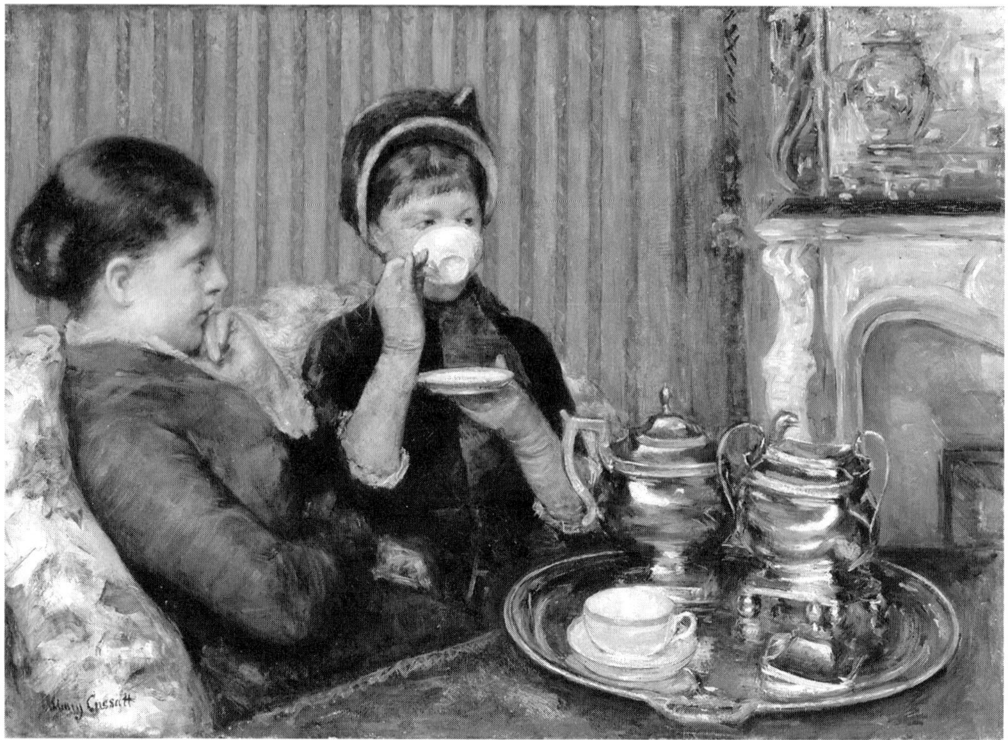

Figure 13.9. Mary Cassatt, *The Tea*, 1879–80. Oil on canvas, 25½ × 36¼ in. Museum of Fine Arts, Boston; M. Theresa B. Hopkins Fund, 42.178. (Photo © 2005 Museum of Fine Arts, Boston.)

subjects—for example, Morisot's *On the Balcony* (1872; Art Institute of Chicago), where mother and daughter are literally confined to the domestic sphere, fenced off from the public life of the city that lies beyond, or Cassatt's *The Tea* (1879–80; fig. 13.9), which has lent itself to similar spatial and social readings.[22] But while such readings have provided a useful way to see these paintings, I would nevertheless caution against relying too heavily on this kind of reductive interpretation, which can ultimately foster an essentialist view of women artists such as Morisot and Cassatt. The issues and attitudes embedded in these images, it seems to me, are far more complicated and far more ambivalent than that. In the case of Cassatt in particular, we are looking at an art that reflects the shifting ideological constructions of gender and femininity within French and American culture during the later decades of the nineteenth century. And there often results from this, in her images of upper-middle-class women going about the

rituals of their comfortable daily domestic lives, a strange ambiguity of meaning and mood and intention, a challenging resistance to any singular or conventional interpretation, which becomes particularly evident and problematic for early-twenty-first-century viewers. Is *The Tea*, for example, a sentimentalized but essentially straightforward view of women's traditional place within the rites of bourgeois domesticity? Or was it meant to be read in the nineteenth century—and should we read it today—as an image of the middle-class woman's narrow imprisonment within the home? Or might we more profitably read it as an image of the modern woman's networks of sociability and the possibilities for empowerment that those networks could provide?

No one would dispute, certainly, that women artists in this era came to maturity in a gender-segregated, power-imbalanced society in which art had traditionally helped to construct women as objects of male desire and possession or as pedestal madonnas whose identities depended almost entirely on the patriarchal notion of the family. But it was also, increasingly, a modern urban world of work and entertainment, in which lower-class and lower-middle-class women were joining the workforce in unprecedented numbers. Women supported commerce and industry not only as producers and sellers of commodities, but also, with increasing and critical economic importance, as consumers. As a result, their appearance in public spaces, though never entirely unproblematic and still resisted, particularly among the upper classes, was nevertheless becoming increasingly commonplace, as we might deduce from several British and French paintings of the 1880s. These would include images of the new woman actively engaged in sports, as in Sir John Lavery's *Tennis Party* (1885; Aberdeen Art Galleries and Museum); or the unchaperoned but respectable young working woman—probably a shop girl—who confronts the busy traffic of a suburban boulevard from the open deck of a horse-drawn omnibus in *A City Atlas*, painted by the British Impressionist Sidney Starr (1889; National Gallery of Canada).[23] Back in France, in such telling images as Jean Béraud's *La Pâtisserie Gloppe* (1889; Musée Carnavalet, Paris), we see unchaperoned but again clearly respectable middle-class women taking refreshments at an elegant patisserie, the kind of establishment that served the needs of the moneyed bourgeois woman who regularly shopped now in the department stores that had sprung up along the new boulevards of Paris during the Second Empire (see also fig. 12.2, p. 236). Even so risqué a place as the bar at the Folies-Bergère, in Manet's famous painting of 1882 (see fig. 12.1, p. 234), was a site that, according to contemporary reports, respectable ladies were known to frequent.[24] I will not dwell too long on this much-contested picture, except to say that critics of the time talked about the serving girl as a prostitute, an epithet that was often applied to respectable working women during this era. In a climate of disorienting social change and backlash, that epithet was an ever-present threat to reputation that could be remarkably effective in containing middle-class women who might now want to venture out into a public sphere that the new

economy was opening up to them. The late nineteenth century, then, was in this sense very much an era of transition, when women of all classes were receiving and had to negotiate mixed messages about their new—and sometimes not so new—places in a modern capitalist society.

In this context, what I do find to be exceptionally truthful among Mary Cassatt's images of women and children are those that deal precisely with this issue of being out in public—a much-contested issue for the respectable woman during the late nineteenth century. In *The Omnibus*, for example, a color print of 1891 (fig. 13.1), a middle-class woman, who has ventured out on a public omnibus with her nursemaid and child, looks watchfully around her, assuming a cautious and protective demeanor. While the class differences between the two women, observable both in their dress and comportment, would have seemed self-evident and probably unremarkable in the nineteenth century, Cassatt displays that difference here in more nuanced social and psychological terms by contrasting the wariness of the middle-class woman, for whom riding on this public conveyance constituted a transgressive act, and the oblivious comfort of the working-class nursemaid, who plays happily with the child on her lap. In this remarkable image, and in the equally telling painting *Woman and Child Driving* (1881; fig. 13.10), we are graphically presented with the ambivalence and the discomfort, the anxiety and the determination with which women of the middle classes during this era embraced the challenges and confronted the pitfalls of the changing moral and political landscape. Both images present familiar Impressionist compositions in which three figures are tightly but asymmetrically massed at the right, while their gazes lead us out into the world beyond the frame. In the painting, the woman driving the open carriage through the park is the active subject. Accompanied by a little girl, representative of the next female generation, she sits assertively, but not, we sense, without some tension and trepidation, in the driver's seat, while the displaced footman sits passively behind. The woman's position—in the driver's seat— is one that metaphorically departs from the normal social order of things, and it may even carry with it a

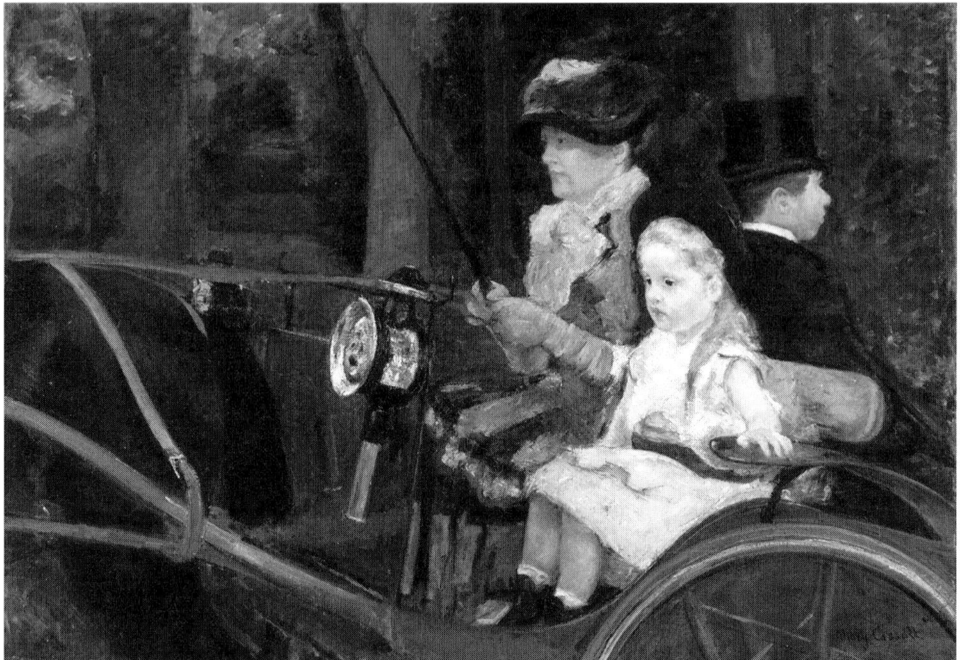

Figure 13.10. Mary Cassatt, *Woman and Child Driving*, 1881. Oil on canvas, 35¼ × 51½ in. Philadelphia Museum of Art; W. P. Wilstach Collection.

veiled challenge to that social order; but at the same time, it is courageously normalized here by the slice-of-life point of view from which Cassatt has chosen to present it.

While Cassatt and other women of her class might not have thought of themselves as political "feminists" during the 1890s, the Woman's Building mural (fig. 13.2) does in fact send a strong feminist message. Its central image, "Young Women Plucking the Fruits of Knowledge and Science," speaks boldly, albeit metaphorically, of the passing down of knowledge from woman to woman—the feminist insistence on empowering modern woman by giving her a public voice. And it was precisely that specter of giving women a public voice that so alarmed the opponents of women's suffrage at the turn of the century. That alarm gave rise to images such as an astounding anti-suffragist postcard of 1909 that shows the suffragist, her voice choked off by a rope tied around her neck and her offending, phallic tongue about to be cut off by a pair of antifeminist scissors; the inscription reads,

"Beware of Suffragists."[25] It was, in fact, precisely around this time that Cassatt herself became outspoken in her support for women's suffrage in the United States. In 1915, to raise money to support the cause, she organized a loan exhibition in New York City with her friend Mrs. Havemeyer that included her own works as well as some by Degas and a variety of old masters. Heavily represented here and in the Havemeyers' holdings of Cassatt's work in general were those increasingly ubiquitous images of children and women shown in intimate caretaking roles, images that would not have been perceived as a challenge to stereotypical ideals of femininity and which would therefore, ironically, have been most effective in helping to support a conservative feminist cause.

In her recent work on Cassatt, Griselda Pollock has connected the unusual concentration of mother and child imagery in Cassatt's late work to a private experience, the death of the artist's mother.[26] She has also provocatively reinterpreted the mother and child images as psychological projections of the only position in this fundamental relationship that the un-married and childless artist herself ever experienced—that of the dependent child, whose gradual efforts to relate to the outside world are launched from within the mother's sheltering embrace and whose point of view, therefore, is what the pictures are said to be about.[27] Writing from the avowed position of her own lived experience as "a motherless daughter,"[28] Pollock sees Cassatt's investment in mother and child images from a position of emotional deprivation, a position, we should note, that was fundamentally different from that of Cassatt, whose empowered sense of self was nurtured by a lifelong relationship with a devoted and supportive mother. Linda Nochlin has astutely characterized Cassatt's images of her mother, such as *The Artist's Mother Reading "Le Figaro,"* as an "homage not to the maternal body, but to the maternal *mind*."[29] That Cassatt's images of her own mother bear no resemblance in these terms to her generic mother and child images, where the conventional beauty and physicality of the mothers as well as the children are normally on display, should make suspect any attempt to locate Cassatt's motives for painting these latter pictures solely or even largely within the realm of her own experience as a woman and a daughter.

But there is a more fundamental issue than intentionality to be dealt with here. For in considering Pollock's contention that Cassatt's identification was not with the mothers but with the children whom she painted, we must ask whether these are in fact the only choices. Or are they the only choices for women? Do we insist that male artists who paint mothers and children be motivated by a personal identification with the social or psychic condition of either one? Or in their case will market forces suffice? Is this insistence for the woman artist an essentialist and essentializing one, further compounding the stereotypical assumptions that made it profitable for Cassatt to paint these pictures in the first place? And why can we not consider the possibility that, in painting mothers and children, Cassatt functioned as a male artist might have done, looking at but not necessarily identifying with a subject that was "Other" to "Self"?

Writing in response to the 1998 Cassatt exhibition, Linda Nochlin quotes and concurs with Pollock's earlier assessment of Cassatt's "modernity," a condition with which both women seem to identify and which they see as rooted and defined, in the most positive sense, by the struggle to reconcile the "feminine" with the "feminist"[30]—what might be described in the contemporary vernacular as the struggle "to have it all." Such a construct, of course, might seem an ahistorical imposition on Cassatt, for it was a notion developed largely for and out of the conflicted situation of women in our own so-called postfeminist era of the late twentieth and now early twenty-first centuries. It describes the presumed goal of the overextended working woman who juggles professional and domestic responsibilities, seeking a precarious truce in a heterosexual world of work and family, where changes in traditional roles and expectations for women, despite feminism, have often been more cosmetic than structural.

But Cassatt, who never chose to marry or have children, clearly never set out to "have it all" in the late-twentieth-century sense of that formulation. And to the extent that she might have thought consciously in those terms, she would appear to have had a very different concept of what having it all might mean for an independent woman in her era: a combination of professional commitment and satisfaction, rewarded by "money and fame," with the close-knit domesticity provided by an extended family and a wide circle of friends—the kind of balanced and fulfilling lifestyle that Cassatt did in fact enjoy and that supported her achievements. In Cassatt's era, however, when the "feminine" and the "feminist" would have been viewed in the larger culture as oppositional terms (and "femininity" and "the cult of true womanhood" functioned as mechanisms for containing feminism), this was a rare and alternative lifestyle, more likely to have been achieved by women who, like Cassatt, maintained their independence from the legal subordination and practical subservience mandated by patriarchal marriage and family, the societal norm for women in her era.

And it remains the societal norm for the "modern

woman" in our own era, whose struggle to have it all, to reconcile and make compatible two still fundamentally incompatible terms—the "feminine" and the "feminist"—suggests the continuing hold exerted over us today by the nineteenth century's crippling myth of the cult of true womanhood. It may suggest, too, why it is that contemporary art historians, even feminist ones, remain reluctant to grant Cassatt the agency that she sought so courageously in her own terms, an agency that was most atypical in her era and even our own.

For Mary Cassatt was an artist and a woman who sought to challenge the phallic public order by actively laying claim to it. To ignore this as the foundation of the choices that supported her work and her life is to practice a binary essentialism that co-opts her and denies her her true voice. As an artist and a woman, she had her goals and priorities and she knew the trade-offs she had to make to achieve them, even seemingly contradictory ones: on the one hand, the refusal to lose her independence, to submit herself personally through marriage to the structure of the patriarchal family, and on the other, the painting of mothers and children for a welcoming market—not because she was uniquely capable as a woman of making these paintings, as nineteenth-century male critics would claim, nor that she did so to express a stifled maternal need or fixation on the mother, as psychologically oriented twentieth-century feminists might say (it strikes me that there is really little difference between the two positions), but because, finally, she was determined to do what needed to be done: to trade off a practical acquiescence to societal expectations in order to gain the success and the fame that she desired.

At the dawn of yet another century, I would therefore enjoin us to see in the work of Mary Cassatt not simply a reification of the nineteenth-century stereotypes and limitations—the spaces of femininity, the happy mothers and children—stereotypes that she and other women artists of her period had to struggle to deal with and overcome. Nor should we attempt to redeem or to glorify those stereotypes, as there is an increasing tendency of late to do, by redefining them as radical feminist positions.[31] Rather, we should look instead and with a sharper eye at the works of these nineteenth-century women for the traces of their self-conscious struggles and ambivalences and, most of all, for their patterns of resistance and complicity; for it is here, I believe, that important lessons for our own, not entirely different time can best be found.

NOTES

1. The title elicited considerable press commentary in Chicago, and the words *Modern Woman* were dropped from the exhibition title in its Washington, D.C., venue.

2. On the organization of this fair and the participation and representation of women in the segregated context of a separate Woman's Building, see Jeanne Madeline Weimann, *The Fair Women: The Story of the Woman's Building, World's Columbian Exposition, Chicago 1893* (Chicago: Academy Chicago), 1981.

3. Letter from Cassatt to Sara Hallowell, reported by the latter in a letter to Bertha Palmer; see Nancy Mowll Mathews, ed., *Cassatt and Her Circle, Selected Letters* (New York: Abbeville, 1984), 254.

4. Letter from Katherine Cassatt to Alexander Cassatt, 1891; ibid., 222.

5. Weimann, *The Fair Women*, 314.

6. Mathews, *Cassatt and Her Circle*, 238.

7. Ibid., 238.

8. On these issues, see the stimulating study by Deirdre David, *Intellectual Women and Victorian Patriarchy: Harriet Martineau, Elizabeth Barrett Browning, George Eliot* (Ithaca, N.Y.: Cornell University Press, 1987).

9. See Joan B. Landes, *Women and the Public Sphere in the Age of the French Revolution* (Ithaca, N.Y.: Cornell University Press, 1988), esp. ch. 6, "The Gendered Republic," 169–89; these quotes, 170 and 175.

10. The presence of the second woman was observed by Kathleen Adler in her paper "Miss Cassatt at the Louvre," presented at the Art Institute of Chicago symposium, 13 November 1998.

11. On the Camille Sée law, see Claire Goldberg Moses, *French Feminism in the Nineteenth Century* (Albany, N.Y.: SUNY Press, 1984), 32–33, 209–10, 233.

12. On the issue of Cassatt's costuming in these images, I am indebted to the observations of Bett Schumacher (Johns Hopkins University) in her unpublished

study, "Mary Cassatt in the Louvre: Freedom in Androgyny."

13. See the discussion in chapter 11, this volume.

14. On the gendered reception of Morisot's work, see Tamar Garb, "'L'Art féminin': The Formation of a Critical Category in Late Nineteenth-Century France," *Art History*, March 1989, 39–65; and Garb, "Berthe Morisot and the Feminizing of Impressionism," in *Perspectives on Morisot*, ed. T. J. Edelstein (New York: Hudson Hills, 1990), 57–66. On the broader role of socially constructed gender distinctions in shaping the reception and interpretation of Impressionist landscape painting in general, from its inception to the present, see chapter 11 above, excerpted from Norma Broude, *Impressionism, A Feminist Reading: The Gendering of Art, Science and Nature in the Nineteenth Century* (New York: Rizzoli, 1991, and Boulder, Colo.: Westview, 1997).

15. As reported by Cassatt in a letter to Homer Saint-Gaudens (director of fine arts at the Carnegie Institute, Pittsburgh), 1922; cited in Mathews, *Cassatt and Her Circle*, 335.

16. Joris Karl Huysmans, "L'Exposition des Indépendants en 1881," in Huysmans, *L'art moderne* (Paris, 1881). On Cassatt's reaction, see William Wiser, "Mary Cassatt," in *The Great Good Place: American Expatriate Women in Paris* (New York: Norton, 1991), 58.

17. As reported by George Biddle, *An American Artist's Story* (Boston: Little, Brown, 1939), cited in Wiser, "Mary Cassatt," 16.

18. See the lists of reproductions compiled by Adelyn Dohne Breeskin, *Mary Cassatt: A Catalogue Raisonné of the Oils, Pastels, Watercolors, and Drawings* (Washington, D.C.: Smithsonian Institution Press, 1970).

19. See Carol Duncan, "Happy Mothers and Other New Ideas in Eighteenth-Century French Art," *Art Bulletin* (1973), reprinted in Norma Broude and Mary D. Garrard, eds., *Feminism and Art History: Questioning the Litany* (New York: Harper and Row, 1982), 200–219.

20. On these issues, see the excellent discussion by Debora Silverman, "The 'New Woman,' Feminism, and the Decorative Arts in Fin-de-Siècle France," in Lynn Hunt, ed., *Eroticism and the Body Politic* (Baltimore: Johns Hopkins University Press, 1991), 148–49.

21. See Rachel G. Fuchs, *Abandoned Children: Foundlings and Child Welfare in Nineteenth-Century France* (Albany, N.Y.: SUNY Press, 1984), esp. ch. 4; and Fuchs, *Poor and Pregnant in Paris: Strategies for Survival in the Nineteenth Century* (New Brunswick, N.J.: Rutgers University Press, 1992), esp. ch. 9. For contemporary voices on the issues of infanticide and abortion, see Ambroise Tardieu, *Etude médico-légale sur l'enfanticide* (Paris, 1868, 1880); Paul Brouardel, *L'Infanticide* (Paris, 1897); Brouardel, *L'Avortement* (Paris, 1901); and Madeleine Pelletier, "Le Droit à l'avortement," in *L'Emancipation sexuelle de la femme* (1911), excerpts trans. and reprinted in Jennifer Waelti-Walters and Steven C. Hause, eds., *Feminisms of the Belle Epoque: A Historical and Literary Anthology* (Lincoln: University of Nebraska Press, 1994), 252–61.

22. See Griselda Pollock, "Modernity and the Spaces of Femininity" (1988), in *The Expanding Discourse. Feminism and Art History*, ed. Norma Broude and Mary D. Garrard (New York: HarperCollins, 1992), 244–67.

23. For reproductions, see Norma Broude, ed., *World Impressionism: The International Movement, 1860–1920* (New York: Abrams, 1990), plates 78 and 86.

24. This according to the disapproving reports of the Goncourt brothers and Louis Veuillot, cited by T. J. Clark, *The Painting of Modern Life: Paris in the Art of Manet and His Followers* (Princeton, N.J.: Princeton University Press, 1984), 207–208. See the discussion by Ruth Iskin, chapter 12, this volume.

25. For reproduction, see Liz McQuiston, *Suffragettes to She-Devils: Women's Liberation and Beyond* (London: Phaidon, 1997), 19.

26. Griselda Pollock, *Mary Cassatt, Painter of Modern Women* (London: Thames and Hudson, 1998), ch. 6.

27. Griselda Pollock, "Some Letters on Feminism, Politics and Modern Art: When Edgar Degas Shared a Space with Mary Cassatt at the Suffrage Benefit Exhibition, New York 1915," in *Differencing the Canon: Feminist Desire and the Writing of Art's Histories* (London: Routledge, 1999), 201–45.

28. Ibid., 204.

29. Linda Nochlin, "Mary Cassatt's Modernity," in *Representing Women* (New York: Thames and Hudson, 1999), 192.

30. Ibid., 181, 215.

31. For variants on this position, see, in addition to Pollock, Harriet Chessman, "Mary Cassatt and the Maternal Body," in *American Iconology*, ed. David C. Miller (New Haven, Conn.: Yale University, 1993), 239–59; and Adam Gopnik, "Cassatt's Children," *New Yorker*, March 1999, 114–20.

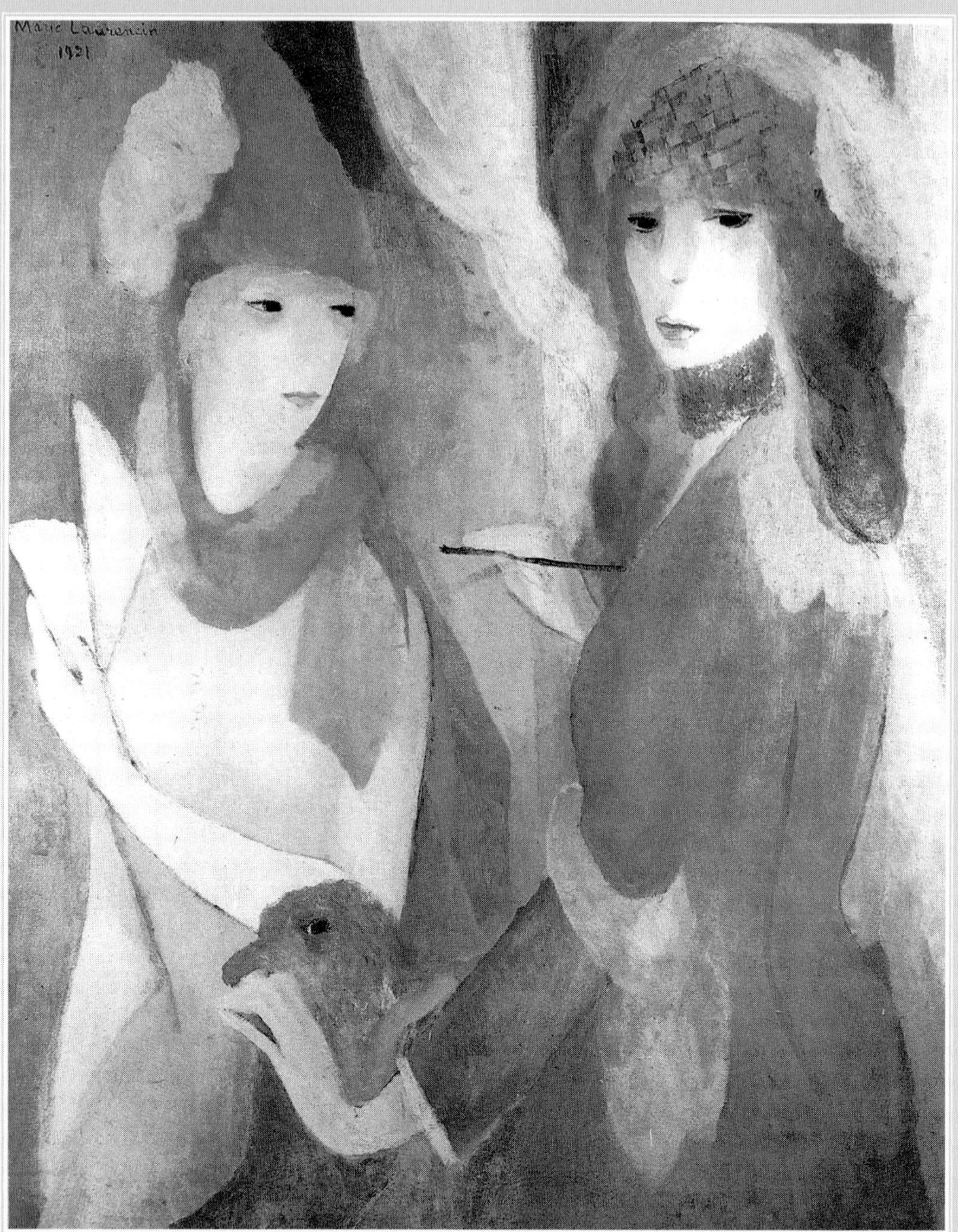

Marie Laurencin
1921

14

THE "STRENGTH OF THE WEAK" AS PORTRAYED BY MARIE LAURENCIN

Bridget Elliott

EVERYTHING ABOUT Marie Laurencin—her artistic practices, her temperament, her appearance, and even her voice—has been saturated with signs of femininity: grace and charm rather than genius, narcissistic self-absorption, surface without substance. Critical discourses on the artist have endlessly echoed Apollinaire's early comments on her work during the opening decades of the twentieth century, when he portrayed her as France's leading exponent of a new, feminine aesthetic characterized by joy, purity, and naiveté, as well as by the expression of emotion and a sense of decorative surfaces. In his words, "Grace is the thoroughly French artistic quality that women like . . . Mlle. Marie Laurencin have maintained in art, even when, as in the last few years, art became severe, and painters, engrossed in new technical experiments that involved mathematics, chemistry, and cinematography no longer cared about charming their admirers."[1]

If Apollinaire found Laurencin charmingly anachronistic, the art critic Roger Allard found her charmingly narcissistic. Discussing Laurencin in the 1920s as a painter of portraits, including numerous self-portraits, Allard conflated the identity of the artist with that of her sitters and models, remarking,

"An egotistical and charming art hers . . . which relates everything to the self. She had scarcely any subject other than herself, nor any curiosity than to know herself better . . . the whole of nature for Marie Laurencin, is but a cabinet of mirrors."[2] Similar sentiments characterized reviews of the artist's work from the 1930s and 1940s, typically beginning with strategically engendering titles, such as "The Capricious Feminine Charm of Marie Laurencin," "The Elfin Maidens of Marie Laurencin," or "A Famous Exponent of Femininity."[3] More recent monographs and exhibition catalogues on the artist have followed suit, often sporting pink covers and titles that stress Laurencin's "undividedly feminine psyche."[4]

On the face of it, such feminine indicators seem to have had a predictable effect on Laurencin's critical stock: in the long term, her success has been rather more popular than avant-garde or academic. During her life, she was generally considered the most famous woman artist of the early-twentieth-century French avant-garde. A typical illustration of such fame was a celebratory banquet lunch organized by the writer Albert Flament in 1930 for the four "queens" of French culture: Colette in literature, Valentine Tessier in theater, Coco Chanel in fashion, and Marie Lau-

This essay was first published in *Genders* 24 (1996): 69–109. It is reprinted here by permission of the author and New York University Press; courtesy of *Genders*.

Figure 14.1. Marie Laurencin, *Femme peintre et son modèle*, 1921. Oil on canvas. Collection of Hervé Odermatt, Paris. © Estate of Marie Laurencin/ADAGP (Paris)/SODRAC (Montreal) 2005.

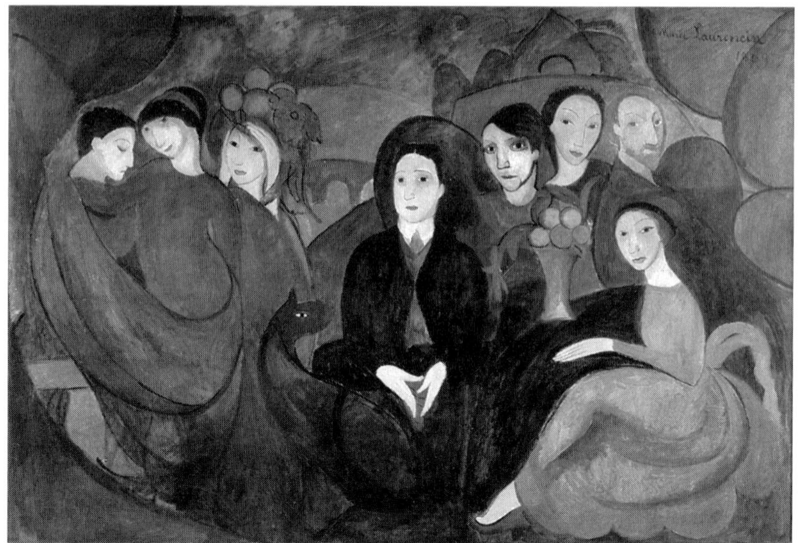

Figure 14.2. Marie Laurencin, *Réunion à la campagne* or *Apollinaire et ses amis*, 1909. Oil on canvas. Musée National d'Art Moderne, Centre Georges Pompidou, Paris. © Estate of Marie Laurencin/ADAGP (Paris)/SODRAC (Montreal) 2005. (Photo: CNAC/MNAM/Dist. Réunion des Musées Nationaux/Art Resource, New York.)

rencin in painting. Another instance from the same year was an article in the French society magazine *Vu*, which published photographs of Laurencin, Colette, and Anna de Noailles, who were identified as "The Three Most Famous Women in France."[5] Such success was more than media hype. By 1925, Laurencin had sold enough work to purchase not only a large, comfortable, and well-appointed Paris apartment on the rue Savoran but also a country house at Champrosay. Her works sold extremely well. Between the years of 1913 and 1940, she maintained a contract with Paul Rosenberg, a leading Parisian dealer who also handled Matisse, Picasso, and Braque. Through Rosenberg, her works were regularly exhibited not only in Paris but also in London, Dusseldorf, and New York.[6]

With few exceptions, recent scholarship on the artist has taken the form of sponsored exhibition catalogues and glossy coffee-table art books. At the same time that a museum devoted to the artist opened outside Tokyo in 1983, there were numerous criticisms of the inflated prices Japanese investors spent in European and North American art markets—the implication being that Laurencin's work was inferior to that of her avant-garde counterparts, such as Rodin or Picasso, who had museums devoted to them in Paris.[7]

In this respect, Laurencin and her work have been figured as the feminized bodies of commodified mass culture—bodies that are highly visible, easily accessible, attractively packaged, and available at (relatively) affordable prices.[8] To be more precise, as Apollinaire pointed out, Laurencin was perceived as occupying the soft and salable margins of the French avant-garde, working in ways that seemed more appealing than the technical and scientific experiments of other painters. Not surprisingly, this image has been a liability in modernist and revisionist accounts of the period, where the worth of the avant-garde has been measured by the "purity" of either its formal innovations or its critical project (depending upon whether one subscribes to the paradigms of Clement Greenberg or Peter Bürger), and in both instances, its distance from the contamination of the marketplace.[9]

Rather more puzzling is the fact that Laurencin has received little attention in recent feminist analyses of the modernist avant-garde.[10] To date, the few serious studies of her work focus on reviving her reputation as a serious painter and advocating her inclusion within the avant-garde canon. For instance, an article by Julia Fagen-King demonstrates that Laurencin was an integral member of the Bateau Lavoir circle and analyzes her group portrait *Réunion à la campagne*

(Apollinaire et ses amis) (fig. 14.2), suggesting it wittily parodied Picasso's *Les Demoiselles d'Avignon* (see fig. 15.1, p. 300).[11] In a similar vein, recent catalogue essays by Daniel Marchesseau and Heather McPherson reassess a number of Laurencin's paintings and stress that, although she is a difficult artist to categorize, her work should be considered part of the School of Paris, along with that of Chagall, Modigliani, Rousseau, Soutine, Pascin, and Utrillo.[12]

I will take a different tack. Instead of arguing that Laurencin be considered a member of the avant-garde, I want to examine how her case reveals certain limitations in feminist theories of avant-gardism—whether, as in the example of Alice Jardine, one wants to celebrate it as a transgressive *écriture/peinture féminine* or, as in the examples of Griselda Pollock and Carol Duncan, one wants to criticize it as a canonical modernist construction that works to exclude women.[13] The case of Laurencin fits into neither paradigm: on the one hand, the hybrid nature of her work, which often bordered on the commercial and formulaic, cannot consistently qualify as transgressive, while on the other, she was hailed by virtually everyone of her generation as an important *female* member of the French avant-garde. Although on some occasions her femininity was mobilized as an exception to prove the rule that women were not serious avant-garde painters, on others her femininity was considered disconcertingly feminist. These latter charges merit investigation, not only because they have been largely overlooked but because they indicate a need for more nuanced feminist frameworks.

Susan Suleiman's *Subversive Intent* provides a useful starting point. As Briony Fer points out in a perceptive review of the book, Suleiman attempts to marry French and Anglo-American perspectives, celebrating a transgressive avant-garde tradition of *écriture féminine* (extending from Surrealism to feminist literary and artistic production of the 1980s and 1990s), which she relates to questions of authorship, agency, and women's cultural marginality.[14] Although she insists on the need for historically grounded readings, Suleiman claims that women in the earlier modernist era were more marginalized and had less agency than women of the postmodern period, who, according to Suleiman, are in the totally new situation of having achieved a critical mass of innovative and outstanding work. While this line of reasoning has a certain pragmatic appeal, I think we should be wary about its implied narrative of liberation. It is worth recalling Michel Foucault's discussion of the ways in which a rather dubious notion of Victorian sexual repression functioned as a rod for measuring twentieth-century sexual liberation.[15] Indeed, Suleiman worries about this issue in a series of cautionary footnotes explaining that recent research on women artists involved with modernist avant-garde movements of the early twentieth century will have to reshape not only our sense of literary and cultural history but also our theories of avant-gardism.[16]

This study of Laurencin contributes to that reshaping by suggesting that she experienced a constantly shifting and ambivalent relationship to the Cubist avant-garde that was both enabling and alienating. By exploring how the signs of Laurencin's femininity were mobilized by the artist as well as by her colleagues, critics, and patrons, I want to question the value of metaphorically gendering avant-garde cultural production as feminine, in the case of Alice Jardine, or as masculine, in the case of Andreas Huyssen. Instead, I will argue that the gendered rhetoric surrounding cultural production was as unstable in the early twentieth century as it is today, leaving even relatively disadvantaged practitioners such as Marie Laurencin a certain room to maneuver. Of course, considering how Laurencin and others manipulated the signs of her femininity necessarily means addressing the ways in which these signs intersected with those of class, occupation, generation, and nationality. As Biddy Martin usefully reminds us, any centering of something called "sexuality" should make us wary of what is being "relegated to the margins or out of sight."[17]

Here, I am using the clichéd notion of "weak sex" counterdiscursively not only to undermine traditional assessments of Laurencin's art, which was generally characterized as feminine, weak, and impure, but also to emphasize the permeability and instability of sexual signifiers. By appropriating Gianni Vattimo's notion of weak thought, I suggest that a certain notion of "weak sex" can describe those forms of poststructuralist feminism that, like Vattimo, reject traditional truth claims in favor of a postmetaphysical experience of truth that is based on a combination of common sense and rhetorical and aesthetic experience, and which is constantly traversed by other sorts of positions.[18] Instead of denigrating the notions of weakness often associated with femininity, I want to explore their unexpected powers of resistance or, to borrow Jean-François Lyotard's expression, the "force des faibles" (the strength of the weak).[19] Utilizing ideas from Michel de Certeau's account of oppositional practices in everyday life, I explore how Marie Laurencin found maneuvering room in and outside avant-garde circles.[20] By making some of her tactical resistances historically visible, I want to further complicate our understanding of the way early-twentieth-century culture has been configured.

FEMININE AND FEMINIST
SPACES OF MODERNITY

Unlike many women artists who adopted avant-garde art practices, Laurencin was *not* seduced by what Griselda Pollock has characterized as cultural modernism's prevailing rhetoric of gender indifference, which seemed to offer women artists an escape from the limiting nineteenth-century sphere of feminine art.[21] By playing with the title of Pollock's well-known essay "Modernity and the Spaces of Femininity," I will explore not only how traditional notions of "respectable" femininity often diverged from the avant-gardism first espoused by critics such as Baudelaire but also how certain artists, such as Laurencin (with varying degrees of success), deliberately tried to manipulate these discrepancies.[22] Evidently, Laurencin harbored few illusions about the freedoms of the modernist community, as she bitterly pointed out in an interview:

> Cubism has poisoned three years of my life, preventing me from doing any work. I never understood it. I get from cubism the same feeling that a book on philosophy or mathematics gives me. Aesthetic problems always make me shiver. As long as I was influenced by the great men surrounding me I could do nothing.[23]

Instead, she repeatedly asserted that her painting practices were thoroughly modern *and* completely feminine. Press interviews stressed that she painted in an apartment with all of the latest conveniences. Moreover, she was carefully represented as a modern woman who preferred movies to the theater and sports clothes and short hair to long skirts and long hair. Reviewers also commented on her passionate support of women's right to work as part of the larger cause of women's emancipation.[24] Over and over, Laurencin insisted on her femininity with a series of remarks that evidently seemed extreme to a number of her contemporaries. For instance, in some autobiographical fragments she observed that if the genius of men intimidated her, she felt "perfectly at ease with everything that is feminine."[25]

On another occasion, responding to the comment that she seldom painted men, Laurencin pointed out that "I am deaf—actually, physically deaf, . . . to the voices of men, my ear is not attuned."[26] She was also quite explicit about how gender related to the practice of painting:

> I conceive of a woman's role to be of a different nature: painting to be essentially a "job" for a woman (one who sits so long quiet on a chair); and a painter's inspiration to be life and that of a natural sensibility rather than the outcome of intellect or reason. There is something incongruous to me in the vision of a strong man sitting all day . . . manipulating small paint brushes, something essentially effeminate.

Dorothy Todd, Laurencin's interviewer, evidently worried that Laurencin's comments needed explaining to the magazine's readers. The ellipsis marks Todd's interjection: "Marie Laurencin always sits to paint—the majority of men painters, as a matter of fact, mostly prefer to stand."[27] It is tempting to read this episode as an instance where Laurencin's naive gender essentialism (after all, she even uses the curiously contradictory phrase "essentially effeminate") led her to justify her presence in the studio by turning the world upside down. But such a reading misses Laurencin's intentional humor—after all, she was highly aware of her anomalous position as one of very few women painters with a significant public profile.

Laurencin's insistence on the female body of the painter presents an interesting contradiction that upsets what Andreas Huyssen has identified as modernism's cultural divide between a mass culture that typically offers up fetishized female bodies and is represented in devalued, feminine terms and a high modernist culture that is valued as masculine—in terms of its heroic practitioners as well as of the difficulty of making critical art forms. But staking a claim to the body of the painter is a project that presents women artists with an impossible choice: denying the importance of gender effaces the particularity of various historical and systemic discriminations women experience, while insisting upon their femininity leads to marginalization. Instead, as Griselda Pollock points out, feminist practices must work toward changing the ways in which the spaces of representation have been configured:

> Feminist practices cannot simply abandon either of these bodies, but whatever constitutes the feminism of the practice results from the necessity to signify a relation to this complex. That is not the same as desiring somehow to have a share in the painter's body while producing new meanings for the feminine body.[28]

Given the complexity of the terrain, how are we to read Laurencin's remarks? Was she simply laying claim to the body of the painter by reinscribing it as feminine, or was she trying to create a more interesting critical space to maneuver?

Again, Dorothy Todd sheds light on this issue when she notes that Laurencin appeared to be playing a role that should not be taken at face value: "To sit on a cushion and sew a fine seam might, it would almost appear, represent the complete ideal of life to this hundred per cent enthusiast of the feminine, but there is another side to the character of Marie Laurencin who is in many respects a typically twentieth-century woman."[29] According to Todd, the issue of Laurencin's femininity was actually quite complicated. As the English editor of *Vogue*, Todd was well aware that nineteenth-century notions of gender difference still had currency, particularly in the pages of the popular press, and that, at least in part, Laurencin's signs of femininity were shaped by conventional expectations that associated women with beauty, nature, and domesticity. Yet, in spite (or perhaps because) of this, Todd felt obliged to point out to her readers: "To Marie Laurencin all the activities of everyday life, all political or economic movements are listed under the general heading of 'masculine affairs'—and yet she is a feminist, probably the strangest feminist the world has ever seen."[30] The shift from feminine to feminist is particularly interesting given the fact that Todd was writing in 1928, well into the modernist period, when, as Pollock explained, many women artists tended to distance themselves from and denounce nineteenth-century femininity (and in some cases feminism) in order to escape the limiting sphere of feminine art. But was it only a limiting sphere? Or is that how it has been retrospectively constructed? Is there something problematic about the assertion in a recent feminist survey of women artists that Florine Stettheimer and Marie Laurencin "embraced the decorative and the fanciful in their work, and both fashioned a myth of the feminine that allowed them to be heard, but that insured they would never be taken as seriously as their male colleagues"?[31] The question I want to explore in Laurencin's case is: taken as seriously by whom? Evidently, even as late as 1928, Todd felt there might be some political purchase in Laurencin's feminine positioning, strange as it seemed.

For the moment leaving aside such questions of intentionality and agency, it cannot be denied that the signs of Laurencin's seemingly inexhaustible femininity were indeed mobilized by many writers who, perpetuating a tradition of nineteenth-century gendered discourse, wanted to reaffirm that women's art—even when produced within twentieth-century avant-garde circles—belonged to a separate (and marginal) artistic sphere.[32] At the start of Laurencin's career, Apollinaire praised the artist for "the greatest possible number of feminine qualities" and freedom from "all masculine short-comings," concluding: "Perhaps the greatest error of most women artists is that they want to surpass their male colleagues, and in attempting to do so, they lose their feminine taste and gracefulness."[33] Or, as John Quinn, an American collector of her work, later put it more crudely: "The thing I like about Marie Laurencin is that she paints like a woman, whereas most women artists seem to want to paint like men and they only succeed in painting like hell."[34] Frank Crowninshield, another American admirer and the editor of *Vanity Fair*, went even further, emphasizing that Laurencin's femininity distanced her not only from men but also from other famous women painters:

> She is the only considerable figure in the annals of art who has painted like a woman; who has, following instinctively the impulses of an undividedly feminine psyche, refused to join that prodigious army of epicene painters—talents that are neither male nor female—headed by such amorphous figures as Vigée Lebrun, Rosa Bonheur, Berthe Morisot and Mary Cassatt.[35]

The reference by this conservative critic to Rosa Bonheur as an amorphous figure was probably based on the intensity of Bonheur's professional commitment, her ambitious animal subjects and scale of painting, as well as a reputation for cross-dressing. However, the inclusion of Vigée-Lebrun, Morisot, and Cassatt seems rather surprising, since Vigée-Lebrun had made her reputation painting portraits of beautiful women and, by the late nineteenth century, Impressionist styles of painting were considered appropriate for women painters, whose natures were deemed spontaneous,

impressionable, and nervous. Morisot in particular was widely praised as an example to be emulated.[36]

This construction of Laurencin as even more feminine than women painters of preceding generations is part of the writer's hyperbolic strategy: he claims Laurencin's femininity is so marked that it overshadows even her most famous eighteenth- and nineteenth-century female predecessors. While one suspects that writers like Crowninshield wanted to gloss over the fundamental changes generated by a growing women's movement, their attitudes also seem to have been shaped, at least in part, by their strong sense of Laurencin's physical presence. Access to the bodies, living spaces, and studios of earlier women was only indirectly available through reminiscences, historical documents, and various sorts of visual representations. In contrast, Laurencin could be visited, scrutinized, and directly questioned. Although writers on art had long been fascinated by the physical appearance of female artists, by the turn of the century, the growing popularity of journalistic interviews with celebrities provided many more opportunities for observing the intimate details of artistic everyday life. In essence, because Laurencin extensively participated in such media interviews—for reasons that will be examined further in a moment—she was more visible than preceding generations of women artists. Important for our purposes is the fact that her perceived femininity (as opposed to masculinity or some form of "deviance") was tirelessly stressed on these occasions.

For instance, a 1925 interview with the *L'Art Vivant* journalist Françoise, entitled "Chez Marie Laurencin," included two photographs of Laurencin's apartment, one of which (fig. 14.3) showed the artist seated amid her ornaments and paintings. Throughout the interview, the artist's living and working space was described as a vision from one of her paintings:

> On a small blue divan in a corner, a model. A graceful blond girl who herself seems to be a part of the decor poses sitting with a tiny guitar in her long white hands. . . . The room is a poem by Francis Jammes. It has the same freshness,

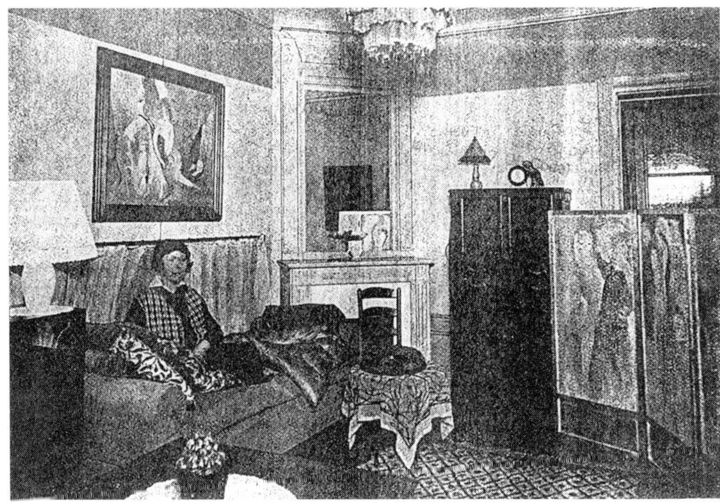

Figure 14.3. Marc Vaux, *Chez Marie Laurencin*. Photograph. From *L'Art Vivant* 3 (1 février 1925): 9. York University Library, Toronto.

the same purity, with all the peaceful and assured naiveté of Marie Laurencin's Art. . . . Two pink ceramic deer lying down on the drawing room mantle seem like the graceful symbol of their mistress. . . . I leave Marie Laurencin filled with a peace that makes me apprehensive of the many noises of Parisian life that will soon darken and then efface the pretty dream of an hour.[37]

In this case, the artist, her model, and her variously displayed paintings and furnishings are all woven into an amazingly consistent image of femininity. The sense of escape into a dreamy and timeless arcadia filled with women playing musical instruments, flowers, pink deer, and other magical animals was characteristic of Laurencin's work during the 1920s, 1930s, and 1940s (e.g., fig. 14.6 below). Even the tools of her trade were described in terms that made them seem like organic outgrowths of her paintings. Another journalist noted that she wore a little bonnet that made her resemble one of La Tour's eighteenth-century personages and held a palette where several colors were spread like "large petals of flowers."[38]

Much was made of the fact that Laurencin painted at home, mostly in her drawing room filled with "gay chintzes and bowls of flowers on every table," rather than in a separate professional studio.[39] Another

source of fascination for reviewers was her meticulous working habits. As one interviewer explained:

> Above all she hates dirt. That is why she goes on wiping her palette with a rag dipped in gasoline while she talks. "I am the only painter in Paris who cleans her palette. You can say that. I also hate dust, which I can date to within a day." The fact is that the furniture is polished and shiny and the study in impeccable order.[40]

References to Laurencin's cultivation and extensive library were mixed with visions of a more cozy domesticity by interviewers who elicited such remarks as: "I should have loved to have had many children, so that I could comb their hair and tie it up with ribbons." Of course these sentiments were hypothetical in this case of a divorced and childless working woman. At various points, Laurencin's remarks made such strategies of rhetorical domestication seem absurd. During one interview, the artist elaborately evoked a domestic scene, which was deliberately viewed from a painter's perspective:

> I was never asked to set up a house, but I could do it well. My house would have a "lived in" look and a refreshing atmosphere. I would serve

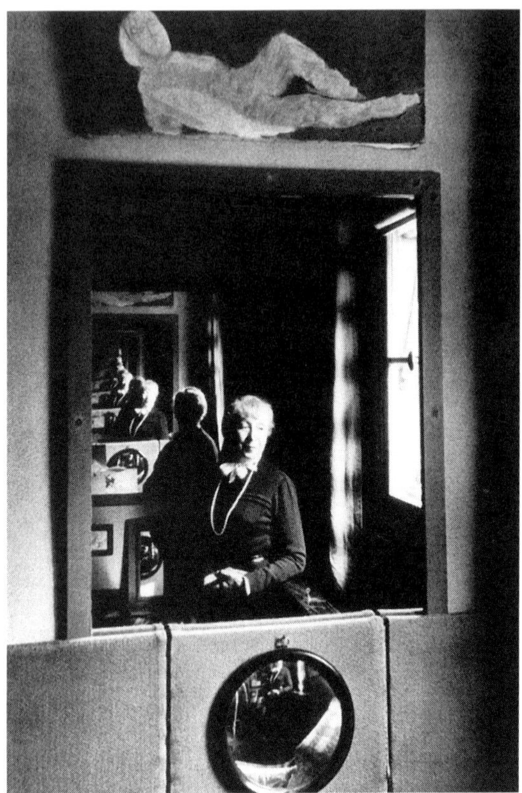

Figure 14.4. Alexander Liberman, untitled photograph of Marie Laurencin, ca. 1950. Research Library, The Getty Research Institute, Los Angeles (2000.R.19).

burning hot coffee in dark blue cups. There would be Kate Greenaway pictures, with clipped gardens and wooden balustrades, and little ladies clad in pink and blue with great big bonnets and muffs. There would be cats and dogs.[41]

Such impressions of a feminine subjectivity that was inwardly domestic and narcissistically self-absorbed were reinforced by photographs of the 1920s showing the artist sitting at her easel in the midst of her drawing room. A later photograph (fig. 14.4), taken in the 1950s by Alexander Liberman, was published with the accompanying commentary: "Only an easel and a few painter's tools intruded on the attractive serenity of her Paris salon."[42] His photograph of Laurencin captures the cabinet-of-mirrors effect that

Roger Allard, among others, ascribed to her paintings. Liberman offers one view of Laurencin's upper torso in a large square mirror and another of her lower body in a smaller round mirror below, both of which are in turn reflected in a larger mirror beyond the picture frame. While the dizzying fracturing and multiplication of Laurencin's image recreate the confusing mirrored space of many famous modernist paintings, such as Manet's *Bar at the Folies-Bergère* (see fig. 12.1, p. 234), it also objectifies and fetishizes the body of the artist.

AVANT-GARDE IMPURITIES

At this point, it is useful to consider the signs of Laurencin's femininity in the context of more particular historical moments and cultural formations. Although for several decades (from when she first started exhibiting in 1907 until her death in 1956) Laurencin was represented as signifying some sort of timeless femininity, such gendered identities were anything but stable categories in the twentieth-century French cultural field. By 1907, much had changed since the 1880s, when members of the Union of Women Painters and Sculptors had mobilized a largely conservative rhetoric of femininity (and occasionally feminism) to justify the admission of women into the Ecole des Beaux-Arts as part of a campaign to defend the historic superiority of French art.[43] As Debora Silverman notes, during the 1890s the emergence of a modern, decorative Art Nouveau movement meant that modernity and femininity were no longer necessarily cast in mutually exclusive terms. The fact that many Art Nouveau initiatives were supported by various state agencies also provided opportunities for public recognition and financial support, which were especially vital to women, since most private networks remained closed to them.[44] Around the turn of the century, a number of modernist women artists, including Laurencin, established careers that were based upon the decorative aesthetics and practices of Art Nouveau and Art Deco, as well as on that of other avant-garde painters.[45] Such careers, which were pursued by both

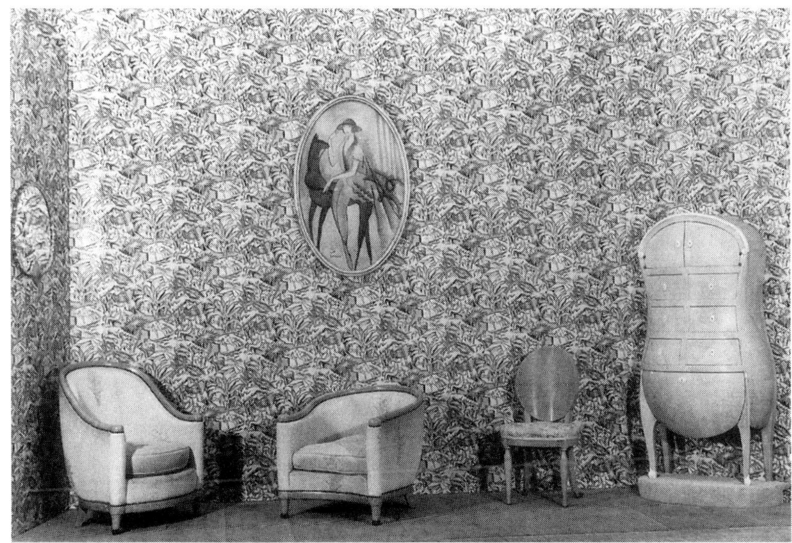

Figure 14.5. André Groult, *La Maison de l'ambassadrice—La Chambre de madame*, 1925. Photograph of installation that includes Marie Laurencin's *Portrait de Nicole Groult* (ca. 1913) on the wall. From Daniel Marchesseau, *Marie Laurencin* (Martigny: Fondation Pierre Gianadda, 1994), 56. © Estate of André Groult/ADAGP (Paris)/SODRAC (Montreal) 2003.

men and women, existed in a curiously hybrid and often contradictory working space, in part allied to the fairly conventional values and institutional networks of official culture and in part connected to groups whose members claimed to be critical outsiders.

By 1912, Apollinaire championed the same sort of artistic hybridity, which he claimed Marie Laurencin best illustrated by producing works that were modern, feminine, primitive, and decorative—all at the same time.

> It seems to me that it would obviously be in the decorators' interest to study carefully the works of today's female artists, who alone possess the charming secret of the gracefulness that is one of the most original traits of French painting. This is true of the works of the so-called French primitives and of the delightful tasteful marvels that could have been produced only in France and that were painted by Watteau, Fragonard, Corot, Berthe Morisot and Seurat. . . . This new delicacy, which is like an innate sense of Hellenism possessed by the French woman, can be found to a high degree in the works that Mlle. Marie Laurencin is currently exhibiting at the Barbazanges Gallery.[46]

To a large extent, Apollinaire was recycling the rhetoric of Art Nouveau when he celebrated an eighteenth-century French decorative tradition that he saw as naturally aligned with the innate Hellenism of the French woman.[47] It is also worth stressing that he was not consigning Laurencin to some sort of feminine ghetto but instead urged artists of both sexes to take up the new decorative aesthetic and its commercial opportunities. His interest in exploring "feminine" creative values can be seen as an extension of his own poetic practice, just as his desire to reach new publics was something he achieved as an art critic. It is easy to see how Laurencin was seduced by Apollinaire's rosy prospect of a new artistic arena that would particularly welcome women's participation.

Furthermore, Laurencin was lured by the financial prospect of extending her market beyond the rather limited confines of the avant-garde. She was glad her paintings were exhibited with the work of interior decorators, as in the case of her portrait of Madame André Groult (née Nicole Poiret) of circa 1913, which was included in a woman's bedroom decoration scheme by André Groult at the Exposition des Arts Décoratifs in Paris in 1925 (fig. 14.5). The installation photograph demonstrates how Laurencin's famous interwoven curvilinear forms and pastel col-

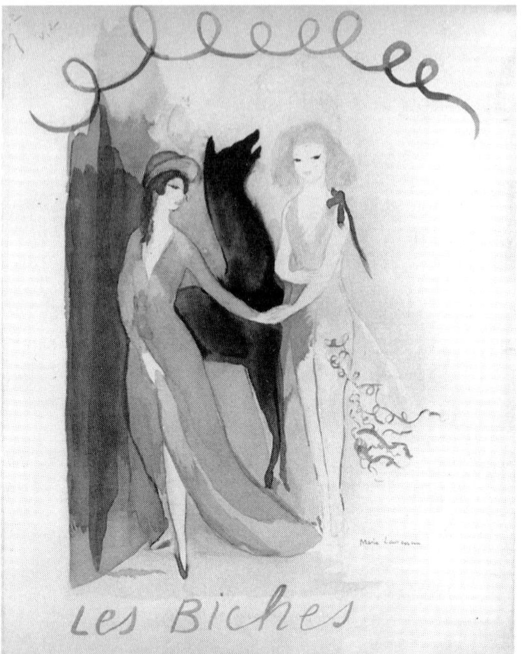

Figure 14.6. Marie Laurencin, frontispiece from *Théâtre Serge Diaghilev: Les Biches*, 2 vols. Illustrations by Marie Laurencin, text by Jean Cocteau, and score by Francis Poulenc (Paris: Editions des Quatres Chemins, 1924). Free Library of Philadelphia. © Estate of Marie Laurencin/ADAGP (Paris)/SODRAC (Montreal) 2003.

ors (in this case, soft pinks, pale blues, and grays) complemented the lines of the furniture and pattern of the wallpaper. Her work for the theater also extended her public, since her costume and set designs were widely perceived as appealingly fashionable rather than austerely shocking. Attending a performance of *Les Biches* by Diaghilev's Ballets Russes, for which Laurencin designed the costumes in 1924 (fig. 14.6), René Gimpel observed: "In the corridor I heard a woman say to a man: 'Look around the house, all the women look as though they were by Marie Laurencin; she has fashioned a type just as Boldini created the eel look fifteen years ago.'"[48] Laurencin revealingly criticized Picasso's ballet designs for *Mercure*, staged at the Cigale the same year, claiming they were too "highbrow" and that Picasso as a Spaniard took himself "too seriously."[49]

Evidently Laurencin was not concerned with de-

fending a reputation for making difficult and challenging art but instead was happy to execute paintings for patrons such as Helena Rubinstein, who ordered three canvases from the artist in 1938 to use as reproductions in her beauty salons.[50] Further proof of the fashionable appeal of Laurencin's portraits was the popularity of a course she offered with Jean-Emile Laboureur and Philippe de Villeneuve during the 1930s, which taught painting, decoration, and drawing to wealthy women. A photograph of Laurencin teaching her section of the course (fig. 14.7) shows a number of society women at their easels, all painting portraits of women in Laurencin's distinctive style.[51] Thus, there is certainly some truth to Apollinaire's assertion that Laurencin wanted to charm her viewers. As early as 1924, the critic Roger Allard had noted that Laurencin's work appealed not only to poets but also to bourgeois and popular muses. In the same year, writing about an exhibition of hers in London, R. H. Wilenski suggested that Laurencin's art would attract even those who normally found modern art "inscrutable" because it "speaks to us in the pictorial language of our day."[52]

Of course, there were those who condemned the more popularly accessible aspects of Laurencin's work as facile and faddish. In 1924, the painter Jean-Louis Forain privately told René Gimpel that he disliked Laurencin's portraits because "there are thousands of people around who can do that sort of thing."[53] But such dismissals were surprisingly rare in the critical literature on the artist from the years 1910 to 1930. The remarks of Allard and Wilenski were made in a positive context, and a number of other critics voiced the hope that Laurencin's decorative work would not obscure her reputation as a painter. Particularly interesting are the 1913 observations of the writer, poet, and art critic André Salmon:

It would be unfortunate if Mlle. Marie Laurencin had no other role to play than that of adjunct to our decorators. May the public, reassured as to her artistic morality, . . . knowing her to be so fragilely associated with wicked demolishers of convenient systems, with the terrorists of modern art, deign

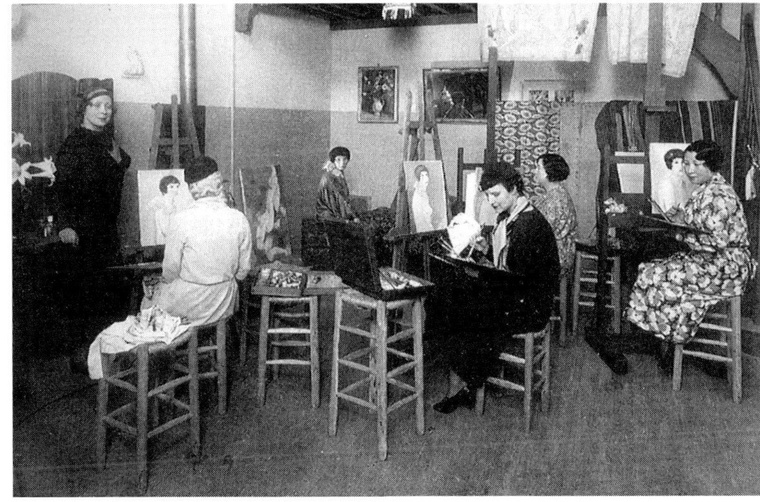

Figure 14.7. Unattributed photograph of "L'Atelier du XVIe": Le cours de Marie Laurencin (ca. 1932). © 1991, Sylvain Laboureur and Ides et Calendes, Neuchâtel.

to take better note of her, and, ultimately, to look at her canvases without preconceived ideas.[54]

Despite Laurencin's precarious position—sandwiched between the frequently contradictory aesthetic demands of decorators and avant-garde painters—Salmon urged his readers to take her art seriously.

At this point, it seems important to start untangling notions of critical and commercial (or popular) success, which need not be mutually exclusive, despite the fact that modernist discourses tend to celebrate only those artists who appear to cultivate the former. For instance, although in relation to Laurencin, Picasso secured higher prices for his canvases from their dealer, Rosenberg, he seldom attracted (or encouraged) clients like Helena Rubinstein, whose exhibition venues were too fashionable to be prestigious. As we have seen, his ballet costumes and stage designs were perceived as avant-garde and difficult, as opposed to Laurencin's, which were more appealingly à la mode. From a modernist perspective, such comparisons have worked to Laurencin's disadvantage, as her work has frequently been measured against less conspicuously commercial artists such as Picasso. But perhaps if one considers the maneuvering room available to each artist, rather different conclusions may be drawn. While Picasso appeared to exercise greater artistic li-

cense in the eyes of the general public, Laurencin criticized how he toadied to dealers like Rosenberg. In 1933, she remarked to René Gimpel, "He [Rosenberg] hasn't got a hold over me as he has over Picasso and Braque. For instance, Helena Rubinstein commissioned me the other day to do a work with Picasso and Braque, and Picasso said to me, confidingly: 'What will Rosenberg say? Rosenberg is in America.' Picasso fills me with pity, he is like a child."[55]

Evidently the popular accessibility of Laurencin's style freed her from totally depending on dealers, since she was able to negotiate many of her own portrait and decorative commissions directly with purchasers. Indeed, the artist seems to have possessed a certain business flair, according to René Gimpel, who described how she dealt with one of her more famous English patrons.

Lady Cunard commissioned her to do her portrait, which she painted with a horse in it, but a fantastic kind of dream horse, the only sort she'll do, and naturally very far from anything seen in England in the way of horses. The lady, who was not satisfied, sent the portrait back from London to Marie Laurencin, and customs imposed a 12 per cent luxury tax on it. She refused to go to their offices, Armand took care of the formalities, and she didn't have to pay anything. The matter, though settled with the customs, was not settled with Marie Laurencin. Her honor as an artist was offended, and she made Lady Cunard get down from her horse and get on a camel; she told the story and showed the picture to everyone. Lady Cunard heard of it and came in all haste to Paris. Lady Cunard, who for years had been trying to scale the last rungs of the English social ladder, Lady Cunard on a camel! What a fall! Absolute horror of seeing the canvas exhibited or reproduced in the *Burlington* or the *Tatler*. She had Armand sit down and think of something and commissioned a whole ballroom from Marie Laurencin. The artist has long since ripped up the canvas.[56]

It should be stressed that Laurencin's business acumen did not stem from a miserly nature—quite the reverse. In fact, she was widely known for her generosity to neighbors, friends, and other artists who had fallen on hard times, and her spending frequently approached the level of her earning.[57] Instead, the artist seems to have wanted artistically and commercially to hedge her bets by working in an accessible and hybrid style that enabled her to move between various constituencies, sometimes playing one off against another.

Having room to maneuver was a priority established early in Laurencin's career, when she chose to continue living at home with her mother throughout her intense affair with Apollinaire. Such a choice has often been attributed to Laurencin's fairly conventional morality since, unlike Fernande Olivier or Jeanne Hébuterne, who were involved with Picasso and Modigliani, Laurencin did not reject her family to embrace the avant-garde. Indeed, many writers have commented on the surprisingly traditional mores of both Apollinaire and Laurencin, who apparently never moved in together or married because both their mothers disapproved of the match. For instance, in her reminiscences published in 1933, Fernande Olivier was especially critical of what she described as Laurencin's bourgeois behavior in Bateau

Lavoir circles. After condemning her for being rather silly, affected, and self-absorbed, Olivier scathingly commented: "She looked like a little girl, and had a little girl's mixture of naïveté and viciousness, and a good deal too naïve to be true. Marie Laurencin, a pupil at an art school on the Boulevard de Clichy, was to become *the* woman painter of the gang."[58]

But Laurencin's decision to live apart from Apollinaire has been read rather differently by others, who have suggested that the artist went home every night so she could get up early and paint without interruption for several hours in the mornings.[59] Unlike Olivier and Hébuterne, Laurencin was interested in securing space for an independent professional career. In fact, and contrary to Olivier's criticisms, during the Bateau Lavoir period (c. 1906–12), Laurencin, the illegitimate daughter of a seamstress, could hardly be described as bourgeois. From an early age, Laurencin's mother had emphasized the merits of a practical vocation, first encouraging her to become a teacher, and when that failed, sending her off to learn the skills of ceramic painting, which was a popular career for artistically oriented working-class girls. If there was anything bourgeois about Laurencin's Bateau Lavoir experience, it was her association with the other members of the group, not her desire to work.[60] One cannot help suspecting that because Olivier's own background was more bourgeois than Laurencin's, the aspirations of the latter made the former decidedly uncomfortable. Because Laurencin refused to play the usual model/lover role allotted to women in the avant-garde, she was dismissively characterized as a young bourgeois girl playing the role of avant-garde painter.[61]

Significantly, Olivier seems to have been more worried about bourgeois forms of femininity (rather than masculinity) infiltrating the avant-garde. By refusing the values of the petit-bourgeois aunt and uncle who had raised her and personally disdaining the sort of upward social mobility and professional status that Laurencin sought, Olivier made herself responsible for legitimating the countercultural claims of the French avant-garde, whereas Picasso and

Braque (also from relatively more prosperous families) were immune to such considerations, neither judged by class criteria nor condemned for ambitious career aspirations.[62] As the assumptions of class and gender difference underpinning Olivier's reminiscences make clear, Laurencin, as a working-class woman, had much less cultural room to maneuver than most of her male counterparts. This was especially true in the early years of her career, when she had not yet established a broader reputation and wider network of social connections. As we have seen, in 1923 she bitterly recalled how Cubism had poisoned three years of her life, the great men paralyzing her work.

One wonders how Olivier might have responded to those women painters outside the Bateau Lavoir who abandoned the notion of "respectable" femininity and adopted the "bohemian" lifestyle that so many male avant-garde painters carefully cultivated. For instance, Suzanne Valadon and Nina Hamnett, neither of whom had any family money, resorted to modeling for other artists in order to make ends meet. Evidently such options did not appeal to Laurencin, at least on a professional level, although numerous friends captured her image. Hamnett, who unlike Laurencin had difficulty producing a large body of salable work, occasionally turned to journalism to supplement her income. Modeling also supported Gwen John, who lived rather meagerly on the margins of various avant-garde communities.[63] Clearly, when compared with these artists, Laurencin was more ambitious for critical recognition and commercial success, but certainly no more so than an artist like Picasso. It seems worth asking whether modeling was any less problematic than producing salable work, given that both activities were frequently denigrated as feminine pursuits.

While it is true that establishing her own cultural and market niches were important to Laurencin, the choice to cultivate a feminine style must also be read (at least early in her career) in terms that Michel de Certeau would call tactical. In *The Practice of Everyday Life*, de Certeau notes that strategies and tactics are differentiated by the position of their users as well as by the types of maneuvers that each involves. Broadly speaking, strategies are formulated by subjects of will and power, or in other words, those who, by virtue of their economic or symbolic capital, can isolate themselves from their environment and secure advantages by deploying their capital over longer periods of time. Typical examples of strategies are the formal systems that govern most Western societies, including political, economic, and scientific rationalities. In contrast, de Certeau locates tactics "in the place of the other," whose inhabitants do not have the resources to wait: "A tactic depends on time—it is always on the watch for opportunities that must be seized 'on the wing.' Whatever it wins, it does not keep. It must constantly manipulate events in order to turn them into 'opportunities.'"[64] According to de Certeau, the weak resort to seizing tactical opportunities in everyday practices such as shopping, walking, cooking, talking, and reading in order to make room for their meanings, transforming the property of others into a transient space they can occupy like that of a rented apartment. The occupation of such borrowed spaces can constitute resistance (at least temporarily) despite the fact that, by its very nature, such resistance remains "hidden" from those in power. Under the guise of social conformity, all sorts of other activities may be taking place because, as de Certeau explains, the accounting systems of capitalist societies deal with "*what* is used, not the ways of *using*" (35).

Taking up de Certeau's ideas, it seems worth exploring some of the less immediately visible aspects of Laurencin's feminine aesthetic. As André Salmon's previously cited comments indicate, Laurencin's work was more often than not taken seriously in avant-garde circles, where early examples of her painting were acquired by Picasso and Gertrude Stein, to name two of her more discerning collectors. Spec-

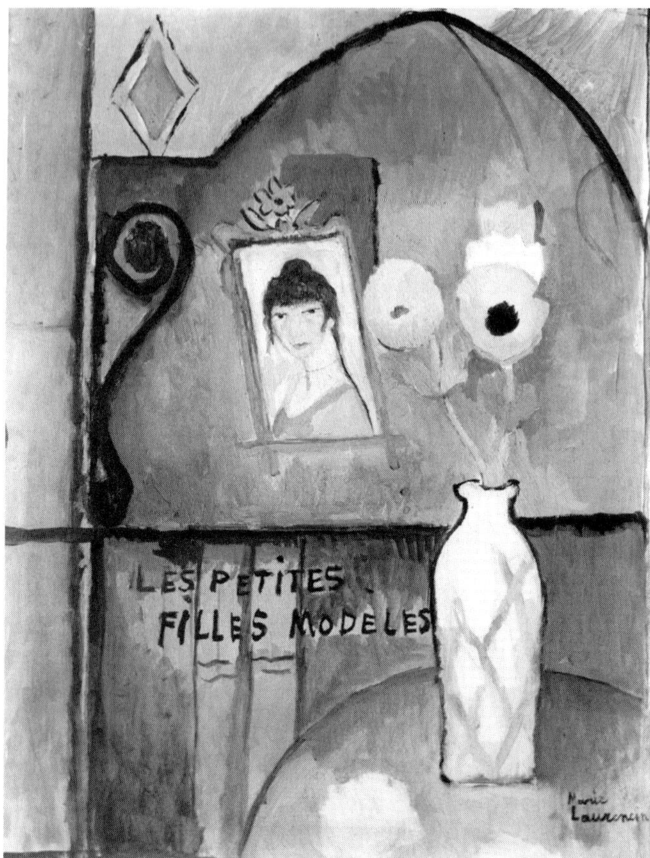

Figure 14.8. Marie Laurencin, *Les Petites Filles modèles*, ca. 1912. Oil on panel. Philadelphia Museum of Art: The A.E. Gallatin Collection. © Estate of Marie Laurencin/ADAGP (Paris)/SODRAC (Montreal) 2003.

ulating on Picasso's reasons for acquiring Laurencin's *La Songeuse*, José Pierre suggests that she brought an important critical perspective to the early Cubist experiments of the Bateau Lavoir. Certainly, the pose and title of Laurencin's *La Songeuse*, which may have been playfully feminizing Rodin's monumental sculpture of the thinker, insistently stresses the sitter's subjective integrity when compared with many of Picasso's and Braque's portraits of women from this period.[65] Furthermore, as the reminiscences of both Gimpel and Olivier repeatedly indicate, Laurencin intensely scrutinized and discussed the work of others. Fagen-King cites the example of Laurencin's etching

Le Pont de Passy of 1908, which mockingly reworked Manet's *Déjeuner sur l'herbe* by replacing the clothed men with animals that the naked woman tames. She also explores how Laurencin's famous *Réunion à la campagne (Apollinaire et ses amis)* of 1909 (fig. 14.2) parodied Picasso's *Les Demoiselles d'Avignon* (fig. 15.1, p. 300) by transforming his figure of Laurencin (at least as the masked and splayed naked body in the lower right had been jokingly identified in Cubist circles) into a demurely dressed and unfragmented woman.[66] Similarly, Pierre has suggested that Laurencin's painting *Dans la forêt* (c. 1915–16) reworked Rousseau's composition of *Le Rêve* by replacing the body of the black male musician with that of a white female painter, which considerably alters the dynamics of looking. Instead of emphasizing the power of the painter's exotic vision, in Laurencin's version both the artist and her model (who sits in the foreground with her back toward the artist) are equally subjected to the gaze of the viewer—a fact that is implied by the painting's other title, *Deux Filles*.[67]

Significantly, when read in an avant-garde context, all of these examples mockingly point out the limits of avant-garde radicality when it came to constructions of gender. Despite using a language that openly problematized conventional bourgeois systems of representation and gender, by and large the horizon structuring the endless puns and jokes about female sexuality was masculine and heterosexual. In this particular context, many of Laurencin's depictions of active and relatively unfragmented female subjects need not be viewed as naively essentialist and compromising, but instead can be seen as tactical incursions into avant-garde space. The notion of a tactic is more appropriate than that of a strategy in this case of a working-class woman who initially had neither the economic nor cultural capital to produce a consistently critical body of work. In order to keep on making art, Laurencin had to regularly sell a substantial number of pictures. Although she occasionally complained about the day-to-day pressures of grinding out commissioned portraits (she could paint about two portraits a month), her resulting financial security not only enabled some measure of independence from dealers like Rosenberg but also conferred a certain immunity from avant-garde orthodoxy and criticism.

As we have seen in the case of her interviews, Laurencin was capable of suddenly uttering remarks that unsettled the image of feminine conformity anticipated by writers and readers. When examined closely, her artistic practice also seems to have taken some unexpected critical turns, particularly when exploring the roles of painter and model. Perhaps irreverently mocking Cubist conceptions of the artist-model relationship, Laurencin's ambiguously titled *Les Petites Filles modèles* (c. 1912, fig. 14.8) carefully reproduces

the major ingredients of a typical Braque or Picasso still life from this period, including a tilted and cropped view of a tabletop in the foreground, a vase of flowers, a portrait, some text directly transposed onto the canvas, and several decorative arabesques that possibly function as abbreviated symbols of interior furnishings. The title, painted just below the center of the composition, emphasizes the gender of the models by doubly underlining the word *filles*. Are the vase of flowers and the framed female portrait young female models or model young girls? In either case, Laurencin gestures to the objectifying tendencies in Cubist painting and collage of the years 1910–20, where the signs of femininity were not only shown to be socially constructed but were also frequently manipulated and rearranged in disconcerting ways. Laurencin leaves the viewer wondering how and why one differentiates between representations of women and those of inanimate objects like vases of flowers.[68]

The relationship between the female painter and model continued to preoccupy Laurencin in numerous self-portraits and depictions of women engaged in the act of painting, as well as in an article she wrote for the *Listener* in 1937, entitled "My Model." A brief foray into this material suggests that part of Laurencin's interest in feminizing the body of the painter involved rethinking the sorts of modernist attitudes toward the model that she had examined in *Les Petites Filles modèles*. By insisting on her own femininity as a painter as well as that of her models (Laurencin often asserted that she disliked and almost never painted men), the artist explored new ways of working.[69] As we have seen, interviewers (evidently encouraged by the artist) tended to wax lyrical on the subject of Laurencin's curiously "feminine" manner of painting, dwelling on her attractively domestic painting space, her cleanliness, the small and detailed scale of her work, its fashionableness, and her tendency to paint sitting rather than standing.

The last observation, which was made by Laurencin herself in the Todd interview and captured in various photographs of the artist, seems to be curiously at odds not only with many of Laurencin's own

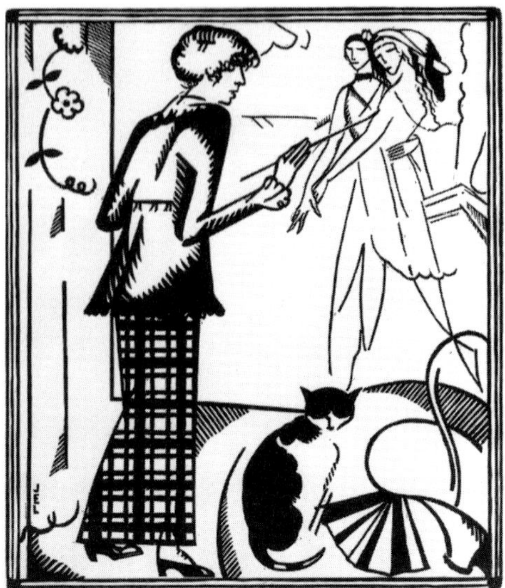

Figure 14.9. J.-E. Laboureur, *Portrait de Marie Laurencin*, 1914. Woodcut. Bibliothèque nationale de France, Cabinet des Estampes, Paris. © Estate of Jean-Émile Laboureur/ ADAGP (Paris)/ SODRAC (Montreal) 2003. (Photo: Bibliothèque nationale de France, Paris.)

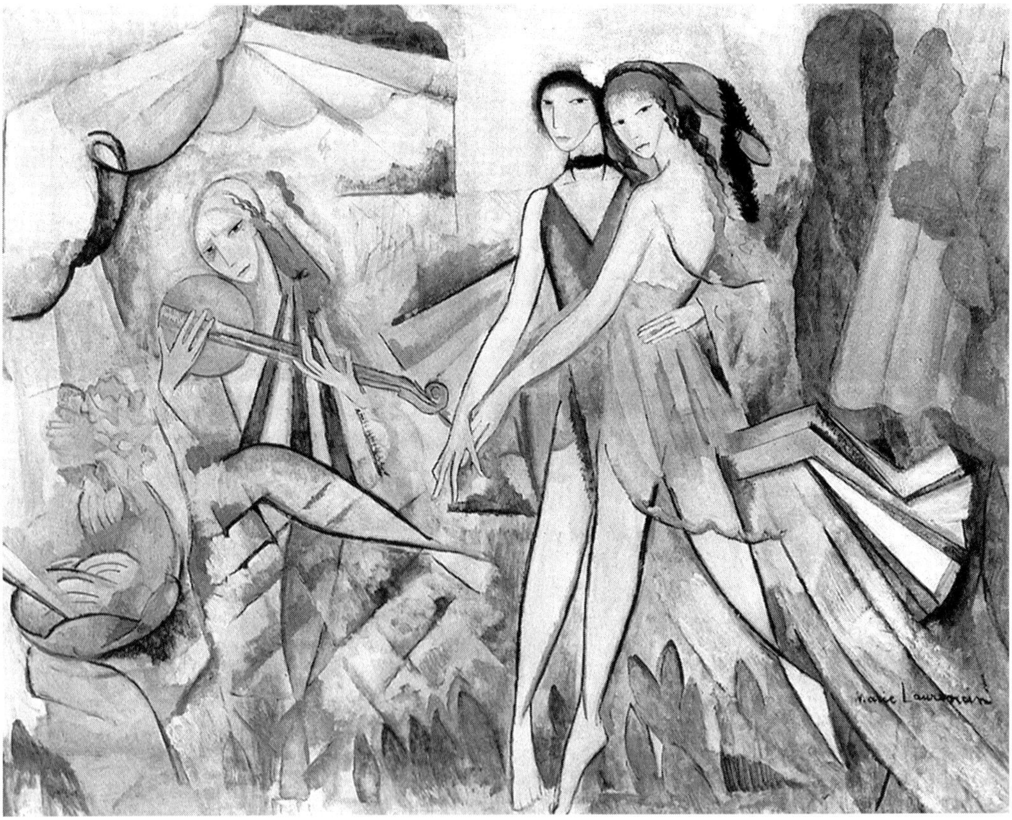

Figure 14.10. Marie Laurencin, *Le Bal élégant / La Danse à la campagne*, 1913. Oil on canvas. © Estate of Marie Laurencin/ ADAGP (Paris)/SODRAC (Montreal) 2003. (Photo: © Musée Marie Laurencin, Japan.)

paintings of woman artists at work (e.g., *Dans la forêt* and *Femme peintre et son modèle*, fig. 14.1) but also with an engraving by her close friend, Jean-Emile Laboureur (fig. 14.9), showing Laurencin in the act of painting her *Le Bal élégant* (sometimes known as *La Danse à la campagne*), which was exhibited at the Salon des Indépendants in 1913 (fig. 14.10). At first glance, the engraving accentuates the differences between the painter and the women she paints—the boldness of Laurencin's fashionably up-to-date plaid skirt and short bobbed hair contrast with the softly floating diaphanous gowns of the arcadian dancers. Yet in spite of these temporal distances, by showing the artist standing to paint, Laboureur draws attention to the long line of the artist's brush and raised arm, which connect the artist and her painted subjects. It seems as if Laurencin could step into the picture, given both its scale and a number of spatial ambiguities that confuse the divisions between the spaces of the studio and canvas, including the curvilinear line in the bottom right that meanders into the painting, the strangely rounded bottom edge of the canvas, and the curiously suspended flower in the upper left, which seems to belong to the flatter two-dimensional space of the canvas but actually hangs in what must logically be the space of the painter. While one could attribute these spatial confusions to an accidental or decorative whim on the part of the engraver, this tendency appears in many of Laurencin's own works.

One of the clearest examples of the reduced distance between artist and model appears in *Femme peintre et son modèle*, painted in 1921 (fig. 14.1). It was probably paintings like this one, with an artist and model who closely resembled each other, that fueled the repeated charges of narcissism that critics such as Roger Allard leveled at Laurencin's work, claiming that such limited and imitative creative abilities were typical of women's work. Yet one cannot help wondering whether such hostility displaced a certain anxiety about the portrayal of what was clearly a romantic and, possibly, an erotic relationship between two women. The similar size of the two women and the fact that they are shown painted in the same flat style and with an equivalent degree of illusionism create the impression that both women are equally real. Reinforcing this impression is the strangely ambivalent position of the gray shape (possibly the artist's palette) that floats between them. A close bond between the two women is established by their similar pink scarves, one of which is tied around the painter's arm like some sort of medieval love token, and by their pose, which suggests the possibility of an embrace.[70] Such depictions of women were hardly surprising given Laurencin's involvement with the lesbian circles of Natalie Barney, for whom she produced a series of Sappho engravings. Whether her involvements with women were platonic or physical remains discreetly suggested and ultimately hidden, perhaps to protect the image of bourgeois respectability that Laurencin cultivated after her return to Paris.[71]

A carefully controlled desire that borders on the erotic and voyeuristic also surfaces in the article Laurencin wrote entitled "My Model," which was translated into English and published in the *Listener* in 1937. Since I have not located an original French version, it is hard to tell whether the chatty journalistic tone of the article was based on a conversation with a translator or whether it accurately captured the tone of an original text. Certainly, there is some evidence suggesting that Laurencin contributed interviews, poems, and other short articles to periodicals in order to supplement her earnings. Accompanied by a specially executed sketch of three entwined dancing women, the article describes Laurencin's relationship with Julia, her model for the past ten years. Laurencin confesses to not really knowing Julia but fantasizing about her domestic life and house. She describes never being invited to Julia's home but at least three or four times a year going past the house and staring at it intently. Later she laments, "Mysterious Julia! I know nothing of where you sleep or of how you spend your days. You come every morning at the same time without question." She also acknowledges the huge social distances between the two of them, noting that her own middle-class neighbors are terrified of Julia and would be even more terrified if they saw Laurencin's paintings of her. Of particular interest to Laurencin is Julia's working-class lifestyle, which includes her Cossack husband, Basil, lots of time squandered drinking in cafés, and the decrepit neighborhood where she lives. Julia's aging beauty is described at length by Laurencin, who claims that it is an essential element of the artist's creative practice. "Her neck is growing thicker, but her hands retain their beauty, and when she takes the pose this commonplace girl becomes a proud sultana. I cannot change my model. She illuminates me like a living lamp which itself only exists in my presence."[72]

Essentially, she describes her role as adorning and complementing the model rather than manipulating and exposing her. While there is, of course, the usual assertion that the artist transforms the commonplace material of everyday life, elsewhere the article critically probes the power relations between artist and model. While Laurencin may have desired her model, this is only indirectly recorded, as in the incident of her repeatedly watching Julia's house. Perhaps in an effort to check her imagination, Laurencin insists on the social and cultural distances that separate herself and Julia. Indeed, there are all sorts of silences between the two of them, which, according to Laurencin, indicate the degree of their mutual respect. Perhaps more than anything else it is this description of disconcerting social distances that lends credibility to Laurencin's initial remark that she really knows nothing about her model because, although Julia has come to her house nearly every day for the past ten years, Laurencin knows her only as an employer in a relationship that is "distant and impersonal."

It is a curiously awkward article, which both raises and finally shies away from the question of whether the model was the object of the painter's desire. Clearly, Laurencin was treading difficult ground given that artist-model relationships were popularly believed to be fraught with erotic possibilities, at least for those male artists who engaged female models, such as Gauguin, Kirchner, or the characters in best-selling novels, such as George Du Maurier's *Trilby*. Was Laurencin merely adopting an artistic convention that poorly served her needs? Or was she suppressing a desire that could not be publicly articulated? The fact that there are no easy answers to these questions makes Laurencin's case an interesting one. In the end, how are we to interpret Laurencin's reticence, good manners, and professionally distant working relationships? Had she simply become a bourgeois woman painter, as Olivier had claimed so many years earlier? Once again straightforward answers prove elusive. Certainly, by 1937 Laurencin's sound business sense had generated a secure income that would have qualified as bourgeois. Nevertheless, as we have seen, it was that income which gave Laurencin at least some degree of control over her working conditions. In many respects, her relationship with her model seems rather more enabling than many—at least from the model's perspective.[73] Laurencin's pragmatic professionalism was hardly the stuff that spawns artistic myth, but perhaps for that very reason she was able to offer some interesting critical insights into the work of other, more famous and self-consciously mythmaking painters and art dealers of her time.

To return to the questions raised at the outset, it is evident that Laurencin *was* interested in laying claim to the painter's body. But by emphatically (and sometimes even absurdly) feminizing that body, she foregrounded women's problematic relationship to modernist artistic production. Her attempt to formulate a feminine visual language was, even during her own day, easily and enthusiastically taken up by those critics and collectors who continued to believe that women's art belonged to a separate sphere. Evidently, Laurencin herself vacillated on this issue— sometimes closing herself off from male colleagues and sometimes directly taking up their work. She produced pictures in a surprisingly consistent style for patrons with diverse interpretative horizons, ranging from John Quinn to Natalie Barney. Clearly each saw what they wanted, whether an essential femininity or a lesbian eroticism. Certain individuals seem to have had some difficulty deciding whether Laurencin's work was conservative or disruptive. For instance, when the artist and critic Marius de Zayas first encountered Laurencin's work in Paris in 1914, he wrote to Alfred Stieglitz that although her work would be easy to get for an exhibition at the 291 Gallery in New York, it was probably not worth bothering, because her work was only a cheap pastiche of modernism. However, de Zayas changed his tune when her work was exhibited at the Modern Gallery in New York in 1917:

> Oh, how the wives of the New Hope Group of Artists would disapprove of the work of Marie Laurencin that is now to be seen in the Modern Gallery. . . . Marie would never do at all in New Hope. Fancy her attending the weekly meetings of the "Lapsed and Lost Society!" It wouldn't do. She'd be too disturbing. She knows too much. It's not good form in Good Hope . . . for a lady to know too much. . . . Marie Laurencin is one of the most conspicuous personalities of modern painting. An adventuress of thought, imbued with the essentially modern spirit.[74]

Perhaps, then, Laurencin and her work offer us examples of de Certeau's tactical indeterminacy, where alternative meanings slip into the system under the guise of social conformity. Not surprisingly, these are just the sort of resistances that get lost over time. Never highly visible in the first place, they easily fade into the background. What remains is only the shell of social conformity that housed them. Such has been the critical fate of Marie Laurencin, who, by and large, has been relegated to history as a woman painter whose feminine style meant she was successful but not serious. In cases like this one, it seems appropriate to conclude with Roland Barthes's comment on "weak myths," which, unlike strong ones, are not depoliticized abruptly. Instead, as Barthes observes, in weak myths, "the political quality of the object has *faded* like a colour, but the slightest thing can bring back its strength brutally."[75]

I would like to thank Lucy Pribas and Adam Stead for research assistance. This work was funded by the Social Sciences and Humanities Research Council of Canada. The notes have been abridged for the present printing.

1. From his essay "Art News: Women Painters," originally published in *Le Petit Bleu* (5 April 1912) and reprinted in translation in *Apollinaire on Art: Essays and Reviews 1902–1908*, ed. Leroy Breunig and trans. Susan Suleiman (New York: Da Capo Press, 1972), 229.

2. Roger Allard, *Marie Laurencin* (Paris: Editions de la Nouvelle Revue Française, 1921), 7.

3. "The Capricious Feminine Charm of Marie Laurencin," *Art Digest*, February 1947, 17; "The Elfin Maidens of Marie Laurencin," *Art Digest*, 15 November 1937, 10; and J. L., "A Famous Exponent of Femininity," *Art News*, 13 November 1937, 18–19.

4. For instance, pink covers were used in the recent paperback editions of Charlotte Gere, *Marie Laurencin* (London: Academy Editions, 1977); Flora Groult, *Marie Laurencin* (Paris: Mercure de France, 1987); and Douglas Hyland and Heather McPherson, *Marie Laurencin: Artist and Muse* (Birmingham, Ala.: Birmingham Museum of Art, 1989), which contains the essay "Marie Laurencin: An Undividedly Feminine Psyche."

5. René Gimpel, *Diary of an Art Dealer*, trans. John Rosenberg (New York: Universe Books, 1987), 399.

6. For example, in 1939 she had eleven solo exhibitions. According to José Pierre, *Marie Laurencin* (Paris: Editions Aimery Somogy, 1988), 80, Daniel Marchesseau noted that in 1921, shortly after Laurencin's return to Paris, few artists were on such a firm financial footing. She apparently had about 35,000 to 40,000 francs in Paris from the sale of her paintings and an equal amount in a Zurich bank. To contextualize these amounts, the rent on her apartment was between 350 and 400 francs per month. Gimpel, her close friend, discusses many details of her financial transactions in his *Diary of an Art Dealer*, noting that in 1923 her contract with Rosenberg paid her about 60,000 francs for a selection of paintings that were shared with Hessel, a German dealer. Laurencin could also produce additional portraits and decorative commissions, for which she charged directly. According to Gimpel, Laurencin

claimed to spend about 100,000 francs a year (243). In 1929, Gimpel noted that "Marie Laurencin is quite well off these days. She must have nearly a million in canvases. She has some good shares, and her two homes which are worth some 800,000 francs" (361). However, Laurencin's relations with Rosenberg were not always harmonious, since she felt he paid her too little (and often irritatingly late), considering what he made on her paintings (see pp. 243, 261, and 376).

7. For speculations about the Japanese investment in Laurencin, see Joseph Roy, "Laurencin au soleil levant," *L'Express*, 16–22 May 1986, 132; and F. D., "Laurencin la muse du Japon," *Le Quotidien de Paris*, 3 May 1984. On Laurencin's secondary status as an avant-garde painter, see Jean-Jacques Leveque, "Marie Laurencin: L'Etat de grâce," *Le Quotidien de Paris*, 8 May 1986.

8. See Andreas Huyssen, "Mass Culture as Woman: Modernism's Other," in *After the Great Divide: Modernism, Mass Culture, Postmodernism* (Bloomington: Indiana University Press, 1986), 44–62.

9. I refer to the classic definitions of the modernist avant-garde by Clement Greenberg in such essays as "Avant-Garde and Kitsch" (1939), reprinted in *Art and Culture* (Boston: Beacon, 1961), 3–21; and "Modernist Painting" (1965), reprinted in *Modern Art and Modernism*, ed. F. Frascina and C. Harrison (New York: Harper and Row, 1984), 5–10. See Peter Bürger, *Theory of the Avant-Garde*, trans. Michael Shaw (Minneapolis: University of Minnesota Press, 1984).

10. While Laurencin is usually included in catalogues or surveys of modernist women artists—see Ann Sutherland Harris and Linda Nochlin, *Women Artists 1550–1950* (Los Angeles: Los Angeles County Museum and New York: Alfred A. Knopf, 1976), 295–96; Elsa Honig Fine, *Women and Art* (Montclair, N.J.: Allanheld and Schram, 1978), 171–73; and Whitney Chadwick, *Women, Art, and Society* (London: Thames and Hudson, 1990), 279, 281, 285—she is either seldom mentioned or discussed disparagingly in more critical studies—see Griselda Pollock and Rozsika Parker, *Old Mistresses: Women, Art, and Ideology* (London: Routledge, 1981); and Gill Perry, *Women Artists and the Parisian Avant-Garde* (Manchester: Manchester University Press, 1995). For a discussion of how Laurencin has made feminist writers uneasy, see Hyland and McPherson, *Marie Laurencin*, 14.

11. Julia Fagen-King, "United on the Threshold of the Twentieth Century Mystic Ideal: Marie Laurencin's Integral Involvement with Guillaume Apollinaire and the Inmates of the Bateau Lavoir," *Art History* 12 (1988): 88–114. See also Renée Sandell, "Marie Laurencin: Cubist Muse or More?" *Woman's Art Journal* 1 (Spring/Summer 1980): 23–27.

12. Hyland and McPherson, *Laurencin*, 39–40; and Daniel Marchesseau, *Marie Laurencin 1883–1956: Catalogue raisonné de l'oeuvre peint* (Tokyo: Editions du Musée Marie Laurencin, 1986).

13. Alice A. Jardine, *Gynesis: Configurations of Woman and Modernity* (Ithaca, N.Y.: Cornell University Press, 1985); and Carol Duncan, "Virility and Domination in Early Twentieth Century Vanguard Painting," *Artforum*, December 1973, 30–39. For Griselda Pollock's work, see notes 21 and 22.

14. Briony Fer, "Knowing the Tropes," *Art History* 15, no. 1 (March 1992): 100.

15. Michel Foucault, *The History of Sexuality*, trans. Robert Hurley (New York: Vintage Books, 1980).

16. Suleiman's claim about the situation of postmodern-period women is made on p. 190 of *Subversive Intent: Gender, Politics, and the Avant-Garde* (Cambridge, Mass.: Harvard University Press, 1990). See also 19 n. 21, 190 n. 23.

17. Biddy Martin, "Sexual Practice and Changing Lesbian Identities," in *Destabilizing Theory: Contemporary Feminist Debates*, ed. Michèle Barrett and Anne Phillips (Stanford, Calif.: Stanford University Press, 1992), 118.

18. Gianni Vattimo, *The End of Modernity*, trans. Jon R. Synder (Cambridge: Polity Press, 1988), 12–13.

19. Jean-François Lyotard, "Sur la force des faibles," *L'Arc*, 1976, 4–12, a version of which has been translated as "On the Strength of the Weak," *Sémiotexte* 3, no. 2 (1978): 204–12.

20. Michel de Certeau, *The Practice of Everyday Life*, trans. Stephen Rendall (Berkeley: University of California Press, 1984).

21. Griselda Pollock, "Painting, Feminism, History," in *Destabilizing Theory*, ed. Michèle Barrett and Anne Phillips (Stanford, Calif.: Stanford University Press, 1992), 161.

22. Griselda Pollock, "Modernity and the Spaces of Femininity," in *Vision and Difference: Femininity, Feminism, and the Histories of Art* (London: Rout-

ledge, 1988), 50–90. Building on Janet Wolff's notion of the "invisible flâneuse," Pollock examines how gendered experiences of public and private urban spaces affected the work of artists such as Morisot and Cassatt. While her case study looks at the impact of gender difference at the level of specific paintings and addresses the way certain spaces and spatial configurations have been privileged in traditional modernist discourses, mine considers how Laurencin consciously mobilized her understanding of gender difference in an attempt to secure artistic space and credibility.

23. Gabrielle Buffet [Picabia], "Marie Laurencin," *Arts*, June 1923, 394.

24. Dorothy Todd, "Exotic Canvases Suited to Modern Decoration," *Arts and Decoration*, January 1928, 64, 92–95. Todd noted numerous details signifying Laurencin's modernity, including the "American complexity and efficiency" of her bathroom and the fact that there were at least six vacuum cleaners in her apartment building. She also devoted considerable attention to Laurencin's support for the women's movement.

25. Marie Laurencin, *Le Carnet des nuits* (1942; repr. Geneva: Pierre Cailler, 1956), 16.

26. Todd, "Exotic Canvases," 92.

27. Ibid., 92.

28. Pollock, "Painting," 153.

29. Todd, "Exotic Canvases," 92.

30. Ibid.

31. Chadwick, *Women, Art, and Society*, 281.

32. On the gendered discourses surrounding women's art in the late nineteenth century, see Tamar Garb, *Sisters of the Brush: Women's Artistic Culture in Late Nineteenth-Century Paris* (New Haven, Conn.: Yale University Press, 1994), 109–112.

33. *Apollinaire on Art*, 44. The review of Laurencin's work appears in his review of the Salon des Indépendants originally published in *La Revue des Lettres et des Arts*, 1 May 1908.

34. B. L. Reid, *The Man from New York: John Quinn and His Friends* (New York: Oxford University Press, 1968), 470.

35. Frank Crowninshield, *Marie Laurencin* (New York: Findlay Galleries, 1937), [2].

36. On the reputation of Vigée-LeBrun, see Pollock and Parker, *Old Mistresses*, 96–98. On Impressionism as an appropriate style for women, consult Garb, *Sisters of the Brush*, 124–27, and on Morisot, see Garb's article, "Berthe Morisot and the Feminizing of Impressionism," in *Perspectives on Morisot*, ed. T. J. Edelstein (New York: Hudson Hills Press, 1990), 57–66.

37. Françoise, "Chez Marie Laurencin," *L'Art Vivant* 3 (1 February 1925): 10.

38. Edmond-Marie Dupuis, "A Visit to Marie Laurencin's Studio" [source and date unidentified], 27–28, press clippings in the Collection of the Bibliothèque Littéraire Jacques Doucet.

39. Todd, "Exotic Canvases," 94. On the "domestication" of women's work and artistic spaces in late-nineteenth-century critical discourses, see Garb, *Sisters of the Brush*, 108–10.

40. Christiane Fournier, "Marie Laurencin" [source, date, and page references unidentified], press clippings in the Collection of the Bibliothèque Littéraire Jacques Doucet. Todd also comments on Laurencin's extremely tidy working habits.

41. Both quotes are from Marie Laurencin, "Art and Life," *Continental Daily Mail*, 30 March 1950.

42. Alexander Liberman, *The Artist in His Studio* (New York: Viking, 1968), 62.

43. See Garb, *Sisters of the Brush*, ch. 6.

44. On the French state's involvement in the promotion of Art Nouveau, see Debora Silverman, *Art Nouveau in Fin-de-Siècle France* (Berkeley: University of California Press, 1989), ch. 10. However, as Silverman notes, those artists who benefited most from state patronage were Emile Gallé, Auguste Rodin, Albert Besnard, Eugène Carrière, and Louis Falize (172).

45. Many parallels can be drawn between the careers of Marie Laurencin and Hermine David, who also cultivated a decidedly feminine artistic identity as a painter of portraits and miniatures as well as a maker of dolls. She, like Laurencin, continued to live at home with her mother despite being involved with Jules Pascin. She was photographed along with Suzanne Duchamp, Hélène Perdriat, and Marie Laurencin for an article by Florence Guillam, "Paris Women and the Arts," *Charm* 4, no. 2 (March 1925): 15–16.

46. *Apollinaire on Art*, 210. The review was entitled "Art News: The Decorative Arts and Female Painting" and originally published in *Le Petit Bleu*, 13 March 1912.

47. On the ways in which femininity was configured in

the critical discourses of Roger Marx, a leading exponent of Art Nouveau, consult Silverman, *Art Nouveau*, 219–28.

48. Gimpel, *Diary*, 260. Laurencin also illustrated a book on the production that included the text by Jean Cocteau and the score by Francis Poulenc; see *Théâtre Serge de Diaghilew: Les Biches*, 2 vols. (Paris: Editions des Quatres Chemins, 1924).

49. Gimpel, *Diary*, 264.

50. Ibid., 428.

51. Sylvain Laboureur, *Catalogue complet de l'oeuvre de Jean-Émile Laboureur*, vols. 2–4 (Neuchâtel: Ides et Calendes, 1991), 20.

52. Roger Allard, "Marie Laurencin," *L'Art d'Aujourd' hui* 2, no. 8 (Winter 1925): 49; and R. H. Wilenski, *Marie Laurencin* (London: Leicester Galleries, 1924), 10–11.

53. Gimpel, *Diary*, 251. Such criticisms increased by the 1930s, as Laurencin continued painting prolifically in what was by then a passé Art Deco style. In 1937 an anonymous critic noted that Laurencin's work was beginning to look dated; see *Studio* 13 (February 1937): 103.

54. André Salmon, "Marie Laurencin," *L'Art Décoratif*, August/September 1913, 116.

55. Gimpel, *Diary*, 418. Gimpel discussed Laurencin's own flaunting of Rosenberg's rules (376) when, outraged by what she regarded as his excessive profiteering, she painted a watercolor of a woman in the guise of a fury with black hair standing on end, which she described as "a woman who isn't afraid of Rosenberg."

56. Armand was Gimpel's nephew and a close friend of Laurencin; see Gimpel, *Diary*, 360–61.

57. On the subject of her spending, see Gimpel, *Diary*, 261–62; on her loans to others, see the example of her generosity to the wife of Laboureur (279).

58. Fernande Olivier, *Picasso and His Friends*, trans. Jane Miller (London: Heinemann, 1964), 43 (italics are in the original).

59. See Pierre, *Laurencin*, 66.

60. On Laurencin's early education, see Groult, *Laurencin*, 48–52. In the interview with Dorothy Todd ("Exotic Canvases," 95), Laurencin noted, "I only like people who work, . . . I have no use for idlers."

61. This has also been noted by Groult, *Laurencin*, 92–93.

62. Olivier quite self-consciously constructed an image of herself as a *declassé* bourgeois from an early age, at

least in her second set of memoirs, *Souvenirs intimes*, where she stresses both her illegitimacy and the fact that she found herself more comfortable with the maids than the family of the petit-bourgeois half-sister of her father who raised her.

63. On Suzanne Valadon, see Rosemary Betterton, "How Do Women Look? The Female Nude in the Work of Suzanne Valadon," *Feminist Review* 19 (March 1985): 3–24; and Patricia Mathews, "Returning the Gaze: Diverse Representations of the Nude in the Art of Suzanne Valadon," *Art Bulletin* 73 (September 1991): 415–30; on Nina Hamnett, see Denise Hooker, *Nina Hamnett: Queen of Bohemia* (London: Constable, 1987); and ch. 5 in Bridget Elliott and Jo-Ann Wallace, *Women Artists and Writers: Modernist (Im)positionings* (London: Routledge, 1994); on Gwen John, see Deborah Cherry and Jane Beckett, "Gwen John," *Art History* 11 (September 1988): 456–62.

64. De Certeau, *Practice*, xix. A summary of these ideas is presented in the "General Introduction," xi–xxiv.

65. Pierre, *Laurencin*, 61–62. Pierre further suggests that *La Songeuse* may well be a self-portrait. Picasso and Braque typically rendered female subjects in a monochromatic and highly fractured style that has frequently been described as analytical Cubism. See Picasso's *Woman with a Mandolin (Fanny Tellier)* of 1910 and *Ma Jolie (Woman with a Guitar)* of 1911–12, as well as Braque's *Woman with a Mandolin* of 1910 and his *Woman with Guitar* of 1913.

66. See the similarly positioned figure of the woman in the lower right of both paintings. Fagen-King, "United on the Threshold," 105–107.

67. Pierre, *Laurencin*, 44–51, 76. The second title is listed in Hyland and McPherson, *Laurencin*, 50.

68. On the differences between painting female models and bowls of fruit, see April F. Masten, "Model into Artist: The Changing Face of Art Historical Biography," *Women Studies* 21, no. 1 (1992): 17–41.

69. See her comments to Todd on this subject (cited above) and in Buffet [Picabia], "Marie Laurencin," 396.

70. Women embracing was a recurring motif for Laurencin; see, for example, *La Danse* (1919), reproduced in Marchesseau, *Marie Laurencin*, no. 153.

71. Laurencin had been much more interested in flamboyantly flouting social convention during the prewar period of her involvement with the Bateau-Lavoir—

ironically, just when Olivier had been so dismissive. While various writers have either hinted or openly suggested that Laurencin had lesbian affairs, those parts of her correspondence and papers that have gone to public collections have been carefully sorted.

72. Marie Laurencin, "My Model" [trans. V. B. Holland], *Listener*, 8 September 1937, 511–12.

73. Writing about *Femme peintre*, Douglas Hyland and Heather McPherson (*Laurencin*, 30) note that Laurencin's handling of the artist and model subject (which was so often painted by Picasso) was given a specifically female twist.

74. De Zayas's condemnation of Laurencin's work is privately expressed in a letter from him to Alfred Stieglitz dated June 30, 1914, preserved in the Alfred Stieglitz Archive, Beinecke Rare Book and Manuscript Library, Yale University. There he writes: "This clever girl is doing exactly what Davies and his bunch did with 'Cubism' at the Montross. She does not express the present, she has the spirit of the XVIII century represented by the formula of modern art." De Zayas's comments on the show at the Modern Gallery appear in "How, When, and Why Modern Art Came to New York" (intro. and notes by Francis Naumann), *Arts* 54, no. 2 (April 1980): 121–22. Thanks to Ernst Birss for drawing my attention to de Zayas's comments.

75. Roland Barthes, *Mythologies*, selected and translated by Annette Lavers (New York: Hill and Wang, 1978), 144.

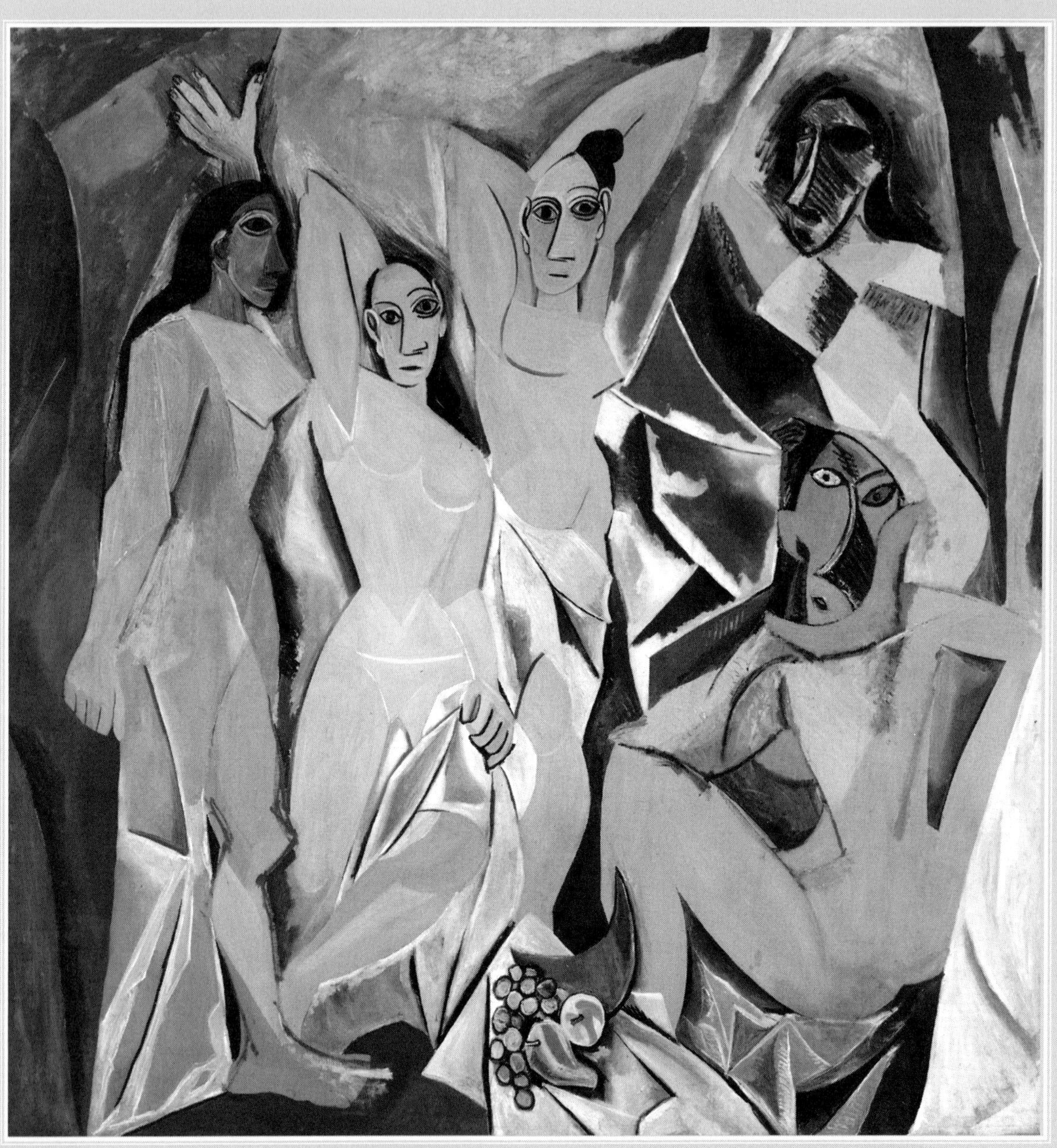

15

NEW ENCOUNTERS
WITH *LES DEMOISELLES D'AVIGNON*

Gender, Race, and the Origins of Cubism

Anna C. Chave

WHAT WAS "the amazing act upon which all the art of our century is built"? What is "the most innovative painting since Giotto," the "harbinger comet of the new century," the very "paradigm of all modern art," no less?[1] What is the modern art-historical equivalent of the Greatest Story Ever Told? What else but the monumental *Demoiselles d'Avignon* (fig. 15.1) painted by Picasso in 1907? In 1988, this single painting, "probably the first truly twentieth-century painting," occasioned a major exhibition at the Musée Picasso in Paris, commemorated by a ponderous two-volume catalogue.[2] The director of the department of painting and sculpture at the Museum of Modern Art in New York swore he would kill himself if the plane transporting the work to that event were to crash.[3] What can account for such hyperbole, for such an unparalleled fixation on a particular picture?

"In mystical terms, with this painting we bid farewell to all the paintings of the past," pronounced André Breton of *Les Demoiselles*.[4] More than any other work of art, Picasso's picture has been held to mark or even to have precipitated the demise of the old visual order and the advent of the new. That art historians should have conscripted *Les Demoiselles* to serve in such a strategic capacity might seem odd, however, if we take into account that the cognoscenti resoundingly rejected the picture at the time it was painted and that it remained all but invisible to the public for three decades thereafter, when it finally found an audience—though at first only in the United States.[5] The painting "seemed to everyone something mad or monstrous," the dealer Daniel-Henry Kahnweiler recalled; "Derain told me that one day Picasso would be found hanging behind his big picture."[6]

Why have historians parlayed this once reviled and ignored image of five rather alien looking prostitutes vying for a client into the decisive site of the downfall of the prevailing visual regime?[7] Undeniably, Picasso violated pictorial convention in *Les Demoiselles d'Avignon*—by his deidealization of the human form, his disuse of illusionistic space, and his deployment of a mixture of visual idioms. In the standard art-historical narratives, however, these violations on the artist's part tend to get conflated with the

This essay was originally published in *Art Bulletin* 76, no. 4 (December 1994): 597–612. Copyright © 1994 by Anna C. Chave. The endnotes have been substantially abridged. Reprinted by permission of the author and courtesy of the College Art Association.

Figure 15.1. Pablo Picasso, *Les Demoiselles d'Avignon*, 1907. Oil on canvas. The Museum of Modern Art, New York. Acquired through the Lillie P. Bliss Bequest. © 2005 Estate of Pablo Picasso/Artists Rights Society (ARS), New York. (Digital image © The Museum of Modern Art/Licensed by SCALA/Art Resource, New York.)

putatively violent aspect of the women he depicted, who often come to assume a kind of autonomous agency. And whereas Picasso's contemporaries fingered *him* as the perpetrator who "attacked" his female figures, later accounts often cast the artist together with the viewing public as the prostitutes' victims.[8] Leo Steinberg experienced the picture as a "tidal wave of female aggression . . . an onslaught"; Robert Rosenblum perceived it as an "explosion" triggered by "five nudes [who] force their eroticized flesh upon us with a primal attack"; and Max Kozloff deemed it simply "a massacre."[9]

Les Demoiselles d'Avignon is generally credited not only with a momentous act of destruction, but also with one of creation. Long designated the first Cubist painting—"the signal for the Cubist revolution" in its full-fledged dismantling of representational conventions[10]—the painting is now more loosely considered a curtain-raiser or trigger to Cubism.[11] Others had pulled crucial triggers before Picasso, however. When Baudelaire told Manet, "You are only the first in the decrepitude of your art," he referred to the scandalously frank picture of a courtesan, *Olympia*, rendered with startling flatness in 1865. For that matter, a compressed or otherwise compromised female form, often that of a prostitute or femme fatale, would come to serve almost as an avatar of modernism.[12] Feminist critics have lately diagnosed this fact, that the avant-garde's testing of cultural limits so often played itself out on the female body, as symptomatic of a visual regime where "Woman" serves as "the very ground of representation, both object and support of a desire which, intimately bound up with power and creativity, is the moving force of culture and history."[13]

The Greatest Story Ever Told was perforce a narrative of exclusion, then: a story told by a heterosexual white male of European descent for an audience answering to the same description; and the stories told ever since about that Greatest Story have mostly been no less narratives told by straight white males for a like public. Virtually every critic who has addressed *Les Demoiselles* has not only assumed what

is indisputable—that the picture's intended viewer is male and heterosexual—but has also elected to consider only the experience of that viewer, as if no one else ever looked at the painting. (Through *Les Demoiselles*, Picasso "tells us what our desires are," one critic declared, peremptorily.)[14] No doubt Picasso's chosen subject dictates this scenario, since today, just as in 1907, prostitution marks an indelible social boundary between the sexes: between men, who can routinely contract for the sexual services of women, and women, who have never had a comparable opportunity.[15]

Among my objectives in the present text, then, is to examine where *Les Demoiselles d'Avignon* positions some of its unanticipated viewers; to explore the painting from, as it were, unauthorized perspectives. What follows is a study in reception, present and past, in short, but one that takes its focus through the critical lenses of gender and race. (Examining the painting's reception history from a given, raking angle, not in a full, even light, will bring some neglected aspects of that history into relief while, admittedly, flattening or obscuring other elements that would figure prominently in a more general or comprehensive kind of reception study.)[16] Poststructuralist and reception theories have shown that all publicly circulated images accrue meanings beyond their makers' intent and control, and that the meanings of works of art are more contingent than immanent, for in the act of interpreting artworks critics shape their significance by shaping how and what the public sees. As for the terms in which *Les Demoiselles* has been read, they have often been incipiently sexist, heterosexist, racist, and neocolonialist: so I will argue. (I should perhaps add plainly that neither Picasso's own intentions for the picture nor his susceptibility to the biases enumerated above are the principal subjects of investigation here.)

To begin with, the place that *Les Demoiselles d'Avignon* conspicuously marks out for a client-viewer is hopelessly unsuited to me—a heterosexual, feminist, female viewer.[17] But I can find some basis to identify with its protagonists. Although my privileged background has insulated me from the desperate straits that have long driven women to toil in the sex industry, like other independent women I nonetheless have an inkling of what it means to be treated as a prostitute. When I traverse the city streets alone I am subject to pestering by strange men who lewdly congratulate me on aspects of my anatomy while ordering me to smile. If I am not mistaken for a prostitute, given my reserved dress and behavior, I remain prey to that pervasive suspicion that a trace of whore lurks in every woman—just as an "honest" woman supposedly lurks in every whore.

As it happens, the streets in my own longtime neighborhood on Manhattan's Lower East Side encompass a major prostitute "stroll." The streetwalkers I encounter there are a lower class of prostitute, more drug-addicted and ill than the type of woman Picasso portrayed, but I occasionally see them assume the poses of the two demoiselles at the center of the painting, their arms crooked over their heads in an age-old formula for seductive femininity. On the Lower East Side, as in Picasso's picture, however, the woodenness of the women's stances and their faces' masklike stolidity make plain that they know they are party to a tiresome artifice. Like virtually all women, I have engaged in such half-hearted acts of simulation, engaged in such a "masquerade,"[18] and this helps me to view the demoiselles empathetically: they seem to me at once to demonstrate and to withdraw from patriarchal stereotypes of femininity, as if in an act of noncooperative cooperation. These women—who are Picasso's fictions no doubt, but fictions founded on his observations of actual disgruntled women and prostitutes—these women can be had, of course, but on another level they are not for the having, and that puts the client-viewer in a position of nerve-wracking uncertainty; of not knowing what lies behind the mask. For women, meanwhile, the price of this strategy is a profound sense of alienation, insofar as "the masquerade . . . is what women do . . . in order to participate in man's desire, but at the cost of giving up [their own]."[19]

A different kind of masquerade, an act not only of mimicry but of minstrelsy is figured by the two boisterous women on the right-hand side of the picture, where Picasso caricatured sacred African masks and employed them in a brazenly disrespectful way.[20] Mimicry is an act of appropriation and "one of the most elusive and effective strategies of colonial power and knowledge," observes Homi Bhabha, adding, "mimicry is at once resemblance and menace."[21] These demoiselles offend me, then—and yet, I confess, they attract me too: not because their outrageous headgear pokes fun at Africans but because it makes fun of the prostitutes' clients, despoiling their sexual appetites. In the boldly squatting figure at the lower right—with her backside turned as if she were "mooning" the johns, while her mask is swiveled forward to terrify them—and in the energy of the woman barging through the curtains above her, I see bodies that educe comparatively natural and confident postures. And I identify with these disruptive figures, who impetuously signal their clientele to get lost, while damning the consequences.

In other critics' accounts, the demoiselles in Africanesque masks have never figured in any way as sympathetic, but only as repellent—indeed as by far the most repellent of all five women, who are generally viewed as disease-ridden harpies. The demoiselles appear not hideous or sickly to me, however, but plain and strong. Their exaggerated, stylized features render them somewhat comical—a bit like the simple figures in the "Little Jimmy" cartoons that Picasso loved at the time he painted this picture—but no more ugly than the artist himself appeared in self-portraits of this period, similarly stylized images that critics do not call grotesque.[22] True, the demoiselles are thick-limbed, angular, and broad-featured, a physiologic type associated with laborers' stock, but Picasso also had a stocky body and critics hardly find it gross.

To my eye, the unmasked faces of the three figures on the left side of the picture suggest not syphilitic monsters but the glazed-over visages of hard-worn pros. The two women at the picture's center appear to direct a jaundiced gaze toward the unending parade of men before them. The woman farthest to the left, the most covered and stiffly restrained of the figures, seems especially businesslike; she evokes a madam holding open the drapery for the patrons' sake while keeping a steady eye on her charges. (I note that her two hands and one of her feet are visible, moreover, whereas, among the other four women, only a single hand and no feet were depicted: thus Picasso symbolically disabled those figures.) Together, the demoiselles might recall the prostitutes and madams in Brassaï's later photographs—unashamed, competent, solid, and tough-looking women trapped in miserable circumstances.

If being the same sex as the demoiselles, the second sex, puts me at a disadvantage in front of this picture, it entails some advantage too—a moral advantage over the men who are supposed to be standing where I stand, men who would readily exploit fellow human beings in this vile way. Instead of letting me bathe in a sense of innocence, however, the picture brings me also a guilty thrill at gaining this close-up view of a tawdry ritual that men ordinarily perform well removed from the curious and censorious gaze of women such as myself. That sense of my anomalousness at the scene of this impending transaction underlines the separation between the demoiselles and myself, driving home the fact that prostitutes were and are far more vulnerable than I. Yet the demoiselles are not, after all, the streetwalkers who are most often the targets of psychopathic Jack the Rippers and Joel Rifkinds; they reside in a brothel under state-regulated conditions,[23] and they appear to me quite unafraid. The terror in this situation has appertained instead, for reasons I shall explore, to the male viewing public.

By no means would I wish to argue that there has been a uniform and univocal response to *Les Demoiselles d'Avignon* among its male audience. Yet I can state that something like a prototypical male response to the picture has emerged, particularly in treatments of it over the last three decades—a response centering on the awfulness and fearsomeness of the depicted prostitutes. Given that prostitution originated and ex-

ists precisely to fulfill male desires, how are we to account for the unmitigated dearth of pleasure expressed by male viewers of the painting? So gripped by anxiety has the (prototypical) male viewer been that he has failed to anticipate any gratification the demoiselles' nude bodies might augur. As Charles Bernheimer portrays him, this viewer quails before the spectacle of women who embody "his worst fears of their atavistic primitivism, animalistic destructiveness, and cold, impersonal eroticism."[24] Such feelings of "deep-seated fear and loathing of the female body" are often attributed equally to the picture's author. And William Rubin comments that such attitudes are "commonplace in male psychology" in any case, so that Picasso's great achievement in *Les Demoiselles* was to make this syndrome emerge as "a new insight—all the more universal for being so commonplace."[25]

That contempt for women is integral to normal male psychology was suggested, predictably, by Freud; noting the prevalence of men's "desire to depreciate" women, he observed that "the curb put upon love by civilization involves a universal [read: male] tendency to debase sexual objects."[26] In this light, we might note the critics' penchant for describing the women Picasso depicted not simply as prostitutes, but as whores, sluts, harlots, strumpets, trollops, and doxies (to take Steinberg's lexicon) or as "a species of bitch goddess" whose bodies "may not even deserve the name human" (as Kozloff calls them).[27] That the psychological mainspring of the response to *Les Demoiselles* has been more contempt and fear than desire surely stems in no small part from the fact that viewers find themselves exposed not to just any brothel, moreover, but to a "brothel reverting to jungle"—one inhabited by more or less exotic-looking women.[28]

Inasmuch as they figure the exotic, the demoiselles' bodies are doubly branded as sexual, for historically the exotic—or, more specifically, the African and the so-called Oriental woman—has often been conflated with the erotic in the European imagination.[29] The prostitute functions too, of course, as evidence of an excess of sexuality. And by the turn of the century, as Western women generally chafed at the bit for more freedom of movement, the "conjunction" of women and the city epitomized by the prostitute "suggest[ed] the potential of an intolerable and dangerous sexuality, a sexuality which is out of bounds precisely as a result of the woman's revised relation to space, her new ability to 'wander' (and hence to 'err')."[30] Fear of the prostitute spilled over into anxiety about the sexual continence of all women, anxiety about distinguishing decent women from indecent ones, and concern that the former may yet vanish.[31]

In the view of some astute observers of modern life, including most notably Walter Benjamin, the prostitute would emerge as a key figure of urban modernity. With the flourishing of capitalism came the ascent of the commodity, and in the prostitute's collapsing of the distinction between the merchandise and the merchant we find (as Benjamin said) the very apotheosis of the commodity.[32] The prostitute could be identified with and blamed for not only the encroaching commodification, the growing coldness or superficiality of social relations, but the very "decline of love" itself.[33] Where images of nude women once stood as tokens of plenitude and joy, pictures of nude prostitutes would stand instead as the specters of a society that no longer makes room for joy or love unless they can be bought and sold. From one feminist perspective then, these figures raise the question: "Does pleasure, for masculine sexuality, consist in anything other than the appropriation of nature, in the desire to make it (re)produce, and in exchanges of its/these products with other members of society? An essentially *economic* pleasure."[34]

In her connection to a peculiarly modern and virulent form of social plague, then, the prostitute made a specially fitting emblem of modernity—which should help explain why *Les Demoiselles d'Avignon* has been singled out as the very "paradigm of all modern art." But such accounts of the prostitute's moment do not explain why this *specific* painting attained a unique prominence surpassing that of, say,

Olympia. After all, since *Olympia* debuted in the Salon and passed after Manet's death into the collection of the state, it could and did serve as a continuing reference point for critics and other artists, whereas for several decades after Picasso completed *Les Demoiselles*, it remained largely unseen and unmentioned.

What made Picasso's painting initially seem less suited for public display than for the studio was that, in deploying disparate visual idioms to render different physiognomic types, he left the work in a disjunctive state, such that historians debated for some time whether it was actually finished. If the disintegration of the great traditions of painting could already be detected in *Olympia*, the evidence of that decrepitude was plainly that much further advanced in *Les Demoiselles*. And insofar as it calls the very notion of a unified style, and so the possibility of finish, into question, the painting's ruptured aspect made it serve the purpose of signifying a moment of rupture particularly well. The evolution of Cubism was impelled by a realization of "the conventional rather than the imitative nature of representation," as Christine Poggi succinctly phrases it; and a corollary of that realization was "that style can be a kind of mask, to be worn at will," so that "there was no reason to observe the law of unity"—an insight clearly at work in *Les Demoiselles d'Avignon*.[35]

On another plane, what separates *Les Demoiselles* from *Olympia* are matters of class and race. Critics saw both Picasso's and Manet's prostitutes as working-class women, owing to their compact muscularity and the perceived coarseness of their features.[36] The superior station of Manet's prostitute is evident, however, from her sumptuous accessories and surroundings; it emerges, too, from the fact that she is quite alone but for the black maid, whose servitude establishes the existence of an underclass compared with which the courtesan enjoys an elevated social standing. By contrast, Picasso's subjects are humble brothel denizens, women who would have been on call, if not always on their feet, from noon until three o'clock in the morning, available to any passerby with a modicum of disposable income (on a busy day they might

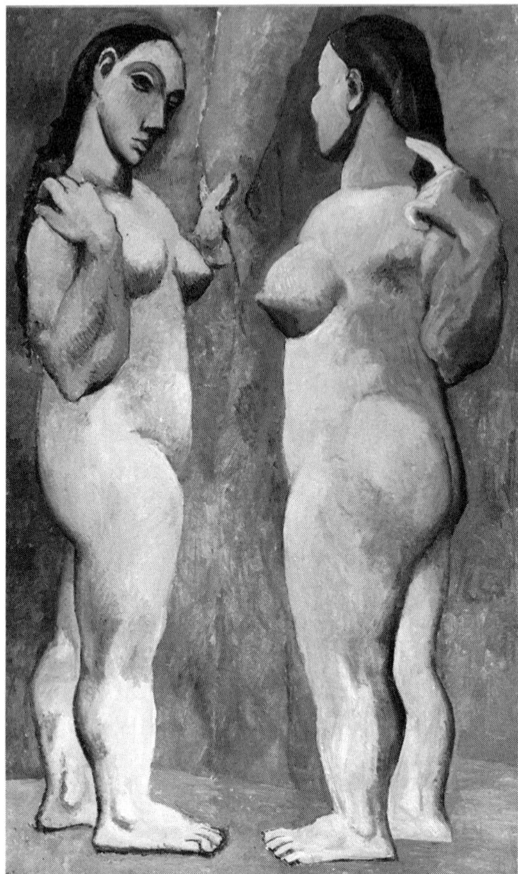

Figure 15.2. Pablo Picasso, *Two Nudes*, 1906. Oil on canvas. The Museum of Modern Art, New York. Gift of G. David Thompson in honor of Alfred H. Barr, Jr. © 2005 Estate of Pablo Picasso/Artists Rights Society (ARS), New York. (Digital image © The Museum of Modern Art/Licensed by SCALA/Art Resource, New York.)

have serviced from sixteen to twenty-five men each, while the courtesan limited her sessions to pre-arranged and costly assignations).[37] Far from having dark-skinned servants to wait upon them, the demoiselles are themselves arguably in a position of some servitude to the woman at the left; and the African-esque masks worn by two of them symbolically elide the distinction, and so the expected discrepancy in social status, between a white woman and a woman of

color. Whereas Manet's picture presumed the viewer to be of the haute bourgeoisie, Picasso's demoted him socially, implying that he procured his sexual goods at the equivalent of, say, K-Mart and not Saks Fifth Avenue; and there were larger signs of social slippage in the implication that the prospective public for a major artwork would be not the elite but the hoi polloi.

Among other, more evident changes, a certain downward mobility might be detected in Picasso's images of women in the period immediately preceding *Les Demoiselles*. In 1906, the artist passed from the wan, Italianate nudes of his Rose period to some bloated, marmoreal, but still classicized figures. In *Two Nudes* of that year (fig. 15.2), the figures face one another, replicate one another, so that almost the entirety of a nude female form is made available to the gaze. The figures' groins are discreetly angled out of view, however, and as with most of Picasso's painted female nudes up to this point, their legs are close together, sealing off their crotches. At the same time, the women peel apart a curtain behind them, opening a space in the pinkish-brown field that might be said to function abstractly as a displaced vagina or transposed female sexual space.[38] In a way, the picture thus subtly demonstrates what Picasso illustrated more literally in a drawing of around 1901 (fig. 15.3): the conventional identity of the body of a woman with the body of the paper or canvas—that space pliantly available to the probing of the painter's phallic pen or brush.

Conventionally, both the act of painting and that of viewing have been described as phallic acts, acts of penetration performed on that passive receptacle, the blank field of the canvas.[39] "I paint with my prick," Renoir supposedly boasted; "A painter has also to paint 'with [his] balls,'" bragged Picasso to his mistress, the painter Françoise Gilot. "I guess that even if a painter fucks a picture to a real climax once a year, it is quite a record," Mark Rothko later estimated. And the critic Jean Clair once pithily proclaimed, "The gaze is the erection of the eye."[40] Such metaphors and the general conceit of penetration as a trope for knowing implicitly exclude the fe-

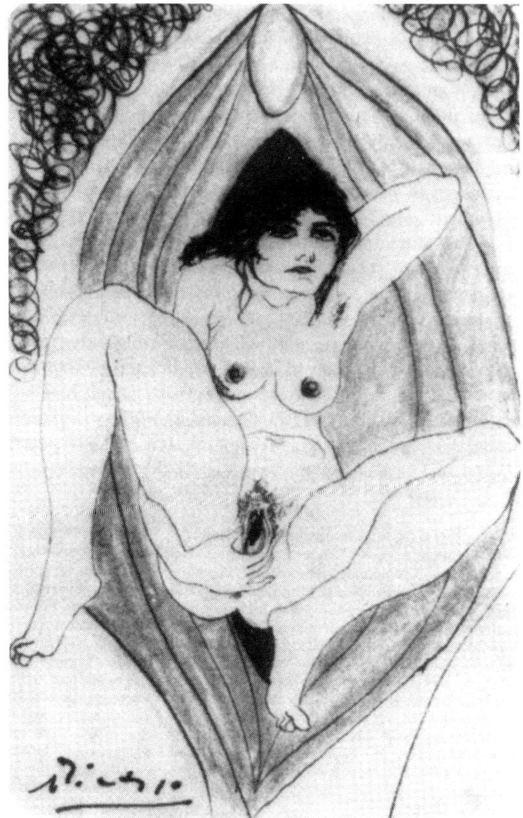

Figure 15.3. Pablo Picasso, *Environnement vaginale*, ca. 1901. Drawing. Private collection. © 2005 Estate of Pablo Picasso/ Artists Rights Society (ARS), New York.

male artist and viewer, of course. But in a less obvious way, these metaphors also exclude the artist and the viewer of color, for dark-skinned peoples of both genders have long been grouped with the feminine as objects for penetration, objects not knowing but subject to being discovered and known. James Olney refers to the colonialist "perception of the [African] countryside as an immense vagina," while Christopher Miller calls the African continent a "blank slate" endlessly inscribed with colonialist desires and fears.[41] These various images converge, for example, in Kandinsky's suggestive recollection of how he mastered his craft:

I learned to battle with the canvas, to come to know it as a being resisting my wish (= dream), and to bend it forcibly to this wish. At first it stands there like a pure chaste virgin with clear eye and heavenly joy. . . . And then comes the willful brush which first here, then there, gradually conquers it with all the energy peculiar to it, like a European colonist, who pushes into the wild virgin nature, hitherto untouched, using axe, spade, hammer, and saw to shape it to his wishes.[42]

Deferring the matter of race for the moment, I wish to pursue another question at this juncture— one that may facilitate a much-needed feminist analysis of Cubism more generally—and that is what the phenomenon of the vaunted new "Cubist space" signified in gendered terms. To this end, I must underline the phallicism endemic to the dialectics of penetration routinely deployed in descriptions of pictorial space and the operations of spectatorship. The type of space that *Les Demoiselles d'Avignon* inaugurated or, rather, prognosticated is a shallow space where voids seal over, becoming solid, while solids flatten and fragment. In Cubist space, movement transpires mostly laterally, through the mechanisms of passage, over borders broken down (perhaps under the pressure—to judge by the evidence of the stranger-looking demoiselles—of foreign influence). How are we to understand this sealing off of that deep pictorial space that had for so long been identified with the feminine sexual body; and how are we to understand the disintegration of those penetrant masses that are readily identified with a masculine sexual presence?[43] ("The radical quality of *Les Demoiselles* lies, above all, in its *threat* to the integrity of mass as distinct from space," Rosenblum declared; and other critics have used comparable phrases.)[44]

One could argue that the space in full-fledged Analytic Cubist paintings is penetrable to a slight degree, but only at the viewer's peril owing to the pictures' shattered aspect; or one could say that a painting such as *Ma Jolie (Woman with a Zither or Guitar)* of 1911–12 (fig. 15.4) is effectively impenetrable and that, in ei-

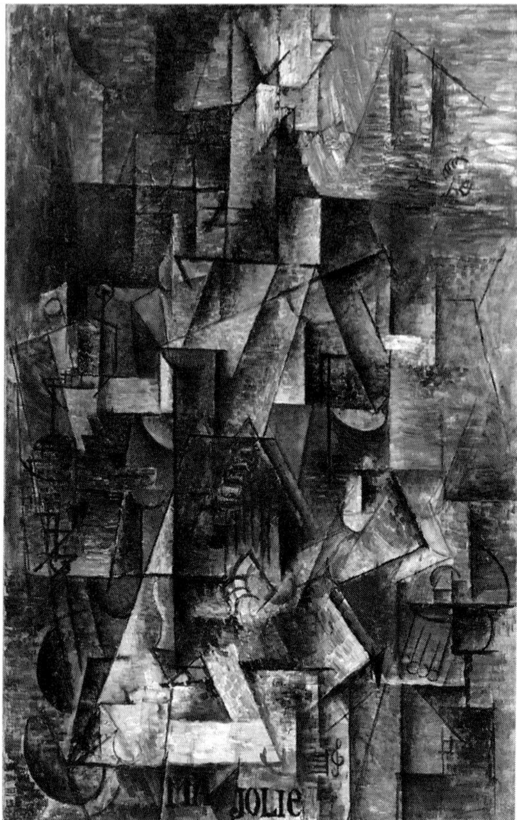

Figure 15.4. Pablo Picasso, *Ma Jolie (Woman with a Zither or Guitar)*, 1911–12. Oil on canvas. The Museum of Modern Art, New York. Acquired through the Lillie P. Bliss Bequest. © 2005 Estate of Pablo Picasso/Artists Rights Society (ARS), New York. (Digital image © The Museum of Modern Art/Licensed by SCALA/Art Resource, New York.)

ther case, this sealing over of the pictorial space has a subtly emasculating or dephallicizing effect on the male viewer. If his penetrant member no longer functions as a passkey to the world of knowledge, with its keyholes newly obstructed, he must prepare to apprehend pictures—and perhaps not pictures alone— in another way.

Some Cubist paintings do allude, obliquely and teasingly, to the canvas as a female sexual space. But they do so with a new focus on female self-penetration, which renders the male organ extraneous. In *Girl with a Mandolin (Fanny Tellier)* of 1910 (fig. 15.5), the nude woman's torso visually echoes the body of an instrument that is (also) at once volume and void, while her hand's placement at the rim of the sound hole carries a mild autoerotic suggestion. In *Ma Jolie*, by contrast, the woman's body melds with the body of the instrument, while both are shattered to the point that the viewer cannot distinguish mass from void. If the canvas remains in any sense a female space, it is no longer a fully available or penetrable one. Rosalind Krauss thus pinpoints *Girl with a Mandolin* as the moment when Picasso "watched depth and touch—what we would call the carnal dimensions—disappear, quite literally from sight."[45]

Picasso's move to seal off the canvas from the penetrating movement of the viewer could be construed as an attempt to protect that viewer from what he had come to perceive as the horrors of the space the canvas once opened up. In 1912, as he began the process of building up forms materially on top of the canvas—in a further move away from opening up spaces behind the picture's surface—he crowed to Braque, "I am in the process of conceiving a guitar and I use a little dust against our horrible canvas."[46] Why the canvas had become horrible in Picasso's sight is the question—though a further question is whether it was more a matter of an artist contriving to be rid of pictorial holes that had become repugnant to him, or whether those holes had, in a sense, already sealed themselves off insofar as artists had been progressively disusing the potentially deep space of the canvas since the latter part of the nineteenth century.[47]

The phenomenon of the gradual and inexorable flattening of pictorial space in the evolution of modernist art has been variously explained. Long established was Clement Greenberg's formalist delineation of an ongoing consolidation of the means unique to each art medium, such that painting (for one) would increasingly reveal its fundamental two-dimensionality. More recently, T. J. Clark has compellingly argued that the shallowing of the picture space may be associated with a shallowing or depleting of the full texture of human experience under capitalism. But neither rationale quite accounts for the utter loathing

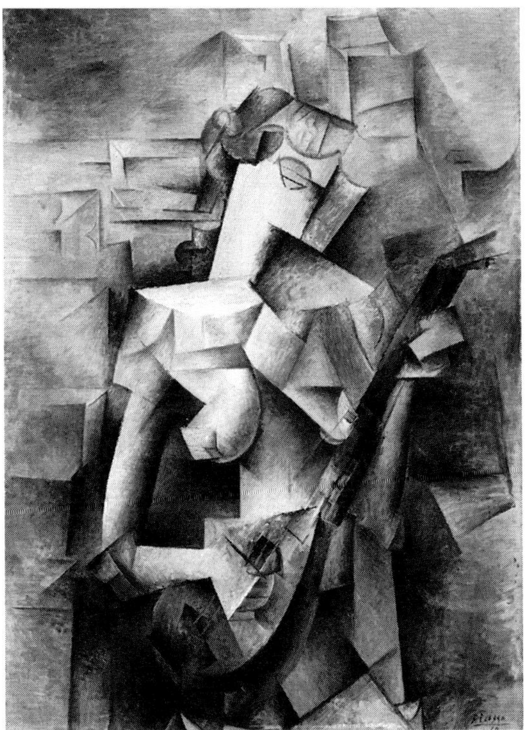

Figure 15.5. Pablo Picasso, *Girl with a Mandolin (Fanny Tellier)*, 1910. Oil on canvas. The Museum of Modern Art, New York. Nelson A. Rockefeller Bequest. © 2005 Estate of Pablo Picasso/ Artists Rights Society (ARS), New York. (Digital image © The Museum of Modern Art/Licensed by SCALA/Art Resource, New York.)

of holes expressed by numerous modernists. I would argue that that element of horror might best be understood in relation to deep-seated and pervasive fears of the feminine body,[48] or (in Freud's formulation) of the "dark continent" more broadly. That horror corresponds, in other words, to what some feminists have diagnosed as a crisis of masculinity brewing in the West by and after the turn of the century, as women and peoples of color increasingly made felt not merely their presence, but also their discontent with their inferiorized and subjugated status. The white male's privileged position was thus threatened by increasing claims for political and social autonomy on the part of European women, and by an influx of intriguing artifacts (such as African masks) that

testified to the existence of impressive though alien visions and values in colonized societies at once derided and admired as "primitive."

To return to *Les Demoiselles d'Avignon*, then: the picture evidences not a full-fledged, almost fully flattened Cubist space, but "depth under stress," as Steinberg aptly put it. "This is an interior space in compression like the inside of pleated bellows, like the feel of an inhabited pocket, a contracting sheath heated by the massed human presence," Steinberg continued, framing the experience of viewing the work almost luridly as an act of coitus. The "very subject [of *Les Demoiselles*] is a connection—a passage from out here inward into the body of the representation," he averred; "Our vision heaves in and out" in "a similitude of sexual energy," as the painting offers us "an interior apprehended on the model of touch and stretch, a nest known by palpation, or by reaching and rolling, by extending one's self with it." Steinberg likewise constructed Picasso's experience in painting the picture as a simulacrum of coitus: the artist, here a Nietzschean figure, "wanted the orgiastic immersion and the Dionysian release," so that "one insistent theme" of *Les Demoiselles* is "the spasmodic action, the explosive release in a constricted space, and the reciprocity of engulfment and penetration."[49]

If *Les Demoiselles* provides a metaphorical sex act for the presumedly heterosexual male viewer, then it may well be the sex act to end all sex acts, an experience too awful to risk repeating. "Doesn't [the prostitutes'] shattering gaze rid us of any desire to enter into the picture's space?" queries Yve-Alain Bois.[50] That the prospective act of coitus in question might be a treacherous one emerges also from Steinberg's account: *Les Demoiselles* "declares that if you wholly accept and undergo the esthetic experience, if you let it engulf and 'frighten' you . . . then you become an insider. It is in the contagion of art that . . . the distinction between outsider and insider falls away. Not every picture is capable of such overriding contagion."[51] Though he used the term "contagion" metaphorically here, elsewhere Steinberg and others have tied the daunting aspect of *Les Demoiselles* and the anger toward women it evinces to Picasso's alleged experience with a sexually transmitted disease. What has helped to frighten some critics, then, is the same (fantasized) prospect of being infected by the demoiselles with an illness that spells at best a chronic nuisance, at worst a slow and grisly death.[52] (To my own eye, the demoiselles do not appear unwell, let alone syphilitic, but my disinclination as a straight female to patronize them immunizes me in any case from the possibility of contracting a disease.)

"Right from the first sketches," *Les Demoiselles* was really a projection of Picasso's "complex and contradictory feelings about women," Rubin asserts, while Bois explains the artist's production of the painting in terms of his rampant castration anxiety: "The Medusa (castration) metaphor . . . best accounts for . . . the apotropaic brutality of the finished picture."[53] Like the Oedipal narrative, the Medusa narrative can indeed be mapped onto many acts of cultural production; but such exercises too often lead in circles, explaining a certain masculinist vision of sexuality by a like vision of sexuality in a way that inevitably debases women. In sustaining a focus on the artist's vulnerable psyche, moreover, we may lose sight of the social ramifications of his acts. If we wish to pursue the hoary tale of castration with the idea of moving in a new direction—one with a view to social and historical realities as well as psychological ones[54]—we might turn our attention to the two figures at the center of the picture with their arms raised in the pose of the Venus Anadyomene.

An image of Venus born of the sea foam, standing and wringing water from her hair was a topos of history painting in the late nineteenth century, realized by Ingres among others.[55] Unsurprisingly, what was not depicted was how the foam that sired the glorious goddess of love flowed from the severed genitals of Uranus, who had been castrated by his son Cronus in revenge for having been jettisoned into the underworld (along with Uranus's other sons, the Titans—the first human race). A buried subtext of *Les Demoiselles d'Avignon*, then, is the story of a woman coming to power at the expense of a patriarch whose authority was unexpectedly and irretrievably revoked. From a masculinist vantage point, this is certainly a horror story, but from a feminist one it could be, to the contrary, a fable or even a good omen of vengeance won against male tyranny.

Although the female body figures in male fantasy as mapped by Freud as a castrated body, it is not thereby simply a figure of impotence; rather, the woman's putative "wound" becomes invested "with such intense negative cathexes that the castrated woman becomes phallic through her association with this powerful fantasmatic energy."[56] As Steinberg and others see them, Picasso's demoiselles are eminently phallic: the prostitute second from left "arrives like a projectile," the one in the center is "a pillar nude," the crouching figure at the right evokes "a jumping jack," and all the women "start up like jerked puppets."[57] To construct the female figure as a phallus is, in Freudian terms, a fetishistic strategy, a gesture at once of recognition and disavowal of the alarming fact that women have no penises. Numerous critics have framed Picasso's act in creating *Les Demoiselles* in related terms, as a self-ministering ploy to exorcise his private "demons," his fear of women and others. "My first exorcism-painting," the artist once called the picture, in an oft-quoted statement.[58]

Picasso's irrational fears would not, of course, die with Picasso. For the past three decades, critics have repeatedly explored and, it seems, empathetically reexperienced the artist's fears while discounting the more justified pain of those his art would exorcise, namely his declared "enemy," women, and his undeclared enemy, peoples of color—whom he erased or diminished in other ways, by denying the influence of their visual culture on his work. "*L'art nègre?* Never heard of it," Picasso reportedly snapped at an interviewer interested in the impact of tribal art on his work. By World War II—that is, at the moment *Les Demoiselles* first emerged into the limelight by entering the collection of the Museum of Modern Art in New York—Picasso was routinely denying that he had been affected by tribal art in composing *Les*

Demoiselles, claims that were until not long ago parroted by historians. In fact, he had seen "examples of *art nègre* here and there for at least six months before he absorbed it into the fabric of the *Demoiselles*," argued Rubin in 1983.[59] It is now a commonplace of the art-historical literature, however, that "'primitive' artefacts were invested with value at the same time as—or even *after*—similar technical innovations appeared within Western art practices" in a phenomenon of sheerly coincidental cultural convergence.[60] Comments Michele Wallace sharply, "Black artists and intellectuals widely assume that a white world is simply unable to admit that art from Africa and elsewhere in the third world had a direct and profound influence on Western art because of an absolutely uncontrollable racism, xenophobia and ethnocentrism."[61]

What is symptomatized by *Les Demoiselles d'Avignon* and by its reception, and symptomatized (more abstractly and indirectly) by the shallowed space of the Cubist canvas, is a fear that spirals through Western society from the late nineteenth century to the present: the fear of women and outsiders, including peoples of color, usurping masculine roles and Western prerogatives, assuming agency. In other words, a fear of the loss of male hegemony together with a fear of the loss of hegemony of the West are at issue in *Les Demoiselles*, so that the painting may be read as a gesture of "recognition and disavowal . . . of the fact that the west—its patriarchal subject and socius—is threatened by loss, by lack, by others," as Hal Foster astutely observes.[62]

If *Les Demoiselles d'Avignon* has functioned historiographically as the preeminent modern site where shifts in the dominant visual order took place, it has held that position not simply because it announced the advent of Cubism, or because it featured prostitutes, those allegorical figures of the modern, but because those prostitutes' physiognomies are more or less foreign-looking, ranging (from left to right) from stylized Egyptian and Iberian to caricatured African types. The hidden shoal on which the ship of mimetic Mediterranean visual ideals is widely said to have foundered is not just the body of a debauched woman, but that of an exotic and debauched woman. And the rhetoric critics used to describe that body (while trying to capture the spirit of Picasso's visual rhetoric) at times seems to betray a fear of the decline of the West spelled by the breaching of Western borders by others—an irrational fear, of course, since Westerners had invaded other continents and not the reverse. A term such as *decivilizing*, for instance, applied to the demoiselles, resonates with an echo of the vocabulary of that colonialist discourse which underpinned sweeping and draconian policies wherein "the other is there only to be reappropriated, recaptured, and destroyed as other," as Hélène Cixous phrases it.[63]

Although the women in *Les Demoiselles d'Avignon* are all light-skinned, critics often differentiate the two with African-looking masks as distinctly ugly, bestial, and dirty or contagion-ridden—that is, with all the scathing stereotypes that have so long dogged dark-skinned peoples. To Western eyes, the African art that engaged Picasso appears "unbearably ugly," pronounces Rosenblum.[64] Rubin refers to "the monstrously distorted heads of the two *whores* on the right," contrasting them with "the comparatively gracious 'Iberian' *courtesans* in the center."[65] And in the view of Rubin and Bernheimer both, *Les Demoiselles* effectively illustrates "the very process of atavistic regression, from the 'normal' heads of the two central figures through the dark metamorphosis of the woman on the left, to the Africanized masks and twisted, disordered anatomies of the two right-hand figures." The painting thus betrays "a fantasy about the active presence in woman's sexual nature of her dark, primitive, degenerate, perhaps diseased biological origins."[66] Frances Frascina actually compares African masks that bear some relation to those concocted by Picasso with medical photographs of figures horribly deformed by the effects of syphilis, claiming (quite unconvincingly, to my eye) that there are similarities between them.[67] Observes Bhabha sagely: "Black skin splits under the racist gaze, displaced into signs of bestiality, genitalia, grotesquerie, which reveal the phobic myth of the undifferentiated whole white body."[68]

The subtext to all these texts on the relation of the more European-looking figures to the two figures in Africanesque masks is a narrative of regression: of normality regressing into deviancy, of well-being degenerating into disease, and of contained eroticism lapsing into raw animality. In this light, I must note that in numerous critics' eyes, the two women whom I describe as wearing African-looking masks do not wear masks at all, but are hybrid creatures instead. (What might justify this reading is the striated, greenish shading on the breast of the figure at the upper right, which echoes the green stripes on her face or mask, though I would maintain that the disjunction between these figures' heads and their bodies is otherwise so marked as to invite us to see them as wearing masks.) That these white women might be metamorphosing into "jungle-nosed nudes" is a cause for terror (as parallel scenarios of humans turning into insects or monsters in later horror movies would be) because mongrels are viewed as impure, degenerate, and corrupting—the notion that indigenous populations are degenerate and savage having been indispensable, of course, to the rationale for colonizing them. What looms in *Les Demoiselles* also is what Mary Ann Doane identifies as "a strong fear that white women are always on the verge of 'slipping back' into a blackness comparable to prostitution. The white woman would be the weak point in the system, the signifier of the always too tenuous hold of civilization."[69]

The identification of the European woman with the figure of the primitive, played out in *Les Demoiselles d'Avignon*, is a familiar one, encapsulated by Freud's allusion to white women as the "dark continent." Freud associated white female sexuality with the sexuality of "races at a low level of civilization," where (as with children) sexuality is allowed "free rein" in a course held to account for the putative evidence of diminished cultural achievement among these populations.[70] In colonialist fantasies, then, the notion of the dark continent "contains the submerged

fear of falling out of the light, down the long coal chute of social and moral regression," as Patrick Brantlinger phrased it, and that

> fear of backsliding has a powerful sexual dimension. . . . In European writings about Africa, [Dominique] Mannoni says, "the savage . . . is identified in the unconscious with a certain image of the instincts. . . . And civilized man is painfully divided between the desire to 'correct' the 'errors' of the savages and the desire to identify himself with them in his search for some lost paradise (a desire which at once casts doubt upon the merit of the very civilization he is trying to transmit to them)."[71]

Like Gauguin, Matisse, and many other modernists, for a time Picasso hoped to pioneer a new vision by looking to a new place, far from Europe. While Matisse would contrive a safe, masculinist utopia or pornotopia set in a France magically refashioned as an Orientalist white North Africa, however, Picasso composed a dangerous, masculinist dystopia set in a Paris abruptly invaded by elements of black Africa. "As the Orientalist dream dies, the surprise is to find Africa within the self," notes Miller, and that surprise was an unpleasant one, for "Africanist discourse is at the least an *unhappy* Orientalism, a discourse of desire unfulfilled and unfulfillable."[72]

From a certain perspective, both Matisse's paradise and Picasso's hell might qualify as regressive visions. But to some, the specter of affluent white men not getting what they wanted or, as it were, getting more than they bargained for from the women and dark-skinned peoples they exploited is at least more heartening than seeing those same men's desires indulged. Traditionally, art-historical narratives construe both Picasso's and Matisse's projects as progressive, of course, on the understanding that the artists' recourse to cultures their own society had deemed primitive implied a critique of that (parent) society's values.[73] Had *Les Demoiselles* been prominently exhibited and discussed in the years after it was painted, it might conceivably have had that impact, so shocked was the reaction to the picture among the small audience it reached. But the painting was effectively suppressed until such time as the potential for critique represented by the "primitive" had been "contravened, absorbed within the body of modern art," so that, from the moment it became the object of sustained attention, *Les Demoiselles* could be vaunted as the greatest achievement of the world's greatest modern artist.[74]

Surely *Les Demoiselles d'Avignon* could never have enjoyed the phenomenal celebrity it has if it did not function in some ways to confirm prevailing social biases. By the time the great icon's retrogressive implications had at last begun to emerge to view, however,[75] its pivotal standing was already subject to question. If the picture's great stature has ostensibly remained undiminished—witness the major homage organized by the Musée Picasso—its position has become increasingly, oddly isolated. As analyses of Cubist practice have recently (and for good reason) shifted to semiologic models that better suit more abstract idioms than Picasso was yet prepared to deploy in 1907, the status of *Les Demoiselles* has become a somewhat separate matter.[76] The move toward isolating the picture well anticipated this methodological shift, however. And I suspect a contributing, though doubtless subliminal, factor in the severing of *Les Demoiselles* from that Cubist corpus it was once said to engender—namely an impulse to, in a sense, quarantine the painting's notoriously "contagion"-ridden body.

Les Demoiselles d'Avignon was hailed as the first Cubist painting during a period when its subject matter was scarcely mentioned.[77] Until the picture's theme became an explicit focus of interest—owing to Steinberg's groundbreaking essay of 1972—the "young ladies" of Avignon enjoyed an exalted status as the virtual mothers of modernist painting. But once they were openly fingered as whores who merely hid behind the flimsy curtain of a euphemistic title,[78] the demoiselles would be sternly and painstakingly stripped of their maternal status.[79] Not only are prostitutes conventionally thought to be barren, but what children they do bear must be of uncertain parentage; and Cubism could not be tainted as an illegitimate production. Worse yet that Cubism should be exposed as a black bastard; yet of the five demoiselles, critics had pinpointed above all the Africanized nudes as the site of Cubism's birth. Steinberg referred to "the intruding savage, deeply recessed, trapped in the cleft of a curtain whose collapsing pleats simulate an impenetrable solidification of space—the famous birthplace of Cubism," while Kahnweiler isolated the figure at the lower right, with her legs spread wide as they would be in giving birth, as "the beginning of Cubism, the first upsurge."[80] No doubt the right-hand side of the painting, which Picasso finished last, is the more innovative part, but that these specific figures should have been isolated as *the* crucial site on *the* crucial site of origin for modernist painting also betrays a Western habit of symbolically pressing Africa into service as the originary realm, together with the habit of leveling the image of Africa into that of an ever penetrable, yet ever unknowable, feminine body.

When we first spy the crouching woman at the lower right of *Les Demoiselles*, our attention is arrested by the frontally poised, vividly drawn, Africanesque mask that serves as her face, and as our gaze travels downward, we expect to find that her whole body faces us with the genitals lewdly exposed between her boldly spread legs (a vision the artist initially considered, as sketches show).[81] But Picasso elected instead to tease us, turning the woman's back to us so that her sexual organs are suppressed, while her mask might be seen (on second thought) as covering the back of her head. Picasso's gesture of withdrawing what he had seemed to promise—a graphic view of the taboo area of the labia and vagina—must be viewed in light of the subsequent sealing-off of pictorial space that Cubism effected. On the one hand, we could construe that shallow Cubist space as implementing metaphorically a wishful recovery of the hymen so as to render the feminine body of the canvas intact, in a sense presexual, and so unthreatening. But sealed female genitalia may also connote what has been regarded as deviant feminine sexuality, that is, lesbianism or barrenness, both of which were associated with the prostitutes' sub-culture (as virginity, needless to say, was not). Numerous critics discern a masculine quality to some or all of the women in *Les Demoiselles d'Avignon*, pointing to their sometimes flattened breasts—which might evoke the virilized form of the New Woman, as well as certain stereotypes about the lesbian body. To other critics, however, the demoiselles' bodies suggest the hypersexualized figure of the femme fatale. Significantly at issue in both these disparate interpretations is a nonprocreative feminine type.[82]

The figures with African-looking masks, once universally accepted as Cubism's mothers, began to be accorded more complicated and more sinister roles in the early 1970s, then, at a moment when African Americans and women generally in the United States were assuming more aggressive roles, including, for women of every color, that of winning and exercising the right to refuse maternity. No longer cast as the harbingers of a great birth, the figures in Africanesque masks became instead the avatars of a ghastly death. To Rubin, the "'African' faces express more . . . than just the 'barbaric' character of pure sexuality . . . their violence alludes to Woman as Destroyer—vestiges of the Symbolist *femme fatale*."[83]

The figure of the femme fatale articulates "fears surrounding the loss of stability and centrality of the self, the 'I,' the ego. These anxieties appear quite explicitly in the process of her representation as castration anxiety," argues Doane.[84] Owing to what were imagined as the devouring mouths and fathomless depths of their vaginas and uteruses, women have been poetically associated with the vertiginous terrors of the abyss;[85] and in many critics' eyes the demoiselles have spelled precisely the threat of that abyss. Though Picasso did not leave gaping holes in the painting's structure, and though he kept the women's mouths drawn closed and their vaginas occluded from view, there remained a nagging doubt: "What secret reserves of space does that jungle-nosed nude, looking in from backstage, leave behind?" as Steinberg anxiously expressed it.[86]

Just as the female body enfolds certain distinct and vital holes or spaces (which are not, of course, generally scary or fully unknowable to women themselves), women have been associated symbolically with the holes or gaps in the epistemological fabric of the culture—and not women alone. Black Africa has had a parallel status in the Western imagination: the very word *Africa* "is practically synonymous with absence in Western discourse."[87] Because the experience of women and peoples of color has historically been discounted under patriarchy, once the paternal order's epistemological fabric began to shred, those missing threads became the subject of increasing anxiety and interrogation.

The crisis of legitimation associated with the advent of modernity entailed a kind of dethroning of the sovereign white male subject. And "discussion of loss of authority inevitably comes around to women," Alice Jardine aptly notes; "'Woman,' 'the feminine,' and so on have come to signify those *processes* that disrupt symbolic structures in the West."[88] Not only women but also dark-skinned peoples "have traditionally been perceived as figures of disorder, 'potential disrupters of [European] masculine boundary systems of all sorts.'" From the dominant perspective, as Elaine Showalter writes (though with a view only to women), these populations' "social or cultural marginality seems to place them on the borderlines of the symbolic order, both the 'frontier between [white] men and chaos' and dangerously part of chaos itself, inhabitants of a mysterious and frightening wild zone outside of patriarchal culture."[89]

To the majority of critics, in *Les Demoiselles d'Avignon* Picasso conjured an exceedingly compelling vision of just such a wild zone. But on finishing that picture, the artist would soon proceed to calmer territory—by moving for a time toward resisting or suppressing the feminine, the bodily, and the foreign. Thus the Analytic Cubist paintings to follow feature tamely banal motifs: still lifes, landscapes, portraits, and (fewest of all) rather chastely abstract nudes.[90] Museum visitors traversing the galleries of the comprehensive "Pioneering Cubism" exhibition at the Museum of Modern Art in 1989—after having been greeted at the show's entrance by the always galvanizing presence of the demoiselles—might well have wondered: What happened to that flagrant, raw nudity as Cubism developed? What happened to those baldly African elements?

Numerous historians would answer that Picasso "purged himself of these barbaric impulses." Subdued by "the disciplining influence of the French tradition" represented by Cézanne and Braque, he turned away from these profound sources of inspiration—African art and Spanish art—and succumbed to "the classicizing influence of Braque."[91] The result was that the African sources of "high" Cubist art would remain comparatively inevident, and scholars would tend to diminish them in any case, the better to qualify Cubism as a classic art.[92] What has been neglected also is that, in retreating from the jarring content of *Les Demoiselles*, Picasso equally retreated from his own heritage, since he had specifically conceived two of the women as Iberian, and southern Spain—his birthplace—lies closer to Africa than anyplace else in Europe.[93] Later in his life, Picasso liked to say that "cubism is Spanish in origin" and that "it was I who invented cubism."[94] But Braque invented it with him in the wake of the storm caused by *Les Demoiselles*, and Braque had no penchant for the dark, bold, sensual, and tragic dramas of Spanish art or for the aspects of tribal art that so gripped Picasso. Braque "was never at all afraid of [the 'Negro pieces']," marveled Picasso, "because he wasn't affected by what I called 'the whole of it,' . . . everything that surrounds us, everything that is not us—he didn't find all of that hostile."[95]

Another answer to the question of what happened to those big-as-life, bawdy women in the aftermath of *Les Demoiselles* is that they got dissected—first by Picasso and, much later, by a legion of art historians who would probe the painting's innards, examining its gestational process in microscopic, and admittedly intriguing, detail. Such was the impetus behind the sedulous and scrupulous scholarship assembled to accompany the Paris exhibition commemorating the

painting, a show praised for having "brilliantly . . . dissected such a point of origin"[96]—or, in a manner of speaking, for performing a successful autopsy on the former prostitute-mothers of modernist painting. (Historically, prostitutes had been the object of dissection in literal ways as well, "for the corpses of destitute prostitutes often served for anatomical dissection, thereby fulfilling the explicit fantasy of numerous nineteenth-century writers to examine female physiology by literally cutting women up.")[97]

As Doane and others have diagnosed it, the urge to plumb the depths of feminine sexuality stemmed from the sense that women harbor a threatening "secret, something which must be aggressively revealed, unmasked, discovered."[98] In this light, the shallow, sealed-off space of Analytic Cubism might be understood to function defensively as a space where almost everything lies on the surface, revealed to view. In its hiddenness, women's interiority was like "the invisibility of nature's interiority . . . threatening precisely because it threatens the balance of power between man and nature, and between men and women," observes the historian of science Evelyn Fox Keller. "To this problem, the culture of modern science has found a truly effective solution. . . . Instead of banishing the Furies underground, out of sight, as did the Greeks, modern science has sought to expose female interiority, to bring it into the light, and thus to dissolve its threat entirely."[99]

Protracted efforts to expose the hidden inner workings of *Les Demoiselles d'Avignon* have not noticeably assuaged the critics' uneasiness, however. The discourse on the picture over the past three decades—since Steinberg substantially redirected the course of discussion—might be said to prove instead its sustained ability to move men to reexperience their deepest anxieties about questions of origins (about the unequaled powers of the mother and the invisibility of the father), to the point where they have hoped to exorcise the "exorcism-painting," to expel it from Cubism's cherished body. Thus, *Les Demoiselles* has gradually assumed the form of a detached preface to a new, improved version of the Greatest

Story Ever Told, which now centers on the relatively de-ethnicized and disembodied corpus of "high" Cubism; for now we are offered a Cubism that commences at ever later dates: in 1908, according to Rubin and as late as 1912 by Bois's account.[100] Though Rubin and Bois continue to insist on *Les Demoiselles'* momentousness, such claims plainly lose some freight once the case is made that the painting did not, in fact, inaugurate Cubism.

Viewers of *Les Demoiselles* have mostly reacted in extreme ways from the very first. An exception was the critic Félix Fénéon, who mildly advised the artist that he really ought to take up caricature.[101] And maybe Fénéon got it right, for *Les Demoiselles* might almost be read as a giant cartoon. What is comical to me are those two mischief-makers in outlandish masks galling their prospective johns as their coworkers coolly take the measure of the (now unnerved) men who dawdle and gawk before them—men as interchangeable as the currency in their wallets, which surely forms their only true appeal. What amuses me no less, however, is the nervous response to this spectacle of feminine effrontery by my fellow historians, for no other modern picture has elicited such widespread and visceral discomfort, mounting at times to a hysterical pitch. For decades, the line of women in *Les Demoiselles* has functioned for many critics like a dreaded dream that will not fade. And the nightmare in question—which these critics think (with reason) is the same bad dream that impelled Picasso to paint the picture—features a file of sturdy, experienced, working women of ambiguous heritage and humble descent, women apparently unimpressed and unbowed by the men who approach them, "women whose independence was clearly menacing," as Pierre Daix describes them.[102] What is humorous, then, is the notion that this dream should rightly petrify us all, while to some of us, of course, such figures— however summarily, distortedly, or abstractly drawn— do not evince aliens, much less monsters: to the contrary, they bear a passing resemblance to ourselves.

Prostitutes and femme fatales admittedly make less than perfect feminist heroines. And white prostitutes sporting goofy pseudo-African masks no doubt make poor heroines for people of African descent: plainly it would be farfetched to construct the demoiselles in heroic terms pure and simple. Doane points out that far from being "the subject of feminism," the femme fatale is rather "a symptom of male fears about feminism"; yet "because she seems to confound power, subjectivity, and agency with the very lack of these attributes, her relevance to feminist discourse is critical."[103] If the demoiselles can never function successfully as models of empowerment, they have nonetheless already functioned effectively as lightning rods for *fear* of the empowerment of women and peoples of color. One story *Les Demoiselles* and its reception teaches is how "a crisis in phallocentric culture was turned into one of its great monuments," as Foster aptly puts it.[104] The sense of crisis or panic that has animated the literature on *Les Demoiselles* and the ongoing efforts to encapsulate the picture in an isolated discursive space prove that it has had some destabilizing or decentering effects on the viewers for whom it was intended. It may, by the same token, be capable of having some more centering effects on the rest of us.

Writing from the position of the so-called exotic woman, perennially subject to the perorations of that "vague entity" Man, who has presumed to speak for all humanity, Trinh T. Minh-ha protests:

> I am profoundly indifferent to his old way of theorizing—of piercing, as he often claims, through the sediments of psychological and epistemological 'depths.' . . . Seeking to perforate meaning by forcing my entry or breaking it open to dissipate what is thought to be its secrets seems to me as crippled an act as verifying the sex of an unborn child by ripping open the mother's womb.[105]

In light of the violence and phallicism of these Western epistemological ideals—of penetrating and dissecting as supreme forms of learning, knowing, and so possessing—the received reading of *Les Demoiselles d'Avignon* as the most apotropaic of all modern

images takes on another valence; for here is a paradoxical case of those most penetrable of all women—
prostitutes—arrayed across that reputedly penetrable
fine-arts vehicle, the canvas, yet being apprehended
widely as the fiercest of warnings *not* to penetrate, but
to stay at a safe, respectful remove.

Those feminists who are leery of further inflating
Picasso's already outsized stature may yet find some
purpose, then, in protecting the iconic status of his
most brazen and motley picture. After all, the viewers this painting specifically addresses—men mostly
used to deriving at the least some basic form of acknowledgment and so reassurance from works of
art—have often found themselves deeply troubled by
Les Demoiselles d'Avignon. What jars them is the
glimpse it seems to afford of a time and circumstance
when the continued primacy, or even viability, of their
habitual modes of perceiving and knowing appear not
merely doubtful, but also distinctly unwelcome.

NOTES

I thank Christine Poggi, Lisa Saltzman, and Lorraine
O'Grady for their comments on earlier versions of
this manuscript.

1. Yve-Alain Bois, "Painting as Trauma," *Art in America* 76, no. 6 (June 1988): 172; John Richardson, *A Life
of Picasso,* vol. 1: *1881–1906* (New York: Random
House, 1991), 475; a phrase of Max Jacob's employed
by Arianna S. Huffington to describe *Les Demoiselles*
(A. S. Huffington, *Picasso: Creator and Destroyer* [New
York: Simon and Schuster, 1988], 93); and Leo Steinberg, "The Philosophical Brothel, Part 1," *Artnews* 71,
no. 5 (September 1972): 20 (Steinberg says that the
painting has come to be regarded in such terms, not
that he himself sees it in that way).

2. Edward F. Fry, *Cubism* (New York: McGraw-Hill,
1966), 12; and Hélène Seckel et al., *Les Demoiselles
d'Avignon,* 2 vols., exh. cat. (Paris: Musée Picasso,
1988).

3. Bois, "Painting as Trauma," 172 n. 14.

4. Cited by Pierre Daix, *Picasso: Life and Art,* trans. O.
Emmet (New York: Icon Editions, 1993), 187. Breton
became a champion of the painting in the 1920s: in

1923 he engineered its (initial) sale, to Jacques Doucet,
and in 1925 he reproduced it in *La Révolution surréa-
liste* (ibid., 69, 252).

5. *Les Demoiselles* was first reproduced in the *Architectural Record* of May 1910. Though it was visible in a
studio photograph published by André Salmon in
1912, it was not properly reproduced in France until
1925 (see note 4 above). The painting was first exhibited by Salmon at the Salon d'Antin in 1916, but it met
"with indifference." In 1939 Alfred Barr acquired it
for the Museum of Modern Art, where it has remained ever since, practically the centerpiece of the
collection. It was not shown again in France until 1953,
when it again "receive[d] very little attention" (Daix,
Picasso, 68–69).

6. Cited in William Rubin, *Picasso and Braque: Pioneering Cubism,* exh. cat. (New York: Museum of Modern Art, 1989), 348. Those openly critical of the picture included Georges Braque, Leo Stein, Guillaume
Apollinaire, Félix Fénéon (ibid., 348, 346), Ambroise
Vollard (Daix, *Picasso,* 79), and the collector Sergei
Shchukin, who appeared at Gertrude Stein's home,
"almost in tears," bemoaning the "loss for French art"
(Gertrude Stein, *Picasso* [New York: Dover, (1938)
1984], 18). Stein supported the picture (Daix, *Picasso,*
79), as did Salmon and Ardengo Soffici (Rubin, *Picasso and Braque,* 348).

7. That this way of narrating the story of modern art
has entailed an overestimation of Picasso at the expense of other modernist pioneers, including some active in centers other than Paris, could easily be, though
it will not be, a subtheme of the present essay.

8. The word is Salmon's, cited in Marilyn McCully, ed.,
*A Picasso Anthology: Documents, Criticism, Reminis-
cences* (London: Thames and Hudson, 1981), 57.

9. Steinberg, "The Philosophical Brothel, 1," 22; Robert
Rosenblum, "The 'Demoiselles d'Avignon' Revisited," *Artnews* 72, no. 4 (April 1973): 45; and Max Kozloff, "Cubism and the Human Comedy," *Artnews* 71,
no. 5 (September 1972): 35. Kozloff does not clarify
whom he regards as the sociopath(s), whether Picasso
(whose "antipathy to his disfigured subjects" is mentioned) or the prostitutes (those "avenging furies of
a new order"), or who would be the victims (ibid.,
38, 37).

10. Salmon's phrase, cited in McCully, ed., *A Picasso Anthology,* 140.

11. The earliest dissenter from the position (promulgated by such authorities as Daniel-Henry Kahnweiler and Alfred Barr) that *Les Demoiselles* was the first Cubist picture was John Golding, who still regarded the picture as "a natural starting-point for the history of Cubism" (John Golding, "The *'Demoiselles d'Avignon,'*" *Burlington Magazine* 100 [1958]: 162–63). Rubin much later took up this point, arguing that the picture "pointed mostly in directions opposite to Cubism's character and structure—although it cleared the path for its development." Further, "none of the earliest references to the *Demoiselles* characterizes it as Cubist; nor did Kahnweiler so qualify it in *'Der Kubismus'* [of 1916]. . . . By 1920, he had apparently changed his mind" (William Rubin, "From Narrative to 'Iconic' in Picasso: The Buried Allegory in Bread and Fruitdish on a Table and the Role of *Les Demoiselles d'Avignon*," *Art Bulletin* 65, no. 4 [1983]: 628, 644). Richardson persists in the view that the picture "established a new pictorial syntax" (Richardson, *A Life* , 475).

12. "From the mid-nineteenth century to the beginning of the twentieth, modernism obsessionally and anxiously displays its innovative desire by fragmenting and disfiguring the female sexual body, epitomized in male fantasy by the prostitute," observes Charles Bernheimer, *Figures of Ill Repute: Representing Prostitution in Nineteenth-Century France* (Cambridge, Mass.: Harvard University Press, 1989), 266. Baudelaire's remark is cited in ibid., 292 n. 51.

13. Teresa de Lauretis, *Alice Doesn't: Feminism, Semiotics, Cinema* (Bloomington: Indiana University Press, 1984), 13. Also, "masculine sexuality and in particular its commercial exchange dominate the works seen as the 'founding mounuments of modern art,'" notes Janet Wolff (who credits Griselda Pollock for this insight); it follows that "the definition of the modern, and the nature of modernism, derived from the experience of men and hence excluded women" (J. Wolff, *Feminine Sentences: Essays on Women and Culture* [Berkeley: University of California Press, 1990], 57, 58).

14. Ronald Johnson, "The 'Demoiselles d'Avignon' and Dionysian Destruction," *Arts*, October 1980, 94; my emphasis.

15. First to remark on the dynamic of exclusion at work in *Les Demoiselles* was Carol Duncan, "The MoMA's Hot Mamas," *Art Journal* 48, no. 2 (Summer 1989): 175–76.

16. A more traditional study of the reception of *Les Demoiselles* may be found in William Rubin, *Les Demoiselles d'Avignon* (New York: Museum of Modern Art, 1994), which was unavailable when the present essay first went to press.

17. Though I do not address the position of the lesbian viewer in this essay, it is an issue worth pursuing, particularly considering that aristocratic lesbian patrons frequented brothels to an extent in turn-of-the-century Paris, and that prostitutes at the better establishments were trained and expected to serve this clientele. See Alain Corbin, *Women for Hire: Prostitution and Sexuality in France after 1850*, trans. A. Sheridan (Cambridge, Mass.: Harvard University Press, 1990), 125.

18. That womanliness and masquerade are in a sense one and the same was initially suggested by the psychoanalyst Joan Riviere (J. Riviere, "Womanliness as a Masquerade" [1929], in *Formations of Fantasy*, ed. Victor Burgin et al. [London: Methuen, 1986], 35–44; see also Stephen Heath, "Joan Riviere and the Masquerade," in ibid., 45–61).

19. Luce Irigaray, cited in ibid., 54.

20. Whether Picasso's intention in giving caricatured African masks to these prostitutes was consciously denigratory or not is a moot point. Patricia Leighten, who was the first to focus on the issue of colonialism in relation to *Les Demoiselles*, has argued strenuously, but I believe unconvincingly, that his gesture was one of fervent solidarity with anticolonial thinking (P. Leighten, "The White Peril and l'Art Nègre: Picasso, Primitivism, and Anticolonialism," *Art Bulletin* 72, no. 4 [1990]: 609–30).

21. Homi Bhabha, "Of Mimicry and Man: The Ambivalence of Colonial Discourse," *October* 28 (Spring 1984): 126–27.

22. See, e.g., Picasso's *Self-Portrait* of 1907, in the National Gallery, Prague, reproduced in *Pablo Picasso*, exh. cat., ed. William Rubin (New York: Museum of Modern Art, 1980), 92. On Picasso's liberal use of cartoons and caricature, see Adam Gopnik, "High and Low: Caricature, Primitivism, and the Cubist Portrait," *Art Journal* 43, no. 4 (Winter 1983): 371–76.

23. See Corbin, *Women for Hire*.

24. Bernheimer, *Figures of Ill Repute*, 269–70.

25. Rubin, "From Narrative to 'Iconic,'" 629. Picasso's "Andalusian misogyny" is mentioned by Richardson, *A Life,* 68; his "obsessive fear of the destructive power of women" is described by Pierre Daix, "Dread, Desire, and the Demoiselles," *Artnews* 87, no. 6 (Summer 1988): 136.

26. Cited in Sarah Kofman, *The Enigma of Women: Woman in Freud's Writings,* trans. C. Porter (Ithaca, N.Y.: Cornell University Press, 1985), 81.

27. Steinberg, "The Philosophical Brothel, 1," and "The Philosophical Brothel, Part 2," *Artnews,* 71, no. 6 (October 1972): 38–47; and Kozloff, "Cubism," 35–36.

28. Steinberg, "The Philosophical Brothel, 1," 24.

29. "The seduction and conquest of the African woman became a metaphor for the conquest of Africa itself . . . to both were attributed the same, irresistable, deadly charm" (Nicolas Monti, cited in Mary Ann Doane, *Femmes Fatales: Feminism, Film Theory, Psychoanalysis* [New York: Routledge, 1991], 213). Regarding the hypersexualization of the black female body, see also Sander L. Gilman, "Black Bodies, White Bodies: Toward an Iconography of Female Sexuality in Late Nineteenth-Century Art, Medicine, and Literature," in Henry Louis Gates, Jr., ed., *"Race," Writing, and Difference* (Chicago: University of Chicago Press, 1986). Gilman stresses the fascination of Europeans with the pronounced buttocks of some women of African descent, a point that bears on the lavish display of buttocks by the woman in the African mask at the lower right of *Les Demoiselles.*

30. Doane, *Femmes Fatales,* 263.

31. See Hollis Clayson, *Painted Love: Prostitution in French Art of the Impressionist Era* (New Haven, Conn.: Yale University Press, 1991).

32. See Clayson's discussion of Benjamin, Baudelaire, and Simmel on the subject of prostitution in ibid., 7–9.

33. An insight credited to Benjamin by Christine Buci-Glucksmann, "Catastrophic Utopia: The Feminine as Allegory of the Modern," in *The Making of the Modern Body: Sexuality and Society in the Nineteenth Century,* ed. Catherine Gallagher and Thomas Laqueur (Berkeley: University of California Press, 1987), 224.

34. Luce Irigaray, "Women on the Market," in *This Sex Which Is Not One,* trans. C. Porter (Ithaca, N.Y.: Cornell University Press, 1985), 184; author's emphasis.

Besides confusing that once basic distinction between the seller and the sold, the prostitute also disturbed the opposition between work and sex that forms the basis for the concept of sublimation. The very possibility of the development of civilization is predicated—so Freud taught—on the systematic instilling of habits of sublimation. From this vantage point, the prostitute marks nothing less than the decline of civilization. See Doane, *Femmes Fatales,* 260–61, 264, on which I rely for this observation.

35. Christine Poggi, *In Defiance of Painting: Cubism, Futurism, and the Invention of Collage* (New Haven, Conn.: Yale University Press, 1992), 45, 32.

36. On the complexities of Olympia's social standing, see T. J. Clark, "Olympia's Choice," in *The Painting of Modern Life: Paris in the Art of Manet and His Followers* (New York: Knopf, 1985).

37. Corbin, *Women for Hire,* 127, 81. Picasso's picture reveals little of the appointments of the brothel that the demoiselles occupy, but the assembling in a salon of "two lines [of prostitutes] in a previously arranged order" was typical of a higher rank of *maison de tolérance* (a term for government-regulated brothels), as opposed to the lowest class of establishment, where the client's "choice was made in the adjoining bar where each woman would solicit the clients in turn." Protocol dictated that the lined-up women could not solicit the client by "a verbal invitation, but they all tried to tempt the visitor with winks, smiles, movements of the tongue, or exciting postures" (ibid., 83).

38. I owe this observation to a former graduate student at Harvard, the critic David Pagel.

39. See Susan Gubar, "'The Blank Page' and the Issues of Female Creativity," in *The New Feminist Criticism: Essays on Women, Literature, and Theory,* ed. Elaine Showalter (New York: Pantheon, 1985), 292–313, which cites Sandra McPherson: "The female genital, like the blank page anticipating the poem, is an absence, a not me, which I occupy" (292). See also Barbara Johnson, "Is Female to Male as Ground Is to Figure?" in *Feminism and Psychoanalysis,* ed. R. Feldstein and J. Roof (Ithaca, N.Y.: Cornell University Press, 1989), 255–68.

40. Sandra M. Gilbert and Susan Gubar, *The Madwoman in the Attic* (New Haven, Conn.: Yale University Press, 1979), 6 (this statement is evidently apocryphal); Rubin, *Picasso and Braque,* 54 n. 1; James E. B. Breslin,

Mark Rothko: A Biography (Chicago: University of Chicago Press, 1993), 360; and Abigail Solomon-Godeau, *Photography at the Dock: Essays on Photographic History, Institutions, and Practices* (Minneapolis: University of Minnesota Press, 1991), 229.

41. Cited in Christopher L. Miller, *Black Darkness: Africanist Discourse in French* (Chicago: University of Chicago Press, 1985), 245, 248. Declared a nineteenth-century French author, "the Black seems to me the female race" (ibid., 244).

42. Wassily Kandinsky, "Reminscences" (1913), in *Modern Artists on Art*, ed. Robert L. Herbert (Englewood Cliffs, N.J.: Prentice-Hall, 1964), 35.

43. Rubin addressed this problem tellingly (though, to my mind, unhelpfully) by distinguishing Picasso's contribution to Cubist practice from Braque's as follows: Braque provided the "passive, feminine side of the formal equation (. . . a vision of Tellus Mater notably open-laned, inviting entry)," while "the vigorous Picasso thrusts his hard, sculptural morphology" into that "syntactical-spatial structure" (William Rubin, "Pablo and Georges and Leo and Bill," *Art in America* 67 [March–April 1978]: 136).

44. Robert Rosenblum, *Cubism and Twentieth-Century Art* (New York: Harry N. Abrams, 1960), 25; my emphasis.

45. Rosalind Krauss, "The Motivation of the Sign," in *Picasso and Braque: A Symposium*, ed. Lynn Zelevansky (New York: Museum of Modern Art, 1992), 271 (my thanks to Christine Poggi for reminding me of this passage). It bears noting that Picasso experienced a kind of crisis in realizing this picture: so many sessions did he demand from the model, whose presence he found "somewhat embarrassing," that she lost patience and declined to return, leaving the artist with what he regarded at the time as an unfinished work (Roland Penrose, *Picasso: His Life and Work*, rev. ed. [New York: Harper and Row, 1973], 169).

46. Cited in Poggi, *In Defiance of Painting*, 5. The holes in the canvas opened by illusionistic or perspectival space had become "of ill repute during the late nineteenth and early twentieth centuries, implying deception about the nature of the medium," Poggi notes, while pursuing the case of a much discussed collage of 1913, *Still-Life: Au Bon Marché*, in which Picasso employed the phrase *un trou ici* in such a way that it apparently alludes to the genitals of a partially visible female figure. "In Picasso's collage, the newspaper text asserts the presence of a *Trou* without, however, creating the illusion of one. The hole remains an effect of writing pasted, with Picasso's characteristic wit, to a slight projection in the wall-like ground, for in a sense, it is a wall that is depicted here" (ibid., 152).

47. Steinberg implies the latter when he argues that "much of the disquiet in the left half of *[Les Demoiselles]* represents Picasso's rage against the solid drop of the canvas" (Steinberg, "The Philosophical Brothel, 1," 25).

48. That such fears emerge with a vengeance in the late nineteenth and early twentieth centuries has been persuasively shown by Elaine Showalter, *Sexual Anarchy: Gender and Culture at the Fin de Siècle* (New York: Viking, 1990); and Sandra M. Gilbert and Susan Gubar, "Tradition and the Female Talent," in *The Poetics of Gender*, ed. Nancy K. Miller (New York: Columbia University Press, 1986); and S. M. Gilbert and S. Gubar, *No Man's Land: The Place of the Woman Writer in the Twentieth Century* (New Haven, Conn.: Yale University Press, 1989).

49. Steinberg, "The Philosophical Brothel, 1," 46, and "The Philosophical Brothel, 2," 23, 25, 40, 46. Richardson pursues this line of thinking about Picasso, noting "the misogynistic pasha's" rendering of his mistress Marie-Thérèse Walter as "a thing of flesh and orifices"; toward the end of his life, "the sexual act and creative act become metaphors for each other, the work gapes with vaginas, which the loaded brush . . . would remorselessly probe" (Richardson, *A Life*, 68).

50. Bois, "Painting as Trauma," 137.

51. Steinberg, "The Philosophical Brothel, 2," 40.

52. Daix, in the minority, argues against this connection, noting that the authorities directed their antivenereal-disease campaign against streetwalkers, while "bordellos were considered clean, regulated places" (Daix, *Picasso*, 67).

53. William Rubin, "Picasso," in *"Primitivism" in Twentieth Century Art: Affinity of the Tribal and the Modern*, 2 vols., exh. cat. (New York: Museum of Modern Art, 1984), 1: 253 (Rubin credits Steinberg for this revelation); and Bois, "Painting as Trauma," 138.

54. "Psychoanalysis gives us sexual identity as construction," but "the terms of that construction" seem "to

fix things for ever in the given, and oppressive, identities, with no connections through to the *social-historical* realities that it also seems accurately to be describing. . . . No doubt it is an articulation of the psychical and the social in the construction of sexuality and sexual identity that we need to break the deadlock" (Heath, "Joan Riviere," 56–57).

55. Frances Frascina identified the type of pose in question and traced its history (F. Frascina, "Realism and Ideology: An Introduction to Semiotics and Cubism," in Charles Harrison, F. Frascina, and Gillian Perry, *Primitivism, Cubism, Abstraction: The Early Twentieth Century* [New Haven, Conn.: Yale University Press, 1993], 112–20).

56. Bernheimer, *Figures of Ill Repute,* 272.

57. Steinberg, "The Philosophical Brothel, 1," 25; "The Philosophical Brothel, 2," 43.

58. André Malraux, *Picasso's Mask,* trans. J. Guicharnaud with J. Guicharnaud (New York: Holt, Rinehart and Winston, 1976), 11. With *Les Demoiselles,* Picasso "succeeded in overpowering the demons that were causing him so much anguish, achieving what William Rubin has called, 'a relentless self-confrontation . . . comparable in this sense only to Freud's solitary self-analysis'" (Daix, "Dread, Desire," 137).

59. See "Appendix VII: Picasso's Equivocations with Respect to *Art Nègre,*" in Rubin, "From Narrative to 'Iconic,'" 632.

60. Gillian Perry, "Primitivism and the 'Modern,'" in Harrison et al., *Primitivism, Cubism, Abstraction,* 3; author's emphasis.

61. Michele Wallace, "Modernism, Postmodernism and the Problem of the Visual in Afro-American Culture," in *Out There: Marginalization and Contemporary Cultures,* ed. Russell Ferguson et al. (Cambridge, Mass.: MIT Press, 1990), 48.

62. Hal Foster, "The 'Primitive' Unconscious of Modern Art, or White Skin Black Masks," in *Recodings: Art, Spectacle, Cultural Politics* (Port Townsend, Wash.: Bay Press, 1985), 182.

63. Hélène Cixous, "Sorties," in H. Cixous and Cathérine Clément, *The Newly Born Woman,* trans. B. Wing (Minneapolis: University of Minnesota Press, 1986), 71.

64. Rosenblum, *Cubism,* 25.

65. Rubin, "From Narrative to 'Iconic,'" 630; my emphasis. The "'African' faces . . . finally conjure something that transcends our sense of civilized experience, something ominous and monstrous such as Kurtz discovered in the heart of darkness" (ibid., 632). (For an insightful reading of Joseph Conrad's *Heart of Darkness* as the paradigmatic Africanist text, see Miller, *Black Darkness,* 170–71.)

66. Bernheimer, *Figures of Ill Repute,* 270; see also Rubin, "From Narrative to 'Iconic,'" 635, which expresses parallel concepts.

67. Frascina, "Realism and Ideology," 128–29.

68. Bhabha, "Of Mimicry," 132–33.

69. Doane, *Femmes Fatales,* 214.

70. Cited in ibid., 210.

71. Patrick Brantlinger, "Victorians and Africans: The Genealogy of the Myth of the Dark Continent," in Gates, ed., *"Race,"* 215.

72. Miller, *Black Darkness,* 150, 23; author's emphasis.

73. Thus, Picasso's primitivism "gestured toward cultures whose transformative powers [he] admiringly offered as escape routes from the stultification of French culture and academic art" (Leighten, "The White Peril," 622).

74. Foster, "The 'Primitive' Unconscious," 194.

75. Foster was the first to wonder publicly, in 1985, "Is this aesthetic breakthrough [represented by *Les Demoiselles*] not also a breakdown, psychologically regressive, politically reactionary?" (ibid., 181). In 1990 Michele Wallace ventured that the painting "seems to represent the desire to both reveal and repress the scene of appropriation as a conjunction of black / female bodies and white culture—a scene of negative instruction between black and white art or black and white culture" (Wallace, "Modernism," 45).

76. Here the pioneers have been Bois, "The Semiology of Cubism," in *Picasso and Braque,* ed. Zelevansky, 169–208; and Poggi, *In Defiance of Painting.*

77. What made *Les Demoiselles* "truly revolutionary" was that "in it Picasso broke away from the two central characteristics of European painting since the Renaissance: the classical norm for the human figure, and the spatial illusionism of one-point perspective," pronounced Fry, *Cubism,* 13, though both those paradigms had long since been disused, as others have by now pointed out.

78. In 1916 Salmon gave the painting the title by which it has always been publicly known (Daix, *Picasso*, 65). Picasso protested in 1933: "'*Les Demoiselles d'Avignon*,' how this title irritates me. . . . You know very well that the original title from the beginning had been *The Brothel of Avignon* (Dore Ashton, ed., *Picasso on Art: A Selection of Views* [New York: Viking, 1972], 153).

79. "The dazzling discoveries of Cubism . . . are nowhere to be found, even in their germinal state in *Les Demoiselles*," Daix could state categorically by 1988 (Daix, "Dread, Desire," 137).

80. Steinberg, "The Philosophical Brothel, 2," 45; McCully, ed., *A Picasso Anthology*, 60.

81. See drawings 46r and 47r in sketchbook 3, as reproduced in Seckel, *Les Demoiselles*, 1: 163.

82. Women become "widely available commodities with the 'massification' of industrial labor and society, simultaneously losing their 'natural' qualities (a feminine essence, a nature determined by child-bearing) and their poetic aura" (Buci-Glucksmann, "Catastrophic Utopia," 222).

83. Rubin, "From Narrative to 'Iconic,'" 632. The modern "woman's body, deprived of its maternal-body, becomes desirable only in its passage to the limit: as death-body, fragmented-body, petrified-body," asserts Buci-Glucksmann, "Catastrophic Utopia," 226.

84. Doane, *Femmes Fatales*, 2.

85. "This Baudelairean abyss—an inclination for chasm-like ruin and nothingness— . . . lives through a continuous metaphor, that of the feminine sex" (Buci-Glucksmann, "Catastrophic Utopia," 228).

86. Steinberg, "The Philosophical Brothel, 2," 41.

87. Miller, *Black Darkness*, 175.

88. Alice A. Jardine, *Gynesis: Configurations of Woman and Modernity* (Ithaca, N.Y.: Cornell University Press, 1985), 67, 42.

89. Showalter, *Sexual Anarchy*, 7–8. "From the earliest times, Black Africa was experienced as the literal end of European knowledge," notes Miller. "Africanist discourse in the West is one in which the head, the voice—the logos, if you will—is missing" (Miller, *Black Darkness*, 22, 27).

90. Further, Picasso scarcely individualized and rarely named his female subjects, whereas he often managed to make his male sitters recognizable, in spite of the difficulties involved (Kozloff, "Cubism," 38–39).

91. Rosenblum, *Cubism*, 26; Rubin, "From Narrative to 'Iconic,'" 636.

92. "At the very crux of MOMAism, analytical cubism in particular must be protected from outside influence; thus tribal art is assigned 'but a residual role' in it" (Foster, "The 'Primitive' Unconscious," 193). Bois separates the ritual from the "purely formal" aspects of African art, and associates the former with *Les Demoiselles*, the latter with Cubist collage (Bois, "The Semiology of Cubism").

93. An argument can be made that Picasso was, however unconsciously, protecting himself as a foreigner in France, where "from the first Moroccan Crisis of 1905, . . . 'nationalism became an atmosphere'" (David Cottingham, "Cubism, Aestheticism, Modernism," in Zelevansky, ed., *Picasso and Braque*, 62). He did not succeed, however, for during the first world war French critics condemned the Cubists as "mostly foreigners" (Patricia Leighten, *Re-Ordering the Universe: Picasso and Anarchism, 1897–1914* [Princeton, N.J.: Princeton University Press, 1989], 99).

94. Cited in Ashton, ed., *Picasso on Art*, 154.

95. Malraux, *Picasso's Mask*, 11. Braque's famous comment to Picasso with regard to *Les Demoiselles* has been variously reported and variously translated: "It's as though you wanted to make us eat tow or drink kerosene," or "It is as if someone had drunk kerosene to spit fire" (cited in Rubin, *Picasso and Braque*, 348).

96. Bois, "Painting as Trauma," 172.

97. Bernheimer, *Figures of Ill Repute*, 270–71. The first serious study of prostitution, done in 1836 by Alexandre Parent-Duchatelet, was impelled "by a fantasy that pervades literary and artistic production in his wake"—that "of knowing female sexuality and defining its essential difference" (ibid., 270). Regarding the urge to dissect female bodies of African descent, see Gilman, "Black Bodies, White Bodies."

98. Doane, *Femmes Fatales*, 1.

99. Evelyn Fox Keller, "Making Gender Visible in Pursuit of Nature's Secrets," in Kauffman, ed., *American Feminist Thought*, 195.

100. Rubin asserts that Braque painted the first Cubist pictures, his l'Estaque landscapes (Rubin, "From Nar-

rative to 'Iconic,'" 643); Bois, "The Semiology of Cubism," 169. If we accept that the issue of when Cubism began is a patently unresolvable one, the fact of the historians' unending quest to determine and claim a point of origin for it—and so to effectively imprint its birth with their own names—assumes a significance all its own.

101. See Seckel, *Les Demoiselles*, 2: 656.

102. Daix, "Dread, Desire," 136.

103. Doane, *Femmes Fatales*, 2–3.

104. Foster, "The 'Primitive' Unconscious," 182.

105. Trinh T. Minh-ha, *Woman, Native, Other: Writing, Postcoloniality and Feminism* (Bloomington: Indiana University Press, 1989), 48–49.

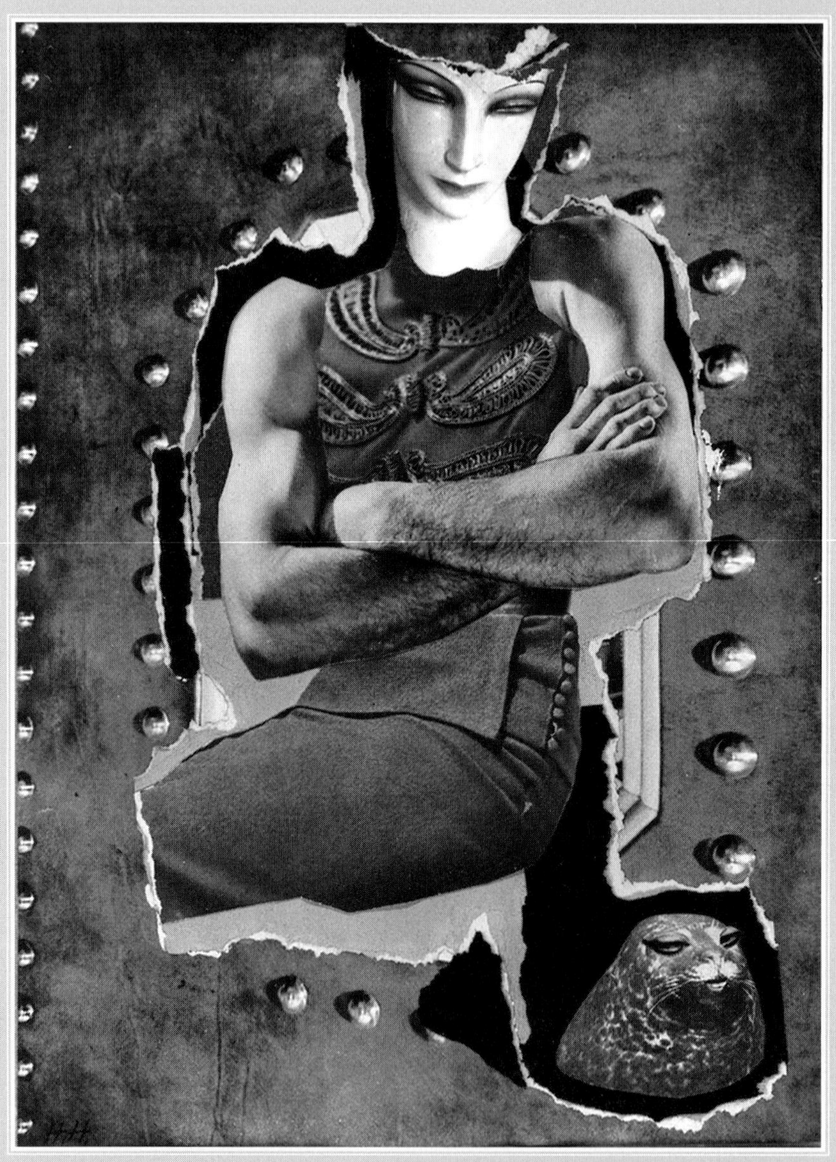

16

THE NEW WOMAN IN HANNAH HÖCH'S PHOTOMONTAGES

Issues of Androgyny, Bisexuality, and Oscillation

Maud Lavin

SHORTLY AFTER World War II, Hannah Höch jotted down some autobiographical notes in which she reflected on the early Berlin Dada years. In these notes she recalled the sexism of many male avant-gardists of her circle: "Enlightened by Freud—in protest against the older generation and [drawn to] . . . the emerging will for freedom of these pioneering women, the New Woman was desirable to him. But [the men] . . . rejected rather brutally that a new orientation was also necessary on their part. This led to those truly Strindbergian dramas that marked the private lives of these men. To complete the [history] . . . many volumes would need to be written telling of these women's fates."[1]

Within Höch's avant-garde subculture and in different ways throughout Weimar German culture, the images and attitudes of modernity were consistently projected onto women. Often these representations signaled greater freedom for women, but they also meant greater risks and some old inequities redesigned in modern packages. For Höch and numerous other women, a selective embrace of the New Woman stereotype would have been useful, and am-

biguity toward the New Woman and what she represented a strategy of survival. Yet ambiguity was rarely foregrounded in the melodramatic images of Weimar films or in the utopian *Lebensfreude* photographs of the *Illustrierte*. In contrast, Höch's Weimar photomontages, particularly those representing androgyny, were engaging and provocative depictions of this ambiguity—and raised questions about the visual culture of sexuality and power as well.

In 1930, the same year that Marlene Dietrich's film *The Blue Angel* was released, Hannah Höch made the photomontage *Marlene* (fig. 16.2). In the montage, two men gaze upward at a pair of gigantic legs adorned with stockings and high heels, mounted upside down on a pedestal. A bright red mouth is positioned in the upper right corner, outside the line of the male gaze. The mouth is instead offered directly as an object of desire to the male or female viewer of the montage. The name *Marlene* is scrawled across the sky in large letters, as if by a fan. With its challenging array of sexual signs and its deliberate allusion to Dietrich, an actress well known for her androgynous

<hr>

This essay is a revised version of material from chapter 6 and the conclusion of my book *Cut with the Kitchen Knife: The Weimar Photomontages of Hannah Höch* (New Haven, Conn.: Yale University Press, 1993). Copyright © 1993 Maud Lavin. Reprinted by permission of the author and courtesy of Yale University Press.

<hr>

Figure 16.1. Hannah Höch, *Dompteuse* (Tamer), ca. 1930. Photomontage, 14 × 10¼ in. Kunsthaus Zürich. © 2005 Artists Rights Society (ARS), New York/VG Bild-Kunst, Bonn.

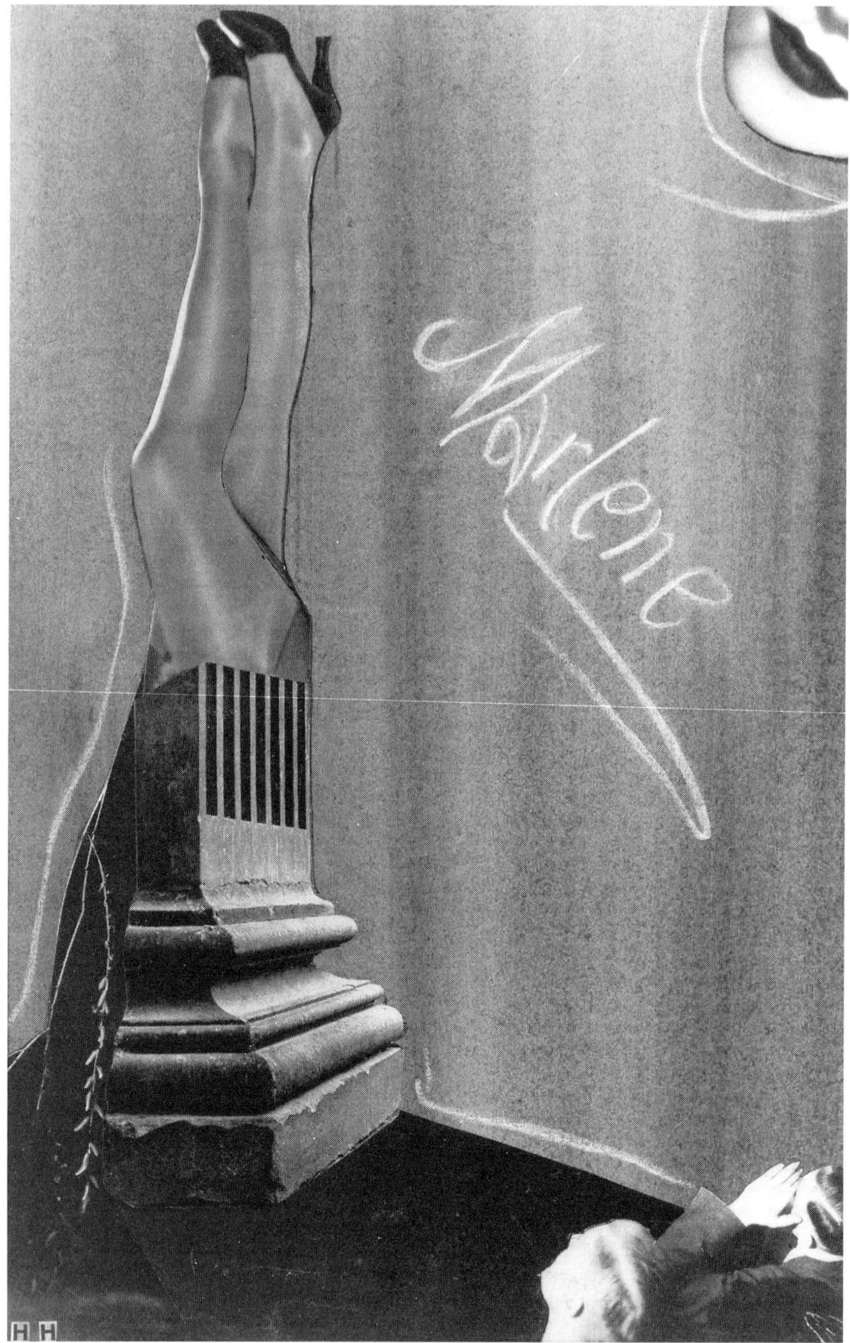

Figure 16.2. Hannah Höch, *Marlene*, 1930. Photomontage, 14½ × 9½ in. Dakis Joannou, Athens. © 2005 Artists Rights Society (ARS), New York / VG Bild-Kunst, Bonn.

image and her ambiguous sexual identity, the photomontage provokes a wealth of questions about gender identity and sexuality, strategies of representation, and the reading of imagery by a Weimar audience. Viewed in its historical context, Höch's image takes its place amid a proliferation of images of androgyny during the Weimar years, produced both by avant-garde artists and by mass culture institutions.

Today, many critical or theoretical treatments of gender promote the androgynous ideal as a liberation from constricting masculine and feminine roles. But in examining the strain of imagery in the historical context of Weimar culture, I have found that representations of androgyny and of ambiguous sexual identity functioned in two fundamentally opposed fashions at that time.[2] For both the producer and the viewer in the Weimar era, images of androgyny could have suggested the possible realization of a utopia of shifting and antihierarchical gender identities. On the other hand, such representations could also have fed reactionary ideologies of hyperindividualism. Only by returning to the social context of such images and by examining their specific strategies of representation can the significance of particular depictions of androgyny be explored.

In representations of the Weimar period, androgyny stood for gender roles and sexual identities that were themselves often blurred in German society, particularly in the depiction of lesbians, bisexual women, or modern (New) women. The prevailing beliefs in Weimar Germany about sexuality generally posited an inherent androgyny or bisexuality as a foundation for understanding heterosexual, homosexual, and bisexual practices. Though the various schools of psychologists conceived of this fundamental bisexuality in radically different ways, the postulate of inherent dualism had wide acceptance among sexologists and psychologists and among nonspecialists as well. Even Freud, in formulating his remarks on the psyche's fundamental bisexuality, strove to dispel belief in the idea of a "third sex," the widely held idea that homosexuals comprised a biological category apart from both men and women. Freud hoped to lead his readers toward his own more

sociological concept of the formation of sexual identity. In contrast, sexologists Otto Weininger and Magnus Hirschfeld were outspoken proponents of the "third sex" concept, even arguing that female homosexuals were biologically more masculine than other women—and that this difference was congenital.[3] This argument, commonly accepted at the time, is most familiar today from British author Radclyffe Hall's 1928 novel, *The Well of Loneliness.*

Today the concept of the third sex seems bizarre, but for homosexual writers of the first decades of the twentieth century it was important in forging an identity and self-acceptance within the homosexual community.[4] Activist homosexual groups such as Hirschfeld's Scientific Humanitarian Committee used the third sex myth as a tool in the fight for legal reform, arguing that as this so-called perversion was a result of nature, not criminality, it should not be punishable by law.[5] Understandably, Hirschfeld's work was greeted with ambivalence by many Weimar homosexuals; although they supported his legal activism for homosexual rights, they resented his definition of homosexuality as a deviation.

The dangerous side of the third sex myth is most apparent in Otto Weininger's work. Theories of congenital sexuality underlie the construction of Weininger's biological hierarchies. He claimed that every individual is constituted with a fixed ratio between masculinity and femininity, thus allowing him or her to be typed accordingly. He held that one is born with this ratio and that this thesis could be extended to a belief in bisexuality. This seemingly benign idea was clearly stated in the 1906 edition of his *Sex and Character:* "In my view all actual organisms have both homosexuality and heterosexuality."[6] Such pronouncements addressed widely perceived anxieties about the ambiguities of gender identity and made this turn-of-the-century book popular during the Weimar era.

Weininger's book also revealed the dark side of its author's ideology. Weininger, a Jewish anti-Semite, was also, in the most exact sense, a misogynist. He argued that a woman's worth depended entirely on the amount of masculinity she possessed: "Manlike women wear their hair short, affect manly dress, study, drink, smoke, are fond of mountaineering, or devote themselves passionately to sport. . . . A woman's demand for emancipation and her qualification for it are in direct proportion to the amount of maleness in her."[7] Weininger rigorously followed this logic to the conclusion that lesbians were superior to other women because they were more masculine. He suggested "the possibility that homosexuality is a higher form than heterosexuality. For the present, it is enough to say that homosexuality in a woman is the outcome of her masculinity and presupposes a higher degree of development."[8] Theories such as Weininger's, then, ascribed bisexuality to a *visible*, physical combination of masculine and feminine attributes. This created a climate in which images of androgyny could refer not only to gender roles but basic sexual identity as well. In this new context, the visual stereotype of the lesbian as androgynous woman could cut two ways: it could promote self-identification, but by the same token it could lock the lesbian into a rigid hierarchical classification.

Though Freud's writings on bisexuality were also based on biology, they aimed at refuting the congenital theory of bisexuality and homosexuality. Freud argued instead that familial and social pressures shaped sexual preference. In his *Three Essays on the Theory of Sexuality* (1905), Freud maintained that manifestations of homosexuality were common in puberty and later developments toward heterosexuality were in part socially determined. Freud saw its "authoritative prohibition by society" as one of the chief factors leading to the renunciation of this juvenile homosexuality.[9]

In his 1920 article "The Psychogenesis of a Case of Homosexuality in a Woman," Freud twice insisted that his subject, a young bourgeois woman sent to him by her parents to "cure" her homosexuality, was in no way neurotic. Indeed, he objected at length to the whole idea of curing homosexuals.[10] He argued that conversion to heterosexuality is not possible; at most, a willing patient could be introduced to her or his inherent bisexuality. Freud did validate the desire to live a heterosexual life, but primarily for such pragmatic

reasons as social acceptability. He wrote: "One must remember that normal sexuality too depends upon a restriction in the choice of object. In general, to undertake to convert a fully developed homosexual into a heterosexual does not offer much more prospect of success than the reverse, except that for good, practical reasons the latter is never attempted."[11]

In the early-twentieth-century German debates on sexuality, Freud's speculations about the beliefs held by his readers are significant for cultural history. The persistence of the congenital third sex myth can be detected even in Freud's text, in his perception of the biases of his hypothetical readers in 1920.[12] There, as usual, Freud addressed potential objections to his arguments, and thus we learn what he assumed to be his readers' prejudices: "The mystery of homosexuality is by no means so simple as it is commonly depicted in popular expositions—'a feminine mind, bound therefore to love a man, but unhappily attached to a masculine body; a masculine mind, irresistibly attracted by women but alas! imprisoned in a feminine body.'"[13] He continued later: "In addition to their manifest heterosexuality, a very considerable measure of latent or unconscious homosexuality can be detected in all normal people. If these findings are taken into account, then, clearly, the supposition that nature in a freakish mood created a 'third sex' falls to the ground."[14] The concept of universal bisexuality, then, seems to have had widespread currency in Weimar Germany, whether in Freud's formulation, or in those of the sexologists he opposed.

According to some theorists, this innate bisexuality was manifest in a person's physical appearance. Any representation of androgyny during Weimar, therefore, had the potential to signify bisexuality or a degree of homosexuality. This potential, however, was unequally distributed between male and female images of androgyny. Male homosexuality remained illegal throughout the Weimar years despite the widespread acceptance of a theory of universal bisexuality.[15] Lesbianism, on the other hand, was never against the law—less an index of toleration than of nonrecognition. This double standard suggests that whereas an image of a feminized man may have ap-

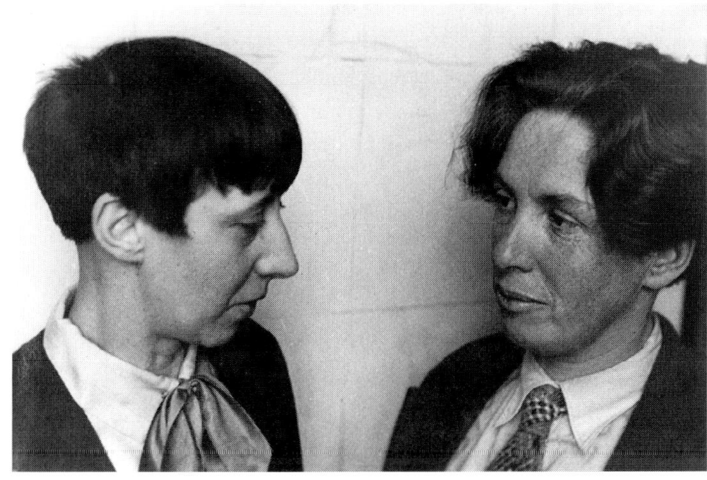

peared to the Weimar viewer as obviously and illegally homosexual, an image of a masculinized woman may not have been so easily categorized. Such images of androgynous women, then, allowed for various significations. The masculine roles newly occupied by women in the labor and political spheres offered another and related set of connotations for female images. A matrix of significations was possible, depending on the image and the arena of reception, linking androgyny, modernism, the New Woman, and a new sexuality.

By the late Weimar period, Hannah Höch's own sexual identity had changed radically. She left Raoul Hausmann in 1922 and by 1926 had begun a lesbian relationship with the Dutch writer Til Brugman, whom she had met through her close friends Kurt and Helma Schwitters. By the fall of 1926, Höch had moved to The Hague to live with Brugman.[16] The two lived together there until 1929, when they moved to Berlin (fig. 16.3). Their relationship lasted nine years, until 1935, making it one of the most enduring and stable bonds of Höch's life.

Höch's relationship with Brugman may have further sensitized her to gender issues, but it is not clear whether Höch identified herself as a lesbian or as bisexual (these distinctions were not as sharply drawn in Weimar times as they are today). Between them-

selves, Höch and Brugman did not seem to feel it necessary or desirable to define their relationship as lesbian; in their letters, they discussed it simply as a private love relationship.[17] In one quite moving letter to her sister Grete, Höch expressed her deep love for Brugman:

> I am and will be very happy with Til. We will be a model of how two women can form a single rich and balanced life. Each day I find out wonderful new things about Til that enrich me and allow me to see life in a new light. My dear Gretelein, you are probably the only one who realized *how* thoroughly the chapter "man" is finished for me. The beautiful and the awful endured, explored, and exhausted. I knew there could not be another man in the world who had something new to offer me, so I began to withdraw and exist only for myself in the purest sense of the term. Besides *you* and your children, no one got close to me—inside— I had ruled out further adventures. I didn't want to give anyone any of myself, and in truth I didn't desire anymore. Now all the gates have been thrown open again, and I stroll happily out from myself and "it" marches back into me. To be closely connected with another woman for me is something totally new, since it means being taken by the spirit of my own spirit, confronted by a very close relative.[18]

Although Höch's relationship with Brugman was eventually accepted by her family and friends, neither Höch nor Brugman was active in homosexual organizations at this time, and outside a small circle, Höch apparently had no public identity as a lesbian. In 1935 Höch began a relationship with Kurt Matthies, a younger man whom she married in 1938; the marriage lasted until 1944.[19]

Höch's shifting sexual preferences were not—with some remarkable exceptions—directly reflected in her paintings and photomontages. I'll note two exceptions here. One is that it's possible to see an increased interest in the erotic landscape of the female body in Höch's scrapbook. The second is her photomontage *Liebe* (Love) of 1931, depicting a part-woman, part-dragonfly-like creature in the air over the genital area of another composite female figure, who wears "Dada shoes," has a languid, white-skinned torso, and has an African woman's face, and who lounges on pillows. *Liebe* seems to me to depict a pleasurable, erotic hovering of one feminine composite figure over another—and implicitly alludes to oral sex. What is more consistently evident than homoerotic representations, though, in Höch's work of the time of her relationship with Brugman, is that her androgynous images—produced with regularity then—depict a pleasure in the movement between gender positions and a deliberate deconstruction of rigid masculine and feminine identities.

In addition, a few works of those years are thought to be portraits of sorts. *Englische Tänzerin* (English Female Dancer) and the monocle-wearing *Russische Tänzerin* (Russian Female Dancer), both photomontages of 1928, are generally believed to represent Höch and Brugman respectively. Höch's photomontage *Vagabunden* (Vagabonds) of 1926 probably alludes to her then-new homosexual relationship with Brugman. In *Vagabunden,* affectionate caricature replaces the stinging irony of the earlier Dada photomontages. Although Höch had previously given male figures female bodies in order to mock them, in this work it is clear that her use of composite male-female figures was changing. In the montage, two women are shown traveling together: one in sports clothes and the other, heavier one in a combination of masculine and feminine attire. This seems to be a double portrait of Höch and Brugman holding hands, arms raised, and may celebrate Höch and Brugman's actual or projected travels.[20]

Höch did not write about her positions on homosexuality. To some degree, however, Höch's attitudes toward the prevalent theories of bisexuality and homosexuality can be inferred from Brugman's early short stories and grotesques, which Höch read and edited between 1926 and 1935.[21] Brugman's position is clearer. Her short story "Warenhaus der Liebe" (Department Store of Love), circa 1934, shares the widespread homosexual ambivalence toward Hirschfeld's sexology. The story is a thinly veiled parody of Hirschfeld's Berlin Institute for Sexology, which was in operation from 1919 to 1933 and provided people of all sexual persuasions with sex counseling and therapy. Brugman makes an analogy with the department store, then a newly arrived mecca of consumerism and entertainment in Germany's big metropolises. Brugman's short story describes a scientific department store where everyone can purchase their favorite fetish objects and achieve complete satisfaction of their desires. But the military objects to the store, claiming that it curtails aggression and that, by making old-fashioned sexual intercourse obsolete, it endangers population growth. As a result, the military closes the department store. Brugman's story derides the National Socialists, but her humor at Hirschfeld's expense is sympathetic. The story was most likely written after May 10, 1933, the date the Nazis plundered the institute, closed it, and burned its books.

An ambiguous and androgynous representation of the New Woman was central to Höch's late Weimar work; her montage techniques encouraged a sense of oscillation between gender roles in her viewers. Ambiguity and oscillation between gender positions do not function uniformly for all spectators, however, and I want to consider specifically what Höch's work may have meant for female viewers. At least in theory, different individuals encounter visual tests in markedly different ways, and part of any female viewer's anxiety in looking at images lies in a conflict between identification with the masculine and the feminine. As feminist film theorists such as Laura Mulvey and Miriam Hansen have pointed out, women in male society, although socialized as feminine, have also generally had to identify with the masculine position as the primary location of action and power.[22] Self-conscious oscillation between the two roles offers women multiple pleasures: first, the possibility or fantasy of occupying both gender positions; second, the perception of both as unfixed or unstable, which is a pleasure certainly to those at the bottom of the gender hierarchy; and third, the destabilization of the hierarchy itself. What is privileged in this case is not oscillation itself but forms of reception in which the personal pleasures derived from viewing are connected to the broader desires to dissolve class and gender hierarchies.

As the degree of ambiguity in Höch's montages increased in her late Weimar representations of androgyny, she used irony and narrative less often and in new ways. In particular, the absence of a distancing irony as a technique of resolution reduces stability in the gender and sexual identities portrayed. *Der Vater* (The Father; 1920), from Höch's Dada period, reads as quite openly ironic. As in her famous *Cut with the Kitchen Knife* of 1919–20, she uses a centrifugal composition that rotates around a central figure, employing many signs of modernity and motion: images of technology, dancers, gymnasts, and boxers, superimposed on packaging and advertising materials, signs of consumer culture. In the center is "the father," a composite figure with a man's head and a woman's body, holding a baby. Around him circulate stretching and leaping athletes, one a black boxer, the others three New Women. These three figures derive from the same stereotype, familiar from the photoweeklies' *Illustrirte*, in which the joy of movement and springing into the air are read as signs of new female emancipation and modernity.[23]

The viewer is not offered an idealized androgynous New Father. Rather, the montage is ironic, and the ineffectual paternal figure bears the brunt of its humor. While the father protectively holds the baby,

in fact, the boxer seems to aim a punch at the baby's eye. The superimposition of cutout eyes formally disrupts the wholeness of the heads of the man and baby. The effect of *Der Vater*'s irony is that the androgynous father appears not so much as a figure of two genders but as a ridiculed man. As has often been noted, the feminization of men is usually used to elicit humor, whereas the masculinization of women has more varied functions.

In general terms, the mechanism of irony can be defined as simultaneously representing a sign and its opposite, reconciling the two through a distancing humor. In other words, irony is saying one thing and meaning its opposite, usually signaling detachment from the statement as a whole. Thus a distanced irony can be seen as overriding potential ambiguity or double readings to produce a unified meaning. Irony can synthesize oppositions; within the dialectical motion between disjunctive photomontage fragments— which variously signify masculine and feminine gender roles—this synthesizing function enables irony to halt the operations of oscillation.[24] By 1925, when Höch painted *Roma* (fig. 16.4), a composition that imitates her photomontages, she employed a less distanced irony and showed greater interest in representing gender ambiguities than during the Dada years. In the painting, the actress Asta Nielsen, dressed in a bathing suit, crouches coquettishly next to Mussolini. Pointing vigorously to the right, Nielsen seems to be ordering Il Duce out of Rome. A theater and film actress particularly popular with women, Nielsen was known for her portrayal of such male roles as Hamlet.[25] In Höch's painting, Nielsen serves as a figure of identification for the viewer. She is shown from the shoulders up in her Hamlet persona. In fact, the image is based on a publicity photograph for a film version of *Hamlet* published in *Berliner Illustrirte Zeitung* in 1920.[26] Mussolini is also presented androgynously in this painting, with his head attached to a woman's body. Ambiguity and contradiction in the echoed pair of women's bodies signify flirtation, athleticism, mockery, and command.

Höch's 1925 photomontage *Liebe im Busch* (Love in the Bush) depicts two figures, composites of mas-

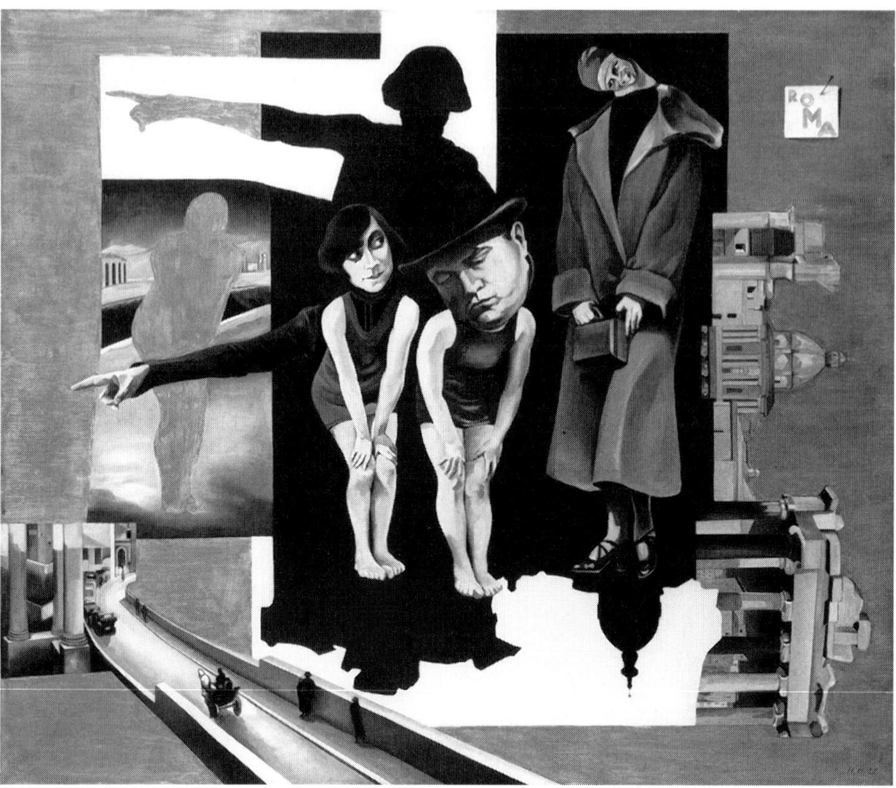

Figure 16.4. Hannah Höch, *Roma*, 1925. Oil on canvas, 35½ × 41¾ in. Berlinische Galerie, Berlin. © 2005 Artists Rights Society (ARS), New York / VG Bild-Kunst, Bonn.

culine and feminine, black and white, romancing in a natural setting. The two figures embrace among oversized stalks of grass; the black figure hugs the white one, who is a montage of jutting arms, trousered legs, and a trunkless head; the white head is a woman's, her hair cut in a short, modern style and her eyes and mouth open in excitement. The montage also connotes primitivism, the jungle *(Busch)*, and the myth of African culture for the German avant-garde (which Höch explored in her Ethnographic Museum series). *Liebe im Busch* was exhibited in the 1931 Berlin Fotomontage exhibition, where it would have contrasted sharply with the rational *Sachlichkeit* (matter-of-factness) of such advertising photomontages as those by Piet Zwart and Paul Schuitema representing mass-produced electrical parts juxtaposed with brand-name logos.[27]

Höch's works produced later in the Weimar era focus increasingly on the pleasure and confusions of gender oscillation. In *Siebenmeilensteifel* (Seven-League Boots), circa 1934, two female legs, naked except for midcalf laced boots, fly in a full straddle leap over a village.[28] Strapped around the crotch (there is no torso) is a spiral-shaped shell whose point faces forward, metaphorically like an erect penis. Male genitalia are also suggested by the bulbous section of the shell that hangs between the legs. The spread-eagled legs and the strapped-on phallus set up for the viewer a reading of this surreal body fragment as not only androgynous but transsexual.

Perhaps Höch's most ambiguous and sophisticated image of androgyny is *Dompteuse* (Tamer), circa 1930 (fig. 16.1). The central figure has a female mannequin's head but masculine, muscular, hairy arms and a flat-chested torso. The figure wears a sleeveless, ornamented top that could be part of a circus costume and a skirt. The mannequin's head is

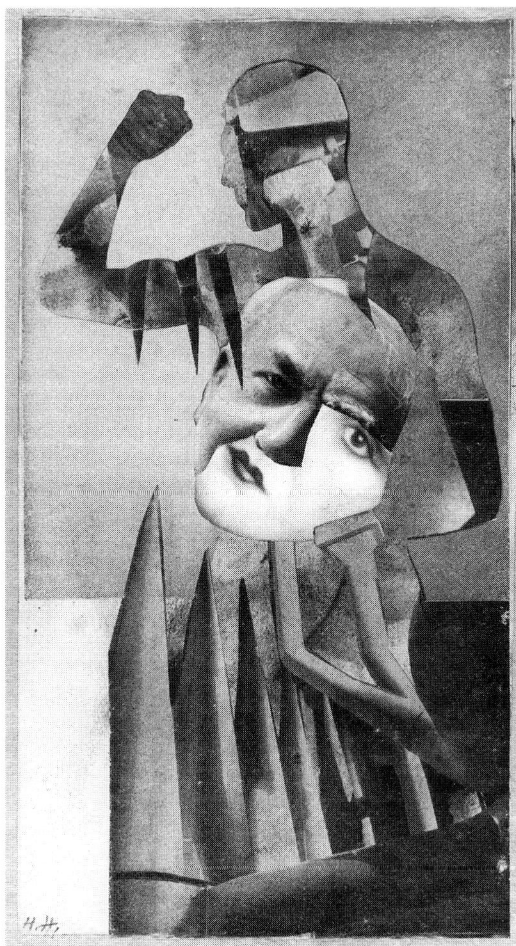

Figure 16.5. Hannah Höch, *Die starken Männer* (The Strong Men), 1931. Photomontage, 9¾ × 5¼ in. Institut für Auslandsbeziehungen, Stuttgart. © 2005 Artists Rights Society (ARS), New York/VG Bild-Kunst, Bonn.

framing device is a contradictory montage of a traditional frame (barely visible behind the figure), surrounded by brass studs and covered by the torn edges of the central montage—signifiers of both containment and overflow, connoting a controlled violence.

The mannequin figure of *Dompteuse* is seated, arms crossed, and seems to look down at the sea lion; along with the title *Dompteuse*, the pose suggests domination. The contrast of scale between the large mannequin and the small sea lion creates a sense of anxiety. Yet the tamer is also strangely beautiful, appearing somewhat meditative, whereas the sea lion looks outward, engaging the viewer with a sly, uncanny gaze. As the viewer looks back and forth between the mannequin and the animal, in fact, it is unclear who is dominant. On a closer look, the mannequin's face appears quite passive. The contradiction between the two faces—the mannequin's blank and porcelain-like, the sea lion's darkened as with makeup—denies a unified, narrative reading and promotes double meanings. Although there is a contrast between the artificial mannequin and the natural animal, the shapes of the two sets of eyes, which echo one another, establish a formal similarity. The androgyny of the mannequin seems to be part of a secret; the figure is inaccessible, enclosed within itself by its self-reflective gaze and folded arms.

Equally complex is Höch's slightly later *Die starken Männer* (the title could mean literally the Strong Men, or, idiomatically, Male Weightlifters), of 1931 (fig. 16.5). In this work, a composite face of an older man and a younger woman is superimposed over the silhouette of the boxer Max Schmeling flexing his biceps. (Schmeling was an athlete much admired and feted by the male avant-garde, including George Grosz and John Heartfield.)[29] The head is surrounded by jagged forms, circled as a precious object, doubly framed yet precariously balanced. Although Höch usually distorts scale and proportion within a face, making one eye too large, for instance, here there is a close fit in the joining of the masculine and feminine faces. Both eyes engage the viewer directly in this central image. Even though both halves match in scale, the photographic facial fragments differ in skin

taken from a black-and-white photograph; the arms, torso, and skirt from color photographs; and the sea lion's eyes in the lower right from a black-and-white photograph tinted sepia. The viewer is always aware of looking at photo fragments, and so the constructed nature of the figure is evident, preventing a reading of the figure as "natural." The pieces are skillfully fitted together and carefully proportioned to avoid any discrepancy of scale. The impossibility of reading a single gender is even more pronounced than in earlier works, like *Roma*. Here, even the remarkable tone and degrees of aging, so that the parts do not quite meld into a whole. For the viewer, the tendency is first to engage one half, then the other, through the different gazes. Thus subject-object confusion can occur in terms of gender, posing the question of whether one is viewing a representation of the self or the Other. The constant shifting is aided by the off-balance position of the head. At the same time, in the middle ground the jagged, phallic forms connote masculinity; two of these forms encroach on the outline of the male face. The background silhouette of Schmeling flexing his arm is painted in with warm red and brown watercolors, and the buttocks are carefully delineated. The focus on these two sites—arm and buttocks—presents the boxer as the object of his own gaze and of others' desire. Although he looks inward at this arm muscle (and thus completes a closed circuit of a narcissistic gaze), his body is turned so the buttocks face outward, emphasizing the crevice, which resembles a feminine sign of availability. Jagged forms continue in a diagonal line beneath the buttocks, creating a juxtaposition of sharply phallic shapes with the dark crevice. Below the waist the athlete's body is feminized, but above the midsection, it is made overtly masculine.

In spite of the fact that feminine elements here are inserted into a frame of primarily masculine attributes, what is exceptional about Höch's montage is that the head can never be resolved into a unity; it is always two genders. Images from Weimar mass media in which androgyny has been commodified as fashion appear, finally, as women who have taken on the attributes of men. In contrast, Höch's *Die starken Männer*, in preserving ambiguity, maintains the radical potential of photomontage at a time when commercial design had emptied that potential through its emphasis on pure form and clean design.

Clearly there is a range of identifications and objects of desire offered here. Through juxtaposition and denial of closure, Höch's representation of androgyny encourages the mechanisms of the fetishizing gaze to shift between masculine and feminine objects. *Die starken Männer* is not only a representation of androgyny but a deliberate destabilizing of the

viewer's gaze. It institutes an oscillation between polarized positions of masculinity and femininity, establishes a bisexual relationship to the object of desire, and shifts between disavowal and recognition of that bisexuality. All of these responses can be described as fundamental conditions of female spectatorship. In the case of Höch's *Die starken Männer*, both male and female viewers are put in the feminine position.

Höch's images differ sharply from most other Weimar representations of androgyny, bisexuality, and lesbianism. The broad array of representations of gender and sexual roles in Weimar is complex and demands a more thorough analysis than is possible here. Certain androgynous images used in Weimar-era advertisements, however, are of particular relevance to Höch's montages—if only by their marked contrast. Body culture images were frequently used to advertise products in the new mass media market, and in these, androgyny could be read as a sign for intensified individualism embodied in a single consumer. It comes as no surprise, for example, that immediately after the release of the enormously popular *Körperkultur* film *Wege zur Kraft und Schönheit* in 1925, stills from the film were used in advertisements in the fashionable Ullstein bimonthly magazine *Die Dame* and elsewhere.[30] These body-as-machine images claim a fantastic plenitude or abundance for the body: that it can be at once masculine and feminine, nature and machine, youth and immortality.

Print media images in Weimar Germany almost always showed women "improved" through masculinization. What was presented as plenitude was actually a subsuming of femininity under masculine signs. And yet not all images in the mass market print media promoted such plenitude. The popular illustrated newspapers often carried jokes about the difficulty of distinguishing between men and women. For example, *Berliner Illustrirte Zeitung* ran a contest in May 1920 called "Bub oder Mädel?" (Guy or Gal?), offering readers a variety of rewards totaling approximately two thousand marks for correctly identifying the gender of young people in six different photographs. The photos were published a second time and answers given on June 18. Thus, both in ads and in contests, some sort of resolution was offered— either through buying a product or naming the correct gender. Although I can guess at the pleasures these images provided by exploring gender confusions, I question, too, how these pleasures were being redirected into easy resolutions.

Despite their limitations, these androgynous images could have provided an important sense of identification for Weimar women involved in new gender roles. This is most clear for the lesbian subculture with regard to images readable not only as androgynous but also as lesbian or bisexual. As Michel Foucault warns in the first volume of his *History of Sexuality*, speaking about alternative sexualities is not necessarily liberating and can, in fact, feed the myth that sexual liberation is integral to political revolution. According to Foucault, the inverse of this myth actually takes place: by obeying the command to speak about sexuality, to represent and explore it constantly, the speaker participates in the promotion of sexuality; this, in turn, contributes to the self-image of the bourgeoisie as all-powerful, life-enhancing, body-intensified, expanding, and eternal.[31] Foucault's warning is particularly apt for images of androgyny circulating within the discourse of *Körperkultur* in early-twentieth-century Germany.

In the case of Weimar's lesbian subculture, however, Foucault's logic fails. Despite the prevalent images of lesbian culture and nightlife in 1920s Berlin, for the most part lesbian life at that time and earlier was marked by invisibility and silence.[32] For lesbians during the early Weimar period, the creation of androgyny as a *fashion* cut two ways, a sign of both acceptance and co-optation or dismissal. This duality confronts the reader in many Weimar mass media photographs. In *Uhu* (also published by Ullstein), for instance, images of androgynous women were often accompanied by ultra-"feminine" signs (such as a model's childish hands-to-mouth gesture) to counter a lesbian "masculine" identification.[33] Thus representations of bisexuality and homosexuality in Weimar cannot be seen simply as a form of repressive toler-

ance in Foucault's sense. For lesbians, such images, however problematic, could enforce the basic and crucial functions of identity and a belief in the right to exist at all.[34]

Both the usefulness and limitations of Foucault's argument are made clear by a famous example of the mass culture representation of homosexuality during Weimar, the lesbian film *Mädchen in Uniform* (Girls in Uniform), which premiered in Berlin in December 1931. Foucault's warning allows us to see how easily this filmic representation of lesbianism was incorporated, legitimized, and sanitized by its critical reception (representing yet another sexual difference collected by the all-encompassing power of the bourgeoisie). At the same time, the limitations of Foucault's thesis are evident when we recognize the tremendous importance of this film for the identity of the lesbian subculture, as well as the overt political radicality of the film's thematic interlacing of antimilitarism and alternative sexualities. At the very least, the film represents the *desire* to link leftist political revolution and homosexuality. Nevertheless, the way *Mädchen in Uniform* represents lesbianism compromises its reception. The film's lack of ambiguity and oscillation contrasts with Höch's aesthetic strategies.

Mädchen in Uniform was the product of the collaboration of a lesbian director, Leontine Sagan, and a lesbian writer, Christa Winsloe. Produced collectively by the Deutsche Film Gemeinschaft, the film is set in a Prussian boarding school for the daughters of military officers. In the film, Manuela (Hertha Thiele) has lost her mother and develops a crush on her teacher, Fräulein von Bernburg (Dorothea Wieck). Though such crushes are not uncommon within the school and are generally tolerated, this crush grows beyond normally accepted limits into a more serious lesbian love, shown explicitly only once—through a kiss. Manuela's love is reciprocated by von Bernburg, who tries, though, to deny her feelings. The narrative builds to a crisis—Manuela's thwarted suicide attempt and the other schoolgirls' and von Bernburg's defiance of the principal.

Since *Mädchen in Uniform* has been discussed at

length elsewhere,[35] here I will focus only on the significance of its narrative and the critical response it received. Upon its release, the film was immediately highly celebrated, particularly as an antimilitaristic, anti-Prussian, and antiauthoritarian statement. But outside homosexual journals, contemporary critics never mentioned the explicit lesbianism, instead referring to the central relationship as merely adolescent.[36] Moreover, as androgynous images are specifically avoided in the film,[37] the issue of naming and speaking about homosexuality (and, conversely, the repression of this speech) is a tension at many levels of *Mädchen in Uniform*, including its production and its critical reception. Ironically, although the film pivots around the crime of publicly naming lesbian passion, lesbianism is never spoken of directly. Rather, such euphemistic expressions as "the great spirit of love that has a thousand forms" or "Manuela's suffering" are used (an elision that Herta Thiele speculated in a 1981 interview was an attempt to make the film acceptable to a broader audience).[38] This pressure to name, which both bursts out and is repressed in the film, cannot be dismissed (as Foucault might suggest) as merely a confession compliant with the bourgeoisie's need to claim sexual investigation and therefore sex itself for its deployment of power. As film critic Ruby Rich has pointed out, the homosexuality in this case is clearly connected to a revolutionary activism and exemplifies an alternative to the principal's definition of the girls: "You are all soldiers' daughters, and God willing, you will all be soldiers' mothers."[39] The audience's understanding of the narrative development is entirely dependent on a reading of Manuela's love as lesbian—why else is she sent to the infirmary after proclaiming it?

But was the proclamation salient enough? Unfortunately, *Mädchen in Uniform* fit easily into contemporary myths that saw lesbianism as schoolgirl crushes, an immature phase on the route to adult heterosexuality. Critics were quick to describe the film in these terms, dwelling on von Bernburg's maternalism or on the idealistic nature of Manuela's crush. Ullstein's *Uhu*, in an advance publicity feature, promoted the movie by focusing on the nonprofessional actresses who played the majority of the boarding school population, stressing that they were all from good bourgeois families and that most had ambitions for nonstage careers.[40] Most tellingly, the film was not banned by the Nazis, despite its antimilitarism. Historian Rosi Kriesche's explanation is twofold: that lesbianism was not officially recognized, and that the heroine Fraeulein von Bernburg inculcates her students with the virtues of work and duty, qualities the party also demanded of its youth, as in the Bund Deutscher Mädchen.[41]

My purpose is not to argue that naming alone—or a more explicit naming—would have been a "better" strategy for the propagation of alternative sexualities and politics. Rather, I find that the stereotypical representation of alternative sexuality in *Mädchen in Uniform* involves limitations that are worth examining. In essence, my question is this: what strategies of representation were most effective in linking gender subjectivity to nonhierarchical societal change?

Höch was not involved in simply representing or propagating homosexuality; her montages instead recombined masculine and feminine gender identities. In this way, her representation of androgyny introduced a radical and nonhierarchical sexual ambiguity. Unlike images of thoroughly masculinized women, as in some forms of fashion photography, her montages suggested fluctuating gender roles. In the context of late Weimar exhibitions, the sexual ambiguity would have had a specific political meaning for the audience, demanding at least temporarily an unsettling oscillation in the gender identity of the engaged viewer. Since these images expressly deny resolution, it is important to consider the effect of this fluidity on the Weimar viewer. A lack of representational resolution could have a particular meaning, for instance, for Weimar women whose economic and sexual roles were in a state of flux. These representations could have the potential to contradict—at least in fantasy— efforts to circumscribe the New Woman's roles, as well as attempts to assure that "new" places were still firmly anchored at the bottom of the social hierarchy.

With this range of connotations in mind, I want to return to the discussion of androgyny in Höch's 1930 photomontage *Marlene* (fig. 16.2). For the female viewer, *Marlene* provokes an oscillation between a male heterosexual position and a female homosexual one. Although the fetishized legs are viewed by two men in the lower right corner, both the mouth and the word "Marlene"—presented frontally, out of the narrative space—are offered directly to the viewer as objects of desire. For female homosexuals in Berlin during the late Weimar years, this montage would have held specific connotations, since any image of Marlene Dietrich would be read as either androgynous or lesbian. As actress Hertha Thiele recalled, Dietrich was a cult figure for lesbians in Berlin: "There was at that time a trend . . . to appear like Dietrich . . . and each would call herself Marlene."[42]

Given this special status accorded Dietrich's image, Höch's highly eroticized representation of a fragmented mouth and legs beneath her name would seem to offer the female viewer a fetishized image of Dietrich as an object of lesbian desire. In fact, the viewer can choose either to engage the name and fragmented body parts as objects of desire or to identify with the two men as surrogates, since the men are defined as spectators. The female viewer faces a choice between a female gaze of homosexual desire (directly confronting the enticing lips and the admired name) and a male gaze of heterosexual desire (represented explicitly if somewhat ironically)—or both. Since the two possibilities are represented alluringly within the montage, the female viewer is encouraged to construct herself as androgynous.

Today, this consideration of the female viewer raises questions concerning the differences between male and female spectatorship, specifically in viewing photographs, and with particular relation to notions of fetishism, an explicit theme of Höch's *Marlene*. Freud described fetishism as a psychic mechanism operating in men and arising from both a disavowal of castration and a substitution, through visualization, of an image for the woman's missing penis. It is significant that this double action—disavowal and substitution—occurs in one crucial moment and is then repeated in future viewings of fetish objects.[43] Referring to Freud's definition, theorist Victor Bur-

gin has made an analogy between the elements of the fetishizing process (such as vision, disavowal, the frozen moment, and repetition) and the mechanisms brought to bear in viewing a photograph. But Burgin introduces the concept of oscillation, placing the viewer in a shifting position: between recognition (of the photograph as representation) and disavowal (a belief that the photograph is in some way real), as well as between an identification with the photographer (the camera's point of view) and with the object photographed.[44] Unfortunately, embedded in Burgin's claim that shifting is inherent in the process of viewing photographs is an idealization of the medium of photography as a privileged site for unmasking fetishistic viewing mechanisms. Certainly, not all photographs and their viewing contexts foreground the process of oscillation. Indeed, many photographs encourage reification; others stimulate an awareness of fetishism's contradictions, while retaining its pleasures. Disparate elements of reception—disavowal, pleasure, and so on—can be either emphasized or suppressed by presenting photographs in different venues (a newspaper, a fan magazine) and in different formats (portrait photography, photomontage).

When these issues of fetishism and representation are applied to female spectatorship, two questions frequently arise: Is the fetishism experienced when viewing photography exclusively a condition of the male viewer? And, conversely, is oscillation between gender positions exclusively female? To both these questions, I would say no. Although it may be desirable to consider fetishism in relation to the phallus and power, I see no reason to keep the concept of fetishism contained wholly within Freud's theory of the castration complex, and therefore maintain it as exclusively male. Jacques Lacan's analysis of fetishism in "Desire and the Interpretation of Desire in *Hamlet*" (an essay underdiscussed in the critical literature) emphasizes a confusion in subject-object relations and a neurotic fixation on time and repetition.[45] While Lacan's remarks focus on the place of fetishism in male fantasy, the rethinking of identity provoked by the Hamlet essay need not be restricted to the male viewer. For the purposes of cultural history, Freud's emphasis on the castration complex may be usefully supplemented by considerations of disavowal and subject-object confusion.

Fetishism in the Freudian sense, however, is more central to a male viewing (or to a neurotic male viewing) than to a female one. Even in this sense, fetishism can be considered part of the female viewing process if one believes that women in our society are required to shift constantly between masculine and feminine positions. And certainly, though masculine and feminine may be binary oppositions in abstract theory, in actual experience there are no pure and completely differentiated gender identities; it is misleading to apply a dichotomized definition of gender to actual individuals and cultural constructs, which are more complex. Oscillation between gender positions can also be experienced by men, of course, but I would assert that while it *can* be experienced by men, it *must* be experienced by women in any relation to forms of societal power gendered as masculine.

The mechanisms of viewing photography—and the degree to which they evince shifting confusion, pleasure, and self-consciousness—bear directly on the reception of photomontage. The fragmented nature of photomontage can encourage, if not an escape from fetishism, an awareness of fetishistic operations and of the viewing mechanism itself. Therefore, when montage is used astutely to represent gender, it can encourage questions in the viewer vis-à-vis the gender identities portrayed. Contrasting the representation of androgyny in photomontage with "straight" photography, the viewer's dialectical assimilation of montage fragments whose connotations are binary opposites can, hopefully, lead to a rethinking of the conventional, monolithic norms of gender identity in society.

One great strength of Höch's photomontages is that they preached ambiguity to the converted. To women consuming images of the New Woman in the 1920s, Höch presented a dialectical rethinking of perceptions of modern femininity. In her Weimar photomontages, there was often a sense of celebration, conveyed by Höch's incorporation of images of liberated New Women—dancers, gymnasts, movie stars. But the euphoric attitude conveyed by such illustrations went hand-in-hand with a recurrent dislocation of subjectivity through her specific disruptions of the female face and body. Höch created alienating effects by using the practice of photomontage to juxtapose the beautiful and the ugly, the feminine and the masculine, the witty and the violent. Hers was a disquieting mix of utopianism and anxiety.

Höch did not oppose the consumerist images of the mass media, nor did she reproduce them unquestioningly. The willful gaps in her representation of the New Woman left room, instead, for viewers of the Weimar years—especially female viewers—to construct their own interpretations. Höch's work disallowed the comfortable closure of even private interpretations. In reading her androgynous montaged figures, for example, it was difficult for viewers to identify them simply as masculine or as feminine. Similarly, in her *Aus einem Ethnographischen Museum* series, Höch's montage compositions of images of modern European women combined with tribal artifacts eluded hierarchical classifications or easy melding.

Mass media representations of the New Woman, often in conjunction with other signs of modernity, created a fantasy site where women could be aligned with bourgeois power. Given the clear class demarcations in Weimar society and the impoverishment of the working class, most visual fantasies of individual empowerment for women adhered to a bourgeois image, a supposedly secure economic identity.[46] Through the mass media, a new norm and consensus about the modern women was in the process of being created during the Weimar era—a representational (if not actual) inclusion in the public sphere. The new images of modern women served a number of purposes for the mass media and for women during this period of transition—encouraging identification with the bourgeoisie, whether the woman was a member of it or not, and a related identification with technology and rationalization, especially as consumers. It is impossible to generalize about whether or not such images were empowering. Through an alliance with modernity, these images represented dreams of individual and sometimes collective freedom. Yet these utopian images also existed in a society that circumscribed women's earning power, political participation, and reproductive freedom.

Still, the wave of wonderfully seductive mass media images of the New Woman that swept over Germany in the 1920s was enticing for women, especially when compared to earlier Wilhelmine stereotypes. Höch re-presented these images of the New Woman with their appeal intact but their contours fractured in order to expose the contradictions of the new female stereotypes. The mass media images of the New Woman that Höch employed were familiar to women in her audience, who were already participating in the mixed blessings of modernism in a changing, yet persistently unequal, Weimar society. Her allegories, with their combination of anger and humor, depended on an audience in the know, particularly other women who went to the movies, read the photo-weeklies, worked hard for little money, wore their hair short, worked at home and in the office, perhaps had had illegal abortions, voiced political concerns, and argued about changing roles in a new society.

Then, as today, questions of feminine subjectivity and external politics were linked. The redefinition of women's roles through representation takes on a political meaning when it challenges the distribution of power in society. The questions Höch addressed in the 1920s remain critical today, though in different contexts; especially pressing are those issues concerning the production and reception of images of women. Höch's work provides important evidence of the necessity—indeed the right—of women to shape those images and even to establish their own new definition of utopia. Tapping the anger and the pleasure associated with femininity and legitimizing ambiguity is crucial to destabilizing societal definitions of femininity and creating the conditions that lead to empowerment.

1. Höch's notes are fragmentary. Höch Nachlass, Berlinische Galerie, Berlin, BG HHC H1569/79.

2. A pioneering analysis of representations of androgyny is Carolyn Heilbrun, *Toward a Recognition of Androgyny* (New York: Knopf, 1964). For an incisive yet ahistorical analysis of androgyny as pre-Oedipal fantasy, see Francette Pacteau, "The Impossible Referent: Representations of the Androgyne," in *Formations of Fantasy,* ed. Victor Burgin et al. (London: Methuen, 1986), 62–84.

3. Otto Weininger, *Sex and Character,* trans. of sixth ed. of *Geschlecht und Charakter* (London: William Heinemann, 1906); Magnus Hirschfeld, *Die Homosexualität des Mannes und des Weibes* (Berlin: Louis Marcus, 1914).

4. See, e.g., the anthology edited by Lillian Faderman and Brigitte Eriksson, *Lesbian-Feminism in Turn-of-the-Century Germany* (Tallahassee, Fla.: Naiad Press, 1980).

5. Manfred Baumgardt, "Das Institut fuer Sexualwissenschaft und der Homosexuellen-Bewegung in der Weimarer Republik," in *Eldorado: Homosexuelle Frauen und Manner in Berlin 1850–1950* (Berlin: Froelich and Kaufmann, 1984), 17–27.

6. Weininger, *Sex and Character,* 48.

7. Ibid., 58, 64.

8. Ibid., 66.

9. Sigmund Freud, *Three Essays on the Theory of Sexuality* (1905) (London: W. W. Norton, 1967), 95.

10. Sigmund Freud, "The Psychogenesis of a Case of Homosexuality in a Woman" (1920), in *The Standard Edition,* ed. and trans. James Strachey, vol. 18 (London: Hogarth Press, 1955), 145–72.

11. Ibid.

12. Freud's role is particularly useful for the construction of a historical spectator, a necessity discussed in Thomas Elsaesser, "Film History and Visual Pleasure: Weimar Cinema," in *Cinema Histories, Cinema Practices,* ed. Patricia Mellencamp and Philip Rosen (Friedrich, Md.: University Publications of America, 1984), 47–84.

13. Freud, "Homosexuality in a Woman," 170.

14. Ibid., 171.

15. James Steakley (in *The Homosexual Emancipation Movement in Germany* [New York: Arno Press, 1975])

notes that during the 1920s some thirty homosexual periodicals flourished, usually free of censorship except for the intermittent application of youth protection laws in late Weimar. Somewhat analogous to today's pornography laws, these statutes were used to close down the magazines (often temporarily) and also sometimes to shut down both male and female bars in Berlin. The most serious consequence, imprisonment, could occur as arbitrarily. Thus our popular image of wild nightlife among homosexuals in Berlin in the 1920s should be tempered by recognition of homosexuality's precarious existence under the law. One must also keep in mind that the participants were born in more conservative Wilhelmine times, when acknowledgment of homosexuality was in its most fledgling state.

16. It seems that Brugman may have had a stronger lesbian identification than Höch. Brugman had had relationships with women before (Kurt Schwitters, letter to Höch, 24 October 1926, from Rettelsdorp b. Schoenberg i. M., BG HHC K438/79), whereas Höch had not, and only Brugman was explicitly referred to as homosexual in others' correspondence, as, for example, by the homophobic Theo van Doesburg. After the war, Brugman was active in the Dutch homosexual organization COC. Myriam Everhard, "Graven: De Dood is de Humor van Heet Leven," *Diva: Lesbisch Tijdschrift* 6 (November 1984): 24–27, 35.

17. Letters from the Höch Nachlass, Murnau, and the Höch Nachlass, Backnang.

18. Höch letter, den Haag, to Grete Koenig, 14 October 1926, Höch Nachlass, Murnau.

19. Theories that her marriage to Kurt Matthies may have been merely masking Höch's homosexuality from the National Socialists are contradicted by Höch's journals of the time, in which she describes a passionate relationship.

20. Travel was central to their relationship. For instance, the two met while Höch was traveling through the Netherlands in 1926, and almost immediately Brugman asked Höch to continue with her to Grenoble. As Höch explained to her biographer: "She persuaded me to come with her to Grenoble. Then we stayed together for nine years." Heinz Ohff, *Hannah Höch* (Berlin: Gebr. Mann, 1968), 25.

21. Til Brugman, "Warenhaus der Liebe," BG HHC H1511/79. I want to thank Myriam Everhard for pointing out that this story reads as a parody of the Institute of Sexology. The collection of unpublished short stories by Brugman is in the Höch Nachlass, Berlinische Galerie, Berlin. In 1935, Höch and Brugman published a book together, with Brugman as author, *Scheingehacktes* (Berlin: Rabenpresse, 1935), which contained stories by Brugman parodying Nazism and consumerism and was illustrated by Höch. Brugman and Höch also collaborated on a descriptive travel article with drawings: Til Brugman, "Von Hollands Blumenfeldern," *Atlantis: Länder/Völker/Reisen* 5 (1933): 429–32.

22. Laura Mulvey, "On *Duel in the Sun:* Afterthoughts on 'Visual Pleasure and Narrative Cinema,'" *Framework* 15–17 (1981): 12–15; and Miriam Hansen, "Pleasure, Ambivalence, Identification: Valentino and Female Spectatorship," *Cinema Journal* 25, no. 4 (Spring 1986): 6–32.

23. Three issues of *Berliner Illustrirte Zeitung* provided mass media sources for *Der Vater:* (1) the single female dancer, cut out from a photograph captioned "Die Tänzerin Maria Leeser in Schevenginen" (*Berliner Illustrirte Zeitung*, 14 August 1921, 500), is the image of a free-spirited New Woman and was used repeatedly in the Ullstein press throughout Weimar in both features and advertisements; (2) the two female dancers from "Tanz im Freien: Die Fliegenden Tänzerinnen," Augn. C. Huenich (*Berliner Illustrirte Zeitung*, 24 July 1921, 456); and (3) the black boxer from "Augenblicksbilder aus berühmten Kämpf um die Weltmeisterschaft in Reno (Amerika) 1910" (*Berliner Illustrirte Zeitung*, 29 August 1920, 399).

24. Soren Kierkegaard, *The Concept of Irony*, trans. Lee M. Capel (Bloomington: Indiana University Press, 1965), 336–42.

25. Miriam Hansen, "Early Silent Cinema: Whose Public Sphere?" *New German Critique* 29 (Spring–Summer 1983): 147–84.

26. "Asta Nielsen als Hamlet," *Berliner Illustrirte Zeitung*, 12 September 1920, 423.

27. *Fotomontage*, Ausstellung im Lichthof des Ehemaligen Kunstgewerbemuseums Prinz Albrechtstr. 7, Berlin, 25 April–31 May 1931.

28. This photomontage is usually dated 1937, but it should be redated c. 1934, concurrent with most of Höch's other androgynous works. It was included in Höch's 1934 photomontage exhibition in Brno, Czechoslova-

kia, and so must have been created that year or earlier. See Höch's handwritten list of works in the Brno exhibition, Collection Museum Brno.

29. David Bathrick, "Max Schmeling on the Canvas: Boxing as an Icon of Weimar Culture," *New German Critique* 51 (Fall 1990): 121.

30. Stills from *Wege zur Kraft und Schönheit* advertised, for example, two health pamphlets, "Licht heilt, Licht schützt von Krankheit" and "Sonne also Heilmittel," *Die Dame* 23 (early August 1925): 46.

31. *History of Sexuality*, vol. 1, trans. Robert Hurley (New York: Vintage Books, 1980).

32. Even later, under National Socialism, though lesbians could be denounced, committed to concentration camps, and killed, lesbianism still was not officially a crime. Ilse Kokula, "Lesbisch leben von Weimar bis zur Nachkriegszeit," in *Eldorado*, 160–61.

33. For example, "Vom Chorgirl zum Buehnenstar: Dolly Haas," Aufn. Elli Marcus, *Uhu*, September 1930, 80.

34. Even this brief speculation on the meaning of androgynous images to the lesbian subculture in Weimar Germany shows how Michel Foucault, in the first volume of *History of Sexuality* (trans. Robert Hurley [New York: Vintage Books, 1980]), elides certain questions of gender identity and subjectivity by oversimplifying previous discourses on sex as concerned only with liberation. He incorrectly subsumes the term *identity* under the term *liberation*. As a feminist, I object to this overriding of investigations on the identity of the gendered subject. Additionally, a contemporary critique of Foucault should consider theories of representation that explore the reception of cultural production and the work of this reception in the positioning of the gendered subject, including, for example, much of recent film theory.

35. Karola Gramann, Heide Schlüpmann, and Amadou Seitz, "Gestern und Heute: Ein Gesprach mit Hertha Thiele," *Frauen und Film* 28 (June 1981): 32–41; Stiftung Deutsche Kinematek, *Hertha Thiele* (Berlin, Stiftung Deutsche Kinematek, 1983), 6–23; Rosi Kriesche, "Lesbische Liebe im Film bis 1950," in *Eldorado*, 187–96; B. Ruby Rich, "From Repressive Tolerance to Erotic Liberation: *Mädchen in Uniform*," in *Re-vision: Essays in Feminist Film Criticism*, ed. Mary Ann Doane, Patricia Mellencamp, and Linda Williams (Frederick, Md.: University Publications of America, 1984), 100–130; and Richard Dyer, "Less and More

than Women and Men: Lesbian and Gay Cinema in Weimar Germany," *New German Critique* 51 (Fall 1990): 5–61.

36. For excerpts of contemporary criticism, see Stiftung Deutsche Kinematek, *Herta Thiele*, 44–51; and Kriesche, "Lesbische Liebe," 187–96. Also see Roland Schacht, "Ein Film setzt sich durch," *Die Dame* 59 (March 1932): 6–8, 52.

37. In an earlier stage version performed in Berlin and also directed by Leontine Sagan, Hertha Thiele had played Manuela opposite Margarete Melzer, but for the film version the artistic director, Carl Froelich, ruled out Melzer as too masculine and chose the more feminine Dorothea Wieck to play von Bernburg (Thiele in Gramann, Schlüpmann, and Seitz, "Gestern und Heute," 32).

38. Thiele in ibid., 41.

39. As quoted in Rich, "Repressive Tolerance," 103.

40. "Von der hoeheren Toechterschule zum Film," *Uhu* 12 (September 1931): 34–42.

41. Kriesche, "Lesbische Liebe," 196.

42. "Es gab damals einen Trend, . . . sich wie Dietrich anzuziehen . . . und jeder nannte sich Marlene, wie sie" (Thiele in Gramann, Schlüpmann, and Seitz, "Gestern und Heute," 40).

43. Sigmund Freud, "Fetishism" (1927), in *The Standard Edition*, ed. and trans. James Strachey, vol. 21 (London: Hogarth Press, 1961), 169–77.

44. Victor Burgin, "Photography, Phantasy, Function," in *Thinking Photography* (London: Macmillan, 1982), 177–216.

45. Jacques Lacan, "Desire and the Interpretation of Desire in *Hamlet*" (1959), *Yale French Studies* 55–56 (1977): 11–52.

46. As film historian Patrice Petro explains, even on the fashion pages of the communist *Arbeiter Illustrierte Zeitung*, the images were more aligned with a bourgeois New Woman than a stereotypical proletariat woman. Patrice Petro, *Joyless Streets: Women and Melodramatic Representation in Weimar Germany* (Princeton, N.J.: Princeton University Press, 1989), 164–69. Narratives of upward class mobility, say from secretary to boss's wife, were common in women's films and novels of the 1920s. Guenter Berghaus, "'Girlkultur': Feminism, Americanism and Popular Entertainment in Weimar Germany," *Journal of Design History* 1, nos. 3–4 (1988): 206–207.

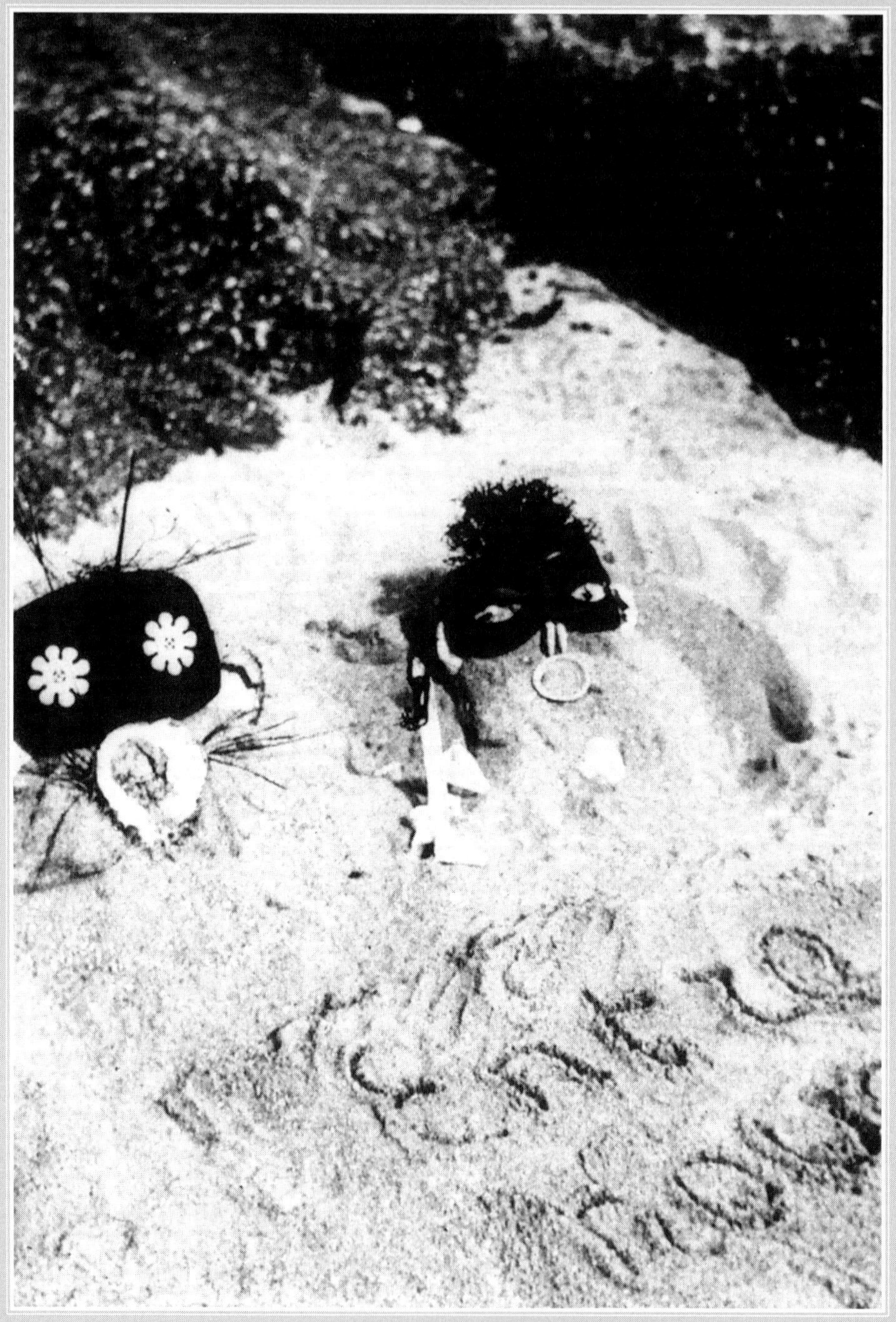

17

CLAUDE CAHUN, MARCEL MOORE, AND THE COLLABORATIVE CONSTRUCTION OF A LESBIAN SUBJECTIVITY

Julie Cole

DURING THE FIRST half of the twentieth century, the young author, artist, and political activist Lucy Schwob temporarily adopted a number of masculine pseudonyms and androgynous identities before becoming the ambiguously gendered entity known as Claude Cahun. As an associate of the Surrealists who signed several of the group's manifestos, Cahun exhibited in international Surrealist shows of the late 1930s, contributed to their publications, and played both male and female roles in experimental theater productions. Cahun also engaged in a variety of politically and artistically subversive activities with her stepsister and lifelong partner Suzanne Malherbe, an artist who changed her own name to the also equivocally gendered Marcel Moore. Following her death, the once well-known Cahun faded into obscurity, and much of the prolific artist's work was lost or destroyed. She reentered art-historical consciousness in the early 1980s, when a portion of her work, including a large number of never-before-seen photographs of the artist, was discovered.

Dubbed "self-portraits," the majority of these recovered works are small, black-and-white, untitled photographs of Cahun posing in a variety of elaborately staged tableaux. Although often masked and costumed to the point of being more or less unrec-

ognizable, the artist/subject of the images almost always stares out of the frame with an intense, straightforward gaze. The extremely theatrical nature of the photographs belies the fact that most of the introspective portraits were highly personal and staged in clearly private, domestic spaces. Indeed, apart from one exceptional work, which appeared in a 1930 edition of the small Paris review *Bifur* (fig. 17.2), and a lithograph based on a second photograph (fig. 17.3), the recently discovered portraits were never exhibited during Cahun's lifetime.[1] Although they eventually became the raw materials for other published pieces, the portraits themselves seem to have been produced as personal objects, not works of art intended for public display.

Since the discovery of the so-called self-portraits, Claude Cahun has been featured in numerous exhibitions, and her work has become a topic of critical discussion among art historians and feminists eager to restore this once forgotten artist to her rightful position within the histories of photography, Surrealism, and women artists. Many scholars, emphasizing Cahun's connections to Surrealism, have discussed her portraits in terms of that movement's interest in the destabilizing of identity and gender. Others, drawing on a perceived affinity between Cahun's use

An earlier version of this essay was delivered at the thirty-second annual Middle Atlantic Symposium in the History of Art, at the National Gallery of Art, Washington, D.C., 13 April 2002. Copyright © 2005 by Julie Cole.

Figure 17.1. Claude Cahun and Marcel Moore, *Entre-nous*, 1926. Black-and-white photograph. Private collection.

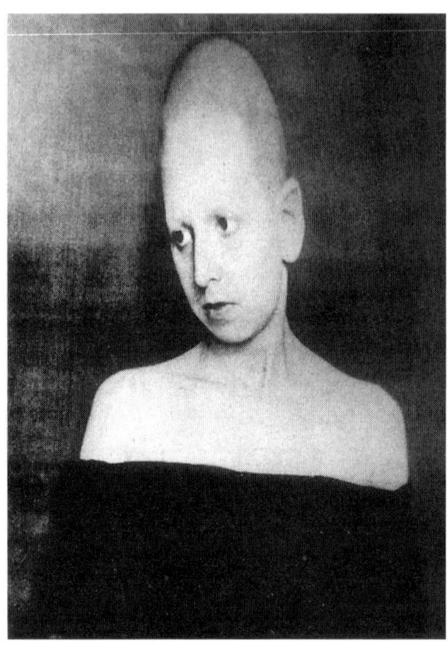

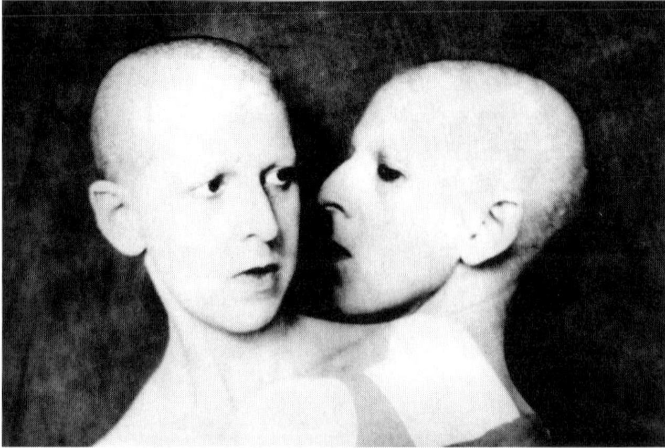

Figure 17.2 (LEFT). Claude Cahun, *Self-Portrait*, 1929. Black-and-white photograph. *Bifur*, no. 5 (1930). Private collection.

Figure 17.3 (ABOVE). Claude Cahun and Marcel Moore, *Que me veux-tu?* 1928. Black-and-white photograph. Private collection.

of her own body in her art and the practice of later feminist artists, such as Cindy Sherman, have seen her work as an almost prophetic feminist interrogation of female subjectivity, performative identity, and the gaze.[2] However, few scholars have approached the photos from an interpretive position that acknowledges both Cahun's personal and creative relationship with her lesbian partner and the fact that the photos in question were produced for them alone. Feminist and Surrealist approaches are to some extent relevant to Cahun's work, but in repositioning her inherently radical photographs within the now mainstream dialogues of artistic identity and Surrealism, modern critics have not only misinterpreted Cahun's art as operating within, rather than outside or against, artistic norms; they have all but eliminated Moore, and all that her involvement in Cahun's production implies, from the discourse.

Marcel Moore, an artist and illustrator in her own right, is known to have collaborated with her stepsister and partner on many political and artistic projects, including Cahun's 1914 book of poetry *Vues et visions*, which Moore illustrated, and Cahun's 1930 quasi-autobiographical book *Aveux non avenus* (which loosely translates as Disavowed Confes-

sions), for which the two artists produced a series of photomontages that appeared as chapter headings.[3] Based on Cahun's preparatory sketches, and composed primarily of images taken from earlier photographic portraits, they were apparently assembled by Moore, who signed the montage accompanying the first chapter.[4] But Moore's involvement in the production of the original photographs often goes underrecognized, even though she was clearly present when many (if not all) of the elaborately staged portraits of Cahun were shot. In fact, it is believed that in most cases Moore, who is almost never visible in any of the surviving portraits, stood behind the camera and made the exposures of Cahun.[5] Moore's presence and her participation in the construction of Cahun's portraits are evidenced by the fact that in one of the few photographs to feature both women, Moore can be seen peering from behind the curtain the two frequently used as a makeshift backdrop.[6]

A series of double portraits from 1926 further embodies the private, collaborative nature of the couple's project (fig. 17.1). Although both women are absent from the scene, their presence is evoked by a pair of masked stand-ins who are composed entirely of sand. The photographs are entitled *Entre nous* (Between Us), after the words written across the bodies in the sand. The humorous tableaux suggest that the phrase refers to a secret or private joke that the sand-women share, but it can also be seen to characterize the very nature of the portraits themselves. The result of shared labor, these photos, like the Cahun portraits, were meant for Cahun and Moore alone, and the play of gazes from photographer to subject to viewer existed only between the two of them.

The writings of Laura Cottingham and Abigail Solomon-Godeau stand as two important exceptions to the scholarly tendency to focus Cahun readings around the poles of Surrealism and female subjectivity alone. Situating Cahun's work within the context of her relationship with Moore and the lesbian subculture to which the couple belonged, Cottingham and Solomon-Godeau each suggest the possibility that Cahun's lesbianism significantly influenced her work.[7] Furthermore, each recognizes the important fact that Moore, whom Cahun referred to as *l'autre moi*, participated in the creation of the "self-portraits," which frequently employ mirrors or feature doubled subjects. Building upon this awareness, I will here examine more specifically how lesbian identity informed the appearance and meaning of the work Cahun produced with Moore.

If one steps outside contemporary theories about female artistic self-representation and looks beyond the Surrealist baffles embedded in her oeuvre, Cahun's relationship with Moore and her identity as one of a pair begin to emerge as major themes of her art. Standing outside the cultural and artistic paradigm of heterosexuality, Cahun worked with Moore both to critique existing constructs—including the misogynist assumptions that the Surrealists shared with mainstream culture—and to envision possible alternatives to the status quo. Their collaborative efforts resulted in the creation of a lesbian subject that appears in the photographs as simultaneously multifaceted and cohesive, stable but unfixed by conventional understanding. To call Cahun a lesbian is not simply to reference her sexual activities, but to invoke an entire series of cultural transgressions, including her personal and professional relationship with Moore, their

mutual refusal to participate in a heterosexual economy (wherein women's bodies and their images are shaped by the needs of heterosexual men, and women's identities are defined solely in terms of their relationships to men), and their production of a deliberately nonconformist visual identity.

The themes of performance, masking, mirroring, and doubling proliferate almost obsessively throughout Cahun's literary and visual oeuvres. Even before adopting the ambiguously gendered identity of Claude Cahun, the young artist began experimenting with the trappings of gender by posing for photographs in drag or in the guises of female archetypes, and her interpretations of even the best-known themes were far from conventional. With rare exceptions, her unwavering gaze, directed at the viewer, remained a constant feature of Cahun's portraits throughout her life. For modern viewers, Cahun's stare confounds expectations when she appears most feminine and underscores her defiance when she adopts the trappings of masculine prerogative; but for Moore, Cahun's original and only intended audience, her even gaze may have registered as engaging and conspiratorial, a sign that photographer and model were closely linked as equal participants in a mutual project, the disruption of gendered stereotypes.

In one of the earliest surviving portraits of Cahun, a photograph from around 1911–12, the teenaged Lucy Schwob appears as a beautiful well-known courtesan.[8] Staring directly at the viewer, her face framed by the curls she would shortly shave off, she foreshadowed many of the portraits to come in her emphasis on the face, her theatrical staging of the scene, and her unflinching gaze, which is simultaneously seductive and self-possessed. Although posing as an exotic courtesan, the young artist eschewed conventions of heterosexual feminine beauty in her refusal to appear demure or to show any part of her body. However, Cahun may have intended for the portrait to be seductive, for it is possible that her love affair with Suzanne Malherbe began around this time; as with many later photographs, this one may have been exposed by Malherbe, who was likely its sole intended audience.[9]

Schwob's wavy hair features prominently in an-

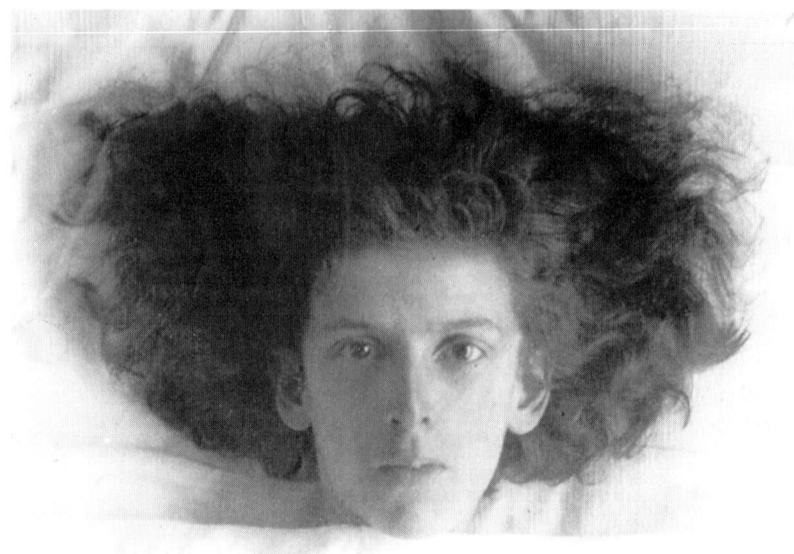

Figure 17.4. Claude Cahun and Marcel Moore, *Portrait of Claude Cahun*, ca. 1915. Black-and-white photograph. Courtesy of the Jersey Heritage Trust Collection.

other image of 1915 (fig. 17.4); like Medusa's crown of snakes, it frames her head, which appears to have been severed from her body by a white sheet (years later, Moore would emphasize this aspect of the portrait by outlining the strands of hair and positioning the decapitated head upside down in a photomontage devoted to the theme of fear).[10] Here Cahun's steady gaze most likely acknowledges Malherbe's presence and alludes to the nature of their relationship, for if the beautiful but grotesque Medusa's head had the power to turn *men* to stone, Schwob's stare posed no threat to the female photographer/viewer who met her eyes, and her visage is beautiful rather than monstrous or frightening. Furthermore, she posed in a bed, the most private of all the interior spaces that appear as backdrops for the Cahun portraits, and lying beneath her photographer.

By 1917, the year Lucy Schwob "became" Claude Cahun, she had shaved her head, but she continued to appear as feminine characters or masked women, and often exhibited both "masculine" and "feminine" traits within a single image. The resulting subject visually transgresses conventional gender boundaries, proving the categories of "man" and "woman" to be unfixed and unnatural. In many of the later portraits, Cahun exaggerated familiar gender signifiers to the point of parody, appearing in heavy makeup or elaborate costumes, some of which were borrowed from the theater productions she played in. In these highly theatrical works, as in those featuring Cahun as a masked female, the artist draws attention to the performative nature of both masculinity and femininity, and the lack of stable meaning behind gender. It is important to note, however, that Cahun's powerful presence and nearly ubiquitous gaze serve to remind viewers that a subjective entity exists behind the gendered mask.[11]

Some debate surrounds the question of whether or not Cahun actually cross-dresses in any of these portraits, and she is often labeled androgynous or bisexual. While a few of the surviving portraits record Cahun's appearance as she performed various male, female, and androgynous roles on stage, others illustrate how she sometimes posed in theatrical costumes for private photographs, thereby transforming an act of public display into one of personal exploration.[12] Through such images, Cahun indicated the performative aspects of her own identity, pictorially equated with that of a character whose being was literally performed. In a few of her earlier portraits, Cahun appeared as male types such as "the dandy" or "the sailor," but aside from the literally theatrical images, she rarely posed in full drag. Rather, she tended to

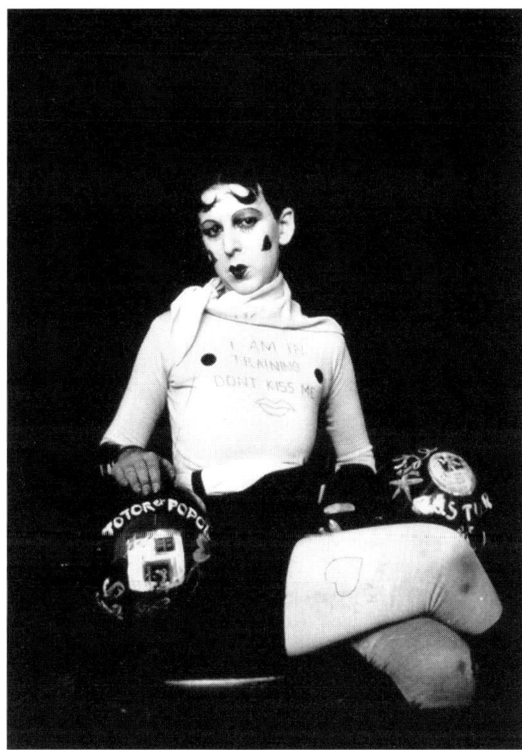

Figure 17.5. Claude Cahun and Marcel Moore, *Portrait of Claude Cahun*, ca. 1927. Black-and-white photograph. Courtesy of the Jersey Heritage Trust Collection.

mix gender signifiers in her costume, and when she posed in masculine dress or with her decidedly "unfeminine" shaved head, she often painted her lips with heavy rouge or adopted a typically "feminine" pout.[13] Furthermore, although difficult to recognize in the black-and-white photographs, Cahun frequently dyed her short hair pink, green, silver, or gold—ornamenting and "feminizing" it—and thus made it difficult to read her cropped hairstyle as purely masculine. Such a treatment may account for the odd, shiny appearance of Cahun's hair in a portrait of 1928 (see fig. 17.8 below). While this particular work is often cited as an example of Cahun's interest in drag, the checkerboard pattern of her garment prevents it from reading as a conventionally masculine suit or jacket, and her dyed or gilded hair further contributes to the idea that here, too, the subject wears a costume that is neither masculine nor feminine. Standing be-

fore a mirror, in a position traditionally assigned to women (particularly vain women), she looks away from her reflection and addresses the viewer, raising further questions about both her gender and her activity.

Cahun's mixing of gendered attributes reached a campy extreme in a 1927 series of images depicting the artist as a circus strong "man" (fig. 17.5). Sporting feminine curls, heart-shaped cheeks, and puckered lips, she donned a shirt decorated with fake nipples, a pair of lips, and the English words "I AM IN TRAINING DON'T KISS ME." If it is difficult to take this admonition seriously, given Cahun's lipsticked, puckered mouth, outrageous posture, and coy expression, both image and message become even more ambiguously playful when we consider that the person snapping the shutter, to whom both the pose and the statement were addressed, was Moore. Although displaying attributes of both a coy, seductive girl and a macho, well-muscled ladies' man, Cahun refused to become a conventionally desirable member of either sex, making her pronouncement of sexual unavailability redundant and unnecessary for all but the one person who potentially could, and might presumably want to, interrupt Cahun's training—or her performance—with a kiss.

Although she portrayed the hypermasculine role of a circus weightlifter, Cahun certainly did not pose as a man in this image. In fact, while the photo has little in common with the "dandy" portraits, it bears a striking resemblance to those recording Cahun's feminized appearance in a 1929 play. As a character called "Elle," she outlined her eyes and lips with makeup, painted hearts on her cheeks, and posed for the photographer with her hips swaying to one side.[14] That she used the same attributes to represent both a weightlifter and a young girl indicates how little stock Cahun placed in conventions of gender, and how willing she was to play with and subvert them.

It is presumably Cahun's doll-like appearance in images such as these, and her tendency to photograph her dressed-up body in numerous staged tableaux, that have led some scholars to draw parallels between her work and that of Hans Bellmer. Bellmer created

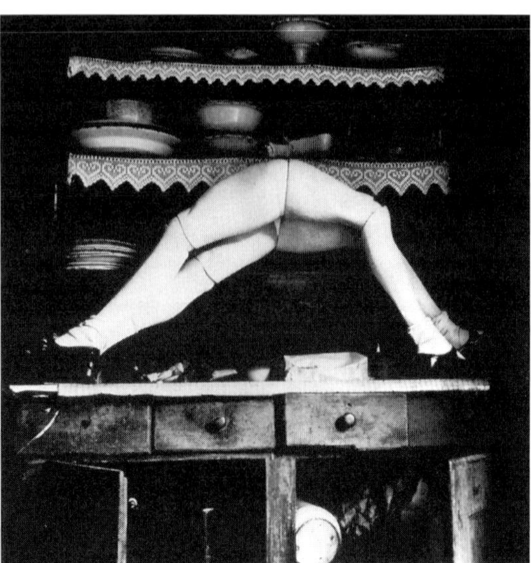

Figure 17.6. Hans Bellmer, *La Poupée*, 1935. Black-and-white photograph. Private collection, Paris. © 2005 Artists Rights Society (ARS), New York/ADAGP, Paris.

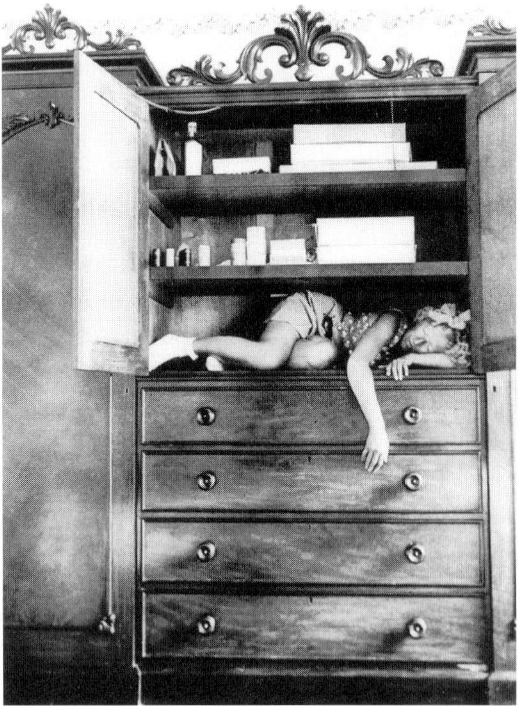

Figure 17.7. Claude Cahun and Marcel Moore, *Portrait of Claude Cahun*, ca. 1932. Black-and-white photograph. Courtesy of the Jersey Heritage Trust Collection.

a female doll from dismembered mannequins, dressed her up, and photographed her in various nightmarish situations that seemingly allude to preceding acts of physical and sexual violence, which would account for the terribly distorted condition of the doll. A particularly notable example of such comparisons, made by Rosalind Krauss, features an image of Bellmer's doll propped before a china cupboard like a headless insect whose four legs serve to index a violent act of dismemberment (fig. 17.6).[15] Harshly lit, surrounded by darkness, and juxtaposed with an article of domestic furniture that is itself in disarray—with distressed finish, open doors and drawers, missing knobs, and items tossed haphazardly on the shelves—the rigid doll is an image of tension and discomfort. In the "corresponding" Cahun photo (fig. 17.7), the image of a costumed adult asleep in a well-ordered cupboard may appear surreal insofar as it creates odd juxtapositions and alludes to the world of dreams, but the tenor of the work is far from frightening. Here the doors open like the cover of a book and flank Cahun like stage wings, triggering associations with theater and fairy tales (Cahun explored both themes), and the soft lighting, which almost dematerializes the paneled walls around the edges of the photo, reinforces the dreamlike (as opposed to nightmarish) nature of the scene. Seen within the context of Cahun's lesbian relationship, the image can be read as a scene of domestic harmony that conveys a childlike sense of security or comfort and references the nurturing environment she and Moore created for each other—one in which it was safe for the female model to appear vulnerable, and for the lesbian artists to produce such heretical images.

Freed (at least to a certain degree) from patriarchal expectations of wifely behavior and motherhood—expectations that often inflected Surrealist scenes of domesticity with uncomfortable, even sinister, overtones[16]—Cahun and Moore were more likely to have seen the home they shared as a haven from, rather than a prison of, social demands of femininity; it was most certainly a site of abundant artistic creativity. Similarly, while the doll's Mary Jane shoes and white socks are fetishized in Bellmer's photo, it is possible to see the incongruous presence of little girl's clothing in Cahun's portrait as a reminder of the artificiality of culturally imposed standards of femininity—such as the Surrealist concept of the passive *femme-enfant* that this image calls to mind— which she and Moore worked to escape. The photo may even contain a highly personal allusion to the fact that their relationship began during the stepsisters' childhood or youth. In any case, the clothing and setting contain playful or humorous elements, and hardly seem designed to shock their viewers (who were, one must recall, Cahun and Moore themselves). While the image now effectively provokes thoughts on themes such as the position of women in both domestic spaces and the world of avant-garde art, the work's greater subversive power lies in its creation of a viable space completely outside the patriarchal structures of heterosexual relationships, enforced femininity, and domestic servitude.

As her chosen name and unconventional appearance illustrate, Cahun was interested in the idea of gender ambiguity, and she understood gender identity to be a cultural construction. The fact that she posed in costume for her portraits, which are themselves highly theatrical, emphasizes the performative and unnatural "nature" of masculinity and femininity. It is significant that Cahun rarely pictured her body, concentrating instead upon the signifying constructions one hangs on it, or her face, another site where identity is worn and read.[17] When she did show her body, as in a nude portrait of 1928, she revealed it as clearly female but refused to conform to expectations about how the nude female body should appear in art.[18] It is also important to note that when she posed as a male character, she usually remained unmasked, drawing attention to her own identity and reminding the viewer that she, Claude Cahun, was a woman in man's clothing (and in a man's name, as Claude often is; Cahun was that of her uncle). Thus her portraits collectively challenge the idea that outward displays of masculinity and femininity are predicated upon a biological sexual difference. Instead,

they represent the individual's ability to transgress artificially imposed, culturally defined boundaries and to lay claim to a variety of oddly gendered identities. Though not depicting her body as androgynous, Cahun portrayed herself as an individual who could perform, literally, a variety of roles and simultaneously possess attributes generally considered mutually exclusive or commonly forbidden to a woman.

Cahun's access to identities beyond those normally considered appropriately feminine may have been due in large part to her lesbianism. As a lesbian, an "unnatural" or "phallic" woman, she was considered by many to be neither female nor male, and Cahun herself, who translated some of Havelock Ellis's controversial writings on the "third sex" into French, seems to have believed that homosexual individuals defied traditional categorization.[19] Existing outside the normative heterosexual paradigm wherein women were defined by and in relation to their male partners, she was no longer required to play the subordinate female role that was as strictly defined among the Surrealists as within the culture at large. Living and working with Moore, Cahun could adopt privately a variety of available identities, and even create new or hybrid ones for herself, but only by removing herself from mainstream culture. This is evidenced by the fact that the Cahun portraits were produced in a domestic setting (she frequently posed before makeshift backdrops of curtains or quilts tacked to walls in her home) and were never widely circulated by her. As negative stereotypes of the lesbian grew during the 1920s and 1930s, Cahun and Moore's public appearances as a couple led to discomfort among the Surrealists (Breton is said to have abandoned his favorite café whenever Cahun and Moore entered, often arm in arm), and much of their art, once discovered, was denounced as immoral and pornographic or destroyed.

Photos showing Cahun in masculinized, but not fully masculine, attire invoke the effort of many of her peers to create a positive lesbian identity or embody a specifically lesbian subject. Cahun's portrait of Sylvia Beach, taken around 1919, shows the famous lesbian standing in her Paris bookstore, Maison des Amis des Livres, a center of the Left Bank lesbian subculture. Posing in the nonfeminine clothing many lesbians of the time adopted as a symbol of their refusal to conform to heterosexual norms of all sorts, and standing in the store she owned and operated on her own, Beach publicly represented several aspects of "the new woman" in her financial freedom and refusal to remain in the home (her refusal to marry, bear children, or assume other heterosexual roles is also implied).[20] Beach's pose and appearance echo those of Cahun as she posed in a pair of portraits from around 1920, but Cahun appears far more masculine than Beach—her shaved head, dandified clothing, clenched fist, and cigarette combine to place these images among the few that can be said to show Cahun dressed "as a man."[21] Unlike Beach, in these images, as in the rest of her portraits, the costumed Cahun was performing. She simultaneously highlighted the artificial nature of the roles she enacted—that of "new woman" or "lesbian," as well as the male role of "dandy"—while gaining access to the privileges and prerogatives associated with them—in this case, the rights to dress as one pleases, to advertise one's sexuality, and to usurp masculine power by adopting the trappings of maleness.

It is important to note that while Beach was photographed in her own clothing and in a public space, Cahun's portraits show her in costume and in a private setting. The private nature of the photos may account for the degree of masculinity Cahun adopted in the images, for cross-dressing was in fact illegal in France at the time and to have appeared in public wearing such a costume would have involved a certain degree of risk. The politics of female drag, cross-dressing, and performance were extremely complex in 1920s France, varying according to factors such as environment, purpose, economic class, and beliefs about the nature of homosexuality, and I do not wish to argue that in these photographs Cahun sartorially aligned herself with any specific group of women. However, in photographing herself as a woman in man's clothing, Cahun performed yet another role,

one with strong ties to the lesbian and intellectual circles both she and Beach, with their partners, traveled in at the time the portraits were made.[22]

Cahun's most insistent references to her relationship with Moore may be found in her frequent use of mirrored or doubled images. Although the introverted artist proclaimed herself a narcissist, her strong identification with Moore, whom she referred to as *l'autre moi*, suggests that her "*self*-love," which she explored in a chapter of *Aveux non avenus* called "Moi-même" (Myself), also took Moore as its object. Recognizing this key fact, one may see Cahun's work and the work she produced in collaboration with Moore as thematizing not only narcissism but also lesbianism. In this context, the 1928 portrait of Cahun before a mirror takes on several layers of ironic meaning (fig. 17.8). Although she had admitted to narcissistic tendencies, when given a mirror Cahun deviated from the script (one determined by mythology, art-historical precedent, and Surrealist concerns) and looked away from her own reflection, gazing instead upon the true object of her affection: her stepsister, collaborator, and lover. Moore presumably returned the affectionate gaze, first as she stood behind the camera and focused it on her partner, and later as she looked upon the finished photograph. That Cahun's identification with Moore was mutual and reciprocal is further illustrated in the few surviving portraits of Moore, particularly two, taken in the same year, that feature the same mirror Cahun posed before. Although these images appear to be almost casual snapshots, they were manipulated in the darkroom (the reflections do not correspond to Moore's actual position before the mirror) and the resulting spatial disjunction, while subtle, is significant. In the double portrait of Moore (fig. 17.9), she too looks away from her reflected profile and addresses Cahun, who had presumably assumed Moore's usual position behind the camera. Standing to the right of the mirror, she reversed Cahun's position; her portrait functions as a virtual mirror-image of Cahun's. Significantly, when placed side by side, the reflected profiles of Moore and Cahun address one another, just as the "real" models ad-

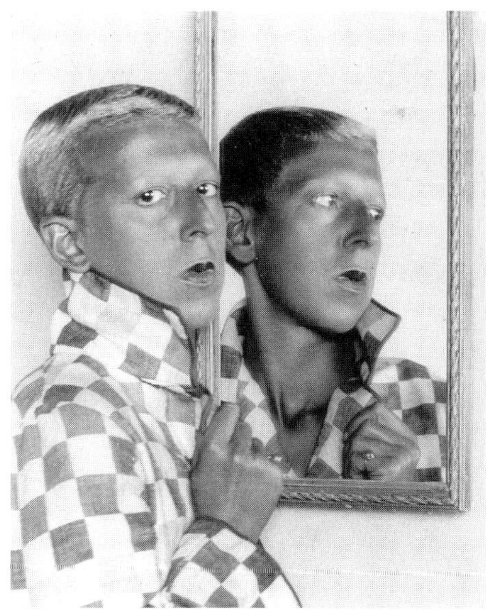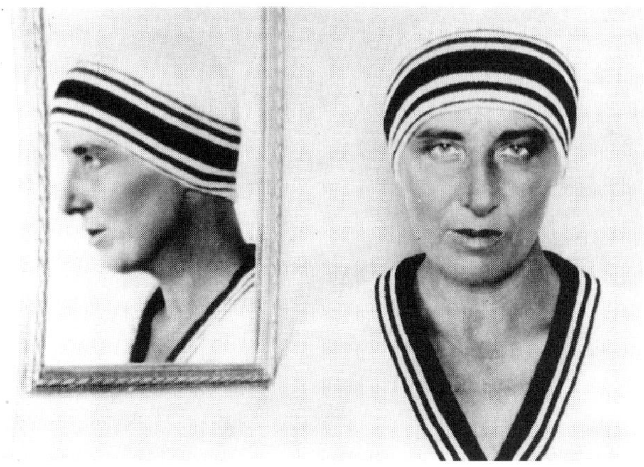

Figure 17.8 (LEFT). Claude Cahun and Marcel Moore, *Portrait of Claude Cahun*, 1928. Black-and-white photograph. Musée des Beaux-Arts, Nantes. (Photo: Réunion des Musées Nationaux/Art Resource, New York.) Figure 17.9 (ABOVE). Claude Cahun, *Suzanne Malherbe*, 1928. Black-and-white photograph. Private collection.

dressed their photographers. The conflation of their reciprocal, reflected identities is taken one step farther in the second photo of Moore (not illustrated here), for this reflection has no object; Cahun, as photographer and viewer, was herself positioned before the depicted mirror. Now looking into it, the lesbian "narcissist" would have seen not her own visage, but that of Moore reflected back at her.

Moore elaborated upon this concept in the *Aveux non avenus* photomontage accompanying the chapter on self-love (fig. 17.10). Anchoring the montage is an axis composed of an eye reflecting Cahun's face and a woman's hand (its palm facing out) holding a mirror that reflects another female hand (palm facing away) holding another mirror, which reflects Cahun's eyes. Unlike the photographic portraits of Cahun, this work was meant to be seen by readers other than Cahun and Moore, both male and female, and the myriad of reflections within reflections appropriately confuse and conflate the identities of subject and object, viewer and viewed. However, acknowledging Cahun's relationship with Moore allows one to recognize the artist's double—whether literally mirrored or appearing in repeated images—as a stand-in for Moore—"the other me" who actually took Cahun's portraits and assembled the seemingly

self-reflective photomontages. Having advertised Moore's authorship with the first signed photomontage, Cahun and Moore repeatedly invoked her presence through reflections and mirrors. The agent organizing and assembling the montage, Moore may be understood to own the hand seen to place a leg and the eye in which Cahun is "seen" or reflected. Furthermore, if in the portraits used to create the montage, Cahun saw Moore instead of her own reflection, here the "viewer" she encountered when she looked out of the mirror was also Moore. And if the position of viewer is traditionally reserved for male subjects, here the spectator's position corresponds to the female whose hand holds the mirror, and "he" sees a woman's face reflected back at "him." The repeated reflections and the women's implicitly reciprocal gazes frustrate the spectator's attempts to locate himself in relation to the image, and he is prevented from fully entering a play of gazes that are not narcissistic but self-sufficient, reciprocal, and lesbian.[23]

The fact that Moore, and not Cahun, signed and assembled the montages indicates the important role Cahun's partner had in shaping her identity, even to the point of becoming part of it, and it is significant that the montages, among the few Cahun works meant for public consumption, foreground Moore's

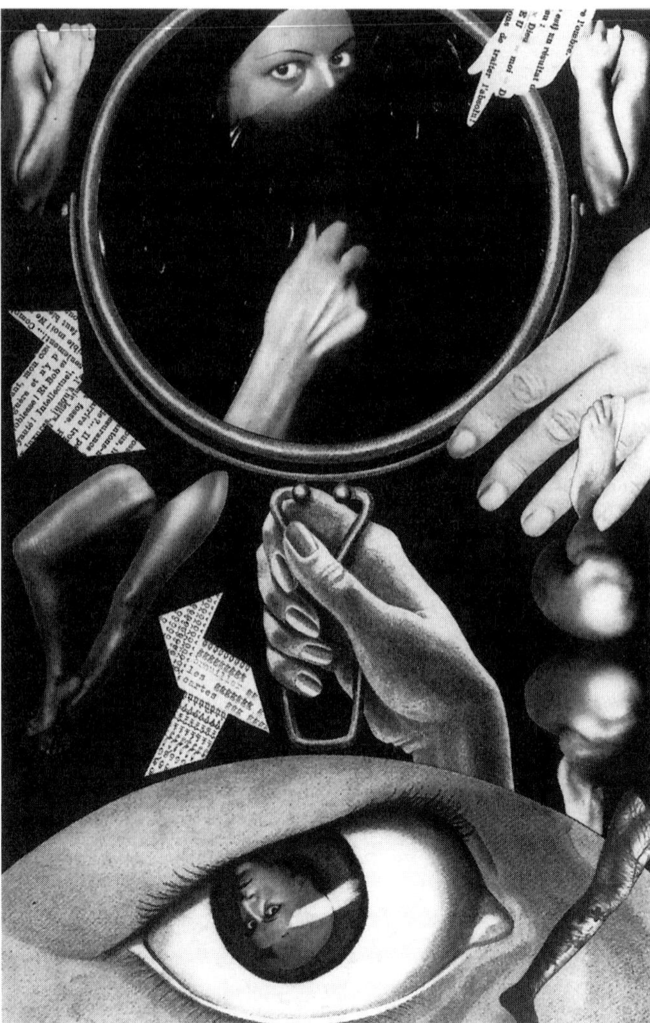

Figure 17.10. Claude Cahun and Marcel Moore, frontispiece for chapter 2, "Moi-meme," in *Aveux non avenus*, 1929–30. Photomontage. Private collection.

participation in the collaborative process. Although Moore rarely appears with Cahun in the photographs that have come down to us, many of the surviving works were manipulated by the artists in order to double Cahun's image, and in several portraits Cahun appears with other figures, who seem to act as stand-ins for Moore. While simultaneously portraying other concepts, on the most basic level these works represent the idea that Cahun apparently saw herself as one of a pair. For example, in a 1928 portrait, Cahun, pale-faced and dressed entirely in white, posed in front of a dark drapery. In the upper left corner of the image, an equally pale full-faced mask hangs near the edge of the curtain. Bearing a striking resemblance to Cahun, who actually wore it in several other photos, the white mask also recalls Moore's appearance behind the curtain in the earlier portrait.[24] Insofar as it features two "Cahuns" and re-creates the formal structure of the earlier double portrait, this picture may constitute a subtle reference to Cahun's personal and artistic involvement with Moore. A similar argument may be made for an image of 1939, in which Cahun and a milliner's mannequin stand in the doorway of the home she and Moore shared.[25] Cahun's body is concealed beneath a cloak similar to the one draped around the model, whose crown of flowers re-creates Cahun's white hair, and both "women" have flowers painted on their cheeks. If the model, along with Cahun's heightened feminine appearance, portrays femininity as something literally constructed, it is also by definition a stand-in for someone who isn't present, in this case Moore, who would have been standing behind the camera rather than in front of it.

Unique among the surviving images of Cahun is the one that appeared in the April 1930 edition of *Bifur* (fig. 17.2). The only photographic portrait of Cahun to be published during the artist's lifetime, it is also the only existing work to feature a surreally distorted image of her face. Cahun, her shaved head unnaturally elongated as if reflected in a fun-house mirror, glances down and to her right; a dark cloth cuts across her chest, baring her shoulders but concealing her breasts, and her bust appears to float in a dark void. The anatomical distortion led Krauss to compare the work to André Kertesz's 1932 photo *Distortion #6*, which also depicts an elongated female figure before a dark background.[26] However, the similarities between the two works end there. Kertesz's anonymous model is nude and faceless, her head is thrown back in a pose that suggests both painful contortion and an ecstatic swoon, and the artist's distortions emphasize the swelling forms of the woman's breasts, buttocks, and thighs. She is overtly sexualized, the object of the artist's desire as well as evidence of his ability to manipulate and control both art and the female body. On the other hand, Cahun presents viewers with an image of her own disembodied face—a symbol of the unique self—and employs distortion in order to draw attention to the cranium, the seat of intellect and Cartesian subjecthood, rather than to the body. Lacking sexualized body parts or conventional gender attributes, the bald Cahun becomes an androgynous image of subjectivity rather than the embodiment of a heterosexual male's ideal of feminine sexuality.

Ironically, in many ways the *Bifur* image portrays Cahun at her most conventionally feminine. By 1930, Cahun's penetrating, straightforward gaze had become a hallmark of her work; appearing in almost all of her portraits, it endows her visage with an intense power. But in both the distorted *Bifur* photo and the original, unmanipulated image from which it was made (fig. 17.11), she averts her eyes; uncharacteristically demure, she appears almost infantile with her bald head and enlarged eyes. Her wary expression underscores the physical vulnerability of her exposed, armless, solitary figure. Also, as David Bate has pointed out, "a Lacanian reading [of the distorted image] might well assert the phallic relation of Cahun's anamorphosis as an 'erection of the head'. . . as phallus: her most and least 'feminine' image."[27] However, it is unlikely that Cahun would have intended either work to be read as conforming to gender conventions or psychoanalytic dogma, and her decision to alter an existing portrait before exhibiting it suggests that differences between her intended audiences influenced both her compositions and their meanings.

The original private image, produced by Cahun and Moore in 1928 or 1929, shows Cahun from the knees up, wrapped in black and white drapery and slouched against a wall. As the object of Moore's gaze, Cahun was in fact the object of romantic desire, but she was also a sister, a beloved childhood playmate, lifelong partner, and artistic collaborator. Neither biologically other to Moore's female body nor mysteriously exotic as lesbian, Cahun's body was real, individualized, and linked to a subjective entity. The artists did not depict it as an anonymous, generalized site for the projection of fantasy, nor as something needing to be defined and controlled according to a male artist's needs.[28] Furthermore, as one of many similar works, this portrays one moment, one aspect of Cahun's being, and there was no danger of the photographer/viewer (roles played by both Moore and Cahun) interpreting this image as an abstract symbol of "woman." Therefore, conventional theories about the relationship between a female model and the artist who "captures" her in art do not operate in this image. In the context of Cahun's relationship with Moore, to display her body in such a way did not mean risking its fetishization, corruption, or colonization by a male artist or viewer, and her apparent vulnerability, which she willingly participated

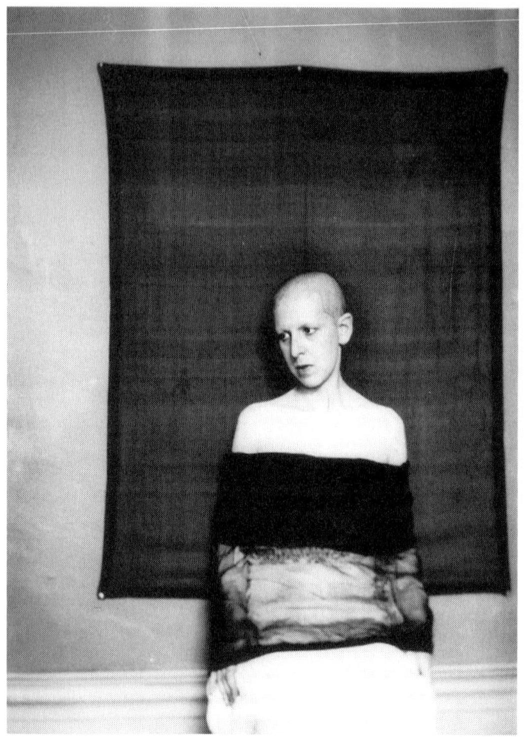

Figure 17.11. Claude Cahun and Marcel Moore, *Portrait of Claude Cahun*, 1928 or 1929. Black-and-white photograph. Courtesy of the Jersey Heritage Trust Collection.

in constructing, may in fact have referenced her feelings of safety and comfort, or signaled her own desire. Unlike Kertesz's unnamed model, who appeared simply as a numbered image, presumably posed and distorted by the artist in order to convey something other than her self (that he was free then to distort the image further underscores this fact), Cahun, in constructing an image of herself, chose to wear these garments, to strike this pose, and to appear before Moore in this way. For her part, Moore allowed Cahun to construct her own presentation and willingly participated in recording the image of Cahun's "self."

Cahun made significant changes to her own image before presenting it to an audience composed, in large part, of male Surrealists. In cropping the photo, she removed her body, the site of male erotic projection and sexual exchange, from public circulation. Although a woman's averted gaze traditionally indexes

her submission, in this case it more likely symbolizes the lesbian artist's refusal to engage the viewer who, in the public realm, was presumably a heterosexual male. And if Cahun's seemingly submissive behavior would have been considered appropriate for a woman (even by many of the avant-garde artists who flaunted a disregard for other forms of propriety), her ambiguously gendered appearance problematizes the notion of what constitutes "proper" behavior for the individual depicted.

While Cahun's use of distortion formally and technically aligns the *Bifur* image with the work of male Surrealists such as Kertesz, her tendency toward subversive parody should discourage one from reading the published image as reiterating Surrealist concepts. Thus, her decision to appear as a "monstrous distortion" may be seen as both a reference to a heterosexist society's perception of the lesbian as a monstrous perversion of the feminine and an illustration of that perception as an unnatural construction—a distortion of reality. In her only published photographic "self-portrait," Cahun publicly refused to conform to accepted standards of femininity, flaunted her refusal to participate in a compulsively heterosexual culture, and announced her identity as lesbian without providing (straight male) viewers with the opportunity to appropriate, sexualize, or exoticize her lesbian body for their own purposes.

The *Bifur* photo was addressed to an audience familiar with Freudian concepts, and readers versed in psychoanalytic theory well may have interpreted Cahun's elongated head as a "phallic projection."[29] Viewers conditioned to fear castration—and the phallic mother who represented both the threat and its repression—possibly found the image frightening and grotesque (as many modern scholars continue to do), and the fact that it was created by a lesbian, an already "unnaturally" phallic woman, may have amplified any threat the photograph posed to those familiar with the artist's sexuality (Breton's homophobia is well attested to, and it was shared by many of the Surrealists). However, the image itself is far from threatening, and even though Cahun seems to have self-consciously played with the archetype of the monstrous lesbian, earnest interpretations of the distorted portrait as such seem to betray the viewer's heterosexist bias, or a fear of lesbianism itself, rather than illuminate the artist's intentions.[30]

A second technically distorted Cahun portrait, labeled *Que me veux-tu?* (fig. 17.3), is closely related to the earlier version of the *Bifur* image and seems to carry similar connotations.[31] The photo portrays Cahun as having two heads—springing from two torsos photographically fused into one entity, the heads face, but do not look at, each other; nor do the bald heads gaze directly out from the picture. One of the few remaining Cahun photos to bear a title, the work asks *"What do you want from me?"* and on one level thematizes Cahun's exploration of multiple selves and shifting identities, but as neither head seems to look at the other, the implication is that the comment is addressed to someone outside the frame—the viewer. That this viewer was understood by Cahun to be someone other than Moore is likely, for the photograph served as the model for a lithograph that appeared on the cover of Georges Ribemont-Dessaignes's book *Frontières humaines*. The image once again portrays Cahun, a lesbian, as "monstrously distorted," and the fact that she also appears doubled—as she does in many of the portraits—may constitute yet another reference to her relationship with Moore. The portrait's title implies the artist's awareness of her status within the photo as something both performed and viewed, and raises questions about the (usually) male viewer's expectations of a work of art depicting a female subject. If, as a lesbian, Cahun was neither conventionally female nor sexually available to the heterosexual male viewer, how should she appear before him, and what function should her image serve? The wary expression of one of the faces and the suspicious sidelong glance of the other impart a degree of tension to the image and make it clear that the subject is uncomfortable with the way she is being viewed. It also implies that the viewer is demanding something of her. Assuming this demand is for her conformity to standard conventions of feminine display and sexual availability, it is not surprising that in both this and the *Bifur* portrait,

Cahun should question the demand, emphasize her relationship with another woman, distort her image in order to make it unattractive by conventional standards, and attempt to evade the viewer by refusing to make direct eye contact.[32]

Since the development of theories surrounding the gaze in filmic media, interpretations of photographic works have been formed in large part around issues of power and subject/object relationships. Endowed with subjectivity and the power of a definitively masculine scopic gaze, a photographer frames and shoots the object before the camera. By virtue of its position as the passive object of the gaze, the subject (which lacks subjectivity) of the photograph is gendered female, whether or not the subject is actually a woman. Played out across the bodies of countless female models, this power dynamic underlies the work of numerous male (and some female) artists, particularly Surrealist artists such as André Kertesz and Hans Bellmer. Given her association with the Surrealists and her frequent use of the female body as photographic subject, it is not surprising that Cahun's photographic portraits have been interpreted as a woman's response to this very dynamic, a woman artist's representation of female subjectivity that adopts the language of Surrealist photography in order to counter or subvert its assumptions.

Such readings assume that Cahun and Moore were operating from a position within the dominant visual discourse of Surrealism. This assumption reveals a number of almost invisible interpretive biases that, when cleared away or at least acknowledged, leave room for a more complete understanding of how Cahun's photographs function. Whether individual images were actually shot by Moore or by Cahun herself, the fact remains that the author(s) of the work was not only an artistic rebel or a woman, but a lesbian whose subject was either herself or her stepsister/lover (perhaps these are one and the same, considering how closely Cahun identified herself with Moore). Furthermore, as the Cahun portraits were never presented to an audience, when Cahun looked at the camera or out from a photograph, she addressed only Moore, her artistic collaborator and lesbian partner. Therefore, the power dynamics generally assumed to be at play in photographic images of women, particularly those by Surrealists, do not apply to Cahun's portraits. In order to understand fully the radical nature of her images and the degree to which they not only challenge and subvert both mainstream and avant-garde conventions but also stand entirely apart from them, one must adopt a completely different viewing paradigm.

The photomontages signed by Marcel Moore present audiences with an image of Cahun constructed by her double from the portraits they produced together, and provide audiences with a new framework for viewing all of Cahun's collaborative works. Viewers must recognize that Marcel Moore, the stepsister, lover, and lifelong partner who, like Cahun, adopted an ambiguously gendered, alliterative pseudonym (the initials of both names are themselves doubled) was an equal contributor to, as well as the primary viewer of, the constructed identity of Claude Cahun—an identity often recognized as doubled by scholars who nevertheless struggle to connect it with a single subjective author. Perhaps this explains the fact that, no matter how hard they try to discover the woman behind the images, readers of Cahun's work are often left feeling as if there were no single "Claude Cahun" to be discovered, for in fact there are two identities at play here, separate but inextricably linked in their exploration of a paired lesbian self existing against the backdrop of early-twentieth-century France.

In assigning authorship of the Cahun portraits and photomontages to Cahun alone, scholars not only demote Moore to the position of helpmate (simultaneously raising Cahun to the level of individual creative force or artistic genius and ridding her work of the "taint" of collaboration); they also remove Moore from behind the camera (or before the photograph, as the case may be) and displace her as Cahun's primary viewer, allowing the theoretical but ubiquitous "male viewer" to occupy Moore's now vacant post and making Cahun the object of a specifically male gaze. In this context, the elements of an empowering outsider identity and lesbian subjectivity, which Moore and Cahun produced and explored together as a private endeavor, become signs of Otherness that transform Cahun's subjective presence into the exotic object of a voyeuristic art-historical fascination with the private snapshots of a mysterious lesbian.

Photography and photomontage were well suited to Cahun and Moore's agenda: the creation of alternative possibilities for the lesbian subject. Photography is a liminal art, one whose indexical nature is simultaneously assumed and denied. Cahun and Moore used this slippage to their advantage, creating alternative worlds and identities that did not really exist but, through their "documentary" photographs, existed as real possibilities. Viewers who look to images of Cahun "in drag" as evidence of her desire to embody lesbian sexuality as masculine are thus missing the point: marginalized to the point of invisibility, Cahun and Moore created from scratch a collection of images that revealed the many possibilities that invisibility afforded the lesbian subject.[33] Neither male nor female, according to cultural definitions, the lesbian was not required to conform to either identity but could draw from each. In fact, as Cahun and Moore have shown, the lesbian subject was not even confined to inhabiting a single body, and could be multifaceted without being dangerously fragmented. While the portraits served as souvenirs or records of a lifelong joint project, in the photomontages the artists went public with the sum total of what they created, the visual representation of a lesbian self that was neither constrained by cultural expectations nor weakened and fragmented by its exploration of possible identities.

NOTES

I am grateful to the editors of this volume for their ongoing advice, support, and encouragement, and extend my particular thanks to Norma Broude for suggesting that I look into the works of Claude Cahun for my M.A. thesis at American University, and for guiding the progress of this paper.

1. A lithograph based on the 1928 Cahun photograph known as *Que me veux-tu?* appeared on the cover of Georges Ribemont-Dessaignes's novel *Frontières humaines* (Paris: Editions du Carrefour, 1929). See François Leperlier, *Claude Cahun: L'Ecart et la métamorphose* (Paris: Jean-Michel Place, 1992), 118–20. Apparently, Cahun occasionally shared the photographs of herself with close friends but never exhibited them. See François Leperlier, "Claude Cahun," trans. Simon Pleasance, in *Mise en Scène* (London: Institute of Contemporary Arts, 1994), 19.

2. First noted in Leperlier, *L'Ecart et la métamorphose*, the Cindy Sherman comparison has been reiterated by several scholars, including Therese Lichtenstein, "A Mutable Mirror: Claude Cahun," *Art Forum* 30, no. 8 (April 1992): 66; and Hal Foster, "L'Amour Faux," *Art in America*, January 1996, 118.

3. *Vues et Visions* (Georges Crès et Cie, 1919) was published by Lucy Schwob under the transitional pseudonym of Claude Courlis. All ten *Aveux non avenus* photomontages are reproduced in Heike Ander and Dirk Snauwaert, eds., *Claude Cahun Bilder*, exh. cat. (Munich: Schirmer/Mosel, 1997), plates 226–35. Unless otherwise noted, all images discussed but not illustrated herein may be found in this catalogue. The title *Aveux non avenus* is deliberately ambiguous.

4. Leperlier, *L'Ecart et la métamorphose*, 235. The title page of *Aveux non avenus* reads "Illustré d'héliogravures composées par Moore d'après les projets de l'auteur." See page 234 for a reproduction of one of Cahun's preparatory sketches.

5. Abigail Solomon-Godeau, "The Equivocal 'I': Claude Cahun as Lesbian Subject," in *Inverted Odysseys: Claude Cahun, Maya Deren, and Cindy Sherman*, exh. cat., ed. Shelley Rice (Cambridge: MIT Press, 1999), 116.

6. See Ander and Snauwaert, *Claude Cahun Bilder*, plate 19. The question of whether or not Cahun ever used a timer or remote to release the shutter of her camera remains unanswered; Moore's appearance in this Cahun portrait seems to support the idea that the couple sometimes used such technology, even as it proves her presence during and participation in the creation of Cahun's images. The complex staging of the portraits may provide a simple answer to the question of why Moore seldom posed with Cahun—she was otherwise occupied with constructing the environment and making the exposures. There is evidence that Cahun and Moore did make other photographs of the two of them together, however. A German officer stationed in Jersey during the occupation noted in his diary that Cahun "had had her head shaved and been thus photographed in the nude from every angle. Thereafter she had worn men's clothes. Further nude photographs showed *both* women practicing sexual perversion, exhibitionism and flagellation" (emphasis mine). See Baron von Aufsess, *The von Aufsess Occupation Diary*, ed. and trans. Kathleen J. Nowlan (Chichester, Sussex: Phillmore, 1985), 61–62, quoted in Lichtenstein, "A Mutable Mirror," 65 n. 5.

7. Solomon-Godeau, "The Equivocal 'I'"; and Laura Cottingham, "Considering Claude Cahun," in *Seeing through the Seventies: Essays on Feminism and Art* (Amsterdam: G+B Arts International, 2000), 189–213 (originally published in German as "Betrachtungen zu Claude Cahun" in Ander and Snauwaert, *Claude Cahun Bilder*, xix–xxix).

8. Ander and Snauwaert, *Claude Cahun Bilder*, plate 1. "In one of her earliest self-portraits, which Leperlier dates 1911, Cahun stages herself as the virtual double of the famously beautiful (and widely photographed) courtesan Cléo de Merode" (Solomon-Godeau, "The Equivocal 'I,'" 122).

9. According to Cahun's biographer, Leperlier, Schwob and Malherbe met as children; Maurice Schwob married Malherbe's mother in 1917, making the young women stepsisters. It is unclear when their friendship became intimate, but by the early 1920s Cahun and Moore were well established as a couple among the Parisian lesbian community.

10. Ander and Snauwaert, *Claude Cahun Bilder*, plate 233.

11. Scholars who see Cahun's photographs as evidence of a shifting identity so unstable it exists only as a void behind a mask often relate them to the theories of psychoanalyst Joan Rivière, who originally published her influential essay "Womanliness as a Masquerade" in 1929 (*International Journal of Psychoanalysis* 10: 303–13). However, Cahun's refusal to conform to any culturally defined identity category need not be read as an annihilation of the artist's self.

12. Solomon-Godeau, "The Equivocal 'I,'" 116–17. For an example of such pairings, see Ander and Snauwaert, *Claude Cahun Bilder*, plates 67 and 281. One photograph, taken in 1929, captured her as she ap-

peared during a performance in which she portrayed a man, while a head-shot of Cahun in her costume from the same production exemplifies how she sometimes transformed a character's clothing into elements of a "self-portrait."

13. Britta Konau discusses this tendency and its effect of raising questions about the validity of strict gender coding, in "Claude Cahun and the Poetics of Contradiction" (paper presented at the University of Connecticut, Stamford, April 2001).

14. Ander and Snauwaert, *Claude Cahun Bilder*, plates 63–66.

15. Rosalind Krauss, *Bachelors* (Cambridge, Mass.: MIT Press, 1999), 37. The photographs are illustrated on pages 38–41. Krauss is not the only author to juxtapose these two particular photos, but her use of them is an excellent example of the problematic nature of the comparison. Others have drawn similar comparisons, including the curators of the Metropolitan Museum of Art's 2002 Surrealism retrospective, who physically and thematically aligned several Cahun portraits with photographs by Bellmer.

16. Pierre Roy's *Danger on the Stairs* (1927), Frida Kahlo's *My Birth* (1932), Toyen's *Relâche* (1943), and Dorothea Tanning's *Maternity* (1946), to name only a few.

17. This is especially important given the Surrealist focus on the body. As David Bate has written, "Her photographs tend to emphasise the cultural *coding* of the body rather than the body itself; costumes, masks, theatrical make-up and facial expression take precedence when compared with those other Surrealist's *[sic]* emphasis on the female body as *torso*" (*Mise en Scène*, 8).

18. Ander and Snauwaert, *Claude Cahun Bilder*, plate 44.

19. The young author also covered trials of interest to homosexuals and wrote both essays and fictional stories on the subject of human sexuality. Havelock Ellis, *La Femme dans la société: I. L'Hygiène sociale*, trans. Lucie Schwob, appeared in *Mercure de France* in 1929. See Leperlier, *L'Ecart et la métamorphose*, 293–95, for a bibliography of relevant literature by Cahun.

20. Artists actively participated in the construction and propagation of this lesbian presence. For example, the lesbian painter Romaine Brooks often portrayed her lesbian sitters in similar garb, and adopted it herself. See the catalogue *Amazons in the Drawing Room:*

The Art of Romaine Brooks, ed. Whitney Chadwick (Berkeley: University of California Press, 2000). Joe Lucchesi has written about the important and complex role clothing played in the fashioning of Brooks's lesbian artistic identity, arguing that while "the dandy in some sense functioned for Brooks as a performative marker of lesbian desire, the signifying range of her sitters' costume and her own was much more fluid and expansive . . . [associated] with a playful homoeroticism and a public persona that may or may not have any relation to an 'essential' self" ("'The Dandy in Me': Romaine Brooks's 1923 Portraits," in *Dandies: Fashion and Finesse in Art and Culture*, ed. Susan Fillin-Yeh [New York: New York University Press, 2001], 155). Cahun's own relation to her clothing, the costumes she posed in, and the artistic identities she fashioned through them were undoubtedly just as complex as Brooks's.

21. Ander and Snauwaert, *Claude Cahun Bilder*, plates 7 and 10.

22. For a discussion of the roles cross-dressing played in the lives of various Paris lesbians during the early decades of the twentieth century, see Shari Benstock, *Women of the Left Bank: Paris 1900–1940* (Austin: University of Texas Press, 1980). Benstock also discusses the implications of the male (aesthete and homosexual) dandy's posturing, including its misogynist subtext. In so far as Cahun evokes the male dandy as well as the lesbian cross-dresser, the photos may function on one level as parodies of those roles as they were *culturally* defined, though Cahun may also be announcing a degree of identification with certain members of both communities.

23. In an essay on the *Aveux non avenus* photomontages, Honor Lasalle and Abigail Solomon-Godeau discuss Cahun's gaze in similar terms, but see it as self-reflexive and existing only between Cahun and her image, thus excluding Moore from the play of gazes. Honor Lasalle and Abigail Solomon-Godeau, "Surrealist Confession: Claude Cahun's Photomontages," *Afterimage* 19, no. 8 (March 1992): 11.

24. Ander and Snauwaert, *Claude Cahun Bilder*, plates 48, 50–53, 19.

25. Ibid., plate 93.

26. Krauss, *Bachelors*, 39.

27. Bate, *Mise en Scène*, 10.

28. For example, it does not represent the heterosexual

male's access to a more authentic state of being, nor does it function as a fetish.

29. Steven Harris, "*Coup d'œil*," *Oxford Art Journal* 24, no. 1 (2001): 99 n. 33.

30. Some modern writers have variously characterized Cahun's personae as vampiric (Katy Kline, "In or Out of the Picture: Claude Cahun and Cindy Sherman," in *Mirror Images: Women, Surrealism, and Self-Representation*, ed. Whitney Chadwick [Cambridge, Mass.: MIT Press, 1998], 67); monstrous and horrifying (Mary Ann Caws, "Doubling: Claude Cahun's Split Self," in *The Surrealist Look: An Erotics of Encounter* [Cambridge, Mass.: MIT Press, 1997], 95–119); terrifying grotesqueries (Lichtenstein, "A Mutable Mirror," 67); perverse, cruel, and in possession of a "pitiless, predatory visage" (Christopher Phillips, "To Imagine That I Am Another," *Art in America* 80, no. 7 [July 1992]: 92–93). While such qualities are often ascribed to Cahun by authors wishing to emphasize the degree to which Cahun was empowered by her departures from convention, and as such are considered somewhat complimentary by those using them, they betray an assumption on the part of scholars that Cahun was posing for an audience she wanted to defy or frighten (that is, men possessing a scopophilic gaze).

31. *Que me veux-tu?* (1928), printed from exposures apparently taken at the same time as the original image used to create the *Bifur* portrait, is one of the small number of surviving works that Cahun apparently altered in the darkroom.

32. It is interesting to note that in the published lithograph, the two bodies maintain their identities as discrete, separate entities, and the heads do appear to address one another. However, the photo's title does not appear on the cover, which instead features the caption "*N'ayez pas peur d'être dévorés*" (Do not fear being devoured).

33. Shelley Rice has discussed the photographs in similar terms. See *Inverted Odysseys*, 2–26.

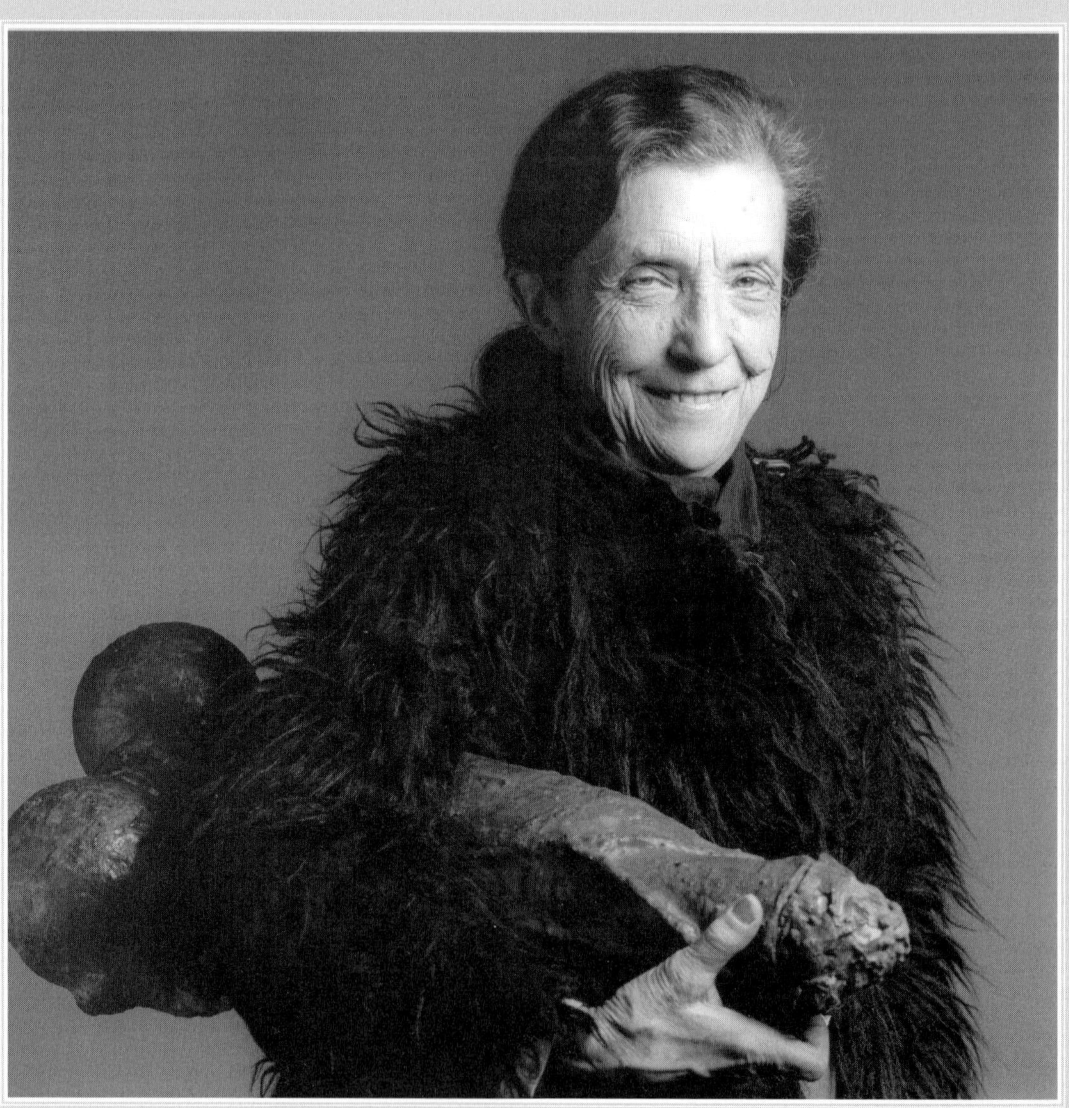

18

LOUISE BOURGEOIS'S *FEMMES-MAISONS*

Confronting Lacan

Julie Nicoletta

AT FIRST GLANCE, Louise Bourgeois's *Femmes-Maisons*, a series of four paintings, each thirty-five by fourteen inches, fill us with puzzlement (figs. 18.2–18.5). They depict nude females whose heads and torsos are replaced by houses. These images were created concurrently between 1945 and 1947, at a time of crucial personal and professional growth for the artist, as well as for New York City's art community. Jerry Gorovoy and Deborah Wye, both of whom have written on the artist, have been quick to relate Bourgeois's unique and intimate works to the artist's troubled childhood. The artist herself has allowed, even promoted, a Freudian psychobiographic interpretation of her work. However, that avenue fails to explore the parallel themes found in Bourgeois's art and in the writings of French psychoanalyst Jacques Lacan. Such a comparison not only allows a Lacanian reading of Bourgeois, but also demonstrates how her work critiques Lacan.

Bourgeois claims that the underlying motives for her art stem from her early years in France, where she was born in 1911. As a young girl, she was caught between "a nurturing, calm, and clear-thinking mother... and a powerful, volatile, and anxiety-causing father."[1]

Paul Gardner, Marsha Pels, and others have focused on the affair that her father had with her live-in English tutor, an affair that Louise's mother knew of and accepted in order to keep the family together. Bourgeois recalled that "she [her tutor] rode in the coupe with him [her father], in the front seat. Maman and I sat in back. I hated her!"[2] Bourgeois has been quite vocal about this period in her life, attributing to it feelings of anxiety and rage that continue to affect her and influence her art.[3]

The story of this affair—whether true or apocryphal—has taken on the aura of myth. No one interested in Bourgeois's work has looked beyond this Freudian idea of a traumatized childhood to see what other factors may have inspired Bourgeois. Her openness about her past and insistence that it is the source of her artistic ideas seem, in some ways, to be not only avowals of this myth but also means to circumvent other issues in her art.

However, the *Femmes-Maisons* beg interpretations beyond that of personal experience. In these early images Bourgeois explores not only her own history but also issues of femininity, psychoanalysis, and communication. Throughout her career she has presented

Figure 18.1. Robert Mapplethorpe, *Louise Bourgeois*, 1982. Gelatin silver print, 20 × 16 in. Copyright © Robert Mapplethorpe Foundation.

ambiguities of gender identity, often through a denial of individuality. Through the duplicity of the *Femmes-Maisons*, the artist explores problems of gender differentiation, particularly when a woman is forced to define her own identity in terms of a man. But perhaps the most overlooked matter in Bourgeois's work is the dilemma of communication. The question is twofold, dealing not only with the theme of communication within a work of art but also with the difficulty of communicating with the viewer. It is this issue that brings Louise Bourgeois and Jacques Lacan together. In fact, Bourgeois has acknowledged that she knew Lacan and long had an interest in his theories. However, her approaches to the feminine and the unconscious are quite different from his. She has expressed her disapproval of the psychoanalyst by calling him a *guerisseur*—a quack doctor.[4]

In the 1940s and 1950s Lacan formulated his ideas concerning human language, studying its structure as a means to understand the unconscious. For Lacan, the patriarchal framework of language provides the key to sexual difference. Language divides male from female, placing the male in a dominant position. Furthermore, language is composed of signifiers that function in terms of figures of speech, primarily metaphor and metonymy. Lacan sees metaphor (a figure of speech in which one object is likened to another by speaking of it as if it were the other) as a privileged, masculine function, and metonymy (the naming of a thing by substituting one of its attributes for the thing itself) as divisive and suggestive of femininity, which therefore prevents clear communication.[5] I suggest Lacan convoluted his own writing style—made it feminine—in order to emphasize this problem.[6]

Bourgeois struggles with the same questions as Lacan, but she transforms verbal examples into visual ones; more important, she reaches different conclusions. As with Lacan, Bourgeois's impenetrability was noted early. In a 1979 interview, Bourgeois recalled that after viewing her first one-woman show at the Peridot Gallery in 1946, Marcel Duchamp claimed he could not understand her work and disliked it for its lack of puns and its excessive emotional content.[7] It is hardly coincidental that Bourgeois's paintings and drawings of the 1940s often parallel the early studies of Lacan. Both knew many of the same members of Surrealist circles in France in the 1930s and later in New York City.[8]

The Surrealists' interest in the work of Freud and psychoanalysis, as seen in their concentration on the omnipotence of the dream and the power of the unconscious, as well as their attraction to non-Western culture and their desire to escape the inhibitions of society, resembles Bourgeois's interest in personal psychology and the influence of childhood on adult actions.[9] Bourgeois's work often draws on the unconscious, producing startling dreamlike images that conform to the Surrealist aesthetic.

Although she developed her own distinct style, in fact Bourgeois had a close relationship to this group. While a student in Paris during the 1930s, she lived in Isadora Duncan's house, above the gallery that served in 1936 as the site of "Gradiva," André Breton's first Surrealist exhibition.[10] This show displayed a variety of objects—mathematical, primitive, natural, found, irrational, readymade, and so forth—which were displayed out of context and in unusual combinations in order to stretch the limits of knowledge.[11] Certainly Bourgeois saw and was influenced by this juxtaposition of curious and normal everyday objects.

In June 1945 at New York's Norlyst Gallery, Bourgeois, with the help of Duchamp, organized "Documents France, 1940–1944: Art-Literature-Press of the French Underground" to inform the American public and draw sympathy for the French avant-garde. Works included anti-Nazi press; poetry by Paul Eluard and Max Jacob; prose by Jean-Paul Sartre, Gertrude Stein, and Andre Gide; and art ranging from Pierre Bonnard to Pablo Picasso. Despite this collaboration and her friendships with many of the Surrealists, Bourgeois thought them "lordly and pontifical."[12]

The Surrealists' interest in psychoanalysis is probably what attracted Lacan to their circle in the 1930s. He published two articles in the Surrealist journal *Minotaure*, one on a case concerning women hysterics.[13] These studies greatly interested the Surrealists; in fact, Paul Eluard later published the "involuntary poetry" of an erotomaniac woman whom Lacan had examined. The idea of the woman hysteric intrigued the Surrealists as much as it did Lacan. Being closer to nature and the "uncivilized," women could instinctively tap into natural drives. For the Surrealists, woman represented the active sexual force in the world and in man's creative life. She served as artistic muse, an object of man's desire, and a seductress.[14] In the Surrealist world, woman existed for man's creativity, not her own.

Lacan also found other sources for artistic style and production. In the first issue of *Minotaure*, his article "Le Problème du style et la conception psychiatrique des formes paranoiaques de l'expérience" (The Problem of Style and the Psychiatric Concept of the Paranoic Forms of Experience) linked symbols of artistic vision to symbols in myth, folklore, and visions of *délirants*—frenzied or mentally disturbed people.[15] The fundamental tendency of a specific symbol to be repeatedly identified with an object is matched by the constant process of *la création poétique*, poetic creation. He goes on to discuss the value of these symbols, noting that their power does not diminish even among *délirants*, because they are grounded in a collective human identity. In this sense, *délirants* resemble women hysterics because they have access to the unconscious. Lacan concludes that the original syntax of these symbols is the basis for understanding the symbolic values of art, as well as the problems of style. Thus, art can be understood through the psychological and anthropological study of individuals and cultures

Lacan linked the symbolic dimension in analysis with the symbolic order that Claude Lévi-Strauss claimed as an organizing principle of the systems of myth, language, kinship, and economic exchange in a culture.[16] Since most cultures are patriarchal, this symbolic order is also patriarchal. It is the pregiven structure of social and sexual roles and relations that make up the family and society. Lacan based all his later theories of language and sexual difference on this order structured around the transcendental signifier, the phallus.

In 1933, when Lacan published his articles in *Minotaure*, Bourgeois was studying math and geom-etry at the Sorbonne (1932–35). Although she did not read the articles, she may have been aware of Lacan's developing ideas on the unconscious and psychoanalysis. It is possible that Bourgeois communicated with Lévi-Strauss and Lacan, particularly after the war, when Bourgeois and Lévi-Strauss were in the United States. However, the artist herself has refused to clarify the existence or extent of any communications.[17] She has said, however, that she began reading Lacan's books in the early 1970s and that they interested her a great deal.[18]

Nevertheless, Bourgeois focuses on issues that also concerned Lacan; her paintings and drawings of the 1940s seem to parallel those early studies in which he began to explore the structure of language as a means of explaining sexual difference. Femininity is the area where Bourgeois deviates most strongly from Lacan. It is also the most pervasive theme in her art, appearing in paintings and sculpture that combine genders or question accepted modes of communication. Although both Bourgeois and Lacan are concerned with issues of gender, Lacan sees sexual difference as grounded in a world in which the phallus is the transcendental signifier. Not only does the phallus divide the male from the female; it also divides the real from the imaginary. On the other hand, Bourgeois seems more interested in overcoming patriarchal dominance through the combination of the sexes and the undermining of language, Lacan's symbolic order.

These issues can be examined best by focusing on Bourgeois's art of the 1940s, especially her *Femmes-Maisons*, which explore two major Lacanian themes: sexual difference, in terms of woman's role in society, and problems of communication. However, these universal concerns never lose their emotional impact because of the personal feeling that comes through to the viewer.

There is no doubt that Bourgeois incorporates her own life into her work. In 1938 she married art historian Robert Goldwater and moved to New York City. Despite Goldwater's contacts in the art world, she remained outside mainstream art movements.[19] Bourgeois also suffered isolation and alienation as a young mother: she gave birth to three sons in quick

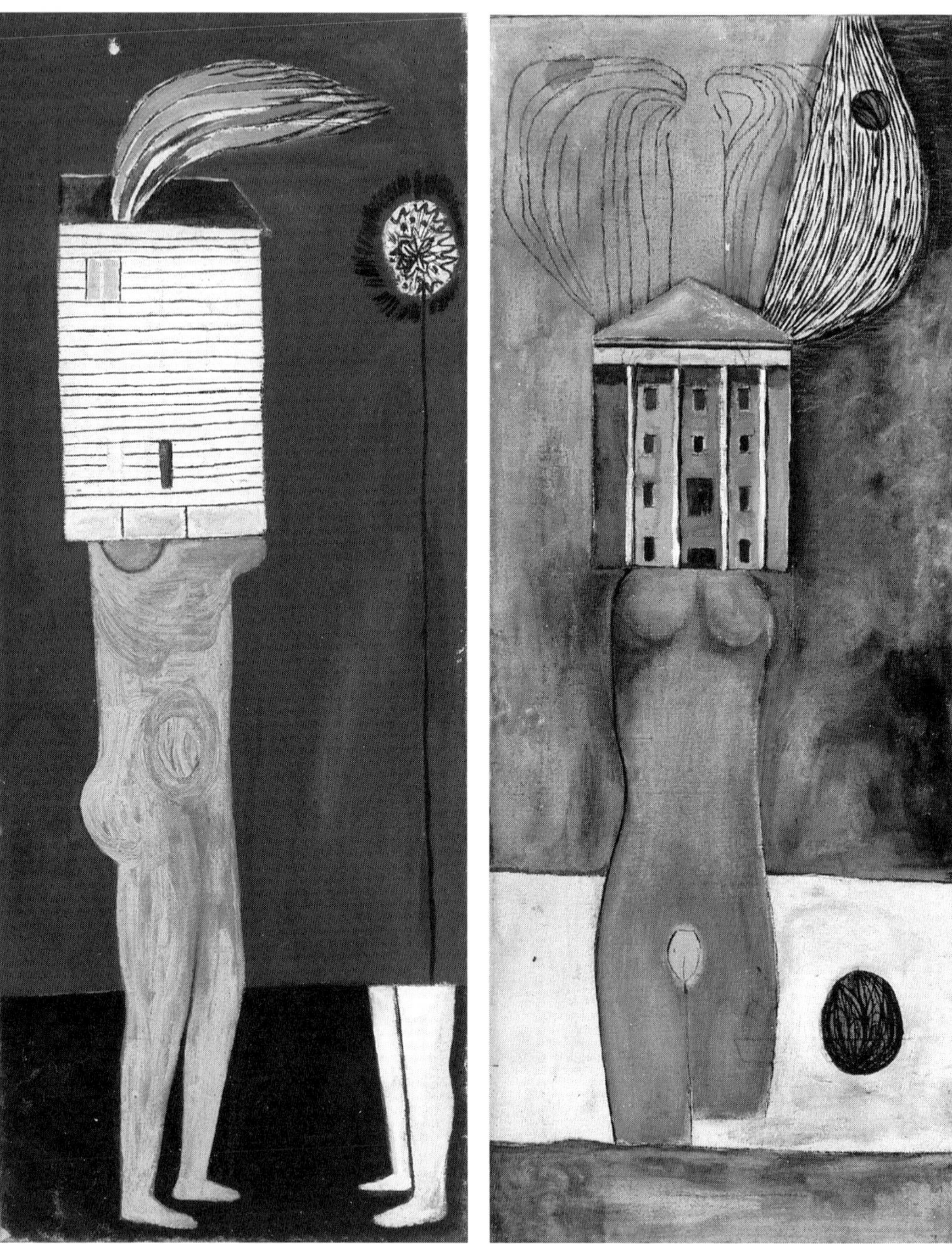

Figure 18.2 (LEFT). Louise Bourgeois, *Femme-Maison*, 1945–47. Oil and ink on canvas, 36 × 14 in. Collection Agnes Gund, New York, courtesy Cheim & Read, New York. (Photo: Donald Greenhaus.)

Figure 18.3 (RIGHT). Louise Bourgeois, *Femme-Maison*, 1946–47. Oil and ink on linen, 36 × 14 in. Collection John D. Kahlbetzer, courtesy Cheim & Read, New York. (Photo: Donald Greenhaus.)

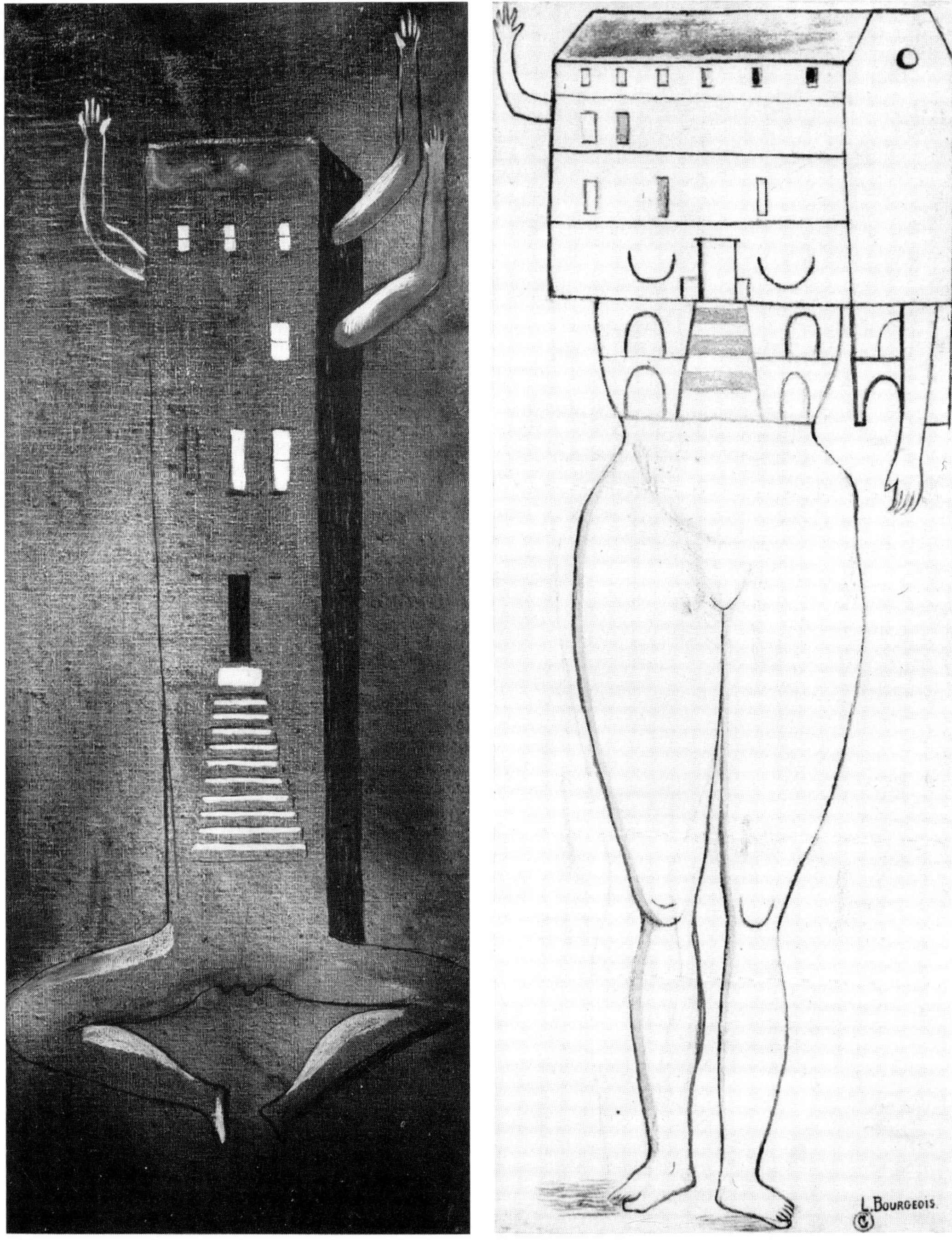

Figure 18.4 (LEFT). Louise Bourgeois, *Femme-Maison*, 1946–47. Oil and ink on linen, 36 × 14 in. Collection John D. Kahlbetzer, courtesy Cheim & Read, New York. (Photo: Donald Greenhaus.)

Figure 18.5 (RIGHT). Louise Bourgeois, *Femme-Maison*, 1946–47. Ink on linen, 36 × 14 in. Private collection, courtesy Cheim & Read, New York. (Photo: Donald Greenhaus.)

succession during the early 1940s.[20] She now recognizes, however, that such feelings are not uncommon for women with young children. In the *Femmes-Maisons,* the artist addresses these sentiments, perhaps to come to terms with them or even to expunge them from her life. Here she universalizes women's domestic and societal roles and their place in the systems of communication.

The *Femmes-Maisons* depict nude female bodies fully exposed except for the houses covering their heads and sometimes their torsos. In some images the arms are trapped within the buildings; in others the arms wave or flail at the viewer. In figure 18.2, a profile of a woman's body is topped by a simple white clapboard building that covers her head and arms and rests on the upper part of her breast. Her hair, flecked with pink, yellow, and brown, flies out of the rooftop, like smoke or fire from a chimney. The woman, whose body is yellow, stands in front of what appears to be a red curtain or backdrop on which is painted a large red and white flower with a long, narrow stem. Below the curtain is a pair of white legs visible from the knees down. The pale coloring of the woman-house and flower contrast with the dark background of the painting's surface. The "housed" woman faces the flower, her hair flowing toward but not touching it, desirous but afraid of its fragile beauty. However, the exposed legs behind the curtain suggest an aspect of deception in that the flower's beauty may be only a lure to further entrapment.

The *Femme-Maison* in figure 18.3 is viewed frontally, her head covered with a classical structure, which, as in the first image, rests on the woman's breasts. Although the upper part of the woman's body and the building blend into the background, the delicately colored genitalia attract the viewer's eye. No arms are evident and the legs are cut off at the knees, reducing the figure to a fragmented torso and adding to the feeling of dependence or lack of freedom. Here Bourgeois presents the female body as an object—a prisoner not only of her home or domestic sphere but also of her sexuality.

In figure 18.4 the body is almost subsumed by the long blocklike building that covers her head, breasts, torso, waist, and hips. Only the genitalia suggest that the body is female. The building not only hides the body but also distorts it, making it appear unnaturally long. The three arms of this *Femme-Maison* protrude from the building, flailing as if trying to free the body of its prison. The legs, too, are bent and cramped in the bottom part of the painting, intensifying the feelings of anxiety and imprisonment. These emotions are heightened by the rough brushwork used on the building and in the background. This work exemplifies what Lucy Lippard calls the "uneasy spaces" that conjure up themes of containment, anxiety, and the desire for escape.[21]

The figure in the fourth *Femme-Maison* (fig. 18.5) seems quite well integrated with her house. As in the other works, Bourgeois uses ink to outline the form of the woman and her house but leaves the figure unmolded by color. Instead of the fiery emotion conveyed by the *Femme-Maison* in figure 18.4, this one presents a calm, composed facade. The lower stories taper smoothly into her waist, and the woman's role as fertility figure is evident in her bare genitalia and rounded hips and thighs. The stairs leading to the door between the woman's breasts signal accessibility without struggle. Her left arm hangs limply by her side; however, the tiny right arm is identical to the flailing one in figure 18.4. Is Bourgeois suggesting here woman's acceptance of her place in society, or is she conveying the tension that arises between contentment in domestic confinement and a desire to break free of traditional roles?

The *Femmes-Maisons* suggest that Bourgeois did not resolve these issues in the 1940s. Her life was not grounded: for her the decade was "a period without feet."[22] Wye has likened Bourgeois's sculpture *Portrait of Jean-Louis* (c. 1947–49; private collection) to the *Femmes-Maisons* in that they both use "anthropomorphized architectural imagery."[23] Indeed, the figures represented in both the paintings and sculpture are recognizably human only in that they have arms or legs. Like the *Femmes-Maisons,* *Portrait of Jean-Louis* conveys instability despite the feelings of comfort commonly associated with a house. The thirty-five-inch-high painted wood figure is narrow and cylindrical, with rough holes to represent windows carved into the skyscraper-like top. Halfway down is a larger hole framed by arches scratched into the wood, signifying the foundation or entrance into the building. This structure stands precariously on two limbs that have rounded ends rather than feet. Bourgeois remarked of the sculpture: "It wasn't grounded. But this is a very important word, this idea of being grounded, because during that period things were not grounded."[24] A year or two after the creation of the *Femmes-Maisons*, Bourgeois still had not found stability.[25]

The ambivalent messages of the *Femme-Maison* paintings can, perhaps, be partly explained by Gaston Bachelard, who, in his *Poetics of Space* (1958), discusses the various meanings of houses. They surround the inside space of the mind, he writes, and are "one of the greatest powers of integration for the thoughts, memories, and dreams of mankind."[26] He later adds that the "room and house are psychological diagrams that guide writers and poets in their analysis of intimacy."[27] Although Bachelard wrote his book years after the *Femmes-Maisons* were created, Bourgeois's images follow similar ideas.[28] The house typically is remembered as a source of warmth and maternal protection. Yet for Bourgeois, at least according to her own accounts, her childhood home was a place of anxiety, pain, and anger. Thus, for her, the house held ambivalent associations.

Bourgeois's interest in Freud cannot be ignored, for the relationship between mother and child has great importance in the discussion of sexual difference in psychoanalysis. Although the *Femmes-Maisons* do not directly relate to the artist's children, as does, for example, *Portrait of Jean-Louis*, named after one of her sons, the traditional role of the woman as homemaker and caretaker is obvious. In Freud's theory of the Oedipus complex, the adoption of gender roles allows the boy and the girl to grow up assuming their predestined positions in society. For Freud, the Oedipus complex set forth the structures of morality, conscience, law, and all forms of social and religious authority. However, all these entities cannot completely wipe out the unruly and unpredictable unconscious,

which is the source of all human desire, repressed or unrepressed. Despite the potential destruction the uncontrolled unconscious could bring into society, Freud believed it held the key to finding ways to expose and subdue problems that arose in individuals and in society.

Where do Lacan and Bourgeois fit into this scheme? Lacan sees the unconscious as being structured like language and so turns to language as a means of probing the inner recesses of the mind. According to Freud, the unconscious mind uses dreams to communicate to the conscious mind, but it couches and distorts meanings, thereby producing a series of symbols that have to be deciphered like a rebus.[29] In language, real objects must be replaced by signifiers, but often this meaning is displaced through metaphor and metonymy. Thus, the very structure of language prevents clear communication and understanding. Metonymy serves only to divide and differentiate identities, a phenomenon Lacan emphasizes by making his own writings convoluted.[30]

Bourgeois explores these problems through visual imagery. Her art is infused with ambiguous meanings that underlie problems of communication. The *Femmes-Maisons* exemplify the difficulties of communication between humans through images rather than words. Without faces, none of the women has an identity. Only the various styles of their houses differentiate them. Some figures seem to fight their containment, while others accept it. In addition, while all the houses have windows and some have doors, implying accessibility, Bourgeois does not tell if the windows and doors are open or closed, locked or unlocked. Although the women's sexual organs are exposed to whoever wishes to exploit them, their minds are closed off from all outsiders by the houses on their heads. Taken together, the images cannot help us decipher their meaning. Just as in Lacan's metonymic chain, we are trapped in a circle of signifiers and signifieds with no single concrete meaning.

Julia Kristeva explained the semiotic as an archaic dimension of language. It is preverbal, linked to bodily contact with the mother. Only when the child is confronted by the paternal order of language is she

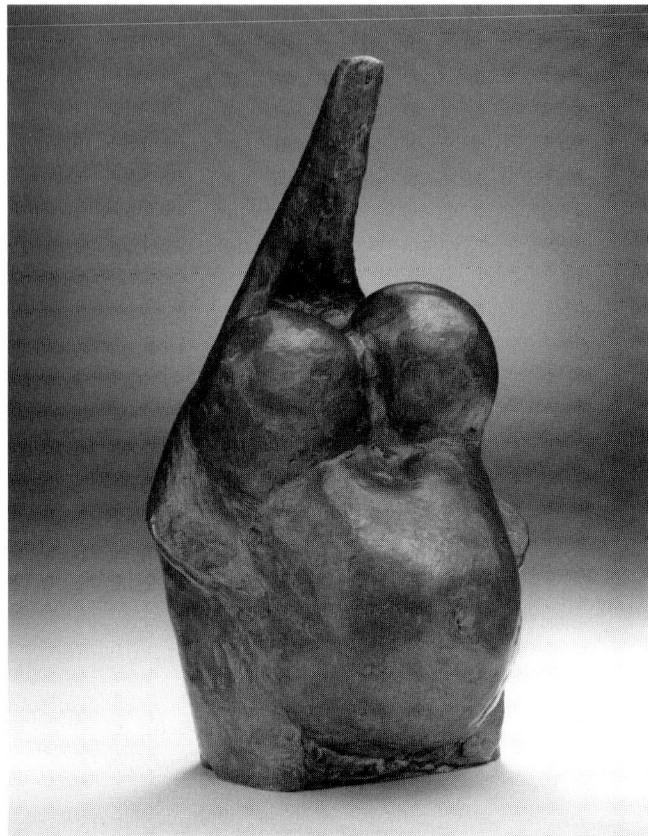

Figure 18.6. Louise Bourgeois, *Fragile Goddess*, 1970. Bronze, 10¼ × 5⅞ × 5⅜ in. Courtesy Cheim & Read, New York. (Photo: Christopher Burke.)

separated from the mother. Thus, the semiotic order exists prior to Lacan's symbolic order and coexists with the pre-Oedipal stage. Art gives the semiotic freer play and, consequently, threatens the dominance of written and spoken language. The semiotic challenges all transcendental signifiers, which, in a phallocentric world, denote signs such as the Father, the Law, and God. By moving away from fixed signs, the semiotic focuses on signifiers that have ambiguous meanings.[31] In addition, since the semiotic is linked with the pre-Oedipal phase and the mother, it is also connected to the feminine. This association, combined with the fluidity of meaning, directs signs toward a sort of bisexuality neither wholly masculine nor wholly feminine. Taken further, the semiotic breaks down all binary oppositions concerning

power and possession in society, decentering the subject and destroying established cultural beliefs and institutions.[32]

Bourgeois's art differs from that of her male counterparts in the New York art world of the 1940s and 1950s because she did not have the advantage of written language. Critics Clement Greenberg and Harold Rosenberg, for example, characterized the paintings of New York School artists Jackson Pollock, Willem de Kooning, and Mark Rothko in masculine terms, focusing on the size and aggressiveness of their work. Although Bourgeois's work had been included in journals of the proto–Abstract Expressionists, she found herself on the fringes of this group. When she turned to sculpture, she moved even farther away from the Abstract Expressionist core. Works in media other than painting or created by artists other than American men with European roots were not given a major place in the Abstract Expressionist movement.[33]

By expressing herself through art rather than language, Bourgeois circumvented the symbolic order of patriarchal society. Since language exists prior to the individual, the child who has acquired language enters into a world of conventions that she has had no role in shaping.[34] Although in the *Femmes-Maisons* Bourgeois shows the loss of control and sense of anxiety that such a situation causes in a woman, she later explores ways in which sexual difference becomes blurred.

In sculptures of the early 1970s, she merged the sexes into forms representing both the male and female genitalia. *Fragile Goddess* (1970; fig. 18.6), a small sculpture of self-hardening clay, recast in bronze, represents both an erect penis and a round fertility goddess. Although each entity shares the same parts, tension is present. It is an aggressive-looking work, but it also appears quite fragile, particularly in the figure's long, narrow penis/neck and thin arms. Bourgeois also searches for a resolution of sexual difference. In *Trani Episode* (c. 1971–72; private collection), a hydrocal and latex work, she rests soft penis/breast forms on top of one another. The calm, flaccid appearance of the work implies a sense of comfort, if not harmony, between the ambiguous shapes. Discussing this sculpture in a 1975 interview, Bourgeois spoke of the merging of opposites and "the problem of survival, having to do with identification with one or the other; with merging and adopting the differences of the father."[35] In an earlier interview she stated, "We are all vulnerable in some way and we are all male-female."[36]

Bourgeois's use of gender ambiguity may be a denunciation not only of phallocentric language and patriarchal society but also of Lacan's definition of the feminine in psychoanalysis. Lacan's theories of absolute sexual difference are based on an inequality of the sexes that begins with the castration complex. Yet he embarked on his own psychoanalytic work by studying women hysterics, as did Freud, and applied the results to male subjects. Lacan never considers the implications of his theories for women; instead he assumes, as did his audience, that the beneficiaries of his explorations into the unconscious would be men.

In her examination of the process of gynesis (the putting into discourse of "woman" as intrinsic to new modes of thinking, writing, and speaking) and its use in literary criticism, Alice Jardine probes Lacan's view of the female body and the male subject.[37] Lacan sees feminine *jouissance* "as an ultimate limit to any discourse articulated by Man," going beyond phallic pleasure.[38] It has to do with the space of the Other—the unfathomable and the ineffable. But there are other limits to discourse—"the Real, the True, and the Unconscious"—all of which are gendered as feminine because they cannot be understood consciously. If the unconscious is feminine, then language and writing must be feminine also. But this cannot be, because Lacan has determined language to be one of the mainstays of patriarchy. Thus, he stops his feminine metonymy at the literary.[39] He must do this, because otherwise woman subverts not only his own theories but the very structures of society. In her analysis of Lacan, Jardine shows that his theories do not hold up to scrutiny. His need to assign everything a gender supports his desire to find absolute sexual difference at all levels of the conscious and unconscious.

Bourgeois may have looked for a female subject in her work of the 1940s, where images focus on the female form and explore problems of femininity through a woman's perspective. By the 1970s, however, the sexes are merged. Perhaps one of the most revealing images of Bourgeois and her art is her 1982 portrait by Robert Mapplethorpe (fig. 18.1). Dressed in a shaggy fur coat, Bourgeois cradles under her arm a large veined phallus with bulbous testicles—a 1968 sculpture incongruously entitled *Fillette*. In keeping with the blatant sexual imagery of the sculpture, we can explicate the photograph in terms of sexuality and gender. Bourgeois, in her black, furry coat, becomes a vagina that engulfs the penis. Her devilish, even lewd expression, as she tickles the head of the penis, leaves little doubt that she is in control. The image has been interpreted as one of castration;[40] however, it can also be seen as one of protectiveness. Indeed, her figure contains the sculpture itself, as if she were protecting it from outside forces. In this photograph Mapplethorpe shows Bourgeois as a mature artist who, though she may not have resolved issues of sexual difference and problems of communication, has gone far beyond Lacan and most feminists by searching for integration of the sexes rather than separation.

NOTES

1. Deborah Wye, *Louise Bourgeois*, exh. cat. (New York: Museum of Modern Art, 1982), 14.

2. Paul Gardner, "The 'Discreet Charm' of Louise Bourgeois," *Art News*, February 1980, 84.

3. Gardner, "Discreet Charm," 82–84; Wye, *Louise Bourgeois*, 14.

4. Author's telephone interview with Louise Bourgeois, October 1989.

5. Jane Gallop, *Reading Lacan* (Ithaca, N.Y.: Cornell University, 1985), 126–27. The definitions of metaphor and metonymy are from *Funk & Wagnalls Standard College Dictionary*.

6. See Terry Eagleton, *Literary Theory: An Introduction* (Minneapolis: University of Minnesota, 1983), 169; Gallop, *Reading Lacan*; and Steve Burnison and Chris Weedon, "Ideology, Subjectivity and the Artistic Text," in *On Ideology*, ed. Bill Schwartz (London: Hutchinson, 1978), 212, for comments on Lacan's impenetrable writing style.

7. See Marsha Pels, "Louise Bourgeois: A Search for Gravity," *Art International*, October 1979, 54.

8. Both Bourgeois and Lacan were part of these circles in France. Bourgeois also knew many Surrealists in New York City during and immediately after the war. However, there is no evidence indicating that Lacan was in New York in the 1940s. Bourgeois is evasive on this issue.

9. Bourgeois published an article on Freud's collection of antiquities. See "Freud's Toys," *Artforum*, January 1990, 111–13.

10. Jerry Gorovoy, "The Iconography of Louise Bourgeois," in *The Iconography of Louise Bourgeois* (New York: Max Hutchinson/Xavier Fourcade, 1980), n.p.

11. Patrick Waldberg, *Surrealism* (London: Thames and Hudson, 1965), 104.

12. Gardner, "Discreet Charm," 84.

13. See Jacques Lacan, "Motifs du crime paranoiaque: Le Crime des soeurs Papin," *Minotaure*, December 1933, 25–28.

14. Whitney Chadwick, *Women of Surrealism* (Boston: Little, Brown, 1985), 103.

15. Jacques Lacan, "Le Probleme du style et la conception psychiatrique des formes paranoiaques de l'experience," *Minotaure*, June 1933, 68–69.

16. See Claude Lévi-Strauss, *The Elementary Structures of Kinship*, trans. James Harle Bell and John Richard von Sturmer (London: Eyre and Spottiswoode, 1969).

17. Author's telephone interview with Louise Bourgeois, October 1989. Robert Pincus-Witten claims that Bourgeois did, indeed, have friendships with Lévi-Strauss and Lacan, but he does not substantiate this statement; see *Bourgeois Truth*, exh. cat. (New York: Robert Miller Gallery, 1982), n.p.

18. Ibid.

19. Robert Storrs, "Louise Bourgeois: Gender and Possession," *Art in America*, April 1983, 128.

20. Pels, "Search for Gravity," 51. Interestingly, Bourgeois's recollections of the period still seem ambivalent. To Pels she revealed memories of not being grounded, but she has told other authors, specifically Deborah Wye, that her studies at the Art Students League in the 1940s provided stability; see Wye, *Bourgeois*, 15.

21. Lucy R. Lippard, "Louise Bourgeois: From the Inside Out," *Artforum*, March 1975, 27.

22. Pels, "Search for Gravity," 50.

23. Wye, *Louise Bourgeois*, 19, and pl. 48. See this catalogue for other works done before 1982, discussed but not illustrated here.

24. Pels, "Search for Gravity," 50.

25. Bourgeois returned to a variation of the *Femme-Maison* theme in the early 1980s. *Femme-Maison '81* (private collection) is a large ($48\frac{1}{8} \times 47 \times 49\frac{7}{8}$ in.) sculpture carved of black marble. Long cylindrical forms cluster around a cliff upon which stands a rectilinear building with a gable roof. A 1983 white marble ($25 \times 19\frac{1}{2} \times 23$ in.) *Femme-Maison* (Robert Miller Gallery, New York) shows a small building

perched atop a mountain of carved drapery. Both sculptures portray the house not as a place that traps women but as an inviting shelter, protected by flexible penile forms or voluptuous drapery. The smooth solidity and volume of the marble contrast with the flatness and fragility of the paintings and offer a stability that the young Bourgeois found impossible to attain.

26. Gaston Bachelard, *The Poetics of Space*, trans. Maria Jolas (New York: Orion, 1964), 6.

27. Ibid., 38.

28. Storrs notes a parallel between Bourgeois and Bachelard and suggests it as an area for further study; see "Gender and Possession," 137.

29. Sigmund Freud, *The Interpretation of Dreams*, in *The Standard Edition of the Complete Psychological Works of Sigmund Freud*, vol. 4, ed. and trans. James Strachey (London: Hogarth Press, 1953–74), 277–78.

30. Eagleton, *Literary Theory*, 169.

31. Julia Kristeva, *Revolution in Poetic Language*, trans. Margaret Waller (New York: Columbia University Press, 1984), 49–50, 62–65, 68–71.

32. Eagleton, *Literary Theory*, 188–90.

33. Ann Gibson, *Issues in Abstract Expressionism: The Artist-Run Periodicals* (Ann Arbor: UMI Research, 1990), 57–58.

34. Rosalind Krauss, "Notes on the Index," *October*, Spring 1977, 70.

35. Lippard, "Bourgeois," 31.

36. Dorothy Seiberling, "The Female View of Erotica," *New York Times*, 11 February 1974, cited in Lippard, "Inside Out," 31.

37. Alice Jardine, *Gynesis* (Ithaca, N.Y.: Cornell University Press, 1985), 25.

38. Ibid., 167.

39. Ibid., 168.

40. Richard Howard, "The Mapplethorpe Effect," in Richard Marshall et al., *Robert Mapplethorpe*, exh. cat. (New York: Whitney Museum of American Art, 1988), 157.

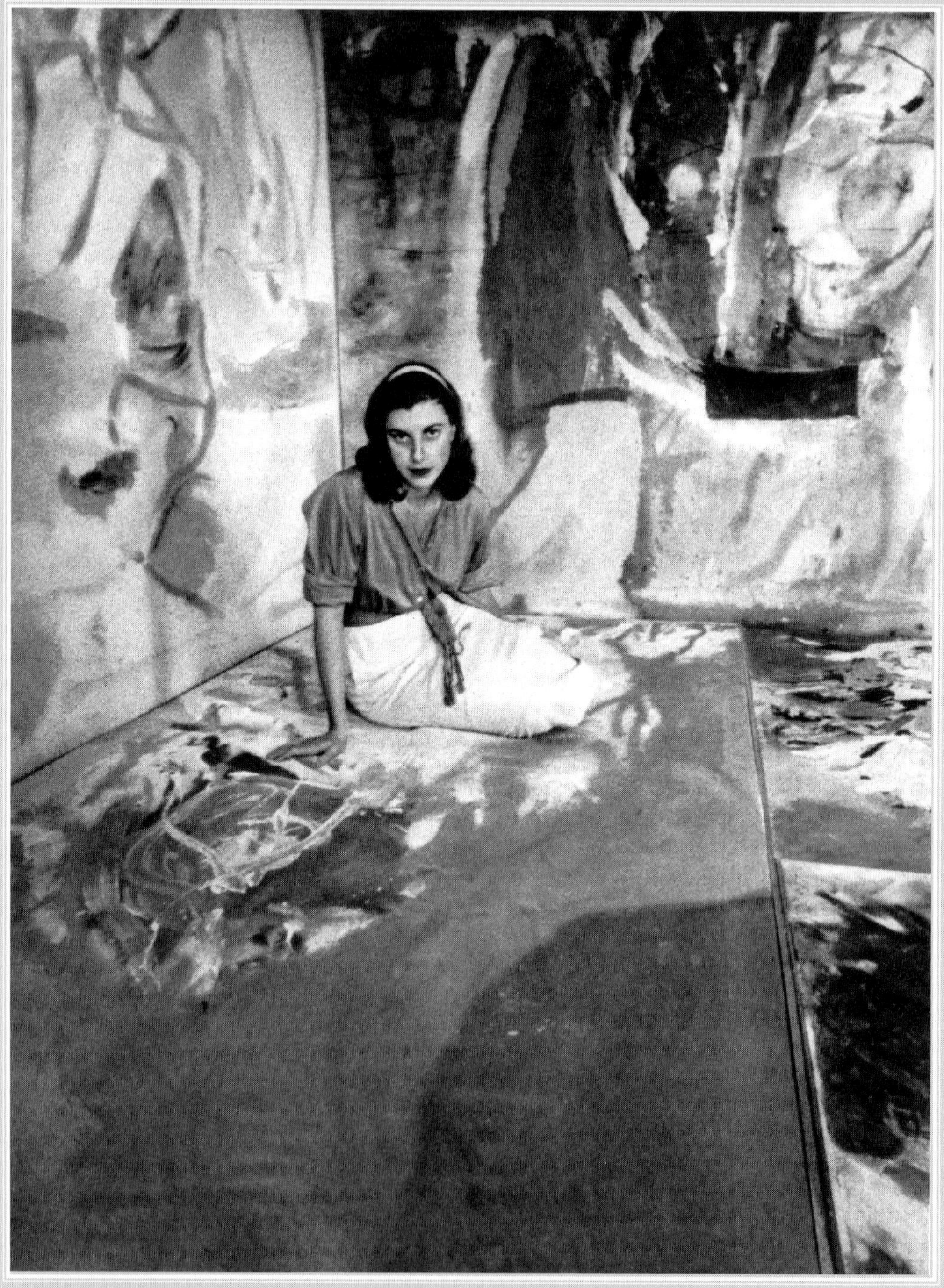

19

RECONSIDERING THE STAIN

On Gender and the Body in Helen Frankenthaler's Painting

Lisa Saltzman

A RETROSPECTIVE GLANCE at the postwar years of American cultural ascendancy reveals that even as Clement Greenberg's formalism posited abstraction as a site of unqualified purity and autonomy, neither painting nor its critics fully acceded to the rigorous regime of renunciation demanded by his aesthetic ethics of pure abstraction. Not only had insistently metaphoric titles ensnared abstraction in a web of meaning and reminded the viewer of the inevitable operations of likeness and analogy to which even the most obdurately abstract surface remained prey; but, as we know from the very first social art-historical accounts of New York School painting, abstraction— particularly gestural abstraction, with its trace signifiers of individuality and personal freedom— had been all too easily co-opted by cultural cold warriors.[1]

If social art historians retrospectively uncovered an idealized American body, or body politic, at play and at stake in the critical and institutional support for and reception of New York School painting, their revisionist account and critique ultimately identified that body as nothing more than the ideological abstraction it was. That is, the body politic at the heart of the revisionists' accounts, a body politic made up of risk takers and individualists imaged and imagined as the "vital center" of Arthur Schlesinger's postwar account, was at once everyman and no man.[2]

Or was it? For at stake as well was the body of woman. That is, as abstract and idealized as the vital center of Schlesinger's liberal ideology may have been, I would contend that the body at issue in the reception of New York School painting was far more particular and far more literal than the interpretations of cold war cultural politics would allow. That body was the gendered body, or bodies, of postwar American society, bodies whose social roles were as blurred by the changes wrought by World War II as was the face of painting.

During the years when New York School painting reigned triumphant, categories of gender and their stabilization were a persistent, if unacknowledged, critical preoccupation. As I will demonstrate,

This is a revised version of the essay "Reconsidering the Stain: On Gender, Identity, and the New York School" published in the catalogue *Friedel Dzubas: Critical Painting*, with essays by Eric M. Rosenberg and Timothy McElreavy and a foreword by John O'Brian (Medford, Mass.: Tufts University Gallery, 1998). Reprinted by permission of the author and by permission of Tufts University and the Tufts University Gallery.

There are no reproductions here of Frankenthaler's works because the artist's permission to reproduce them could not be secured.

Figure 19.1. Gordon Parks, *Helen Frankenthaler*. From *Life* 42, no. 10 (13 May 1957). Time Life Pictures/Getty Images.

one pictorial form, one painterly process, garnered a great deal of critical attention—namely, the stain. And, as a close analysis of the critical reception of color-field painting reveals, it was the stain that served as an available sign through which to delineate categories of gender. Although it could be argued that gender was simply an available metaphor with which to describe abstract painting, or that characteristics associated with masculinity and femininity were simply appropriate and evocative adjectives with which to give critical voice to the mute surfaces of abstraction, I would suggest that the recurrent critical discourse of gender and corporeality surrounding New York School painting signaled something more particular and significant about both postwar American painting and postwar American society.

That is, if the language of emergent formalist criticism is taken at its word, criticism would seem to have found in these purportedly autonomous, self-reflexive, and hermetic paintings not pure abstraction but a legible subject—namely, the artistic self and, more pointedly, the artist's body. As such, the gendered language of emergent formalist criticism would seem to echo in its response to the radically dispersed, diffuse, all-over surfaces of New York School painting something of a broader societal anxiety about the dissolution of gender boundaries in postwar America.

Despite the prevalence of a gendered metaphorics in the reception of abstraction, very little has been done to analyze its implications, either for New York School painting or for the interpretation of abstraction more generally.[3] Even in the work of the first generation of feminist art historians who explicitly took on questions of gender, the interpretation of abstraction was never the primary object of inquiry. This resistance to re-reading abstraction lies in part in the enduring legacy of Greenberg's modernist paradigm for many art historians of the postwar period. But it results as well from the grounding methodological practice of Anglo-American feminist art history, whose materialist hermeneutic typically privileged the analysis of figuration over abstraction.

This essay, then, is fueled by the conviction that feminist scholars of modernist painting are faced with a doubly important challenge. Furthermore, it is grounded in the belief that we can begin to redress this art-historical lacuna regarding questions of gender and abstraction by looking back at the historical context in which both New York School painting and its criticism emerged—namely, postwar America—and directing a particularly focused gaze on the critical reception of color-field painting. For in that critical reception, we can begin to isolate and attend to the marked tendency to insist upon gender, identity, and difference. And we can begin to theorize something like the following: in the face of radical societal transformation, as well as radical artistic developments, art criticism turned these complex paintings into either heroic symbols of masculinity or denigrated emblems of femininity.

The demographic shifts that took place throughout America during and after the war saw their reproduction in the aesthetic microcosm of New York School painting, where women emerged alongside men as principal practitioners. Although women artists did not perform the same vital function for the national economy as Rosie the Riveter, the war did afford women artists opportunities they might not otherwise have had. As John Elderfield would note years later in his monographic study of Helen Frankenthaler, one of the factors that contributed to her artistic development in the 1940s was precisely "her sex, which spared her military service."[4] As in other industries and professions, once established in their careers, Frankenthaler and other women artists did not retreat from their newly attained positions, nor did their continued presence in the artistic sphere after the war go unnoticed.

During the 1950s, as the careers of these women artists took shape, a number of articles appeared in the popular press, in such magazines as *Life*, *Time*, and *Cosmopolitan*.[5] These articles, which typically focused on Helen Frankenthaler, Grace Hartigan, Lee

Krasner, and Joan Mitchell, highlighted and even celebrated the ascendance of women artists within the ranks of the New York School. Nevertheless, despite the congratulatory premise and tenor of these articles, they articulated a very different message about the "lady artists" and "vocal girls." The art world was described as "under siege," threatened by a "feminine invasion,"[6] such anxious language reflecting the broader societal message that the former preserves of men were rapidly losing their insularity or, more pointedly, that a woman's true place was not in the studio but in the home.

At the same time that these articles treated the social phenomenon of the changing face of the art world, they described the changing face of painting itself. In an era of painting characterized as "dealing more directly with emotions and intuitions,"[7] these articles offered up descriptions of the canvases that ascribed to their surfaces the very characteristics attributed to their female makers. For example, a *Cosmopolitan* reader learned that "the slender, chestnut-haired Helen Frankenthaler, born in New York City thirty-two years ago, is the wife of abstract painter Robert Motherwell," as a prelude to a similarly indexed description of her "impetuous technique" and her "delicate and subtle" paintings.[8] Within the popular press, abstract painting in the hands of these "lady artists" and "vocal girls" became a site for the painterly inscription of femininity. In the perceived impetuosity of this emotional and intuitive form of painting, women were regarded as perhaps uniquely suited to its formal demands. Moreover, the perceived subtlety and delicacy achieved in their work was seen as inextricably linked to their identity as women.

It is this tendency to ascribe femininity to the canvases of female abstract painters that unites the writing in the popular press with the more rarified discourses of academic art criticism, as is demonstrated quite dramatically in the reception of Helen Frankenthaler. Consider, for example, the following discussion of Frankenthaler's unique contribution to the history of Western painting in an article in *Art International* by E. C. Goossen:

Frankenthaler's painting is manifestly that of a woman. . . . Without Pollock's painting hers is unthinkable. What she took from him was masculine; the almost hard-edged, linear splashes of duco enamel. What she made with it was distinctly feminine, the broad, bleeding-edged stain on raw linen. With this translation she added a new candidate for the dictionary of plastic forms, the stain.[9]

If the passage is interesting for its attention to patterns of influence, positioning Frankenthaler's work as distinct from yet inextricably bound to Jackson Pollock's innovations, it is even more noteworthy for its establishment of sexual difference as determinative of artistic product. Frankenthaler's painting may have been indebted to Pollock's, but, at the same time, it was "manifestly that of a woman." Their painting is distinguished, and distinguishable, according to culturally constructed notions of gender. Pollock's painting is masculine, as characterized by a linear, hard-edged splash. Frankenthaler's is feminine, as characterized by a seeping, bleeding-edged stain.[10] In focusing exclusively on the "stain," on the fluid and coloristic aspects of her work, critics like Goossen leveled the diffuse, complex, and varied surfaces into monolithic entities.

If we turn, for a moment, not to criticism but to its purported subject, the actual paintings, we might note that Frankenthaler's work was characterized by more than the fluid emblem of the stain. In what was considered her breakthrough painting, *Mountains and Sea* of 1952, conceived and painted after Greenberg introduced her to Pollock and his paintings, it is undeniable that distinct, dark lines trace or subdivide areas of color, the so-called stains.[11] Yet despite this dialectical pull between wide pools of colored pigment and thin lines of black paint, between automatism and rigorous control, it was the aspect of the liquid areas of color, the perceived fluidity of Frankenthaler's soak-stain technique, that endlessly captured the imaginations of the critics. In other words, it was less the thematic and formal invocation of the rugged terrain and outline of the mountains than the watery depths of the sea to which critics were drawn.

It was this fluidity, specifically the emblematic form of the stain as seen in *Mountains and Sea* and in other examples of this period, such as *Basque Beach* (1958), that provided the touchstone for what became a significantly gendered discourse, one that set Frankenthaler's work apart from that of her modernist male colleagues, past and present. In Frankenthaler's case, the metaphor of the stain was given a particular valence. As Goossen's criticism suggests, Frankenthaler did more than pour paint onto the canvas. She bled on the raw "linen," she stained the sheets. In the slippage between literal and metaphorical language that pervaded the majority of the criticism surrounding Frankenthaler's painting, and which I take this passage by Goossen to bring into particularly sharp focus, Frankenthaler's painting became an extension of her differently female body. Insofar as the stain was also culturally coded as menstrual,[12] its invocation functioned as an index of a thwarted or ineffectual creative process, signifying not creative inception or biological conception, but their refusal, the flushing of an empty womb. Moreover, her menstrual painterly fluids came to signify the trace of an involuntary bodily function, of uncontrolled nature, turning painting into the record of an accident.[13]

This metaphor of automatism, of relinquishing control, of accident, became central to the critical reception of Frankenthaler's creative process. As Harold Rosenberg wrote of Frankenthaler, referring first, as a point of comparison, to those occasional male stainers, Jackson Pollock, Arshile Gorky, and Wassily Kandinsky:

> The early paintings with their borrowing from Pollock, Gorky, Kandinsky and other occasional stainers, are sensitive, but more timid than sensitive . . . with Frankenthaler, the artist's action is at a minimum; it is the paint that is active. The artist is the medium of her medium; her part is

limited to selecting aesthetically acceptable effects from the purely accidental behavior of her color. Apparently, Miss Frankenthaler has never grasped the moral and metaphysical basis of Action painting, and since she is content to let the pigment do most of the acting, her paintings fail to develop resistances against which a creative act can take place.[14]

In this passage, the presence of the stain is acknowledged in work by male artists. In contrast to Frankenthaler, however, in the hands of Pollock, or Gorky and Kandinsky before him, the stain, if only the occasional stain, could still be redeemed for art, the actions of these men taking place under the aegis of masculinity that protects and defines their work.

As the passage continues, radically different portraits of Pollock and Frankenthaler emerge. Pollock may have flung paint about in a bacchanalian frenzy, but that was part of his mythic, male genius, his actively creative artistic persona, impregnating the virgin canvas with his life-giving seed. Frankenthaler, in contrast, merely allowed accidents to happen, passively staining the linen canvases with the seep and ooze of bodily fluids.

Rosenberg's descriptive summation of the divergent painterly processes of Pollock and Frankenthaler finds its visualization in various photographs of the artists in their studio spaces. For example, in the now iconic Hans Namuth photographs of Pollock at work, Pollock emerges as active, stilled only by the camera shutter in his rhythmic dance of creation, can and brush in hand, paint, like artist, arrested in flight. In contrast, in a shot by Gordon Parks accompanying an article in *Life*, Frankenthaler is depicted sitting demurely atop a canvas, posed against her work less as artist than as mere vessel for the fluids that seep from her body onto the material spread beneath her (fig. 19.1).

Both Rosenberg's critical description of Frankenthaler's painterly process and the photographic image of Frankenthaler in her studio deny her self-consciousness and agency in the symbolic field, the arena of language, be it written or painterly. If there was some thought or agency recognized or acknowledged in Frankenthaler's work, it was seen simply in her selection of "aesthetically acceptable effects," suggesting the affinity of her practice to the historical and stereotypical female domain of the decorative arts, to the tasks of choosing colors and dyeing fabric. Such work had little, on Rosenberg's account, to do with the "moral and metaphysical" project of painting.[15]

The critical gendering of the stain becomes more problematic when it is taken up as a frequent rather than occasional form by a male artist, as was the case with Morris Louis. For no sooner had Frankenthaler begun working with her stain technique than Greenberg took Louis and Kenneth Noland away from their studios in Washington, D.C., into New York to see her work. Louis's ensuing paintings, dubbed the veils and florals, created delicately fluid and watery surfaces that, were I to invoke the same metaphors as the critics whom I have been citing, might be described as equally if not far more "feminine" than Frankenthaler's characteristically bolder, more saturated paintings. Yet despite the undisputed artistic lineage of Louis's paintings, the acknowledged formal similarities between Louis's and Frankenthaler's work, and what I take to be overall the more stereotypical "femininity" of Louis's paintings, his work was received in thoroughly different terms than was Frankenthaler's.

Typically described as "massive," "solid," "hard," and "sharp," Louis's paintings were seen to demonstrate "control," "strength," "clarity," and "firmness," quite a departure from Frankenthaler's accidental, soft, watery, decorative forms.[16] As if responding directly to Rosenberg's diagnosis of the absence of a deliberate "creative act" in Frankenthaler's stain paintings, one critic came to describe Louis's stain paintings as "stiffened by intelligence and consistent formality."[17] In the most decisive ascription of masculinity to Louis's formal project, Noland referred to Louis's paintings as "single-shot" images,[18] in effect reducing and transforming the complex, temporally durational,

additive process of the soak-stain method into an enactment of male orgasm, allowing Louis—the painter of veils and florals—to join the ranks of the virile New York School painters.[19]

At times, the critical attempt to maintain aesthetic differences between the canvases of male and female artists produced a confused critical language, one that reveals the utter instability, or so I would suggest, of the gendered categories upon which it so heavily relied. Take, for example, another passage from Goossen's *Art International* piece, in which he sets Frankenthaler's work against Gorky's at the same time that he establishes her contribution of the stain:

> The thin curvaceous, form-suggesting line in her early canvases (ca. 1952–53) comes directly from Gorky's mid-40s work. During that period Frankenthaler's colors, similar to Gorky's in their dry feel and tone, were yet paler and more feminine than Gorky's hues. This sounds like a totally unnecessary remark but it is true that many of his later pictures *Agony* (1947) and *The Calendars* (1946–47), for example, have a feminine delicacy in the sensuous line that only a man could have produced.[20]

In stating that a picture could have "feminine delicacy . . . that only a man could have produced," Goossen makes the claim that if a painting by a man displays "feminine" aspects, it does not mean he is innately feminine, but instead, that he is solely capable, in his masculinity, of enacting femininity, of taking its culturally coded trappings and representing them with admirable, if not superior, skill.

I do not mean to suggest that such criticism posits "feminine" painting in the hands of a male artist as an act of transvestism, camp, or travesty, even if such language begs for such a reading.[21] Nor do I mean to imply that such criticism anticipates something of French feminist criticism in its valorizing of the feminine within modernist practice,[22] even as such criticism makes all too clear the ways in which such feminist theoretical work would prove enormously productive for interpreting the painterly fields of modernist abstraction.[23] Rather, I am suggesting that its seeming illogic reveals the difficult task criticism took on in rendering stable such fundamentally unstable paintings, such fundamentally unstable categories. It would seem that the only way to conceptualize and control these slippages between categories of gender was to somehow redeem them by incorporating them back into traditional narratives of artistic mastery. Never "unnecessary remarks," I would suggest that such remarks were instead of the utmost urgency during the years when the changing face of abstract painting (as well as the faces of its practitioners) undermined the binary logic that had previously afforded clearer demarcations between masculinity and femininity.

That Louis's painting, despite its fundamental indebtedness and similarity to Frankenthaler's stain painting, could be constructed as supremely and singularly different, and ultimately, supremely and singularly masculine, was a critical fiction that persisted despite the more nuanced interpretations of later critics. For example, in 1971, Michael Fried, heir apparent to the Greenbergian legacy, would at once avow and disavow the dualities of Louis's painting:

> *Intrigue* ravishes the beholder with its fullness of something like detail: the subtle, modulating color, simultaneously metallic and floral, the warm soft sepia graining of what may have been the last wave of pigment, the delicate irregular, fugitive pattern of the overlapping configurations, the fragile, cloud-like crests of those configurations, aureoled by faint bleeds of thinner, evoking distance. . . . *Terranean* on the other hand strikes one as wholly devoid of incidental felicities. The stained portion looms as though just risen, its proportions together with the dense brown tonality of the whole connoting overwhelming mass, its internal figuration stark, sharp, almost menacing, at once flame-like and mineral in character. And yet, for reasons I have tried to make clear, one's perception of the stained area as a whole and of the figuration it contains is not of

things that are precisely tangible. Rather, it is as though the apparent massiveness and solidity of the one and the apparent hardness and sharpness of the other are experienced by eyesight alone, without reference to the sense of touch; as though, one might say, massiveness and solidity and hardness and sharpness as such were known to eyesight alone and not to touch; as though the sense of touch itself were strictly visual.[24]

If the formal dualities of Louis's paintings are acknowledged in Fried's treatment of *Intrigue*, a painting that is at once "metallic and floral," "flame-like and mineral," these elements of difference are ultimately leveled in the interest of establishing, for Louis, a certain conquest of the "incidental felicities" of the stain, enabling Fried to then put forth *Terranean* as the painting that "establishes a magnitude of realized ambition that only Pollock, perhaps, among Americans had previously achieved."[25] In *Terranean*, the stain no longer is a form that bleeds onto raw linen but, instead, "looms as though just risen," firmly reinscribed within a gendered metaphorics of masculinity, devoid of its previously feminine associations.

Fried's 1971 text on Louis thus displays in the metaphorics of its prose the unacknowledged preoccupation with gender that pervaded discussions of abstraction following its reemergence in America after the war and, moreover, the unacknowledged preoccupation with controlling, through endless categorization, the threat of the feminine. Albeit in quite elegant and sophisticated terms, the move Fried makes in celebrating Louis's handling of the stain in the name of opticality, in redeeming the feminine in the name of the masculine, is in the end altogether typical of an entire era of formalist criticism. For although painting, rather than the painter, was the expressed subject of nascent formalist criticism, and opticality, rather than corporeality, was its privileged object, it seems that the analysis of modernist painting was in fact repeatedly suffused with discussions of the body, of masculinity and femininity, locating and displacing gender and artistic subjectivity in and upon the purportedly pure, self-reflexive, autonomous surfaces of high modernist painting. Moreover, in linking artistic practice to the male and female body, critics inscribed gender within and ascribed essentialized gender difference to a school of painting whose shared formal practices rigorously undermined the rigid boundaries of codified sexual difference.[26]

I have sought with my examples from criticism and painting to reveal that very few of these New York School canvases are exclusively masculine or feminine in their characteristics; nor, if they seem to be, is one set of traits necessarily linked to either the male or the female artist. Whether through metaphors of urination, ejaculation, or menstruation, the body, male and female, is inscribed in multiple and various ways in the drips, spills, sprays, and stains that coat the majority of the canvases of the New York School painters. And it is precisely this intermingling and breakdown of properties of line and color, this breakdown of boundaries, that I believe led critics to at least try to assert, ascribe, and inscribe a sense of normative order.

Perhaps even more important, I would suggest that criticism embodied a response not simply to painterly change but, indeed, to societal transformation as well. The critical tendency to perceive and locate gender in the all-over canvases of the New York School painters can be read as an almost desperate, albeit unacknowledged, attempt to identify and establish difference and maintain order, at precisely a moment when aesthetic practice and social structures emerged radically altered from the Second World War. I have suggested that the strictly delineated gender metaphorics of critical language—its seeking and establishing of order—masked and controlled what was, in artistic practice and the social sphere, a shifting terrain, far less fixed and stable than the criticism would initially seem to allow. I have suggested that the diffuse, dehierarchized, all-over can-

vases of the New York School, in evincing some combination of masculine and feminine characteristics, would seem to have transgressed the normative, stabilizing principles of modernist painting, of modernist purity, principles already under siege in society at large.

In their attribution of masculinity to canvases painted by male artists and femininity to those painted by female artists, critics asserted the fundamental primacy of sexual difference, and did so at precisely the moment when gender boundaries were seen as being in danger of disappearing, both artistically and socially. More specifically, in the deeply gendered and fundamentally conservative critical language with which postwar abstraction was received, it was the metaphoric invocation of the stain that was instrumentalized to serve as a particularly powerful signifier of gender, and through that, of difference. Unlike the fluidity that was celebrated in subsequent decades by French feminist theorists, whose concept of *écriture feminine* might be transported into the realm of art history to describe something like a *peinture feminine*, there is no valorization of female bodily functions or libidinal economies in the writing of such art critics. Instead, their writing is a means of segregating, rather than celebrating, certain forms of painting practiced by women.

In many respects, this anxious critical response should not surprise us. Feminist readings of social and cultural history have sought to demonstrate that when a threat to patriarchal society is perceived, an attempt is made to preserve the social order, to reconstitute its boundaries and hierarchies.[27] Similarly, and perhaps more broadly, anthropological writings have analyzed and theorized how the establishment of difference or the creation of hierarchical distinctions, both of which can be conceptualized as making order out of disorder, are basic characteristics of human behavior. As Mary Douglas wrote in 1966, "It is only by exaggerating the difference between within and without, above and below, male and female, with and against, that a semblance of order is created."[28]

Although from our position in the present, we might now want to recognize and valorize, in their combinations of tangles, skeins of paint, drips, and stains, the painterly invocation and intermingling of gender-coded forms, we must acknowledge that we face New York School painting in a fundamentally different moment than did its original critics. Our critical preoccupations, some acknowledged and others still unacknowledged, have changed. So too, I might add, has the practice of abstraction.

Contemporary abstract practice makes visible, even quite material, the metaphors of the body so pervasive in the criticism surrounding New York School painting. In the work of Ghada Amer, Cecily Brown, Barbara Takanaga, and Sue Williams, the body emerges and recedes upon the picture plane, presence and absence at play in surfaces at once figurative and abstract. Moreover, if we look to contemporary practice more broadly, we see, often in exacting and even microscopic detail, the body and its essential fluids. In the work of such artists as Kiki Smith, Mike Kelley, Curtis Mitchell, and Andres Serrano, for example, liquid traces of the body are duly evoked, inscribed, contained, or rendered, in pieces ranging from the sculptural and the painted to the printed and the photographic. A vivid testimonial to the emancipatory politics and concomitant artistic practices of the late 1960s and 1970s, the work of the 1980s and later also marks a departure. For although contemporary artists have returned to the representation of the body and identity, the invocation of the corporeal is less to celebrate difference in the name of creating equality, as it was circa 1968, than to expose similarity in the name of dismantling the patriarchal logic that produced such inequalities in the first place. In other words, contemporary artists use the body, its pieces and its fluids, to explore the very instability of categories of gender and difference. In works that range across painting, photography, and installation, it is often the stain, the fluid trace of the body, male and female, that serves as an available form, an available sign, through which to screen, artistically and theoretically, a deconstruction of gender.[29]

During the era of New York School painting, neither painting nor its criticism was armed with the kinds of political or theoretical knowledge, or self-knowledge, with which many artists and critics now practice their respective crafts. In those years, the stain served as an available sign through which to reconstruct, rather than deconstruct, categories of gender. Within the male bastions of the art world, it was art criticism that assumed the task of preserving tradition, of critically constructing, or reconstructing, through the use of gendered metaphor, a form of painting where men could be men and women could be women. And that critical practice had a particular urgency, if not poignancy. For its reconstruction of gender difference was achieved by locating and asserting difference at precisely a moment when painting and society seemed on the brink of blurring and effacing those formerly rigid boundaries, a moment when painting may have been envisioning not so much its social present as its future.

NOTES

This essay has had many incarnations. First written for Alice Jardine's seminar on French feminist criticism at Harvard University in 1989, it was revised for presentation in Anna Chave's session on modern art at the College Art Association in Chicago in February 1992 and at the Whitney Symposium on American Art in April 1992. Some years later, it was solicited and expanded for the catalogue *Friedel Dzubas: Critical Painting*. The present revised version attempts to reintegrate some of the founding feminist concerns of that 1992 CAA paper with subsequent iterations of the project. I am grateful to Norma Broude and Mary Garrard for their sustained, and sustaining, interest in the piece.

1. See Serge Guilbaut, *How New York Stole the Idea of Modern Art: Abstract Expressionism, Freedom and the Cold War*, trans. Arthur Goldhammer (Chicago: University of Chicago Press, 1983); and Francis Frascina, ed., *Pollock and After: The Critical Debates* (New

York: Harper and Row, 1985), 107–51. Central to Guilbaut's account in particular is Arthur Schlesinger, *The Vital Center: Our Purposes and Perils on the Tightrope of American Liberalism* (Cambridge, Mass.: Riverside Press, 1949).

2. That the body politic is, metaphorically, a male/masculine body, is taken up by Moira Gatens in her "Corporeal Representation in/and the Body Politic," in *Writing on the Body: Female Embodiment and Feminist Theory*, ed. Katie Conboy, Nadia Medina, and Sarah Stanbury (New York: Columbia University Press, 1997), 80–89.

3. There has been an emergent body of work within the discipline of art history that addresses questions of gender in relation to abstraction. See Anna C. Chave, "Pollock and Krasner: Script and Postscript," *Res* 24 (Autumn 1993): 95–111; Michael Leja, "Barnett Newman's Solo Tango," *Critical Inquiry* 21, no. 3 (Spring 1995): 556–80; and Anne M. Wagner, "Lee Krasner as L.K.," *Representations* 25 (Winter 1989): 42–57. Since my essay first took shape, see also Griselda Pollock, "Killing Men and Dying Women: A Woman's Touch in the Cold Zone of American Painting in the 1950s," in *Avant-Gardes and Partisans Reviewed*, ed. Fred Orton and Griselda Pollock (Manchester: Manchester University Press, 1996), 219–94; and Anne M. Wagner's "Pollock's Nature, Frankenthaler's Culture," in *Jackson Pollock: New Approaches*, ed. Kirk Varnedoe and Pepe Karmel (New York: Museum of Modern Art, 1999), 181–99.

4. John Elderfield, *Frankenthaler* (New York: Harry N. Abrams, 1989), 12. Of course, there had been a long and varied history of women artists, which might suggest that the presence and concomitant treatment of women artists represent more an instance of historical and critical repetition than uniqueness. See Griselda Pollock and Rozsicka Parker, *Old Mistresses: Women, Art and Ideology* (New York: Routledge and Kegan Paul, 1981). But, such studies notwithstanding, the level of emancipation occasioned by the war afforded women heretofore unprecedented opportunities in the public sphere, including the arena of artistic practice.

5. See "Laurels for Lady Artists: Women Artists in Ascendance: Young Group Reflects Lively Virtues of U.S. Painting," *Life* 42, no. 19 (13 May 1957): 74–77; "The Vocal Girls," *Time* 75, no. 18 (2 May 1960); and Jean Lipman and Cleve Gray, "The Amazing Inventiveness of Women Painters," *Cosmopolitan* 151, no. 4 (October 1960): 62–66.

6. Lipman and Gray, "The Amazing Inventiveness of Women Painters," 62.

7. Ibid.

8. Ibid., 66.

9. E. C. Goossen, "Helen Frankenthaler," *Art International* 5, no. 8 (20 October 1961): 78.

10. Of course, men too, including Pollock and, more notably, Morris Louis, could be "stainers." The stain—in French, *la tache*—had been an operative term in modernist criticism since the time of Manet and the Impressionists, and was taken up to describe the importation of Abstract Expressionism into France as Tachisme. Also, as Thierry de Duve notes in his "Time Exposure and the Snapshot: The Photograph as Paradox," *October* 5 (Summer 1978). 116, the German word *Mal* (which yields *malen*, to paint) comes from the Latin *macula*, stain. As such, painting is, at its etymological if not ontological essence, staining.

In regard to the first generation of New York School painters, Michael Fried employs the term *stain* to describe a form in Pollock's work of the early 1950s. But it is done in the name of identifying a form that overcomes the opposition of line and color. See Fried, *Three American Painters: Kenneth Noland, Jules Olitski, Frank Stella*, exh. cat. (Cambridge, Mass.: Fogg Art Museum, 1965), 19. In opposition to Fried, Rosalind Krauss points out, in her repudiation of a rigorously formalist reading of a presumptively autonomous modernist practice, that Andy Warhol's Oxidation Paintings reveal to us that the liquid gesture in the work of "Jack the Dripper" always encoded a certain masculine potency. See Krauss, *The Optical Unconscious* (Cambridge, Mass.: MIT Press, 1993), 269–77.

11. Reproductions of Frankenthaler's paintings may be found in John Elderfield, *Helen Frankenthaler* (New York: Abrams, 1989).

12. See Janice Delaney, Mary Jane Lupton, and Emily Toth, eds., *The Curse: A Cultural History of Menstruation* (Urbana: University of Illinois Press, 1988); and Emily Martin, "Medical Metaphors of Women's Bodies: Menstruation and Menopause," in *The Woman in the Body* (Boston: Beacon Press, 1987).

13. I should point out that my intent in excavating and interrogating a shifting metaphorics of gender in the critical reception of New York School painting is certainly not to deny the way in which these paintings can or do function as expressions of an artist's experience of his or her body. For examples of Frankenthaler's understanding of her painting and its relation to her identity as a woman, see Henry Geldzahler, "An Interview with Helen Frankenthaler," *Artforum* 4, no. 2 (October 1965): 38; and Cindy Nemser, "An Interview with Helen Frankenthaler," *Arts* 46, no. 2 (November 1971): 54.

14. Harold Rosenberg, "Art and Words," in *The Re-Definition of Art* (New York: Horizon Press, 1972), 64.

15. In similar terms, although Frankenthaler worked on an extremely large scale typical of the postwar abstract painters and used oil and acrylics—and bore the legacy not just of Pollock and Hans Hofmann before him, but of André Masson, Joan Miró, and Arshile Gorky—her technique was seen to bear a resemblance to that of watercolor. As such, critics were able to link her work to such American landscape artists as Arthur Dove, John Marin, and Georgia O'Keeffe, establishing a lineage outside of European modernism and implying an intimacy and softness in her paintings despite their monumental scale, which could then be linked specifically to her identity as a woman, providing another means by which to isolate her, not just from a tradition of early-twentieth-century European modernism but from postwar American high modernism.

16. The articles on Louis to which I refer were published in *Art International*, *Arts*, and *Art News* during the 1950s and 1960s, as well as in exhibition catalogues.

17. Elizabeth C. Baker, "Morris Louis: Veiled Illusions," *Art News* 69, no. 2 (April 1970): 36.

18. As cited in E. A. Carmean, Jr., "Morris Louis and the Modern Tradition: I. Abstract Expressionism," *Arts* 51, no. 1 (September 1976): 75.

19. Here we might think specifically of the critical and biographical construction of Jackson Pollock, who came to be seen as a sort of cowboy figure, arriving in New York from the American West and reinvigorating American painting. His paintings were described in ways that furthered and celebrated his virility and masculinity, an act of "casting paint like seed . . . onto the canvas at his feet. This was no

sissy . . . it was, demonstrably, the real thing . . . painting composed of (a) . . . manly ejaculatory splat." See William Feaver, "The Kid from Cody," review of the "Jackson Pollock: Drawing into Painting" exhibition in its Oxford, England, Museum of Modern Art venue, 1979, as recorded in Pollock's artist's file at the Museum of Modern Art New York library. These quotations, as well their incisive critique, are found in Anna Chave's article "Pollock and Krasner: Script and Postscript," 95–111.

20. Goossen, "Helen Frankenthaler," 77–78.

21. It is interesting to reflect for a moment here on Clement Greenberg's critical assessment of "the travesty that was cubism" in "Towards a Newer Laocoön" (1940), repr. in Frascina, *Pollock and After,* 44. For is not the "travesty" that was Cubism perhaps Analytic Cubism's quite literal effacing of the recognizable signifiers of the differently male and female body?

22. I refer here to the work of the French theorists Hélène Cixous, Catherine Clément, Luce Irigaray, and Julia Kristeva, among others, each of whom posits, though in fundamentally different ways, the emergence or eruption of a "feminine" impulse in modernist writing.

23. Certainly, the aforementioned work of Chave has done much to forge a productive relation between aspects of French feminist theory and the art-historical enterprise vis-à-vis the interpretation of abstraction.

24. Michael Fried, *Morris Louis* (New York: Harry N. Abrams, 1971), 25–26.

25. Ibid.

26. On the issue, or the question, of essentialism, see the special issue of *differences*, "The Essential Difference: Another Look at Essentialism," vol. 1, no. 2 (Summer 1989), reissued in book form as *The Essential Difference*, ed. Naomi Schor and Elizabeth Woods (Bloomington: University of Indiana Press, 1994); and the special issue of *Critical Inquiry*, "Writing and Sexual Difference," vol. 8, no. 2 (Winter 1981).

27. See Betty Friedan, *The Feminine Mystique* (New York: Norton, 1963); Elaine Tyler May, *Homeward Bound: American Families in the Cold War Era* (New York: Basic Books, 1988); and Susan Faludi's *Backlash: The Undeclared War against American Women* (New York: Anchor Books, 1991).

28. Mary Douglas, *Purity and Danger: An Analysis of*

Concepts of Pollution and Taboo (New York: Praeger, 1966), 4.

29. See Catherine Gallagher and Thomas Laqueur, eds., *The Making of the Modern Body: Sexuality and Society in the Nineteenth Century* (Berkeley: University of California Press, 1987); Thomas Laqueur, *Making Sex: Body and Gender from the Greeks to Freud* (Cambridge, Mass.: Harvard University Press, 1990); and Judith Butler, *Gender Trouble: Feminism and the Subversion of Identity* (New York: Routledge, 1990).

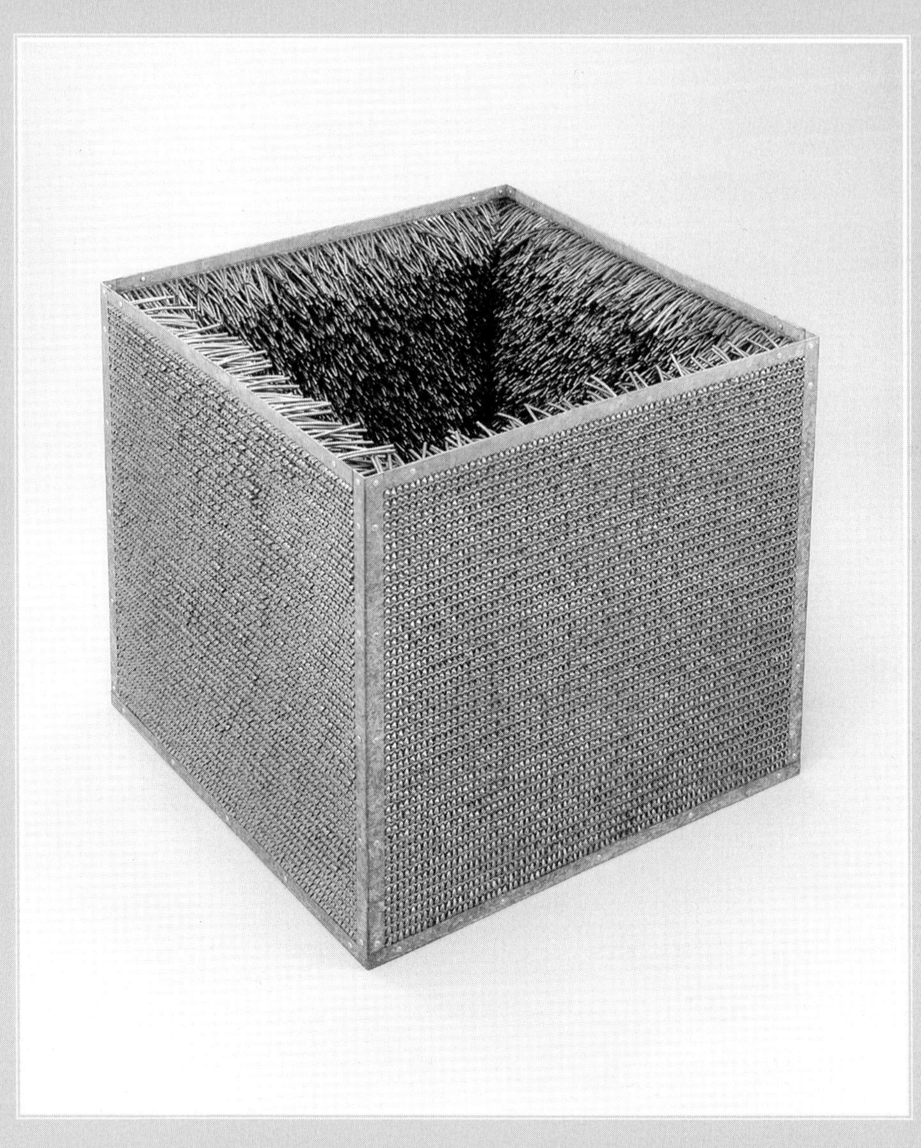

20

MINIMALISM AND BIOGRAPHY

Anna C. Chave

EVER GREATER, apparently indelible, claims are being made for Minimalism as a movement occupying "a place in the second half of our century akin to the one held by Cubism in the first half,"[1] or as crucially defining the very cusp between late modernism and the postmodern and, as such, a key site of origin for postmodern practices in the visual arts.[2] Where the identity of the Minimalist movement is concerned, there can be no indelible ink and no orthodoxy, however, for there have been all along not one but multiple Minimalisms, different discursive configurations describing differing movements: some medium- and period-specific, others not; the majority New York–based, but some bicoastal or global; most with an all-white, male membership, but others encompassing some white women. This is not to deny that there has emerged a formidable Minimalist canon—an area of consensus surrounding particular bodies of work by specific figures—though it bears underlining that none of the New York–based males usually assigned to this elite was self-identified as a Minimalist. The Minimalism that I construct in what follows isolates for case study certain figures commonly regarded as peripheral to the Minimalist canon, such as Simone

Forti, Yvonne Rainer, and Eva Hesse, alongside some figures considered indispensable to it, namely, Robert Morris and Carl Andre. All these figures are here subjected to examination through what is, for Morris and Andre at least, a rather unexpected critical lens: that of biography. By bringing into focus more specifically these figures' relations to one another, as well as to other intimates who had a professional stake in the critical and material fortunes of the Minimalist movement, I mean to help clarify how the Minimalist canon came to assume its present shape. In the process, I call into question the inevitability and the continued viability of that shape, in part by problematizing the claims now being staked over a privileged locus: the site of origin for Minimalism as a movement.

Representative of the kind of object persistently designated as "Minimalist" is *Lever* (fig. 20.2), with its row of 137 firebricks neatly lined up by Carl Andre in a considered relation to a given location, initially a room in the groundbreaking 1966 show *Primary Structures* at the Jewish Museum in New York. By its industrial material, its geometrically standardized components, its serialized composition, and its affecting an ultimate elementariness of form, order,

This essay was originally published in the *Art Bulletin* 82, no. 1 (March 2000): 149–63. Copyright © 2000 by Anna C. Chave. The endnotes have been abridged. Reprinted by permission of the author and courtesy of the College Art Association.

Figure 20.1. Eva Hesse, *Accession II*, 1967. Galvanized steel and plastic tubing. The Detroit Institute of Arts. Founders Society Purchase, Friends of Modern Art Fund and Miscellaneous Gifts Fund. © The Estate of Eva Hesse. Hauser & Wirth Zürich/London. (Photo: © 1987 The Detroit Institute of Arts.)

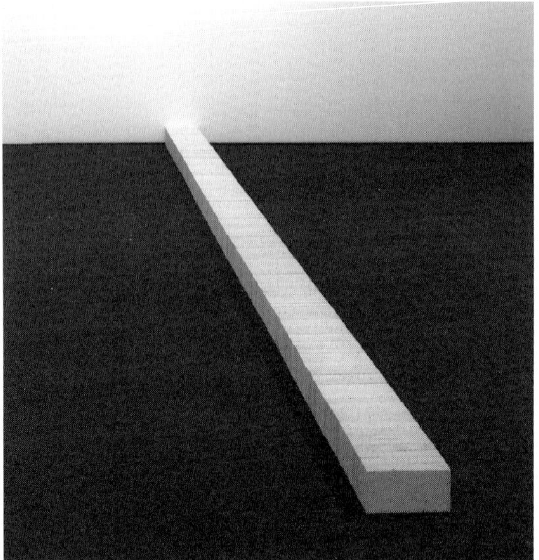

Figure 20.2. Carl Andre, *Lever, New York, 1966*. 137 firebricks. The National Gallery of Canada, Ottawa. Art © Carl Andre/ Licensed by VAGA, New York, N.Y.

material, and facture, *Lever* appeared to test the very boundaries that distinguish art objects from all other objects in the general culture. Further, by withholding any trace of the touch of his hand or other patent expression of his subjectivity, Andre initially appeared to be placing his own status as an artist in some question and, by the same stroke, to be rebuffing the art public. By calculating *Lever*'s design and placement in relation to a given art-institutional site with a view to the public's eventual circulation through that site, however, Andre implicitly accepted the mantle of the artist and took the art public into consideration in another way.[3]

Early proponents of Minimalism, such as Hunter College professor Eugene Goossen, lauded the art of Andre and his peers for affording a "direct, unadulterated experience . . . minus messages" and free of any "boring display of personality."[4] German philosopher Edmund Husserl's directive—"Go to the things themselves"—led off an essay by Mel Bochner, who paradoxically described the work of Andre and others as rigorously excluding individual personality while being profoundly "solipsistic."[5] "Matter mat-

ters" was the maxim Andre used to encapsulate work that evidently, taciturnly insists on its strict facticity or sheer materiality. There is further and conflicting evidence, however: that of Andre's imagistic title, *Lever*, which points to a metaphorical aspect in the work, and that of the sculptor's invoking, and simultaneously denying, a relation between the work's elongated form and that of "the male organ."[6] The absence of the imprint of the artist's hand apparently discourages reading into *Lever* any additional, more personal meanings on his part—I say "apparently" because Andre would in fact regale audiences with the tale of his paternal grandfather, a bricklayer who built his boyhood home in Quincy, Massachusetts. The sculptor further characterized bricks as "almost a personal emblem, or a psychological emblem, that relates to earliest experiences."[7] In short, if Minimalism is more emphatically depersonalized than any prior visual art idiom, Minimalism and biography, nevertheless, are not such utterly incommensurable terms as they at first appear.

That the artists associated with Minimalism were mostly spared extensive biographical inquiries is unsurprising, not only because of the intently impersonal aspects of their practices but also because the period of their work's ascendancy overlapped with the broaching of certain critical paradigms entailing the diminishment or outright erasure of considerations of artistic subjectivity. In the radicalized 1960s, neo-Marxists, including partisans of Louis Althusser, elevated the categories of the material and the social over those of the individual or the subjective. For Marxists generally—as indeed for capitalism also— personal and expressive values have historically been derogated as secondary and, tacitly or otherwise, feminine, since women have ordinarily been acculturated to assume these arenas as their proper domains. Feminist critics may counter that the categories of the personal and the social are irrevocably intertwined such that the "so-called private sphere" has all along been "radically implicated in patterns of modernization and processes of social change."[8] But Marxist-informed criticism has largely persisted in depreciating the biographical, in so doing finding common cause at once with much poststructuralist art criticism as well as with the deindividualizing impetus underlying key Minimalist initiatives. Thus, Hal Foster, for one, could argue that by its antiexpressive procedures Minimalism "sever[ed] art . . . from the subjectivity of the artist," opening up "a new space of 'object/subject terms,'" one predicated on a "'death of the author' (as Roland Barthes would call it [in 1968]) that is at the same time a birth of the reader" or perceiver.[9]

The unseating of the author or artist as transcendent, self-present subject and authentic locus of meaning held, from this vantage point, above all liberatory prospects. It effectively licensed a shift from a history of art narrowly focused on a succession of individuals whose lives have been overglorified in a veritable cult of personality to a history of art concerned more broadly with the roles the visual arts play in society. So far, so good. But in actuality, the leading Minimalists have been hardly less heroized than prior members of the elite of art-historical canons. What their former fellow traveler Yvonne Rainer has observed about John Cage and his use of the ostensibly antiauthorial mechanisms of chance procedures might, by extension, be applied to the Minimalists themselves:

> If the avowed goal of a work is a succession of "nonsignifying signifiers," one is left with an impenetrable web of undifferentiated events set in motion by and referring back to the original flamboyant artist-gesture, in this case the abandonment of personal taste. The work thus places an audience in the "mindless" (sensual?) position of appreciating a manifestation of yet one more Artist as Transcendental Ego and excludes it from participation in the forming of the meanings of that manifestation just as surely as any monolithic, unassailable, and properly validated masterpiece.[10]

If the deployment of biographical modes of inquiry has mainly led the discipline in habitual and conservative directions, toward enlarging or embellishing the achievements of an already glorified canon of masters, the suspension of explicitly personal speech on the artists' part and of answering biographical modes of inquiry on the critics' part has not necessarily redounded in progressive ways. Assuming as a premise that art and experience must be linked, that artistic as well as critical practices and positions, interests, and privileges are invariably colored by personal factors that may reward examination, the present essay proposes to turn biography to oppositional ends, exploring what has been at stake, and for whom, in the exempting of certain artists from biographical scrutiny.[11] At issue are the consequences not only of the discounting or disuse of biography but also of a partial or uneven use of biographical information relative to the male and female artists in question, and relative to certain of the critics who bear responsibility for the imposing face, or facelessness, that Minimalism has come to assume in the public eye.

Most of the critics who built their own reputations by building the reputations of artists in Minimalism's inner and outer circles were friends and, at times, lovers or spouses of those same artists, a fact that is a matter of record on a piecemeal basis at best and thus is widely unknown outside the circles in question. One critic who has been relatively forthcoming about her at once personal and professional involvement with artists in the Minimalist group is Lucy Lippard, who lived with Robert Ryman from 1960 to 1967 and who counted Sol LeWitt both a close friend and her "major intellectual influence" during that period.[12] In a 1966 essay, Lippard assumed a position consonant with Goossen's, questioning the need for art to be "obscured by everyday emotional and associative obsessions, by definite pasts, presents, and futures, by 'human' experience." A decade later, she was "shudder[ing]" at the "narrowness" of this passage while contending that she had honored its implications only in the breach: "I never could resist puns, associative and psychological readings, and snuck them in when I could."[13]

The women's movement had by then guided Lippard toward a more explicitly subjective criticism. She recalled having been inducted in 1970 from the ranks of antiwar activists in the New York art community (which included the Minimalists Andre, Morris, and Donald Judd, among others) to join an added cause: "I used to compare becoming a feminist to jumping off a building and deciding halfway down that it wasn't such a good idea," she remarked drily. Openly assuming a female subject position seemed a bad idea because "women were cut out of a lot of the action, and perceived as inferior. So I didn't really think I was one of *them*."[14]

An early initiative that Lippard joined was the Women's Art Registry, a slide archive. And she recalled that much of the work submitted to WAR was abstract, although "it turned out sometimes that the same women also did much more private, personal, less neutral work, but didn't show it, didn't send it out."[15] Among a generation bent on separating itself from the heroic individualism of Abstract Expressionism, depersonalized visual modalities had come to the fore. For a woman to resist the example of Pop and Minimalism by overtly personalizing her art was to risk branding her work as retrogressive and, by the same stroke, to risk reinforcing that tacitly invidious division of labor that presupposes that women will assume "expressive roles and orientations" while men adopt "instrumental" ones.[16] Judy Chicago, who had earned notice as a Minimalist especially in her professional home base of Los Angeles, recalled facing just such a dilemma around 1970:

> I could not be content with having my work seen as trivial, limited, or "unimportant" if it dealt openly with my experiences as a woman, something I had seen happen to women who had not neutralized their subject matter. I also could no longer accept denying my experiences as a woman in order to be considered a "serious" artist, especially if my stature was going to be diminished anyway by the male-dominated community.[17]

Chicago sacrificed some hard-won critical credibility as she steered her work in the 1970s away from Minimalism toward idioms accommodating a more explicit visualization of women's experience.

The hesitation that Lippard and Chicago felt at the prospect of openly claiming their identities as women at this historical juncture also surfaced among the sixteen female artists whom Cindy Nemser approached for inclusion in a book of interviews, a project that she eventually framed in part as a rebuttal to Linda Nochlin's pioneering feminist tract of 1971, "Why Have There Been No Great Women Artists?" Four of Nemser's would-be subjects declined her invitation (the more commercially established, ergo least publicity-starved of the women, namely, Georgia O'Keeffe, Helen Frankenthaler, Joan Mitchell, and Bridget Riley), and Nemser met with some uneasiness even among the participants.[18] In the case of Eva Hesse, force of circumstance may have helped impel her to cooperate: facing imminent death from brain tumors and intent on securing a place in posterity for a body of work that barely spanned a decade, she had incentives to respond to whatever critical attention came her way.

Eva Hesse's mature work was in certain respects not unlike that of her peer and sometime intimate, Carl Andre.[19] Employing at times such geometric fundaments as the grid and the cube, Hesse's sculpture often explored seriality and repetition through the deployment of industrial materials and modes of facture. Consider *Accession II* of 1967 (fig. 20.1), an industrially fabricated, gridded, galvanized steel cube that would seem to exemplify Minimalist-identified practices perfectly were it not for the bits of plastic tubing looped by hand through the tens of thousands of holes comprising the grid, thereby endowing the cube with a randomly ordered, hirsute-looking interior. When Nemser suggested to Hesse that works such as *Accession II* might be less typically Minimalist than parodistic of Minimalism, Hesse demurred, professing instead her sense of closeness to Andre's art in particular. Hesse, a German-Jewish refugee, observed of Andre's work, "It does something to my insides. His metal plates were the concentration camp for me. [T]hey were those showers that they put on the gas." When asked how Andre would react to such a description, Hesse admitted that it would probably repel him, for he believed "you can't confuse life and art." "Exactly," replied Nemser in her turn, bemoaning "this whole attitude" and adding, "if you wanted to know why people have stayed away from you [. . .] certain critics [. . . that] is probably one of the reasons. You scare them. Sure you scare them. You know you talking like [that] is terribly frightening."[20]

Hesse's preoccupation with the harrowing life story that she readily detailed to Nemser, in tandem with the stress on the personal that was abstractly manifest in the eccentric operations she had been defiantly performing on the standardized Minimalist grid, were, as Nemser sensed, to exact a steep critical price. While she aspired to equal critical standing with such friends as Andre, LeWitt, and Robert Smithson, Hesse was instead fated, figuratively speaking, to be cast to the likes of Lippard and Nemser, to feminists whose early credo was "The personal is political."[21] What specially marked feminism's so-called second wave in the United States was this very belief that "the ubiquity of sexism . . . demanded a movement for sexual liberation that was every bit as encompassing as the structure of domination against which it was obliged to struggle"; therefore, the liberation of women would require "challenging the way in which male domination manifests itself and is reproduced within our most intimate, even unconscious activities."[22] Hesse's case seemed ripe for analysis in such terms, not only because of her art's personal dimensions but because she left as part of her legacy an extended series of eminently revealing diaries. Primed by reading Simone de Beauvoir's *The Second Sex* (in 1964), the Hesse who emerges in those diaries was keenly aware of the forces within her personal and domestic, as well as public and professional, life conspiring to admit her to, at most, secondary standing as an artist.[23]

Several decades after the opening, sweeping,

blustering sallies of second-wave feminism—in a society notably less monolithically patriarchal—poststructuralist feminist theorists have left behind militant, pragmatic dissertations on the politics of housework and the like and moved their more ambivalent discussions to more rarefied planes. As Barbara Johnson frames it: "Deconstruction introduces a fissure between 'woman' as a concept that can never be a proper name for all women and 'feminism' as a movement that must—but *cannot*—consider 'woman' as an epistemological ground for action."[24] Those scholars who are more impelled by the "must" than the "cannot" in Johnson's formulation—I count myself among them—may proceed on the basis that long-standing discrepancies in the social treatment, and so the histories, experience, and social possibilities of men and women (patriarchy, in a word), compounded by more and less profound differences in the biological realities of male and female beings, mean that "women's interests and needs" are bound to "differ in fundamental ways from those of men, and that these conflicting interests cannot be addressed within the category of a universal subject."[25] Other scholars are more impelled by the "cannot" than the "must" in the dilemma Johnson outlines, however, among them some female critics who have staged a kind of rescue mission around the legacy of Hesse, intent on framing it as broadly human rather than particularly female.[26] Such initiatives are undoubtedly necessary if Hesse's distinctive achievements are to be duly validated under the present dominant critical regime.

Something akin to the sway that Clement Greenberg held over United States art critical discourse in Hesse's day came, arguably, to be held by his former disciple Rosalind Krauss. In Krauss's view, "The significance of the art that emerged in this country in the early 1960s is that it staked everything on the accuracy of a model of meaning severed from the legitimizing claims of a private self."[27] What underlies Hesse's eccentric art, as Krauss interpreted it, is precisely "the message of privacy . . . of a withdrawal into those extremely personal reaches of

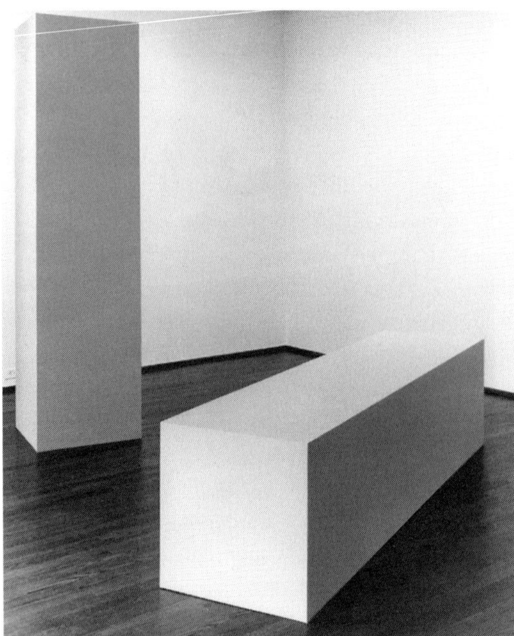

Figure 20.3. Robert Morris, *Columns*, painted aluminum refabrication, 1973, of painted plywood original, 1961–63. Teheran Museum of Contemporary Art, Teheran. © 2005 Robert Morris/Artists Rights Society (ARS), New York.

experience which are beyond, or beneath speech."[28] Unsurprisingly then, in Krauss's widely assigned 1977 textbook *Passages in Modern Sculpture*, Hesse's name would figure in a mere two sentences.[29] Following her early fealty to Greenberg, Krauss's vision of the history of modern sculpture, and of sculpture's eventual primacy over painting, had been heavily colored by her deepening acquaintance with one of her colleagues in the Art Department at Hunter College, Robert Morris. Spurred by an interest in Marcel Duchamp and an involvement with the pioneering, prop-based choreography of Simone Forti, his first wife, Morris had quit painting to stake out some areas in the practice of sculpture (fig. 20.3)—including a deaestheticized, antiexpressive visual mode, now classified as Minimalist, a mode that "takes relationships out of the work and makes them a function of space, light, and the

viewer's field of vision," as he theorized it in 1966.[30] In the writings of Krauss and of her former student Hal Foster, among others, Morris's Minimalist initiatives particularly have come to serve as a very pivot of a paradigm shift in twentieth-century art, the shift that is said to have opened up "a new space of 'object/subject terms'" and eventuated "'a death of the author' . . . that is at the same time a birth of the reader."[31]

Krauss and another of her former students, Maurice Berger (who became for a time also a colleague at Hunter College), are conspicuous among the readers "birthed" by Morris's work. Further, around the time when Krauss first advanced the importance of a "model of meaning . . . severed from the legitimizing claims of a private self"—in a 1973 essay entitled "Sense and Sensibility," which featured Morris, among others—her "private self" was reputedly entering into an intimate as well as professional relationship with Morris.[32] A potential for overidentification with a subject of her criticism could have contributed to Krauss's receptivity to a critical position that debarred all inquiry into the private, then, for she would surely have wished to deflect the suggestions that typically arise when such cases become a matter of public knowledge. Typically, the suspicion is that a critic's judgment may be prejudiced or impaired by a deep, intimate connection to an artist, and that self-interest may fuel a critic's enthusiasm for an artist whose works became well represented in the critic's private collection as a benefit of that liaison. The tenure of the romantic relationship is difficult to pinpoint in Krauss and Morris's case, given the principals' disinclination to go on record on the matter, but the two figures' lives would in any case remain intertwined: they bought a SoHo building together around 1976, for instance, where they remain to this day close neighbors.

Krauss's liaison with her artist colleague was complicated from the outset by his collaboration with another, erstwhile Hunter College professor, Lynda Benglis, or so Benglis and some others perceived.[33] In a sequence of publicity photographs,

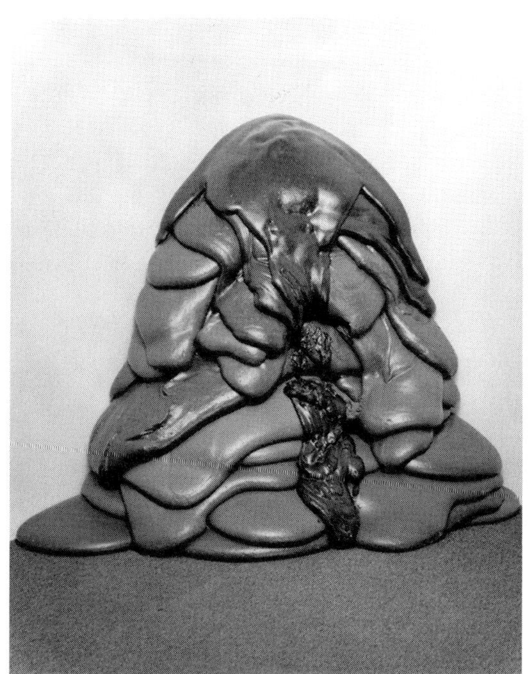

Figure 20.4. Lynda Benglis, *For Carl Andre*, 1970. Pigmented polyurethane foam. Collection of the Modern Art Museum of Fort Worth: Museum Purchase, The Benjamin J. Tillar Memorial Trust. © Lynda Benglis/Licensed by VAGA, New York, N.Y.

Benglis entered into a tacit, antic contest of exhibitionism and machismo with Morris in 1974, culminating in her vampy, nude self-portrait with double dildo published in the November issue of *Artforum*, at Morris's encouragement.[34] The following month, Krauss and others on *Artforum*'s masthead vituperatively attacked Benglis's gambit as "exploitative" and "brutalizing."[35] Meanwhile, Morris's comparably outrageous image of the bare-chested artist sinisterly clad in helmet, sunglasses, and chains (a picture issued by the Sonnabend Gallery as a promotional poster) entirely escaped censure—certainly from Krauss, who seems indeed to have been responsible for taking the photograph.[36] Besides her mischievous publicity campaign, the versatile Benglis produced an exceptionally fresh and experimental body of work from the mid 1960s through the mid 1970s. Some of that work irrever-

ently and theatrically engaged certain of the premises underlying Minimalist sculpture, in part through objects that articulated a kind of liquidation of painting as a medium, including rainbow-hued, carpet-like works of poured pigmented latex rubber, or the big, cornered, hardened pile of oozing brown polyurethane foam of 1970 that Benglis designated *For Carl Andre* (fig. 20.4). Such a vision (of painting's demise) could be construed as compatible with Krauss's own, yet Krauss ignored Benglis entirely in her 1977 sculpture textbook.

A certain overweighting of Morris's role as progenitor or "intellectual superman"[37] has served to occlude or subsume the initiatives of other generative and engaging figures of this era with differing reference points, emphases, and values, in short. Inasmuch as the act of writing history implicitly entails constructing a relationship to the past, whether recent or distant, it is an act "always already invested with interests and prejudice (prejudgment) rather than embodying the creation of value-free science."[38] Morris blithely observed, "Art has always been dependent upon and served one set of forces or another with little regard for the morality of those forces. . . . Art is always propaganda—for someone."[39] And seen from that vantage point, he and Krauss have served as deft propagandists, one for the other. But the lionizing of Morris by Krauss and others has not only functioned indirectly to slight other individuals whose achievements and scope of influence might render them equally or more deserving of such attention; it has also traduced much that was most radical—because at least incipiently communitarian—about the creative ferment at this historical juncture in the United States (that is, around the waning of the New York School's star).

The discounting of Morris's personal history—including the contributions to the most lauded chapters in his career by a succession of women deeply involved in his life, from Forti and Rainer to Benglis and Krauss—has served to elevate his art-historical profile by feeding some old-time myths of artistic greatness: that the genius realizes his masterworks, which must transcend the vicissitudes of his life, and attains fame all on his own striving and merit. Such a selective construction of history was never available to Hesse, whose critical fortunes have all along been colored by attention to her biography. Accounts of Hesse's career habitually extend credit to a network of enabling colleagues, usually without acknowledging the extent to which the stream of influence ran both ways: "Eva influenced her male friends as much as they influenced her. LeWitt, Andre, Smithson, myself . . . were all influenced by her," Mel Bochner has remarked—and he could have added some peers who were not friends to the list, including Morris and Serra. Bochner observed, too, that "certain developments" since the 1960s have rendered the metaphoric dimensions of Hesse's work more apparent: "What strikes me as a central issue seems to be her involvement with the phenomenology of being Eva Hesse—physically, emotionally, and intellectually."[40] The erasure of artistic subjectivity that seemed such a radical prospect to certain male artists in the 1960s could hardly portend the same for their female contemporaries, for whom erasure was almost a given. With women all but invisible as creative subjects or agents, the very act of constituting them as such—Hesse's act and Nemser's act—held another kind of deeply radical potential. The deployment of personal material by or about a female artist would have an additional, often inadvertent effect, however, insofar as it was and is liable to being taken as corroborating invidious stereotypes of the narrowly confessional and autobiographical impulses underlying women's creative processes.

By liberally sharing her life story, by leaving her diaries to posterity, and by playing to the camera's lens, Hesse would seem to have invited personalized critical treatment.[41] But the pronounced camera-shyness of Andre and Judd, for example, was seemingly immaterial to the kind of privacy these men were reflexively accorded by critics. For years, Morris (a.k.a. "Body Bob") deployed even his stripped body in the process of building his career without its having been construed as in any meaningful re-spect an exposure of a private self. Morris's 1962 relief *I-Box,* with its frontal nude, photographic self-portrait, adorned the cover and first page of the catalogue of the retrospective organized by Krauss and Thomas Krens at the Solomon R. Guggenheim Museum in New York in 1994, and the next four pages also featured full-page photographs of Morris at and with his work. But the figure described in the ensuing essays remains—more like the *I-Box,* with its little pink I-shaped door swung shut—a man oddly without a body or a biography, and certainly without any private history with one of the show's chief architects (unless we read between the lines to the works variously on loan from and dedicated to her).[42]

The depersonalized view of Morris prevalent in the Guggenheim catalogue (which lacks even the most skeletal chronology, that indispensable scholarly amenity of the standard retrospective catalogue) must devolve in part from the fact that his own copious statements mostly forgo the autobiographical. In 1989, however (that is, in a moment remote from his Minimalist past, when issues concerning identity had newly acquired a critical cachet in some circles), Morris published some "autobiographical asides," divulging, for instance, that the first Minimalist works that he had made, starting in 1961, "those gray columns and slabs I copied directly from the photographs of the ruins of the King Zoser complex at Saqqâra, Egypt," had engrossed him as a boy at the Nelson Gallery in Kansas City, Missouri. He told also of the childhood lure of the sadistic, hypermasculine atmosphere of the stockyards, that "dense and stressful labyrinth" where his father worked and, "like Virgil, guided me through its noxious circles."[43] In that light, it is noteworthy that Morris's sadomasochistic self-portrait was realized as an advertising poster for a 1974 show involving labyrinths, the built version of which had eight-foot-high walls and claustrophobia-inducing corridors too narrow for two adults to pass easily.

Such personal anecdotes do not provide sufficient accounts of the works in question, of course: biog-

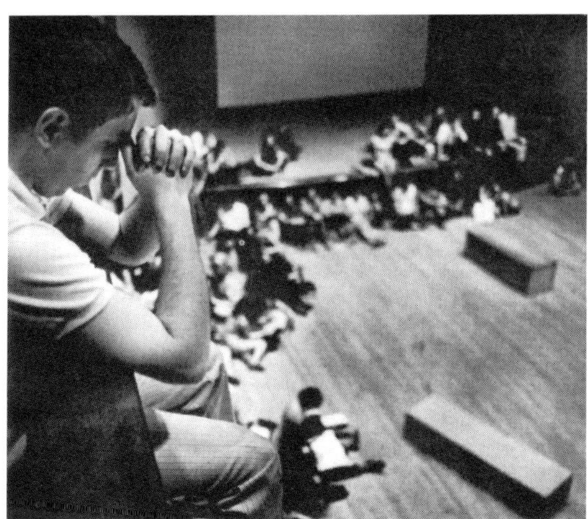

Figure 20.5. Simone Forti, *Platforms*, 1967 performance of 1961 dance construction. Loeb Student Center, New York University, New York. (Photo: Peter Moore, © Estate of Peter Moore/ VAGA, New York, N.Y.)

raphy can never presume to accomplish that. A glaring omission at the center of Morris's account of what have lately been cited as the first Minimalist objects bears underlining, for that matter, for the gray, elongated, wooden box that marked the ex-painter, sometime dancer-choreographer Morris's debut as a sculptor—a column that served in 1962 as a prop in a performance he contrived, a column that he later paired with a twin and exhibited as sculpture—plainly owed less to Egyptian artifacts glimpsed in photographs during boyhood than it, or they, did to the two elongated wooden boxes that Forti designed for her "dance construction" *Platforms* (fig. 20.5), which debuted at Yoko Ono's Chambers Street loft in May 1961, a year when Morris and Forti shared a studio, as well as the year they divorced. *Platforms* entailed having two performers, "preferably a man and a woman," perform simple tasks, in part while sequestered inside two wooden boxes, each open on one side and "long enough and high enough to hide a person" but "not . . . exactly alike."[44] Morris's pair of wooden columns, which were alike in dimensions, one to another (each eight feet by two feet by two feet), incorporated (or entailed refabricating) the single column

used in a February 1962 performance by Morris at New York's Living Theater, where it stood on end for three and a half minutes before he toppled it, by pulling a string from offstage, and left it lying for another three and a half minutes. The initial plan, for Morris to fell the column by standing inside it and tipping it over bodily, was foiled when he sustained an injury during rehearsal. The pair of columns he realized later, arranged with one erect and one prone, would "synchronously restage the two positions successively taken by the column in the Living Theater performance."[45]

The claims being made for the seminal status of Morris's early work, and with it for a canonical strain of Minimalism—the notion that these artists definitively put "the question of the subject in play" by arranging performative situations—would be better displaced to Forti's work of 1960–61, then. Whereas Morris's work apparently evidenced and addressed a kind of neutral or generically interchangeable viewing subject, Forti's subjects were sometimes marked by gender-coded traits (as in *Platforms*). Prior to *Platforms*, she employed Minimal or rudimentary wooden props in her 1960 *See Saw*—with Morris reading aloud from *Artnews* "in a monotonous self-contained voice" while Rainer was "throwing herself around and shrieking"—and in her 1960 *Rollers*, which involved two wooden boxes with ropes attached, serving as makeshift wagons for towing performers.[46] Forti's dance constructions, however, have been mentioned in only one of the monographs on the Minimalist movement—tellingly, the one authored by a historian not of art but of music.[47]

Morris's fall 1963 Green Gallery show was "the effective advent of Minimalism," pronounced Thomas Crow in a recent textbook on art of the 1960s.[48] Crow does mention that Morris had earlier been building objects akin to those featured in the show as props for Forti; indeed, while separately discussing her work, Crow labels a reproduction of her *Slant Board* as involving a "prop by Robert Morris."[49] By this account, the theatrical props she designed remain mere props or, worse, proto-Morris sculptures, while the theatrical props that he based on her initiatives—that boxy column and its successors—are assimilated to an autonomous history of sculpture and canonized as the point of origin for Minimalism. Venue is an issue in the segregation of a history of Minimalism from a history of dance, of course, as Crow observes that the Minimalists "transferred the aesthetic of task and function from Judson-style dance to the gallery."[50] But the venue for Forti's 1960 dance constructions was the Reuben Gallery, and the original venues for what are now called Morris's first Minimalist sculptures were performance spaces. Further, by relegating Forti's dance constructions to the status of minor previews of the main event, critics generally have perpetuated a gendered division of labor whereby dance is coded as a marginal and feminine (or effeminate) province while sculpture is central and masculine. Such divisions traduce the category-shaking radicality of Forti's and Morris's early efforts, however, and unjustifiably narrow the parameters of Minimalism as a movement.[51] (Not only for Morris but for Hesse also, experimental dance catalyzed a departure from painting: her first three-dimensional work was made as an inhabited prop for a *Sculpture Dance*, part of a series of happenings organized by Allan Kaprow, Walter De Maria, and others at Woodstock in 1962, and even occasionally in her mature work, she toyed with the link between sculpture and theatrical prop.)[52]

The integration of Morris's personal and professional histories, in this case through a focus on his working relationship with his first wife, may afford an inroad toward correcting the critical asymmetry that allows his production to figure as an impersonal, towering cultural force, while Forti's pathbreaking experiments are eclipsed to little more than footnotes, and Hesse's hugely influential enterprise is still considered liable to being depreciated as "purely personal."[53] Compounding this asymmetry is an influential critical account that goes so far as to argue that the burgeoning feminist art practices of the 1970s and after—with their embrace of the body, subjectivity, biography, and expressivity—owe the very possibility of their existence to the famously depersonalized, or (as I have characterized it in another place) distinctly masculinist, movement of Minimalism,[54] that "feminist art begins where minimalism ends," as Foster frames it, pointing to Minimalism's alleged role, again, in putting the "subject in play." Distinctly unlike the subject of and for feminist art, however, the subject entailed in canonical Minimalist sculpture was "somehow before or outside history, language, sexuality, and power," as Foster himself acknowledges.[55]

Unlike any of the male artists engaged with Minimalism in the 1960s, Hesse's example lends itself to being described as protofeminist, and as fecund for the unfolding of certain of those feminist art practices that would so radically undermine the premises of high modernism.[56] Hesse escalated Minimalism's impetus toward the birth or mobilizing of the perceiver—by making works whose detached or dangling components, informal-looking organization, and pronounced tactility tended to invite the touch of spectators[57]—but not at the cost of staging a death of the artist. In lieu of the apparently neutral and neutered forms commonly identified with Minimalism, Hesse tendered forms more idiosyncratic, more suggestive of the body, and more patently open to those metaphoric valences that the Minimalists claimed to abhor—forms more expressive, in a word, and in that sense, more aligned with values the society codes as feminine. Where the canonical Minimalist object typically had an alienating or distancing effect on viewers, Hesse's sculpture generally compelled a more complex dialectic, as of attraction and repulsion or seduction and alienation.

An unprecedented foregrounding of the role or status of the viewer is increasingly cited as the most radical innovation, even the keystone, of Minimalism. "Your work and that of some others made the role of viewer more 'open-ended'—at least it made me more self-conscious, more aware of my own presence alongside your sculpture," declaimed Ian Burn and Karl Beveridge, in 1975, of and to Donald Judd.

Perhaps this was a function of the sculpture's alienating effect; the art object, being (as it were) exclusive of me, forced me self-reflectively to deal with my own presence. This focused attention anew on the subject-object relation . . . made the relation explicit . . . made it conscious again. This became important for a lot of us. It encouraged me to view myself as object-and-subject. For a moment, this seemed radical, even revolutionary. It was radical. It touched the very alienating structure of modern art.[58]

Given the marginality and relative meagerness of the historical record on modern dance, it remains underrecognized that the Minimalist sculptors' initiative in putting a subject in play in relation to their objects stemmed largely from exchanges with such pioneers as Forti and Rainer. Of Forti's prescient 1961 *Evening of Dance Constructions,* Rainer mused ruefully, "I sometimes wonder if more feedback would have prevented her retirement. . . . [I]t was as though a vacuum sealed that event. Nothing was written about it. . . . It would be another two and a half years before the idea of a 'construction' to generate movement or situation would take hold."[59] Rainer has acknowledged her own debt to Forti, whose studio she shared for a time when it was Morris's studio as well. And Rainer would come to number among Forti's successors as Morris's domestic partner.[60] Lippard recalled first seeing Rainer dance at the Judson Church during the winter of 1963–64: "I was particularly turned on by those elements [of the dance] bounding on so-called Minimal Art, with which I was coming of age as an art critic. Since then, I have gradually become aware of how crucial these ideas have been to the 'advanced' art, dance, film, and performance that have followed."[61]

In an incisive essay of 1966, Rainer explained how her own practices paralleled those of Minimalist sculptors.[62] While the sculptors were exploring ordinary materials and commonplace principles of order, she (like Forti before her) was investigating ordinary or nondance movement, sometimes drawn from the

body's interactions with simple props or commonplace objects. To better explore unstylized or deskilled modes of movement, Rainer's troupes routinely positioned professionally trained dancers such as Julie Judd (wife of Donald Judd) alongside amateurs such as Morris, Andre, and the sculptor Rosemarie Castoro (who was Andre's wife).[63] Rainer would decline to be constrained by Minimalism's "anti-metaphorical strategies," however, and she all along interjected autobiographical material into her work.[64] Plagued throughout her adult life by ill health, she staged a *Convalescent Dance* in 1967, for instance, performing her *Trio A* with a body gravely weakened by a recent hospital stay. For Hesse (who was a fan of Rainer's work), illness was no less familiar a realm of experience, and she also found means to explore it in her work.[65]

By portraying Rainer and Hesse as artistic autobiographers of a kind and as plagued by illness, it may seem that I am bound to reinforce stereotypical gender divisions, between men who would transcend their private lives in their art and women who compound the two, between hale men and frail women.[66] But while Rainer and Hesse conspicuously endured more serious medical problems than their male peers, further scrutiny yields a more complicated perspective, for Morris in fact shared Rainer's penchant for encrypting personal material, at times of a medical nature, into his work, albeit with a wry consciousness of the artist's self as a "self," a willful construction. Berger has summed up the autobiographical subject at issue in Morris's work with a line of Samuel Beckett's: "I seem to speak, it is not I, about me, it is not about me."[67] In a 1963 Green Gallery show—in the same year and at the same site where he is said to have inaugurated Minimalism—Morris exhibited, alongside his *I-Box,* two other ironic self-portraits. *Portrait* (1963) is a wooden rack holding a row of identical small, opaque gray bottles said to contain samples of his own blood, sweat, sperm, saliva, phlegm, tears, urine, and feces; *Self-Portrait (EEG)* (1963) incorporates an electroencephalograph done while, he has said, he focused on himself for the amount of time it took to produce a record of his brain waves measuring as long as his body is tall.[68] Using autobiography as a "found object," Rainer, for her part, integrated in the solo *Ordinary Dance* of 1962, for instance, a "litany of street names and grade school teachers": lists whose autobiographical character would have been recognizable to few besides herself.[69] "My work in a broad sense has always been autobiographical," she has noted. But while "interested in private experience and the problems of projecting and transforming it," she cared further about how to "link it all up with the kinds of conditioning and power structures that govern our lives." And she drew a line at lapsing into what she disparaged as the "*merely* personal."[70]

The "I" that Morris articulated in his "early objects and dances is always rhetorical, always institutionally grounded, deflected away from the private personality or history of the speaker," Berger has argued. "The 'I' who mocks the notion of the self-portrait in *I-Box* exists *not* as expressions of personality or ego but as constantly shifting surrogate."[71] All biography is rhetorically constructed, of course, but as a representation of an actual historical being. In my view, Morris's "I" is best understood as both rhetorical and autobiographical, then, and certainly as evidence of a specific personality and ego. In their recourse to autobiographical material, Rainer and Morris would share an emphasis on the constructed character of the artistic subject, however.[72] And that contention would notably separate them from Hesse—whose work was no more transparently (or "merely") autobiographical than theirs but who cherished a troubled dream of an ideal unity or continuum between art and life—as well as from Andre, who conceived his sculptures as being "of very subjective origin—infantile origin."[73]

Through intermittent interviews and the published recollections of selected old friends (including Barbara Rose and Hollis Frampton), Andre has steadily crafted and polished a certain unilinear, teleological life story. Nearly all substantive catalogues of his work for the past three decades have, accordingly, proffered a point-by-point source for almost all of his signature materials, forms, and practices (working with bricks, metal plates, granite, and timbers and writing poetry) in an oft-told tale: that of the overall-clad grandson of a humble but proud Swedish bricklayer and son of a marine draftsman and housewife-poetess, who grew up by the shipbuilding yards and the granite quarries of historic, blue-collar Quincy, Massachusetts, and took further vital aesthetic sustenance from a stint in the early 1960s working on the railroads. A tale is often recycled, too, of an epiphany experienced just prior to his first New York solo show while canoeing on a New Hampshire lake in 1965: that his work should be as level as water. Thus, a mix of innocently pastoral and industrial images came appended to the sculptures that Andre referred to, also in a pastoral way, as "plains."[74]

The brutal aspect of Andre's work—the fact that his plains could remind as alert an observer as Hesse of the floors of Nazi gas chambers—is nowhere explained by this tidy idyll. And here we may see why some feminists have welcomed the tidings of Michel Foucault and Roland Barthes that it does not matter who is speaking, or that the author has expired, for Andre would return us to a familiar biographical model, to a would-be definitive, yet highly partial, mythologized, and virilized portrait of the artist. As early as 1968 he prepared a self-interview for the catalogue to his Mönchengladbach solo show, replete with Whitmanesque paean to his native Quincy, "CITY OF GRANITE QUARRIES AND SHIP BUILDING YARDS GREAT UNCUT BLOCKS OF STONE ACRES OF STEEL PLATES." Yet Dan Graham would characterize Andre's art around the same time as "disencumber[ed] . . . of the weight of personal and historically evolutionary determination."[75] And Andre's pithy life story would largely be ignored in those (many) accounts bent on integrating his work into the Minimalist canon. That omission may be attributed to the depreciation of the biographical under the critical paradigms that have prevailed over the course of his career, as well as to his own conflicting directives on the correct approach to his art. Thus, in the catalogue for a vast retrospective in Germany—entitled by the artist *Carl Andre / Sculptor 1996*—the chief curator, guided by Andre's directives, talked paradoxically about Quincy and the railroad as "place[s] that opened up possibilities for his sculpture, fertilized it" but have had "no direct influence on [the] content" of the work.[76] Absent from her narrative, or any provided by Andre, meantime, is an accounting of a personal past evidently instrumental to the course of his career, namely, his connections with women from Rose, Castoro, Lippard, Hesse, and Angela Westwater to Ana Mendieta—who notoriously expired in a plunge from Andre's thirty-fourth-story apartment window in 1985.[77] Whatever the unknowable facts of that case, Andre, forever the artistic autobiographer, followed the trial with a singular semiprivate exhibition featuring a wooden window frame of approximately Mendieta's height stretched with metal screening torn in the lower part of the frame.[78]

In a 1994 roundtable on the "Reception of the Sixties" in *October,* a magazine cofounded and coedited by Krauss, she summoned former students Foster and Benjamin Buchloh, among others, to rally in defense of Morris against what she deemed an unacceptable response from the general press to the Guggenheim retrospective's claims of preeminence for Morris.[79] Krauss, on this occasion, upheld her conceit of Minimalism as signaling the advent of an "artistic personality . . . voided by industrialized production." But Denis Hollier (her current domestic partner) reflected that, for him,

> the distance and the proximity of the 1960s is best emblematized by the effect of estrangement induced by the fact that today an autobiography by Althusser exists. . . . [T]hat the name of Althusser can—or has to—bear responsibility for such a book today . . . might be consonant with the return of the body, the return to expressivity, the return to the biographical, to the subject. Somehow, all the values against which,

precisely, Althusser became an author, making him one of the heroic figures in the fight for the suppression of the centered subject, are now back. . . . Suddenly, the promoter of the concept of *procès sans sujet* turns out to be a *sujet sans procès*; he becomes a subject precisely because he is deprived of a *procès*, in that he was not allowed to stand trial, as a subject, for his wife's murder.[80]

Some fissures in the argument for the author's removal here become starkly visible: in the matter of accountability, of needing an embodied author to interrogate, on the one hand, and on the other, in that telling formulation of the "heroic figures in the fight for the suppression of the centered subject." This formulation parallels passages in the 1996 Andre retrospective catalogue, for instance, that herald him and his peers for being "self-effacing," refusing "personal 'touch,'" yet "us[ing] a distinctive, personal language" and "add[ing] to the world something that makes them unique and identifiable."[81] Here the deprivileged author envisioned by revisionist critics comes unmasked as an author doubly privileged, basking in the glory, not to mention the economic advantages, of the prior, "unique," and "heroic" author while enjoying some powerful new prerogatives or protections; here we glimpse a form of "authoritarianism masquerading as antiauthoritarian," to borrow a phrase from Craig Owens.[82] The return to the subject that Hollier implicitly mourns can better be seen not as a 1990s retreat from 1960s radicality, then, but as a newly framed initiative from that very—activist—decade of the rekindling feminist movement, as well as of such protofeminist figures as Hesse, Forti, and Rainer.[83]

Homi Bhabha insightfully observes that "'masculinism' as a position of social authority is not simply about the power invested in the recognizable 'persons' of men." In fact, "it would be perfectly possible for a woman to occupy the role of a representative man, in the sense I am giving to that term." Masculinism is instead "about the subsumption or sublation of social antagonism; it is about the re-pression of social divisions; it is about the power to authorize an 'impersonal' holistic or universal dis-course on the representation of the social that natu-ralizes cultural difference and turns it into a 'second'-nature argument."[84]

In their aim to address broadly the state of culture under capitalism, would-be revisionist, Marxist-identified historians, such as Crow (and Buchloh), who have trained their sights on the 1960s, have gen-erally come to occupy a rhetorical space as problem-atic as that staked out by the poststructuralists Krauss and Foster—namely, the all-too-familiar space of the normative authority (read: straight white male) who speaks from an unmarked subject position as if speaking neutrally or universally for or on behalf of the good of us all. But this cloak of impersonality—long assumed as the art-historical authorities' garb and widely draped by said authorities over the shoul-ders of the canonical Minimalists—can only ever have passed for radical raiment among those secure in their entitlement to speak. For those unacculturated to the prerogatives of speaking, unused to holding the floor, anonymity is but regulation wear; hence the feminist epigram, drawn from Virginia Woolf, "Anonymous was a woman." And insofar as imper-sonal speech coincides with institutional speech, to the less or disempowered generally, the specter of the anonymous author/ity hardly augurs emancipation. In this light, the answer to Foucault's blithe, Beckett-derived 1960s question, "What does it matter who is speaking?" was and is: it matters crucially.[85] And as for who is *not* speaking: that matters even more.

Not many female artists in or prior to the 1960s managed to "speak" or, in any case, to attain the au-thority to speak and be heard. All the more reason, then, why the speech of Eva Hesse signaled a new quarter heard from, a quarter that has in due course shaken the indifferently male textual monolith of the history of art. The reasons that Hesse (more than, say, Frankenthaler or Mitchell) helped disrupt the discur-sive proceedings-as-usual have to do with the risk she took in insinuating into an ostensibly desubjectivized,

sexually neutral, or indifferent visual modality an em-phasis on the personal, implicitly including that mark of difference: her identity as a woman. In Hesse's wake, feminism "infiltrated or overtly influenced every art- (or un-art-) making process of [the 1970s] in distinct and irreversible ways," as Mary Kelly phrased it, "notably, by transforming the phenom-enological presence of the body into an image of sex-ual difference, extending the interrogation of the object to include the subjective conditions of its exis-tence, turning political intent into personal account-ability, and translating institutional critique into the question of authority."[86]

If by its (and her) very character, Hesse's art is and has been subject to investigation in relation to her biography, then her male peers' more reticent pro-duction should no longer be exempted. From the in-side view of Lippard in 1968, Minimalism's vaunted impersonalism already seemed to be "just a new kind of personalism."[87] From my view as outlined in 1990, that impersonalism, rather than being so neutral, as was generally said, smacked of certain tropes of mas-culinism as they intersect with tropes of power: both the power of the virile body and that of the realms of industry and technology, with their governing prin-ciples of rationality, systematism, regularity, and instrumentality—realms that may indeed at once affirm and threaten the privileged status of the virile body.[88] Too little has yet been said on this subject of masculinism and of heterosexual masculinities, however—or too little that takes exception to the pre-vailing "order of discourse."[89] By particularizing, deidealizing, and complicating the construction of masculinity, we can move toward foiling the norma-tivizing yardsticks against which those who are counted "different"—by virtue of gender, sexuality, skin color, or other attributes—are always implicitly measured and found to be stunted, peculiar, other. By restoring to men—in critically conscious ways—their private and family lives and their embeddedness in their bodies and in nature, we can also move, im-portantly, toward defeminizing and so upwardly revaluing those realms of experience; we can move toward a society where what is coded as feminine will not reflexively be counted as secondary.

NOTES

Christopher McAuliffe, Jo Anna Isaak, and Maurice Berger came to my aid in various ways with this essay. So, too, did audiences at the 1997 "Sculpting Words" conference at University College, London; at the 1997 Mount Holyoke College symposium on "The Future of the Social History of Art"; at Dartmouth College; and at the University of Leeds, where I delivered an earlier version of this essay. The Mount Holyoke event honored Robert L. Herbert, to whom I dedicate this essay.

1. Lynn Zelevansky, *Sense and Sensibility: Women Artists and Minimalism in the Nineties,* exh. cat. (New York: Museum of Modern Art, 1994), 7.

2. Hal Foster, "The Crux of Minimalism," in *The Return of the Real* (Cambridge, Mass.: MIT Press, 1996), 54, and passim. The present essay particularly questions certain aspects of the version of Minimalism synthesized by Foster in this article—a version that is increasingly acquiring a canonical status.

3. "The piece was designed for a specific space so that viewers in two neighboring galleries would have distinctly different views of it," either as a kind of "horizon line" or "in receding perspective," noted David Bourdon, *Carl Andre: Sculpture, 1959–1977* (New York: Jaap Rietman, 1978), 27. *Lever* figured in the catalogue for the Jewish Museum show as a drawing by Andre, labeled a "proposal" for a piece involving one hundred firebricks in a line extending from a position flush with the wall of one room through a doorway into a second room (in Kynaston McShine, *Primary Structures: Younger American and British Sculptors,* exh. cat. [New York: Jewish Museum, 1966], n.p.). As it was ultimately realized, the work consisted of a row of 137 bricks that did not penetrate but "stopp[ed] short" of a doorway (David Bourdon, "The Razed Sites of Carl Andre" [1966], in *Minimal Art: A Critical Anthology,* ed. Gregory Battcock [1968; reprint, Berkeley: University of California Press, 1995], 103). Note that in this firsthand account Bourdon places the number of bricks at 139, though subsequent reckonings by Bourdon and oth-

ers consistently use the figure 137. The move to confine the work within a single room reportedly stemmed from issues of artistic territoriality that came to be endemic in group shows involving so-called site-specific work. Lately, Minimalist art's tacitly theatrical or performative dimension (of which Michael Fried famously complained in his 1967 "Art and Objecthood," reprinted in Battcock, *Minimal Art,* 116–47) has been emphasized as a distinct achievement of the movement by numerous critics, including Hal Foster. Views of the Minimalist movement as having newly foregrounded the role of the spectator, and thus as having (generously) mobilized or empowered a viewing public, would appear at odds with the experience of the lay public, at least, for whom Minimalism's perceived withholding of the (expected) fruits of an aesthetic experience has seemed to be paramount. A once outspoken ally of the Minimalists, Lucy Lippard, recently observed of the movement, "What I didn't like was the exclusivity, the inaccessibility, the disregard for the audience" (quoted in Susan L. Stoops, "From Eccentric to Sensuous Abstraction: An Interview with Lucy Lippard," in *More than Minimal: Feminism and Abstraction in the '70s,* exh. cat. [Waltham, Mass.: Rose Art Museum, Brandeis University, 1996], 28). Spectators differ one from the next, then as now, however, and I have argued that Minimalism may afford radically different kinds of experiences for different viewers, in Anna C. Chave, "Minimalism and the Rhetoric of Power," *Arts* 64 (January 1990): 44–63.

4. E. C. Goossen, "Two Exhibitions," in Battcock, *Minimal Art,* 169, 168. When Gregory Battcock's key early attempt at gathering a canonical body of Minimalist criticism first appeared, in 1968, he held the title of lecturer in the Art Department at the City University of New York's Hunter College, a department that, over time, housed numerous individuals instrumental in forming or defining the Minimalist movement and in making one another (key or bit) players within it, including Goossen, a longtime department chair, Tony Smith, Ad Reinhardt, and later, Robert Morris, Rosalind Krauss, Maurice Berger, and Phyllis Tuchman, among others. (Full disclosure: I was curator of the Hunter College Art Gallery from 1981 to 1983 and visiting associate professor in the Art Department there from 1991 to 1993.) The second of the

two phrases cited here derives from Goossen's text for "probably the first exhibition devoted to . . . 'Minimal' art," the 1964 *Eight Young Artists* show he curated at the Hudson River Museum (ibid., 165).

5. Mel Bochner, "Serial Art, Systems, Solipsism," in Battcock, *Minimal Art*, 92–102.

6. Bourdon, *Carl Andre*, 104: "'All I'm doing,' says Andre, 'is putting Brancusi's *Endless Column* on the ground instead of in the sky. Most sculpture is priapic with the male organ in the air. In my work, Priapus is down on the floor. The engaged position is to run along the earth.' Rhetoric aside, he denies emphatically that his work has even implicit sexual meaning." A certain would-be orthodox view of Minimalism has it that to view works such as *Lever* in terms of metaphor or reference, as Andre and his contemporaries did, and as I have done elsewhere, is to perform incongruously an iconographic exercise on art that was conceived precisely to defeat such exercises, art that would exemplify pure materiality, and thus pure nonreferentiality. For accounts specifically taking me to task, see Foster, "The Crux," 247 n. 37; and David Batchelor, *Minimalism* (Cambridge: Cambridge University Press, 1997), 71–72. Even were I to concur that the artists' view of their enterprise must dictate the parameters of any valid reading of it, this criticism presupposes a singleness of purpose on the part of the Minimalists with respect to matters of iconicity and indexicality that they manifestly did not possess, while implicitly consigning present-day critics to an untenable fiction: that of the artwork that can escape not merely fixed symbol systems—the usual domain of iconographic modes of inquiry, which the Minimalists did indeed defeat, and which I in fact forgo—but all metaphor and reference. In time, Andre publicly acknowledged the futility of that aim. In a 1978 interview, he said, "I was both naive and being polemical. . . . I now realise that one cannot purge the human environment from the significance we give it" (cited in Peter Fuller, "Carl Andre on His Sculpture, II," *Art Monthly* 17 [June 1978]: 10).

7. Ibid.

8. Rita Felski, *The Gender of Modernity* (Cambridge, Mass.: Harvard University Press, 1995), 3. (In context, Felski uses this phrase in summarizing an argument of the literary theorist Gail Finney.)

9. Hal Foster, "The Crux of Minimalism," in *Individuals: A Selected History of Contemporary Art, 1945–1986*, ed. Howard Singerman, exh. cat. (Los Angeles: Museum of Contemporary Art, 1986), 172–73 (the first published version of this previously cited essay).

10. Yvonne Rainer, "Looking Myself in the Mouth," *October* 17 (Summer 1981): 69–70.

11. "Any True Discourse that relies on a *disembodied* founding subject does indeed both mask and justify the authoritarian process by means of which such a subject has (at least in part) been formed," Balbus observed in his critique of Michel Foucault; therefore, "a True Discourse that posits an embodied founding subject is a prerequisite for any material appeal against this very process." Isaac Balbus, "Disciplining Women: Michel Foucault and the Power of Feminist Discourse," in *Feminism as Critique*, ed. Seyla Benhabib and Drucilla Cornell (Minneapolis: University of Minnesota Press, 1987), 125.

12. Lucy R. Lippard, ed. and annot., *Six Years: The Dematerialization of the Art Object from 1966 to 1972* (1973; reprint, Berkeley: University of California Press, 1997), viii.

13. Lucy Lippard, *From the Center: Feminist Essays on Women's Art* (New York: E. P. Dutton, 1976), 3.

14. Lucy Lippard, quoted in Stoops, *More than Minimal*, 27, 26.

15. Ibid., 27.

16. Isaac D. Balbus, *Marxism and Domination: A Neo-Hegelian, Feminist, Psychoanalytic Theory of Sexual, Political, and Technological Liberation* (Princeton, N.J.: Princeton University Press, 1982), 78.

17. Judy Chicago, *Through the Flower: My Struggles as a Woman Artist* (1975), rev. ed. (Garden City, N.Y.: Anchor/Doubleday, 1982), 65–66. Exhibiting under her given name, Judy Gerowitz, Chicago was (with Tina Matkovic and Anne Truitt) one of three women out of forty-two artists in the 1966 *Primary Structures* show. *Through the Flower* is the first of two volumes that cast her life's work in autobiographical terms. Truitt, who by contrast has sustained a kind of Minimalist vision, eventually published three volumes of edited journal entries, starting with *Daybook: The Journal of an Artist* (New York: Pantheon, 1982).

18. See Cindy Nemser, *Art Talk: Conversations with Twelve Women Artists* (New York: Charles Scribner's Sons, 1975), 4–5. The risks of being marked as a "woman artist"—of being stigmatized as secondary, of ghet-

toization, of being held accountable to an insufficiently flexible or considered feminist "party line"—were more apparent to many or most female artists and critics in the 1960s and 1970s (and, arguably, ever since) than the potential benefits attaching to such identification. Those who aligned themselves with a feminist ideology generally took that step with a degree of ambivalence. The preponderant desire, although a fantasy then as now, was to do work in and for a world where an artist's gender would never count against her.

19. Hesse noted once that she had "a thing going" with Carl Andre: "I spend time going where I know he will be but he is never (almost) there. We have a date tomorrow eve.—I doubt he will keep date. He is a strange one." The note, dated May 7, 1967, is in a ledger given to her by a more faithful friend, LeWitt (Eva Hesse Archives, Allen Memorial Art Museum, Oberlin College, Oberlin, Ohio). Hesse is often called a Postminimalist, a term coined by Robert Pincus-Witten, in essays collected in Pincus-Witten, *Postminimalism* (New York: Out of London Press, 1977). Insofar as the Postminimalist rubric evokes figures distinctly junior to the Minimalists, it somewhat misleads in Hesse's case, however. Hesse (born in 1936) was younger than Andre by only four months, and, although she arrived at a Minimalist idiom some years after he and others did, the work she did that was in dialogue with Minimalism began emerging into public view in New York City not long after Minimalism first visibly coalesced as a movement there. Lippard included Hesse's work in the important *Eccentric Abstraction* show at the Fischbach Gallery in New York in 1966, the same year as the Jewish Museum's *Primary Structures* exhibition. (Only after the *Primary Structures* show did the adjective *minimal* begin to enter general critical usage to describe the work that is now so categorized; see Frances Colpitt, *Minimal Art: The Critical Perspective* [Seattle: University of Washington Press, 1993], 3.) Hesse's mature work is best understood, in my view, as occupying a position complexly both inside and outside of what is now viewed as canonical Minimalism—a position parallel in certain respects to those of her friend Robert Smithson (born in 1938), Richard Serra (born in 1939, arrived in New York in 1966), or Dan Graham (born in 1942).

20. Hesse, who would elsewhere in this interview stress that she viewed art and life as ideally unified and inseparable, admits at this juncture to torn feelings, saying that she cannot abide "romanticism"; it was a contradiction, she allowed: "I can't give you a statement to satisfy it." Cindy Nemser, transcripts of interview with Eva Hesse, Eva Hesse Archives, Archives of American Art, reel no. 1475, frame nos. 20, 40, 41, 94 (brackets indicate correction of orthography as found in the original manuscript).

21. This is not to suggest that Hesse drew no notice from nonfeminist critics: to the contrary. But Lippard and Nemser initially gave her by far more sustained support and attention than others, and female, if not feminist, museum curators have from the outset been the stalwarts behind the organization of Hesse exhibitions. I was commissioned to provide a contemporary feminist perspective on Hesse for a 1992 survey exhibition of her work; see Chave, "Eva Hesse: A 'Girl Being a Sculpture,'" in *Eva Hesse: A Retrospective*, ed. Helen Cooper, exh. cat. (New Haven: Yale University Art Gallery, 1992), 99–117; as well as Chave, "Striking Poses: The Absurdist Theatrics of Eva Hesse," in *Sculpture and Photography*, ed. Geraldine A. Johnson (New York: Cambridge University Press, 1998), 166–80, which serves in part as a corrective to a certain imbalance of emphasis in the earlier essay.

22. Balbus, *Marxism and Domination*, 61. See also Rita Felski, *Beyond Feminist Aesthetics: Feminist Literature and Social Change* (Cambridge, Mass.: Harvard University Press, 1989), ch. 2, 51–85.

23. Hesse was evidently of two minds, however, about whether she wanted strictly to make important art or purposely to make important art "as a woman." In 1965, she worried, "Do I have a right to womanliness? Can I achieve an artistic endeavor and can they coincide?" and noted that "there are handfuls [of women] that succeeded, but less when one separates the women from the women that assumed the masculine role" (see Chave, "Eva Hesse," 99). Five years later, she remarked that "excellence has no sex" (jotted by Hesse on a letter of 6 January 1970, from Cindy Nemser, Eva Hesse Archives, Archives of American Art, reel no. 1475, frame no. 19), though she acceded to Nemser's request to participate in a book of interviews with female artists. Extracts from Hesse's diaries were first published in Robert Pincus-Witten,

"Eva Hesse: Last Words," *Artforum* 11, no. 3 (November 1972): 74–76.

24. Barbara Johnson, *The Feminist Difference: Literature, Psychoanalysis, Race, and Gender* (Cambridge, Mass.: Harvard University Press, 1998), 7. This paradox, whose ramifications have sharply divided feminists, is often framed in terms of (the risk of) "essentialism"; useful discussions of the problem include Diane Fuss, *Essentially Speaking: Feminism, Nature and Difference* (New York: Routledge, 1989); Elizabeth Grosz, "Sexual Difference and the Problem of Essentialism," in *The Essential Difference*, ed. Naomi Schor and Elizabeth Weed (Bloomington: Indiana University Press, 1994), 82–97; and Griselda Pollock, "Inscriptions in the Visible," in *Inside the Visible: An Elliptical Traverse of 20th Century Art / In, of, and from the Feminine*, ed. M. Catherine de Zegher, exh. cat. (Boston: Institute of Contemporary Art, 1996), 67–87.

25. Felski, *Beyond Feminist Aesthetics*, 70.

26. See Briony Fer, "Bordering on Blank: Eva Hesse and Minimalism," *Art History* 17, no. 3 (September 1994): 424–49; and Anne M. Wagner, "Another Hesse," *October* 69 (Summer 1994): 49–84. Wagner's essay takes my 1992 essay on Hesse to task for being an overly personalized, overly biographical, and insufficiently historical reading of the artist's work. Oddly enough, her own account of Hesse relies throughout on evidence culled from the diaries, whose accessibility she laments. Heavily biographical, if in a way different from my own account, Wagner's reading also relies crucially on a fact drawn (without acknowledgment) from my historical findings concerning the means by which Hesse's mother committed suicide. For my (abridged) reply to Wagner, see Anna C. Chave, Letter to the Editor, *October* 71 (Winter 1995): 146–48. For Wagner's revision of her own essay, see Wagner, *Three Artists (Three Women): Modernism and the Art of Hesse, Krasner, and O'Keeffe* (Berkeley: University of California Press, 1996).

27. Rosalind E. Krauss, *Passages in Modern Sculpture* (Cambridge, Mass.: MIT Press, 1977), 266.

28. Rosalind E. Krauss, "Eva Hesse," in *Eva Hesse: Sculpture, 1963–1970*, exh. cat. (London: Whitechapel Art Gallery, 1979), n.p.

29. Krauss, *Passages*. Returning to Hesse's case in the final chapter of a recent book, Krauss opens with an elliptical private reference of her own, citing a slur that Greenberg had long ago muttered in her presence against "smart Jewish girls with their typewriters." With her obedience to Greenberg decidedly behind her, Krauss proceeds to diminish another smart Jewish girl whom she views as having been constrained specifically by a sense of obedience, namely Hesse, who is charged with sustaining a putatively anachronistic obedience to the authority of the medium of painting. See Rosalind E. Krauss, *The Optical Unconscious* (Cambridge, Mass.: MIT Press, 1993), 309, 313–14.

30. Robert Morris, "Notes on Sculpture" (1966), in Battcock, *Minimal Art*, 232. That some critics have taken to isolating this sentence of Morris's text as a credo for the Minimalists generally is misleading insofar as elsewhere in his and his peers' writings of this period relatively little heed was given to the role of the viewer, who—as in the Morris passage cited here—tends to figure at best as possessed of no more than a "field of vision."

31. Foster, "The Crux of Minimalism" (as in n. 9), 172–73.

32. Rosalind Krauss, "Sense and Sensibility: Reflection on Post '60s Sculpture," *Artforum* 12, no. 3 (November 1973): 48.

33. Lynda Benglis, conversation with author, winter (Feb.?) of 1991. Though it has been stated in print that Benglis had an affair with Morris at the time of their collaboration, in conversation with me she denied having had such a relationship with him. Benglis and Morris's collaboration began in 1971 and led to her making a video *(Mumble)* in 1972, and to his making one *(Exchange)* the following year. Robert Pincus-Witten discusses the autobiographical dimension to these videos, which dealt with "the frustration and confusion of physical desire with artistic creation," and cites Morris's stating in one of them, "The maniacal pursuit of art has led me to hurt women" (cited in Pincus-Witten, "Benglis' Video: Medium to Media," in *Postminimalism*, 160–61).

34. Benglis reports that Morris and Robert Pincus-Witten "kind of gave me permission" to publish the picture in question. Initially, she considered including a man, possibly Morris, in the image—"Morris came with me to buy the dildo and we had different poses"—but finally she determined that the dildo rendered her a figure "both male and female so I didn't

really need a male." Quoted in France Morin, "Lynda Benglis: Conversation with France Morin" (1977), in *Theories and Documents of Contemporary Art: A Sourcebook of Artists' Writings*, ed. Kristine Stiles and Peter Selz (Berkeley: University of California Press, 1996), 621.

35. Lawrence Alloway, Max Kozloff, Rosalind Krauss, Joseph Masheck, Annette Michelson, "Letters," *Artforum* 13, no. 4 (December 1974): 9.

36. See the tiny print in the photograph credits of Thomas Krens, Rosalind Krauss, et al., *Robert Morris: The Mind/Body Problem*, exh. cat. (New York: Solomon R. Guggenheim Museum, 1994), viii. Benglis's and Morris's oft-reproduced images may be found side by side in, for instance, Susan Krane, *Lynda Benglis: Dual Natures*, exh. cat. (Atlanta: High Museum of Art, 1991), 40–41.

37. This is how Morris is said to regard himself, by Krens, in Krens and Krauss, *Robert Morris*, xxix, but this self-evaluation seems in keeping with the assessment of the catalogue's principal coauthors.

38. Felski, *Gender of Modernity*, 207. (In context, Felski used these phrases to characterize a position attributed to Friedrich Nietzsche.)

39. Robert Morris, "Notes on Art as/and Land Reclamation" (1980), in *Continuous Project Altered Daily: The Writings of Robert Morris* (Cambridge, Mass.: MIT Press, 1993), 229–30.

40. Mel Bochner, quoted in Joan Simon, "Mel Bochner Interviewed by Joan Simon: About Eva Hesse," in *Eva Hesse: Drawing in Space* by Brigitte Reinhardt, Klaus Bussmann, and Erich Franz, exh. cat. (Münster: Ulmer Museum and Westfälisches Landesmuseum, 1994), 91–93.

41. On Hesse's history of posing for photographs, see Chave, "Striking Poses."

42. The exception to the unmitigatedly antibiographical slant of the catalogue is Maurice Berger's contribution, mentioned below.

43. Robert Morris, "Three Folds in the Fabric and Four Autobiographical Asides as Allegories (or Interruptions)," *Art in America* 77, no. 9 (November 1989): 144, 148.

44. Simone Forti, *Handbook in Motion* (Halifax: Press of the Nova Scotia College of Art and Design, 1974), 62: "The man helps the woman get under her platform, walks over to his, and gets under it. Under the plat-

forms, the two gently whistle. . . . It is important that the performers listen to each other. . . . The piece goes on for about fifteen minutes. The man should wear a watch so that he knows when the designated time is up. He emerges from under his platform, and helps the woman from under hers."

45. Kimberly Paice, catalogue entry on *Columns, 1961*, in Krens and Krauss, *Robert Morris*, 90. Morris observed the importance of Forti's 1961 concert in a little-noted, unreprinted essay of 1965 (at which time Forti's name was Simone Whitman after her marriage to Robert Whitman); see Robert Morris, "Notes on Dance," *Tulane Dance Review* 10, no. 2 (Winter 1965): 179. Maurice Berger deserves credit for insisting on the significance of Forti to Morris's subsequent production, though he did so (without illustrating Forti's work) in a monographic context in which Morris necessarily remains the primary, and heroized, subject of investigation (see Berger, *Labyrinths: Robert Morris, Minimalism, and the 1960s* [New York: Harper and Row, 1989], 26, 49, 83). In her catalogue entry on Morris's *Columns*, Paice relayed confirmation from Morris of the significance of Forti's 1961 concert but without mentioning, much less illustrating, *Platforms*. Further, Paice claimed that Morris's first column was built in 1960 and dated the pair of columns 1961 (Paice in Krens and Krauss, *Robert Morris*, 90), whereas Edward Strickland's more meticulous chronology asserts that the column was conceived in 1960 or 1961, realized in 1961, used as a prop in 1962 (not 1961, contrary to Berger, *Labyrinths*), and first exhibited at the Green Gallery as sculpture in 1963, after which it acquired its twin (see Strickland, *Minimalism: Origins* [Bloomington: Indiana University Press, 1993], 261–64).

46. Forti, *Handbook*, 39–46.

47. Colpitt, *Minimal Art*; Batchelor, *Minimalism*; and Kenneth Baker, *Minimalism* (New York: Abbeville, 1988) neglect to discuss Forti's work, nor was it mentioned in Battcock, *Minimal Art*, or Foster, "The Crux." The exception is Strickland, *Minimalism*. Forti is mentioned only incidentally in James Meyer, *Minimalism: Art and Polemics in the Sixties* (New Haven, Conn.: Yale University Press, 2001), which appeared after the first appearance of the present article.

48. Thomas Crow, *The Rise of the Sixties: American and European Art in the Era of Dissent* (New York: Harry

N. Abrams, 1996), 139. It bears underlining that the case for Morris as Minimalism's founder, on which current claims for his stature in part rest, depends on a narrowly selective notion of what qualifies as a Minimalist object, one that ignores not only monochrome painting and prop-based dance but also such initiatives as the *Elements* series that Andre conceived in 1960, without executing it until a later date; Tony Smith's *Die*, conceived in 1961 or 1962 and realized in 1962; and Walter De Maria's four-by-eight-foot plywood box of 1961—the first three-dimensional Minimalist object to be exhibited in a gallery as sculpture, as Strickland (*Minimalism*, 261) and Barbara Haskell have noted (Haskell, *Blam!: The Explosion of Pop, Minimalism, and Performance, 1958–1964*, exh. cat. [New York: Whitney Museum of American Art, 1984], 99). Truitt's February 1963 show at the Andre Emmerich Gallery, reviewed by Judd and Michael Fried, is deemed "the first identifiably Minimal show" by Colpitt (*Minimal Art*, 1).

49. Crow, *Rise of the Sixties*, 124. Inappropriately for the kind of aesthetic at issue here, Crow thus effectively introduced the conventional authorial matter of who held the tools that produced a given object and, by the same stroke, tacitly underlined the fact that Forti lacked the master tool (or phallus), inasmuch as she lacked command of the requisite tools of the building trade—almost inevitably so, of course, since girls were routinely debarred from shop classes and their fathers' tool benches. Like theatrical props generally, the tacitly sculptural objects that anchored Forti's dance constructions were destroyed and rebuilt as needed for particular performances, but such was also the fate of Morris's earliest props, which came to assume more fixed versions and an institutional presence only because, and as, there came to exist a market for them and a history canonizing them. Forti in fact contemplated producing sculpture but could not envision finding an outlet for it; next to an undated sketch in a notebook, she remarked that she had "an idea for a sculpture but if I make it then what will I do with it?" (Forti, *Handbook*, 49).

50. Crow, *Rise of the Sixties*, 142.

51. Haskell, *Blam!*, was perhaps the first to argue for a broadened view of Minimalism as integral from the outset with performance art. Berger has also consistently framed Minimalism in such terms. And Crow's account of the 1960s, too, encompasses a wide range of media and practices.

52. See Chave, "Striking Poses."

53. Framing her own reading of Hesse as a counter to those readings that would ascribe to her work a "purely personal range of meanings," Anne Wagner proclaims, in the concluding sentences of her essay on Hesse, that her art "can never be only or simply personal" (Wagner, *Three Artists*, 272, 282). Indeed, no substantive reading of Hesse's work has ever claimed otherwise, and concerns about an excessively biographical approach to the artist have marked the Hesse literature since her death, but it remains telling that such a narrowly personalized account of her art should continue to be regarded as a threat to her attaining her full due stature as an artist.

54. See Chave, "Minimalism and the Rhetoric of Power." Though I would modify some of its arguments were I to write it today, this much discussed but not closely read essay does not caricature or categorically condemn Minimalism as a "macho" enterprise, as some critics have complained and some others have applauded. Rather, it suggests that the insistent visual rhetoric of power that typifies the art of the Minimalist canon, and which is more suggestively, subtly, or constructively deployed by some of its members in certain works than in others, may be understood as a form of decompensation bespeaking a "sense of impotence visited on the once sovereign (read: male) subject by the ascendency of technology" (ibid., 45). An argument has recently been made for the deceptive fragility of Judd's work—an argument wrongly framed as if it were decisively in opposition to my own views; see Briony Fer, *On Abstract Art* (New Haven, Conn.: Yale University Press, 1997), ch. 7, 131–51, esp. 151.

55. Foster, "The Crux," 247 nn. 37, 43. "To ask minimalism for a full critique of the subject may be anachronistic." Foster continues, "It may be to read it too much in terms of subsequent art and theory" (43–44). There is logic here, no doubt, but contemporary identity politics are rooted in 1960s activism and discourses. Betty Friedan's *The Feminine Mystique* was published in 1963, for instance, while the first English edition of Simone de Beauvoir's *The Second Sex*, which appeared in 1953, had been reprinted twenty times by 1970.

56. See Chave, "Eva Hesse," for one reading of Hesse's work (including *Accession II*) as protofeminist.

57. Of the first version of the work by Hesse illustrated here (fig. 20.1), with its 1960s shag rug–like interior, she stated, "I don't ask that *Accession* be participated with other than thought. There is no option in arrangement in *Accession*" (quoted in Bill Barrette, *Eva Hesse: Sculpture* [New York: Timken, 1989], 140). The public defied her, however, and soon destroyed the work by handling it excessively and clambering into it; its successor, shown here, has had to be placed under protective glass to fend off similar treatment by present-day museum patrons. In some cases, Hesse explicitly accepted that viewers would participate with her work and, given the unfixed arrangement of much of her sculpture, collectors and curators engage with it of necessity simply in the act of installing it (see Chave, "Striking Poses").

58. Karl Beveridge and Ian Burn, "Don Judd," *Fox* 2 (1975): 132.

59. Yvonne Rainer, *Work 1961–73* (Halifax: Press of the Nova Scotia College of Art and Design, 1974), 7. Without truly retiring, Forti would dedicate herself for some years to the performance work of her second husband, Robert Whitman, before returning to dance. There is scant literature on Forti, but her 1974 *Handbook*, besides providing descriptions of her various choreographic projects, incorporates diary entries, personal reminiscences and reflections, autobiographical vignettes, sketches, poems, and koanlike formulations.

60. Rainer, *Work*, 5, 7. Forti and Rainer have in turn acknowledged the example set by San Francisco–based choreographer Ann Halprin. Rainer and Morris began to live together early in 1964, but the following year, stung by some favoritism shown his work by the press, she urged him to renounce either his dance experiments or her (he chose to renounce the former). Ibid., 9–10.

61. Lippard, *From the Center*, 265.

62. Yvonne Rainer, "A Quasi Survey of Some 'Minimalist' Tendencies in the Quantitively Minimal Dance Activity midst the Plethora, or an Analysis of Trio A" (1966), in Battcock, *Minimal Art*, 263–73.

63. Andre, Castoro, Julie Judd, and others participated in a 1966 Rainer dance, *Carriage Discreteness*, which involved many props, including "Andre's styrofoam beam." A 1969 performance of a 1966 Rainer work (*Trio A, or, The Mind Is a Muscle*) included Castoro and Julie Judd. *Rose Fractions*, on the same program, garnered Rainer an affectionate fan letter from Andre; Rainer, *Work*, 303–5, 117, 158. (Andre was married to Castoro by 1964, according to Robert Katz, *Naked by the Window: The Fatal Marriage of Carl Andre and Ana Mendieta* [New York: Atlantic Monthly Press, 1990], 78, 104; it is unclear when the marriage dissolved.)

64. See Thyrza Nichols Goodeve, "Rainer Talking Pictures," *Art in America* 85, no. 7 (July 1997): 58.

65. See Rainer, *Work*, 79, 317. And, regarding Hesse's identity and self-identity as an ill woman, see Chave, "Eva Hesse." Bochner has also underlined "the metaphor of the hospital" at play in Hesse's sculpture and "the side of her work that alludes to the body as a sewer system" (Simon, "Mel Bochner Interviewed," 93).

66. The stereotype in question, though it contravenes ways in which women's bodies tend to prove hardier than men's, also correlates importantly with certain realities—namely, that women are more susceptible to illness during the years when relative youthfulness would seem to warrant good health, and that women are differently, often more, susceptible to certain illnesses throughout their lives. See Anna C. Chave, "'Normal Ills': On Feminism, Embodiment, and the Origins of Feminist Art," in *Trauma and Visuality in Modernity*, ed. Eric Rosenberg and Lisa Saltzman (Hanover, N.H.: University Press of New England, 2005).

67. Beckett's line serves as the epigraph to Berger, "Wayward Landscapes," in Krens and Krauss, *Robert Morris*, 18. Berger discerned a shift in Morris's work of the mid 1970s, at which point the artist's "I" becomes "decidedly autobiographical" (ibid., 29).

68. Krens and Krauss, *Robert Morris*, 142.

69. Rainer, *Work*, 79; Goodeve, "Rainer Talking," 58.

70. Rainer, *Work*, 275; Rainer, cited in Lippard, *From the Center*, 279; Rainer, *Work*, 276.

71. Berger, *Labyrinths*, 43.

72. For Morris's strongest statement on this issue, see "Robert Morris Replies to Roger Denson (Or Is That a Mouse in My *Paragone?*)," in Morris, *Continuous Project*, 312–13, and passim.

73. Carl Andre, quoted in Paul Cummings, *Artists in*

Their Own Words: Conversations with Twelve American Artists (New York: St. Martin's Press, 1979), 183. The interview in question was conducted in 1972. "Art has to do with early sexual traumas and weaning and toilet training and reading," Andre added (ibid., 194). In response to the question, "What would you say to the view that your obsession with materials which have been 'digested' into similar units, but not fully refined by industrial production, can be correlated with a fascination with shit?" Andre replied, "Yes, of course. Absolutely." (See Fuller, "Carl Andre, II," 10–11.) As for the canonical Minimalists not discussed in the present essay, De Maria, Judd, and LeWitt have generally been closemouthed about their personal histories, while Flavin was prone to autobiographical reflections.

74. Besides Cummings, *Artists*, see Bourdon, *Carl Andre*; Fuller, "Carl Andre, II"; and Diane Waldman, *Carl Andre*, exh. cat. (New York: Solomon R. Guggenheim Museum, 1970), 15, 13.

75. Carl Andre, "Artist Interviews Himself," in *Carl Andre*, exh. cat. (Städtisches Museum Mönchengladbach, 1968), cited (in capital letters) in Phyllis Tuchman, "Background of a Minimalist: Carl Andre," *Artforum* 16, no. 7 (March 1978): 30; Dan Graham, "Carl Andre," *Arts* 42, no. 3 (December 1967–January 1968): 34. In 1973, Andre would publish his *Quincy Book*, forty-eight pages of uncaptioned photographs of Quincy's cemetery, quarry, scrap yard, and so forth, taken by a photographer under Andre's direction.

76. Eva Meyer-Hermann, *Carl Andre / Sculptor 1996*, exh. cat. (Krefeld, Germany: Haus Lange und Haus Esters Krefeld and Wolfsburg, Germany: Kunstmuseum Wolfsburg, 1996), 33. Also, "The importance of Quincy in his work is hard to overestimate" (ibid., 32).

77. Andre was tried for and acquitted of the murder of his wife. According to Katz's account, the evidence in the case was bungled by the police. The judge who decided to acquit Andre, Alvin Schlesinger, reflected afterward in an interview with Katz, paraphrased by the latter: "Odd sort of person, Carl. He probably did it. Fifteen years was the least he would have to serve, if found guilty. Interesting case. Very close call" (Katz, *Naked*, 370). Katz reported that Andre had a liaison with Lippard during the 1960s and with Westwater— who went from being managing editor of *Artforum* to being for a time Andre's dealer—during the 1970s;

the marriage to Mendieta occurred in 1985 (ibid., 127, 78, 163).

78. Ibid., 381–82.

79. Specifically, the Morris show came under attack in Roberta Smith, "A Robert Morris Tour of Contemporary History," *New York Times*, 4 February 1994, C24; and in Peter Schjeldahl, "The Smartass Problem," *Village Voice*, 1 March 1994.

80. Dennis Hollier, quoted in "The Reception of the Sixties," *October* 69 (Summer 1994): 3, 13, 20–21.

81. Meyer-Hermann, *Carl Andre*, 38.

82. Craig Owens, "The Discourse of Others: Feminists and Postmodernism," in *Beyond Recognition: Representation, Power, and Culture* (Berkeley: University of California Press, 1992), 149.

83. Rainer would come to acquire her present identity as a feminist by fits and starts; see Lippard, *From the Center*, 269.

84. Homi K. Bhabha, "A Good Judge of Character: Men, Metaphors, and the Common Culture," in *Race-ing, Justice, En-gendering Power: Essays on Anita Hill, Clarence Thomas, and the Construction of Social Reality*, ed. Toni Morrison (New York: Pantheon, 1992), 242.

85. See Michel Foucault, "What Is an Author?" in *Textual Strategies*, ed. Josue V. Harari (Ithaca, N.Y.: Cornell University Press, 1979), 141, and the last line of that essay ("What difference does it make who is speaking?"), 160.

86. Mary Kelly, "Remembering, Repeating, and Working-Through," in *Imaging Desire* (Cambridge, Mass.: MIT Press, 1996), xxiii.

87. Lucy Lippard, "Ten Structurists in Twenty Paragraphs" (1968), in *Theories of Contemporary Art*, ed. Richard Hertz (Englewood Cliffs, N.J.: Prentice-Hall, 1985), 214. Also: just as Reinhardt "made of impersonality one of the most easily recognized styles in New York, so the new blandness is likely to result in similarly easy identification, despite all the use of standard units and programmatic suppression of individuality," remarked another insider, critic Barbara Rose (married in 1961 to Stella), in "A B C Art" (1965), in Battcock, *Minimal Art*, 286.

88. See Chave, "Minimalism and the Rhetoric of Power." "The technologization of work and war . . . has diminished the importance of the male body as a productive or heroic figure and thereby undermined traditional male identities. . . . Not surpris-

ingly, much of the present cultural anxiety about the erosion of masculinity (really, the erosion of patriarchy) focuses on the male body," observed Harry Brod, "Masculinity as Masquerade," in *The Masculine Masquerade: Masculinity and Representation*, ed. Andrew Perchuk and Helaine Posner, exh. cat. (Cambridge, Mass.: MIT List Visual Arts Center, 1995), 19.

89. The phrase comes from Michel Foucault, "The Order of Discourse" (1970), in *Untying the Text: A Post-Structuralist Reader*, ed. Robert Young (Boston: Routledge and Kegan Paul, 1981).

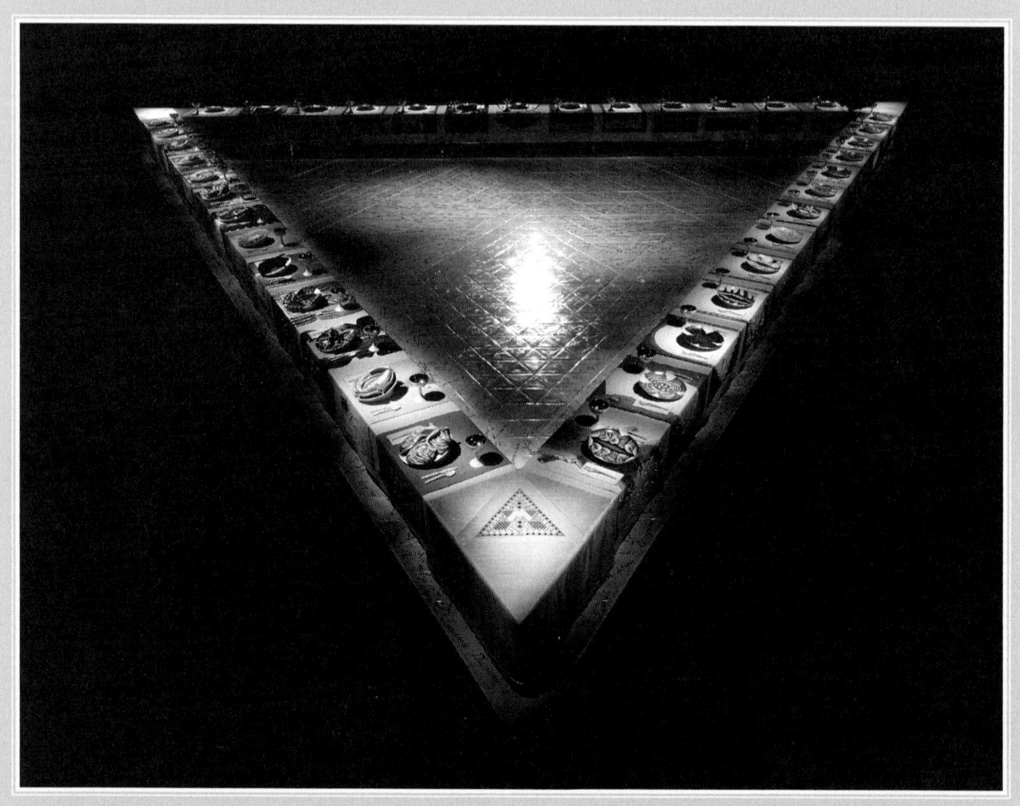

21

THE "SEXUAL POLITICS" OF *THE DINNER PARTY*

A Critical Context

Amelia Jones

> Within feminist debate, an increasing problem has been to reconcile the apparent need to formulate a politics which assumes the category of "women" with the demand, often politically articulated, to problematize the category, interrogate its incoherence, its internal dissonance, its constitutive exclusions.
>
> JUDITH BUTLER

SINCE ITS PREMIERE at the San Francisco Museum of Modern Art in 1979, Judy Chicago's *Dinner Party* (fig. 21.1) has engendered vehement responses, both positive and negative. In 1980 John Perreault described the piece as "magnificent," stating: "It is an important work; it is a key work. Certain conservative journalistic critics may call it kitsch to their dying day, may puritanically rage against its sexual imagery, may imply over and over again that it can't be good art because it's too popular; but I know it's great. I was profoundly moved."[1] Kay Larson, conversely, insisted that *The Dinner Party* "manages to be brutal, baroque, and banal all at once," and Hilton Kramer intoned, notoriously, that "'The Dinner Party' reiterates its theme . . . with an insistence and vulgarity more appropriate . . . to an advertising campaign than to a work of art."[2]

In spite of these conflicting readings—or perhaps because of them—*The Dinner Party*, which was in storage from 1988 to 2002,[3] has come to be seen as a central icon of a certain period of feminist art. It has been positively viewed, by Perreault and populist feminists such as Lucy Lippard, as paradigmatic of feminism's triumphant and uplifting celebration of female artistic expression. It has been negatively evaluated by modernist critics such as Kramer as epitomizing a loss of "artistic standards."[4] Feminist commentators have criticized it as exemplary of 1970s feminism's supposed naiveté, essentialism, universalism, and failure to establish collaborative alterna-

This is an abridged, slightly revised, and updated version of an essay originally published in Amelia Jones, ed., *Sexual Politics: Judy Chicago's* Dinner Party *in Feminist Art History* (Los Angeles: UCLA at the Armand Hammer Museum of Art and Cultural Center; Berkeley and Los Angeles: University of California Press, 1996), 84–118. Copyright © 1996 by The Regents of the University of California. Reprinted with permission.

Figure 21.1. Judy Chicago, *The Dinner Party*, 1979. Mixed media. © Judy Chicago 1979. Collection of The Brooklyn Museum of Art, Gift of The Elizabeth A. Sackler Foundation. (Photo: © Donald Woodman.)

tives to the unified (and masculinist) authorial structures of modernist art production. Indeed, the very intensity of these responses to *The Dinner Party* and the extreme polarization of opinion seen in evaluations of the piece testify to its importance as a cultural monument with which all historians of contemporary art, and perhaps especially feminist art historians, must come to terms. *The Dinner Party* and the issues it raises are central to an understanding of the politics of modernist, postmodernist, and feminist art theory and art history.

The reception of *The Dinner Party* highlights unexpected intersections among critical models thought to be opposed; for example, some feminist responses to the piece converge uncomfortably with conventional modernist evaluations. Here I would like first to outline the parameters of modernist critiques of the piece and then to explore its position within feminist arguments in order to highlight what the artwork can teach us about the ideological assumptions motivating critical thought about contemporary art. The history of *The Dinner Party*'s reception can tell us a great deal about the politics of art criticism and of feminism itself, foregrounding, in particular, the complexity of the feminist project, which attempts—as Judith Butler notes in the epigraph above—both to construct a coalition of women and to contest the exclusions that such a unification of subjects entails.

Returning *The Dinner Party* to a complex historical and political matrix is a crucial step in attempting to understand the "sexual politics" of feminist art theory and practice and, by extension, the politics of identity in the 1990s and later. Today there appears to be little understanding of the complexities of 1970s feminism and its historical context. The results of this loss of history are damaging: younger generations of feminists have little access to the wealth of insights that were painfully developed in the art and theory of this period and waste time reinventing what has already been extensively theorized,[5] and writers such as Camille Paglia and Katie Roiphe have capitalized on this lost history by dismissing earlier feminisms in order to pose themselves as the avatars of a "postfeminist" (and, I would argue, misogynist) viewpoint.[6] Furthermore, this erasure has encouraged the tendency of mainstream nonfeminist historical accounts of the 1970s to ignore the feminist advances that took place during this period, to emphasize male movements and conceptions of radicality over the explosively disruptive effects of feminist art, theory, and activism.[7] The charged reception of *The Dinner Party* has much to teach us about the complexities of feminist and contemporary art history.

Hilton Kramer's account of *The Dinner Party*, which sticks obsessively on its populism, confirms the transgressiveness of the piece within the conservative codes of modernist art discourse. The hysteria with which modernist art critics have accused *The Dinner Party* of being kitsch testifies to its enormous threat to these ostensibly disinterested discourses, which take their authority from the assumed inherence of artistic value. Through its overt celebration of craft and its explicit politicization of the history of Western culture, the piece blatantly subverts modernist value systems, which privilege the "pure" aesthetic object over the debased sentimentality of the domestic and popular arts.

The Dinner Party revises the history of Western culture by naming and symbolizing in visual form 1,038 women from various historical periods. Nine hundred ninety-nine of them are named on luminous porcelain floor tiles, and the thirty-nine honorees at the dinner table itself are symbolically represented through elaborate needlepoint runners, in large part worked in techniques drawn from the period in which each woman lived, and ceramic plates with centralized motifs and vulvar imagery. Chicago's integration of media associated with women's labor in the domestic sphere (needlework, ceramics, and china painting) into this monumental artwork produces an explosive collision between aesthetics (the public domain of the high art museum) and domestic kitsch (the private domain of women's space, the home).[8]

The judgments of modernist art criticism in its

hegemonic form, as epitomized by the later writings of Clement Greenberg, are predicated on the notion that visual art must, in Greenberg's words, "confine itself to what is given in visual experience and make no reference to any other orders of experience."[9] From the perspective of Chicago and other feminist artists and artists of color working in the 1960s and 1970s, Greenberg's insistence on the autonomy of art (especially as his more complex arguments were reductively deployed by writers such as Kramer) was perceived as motivated by a reactionary apoliticism that supported the status quo, excluding from the privileged domain of "high art" elements of popular culture and work by women and other groups of people marginalized by elitist institutions of high art. Greenberg's formalism came to be seen as synonymous with modernism's conservative privileging of masculine values and white male artists.

In Greenberg's late, formulaic view of high art, the "essence" of modernism lies in the artwork's "purity" and "self-definition," its truthfulness to its medium; from the mid nineteenth century onward, "all ambitious tendencies in painting were converging . . . in an anti-sculptural direction." The modernist work of art must "exclude the representational or the 'literary,'" must be abstract, must be "a question of purely optical experience."[10] In a 1939 essay he demanded that a strict boundary be maintained between "avant-garde" (high modernist) art and low culture, or "kitsch." Kitsch is all that formalist, modernist art history is not: it is popular, loved by the masses; it is literary; it is associated with women's tastes and with domestic crafts.[11]

Clearly Greenberg's seemingly "disinterested" criteria for judging works of art—inherited by Kramer—have a distinct gender bias. Kramer's response to *The Dinner Party* is paradigmatic of a modernist and still-masculinist mode of critical evaluation that could view the piece only as a threat to post-Enlightenment definitions of artistic "quality." Notions of "quality" and "greatness," as 1970s feminist artists and art theorists had already begun to argue when *The Dinner Party* appeared on the scene, always harbor ideological investments.[12] Thus, Kramer's his-

trionic rejection of *The Dinner Party* can be seen as the response of a critic whose system of values is being threatened. *The Dinner Party* is a blast in the face of modernist criticism: it is literary; it is aggressively handmade, using "feminine" crafts techniques; it is painting and embroidery made blatantly sculptural. Through its flamboyant activation of kitsch—the prohibited desire of modernism—*The Dinner Party* explodes the boundaries of aesthetic value so carefully policed by modernist criticism.

It is difficult, however, to align *The Dinner Party* with the radical feminist goal of merging high and low so as to collapse the masculinist hierarchy of value that dichotomizes "avant-garde" and "kitsch," especially if one reads the piece through Chicago's own public statements about her introduction of craft into the high-art realm.[13] She has made it clear that she wants *The Dinner Party* to be viewed as high-art, that she still subscribes to this structure of value: "I'm not willing to say a painting and a pot are the same thing," she has stated. "It has to do with intent. I want to make art."[14] Chicago was ambivalent about whether china painting could be considered an aesthetic pursuit. She wrote that the women in her china-painting class were "primarily housewives interested in filling their spare time," whereas she herself had been a "'serious' art student" from the time she was young.[15] Rather than attempting to break down the distinction between high and low, Chicago has openly acknowledged her continued investment in upholding such an opposition.

Here again, *The Dinner Party* teaches us something about conflicts endemic to feminist art theory: Chicago is by no means the only feminist to have maintained a desire to have her work exhibited and discussed within high-art institutions and discourses while attempting to critique them at the same time. In fact, as I have argued elsewhere, this contradiction is common to almost all feminist practice from 1970 to the present.[16] At the same time it is clear from Kramer's response that, in spite of Chicago's investment in a hierarchical and ultimately masculinist modernist conception of "high" art, *The Dinner Party* clearly disrupted modernist value systems.

It is clear that Chicago's decision to use many different techniques and styles of needlework as well as china painting to "call . . . attention to women's unrecognized heritage" challenged the prevailing modernist structures of critical judgment.[17] For it is precisely its use of women's crafts, combined with its style and content, that aligned *The Dinner Party* with kitsch in the eyes of conservative critics. A photograph accompanying a *People* magazine article headlined "Sassy Judy Chicago Throws a Dinner Party but the Art World Mostly Sends Regrets" (December 8, 1980) depicts the artist sitting in front of the piece and sticking out her tongue (presumably at Kramer, who is cited in the article); this is a particularly apt visualization of her self-defined, contradictory position—both at odds with and on top of the modernist critical system.

THE POPULISM OF *THE DINNER PARTY*: AN ART WORLD CONUNDRUM

As we have seen, *The Dinner Party* has provoked vehement responses, both pro and con. The very qualities for which the piece is lauded by the general public and by some populist feminists are largely those for which it is criticized by the majority of poststructuralist feminist art theorists and vilified by conservative modernist critics. Indeed, *The Dinner Party*'s massive popularity has made it problematic for many within the art world. *Artforum* critic Hal Fischer, for example, condemned the piece for "playing down to the public."[18] His comment says a great deal about his own elitism: his desire to speak for the "public" and to control the parameters of value within art exhibition structures— and that of the critical establishment in general.

The unprecedented attendance figures for each of its fourteen showings from 1979 to 1988 testify to *The Dinner Party*'s popularity. In San Francisco, for example, one hundred thousand people saw the exhibition, and twenty thousand hardcover copies of *The Dinner Party: A Symbol of Our Heritage* were sold in the first two weeks of its release.[19] In addition to the hundreds of positive comments written in the guest books at each venue, hundreds of fan letters poured in to Judy Chicago from all over the world over the decade in which the piece was on view. The guest books and letters include rapturous statements describing the awe visitors (primarily women) felt on viewing the piece.

Many critics have seen some significance in *The Dinner Party*'s appeal for the nonspecialist audience. For Kramer the piece's popularity was evidence of its degradation and lack of "quality," whereas Lucy Lippard saw it as an aspect of its indisputable success as a feminist monument.[20] Kramer regarded the piece's ideological content as the source of its popular appeal and, by extension, its lack of artistic merit: "For the many followers of the Feminist art movement nothing more need be said [than that *The Dinner Party* is opening in Brooklyn]. This is news—and indeed, review—enough. . . . For the rest of us—or for anyone more interested in art than in ideology . . . the esthetic pleasure to be derived from 'The Dinner Party' may prove to be more elusive."[21] Maureen Mullarkey, whose description of the appreciative crowds drips with condescension, clearly found the popular acclaim of the piece an obstacle to her need to justify her own revulsion: "The women who file worshipfully past this cunnilingus-as-communion table see nothing askew in Chicago's decision to represent the stature and variety of women's accomplishments by genitals only." She snidely commented on the "litany of ecstatic manifestations" written by visitors in the comment book, which, she argued, simply "tells a tale about the gullibility, the insensitivity to nuance and the need of Chicago's audience."[22] Perhaps even more disturbingly, feminist theorist Clara Weyergraf sneered at the "brash vulgarity of *The Dinner Party*," whose degradation is confirmed by its appeal "to the taste of the middle-class housewife."[23]

Mullarkey's description of Chicago's audience as "gullible," "insensitive," and "needy" and Weyergraf's dismissal of the (presumably helplessly seduced) "middle-class housewife" dovetail in a disconcerting way with both the elitism of Kramer, who clearly has contempt for the "followers of the Feminist art movement," and the antipleasure rhetoric of the sophisticated avant-gardist theories of representation that characterize poststructuralist feminist theory. Griselda Pollock, one of the key formulators of this body of theory, thus stated in 1988 that "feminist critical practice [in the visual arts] must resist . . . specularity especially when the visible object *par excellence* is the image of woman. It has to create an entirely new kind of spectator as part and parcel of its representational strategies."[24] The radical feminist artist must strive to resist visual pleasure, according to Pollock, by implementing Bertolt Brecht's theories of "distanciation" to break the seductive bond between the spectator and the image, to "liberate the viewer from the state of being captured by illusions of art which encourages passive identification with fictional worlds." In Marxian terms, distanciation, or "dis-identificatory practices," erodes "the dominant structures of cultural consumption" that make the viewer a passive victim of capitalist ideologies.[25]

While Pollock's model obviously comes from a vastly different (one might even say diametrically opposed) political basis from that of Kramer, in her privileging of the artwork that refuses spectatorial engagement while challenging the viewer to greater heights of self-awareness, she unwittingly parallels his antikitsch, avant-gardist value system. She effectively sets up a new value system that privileges artwork that operates through "dis-identificatory" strategies over populist works such as *The Dinner Party*, denying that such populism can have any potential benefit. Yet Chicago's recent recapitulation of her goals persuasively outlines the progressive aspect of work that reaches a broad audience: "The whole notion of feminist art, as I was trying to articulate it, is that the form-code of contemporary art has to be broken in order to broaden the audience base. . . . What I have been after from the beginning is a redefinition of the role of the artist, a reexamination of the relation of art and community, and a broadening of the definitions of who controls art and, in fact, an enlarged dialogue about art, with new and more diverse participants."[26]

The point here, however, is not to privilege Chicago over Pollock, forcing the latter to play the role of scapegoat for contradictions within poststructuralist feminism; it is certainly thanks to the advances made both by Chicago and her colleagues and by Pollock

and other "antiessentialist" feminists that I can raise such questions. What is at issue, rather, are the ways in which *The Dinner Party* forces the question of *address* into the feminist debate. Since feminism has an interest in challenging exclusionary and elitist systems of value (which have conventionally worked to exclude the work of women artists), it behooves feminists to take seriously the impact this piece has had on a broad-based public. Today it is useful to ask what it means for feminism to promote a Brechtian theory of representation that—while clearly enabling for a specialized audience of feminist critics, historians, and theorists in the particular political context of the 1980s—ultimately forecloses the potential political effects of feminist artworks that are more accessible and enjoyable to a wider spectrum of viewers.

Lippard has insightfully noted that the art world's negative responses to the populism of *The Dinner Party* had everything to do with its specificity of content, its explicit presentation of the kind of allusive ("literary" and "wholly interpretable") imagery that is anathema to the ideology of the avant-garde (evident in both Kramer's rejection of the piece for its "vulgar" accessibility and Pollock's dismissal of feminist art that is "realist in an uncritical way").[27] What has made the debate even more highly charged is that the "wholly interpretable imagery" of *The Dinner Party*—that is, that aspect of the piece most frequently mentioned in discussions of its success or failure as an artwork—is clearly identifiable as a symbolic representation of a part of the body that is conventionally veiled: the female sex.

"WHAT IS FEMALE IMAGERY?" FEMINIST RESPONSES TO *THE DINNER PARTY* AND THE POLITICS OF "CUNT ART"

Criticism of *The Dinner Party* has often focused on the plates, the majority of which are constructed out of labial folds of clay and decorated with painted vulvar patterns (see fig. 21.2).[28] This is certainly due at least in part to their transgression of the prohibition against such direct representation. The iconography

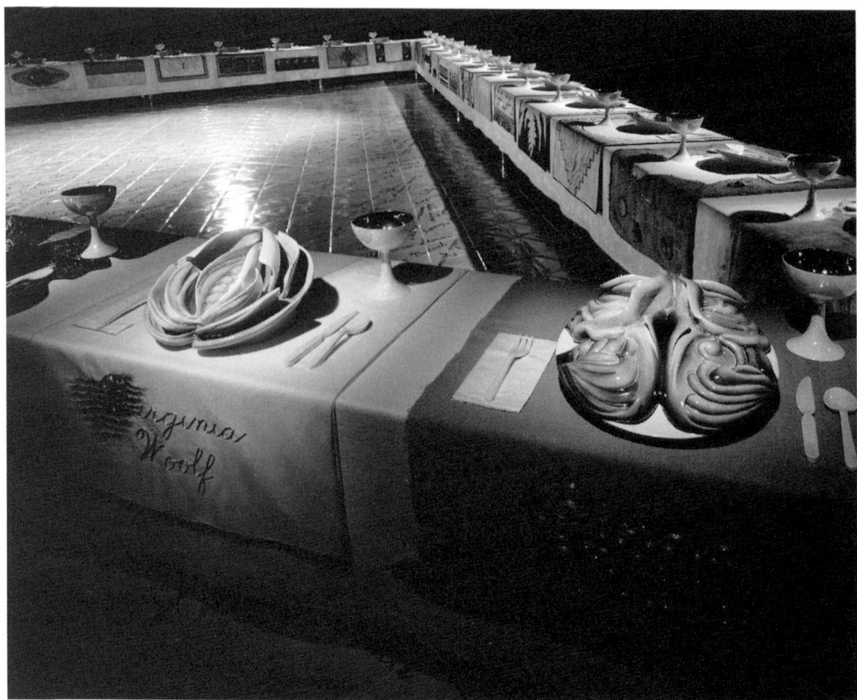

Figure 21.2. Judy Chicago, *The Dinner Party*, with the *Virginia Woolf* and *Georgia O'Keeffe* place settings, 1979. Mixed media. © Judy Chicago 1979. Collection of The Brooklyn Museum of Art, Gift of The Elizabeth A. Sackler Foundation. (Photo: © Donald Woodman.)

of the plates developed out of Chicago's extended experimentation with centralized imagery in her work from the late 1960s onward and her interest in using "butterfly," "flower," or "cunt" forms as metaphors for women's experience.[29] Kramer and Hughes thus reviled *The Dinner Party* not only because of its threat to the modernist system of determining aesthetic value but also because of, in Hughes's words, its "relentless concentration on the pudenda," which clearly threatens the (male) modernist critic's belief in the propriety of the phallus as the proper symbol of creative impulse.

The use of what Kramer called "vulviform image(s)" on the plates also threatened the Western aesthetic conventions that privilege images of the female body as fetishistic objects for male spectatorial pleasure but prohibit direct representation of the female genitalia. As I have noted elsewhere, by overtly representing the female sex, the artist endangers the system of aesthetic judgment, since the clearly "ob-

scene" female body is that which must remain outside the realm of high art (since the obscene is that against which high art confirms its purity).[30] Chicago's "relentless" symbolization of the female sex threatens the masculinist modernist critic's claims of "disinterestedness." The fact that right-wing members of the United States Congress, debating the proposed gift of *The Dinner Party* to the federally supported University of the District of Columbia in 1991, hysterically denounced the piece for its obscenity only confirms this. Notably Robert K. Dornan derided the piece as "ceramic 3-D pornography," and Dana Rohrbacher called it "weird sexual art" (both are Republicans from California).[31] The convergence of these politicians' reactions with that of Kramer suggests that, in fact, the piece has some very empowering feminist effects in challenging the modernist, masculinist boundaries between art and pornography.

Ironically, however, feminist criticism of *The Dinner Party* has also tended to focus on the plates, with their vulvar, or "cunt," imagery. It was through its deployment of this imagery that *The Dinner Party* came to be seen by many feminists as paradigmatic of all that was problematic about certain strands of 1970s feminism. Although East Coast artists such as Hannah Wilke explored cunt imagery in the 1960s, historically it has been associated with Los Angeles–based feminism—and especially with the writings of Chicago, Arlene Raven, Miriam Schapiro, and Lucy Lippard (then from New York but sympathetic to the Los Angeles feminist art scene). The use of centralized "female" imagery was, from the beginning, challenged by other feminists. Thus, New York critic Cindy Nemser, in an essay published in the *Feminist Art Journal* in 1973–74, described Chicago as the originator of a notion of "cunt art," which "made a case for an intrinsic female imagery created out of round, pulsating, 'womb-like' forms. This 'inner space' ideology," she concludes, "reduces the work of women artists to a simplistic biological formula."[32]

It is important to distinguish between Chicago's use of centralized imagery in her own work and her notion that a "hidden content" could be found in the work of other women artists, many of whom predated feminism or were antagonistic to it.[33] It was this "hidden content" theory that caused the most consternation among feminist critics, since it seemed to imply that women were biologically driven to produce imagery that mimicked the structure of their own sexual anatomy.

Around 1970 Chicago, motivated by her own developing identity as a woman artist, not only began producing overtly centralized imagery, often overlaid with explicitly feminist texts, but also began to recognize her own earlier works as subconsciously "female-oriented": "I began to realize," she wrote in her autobiography, "that my real sexual identity had been denied by my culture, and this somehow represented the entire sense of denial I had been experiencing as a woman artist. I felt that if I could symbolize my true sexual nature, I could open up the issue of the nature of my identity as a woman through that symbolic statement." Looking back at her 1968 *Dome* pieces, small acrylic mounds spray-painted with glowing layers of colored lacquer, Chicago described them as evidence of the return of "female body references . . . reminiscent of the Venus of Willendorf and other early goddesses."[34]

Chicago's *Atmospheres*, environmental pieces begun in 1969 and continued into the early 1970s, oscillated between abstracted conceptual explorations of the interrelationship of "flesh and landscape" and specifically feminist interventions into the environment through the inclusion of goddess figures.[35] She introduced women performers into the *Atmospheres* as signs of female power, to actualize her desire for the pieces "to transform and soften (i.e. feminize) the environment."[36] Her interest in the goddess, which she shared with feminist artists such as Faith Wilding, Mary Beth Edelson, and Carolee Schneemann, extensively informed *The Dinner Party*—not only in its inclusion of a number of goddess place settings but also in its overall revisionist impulse toward history. Chicago's belief in a prepatriarchal, utopian matriarchal culture, explicitly outlined in the first *Dinner Party* book and concretized in the idealizing, abstract representations of the goddess plates and runners, has been criticized as naive.[37] But the *idea* of the mythical goddess was clearly powerfully enabling for these artists, serving as a site of projection that allowed them to actualize their own attempts to attain the kind of transcendence conventionally reserved for men (the "central core" image played the same empowering role).[38]

By 1973 Chicago had fully established in two and three dimensions this centralized imagery—radiating, pulsating rings and folds of brilliantly colored, airbrushed paint—which she would develop into the sculptural vulvar forms of the *Dinner Party* plates. Whereas her *Domes* "subconsciously" suggested the rounded, centralized forms of the breasts or womb, Chicago's pictorial forays into the "central core" are much more literal. In *Female Rejection Drawing #3* (fig. 21.3), also known as *Peeling Back*, a particularly dramatic and evocative image from the *Rejection Quintet* of 1974, she combined the formal structure of the central core, here a delicately colored series of labial folds emerging from a painfully torn contain-

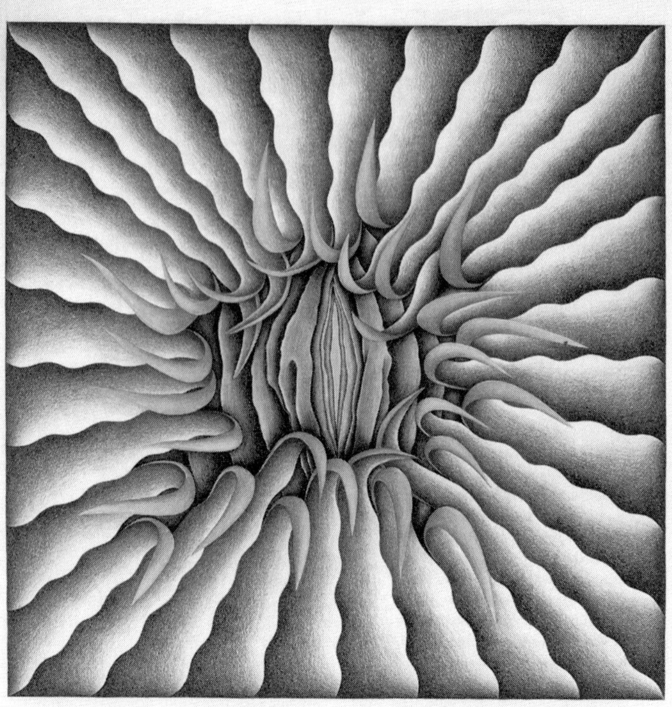

Figure 21.3. Judy Chicago, *Female Rejection Drawing #3 (Peeling Back)*, from the *Rejection Quintet*, 1974. Prismacolor on rag paper. © Judy Chicago 1974. Collection of the San Francisco Museum of Modern Art. (Photo: © Donald Woodman.)

ing surface, with an extensive handwritten text describing her feelings of exposure, fear, and anguish at being judged and rejected by the male-dominated art world.[39]

Female Rejection Drawing, one of Chicago's most explicitly autobiographical images, seems to sum up in vibrant, material terms both her commitment to the notion of a centralized form as a means of reclaiming the female body from patriarchy in an empower-

ing way and her insistence, common in the women's movement in general at this time, on the importance of expressing personal issues in political terms. A central component of Chicago's coming to consciousness as a feminist artist in the 1970s was her desire to "peel back" the repressed content of her work, to "put together the sophisticated formal language of contemporary art with the rather raw and unexpressed subject matter I wanted to begin to deal with. . . . I peeled back my coded imagery and finally broke through to the beginning of new imagery and the reappearance of the butterfly. . . . This became pivotal in the imagery of *The Dinner Party*."[40] *Female Rejection Drawing* exemplifies Chicago's desire to transform the female sex from a locus of objectification to a powerful sign of subjectivity through imagery that visualized the "orgiastic throbbing [and] . . . highly focussed feeling of clitoral sensation" that signaled women as desiring subjects rather than mere objects of desire.[41]

Chicago's theory of the central-core image as the reflection of a "female sensibility" became more problematic when she extended this formal symbology to the work of other artists. In "Female Imagery" Chicago and Schapiro solidified this theory, asking: "What does it feel like to be a woman? To be formed around a central core and have a secret place which can be entered and which is also a passageway from which life emerges?" They concluded by suggesting that "women artists have used the central cavity which defines them as women as the framework for an imagery which allows for the complete reversal of the way in which women are seen by the culture. That is, to be a woman is to be an object of contempt and the vagina, stamp of femaleness, is devalued. The woman artists /sic/, seeing herself as loathed, takes that very mark of her otherness and by asserting it as the hallmark of her iconography, establishes a vehicle by which to state the truth and beauty of her identity."[42]

In the early essays on this subject, a hesitancy in defining the sources of this "female sensibility" is apparent. While they saw the crucial political importance of defining a particular female approach to artistic form, feminists such as Chicago and Schapiro were loath to fix this form, its sources or meanings, in any determinate way. Thus, they explicitly state that "the visual symbology we have been describing must not be seen in a simplistic sense as 'vaginal or womb art'" and stress that it is the "way in which women are seen by the culture" that is at issue. Likewise, Raven insisted in 1975 that the "female experience . . . is socially defined and cultural rather than biological, innate, or personal."[43] In an earlier essay she also underlined the importance of the feminist insistence on *content* (that is, the representation or evocation of "female experience") as an attack on modernist formalism and the capitalist structure it serves.[44] She questioned the "very word *feminine*," which, she argued, "refers to the characteristics of a biological female . . . [and] is a fluid term which is effected /sic/ by the historical moment to which it is applied. 'Feminine' characteristics change according to the political, economic and social needs of a world which demands a woman to display them." Raven expanded this argument, which is clearly not biologically essentialist: "When we notice a tendency for women to construct forms in a circular manner, which is different from a man's constructive sense, we cannot conclude that the female image is the circle, because women's tendency toward circular construction can take any number of visual forms. . . . Female forms are not stationary in art unless the forms we know to be 'female' at this time are fixed into symbolic conventions, or signs. This is biological determinism— an idea to which feminism is opposed."[45]

Generally speaking, then, the goal of feminists exploring the notion of a "female imagery" in women's art was to identify a positive mode of representing the female body in order to *reclaim* it from its patriarchal construction as passive object, fetishized through structures of male desire.[46] While the question of whether this gesture was successful will always be open to debate, it has undeniably been productive in generating discussion about strategies of feminist production and modes of female subjectivity in general. The actual form this representation took was often complex and multidimensional, establishing such symbolism as ambiguous rather than secure or fixed. Even the forms of *The Dinner Party* plates are not the simple holes (or "vaginas") they are usually reductively described as being. Developing from the flat, centralized patterns symbolizing ancient goddesses to the sculptural folds, crevices, and thrusting lips emblematic of twentieth-century figures such as Virginia Woolf and Georgia O'Keeffe (see fig. 21.2), the plates also represent the relative restraint and containment of creative female subjects throughout history.[47] Through the muscular three-dimensionality of the plates representing modern women, Chicago aimed to subvert the patriarchal obsession with phallic forms by developing "an active vaginal form."[48]

Revolting against the masculinist formalist doctrine of modernist criticism, which excluded content from discussions of art and thus placed issues of gender, sexual, class, or racial politics outside the purview of the aesthetic, feminists such as Chicago insisted on returning explicit sexual content to artistic practice. Female sexuality became an obvious focus of exploration since sexuality has historically been the site of women's oppression.[49] As Wilding, who was a colleague of Chicago's in the Feminist Art Program, has argued, the notion "cunt is beautiful," like the civil rights mantra "black is beautiful," was about "claiming what has been most derogated as your strength."[50]

The subtleties and complexities of the feminist debates of the 1970s are generally lost in accounts that regard feminist art of the period as simply and reductively essentialist. At the risk of oversimplifying "1980s" feminism, I would like to define loosely a set of concerns that became dominant in feminist art criticism from this period. From the late 1970s on, a broad shift occurred in feminist art theory and practice. The emphasis on activism, collaboration, and the notion of feminist art as an articulation of female experience gave way to an examination of femininity as constructed through representation and a critique of the "male gaze" (the means through which images of women are structured—as objects of male desire to palliate male fear of symbolic castration—in patriarchal culture).[51] While 1970s feminists had, as noted above, asserted that femininity was not biological but culturally constructed, this position was often viewed narrowly through Chicago's work and criticized as essentialist; earlier feminists' generally celebratory view of the female body and female experience and their highly personal approach to art-making were also frequently singled out for criticism in the 1980s. The differences of opinion among them were lost in this general move toward the promotion of feminist art that "deconstructed" the pleasure that men in patriarchal culture take in representations of the female body.

As noted above, Griselda Pollock has articulated a theory of feminist critical practice that demands resistance of visual pleasure, "especially when the visible object *par excellence* is the image of woman." Following Brechtian strategies of distanciation, feminist art then must specifically avoid the representation of the female body and must resist the "realist myth," that is, the notion that simply representing something transparently relates its essential meaning, that making something visible produces empowerment or ensures access to knowledge.[52]

Typical of the poststructuralist feminist emphasis on *critiquing* patriarchal formations of viewing pleasure rather than presenting positive images of femininity is Pollock's insistence that feminist art practice *must* resist the dominating scopophilic and fetishizing effects of the "male gaze."[53] For, as Lisa Tickner—also a British feminist art historian—wrote in a 1984 essay, women "have an investment in the deconstruction of 'femininity' and compensatory pleasures." Perhaps not surprisingly, Tickner ends this essay with an explicit reference to *The Dinner Party,* suggesting that the piece had come to epitomize for antiessentialist feminist theorists all that they rejected in 1970s feminist art from the United States. Hence, she argues that its "deployment of the fixed signs of femininity produces a reverse discourse, a political/aesthetic strategy founded on the same terms in which 'difference' has already been laid down." She opposes this diametrically to postmodern work, which "is rather an interrogation of an unfixed femininity produced in specific systems of signification."[54]

Tickner's argument makes clear that the development of a poststructuralist feminist art theory in the 1980s in some senses took place at the expense of the kind of feminist art from the 1970s that attempted to represent the female body in order to reclaim it from patriarchy, and that, furthermore, this vast range of body-oriented, utopian, transformative work was often collapsed into *The Dinner Party,* which was then cited as exemplary of its problems. The shift in paradigm, which entailed the reduction of 1970s feminism to a relatively narrow set of issues that could easily be dismissed, seems to reflect a kind of generational (and even uncomfortably "Oedipal"-seeming) anxiety. As Mira Schor argued in her critique of this dismissal of 1970s feminism, "Essentialism in this context was a category created by its opposition"; it is an unfair label to the extent that women artists dealing with gender representation have always operated in a complex zone between "the polarities of 'essence' and 'culture.'"[55] Generational differences and the particularities of local cultural politics (most of the feminists who articulated the poststructuralist arguments dominant in the 1980s were from Britain) motivated the oppositional stance taken toward so-called 1970s essentialist feminism in the United States (with *The Dinner Party* viewed as paradigmatic). By identifying, defining, and rejecting earlier assumptions, a new generation of feminists moved the discussion in a new direction. At the same time such a strategy inevitably oversimplified and misrepresented certain aspects of feminist theory and practice from the 1970s.

In looking again at *The Dinner Party*, it may be useful to reexamine the context in which it developed, in particular, to look more closely at the *political* reasons for the formulation of a theory of a "female imagery" linked to female experience. While I do not wish to use Chicago's own statements simplistically to "prove" that this theory wasn't as naive and self-defeating as it was later accused of being, there seems to be a real need to open up the question of "female experience" again and to try to understand the role that it played for Chicago and her contemporaries. At the very least, this should provide a richer historical and theoretical context in which to view *The Dinner Party*.

"FEMALE IMAGERY":
A POLITICAL STRATEGY

Poststructuralist feminist theorists have been responsible for radically rethinking the ideological effects of representations of female bodies and for making feminism respectable within mainstream (that is, male-dominated) academic discourse. They have also, however, tended to oversimplify the theories and practices of the supposedly "essentialist" artists and

writers of the 1970s and to narrow considerably the possible strategies for a feminist art practice by calling polemically for feminist art to resist the male gaze and to avoid at all costs an "essentializing" notion of femininity. In hindsight one sees clearly how *prescriptive* this antiessentialist feminist theory has often been. (Note, for example, Pollock's insistence that feminism "must" resist specularity and "has to" create a new spectator.) One might ask in this regard: isn't feminism, on the contrary, more productive when it embraces multiple politics, multiple points of view, multiple modes of artistic production and styles and forms of art? Chicago's notion of "female imagery" was criticized precisely for its narrowing of the definition of women's art, in Nemser's terms, "to a simplistic biological formula"; antiessentialist approaches to feminist art and theories of representation are perhaps just as "essentializing" and confining in their own way.

In her book *Essentially Speaking: Feminism, Nature, and Difference*, Diana Fuss points out that essentialism is in fact central to the "antiessentialist" theories of social construction that claim that components of identity are socially determined rather than biologically so. In its eagerness to transcend biological essentialism, antiessentialism ends up simply displacing the concept of origins from the body onto society: "Essentialism is embedded in the idea of the social and lodged in the problem of social determination."[56] Thus, for example, Pollock's claim in her important essay "Modernity and the Spaces of Femininity" that the work of late-nineteenth-century women painters in France differed from that of their male colleagues because of their particular experience of modernity as women seems on one level as "essentialist" as Chicago and Schapiro's claim, in "Female Imagery," that the works of modernist women artists such as Lee Bontecou, Louise Nevelson, and Georgia O'Keeffe were informed by their particular "perception of reality" as women, or as Norma Broude and Mary Garrard's assertion that "the definitive assignment of sex roles in history has created fundamental differences between the sexes in their perception, experience, and expectations of the world. . . ."

[These differences] cannot help but have been carried over into the creative process."[57]

As Fuss points out, a certain "essentialism"—that is, the claiming of identifiably similar experiences among particular groups of people—is a crucial component of any "coalition politics" and must be accommodated within any politics of representation (certainly Pollock herself is assuming a particular coalition among women in general in her polemical critiques of essentialism). At the same time Fuss is careful to point out—in a comment that would apply to Pollock's theory as well as to Chicago's—that "the problem with positing the category of experience as the basis of a feminist pedagogy is that the very object of our inquiry, 'female experience,' is never as unified, as knowable, as universal, and as stable as we presume it to be. . . . The appeal to experience, as the ultimate test of all knowledge, merely subtends the subject in its fantasy of autonomy and control. Belief in the truth of Experience is as much an ideological production as belief in the experience of Truth." Fuss's critique of essentialism is valuable for its insightful recognition of the inevitability of essentializing logic in any sexual or, for that matter, racial politics. Essentialism, she notes, is a key element of identity politics, allowing experience "to be politicized." The "determining factor in deciding essentialism's political or strategic value is," she argues, "dependent on who practices it"—and, I would add, when, where, and how they practice it and on what terms the foundational identity is defined.[58]

Chicago's "essentialism," like that of her colleagues Ruth Iskin, Lucy Lippard, Arlene Raven, Miriam Schapiro, and others, was a crucial component of 1970s identity politics: it enabled the development of a feminist politics of art and art history. As Broude and Garrard have argued, the "body based female aesthetic" of the early 1970s (or what Lippard described at the time as the use of "gyno-sensuous imagery") was equally "an enabling myth." The use of centralized imagery and craft techniques in 1970s feminist art "was a *political act,* a defiance of the conventions that had made it death for earlier women artists to associate themselves with forms and iconography that had been stereotypically and pejoratively deemed 'feminine.'"[59] Using these forms and materials was a way, again, of *reclaiming* them and valuing the femininity with which they were associated. Thus, just as poststructuralist feminists have taken an extreme position in rejecting any artwork that does not resist specularity or forcefully deconstruct patriarchal notions of "femininity" in order to produce what Pollock terms a "feminist critical practice," so Chicago and other advocates of "centralized" or "gyno-sensuous" imagery had a specifically *political* goal in arguing—at that particular moment—for a "female imagery" (just as I have a particular agenda in rethinking these evaluations).

The definition of a female sensibility, furthermore, was necessary in order to counter, in Chicago's words, the art world's view that gender has nothing to do with art and to assert "that a woman might have a different point of view than a man."[60] It was a crucial step for feminism to mark gender as informative of cultural practice, to refuse the masculinist notion of "universality" that guaranteed the privileging of male-invented forms and themes as neutrally aesthetic (as beyond race, gender, sexuality, and class). "Women's art" became a unifying factor, a means of binding together an infinitely variable group of practices. Michele Barrett, who was respectfully critical of *The Dinner Party*'s "vaginal imagery," which she saw as indicative of Chicago's "somewhat biologistic approach to feminism," also recognized that "women's shared experience of oppression" is crucial to the construction of a feminist cultural politics. Ultimately it is in part the difficulty of, in Barrett's words, "arriving at a consensus among feminists as to what constitutes 'feminist' art"[61] and the impossibility of ensuring an empowering rather than objectifying reading of centralized imagery that explain the mixed reception of *The Dinner Party.*

"FEMALE IMAGERY": UNIVERSALISM, RACISM, HETEROSEXISM

Perhaps the most compelling critiques of the notion of a "female imagery" so central to the work of

Chicago and others in the 1970s have been articulated by feminists of color and lesbian feminists who have taken issue with the tendency of those defining this imagery to assume that there is such a thing as a unified—implicitly heterosexual and white (not to mention middle-class)—female experience. For example, poet Audre Lorde, who described herself as a "Black lesbian feminist socialist mother of two," wrote succinctly that "white women ignore their built-in privilege of whiteness and define woman in terms of their own experience alone."[62] Once the coalition of "oppressed women" had been formulated in a general way in the late 1960s and early 1970s, it was a crucial step for writers such as Lorde to intervene in this discourse and call into question the notion of a universal "female experience."

Two passionate and convincing critiques were made of *The Dinner Party*'s perceived claim of narrating a comprehensive women's history. In 1978 a group of Hispanic women from the National Women's Political Caucus visited the *Dinner Party* studio; following their visit, a member of the group, Estelle Chacon, sent Chicago a rough draft of an article she had written that was to appear in a Hispanic magazine.[63] In this article, which is an impassioned complaint about discrimination against Hispanics in Los Angeles, Chacon praised *The Dinner Party* as a "magnificent work of art and history of women," and an "original" forum for women's achievements. At the same time, however, she expressed her disappointment at finding that, while the 999 names of prominent women on the porcelain floor tiles included several Hispanas, no "pre-conquest New World heroines were honored guests" at the table itself. Chacon writes,

> The Hispanas do not have a role model in this art project that through the genius of a Feminist Artist, combines art, history, and politics. . . . I am truly sad that like men historians that have constantly overlooked the achievements of our Chicanos . . . Chicago, who claims to hurt about the omission of women in history, turns and hurts millions of Hispanas by not considering, not even one of us, to be an honored guest at her Dinner Party. Like most Anglos she thinks the New World ends at the Rio Grande . . . [and she believes that] Hispanics are not important enough to be considered in History or in art.

Chacon concluded by calling for a boycott of the piece and a letter-writing campaign to protest its exclusion of "Hispanas."

In an essay originally published in *Ms.* magazine, Alice Walker also pointed to Chicago's ignorance of women of color in history (specifically black women painters), focusing in particular on *The Dinner Party*'s representation of black female subjectivity in the one plate devoted to a black woman, the Sojourner Truth plate (fig. 21.4). Although she "loved Chicago's art and audacity," Walker was clear about her disapproval of Chicago's design for the Sojourner Truth plate: "All of the other plates are creatively imagined vaginas. . . . The Sojourner Truth plate is the only one in the collection that shows—instead of a vagina—a face. In fact, *three* faces. . . . It occurred to me that perhaps white women feminists, no less than white women generally, can not imagine black women have vaginas. Or if they can, where imagination leads them is too far to go." (Artist Lorraine O'Grady has elaborated upon Walker's critique, noting that "Sojourner Truth, the only black guest, must make it without a pussy.")[64]

Ironically Walker criticizes *The Dinner Party* for *not* producing an image of black female subjectivity through vulvar symbology. While certainly the obvious criticism—as per the general opprobrium heaped upon Chicago's so-called vaginal imagery—would have been of the *sexualization* and *objectification* of (white) femininity and the collapsing of difference into a unified symbol of femaleness, Walker brilliantly exposes the hesitancy white feminists tend to exhibit in relation to black female sexuality. Rather than acknowledging the threat of the sexuality and maternity of black women, the white woman prefers to "deny that the black woman has a vagina. Is capable of motherhood. Is a woman." Finally, Walker concludes, *The Dinner Party* exemplifies the fact that "white women feminists [have] revealed themselves

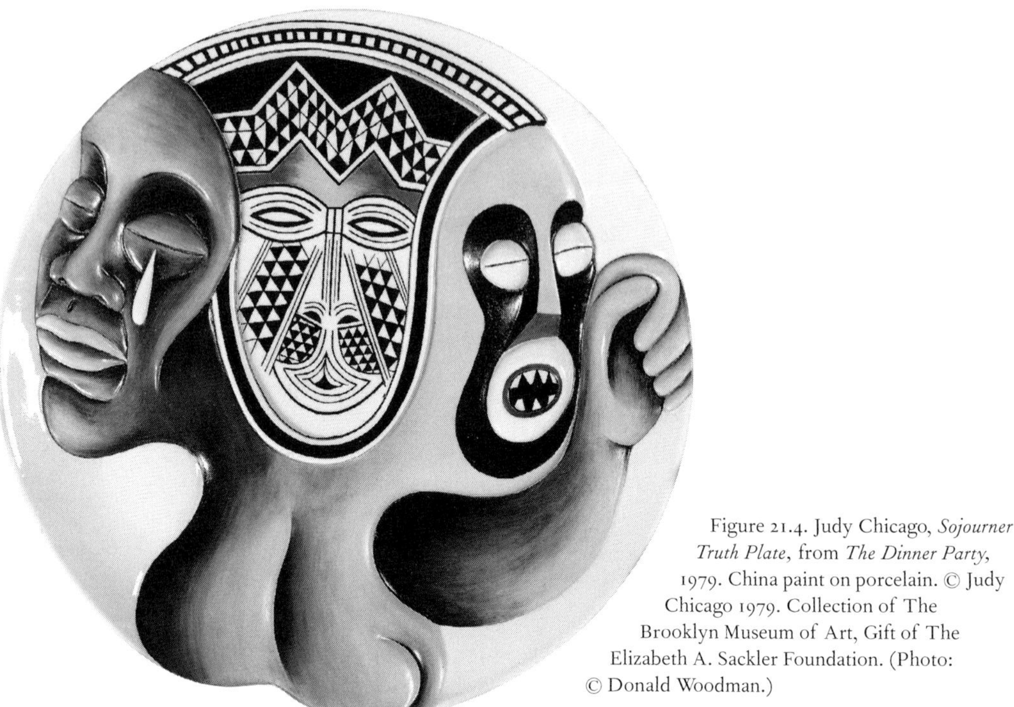

Figure 21.4. Judy Chicago, *Sojourner Truth Plate*, from *The Dinner Party*, 1979. China paint on porcelain. © Judy Chicago 1979. Collection of The Brooklyn Museum of Art, Gift of The Elizabeth A. Sackler Foundation. (Photo: © Donald Woodman.)

as incapable as white and black men of comprehending blackness and feminism in the same body."[65]

I count myself, a white feminist, among those Walker accuses of a certain blindness (and, in general, I think she is on the mark for white feminists, who have trouble comprehending the inevitability of race just as black men often seem to have trouble comprehending the inevitability of gender—as a constitutive element in the oppression of nonmale, nonwhite people). Those of us who have benefited from being white—like Chicago, like myself—don't tend to see race as an aspect of our femininity. As Richard Dyer has written: "Black is always marked as a colour . . . and is always particularizing; whereas white is not anything really, not an identity, not a particularizing quality. . . . White people's inability to see whiteness appears intractable."[66] Just as gallery owners and museum curators have for years defended the lack of exhibitions of women's work through recourse to the naturalizing idea that they are "gender blind" and interested only in "quality" art (thus implying that women's art simply isn't as "good" as

men's), so art world feminism (that is, the feminism that is dominated by white women artists, critics, and historians) has tended to naturalize race, failing to see its constitutive role in (sexual) identity.

The overall points that Walker and Chacon make about feminism's race blindness are crucial to the rethinking of the notion of female imagery, with its supposed grounding in "female experience."[67] Chicago's emphasis in *The Dinner Party* on (white) women's history at the expense of a broader, more complex vision of who makes up the coalition "women" epitomizes the general tendency of white feminists to focus on gender to the exclusion of other components of subjectivity. At the same time it should be stressed that the now commonly held assumption that 1970s feminism simply ignored issues of race is not accurate. While most historical narratives of the period suggest that feminists were oblivious to race (and, until recently, most feminist art historians have focused almost exclusively on white women artists), in fact, the 1970s feminist art community often debated issues of race, as Sheila de Bretteville's 1977 design for the cover of the Los Angeles–based feminist journal *Chrysalis* suggests. Black feminists have been central to the movement from the beginning; women such as Faith Ringgold and Betye Saar were and continue to be extremely active and important figures in the art world.[68]

Just as it is incorrect to suggest that 1970s feminism ignored race entirely, so it is inaccurate to dismiss feminism from this period as having been blindly heterosexist. While issues of sexuality and sexual practice were certainly not understood in the way that we comprehend them today, they were central to consciousness-raising within the feminist art movement and, thus, to the bases of feminist art practice. Sexual orientation was often discussed during consciousness-raising sessions. Panels, lectures, exhibitions, and articles considered the question of "lesbian sensibilities in art."[69] All the same, although periodic expressions of frustration on the part of lesbians in consciousness-raising groups at the Feminist Art Program and in the *Dinner Party* project were discussed within these groups, sexual orientation was generally not regarded as a fundamental component of identity politics the way it came to be with the rise of queer theory in the 1980s.[70] While creating a community of women was a goal of feminism in this period, the sexual implications of this were often veiled.[71] The "female experience" that was so central to Chicago and her colleagues' development of a feminist art practice was clearly about the "common oppression [of women] based on . . . gender," and not about race or the sexual identification of the feminists involved.[72]

The Dinner Party, however, was open to being understood as a monument to lesbianism. In a homophobic 1979 review Kay Larson, oddly enough, identified the entire project as having a "gay woman theme," describing it acerbically as "a ritual of oral consumption, a communion of the spirit in the flesh, a cultural cannibalism in which we're invited to eat from the labia of mythical women and ingest their power." Jan Adams responded more appreciatively in *The Lesbian Tide,* noting that, while "a charge that lesbians are treated as tokens [in the piece] seems justified, I feel a lesbian sensibility in the imagery." Unifying lesbian politics with those of women in general, she concluded that the work "advances every woman's struggle against erasure in a woman-hating world" and noted the presence of lesbians in Chicago's "her-story": "We are there, highlighted by Sappho's green and lavender floral plate and an exquisite lily motif portraying Natalie Barney."[73]

Names on the floor tiles and documentary panels grouped around Barney include a number of lesbian artists and writers: Romaine Brooks, Radclyffe Hall, and Gertrude Stein. At the same time neither Sappho nor Woolf, who are also represented at the table, are explicitly identified—either through the iconography of the place settings or in the biographical descriptions in the *Dinner Party* book—as lesbians. It is Barney who is explicitly identified there as a lesbian: "Lesbianism is—in the context of those grouped around Barney—presented not only as a sexual preference, but also as a political choice, one which refutes the heterosexual bias of the culture." The book explains the logic by which the project workers chose the names included around Barney: "In addition to avowed lesbians, other women in this section include those who chose women as companions, with or without a sexual relationship; women who refused to allow their identities to be submerged by the men with whom they were involved; and other women of the French salons."[74]

The pitfalls of identity politics, which have become increasingly evident to feminists since the mid 1980s, are exposed both in Adams's ambivalent and partially thwarted desire to identify with the labial forms of the plates and in Chicago's inevitably clumsy attempt to address lesbianism by seeking to name it—by labeling Barney, but not Woolf or Sappho, as a lesbian. Again, *The Dinner Party* enables us to open up important questions about identity: What, after all, is a lesbian? Any woman who has sex with another woman? Or only a woman who identifies herself with the politics of lesbianism as they are constituted at a particular moment? Or a woman identified as such by Chicago and others? And how does one represent or symbolize in visual form a particular identity without implicitly fixing its signification, implying that lived identity is codifiable in formal terms?

In this light Chicago's painful attempt to name the lesbian can be seen as a valiant but perhaps doomed effort to expand the notion of "female experience" to include the experiences of lesbians ("or other women of the French salons"). This failure is endemic to a particular phase of feminist thought; through its very failure this attempt to *name* enabled feminists subsequently to rethink identity politics. Chicago's own later insight—"We cast the dialogue incorrectly in the seventies. We cast it around gender, and we were also simplistic about the nature of identity. Identity is multiple"—resonates with revisionist theories of identity informed by poststructuralism.[75] Thus, in her important essay from the mid 1980s, "A Cyborg Manifesto," Donna Haraway points out that "it has become difficult to name one's feminism by a single adjective. . . . Consciousness of exclusion through naming is acute. Identities seem contradictory, partial, and strategic. . . . There is nothing about being 'female' that naturally binds women."[76] In spite of Chicago's interest in including many kinds of women within the renovated historical narrative of *The Dinner Party* (expressed in interviews, in the *Dinner Party* book, and through her inclusion of figures such as Barney and Sojourner Truth), the project has been interpreted by many as reinforcing traditional exclusions through its attempt at naming. It has in fact been seen as epitomizing the problematic logic of a particular stereotype of 1970s feminism, with its utopian and ultimately universalizing tendencies. One has to take seriously these interpretations of the piece, which inform its meanings within art history, while acknowledging that it is a product of a particular moment in feminist politics and of a particular person's negotiation of these politics.[77]

FEMINIST CRITIQUES OF *THE DINNER PARTY:* A "COLLABORATIVE" OR "COOPERATIVE" PROJECT?

At least in part because of Chicago's success in marketing her ideas and projects, especially *The Dinner Party,* they have come to be seen as paradigmatic of either the triumph or the failure of 1970s feminism, according to the evaluator's point of view. The alternative mode of production Chicago practiced in the *Dinner Party* studio, for example, has been judged a success or failure according to certain ideas regarding what feminist collaboration was about during the first decade of feminist art practice.

In the June 1979 issue of *Ms.* magazine, April Kingsley wrote a short essay on the piece that carefully but clearly distanced the magazine from Chicago's mode of production. *The Dinner Party,* Kingsley stated, was "completely one woman's conception, and therefore not typical of feminist collective projects."[78] Her implicit disapproval indicates a discomfort with Chicago's methods that has been expressed more directly by feminist scholars and art critics. For example, Barrett noted that Chicago's work process entailed "principles of collective work . . . not so much . . . ones I might recognize as a feminist but an attempt to recreate the 'school' or studio of an 'Artistic Genius' like Michelangelo. Although hundreds of people gave much time and work to the project it is Judy Chicago personally who has, apparently not unwillingly, made an international reputation from it."[79] Indeed, seemingly confirming this harsh judgment, in the *Dinner Party* book Chicago explicitly identified herself with the Italian Renaissance master, remarking, "I can imagine how Michelangelo must have felt—twelve years at that ceiling."[80]

Clearly *The Dinner Party* did not fulfill the utopian ideals of nonhierarchical collaboration that are understood as having been central to the mainstream women's movement in the 1970s. As all of the participants in the project have stressed (including Chicago herself), she controlled the studio, determined the design of the runners and banners, and designed and painted the plates. Although she scrupulously documented the contributions of participants in each portion of the project (and honored them through photographs on panels mounted during the exhibition of the piece as well as in the *Dinner Party* book), Chicago clearly took full credit for the conception and creation of the piece. This is hardly hypocritical, however, since she has never subscribed to the notion, often held to be common to all feminists, that feminism entails a complete abdication of authorial identity and authority in general.

It must, however, be stressed that Chicago has never made exorbitant claims for the "collaborative" or nonhierarchical nature of the project. She has insisted that it was never conceived or presented as a "collaborative" project as this notion is generally understood (although she has expressed hopes that the piece would "demonstrate another [alternative] mode of art-making for a woman artist").[81] Instead, she proposed the notion of a "flexible" or "benevolent" hierarchy, "where people get recognized for their work but one person is in charge."[82] The *Dinner Party* project, she insisted throughout, was *cooperative*, not collaborative, in the sense that it involved a clear hierarchy but cooperative effort to ensure its successful completion.[83]

Chicago was clear from the beginning about what was expected of participants in the project, and generally speaking, those who remained on a long-term basis have been positive or at worst ambivalently appreciative in their accounts of their experiences.[84] As weaver Elaine Ireland recalled, the project was "exciting and horrendous all the time. We could have grown more easily, not been devastated so often, been coddled as well as challenged, been given more explicit credit. But I have to admit that I would probably do it again."[85] While working on Chicago's project was clearly a challenge on both a personal and professional level, everyone involved was there presumably because she or he wanted to be. But the situation inevitably created feelings of resentment and ambivalence toward Chicago, who was empowered—within a context that at least some of the participants interpreted as unsuccessfully "collaborative"—to make all the rules and who ultimately received the authorial credit for the piece. The problem of Chicago's "authority" (and, arguably, authoritarianism) remains a sticking point in the reception of *The Dinner Party* and consequently must continue to be negotiated in any attempt to understand its position in feminist art history.

Finally it is difficult to ignore the seeming contradictions apparent in the contrast between Chicago's identification with Michelangelo (her desire to be, in Maureen Mullarkey's words, "bound in morocco")[86] and the critique, developed by poststructuralist feminist art historians and seemingly implicit in *The Dinner Party*'s subversive insistence on a feminization of historical narrative and art production, of masculinist conceptions of greatness or genius.[87] Beyond the question of its putative essentialism, then, it is the contradiction between Chicago's critique of masculinist historical narrative and modernist formalism and her adherence to conventional notions of genius—her desire to be a great artist within terms that are structurally masculinist—that makes *The Dinner Party* as controversial as it is within debates about feminist art. *The Dinner Party* aims to *elevate* women—including, many have argued, Chicago herself—to a state of transcendence or genius usually reserved for male subjects but does not question the exclusions that a belief in transcendence necessarily implies.

BY WAY OF A PROVISIONAL
CONCLUSION: FEMINISM AND HISTORY

The Dinner Party subverts mainstream modernism's proscription against symbolic allusion with a sexually charged theme; it also blatantly feminizes historical narrative. The piece is, in Chicago's words, a reinterpretation of the Last Supper from the point of view of "the people who have done the cooking throughout history."[88] Like Mary Beth Edelson's 1972 version of the Last Supper, titled *Some Living American Women Artists*, in which the faces of the male protagonists of Leonardo's famous painting are replaced by those of women artists, it is a feminized restaging and expansion of the all-male club of Christ and his twelve disciples—in Chicago's case, with three groups of thirteen women.[89] Presenting this "herstory" in a populist form—one that is didactically and decoratively accessible ("kitsch," in the terms of modernist art criticism)—the piece attempts to reach the largest possible audience with its utopian message of women's greatness. By creating a monumental structure heroizing "great ladies," however, Chicago both challenged and reinforced conventional patriarchal conceptions of history. The piece undermines male historical narrative by insisting on reinserting important women and yet reinforces the problematic, masculinist notion of "greatness." Moreover, as Michele Barrett has argued, it creates a hierarchical structure of women that inevitably privileges some (the 39 at the table) over others (the 999 on the floor, as well as those left out entirely).[90]

Chicago's investment in greatness informs *The Dinner Party*—in its ambivalent attempt to raise craft to high-art status; its modified, "cooperative" model of authorship (which maintains Chicago as primary author); and its presentation as an isolated "masterpiece" within the museum setting. In the *Dinner Party* book, Chicago published a journal entry from 1975 stating her desire to "make a piece so far beyond judgment that it will enter the cultural pool and never be erased from history, as women's work has been erased before."[91] The poignancy of this desire lies in its inevitable failure. The conflict between wanting to revise history to include women and aspiring to transcend it altogether has followed *The Dinner Party* through its public existence so far, just as has the tension, identified by Judith Butler, between the desire to represent female subjectivity in a positive way and the need to avoid fixing it through limiting and universalizing bodily signifiers.

The burgeoning (or reburgeoning) of feminist interest in the body, women's sexualities, and female desire in 1990s art practice and theory alerts us to the fact that these conflicts—still unresolved and problematic—still offer much to compel feminist thought. While artists such as Mary Beth Edelson, Harmony Hammond, Mira Schor, and Faith Wilding have sustained their commitment to exploring female sexual forms in their work since the 1970s, a new generation of feminists—including Judie Bamber, Lauren Lesko, and Millie Wilson—have turned with a vengeance to the type of vulvar, labial, and orificial forms that were so central to the explorations of Chicago and other feminists in the 1970s. And yet, as Susan Kandel points out,[92] conditioned by the critical awareness of poststructuralist feminist theory

(if unfortunately sometimes ignorant of 1970s feminist art and theory), they approach these forms from a different perspective.

Acknowledging the inevitable oversimplification that such comparisons entail, it is nonetheless provocative to suggest that the difference between work produced by feminists in the 1970s and that produced today is one of both *attitude* and *emphasis*. No longer utopian, feminist artists today tend to conceptualize the female body—which they often render in fragmented form or through substitutes such as clothing—as radically polymorphous rather than representing it through the unified symbol of a definable "female imagery." This body is not *only* and perhaps not even *primarily* female: its "femaleness" (and what that may be is open to question) is interrelated with its ethnicity, its economic status, its sexuality.

Although Chicago and her colleagues recognized these other aspects of identity, they emphasized *femaleness* in an idealizing way; it was the constituent factor of their coalition politics. As I have attempted to make clear here, they were never committed to a simplistic notion of "biological essentialism," although they were clearly hopeful about the possibilities of combating discrimination through the recuperation of women's bodies through representation. Today such hopefulness, for better or for worse, holds no authority and, in fact—as the fate of *The Dinner Party* within art world discourse makes clear—engenders a certain amount of condescension and even hostility.

With all of its shortcomings and contradictions, however, the diverse, complex feminist art of the 1970s, its theory and practice, has been fundamental to subsequent developments in feminist art and art history (which themselves suffer from internal contradictions). While feminism has moved to a new place and has come to acknowledge and emphasize the complexities of sexual politics and the conflicted vicissitudes of identification, it has been able to do so only because of the foundations laid by feminists such as Chicago, Hammond, Schapiro, Wilding, and their colleagues and through works as controversial as *The Dinner Party*. Whether subsequent feminist theorists and artists wish to continue within the utopian vein mined by Chicago and her colleagues or to react critically against it, in my view we would benefit from respecting these important "mother figures" for the chances they took at a time when no one took women artists or women's issues seriously and, perhaps especially, for the mistakes they weren't afraid of making.

NOTES

Epigraph from Judith Butler, *Bodies That Matter: On the Discursive Limits of "Sex"* (New York: Routledge, 1994), 188.

1. John Perreault, "No Reservations," *Soho News*, 22 October 1980, 19.

2. Kay Larson, "Under the Table: Duplicity, Alienation," *Village Voice*, 11 June 1979, 51; Hilton Kramer, "Judy Chicago's 'Dinner Party' Comes to Brooklyn Museum," *New York Times*, 17 October 1980.

3. Following a five-month exhibition at the Brooklyn Museum that began in September 2002, *The Dinner Party* is now permanently housed at that museum in its own gallery, thanks to the generous support of Elizabeth A. Sackler.

4. See Hilton Kramer, "Does Feminism Conflict with Artistic Standards?" *New York Times*, 27 January 1980, sec. 2, in which he implies, of course, that it does.

5. As Lucy Lippard has pointed out, in much of the new feminist work from the 1990s, "it feels as though the wheel is being reinvented by those who don't know the feminist art history of 'transgression'" ("Moving Targets/Concentric Circles: Notes from the Radical Whirlwind," introduction to Lippard's *The Pink Glass Swan: Selected Feminist Essays on Art* [New York: New Press, 1995], 3–28). I am indebted to Lippard, who has been the single most consistent champion of 1970s feminist art for decades, for sharing her thoughts on an early version of this text with me.

6. For Paglia's offensive "postfeminist" views (e.g., her dismissal of "endlessly complaining feminists" [9]), see her *Sex, Art, and American Culture* (New York: Vintage Books, 1992). Roiphe most clearly demonstrates the dangers of losing this history in her excoriation of "fashionable feminists" and "rape crisis feminists"; see her disturbing *The Morning After: Sex, Fear, and Feminism on Campus* (Boston: Little, Brown, 1993). Given the striking parallels between their positions and those of traditional patriarchy, it is no surprise that both women have been given enormous media attention.

7. A perfect example of this erasure is the revisionist history of the California Institute of the Arts, Valencia (known as CalArts), as a site for the development of radical postmodern practice in the early 1970s— accounts that completely ignore the motivating presence of the Feminist Art Program run by Chicago and Miriam Schapiro in the early 1970s. For example, in the 1987 exhibition *CalArts: Skeptical Belief(s)*, only one passing reference is made to the Feminist Art Program in the seven essays in the catalogue, and none of the artists from the program was included in the exhibition (see *CalArts: Skeptical Beliefs* [Chicago: Renaissance Society, University of Chicago; Newport, Calif.: Newport Harbor Art Museum, 1987]).

8. The needlework loft was run by Susan Hill, who cowrote (with Chicago) the second *Dinner Party* book, *Embroidering Our Heritage: The Dinner Party Needlework* (New York: Anchor Press/Doubleday, 1980).

9. Clement Greenberg, "Modernist Painting" (1965), in *The New Art: A Critical Anthology*, ed. Gregory Battcock (New York: Dutton, 1966), 74.

10. Greenberg, "Modernist Painting," 68–69, 70, 71.

11. Clement Greenberg, "Avant-Garde and Kitsch" (1939), in *Art and Culture: Critical Essays* (Boston: Beacon Press, 1961), 10. Greenberg specifically notes that the appreciator of kitsch culture is "more usually" a woman, in "Present Prospects in American Painting" (1947), in *Clement Greenberg: The Collected Essays and Criticism*, vol. 2: *Arrogant Purpose, 1945–1949*, ed. John O'Brian (Chicago: University of Chicago Press, 1986), 161.

12. See Carol Duncan, "When Greatness Is a Box of Wheaties" (1975), in *The Aesthetics of Power: Essays in Critical Art History* (Cambridge: Cambridge University Press, 1993), 121–32.

13. On the use of craft to "feminize" art practice and subvert modernism, see Norma Broude, "Miriam Schapiro and 'Femmage': Reflections on the Conflict between Decoration and Abstraction in Twentieth-Century Art" (1980), in *Feminism and Art History: Questioning the Litany*, ed. Norma Broude and

Mary D. Garrard (New York: Harper and Row, 1982), 315–29; and idem, "The Pattern and Decoration Movement," in *The Power of Feminist Art: The American Movement of the 1970s, History and Impact*, ed. Norma Broude and Mary D. Garrard (New York: Harry N. Abrams, 1994), 208–25.

14. Cited in Lucy Lippard, "Judy Chicago's 'Dinner Party,'" *Art in America* 68 (April 1980): 124.

15. Judy Chicago, *The Dinner Party: A Symbol of Our Heritage* (Garden City, N.Y.: Doubleday, 1979), 8–9.

16. For example, see my critique of the contradictory privileging and heroizing of artists such as Barbara Kruger for their supposed deconstruction of conceptions of artistic genius, in my book review, "Modernist Logic in Feminist Histories of Art," *Camera Obscura* 27 (1991–92): 149–65.

17. Chicago, *Embroidering Our Heritage*, 15.

18. Hal Fischer, "Judy Chicago, San Francisco Museum of Art," *Artforum* 17 (Summer 1979): 77.

19. According to Diana Ketcham, roughly one thousand people a day saw *The Dinner Party* at the San Francisco Museum of Modern Art, in contrast to the four to five hundred a day who saw the museum's Jasper Johns and Robert Rauschenberg shows ("On the Table: Joyous Celebration," *Village Voice*, 11 June 1979, 47). On the demographics of *Dinner Party* visitors, see Estelle Inman, "The Dinner Party: Visitor Demography and Reactions," an unpublished study of attendance at the showing at the Glenbow Museum in Calgary (Judy Chicago archives).

20. See Lucy Lippard, "*Dinner Party* a Four-Star Treat," *Seven Days*, 27 April 1979, 27–29.

21. Kramer, "Judy Chicago's 'Dinner Party'" See also Thomas Albright's snide comments about Chicago's "less beautiful followers" in his condescending and scathing attack on the piece in "The Era of Conceptualized Schlock," *San Francisco Chronicle*, 5 July 1979. Lisa H. Jensen examines this and other criticisms of *The Dinner Party* in an interesting analytical essay, "Responses to a Feminist Perspective in Art: Judy Chicago's 'Dinner Party' and the Language of Its Critics" (1980, Judy Chicago archives).

22. Maureen Mullarkey, "Dishing It Out: Judy Chicago's 'Dinner Party,'" *Commonweal* 108 (April 1981): 210–11. The guest book included ecstatic remarks such as: "What a gift! What a joy! I'll always see things differently now," and "For the first time I've been in touch with my own sexuality (I'm a male). Thank you." These are cited with derision by Mullarkey.

23. Clara Weyergraf, "The Holy Alliance: Populism and Feminism," *October* 16 (Spring 1981): 31. For someone who assumes a Marxist approach, Weyergraf seems extraordinarily condescending to working housewives.

24. Griselda Pollock, "Screening the Seventies: Sexuality and Representation in Feminist Practice—a Brechtian Perspective," in *Vision and Difference: Femininity, Feminism, and the Histories of Art* (New York: Routledge, 1988), 181; see Pollock's specific criticism of *The Dinner Party* (coauthored with Rozsika Parker) in *Old Mistresses: Women, Art, and Ideology* (New York: Pantheon Books, 1981), esp. 137–40.

25. Pollock, "Screening the Seventies," 163, 165.

26. In Norma Broude and Mary D. Garrard, "Conversation with Judy Chicago," in *The Power of Feminist Art*, 70–71.

27. Lippard, "Judy Chicago's 'Dinner Party,'" 118; Kramer, "Judy Chicago's 'Dinner Party'"; Pollock, "Screening the Seventies," 165.

28. My heading for this section, "What Is Female Imagery?" comes from the title of a debate among feminist artists and critics, including Lippard, Susan Hall, Linda Nochlin, Joan Snyder, and Susana Torre, originally published in *Ms.* magazine (May 1975) and reprinted in Lucy Lippard, *From the Center: Feminist Essays on Women's Art* (New York: Dutton, 1976), 80–89; "cunt art" is Cindy Nemser's term in "The Women Artists' Movement," *Feminist Art Journal* 2 (Winter 1973–74): 9. Many other terms have been used to describe visual expression characteristic of women subjects; I tend to use either "female imagery" or "female sensibility" since Chicago herself has used these; see esp. Judy Chicago and Miriam Schapiro, "Female Imagery," *Womanspace Journal* 1 (Summer 1973): 11–17.

29. *Through the Flower*, the title of a painting by Chicago and of her autobiography, is a metaphor for this experience of coming to consciousness: "Moving 'through the flower,'" she writes, "is a process that is available to all of us, a process that can lead us to a place where we can express our humanity and values as women through our work and in our lives" (*Through the Flower: My Struggle as a Woman Artist* [New York: Penguin, 1975], 206).

30. See my "Interpreting Feminist Bodies: The Unframeability of Desire," in *The Rhetoric of the Frame: Essays toward a Critical Theory of the Frame in Art*, ed. Paul Duro (New York: Cambridge University Press, 1996).

31. For an extended discussion of these debates and the campaign to punish the University of the District of Columbia for encouraging Chicago's donation of the piece, see Lucy R. Lippard, "Uninvited Guests: How Washington Lost 'The Dinner Party,'" *Art in America* 79 (December 1991): 39–49.

32. Nemser, "The Women Artists' Movement," 9. See also Patricia Mainardi's "Feminine Sensibility: An Analysis," *Feminist Art Journal* 3 (April 1972): 9, 22; and "A Feminine Sensibility: Two Views" (written with Janet Sawyer), *Feminist Art Journal* 3 (Fall 1972): 4–25.

33. On "hidden content," see Chicago, *Through the Flower*, 143. The most obvious figure in this regard is Georgia O'Keeffe. Chicago greatly admired her and gave her the final seat at *The Dinner Party*, but throughout her life O'Keeffe strenuously denied that there was anything particularly "female" about her paintings. [Ed. note: see Barbara Buhler Lynes, "Georgia O'Keeffe and Feminism: A Problem of Position," in *The Expanding Discourse: Feminism and Art History*, ed. Norma Broude and Mary D. Garrard (New York: HarperCollins, 1992), 437–50.]

34. Chicago, *Through the Flower*, 80, 52, following 72.

35. Chicago described the environments to me in these terms in conversation, 31 August 1994.

36. Chicago, *Through the Flower*, following 72.

37. See, e.g., Mark Stevens, "Guess Who's Coming to Dinner," *Newsweek*, 2 April 1979, 93. Chicago discusses matriarchies and the role of the goddess in *The Dinner Party: A Symbol*, 57–61. For an excellent and intelligent explanation of the role of the goddess for 1970s feminist artists, see Mary Beth Edelson, "An Open Letter to Thomas McEvilley," *New Art Examiner* 16 (April 1989): 34–38. See also *Heresies*, no. 5 (1978), titled "The Great Goddess"; and Gloria Feman Orenstein, "Recovering Her Story: Feminist Artists Reclaim the Great Goddess," in *The Power of Feminist Art*, ed. Broude and Garrard, 174–89.

38. I use *transcendence* here in the sense in which Simone de Beauvoir employed it in *The Second Sex*, where she points out how patriarchy refuses women the "transcendence" granted to men, containing them within a biological structure of "immanence" (*The Second Sex*, trans. and ed. H. M. Parshley [New York: Alfred A. Knopf, 1953]). See also Josephine Withers's discussion of transcendence in relation to *The Dinner Party* in "Judy Chicago's Dinner Party: A Personal Vision of Women's History" (1981), in *The Expanding Discourse*, ed. Broude and Garrard, 454–55.

39. Chicago has observed that her method of painting the canvas from the inside outward was anathema to the art world at the time, which subscribed to the Greenbergian dictum that the forms of a painting be constructed in relation to the edges of the canvas rather than the center (interview with the author, 21 June 1994).

40. Broude and Garrard, "Conversation with Judy Chicago," 70. According to Chicago, the notion of "peeling back" came out of a discussion with Lippard, who suggested that Chicago open up her imagery, that she "peel it back and see what happens" (Natalie Veiner Freeman, "A Dream of a Dinner Party: Judy Chicago," *City Woman*, Spring 1982, 62).

41. Chicago and Schapiro, "Female Imagery," 11. The authors are describing the feelings they believe are conveyed by an O'Keeffe painting. It is precisely their suggestion that the centralized image "establishes a vehicle by which to state the truth and beauty of [a woman's] . . . identity" (ibid., 14)—and the corollary implication that this nature can be extrapolated to all women—that Pollock criticizes in her argument that feminism "must" resist such idealistic recourse to a realist ideology ("Screening the Seventies," 165). See also Pollock's specific rejection of "vaginal imagery" as recuperable to patriarchal readings, in "What's Wrong with Images of Women?" *Screen Education*, no. 24 (Autumn 1977): 30–31.

42. Chicago and Schapiro, "Female Imagery" 11, 14.

43. Ibid., 14, 13 (emphasis added); Arlene Raven, "Feminist Content in Current Female Art," *Sister* 6 (October–November 1975): 10. Elsewhere Chicago stated, regarding how masculinity and femininity are defined, "My suspicion is that it's a result of culture not biology" (interview with Judith Dancoff, "A Feminist Art Program," *Art Journal* 31 [Fall 1971]: 48).

44. Arlene Raven, "Women's Art: The Development of a Theoretical Perspective," *Womanspace Journal* 1 (February–March 1973): 14. See also Ruth Iskin, "Sex-

ual and Self-Imagery in Art—Male and Female," *Womanspace Journal* 1 (Summer 1973): 4–10.

45. Raven, "Women's Art," 14, 20.

46. On this point, see Joanna Frueh, "The Body through Women's Eyes," in *The Power of Feminist Art*, 190–207.

47. As Chicago puts it: "No matter how strong we are and how beautiful we are, we are contained. And that is the basis of *The Dinner Party*" (quoted by Jan Butterfield, in "Guess Who's Coming to Dinner?" *Mother Jones*, January 1979, 23).

48. Broude and Garrard, "Conversation with Judy Chicago," 71; see also note 41 above. The "Cunt Cheerleaders," a group of Chicago's Fresno students who dressed as cheerleaders with letter sweaters spelling "C-U-N-T" and performed cheers in public, exemplify the empowering aspect of the "cunt" for these women as well as the humor that accompanied its recuperation (a humor that is largely ignored by theorists who dismiss "cunt imagery" as essentialist).

49. Lucy Lippard adds to this: "Sex is bound to be a factor in women's work precisely because women have been sex objects and are much more aware of their bodies than men. Men are aware of their pricks. Women are aware that every movement they make in public is supposed to have sexual content for the opposite sex. Some of that has to come out in the work" ("Six" [1974], reprinted in *From the Center*, 93). See also Joan Semmel and April Kingsley, "Sexual Imagery in Women's Art," *Woman's Art Journal* 1 (Spring–Summer 1980): 1.

50. Faith Wilding, interview with the author, 13 July 1994. Wilding described the importance of consciousness-raising in the development of the "central core" concept: it was in consciousness-raising sessions that women opened up to discuss negative labels for the female sex—such as "gash" and "hole"—and the effects that these labels had on their senses of self.

51. For a more extended discussion of this politics of 1980s feminist theory, see my "Postfeminism, Feminist Pleasures, and Embodied Theories of Art," in *New Feminist Criticism: Art, Identity, Action*, ed. Joanna Frueh, Cassandra Langer, and Arlene Raven (New York: HarperCollins, 1994), esp. 25–29. See also Thalia Gouma-Peterson and Patricia Mathews, "The Feminist Critique of Art History," *Art Bulletin* 69 (September 1987): 326–57. The dangers of an over-simplistic division of feminist art theory into "generations" are made clear by Griselda Pollock in her pointed critique of Gouma-Peterson and Mathews's privileging of her work as "second generation" even though she (along with Mary Kelly and other "1980s" feminists) had been active throughout the 1970s; see Griselda Pollock, "The Politics of Theory: Generations and Geographies: Feminist Theory and the Histories of Art Histories," *Genders*, no. 17 (Fall 1993): esp. 108–15. While Pollock is certainly right to point out that the literal age of the feminist in question is not necessarily a factor in defining her position in relation to feminist ideologies of representation, I would argue that generational politics are at work in the discursive rejection of "1970s" U.S. feminism by Pollock and others. That is, the strategic critique by British feminists of the central-core phenomenon clearly operates to position them as "beyond" the implicitly old-fashioned assumptions that they identify as underlying it. Furthermore, in a historical sense it is quite clear that a shift in hegemony occurred from the 1970s, when figures such as Chicago dominated the scene, to the 1980s, when the work of Pollock and other poststructuralist feminists began to be seen as authoritative.

52. Pollock, "Screening the Seventies," 181, 163, 165. See also Mary Kelly's pointed attack on essentialism in her conversation with Paul Smith, "No Essential Femininity," *Parachute* 37 (Spring 1982): 31–35. Kelly's visual art has been constructed by Pollock and others as paradigmatic of radical ("Brechtian") postmodern feminist practice.

53. Laura Mulvey's important polemic in "Visual Pleasure and Narrative Cinema" (1975; reprinted in *The Feminism and Visual Culture Reader*, ed. Amelia Jones [New York: Routledge, 2003], 44–52) was central to the deconstructive theory of the "male gaze." Pollock and other British feminists were working through this notion around the same time in relation to the visual arts.

54. Lisa Tickner, "Sexuality and/in Representation: Five British Artists," in *Difference: On Representation and Sexuality*, exh. cat. (New York: New Museum of Contemporary Art, 1984), 28, 29.

55. Mira Schor, "Backlash and Appropriation," 254, 259. In this essay Schor also savages *The Dinner Party*, singling it out as epitomizing the weaknesses in 1970s

feminism that "justified" some aspects of the backlash.

56. Diana Fuss, *Essentially Speaking: Feminism, Nature, and Difference* (New York: Routledge, 1989), 6. For an excellent collection of essays on the question of essentialism, see *The Essential Difference*, a special issue of *differences* 1 (Summer 1989).

57. Pollock, "Modernity and the Spaces of Femininity," in *Vision and Difference*, 55; Chicago and Schapiro, "Female Imagery," 14; Broude and Garrard, eds., *Feminism and Art History*, 161. There are many further examples of essentialism in poststructuralist feminism. The notion of closeness as particular to the maternal relationship and of a specifically "female voice" (*écriture feminine*), drawn from French feminist theorists such as Hélène Cixous and Julia Kristeva and taken up by many antiessentialist feminist theorists (especially in literary theory), is arguably as "essentializing" as Chicago's notion of a "body identification" in women's painting. Gouma-Peterson and Mathews point this out in "The Feminist Critique," 335.

58. Fuss, *Essentially Speaking*, 114, 68, 32 (with "to be politicized" Fuss cites Luce Irigaray, in *This Sex Which Is Not One*).

59. Broude and Garrard, "Introduction: Feminism and Art in the Twentieth Century," in *The Power of Feminist Art*, 28, 24 (emphasis added). Lippard uses the term *gyno-sensuous imagery* in "Excerpt from the Catalogues of Three Women's Exhibitions" (1975), in *From the Center*, 51.

60. Chicago, *Through the Flower*, 63.

61. Michele Barrett, "Feminism and the Definition of Cultural Politics," in *Feminism, Culture and Politics*, ed. Rosalind Brunt and Caroline Rowan (London: Lawrence and Wishart, 1982), 46, 47.

62. Audre Lorde, "Age, Race, Class, and Sex: Women Redefining Difference," in *Sister Outsider: Essays and Speeches* (Freedom, Calif.: Crossing Press, 1984), 114, 117.

63. I obtained a copy of this letter, dated 29 September 1978, and the article draft from Judy Chicago's archives; there is no specific reference to the magazine in which the article was to appear. The author refers to herself and her group as "Hispanas" or "Hispanics"; hence my use of this term here. Subsequent quotes are from this article draft.

64. Alice Walker, "One Child of One's Own: A Mean-ingful Digression within the Work(s)" (1979), in *In Search of Our Mothers' Gardens: Womanist Prose* (San Diego: Harcourt Brace Jovanovich, 1983), 383; Lorraine O'Grady, "The Cave," *Artforum* 30 (January 1992): 22.

65. Walker, "One Child of One's Own," 384.

66. Richard Dyer, "White," *Screen* 29 (Autumn 1988): 45, 46.

67. Chicago herself has recognized the limitations of her approach in the *Dinner Party* project, stating that she hoped to "involve an even wider range of people [in the later Birth Project], particularly Blacks and Hispanics, than was the case in *The Dinner Party*." "Unfortunately," she continues, "the people in this country who have the time—that is, the privilege of time—to make art are mostly white and middle-class. . . . I can't make that go away" (cited in Blair, "The Womanly Art of Judy Chicago," *Madmoiselle*, January 1982, 153).

68. Saar was active in Los Angeles, participating in feminist workshops and exhibitions, and in shows of black women artists, such as *Black Mirror* at Womanspace in 1973 (reviewed by Claudia Chapline, *Womanspace Journal* 1 [Summer 1973]: 20–21). Ringgold, a New York–based artist, was a founder—along with her daughter Michelle Wallace, a feminist theorist—of Women, Students, and Artists for Black Art Liberation and was a central force in the establishment of the black women artists' activist group Where We At, both in the early 1970s. Panel discussions on issues of race were held at the Woman's Building in Los Angeles, and in the 1980s an issue of *Heresies*, entitled *Racism Is the Issue*, was devoted to the interconnected politics of race, sexuality, and art (of course, the fact that separate panels and publications had to be devoted to women of color and their art in relation to issues of racism indicates the marked nature of "nonwhite" as "race").

69. Notably, in 1973 Womanspace sponsored "Lesbian Week," devoted to "an examination of Lesbian Sensibilities in Art" and including performances, films, and gay-straight dialogues; see *Womanspace Journal* 1 (February–March 1973). See also the astute writings of Harmony Hammond on lesbian feminist issues in art, most of which are reprinted in *Wrappings: Essays on Feminism, Art, and the Martial Arts* (New York: Mussmann Bruce, 1984), and the third issue of *Here-*

sies on "Lesbian Art and Artists" (1977). Laura Cottingham and Tee Corinne, a lesbian photographer who has made a wide range of "cunt art" since the early 1970s, have alerted me to the wide range of art-making and publishing activities by lesbian artists during the 1970s.

70. For insight on this issue, I am indebted to conversations with Juliet Myers and Arlene Raven.

71. As Flora Davis and other historians have pointed out, in debates within the women's movement in the 1970s, the question of sexual orientation was central but often veiled. The infamous "Lavender Menace," a group of lesbian-identified women frustrated with the tendency in mainstream feminist groups such as NOW to downplay or suppress lesbianism in an attempt to make feminism palatable to a broader public, interrupted the 1970 Congress to Unite Women in New York City with a call for an "outing" of the centrality of lesbianism to feminist politics and personal practice (Flora Davis, *Moving the Mountain: The Women's Movement in America since 1960* [New York: Simon and Schuster, 1991], 264–65). For a specific example of this veiling, note Chicago's adoption of a "butch" persona in several of her exhibition advertisements from the early 1970s. I discuss these in my article "Dis/Playing the Phallus: Male Artists Perform Their Masculinities," *Art History* 17 (December 1994): 551–52. On the problematic tendency of heterosexual feminists to appropriate the tropes of lesbianism in order to radicalize feminism, see Teresa De Lauretis, "The Seductions of Lesbianism: Feminist Psychoanalytic Theory and the Maternal Imaginary," in *The Practice of Love: Lesbian Sexuality and Perverse Desire* (Bloomington: Indiana University Press, 1994), 149–202.

72. Wilding, "The Feminist Art Programs at Fresno and CalArts, 1970–75," in *The Power of Feminist Art*, ed. Broude and Garrard, 35.

73. Kay Larson, "More (or Less) Awful Rowing toward God," *Village Voice*, 17 December 1979, 113; idem, "Under the Table," 49; Jan Adams, "Perspectives: Chicago's Dinner Party/A Feminist Feast," *Lesbian Tide*, May–June 1979, 4, 5.

74. Chicago, *The Dinner Party: A Symbol*, 204.

75. Broude and Garrard, "Conversation with Judy Chicago," 72.

76. Donna Haraway, "A Cyborg Manifesto: Science, Technology, and Socialist-Feminism in the Late Twentieth Century" (1985), in *Simians, Cyborgs, and Women: The Reinvention of Nature* (New York: Routledge, 1991), 155.

77. As Chicago once stated in exasperation in answer to a question about why she included only women from Western civilization: "That's like asking, when you're invited to someone's house for supper, 'If you made dinner why didn't you make breakfast and lunch too?' I set out to recast Western civilization from a female perspective. . . . I did not set out to recast all of human civilization" (in Susan Rennie and Arlene Raven, "The Dinner Party Project: An Interview with Judy Chicago," *Chrysalis*, no. 4 [1977]: 98).

78. April Kingsley, "The I-Hate-to-Cook 'Dinner Party,'" *Ms.*, June 1979, 30–31.

79. Barrett, "Feminism and the Definition of Cultural Politics," 44. See also Karen Woodley's harsh assessment of Chicago's "use of thousands of unpaid volunteers," in "The Inner Sanctum: The Dinner Party," in *Visibly Female: Feminism and Art Today*, ed. Hilary Robinson (New York: Universe, 1988), 97.

80. Chicago, *The Dinner Party: A Symbol*, 29.

81. Rennie and Raven, "The Dinner Party Project," 100.

82. Chicago, in Blair, "The Womanly Art," 153. On "benevolent" hierarchy, see Lippard, "Dinner Party a Four-Star Treat," 28.

83. Chicago is clear on her position in Rennie and Raven, "The Dinner Party Project," 99.

84. See, e.g., Jan Castro's interview with participants Kate Amend and Ann Isolde, "The Dinner Party Talks," *River Styx*, no. 9 (1981): 58–69.

85. Cited in Blair, "The Womanly Art," 153.

86. This expectation, Mullarkey argues, "is fatal to [*The Dinner Party*'s] . . . stated feminist aim" ("Dishing It Out," 21).

87. See Griselda Pollock and Rozsika Parker, "God's Little Artist," in *Old Mistresses*, 82–113; and Duncan, "When Greatness Is a Box of Wheaties." Notably, Linda Nochlin's ground-breaking essay "Why Have There Been No Great Women Artists?" (1971) also assumes a notion of greatness rather than critiquing it (in *Art and Sexual Politics*, ed. Thomas B. Hess and Elizabeth C. Baker [New York: Macmillan, 1973], 1–43).

88. Cited in Lee Wohlfert, "Sassy Judy Chicago Throws a Dinner Party, but the Art World Mostly Sends Regrets," *People*, 8 December 1980, 156.

89. Edelson's piece is reproduced in Broude and Garrard, eds., *The Power of Feminist Art*, 17. In an interview published in 1979, Chicago expressed her discomfort with the hierarchical structure of the Last Supper theme, with Christ obviously privileged over his disciples, as a motivating factor in her desire to expand the "party." She also notes that the thirteen guests along each side of the table, obviously a reference to the thirteen men at the Last Supper, is also a subversive allusion to the number of participants at a witch's coven (Butterfield, "Guess Who's Coming to Dinner?" 22–23).

90. Barrett, "Feminism and the Definition of Cultural Politics," 45. As Carrie Rickey argues of *The Dinner Party*'s retelling of history: "This is history using the Great Women theory; what happened to the anonymous women?" (review of *The Dinner Party*, *Artforum* 19 [January 1981]: 73).

91. Chicago, *The Dinner Party: A Symbol*, 29.

92. Susan Kandel, "Beneath the Green Veil: The Body in/of New Feminist Art," in *Sexual Politics: Judy Chicago's Dinner Party in Feminist Art History*, ed. Amelia Jones (Los Angeles: UCLA at the Armand Hammer Museum of Art and Cultural Center; Berkeley and Los Angeles: University of California Press, 1996), 184–207.

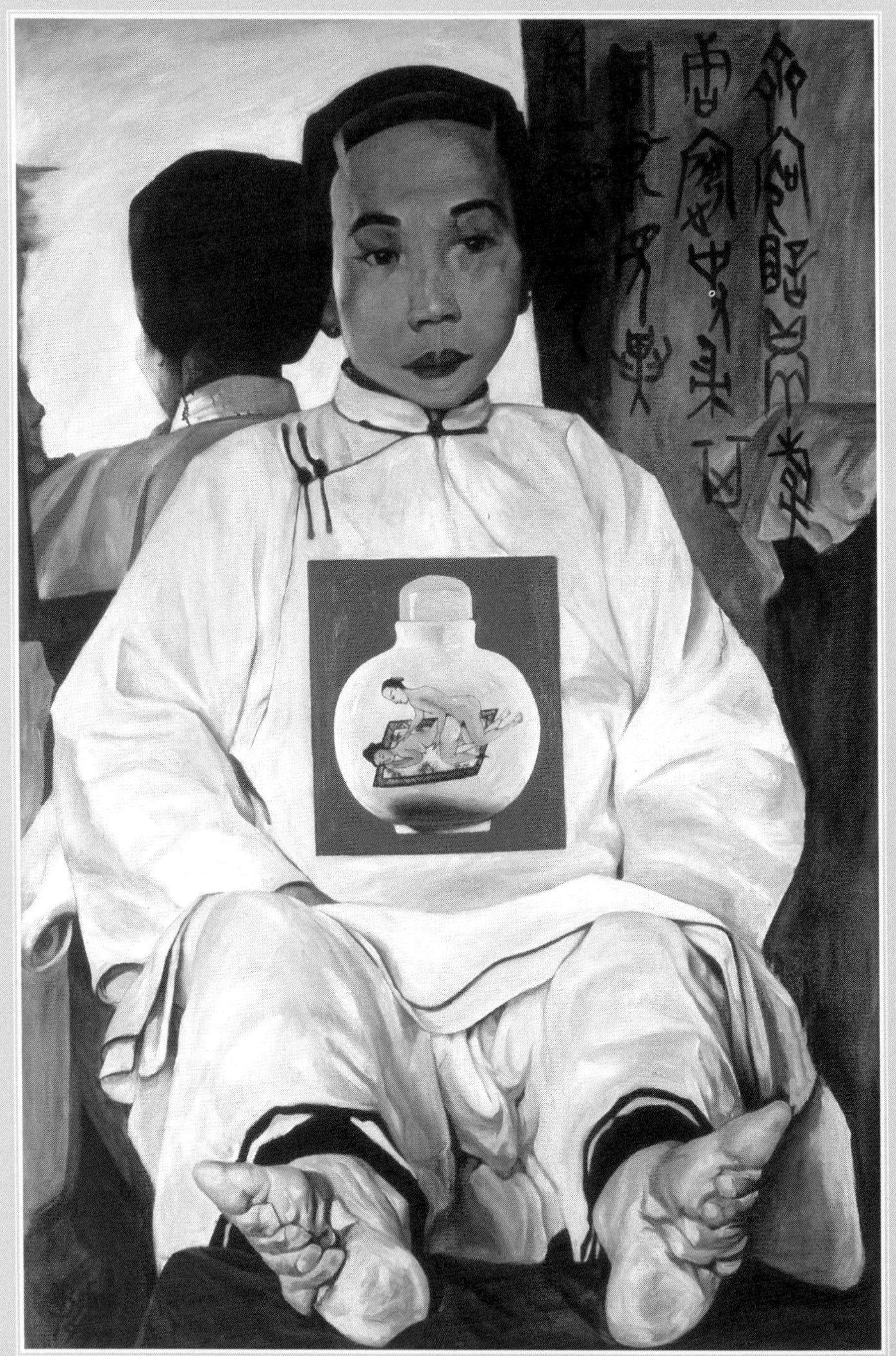

22

CULTURAL COLLISIONS

Identity and History in the Work of Hung Liu

Allison Arieff

DECEPTIVELY SIMPLE, Hung Liu's paintings address such diverse and complex issues as footbinding and Western art-historical tradition. The tension inherent in her conflicted personal identity as a Chinese-born woman artist living in the West informs her art. Liu's images of women form a cultural critique, simultaneously referring to and challenging artistic and social traditions of East and West. In basing her subject matter on Western-influenced photographs of turn-of-the-century Chinese prostitutes, Liu further objectifies representations of women as a basis for criticizing both the way "we" (Westerners) view Chinese culture and the way Chinese culture has looked at women. She assumes the difficult task of critiquing China's oppressive patriarchal system, alerting her audience to past transgressions in the hope that knowledge and awareness may serve as an impetus for change.

Political content notwithstanding, the artist's work, as Lisa Corrin points out, "cannot be reduced to the cliché of an artist longing for democracy."[1] Liu's painting style both reflects and subverts her traditional art training. Her canvases are deliberately flattened and distorted, simulating the photographic images she appropriates, while at the same time rebelling against stringent academic rendering. Forced to paint in a Social Realist style in China, she now eagerly embraces the techniques of collage, installation, and assemblage. Liu also mocks traditional Western portrayals of women by referencing the iconography and using the titles of canonical artworks such as her *Mona Lisa I*, *Madonna*, and *La Grande Odalisque*.

Liu's paintings can perhaps best be read as allegories, given their metatextuality: one text is read through another. She does not invent her imagery but rather confiscates or appropriates it from other sources. At times she may even project the photographic image onto the canvas and paint from there. In her hands, then, the image becomes something other than it was originally intended to be. Liu's manipulation of the original images lessens their intent and authoritative claim to meaning. By generating images through the reproduction of found photographs, Liu alters their significance. The women in her paintings can be viewed as more than objects for the male gaze. Her representation of prostitutes and concubines and, more recently, Qing Dynasty court figures, allows for new ways of seeing.

Figure 22.1. Hung Liu, *Virgin/Vessel*, 1990. Oil on canvas. Courtesy Bernice Stembaum Gallery, Miami, Florida.

Liu, writes Moira Roth, has "developed more fully and consciously her presentation of the interplay of gazes: European and Chinese, male and female, past and present, artist's and viewer's."[2] The struggle between opposing elements is continual. The artist explains, "Sometimes I feel more labeled than embraced, . . . labeled . . . as a minority artist, . . . an artist of color, a woman artist (feminist?). . . . I am an artist from China and in China the terms by which I am defined here make little sense."[3] She compares the process of her work to an excavation where there are so many layers that she is still trying to understand and analyze them all. Liu's move to the United States and the shift in her work from Socialist Realism to Social Realism resulted in what she describes as "a crisis of cultural collision." Perhaps out of necessity, Liu's is an art of subversion. She is attempting to invent for herself a way to practice as a Chinese artist outside of Chinese culture. The shift from her classical training in Chinese art to contemporary Western art practice has in effect become the subject of her work. She challenges and reinterprets existing social and cultural conventions so as to forge her own personal and artistic identity.

Hung Liu was born in the city of Chang Chung in northeastern China in 1948. Her father, a military officer in the Nationalist army of Chiang Kai-shek, was captured and jailed by the Communists when she was only six months old. Liu's mother was forced to divorce her husband, who had fought on the "wrong side" and was considered the enemy. Liu, an only child, met her father for the first time in 1994. Her mother still lives in China. Liu received most of her education in Beijing. In 1966, when she was just eighteen and looking forward to college, the Cultural Revolution began. For years the schools were closed. Considered an intellectual because of her high school education, Liu was sent to a military farm in the countryside for reeducation. There, with other "intellectuals," a diverse group that ran the gamut from actors to junior high school students, she was forced to work in rice, corn, and wheat fields and to take care of horses as a means of ridding her of elitist thought. Later, as an artist she was perceived as too independent and was thus periodically subjected to reeducation programs aimed at eradicating politically unpopular ideas. She never stopped thinking about art, though. She made the best of her circumstances, befriending peasants who realized that she and other girls had been sent to the fields as punishment not for bad behavior but simply for being from the city. Ironically, her forced peasant status worked to her advantage. In 1972, toward the end of the Cultural Revolution, she was able to enter the Revolutionary Entertainment Department at Beijing Teachers College under a policy that provided education to the working class.

As an art student at college, Liu had no creative freedom. Under Communist rule, art was not about individual expression or inspiration. The true purpose of art, according to Mao Tse-tung, was to serve the masses. The "rich legacy and the good traditions" from China's past were to be reappropriated for the people and transformed into something revolutionary. Art has an assigned position in Communist Party politics. Cultural and artistic policy is still set by the Department of Propaganda. All art publicly exhibited or reproduced is required to meet current art policy standards. "When I was in China," Liu explains, "artists were expected to be the tools of propaganda. Abstract and individualistic paintings are not acceptable in schools or for public exhibition."[4]

But Liu drew secretly using a small hidden paint box. She was subsequently criticized for paying too much attention to art and not enough to politics. Her first job upon graduation was teaching art at an experimental school where her young students were instructed how to paint the red flag of Communism. She wanted to continue her education, but only classes related to the revolution were offered. She studied books on Western and Chinese art history and criticism on her own, eventually making her eligible to attend the Central Academy of Fine Arts in Beijing.

Once at the academy, Liu wanted to study mural painting. Because of its roots in Buddhist and Taoist traditions, mural painting seemed at first to allow for some measure of artistic freedom and individual style. However, the muralists, too, came to be considered a

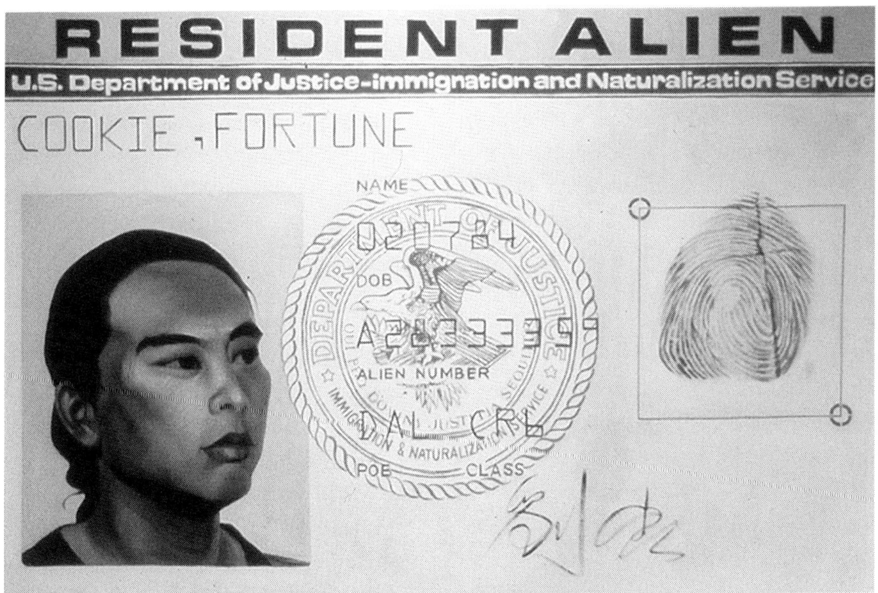

Figure 22.2. Hung Liu, *Resident Alien*, 1988. Oil on canvas. Courtesy of the artist. (Photo: Ben Blackwell.)

threat to the officially entrenched styles of Socialist Realism and Chinese ink painting, and were forced to produce propaganda.[5] "Everybody hated politics because it meant we had to obey everything the government, the party said. We tried to get as far away from politics as we could," Liu indicates.[6] Although pressured to glorify party leadership, she instead produced a mural celebrating Chinese music—a little personal rebellion against authority that would come to characterize her later work. The mural still stands at the Central Academy. Unhappy with the People's Republic of China's requirements for art—that it be completely politicized, its messages blatantly obvious and propagandizing, and anonymous[7]—Liu applied and was accepted to graduate school at the University of California, San Diego, in 1981.

It took nearly four years for Liu to get a passport and permission to leave. It was difficult for her Chinese friends to understand why she would want to go to the United States, since Western art was "degenerate." But she persisted, saying that she just wanted an opportunity to look and learn. Meanwhile, in San Diego, the university waited for the

"Chinese artist who never showed up." Arriving at last in the United States in 1984, she found the transition somewhat eased because she had learned some English in elementary school. But once given the freedom of expression she had so wished for, Liu realized she did not really know what she wanted to do with it. She continued doing what she knew best—murals—and waited to see how her work would evolve.[8] Liu credits her advisor, artist and critic Allan Kaprow, for changing the way she thought about and approached art.

Liu's first major work in the United States was a mural and site-specific installation at the Capp Street Project art gallery in San Francisco. This 1988 work was a turning point for the artist. She had become interested in historical photographs of Chinese immigrants in San Francisco's Chinatown and wanted to relate their experiences to her own. One result was *Resident Alien* (1988; fig. 22.2), a self-portrait constructed around a green card belonging to the immigrant "Fortune Cookie" (alias Hung Liu). Text accompanying the piece reads: "Five-thousand-year-old culture on my back. Late-twentieth-century world in my face." The themes and styles she explored in this work, which combined the traditional medium of painting with the display of objects to create complete environments, were pursued through the early 1990s. Although this juxtaposition of elements is common to much postmodern art, in Liu's work it resonates with personal conflicts of identity. In *Resident Alien* the image on the green card reappropriates her own identification card photo, and her ironic use of the name "Fortune Cookie" is sexually connotative and signifies Western manipulations of Chinese culture. Liu views the fortune cookie as an apt symbol of her status because "it is a hybrid— it exists between cultures . . . it's not Chinese and it's not American."[9] (The fortune cookies reappear later, piled atop railroad tracks, in her 1994 mixed-media installation *Jiu Jin Shan: Old Gold Mountain* at the M. H. De Young Memorial Museum in San Francisco.)

Resident Alien also signals the beginning of the incorporation of photography in her art. Working from photographs rather than live models was discouraged in China, and Liu views her use of photography as artistic defiance, a rebellion against the academy and her education. Liu's primary source of imagery comes from books of photographs. One such book, *The Face of China*, published in the United States, features images taken by foreign tourists in China between 1860 and 1912 (these pictures have never been seen in China). Two other books, which she found in China during a 1991 visit, contained images of famous prostitutes, a kind of catalogue of availability; they had amazingly survived the Cultural Revolution's book burnings. She mines the old photographs for information and insight: "I put them through rituals. I see it almost like research or some kind of scientific observation. I move from square inch to square inch. I find out a lot of things."[10] Liu returned again to China in the summer of 1993, discovering more pictures, some from magazines dating from the 1920s to the 1940s. Her 1995 exhibition *The Last Dynasty*, at the Steinbaum Krauss Gallery in New York, featured imagery culled from historic photographs documenting Qing courtiers (1644–1911).

Liu's found images of China are reprocessed with contemporary Western materials and modes of display but at the same time refer to traditional Chinese art-making processes, such as copying as an act of homage. Her simulation of photography allows the works to preserve their documentary status even when they are being interpreted formally. Whereas the paintings of the early 1990s were often quite finished, truer to their photographic source, later pieces give increasing primacy to the painterly gesture. "Saturated with oil and mediums, my paintings sort of perform themselves," she explains. "They drip, they stain, and wash the images in a way that opens them to time, the literal time of gravity pulling oil to the bottom edge of the canvas."[11]

Liu seeks to amplify "the historical moment, bringing it into focus, exposing its . . . humanness" to ensure that the viewer understands that these images reflect reality.[12] She feels that her images of nineteenth- and twentieth-century Chinese women reveal the sufferings of these women through centuries of spiritual and physical oppression. Her desire is to expose the generations-old wounds of her mother, grandmother, and great-grandmother. "Although I do not have bound feet, the invisible spiritual burdens fall heavy on me," she notes. "I communicate with the characters in my paintings, prostitutes—these completely subjugated people—with reverence, sympathy and awe. They had no real names. Probably no children. I want to make up stories for them. Who were they? Did they leave any trace in history?"[13]

Liu's desire is to give these women their place in history. Her paintings expose the pain of the traditional roles women were assigned, regardless of their status, according to the "three obediences" of Confucianism—to father, to husband, and to son. Before Communism, Confucianism had provided the model for proper family life. It prescribed a patriarchal, patrilineal, and patrilocal family system. The roles, privileges, duties, and responsibilities of the individual were dictated by sex, age, and generation. Confucianism officially sanctioned the dominance of men over women and old over young. Individual identity was virtually a nonissue: one's needs

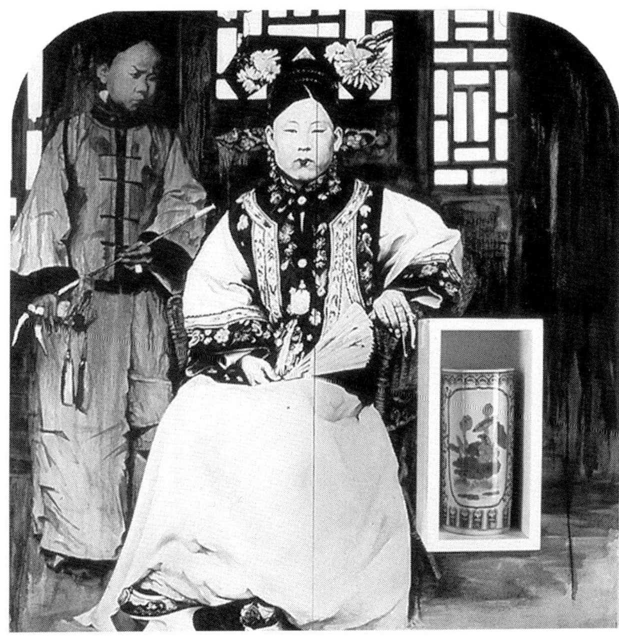

Figure 22.3. Hung Liu, *Half of the Sky*, 1991. Oil on canvas, lacquered wood, and ceramic. Collection of Garen and Shari Staglin, Rutherford, California. (Photo: Ben Blackwell.)

were subordinated to those of the family group.[14] Females suffered greatly under this system: often they were not named. Their lack of autonomy and their exclusion from public life were considered essential for the preservation of civilization itself.[15] An ancient ode confirms this: "The wise man founded the city; but the wise woman destroys it. . . . Disaster does not descend from Heaven; it comes from Woman."[16]

Conditions were supposed to change under Communism. Although Mao once commented that "women can hold up half the sky," women were granted little power or autonomy under the Communist regime. In *Half of the Sky* (1991; fig. 22.3), Liu responds with irony to the contradiction between what is said and what is actually meant. The Manchu woman, who appears to be a concubine, has bound feet and long fingernails and is garishly made up. Her formal attire immobilizes her—she appears unable to rise from her chair. The servant to her left symbolizes the woman's wealth and status. Regardless of her social standing, she possesses no power or autonomy. She is as elaborately decorated and objectified as the vase to her left. The work's monochromatic rendering in tones

of blue adds to its status as a historical document. The blue is cold and distant, echoing the icy stare on the woman's face.

Nowhere was women's subjugation more explicitly expressed than in the practice of footbinding. Popularized in the Sung Dynasty (960–1279), footbinding is chilling in its associations of manipulation and confinement. Liu views bound feet as a vivid metaphor for both the shaping of women as objects of male desire and the distortion of the larger society through various forms of domination. Disturbing as the practice now seems, for centuries footbinding was easily justified. Initially, its appeal was purely aesthetic. Courtesans and wealthy women had bound feet, women who worked did not: it was a marker of class, a symbol of conspicuous leisure. But as the treatment of women became increasingly oppressive, footbinding was tied to a wide range of behavioral expectations. It was an indicator of good breeding and became necessary for obtaining suitable marriage proposals.[17] Men were thus guaranteed subservient sex objects, while women were left with a pair of three-inch stumps that caused lifelong pain and

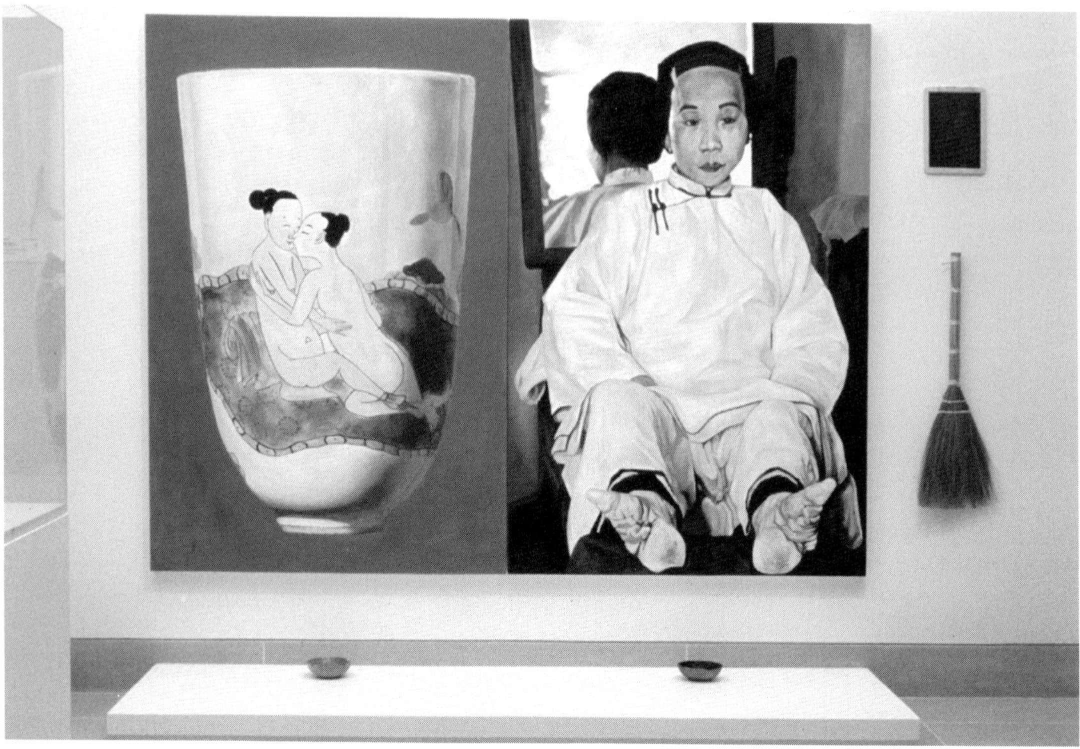

Figure 22.4. Hung Liu, *Goddess of Love/Goddess of Liberty*, 1989. Oil on canvas and mixed media. Dallas Museum of Art, Dallas, Texas. (Photo: Tom Jenkins.)

made even the simple act of walking excruciating.

Footbinding transformed woman into a fetish and thus a pure object of desire. Liu's paintings of prostitutes or concubines with startlingly tiny feet (termed "golden lilies" or "lotus petals") posing for clients document this phenomenon. Freud saw the custom of footbinding as a symbolic castration of women, a claim that, according to French philosopher Julia Kristeva, Chinese civilization was unique in admitting.[18] Kristeva takes this idea further, explaining that "if by castration we understand the necessity for something to be excluded so that a socio-symbolic order may be built—the cutting off of one part of the whole so that the whole as such may be constituted as an alliance of homogeneous parts—it is interesting to note that for Chinese civilization, this superfluous quantity was found in women."[19] The various oppressive practices directed at the female population—

female infanticide, filial piety, chaste widowhood, namelessness, lack of educational opportunities—sustained China's long-established male hierarchical system.

Most of the women Liu depicts have bound feet. But in *Goddess of Love/Goddess of Liberty* (1989; fig. 22.4), she takes an especially rebellious swing at her country's authoritarianism by showing a woman with her bound feet exposed. The two-paneled painting juxtaposes a Ming vase decorated with a nude couple making love on the left with a seated woman, solitary and complacent, as if resigned to her fate, on the right. The vivid red of the background is the color of fertility and of happiness in traditional China but also the symbolic color of Communism. The vase (or vessel) is a recurrent form in Liu's work and is either incorporated in painted form or as an actual object placed near the canvas. For her, the vases/vessels "symbolize the fact that women, especially prostitutes, were treated as mere decorations, inhuman objects, beautifully made up, but empty and useless, placed passively in the corner of the room." These containers are often empty, in keeping with the ancient Chinese proverb "To be empty of knowledge is a female virtue." The objects that hang on the wall to the right of the canvas further affirm the position of women in China. A child's chalkboard is blank—a symbol of the blank slate of female education. The small broom beneath it represents women's work but can also be read as "a symbolic tool used to sweep away disorder and memory."[20] A figure with a broom was also a traditional Chinese character for wife.[21] The woman is depicted in monochromatic sepia tones, again enhancing the historicity of the work. Clearly something about this woman resonated for Liu. Her image appears again in *Virgin/Vessel* (1990; fig. 22.1), her chest emblazoned with a symbolically charged scarlet square. Set within the square is a blue vase painted with an erotic scene. The woman is featured yet again in *Bonsai* (1992), juxtaposed against Liu's re-creation of an ancient Chinese medical illustration.

The woman's mangled feet carry the most profound message here. Never revealed, the bound foot was considered the most erotic part of the body. A special stocking covered it at all times—even during intercourse. Chinese artists might have depicted female genitalia but never a naked, crippled foot.[22] Liu subverts this false sense of propriety by metaphorically unwrapping the bandages. In exposing the feet, she exposes the woman's pain. Liu's paintings are didactic in their efforts to inform the viewer of the roles and representations of women in Chinese history. "I'm glad I didn't have to bind my feet," she explains, "but inequality is still there." Some viewers do not appreciate Liu's efforts. An elderly Chinese man stormed out of an exhibition in San Francisco after inquiring at the front desk why Liu had exposed only the ugly aspects of old China and not its tradition of beautiful landscape and flower paintings. Liu was not surprised by this reaction. "I don't expect the gentlemen of our traditionally patriarchal society, who are

so used to treating women as inferiors, to be happy to see the pain that (was) caused those women."[23]

With their references to European art-historical tradition, Liu's paintings also form a critique of the way women are represented in Western culture. Some titles, and the passive, reclining poses she uses, play on "masterpieces" such as Leonardo's *Mona Lisa*, Ingres's *Grande Odalisque* (see fig. 9.2, p. 188), and Manet's *Olympia*. Such depictions of passive women are not part of Chinese tradition. Although women are often idealized, they usually are engaged in some activity—palace-style beauties swatting butterflies or enthusiastic Communist Party members working in the field.

The image of the woman in *La Grande Odalisque* (1992; fig. 22.5) is taken from the book *The Face of China*. Liu makes the photograph her own by her use of color, objects, and the gestural paint drips at the bottom of the canvas. She presents here an elaborate stage set, adding an element of theatricality to the work. The canvas rests on a painted platform with generic "Oriental" vases filled with gilt flowers at either end and a long-stemmed gilded calla lily placed in front. The inanimate objects contrast with the sexually animated woman, but parallels can be drawn between the two as well. Both the woman and the objects are viewed as possessions; both are used for decorative and utilitarian purposes. "These kinds of flowers don't have a life," Liu says. "They're so highly polished and decorative, but cold and detached."[24] The same could be said for the young woman in the photograph. In Chinese culture, flowers are associated with women and beauty. Ellen Johnston Laing has described, for example, how butterflies (associated with males) landing on flowers became a way of choosing sexual partners during the traditional Flower Morning Festival.[25] Flowers symbolize fertility and sexuality and often represent female genitalia. Prostitutes were frequently assigned "flower" names such as White Orchard or Sweet Lily. Most important, every element in this work— the vases, the flowers, and the woman—is put on display. Liu's *Olympia* (1992) is similar to her *Odalisque* with its reclining subject and floral display. It makes

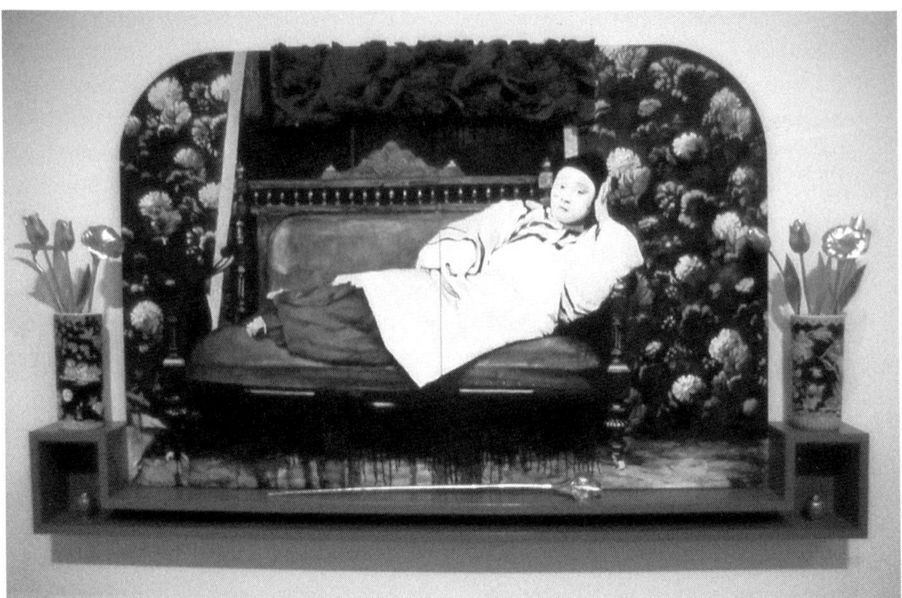

Figure 22.5. Hung Liu, *La Grande Odalisque*, 1992. Oil on canvas, lacquered wood, ceramic, and antiques. Collection of Eric and Barbara Dobkin, New York. (Photo: Ben Blackwell.)

reference, of course, to Manet's scandalous study of Victorine Meurent, whose confrontational gaze caused an uproar in the staid French salons.

At first glance, Liu's passive images seem to cater to the male gaze, as did the paintings on which they are based. The confrontational expressions of her subjects, however, subvert that gaze, as does the fact that these works have been painted by a woman. Witness the confrontational sexuality of the 1995 painting *Cherry Lips* (fig. 22.6). "The women look directly at the camera, which means that when I look at them they look back at me," Liu explains. "A man put them there on a couch, a chair, with the intention to sell them as products. The women had no control. But now that man is gone, yet the imagery of these women is left. It has survived through time and space, even a revolution. When I felt the women looking at me, somehow I just wanted to empower them."[26] In reappropriating or "taking" these images from the patriarchal gaze, Liu gives something back to the passive women who have been objectified throughout history. She catalogues past transgressions in an effort to avoid their recurrence.

Liu's work attempts to mount "a sustained and far-reaching political critique of contemporary representational systems, which have had an over-determined effect in the social production of sexual difference," as espoused by Griselda Pollock.[27] Ways must be discovered to address women as subjects rather than as objects of male desire, fantasy, and hatred. Sexual divisions have resulted from the construction of sexual difference as a socially significant axis of meaning. Pollock explains that these constructions are constantly enforced by representations created in the ideological practices we call culture. Pictures, photographs, films, and so forth are addressed to us, the viewer, in an attempt to win our identification with the represented versions of masculinity and femininity.[28] These representations perpetuate existing roles. The need, therefore, is to deconstruct those roles and create new representations of gender and identity. I believe that Liu's work takes positive steps toward that goal.

A symposium titled "(re) Orienting: Self Representations of Asian American Women through the Visual Arts," held in New York City in 1991, raised

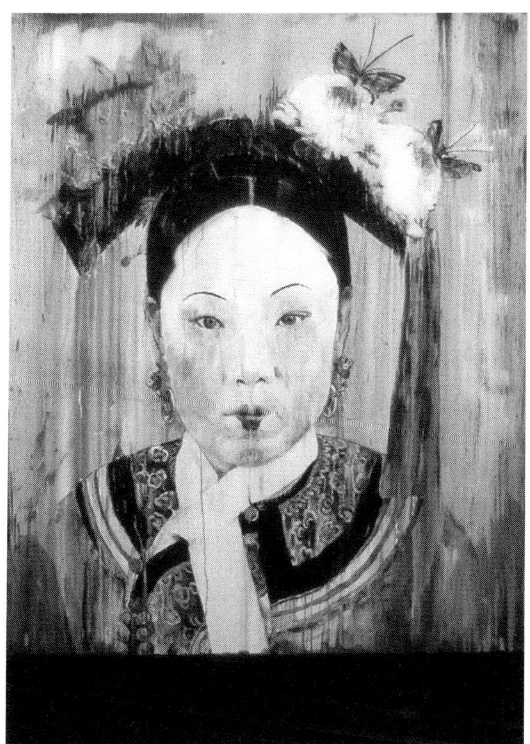

Figure 22.6. Hung Liu, *Cherry Lips*, 1995. Oil on canvas. Collection of Nancy and Peter Gennet, Napa, California. (Photo: Ben Blackwell.)

the issue that for Asian women in a predominantly white society, it is race, not gender that is often seen as the primary area of conflict and concern. Panel members commented that the objectification of Asian women, based not just on gender but even more significantly on race, highlights the need for a feminist and multicultural agenda more sensitive to the needs of various groups.[29] Liu has, of course, experienced this dilemma firsthand. In *Women of Color* (1991), she interprets the politically correct cliché literally. Three bust-length images of Asian women, one red, one yellow, and one blue, are placed frieze-like on the canvas. A shelf holding three vessels in the corresponding colors is installed below the painting. Color here becomes an arbitrary, meaningless distinction. Approaching such a volatile issue with humor challenges the viewer to consider the issue of multiculturalism as more than skin deep.

Just as Liu's paintings examine how the concept of femininity is socially constructed, they also explore how the West has constructed "the Orient." Edward Said explains that the outsider's knowledge of the Orient consists merely of that outsider's representation of it. The Orient has been presented in binary opposition to the Occident and has provided the most recurring images of the "other." The relationship between the two cultures, like the relationship between men and women, has been one of power, of domination, and of varying degrees of a complex hegemony.[30] By positing the Orient as "different" and therefore culturally inferior, the West assumed a sense of authority over it.

"The Orient," Said writes, "was almost a European invention, and had been since antiquity a place of romance, exotic beings, haunting memories and landscapes, remarkable experiences."[31] Numerous European artists, among them Gérôme, Delacroix, Ingres, and Manet, invented their own versions of an exotic Orient. Linda Nochlin has suggested that for Western artists, the Orient existed either "as an actual place to be mystified with effects of realness" or as "a project of the imagination, a fantasy space or screen onto which strong desires—erotic, sadistic, or both—could be projected with impunity." The function of such representations was to assure the viewer that the "Orientals" depicted were "irredeemably different from, more backward than, and culturally inferior to those who constructed and consumed the product."[32]

Liu's found photographs further reveal this fascination with the exoticism and difference of "the Orient." Depicted in the images are scenes of torture and field labor, veiled brides and rigidly posed aging dowagers. Everyday life is selectively filtered to distance East from West, voiding shared viewpoints. Present are images of "bad women" (the title of one of Liu's exhibitions)—prostitutes or courtesans who also serve to reinforce the moral superiority of the Western photographer. Images of Asian women have long occupied a place in Western imagination, be they "exotic" sex object, Dragon Lady, or today's submissive mail-order bride. Liu and other Asian American women have attempted to respond to these stereotypical representations by finding alternate ways to "name" themselves in a culture unable to encompass the complexity of their experience.[33]

Liu's images do not always succeed on a visual and emotional level. At times the work is too didactic, weighted down perhaps by her anger and the sheer volume of information the viewer needs to process. At times, her message seems imperceptible, especially to those who know nothing of the artist's history. Her use of various mediums and modes of display is at times too referential to the works of other postmodern artists. But, in general, Liu has successfully fused Eastern and Western traditions, combining the graceful elements of traditional Chinese painting with Western style. The juxtaposition seems inevitable. "I am trying to invent a way of allowing myself to practice as a Chinese artist outside of Chinese culture," she explains. "Perhaps the displaced meanings of that practice—reframed within this culture—are meaningful *because* they are displaced."[34]

Liu's work can be read as a struggle for artistic identity but, even more important, as a struggle to define her conflicted personal identity: "I often feel suspended between the two cultures, but I see this as a unique position, hopefully a situation that will energize me," she says. "I can look at things from multiple points of view. It is a position I embrace rather than feel bitterness about."[35]

Liu's paintings of Chinese women focus on the persistence of memory. It is of paramount importance to her that the experiences of her subjects not be forgotten. Recovering the history of these women acknowledges their relevance both then and now in the female struggle for equality. It also aids in forging a place for contemporary Asian American women. Liu continues to work toward her goal of functioning "much as the ancient scholar-painters of my homeland did, so that my art is the consequence of a research process in which images from the past are recovered, re-evaluated, recognized, and re-presented in terms relevant to my own and I believe to our multicultural experience today."[36]

NOTES

1. Lisa G. Corrin, "In Search of Miss Sallie Chu," in *Canton: The Baltimore Series*, exh. cat. (Baltimore: Contemporary, 1995), n.p.

2. Moira Roth, "Interactions and Collisions: Reflections on the Art of Hung Liu," in announcement for exhibit of the same name at the Bernice Steinbaum Gallery, New York, May 23–June 27, 1992.

3. Cited in Margo Machida, "(re) Orienting," *Harbour* 1, no. 3 (August–October 1991): 37–43.

4. Cited in Xiarorong Li, "Painting the Pain," *Human Rights Tribune* 3, no. 1 (Spring 1992): 12.

5. Joan Lebold Cohen, "Art in China Today," *Art News*, Summer 1980, 64.

6. Interview with Hung Liu, September 1993.

7. Ellen Johnston Laing, *The Winking Owl: Art in the People's Republic of China* (Berkeley: University of California Press, 1988), 64.

8. Interview with Hung Liu, *Society for the Encouragement of Contemporary Art (SECA) Award* (San Francisco: Museum of Modern Art, 1992), n.p.

9. Cited in Robin Cembalest, "Goodbye, Columbus?" *Art News*, October 1991, 108.

10. Liu, in *SECA Award*, exh. brochure (San Francisco: San Francisco Museum of Modern Art, 1992).

11. Hung Liu, Artist Statement, *The Last Dynasty* (New York: Steinbaum-Krauss Gallery, 1995), n.p.

12. Jim Edwards, *Precarious Links* (San Antonio, Tex.: San Antonio Museum of Art, 1990), 26.

13. Cited in Li, "Painting the Pain," 10.

14. Judith Stacey, *Patriarchy and Socialist Revolution in China* (Berkeley: University of California Press, 1983), 32–33.

15. Ibid., 39.

16. Hu Shih, "Women's Place in Chinese History," in *Chinese Women through Chinese Eyes*, ed. Li Yu-ning (Armonk, N.Y.: M. E. Sharpe, 1992), 5.

17. Alison R. Drucker, "The Influence of Western Women on the Anti-Footbinding Movement: 1840–1911," in *Women in China: Current Directions in Historical Scholarship*, ed. R. W. Guisso and S. Johanessen (Youngstown, N.Y.: Philo Press, 1981), 179–80.

18. Julia Kristeva refers to Freud's perception of footbinding in *About Chinese Women* (London: Marion Boyars, 1977).

19. Ibid., 83.

20. Edwards, *Precarious Links*, 27.

21. Stacey, *Patriarchy and Socialist Revolution in China*, 39.

22. Kristeva, *About Chinese Women*, 82.

23. Cited in Li, "Painting the Pain," 11.

24. Liu, *SECA Art Award*.

25. Ellen Johnston Laing, "Notes on Ladies Wearing Flowers in Their Hair," *Orientations* 21, no. 2 (February 1990): 37.

26. Personal interview with Hung Liu, September 1993.

27. Griselda Pollock, *Vision and Difference: Femininity, Feminism and the Histories of Art* (London: Routledge, 1988), 15.

28. Ibid., 33–34.

29. See Margo Machida's summary of the event in "(re) Orienting," 42.

30. Edward W. Said, *Orientalism* (New York: Random House, 1979), 1–5.

31. Ibid., 3–5

32. Linda Nochlin, "The Imaginary Orient," in *The Politics of Vision* (New York: Icon, 1989), 51.

33. Machida, "(re) Orienting," 37.

34. Lucy Lippard, *Mixed Blessings: New Art in a Multicultural America* (New York: Pantheon, 1990), 137.

35. Interview with Hung Liu, September 1993.

36. Hung Lui, Artist's Statement, Capp Street Project, San Francisco, 1988.

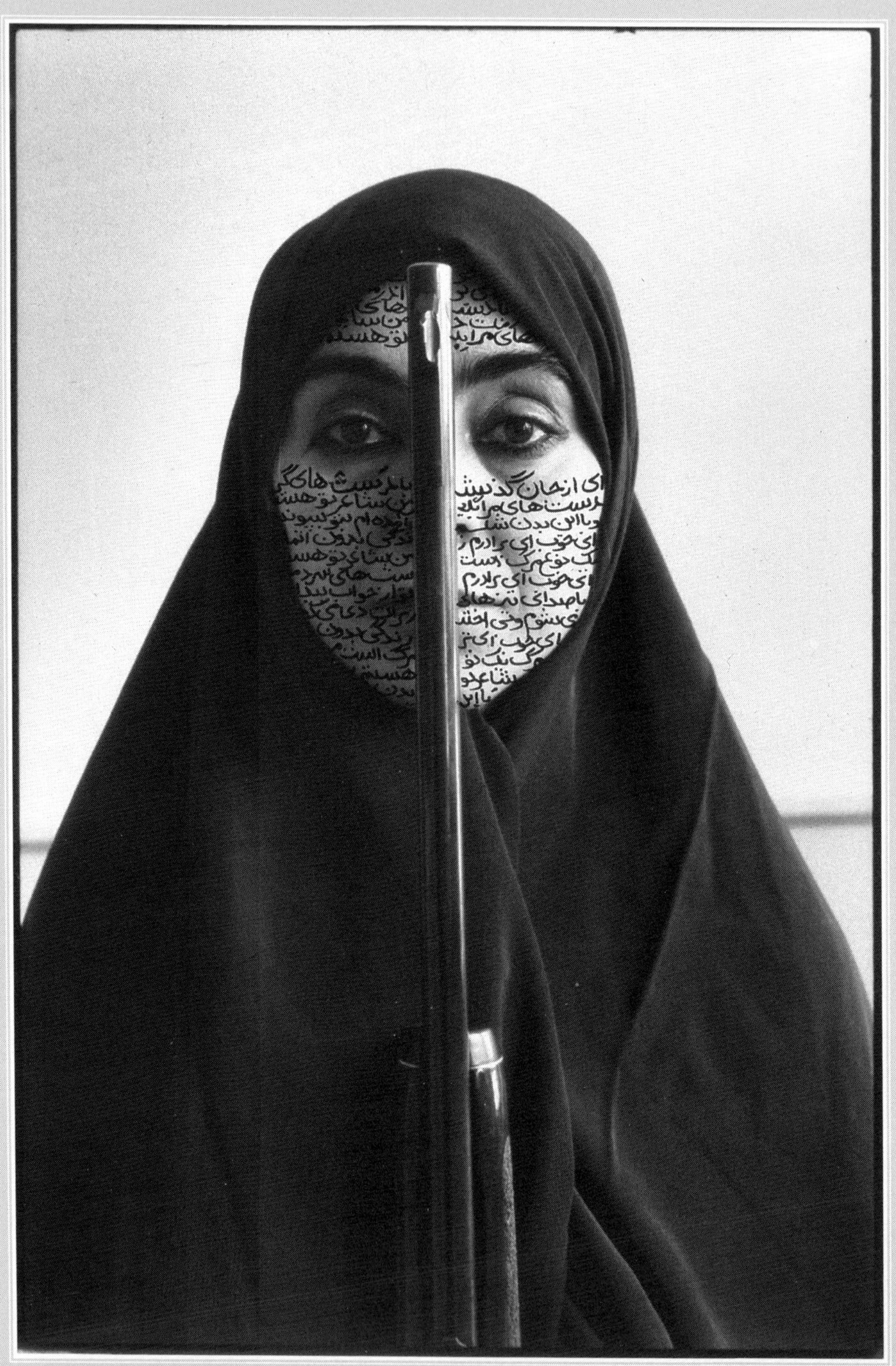

23

SHIRIN NESHAT

Double Vision

John B. Ravenal

SHIRIN NESHAT'S first video trilogy—*Turbulent, Rapture,* and *Fervor*—represents a sophisticated meditation on gender and culture, and on the central role of vision in constructing identity. Made between 1998 and 2000, these works build on several decades of feminist and postcolonial theory whose critiques of patriarchy and imperialism have profoundly affected the definition of subjectivity. One of the main issues linking these critical theories is representation: who is represented, how, and by whom? Neshat's work creates a subtle and far reaching narrative of women in Islamic society, made from the perspective of an Iranian-born artist living in the United States. Appearing to flirt with discredited notions of exoticism, essentialism, and binary opposition (us/them, male/female), she grounds her pieces in these familiar tropes, only to subvert their authority.

Recognized today as one of the premier figures working in video art, Neshat first became known in the mid 1990s for her controversial photographs of veiled, gun-toting Middle Eastern women (frequently the artist herself). These images conflated ambivalent Western views of the Orient as exotic and spiritual yet also irrational and violent—a split perspective that has only intensified over the past decade.[1] Neshat's

stark but artfully composed works with titles such as *Faceless, Rebellious Silence* (fig. 23.1) and *Seeking Martyrdom* posed a challenge.[2] Rather than reject deep-seated stereotypes, they seemed to embrace prevailing Western views of the Middle East. Inhabiting the stereotypes allowed Neshat to explore the close connection among violence, politics, religion, and spirituality in extremist Islamic practice, as well as the contradictory status of women: subservient to men in most public spheres but compelled to participate fully in revolution and war. Neshat's work offered no clear road map to unravel these complex issues. Instead, she packed multiple themes into single images, encapsulating the larger, combustible debate. As she has said, "I see my work as a visual discourse on the subjects of feminism and contemporary Islam—a discourse that puts certain myths and realities to the test, claiming that they are far more complex than most of us have imagined. . . . I prefer raising questions as opposed to answering them as I am totally unable to do otherwise, and I am not interested in creating works that simply state my personal political point of view."[3]

Neshat's photographs grew out of her experience as a displaced Iranian viewing her country through the filter of cultural homelessness. She was born in

This essay builds upon a text published in *Outer and Inner Space: Pipilotti Rist, Shirin Neshat, Jane and Louise Wilson, and the History of Video Art* (Richmond: Virginia Museum of Fine Arts, 2002). By permission of the author and the Virginia Museum of Fine Arts.

Figure 23.1. Shirin Neshat, *Rebellious Silence,* 1994. Black-and-white RC print and ink. © Shirin Neshat. Courtesy Barbara Gladstone Gallery. (Photo: Larry Barns.)

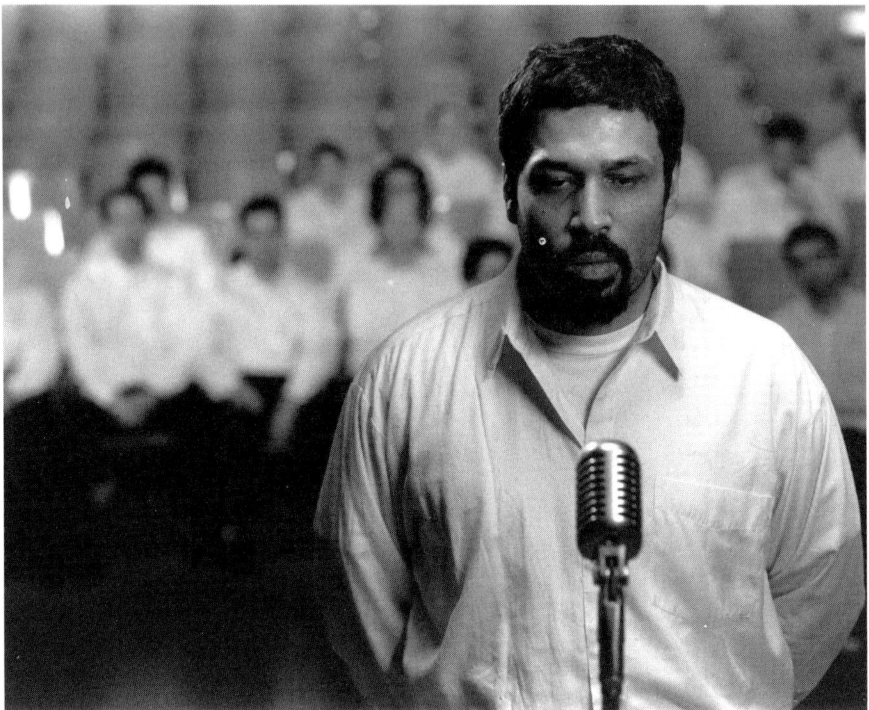

Figure 23.2. Shirin Neshat, *Turbulent*, 1998. Production still. © Shirin Neshat. Courtesy Barbara Gladstone Gallery. (Photo: Larry Barns.)

Qazvin in 1957 and at age seventeen was sent abroad to finish her studies, like many children of educated families at the height of Iran's modernization drive. She majored in art at the University of California at Berkeley, where she earned both undergraduate and graduate degrees. In 1979, the Iranian Revolution stranded her in the United States when it transformed her homeland from a secular society led by a Western-educated but autocratic shah to an Islamic society led by a fundamentalist cleric. Not until 1990, the year after Ayatollah Khomeini's death, was Neshat finally able to return for a visit. She was stunned by the transformation, saying, "I had never been in a country that was so ideologically based,"[4] and further, "It was shocking. Everyone had gone through this major identity crisis. Before I left they were Iranian-Persians, and now they were strict Muslims. Visually everything was black and white, and women had to be in dark clothes."[5] That visit inspired Neshat to begin making art again, a practice she had abandoned

around the time that she moved to New York in 1983. Her photographs represented a way for the artist, who had now lived half her life outside Iran, to try to understand the transformation of her homeland, the changed role of women, and her status in relation to the loss of a culture that had formed her.

Soon Neshat sought ways to extend her photographic practice by making time-based sequences of images using video. The first, a four-minute single projection called *Anchorage* (1996), continued Neshat's interest in extremist Islam. Like her photographs, it shows the artist standing in darkness with all body parts covered except for her face, hands, and feet. She engages in three sequential actions, each an iconic gesture associated with contemporary Middle Eastern culture: prayer and recitation from the Quran, firing a gun pointed directly at the viewer, and a meditative dance based on the whirling of Sufi dervishes. The following year, Neshat produced *The Shadow under the Web*, a simultaneous projection of

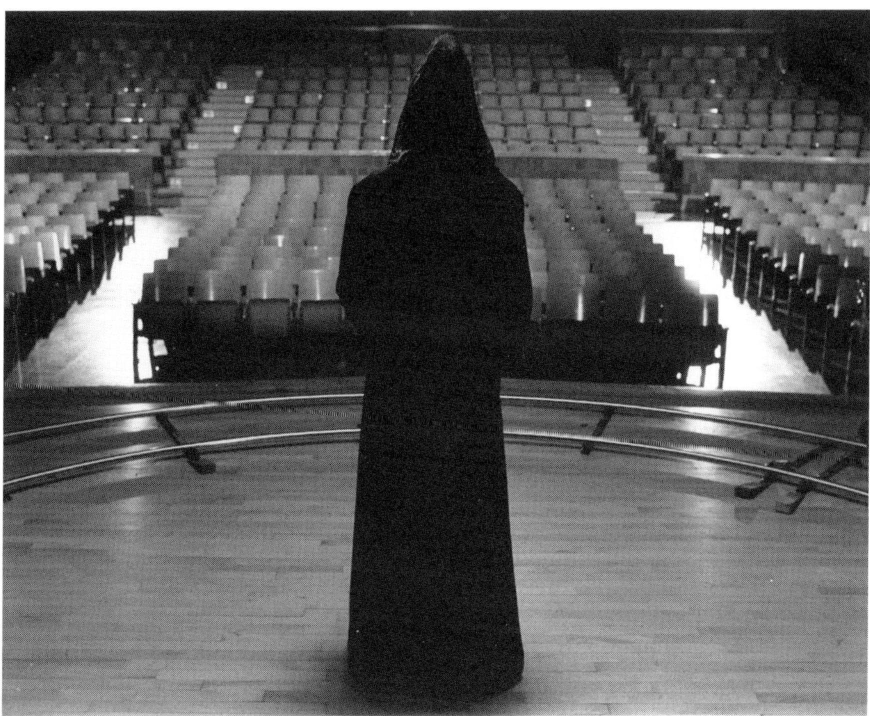

Figure 23.3. Shirin Neshat, *Turbulent*, 1998. Production still. © Shirin Neshat. Courtesy Barbara Gladstone Gallery. (Photo: Larry Barns.)

four videos on separate walls around a room.[6] Recorded in Istanbul, Turkey, they show the veiled artist running endlessly through different sites representing the conflict between tradition and modernity, sacred and profane, public and private. With this work, Neshat's focus shifted from the poetics of Islamic extremism to issues of cultural uprootedness and of gender in relation to spatial boundaries—themes that have taken the central place in her subsequent work.

With the appearance of her next video installation, *Turbulent* (1998), Neshat established a reputation as one of the top artists working in a medium that had blossomed during the 1990s to become a dominant international art form.[7] Although conceived as a stand-alone project, *Turbulent* came to be seen by the artist as the first in a trilogy of two-screen video installations that also includes *Rapture* (1999) and *Fervor* (2000).[8] Each of these short (ten to thirteen minutes long) black-and-white pieces explores a different facet of fundamentalist Islam's social segregation of

men and women. Unable to work in Iran, however, Neshat filmed in the Moroccan port town of Essaouira. She used 16mm film on location, achieving the pearly, saturated tones of early cinema, and then transferred the film to video to make the precisely synchronized installations of paired projections.

The works in the trilogy are united by a fascination with relationships: between men and women, between individuals and culture, and between people and space. Each of the works is constructed around a set of paired oppositions that serves as its formal structure and as a pervasive metaphor. In *Turbulent* (figs. 23.2 and 23.3), cultural and gender oppositions are suggested by the English and Farsi (Persian) titles on facing screens, then by the unfolding events in two theaters, one half filled with an audience of men dressed in black pants and white shirts, the other empty. The viewer's perspective is from the rear of each stage, looking past vintage 1950s-type microphones toward the seats. When the solo performers enter, one male, the other female, they appear with their backs to the viewer. The men clap and the male singer turns away from them to face out, performing across the room toward the woman, but also appearing to address the viewer in between the two projections. His impassioned song is a traditional expression of divine love based on a thirteenth-century Sufi poem by Persian mystic Jalal al-Din Rumi.[9] The woman remains turned away and motionless throughout, a mysterious specter whose black-clad form reveals nothing.

As the first song concludes and the applause dies down, a deep and earthy sound begins from the opposite wall. The male performer returns from bowing to his audience and again looks out across the space, now with an expression of curiosity. The camera on the woman's side begins to slowly circle, revealing the side of her face. As her song gathers momentum, the camera circulates more actively and zooms and retreats, in contrast to the ever-fixed view on the male side. Her song is a dynamic sound collage of layered, reverberating vocalizations, mixing ancient forms of expression such as ululating with contemporary experimentation.[10] Wordless and universal, it erupts with a range of voices and depth of emotion that seem to express all women's experience under oppressive regimes. The camera's movements continually remind us that she sings to an empty theater. But her audience extends to the spellbound men across the room and incorporates viewers of the installation, who become her real-time audience. In its final phase, her song erupts in an electronically enhanced, all-consuming shriek like a low-flying flock of birds, then all is calm. No applause greets her, but the men's stunned silence conveys awareness of having encountered a profound truth in the guise of the unfettered female voice.

The cathartic nature of the female singer's expression and the men's awed and alarmed response underscore a widespread view, shared by Neshat, that the discourse of religious, political, and cultural identity in fundamentalist Islam is centered on the visibility of women.[11] Shiite Muslim law forbids women to sing in public, and the female character's performance in *Turbulent* is a brave act of rebellion. At the same time, she has waited for the male singer to finish before taking her turn and she remains properly clad in the *chador,* the Iranian version of the veil required by strict Islam. Covering the female body with a large square of black cloth, the *chador* is a tent (the word's literal translation), which one scholar describes as a portable house to fence off the female, setting close limits to her space and neutralizing her threat when she appears in male-dominated public spaces.[12] The veil has another side, however. Prohibited in 1936 by Reza Shah Pahlavi in his drive toward Western modernization, it was officially reinstituted in 1983 as a revolutionary gesture rejecting the secular values of colonialism and global capitalism. Variously welcomed and reviled among Iranian women, the veil protects them from the objectifying male gaze but serves as an outward symbol of female oppression by enforcing public invisibility. For Westerners, the veil also has contradictory implications, as its connotations have shifted from erotic submissiveness to fanaticism and violence.

The combination of deference and resistance displayed by Neshat's female character reflects a survival strategy of women under Islamic law. It is also an approach adopted by postrevolutionary Iranian filmmakers to slide under the radar of censorship while addressing their culture and maintaining artistic integrity. Neshat became familiar with Iranian cinema, in particular the work of Abbas Kiarostami, from her home in the United States. She found it to be a major inspiration, admiring the way "it created a language that, although remaining within the confines of the social codes, so profoundly expresses the cultural subtleties that would have been otherwise extremely difficult to detect."[13] Neshat was further impressed by qualities that she describes as "simple, concise, poetic, minimalist, and powerful" (terms that also apply to her own work) and the way that "it criticizes society without claiming to do so."[14] Neshat, too, decided to work within boundaries of Islamic culture, embracing its social conventions and reduced number of visual elements as the materials with which to create her art.

Rapture (figs. 23.4 and 23.5), the second work in the trilogy, continues Neshat's exploration of the opposition between men and women in strict Islamic cultures, now in a more complex interplay between the two sides. Again the films play simultaneously on facing walls. On one side, some one hundred men march through town streets and then inhabit an open-air fortress (built by the Portuguese in the fifteenth century). They spend their time performing ritualized drills of clapping, ladder raising, hand washing, and pushing against each other in rough sport, activities that mostly suggest rehearsal of tradition or release of aggressive tension. Dressed, like the men in *Turbulent*, in uniforms of black pants and white shirts, they resemble a regiment of Westernized bureaucrats, underscoring their groupthink mentality (and perhaps their lot of occupying themselves in the remains of a colonial fortification). They are masters of their structure, but their ardent embrace of its boundaries suggests imprisonment in its confines.

The opposite wall shows a similar-sized group of women, veiled head to toe. They emerge over the horizon of a desert landscape and move toward the viewer. Once assembled, they spend much of the first part of the work staring silently into the camera. This gives the impression that they are looking across the room at the men, observing their empty gestures and futile activities. At one point, the women let out a startling *kell*, a high-pitched ululating sound used in Middle Eastern cultures as either warning or applause. The men immediately stop their fighting and look across to the women, who turn away from the camera and begin a journey back across the desert to the sea. Once there, they struggle to launch a wooden boat, and six of them set out upon the waves.[15]

The women's movements have an epic quality, conveying a sense of purpose, endurance, and tragedy. It is uncertain whether those in the boat head toward liberation or drowning, or whether the two options have finally become the same. A parting view of the men shows them waving from the ramparts. It is their first gesture of any kind toward the women. But the apparent goodwill could also signal distress, indicating awareness of their entrapment and of the

freedom found by the women in their exile. The opposing behavior of the men and the women illustrates Neshat's contention that women in Iran (and, by implication, in general)—although subject to greater social restrictions, or precisely because of their greater hardships—perform actions of real consequence, in contrast to men's displays of mock power and control. As Neshat describes it, "This all ties back to what I believe is a type of feminism that comes from such cultures; on a daily basis the resistance you sense from the women is far higher than that of the men. Why? Because the women are the ones who are under extreme pressure; they are repressed and therefore they are more likely to resist and ultimately to break free."[16]

As in *Turbulent*, *Rapture*'s placement of the men and the women on opposite walls underlines their segregation in fundamentalist Islam. It allows Neshat to separate them across a gulf they can only bridge by exchanged gazes, reflecting the prohibition against physical contact between the sexes unless they are married or related. In *Rapture* especially, Neshat emphasizes the different conditions they experience by coding the opposing spaces with distinctly different gender characteristics. Men inhabit the architectural space of authority and tradition; women inhabit the exposed desert space of human vulnerability. Men control the center; women exist at the margin. Yet the men appear trapped, while the women are free to wander.[17] An emotionally charged soundtrack by Sussan Deyhim (the female performer in *Turbulent*) underscores these gender-based spatial distinctions between the two sides. During the men's activities, the music pulsates with a virile, regimented beat and the traditional call to prayer. The women's journey to the sea, by contrast, is accompanied by Deyhim's free-form, ethereal vocals.

The interaction of the two projections on opposite walls also opens up a third arena of action and experience in the space contained between them. Unlike the generally passive viewing conventions of film and television, *Turbulent* and *Rapture* activate the viewer's space, involving their audiences both physically and psychologically. Encouraged by the

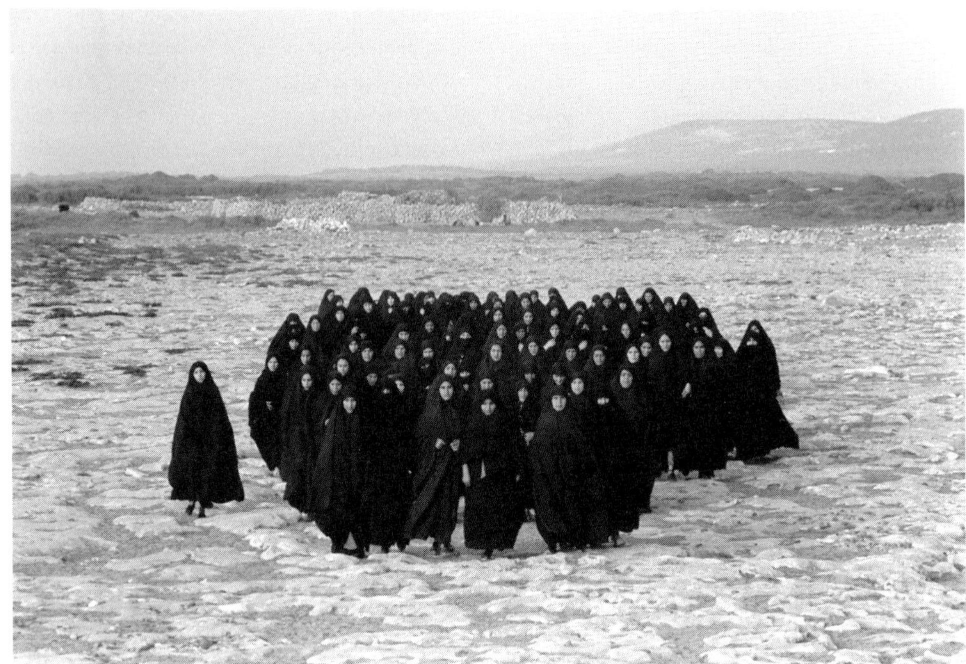

Figure 23.4. Shirin Neshat, *Rapture*, 1999. Production still. © Shirin Neshat. Courtesy Barbara Gladstone Gallery. (Photo: Larry Barns.)

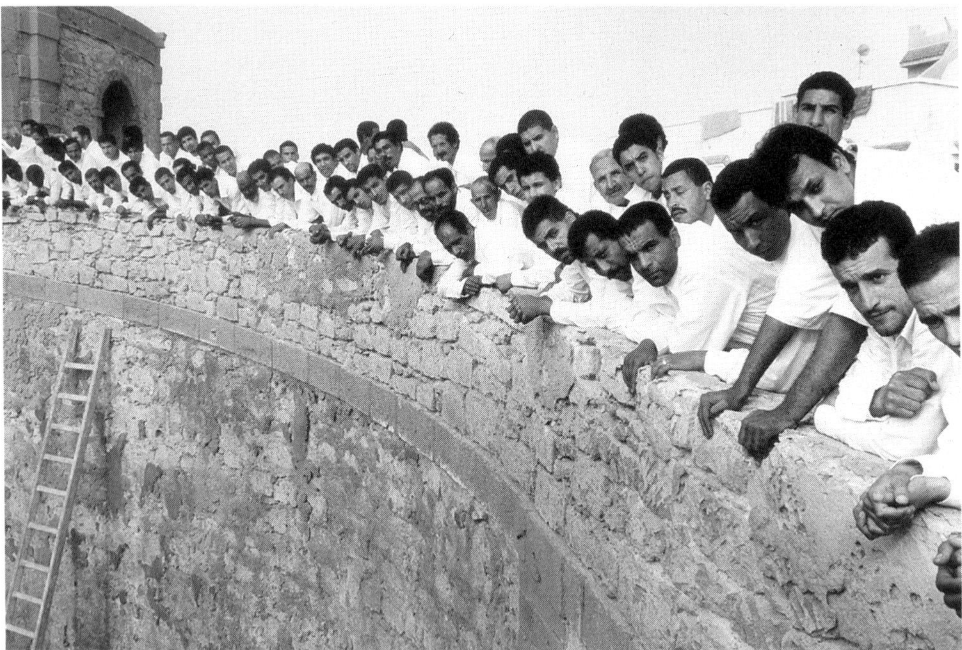

Figure 23.5. Shirin Neshat, *Rapture*, 1999. Production still. © Shirin Neshat. Courtesy Barbara Gladstone Gallery. (Photo: Larry Barns.)

synchronization of the projections and the fact that the two walls cannot be seen at the same time, viewers must shift their attention back and forth along with the men and women who take turns watching each other. *Turbulent* defines its viewers as an audience to the sequential performances, but also as frequent monitors of the response from the other wall. In *Rapture,* the increased interaction between the men and women requires an even more kinetic observer. These physical demands are matched by an emotional pull between the two sides, as viewers form allegiances based on gender, or perhaps maintain a fluid identification with whichever group appears active or passive (depending on one's self-perception). Moreover, the experience of being caught between facing projections suggests that viewers are not only observers but also observed—as much objects of the men's and women's gazes as they are of the viewers'.

Neshat's emphasis on actively involving viewers recalls the importance of direct audience address in the early history of video art. Works from the 1970s by artists such as Vito Acconci, Lynda Benglis, and Hannah Wilke frequently acknowledge the presence of their observers by casting them in specific roles: voyeur, witness, confidant.[18] Early video art's urge to speak directly to its viewers and to incorporate them into the work grew in part out of an intense focus in art of the 1960s on the relationship between the work and its audience. Minimalist sculpture used its reduced, geometric forms to draw attention to the phenomenology of viewing. By resisting illusionism, the obdurate presence of Minimalist objects put pressure on the spaces they inhabited, heightening observers' awareness of their own position in relation to the work (an emphasis on viewing conditions that led art critic Michael Fried to famously criticize Minimalist art as theatrical).[19] Following on the heels of Minimalism, Conceptual Art embraced viewers as active participants in "making" the work, often presenting scenarios, instructions, or methodologies that engaged them as mental collaborators. The medium of video installation had its origins in this period, and over the past three decades it has built upon the shifting relationship between viewer and work by situat-

ing its beholders in room-sized environments of projected moving images that incorporate their presence as an inherent part of the work.

This redefinition of the viewer is one of the most salient features of late-twentieth-century art and theory. Since the invention of single-point perspective in the Renaissance, the viewing subject was traditionally theorized as a disembodied eye from which rays of vision emanated to measure and systematize the world of inert objects. Soon elevated to a philosophical model of human subjectivity, this rationalist model of vision (called Cartesian perspectivalism by contemporary theorists) posited "man's" place in the world as master of all that his gaze encompassed. The privileged position assigned to the observer— as pure consciousness separated from the matter he seeks to know—was thought to yield a comprehensive, systematic, and above all, objective picture of external reality.[20]

The implications of this perspective, which dominated Western thought well into the twentieth century, permeated all aspects of culture, including science and international affairs, reinforcing a wide range of asymmetrical relationships in which lesser beings (women, non-Westerners) could be objectified by the dominant observer. Only in the 1970s did this model of subject-object relations come under direct attack in art and art theory. While the self-reflexivity of Minimalism and Conceptual Art provided one opening wedge, feminism, especially feminist film theory, represents one of the earliest attempts to actively deconstruct the patriarchal view. Although at first centered on revising stereotypical images of women in Hollywood films, feminist film theory soon developed an alternative focus on the mechanisms that created the images. Using the methods of semiotics and psychoanalytic theory, feminist critiques analyzed the gaze and its role in constructing the identity of its viewing subject, in particular the female spectator.[21]

The emphasis on vision, visibility, and representation in feminist theory soon found parallels in critiques of other discourses of power, as in the developing field of postcolonial studies. Edward Said's

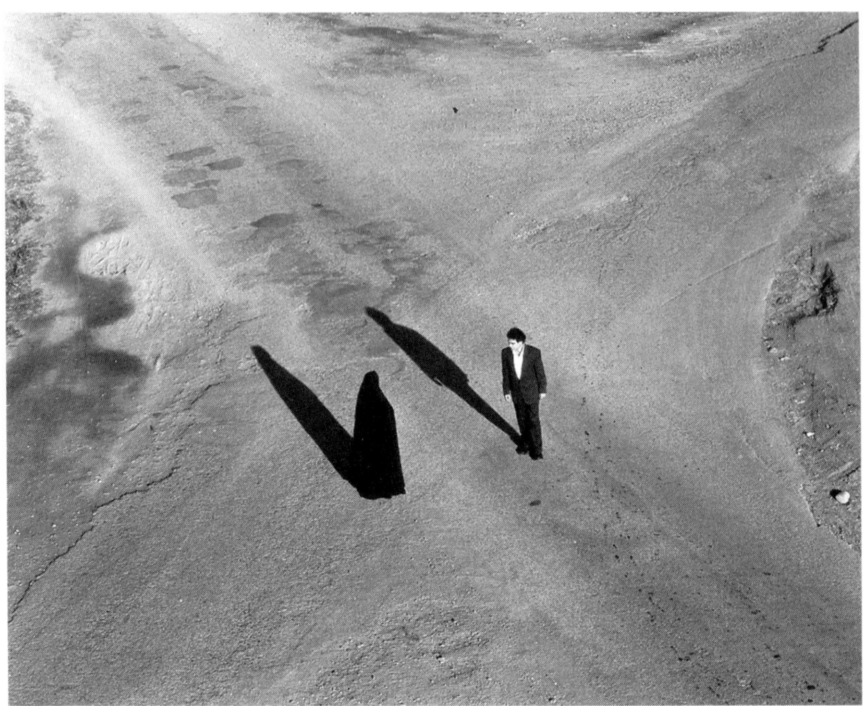

Figure 23.6. Shirin Neshat, *Fervor*, 2000. Production still. © Shirin Neshat. Courtesy Barbara Gladstone Gallery. (Photo: Larry Barns.)

Orientalism (1978) marks a seminal moment in the analysis of Western cultural imperialism, calling for a replacement of the master narratives that created the Orient and Oriental as subjects "suitable for study in the academy, for display in the museum, for reconstruction in the colonial office, for theoretical illustration in anthropological, biological, linguistic, racial, and historical theses about mankind and the universe."[22] Said defines Orientalism as a European invention "of one of its deepest and most recurring images of the Other."[23] (At first primarily identified with the Middle East and South Asia, the Orient was synonymous with those lands subjected to Western colonization, especially by Britain and France, in the eighteenth and nineteenth centuries.) Fundamental to Said's thesis is the importance of self-representation—of colonized peoples regaining and controlling their visibility.

Neshat's creation of a visual poetics of gender and culture shows the influence of feminist and postcolo-nial discourses. Her trilogy can be understood as fulfilling their call for localized narratives grounded in the details of a particular group or culture and giving voice to its representatives. At the same time, her work reflects the difficulty, or perhaps impossibility, of creating authoritative narratives from any vantage point, given the complexity of also accounting for the perspectives of viewer and maker. In *Rapture*, at those moments when the groups of men or women appear to look directly out from the wall, viewers might imagine themselves as able to engage their attention, to access a human interior through the portal of the eyes. But further engagement reveals how they distance the viewer with their watchfulness, denying access to the interior—to what they are thinking, to the physical space in which they exist, to their experience. The viewers' position as cultural outsiders is made apparent—as an "'other' among others."[24]

This shifting relationship between subject and object speaks also to the artist's own relationship with a

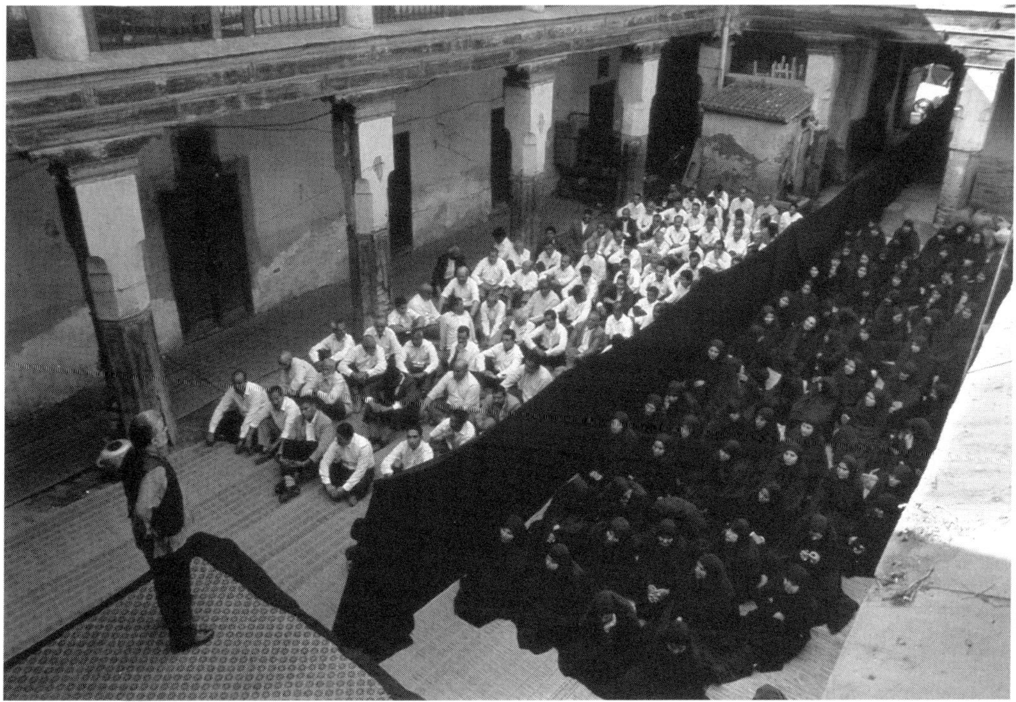

Figure 23.7. Shirin Neshat, *Fervor*, 2000. Production still. © Shirin Neshat. Courtesy Barbara Gladstone Gallery. (Photo: Larry Barns.)

culture to which she does and does not belong. Iran's transformation during Neshat's absence deprived her of a home. As she describes it, "Leaving has offered me incredible personal development, a sense of independence that I don't think I would have had. But there's also a great sense of isolation. And I've permanently lost a complete sense of center. I can never call any place home. I will forever be in a state of in-between. One constantly has to negotiate back and forth between one culture and the other and often they're not just different, they're in complete conflict."[25] Neshat's work questions the place of the artist-observer in relation to a culture that represents "home" but to which she can longer return.[26] Placing viewers in the crossfire between the projections reflects the artist's own experience of perpetual in-between, a condition that Said, in his writings on exile, has called a "contrapuntal" state of existence.[27]

In *Fervor* (figs. 23.6 and 23.7), the final work in the trilogy, Neshat replaces the contrapuntal format with a stereoscopic model: two projections placed side by side. The gaze again serves as the primary means of exchange between genders, but their relationship shifts from opposition to coexistence under a shared social restriction that both unites and divides them: the prohibitions on sexuality and romantic love. *Fervor* begins with two figures walking on parallel roads, one per screen, the woman advancing, the man receding. The roads soon converge and both figures approach. With the projections placed beside each other, Neshat's exquisite choreography of synchronized forms, patterns, and movements becomes especially apparent. As the camera pulls back, the two paths cross in a no-man's-land. Hardly breaking stride, the figures pass closely, exchange glances, then continue on their way. Later they meet again by chance while entering an open-air courtyard for a public ceremony. Men and women are seated on either side of a black curtain running the length of the space. The speaker begins his oration, using a painted image for illustration. It is the story from the Quran of Zuleikha's attempt to seduce Youssef, a well-known moral lesson about desire, sin, and obedience to God.[28] Delivered in Farsi, the exact content of the oration is unavailable to most Westerners, but the tone of strident warning is clear. Meanwhile, the protagonists cast tender looks to where the other might be seated, projecting their fantasies of longing onto the curtain that separates them.

As the speaker's delivery escalates and the audience begins a fervent chant, the sense of struggle between human desire and social conditioning comes to a climax. The woman, who has become increasingly alarmed, rises and flees, reflecting Neshat's contention that although "the notion of 'taboo' in relation to sexuality and romantic love in Islamic societies is equally shared by men and women . . . it is often women who are sanctioned" and thus bear the responsibility for desire.[29] The film ends with a double image of the man and woman walking away from each other down a narrow street, unaware of the other's presence and having made no further contact. Viewers are left to form their own conclusion: a tragic tale of an aborted love affair, an illustration of moral virtue like the lesson of Zuleikha and Youssef, or merely one story among many from an everyday state of affairs that pits religious fervor against romantic fervor and individual desire against communal values.

The relationship of the projections as close but never touching underscores the painful unlikelihood of the protagonists ever coming together. Like a stereoscopic photograph for which the viewing apparatus has become lost, the adjacency of the projections also calls attention to vision itself by frustrating its usual functioning. It replicates the physical fact of sight as emanating from two eyes located at slightly different vantage points whose views must unite to form a single coherent picture. But kept apart, as in *Fervor,* the dual images heighten viewers' self-awareness and defeat the transparency of the Western gaze that paradoxically sees from afar and maintains the illusion of penetration into fully revealed spaces. This model of vision is no more natural, Neshat seems to say, than the cultural, political, and re-

ligious conditioning of vision that viewers observe in the film, where a simple gaze is considered a sin.

By her sophisticated ability to attend to both the narrative and the mechanism of its presentation, Neshat convincingly moves from the specific to the general without sacrificing credibility. For ultimately, Neshat's goal is to speak on a universal plane, addressing, she says, "the more philosophical aspects that interest me as well—the desire of all human beings to be free, to escape conditioning, be it social, cultural, or political, and how we're trapped by all kinds of iconographies and social codes."[30] Neshat's position as both insider and outsider in relation to Eastern and Western cultures allows her the double vision to do this—creating a global picture grounded in local perception, while addressing the perspectives of both maker and viewer.

NOTES

1. For an in-depth exploration of the Middle East as "Orient," see Edward Said, *Orientalism* (New York: Pantheon Books, 1978).

2. These works belong to the *Women of Allah* series (1993–97), which references notions of martyrdom and faith in relation to the Iranian Revolution. See Francesco Bonami, Hamid Dabashi, and Octavio Zaya, *Shirin Neshat: Women of Allah* (Turin, Italy: Marco Noire Editore, 1997).

3. Gerald Matt, "In Conversation with Shirin Neshat," in *Shirin Neshat* (Vienna: Kunsthalle Wien and London: Serpentine Gallery, 2000), 13.

4. Lina Bertucci, "Shirin Neshat: Eastern Values," *Flash Art* 30, no. 197 (November–December 1997): 84–87.

5. Deborah Solomon, "Prudence of the Chador," *New York Times Magazine,* 25 March 2001, 42.

6. For illustrations of *Anchorage* and *The Shadow under the Web,* see Giorgio Verzotti, ed., *Shirin Neshat* (Milan: Charta and Turin: Castello di Rivoli Museo d'Arte Contemporanea, 2002), 89–97.

7. *Turbulent* (1998) was shown at the Venice Biennale in 1999, where Neshat was awarded the Golden Lion for best international work. Like most video installations, Neshat's work is projected directly on the walls in continuous cycle, with little or no seating, encourag-

ing viewers to move freely around the space. For further information about the development of video installation during the 1990s, see John B. Ravenal, *Outer and Inner Space: Pipilotti Rist, Shirin Neshat, Jane and Louise Wilson, and the History of Video Art* (Richmond: Virginia Museum of Fine Arts, 2002).

8. Matt, "In Conversation," 29; and Arthur Danto, "Shirin Neshat," *Bomb* 73 (Fall 2000): 64.

9. The male singer is acted by Shoja Azari, who lip-synchs to the popular Kurdish Iranian singer Shahram Nazeri.

10. The female role is performed by Sussan Deyhim, an Iranian-born experimental vocalist based in the United States. An original composition, it mixes Deyhim's extraordinary vocal capabilities with electronic editing.

11. See, for example, the writings of Fatima Mernissi, a feminist scholar whose work Neshat acknowledges as an influence.

12. Farzeneh Milani, "The Visual Poetry of Shirin Neshat," in *Shirin Neshat* (Milan: Charta, 2001), 9.

13. Matt, "In Conversation," 13.

14. Ibid.

15. The story is inspired by contemporary Iranian writer Moniru Ravanipur's 1989 novel *Ahl-i-gharq* (Brave Enough to Drown).

16. Danto, "Shirin Neshat," 65. Because of its feminist content, Neshat's work was not shown in Iran until 2002 (in "New Art Exhibition" at the Tehran Museum of Contemporary Art) and the piece selected, *Tooba* (filmed in Mexico), is her most removed from commentary on Islamic culture.

17. Neshat credits her interest in the relationship between space and ideology, including the controlling and coding of the female body, in part to her involvement with the Storefront for Art and Architecture, an alternative arts space at 97 Kenmare Street in Lower Manhattan, which she codirected from around 1986 to 1996 with her former husband Kyong Park (see Matt, "In Conversation," 15).

18. See Acconci's *Theme Song* (1973), Benglis's *Now* (1973), and Wilke's *Through the Large Glass* (1976). The experience of being caught in the crossfire of gazes also suggests an affinity with early single-channel works whose primary focus is on the subjects of space and attention rather than viewer/artist dynamics, such as Joan Jonas's *Vertical Roll* (1972) and Bill Viola's *Chott el-Djerid* (1979). Another early

video art precedent for Neshat's work appears in the exploration of gender dynamics, such as in Abramovic and Ulay's *Relation Work* (1976–88), Acconci's *Pryings* (1971), and Klaus vom Bruch's *The West Is Alive* (1983–84).

19. See Fried, "Art and Objecthood," in Gregory Battcock, *Minimalism, A Critical Anthology* (New York: E. P. Dutton, 1968), 116–47.

20. For a brief introduction to the vast literature on perception and perspective, see essays by Jonathan Crary, Martin Jay, and Norman Bryson in Hal Foster, ed., *Vision and Visuality: Discussion in Contemporary Culture* (New York: Dia Art Foundation, 1988). For further references and for an application of these theories to the work of a contemporary sculptor, see John B. Ravenal, *robert lazzarini* (Richmond: Virginia Museum of Fine Arts, 2003).

21. For one brief overview of the enormous literature on feminist film theory, see Anneke Smelik, "Feminist Film Theory," in Pam Cook and Mieke Bernink, eds., *The Cinema Book*, 2d ed. (London: British Film Institute Publishing, 1999) and online at www.let.uu.nl/womens_studies/anneke/filmtheory.html. Also see Laura Mulvey, "Visual Pleasure and Narrative Cinema," and Constance Penley, "'A Certain Refusal of Difference': Feminism and Film Theory," both in *Art after Modernism: Rethinking Representation*, ed. Brian Wallis (New York: New Museum of Contemporary Art, 1984); Kate Linker, "Engaging Perspectives: Film, Feminism, Psychoanalysis, and the Problem of Vision," in *Art and Film since 1945: Hall of Mirrors*, ed. Kerry Brougher and Russell Ferguson (Los Angeles: Museum of Contemporary Art, 1996); and Teresa de Lauretis, "Aesthetic and Feminist Theory: Rethinking Women's Cinema," in *Feminist Art Criticism: An Anthology*, ed. Arlene Raven, Cassandra L. Langer, and Joanna Frueh (Ann Arbor: UMI Research Press, 1988).

22. Said, *Orientalism*, 7.

23. Ibid., 1.

24. Paul Ricoeur's term, quoted in Craig Owens, "The Discourse of Other: Feminists and Post-Modernism," in Hal Foster, ed., *The Anti-Aesthetic: Essays on Postmodern Culture* (Port Townsend, Wash.: Bay Press, 1983), 57.

25. Susan Horsburgh, "Middle East Daily," *Time Europe*, 31 January 2001 (online at www.time.com/time/

europe/webonly/mideast/2000/08/neshat.html).

26. Cultural identity emerged as a major theme in art of the 1990s. However, several video artists working in the 1970s and early 1980s form a significant precedent for Neshat by looking at cultures from which they have been displaced and raising the issue of how one can form a perspective as both an insider and outsider. These include Juan Downey in *Video Trans America* series (1971–c. 1993), Mona Hatoum in *Changing Parts* (1984), and Edin Velez in *Meta Mayan II* (1981).

27. Edward Said, *Reflections on Exile and Other Essays* (Cambridge, Mass.: Harvard University Press, 1984), 186.

28. This is also the Old Testament story of Joseph and Potiphar's wife.

29. Matt, "In Conversation," 29.

30. Octavio Zaya, "Shirin Neshat," *Interview*, September 1999, 167.

ALLISON ARIEFF is Editor in Chief of *Dwell* and was the magazine's founding Senior Editor. She is the author of three books, *Prefab*; *Trailer Travel: A Visual History of Mobile America*; and *SPA*, and the editor of numerous books on art and popular culture, including *Airstream: The History of the Land Yacht; Cheap Hotels; Gilded Edge: The Art of the Picture Frame;* and *Hatch Show Print: The History of a Great American Poster Shop*. Before leaving academia to work in publishing in 1996, she completed coursework for a Ph.D. in American Studies at New York University. The essay in this volume was written at the University of California, Davis, where Arieff received her M.A. in art history in 1994.

JANIS BERGMAN-CARTON, Associate Professor of Art History at Southern Methodist University, has published numerous articles on nineteenth-century French visual culture and contemporary Latin American art. She is the author of *The Woman of Ideas in French Art, 1830–1848* (1995) and is at work on a new study of *La Revue Blanche* and late-nineteenth-century European art culture.

BABETTE BOHN is Professor of Art History at Texas Christian University. A specialist in Bolognese art, she is the author of two volumes in *The Illustrated Bartsch* series, many articles on the Carracci and their school, and a forthcoming book, *Ludovico Carracci and the Art of Drawing*. She is currently working on a book project, *Elisabetta Sirani and the Women Artists of Bologna*.

NORMA BROUDE, Professor of Art History at American University in Washington, D.C., is the author of *The Macchiaioli: Italian Painters of the Nineteenth Century* (1987), *Impressionism, A Feminist Reading: The Gendering of Art, Science, and Nature in the Nineteenth Century* (1991), and *Edgar Degas* (1993). Broude also edited and contributed to *World Impressionism: The International Movement* (1990) and *Gustave*

Caillebotte and the Fashioning of Identity in Impressionist Paris (2002). With Mary D. Garrard, she was co-editor and a contributor to *Feminism and Art History: Questioning the Litany* (1982), *The Expanding Discourse: Feminism and Art History* (1992), and *The Power of Feminist Art: The American Movement of the 1970s, History and Impact* (1994).

ANNA C. CHAVE is Professor of Art History at Queens College and the Graduate Center, City University of New York. She has authored studies of Rothko (1989) and Brancusi (1993), as well as numerous articles concerned with how modern art (especially Minimalism and the works of Eva Hesse, Agnes Martin, Georgia O'Keeffe, Jackson Pollock, and Lee Krasner) may be sexually and ideologically inscribed.

JULIE COLE earned her M.A. degree in the history of art at American University and is currently a teacher of art and art history at Colorado College and the University of Colorado in Colorado Springs. The essay included here is her first publication.

BRIDGET ELLIOTT is Professor of Visual Arts at the University of Western Ontario. Her recent books include *Women Artists and Writers: Modernist (Im)Positionings*, co-authored with Jo-Ann Wallace (1994); *Architecture and Allegory: The Cinema of Peter Greenaway*, co-authored with Anthony Purdy (1997); and *Women Artists and the Decorative Arts, 1880–1935: The Gender of Ornament*, co-edited with Janice Helland (2002).

SHEILA FFOLLIOTT is Professor in the Department of History and Art History at George Mason University in Fairfax, Virginia. Her publications concern the role of art in the political arena, art patronage and collecting, and issues of gender, primarily regarding sixteenth-century France and Italy. She is a Trustee of the National Museum of Women in the Arts in Washington, D.C., and has served as President of the Society for the Study of Early Modern Women (1998).

MARY D. GARRARD is Professor Emerita of Art History at American University, Washington, D.C. She is the author of *Artemisia Gentileschi: The Image of the Female Hero in Italian Baroque Art* (1989); *Artemisia Gentileschi circa 1622: The Shaping and Reshaping of an Artistic Identity* (2001); and articles and reviews on Jacopo Sansovino, Michelangelo, Raphael, Leonardo da Vinci, Titian, and feminist art theory. With Norma Broude, Garrard edited and contributed to *Feminism and Art History: Questioning the Litany* (1982); *The Expanding Discourse: Feminism and Art History* (1992); and *The Power of Feminist Art: The American Movement of the 1970s, History and Impact* (1994).

DARCY GRIMALDO GRIGSBY is Associate Professor of the History of Art at the University of California, Berkeley, and author of *Extremities: Painting Empire in Post-Revolutionary France* (2002). Her 2003 essay "Geometry/Labor = Volume/Mass?" stems from a book-in-progress entitled *Colossal Engineering: Reconnecting the Suez Canal, Statue of Liberty, Eiffel Tower and Panama Canal*. Her 2002 article "Revolutionary Sons, White Fathers and Creole Difference: Guillaume Guillon Lethière's Oath of the Ancestors of 1822" is part of another book-in-progress, called *Creole Looking*.

RUTH E. ISKIN's book on Impressionism, *Parisian Consumer Culture and Modern Women*, is forthcoming from Cambridge University Press. Her work has been supported by a Mellon grant at the Penn Humanities Forum, the Ahmanson-Getty grant at UCLA's Center for Seventeenth and Eighteenth Centuries Studies, and the Izaak Walton Memorial Postdoctoral Fellowship at the University of British Columbia. Currently teaching at Ben Gurion University, she has published essays in the *Art Bulletin*, *Discourse*, and *Nineteenth Century Contexts*.

GERALDINE A. JOHNSON is University Lecturer in the History of Art at the University of Oxford and a Fellow of Christ Church. She has published on the history of sculpture from the late medieval period to the present day, the role played by gender in the production and reception of art, the history of photography, and the historiography of art history as a discipline. For Cambridge University Press, she edited *Sculpture and Photography: Envisioning the Third Dimension* (1998) and co-edited *Picturing Women in Renaissance and Baroque Italy* (1997). At present, she is completing a book on the visual and tactile reception of sculpture in early modern Italy.

AMELIA JONES is Professor and Pilkington Chair in the History of Art at the University of Manchester. She has written numerous articles in anthologies and journals and has organized exhibitions, including *Sexual Politics: Judy Chicago's 'Dinner Party' in Feminist Art History* (1996). Jones co-edited the anthology *Performing the Body/Performing the Text* with Andrew Stephenson (1999), edited the volume *Feminism and Visual Culture Reader* (2003), and authored *Post-Modernism and the En-Gendering of Marcel Duchamp* (1994) and *Body Art/Performing the Subject* (1998). Her book *Irrational Modernism: A Neurasthenic History of New York Dada* is forthcoming. Jones has received ACLS, NEH, and Guggenheim fellowships.

MAUD LAVIN is an Associate Professor of Visual and Critical Studies and Art History, Theory, and Criticism at the School of the Art Institute of Chicago. She is the author of *Cut with the Kitchen Knife: The Weimar Photomontages of Hannah Höch* (1993) and *Clean New World: Culture, Politics, and Graphic Design* (2001) and the editor and co-author of *The Business of Holidays* (2004). Her criticism has appeared in the *New York Times Book Review*, *Print*, *Art in America*, *Artforum*, the *Nation*, and numerous anthologies and museum catalogues, including *Montage and Modern Life*, *Graphic Design in America*, and *Citizen Designers*.

JULIE NICOLETTA is Associate Professor in the Interdisciplinary Arts and Sciences Program at the University of Washington, Tacoma. She has written numerous books and articles on topics ranging from American architecture to gender studies, including *The Architecture of the Shakers* (1995) and *Buildings of Nevada* (2000). Another book, *Unisphere: Architecture and Globalization at the New York World's Fair of 1964–1965*, is in progress.

CAROL OCKMAN is Professor of Art History at Williams College. She is the author of *Ingres's Eroticized Bodies: Retracing the Serpentine Line* (1995). Her essays include "When Is a Jewish Star Just a Star? Interpreting Images of Sarah Bernhardt," in *The Jew in the Text: Modernity and the Politics of Identity*, edited by Linda Nochlin and Tamar Garb (1995); "Barbie Meets Bouguereau: Constructing an Ideal Body for the Late Twentieth Century," in *The Barbie Chronicles: An American Doll Turns Forty*, edited by Yona Zeldis McDonough (1999); and "Women, Icons and Power," in *Self and History: A Festschrift in Honor of Linda Nochlin*, edited by Aruna D'Souza (2001). Ockman and Kenneth E. Silver of New York University are curating and preparing the catalogue for a major loan exhibition on Sarah Bernhardt to open at the Jewish Museum in New York in December 2005.

ERICA RAND teaches at Bates College in the Art Department and in the Program in Women and Gender Studies. Her writings include *Barbie's Queer Accessories* (1995), essays on gender coercion and activist visuals, and collaborative projects on sex and censorship, teaching about consumption, and anti-racist classroom practices. Recent publications include "Breeders on a Golf Ball: Looking for Sex at Ellis Island" (2003), related to *The Ellis Island Snow Globe: Sex, Money, Products, Nation* (forthcoming); and "Hate Crimes, Big Dykes, and Other Problems in Academic Freedom" (2003). She serves on the Editorial Board of the journal *Radical Teacher*.

JOHN B. RAVENAL is Curator of Modern and Contemporary Art at the Virginia Museum of Fine Arts, Richmond. His recent exhibitions and accompanying publications include *Vanitas: Meditation on Life and Death in Contemporary Art* (2000), *Outer & Inner Space: A Video Exhibition in Three Parts* (2002), and *robert lazzarini* (2003).

LISA SALTZMAN is Associate Professor of the History of Art and Director of the Center for Visual Culture at Bryn Mawr College. She is the author of *Anselm Kiefer and Art after Auschwitz* (1999) and the co-editor, with Eric Rosenberg, of *Trauma and Visuality in Modernity* (2004). She is currently at work on a new book project, *Mnemonic Devices: Strategies of Remembrance in Contemporary Art*.

MARY D. SHERIFF is Daniel W. Patterson Distinguished Term Professor and Chair of the Department of Art at the University of North Carolina, Chapel Hill. She is the author of *J. H. Fragonard: Art and Eroticism* (1990); *The Exceptional Woman: Elisabeth Vigée-Lebrun and the Cultural Politics of Art* (1996); and *Moved by Love: Inspired Artists and Deviant Women in Eighteenth-Century France* (2003).

Note: Page numbers in italics refer to illustrations.

289–91, 298n65, 308, 315, 317n6, 320n43, 322nn94, 100

Braquemond, Marie, 264

Brassai, 304

Braunschweig, Duchess of, 84–85

breasts, in Rubens's visual rhetoric, 103–6, 108, 111

"breathing likenesses," 27

Brecht, Bertolt, 413, 418

Brenet, Nicholas-Guy, *Piety and Generosity of Roman Women*, 183n33

Breton, André, 301, 317n4, 349, 354, 362

Bril, Paul, *Self-Portrait*, 65

Brisson, Adolphe, 207

Brod, Harry, 407n88

Bronzino, Agnolo, 65; *Portrait of a Young Man*, 194

Brooks, Romaine, 358n20, 423

Broude, Norma, 459; on Cassatt, 18, 259–75; on female agency, 1–25, 419–20; on Impressionism, 15–17, 18, 217–33

Broussonet, Victor, 168

Brown, Cecily, 380

Bruch, Klaus vom, *The West Is Alive*, 457n18

Brugman, Til, *329*, 329–30, 340nn16, 20; *Scheingehacktes*, 340n21; "Warenhaus der Liebe," 330, 340n21

Bruni, Leonardo, 88

Bryson, Norman, 153–54

Buchloh, Benjamin, 397, 398

Buci-Glucksmann, Christine, 322nn82, 83, 85

Buddhism, 436

Buffon, Georges-Louis Leclerc de, 208

Bulwer, John, *Chirologia*, 75

Bund Deutscher Mädchen, 336

Bürger, Peter, 278

Burgin, Victor, 337

Burn, Ian, 394–95

Burrini, Giovanni Antonio, 84

Butler, Judith, 2, 409, 410, 426

Cabinet des Modes, 121

Cage, John, 387

Cagnacci, Guido, *Cleopatra*, 90

Cahun, Claude, 14–15, 343–59; contrast between Bellmer and, 347–48; gaze of, 353; lesbian relation-ship with Moore, 343–45, 347–50, 353, 356; transgression of gender boundaries by, 345–46, 349

WORKS: *Aveux non avenus*, 344, 350, 351, *352*, 357nn3, 4, 358n23; *Entre nous*, *342*, 344–45; *Portraits of Claude Cahun*, 345–53, *346–48*, *351*, *354*; *Que me veux-tu?*, *344*, 355, 357n1, 359n31; *Self-Portrait* (Bifur), *344*, 353–55; *Suzanne Malherbe*, 350, *351*; *Vues et visions*, 344, 357n3

Caillebotte, Gustave, 220, 221

California Institute of the Arts (CalArts), Feminist Art Program at, 418, 423, 427n7

Callamard, Charles-Antoine, *The Wounded Hyacinth*, 196

Camilla, 34, 86

Camondo, Isaac de, 225

Campan, Rose, 135, 136

Campaspe, 31

Campbell, Jan, 23n9

Campi, Bernardino, 4, 28–30, *30*, 32–34, 40, 43, 44n7; *see also* Anguissola, Sofonisba: *Bernardino Campi Painting Sofonisba Anguissola*

Campi, Giulio, 38–39, 46n67; *The Chess Game*, 38, *39*

Canova, Antonio, 12, 189–90, 192–98; *Boxer*, 198; *Cupid and Psyche*, 187, 189, 196, 197; *Cupid in Flight*, *261*; *Dancer*, 197; *Hebe*, 197; *Hercules and Lycas*, 198; *Paolina Borghese as Venus Victrix*, 189–90, *190*, 191–95; *Paris*, 197; *Penitent Magdalene*, 196; *Three Graces*, 192; *Venere Italica*, 196

Cantaro, Maria Teresa, 45nn47, 56

Cantofoli, Ginevra, 84, 95n32, 97n79, 98n89

Canuti, Domenico Maria, 84

Canuti, Giulia, 93n3

Caravaggio, 41, 53, 59n36, 71; *Boy Bitten by a Lizard*, 47n72

Caricature, La (journal), 204

Caro, Annibale, 30–33

Carracci, Annibale, 55

Carracci family, 83, 84

Cartellier, Pierre, *Modesty*, 197

Cassatt, Alexander J., 266

Cassatt, Mary, 2, 17–18, 245, 254nn32, 35, 259–75, 282, 297n22; and "cult of true womanhood," 262–63; and gendered concepts of artistic style, 264–65; mother's description of, 259, 261; and patri-archal values, 261–62; social and market contexts of, 266, 268–72

WORKS: *The Artist's Mother Reading "Le Figaro,"* 262, 273; *At the Opera*, 262; *The Caress*, 266, *267*; *In the Omnibus*, 258, 271; *Lydia Reading in the Garden*, 262; *Modern Woman*, 17–18, 259–60, *260–61*, 272; *Self-Portrait*, 263, *264*; *The Tea*, 270, *270*; *Woman and Child Driving*, 271–72, *272*

Cassatt, Robert, 266

Castellane, Louis-Joseph-Alphonse-Jules de, 210, 215n34

Castiglione, Baldassare, *Il Cortegiano*, 35

Castiglione, Giovanni Benedetto, 31, 39, 44n21

Castle, Terry, 137

Castoro, Rosemarie, 395, 397, 405n63

Catena sexaginta quinque graecorum patrium in S. Lucam, 107

Cattalani, Andrea, 85, 87, 88

Cavaignac, Mme, 193

Cavalieri, Tommaso, 47n71

Cavalli, Joseph, *30*

Cavazzini, Patrizia, 51

Cecilia, Saint, 37

centralized/"central core" imagery, 413–17, 420, 426, 429n42, 430n50

Certeau, Michel de, 19, 280, 289, 295

Cervi, Valentina, *48*, 52, *54*

Cézanne, Paul, 223, 315

Chabot, François, 149

Chacon, Estelle, 421, 422

Chadwick, Whitney, 27

Chagall, Marc, 279

Cham (Amédée de Noé), 204

Champfleury (Jules Husson), 246

Chanel, Coco, 18, 277

Chapelle, Madeleine, 192

Charivari, Le (journal), 204–8, 210–12, 213n9, 214n24, 215nn30, 34

Charlemagne, 183n40

Charpentier, Auguste, 207

chastity, 107; association of intellect and, 34–35; musical instruments identified with, 36–37

Guarini, Battista, *Il Pastor Fido*, 75
Guercino (Gian-Francesco Barbieri),
    73; *Cleopatra*, 90
Guérin, Pierre-Narcisse, *Anacreon
    Rekindling Love*, 197
Guidorf, Reine, 205
Guidotti family, 85
Gutwirth, Madelyn, 134, 139
Guyon, Abbé, 134
gynesis, 369

Habermas, Jurgen, 255n43
hairstyles. *See* fashion
Hall, Radclyffe, 327, 423
Hall, Susan, 428n28
Halprin, Ann, 405n60
Hamelin, Fortunée, 168, 172, 173
Hamer, Mary, 89, 91
Hamilton, George Heard, 217, 218,
    257n70
Hammond, Harmony, 426
Hamnett, Nina, 289
hands, 5, 63–75; of artists, 71–73; asso-
    ciation of intellect and, 71; class
    and, 71; in connoisseurship, 63;
    gendered dimension of, 64, 66,
    71–72; as objects of beauty, 65, 73
Hansen, Miriam, 331
Hapsburgs, 6, 131, 132, 137, 138
Haraway, Donna, 424
Harriet, E. J., *The Parisian Tea*, *170*
Harris, Ann Sutherland, 70
Hartigan, Grace, 16, 374
Haskell, Barbara, 404n51
Hatoum, Mona, *Changing Parts*, 458n26
Hausmann, Raoul, 329
Haussmann, Baron, 226
Havemeyer, Louisine, 268, 272
Heartfield, John, 333
Heath, Stephen, 23nn9, 18, 321n54
Hébuterne, Jeanne, 288
Helmholtz, Hermann von, 218
Hemessen, Caterina van, 36
Henri IV, King of France, 5, 101–2, 108,
    111, 112, 128
Henrietta Maria, Queen of England, 51
Herbert, Robert, 253n2
Heresies (journal), 431n68
heroic women, depictions of, 4–5; bare
    breasts in, 103–5; by Bolognese
    women artists, 81–93; by David,
    143, 151–52; as female "worthies,"
    106–7

Hersilia, 152, 163, 165, 167, 172–75, 180
Hertz, Neil, 155n2
Hesse, Eva, 17, 385, 388–89, 392,
    394–98, 401nn19–21, 23,
    402nn26, 29, 404n53, 405nn57,
    65; *Accession*, 405n57; *Accession
    II*, *384*, 388; *Sculpture Dance*, 394
Hewitt, Lleyton, 70
Hibri, Azizah Y. al-, 21
Hill, Susan, 427n8
Hirschfeld, Magnus, 327, 330
Hispanics, 421, 431n67
history paintings, 83–84, 144, 310; by
    David, 143–44, 147–54, 159–81;
    by Sirani, 84–99
Höch, Grete, 329
Höch, Hannah, 14, 325–41, *329;*
    androgynous representations by,
    325, 327, 330–34, 336–38;
    lesbianism of, 329–30; and mass
    media images of New Woman,
    338–39
  WORKS: *Aus einem Ethnographischen
    Museum* series, 332, 338; *Cut with
    the Kitchen Knife*, 331; *Dompteuse
    (Tamer)*, *324*, 332–33; *Englische
    Tänzerin*, 330; *Liebe*, 330; *Liebe
    im Busch* (Love in the Bush),
    331–32; *Marlene*, 325, *326*, 337;
    Roma, 331, *332*, 333; *Sieben-
    meilensteifel*, 332; *Die starken
    Männer* (The Strong Men), *333*,
    333–34; *Vagabunden*, 330; *Der
    Vater* (The Father), 331, 340n23
Hoff, Joan, 22n2
Hoffman, Dustin, 24n32
Hofmann, Hans, 382n15
Hollander, Anne, 117n27
Hollier, Denis, 397
Homer, 73
homosexuality, 327–30; Surrealists'
    fear of, 354; *see also* lesbianism
Honthorst, Gerard, *Merry Flea Hunt*, 55
Horney, Karen, 23n16
Hoschedé, Ernest, 225
Houssaye, Henri, 237
Hubert, Gérard, 189–90
Hughes, Robert, 414
Hunt, Lynn, 127, 134, 139, 152, 164
Husserl, Edmund, 386
Huysmans, Joris Karl, 266
Huyssen, Andreas, 235, 279, 281
Hyland, Douglas, 299n73

identity politics, 423
Illustration, L' (journal), 269, *269*
Impressionism, 15–16, 21, 217–33, 248,
    250, 271, 381n10; and discourse of
    mass consumption, 252; modern-
    ism and, 227–30; remasculiniza-
    tion of, 16, 224–27; Romantic
    roots of, 15, 218–21; Symbolism
    and, 15–16, 217–18, 221–24; and
    women painters, 264, 265, 282;
    see also specific artists
industrialization, 204, 226
Ingres, Jean-Auguste-Dominique,
    11–12, 187–201, 443; anacreon-
    tism of, 195–98; classicism of, 15;
    and iconography of odalisques,
    191; portrayals of monarchs by,
    193–94
  WORKS: *Achilles Receiving the Ambas-
    sadors of Agamemnon*, 198; *Bather
    of Valpinçon*, 192; *Betrothal of
    Raphael*, 197; *The Golden Age*,
    198; *Grande Odalisque*, 11–12,
    187, *188*, 189–95, 198, 201n40,
    441; *The Iron Age*, 198; *Jupiter
    and Thetis*, 198, 201n42; *Napoléon
    Bonaparte, First Consul*, 193, *194;*
    Odalisque with Slave, 198; *Paolo
    and Francesca*, 197, *197; Queen
    Caroline Murat*, *186*, 193, 197;
    Reclining Odalisque, *188; Saint
    Symphorian*, 198; *Sleeper of
    Naples*, 12, 187, 189, 192, 195,
    198, 201n40
intellectuals, female, 8, 33, 36; in
    Bologna in sixteenth and seven-
    teenth centuries, 81–83, 93;
    Daumier and his contemporaries
    on, 203–13, 214nn21, 24; sexualiz-
    ing of, 36
International Exhibition (Paris, 1867),
    244; *International Cafés in the
    Park*, *244*
Internet Movie Database (IMDb), 50
Intervention of the Sabine Women
    (David), 7–8, *144*, 152–54, *158*,
    159–61, *162*, 168; Chaussard
    on, 143, 152, 154, 163, 178, 180;
    iconography of female dress
    in, 166, 172–74; male nudity in,
    165–66, 175
Iranian Revolution, 448, 456n2
Ireland, Elaine, 425

SPONSORING EDITOR
Stephanie Fay

ASSISTANT ACQUISITIONS EDITORS
Erin Marietta, Sigi Nacson

PROJECT EDITOR
Sue Heinemann

EDITORIAL ASSISTANT
Lynn Meinhardt

COPYEDITOR
Elizabeth Berg

INDEXER
Ruth Elwell

DESIGNER
Victoria Kuskowski

PRODUCTION COORDINATOR
John Cronin

TEXT
10.5/12.75 Fournier

DISPLAY
Bauer Text Initials, Interstate Light, Fournier

COMPOSITOR
Integrated Composition Systems

PRINTER AND BINDER
Friesens